12e

PRINCIPLES OF ORGANIZATIONAL BEHAVIOR

John W. Slocum, Jr.
Southern Methodist University

Don Hellriegel
Texas A & M University

SOUTH-WESTERN
CENGAGE Learning™

SOUTH-WESTERN
CENGAGE Learning™

Principles of Organizational Behavior, 12/e
John W. Slocum, Jr. and Don Hellriegel

Vice President of Editorial, Business: Jack W. Calhoun

Editor-in-Chief: Melissa S. Acuña

Sr. Acquisitions Editor: Michele Rhoades

Developmental Editor: Erin Berger

Executive Marketing Manager: Kimberly Kanakes / Clint Kernen

Sr. Marketing Coordinator: Sarah Rose

Content Project Manager: Pat Cosgrove / Margaret M. Bril

Manager of Technology, Editorial: Kristen Meere / Rob Ellington

Technology Project Editor: Erin Donohoe / Adam Grafa

Website Project Manager: Brian Courter

Sr. Manufacturing Coordinator: Doug Wilke

Production Service: Newgen–Austin Publishing and Data Services

Copyeditor: Lorretta Palagi

Sr. Art Director: Tippy McIntosh

Internal Designer: Grannan Graphic Design, Brenda Grannan

Photography Manager: Deanna Ettinger

Photo Researcher: Charlotte Goldman

Library of Congress Control Number: 2007941716

International Student Edition:

ISBN-13: 978-0-324-58115-7

ISBN-10: 0-324-58115-7

Student Edition Pkg ISBN 13: 978-0-324-58115-7

Student Edition Pkg ISBN 10: 0-324-58115-7

Cengage Learning International Offices

Asia
cengageasia.com
tel: (65) 6410 1200

Australia/New Zealand
cengage.com.au
tel: (61) 3 9685 4111

Brazil
cengage.com.br
tel: (011) 3665 9900

India
cengage.co.in
tel: (91) 11 30484837/38

Latin America
cengage.com.mx
tel: +52 (55) 1500 6000

UK/Europe/Middle East/Africa
cengage.co.uk
tel: (44) 207 067 2500

Represented in Canada by Nelson Education, Ltd.
tel: (416) 752 9100 / (800) 668 0671
nelson.com

Cengage Learning products are represented in Canada by Nelson Education, Ltd.

Printed in China
1 2 3 4 5 6 7 12 11 10 09 08

To Christopher, Bradley, and Jonathan (JWS)
Jill, Kim, and Lori (DH)

BRIEF CONTENTS

CONTENTS

Part 2: The Individual in Organizations 33

PREFACE

This 12th edition continues our legacy of thoughtfully and meaningfully revising our book to assist users to learn and apply core organizational behavior concepts, models, and competencies to the management of others. As with previous editions, we have been responsive to excellent feedback from our users. This preface provides you with a number of insights to the text and the supplements that support instructors and the learners who read this edition.

Snapshot of What's New

What's new? Here is a brief snapshot of the **NEW** features, concepts, and thought-provoking issues in this edition:

- Each chapter opens with a **NEW** feature called *Learning from Experience*. It presents actual situations experienced by leaders, employees, teams, and organizations. Throughout the chapters, we return to this feature to illustrate various concepts and issues within the chapter. All 16 *Learning from Experience* features are **NEW** to this edition.
- Each chapter includes a minimum of four competency features, 79 percent of which are **NEW** to this edition. All carryover competency features have been updated and revised.
- Each chapter includes a **NEW** feature called *Leader Insight*. It provides a brief insight by a leader that is directly related to the content of the chapter section where it appears. There are two **NEW** *Leader Insights* in each chapter.
- Each chapter includes **NEW** or revised concepts, issues, and models. Examples of **NEW** concepts, issues, or models include (1) managing emotions at work, (2) reasons why employees who take assignments in foreign countries often fail, (3) bullying at work, (4) active listening, (5) impact of e-mail and body language on communications, (6) GLOBE leadership model, (7) five potential team dysfunctions, (8) principled negotiations, (9) evidence-based management, and (10) impact of generational differences on the ability to manage change.
- Each chapter includes **NEW** sections entitled *Managerial Guidelines* and/or *Individual Guidelines*. These sections, which often appear in several places within each chapter, present suggested managerial actions that can be used to improve the effectiveness of the implementation of the model under discussion.
- Each chapter includes a **NEW** experiential exercise and/or case at the end of the chapter.
- Each chapter includes 8 to 10 discussion questions at the end of the chapter, 75 percent of which are **NEW** to this edition.
- Each chapter has been revised to reflect the **NEW** and best thinking related to the chapter's content.
- Five of the nine integrating and more comprehensive cases that appear at the end of the book are **NEW** to this edition.
- **NEW** photos have been added to the text. Concepts are clearer and more easily understood with colorful, engaging photography.

Snapshot of What Stayed the Same

What stayed the same? First, as in all previous editions, we pursued the goal of presenting core concepts and models in the field of organizational behavior that are fundamental to individual and managerial effectiveness. These are illustrated through contemporary examples, issues, and management practices. Second, to actively engage readers in the learning process and to assist them in developing their individual and managerial competencies, there are numerous self-assessment instruments for them to complete. These instruments assist readers in assessing their own behaviors and experiences and in developing the competencies they will need to become successful employees, managers, and leaders. A third goal is to present timely real-life examples to encourage, stimulate, and support learning.

The effective management and leadership of organizations requires thoughtful application of the competencies related to people at work. Few, if any, of the dramatic challenges facing organizations can be handled effectively without a solid understanding of human behavior at work. Highly motivated and committed employees and leaders are critical for organizational success and effectiveness. Organizations fail or succeed, decline or prosper because of what people do or do not do every day on the job. Effective organizational behavior is the bedrock on which effectiveness rests. Long-term competitive advantage comes from the rich portfolio of individual, managerial, and team-based competencies learned by members of an organization.

LEARNING PROCESS

Our road map to the learning process starts in Chapter 1. In this chapter, we detail the seven key competencies that all employees, managers, and leaders need to master. There is much research to suggest that these seven competencies are essential for improving individual, team, and managerial effectiveness.

Key Competencies

Performance is related to how well organizational members practice the competencies and concepts that are incorporated in our book. What are these? Chapter 1 presents them in depth. We briefly identify and describe them here:

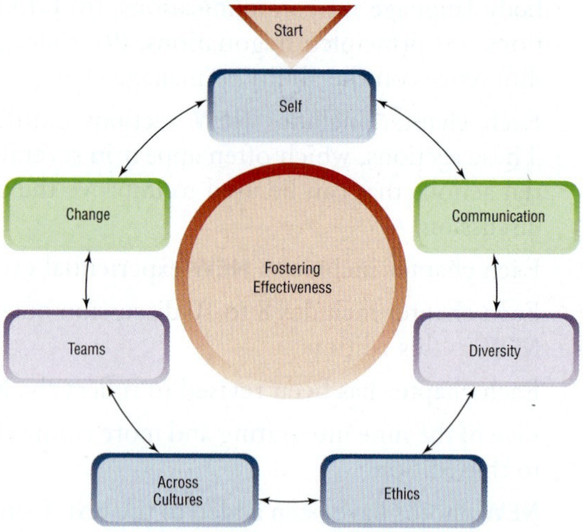

- ***Self Competency*** includes the knowledge, skills, and abilities to assess your own strengths and weaknesses, set and pursue professional goals, balance work and personal life, and engage in new learning—including new or modified skills, behaviors, and attitudes.
- ***Communication Competency*** includes the knowledge, skills, and abilities to use all the modes of transmitting, understanding, and receiving ideas, thoughts, and feelings—verbal, listening, nonverbal, written, and electronic—to accurately transfer and exchange information and emotions.
- ***Diversity Competency*** includes the knowledge, skills, and abilities to value unique individual and group characteristics found in organizations, embrace such characteristics as potential sources of organizational strength, and appreciate the uniqueness of each individual.
- ***Ethics Competency*** includes the knowledge, skills, and abilities to incorporate values and principles that distinguish right and wrong when making decisions and choosing actions.
- ***Across Cultures Competency*** includes the knowledge, skills, and abilities to recognize and embrace the similarities and differences among nations and cultures and then approach key organizational and strategic issues with an open and curious mind.
- ***Teams Competency*** includes the knowledge, skills, and abilities to develop, support, facilitate, and lead groups to achieve organizational goals.

- ***Change Competency*** includes the knowledge, skills, and abilities to recognize and implement needed adaptations or entirely new transformations in the people, tasks, strategies, structures, or technologies in a person's area of responsibility.

Action Learning

We provide a rich portfolio of action learning opportunities to develop these seven competencies. These opportunities include self-assessment instruments, experiential exercises, case studies, and discussion questions. Self-assessment instruments, such as the one at the end of Chapter 1, provide benchmarks against which learners can gauge their competencies independently and compare their levels with those of other students and practicing managers.

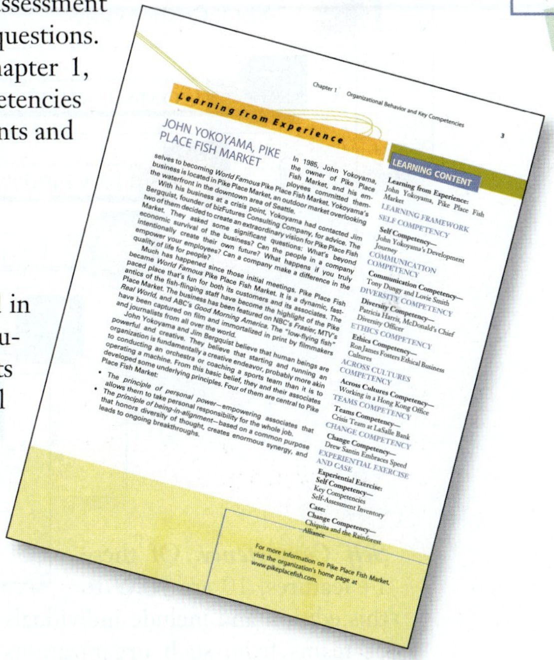
Chapter 1 Organizational Behavior and Key Competencies 3

Learning from Experience

JOHN YOKOYAMA, PIKE PLACE FISH MARKET

In 1985, John Yokoyama, the owner of Pike Place Fish Market, and his employees committed themselves to becoming *World Famous* Pike Place Fish Market. Yokoyama's business is located in Pike Place Market, an outdoor market overlooking the waterfront in the downtown area of Seattle.

With his business at a crisis point, Yokoyama had contacted Jim Bergquist, founder of bizFutures Consulting Company, for advice. The two of them decided to create an extraordinary vision for Pike Place Fish Market. They asked some significant questions: What's beyond economic survival of the business? Can the people in a company intentionally create their own future? What happens if you truly empower your employees? Can a company make a difference in the quality of life for people?

Much has happened since those initial meetings. Pike Place Fish became *World Famous* Pike Place Fish Market. It is a dynamic, fast-paced place that's fun for both its customers and its associates. The antics of the fish-flinging staff have become the highlight of the Pike Place Market. The business has been featured on NBC's *Frasier*, MTV's *Real World*, and ABC's *Good Morning America*. The "low-flying fish" have been captured on film and immortalized in print by filmmakers and journalists from all over the world.

John Yokoyama and Jim Bergquist believe that human beings are powerful and creative. They believe that starting and running an organization is fundamentally a creative endeavor, probably more akin to conducting an orchestra or coaching a sports team than it is to operating a machine. From this basic belief, they and their associates developed some underlying principles. Four of them are central to Pike Place Fish Market:

- The *principle of personal power*—empowering associates that allows them to take personal responsibility for the whole job.
- The *principle of being-in-alignment*—based on a common purpose that honors diversity of thought, creates enormous synergy, and leads to ongoing breakthroughs.

LEARNING CONTENT

Learning from Experience: John Yokoyama, Pike Place Fish Market

LEARNING FRAMEWORK

SELF COMPETENCY

Self Competency— John Yokoyama's Development Journey

COMMUNICATION COMPETENCY

Communication Competency— Tony Dungy and Lovie Smith

DIVERSITY COMPETENCY

Diversity Competency— Patricia Harris, McDonald's Chief Diversity Officer

ETHICS COMPETENCY

Ethics Competency— Ron James Fosters Ethical Business Cultures

ACROSS CULTURES COMPETENCY

Across Cultures Competency— Working in a Hong Kong Office

TEAMS COMPETENCY

Teams Competency— Crisis Team at LaSalle Bank

CHANGE COMPETENCY

Change Competency— Drew Santin Embraces Speed

EXPERIENTIAL EXERCISE AND CASE

Experiential Exercise:
Self Competency— Key Competencies Self-Assessment Inventory

Case:
Change Competency— Chiquita and the Rainforest Alliance

For more information on Pike Place Fish Market, visit the organization's home page at www.pikeplacefish.com.

Learning from Experience Feature

Our purpose is to engage the learner with the themes illustrated in the chapter. To do so, we often use the experiences of individuals who are employed in organizations with which most students are familiar, such as Virgin Group, Estée Lauder, Continental Airlines, Google, GE, UPS, Costco, and Microsoft. Typically, the *Learning from Experience* feature illustrates effective or ineffective applications of one or more of the seven key competencies. Within the chapter, there are flashbacks to how the *Learning from Experience* feature illustrates particular concepts, issues, or practices.

Leader Insight Feature

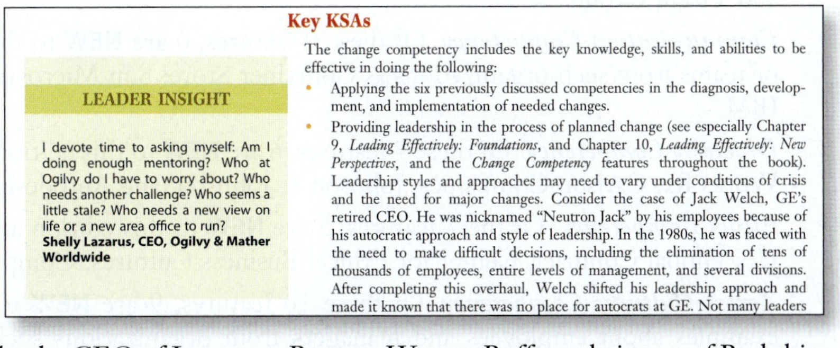
Key KSAs

The change competency includes the key knowledge, skills, and abilities to be effective in doing the following:

- Applying the six previously discussed competencies in the diagnosis, development, and implementation of needed changes.
- Providing leadership in the process of planned change (see especially Chapter 9, *Leading Effectively: Foundations*, and Chapter 10, *Leading Effectively: New Perspectives*, and the *Change Competency* features throughout the book). Leadership styles and approaches may need to vary under conditions of crisis and the need for major changes. Consider the case of Jack Welch, GE's retired CEO. He was nicknamed "Neutron Jack" by his employees because of his autocratic approach and style of leadership. In the 1980s, he was faced with the need to make difficult decisions, including the elimination of tens of thousands of employees, entire levels of management, and several divisions. After completing this overhaul, Welch shifted his leadership approach and made it known that there was no place for autocrats at GE. Not many leaders

LEADER INSIGHT

I devote time to asking myself: Am I doing enough mentoring? Who at Ogilvy do I have to worry about? Who needs another challenge? Who seems a little stale? Who needs a new view on life or a new area office to run?

Shelly Lazarus, CEO, Ogilvy & Mather Worldwide

This feature provides insights that are related to the content of the chapter sections where it appears. A few of the leader insights are from Shelly Lazarus, CEO of Ogilvy & Mather Worldwide; Andrea Doelling, senior vice president of sales at AT&T Wireless; Jack Gustin, president of Lakewood Hospital; Carlos Sepulveda, CEO of Interstate Battery; Warren Buffett, chairman of Berkshire Hathaway; and David Radcliffe, CEO of Hagg and Robinson Ltd (United Kingdom).

Competency Feature

Following the tradition we started several editions ago, we have at least four competency features in each chapter. These features aid teaching, learning, and reinforcing of each chapter's content. They lend a real-world flavor to the materials. We have chosen these 67 competency features to provide additional examples and applications to help you develop your competencies. Seventy-nine percent of these are **NEW** to this edition. Those that we have retained have been updated and revised. In many instances, learners are challenged to analyze and evaluate the competency being presented. Let's briefly highlight some of the organizations of the managers, teams, or individuals that are illustrated for learners in these competency features:

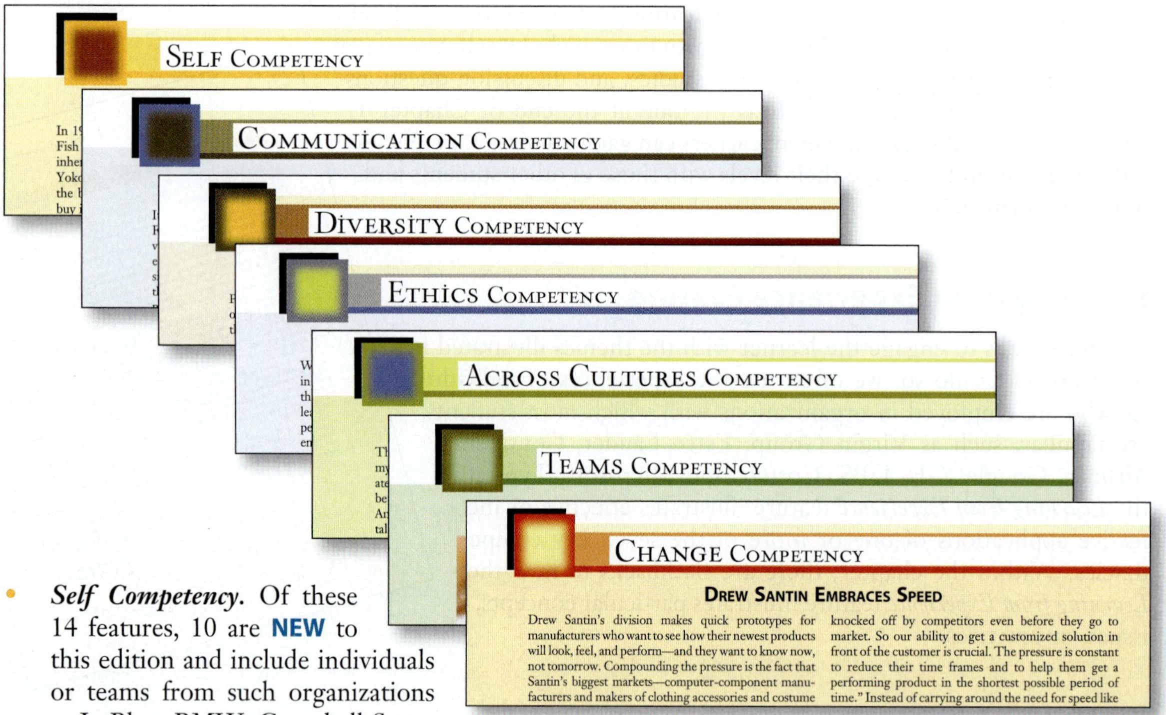
SELF COMPETENCY
COMMUNICATION COMPETENCY
DIVERSITY COMPETENCY
ETHICS COMPETENCY
ACROSS CULTURES COMPETENCY
TEAMS COMPETENCY
CHANGE COMPETENCY
DREW SANTIN EMBRACES SPEED
Drew Santin's division makes quick prototypes for manufacturers who want to see how their newest products will look, feel, and perform—and they want to know now, not tomorrow. Compounding the pressure is the fact that Santin's biggest markets—computer-component manufacturers and makers of clothing accessories and costume
knocked off by competitors even before they go to market. So our ability to get a customized solution in front of the customer is crucial. The pressure is constant to reduce their time frames and to help them get a performing product in the shortest possible period of time." Instead of carrying around the need for speed like

- ***Self Competency.*** Of these 14 features, 10 are **NEW** to this edition and include individuals or teams from such organizations as JetBlue, BMW, Campbell Soup, and Virgin Group.
- ***Communication Competency.*** Of these 9 features, 6 are **NEW** to this edition and include individuals or teams from such organizations as Container Store, Sun Microsystems, Walgreens, Starbucks, and IBM.
- ***Diversity Competency.*** Of these 7 features, 6 are **NEW** to this edition and include insights from Office Works Rx, Carlson Companies, Johnson & Johnson, and Autodesk.
- ***Ethics Competency.*** Of the 7 features, 5 are **NEW** to this edition and are from such organizations as UN Global Compact, Center for Ethical Business Cultures, Computer Associates, and The Gap.
- ***Across Cultures Competency.*** Of these 10 features, 9 are **NEW** to this edition. We have included examples about employees and managers from organizations such as Logitech, Hewlett-Packard, Mercedes-Benz, *Wall Street Journal*, Nokia, and Nike.
- ***Teams Competency.*** Of these 9 features, 8 are **NEW** to this edition. We include features from teams working at such organizations as LaSalle Bank, Starbucks, Steelcase, Toyota, IBM, and FedEx.
- ***Change Competency.*** Of these 11 features, 8 are **NEW** to this edition. Managers and teams are included from such organizations as Cianbro, Home Depot, Procter & Gamble, Harley-Davidson, and Crocs.

Key Terms and Concepts

Key terms and concepts appear in blue in the text, making it easy for readers to check their understanding. The definition of each term and concept is in italics to enhance clarity and student learning. A list of these terms and concepts appears at the end of each chapter.

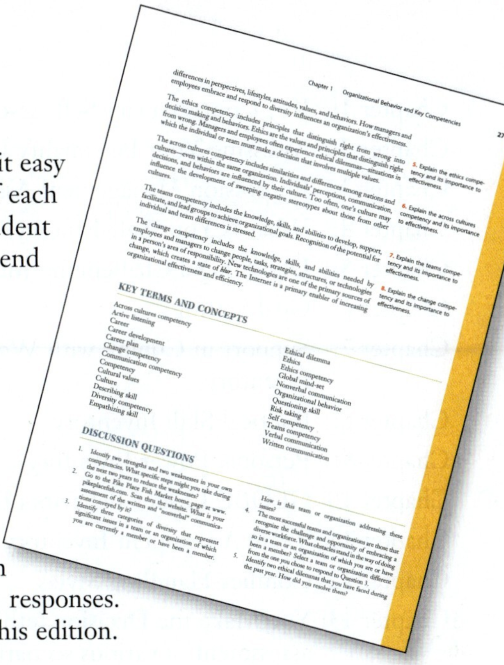

Discussion Questions

These questions require students to apply, analyze, discover, and think about important chapter concepts and related competencies. At least one question requires the student to search the Internet for an answer. These questions also require students to build their communication competencies because they ask for thoughtful, focused responses. The majority of the more than 150 questions are **NEW** to this edition.

Experiential Exercises and Cases

Each chapter contains one experiential exercise and case, each of which emphasizes one of the seven key competencies. These end-of-chapter features provide additional means for learners to actively develop their depth of comprehension and to further enhance their competencies. Some of the experiential exercises include the Foundation Competencies Self-Assessment Inventory, What's Your Emotional IQ?, Interpersonal Communication Styles, Personal Power Inventory, and Team Assessment Inventory. A few organizations featured in the end-of-chapter cases are Chiquita, Allstate Insurance Company, PWC, eBay, Novartis Brazil, Ford Motor, and DriveCam. We pose questions that stimulate learners to become insightful and critical thinkers.

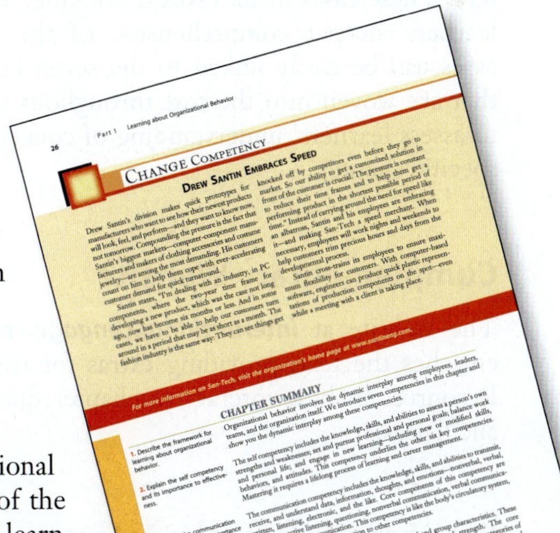

Chapter Summaries

Every chapter ends with a summary that distills the chapter's main points. These summaries are organized around the chapter's *Learning Goals*. Readers can use these summaries to readily assess their mastery of the material presented for each of these goals.

Assessment Instruments

Throughout the book, we present 37 self, team, and organizational assessment instruments that typically focus on one or more of the key competencies in the chapter. They are aimed at helping learners to (1) gain self-insights, (2) gain insights about teams they have served on, (3) gain insights about organizations they have worked for, (4) more readily learn concepts, (5) identify their own strengths and weaknesses, and (6) effectively lead others. These instruments were chosen because they have been proven to enhance individual learning, develop competencies, and stimulate classroom discussion. A sample of these instruments include:

- Chapter 1: Key Competencies Self-Assessment Inventory
- Chapter 2: Assessing Your Personality Using the Big Five
- Chapter 3: Impression Management Assessment
- Chapter 4: What Is Your Self-Efficacy?
- Chapter 5: Designing a Challenging Job
- Chapter 6: Goal Setting
- Chapter 7: Support in Coping with Work-Related Stress Inventory
- Chapter 8: Political Skill Inventory
- Chapter 9: Personal Power Inventory
- Chapter 10: GLOBE Leader Behaviors Instrument
- Chapter 11: Team Assessment Inventory
- Chapter 12: Conflict-Handling Styles
- Chapter 13: You Make the Decision (ethical assessment of various scenarios)
- Chapter 14: Analyzing Your Organization's Design
- Chapter 15: Assessing the Culture of Your Organization
- Chapter 16: Assessing an Organization's Readiness for Change

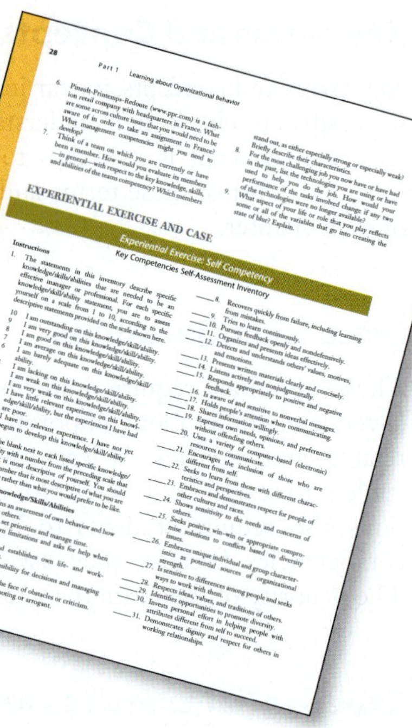
EXPERIENTIAL EXERCISE AND CASE

Experiential Exercise: Self Competency

Key Competencies Self-Assessment Inventory

Integrating Cases

Each case poses questions that require learners to draw from a variety of concepts presented in various chapters. These cases foster critical thinking. They challenge learners' deeper comprehension of the materials. The cases can be easily linked to the seven key competencies that are woven into the text throughout the book or used to assess learners' understanding of concepts presented in a specific chapter.

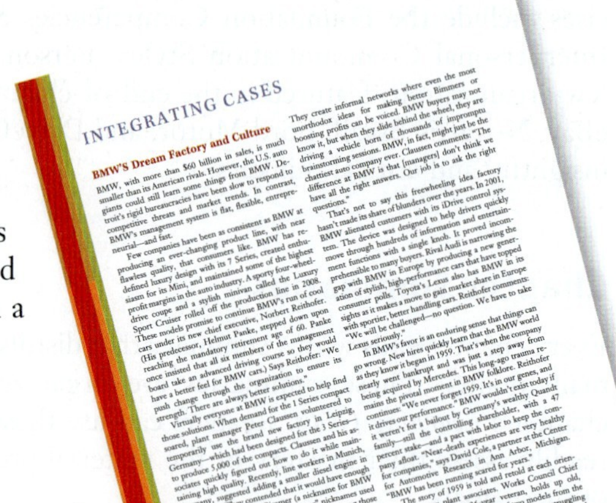
INTEGRATING CASES

BMW's Dream Factory and Culture

Complementary Website

The website at ***international.cengage.com*** complements and enriches the text, providing extras for learners and instructors. Resources include interactive chapter quizzes and downloadable ancillaries.

Enriching Competency Instrument

An access card bound into every new copy of the book allows online access to a detailed self-assessment competency instrument for learners to use and reuse as their competencies develop. Individual ratings can be compared with those of practicing professionals as well as with those of others. These comparisons give learners feedback on their developmental needs. In addition, videos, glossaries, and links to other online resources complete this collection of technology-based tools and content.

LEARNING FRAMEWORK

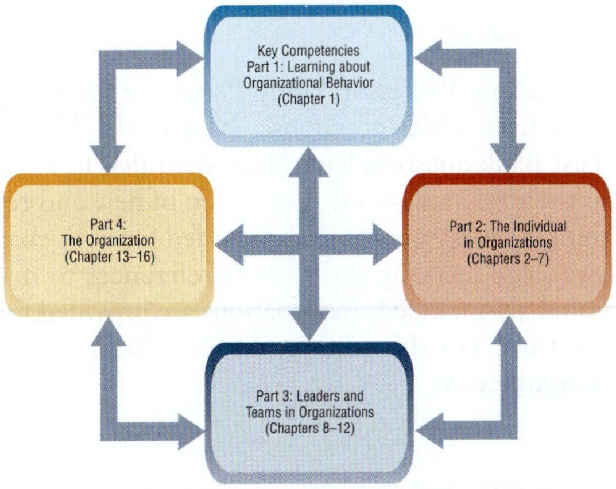

The framework for learning about organizational behavior and developing competencies is fully presented in Chapter 1, titled *Organizational Behavior and Key Competencies*. As shown in Figure 1.1, our learning framework for increasing learner effectiveness moves from the individual level, to the leader and team level, to the organizational level.

Part 2 of the book focuses on key aspects of the individual by discussing individual differences, workforce diversity and cultural values, the psychological nature of people, elements of personality, how emotions affect employee behaviors, how people form attitudes, perceptual and attribution processes, how people learn, motivation, goal setting, reward systems, workplace stress and aggression, and much more. The six chapters in Part 2 are full of real-world examples of how today's leaders and organizations are using these concepts to lead and manage others.

The third part of the book moves learners from individual aspects of organizational behavior to the interpersonal processes that often impact the effectiveness of organizations. We start with a discussion of the multiple facets of interpersonal communication. Leadership is presented in a two-chapter sequence, covering the foundations in one chapter and contemporary leadership models the following chapter. This is followed by a presentation on developing and leading teams. We conclude this part with a discussion of managing conflict and negotiating effectively.

In Part 4, we address more macro and system-wide aspects of organizational behavior. We start with a focus on making ethical and managerial decisions. This is followed by presentation of the issues and concepts needed for effectively designing organizations. The importance of cultivating organizational culture is examined to set the context for how organizational behavior operates in practice. We end this part with a discussion of how to guide organizational change, which serves as a capstone and integrating presentation for a number of the concepts, models, and issues presented in previous chapters.

RESOURCES FOR INSTRUCTORS

A full range of teaching and learning supplements and resources are available for use with the 12th edition of ***Principle of Organizational Behavior***.

Instructor's Manual

Written by Professor Susan Leshnower of Midland College, the *Instructor's Manual* contains comprehensive resource materials for lectures, including enrichment modules for enhancing and extending relevant chapter concepts. It includes a variety of enrichment modules, including the use of jazz bands as a metaphor for exploring the many facets of organizational behavior. This supplement also presents suggested answers to all end-of-chapter discussion questions. It includes notes on using the end-of-chapter *Experiential Exercise and Case* features, including suggested answers to case questions and notes for the integrating cases. Finally, the *Instructor's Manual* contains a guide to the videos available for use with the text. For this edition, this manual is available only on the product support website, ***international.cengage.com***.

Test Bank

Written by Professor Molly Pepper of Gonzaga University, the Test Bank contains almost 4,000 questions from which to choose. New to the 12th edition, the AACSB learning standards reflected in each Test Bank question have been identified to allow for the assessment of student achievement as it relates to these key measures. A selection of new and revised true/false, multiple-choice, short essay, and critical thinking essay questions is provided for each chapter. Questions are classified according to type, difficulty level, and learning goal. Cross-references to materials in the textbook and pages where answers can be found are included. Explanations are provided for why statements are false in the true/false sections of the test bank. For this edition, the Test Bank is available only on the product support website, ***international.cengage.com***.

ExamView®

Available on the website ***international.cengage.com***, ExamView contains all of the questions in the printed Test Bank. This program is easy-to-use test creation software that is compatible with Microsoft® Windows®. Instructors can add or edit questions, instructions, and answers, and select questions (randomly or numerically) by previewing them on the screen. Instructors can also create and administer quizzes online, whether over the Internet, a local-area network (LAN), or a wide-area network (WAN).

PowerPoint® Presentation Slides

Developed by Argie Butler of Texas A&M University and prepared in conjunction with the *Instructor's Manual*, more than 400 PowerPoint slides are available to supplement course content, adding structure and a visual dimension to the learning experience. With an improved design, these PowerPoint slides present the dynamic nature of the materials presented. Available on the website ***international.cengage.com***, all of the PowerPoint slides include meaningful captions that tie in directly to the concepts in the book. Material is organized by chapter and can be modified or expanded for individual classroom use. PowerPoint slides are easily printed to create customized transparency masters. We want learners to engage with their classroom experience and grow from it.

Video DVD

A video library is available to users of the 12th edition to show how real organizations and managers deal with organizational behavior issues. This unique video package is available on DVD.

One offering, entitled *BizFlix*, is compromised of 16 short film scenes from popular Hollywood films, such as *Apollo 13*, *The Breakfast Club*, and *8 Mile*, to illustrate organizational behavior concepts from the text. These film scenes help learners synthesize and reflect on key concepts. Many clips draw insights from two or more chapters and its application to chapter content. The 16 *BizFlix* incidents are presented in brief form, along with key questions, in Appendix A of the text.

On the Job videos are from organizations such as Yahoo!, McDonald's, and Cold Stone Creamery. They give learners an insider's look at the situations faced by organizations and their subsequent solutions.

TextChoice: Management Exercises and Cases

TextChoice is the home of Cengage Learning's online digital content. TextChoice provides the fastest, easiest way for instructors to create their own learning materials. South-Western's Management Exercises and Cases database includes a variety of experiential exercises, classroom activities, management in film exercises, and cases that can be used to enhance any course. Instructors can select as many exercises as they like and even add their own material to create a supplement tailored to fit their course. Contact your South-Western/Cengage Learning sales representative for more information.

LEARNER AND INSTRUCTOR RESOURCES

WebTutor™

WebTutor is an interactive, web-based learner supplement on WebCT and/or BlackBoard that harnesses the power of the Internet to deliver innovative learning aids that actively engage learners. Instructors can incorporate WebTutor as an integral part of their courses, or learners can use it on their own as a study guide. Benefits to learners include automatic feedback from quizzes and exams; interactive, multimedia-rich explanation of concepts; online exercises that reinforce what they have learned; flash cards that include audio support; and greater interaction and involvement through online discussion forums.

The Business & Company Resource Center

The Business & Company Resource Center (BCRC) puts a business library at the learner's fingertips. The BCRC is a premier online business research tool that allows learners to seamlessly search thousands of periodicals, journals, references, financial information, industry reports, company histories, and much more. This all-in-one reference tool is invaluable to learners, helping them to quickly research their case analysis, presentation, or business plan. Learners can save time and money by building an online coursepack using BCRC InfoMarks. It links learners directly to the assigned reading without the inconvenience of library reserves, permissions, or printed materials.

Visit **http://bcrc.swlearning.com** or contact your local Cengage Learning sales representative to learn more about this powerful tool and how the BCRC can save valuable time for both instructors and learners.

CengageNOW

This powerful and fully integrated online teaching and learning system provides you with flexibility and control; saves valuable time and improves outcomes. Students benefit by having choices in the way they learn through our unique personalized learning path. All this is made possible by CengageNOW!

- Homework, assignable and automatically graded
- Integrated eBook
- Personalized Learning Paths
- Interactive Course Assignments
- Assessment Options including **AACSB learning standards achievement reporting**
- Test Delivery
- Course Management Tools, including Grade Book
- WebCT and Blackboard Integration

Speak with your South-Western/Cengage sales representative about integrating CengageNOW into your courses!

ACKNOWLEDGMENTS

We express our sincere and grateful appreciation to the following individuals who provided thoughtful reviews and useful suggestions for improving this edition of *Principle of Organizational Behavior*. Their insights were critical in making a number of important revisions.

Eileen Albright, *Cinemark Theaters*
Lucinda Blue, *Strayer University*
Alicia Boisnier, *State University of New York at Buffalo*
Rupert Campbell, *St. Joseph's College*
Robin Cheramie, *Kennesaw State University*
Cecily Cooper, *University of Miami*
David Ford, *University of Texas at Dallas*
Lynda Fuller, *Wilmington College*
Mary Rose Hart, *Rogers State College*
Amy Henley, *Kennesaw State University*
Peter Heslin, *Southern Methodist University*
Homer Johnson, *Loyola University, Chicago*
Howard Johnson, *Loew's Corporation*
Bill Joyce, *Dartmouth College*
David Lei, *Southern Methodist University*
Morgan R. Milner, *Eastern Michigan University*

Padmakuma Nair, *University of Texas at Dallas*
Rhonda Palladi, *Georgia State University*
William Reisel, *St. John's University*
Ralph Sorrentino, *Deloitte Consulting*
Alesia Stanley, *Wayland Baptist University*
Barbara Thomas, *Hewlett-Packard*
Roger Volkema, *American University*
William Walker, *University of Houston*

For their assistance with the previous edition, we would like to thank the following individuals:

Jason Colquitt, *University of Florida*
Humberto Gutierrez-Olvera, *CompUSA*
Sue Hammond, *Thin Book Publishing*
Karl O. Magnusen, *Florida International University*
Tom Nevant, *Deep South Insurance Company*
Stephen D. Schuster, *California State University, Northridge*
J. Daniel Sherman, *University of Alabama, Huntsville*
Sydne W. Tustison, *Columbia College*
Don VandeWalle, *Southern Methodist University*

For their valuable professional guidance and collegial support, we sincerely thank the following individuals who served on the team responsible for this edition:

- Michele Rhoades, our excellent editor, who worked with us in framing the revisions for this edition
- Erin Berger, our talented and dedicated developmental editor, who worked with us on all facets of this edition and also provided a key interface with the authors of the various supplements
- Lorretta Palagi, our outstanding copyeditor, who improved the flow and readability of the text
- Pat Cosgrove and Marge Bril, our production editors, who so deftly handled the myriad issues in the production process
- Clint Kernen, our marketing manager, who provided the fine leadership in presenting this edition to potential adopters
- Tina Potter, John Slocum's associate at Southern Methodist University, who superbly supported manuscript preparation
- Argie Butler, Don Hellriegel's associate at Texas A&M University, who creatively designed and developed the PowerPoint slides for this edition and superbly supported manuscript preparation.

John Slocum acknowledges his colleagues at Southern Methodist University, especially Tom (aka "The Lion") Perkowski, for their constructive inputs and reviews. Also, special thanks are extended to Al Niemi, dean of the Cox School, for his intellectual support and warm friendship. To all of the executive MBA students who listened to countless stories and wrote some cases for this book, John is forever grateful. John also thanks his golfing group at Stonebriar Country Club (Cecil Ewell, Jack Kennedy, Ken Haigler, and Barry Sullivan) for delaying tee-times so that he could finish this project.

Finally, we celebrate the 12th edition, some 32 years after the publication of our first edition in 1976. We thank the many hundreds of reviewers, adopters, students, and others who have supported the development of these 12 editions for the past three decades. Moreover, Don and John thank each other for being close friends since 1962. We met each other in an industrial relations course during our master's days at Kent State University in 1962 and are still close and special friends. It's been a unique and remarkable lifetime of experiences for both of us. During that time, Don and Lois raised three daughters who now are raising 12 children. Don remains happily married to Lois, his first love. John and Gail raised three sons who are now raising seven children. John remains happily married to Gail. We are grateful for their love and support over these many years.

Don Hellriegel expresses his appreciation to his colleagues at Texas A&M University who collectively create a work environment that nurtures his continued learning and professional development. In particular, the learning environment fostered by Jerry Strawser, now Interim Executive Vice President and Provost, and by Duane Ireland, former head of the Management Department and now editor of the *Academy of Management Journal*, is gratefully acknowledged. In the latter months of developing this revision, Murray Barrick, head of the Management Department, and Ricky Griffin, Interim Dean, continued to nourish a positive and learning-based work environment.

John W. Slocum, Jr., *Southern Methodist University*

Don Hellriegel, *Texas A&M University*

John W. Slocum, Jr.

John W. Slocum, Jr., is the O. Paul Corley Professor of Organizational Behavior at the Edwin L. Cox School of Business, Southern Methodist University, Dallas, Texas. He has also taught on the faculties of the University of Washington, Penn State University, the Ohio State University, the International University of Japan, and Dartmouth's Amos Tuck School. He holds a B.B.A. from Westminster College, a M.B.A. from Kent State University, and a Ph.D. in organizational behavior from the University of Washington.

Professor Slocum has held a number of positions in professional societies, including President of the Eastern Academy of Management in 1973-1974, the 39th President of the Academy of Management in 1983-1984, and Editor of the *Academy of Management Journal* from 1979-1981. He is a Fellow of the Academy of Management, Decision Science Institute, and the Pan-Pacific Institute. He has been awarded the Alumni Citation for Professional Accomplishment by Westminster College, and the Nicolas Salgo, Rotunda, and Executive MBA Outstanding Teaching Awards at SMU. Currently he serves as Co-Editor of the *Journal of World Business* and the *Journal of Leadership and Organizational Behavior*, Associate Editor for *Organizational Dynamics*, and is a member of the editorial review board of the *Leadership Quarterly*. He has authored or co-authored more than 127 journal articles.

Professor Slocum has served as a consultant to such organizations as Aramark, OxyChem, Southwest Real Estate Corporation, Celanese, Pier 1, NASA, Pfizer Corporation, Bayer Corporation, Brakke Consulting, and KeySpan Energy. He is a regular speaker in senior executive development programs sponsored by Lockheed Martin Corporation, the Governor of Texas, Oklahoma State University, University of Oklahoma, and Wuhan University, among others. He is currently on the Board of Directors of Kisco Senior Living, The Winston School of Dallas, GoToLearn (a nonprofit corporation), ViewCast Corporation of Plano, Texas, and the School of Business Management at the Bandung Institute of Technology in Indonesia.

Don Hellriegel

Don Hellriegel is Emeritus Professor of Management within the Mays Business School at Texas A&M University. He received his B.S. and M.B.A. from Kent State University and his Ph.D. from the University of Washington. Dr. Hellriegel has been a member of the faculty at Texas A&M since 1975 and has served on the faculties of the Pennsylvania State University and the University of Colorado.

His research interests include corporate entrepreneurship, the effects of organizational environments, managerial cognitive styles, and organizational innovation and strategic management processes. His research has been published in a number of leading journals.

Professor Hellriegel served as Vice President and Program Chair of the Academy of Management (1986), President Elect (1987), President (1988), and Past President (1989). In September 1999, he was elected to a three-year term as Dean of the Fellows Group of the Academy of Management. He served a term as Editor of the *Academy of Management Review* and served as a member of the Board of Governors of the Academy of Management (1979-1981 and 1982-1989). Dr. Hellriegel has performed many other leadership roles, among which include President, Eastern Academy of Management; Division Chair, Organization and Management Theory Division; President, Brazos County United Way; Co-Consulting Editor, *West Series in Management*; Head (1976-1980 and 1989-1994), Department of Management (TAMU); Interim Dean, Executive Associate Dean (1995-2000), Mays School of Business (TAMU); and Interim Executive Vice Chancellor (TAMUS).

He has consulted with a variety of groups and organizations, including 3DI, Sun Ship Building, Penn Mutual Life Insurance, Texas A&M University System, Ministry of Industry and Commerce (Nation of Kuwait), Ministry of Agriculture (Nation of Dominican Republic), AACSB, and Texas Innovation Group.

PART 1

LEARNING ABOUT ORGANIZATIONAL BEHAVIOR

CHAPTER 1 **Organizational Behavior and Key Competencies**

CHAPTER

1

Organizational Behavior and Key Competencies

Learning Goals

When you have finished studying the chapter, you should be able to:

1. Describe the framework for learning about organizational behavior.
2. Explain the self competency and its importance to effectiveness.
3. Explain the communication competency and its importance to effectiveness.
4. Explain the diversity competency and its contribution to effectiveness.
5. Explain the ethics competency and its importance to effectiveness.
6. Explain the across cultures competency and its importance to effectiveness.
7. Explain the teams competency and its importance to effectiveness.
8. Explain the change competency and its importance to effectiveness.

Learning from Experience

JOHN YOKOYAMA, PIKE PLACE FISH MARKET

In 1985, John Yokoyama, the owner of Pike Place Fish Market, and his employees committed themselves to becoming *World Famous* Pike Place Fish Market. Yokoyama's business is located in Pike Place Market, an outdoor market overlooking the waterfront in the downtown area of Seattle.

With his business at a crisis point, Yokoyama had contacted Jim Bergquist, founder of bizFutures Consulting Company, for advice. The two of them decided to create an extraordinary vision for Pike Place Fish Market. They asked some significant questions: What's beyond economic survival of the business? Can the people in a company intentionally create their own future? What happens if you truly empower your employees? Can a company make a difference in the quality of life for people?

Much has happened since those initial meetings. Pike Place Fish became *World Famous* Pike Place Fish Market. It is a dynamic, fast-paced place that's fun for both its customers and its associates. The antics of the fish-flinging staff have become the highlight of the Pike Place Market. The business has been featured on NBC's *Frasier*, MTV's *Real World*, and ABC's *Good Morning America*. The "low-flying fish" have been captured on film and immortalized in print by filmmakers and journalists from all over the world.

John Yokoyama and Jim Bergquist believe that human beings are powerful and creative. They believe that starting and running an organization is fundamentally a creative endeavor, probably more akin to conducting an orchestra or coaching a sports team than it is to operating a machine. From this basic belief, they and their associates developed some underlying principles. Four of them are central to Pike Place Fish Market:

- The *principle of personal power*—empowering associates that allows them to take personal responsibility for the whole job.
- The *principle of being-in-alignment*—based on a common purpose that honors diversity of thought, creates enormous synergy, and leads to ongoing breakthroughs.

LEARNING CONTENT

For more information on Pike Place Fish Market, visit the organization's home page at www.pikeplacefish.com.

- The *principles of vision-in-action*—being guided by a vision of possibility; having a powerful purpose that gives meaning to people's lives and work; the soul of our organization.
- The *principle of transformation*—our situations and circumstances may not be nearly as set in stone as we think they are. They may in fact be far more malleable than we ever realized.

These principles can be applied in many organizations, both small and large.

The company is very profitable and now has a successful and inviting online store (www.pikeplacefish.com/store). Over a 20-year period, its sales volume has increased by a factor of 4, and its employees are working in the same 1,200 square feet they've always occupied. In terms of sales per square foot, finding a comparable retail operation anywhere would be difficult. Since John Yokoyama committed to empowering his employees and including them in the running of Pike Place Fish Market, his cost of doing business has dropped nearly 25 percent. Each individual in the company has taken personal responsibility for company profitability, and they share in it. They like to win. They take it personally.[1]

John Yokoyama is a unique person and Pike Place Fish Market is a unique organization. We point out in this chapter and throughout the book that the principles and practices of Yokoyama and this firm reflect the latest thinking and perspectives in organizational behavior.

One theme of this book is to demonstrate that there are no easy or complete answers as to why people and organizations function smoothly or fail to do so. Our goal is to assist you in learning how to understand the behavior of individuals in organizations. This will guide you through your career in addressing organizational and behavioral issues and developing ways to resolve them.

Organizational behavior *is the study of individuals and groups within an organizational context, and the study of internal processes and practices as they influence the effectiveness of individuals, teams, and organizations.* The Organizational Behavior Division of the Academy of Management, the leading professional association dedicated to creating and disseminating knowledge about management and organizations, identifies the major topics of organizational behavior as follows:

> *individual characteristics such as beliefs, values and personality; individual processes such as perception, motivation, decision making, judgment, commitment and control; group characteristics such as size, composition and structural properties; group processes such as decision making and leadership; organizational processes and practices such as goal setting, appraisal, feedback, rewards, and performance, turnover, absenteeism, and stress.*[2]

We address all of these topics and more in this book.

An overarching theme of this book is to demonstrate the importance of organizational behavior to you and your own effectiveness. You are or probably will be an employee of an organization—and in all likelihood of several organizations—during your career. You may eventually become a team leader, a manager, or an executive. Studying organizational behavior will help you attain the knowledge and competencies needed to be an effective employee, team leader, manager, and/or executive. The knowledge and competencies that you acquire will help you diagnose, understand, explain, and act on what is happening around you in your job.

In the first section of this chapter, we introduce our general learning framework for enhancing individual, leader, team, and organizational effectiveness. In the remaining sections of this chapter, we explain each of the seven key competencies that are woven into the chapters throughout the book.

LEARNING FRAMEWORK

Learning Goal

1. Describe the framework for learning about organizational behavior.

The long-term effectiveness of an organization is determined by its ability to anticipate, manage, and respond to changes in its environment. Shareholders, unions, employees, financial institutions, and government agencies, among others, exert numerous and ever-changing pressures, demands, and expectations on the organization. The seven competencies presented in this chapter are linked to the actions of managers and employees. Throughout this book, therefore, we discuss the relationships among these various competencies and organizational behavior in general.

The framework for learning about organizational behavior and improving the effectiveness of employees, teams, and organizations consists of four basic components: (1) the key competencies that underlie and integrate the next three components, (2) the individual in organizations, (3) leaders and teams in organizations, and (4) the organization itself, as shown in Figure 1.1. This figure suggests that these components are not independent of each other. The relationships among them are much too dynamic—in terms of variety and change—to define them as laws or rules. As we discuss each component here and throughout this book, the dynamics and complexities of organizational behavior will become clear. Most of this chapter, which represents Part 1, focuses on explaining each of the seven key competencies that are developed and illustrated throughout the book.

FIGURE 1.1 Learning Framework for Increasing Your Effectiveness

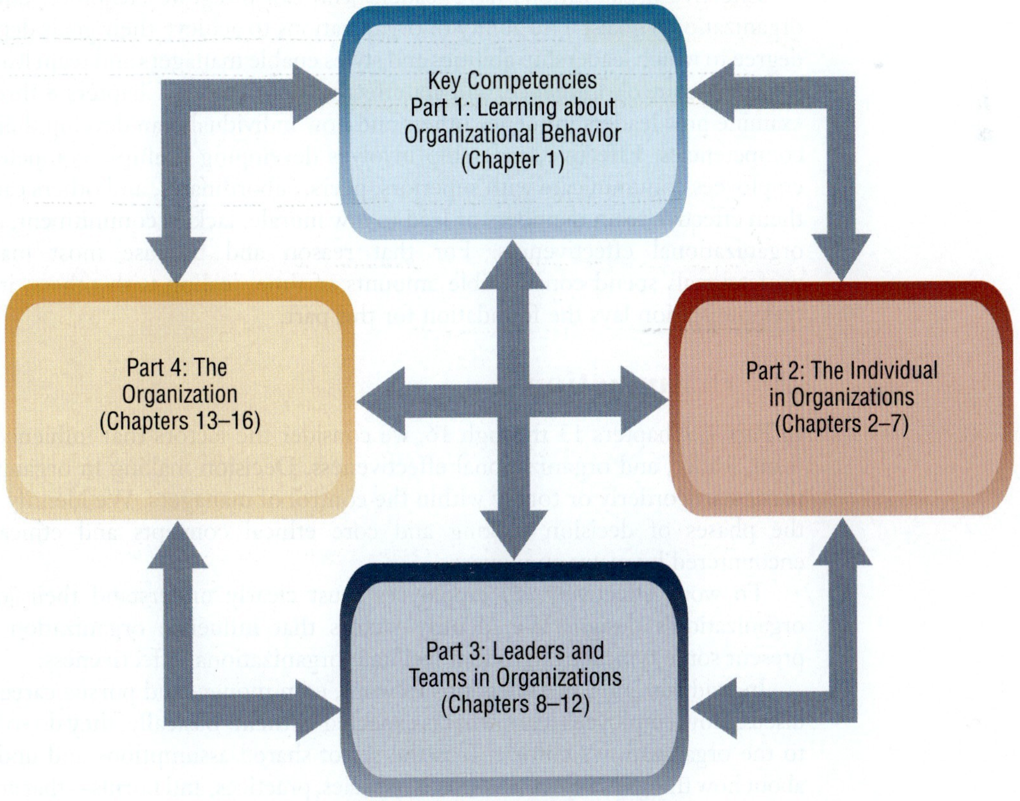

The Individual in Organizations

Each individual makes assumptions about those with whom she or he works or spends time in leisure activities. To some extent, these assumptions influence a person's behavior toward others. An effective employee understands what affects her or his own behavior before attempting to influence the behaviors of others. In Part 2, Chapters 2 through 7, we focus on the behavior, decisions, attitudes, personality, and effectiveness of each individual. The individual is the starting point of organizational effectiveness. Understanding the individual is crucial for enhancing personal, team, leadership, and organizational effectiveness. Each person is a physiological system composed of various subsystems—digestive, nervous, circulatory, and reproductive—and a psychological system composed of various subsystems—attitudes, perceptions, learning capabilities, personality, needs, feelings, and values. In Part 2, we concentrate on the individual's psychological system. Both internal and external factors shape a person's behavior on the job. Among others, internal factors include learning ability, motivation, perception, attitudes, personality, and values. Among the external factors that affect a person's behavior are the organization's reward system, groups and teams, managerial leadership styles, organizational culture and the organization's design. We examine these and other factors in Parts 3 and 4.

Leaders and Teams in Organizations

Being inherently social, an individual generally doesn't choose to live or work alone. Most of the individual's time is spent interacting with others. Each person is born into a family, worships in groups, works in teams, and plays in groups. Much of a person's identity is based on the ways in which other people and groups perceive and treat that person. For these reasons—and because many managers and employees spend considerable amounts of time interacting with others—a variety of competencies are usually vital to each person in an organization.

Effective organizations have leaders who can integrate customer, employee, and organizational goals. The ability of organizations to achieve their goals depends on the degree to which leadership abilities and styles enable managers and team leaders to plan, organize, control, influence, and act effectively. In Part 3, Chapters 8 through 12, we examine how leaders influence others and how individuals can develop their leadership competencies. Effective leadership involves developing multiple competencies. How employees communicate with superiors, peers, subordinates, and others can help make them effective team members or lead to low morale, lack of commitment, and reduced organizational effectiveness. For that reason and because most managers and professionals spend considerable amounts of time dealing with others, interpersonal communication lays the foundation for this part.

The Organization

In Part 4, Chapters 13 through 16, we consider the factors that influence individual, team, leader, and organizational effectiveness. Decision making in organizations isn't particularly orderly or totally within the control of managers. We identify and explore the phases of decision making and core ethical concepts and ethical dilemmas encountered by many employees.

To work effectively, all employees must clearly understand their jobs and the organization's design. We identify factors that influence organization design and present some typical designs that facilitate organizational effectiveness.

Individuals enter organizations to work, earn money, and pursue career goals. We discuss how employees learn what is expected of them. Basically, they do so by exposure to the organization's culture. It is the set of shared assumptions and understandings about how things really work—that is, policies, practices, and norms—that are important to supporting, or perhaps diminishing, individual, team, or organizational effectiveness.

The management of change involves adapting an organization to the demands of the environment and modifying the actual behaviors of employees. We explore the dynamics of organizational change and present several basic strategies for achieving change to improve organizational effectiveness.

Key Competencies

Our first component in Figure 1.1 is key competencies. These competencies are the focus of this chapter. The seven competencies presented serve as an underlying foundation to the other three components and means of integrating them throughout the book.

John Yokoyama developed a mosaic of competencies over time that enabled him to successfully lead Pike Place Fish Market. A **competency** *is an interrelated cluster of knowledge, skills, and abilities needed by an individual to be effective.* A number of competencies can be identified as important to the effectiveness of most organizations.[3] We focus on seven key competencies that significantly affect the behavior and effectiveness of each individual, team, and organization. These particular competencies are important to the effectiveness of virtually all employees, not just those in managerial and leadership roles. One of the goals of this book is to define, describe, and illustrate how the seven key competencies can be used by you and others in organizations. We weave these ideas into the discussion of organizational behavior and effectiveness throughout.

One goal of this book is to help you further develop these seven competencies, which are identified in Figure 1.2. Before reading further, we invite you to assess yourself in

FIGURE 1.2 Key Competencies for Effectiveness

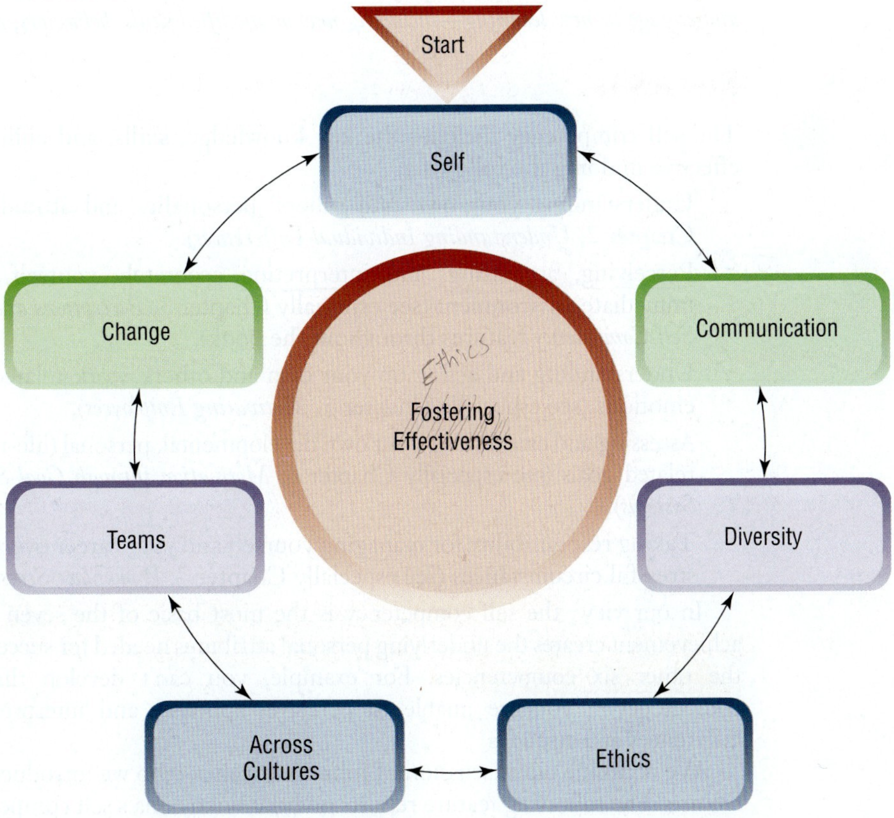

these seven key competencies. Go to the end of this chapter and complete the Key Competencies Self-Assessment Inventory on pages 28–30. The double-headed arrows in Figure 1.2 indicate that these competencies are interrelated and that drawing rigid boundaries between them isn't feasible. We discuss them in considerable depth in specific chapters.

Many leading organizations use individual-based competency frameworks, including the types of competencies we present here. They are used to select, develop, assess, and promote employees. A few of these organizations include American Express, Bank of America, Exxon-Mobil, John Hancock, Merck & Co., and AT&T.[4] Why do they use competency models? For years, many top-level managers believed that there were two ways to think about identifying successful individuals. From a selection perspective, the approach was to identify the common characteristics of effective managers and professionals and try to identify the employees who possessed these characteristics early in their career. The other perspective was to identify those employees who management thought were best able to take advantage of developmental opportunities, if provided. The competency-based approach identifies individuals who can develop or possess key competencies and provides them with challenging opportunities to learn. This is what we have tried to do in this edition of our book. Throughout the book, we give you opportunities to learn how successful leaders, employees, and organizations use these seven key competencies. The successful outcome of using this book is your development of the competencies needed for you to be an effective professional or manager.

Learning Goal

2. Explain the self competency and its importance to effectiveness.

SELF COMPETENCY

The self competency *includes the knowledge, skills, and abilities to assess your own strengths and weaknesses, set and pursue professional and personal goals; balance work and personal life; and engage in new learning—including new or modified skills, behaviors, and attitudes.*

Key KSAs

The self competency includes the key **k**nowledge, **s**kills, and **a**bilities (KSAs) to be effective in doing the following:

- Understanding your own and others' personality and attitudes (see especially Chapter 2, *Understanding Individual Differences*).
- Perceiving, appraising, and interpreting accurately yourself, others, and the immediate environment (see especially Chapter 3, *Perceptions and Attributions*, and *Self Competency* features throughout the book).
- Understanding and acting on your own and others' work-related motivations and emotions (see especially Chapter 5, *Motivating Employees*).
- Assessing and establishing your own developmental, personal (life-related), and work-related goals (see especially Chapter 6, *Motivation through Goal Setting and Reward Systems*).
- Taking responsibility for managing yourself and your career over time and through stressful circumstances (see especially Chapter 7, *Workplace Stress and Aggression*).

In our view, the self competency is the most basic of the seven competencies. Its achievement creates the underlying personal attributes needed for successfully developing the other six competencies. For example, you can't develop the communication competency if you are unable to perceive, appraise, and interpret your individual differences and attitudes.

We continue our discussion of John Yokoyama, who we introduced in the opening feature. The following feature reports on how Yokoyama's self competency was formed by him over time. As you will see, he was not always effective.[5]

Self Competency

John Yokoyama's Development Journey

In 1958, John Yokoyama began working at Pike Place Fish Market. In 1965, owner Bill Constantine, who had inherited the business from his father, offered to sell it to Yokoyama. Yokoyama states: "[Constantine] didn't like the business and really wanted out, but no one would buy it from him. He tried to sell it for $10,000 for four years, and finally offered it to me for $3,500; $350 down and $350 a month, because that was all I had."

Yokoyama became a business owner at 25, and was in competition with five other fish markets at Pike Place. He knew that his market was third in volume of sales, which wasn't good. He states: "At first, I ran it the only way I knew, by yelling and screaming at employees, like my father did. Then I almost went into bankruptcy and I had to sell everything I owned to get out of a $300,000 hole."

By 1990, Yokoyama wasn't financially able to hire any new employees, but was unable to resist the offer of business consultant Jim Bergquist. Yokoyama comments: "He proposed that I hire him to create a new philosophy for Pike Place Fish Market, and he wanted $2,000 a month. Then he said that if he didn't earn us [the fish market] his wages within a year or so, we could fire him. He's still with us today."

Bergquist and Yokoyama brainstormed with all the employees to see what they thought the company should do. "One guy said: 'Let's be world famous!' and we thought he was crazy," said Yokoyama. "But then we said, 'Why not go for it?" so we started writing 'world famous' on all our bags and boxes. In order to create the possibility of success, you have to work from the future to the present."

Yokoyama said he started making a 180-degree turn from being a yeller and a screamer to being a listener. "It was tough, and took me a year to transform from who I was as a human being. It was a process for the whole business and employees, because you can't force people to change; it's up to them. We noticed that the people who didn't commit to our vision left on their own."

Yokoyama admits that before this transformation he behaved like an angry dictator and created a hostile work environment that caused high turnover. Once he understood the creative power of his people and the importance of offering a place where they could make a difference, the fish market's mediocre profits began to soar. People were attracted to the fun, energetic atmosphere.

For more information on John Yokoyama and the Pike Place Fish Market, visit the organization's home page at www.pikeplacefish.com.

Career Development

A career *is a sequence of work-related experiences occupied by a person during a lifetime.*[6] It embraces attitudes and behaviors that are part of ongoing work-related tasks and experiences. The popular view of a career usually is restricted to the idea of moving up the ladder in an organization. At times, this opportunity is no longer available to many people because of downsizing, mergers, and the increasing tendency of management to place the responsibility on employees to develop their own competencies. A person may remain at the same level, acquiring and developing new competencies, and have a successful career without ever being promoted. A person also can build a career by moving among various jobs in different fields, such as accounting, management information systems, and marketing, or among organizations such as Toyota, IBM, and Nike. Thus, a career encompasses not only traditional work experiences but also the opportunity for career alternatives, individual choices, and individual experiences.[7] Let's briefly consider five aspects of a career:

- The nature of a career in itself doesn't imply success or failure or fast or slow advancement. Career success or failure is best determined by the individual, rather than by others.

- No absolute standards exist for evaluating a career. Career success or failure is related to a person's self-concept, goals, and competencies. An individual should evaluate her own career goals and progress in terms of what is personally meaningful and satisfying. Unfortunately, too often the individual falls into the trap of comparing his own career progress to that of others. This can undermine the person's experience of career success.
- An individual should examine a career both subjectively and objectively. Subjective elements of a career include one's values, attitudes, personality, and motivations, which may change over time. Objective elements of a career include job choices, positions held, income earned, challenges overcome, and competencies developed.
- Career development *involves making decisions about an occupation and engaging in activities to attain career goals.* The central idea in the career development process is time. The shape and direction of a person's career over time are influenced by many factors (e.g., the economy, availability of jobs, skill acquisition, personal characteristics, family status, and job history).[8]
- Cultural factors play a role in careers. Cultural norms in countries such as Japan, the Philippines, and Mexico also influence the direction of a person's career. By U.S. standards, women are discriminated against as managers in these cultures. In India and South Korea, social status and educational background largely determine an individual's career paths.

Ralph Waldo Emerson's classic essay "Self-Reliance" offers good advice for a person's career: "Trust thyself." To be successful, you need to commit yourself to a lifetime of learning, including the development of a career plan. A career plan *is the individual's choice of occupation, organization, and career path.*

LEADER INSIGHT

I devote time to asking myself: Am I doing enough mentoring? Who at Ogilvy do I have to worry about? Who needs another challenge? Who seems a little stale? Who needs a new view on life or a new area office to run?
Shelly Lazarus, CEO, Ogilvy & Mather Worldwide

Learning Goal

3. Explain the communication competency and its importance to effectiveness.

COMMUNICATION COMPETENCY

The communication competency *includes the knowledge, skills, and abilities to use all the modes of transmitting, understanding, and receiving ideas, thoughts, and feelings—verbal, listening, nonverbal, written, electronic, and the like—for accurately transferring and exchanging information and emotions.*[9] This competency may be thought of as the circulatory system that nourishes the other competencies. Just as arteries and veins provide for the movement of blood in a person, communication allows the exchange of information, thoughts, ideas, and feelings.

The communication competency became one of the strengths that John Yokoyama developed over time. You will recall that early in his career it had been a major weakness. Yokoyama commented, "At first, I ran it the only way I knew by yelling and screaming at employees, like my father did.[10]

Key KSAs

The communication competency includes the key knowledge, skills, and abilities to be effective in doing the following:

- Conveying information, ideas, and emotions to others in such a way that they are received as intended. This ability is strongly influenced by the describing skill—*identifying concrete, specific examples of behavior and its effects.* This skill also includes recognizing that too often individuals don't realize that they are not being clear and accurate in what they say, resulting from a tendency to jump quickly to generalizations and judgments (see especially Chapter 8, *Fostering Interpersonal Communication in Organizations*, and *Communication Competency* features throughout the book).

- Providing constructive feedback to others (see especially Chapter 8).
- Engaging in active listening—*the process of integrating information and emotions in a search for shared meaning and understanding*. Active listening requires the use of the questioning skill—*the ability to ask for information and opinions in a way that gets relevant, honest, and appropriate responses*. This skill helps to bring relevant information and emotions into the dialogue and reduce misunderstandings, regardless of whether the parties agree (see especially Chapters 8 and 12, *Managing Conflict and Negotiating Effectively*).
- Using and interpreting nonverbal communication—*facial expressions, body movements, and physical contact that are often used to send messages*. The empathizing skill *refers to detecting and understanding another person's values, motives, and emotions*. It is especially important in nonverbal communication and active listening. The empathizing skill helps to reduce tension and increase trust and sharing (see especially Chapter 3, *Perceptions and Attributions*, and Chapter 8).
- Engaging in verbal communication *effectively—presenting ideas, information and emotions to others, either one-to-one or in groups*. Recall John Yokoyama's discussion of his ineffective communication with his employees and his hard work to improve his verbal communications. We provide the opportunity for you to apply this skill in the Experiential Exercise and Case section at the end of many chapters.
- Engaging in written communication *effectively—the ability to transfer data, information, ideas, and emotions by means of reports, letters, memos, notes, e-mail messages, and the like*.
- Using a variety of computer-based (electronic) resources, such as e-mail and the Internet. Through an array of computer-based information technologies, the Internet directly links organizations and their employees to customers, suppliers, information sources, the public, and millions of individuals worldwide. We help you develop this skill throughout the book by presenting numerous Internet addresses and encouraging you to learn more about the organizations, issues, and people discussed.

In the following feature, we provide insight into the communication of Tony Dungy and Lovie Smith, both head football coaches in the National Football League.[11]

Communication Competency

Tony Dungy and Lovie Smith

It has been suggested that the 2007 National Football League Super Bowl should be required viewing for managers who think screaming at employees is the best way to motivate them—or simply their prerogative as bosses. They didn't see that kind of behavior, as the Indianapolis Colts played the Chicago Bears for football's highest trophy. The Colts' head coach, Tony Dungy, and the Bears' Lovie Smith don't curse or sarcastically chew out players, which makes them stand out in the National Football League.

The two men—the first African Americans to lead Super Bowl teams—became close friends when Dungy, formerly head coach for the Tampa Bay Buccaneers, hired Smith as an assistant. Both believe they can get their teams to compete more fiercely and score more

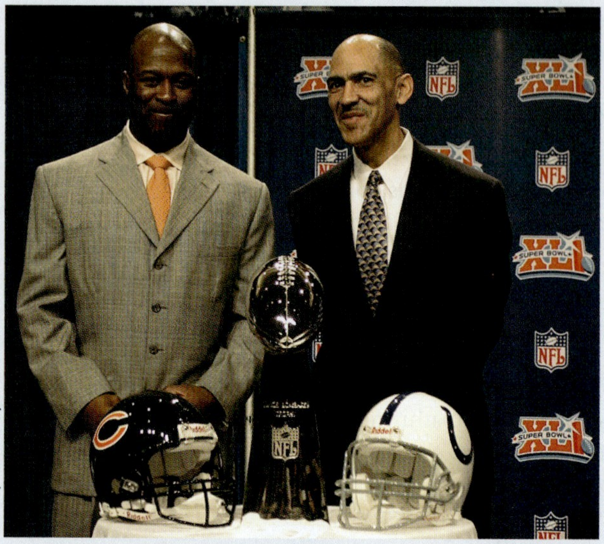

© Gary C. Caskey/UPI/Landov

Chicago Bears head coach Lovie Smith (L) and Indianapolis Colts head coach Tony Dungy (R) believe they can get better team performance by treating players with respect.

touchdowns by giving directives calmly and treating players with respect.

This doesn't mean they aren't demanding or don't push hard. Dungy has a grading system that counts players' "loafs." If someone isn't running at full speed, or eases up or fails to hit an opponent when he could have, those are loafs, and it's hard to get through a game without getting at least one.

When Smith, who uses the same system, became the Bears' head coach, he told players to lift more weights and eat better because he wanted a slimmer, faster team. When Smith gets mad, he stares straight ahead in silence. His players call it "the Lovie Look" and say it's more frightening—and more of a warning to play better—than a torrent of angry words.

During one interview for a head coaching position when an owner asked if Dungy would make the team the most important thing in his life, he said no, "I figured I probably wouldn't get that job, and I didn't. I think your faith is more important than your job, family is more important than your job. We all know that's the way it should be, but we're kind of afraid to say that sometimes." Dungy continues "Lovie Smith and I aren't afraid to say it. Both of us run our teams in the same way. The Colts and Bears play tough, disciplined football even though there's not a lot of profanity from the coaches, there's none of the win-at-all-costs atmosphere. I think for two guys to show you can win that way is important for the country to see."

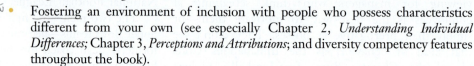

For more information on Lovie Smith of the Bears and Tony Dungy of the Indianapolis Colts, visit the organizations' home pages at www.chicagobears.com and www.colts.com.

Learning Goal

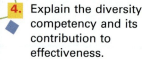

4. Explain the diversity competency and its contribution to effectiveness.

DIVERSITY COMPETENCY

The diversity competency *includes the knowledge, skills, and abilities to value unique individual and group characteristics, embrace such characteristics as potential sources of organizational strength, and appreciate the uniqueness of each individual.*[12] This competency also involves the ability to help people work effectively together even though their interests and backgrounds may be quite different. At Pike Place Fish Market, the diversity competency is based on a common purpose that honors diversity of thought.

Key KSAs

The diversity competency includes the key knowledge, skills, and abilities to be effective in doing the following:

- Fostering an environment of inclusion with people who possess characteristics different from your own (see especially Chapter 2, *Understanding Individual Differences;* Chapter 3, *Perceptions and Attributions*; and diversity competency features throughout the book).
- Learning from those with different characteristics, experiences, perspectives, and backgrounds. Diversity of thought and behavior is vital to stimulating creativity and

innovation (see especially Chapter 13, *Making Ethical and Managerial Decisions*, and Chapter 16, *Guiding Organizational Change*).

- Embracing and developing personal tendencies—such as conscientiousness and attitudes that demonstrate respect for people of other cultures and races—that support diversity in the workplace and elsewhere (see especially Chapter 2).
- Communicating and personally practicing a commitment to work with individuals and team members because of their talents and contributions, regardless of their personal attributes (see especially Chapter 11, *Developing and Leading Teams*).
- Providing leadership—*walk the talk*—in confronting obvious bias, promoting inclusion, and seeking win–win or compromise solutions to power struggles and conflicts that appear to be based on diversity issues (see especially Chapter 10, *Leading Effectively: New Perspectives*, and Chapter 12, *Managing Conflict and Negotiating Effectively*).
- Applying governmental laws and regulations as well as organizational policies and regulations concerning diversity as they relate to a person's position.

The case for the diversity competency within the United States is well stated by Elizabeth Pathy Salett, president of the National MultiCultural Institute, headquartered in Washington, D.C. She comments:

> *Multiculturalism is an acknowledgment that the United States is a diverse nation and does not assume that any cultural tradition is ideal or perfect. It looks to the equitable participation of all individuals in society. It assumes that our nation can be both unified and diverse, that we can be proud of our heritage and of our individual group identities while at the same time working together on common goals. It is a reciprocal process based on democratic principles and a shared value system.*[13]

Categories of Diversity

As suggested in Figure 1.3, diversity includes many categories and characteristics.[14] Even a single aspect of diversity, such as physical abilities and qualities, contains various characteristics that may affect individual or team behaviors. One challenge for managers is to determine whether those effects (1) deny opportunity and are wasteful and counterproductive, (2) simply reflect a tolerance of differences, or (3) lead to embracing diversity as a value-added organizational resource. A second challenge is to assist in developing individual, team, and organizational competencies—including learning new KSAs and methods of intervention—to value and embrace diversity as a source of creativity and strength.

Figure 1.3 identifies the more common categories of diversity dealt with in organizations. They are subdivided into *primary categories*—genetic characteristics that affect a person's self-image and socialization—and *secondary categories*—learned characteristics that a person acquires and modifies throughout life. As suggested by the arrows, these categories aren't independent. For example, a woman (gender) with children (parental status) is likely to be directly affected by an organization with *family-friendly* or *family-unfriendly* policies and attitudes. An example of a family-unfriendly attitude would be "Your job must always come first if you are to get ahead in this organization."

Primary Categories. The following are brief explanations of the primary categories of diversity. Individuals have relatively little influence over these characteristics.

- *Age*: the number of years a person has been alive and the generation into which the individual was born in the United States (e.g., depression era, baby boomers, generation X born between 1965 and 1977, or generation Y born between 1978 and 1998).

FIGURE 1.3 Selected Categories of Diversity

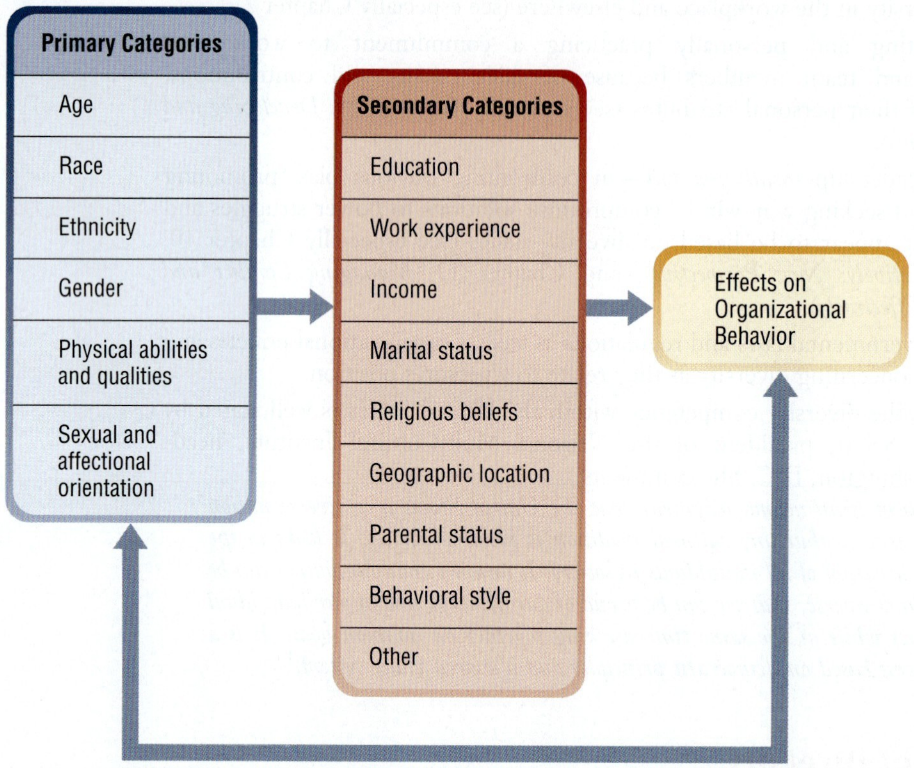

Source: Adapted from Bradford, S. Fourteen dimensions of diversity: Understanding and appreciating differences in the workplace. In J. W. Pfeiffer (ed.), 1996 *Annual: Volume 2, Consulting*. San Diego: Pfeiffer and Associates, 1996, 9–17.

- *Race*: the biological groupings within humankind, representing superficial physical differences, such as eye shape and skin color. Race accounts for less than 1 percent of the difference in a person's genetic heredity.
- *Ethnicity*: identification with a cultural group that has shared traditions and heritage, including national origin, language, religion, food, and customs. Some people identify strongly with these cultural roots; others do not.
- *Gender*: biological sex as determined by XX (female) or XY (male) chromosomes.
- *Physical abilities and qualities*: a variety of characteristics, including body type, physical size, facial features, specific abilities or disabilities, and visible and invisible physical and mental talents or limitations.
- *Sexual and affectional orientation*: feelings of sexual attraction toward members of the same or opposite gender, such as heterosexual, homosexual, or bisexual.

GENERATION GAP STEREOTYPES Let's consider several insights related to generation (age)-related diversity from research published by the Center for Creative Leadership in Greensboro, North Carolina. This research challenges 10 of the stereotypes regarding presumed conflicts between generations. We present 3 of the 10 generation gap stereotypes identified here.[15]

First, the various generations have similar levels of trust in their organization and in upper management: They don't trust them much. Employees of all generations and at all levels trust the people they work with directly (managers, peers, and direct reports) more than they trust higher management in their organizations.

Second, employees from all generations are concerned about the effects of organizational politics on their careers. They are concerned with being recognized for the work they are doing and for getting access to the resources they need to do their job. At the same time, employees know that political skills are a critical component in being able to move up and be effective at higher levels of management.

Third, the stereotype that older employees only want stability in their workplace and younger employees love change is not true. In general, employees from all generations are uncomfortable with change. Only a very few people in the study said they actually liked change! Resistance to change has nothing to do with age. It is all about how they see themselves being impacted by the change.

We are not claiming there are no differences between the generations.[16] Rather, on a number of important workplace issues, the presumed conflicts and differences are more stereotypes than real.

Secondary Categories. The following are brief explanations of the secondary categories of diversity. Individuals have relatively more influence over them during their lifetimes by making choices.

- *Education:* the individual's formal and informal learning and training.
- *Work experience:* the employment and volunteer positions the person has held and the variety of organizations for which the person has worked.
- *Income:* the economic conditions in which people grow up and their current economic status.
- *Marital status:* the person's situation as never married, married, widowed, or divorced.
- *Religious beliefs:* fundamental teachings received about deities and values acquired from formal or informal religious practices.
- *Geographic location:* the location(s) in which the person was raised or spent a significant part of her life, including types of communities and urban areas versus rural areas.
- *Parental status:* having or not having children and the circumstances in which the children are raised, such as single parenting and two-adult parenting.
- *Behavioral style:* tendency of the individual to think, feel, or act in a particular way.

We discuss many of the primary categories of diversity throughout the book. In addition, Diversity Competency features are presented in various chapters throughout the book. In the following feature, we discuss the diversity competency of Patricia Harris and how she leads efforts to foster it throughout McDonald's.[17] There are more than 31,000 local McDonald's restaurants in 100 countries.

Diversity Competency

Patricia Harris, McDonald's Chief Diversity Officer

Patricia Harris has been employed by McDonald's for over 35 years, having started in a secretarial position for the legal department in 1976. She soon applied and was hired for an opening in the human resources department. By 1979, she completed her degree and was offered the position of affirmative action manager. She has been promoted into a number of positions, including vice president of McDonald's USA and global chief diversity officer of McDonald's Corporation in 2006. We review some of her diversity leadership contributions.

Harris is particularly proud that McDonald's received an Equal Employment Opportunity Commission (EEOC) "Freedom to Compete Award" in 2006 as recognition of the company's diversity and inclusion initiatives. The EEOC specifically cited McDonald's employee networks, which include the African-American Council, the Hispanic Employee Network, the Asian Employee Network, the Women's Leadership Network (which is global now), and the Gays, Lesbians and Allies at McDonald's. Each group provides networking opportunities for its members and offers them a way to share ideas with management.

Harris still remembers the first networking meetings she attended as a new employee. Those early sessions were somewhat ad hoc and casual, she says, but they started becoming more formal in the early 1980s. Harris notes: "We're in a different place today. The networks are continuing to evolve. They offer seminars on career management and leadership skills development as well as provide opportunities to network and to share best practices."

McDonald's recognized Harris's work by creating the Pat Harris Diversity Award—only the third time in 50 years at McDonald's that an award has been named for an employee. Given for the first time in 2006, the new award goes to the McDonald's leader each year who has achieved the highest results in meeting his or her department's diversity goals.

In her role as global chief diversity officer, Harris meets with HR leaders from McDonald's restaurants around the world to enlist their help in ensuring that diversity reaches all levels of the organization across the globe. Harris comments: "Diversity has so many dimensions. It means different things in different countries." Harris reports to Rich Floersch, McDonald's executive vice president for human resources. He remarks: "Pat Harris is very well informed, a true student of diversity. She is good at analyzing U.S. diversity principles and applying them in the international market. She's also a good listener who understands the business and the culture very well."

For more information on McDonald's, visit the organization's home page at www.mcdonalds.com/corp.

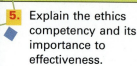

Learning Goal

5. Explain the ethics competency and its importance to effectiveness.

ETHICS COMPETENCY

The ethics competency *includes the knowledge, skills and abilities to incorporate values and principles that distinguish right from wrong in making decisions and choosing behaviors.* Ethics *are the values and principles that distinguish right from wrong.*[18]

Key KSAs

The ethics competency includes the key knowledge, skills and abilities to be effective in doing the following:

- Identifying and describing the principles of ethical decision making and behavior (see especially Chapter 13, *Making Ethical and Managerial Decisions*, and the ethics competency features throughout this book).
- Assessing the importance of ethical issues in considering alternative courses of action. The decision to shop at Sears versus Target is not related to any ethical issue of consequence for most individuals. In contrast, when purchasing a new car, some individuals consider the gasoline mileage an important ethical issue that allows them to make a decision to help reduce air pollution.
- Applying governmental laws and regulations, as well as the employer's rules of conduct, in making decisions. In general, the greater a person's level of responsibilities and authority, the more the person is likely to face increasingly complex and ambiguous ethical issues and dilemmas. For example, an associate at a Target store does not make purchasing decisions from foreign countries that often

involve ethical issues (see especially Chapter 9, *Leading Effectively: Foundations*). The associate has no authority and responsibility in this decision-making area at Target.

- Demonstrating dignity and respect for others in working relationships, such as taking action against discriminatory practices as individually feasible and in terms of a person's position. The manager at a Sears store is more able to stop an employee from showing disrespect to members of a minority group than is a checkout associate in the store (see especially Chapter 10, *Leading Effectively: New Perspectives*).
- Being honest and open in communication, limited only by legal, privacy, and competitive considerations (e.g., do what you say and say what you do). (See especially Chapter 12, *Managing Conflict and Negotiating Effectively*, and Chapter 8, *Fostering Interpersonal Communication in Organizations*).

Top-management leadership, policies and rules, and the prevailing organizational culture can do much to reduce, guide, and help the individual confront and resolve ethical dilemmas.[19] Table 1.1 provides a brief questionnaire that asks you to assess an organization (or manager) that you have worked for with respect to its commitment to various ethical behaviors, practices, and policies.

Table 1.1 **Ethical Practices Questionnaire**

Instructions: Think of an organization for which you have worked or currently work. Respond to the 10 statements that follow the scale in terms of the degree to which you think the organization reflects the behavior, policy, and/or practice in each statement. Use the following 10-point scale, which ranges from 10 (highly descriptive of the organization) to 1 (not at all descriptive). The middle point in the scale, 5, indicates that you are neutral or undecided.

NOT AT ALL DESCRIPTIVE				NEUTRAL					HIGHLY DESCRIPTIVE
1	2	3	4	5	6	7	8	9	10

Record your number next to each statement.

_____ 1. I did not fear retaliation from higher management for reporting misconduct by others.
_____ 2. Management was trusted to do the right thing by me and other employees.
_____ 3. When making important decisions, managers and other employees considered the ethical implications of the alternatives being considered.
_____ 4. There were well-established policies and practices by higher management for dealing honestly with customers.
_____ 5. The core abilities in the managing ethics competency were seen as important and applied consistently by higher management.
_____ 6. I and my coworkers never felt pressured to engage in practices that we found to be questionable or unethical.
_____ 7. My organization had a practice of doing what was right, not just what brought quick profits or other benefits.
_____ 8. The organization's ethics policies and expected behaviors were effectively communicated to all employees.
_____ 9. There were clearly communicated consequences for deviations from or violations of ethics policies and expected behaviors—which were backed up by action in the case of such violations.
_____ 10. High levels of individual performance that were achieved by violating or distorting the organization's ethics policies and expected behaviors were not tolerated.

Results and Interpretation: Sum the point values for items 1 through 10. Totals of 80 to 100 provide indicators of a highly ethical organization. Totals of 61 to 79 suggest needed improvements. Totals of 40 to 60 may suggest confusing and inconsistent ethical signals and practices. Scores of 10 to 40 suggest a highly unethical organization that requires a major transformation.

Ethical Dilemmas

The ethical issues facing managers and other employees have grown significantly in recent years, fueled by public concern about how business is conducted. We develop this point through *Ethics Competency* features throughout the book. Ethical behavior can be difficult to define, especially in a global economy with its varied beliefs and practices. Although ethical behavior in business clearly has a legal component, it involves more than that. Absolutes in one country aren't always applicable in another country.

Managers and employees alike face situations in which there are no clear right or wrong answers. Often, the burden is on each individual to make ethical decisions. An ethical dilemma *occurs when an individual or team must make a decision that involves multiple values*. An ethical dilemma doesn't always involve choosing right over wrong because there may be several competing values. Some ethical dilemmas arise from competitive and time pressures, among other factors.[20] Consider these three real-life examples of ethical dilemmas:

- A customer asked for a product from us today. After telling him our price, he said he couldn't afford it. I know he could get it cheaper from a competitor. Should I tell him about the competitor—or let him go without getting what he needs? What should I do?
- A fellow employee told me that he plans to quit the company in two months and start a new job that has been guaranteed to him. Meanwhile, my manager told me that she wasn't going to give me a new opportunity in our company because she was going to give it to my fellow employee now. What should I do?
- The vice president told me that one of my subordinates is among several to be laid off soon and that I'm not to tell him yet or he might tell the whole organization, which would soon be in an uproar. Meanwhile, I heard from my subordinate that he plans to buy braces for his daughter and new carpet for his house. What should I do?[21]

Ron James is CEO of the Center for Ethical Business Cultures, which is an independent nonprofit organization headquartered in Minneapolis, Minnesota. The center assists business leaders in creating ethical and profitable business cultures. James has served in a variety of executive positions and currently is a member of the board of directors of Best Buy Corporation, Tamarack Funds, Bremer Financial Corporation, and Allina Hospitals and Clinics. The following Ethics Competency feature presents a few of James's perspectives on a corporate ethics survey of more than ten thousand employees at about 3,500 companies.[22]

Ethics Competency

Ron James Fosters Ethical Business Cultures

While senior leaders often establish ethical guidelines, in reality they aren't always reinforcing the norms that they are supposed to be setting. For example, senior leaders tend to consistently emphasize the importance of performance and the bottom line. But if you aren't also emphasizing ethical behavioral messages, then all employees hear is that it's all about the numbers. Get the numbers at all costs, they think—and that causes some to compromise ethics.

Second, compensation, appraisals, and promotions are all based on quantitative results—again, numbers. So employees will think: "If I want to get promoted, then I have to focus on the numbers and not necessarily the behavioral standards." Evidence of that is embodied in our research, where employees answered the question: Can I get ahead in this organization even if I don't live up to the values? About 6 out of 10 employees said yes. Leaders may be *saying* that you have to live up to the values, but the way too many leaders run their companies gives employees the impression that it isn't about how you behave—it's about what you bring in.

There are some companies that say, "Let's do whatever it takes to meet the requirements of the law." There's nothing wrong with that, but you have to recognize that the laws are made up of rules that have been made to address previous situations. It's tough to anticipate future violations that might occur. Companies that invest in building an ethical culture recognize that when new issues arise, people will need an ethical compass that will help them make the right call or at least get help in a gray area. Then, too, ethics are good for the business.

Our research shows that companies that we've identified as having a strong ethical culture have a greater number of employees who have said that they intend to stay at the organization. Besides retention, we found workers at ethical companies to be many times more likely to recommend stock purchases in their companies. Other factors such as teamwork, communication, pride, and emphasis on quality were also found to be rated higher by employees at ethical organizations.

For more information on the Center for Ethical Business Cultures, visit the organization's home page at www.cebcglobal.org.

ACROSS CULTURES COMPETENCY

Learning Goal

6. Explain the across cultures competency and its importance to effectiveness.

The across cultures competency *includes the knowledge, skills, and abilities to recognize and embrace similarities and differences among nations and cultures and then approach key organizational and strategic issues with an open and curious mind.* Culture *is the dominant pattern of living, thinking, feeling, and believing that is developed and transmitted by people, consciously or unconsciously, to subsequent generations.*[23] For a culture to exist, it must

- be shared by the vast majority of the members of a major group or entire society;
- be passed on from generation to generation; and
- shape perceptions, judgments, and feelings as well as subsequent decisions and behavior.[24]

As discussed further in Chapter 2, a key feature of a culture is its cultural values—*those deeply held beliefs that specify general preferences and behaviors and define what is right and wrong.* Cultural values are reflected in a society's morals, customs, and established practices.

Key KSAs

The across cultures competency includes the key knowledge, skills, and abilities to be effective in doing the following:

- Understanding, appreciating, and using the characteristics that make a particular culture unique and are likely to influence a person's behaviors (see especially Chapter 2, *Understanding Individual Differences*, and the *Across Cultures Competency* features throughout the book).
- Identifying and understanding how work-related values, such as individualism and collectivism, influence the choices of individuals and groups in making decisions.
- Understanding and motivating employees with different values and attitudes. These may range from the more individualistic, Western style of work, to paternalistic, non-Western attitudes, to the extreme "the state-will-take-care-of-me" collectivist mind-set.
- Communicating in the language of the country with which the individual has working relationships. This ability is crucial for employees who have ongoing

communications with people whose native language is different from their own.

- Taking assignments in a foreign country or effectively working with those from foreign countries. This ability applies even if the assignment is short term or the person has international responsibilities from the home office.
- Addressing managerial and other issues through a global mind-set—*viewing the environment from a worldwide perspective, always looking for unexpected trends that may create threats or opportunities for a unit or an entire organization*. Some call this the ability to think globally, act locally.

Avoiding Stereotypes

The development of the across cultures competency is useful for explaining, understanding, and relating to individuals or groups with cultural values different than your own. We caution that there are often wide variations of behavior and values by various individuals and groups within a given society.

You need to be wary of stereotyping individuals or groups in a particular society in simple terms and thus glossing over the nuances and complexities of a culture.[25] Furthermore, the specific issues and situations—such as work, family, friends, and recreation—can play a significant role in understanding the impact of different cultural values on behaviors. For example, when Japanese businesspeople develop contracts, they want them to be more general than detailed, as preferred by U.S. managers. They believe that those entering into an agreement are joined together and share something in common; thus they should rely on and trust one another.

The following Across Cultures competency reports on a few of the office experiences of Geoffrey Fowler, a journalist for the *Wall Street Journal* at its Asian headquarters in Hong Kong. Fowler, an American, demonstrates the ability to understand and work in an office culture and setting that is quite different than that found in the United States. We provide excerpts from Fowler's insights.[26]

Across Cultures Competency

Working in a Hong Kong Office

There's a lot that goes on in Chinese workplaces that mystifies—and occasionally embarrasses—the expatriates pouring into China. Chinese people draw the lines between personal and work space differently from Americans. Beyond weight and body shape, office small talk here often includes the size of your apartment and your salary. Sometimes, my Chinese colleagues nap at their desks during lunch.

Some Chinese office characteristics came about because corporations here embrace the idea of company as surrogate family. Many offices have a "tea lady," who spends all day making tea and heating lunches—kind of an office nanny. For Lunar New Year, starting February 18 in 2007, managers give employees red envelopes filled with money, as family elders do, and host a banquet complete with games, prizes and karaoke.

Chinese offices tend to be hierarchical. Employees wouldn't think of calling their manager by his or her first name. So while there are often close relationships between Chinese co-workers, American managers' efforts to get too close to their Chinese subordinates can backfire. Justine Lee, who works for an American manufacturer in Hong Kong, says her American manager caused havoc with an annual ritual of meeting with each of his subordinates individually. His subordinates tried to work out their 'smartest' question a month in advance. It became a big project for the Chinese staff every year, she says. After a couple years, her boss dropped the practice.

© Keith Brofsky/Photodisc/Getty Images

Expatriates working in China should be aware of cultural differences that create unique expectations for office etiquette and behavior.

Of course, there's plenty about American office culture that confuses Chinese employees who join U.S. companies located here. They're baffled by "brown-bag lunch' conferences, during which employees rudely eat while somebody senior is giving a talk. It's rude because it mixes a social event with an official one. "Chinese law firms would not have this kind of lunch," says Qian Wei, who works at a U.S. law firm in Beijing. "Maybe we would go outside to a really good restaurant to drink and chat for a while. But in the U.S., people pay much more attention to efficiency."

For more information on the Wall Street Journal Asia, visit the organization's home page at www.wsj-asia.com.

TEAMS COMPETENCY

Learning Goal

7. Explain the teams competency and its importance to effectiveness.

The teams competency *includes the knowledge, skills, and abilities to develop, support, facilitate, and lead groups to achieve organizational goals.*[27] The components of this competency are developed in several chapters, especially Chapter 11, *Developing and Leading Teams*, and Chapter 12, *Managing Conflict and Negotiating Effectively*, and the *Teams Competency* features presented throughout the book. Of course, the other competencies reviewed in this chapter contribute to the variety of abilities needed to be effective as a team member or leader (as suggested previously in Figure 1.2).

John Yokoyama of Pike Place Fish Market places great emphasis on teamwork. Always mindful of the commitment that each person has made to the company's vision, the employees at Pike Place Fish coach each other. As one fish seller explains:

> *You act differently when you're "being" world famous; you coach each other differently. Any action that's inconsistent with the vision—being grouchy or pessimistic, leaving a knife on the counter, becoming distracted, or throwing a fish improperly—is reviewed in light of the vision and coached accordingly. Everyone coaches and everyone, including the owner, can be coached, even by the newest employee. It's not just about making Pike Place Fish Market a better place; it's also about becoming people of integrity. The employees respect and care about each other enough to remind each other continually of the possibilities and purpose they've declared for themselves.*[28]

Key KSAs

The teams competency includes the key knowledge, skills, and abilities to be effective in doing the following:

- Determining the circumstances in which a team approach is appropriate and, if using a team is appropriate, the type of team to use.
- Engaging in and/or leading the process of setting clear performance goals for the team.
- Participating in and/or providing the leadership in defining responsibilities and tasks for the team as a whole, as well as its individual members.
- Demonstrating a sense of mutual and personal accountability for the achievement of team goals, not just an individual's own goals. That is, the individual doesn't approach problems and issues with a mind-set of "That's not my responsibility or concern."
- Applying decision-making methods and technologies that are appropriate to the goals, issues, and tasks confronting the team.
- Resolving personal and task-related conflicts among team members before they become too disruptive.
- Assessing a person's own performance and that of the team in relating to goals, including the ability to take corrective action as needed.

Teams and Individualism

People in some countries strongly believe in the importance and centrality of the individual. In the United States, the United Kingdom, and Canada, educational, governmental, and business institutions frequently state that they exist to serve individual goals. As we discuss further in Chapter 2, two cultural values that strongly affect decisions about whether to use teams and groups in organizations are *individualism* and *collectivism*.

Employees in individualistic cultures are expected to act on the basis of their personal goals and self-interest. In collectivistic countries, such as China and South Korea, the use of teams by organizations is a natural extension of their nations' cultural values. Uneasiness revolves around the relative influence of individuals in teams. Thus, we might characterize the basic difference as "fitting into the team" versus "standing out from the team." Even in societies that value individualism, the use of teams is substantial in such firms as J. C. Penney, General Electric, and PepsiCo.

The potential for teams and individuals to have incompatible goals clearly exists, but these goals need not always conflict; in fact, they often are compatible.[29] The potential strengths and weaknesses of teams is captured in the following statements:

- Teams do exist, and employees need to take them into account.
- Teams mobilize powerful forces that create important effects for individuals.
- Teams may create both good and bad results.
- Teams can be managed to increase the benefits from them.

The circumstances under which teams should be used versus sole reliance on the individual—that is, a single employee or manager taking primary control and personal accountability for performing a task, resolving an issue, or solving a problem—should be assessed continually and are discussed further in Chapter 11.

Larry Richman is the president and chief executive officer of Chicago-based LaSalle Bank Corporation. It has a number of subsidiaries and retail locations. Upon appointment to this position in 2007 after 25 years of service with LaSalle Bank, he commented: "We have such a talented and dedicated executive management team, which has been responsible for growing the bank to what it is today. I'm looking forward to continuing our legacy and working together to build towards even greater success."[30] In December 2004, LaSalle Bank was faced with a crisis—a major fire that started on the 29th floor of the 45-story LaSalle Bank Building in the financial district of Chicago. No lives were lost. Thirty-four people were injured, mostly from smoke inhalation. More than a million gallons of water were used to fight this fire. Amazingly, several key bank functions were up and running the next morning, with the majority of them operational within 48 hours of the fire.

The following feature reports on the positive impact of the widely shared team competency among numerous bank employees in the quick recovery from this crisis. It primarily reflects the perspectives of Larry Richman, who consistently emphasizes and demonstrates the importance of the teams competency and a team-based culture.[31]

Teams Competency

Crisis Team at LaSalle Bank

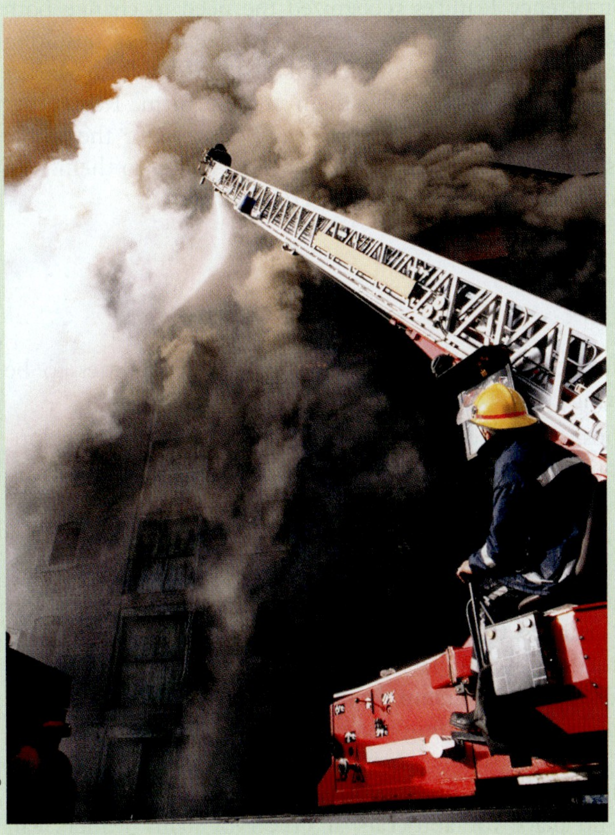

© Nigel Shuttleworth/Life File/Photodisc/Getty Images

The crisis team at LaSalle Bank used a team-based system to deal with a disastrous fire in their Chicago office.

I was in the office in Chicago at the time of the fire. I saw it and lived it. So much of the response to this crisis can be attributed to great people within the organization, who were prepared to deal with such things and immediately knew the proper actions to take. We had a team-based system and a capability in place, which was invaluable. That was the first step in the process: level-headed people who knew what to do. Second, we had officers and staff who were willing to roll up their sleeves in an effort to get us back on track. Everyone really rallied together and thank heavens no one was hurt. It was phenomenal, and one of those experiences that, despite being something you never want to endure again, was amazing in that it created a unique bond amongst those who went through it together. That shared relationship is something that will be remembered.

Despite everything, we remained very focused on the client. Further, we concentrated on doing the right thing, working together, and helping each other. It turned into a very remarkable experience and I think we've learned a lot from it, not only in terms of future practice but also regarding lessons that we learned long ago and that we can now pass along to others.

The first lesson would be to proactively develop and maintain both a dedicated disaster recovery team, made up of members who actively know their roles, and a crisis management plan. Fortunately, we had this in place. Related to this point, I would emphasize the importance of practicing the plan on a regular basis in order to help facilitate smooth implementation when or if a crisis does occur. We had this.

The second lesson would be to educate the senior management team and officers as to the roles and responsibilities they would be expected to carry out in times of crisis. We had this.

The third lesson would be to have technology, such as Blackberry devices, available to all key players in order to facilitate communication throughout a crisis. We had this. This technology component is essential. When we experienced the fire at LaSalle headquarters, in less than 24 hours all of our customers had been contacted and everyone in the organization knew where to go and what to do.

We had 15 assigned emergency remote locations. By being able to contact everyone within the morning after the fire, we were able to transact business the next day. Some individuals worked out of the dedicated locations, others were able to work remotely from home. But, everyone knew where everyone else was. The process I have described enabled us all to roll up our sleeves and demonstrate our commitment to serving our clients, no matter what.

For more information on LaSalle Bank Corporation, visit the organization's home page at www.lasallebank.com.

Learning Goal

8. Explain the change competency and its importance to effectiveness.

CHANGE COMPETENCY

The change competency *includes the knowledge, skills, and abilities to recognize and implement needed adaptations or entirely new transformations in the people, tasks, strategies, structures, or technologies in a person's area of responsibility.*[32] John Yokoyama, the focus of our Learning from Experience and Self Competency features recognized the need to change both personally and professionally when he employed Jim Bergquist of bizFutures Consulting Company. As you will recall, Bergquist assisted Yokoyama and the Pike Place Fish Market employees to engage in a major transformation by them and the firm. Remember Yokoyama's remark in the Self Competency feature: "It was a process for the whole business and employees because you can't force people to change; it's up to them. We noticed that the people who didn't commit to our vision left on their own."

LEADER INSIGHT

Stories are among the tools of leadership. Sometimes the stories are heroic in nature (you probably couldn't do this), sometimes cautionary (never do this), sometimes motivational (you should try to do this), sometimes exhortative (always do this), and sometimes expository (I did this and this is what I learned).

Jack Harris, VP Medical, Eli Lilly & Company

Key KSAs

The change competency includes the key knowledge, skills, and abilities to be effective in doing the following:

- Applying the six previously discussed competencies in the diagnosis, development, and implementation of needed changes.
- Providing leadership in the process of planned change (see especially Chapter 9, *Leading Effectively: Foundations*, and Chapter 10, *Leading Effectively: New Perspectives*, and the *Change Competency* features throughout the book). Leadership styles and approaches may need to vary under conditions of crisis and the need for major changes. Consider the case of Jack Welch, GE's retired CEO. He was nicknamed "Neutron Jack" by his employees because of his autocratic approach and style of leadership. In the 1980s, he was faced with the need to make difficult decisions, including the elimination of tens of thousands of employees, entire levels of management, and several divisions. After completing this overhaul, Welch shifted his leadership approach and made it known that there was no place for autocrats at GE. Not many leaders can change their behaviors as dramatically as Welch. In many instances, the directive autocrat needs to be replaced by a more supportive leader or become more so themselves when a crisis has passed.[33]
- Diagnosing pressure for and resistance to change in specific situations. These pressures may be internal—such as the organizational culture—or external—such as new technologies or competitors (see especially Chapter 15, *Cultivating Organizational Culture*, and Chapter 16, *Guiding Organizational Change*).
- Applying the systems model of change and other processes to introduce and achieve organizational change. Individuals with this ability are able to identify key issues and diagnose them by examining the basic factors of *who*, *what*, *why*, *when*, *where*, and

how (see especially Chapter 16). We provide insights for developing this ability in a number of the chapters.

- Seeking, gaining, sharing, and applying new knowledge in the pursuit of constant improvement, creativity, and entirely new approaches or goals. These behaviors require risk taking or *the willingness to take reasonable chances by recognizing and capitalizing on opportunities while also recognizing their potential negative outcomes and monitoring progress toward goals.*[34]

Technological Forces

Technological forces, especially computer-based information technologies and the Internet, continue to revolutionize how customers are served; employees communicate and network with one another and external stakeholders, such as customers, suppliers, competitors, and governmental agencies; tasks are performed; organizations are structured; human resources are led and managed; and so on.[35] Many readers of this book may not be able to think of their lives before the Internet, e-mail, MySpace, YouTube, text messaging, and cell phones.

Technological change may have positive effects, including products and services of higher quality and lower costs. But it also may have negative effects, including erosion of personal privacy, work-related stress, and health problems (e.g., eyestrain, carpal tunnel syndrome, and exposure to toxic substances). The revolution in technologies is a driving force in creating the need to actively manage change.

Constant Change: Blur

New technologies are increasing the need for constant learning, adaptation, and innovation by individuals, teams, and entire organizations. In *Blur: The Speed of Change in the Connected Economy*, S. Davis and C. Meyer proposed a formula to represent the rapidly accelerating rate of technological and other changes:

$$\text{Speed} \times \text{connectivity} \times \text{intangibles} = \text{blur.}$$

Speed Every aspect of how organizations operate and change in real time.

Connectivity Everything is becoming electronically connected to everything else: products, people, companies, countries—everything.

Intangibles Every transaction has both tangible (e.g., monetary) and intangible (e.g., reputational) value. The intangible is growing faster; it is the increasing role of personal services for many organizations and the economy as a whole.

Blur The new world in which we will come to live and work.[36]

The revolution in technologies is a driving force in creating the state of *blur* and the need to actively manage change. Throughout this book, we discuss topics that are related to the introduction and use of technology and which, in turn, are affected by it.

The rapid rise in use of the Internet throughout the world is the most obvious expression of economies and businesses that focus on technology. The Internet seems to bring the entire world to a person's desktop, laptop, or personal digital assistant instantaneously and to satisfy quickly any query or curiosity. The ever-expanding online World Wide Web is but the most recent indication of a trend during the past few decades that has brought businesses, customers, and others continually closer in real time. Technologies have shaped our expectations about acceptable time frames for communicating, performing tasks, and seeing results.

Drew Santin is the president of San-Tech, a division of Res-Tech Corporation, with headquarters in Peabody, Massachusetts. The following Change Competency feature reveals how Drew Santin and his employees increased speed to meet the needs of their clients.[37]

Change Competency

Drew Santin Embraces Speed

Drew Santin's division makes quick prototypes for manufacturers who want to see how their newest products will look, feel, and perform—and they want to know now, not tomorrow. Compounding the pressure is the fact that Santin's biggest markets—computer-component manufacturers and makers of clothing accessories and costume jewelry—are among the most demanding. His customers count on him to help them cope with ever-accelerating customer demand for quick turnaround.

Santin states, "I'm dealing with an industry, in PC components, where the two-year time frame for developing a new product, which was the case not long ago, now has become six months or less. And in some cases, we have to be able to help our customers turn around in a period that may be as short as a month. The fashion industry is the same way: They can see things get knocked off by competitors even before they go to market. So our ability to get a customized solution in front of the customer is crucial. The pressure is constant to reduce their time frames and to help them get a performing product in the shortest possible period of time." Instead of carrying around the need for speed like an albatross, Santin and his employees are embracing it—and making San-Tech a speed merchant. When necessary, employees will work nights and weekends to help customers trim precious hours and days from the developmental process.

Santin cross-trains its employees to ensure maximum flexibility for customers. With computer-based software, engineers can produce quick plastic representations of production components on the spot—even while a meeting with a client is taking place.

For more information on San-Tech, visit the organization's home page at www.santineng.com.

CHAPTER SUMMARY

1. Describe the framework for learning about organizational behavior.

Organizational behavior involves the dynamic interplay among employees, leaders, teams, and the organization itself. We introduce seven competencies in this chapter and show you the dynamic interplay among these competencies.

2. Explain the self competency and its importance to effectiveness.

The self competency includes the knowledge, skills, and abilities to assess a person's own strengths and weaknesses; set and pursue professional and personal goals; balance work and personal life; and engage in new learning—including new or modified skills, behaviors, and attitudes. This competency underlies the other six key competencies. Mastering it requires a lifelong process of learning and career management.

3. Explain the communication competency and its importance to effectiveness.

The communication competency includes the knowledge, skills, and abilities to transmit, receive, and understand data, information, thoughts, and emotions—nonverbal, verbal, written, listening, electronic, and the like. Core components of this competency are describing, active listening, questioning, nonverbal communication, verbal communication, and written communication. This competency is like the body's circulatory system, nourishing and carrying information to other competencies.

4. Explain the diversity competency and its contribution to effectiveness.

The diversity competency includes unique individual and group characteristics. These characteristics can act as potential sources of organizational strength. The core components of this competency are related to a framework of six primary categories of diversity: age, race, ethnicity, gender, physical abilities and qualities, and sexual orientation. Eight secondary categories of diversity include education, work background, and religious beliefs. These types of diversity are important because they often reflect differences in perspectives, lifestyles, attitudes, values, and behaviors. How managers and employees embrace and respond to diversity influences an organization's effectiveness.

The ethics competency includes principles that distinguish right from wrong into decision making and behaviors. Ethics are the values and principles that distinguish right from wrong. Managers and employees often experience ethical dilemmas—situations in which the individual or team must make a decision that involves multiple values.

5. Explain the ethics competency and its importance to effectiveness.

The across cultures competency includes similarities and differences among nations and cultures—even within the same organization. Individuals' perceptions, communication, decisions, and behaviors are influenced by their culture. Too often, one's culture may influence the development of sweeping negative stereotypes about those from other cultures.

6. Explain the across cultures competency and its importance to effectiveness.

The teams competency includes the knowledge, skills, and abilities to develop, support, facilitate, and lead groups to achieve organizational goals. Recognition of the potential for individual and team differences is stressed.

7. Explain the teams competency and its importance to effectiveness.

The change competency includes the knowledge, skills, and abilities needed by employees and managers to change people, tasks, strategies, structures, or technologies in a person's area of responsibility. New technologies are one of the primary sources of change, which creates a state of *blur*. The Internet is a primary enabler of increasing organizational effectiveness and efficiency.

8. Explain the change competency and its importance to effectiveness.

KEY TERMS AND CONCEPTS

Across cultures competency
Active listening
Career
Career development
Career plan
Change competency
Communication competency
Competency
Cultural values
Culture
Describing skill
Diversity competency
Empathizing skill
Ethical dilemma
Ethics
Ethics competency
Global mind-set
Nonverbal communication
Organizational behavior
Questioning skill
Risk taking
Self competency
Teams competency
Verbal communication
Written communication

DISCUSSION QUESTIONS

1. Identify two ethical dilemmas that you have faced during the past year. How did you resolve them?
2. What aspect of your life or role that you play reflects some or all of the variables that go into creating the state of blur? Explain.
3. The most successful teams and organizations are those that recognize the challenge and opportunity of embracing a diverse workforce. What obstacles stand in the way of doing so in a team or an organization of which you are or have been a member? Select a team or organization different from the one you chose to respond to Question 3.
4. For the most challenging job you now have or have had in the past, list the technologies you are using or have used to help you do the job. How would your performance of the tasks involved change if any two of the technologies were no longer available?
5. Identify three categories of diversity that represent significant issues in a team or an organization of which you are currently a member or have been a member.

How is this team or organization addressing these issues?

6. Think of a team on which you are currently or have been a member. How would you evaluate its members —in general—with respect to the key knowledge, skills, and abilities of the teams competency? Which members stand out, as either especially strong or especially weak? Briefly describe their characteristics.
7. Go to the Pike Place Fish Market home page at www.pikeplacefish.com. Scan thru the website. What is your assessment of the written and "nonverbal" communications conveyed by it?
8. Pinault-Printemps-Redoute (www.ppr.com) is a fashion retail company with headquarters in France. What are some across culture issues that you would need to be aware of in order to take an assignment in France? What management competencies might you need to develop?
9. Identify two strengths and two weaknesses in your own competencies. What specific steps might you take during the next two years to reduce the weaknesses?

EXPERIENTIAL EXERCISE AND CASE

Experiential Exercise: Self Competency

Key Competencies Self-Assessment Inventory

Instructions

1. The statements in this inventory describe specific knowledge/skills/abilities that are needed to be an effective manager or professional. For each specific knowledge/skill/ability statement, you are to assess yourself on a scale from 1 to 10, according to the descriptive statements provided on the scale shown here.

   10 I am outstanding on this knowledge/skill/ability.
   9 I am very good on this knowledge/skill/ability.
   8 I am good on this knowledge/skill/ability.
   7 I am average on this knowledge/skill/ability.
   6 I am barely adequate on this knowledge/skill/ability.
   5 I am lacking on this knowledge/skill/ability.
   4 I am weak on this knowledge/skill/ability.
   3 I am very weak on this knowledge/skill/ability.
   2 I have little relevant experience on this knowledge/skill/ability, but the experiences I have had are poor.
   1 I have no relevant experience. I have not yet begun to develop this knowledge/skill/ability.

2. Fill in the blank next to each listed specific knowledge/skill/ability with a number from the preceding scale that you think is most descriptive of yourself. You should choose a number that is most descriptive of what you are actually like rather than what you would prefer to be like.

Statements of Knowledge/Skills/Abilities

_____ 1. Maintains an awareness of own behavior and how it affects others.
_____ 2. Is able to set priorities and manage time.
_____ 3. Knows own limitations and asks for help when necessary.
_____ 4. Assesses and establishes own life- and work-related goals.
_____ 5. Takes responsibility for decisions and managing self.
_____ 6. Perseveres in the face of obstacles or criticism.
_____ 7. Is not self-promoting or arrogant.
_____ 8. Recovers quickly from failure, including learning from mistakes.
_____ 9. Tries to learn continuously.
_____ 10. Pursues feedback openly and nondefensively.
_____ 11. Organizes and presents ideas effectively.
_____ 12. Detects and understands others' values, motives, and emotions.
_____ 13. Presents written materials clearly and concisely.
_____ 14. Listens actively and nonjudgmentally.
_____ 15. Responds appropriately to positive and negative feedback.
_____ 16. Is aware of and sensitive to nonverbal messages.
_____ 17. Holds people's attention when communicating.
_____ 18. Shares information willingly.
_____ 19. Expresses own needs, opinions, and preferences without offending others.
_____ 20. Uses a variety of computer-based (electronic) resources to communicate.
_____ 21. Encourages the inclusion of those who are different from self.
_____ 22. Seeks to learn from those with different characteristics and perspectives.
_____ 23. Embraces and demonstrates respect for people of other cultures and races.
_____ 24. Shows sensitivity to the needs and concerns of others.
_____ 25. Seeks positive win–win or appropriate compromise solutions to conflicts based on diversity issues.
_____ 26. Embraces unique individual and group characteristics as potential sources of organizational strength.
_____ 27. Is sensitive to differences among people and seeks ways to work with them.
_____ 28. Respects ideas, values, and traditions of others.
_____ 29. Identifies opportunities to promote diversity.
_____ 30. Invests personal effort in helping people with attributes different from self to succeed.
_____ 31. Demonstrates dignity and respect for others in working relationships.

_____ 32. Is honest and open in communication, limited only by privacy, legal, and competitive considerations.
_____ 33. Assesses the right or wrong in own decisions and behaviors.
_____ 34. Adheres to professional and organizational codes of conduct.
_____ 35. Resists pressures from others to engage in unethical conduct.
_____ 36. Understands ethical principles and rules.
_____ 37. Is seen by others as a person of integrity.
_____ 38. Sets clear expectations of ethical behavior and regularly reinforces this expectation with others.
_____ 39. Is sensitive to the rights of others.
_____ 40. Takes responsibility for own decisions and actions —doesn't place blame on others to escape responsibility.
_____ 41. Seeks to understand and appreciate the characteristics that make a particular culture unique.
_____ 42. Treats people from different cultures with respect.
_____ 43. Considers managerial and other issues from a worldwide perspective, that is, the ability to think globally, act locally.
_____ 44. Works effectively with members from different cultures.
_____ 45. Likes to experience different cultures.
_____ 46. Learns from those with different cultural backgrounds.
_____ 47. Knows which cultures have the expectation that individuals are to take care of themselves.
_____ 48. Possesses firsthand knowledge that different cultures are risk adverse and use rules to minimize trying to deal with uncertainty.
_____ 49. Knows how masculinity and femininity in different societies affect interpersonal relationships.
_____ 50. Works effectively with people from different cultures who value unequal distribution of power in society.
_____ 51. Works effectively in team situations.
_____ 52. Encourages teams to celebrate accomplishments.
_____ 53. Demonstrates mutual and personal responsibility for achieving team goals.
_____ 54. Observes dynamics when working with groups and raises relevant issues for discussion.
_____ 55. Promotes teamwork among groups, discourages "we versus they" thinking.
_____ 56. Supports and praises others for reaching goals and accomplishing tasks.
_____ 57. Encourages and supports creativity in teams.
_____ 58. Shares credit with others.
_____ 59. Motivates team members to work toward common goals.
_____ 60. Is able to use groupware and related information technologies to achieve team goals.
_____ 61. Demonstrates the leadership skills to implement planned change.
_____ 62. Understands how to diagnose pressures for and resistances to change.
_____ 63. Prepares people to manage change.
_____ 64. Learns, shares, and applies new knowledge to improve a team, department, or whole organization.
_____ 65. Knows how to diagnose a firm's culture.
_____ 66. Uses a variety of technologies to achieve successful change.
_____ 67. Understands how various organizational designs can be used to bring about successful organizational change.
_____ 68. Possesses a positive attitude toward considering changes and new ideas.
_____ 69. Is able to negotiate and resolve conflicts that are often part of any significant change.
_____ 70. Understands how organizational cultures influence organizational change.

Scoring and Interpretation

The *Key Competencies Self-Assessment Inventory* seeks your self-perceptions on characteristics and dimensions that are representative of seven key competencies. Total your responses for each competency as instructed. The sum of your responses is your score. The maximum score is 100 points for each competency.

Self Competency:

Includes the knowledge, skills, and abilities to assess your own strengths and weaknesses; set and pursue professional and personal goals; balance work and personal life; and engage in new learning—including new or changed skills, behaviors, and attitudes.

- Add your responses for items 1 through 10 = _____, which is your self-assessment on the self competency.

Communication Competency:

Includes the knowledge, skills, and abilities to use all of the modes of transmitting, understanding, and receiving ideas, thoughts, and feelings—verbal, listening, nonverbal, written, electronic, and the like—for transferring and exchanging information and emotions.

- Add your responses for items 11 through 20 = _____, which is your self-assessment on the communication competency.

Diversity Competency:

Includes the knowledge, skills, and abilities to value unique individual and group characteristics, embrace such characteristics as potential sources of organizational strength, and appreciate the uniqueness of each individual.

- Add your responses for items 21 through 30 = _____, which is your self-assessment on the diversity competency.

Ethics Competency:

Includes the knowledge, skills, and abilities to incorporate values and principles that distinguish right from wrong in making decisions and choosing behaviors.

- Add your responses for items 31 through 40 = _____, which is your self-assessment on the ethics competency.

Across Cultures Competency:

Includes the knowledge, skills, and abilities to recognize and embrace similarities and differences among nations and cultures and then to approach key organizational and strategic issues with an open and curious mind.

- Add your responses for items 41 through 50 = _____, which is your self-assessment on the across cultures competency.

Teams Competency:
Includes the knowledge, skills, and abilities to develop, support, facilitate, or lead groups to achieve organizational goals.

- Add your responses for 51 through 60 = _____, which is your self-assessment on the teams competency.

Change Competency:
Includes the knowledge, skills, and abilities to recognize and implement needed adaptations or entirely new transformations in the people, tasks, strategies, structures, or technologies in the person's area of responsibility.

- Add your responses for items 61 through 70 = _____, which is your self-assessment on the change competency.

Your Overall Profile and Comparisons

Determine your overall profile of competencies by using the summary (total) score for each competency. Compare and contrast your scores with those of two sample populations: (1) experienced managers and professionals (shown on the first table below) and (2) undergraduate students at colleges and universities (shown on the second table below). Mean scores and standard deviations are based on a sample of more than 300 individuals. One standard deviation from the mean covers 68 percent of the sample population; that is, if your score falls within one standard deviation of the mean score of either the managerial or the student population, your score is similar to the scores of 68 percent of that population.

Managerial Sample Population

Competency	Mean	One Standard Deviation from Mean	Numerical Range for 68% of Population (High and Low)
Self	78	9	87–69
Communication	75	9	84–66
Diversity	75	11	87–63
Ethics	84	9	93–75
Across Cultures	72	14	86–58
Teams	77	12	89–65
Change	69	14	83–52

Student Sample Population

Competency	Mean	One Standard Deviation from Mean	Numerical Range for 68% of Population (High and Low)
Self	77	8	85–69
Communication	74	9	84–65
Diversity	75	12	88–63
Ethics	83	8	91–75
Across Cultures	66	16	84–50
Teams	79	11	90–68
Change	67	16	84–52

Overall Interpretations

Scores	Meaning
20–39	You see yourself as having little relevant experience and are deficient on this competency.
40–59	You see yourself as generally lacking on this competency but may be satisfactory or better on a few of its knowledge/skill/ability components.
60–74	You see yourself as average on this competency—probably below average on some its knowledge/skill/ability components.
75–89	You see yourself as generally above average on this competency and very good on a number of its knowledge/skill/ability components.
90–100	You see yourself as generally outstanding on this competency.

Questions

1. What does your overall profile suggest in relation to your needs for personal and professional development?
2. Based on the competency most in need of development, identify three possible actions that you might take to reduce the gap between your current and desired level for that competency.
3. Would others who work with you closely or know you well agree with your self-assessment profile? In what dimensions might their assessments of you be similar to your own? Why? In what dimensions might they differ? Why?

Case: Change Competency

Chiquita and the Rainforest Alliance[38]

David McLaughlin, senior director of environmental affairs for Chiquita, and Tensie Whelan, executive director of the Rainforest Alliance, like to tell this story. It begins in the 1990s, when, as McLaughlin says, "our license to operate was being severely questioned by a lot of environmental activists."

Chiquita is a company with a long history. More than 100 years ago, Captain Lorenzo Dow Baker bought 160 bunches of bananas in Jamaica. He brought them to Jersey City and sold the bananas for a profit. Since then, Chiquita has expanded operations into some 60 countries. Panama, Cost Rica, Colombia, Guatemala, and Honduras provide the bulk of the company's $4 billion in global sales. The company is headquartered in Cincinnati, Ohio, and has 26,000 employees.

Historically, the company operated in countries with limited social infrastructures. Consequently, Chiquita established a patriarchal base in these countries, taking care of everything from telecommunications to road maintenance. Formerly the United Fruit Company, Chiquita was seen as a corporate imperialist, establishing jungle fiefdoms and banana republics in Central and South America. In 2001, Chiquita took the unprecedented step of admitting instances of past brutality toward its workers.

In the 1990s, Chiquita faced serious challenges to its practices and recognized the need to sit down with its adversaries to understand their grievances. Instead of reacting to them in isolation, Chiquita's management opened the door to the Rainforest Alliance, a New York-based nongovernmental organization (NGO). It is committed to protecting ecosystems and the people and wildlife that depend on them. The Rainforest Alliance focuses on transforming land-use practices, business practices, and consumer behavior.

McLaughlin, a 28-year veteran of Chiquita, comments: "We really had to go beyond any traditional boundaries that we had in our corporate culture. We had to change our decision framework, completely open up, accept these viewpoints, and figure out whether we could accept them and fit them into our production process. We also recognized the need for a credible standard."

This engagement between the two organizations, while at times uncomfortable and confrontational, led Chiquita's management to a greater understanding of the issues and grievances at play. It also led to one of the most successful company–NGO partnerships of the past decade.

The partnership is founded on what was originally called the Better Banana Program (BBP), the Rainforest Alliance's certification standard. Broad areas covered by the certification standards include wildlife conservation, ecosystem considerations, soil erosion, water conservation, integrated waste management, integrated pest management, fair treatment and good conditions for workers, and the establishment of strong community relations.

Complying with these exacting standards was expensive for Chiquita. The company spent over $20 million from 1992 to 2000 to certify the environmental performance of its farms in Latin America. Given the costs involved, Chiquita's management wanted to establish a clear-cut business case before fully signing on to the certification standards. Thus, began an in-depth 18-month pilot project involving two Chiquita farms that adopted the standards. Conservation International, another environmental NGO, was retained to measure differences in performance between Chiquita's pilot farms and the noncertified farms.

Certification has contributed to increased productivity and reduced costs, according to Chiquita. For all its farm operations from 1997 to 2006, the company has seen productivity increased by 27 percent and costs reduced by 12 percent. In terms of environmental performance, agrichemical use was greatly reduced and the incidence of pallet recycling increased. There was, it seemed, a clear-cut business case for better social and environmental practices, as enshrined in the Rainforest Alliance certification, to be rolled out more widely across Chiquita's farms.

Signing on to the standard drove a process of change in Chiquita. Managers were held accountable for adherence to tangible criteria that had proven long-term value for the business, society, and the environment. The company is regularly praised by NGOs in Europe for the way in which it approaches stakeholder engagement. Clear accountability to social and environmental issues has been established. There is, consequently, a lower risk of NGO and consumer activism. Reputational pluses have been quick to follow.

Recognizing the increasing importance of social and environmental issues for consumers, in 2005 the company started a high-profile consumer campaign with the Rainforest Alliance to raise awareness for the Rainforest Alliance standards. Ninety-three percent of all bananas Chiquita produces are now Rainforest Alliance certified and can display the Rainforest Alliance green frog on the banana stickers.

In 2007, Chiquita agreed to a $25 million fine after admitting it paid terrorists for protection in a volatile farming region of Colombia. The settlement resolved a lengthy Justice Department investigation into the company's financial dealings with right-wing paramilitaries and leftist rebels the U.S. government deems terrorist groups. In court documents, federal prosecutors said the Cincinnati-based company and several unnamed high-ranking corporate officers paid about $1.7 million between 1997 and 2004 to the United Self-Defense Forces of Colombia, known as AUC for its Spanish initials. The AUC has been responsible for some of the worst massacres in Colombia's civil conflict and for a sizable percentage of the country's cocaine exports. The U.S. government designated the right-wing militia a terrorist organization in September 2001.

Prosecutors said the company made the payments in exchange for protection for its workers. In addition to paying the AUC, prosecutors said, Chiquita made payments to the National Liberation Army, or ELN, and the leftist Revolutionary Armed Forces of Colombia, or FARC, as control of the company's banana-growing area shifted. Leftist rebels and far-right paramilitaries have fought viciously over Colombia's banana-growing region, though the victims are most often noncombatants. Most companies in the area have extensive security operations to protect employees.

"The information filed is part of a plea agreement, which we view as a reasoned solution to the dilemma the company faced several years ago," Chiquita's chief executive, Fernando Aguirre, said in a statement. "The payments made by the company were always motivated by our good faith concern for the safety of our employees." Chiquita sold its Colombian banana operations in June 2004.

For more information on Chiquita Brands, Inc., visit the organization's home page at ***www.chiquita.com***.

Questions

1. What components of the communication competency are illustrated in this case? Give a specific example of each component identified.

2. What components of the teams competency are illustrated in this case? Give a specific example of each component identified.
3. What components of the change competency are illustrated in this case? Give a specific example of each component identified.
4. What components of the ethics competency are illustrated in this case? Give a specific example of each component identified.

PART 2

THE INDIVIDUAL IN ORGANIZATIONS

CHAPTER

2

Understanding Individual Differences

Learning Goals

When you have finished studying the chapter, you should be able to:

1. Explain the basic sources of personality determinants.
2. Identify a set of personality characteristics that affect behavior.
3. Describe how attitudes influence performance.
4. Explain how emotions impact performance.

Learning from Experience

RICHARD BRANSON, CEO, VIRGIN GROUP, LTD.

Richard Branson, founder and chairman of the London-based Virgin Group Ltd., has turned a lifelong disdain for conventional business wisdom into a multibillion-dollar international conglomerate and one of the world's most recognizable brands. The Virgin Group has ventured into businesses ranging from retail stores to travel to financial services.

His personal trademark is doing outlandish publicity stunts. Branson will do almost anything to promote the Virgin brand, including driving a tank down Fifth Avenue in New York to introducing Virgin Cola to the United States and engaging in high-profile hot-air balloon adventures. Branson sets aside about 25 percent of his time for public relations activities. He has a staff member whose sole responsibility is devising headline-catching publicity stunts. Branson states, "Using yourself to get out and talk about it is a lot cheaper and more effective than a lot of advertising. In fact, if you do it correctly, it can beat advertising hands down and save tens of millions of dollars."

Another aspect of Branson's philosophy is centered on finding the best people to run the diverse businesses in the Virgin Group. He is not as much concerned about industry-specific expertise as he is with recruiting employees with strong communication and teamwork competencies that mesh with the Virgin culture. Branson states, "What makes somebody good is how good they are at dealing with people. If you can find people who are good at motivating others and getting the best out of people, they are the ones you want. There are plenty of so-called experts, but not as many great motivators of people." Virgin tends to promote from within. The desired profile, not surprisingly, is someone like Branson: someone who gets charged up when told that something cannot be done; someone who is unafraid of industry barriers and will not take no for an answer.

Many executives devote their attention primarily to serving customers and shareholders. Branson thinks that the correct pecking order is employees first, customers next, and then shareholders last. His logic is this: If your employees are happy, they will do a better job. If they do a better job, the customers will be happy, and thus business will be good and the shareholders will be rewarded.

LEARNING CONTENT

Learning from Experience:
Richard Branson, CEO, Virgin Group, Ltd.

PERSONALITY DETERMINANTS

Self Competency—
David Neeleman of JetBlue

PERSONALITY AND BEHAVIOR

Teams Competency—
Why Personality Is Important at Starbucks

WORK ATTITUDES AND BEHAVIOR

Communication Competency—
Creating Positive Attitudes at The Container Store

MANAGING EMOTIONS AT WORK

Across Cultures Competency—
Emotions in Japan

EXPERIENTIAL EXERCISES

Experiential Exercise:
Self Competency—
What Are Your Cultural Values?

Experiential Exercise:
Self Competency—
What's Your Emotional IQ?

For more information on Virgin Group, Ltd., visit the organization's home page at www.virgin.com.

Branson is frequently on the road to visit Virgin businesses, talking with employees and customers. He is known for his ever-present notebook and pen, which he pulls out whenever he chats with employees and customers. Branson insists that this is a crucial element in his role as chairman. By writing things down, he creates a regular list of items for immediate action. He reads mail from employees every morning before he does anything else. This habit, which he started in Virgin's early days, influences company–employee dynamics. Employees do not hesitate to air their grievances directly to him. Branson has proved with his actions that he actively listens. Although Virgin has more than 40,000 employees around the world, he gets only about 50 e-mails or letters each day from nonmanagerial employees. They vary from small ideas to frustrations with middle management to significant proposals. He addresses every one by answering personally or by initiating some action. Branson states, "Instead of needing a union when they have a problem, they come to me. I will give the employee the benefit of the doubt on most occasions."

For Branson, retaining the standards he has instilled as the company grows is his major task. He states, "You've got to treat people as human beings—even more so as the company gets bigger. The moment I start to think 'I've made lots of money, I'm comfortable. I don't need to bother with these things anymore,' that's when Virgin will be at risk."[1]

As the *Learning from Experience* feature indicates, people react to how they are treated by others. You might ask yourself whether you would be willing to work for Branson. Depending on your personality, preferences, and goals, your answer might be either *yes* or *no.* As an employee and future manager, you must recognize and appreciate individual differences in order to understand and respond appropriately to the behavior of people in organizations.[2]

In Part 2 of this book, we cover individual processes in organizations. In this chapter, we focus first on the individual to help you develop an understanding of organizational behavior.

Individual differences *are the personal attributes that vary from one person to another.* Individual differences may be physical, psychological, or emotional. What are some individual differences about Richard Branson that stand out for you? What are your individual differences? The individual differences that characterize you make you unique. Perhaps you have a dynamic personality and enjoy being the center of attention, whereas others you know avoid crowds and do not have the same energy level as you. Is that good or bad? The answer, of course, is that it depends on the situation. Whenever you attempt to understand individual differences, you must also analyze the situation in which the behavior occurs. A good starting point in developing this understanding is to appreciate the role of personality in organizations. In this chapter, we discuss individual differences in personality attitudes and emotions. We begin by addressing the concept of personality. Later in the chapter, we explore the role of attitudes and emotions in organizational behavior.

PERSONALITY DETERMINANTS

Learning Goal

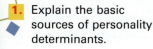

1. Explain the basic sources of personality determinants.

Behavior always involves a complex interaction between the person and the situation. Events in the surrounding environment (including the presence and behavior of others) strongly influence the way people behave at any particular time; yet people always bring something of themselves to the situation. This "something," which represents the unique qualities of the individual, is *personality.*[3] No single definition of personality is accepted universally. However, one key idea is that personality represents personal characteristics that lead to consistent patterns of behavior. People quite naturally seek to understand these behavioral patterns in interactions with others.

Personality *represents the overall profile or combination of stable psychological attributes that capture the unique nature of a person*. Therefore, personality combines a set of physical and mental characteristics that reflect how a person looks, thinks, acts, and feels. This definition contains two important ideas.

First, theories of personality often describe what people have in common and what sets them apart. To understand the personality of an individual, then, is to understand both what that individual has in common with others and what makes that particular individual unique. Thus, each employee in an organization is unique and may or may not act like someone else will act in a similar situation. This uniqueness makes managing and working with people extremely challenging.

Second, our definition refers to personality as being "stable," meaning that it remains somewhat the same through time. Most people intuitively recognize this stability. If your entire personality could change suddenly and dramatically, your family and friends would confront a stranger. Although significant changes normally don't occur suddenly, an individual's personality may change over time. Personality development occurs to a certain extent throughout life, but the greatest changes occur in early childhood.

How is an individual's personality determined? Is personality inherited or genetically determined, or is it formed after years of experience? There are no simple answers because too many variables contribute to the development of each individual's personality. As Figure 2.1 shows, two primary sources shape personality differences: heredity and environment. An examination of these sources helps explain why individuals are different.

> **LEADER INSIGHT**
>
> Personality is like a tree and reputation like its shadow. The shadow is what we think of it; the tree is the real thing.
>
> **Robert Eccles, Founder, Perception Partners.**

Heredity

Deeply ingrained in many people's notions of personality is a belief in its genetic basis. Expressions such as "She is just like her father" or "He gets those irritating qualities from your side of the family, dear" reflect such beliefs. Genes determine height, eye color, size of hands, and other basic physical characteristics. Some people believe that

FIGURE 2.1 Sources of Personality Differences

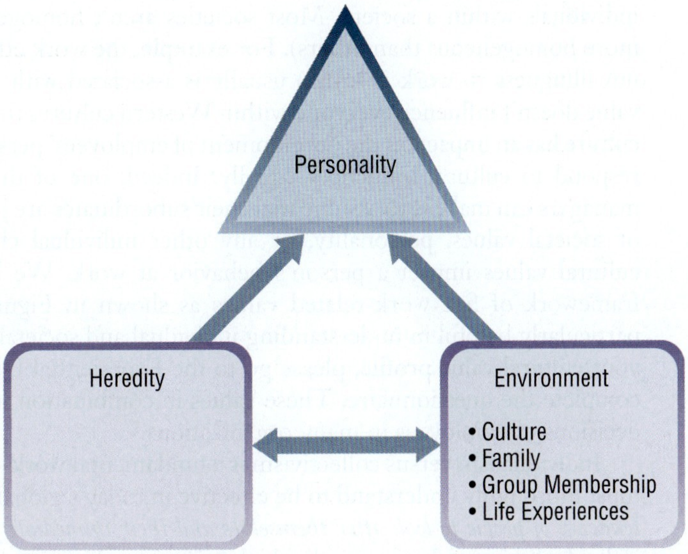

personality is inherited; others believe that a person's experiences determine personality. Our thinking is balanced—both heredity (genes) and environment (experiences) are important. Of course, some personality characteristics may be influenced more by one factor than the other. Some personality traits seem to have a strong genetic component, whereas other traits seem to be largely learned (based on experiences).[4]

Heredity sets limits on the range of development of characteristics, and within this range environmental forces influence personality characteristics. However, recent research on the personalities of twins who have been raised apart indicates that genetic determinants may play a larger role than many experts had believed. Some studies of twins suggest that as much as 50 to 55 percent of personality traits may be inherited. Further, inherited personality traits seem to explain about 50 percent of the variance in occupational choice. In other words, you probably inherited some traits that will influence your career choices. Furthermore, there is not one single gene that determines a person's personality but a combination of genes.[5]

Environment

Other people think that the environment plays a large role in shaping personality; in fact, the environment may have a more important role than inherited characteristics. That is, beyond what genes are inherited from your parents, the environment a person experiences as a child has an important role in molding one's personality. How a child is treated by adults and playmates and others influences the child's personality. A person growing up in a warm and nurturing household is much more likely to be a well-adjusted person than a child growing up in a cold and sterile environment. Aspects of the environment that influence personality formation include culture, family, group membership, and life experiences.

Culture. Anthropologists have clearly demonstrated the important role that culture plays in personality development.[6] Individuals born into a particular society are exposed to family and societal values and to norms of acceptable or unacceptable behavior—the culture of that society. Culture also defines how various roles in that society are to be performed. For example, U.S. culture generally rewards people for being independent and competitive, whereas Japanese culture generally rewards individuals for being cooperative and group oriented.[7]

Culture helps determine broad patterns of behavioral similarity among people. However, differences in behavior—which at times can be extreme—usually exist among individuals within a society. Most societies aren't homogeneous (although some are more homogeneous than others). For example, the work ethic (hard work is valued; an unwillingness to work is sinful) usually is associated with Western cultures. But this value doesn't influence everyone within Western cultures to the same degree. Although culture has an impact on the development of employees' personalities, not all individuals respond to cultural influences equally. Indeed, one of the most serious errors that managers can make is to assume that their subordinates are just like themselves in terms of societal values, personality, or any other individual characteristic. A number of cultural values impact a person's behavior at work. We briefly introduce you to a framework of five work-related values as shown in Figure 2.2. We believe that is particularly helpful in understanding individual and societal differences. To determine your cultural value profile, please go to the Experiential Exercise on pages 63–64 and complete the questionnaire. These values in combination influence the behaviors and decisions of employees in many organizations.[8]

Individualism versus collectivism is a fundamental work-related value that managers must thoroughly understand to be effective in today's global world. Individualism *is the tendency of people to look after themselves and their immediate families.* A culture high on individualism emphasizes individual initiative, decision making, and achievement.

FIGURE 2.2 Influence of Culturally Based Work-Related Values

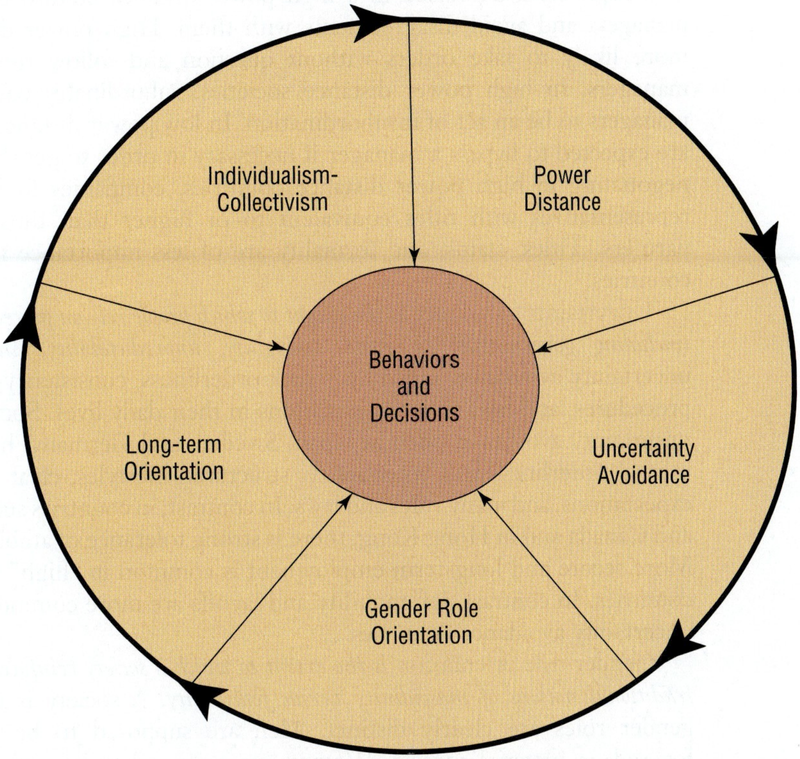

Everybody is believed to have the right to privacy and personal freedom of expression. Individuals in these countries generally do not believe that they share a common fate with others. They view themselves as independent, unique, and special. They are less likely to conform to the expectations of others. When group goals conflict with personal goals, individuals commonly pursue their own goals. In addition, seeking personal identity is highly valued in individualistic cultures. Personal achievement, pleasure, and competition are all highly valued. Countries characterized by an emphasis on individualism include the United States, Canada, New Zealand, the United Kingdom, and Australia.

At the other end of the continuum, collectivism *is the tendency of people to emphasize their belonging to groups and to look after each other in exchange for loyalty*. Groups (relatives, communities, and organizations) focus on their common welfare. Collectivism usually involves emotional dependence of the individual on groups, organizations, and institutions. The sense of belonging and "we" versus "I" in relationships is fundamental. Individuals' private lives are shaped by the groups and organizations to which they belong. Group goals are generally thought to be more important than the individual's personal goals. Individuals in China, Japan, Taiwan, and South Korea care about whether their behavior would be considered shameful by the other members of their groups. They also avoid pointing out other people's mistakes in public so that the others won't lose face and harmony is maintained. Face-saving is important in these cultures because it allows people to retain their dignity and status.

Power distance *is the extent to which people in a society accept status and power inequalities as a normal and functional aspect of life*. Countries that are "high in power distance" are those whose citizens generally accept status and power inequalities; those "low in power distance" are those whose citizens generally do *not*. Countries that are high in power distance include Argentina, India, Malaysia, Mexico, the Philippines, and the Commonwealth of Puerto Rico. At the opposite extreme, countries that are low in power distance include Finland, Israel, Norway, and Sweden. (The United States is moderately low.)

People who are raised in a high power distance culture behave submissively to managers and avoid disagreements with them. High power distance employees are more likely to take orders without question and follow the instructions of their managers. In high power distance societies, subordinates consider bypassing their managers to be an act of insubordination. In low power distance countries, employees are expected to bypass a manager if necessary in order to get their work done. When negotiating in high power distance countries, companies find it necessary to send representatives with titles equivalent to or higher than those of their bargaining partners. Titles, status, and formality are of less importance in low power distance countries.

Uncertainty avoidance *is the extent to which people rely on procedures, and organizations (including government) to avoid ambiguity, unpredictability, and risk.* With "high" uncertainty avoidance, individuals seek orderliness, consistency, structure, formalized procedures, and laws to cover situations in their daily lives. Societies that are high on uncertainty avoidance, such as Japan, Sweden, and Germany, have a strong tendency toward orderliness and consistency, structured lifestyles, clear specification of social expectations, and many rules and laws. In contrast, in countries such as the United States and Canada and in Hong Kong, there is strong tolerance of ambiguity and uncertainty. More secure and long-term employment is common in "high" uncertainty avoidance countries. In contrast, job mobility and layoffs are more commonly accepted in "low" uncertainty avoidance countries.

Gender role orientation *is the extent to which a society reinforces, or does not reinforce, traditional notions of masculinity versus femininity.* A society is called *masculine* when gender roles are clearly distinct. Men are supposed to be assertive, tough, and focused on material success. Women are supposed to be more modest, tender, and concerned with the quality of life. In masculine-dominated cultures, gender roles are clearly distinct. Japan, Austria, Italy, Mexico, and Ireland are a few of the countries ranked as high in masculinity. Dominant values are material success and progress and money. A society is called *feminine* when gender roles overlap: Both men and women are supposed to be modest, tender, and concerned with the quality of life. In feminine-dominated societies, roles are often merged or overlap for sexes. A few of the countries ranked high on femininity are Denmark, Costa Rica, Finland, and Portugal. Dominant values include caring for others, emphasizing the importance of people and relationships, accepting that both men and women can be gentle, stressing the quality of work life, and resolving conflict by compromise and negotiation.

Long-term orientation *is the extent to which the society embraces the virtues oriented toward future rewards.* A long-term orientation ranking indicates that the society prescribes to the values of sustained commitments, perseverance, and thrift. This is thought to support a strong work ethic where long-term rewards are expected as a result of today's hard work. A few of the countries with a long-term orientation are China, Japan, India, and the Netherlands. These countries include characteristics such as adaptation of traditions to the modern context, respect for tradition and obligation within limits, thrift (saving resources), perseverance toward slow results, willingness to subordinate oneself for a purpose, and concern with virtue.

A short-term orientation stands for societies that expect and reward quick results, view leisure time as important, have little respect for old-time traditions, and reward the risk-taking and adaptability exhibited by entrepreneurs. A few of the societies with a short-term orientation include Canada, Czech Republic, Pakistan, Spain, and the

United States. From a business perspective, several of the features of a strong short-term orientation include the following:

- The main work values are freedom, individual rights, achievement, and thinking for oneself.
- The focus is on the bottom line with an emphasis on the importance of this year's profits.
- Managers and workers view themselves as highly distinct groups.
- Personal loyalties vary with business needs (versus investment in lifelong personal networks).[9]

Family. The primary vehicle for socializing an individual into a particular culture is the person's immediate family. Both parents and siblings play important roles in the personality development of most individuals. Members of an extended family—grandparents, aunts, uncles, and cousins—also can influence personality formation. In particular, parents (or a single parent) influence their children's development in three important ways:

- Through their own behaviors, they present situations that bring out certain behaviors in children.
- They serve as role models with which children often strongly identify.
- They selectively reward and punish certain behaviors.[10]

The family's situation also is an important source of personality differences. Situational influences include the family's size, socioeconomic level, race, religion, and geographic location; birth order within the family; parents' educational level; and so on. For example, a person raised in a poor family simply has different experiences and opportunities than does a person raised in a wealthy family. Being an only child is different in some important respects from being raised with several brothers and sisters.

Group Membership. The first group to which most individuals belong is the family. People also participate in various groups during their lives, beginning with their childhood playmates and continuing through teenaged schoolmates and sports teams to adult work and social groups. The numerous roles and experiences that people have as members of groups represent another important source of personality differences. Although playmates and school groups early in life may have the strongest influences on personality formation, social and group experiences in later life continue to influence and shape personality. Understanding someone's personality requires understanding the groups to which that person belongs or has belonged in the past.

Life Experiences. Each person's life also is unique in terms of specific events and experiences, which can serve as important determinants of personality. For example, the development of self-esteem (a personality dimension that we discuss shortly) depends on a series of experiences that include the opportunity to achieve goals and meet expectations, evidence of the ability to influence others, and a clear sense of being valued by others. Thus, a complex series of events and interactions with other people helps shape the adult's level of self-esteem.

As we weave an understanding of personality and other individual differences into our exploration of a variety of topics in organizational behavior, we hope that you will come to understand the crucial role that personality plays in explaining behavior. People clearly pay a great deal of attention to the attributes of the personalities of the coworkers with whom they interact. The following Self Competency feature shows how JetBlue's former CEO David Neeleman's personality was shaped by various forces.[11]

Self Competency

David Neeleman of JetBlue

© Photo courtesy JetBlue Airways

David Neeleman, founder and former CEO of JetBlue, believes in maintaining equality among employees and providing customers with personal service.

If you want to understand the culture of a company that is led by its founder, it helps to understand the personality of the founder and former CEO. Neeleman spent the first five years of his life in Brazil where his father was a journalist. His family moved from Brazil, but he visited every summer. Brazil is a country that is divided between the haves and haves-not. He grew up in the rich part of the country and enjoyed a big house, a membership in country clubs, and so forth. During his junior year in Utah, he decided to return to Brazil to go on a mission for his church and ended up living in the slums or "favelas" of Brazil. The slums are where the desperately poor people live behind barbed wire fences in cardboard shacks.

He was struck by a few things living in the slums. First, most wealthy people have a sense of entitlement. They thought that they were better than the people in the slums. This bothered him tremendously. Second, most of the poor people were happier than the rich people and they generously shared what little they had. He experienced enormous pleasures and satisfactions from working with these people.

These experiences had a tremendous impact on the formation of his personality and his drive to manage JetBlue differently. When he travels on a business trip, he flies coach class. There is no Lincoln Town Car waiting for him at the airport. At JetBlue, there are no reserved parking places. The coffee in the kitchen down the hall from his work space is the same as that in the employee lounge at J. F. Kennedy airport. There is only one class on JetBlue planes. The seats at the back have slightly more legroom, so people who get off the plane last actually have roomier seats in-flight. The desk and other furniture in his office are the same as that used by everyone else. He tells his pilots: "There are people who make more money at this company than others, but that doesn't mean they should flaunt it."

He can be seen frequently on flights from Florida to New York City. Once the plane settles into its cruising altitude, Neeleman walks to the front of the cabin, grabs the microphone, and introduces himself. He explains that he'll be coming through the cabin serving drinks and snacks along with the crew. He also takes out the garbage when the flight is over. It's his chance to speak directly to JetBlue's customers. JetBlue also has a Crewmember Crisis fund. Everyone donates to it and it's used to help employees in crisis. If someone at JetBlue gets cancer, they have health benefits, but they might tap the fund to pay a babysitter while at chemotherapy.

Employees and customers like the "touchy-feely" aspect of JetBlue. "When you have a leader who's so friendly, it makes everybody feel good about what they're doing," says Jim Small, a general manager for JetBlue in San Juan. JetBlue is also generous with travel vouchers when passengers are inconvenienced. Neeleman himself once drove an elderly couple from JFK to Connecticut, where he lives and they were headed, rather then let them spend $200 on a taxi.

For more information on JetBlue, visit the organization's home page at www.jetblue.com.

PERSONALITY AND BEHAVIOR

Learning Goal

2. Identify a set of personality characteristics that affect behavior.

You don't see a person's personality, but rather you see behaviors that reflect these internal characteristics.[12] For our purposes, personality describes a person's most dominant characteristics—shy, sensitive, reliable, creative, and the like. This meaning of personality is useful to employees because it contains a profile of characteristics that tell the employee about the behaviors they can expect from his or her manager. This profile also serves as a guide for how we might communicate with the manager or fellow employee. The main reason that we are interested in individual personality in the study of organizational behavior is because of the link between personality and individuals' competencies. Most people believe that there is a relationship between personality traits and behavior. However, as Hewlett-Packard discovered, just because a person has the right "personality," that doesn't mean they will be successful on the job. Carly Fiorina, the former CEO of HP took a 900-item personality questionnaire. The results indicated she had the right personality to handle the CEO position at HP. But how she expressed her basic personality traits through her self-management and other competencies didn't result in effective performance at HP as seen by HP's board and many other employees.[13]

The vast number and variety of specific personality traits or dimensions are bewildering. The term personality trait *refers to the basic components of personality.* Researchers of personality have identified literally *thousands* of traits over the years. Trait names simply represent the terms that people use to describe each other. However, a list containing hundreds or thousands of terms isn't very useful either in understanding the profile of personality in a scientific sense or in describing individual differences in a practical sense. To be useful, these terms need to be organized into a small set of concepts or factors. Recent research has done just that, identifying several general factors that can be used to describe a personality.[14] Before reading any further, please take time to complete the questionnaire in Table 2.1.

Table 2.1 **Assessing Your Personality Using the Big Five**

The following questionnaire gives you a chance to gain insights into your Big Five personality dimensions. Please answer the following 25 statements using the following scale:

5 = Strongly agree

4 = Agree

3 = Moderate

2 = Disagree

1 = Strongly disagree

STATEMENTS

_____ 1. I am the life of the party.

_____ 2. I sympathize with others' feelings.

_____ 3. I get chores done right away.

_____ 4. I have frequent mood swings.

_____ 5. I have a vivid imagination.

_____ 6. I don't talk a lot. (R)

_____ 7. I am not interested in other people's problems. (R)

_____ 8. I often forget to put things back in their proper place. (R)

_____ 9. I am relaxed most of the time. (R)

_____ 10. I am not interested in abstract ideas. (R)

_____ 11. I talk to a lot of different people at parties.

_____ 12. I feel others' emotions.

_____ 13. I like order.
_____ 14. I get upset easily.
_____ 15. I have difficulty understanding abstract ideas. (R)
_____ 16. I keep in the background. (R)
_____ 17. I am not really interested in others. (R)
_____ 18. I make a mess of things. (R)
_____ 19. I seldom feel blue. (R)
_____ 20. I do not have a good imagination. (R)
_____ 21. I don't mind being the center of attention.
_____ 22. I make people feel at ease.
_____ 23. I pay attention to details.
_____ 24. I am easily disturbed. (R)
_____ 25. I am full of ideas.

SCORING

NOTE: If a statement has an "(R)" at the end of it, the scoring for that statement is reversed. That is, strongly agree is worth 1 point, agree is worth 2 points, etc.

1. Add your score for statements 1, 6, 11, 16, and 21: _________. This is your score for extraversion. The higher the score, the more likely you are to be energetic, outgoing, and gregarious.
2. Add your score for statements 2, 7, 12, 17, and 22: _________. This is your score for agreeableness. The higher the score, the more warm, tactful, and considerate you are toward others.
3. Add your score for statements 3, 8, 13, 18, and 23: _________. This is your score for conscientiousness. The higher the score, the more careful, neat, and dependable you are likely to be.
4. Add your score for statements 4, 9, 14, 19, and 24: _________. This is your score for emotional stability. The higher the score, the more stable, confident, and effective you are likely to be.
5. Add your score for statements 5, 10, 15, 20, and 25: _________. This is your score for openness. The higher the score, the more imaginative, curious, and original you are likely to be.

Big Five Personality Factors

The "Big Five" personality factors, as they often are referred to, describe the individual's emotional stability, agreeableness, extraversion, conscientiousness, and openness.[15] As shown in Figure 2.3, each factor includes a potentially large number and range of specific traits. That is, each factor is both a collection of related traits and a continuum.

Researchers have investigated extensively the relationships between the Big Five personality factors and job performance. Their findings indicate that employees who have emotional stability, agreeableness, and conscientiousness perform better than those who lack these traits (the extremes of the *conscientiousness* continuum in Figure 2.3). An individual with a personality at one extreme of the *agreeableness* factor continuum might be described as warm and considerate. But with a personality at this factor's other extreme, the person would be considered cold or rude. We next define the terms used for the Big Five traits.

Emotional stability *is the degree to which a person is calm, secure, and free from persistent negative feelings.* People who are emotionally stable are relaxed, poised, slow to show anger, handle crises well, resilient, and secure in their interpersonal dealings with others. People with less emotional stability are more excitable, insecure in their dealings with others, reactive, and subject to extreme swings of moods. Teams composed of emotionally unstable individuals usually come up with relatively fewer creative ideas

FIGURE 2.3 The "Big Five" Personality Factors

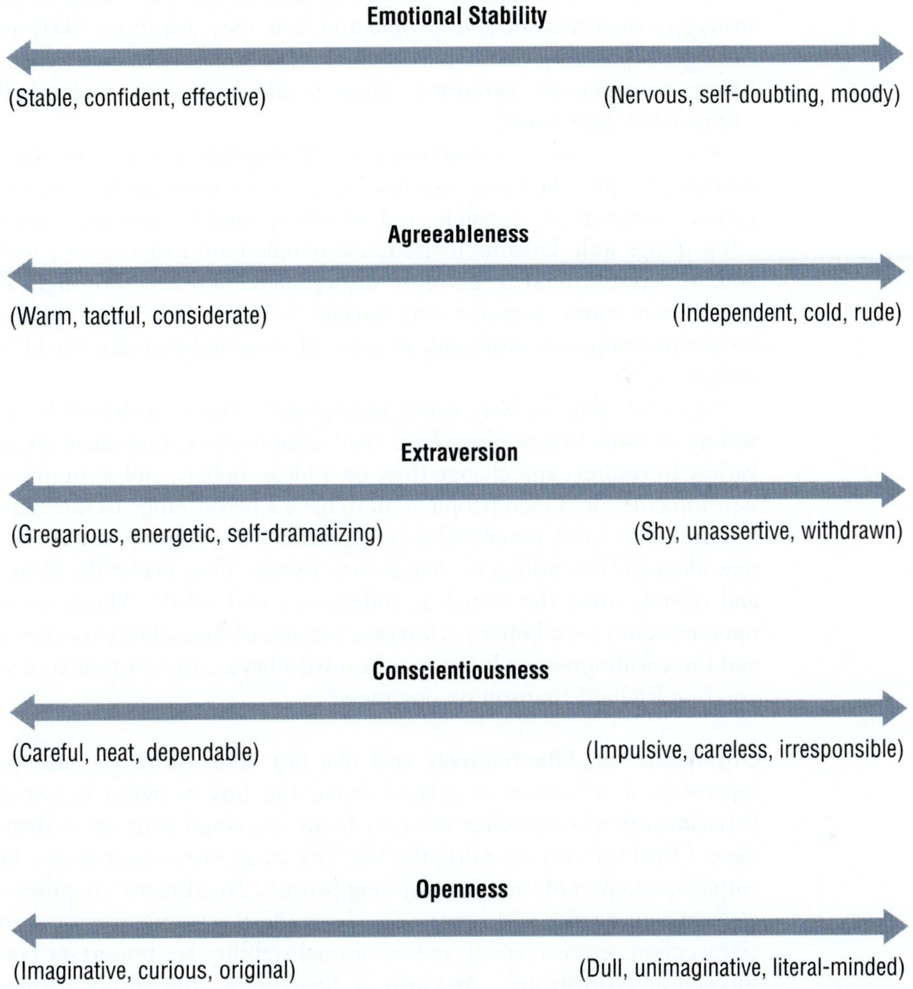

than teams composed of emotionally stable individuals. People with emotional stability handle the stress of managing others better than those who are less emotionally stable. How would you rate David Neeleman's emotional stability?

Agreeableness *is a person's ability to get along with others.* Agreeable individuals value getting along with others. They are considerate, friendly, helpful, and willing to compromise their interests. Agreeable people also have an optimistic view of human nature. They believe people are basically honest, decent, and trustworthy. People who demonstrate low agreeableness are often described as short tempered, uncooperative, and irritable. They are generally unconcerned with others' well-being and are unlikely to extend themselves for other people. Highly agreeable people are better at developing and maintaining close relationships with others at work, whereas less agreeable people are not likely to have particularly close working relationships with others, including customers and suppliers. How would you rate Richard Branson on the agreeableness dimension?

Extraversion *is the degree to which a person seeks the company of others.* Extraverts enjoy being with people, are full of energy, and often experience positive emotions. Sociable people are extraverts. Extraverts are comfortable talking with others, speak up in a group, and are assertive, talkative, and open to establishing new interpersonal relationships. Less sociable people are usually called *introverts.* They tend to be low key, quiet, and deliberate. Their lack of social involvement should not be interpreted as shyness; the introvert simply needs less stimulation and more time alone to recharge his or her batteries. Research has shown that sociable people tend to be higher performing managers than less sociable people and that they are more likely to be attracted to managerial positions that require good interpersonal skills, such as marketing, sales, and senior management positions. How would you rate Richard Branson on the extraversion dimension?

Conscientiousness *is concerned with self-discipline, acting responsibly, and directing our behavior*. People who focus on a few key goals are more likely to be organized, reliable, careful, thorough, responsible, and self-disciplined because they concentrate on doing a few things well. Unconscientiousness people tend to focus on a wider array of goals and, as a result, tend to be more disorganized and less thorough. Researchers have found that more conscientious people tend to be higher performers than less conscientious people, especially in sales. How would you rate David Neeleman on this dimension?

Openness *describes imagination and creativity*. People with high levels of openness are willing to listen to new ideas, have vivid imaginations, appreciate art and beauty, prefer variety to routine, and change their own ideas, beliefs, and assumptions in response to new information. Open people tend to have a broad range of interests and be creative. On the other hand, people who demonstrate low openness tend to be less receptive to new ideas and less willing to change their minds. They prefer the plain, straightforward, and obvious over the complex, ambiguous, and subtle. Managers who are high on openness tend to be better performers because of their ability to adapt to new situations and their willingness to listen to others who have different points of view. How would you rate Richard Branson on openness?

Organizational Effectiveness and the Big Five. Although each personality factor represents a collection of related traits, the link between personality and specific behaviors often is most clear when we focus on a single trait rather than all five factors at once. Organizations are using the Big Five as an assessment device for screening new employees as part of their interviewing process. Nordstrom's requires salespeople to be cheerful, energetic, and serve very demanding customers with a smile. Therefore, extraversion, agreeableness, and emotional stability are important personality traits to succeed at Nordstrom's. At Outback Steakhouse, the turnover of employees varies between 40 and 60 percent a year. Using the Big Five inventory, Outback managers found that by recruiting employees who were extraverted and agreeable, they were able to cut down on turnover and increase customers' satisfaction with their dining experiences. Similarly, Outsourcing Solutions, a debt collection firm, found that those employees high in conscientiousness and introversion were able to sit for hours by themselves to make calls regarding past-due accounts and stayed with the organization longer than those employees who did not demonstrate these traits. New Horizons Computer Learning Centers also faced high turnover until it discovered that those employees who were high in conscientiousness and extraversion made the best employees for them.[16]

Some individuals question these findings noting that one's personality traits can undergo change. We believe that one's personality can evolve over time as a person becomes exposed to new experiences and situations. Graduating from college, breaking away from one's parents, starting a career, getting married, raising children, being managed by various "bosses" can all shape a person's personality. Also by examining our own behavior, we may learn to behave differently from situation to situation. Have you ever noticed how your behavior at a Super Bowl party is different than your behavior at work?

Self-Esteem

Self-esteem *is the extent to which a person believes that he or she is a worthwhile and deserving individual.* In other words, people develop, hold, and sometimes modify opinions of their own behaviors, abilities, appearance, and worth. These general self-assessments reflect responses to people and situations, successes and failures, and the opinions of others. Such self-evaluations are sufficiently accurate and stable to be widely regarded as a basic personality trait or dimension. In terms of the Big Five personality factors, self-esteem most likely would be part of the *emotional stability* factor (see Figure 2.3).

Self-esteem affects behavior in organizations and other social settings in several important ways. It influences initial vocational choice. For example, individuals with high self-esteem are more likely to take risks in job selection, to seek out high-status occupations (e.g., medicine or law), and are more likely to choose unconventional or nontraditional jobs (e.g., forest ranger or jet pilot) than are individuals with low self-esteem. A study of college students looking for jobs reported that those with high self-esteem (1) received more favorable evaluations from recruiters, (2) were more satisfied with the job search, (3) received more job offers, and (4) were more likely to accept jobs before graduation than were students with low self-esteem.[17]

Self-esteem appears to influence numerous behaviors. Employees with low self-esteem are more easily swayed by the opinions of other workers than are employees with high self-esteem. Employees with low self-esteem set lower goals for themselves than do employees with high self-esteem. Employees with high self-esteem place more value on actually attaining their goals than do employees with low self-esteem. That is, high self-esteem people break down jobs into specific tasks and prioritize their work so they can accomplish their jobs. Employees with low self-esteem are more susceptible than employees with high self-esteem to procrastinate, suffer stress, conflict, ambiguity, poor supervision, poor working conditions, and the like. In brief, high self-esteem is positively related to achievement and a willingness to expend effort to accomplish tasks. Clearly, self-esteem is an important individual difference in terms of work behavior. Both Richard Branson and David Neeleman appear to be individuals with high self-esteem.

Locus of Control

Locus of control *is the extent to which individuals believe that they can control events affecting them.*[18] Individuals who have a high internal locus of control (internals) *believe that their own behavior and actions primarily, but not necessarily totally, determine many of the events in their lives.* On the other hand, individuals who have a high external locus of control (externals) *believe that chance, fate, or other people primarily determine what happens to them.* Locus of control typically is considered to be a part of the *conscientiousness* factor (see Figure 2.3). What is your locus of control? Table 2.2 contains a measure that you can use to assess your own locus of control beliefs.

Many differences between internals and externals are significant in explaining aspects of behavior in organizations and other social settings.[19] Internals control their own behavior better, are more active politically and socially, and seek information about their situations more actively than do externals. Compared to externals, internals are more likely to try to influence or persuade others and are less likely to be influenced by others. Internals often are more achievement oriented than are externals. Compared to internals, externals appear to prefer a more structured, directive style of supervision. As we pointed out in Chapter 1, the ability to manage effectively in the global environment is an increasingly important competency. Individuals with a high internal locus of control often adjust more readily to international assignments than do those with a high external locus of control. What do you think David Neeleman's locus of control score is?

Table 2.2 A Locus of Control Measure

For each of these 10 questions, indicate the extent to which you agree or disagree, using the following scale.

1 = strongly disagree	5 = slightly agree
2 = disagree	6 = agree
3 = slightly disagree	7 = strongly agree
4 = neither disagree nor agree	

_____ 1. When I get what I want it's usually because I worked hard for it.

_____ 2. When I make plans I am almost certain to make them work.

_____ 3. I prefer games involving some luck over games requiring pure skill.

_____ 4. I can learn almost anything if I set my mind to it.

_____ 5. My major accomplishments are entirely due to my hard work and ability.

_____ 6. I usually don't set goals, because I have a hard time following through on them.

_____ 7. Competition discourages excellence.

_____ 8. Often people get ahead just by being lucky.

_____ 9. On any sort of exam or competition I like to know how well I do relative to everyone else.

_____ 10. It's pointless to keep working on something that's too difficult for me.

To determine your score, reverse the values you selected for questions 3, 6, 7, 8, and 10 (1 = 7, 2 = 6, 3 = 5, 4 = 4, 5 = 3, 6 = 2, 7 = 1). For example, if you strongly disagreed with the statement in question 3, you would have given it a value of "1." Change this value to a "7." Reverse the scores in a similar manner for questions 6, 7, 8, and 10. Now add the 10 point values together.

Your score: _____

A study of college students found a mean of 51.8 for men and 52.2 for women using this questionnaire. The higher your score, the higher your internal locus of control. Low scores are associated with external locus of control.

Source: Adapted from Burger, J. M. *Personality: Theory and Research.* Belmont, Calif.: Wadsworth, 1986, pp. 400–401.

Figure 2.4 shows some of the important relationships between locus of control and job performance.

Emotional Intelligence

Psychologist Daniel Goleman contends that emotional intelligence (EQ) is actually more crucial than general intelligence (IQ) in terms of career success.[20] Emotional intelligence *refers to how well an individual handles oneself and others rather than how smart or how capable the individual is in terms of technical skills.* Goleman suggests that leaders need a high EQ to be effective in their leadership positions. A high EQ enables a leader to accurately assess his subordinates' needs, analyze the situation, and then suggest the proper course of action. The leader processes this information to tailor his behaviors to fit the situation. To assess your emotional intelligence, turn to pages 64–65 and complete the questionnaire. Emotional intelligence includes the attributes of self-awareness, social empathy, self-motivation, and social skills:

- Self-awareness *refers to recognizing one's emotions, strengths and limitations, and capabilities and how these affect others.* People with high self-awareness know their emotional state, recognize the links between their feelings and what they are thinking, are open to feedback from others on how to continuously improve, and are able to make sound decisions despite uncertainties and pressures. They are able to show a sense of humor. How would you rate Richard Branson on this dimension?
- Social empathy *refers to sensing what others need in order for them to develop.* Individuals who are socially aware of themselves show sensitivity, understand other people's

FIGURE 2.4 The Effects of Locus of Control on Performance

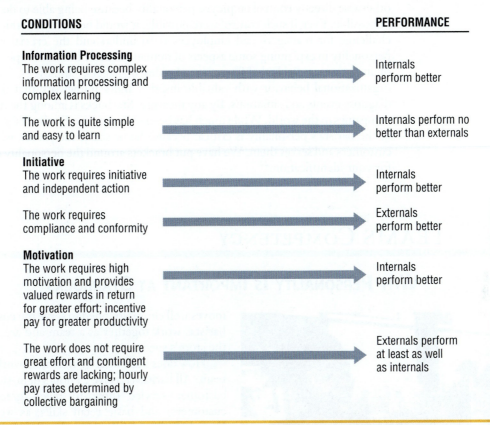

CONDITIONS	PERFORMANCE
Information Processing The work requires complex information processing and complex learning	Internals perform better
The work is quite simple and easy to learn	Internals perform no better than externals
Initiative The work requires initiative and independent action	Internals perform better
The work requires compliance and conformity	Externals perform better
Motivation The work requires high motivation and provides valued rewards in return for greater effort; incentive pay for greater productivity	Internals perform better
The work does not require great effort and contingent rewards are lacking; hourly pay rates determined by collective bargaining	Externals perform at least as well as internals

From J. B. Miner, *Industrial-Organizational Psychology.* McGraw-Hill, 1992, 151.

needs and feelings, challenge bias and intolerance, and act as trusted advisers to others. They are good at acknowledging people's strengths, accomplishments, and development. As a mentor, they give timely coaching advice and offer assignments that challenge a person's competencies.

- Self-motivation *refers to being results oriented and pursuing goals beyond what is required.* Highly self-motivated people set challenging goals for themselves and others, seek ways to improve their performance, and readily make personal sacrifices to meet the organization's goals. They operate from hope of success rather than a fear of failure. How would you rate David Neeleman on this dimension?
- Social skills *refer to the ability of a person to influence others.* A person with effective social skills is good at persuading others to share her vision; stepping forward as a leader, regardless of her position in the organization; leading by example; and dealing with difficult interpersonal situations in a straightforward manner. How would you rate Richard Branson on this dimension?

Think of EQ as being the social equivalent of IQ. In organizations undergoing rapid change, emotional intelligence may determine who gets promoted and who gets passed over or who gets laid off and who stays. Studies have consistently shown, for example, that the competencies associated with emotional intelligence (e.g., the ability to persuade others, the ability to understand others, and so on) are twice as important for career success as intelligence (IQ) or technical competencies.[21]

Role of Personality in Organizations

It should be evident by now that the personality dimensions have important implications for understanding behavior. However, managers or groups should not try to change or otherwise directly control employee personality because being able to do so is generally impossible. Even if such control were possible, it would be highly unethical. Rather, the challenge for managers and employees is to understand the crucial role played by personality in explaining some aspects of human behavior in the workplace. Knowledge of important individual differences provides managers, employees, and students of organizational behavior with valuable insights and a framework that they can use to diagnose events and situations. By any measure, Starbucks is among the most successful companies in the world. While much has been written about Starbucks' success, the role of the barista's personality is critical because he or she is the person who talks to the customers and serves them. We have put brackets around the personality characteristics for your identification.[22]

Teams Competency

Why Personality Is Important at Starbucks

© AP Images

When hiring a barista, Starbucks looks for an individual with high self-esteem, who is sensitive to the feelings of others, and who wants to participate in the success of all team members.

Enter any Starbucks and you'll see baristas (the associates who take orders and make and serve coffee and food) at work. They work like a well-oiled machine with all moves well choreographed to serve the customer. These baristas work together as a team and are important for the store's success.

How does Starbucks train them to work together as a team? All baristas receive 24 hours of in-store training in customer service (how to meet, greet, and serve customers) and basic retail skills, as well as "Coffee Knowledge" and "Brewing the Perfect Cup" classes. Baristas are taught to anticipate the customer's needs, and to make eye contact while carefully explaining the various flavors and blends. They are also trained in the care and maintenance of the machinery and how to treat each other.

One of the guiding principles at Starbucks is to provide a great working environment and to employ people who treat each other with high respect and dignity [emotional stability]. A company survey found the top two reasons people want to work for Starbucks are "the opportunity to work with an enthusiastic team" and "to work in a place where I feel I have value" [agreeableness]. Therefore, Starbucks looks to hire people with high self-esteem, who are sensitive to the feelings of others and who want the participation and success for all team members. Highly effective baristas are also stable individuals who do not show anxiousness or hostility to others even under stressful conditions. Finally, Starbucks wants barista partners who combine their passion for great coffee and quality customer service, listen to others, are reliable, organized, and can focus on completing their tasks.

For more information on Starbucks, visit the organization's home page at www.starbucks.com.

Managerial Guidelines

Although understanding differences in personality is important, behavior always involves an interaction of the person and the situation. Sometimes the demands of the situation may be so overwhelming that individual differences are relatively unimportant. For example, if an office building is burning, everyone in it will try to flee. However, the fact that all employees behaved the same way says nothing about the personalities of those individuals. In other situations, individual differences may explain more about behavior.

Under normal working conditions, a person's personality has a major role in determining how he behaves at work. Just reflect on how Richard Branson's personality affects others at Virgin, or the characteristics of baristas that Starbucks looks for when hiring new employees. We believe that considering both the personality of the individual and the demands of the job are needed to help you understand behavior in organizations. When an individual's personality does not fit the demands of the job, she will be less satisfied and productive. Job applicants should assess the fit between their personal characteristics and the demands of the job and organization. However, if all individuals share common characteristics and preferences, the organization might be quite resistant to change. To remain competitive over the long term, organizations are probably well served to hire some people who do not fit the mold. For that reason, this perspective is consistently used throughout this book. You will discover that many of the topics covered, such as leadership, interpersonal communication, conflict management, stress, and resistance to change, examine both *personal* and *situational causes* for the organizational behavior discussed. Both *interact* to determine behavior.

WORK ATTITUDES AND BEHAVIOR

Learning Goal

3. Describe how attitudes influence performance.

It is often very difficult to separate personality and attitudes. You cannot see either one, but you can see the results of each through a person's behavior. Attitudes are another type of *individual difference* that affects an individual's behavior in organizations. Attitudes *are relatively lasting feelings, beliefs, and behavioral tendencies aimed at specific people, groups, ideas, issues, or objects.*[23] Attitudes reflect an individual's background and experiences and are formed by a variety of forces, including their personal values, experiences, and personalities. Attitudes are important for three reasons. First, attitudes are reasonably stable over time. Unless people have strong reasons to change, they will persist. People who have a favorable attitude toward buying domestic cars will probably like domestic cars in the future, unless important reasons occur to change their automobile preferences. Second, people hold attitudes that are directed toward some object—job, supervisor, company, college. If a barista likes coffee and serving people, they probably won't have a negative attitude toward working at Starbucks as a barista. Third, attitudes influence our behavior. That is, people tend to behave in ways that are consistent with their feelings. If we have a specific attitude toward an object or person, we tend to form other consistent attitudes toward related objects or people. Therefore, to change a person's attitude, you need to change a person's behavior.

Components of Attitudes

A person might decide to join an organization for a variety of reasons. Once she joins that organization, we would expect that person to express a consistently positive attitude toward that organization by telling others about her decision to join, what outstanding products or services the organization offers, and what great challenges the organization will offer her to develop as a professional. Individuals often think of attitudes as a simple concept. In reality, attitudes and their effects on behavior can be extremely complex. An attitude consists of

- an *affective* component—the feelings, sentiments, moods, and emotions about some person, idea, event, or object;

- a *cognitive* component—the thoughts, opinions, knowledge, or information held by the individual; and
- a *behavioral* component—the predisposition to act on a favorable or unfavorable evaluation of something.

These components don't exist or function separately. An attitude represents the *interplay* of a person's affective, cognitive, and behavioral tendencies with regard to something—another person or group, an event, or an issue. For example, suppose that a college student has a negative attitude about the use of tobacco. During a job interview with the representative of Oscar Mayer, he discovers that Oscar Mayer is owned by Kraft Foods, which is a major division of Philip Morris, a major supplier of cigarettes. He might feel a sudden intense dislike for the company's interviewer (the affective component). He might form a negative opinion of the interviewer based on beliefs and opinions about the type of person who would work for such a company (the cognitive component). He might even be tempted to make an unkind remark to the interviewer or suddenly terminate the interview (the behavioral component). However, the person's *actual* behavior may or may not be easy to predict and will depend on several factors that we discuss shortly.

LEADER INSIGHT

I really think there's only one thing in your life you have control over, and that's your attitude.
Susan Mead, Partner, Jackson Walker, LLP

Key Work-Related Attitudes: Hope, Job Satisfaction, and Organizational Commitment

Individuals form attitudes about many things. Employees have attitudes about their manager, pay, working conditions, promotions, where they park, coworkers, and the like. Some of these attitudes are more important than others because they are more closely linked to performance. Especially important are attitudes of hope, job satisfaction, and organizational commitment.

Hope. Hope *involves a person's mental willpower (determination) and waypower (road map) to achieve goals.*[24] Simply wishing for something isn't enough; a person must have the means to make it happen. However, all the knowledge and skills needed to solve a problem won't help if the person doesn't have the willpower to do so. Therefore, a simple definition of hope is

$$\text{Hope} = \text{mental willpower} + \text{waypower to achieve goals.}$$

Answering the questions in Table 2.3 on page 53 will help you understand this definition of *hope*. The value of this concept is that it applies to a variety of work-related attitudes. The high-hope person enjoys the pursuit of challenging goals and pursues them with a positive attitude. High-hope people engage in self-talk, such as "This should be an interesting task" or "I am ready for this challenge." The high-hope person is attentive and focused on the appropriate behaviors for the situation. High-hope people commit themselves to desired positive work outcomes (e.g., good performance) and distance themselves from negative outcomes.

High-hope individuals establish clear goals, imagine pathways to those goals, and motivate themselves to follow such pathways. High-hope individuals are likely to be characterized as being high in self-esteem, having an internal locus of control, and exhibiting the Big Five personality dimensions of conscientiousness and openness. In contrast, the low-hope person is apprehensive about what is to come. Their attention is quickly diverted from task-relevant behavior to such thoughts as "I'm not doing well very." Quickly the low-hope person may feel a lot of negative emotions. Low-hope people are especially susceptible to feeling great amounts of stress in their jobs and becoming easily derailed by issues in their pursuit of goals. With such derailments, low-hope people perceive that they are not going to reach their desired goals. Their natural tendency is to

Table 2.3 **Hope Scale**

Read each item carefully. For each item, what number best describes you?

1 = definitely false

2 = mostly false

3 = mostly true

4 = definitely true

_____ 1. I energetically pursue my work (academic) goals.

_____ 2. I can think of many ways to get out of a jam.

_____ 3. My past experiences have prepared me well for my future.

_____ 4. There are lots of ways around any problem.

_____ 5. I've been pretty successful in life.

_____ 6. I can think of many ways to get things in life that are most important to me.

_____ 7. I meet the goals (work/academic) that I set for myself.

_____ 8. Even when others get discouraged, I know I can find a way to solve the problem.

Scoring: Total the eight numbers. If you score higher than 24, you are a hopeful person. If you score less than 24, you probably aren't hopeful. Items 1, 3, 5, and 7 relate to willpower, and items 2, 4, 6, and 8 relate to waypower.

Source: Adapted from Snyder, C. R. Managing for high hope. *R & D Innovator*, 1995, 4(6), 6–7; Snyder, C. R., LaPointe, A. B., Crowson, J. J., and Early, S. Preferences of high- and low-hope people for self-referential input. *Cognition and Emotion*, 1998, 12, 807–823.

withdraw from friends and become "loners." For a high-hope person, however, the stressor is seen as a challenge that needs to be worked around. Should the high-hope person be truly blocked in the pursuit of a goal, instead of being full of anger, self-pity, and negative emotions, as is the case for low-hope individuals in similar circumstances, high-hope individuals will find another goal that will fulfill similar needs. This is because high-hope individuals have several goals that can bring them happiness. Managers who are hopeful spend more time with employees, establish open lines of communication with employees and others, and help employees set difficult, but achievable, goals. High-hope individuals tend to be more certain of their goals, value progress toward achieving those goals, enjoy interacting with people, readily adapt to new relationships, and are less anxious in stressful situations than are low-hope individuals.

Managers can help employees increase their level of hope in at least three ways.[25] First, they can help employees set clear *goals* that have benchmarks so that the employees can track their progress toward the goal; vague goals may actually lessen hope because the result sought is unclear and tracking progress therefore is difficult, if not impossible. Employees who set goals that are slightly higher than previous levels of performance learn to expand their range of hope. They also learn a great deal about which goals are best for them. Second, managers can help employees break overall, long-term goals into *small subgoals* or *steps*. Remember how you learned to ride a bike? Through many falls and wobbles, you learned that each consecutive subgoal (moving the pedals, balancing, going a block without falling) is a stretch. These small steps provided you with positive mental maps about how to reach your goal—riding a bike. Third, managers can help employees figure out how to *motivate* themselves to reach their goals.

Job Satisfaction. An attitude of great interest to managers and team leaders is job satisfaction.[26] Job satisfaction *reflects the extent to which people find fulfillment in their work*. Job satisfaction has been linked to employees staying on the job and low job turnover. With the cost of replacing employees being about 30 to 40 percent of their salary, job turnover can become quite expensive. Similarly, employees who are highly satisfied with their jobs come to work regularly and are less likely to take sick days.

Do employees generally like their jobs? Despite what you may hear in the news about dissatisfied employees going on strike or even acting violently toward their coworkers and/or managers, they are generally quite satisfied with their jobs. These feelings, reflecting attitudes toward a job, are known as job satisfaction. Low job satisfaction can result in costly turnover, absenteeism, tardiness, and even poor mental health. Because job satisfaction is important to organizations, we need to look at the factors that contribute to it.

A popular measure of job satisfaction used by organizations is shown in Table 2.4. It measures five facets of job satisfaction: pay, security, social, supervisory, and growth satisfaction. Take a minute now to complete it. Obviously, you may be satisfied with some aspects of your job and, at the same time, be dissatisfied with others.

Table 2.4 **Measuring Job Satisfaction**

Think of the job you have now, or a job you've had in the past. Indicate how satisfied you are with each aspect of your job below, using the following scale:

1 = Extremely dissatisfied
2 = Dissatisfied
3 = Slightly dissatisfied
4 = Neutral
5 = Slightly satisfied
6 = Satisfied
7 = Extremely satisfied

_____ 1. The amount of job security I have.
_____ 2. The amount of pay and fringe benefits I receive.
_____ 3. The amount of personal growth and development I get in doing my job.
_____ 4. The people I talk to and work with on my job.
_____ 5. The degree of respect and fair treatment I receive from my boss.
_____ 6. The feeling of worthwhile accomplishment I get from doing my job.
_____ 7. The chance to get to know other people while on the job.
_____ 8. The amount of support and guidance I receive from my supervisor.
_____ 9. The degree to which I am fairly paid for what I contribute to this organization.
_____ 10. The amount of independent thought and action I can exercise in my job.
_____ 11. How secure things look for me in the future in this organization.
_____ 12. The chance to help other people while at work.
_____ 13. The amount of challenge in my job.
_____ 14. The overall quality of the supervision I receive on my work.

Now, compute your scores for the facets of job satisfaction.

Pay Satisfaction:
Q2 + Q9 = _____ Divided by 2:
Security Satisfaction:
Q1 + Q11 = _____ Divided by 2:
Social Satisfaction:
Q4 + Q7 + Q12 = _____ Divided by 3:
Supervisory Satisfaction:
Q5 + Q8 + Q14 = _____ Divided by 3:
Growth Satisfaction:
Q3 + Q6 + Q10 + Q13 = _____ Divided by 4:

Scores on the facets range from 1 to 7. (Scores lower than 4 suggest there is room for change.) This questionnaire is an abbreviated version of the Job Diagnostic Survey, a widely used tool for assessing individuals' attitudes about their jobs.

Source: J. Richard Hackman & Greg R. Oldham, WORK REDESIGN, © 1980. Reprinted by permission of Pearson Education, Inc., Upper Saddle River, NJ.

Table 2.5 Effects of Various Work Factors on Job Satisfaction

WORK FACTORS	EFFECTS
Work itself	
Challenge	Mentally challenging work that the individual can successfully accomplish is satisfying.
Physical demands	Tiring work is dissatisfying.
Personal interest	Personally interesting work is satisfying.
Reward structure	Rewards that are equitable and that provide accurate feedback for performance are satisfying.
Working conditions	
Physical	Satisfaction depends on the match between working conditions and physical needs.
Goal attainment	Working conditions that promote goal attainment are satisfying.
Self	High self-esteem is conducive to job satisfaction.
Others in the organization	Individuals will be satisfied with supervisors, coworkers, or subordinates who help them attain rewards. Also, individuals will be more satisfied with colleagues who see things the same way they do.
Organization and management	Individuals will be satisfied with organizations that have policies and procedures designed to help them attain rewards. Individuals will be dissatisfied with conflicting roles and/or ambiguous roles imposed by the organization.
Fringe benefits	Benefits do not have a strong influence on job satisfaction for most workers.

Source: Adapted from Landy, F. J. Psychology of Work Behavior, 4th ed. Pacific Grove, Calif.: Brooks/Cole, 1989, 470.

The sources of job satisfaction and dissatisfaction vary from person to person. Sources important for many employees include the challenge of the job, the interest that the work holds for them, the physical activity required, working conditions, rewards available from the organization, the nature of coworkers, and the like. Table 2.5 lists work factors that often are related to levels of employee job satisfaction. An important implication suggested is that job satisfaction be considered an outcome of an individual's work experience. Thus, high levels of dissatisfaction should indicate to managers that problems exist, say, with working conditions, the reward system, or the employee's role in the organization.

Of special interest to managers and employees are the possible relationships between job satisfaction and various job behaviors and other outcomes in the workplace. A commonsense notion is that job satisfaction leads directly to effective performance. (A happy worker is a good worker.) Yet, numerous studies have shown that a simple, direct link between job satisfaction and job performance often doesn't exist.[27] Research has shown that job satisfaction and job performance are mediated by one's personality. That is, a person's locus of control and Big Five personality characteristics affect the relationship between job satisfaction and job performance. The difficulty of relating attitudes to behavior is important. For example, people who hold a positive attitude toward their job but are low in conscientiousness may not necessarily work harder because they come late to work, fail to show up, are unorganized, and the like. General attitudes best predict general behaviors, and specific attitudes are related most strongly to specific behaviors. These principles explain, at least in part, why the expected relationships often don't exist. Job satisfaction is a collection of numerous attitudes toward various aspects of the job and represents a general attitude. Performance of a specific task, such as preparing a particular monthly report, can't necessarily be predicted on the basis of a general attitude. However, studies have shown that the level of overall workforce job satisfaction and organizational performance are linked. That is, organizations with satisfied employees tend to be more effective than organizations with unsatisfied employees. Further, management in many organizations recognizes the important link between customer satisfaction and the satisfaction of employees who interact with their customers. Examples of this link are apparent in the following Communication Competency feature.[28]

Communication Competency

Creating Positive Attitudes at The Container Store

© Andreas Pollok/Digital Vision/Getty Images

New employees at The Container Store go through extensive training to learn about the store's products, processes, and values.

Employee turnover is greater than 100 percent in most retail stores. In contrast, it is only 30 percent at The Container Store. Let's consider how its managers attract and retain employees.

The Container Store recently was named by *Fortune* magazine and the Great Places to Work Institute as one of America's top 10 best places to work. Sales exceed $500 million for its 39 stores. What goes into this ranking? Great Places uses five criteria to judge a company: (1) credibility—open communications, integrity; (2) respect—caring for employees as individuals with personal lives; (3) fairness—absence of favoritism in hiring and promotions; (4) pride—the organization's reputation in the community; and (5) camaraderie—a sense of family or team.

How does The Container Store rate? First, it practices what it preaches. Every first-year full-time employee gets about 241 hours of training (the norm for the retail industry is 7 hours). All new employees in the stores, distribution center, and headquarters (full-time and seasonal employees) go through Foundation Week—five days dedicated to learning information about The Container Store's products, processes, and values, plus extra human resources reading. Second, new employees assume regular work schedules only after having completed five full days of training. Third, employees spend time in different functions and units to gain a broader perspective and to learn about the company's strategic challenges. Each store has a back room where new products are housed prior to display. Employees receive formal training on how to display these new products and how to communicate their benefits. According to Chairman Garrett Boone and CEO Kip Tindell, "Nothing goes out on the sales floor until our people are ready for it." This program is coupled with extensive training programs designed to develop individual competencies for various job functions. A "super sales trainer" serves each store. These trainers are top sales performers who know how to sell the hard stuff and who have an aptitude for leadership and strong communication and presentation skills. These people give on-the-spot help to employees who ask, but employees are encouraged to take responsibility for their own development.

The Container Store pays above-industry salaries to employees. Employees earn 50 to 100 percent more than employees earn at other retailers, such as the Gap, Sample House, and Borders. Employees do not sell on a commission basis. Rather a team-based incentive system is used. The company is also attractive to employees because it offers flexible shifts, allowing college students to earn some cash between classes and mothers to work while their kids are in school (9 A.M. to 2 P.M.). Some of the free perks include yoga classes three times a week, on-site dry cleaning, chair massages once a week, a subsidized cafeteria, car washes, and the full use of a postal and packaging center. According to a recent survey, 97 percent of the employees agreed with the statement "People really care about each other here."

Guided by what Boone and Tindell call a "do-unto-others" philosophy, The Container Store's more than 4,000 employees, of whom 27 percent are minority and 60 percent are women, work in an environment that ensures open communication throughout the company. This includes regular discussions of store sales, company goals, and expansion plans. Another guiding principle is to offer the best selection, the best price, and the best service. All employees are encouraged to treat customers like they would treat visitors in their homes. Boone and Tindell empathize with those who must cope with multiple demands on their time and energy and need to bring some order to their lives. Balancing both work and motherhood symbolizes their clientele—85 percent of whom are well-educated females from households with annual incomes of more than $100,000.

For more information on The Container Store, visit the organization's home page at www.containerstore.com.

Organizational Commitment. Like job satisfaction, organizational commitment influences whether a person stays on the job. Organizational commitment *is the strength of an employee's involvement in the organization and identification with it.*[29] Employees who stay with their organization for a long period of time tend to be much more committed to the organization than those who worked for shorter periods of time. For long-time employees, simply the thought of packing up and moving on is too much. Strong organizational commitment is characterized by

- a support of and acceptance of the organization's goals and values,
- a willingness to exert considerable effort on behalf of the organization, and
- a desire to remain with the organization.[30]

Highly committed employees will probably see themselves as dedicated members of the organization, referring to the organization in personal terms, such as "we make high-quality products." They will overlook minor sources of job dissatisfaction and have a long tenure with the organization. In contrast, less committed employees will view their relationship with the organization in less personal terms ("They don't offer quality service"), will express their dissatisfaction more openly about things, and will have a short tenure with the organization.

Organizational commitment goes beyond loyalty to include an active contribution to accomplishing organizational goals. Organizational commitment represents a broader work attitude than job satisfaction because it applies to the entire organization rather than just to the job. Further, commitment typically is more stable than satisfaction because day-to-day events are less likely to change it.

As with job satisfaction, the sources of organizational commitment may vary from person to person. Employees' initial commitment to an organization is determined largely by their individual characteristics (e.g., cultural values, personality, attitudes) and how well their early job experiences match their expectations. As we discussed in Chapter 1, employees like working for John Yokoyama at the Pike Place Fish Market in Seattle because he encourages them to work hard, have fun, be kind, and develop positive attitudes. Tossing the fish and joking with customers, practices that may not work at IBM, seem to work at Yokoyama's fish market. Organizational commitment continues to be influenced by job experiences, with many of the same factors that lead to job satisfaction also contributing to organizational commitment or lack of commitment: pay, relationships with supervisors and coworkers, working conditions, opportunities for advancement, and so on. Over time, organizational commitment tends to become stronger because (1) individuals develop deeper ties to the organization and their coworkers as they spend more time with them, (2) seniority often brings advantages that tend to develop more positive work attitudes, and (3) opportunities in the job market may decrease with age, causing employees to become more strongly attached to their current organization.

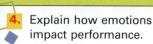

Learning Goal

4. Explain how emotions impact performance.

MANAGING EMOTIONS AT WORK

Anger, jealousy, guilt, shame, happiness, and relief are all feelings that you have probably experienced in organizations. These feelings are all part of your emotions. Emotions *are the complex patterns of feelings toward an object or person.* We have all seen how emotions affect workplace attitudes and behaviors. When performing your job, you experience a variety of emotions during the day. You also know that how employees and managers handle their emotions at work has a tremendous impact on their productivity.[31] The more emotions that are positive, the more we form positive attitudes toward the organization. Positive emotions, such as joy, affection, and happiness, serve many purposes. When employees experience these positive emotions, they tend to think more creatively, seek out new information and experiences, behave more flexibly, have greater confidence in their competencies, and be more persistent. Positive emotions can help individuals bounce back from adversity and live longer and healthier lives. Individuals who experience positive emotions, especially during stressful times, tend to tolerate pain better, cope with and recover from illness faster, and experience less depression. In contrast, negative emotions, such as anger, disgust, and sadness, tend to narrow an individual's focus and limit their options to seek alternatives. For example, anger tends to lead to a desire to escape, attack, or take revenge, and guilt/shame can result in a person's desire to withdraw from the situation rather than creatively problem solve. Negative emotions also tend to produce larger, more long-lasting effects than positive emotions. That is, negative emotions tend to stay with individuals longer than positive ones.

The distinction between positive and negative emotions is shown in Figure 2.5. Negative emotions are incongruent with the goal you are striving to achieve. For example, which of the six emotions are you likely to experience if you fail the final exam for this course, or if you are dismissed from your job? Failing the exam or losing your job would be incongruent with your goal of graduating or being perceived as an accomplished professional. On the other hand, which of the four positive emotions, shown in Figure 2.5, will you likely experience if you graduate with honors or receive a promotion? The emotions that you would experience in these situations are positive because these are congruent with your goals. Therefore, emotions are goal directed.

Positive emotions have been linked to organizational effectiveness. Leaders who express positive emotions encourage employees to feel positive emotions as well. When individuals have positive emotions, they are more likely to set high goals, see and fix mistakes, feel more competent, and have greater problem-solving capabilities. In organizations that recently cut staff, those organizations that had leaders who displayed positive emotions even in such trying times had significantly higher productivity, higher quality, and lower voluntary employee turnover than those leaders who displayed

FIGURE 2.5 Positive and Negative Emotions

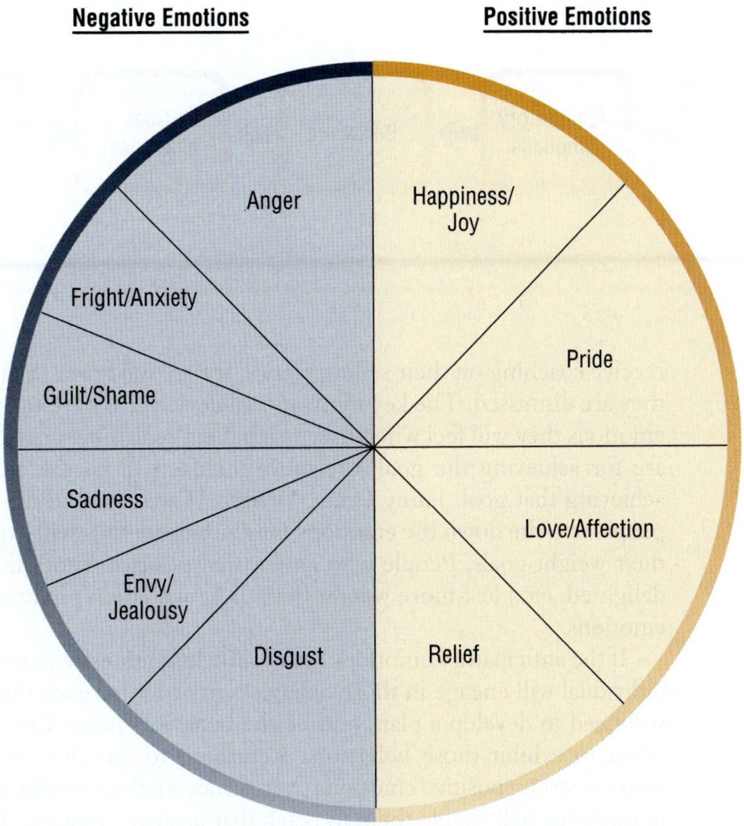

negative emotions. After the Twin Towers toppled as a result of terrorist attacks on September 11, 2001, employees at a Starbucks near the Towers were told by their manager that they could leave to protect their safety. Instead, employees and the store managers chose to stay and literally pulled stunned people passing by into the store, giving them food, drink, shelter, and emotional support. As one reporter said: "Embedded in a crisis is an opportunity for employers to build loyalty and wholeheartedly supply positive emotions."

A Model of Emotions

A model of how emotions affect behavior is shown in Figure 2.6.[32] The process starts with a goal. A goal *refers to what an individual is trying to accomplish*. That is, a goal is your purpose or intent. An eye doctor may have a goal of serving 30 patients a week. Anticipatory emotions *refer to the emotions that individual's believe they will feel after achievement or failure of reaching their goal*. For example, at Sewell Automotive in Dallas, Texas, a salesperson's goal is to sell 9 cars a month. If they sell between 9 and 19 cars, they receive special recognition (e.g., flowers, round of golf, choice of cars to drive for the next month) from their manager. If they sell more than 20 cars in any month, they receive a special letter from Carl Sewell, a weekend package at a local hotel with all expenses paid, as well as flowers, golf, etc. If they sell fewer than 9 cars a month, they will

FIGURE 2.6 Role of Emotions in Performance

receive coaching on their selling tactics. If they sell fewer than 27 cars in three months, they are dismissed. The key motivational device is to have each salesperson imagine the emotions they will feel when they reach their goal. The more desirable the implications are for achieving the goal, the more intense will be the anticipated emotions from achieving that goal. Jenny Craig, Weight Watchers, and other diet organizations ask people to write down the emotions they anticipate they will experience when they reach their weight goals. People who anticipated positive emotions (e.g., I will feel excited, delighted, etc.) lost more weight than those who didn't have such positive anticipatory emotions.

If the anticipatory emotions are of sufficient intensity to motivate the individual, the individual will engage in those behaviors in order to reach their goal. That is, a person will need to develop a plan, outline the behaviors needed to reach her plan, and exert effort to exhibit those behaviors. Returning to our diet example, if individuals can imagine strong positive emotions from achieving their weight goals, they need to behave in ways that will enable them to reach that positive emotion. That is, they need to start exercising and dieting. Both of these behaviors are linked to loss of weight. As shown in Figure 2.6, goal attainment is the next step. Did they reach their goal? Yes or no? If yes, then they would experience positive emotions; if no, then they would experience negative emotions. In our dietary plan, researchers found that those people who could anticipate positive emotions from achieving their goal were more likely to diet and exercise and reach their goal than those individuals who didn't engage in these behaviors.

On any given Saturday, the Magnolia Cafe in Austin, Texas, is packed with noisy customers. Customers wait outside for tables and parking is limited. A customer asks for a menu and some water because he has been waiting for some time and the waiter yells to a customer: "If you want fast service, go to McDonald's." To a new customer, this sort of rude behavior is unusual. But the Magnolia Cafe is a place where both customers and the waitstaff play out their emotions. Customers come to the Magnolia Cafe to be "insulted" and treated "rudely" and they are usually treated that way. Such emotional displays are unusual because employees are expected to manage their emotions in the workplace. At the Ritz-Carlton Hotel chain, employees are told to smile and hold their negative emotions in check at all times.

There are cross-cultural differences in the display of emotions. Most Japanese managers believe that it is inappropriate to get emotional doing business, compared with 40 percent of Americans, 34 percent of the French, and 29 percent of the Italians. Italians, for example, are more likely to accept people who display their emotions at work, whereas this would be considered rude in Japan. The following Across Cultures Competency feature illustrates how companies in Japan teach employees to display proper emotions.[33]

Across Cultures Competency

Emotions in Japan

Hiroshi Ieyoshi and other gas station attendants are gathered for a three-hour training session on learning how to smile. "It's easy to say you should smile at customers," says Leyoshi, a 39-year-old gas attendant after the seminar. "But to be honest, it all depends on how I feel at the moment." Leyoshi isn't the only person who has trouble smiling at customers.

In the Japanese culture, hiding one's emotions is considered a virtue because the lack of expression minimizes conflict and avoids drawing attention to the individual. Tomoko Yoshida is a customer relations training expert who works at the Sheraton Hotels in Japan. He teaches hotel employees never to show emotions while talking with a guest. In particular, even if the employee is upset, they are instructed never to point with their finger. Pointing is considered rude. Using one's whole hand shows more effort and is considered more polite and business-like. Similarly, if a customer is sitting in a restaurant and the waiter raises his or her voice, it signals to the customer that the waiter wants the guest to leave and isn't welcome any longer. Yoshida also instructs bellmen not to use their feet to close a door or move a customer's bags or toys even if the bellman is upset. Why? In Japan, people believe that the ground is where they walk in shoes. When they go home, they take their shoes off because they don't want to mix the outside ground with the inside ground.

Yoshikihiko Kadokawa, author of *The Power of Laughing Face*, found that even in Japan's culture, the friendliest clerks in some of Japan's biggest retail stores consistently rang up the highest sales. His research found that smiling salesclerks reported 20 percent more sales than nonsmiling salesclerks.

McDonald's Corporation is using Kadokawa's techniques to screen applicants. The company screens out people who are too poker faced. When asked by the company to describe a pleasant experience, those applicants who don't smile and indicate that they find pleasure in what they're discussing aren't hired. McDonald's wants all of their employees to provide the friendly service at the price stated on its menu: "Smiles, 0 yen."

Managerial Guidelines

Let's consider seven ways by which managers can create positive emotions in their organization:

- Express positive emotions—gratitude, generosity, optimism, trust—regularly at work. Start meetings with sincere words of appreciation. Remember that positive emotions are contagious, especially when expressed by direct supervisors and organizational leaders.
- A rule of thumb is that the number of positive communications sent by the manager must outnumber the number of negative communications by a ratio of 5:1 if the employee is to have positive emotions at work.
- Give unexpected kindness and reach out to others when it is least expected. When you engage in positive emotions and behaviors when it goes against the norm, the element of surprise and courage becomes a powerful example to others, both strengthening people's trust in you and role-modeling behavior for others to follow.
- Help people find positive meaning in their day-to-day work lives. Help employees see how their work contributes to a greater good and whom they are helping through their efforts.

- Provide opportunities for people to help each other and to express appreciation for the help they receive from others.
- Celebrate small wins so that employees experience ongoing success and the associated positive emotions.
- In a crisis, enable employees to experience and express what it feels like to rise to the occasion and find the strength and resources they never knew they had.[34]

CHAPTER SUMMARY

1. Explain the basic sources of personality determinants.

Personality is a person's set of relatively stable characteristics and traits that account for consistent patterns of behavior in various situations. Each individual is like other people in some ways and in some ways is unique. An individual's personality is determined by inherited genes and the environment. Experiences occur within the framework of the individual's biological, physical, and social environment—all of which are modified by the culture, family, and other groups to which the person belongs. We review five basic culture values—individualism and collectivism, power distance, uncertainty avoidance, gender role orientation, and long-term orientation—that impact the development of a person's personality.

2. Identify a set of personality characteristics that affect behavior.

An individual's personality may be described by a set of factors known as the Big Five personality factors. Specifically, these personality factors describe an individual's degree of emotional stability, agreeableness, extraversion, conscientiousness, and openness. We hope that you took the opportunity to assess your own Big Five personality dimensions in Table 2.1. Many specific personality dimensions, including self-esteem, locus of control, and emotional intelligence, have important relationships to work behavior and outcomes. In addition, an understanding of interactions between the person and the situation is important for comprehending organizational behavior.

3. Describe how attitudes influence performance.

Attitudes are patterns of feelings, beliefs, and behavioral tendencies directed toward specific people, groups, ideas, issues, or objects. Attitudes have affective (feelings, emotions), cognitive (beliefs, knowledge), and behavioral (a predisposition to act in a particular way) components. The relationship between attitudes and behavior isn't always clear, although important relationships exist. We reviewed how the attitudes of hope, job satisfaction, and organizational commitment affect behavior in many organizations.

4. Explain how emotions impact performance.

Employees show a variety of emotions during the day. Some of these are positive and can lead to more effective performance, whereas others are negative and can lead to poor performance. We introduced how emotions can influence the productivity of employees.

KEY TERMS AND CONCEPTS

Agreeableness
Anticipatory emotions
Attitudes
Collectivism
Conscientiousness
Emotional intelligence
Emotional stability
Emotions
External locus of control
Extraversion
Gender role orientation
Goal
Hope
Individual differences
Individualism
Internal locus of control

Job satisfaction
Locus of control
Long-term orientation
Openness
Organizational commitment
Personality
Personality trait
Power distance
Self-awareness
Self-esteem
Self-motivation
Social empathy
Social skills
Uncertainty avoidance

DISCUSSION QUESTIONS

1. How can you use the model of emotions to increase your performance?
2. Using the Big Five personality factors, describe the personality of (a) a close family member and (b) a person for whom you have worked. How did these factors affect your behavior toward them?
3. Think of an organization that you have worked for. What factors seemed to influence your commitment to this organization?
4. Identify a specific personality factor that seems particularly interesting to you. Provide an example from your own work or other experience of an instance when this factor seemed strongly related to your behavior or that of another person.
5. Describe how you can develop your hope attitude to improve your performance.
6. What influences on personality development seem most important to you? Why?
7. Don Tuttle, CEO of Top Gun Ventures, believes that satisfied workers are more productive than less satisfied workers. Do you agree or disagree with him? Explain.
8. How might a culture impact the development of a person's personality? What cultural dimensions seem to have the most influence on this developmental process?
9. Can a person change his attitude without changing his behavior? Give an example?
10. Visit Virgin's website (www.virgin.com) and click on the Jobs icon. Then click on the feature "What we are like." Using the dimensions found in the Big Five personality profile, how do the job descriptions match the personality of Richard Branson?

EXPERIENTIAL EXERCISES

Experiential Exercise: Self Competency

What Are Your Cultural Values?[35]

Instructions

1. In the following questionnaire, please indicate the extent to which you agree or disagree with each statement. For example, if you ***strongly agree*** with a particular statement, write ***5*** next to that statement.

1 = Strongly disagree
2 = Disagree
3 = Neither agree nor disagree
4 = Agree
5 = Strongly agree

Questions

_____ 1. It is important to have job requirements and instructions spelled out in detail so that employees always know what they are expected to do. 1 2 3 4 5

_____ 2. Managers expect employees to follow instructions and procedures closely. 1 2 3 4 5

_____ 3. Rules and regulations are important because they inform employees about what the organization expects of them. 1 2 3 4 5

_____ 4. Standard operating procedures are helpful to employees on the job. 1 2 3 4 5

_____ 5. Instructions for completing job tasks are important for employees on the job. 1 2 3 4 5

_____ 6. Group welfare is more important than individual rewards. 1 2 3 4 5

_____ 7. Group success is more important than individual success. 1 2 3 4 5

_____ 8. Being accepted by the members of the work group is very important. 1 2 3 4 5

_____ 9. Employees should only pursue their goals after considering the welfare of the group. 1 2 3 4 5

_____ 10. Managers should encourage group loyalty even if individual goals suffer. 1 2 3 4 5

_____ 11. Individuals should be expected to give up their goals in order to benefit group success. 1 2 3 4 5

_____ 12. Managers should make most decisions without consulting subordinates. 1 2 3 4 5

_____ 13. Managers must often use authority and power when dealing with subordinates. 1 2 3 4 5

_____ 14. Managers should seldom ask for the opinions of employees. 1 2 3 4 5
_____ 15. Managers should avoid off-the-job social contacts with employees. 1 2 3 4 5
_____ 16. Employees should not disagree with management decisions. 1 2 3 4 5
_____ 17. Managers should not delegate important tasks to employees. 1 2 3 4 5
_____ 18. Managers should help employees with their family problems. 1 2 3 4 5
_____ 19. Management should see to it that workers are adequately clothed and fed. 1 2 3 4 5
_____ 20. Managers should help employees solve their personal problems. 1 2 3 4 5
_____ 21. Managers should see that health care is provided to all employees. 1 2 3 4 5
_____ 22. Management should see that children of employees have an adequate education. 1 2 3 4 5
_____ 23. Management should provide legal assistance for employees who get in trouble with the law. 1 2 3 4 5
_____ 24. Management should take care of employees as they would treat their children. 1 2 3 4 5
_____ 25. Meetings are usually run more effectively when they are chaired by a man. 1 2 3 4 5
_____ 26. It is more important for men to have professional careers than it is for women to have professional careers. 1 2 3 4 5
_____ 27. Men usually solve problems with logical analysis; women usually solve problems with intuition. 1 2 3 4 5
_____ 28. Solving organizational problems usually requires an active, forcible approach typical of men. 1 2 3 4 5
_____ 29. It is preferable to have a man in a high-level position rather than a woman. 1 2 3 4 5

Interpretation

1. The questionnaire measures each of the five basic culture dimensions. Your score can range from 5 to 35. The numbers in parentheses that follow the title of the value are the question numbers. Add the scores for these questions to arrive at your total score for each cultural value. The higher your score, the more you demonstrate the cultural value.

Value 1: Uncertainty Avoidance (1, 2, 3, 4, 5). Your score ____. A high score indicates a culture in which people often try to make the future predictable by closely following rules and regulations. Organizations try to avoid uncertainty by creating rules and rituals that give the illusion of stability.

Value 2: Individualism–Collectivism (6, 7, 8, 9, 10, 11). Your score _____. A high score indicates collectivism, or a culture in which people believe that group success is more important than individual achievement. Loyalty to the group comes before all else. Employees are loyal and emotionally dependent on their organization.

Value 3: Power Distance (12, 13, 14, 15, 16, 17). Your score _____. A high score indicates a culture in which people believe in the unequal distribution of power among segments of the culture. Employees fear disagreeing with their bosses and are seldom asked for their opinions by their bosses.

Value 4: Long-Term Orientation (18, 19, 20, 21, 22, 23, 24). Your score ____. A high score indicates a culture in which people value persistence, thrift, and respect for tradition. Young employees are expected to follow orders given to them by their elders and delay gratification of their material, social, and emotional needs.

Value 5: Gender Role Orientation (25, 26, 27, 28, 29). Your score _____. A high score indicates masculinity, or a culture in which people value the acquisition of money and other material things. Successful managers are viewed as aggressive, tough, and competitive. Earnings, recognition, and advancement are important. Quality of life and cooperation are not as highly prized.

Experiential Exercise: Self Competency

What's Your Emotional IQ?[36]

An individual difference that has recently received a great deal of interest is *emotional intelligence* You can assess your EQ by using the following scale.

Instructions

Using a scale of 1 through 4, where 1 = strongly disagree, 2 = somewhat disagree, 3 = somewhat agree, and 4 = strongly agree, respond to the 32 statements.

_____ 1. I know when to speak about my personal problems to others.
_____ 2. When I'm faced with obstacles, I remember times I faced similar obstacles and overcame them.
_____ 3. I expect that I will do well on most things.
_____ 4. Other people find it easy to confide in me.
_____ 5. I find it easy to understand the nonverbal messages of other people.
_____ 6. Some of the major events of my life have led me to reevaluate what is important and not important.
_____ 7. When my mood changes, I see new possibilities.
_____ 8. Emotions are one of the things that make life worth living.
_____ 9. I am aware of my emotions as I experience them.
_____ 10. I expect good things to happen.

_____ 11. I like to share my emotions with other people.
_____ 12. When I experience a positive emotion, I know how to make it last.
_____ 13. I arrange events others enjoy.
_____ 14. I seek out activities that make me happy.
_____ 15. I am aware of the nonverbal messages I send to others.
_____ 16. I present myself in a way that makes a good impression on others.
_____ 17. When I am in a positive mood, solving problems is easy for me.
_____ 18. By looking at facial expressions, I can recognize the emotions that others are feeling.
_____ 19. I know why my emotions change.
_____ 20. When I am in a positive mood, I am able to come up with new ideas.
_____ 21. I have control over my emotions.
_____ 22. I easily recognize my emotions as I experience them.
_____ 23. I motivate myself by imagining a good outcome to the tasks I do.
_____ 24. I compliment others when they have done something well.
_____ 25. I am aware of the nonverbal messages other people send.
_____ 26. When another person tells me about an important event in their life, I almost feel as though I have experienced this event myself.
_____ 27. When I feel a change in emotions, I tend to come up with new ideas.
_____ 28. When I am faced with a challenge, I usually rise to the occasion.
_____ 29. I know what other people are feeling just by looking at them.
_____ 30. I help other people feel better when they are down.
_____ 31. I use good moods to help myself keep trying in the face of obstacles.
_____ 32. I can tell how people are feeling by listening to the tone of their voices.

Scoring

1. Add your responses to questions 1, 6, 7, 8, 12, 14, 17, 19, 20, 22, 23, and 27. Put this total here____. This is your *self-awareness* score.
2. Add your responses to questions 4, 15, 18, 25, 29, and 32. Put this total here____. This is your *social empathy* score.
3. Add your responses to questions 2, 3, 9, 10, 16, 21, 28, and 31. Put this total here____. This is your *self-motivation* score.
4. Add your responses to questions 5, 11, 13, 24, 26, and 30. Put this total here____. This is your *social skills* score.

Discussion and Interpretation

The higher your score is in each of these four areas, the more emotionally intelligent you are. Individuals who score high (greater than 36) in *self-awareness* recognize how their feelings, beliefs, and behavior affect others. They accurately assess their strengths and limitations, and have a strong sense of their self-worth and capabilities.

Individuals who score high (greater than 18) in *social empathy* are thoughtful and consider others' feelings when making decisions and weigh those feelings along with other factors when making a decision. They are good at understanding others, taking an active interest in their concerns, empathizing with them, and recognizing the needs of others.

Individuals who score high (greater than 24) in *self-motivation* can keep their disruptive emotions and impulses under control, maintain standards of integrity and honesty, are conscientious, adapt their behaviors to changing situations, and have internal standards of excellence that guide their behaviors. That is, these people always want to do things better and seek out feedback from others about their performance. They are passionate about their work.

Individuals who have high (greater than 18) *social skills* sense others' developmental needs, inspire and lead groups, send clear and convincing messages, build effective interpersonal relationships, and work well with others to achieve shared goals. They build effective bonds between people. Often, they appear to be socializing with coworkers, but they are actually working to build solid relationships at work.

Questions

1. Use EQ to describe a friend. What are this person's strengths and weaknesses?
2. Is EQ genetic or shaped by experience?

CHAPTER 3

Perceptions and Attributions

Learning Goals

When you have finished studying the chapter, you should be able to:

1. Describe the major elements in the perceptual process.
2. Identify the main factors that influence what individuals perceive.
3. Identify the factors that determine how one person perceives another.
4. Describe the primary errors in perception that people make.
5. Explain how attributions influence behavior.

Learning from Experience

THIA BREEN, PRESIDENT, ESTÉE LAUDER AMERICAS AND GLOBAL BUSINESS DEVELOPMENT

Thia Breen has described three critical factors that have enabled her to advance to one of the most powerful positions in the retail market: "people, passion and performance."

As a graduate of the University of Minnesota, Breen took a job at Marshall Field's in the toy department. It was a two-person department and her job was to stock toys for the department. The job was physically demanding. When the truck arrived at the loading dock, she had to unload the stock in the truck and move it to shelves. After six months, her department became the best-performing department in the store and she wanted some recognition. The woman she worked for was quiet and didn't say anything when Breen asked about a promotion. Not satisfied, Breen went to the human resource manager. She was told "nobody gets promoted out of that department. The woman you work for just doesn't do promotions. Ever." He then added "I think you're going to be fired, anyway." Breen was stunned and asked him why, noting that the department's numbers had gone up. His response was: "The women in the regional office just do not like you. The decision has been made."

As she was preparing to leave the store, the store manager asked her what she knew about cosmetics. Instead of saying "Not much," she said "I know I can learn everything I have to know within three months." She had learned her first lesson working in corporations: "There will be times when life is unfair, but navigating those times will be the most important thing you can do."

To continue working at Marshall Field's soon meant relocating to Los Angeles. Her new assignment was to organize sales teams to sell Clinique cosmetics. It was during that assignment that she learned her next two management lessons. She learned that success was about putting together a high-performance team. Working with people who are passionate about a product was an important part of building a team. Her team's passion was helping customers get great skin through great products and great service. Learning how to let others take credit for success was also a valuable lesson. Remembering how she was

LEARNING CONTENT

For more information on Thia Breen, visit the organization's home page at www.esteelauder.com.

treated in the toy department, she was determined never to make another person go through that. Therefore, she provided team members with honest, direct feedback and let them know what they were doing right and what needed improvement. She believes that "how well you work with your people will make or break your career."

After several more career moves, she was lured to Estée Lauder. As president and head of Lauder's global business development, she reflects that her career has been all work and little else. Although she doesn't work seven days a week, her global travels to such places as Dubai, Japan, Korea, Paris, and London are exhausting. She knows that competition in the cosmetics industry is no longer local and that Estée Lauder and other companies need to get rid of the one-size-fits-all approach. The market in Asia is huge, but Asian women have different needs than American or European women. "Building brand equity through strategic decisions and building teams and partnerships" is what Breen's job is all about.[1]

The Learning from Experience feature illustrates the importance of how managers' perceptions of their employees influence their behavior. People base their behaviors on what they *perceive*, not necessarily on what reality *is*. The human resource manager's belief that "nobody gets promoted out of that department" influenced how he answered Breen's request for a promotion. This kind of perception keeps stereotypes alive about departments and people.

In this chapter, we explore the importance of *perception* and *attribution*. First, we describe the perceptual process. Then, we examine the external and internal factors that influence perception, the ways that people organize perceptions, the process of *person perception*, and various errors in the perceptual process. Finally, we explore the attributions that people make to explain the behaviors of themselves and others.

THE PERCEPTUAL PROCESS

Learning Goal

1. Describe the major elements in the perceptual process.

As you learned from Thia Breen's experiences, if managers do not perceive people and performance accurately, these inaccurate perceptions will be used as the basis for their judgments. As Thia Breen discovered, it is the *perception* of reality—not reality—that influences behavior. Perception *is the process by which people select, organize, interpret, and respond to information from the world around them*. Employees are constantly exposed to a variety of information. This information is processed in a person's mind and organized to form concepts pertaining to what is sensed or experienced. What happens when Tina Potter wants to buy Estée Lauder lip gloss? Before buying it, she touches the product, looks at its size and shape, smells it, and tries it on to see how it looks before buying. Her mind processes all of this information and helps her form ideas and attitudes about lip gloss. She gathers this information by using her three senses—touch, sight, and smell. This represents the psychological process whereby people take information from the environment and make sense of their worlds.[2]

The key words in the definition of perception are *select* and *organize*. Different people often perceive a situation differently, both in terms of what they selectively perceive and how they organize and interpret the things perceived. Figure 3.1 summarizes the basic elements in the perceptual process from initial observation to final response.

Everyone selectively pays attention to some aspects of the environment and selectively ignores other aspects. For example, when shoppers pull into the parking lot at 7-Eleven, what objects in their environment are they paying attention to and what do they ignore? What do they observe? A well-lit convenience store, clean areas to pump

FIGURE 3.1 The Perceptual Process

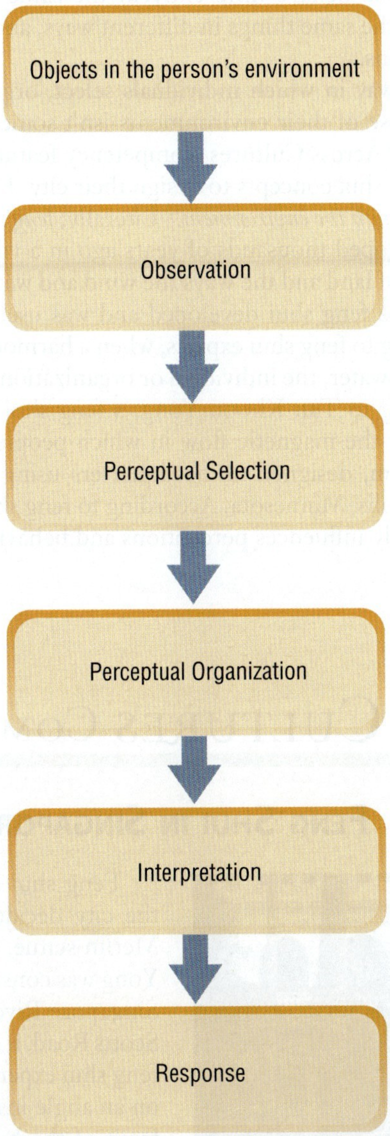

gas, fully stocked paper towel dispensers with squeegees to wipe and clean windshields, etc., are objects people notice when they pull into a gas line at a convenience store. They might ignore signs advertising freshly brewed coffee or the price of Coke. A person's selection process involves both external and internal factors. In other words, a complex set of factors, some internal to the person (attitudes) and some in the external environment, combine to determine what the person perceives. We discuss this important process in more detail shortly.

The individual organizes the stimuli selected into meaningful patterns. How people interpret what they perceive also varies considerably. The Experiential Exercise at the end of this chapter titled *The Perception Process* permits you to test your current level of perceptual skills. For example, a wave of the hand may be interpreted as a friendly gesture or as a threat, depending on the circumstances and the state of mind of those involved. In organizations managers and employees need to recognize that perceptions of events and behaviors may vary among individuals and be inaccurate.

As suggested in Figure 3.1, people's interpretations of their environments affect their responses. Everyone selects and organizes things differently, which is one reason why people behave differently in the same situation. In other words, people often perceive the same things in different ways, and their behaviors depend, in part, on their perceptions.

The way in which individuals select, organize, and interpret their perceptions to make sense of their environments isn't something that managers should ignore. The following Across Cultures Competency feature shows how city managers in Singapore used feng shui concepts to design their city. Feng shui *is the belief that space needs to be in harmony with the environment.*[3] Literally, *feng* means "wind" and *shui* "water." Feng shui was developed thousands of years ago in a village in China. Villagers studied the formations of land and the ways the wind and water worked together to help them survive. Over time feng shui developed and was used by emperors to ensure their successes. According to feng shui experts, when a harmonious arrangement is created between the wind and water, the individual or organization prospers and the quality of life improves. According to Tan Khoon Yong, a feng shui master, this balance can be achieved by balancing the magnetic flow in which people live. Nortel, a Canadian telecommunication firm, designed its headquarters using feng shui concepts, as did Best Buy in Minneapolis, Minnesota. According to feng shui, what is being perceived may be subtle and greatly influences perceptions and behaviors.[4]

Across Cultures Competency

Feng Shui in Singapore

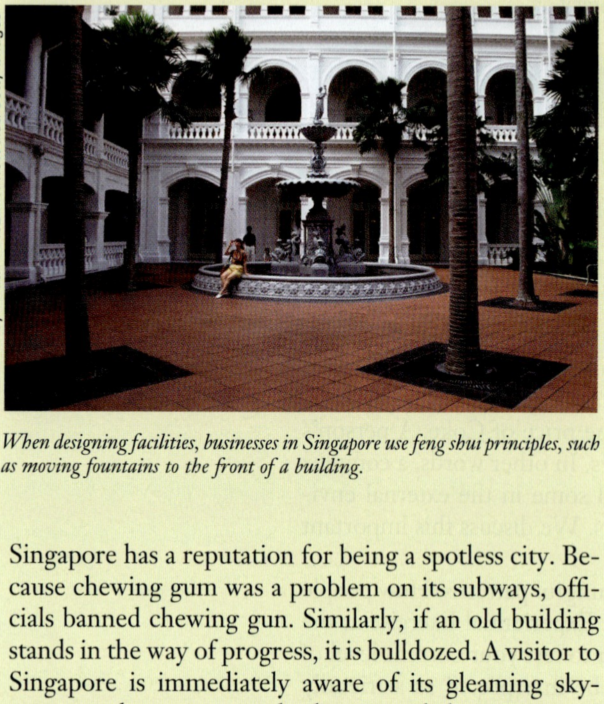
© Annie Reynolds/PhotoLink/Photodisc/Getty Images

When designing facilities, businesses in Singapore use feng shui principles, such as moving fountains to the front of a building.

Singapore has a reputation for being a spotless city. Because chewing gum was a problem on its subways, officials banned chewing gun. Similarly, if an old building stands in the way of progress, it is bulldozed. A visitor to Singapore is immediately aware of its gleaming skyscrapers, clean streets and subways, and clear waters.

Feng shui is widely practiced in Singapore. When the city decided to move Singapore's great icon, the Merlin statue, to its new location in 1985, Tan Khoon Yong was consulted. It is now located on the bank of the Singapore River. When the Grand Hyatt was built on Scotts Road, it experienced slow patronage. It called on a feng shui expert who suggested that placing lobby doors on an angle instead of straight, moving fountains to the front of the building, and installing a flag pole on the fourth floor would improve results. Indeed, business picked up immediately after the changes. When designing Singapore's Suntec City, the architects designed a building in a circular fashion to indicate the oneness of all people. The architects also recommended that the site not be near a cemetery or hospital because of the magnetic flow around such places.

The Sheraton, Marriott, and Mandarin hotels have used feng shui colors to improve their business in Singapore. For example, in hallways between rooms, warm gold colors are used because this stands for health and balance. Play rooms for kids are decorated in pastels, which are associated with children and creativity. Gray and metallic colors are used near customer service areas because these colors are associated with helpful friends and travel. In designing the in-house hotel convenience stores, the front right corner of the store is the preferred location for travel and other helpful items for people and this is where the customer service desk is located. The back left corner is the wealth area and anything to do with money is placed there.

For more information on Feng Shui, visit www.fengshuisociety.org.uk.

PERCEPTUAL SELECTION

Learning Goal

2. Identify the main factors that influence what individuals perceive.

The phone is ringing, your TV is blaring, a dog is barking outside, your PC is making a strange noise, and you smell coffee brewing. Which of these events will you ignore? Which will you pay attention to? Can you predict or explain why one of these events grabs your attention at a particular time?

Selective screening *is the process by which people filter out most information so that they can deal with the most important matters.* Perceptual selection depends on several factors, some of which are in the external environment and some of which are internal to the perceiver.

External Factors

As we noted in Chapter 2, one of the most common external forces affecting behavior is culture. Different cultures train people to respond to different cues. Do the French and Chinese see the world in the same way? No. In fact, no two national groups see the world in exactly the same way. When Mexican children simultaneously see a picture of a bullfight and a baseball game, they generally remember only seeing the bullfight. American children, on the other hand, remember seeing only the baseball game. Why do the children not see both pictures? This is the nature of perception. Perceptual patterns are not absolute. Misperceptions cause many managers to fail in their international assignments. Many U.S. firms, such as Estée Lauder, Microsoft, and PepsiCo, are competing in global markets where English is not the first language either read or spoken. Therefore, language is becoming an increasingly important consideration in product names and slogans.

Frito-Lay, a division of PepsiCo, is trying to become a dominant supplier of salty nuts and chips to China's $400 million market. Frito-Lay's senior management believes that China has tremendous growth potential. However, its managers realize that Chinese consumers have different perceptions of their product depending on where they live. People in Hong Kong like salty chips, in Beijing they like meaty ones, and in Xian, they like spicy flavors. Frito-Lay recently introduced "cool lemon" potato chips. These yellow, strongly lemon-scented chips are dotted with greenish lime specks and mint and are sold in a package featuring images of breezy blue skies and rolling green grass. Why "cool lemon"? Chinese people consider fried foods hot and therefore do not eat them in the summer months. Cool is better in the summer months.[5]

What are some other external factors that influence our perceptual process? What does Thia Breen want customers to notice when they arrive in the cosmetics department of a department store? Factors present in the department store can affect whether customers sense important information and these factors can influence whether this information is used in perceptions. Let's review some external factors that may affect perception. In each case we present an example to illustrate the principle.

- *Size.* The larger the object, the more likely it is to be perceived. The space and the new buildings to be built where the Twin Towers in New York City were destroyed by terrorist attacks on September 11, 2001, will get noticed more than an alleyway on 42nd street.

- *Intensity.* The more intense an external factor (bright lights, loud noises, and the like), the more likely it is to be perceived. The language in an e-mail message from a manager to an employee can reflect the intensity principle. For example, an e-mail message that reads "Please stop by my office at your convenience" wouldn't fill you with the same sense of urgency as an e-mail message that reads "Report to my office immediately!"
- *Contrast.* External factors that stand out against the background or that aren't what people expect are the most likely to be noticed. In addition, the contrast of objects with others or with their backgrounds may influence how they are perceived. Figure 3.2 illustrates this aspect of the contrast principle. Which of the solid center circles is larger? The one on the right appears to be larger, but it isn't: The two circles are the same size. The solid circle on the right appears to be larger because its background, or frame of reference, is composed of much smaller circles. The solid circle on the left appears to be smaller because its background consists of larger surrounding circles.

FIGURE 3.2 Contrast Principle of Perception

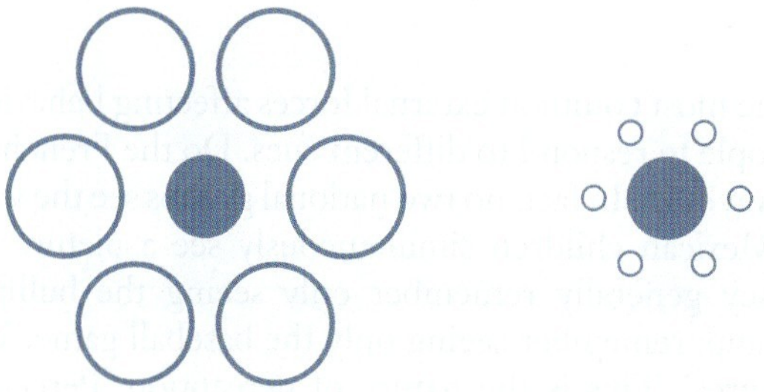

- *Motion.* A moving factor is more likely to be perceived than a stationary factor. Play Station games use this to attract people to play them.
- *Repetition.* A repeated factor is more likely to be noticed than a single factor. Marketing managers use this principle in trying to get the attention of prospective customers. An advertisement may repeat key ideas. The ad itself may be presented many times for greater effectiveness. Marketing managers at Nike have developed the Nike "swoosh" symbol that is used consistently worldwide on all of its products. Similarly, Frito-Lay's ad claiming "Bet you can't eat just one" is repeated around the globe in different languages.
- *Novelty and familiarity.* Either a familiar or a novel factor in the environment can attract attention, depending on the circumstances. A Korean businessman entered a client's office in Stockholm and was greeted by a woman sitting behind a desk. He asked to see the president. The woman responded by saying that she (the president) would be glad to see him. The Korean became confused because he assumed that most women are secretaries and not presidents of a company. His misinterpretation of the situation was caused by a novel situation.[6]

A combination of these or similar factors may be operating at any time to affect perception. Along with a person's internal factors, they determine whether any particular stimulus is more or less likely to be noticed.

Nowadays the visual aspects of a corporation's marketing materials are receiving increasing attention. Typeface designs of advertised brands influence readability and memorability. The following Communication Competency feature illustrates how typefaces (fonts) you use send messages to others about you. Oftentimes, these messages are subtle, but affect how others perceive you and your message.[7]

Communication Competency

Just My Type

The "one picture is worth a thousand words" saying is an old wives' tale that has been used by marketing and advertising companies for decades because people can remember pictures better than words. Similarly, organizations need design styles that are pleasing, engaging, reassuring, and prominent to catch the attention of their customers. Typestyles (fonts) suit the images that they want to send to their customers.

If you chose B, these fonts convey interest, emotion, excitement, and innovation. They are also unsettling and unfamiliar to most people.

If you chose C, these individuals are generally considered to be cold, unattractive, uninteresting, and unemotional. Companies use these to display characteristics or claims of being countercultural.

A Informal Roman, AncientScript, Enviro, Pepita MT

B Baphomet, Edda, Stonehenge, Paintbrush

C Playbill, Logan, Industria Inline, StencilSet

D NewYorkDeco, Bandstand, SunSplash, Middle Ages

E AluminumShred, BigDaddy, Ransom, Amazon

We present you with five different fonts. Circle the letter in front of the font that reflects the image you want to convey to others.

If you chose A, these fonts are considered likable, warm, attractive, interesting, emotional, feminine, and delicate. They do not convey strength, but are reassuring and pleasing.

If you chose D, these fonts represent strength and masculinity. The weighty lines suggest a forcefulness and solidity.

If you chose E, these fonts get high marks for being interesting, elaborate, emotional, exciting, and informal. These fonts could also be considered dishonest, cold, and unattractive.

Internal Factors

The perception process is also influenced by several factors that are related to the perceiver. These are internal factors that influence what people see. Effective managers are able to develop complete and accurate perceptions of various situations and people with whom they communicate. An effective manager knows when people are sincere, honest, and dependable. These accurate perceptions are crucial to be an effective manager. The powerful role that internal factors play in perception shows itself in many ways. We will review how personality, learning, and motivation influence the process of perceiving other people.

Personality. Personality has an interesting influence on what and how people perceive. Any of the several personality dimensions that we discussed in Chapter 2, along with numerous other traits, may influence the perceptual process. Personality appears to affect strongly how an individual perceives other people. In Chapter 2, we introduced you to the Big Five personality factors. To illustrate how personality can influence perception, let's examine one of the Big Five factors, conscientiousness. A conscientious person tends to pay more attention to external environmental cues than does a less conscientious person. On the one hand, less conscientious people are impulsive, careless, and irresponsible. They see their environment as hectic and unstable, which affects the way in which they make perceptual selections. On the other hand, more conscientious people organize their perceptions into neat categories, allowing themselves to retrieve data quickly and in an organized manner. In other words they are careful, methodical, and disciplined in making perceptual selections.

LEADER INSIGHT

A focus on personality characteristics, rather than particular work experiences, allows our company to hire people who will naturally bring the right qualities to the job.
Chet Cadieux, CEO, QuikTrip

Learning. Another internal factor affecting perceptual selection is learning. Among other things, learning determines the development of perceptual sets. A perceptual set *is an expectation of a particular interpretation based on past experience with the same or a similar object*. What do you see in Figure 3.3? If you see an attractive, elegantly dressed woman, your perception concurs with the majority of first-time viewers. However, you may agree with a sizable minority and see an ugly, old woman. The woman you first see depends, in large part, on your perceptual set.

In organizations, managers' and employees' past experiences and learning strongly influence their perceptions. Managers are influenced by their functional backgrounds (e.g., accounting, engineering, marketing, or production) when making decisions. Because perceptions influence how employees and managers behave toward one another, it is important to understand a manager's perceptual set. When Thia Breen was told by the human resource manager that her boss "just doesn't do promotions. Ever," this statement was based on the fact that no employee had ever been promoted out of the toy department to his knowledge. That is, his perceptual set was that since no person had ever been promoted, Breen's chances of being the first person were small.

Motivation. Motivation also plays an important role in determining what a person perceives. A person's most urgent needs and desires at any particular time can influence perception. For example, imagine that, while taking a shower, you faintly hear what sounds like the telephone ringing. Do you get out of the shower, dripping wet, to answer it? Or do you conclude that it is only your imagination? Your behavior in this situation may depend on factors other than the loudness of the ringing. If you are expecting an important call, you're likely to leap from the shower. If you aren't expecting a call, you're more likely to attribute the ringing sound to shower noises. Your decision, then, has been influenced by your expectations and motivations.

FIGURE 3.3 Test of Perceptual Set

In general, people perceive things that promise to help satisfy their needs and that they have found rewarding in the past. They tend to ignore mildly disturbing events (a barking dog), but will react to dangerous events (the house being on fire). Summarizing an important aspect of the relationship between motivation and perception is the Pollyanna principle, *which states that people process pleasant events more efficiently and accurately than they do unpleasant events*. For example, an employee who receives both positive and negative feedback during a performance appraisal session may more easily and clearly remember the positive statements than the negative statements.[8]

PERSON PERCEPTION

Learning Goal

3. Identify the factors that determine how one person perceives another.

The preceding discussion shows that perceiving others accurately can be challenging. Because perceptions influence how people behave toward one another, it is important for you to understand the factors that influence both the perceiver and the situation in general.

Person perception *is the process by which individuals attribute characteristics or traits to other people*. The person perception process relies on the same general process of perception shown in Figure 3.1. That is, the process follows the same sequence of observation, selection, organization, interpretation, and response. However, the object being perceived is another person. Perceptions of situations, events, and objects are important, but individual differences in perceptions of other people are crucial at work. For example, suppose that you meet a new employee. To get acquainted and make him feel at ease, you invite him to lunch. During lunch, he begins to tell you his life history and focuses on his accomplishments. Because he talks only about himself (he asks you no questions about yourself), your first impression is that he is very self-centered.

In general, the factors influencing person perception are the same as those that influence perceptual selection: Both external and internal factors affect person perception. However, we may usefully categorize factors that influence how a person perceives another as

- characteristics of the perceived,
- characteristics of the perceiver, and
- the situation or context within which the perception takes place.

The Perceived

When perceiving someone else, you need to be aware of various cues given by that person: facial expressions, general appearance, skin color, posture, age, gender, voice quality, personality traits, behaviors, and the like. Such cues usually provide important information about the person. People seem to have implicit theories about the relationships among physical characteristics, personality traits, and specific behaviors.[9] Implicit personality theory *is a person's beliefs about the relationships between another's physical characteristics and personality.* Table 3.1 illustrates implicit personality theory in action. People often seem to believe that some voice-quality characteristics indicate that the speaker has certain personality traits. However, the relationships presented in Table 3.1 have no scientific basis. Similarly, think about your first contact with someone you met on MySpace, Facebook, or an online dating service. It is not the person's voice that you consider, but his or her physical appearance. Later, on meeting, did that person look and act as you expected?

Table 3.1 **Personality Judgments on the Basis of Voice Quality**

VOICE QUALITY: HIGH IN	MALE VOICE	FEMALE VOICE
Breathiness	Younger, artistic	Feminine, pretty, petite, shallow
Flatness	Similar results for both sexes:	Masculine, cold, withdrawn
Nasality	Similar results for both sexes:	Having many socially undesirable characteristics
Tenseness	Cantankerous (old, unyielding)	Young, emotional, high-strung, not highly intelligent

Source: Adapted from Hinton, P. R. *The Psychology of Interpersonal Perception*, London: Routledge, 1993, 16.

The Perceiver

Listening to an employee describe the personality of a coworker may tell you as much about the employee's personality as it does about that of the person being described. That shouldn't surprise you if you recall that factors internal to the perceiver, including personality, learning, and motivation, influence perception. A person's own personality traits, values, attitudes, current mood, past experiences, and so on, determine, in part, how that person perceives someone else.

Accurately perceiving an individual raised in another culture often is difficult. In China, for example, the communication style is generally indirect. Chinese may talk around the point and hedge their speech using words such as *maybe* or *perhaps* because they must protect their social face and respect social roles (e.g., manager, employee). The Chinese will lose social face if they fail to understand what is being asked or cannot do what is requested. Therefore, by being vague, Chinese businesspeople save face and can continue to build and maintain relationships. Rick Linck, CEO of Asia Pacific for Heineken Brewing Company, has learned that when communicating with beer distributors in China, distributors frequently say "Let me look into this further" to avoid a direct no or to avoid admitting that they cannot do what he asked. Linck has learned to communicate with distributors by saying "What do you think about this?" instead of saying "Is this acceptable?"[10]

Cross-cultural negotiations are an important part of every global manager's job. The dynamics of negotiating, however, reflects each culture's value and beliefs. In Mexico, personal qualities and social connections influence the selection of a negotiator, whereas in the United States, many companies select negotiators on the basis of position and competence. In U.S.–Chinese negotiations, U.S. companies often prefer to send a small team or only a single person to represent them, whereas the Chinese prefer to send a large group. The large group allows them to have representatives from different areas of the organization present at the negotiations.

The Situation in Foreign Assignments

As more and more employees are asked to take assignments in foreign countries, opportunities for living and working in different countries arise. Siemens, the German electronics firm with headquarters in Munich, Germany, estimates that almost 25 percent of its managers take expatriate assignments. Expatriates *are employees who live and work outside of their home country.*[11] There are now more than 400,000 U.S. expatriate managers living around the globe. Because of the high cost of sending employees and their families to foreign countries for extended periods of time (usually three years), it is important for this experience to be successful. Unfortunately, many expatriates cannot adapt to the new situation (culture) and fail in their assignments. Why do people fail? According to Global Relation Services, the top reasons for expatriate failure are as follows:

- Lowered security and safety,
- Lower quality of life,
- Job doesn't meet expectations,
- Inability to adapt to new situation,
- Family concerns, and
- Spouse/partner dissatisfaction.[12]

Running down the list, the reasons for failure are personal and not related to technical competence. China and India were the two countries that presented expatriates with the greatest challenge. Why do you think these two countries were singled out?

What are some characteristics that human resource managers are looking for in the person who takes a foreign assignment? Patience, flexibility, openness to new experiences, and tolerance for other beliefs are among the top characteristics.[13] Making sure that the family supports the foreign assignment, developing foreign language competencies, getting strong support from your manager, and making sure that your accomplishments are widely visible are tips for successfully handling a foreign assignment.

Are women more likely to succeed or fail in expatriate assignments? A number of male managers still think that women aren't interested in overseas jobs or won't be effective in them. These managers typically cite dual career issues, a presumed heightened risk of sexual harassment, and gender prejudices in many countries as reasons why their female employees often aren't seriously considered for international assignments. In contrast, a recent survey of female expatriates and their managers revealed that women, on average, are just as interested as men in foreign assignments and every bit as effective once there.[14] Indeed, some of the traits considered crucial for success overseas—such as knowing when to keep your mouth shut, being a strong team player, and soliciting a variety of opinions and perspectives when solving problems—are more often associated with women's management styles than with men's.

Misinterpretation of the situation occurs when an individual gives certain meaning to observations and their relationships. Interpretation organizes our experience and guides our behavior. Read the following sentence and quickly count the number of Fs:

FINISHED FILES ARE THE RESULT OF YEARS OF SCIENTIFIC STUDY COMBINED WITH THE EXPERIENCE OF YEARS.

Most people who do not speak English see all six Fs. By contrast, many English speakers see only three Fs; they do not see the Fs in the word *of.* Why? Because English-speaking people do not think that the word *of* is important for them to understand the meaning of the sentence. We selectively see those words that are important according to our cultural upbringing.

A way to understand the norms and values of a culture is to pay attention to the behaviors that are rewarded in that society. The following Self Competency feature illustrates a sample of important behaviors that you should be aware of when conducting business in Arab countries.[15]

Self Competency

Doing Business in Arab Countries

© The Studio Dog/Photodisc/Getty Images

It is important to understand the norms of a culture when conducting business in another country. In an Arab country, for example, the majority of men wear a long-sleeved, one-piece dress called a thoub.

- *Greeting women.* When you are introduced to a female employee, never greet her with a kiss. If the employee extends her hand to greet you, you may shake it; otherwise greeting with words is appropriate. Do not compliment your host on the beauty of his wife, sister, or daughter. Such statements will not be taken as compliments.
- *Gift giving.* When Arab businesspeople receive a gift, it is not customary to open it in front of the giver. Never give alcohol or products made out of pigs.
- *Face concept.* The Arabian culture is a nonconfrontational one. Saving face involves holding one's reactions to give the other party a way to exit the situation with minimal discomfort. It involves compromise, patience, and sometimes looking the other way to allow things time to get back to normal. Pressure sales tactics should be avoided because the Arab managers will associate you with an unpleasant experience.
- *Dress.* The majority of men wear a long-sleeved, one-piece dress called a *thoub* that covers the entire body. This garment allows air to circulate in hot summer days. Women dress conservatively in a garment called an *abayah.* This is a long black garment that covers a woman's body from the shoulders down to her feet.
- *Social duties.* Managers perform a variety of social duties, including greeting an employee who returns from a trip, visiting an employee who is ill, bringing a gift to a newly wed couple, and visiting the husband and wife after the wife has delivered a new baby.
- *Privacy.* Privacy is important in Arabian societies. Therefore, houses and offices are built with walls that maintain privacy from others. People are not permitted to enter until the manager or host extends his right hand with his palm up saying "Tafaddal," which means come in.
- *Social gatherings.* Men and women may meet in separate rooms in some Arab countries. Men gather in rooms that are outside the main entrance of a home, away from the rest of the house. Women guests meet in a room inside the house and go through an entrance specifically assigned for female visitors.

For more information on Arab countries, visit www.montclair.edu/orgs/aso/arab6.html.

PERCEPTUAL ERRORS

Learning Goal

4. Describe the primary errors in perception that people make.

The perceptual process may result in errors in judgment or understanding. An important part of understanding individual differences in perception is knowing the source of these errors. First, we examine the notion of accuracy of judgment in person perception. Then, we explore five of the most common types of perceptual errors: perceptual defense, stereotyping, the halo effect, projection, and impression management.

Perceptual Accuracy

How accurate are people in their perceptions of others? This question is important in organizational behavior. For example, misjudging the characteristics, abilities, or behaviors of an employee during a performance appraisal review could result in an inaccurate assessment of the employee's current and future value to the firm. Another example of the importance of accurate person perception comes from the employment interview. Considerable evidence suggests that interviewers can easily make errors in judgment and perceptions when basing employment decisions on information gathered in face-to-face interviews. In fact, most managers make a decision about hiring a person within the first 10 minutes of an interview and spend the remainder of the interview just confirming their first impressions.[16] After reading the following types of errors, can you identify those made by the human resources manager communicating with Thia Breen in the Learning from Experience feature?

- *Similarity error.* Interviewers are positively predisposed toward job candidates who are similar to them (in terms of background, interests, hobbies, jobs, and the like) and negatively biased against job candidates who are unlike them.
- *Contrast error.* Interviewers have a tendency to compare job candidates to other candidates interviewed at about the same time, rather than to some absolute standard. For example, an average candidate might be rated too highly if preceded by several mediocre candidates; however, an average candidate might be scored too low if preceded by an outstanding applicant.
- *Overweighting of negative information.* Interviewers tend to overreact to negative information as though looking for an excuse to disqualify a job candidate.
- *Race, gender, and age bias.* Interviewers may be more or less positive about a candidate on the basis of the candidate's race, gender, or age.
- *First-impression error.* The primacy effect may play a role in the job interview, because some interviewers are quick to form impressions that are resistant to change.

There are no easy answers to the general problem of ensuring accuracy. Some people accurately judge and assess others, and some people do so poorly. You can learn to make more accurate judgments by following some basic guidelines: (1) Avoid generalizing from an observation of a single trait (e.g., tactful) to other traits (e.g., stable, confident, energetic, dependable); (2) avoid assuming that a behavior will be repeated in all situations; and (3) avoid placing too much reliance on physical appearance. Your accuracy in person perception can be improved when you understand these potential biases.

Perceptual Defense

Perceptual defense *is the tendency for people to protect themselves against ideas, objects, or situations that are threatening.* A well-known folk song suggests that we "hear what we want to hear and disregard the rest." Once established, an individual's way of viewing the world may become highly resistant to change. Sometimes perceptual defense may have negative consequences. This perceptual error can result in a manager's inability to perceive the need to be creative in solving problems. As a result, the individual simply proceeds as in the past even in the face of evidence that "business as usual" isn't accomplishing anything.

Stereotyping

Stereotyping *is the belief that all members of specific groups share similar traits and behaviors.* The use of stereotypes can have powerful effects on the decisions that managers make. There are many exceptions to any stereotype. In a study of *Fortune* magazine's top 500 CEOs, researchers found that CEOs are mostly white males. The study also found that on the average, male CEOs were almost six feet tall, which reflects a kind of implicit stereotype of the height of CEOs. Given that the average American male is five foot nine, it means that CEOs as a group are about three inches taller. In the United States, about 14.5 percent of all men are six feet or taller and 3.9 percent of white males are six foot two or taller. In this sample, almost a third were six foot two or taller. Furthermore, it was calculated that each inch of height is worth $789 a year in salary.[17] That means an individual who is six feet tall but otherwise identical to someone who is five foot five will make on average $5,525 more per year. Over a career, the difference is hundreds of thousands of dollars. In another study, the authors found that attractive people earn about 5 percent more than do average-looking employees, who in turn earn 9 percent more than plain-looking employees. That means that if an average-looking college graduate starts at $47,000, their good-looking friends start at $49,350, while their least attractive friends start at $42,770. Plain-looking employees may also receive fewer promotions than those awarded to their better looking colleagues.[18]

An interesting challenge for organizations is to determine in what ways women managers essentially are like their male counterparts. To the extent they are alike, gender differences should be only a marginal concern. However, a debate is raging in scientific and management circles around the world with regard to gender differences in thought, emotions, and information processing styles. Some evidence from the research being conducted suggests that women are, on average, superior to men in many organizational roles. Such roles include interacting with customers or clients, facilitating discussions, and smoothing conflicts. With regard to the latter two roles, one study indicated that female project team leaders were more effective, on average, than males in leading cross-functional teams designed to foster high rates of innovation.[19]

Halo Effect

The halo effect *refers to evaluating another person solely on the basis of one attribute, either favorable or unfavorable.* The halo effect is based on general assessments of the overall person. That is, if the manager regards the person as "good," that manager will tend to review that person's performance in a positive way. In other words, a halo blinds the perceiver to other attributes that also should be evaluated to obtain a complete, accurate impression of the other person. Managers have to guard against the halo effect when rating employee performance. A manager may single out one trait and use it as the basis for judging all other performance measures. Students have been known to evaluate the overall effectiveness of a faculty member in just the first two seconds of the first class. The ratings they gave after these two seconds were almost identical to rankings made after sitting through the instructor's course the entire semester. That's the power of the halo effect.

An important aspect of the halo effect is the self-fulfilling prophecy. The self-fulfilling prophecy *is the tendency for someone's expectations about another to cause that individual to behave in a manner consistent with those expectations.*[20] Expecting certain things to happen shapes the behavior of the perceiver in such a way that the expected is more likely to happen. Self-fulfilling prophecies can take both positive and negative forms. In the positive case, *holding high expectations of another tends to improve the individual's performance*, which is known as the Pygmalion effect. The Pygmalion effect has its roots in Greek mythology. According to mythology, Pygmalion was a sculptor who hated women yet fell in love with a statue he carved of a beautiful woman. He became so infatuated with the statue that he prayed to a goddess to bring her to life. The goddess granted him his wish. The essence of the Pygmalion effect is that people's expectations determine their behavior or performance, thus serving to make their expectations come true. In other words, we strive to validate our perceptions of reality no matter how faulty they may be. Subordinates whose managers expect them to perform well do perform well. Subordinates whose managers expect them to perform poorly do in fact perform poorly. Obviously, this effect can be quite devastating.[21] At Citibank, for example, some top executives believe that a manager who puts in long hours and works on Saturday is a better performer than those who do not put in these hours. Because Citibank has an industry reputation for meeting deadlines, long hour expectations help create and foster a reward system that uses long hours as one criterion for a manager's success.

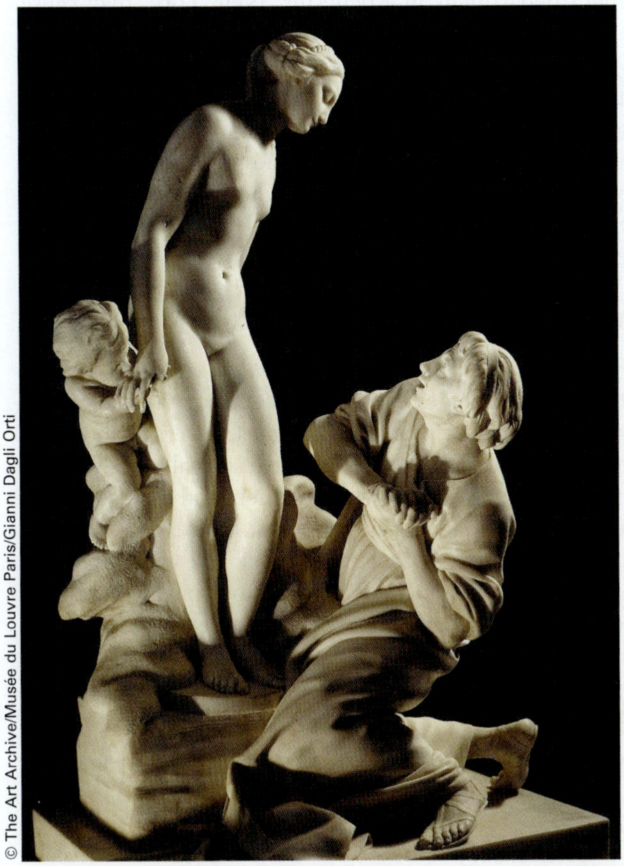

This sculpture is of the mythological Pygmalion. The Pygmalion effect is when people's expectations determine their behavior or performance, serving to make their expectations come true.

The Golem effect *refers to the loss in performance resulting from low expectations on the boss's part.*[22] If a manager notices that a subordinate's sales reports are always late, this leads the manager to doubt whether the employee is committed to being a high achiever. This results in the manager watching the employee more closely, and the employee becomes afraid to make suggestions that could improve the report for fear of turning the report in late. The manager then interprets this as a lack of initiative.

How can managers create positive performance expectations? We believe that managers need to consider three things:

1. *Individuals behave toward others consistent with others' expectations of them.* Managers who have high expectations of their employees are supportive and generally give employees more training and challenging jobs. By contrast, managers who have low expectations of their employees aren't supportive and generally won't give employees training and challenging jobs.
2. *A person's behavior affects others.* Not only will those treated positively benefit from special opportunities, but these opportunities will also bolster their self-esteem.
3. *People behave in response to how they are treated.* People who have benefited from special treatment and who have confidence in their abilities are likely to be high performers.

LEADER INSIGHT

Anytime anyone sold something, they rang a bell—and even though it sounded hokey at first, it made people feel like winners.
Andrea Doelling, Senior Vice President of Sales, AT&T Wireless

Projection

Projection *is the tendency for people to see their own traits in other people.* That is, they project their own feelings, personality characteristics, attitudes, or motives onto others. For example, Kodak's decision to lay off employees in its analog camera department in Rochester, New York, may cause employees in its copier department in Texas not only to judge others as more frightened than they are but also to assess various job changes to be more threatening than need be. Of course, this may be an inaccurate perception. Falsely believing that others share ours beliefs can lead to poor performance. Projection may be especially strong for undesirable traits that perceivers possess but fail to recognize in themselves. People whose personality traits include stinginess, obstinacy, and disorderliness tend to rate others higher on these traits than do people who don't have these personality traits.

Impression Management

Impression management *is an attempt by an individual to manipulate or control the impressions that others form about them.* This includes everything from how people talk to how they dress and how they walk. Employees in organizations use several impression management tactics to affect how others perceive them. They are especially likely to use these tactics when talking with managers who have power over them and on whom they are dependent for raises, promotions, and good job assignments. Impression management is used by individuals at all organizational levels when they talk with suppliers, coworkers, managers, and others—and vice versa. To determine how much you rely on impression management tactics, take a moment and complete the self-assessment questionnaire in Table 3.2.[23]

Table 3.2 **Impression Management Assessment**

To assess the impression tactics you use, please answer the following 22 questions using the following scale:

How often do you behave this way?

Never		Occasionally		Often
1	2	3	4	5

_____ 1. Talk proudly about your experience or education.
_____ 2. Make people aware of your talents.
_____ 3. Let others know how valuable you are to the organization.
_____ 4. Make people aware of your accomplishments.
_____ 5. Compliment your colleagues so they will see you as likable.
_____ 6. Take an interest in your colleagues' personal lives to show them that you are friendly.

_____ 7. Praise your colleagues for their accomplishments so they will consider you a nice person.
_____ 8. Do personal favors for others to show them that you are friendly.
_____ 9. Be pushy with coworkers when it will help you get your job done.
_____ 10. Let others know you can make things difficult for them if they push you too far.
_____ 11. Deal forcefully with others when they hamper your ability to get the job done.
_____ 12. Deal aggressively with others who interfere in your business.
_____ 13. Use intimidation to get others to behave appropriately.
_____ 14. Act like you know less than you do so people will help you out.
_____ 15. Try to gain sympathy from people by appearing needy in some areas.
_____ 16. Pretend not to understand something to gain someone's help.
_____ 17. Act like you need assistance so people will help you out.
_____ 18. Pretend to know less than you do so you can avoid an unpleasant assignment.
_____ 19. Stay late so people will know you are working hard.
_____ 20. Try to appear busy, even at times when things are slow.
_____ 21. Arrive early to work to look dedicated.
_____ 22. Come to the office at night or on weekends to show that you are dedicated.

Scoring:
To determine your impression management tactics, please add your answers to decide your score.

Questions:

1–4	_____	This is your *self-promotion score.* The higher your score, the more likely you are to use this tactic.
5–8	_____	This is your *ingratiation score.* The higher your score, the more likely you are to use this tactic.
9–13	_____	This is your *intimidation score.* The higher your score, the more likely you are to use this tactic.
14–18	_____	This is your *supplication score.* The higher your score, the more likely you are to use this tactic.
19–22	_____	This is your *exemplification score.* The higher your score, the more likely you are to use this tactic.

Source: Adapted from Bolino, M. C., and Turnley, W. H. Measuring impression management in organizations: A scale development based on Jones & Pittman taxonomy. *Organizational Research Methods,* 1999, 2, 187–206.

Impression management involves the systematic manipulation of the perceptual process. Jeff Skilling and others at Enron tried to look good to Wall Street investors by encouraging investors to attribute Enron's success to their efforts and attribute problems or failures to others beyond their control. Table 3.3 describes five common impression management tactics: self-promotion, ingratiation, intimidation, supplication, and exemplification.

Table 3.3 **Impression Management Tactics**

TACTIC	DESCRIPTION	EXAMPLE
Self-promotion	The person tries to present himself in a positive light	Employee reminds boss about accomplishments
Ingratiation	The person flatters others so they will see the person as likable	Employee compliments manager on good customer service after the manager handled a complaint from an irate customer
Intimidation	The person lets others know that she can make life difficult for them if they push her	Employee tries to push others to get things done on schedule or else

TACTIC	DESCRIPTION	EXAMPLE
Supplication	The person acts like he needs help so others will help him	Employee asks for help on a task that he could perform himself
Exemplification	The person stays late so others know she is working hard	Employee is the last one to leave the parking lot and the first one to arrive

Source: Harris, K. J. , Zivnuska, S. , Kacmar, K. M. , and Shaw, J. D. The impact of political skill on impression management effectiveness. *Journal of Applied Psychology*, 2007, 92, 278–285.

These five impression tactics can lead to either positive or negative perceptions depending on how the individual uses them. Employees who are high in political skills have the ability to create better managerial impressions when they use these tactics frequently. On the other hand, employees who use these impression management tactics and have low political skills are less likely to be viewed favorably and should avoid using these tactics. Also, if superior performance evaluations are used to make key organizational decisions (e.g., pay raises, promotions, job assignments), there is a potential for employees to receive these outcomes because of their ability to use impression management tactics rather than more job-related criteria.[24]

Learning Goal

5. Explain how attributions influence behavior.

ATTRIBUTIONS: WHY PEOPLE BEHAVE AS THEY DO

A question often asked about others is "Why?" "Why did this engineer use these data in his report?" or "Why did Howard Schultz, CEO and founder of Starbucks, start Starbucks?" Such questions are an attempt to get at why a person behaved in a particular way. The attribution process *refers to the ways in which people come to understand the causes of their own and others' behaviors.*[25] In essence, the attribution process reflects people's need to explain events through the deliberate actions of others rather than viewing them as random events. To maintain the illusion of control, people need to create causal attributions for events. Attributions also play an important role in perceptions. Attributions made about the reasons for someone's behavior may affect judgments about that individual's basic characteristics (that is, what that person is really like).

The attributions that employees and managers make concerning the causes of behavior are important for understanding behavior. For example, managers who attribute poor performance directly to their subordinates tend to behave more punitively than do managers who attribute poor performance to circumstances beyond their subordinates' control. A manager who believes that an employee failed to perform a task correctly because he lacked proper training might be understanding and give the employee better instructions or more training. The same manager might be quite angry if he believes that the subordinate made mistakes simply because he didn't try very hard.

Responses to the same outcome can be dramatically different, depending on the attributions made about the reasons for that outcome. Table 3.4 lists some of the possible differences in managerial behavior when employees are perceived positively versus when they are perceived negatively. The relationships between attributions and behavior will become clearer as we examine the attribution process.

The Attribution Process

People make attributions in an attempt to understand why others behave as they do and to make better sense of their situations. Individuals don't consciously make attributions all the time (although they may do so unconsciously much of the time).[26] However, under certain circumstances people are likely to make causal attributions consciously. For example, causal attributions are common in the following situations:

Table 3.4 Possible Results Stemming from Differences in Perceptions of Performance

BOSS'S BEHAVIOR TOWARD PERCEIVED STRONG PERFORMERS	BOSS'S BEHAVIOR TOWARD PERCEIVED WEAK PERFORMERS
Discusses project objectives. Gives subordinate the freedom to choose own approach to solving problems or reaching goals.	Gives specific directives when discussing tasks and goals.
Treats mistakes or incorrect judgments as learning opportunities.	Pays close attention to mistakes and incorrect judgments. Quick to emphasize what subordinate is doing wrong.
Is open to subordinate's suggestions. Solicits opinions from subordinate.	Pays little attention to subordinate's suggestions. Rarely asks subordinate for input.
Gives subordinate interesting and challenging assignments.	Gives subordinate routine assignments.
May frequently defer to subordinate's opinions in disagreements.	Usually imposes own views in disagreements.

- The perceiver has been asked an explicit question about another's behavior. (Why did she do that?)
- An unexpected event occurs. (I've never seen him behave that way. I wonder what's going on?)
- The perceiver depends on another person for a desired outcome. (I wonder why my manager made that comment about my expense account?)
- The perceiver experiences feelings of failure or loss of control. (I can't believe I failed my midterm exam!)

Figure 3.4 presents a schematic model of the attribution process. People infer "causes" to behaviors that they observe in others, and these interpretations often largely

FIGURE 3.4 The Attribution Process

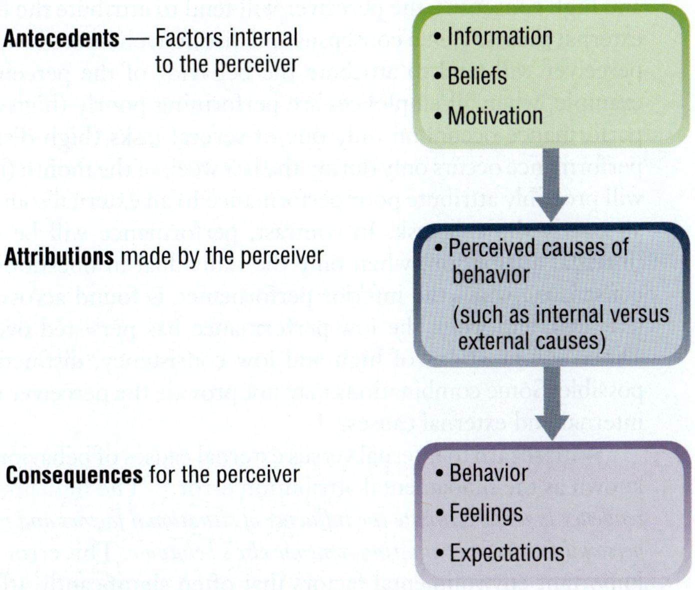

determine their reactions to those behaviors. The perceived causes of behavior reflect several antecedents: (1) the amount of information the perceiver has about the people and the situation and how that information is organized by the perceiver; (2) the perceiver's beliefs (implicit personality theories, what other people might do in a similar situation, and so on); and (3) the motivation of the perceiver (e.g., the importance to the perceiver of making an accurate assessment). Recall our discussion of internal factors that influence perception—learning, personality, and motivation. These same internal factors influence the attribution process. The perceiver's information and beliefs depend on previous experience and are influenced by the perceiver's personality.

Internal versus External Causes of Behavior

In applying attribution theory, you should be especially concerned with whether a person's behavior has been internally or externally caused. Internal causes are believed to be under an individual's control—you believe that your website designer's performance is poor because she's often late to work. External causes are believed to be beyond a person's control—you believe that her performance is poor because her Windows operating system is old. According to attribution theory, three factors influence the determination of internal or external cause:

- *Consistency*—the extent to which the person perceived behaves in the same manner on other occasions when faced with the same situation. If your website designer's behavior has been poor for several months, you would tend to attribute it to an internal cause. If her performance is an isolated incident, you would tend to attribute it to an external cause.
- *Distinctiveness*—the extent to which the person perceived acts in the same manner in different situations. If your website designer's performance is poor, regardless of the computer program with which she's working, you would tend to make an internal attribution; if her poor performance is unusual, you would tend to make an external attribution.
- *Consensus*—the extent to which others, faced with the same situation, behave in a manner similar to the person perceived. If all the employees in your website designer's team perform poorly, you would tend to make an external attribution. If other members of her team are performing well, you would tend to make an internal attribution.[27]

As Figure 3.5 suggests, under conditions of low consistency, high distinctiveness, and high consensus, the perceiver will tend to attribute the behavior of the perceived to external causes. When consensus and distinctiveness are low, but consistency is high, the perceiver will tend to attribute the behavior of the perceived to internal causes. For example, when all employees are performing poorly (high consensus), when the poor performance occurs on only one of several tasks (high distinctiveness), and the poor performance occurs only during the last week of the month (low consistency), a manager will probably attribute poor performance to an external source, such as peer pressure or an overly difficult task. In contrast, performance will be attributed to an employee (internal attribution) when only the individual in question is performing poorly (low consensus), when the inferior performance is found across several tasks (low distinctiveness), and when the low performance has persisted over time (high consistency). Other combinations of high and low consistency, distinctiveness, and consensus are possible. Some combinations may not provide the perceiver with a clear choice between internal and external causes.

With regard to internal versus external causes of behavior, people often make what is known as the fundamental attribution error.[28] The fundamental attribution error *is the tendency to underestimate the influence of situational factors and to overestimate the influence of personal factors in evaluating someone else's behavior*. This error causes perceivers to ignore important environmental factors that often significantly affect a person's behavior. In

FIGURE 3.5 Example of Attribution Process

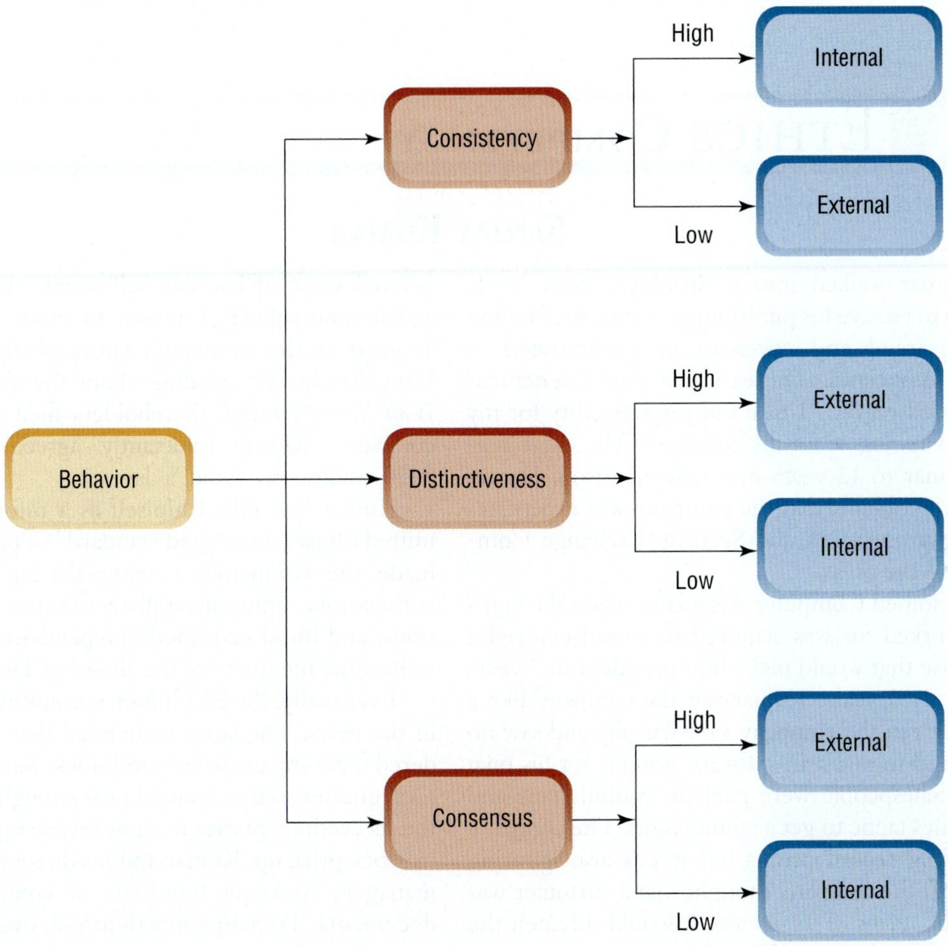

organizations, employees often tend to assign blame to other departments or individuals and fail to recognize the effect of the situation. For example, a CEO might attribute a high level of political behavior on the part of her vice presidents to aspects of their personalities, not recognizing that competition for scarce resources is causing much of the political behavior.

Some cultural differences exist in the fundamental attribution error. For example, in North America, this type of error would be as just described (underestimating external causes and overestimating internal causes). In India, however, the more common attribution error is for managers to overestimate situational or external causes for the observed behavior. This difference in attributions may reflect the way that people view personal responsibility or perhaps differences in "average" locus of control beliefs in the different societies.

The fundamental attribution error isn't the only bias that can influence judgments concerning internal versus external causes of behavior. A study of supervisors showed that they were more likely to attribute effective performance to internal causes for high-status employees and less likely to attribute success to internal causes for low-status employees. Similarly, supervisors were more likely to attribute ineffective performance to internal causes for low-status employees and less likely to attribute failure to internal causes for high-status employees.[29]

Perceptions of people and their behaviors are subjective. How others perceive you has important implications as the following Ethics Competency feature illustrates.[30] After reading this feature, how do you perceive Kumar? What aspects of this feature did you rely on to make your attributions?

Ethics Competency

Sanjay Kumar

Sanjay Kumar walked into a Brooklyn, New York, courtroom to receive his punishment for the $2.2 billion accounting fraud and cover-up he orchestrated at Computer Associates. The ex-CEO read a statement that expressed regret: "I take full responsibility for my actions and apologize for my conduct." The judge sentenced Kumar to 12 years in a federal prison. Kumar blamed the problems that the company was experiencing on the prosecutors, the Security Exchange Commission, and the press.

Kumar joined Computer Associates when the company he worked for was acquired by it and enjoyed a meteoric rise that would make him president in 7 years and CEO in 15 years. Kumar ran the company like a start-up. He ran the company very frugally and saw no pressing need to invest in software systems for his own company. Salespeople were paid on commissions and used any sales tactic to get a commission. The company was recording record profits but it was also ignoring customers. If the company thought that a customer was violating the terms of its license, it would threaten the customer with a lawsuit. Why did customers stay with Computer Associates? Because the company specialized in developing software for giant mainframe computers that permitted information managers to monitor, diagnose, and manage other systems and software. They also found out that once its software had been installed in the company's system, it was almost impossible to pull out. Many *Fortune* 500 companies used its software.

Customers described Computer Associates as very successful but arrogant and that Kumar had an exaggerated sense of his own self-worth. As CEO, he and a colleague split $1.1 billion in stock, a figure nearly as great as the company's entire profits for the year. Immediately after reading about the stock deal in the *Wall Street Journal*, shareholders filed suit against the company. Kumar reluctantly agreed to give back $250 million to avoid a lawsuit.

Kumar had billed himself as a reformer and committed himself to a "gold standard" of performance. He made the company's revenue-sharing program very conservative, announced plans to repair customer relations, and hired respected independent businesspeople to become members of the Board of Directors.

Eventually, the $2.2 billion accounting scandal broke in the news. The story contended that Kumar had ordered the company to keep its books open after the end of each quarter so that it could post enough revenues from the succeeding quarter to show increasing sales and keep its stock price up. Kumar and his direct reports also had managers backdate hundreds of contracts and alter documents. To maintain a tight rein over the company, Kumar and his top managers hoarded key information needed to make strategic decisions. The company's internal systems were not updated and integrated. Therefore, when its 4,000 salespeople's commissions were due, employees in the finance department had to individually calculate commissions, verify them, and then manually enter these back into the system. Employees working at the company were so used to blindly doing what they were told to do that many didn't even know how to respond when he was indicted.

Attributions of Success and Failure

The attributions that employees and managers make regarding success or failure are very important. Managers may base decisions about rewards and punishments on their perceptions of why subordinates have succeeded or failed at some task. In general, individuals often attribute their own and others' success or failure to four causal factors —ability, effort, task difficulty, and luck[31]:

- I succeeded (or failed) because I had the competencies to do the task (or because I did not have the competencies to do the task). Such statements are ability attributions.
- I succeeded (or failed) because I worked hard at the task (or because I did not work hard at the task). Such statements are effort attributions.
- I succeeded (or failed) because the task was easy (or because the task was too hard). Such statements are attributions about task difficulty.
- I succeeded (or failed) at the task because I was lucky (or unlucky). Such statements are attributions about luck or the circumstances surrounding the task.

Causal attributions of ability and effort are internal, whereas causal attributions of task difficulty and luck are external. These attributions about success or failure reflect differences in self-esteem and locus of control—personality dimensions discussed in Chapter 2. Accordingly, the self-serving bias *refers to individuals attributing their success to internal factors (ability or effort) and attributing their failure to external factors (task difficulty or luck)*. For example, individuals with high self-esteem and high internal locus of control are likely to assess their own performance positively and to attribute their good performance to internal causes.

The tendency of employees to accept responsibility for good performance but to deny responsibility for poor performance often presents a serious challenge for managers during performance appraisals.[32] A self-serving bias may also create other types of problems. For example, it prevents individuals from accurately assessing their own performance and abilities and makes it more difficult to determine why a course of action has failed. The general tendency to blame others for a person's own failures often is associated with poor performance and an inability to establish satisfying interpersonal relationships at work and in other social settings. In general, a version of the self-serving bias seems to operate when people are asked to compare themselves to others in the work setting. That is, managers and employees often view themselves to be more ethical, more effective, better performing, and so on, than the "average" other person.

One of the more traumatic events that can occur to anyone is being fired.[33] Today losing a job doesn't carry the stigma that it once did. But—it still hurts! Inevitably the person asks himself: What went wrong? What could I have done differently? And, perhaps most important: What am I going to do now?

For most people, undertaking a job search at any time is always stressful. Undertaking a job search *after* suffering the psychological blow of being fired can be a formidable challenge for anyone. Suppose that you have just been fired. You can take certain constructive actions to increase your chances of success and even end up with a more satisfying job.

1. *Work through the firing psychologically.* Emotionally, you might feel like hiding or taking a sabbatical. But, experts suggest that beginning the search for a new job immediately is crucial. The first contact or two may be hard, but the sooner you get started and the more people you talk to, the quicker you will find another position. Of course, reestablishing your normal good spirits may be either a long or slow process, depending on your ability to bounce back. Maintaining a sense of humor helps. Hal Lancaster, of the *Wall Street Journal*, suggests that "getting fired is nature's way of telling you that you had the wrong job in the first place."
2. *Figure out what went wrong.* This step is an important part of coming to grips, psychologically, with the situation. If you don't understand what led to your being fired, you're likely to repeat the same mistakes in the future. Moreover, you need to talk to your former employer, coworkers, and friends and seek honest feedback to help you understand your strengths and weaknesses. Doing so may well be difficult. Many firms' human resource professionals prefer to say as little as possible at the time of dismissal in order to minimize lawsuits. If you can't get insights from your former employer, experts suggest utilizing a career counselor to help you make the same evaluation.

3. *Work with your former employer to develop an exit statement.* If possible, you should have something in writing from your former employer that will be an asset in your job search. Specific suggestions include having a paragraph that describes what you accomplished in your former job followed by a paragraph that explains why you are no longer with the firm. There are lots of "socially acceptable" reasons that can be given in such a document: a change in management style, a change in strategy, the desire to pursue interests that no longer fit what the employer wants, and so on. Surprisingly, the fired employee can often get a former manager or a senior manager to sign such a document. Managers often want to be helpful, and if such a request is approached in a constructive, problem-solving manner, many times the former manager is willing to help create a letter or other document that does not condemn the company or you. This approach has the advantage of creating a situation where prospective future employers hear the same "story" from both the former employer and you.
4. *Avoid negative attributions as part of your explanation.* Experts say that you should never say anything bad about your former employer. Don't make excuses, don't trash the people you used to work for, and don't blame everything on others. Focus on the positive aspects of any written understanding that you have obtained. Accept responsibility for both your failures and successes. Quickly move the discussion to the future, stressing what you've learned from previous jobs and focusing on what you can do for a new employer.

CHAPTER SUMMARY

1. Describe the major elements in the perceptual process.

Perception is the psychological process whereby people select information from the environment and organize it to make sense of their worlds. Environmental stimuli are observed, selected, organized, interpreted, and responded to as a result of the perceptual process. Understanding the two major components of this process—selection and organization—is particularly important.

2. Identify the main factors that influence what individuals perceive.

People use perceptual selection to filter out less important information in order to focus on more important environmental cues. Both external factors in the environment and factors internal to the perceiver influence perceptual selection. External factors can be thought of as characteristics of the perceived event that influence whether it is likely to be noticed. Internal factors include personality, learning, and motivation.

3. Identify the factors that determine how one person perceives another.

How people perceive each other is particularly important for organizational behavior. Person perception is a function of the characteristics of the person perceived, the characteristics of the perceiver, and the situation within which the perception takes place. People may go to great lengths to manage the impressions that others form about them.

4. Describe the primary errors in perception that people make.

The perceptual process may result in errors of judgment or understanding in various ways. The more important and common perceptual errors include perceptual defense, stereotyping, the halo effect, projection, and impression management. However, through training and experience, individuals can learn to judge or perceive others more accurately.

5. Explain how attributions influence behavior.

Attribution deals with the perceived causes of behavior. People infer causes for the behavior of others, and their perceptions of why certain behaviors occur influence their own subsequent behavioral responses and feelings. Whether behavior is internally caused by the nature of the person or externally caused by circumstances is an important attribution that people make about the behaviors of others. Individuals also make attributions concerning task success and failure that have important implications for organizational behavior.

KEY TERMS AND CONCEPTS

Attribution process
Expatriates
Feng shui
Fundamental attribution error
Golem effect
Halo effect
Implicit personality theory
Impression management
Perception
Perceptual defense
Perceptual set
Person perception
Pollyanna principle
Projection
Pygmalion effect
Selective screening
Self-fulfilling prophecy
Self-serving bias
Stereotyping

DISCUSSION QUESTIONS

1. Are people who have been laid off from their jobs victims of a fundamental attribution error?
2. If you take an assignment with an organization in a foreign country, what are some of the perceptual errors that you should avoid making in order for your assignment to be successful?
3. Which type of stereotype do you believe is most persuasive in organizations? Why?
4. Give three examples of the halo effect that you have observed personally.
5. Describe an important task at which you failed. Describe a second important task at which you succeeded. Identify the attributions that you made to explain your failure and your success.
6. Using the scores you gained from the *Impression Management Assessment* questionnaire in Table 3.2, how might the overuse of such tactics backfire on you and hurt your career advancement?
7. Provide two real examples of the Pygmalion effect.
8. What style of font are you using on your PC? What hidden message does that send to others about you?
9. Give an example of a situation in which you attributed someone's behavior to internal or external factors. What influenced your attribution?
10. Visit Estée Lauder's website (www.ELcompanies.com) and click on the box for "Company," then "Our Workplace," then "Our Principles." Are the principles mainly internal or external attributions? What does this mean for a manager's evaluation of a subordinate's performance?

EXPERIENTIAL EXERCISE AND CASE

Experiential Exercise: Self Competency

The Perception Process[34]

The *Perception Process Questionnaire* (PPQ) is designed to help you evaluate your current level of perceptual skills. If you do not have experience in a management-level position, consider a project you have worked on either in the classroom or in an organization such as a fraternity, sorority, club, church, or service group. You will find that the questions are applicable to your own experience even if you are not yet a manager.

Use the following scale to rate the frequency with which you perform the behaviors described in each question. Place the corresponding number (1–7) in the blank space preceding the statement.

1 = Rarely
2 = Irregularly
3 = Occasionally
4 = Usually
5 = Frequently
6 = Almost Always
7 = Consistently

_____1. I search for verified facts and observations to support inferences or conclusions.

_____2. I examine available information related to my area of job responsibility.

_____3. I note organizational changes and policies that might affect my information.

_____4. I ask others for their opinions and observations to get access to more information.

_____5. I note inconsistencies and seek explanations for them.

_____6. I look at information in terms of similarities and differences.

_____7. I generate possible explanations for available information.

_____8. I check for omissions, distortions, or exaggerations in available information.

_____9. I verbally summarize data that are not completely quantified (e.g., trends).

______ 10. I distinguish facts from opinions.

______ 11. I am aware of my own style of approaching problems and how this might affect the way I process information.

______ 12. I put quantitative information in tables, charts, and graphs.

______ 13. I am aware of the personality characteristics of my peers, colleagues, subordinates, and superiors.

______ 14. I am aware of my own biases and value systems that influence the way I see people.

______ 15. I am aware of patterns of people's performance and how these patterns might indicate characteristics.

______ 16. I recognize differences and similarities among people.

______ 17. I actively seek to determine how pieces of information might be related.

______ 18. I relate current information to past experiences.

______ 19. I relate my own attitudes and feelings and those of others to job performance.

______ 20. I relate work methods to outcomes.

PPQ Scoring

The PPQ Scoring Sheet summarizes your responses for the PPQ. It will help you identify your existing strengths and pinpoint areas that need improvement. Add the five category scores to obtain a total score. Enter that total score in the space indicated.

PPQ Scoring Sheet

Skill Area	Items	Assessment
Searching for information	1, 2, 3, 4	
Interpreting and comprehending information	5, 6, 7, 8	
Determining essential factors	9, 10, 11, 12	
Recognizing characteristics of people	13, 14, 15, 16	
Identifying relationships	17, 18, 19, 20	
TOTAL SCORE		

PPQ Evaluation

The PPQ Evaluation (see below) shows scoring lines for your total score and for each category measured on the PPQ. Each line shows a continuum from the lowest possible score to the highest. Place a B (before-practice) where your personal score falls on each of these lines. The score lines in the PPQ Evaluation show graphically where you stand with regard to five areas of perception. If you have been honest with yourself, you now have a better idea of your relative strengths and weaknesses in the categories of behavior that make up perception skills.

PPQ Evaluation

Total Score

Lowest score ______________________________ Highest score

20 50 80 110 140

Category Scores

Searching for information

4 10 16 22 28

Interpreting and comprehending information

4 10 16 22 28

Determining essential factors

4 10 16 22 28

Recognizing characteristics of people

4 10 16 22 28

Identifying relationships

4 10 16 22 28

Questions

1. What managerial competencies can you draw on to improve your perceptual skills?
2. How has your score affected your communications with others?

Case: Self Competency

John Kerner[35]

Instructions

John Kerner is a computer engineering programmer for the aerospace division of Mitsubishi International Company. Please read the case and then identify the causes of his behavior by answering the questions following the case. Then determine whether you made an internal or external attribution. After completing this task, decide on the appropriateness of various forms of corrective action. A list of potential recommendations has been developed. The list is divided into four categories. Read each action, and evaluate its appropriateness by using the scale provided. Next, compute a total score for each of the four categories.

The Case

John Kerner, 42, received his baccalaureate degree in aerospace engineering from a school in the Midwest. He graduated with a 3.4 GPA and had a minor in international relations. During the summer between his junior and senior years, he took an internship with Mitsubishi International in Kyoto, Japan. Immediately upon graduation, he took a permanent position with Mitsubishi International and was assigned to its Los Angeles division. John is currently working in the aerospace engineering department as a senior engineer. During the past year, he has missed 12 days of work. He seems unmotivated and rarely has his assignments completed on time. John is usually given the harder engineering designs to work on because of his technical competency.

Past records indicate John, on average, completes programs classified as "routine" in about 45 hours. His coworkers, on the other hand, complete "routine" programs in an average time of 32 hours. Further, he finishes programs considered "major problems," on average, in about 115 hours. His coworkers, however, finish these same "major problems" assignments, on average, in about 100 hours. When he has worked in engineering teams, his peer performance reviews are generally average to marginal. His peers have noted he is not creative in attacking problems and he is difficult to work with.

The aerospace engineering department recently sent a questionnaire to all customers to evaluate the usefulness and accuracy of its designs. The results indicate many departments are not using its designs because they cannot understand the reports. It was also determined that many customers found John's work unorganized and they could not use his work unless someone redid it.

Causes of Performance

To what extent was each of the following a cause of John's performance? Use the following scale:

	Very Little			**Very Much**	
	1	2	3	4	5
a. High ability	1	2	3	4	5
b. Low ability	1	2	3	4	5
c. Low effort	1	2	3	4	5
d. Difficult job	1	2	3	4	5
e. Unproductive coworkers	1	2	3	4	5
f. Bad luck	1	2	3	4	5

Internal attribution (total score for causes a, b, and c)

____

External attribution (total score for causes d, e, and f)

____

Appropriateness of Corrective Action

Evaluate the following courses of action by using the scale below:

Very Inappropriate			**Very Appropriate**	
1	2	3	4	5

Coercive Actions

a. Reprimand John for his performance.
1 2 3 4 5

b. Threaten to fire John if his performance does not improve.
1 2 3 4 5

Change Job

c. Transfer John to another job.
1 2 3 4 5

d. Demote John to a less demanding job.
1 2 3 4 5

Coaching Actions

e. Work with him to help him do the job better.
1 2 3 4 5

f. Offer him encouragement to help him improve.
1 2 3 4 5

No Immediate Actions

g. Do nothing.
1 2 3 4 5

h. Promise him a pay raise if he improves.
1 2 3 4 5

Compute a score for the four categories:

Coercive actions = a + b = ______

Change job = c + d = ______

Coaching actions = e + f = ______
No immediate actions = g + h = ______

Questions

1. How would you evaluate John's performance in terms of consistency, distinctiveness, and consensus?
2. Would you attribute John's performance to internal or external causes? What is the rational for your decision?
3. Which of the four types of corrective action do you think is most appropriate? Explain. Can you identify any negative consequences of this choice?

CHAPTER 4

Applying Reinforcement and Social Learning Concepts to Improve Effectiveness

Learning Goals

When you have finished studying the chapter, you should be able to:

1. Explain the role of classical and operant conditioning in fostering learning.
2. Describe the contingencies of reinforcement that influence behavior.
3. Explain how positive reinforcement, negative reinforcement, punishment, and extinction can affect learning.
4. Describe how social learning theory can be used by individuals to learn new behaviors.

Learning from Experience

WORKING AT UNITED PARCEL SERVICE

For United Parcel Service (UPS), the slogan "What Can Brown Do for You?" is gospel. With revenues of more than $42.6 billion dollars, 407,200 employees worldwide, and 1,788 locations, UPS is the world's largest package-delivery company. UPS transports 15 million packages and documents per business day throughout the United States and to more than 200 countries and territories. Its delivery operations use a fleet of about 92,000 motor vehicles and nearly 600 aircraft. How does UPS deliver?

It all starts with a computer-generated shipping label that goes onto all of the packages in the UPS system. The label has a unique tracking number, a bar code, and a UPS maxicode that contains all of the information pertinent to your shipment. At 4:00 A.M. every morning after the feeder trucks bring the packages into the UPS centers for the "presort," they go out for final delivery. Service providers carry a delivery information acquisition device (DIAD) that will upload delivery information to the UPS network. The DIAD even includes digital images of a recipient's signature, giving shippers quicker confirmation of final delivery and allowing drivers to stay in contact with their operational centers. Every route has been planned out for maximum efficiency in terms of time commitments. Routes are even optimized to avoid left turns where possible so drivers don't have to wait in traffic as long. Service providers are trained to perform their tasks over and over again without wasted effort. Veteran service providers earn $29 per hour and can earn more with overtime. They are told to keep the DIAD under the right arm and the package under the left. Keys are on the pinky finger. They are told to look at the package only once to fix the address in their mind. They walk to the customer's place of business or home at three feet a second. The service provider's left foot should hit the truck's first step. They are told to put their seat belt on with their left hand, while at the same time turning on the ignition with their right hand. During an average day, a service provider will make about 100 stops to deliver 246 packages and pick up 70 others. Each service provider participates in hours and hours of classroom and on-the-road training during which they learn the Five Seeing Habits: (1) look down the road to uncover traffic patterns, (2) maintain the proper following distance,

For more information on UPS, visit the organization's home page at www.ups.com.

LEARNING CONTENT

(3) constantly keep your eyes on the road, (4) make sure that the truck has an escape route, and (5) communicate in traffic with your horn, lights, and signals. Those service providers who use these Five Seeing Habits effectively are rewarded with T-shirts, free lunches, and the like.

United Parcel Service gives its supervisors personal digital assistants (PDAs) to use in on-road driver evaluations. The PDAs are equipped with proprietary software that standardizes the evaluation process, helping to ensure that each driver review is as objective as possible. "Our supervisors do ride-alongs to see if the service provider is following procedures and adhering to our health and safety policies," says Cathy Callagee, vice president of applications development for UPS's operations portfolio. "But this was problematic because supervisors used to have to write notes on paper, and then bring their notes back to the office and type them into reports."

Paper is eliminated with the help of PDAs, which display a series of checklists for the supervisor to use during the evaluation. The checklists guide the supervisors through a list of duties the service provider should be performing. The supervisor simply checks off each duty as the service provider completes it. Additionally, the checklists are uniform across the UPS network, so each service provider receives the same evaluation, regardless of who is conducting the review. The PDAs also identify training needs to help make service providers safer and provide better customer service. The PDAs also permit the supervisor to immediately reward an employee for excellent service with a congratulatory note.

The new PDAs also are helpful for supervisors because they serve as a remote office, allowing supervisors to receive e-mail and check the status of other activities while they are on the road with drivers. Currently, UPS has thousands of PDAs in the field. "Supervisors can now electronically write how their drivers are doing and [whether] they are following procedures," Callagee says. "If [they're] not, the supervisor can bring the applied methods right up on the PDA and walk the driver through it."[1]

Companies in all industries are recognizing the importance of customer satisfaction and how the quality of frontline customer service providers can make or break a company. Turnover and competition are pushing organizations to focus on ways to keep top-quality employees satisfied and motivated. A recent survey conducted by WorldatWork found that recognition and reward programs remain a top priority for all managers.[2] As you read in the feature on UPS, managers have in place opportunities to recognize and reward good performance. UPS asks service providers, via surveys and team meetings, what they value most in terms of recognition and rewards and then designs their motivational program around these employee expectations and values. UPS also knows that unless there is a consistent way to track and recognize superior performance, such motivational programs lose their effectiveness.

UPS managerial practices are based on specific principles drawn from an area of psychology called *learning*. Learning *is a relatively permanent change in knowledge or observable behavior that results from practice or experience*.[3] Desirable work behaviors contribute to achievement of organizational goals; conversely, undesirable work behaviors hinder achievement of these goals. Labeling behavior as *desirable* or *undesirable* may be somewhat subjective and depends on the value systems of the organization (most often represented by an employee's manager) and the employee exhibiting the behavior. For example, a service provider at UPS who returns late from lunch exhibits undesirable behavior from the supervisor's viewpoint, desirable behavior from the viewpoint of friends with whom the worker chats during the break, and desirable behavior from the worker's viewpoint because of the satisfaction of social needs. Employees quickly learn whether their behavior is desirable or undesirable based on the manager's reaction to the behavior and how to change an undesirable to a desirable (from the manager's viewpoint) behavior.

Usually, however, the work setting and organizational norms provide objective bases for determining whether a behavior is desirable or undesirable. The more a behavior deviates from organizational expectations, the more undesirable it is. At UPS, undesirable behavior includes anything that results in lost packages and late or missed deliveries. Expectations vary considerably from one organization to another. For example, at Microsoft's research and development laboratory, engineers and scientists are encouraged to question top management's directives because innovation and professional judgment are crucial to the organization's success.

Effective managers do not try to change employees' personalities or basic beliefs. As we pointed out in Chapters 2 and 3, an individual's personality, emotions, and perceptual processes influence his behavior and directly influencing those traits is often difficult, if not impossible. Rather, effective managers focus on identifying observable employee behaviors and the environmental conditions that affect these behaviors. They then attempt to influence external events in order to guide employee behaviors—to help employees learn and exhibit desirable behaviors. In this chapter, we explore three major concepts of learning: classical conditioning, operant conditioning, and social learning theory. Each theory proposes a different way by which people learn, but focusing on observable behaviors is common to all three.

LEARNING THROUGH REWARDS AND PUNISHMENTS

Learning Goal

1. Explain the role of classical and operant conditioning in fostering learning.

Employees need to learn and practice productive work behaviors. Learning new work often depends on many factors. The manager's task, then, is to provide learning experiences in an environment that will simplify the learning process and promote the employee behaviors desired by the organization. For learning to occur, some types of behavioral change are required. In the sterile processing department at Children's Hospital in Denver, Colorado, good attendance is critical. Absenteeism impacts the entire department because the work must get done regardless, so team members have to pick up the slack for their colleagues. To encourage perfect attendance, staff members who have not missed work in the previous three months are announced at the department's meetings. Various rewards are handed out, such as ribbons, perfect attendance pins, prizes, tote bags, alarm clocks, and the like. As an added incentive, the person with the longest record of perfect attendance is allowed to choose first from the list of "gifts." In addition, each quarter a list of employees who have not missed any days of work is posted in the staff lounge along with the length of their perfect attendance. If the entire department has perfect attendance for a quarter, the whole department celebrates with events like an ice cream social or root beer float party to acknowledge everyone's efforts and accomplishments.[4]

Classical Conditioning

Classical conditioning *is the process by which individuals learn to link the information from a neutral stimulus to a stimulus that causes a response.* This response may not be under an individual's conscious control.[5] In the classical conditioning process, an unconditioned stimulus (environmental event) brings out a natural response. Then a neutral environmental event, called a *conditioned stimulus*, is paired with the unconditioned stimulus that brings out the behavior. Eventually, the conditioned stimulus alone brings out the behavior, which is called a *conditional response*.

The person most frequently associated with classical conditioning is Ivan Pavlov, the Russian physiologist whose experiments with dogs led to the early formulations of classical conditioning theory. In Pavlov's famous experiment, the sound of a metronome (the conditioned stimulus) was paired with food (the unconditioned stimulus). The dogs eventually exhibited a salivation response (conditioned response) to the sound of the metronome alone. The classical conditioning process is illustrated in Figure 4.1.

The classical conditioning process helps explain a variety of behaviors that occur in everyday organizational life. At Presbyterian Hospital's emergency room in Plano,

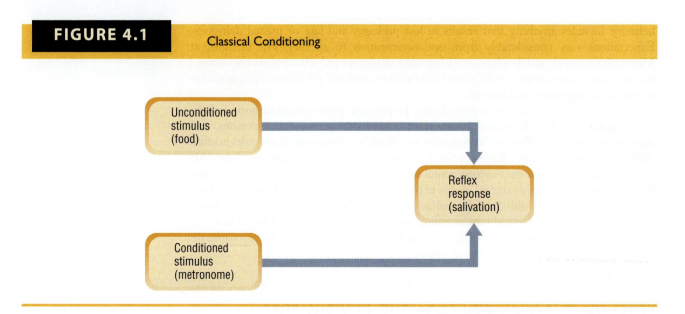

FIGURE 4.1 Classical Conditioning

Texas, special lights in the hallway indicate that a patient who needs treatment has just arrived. Nurses and other hospital staff report that they feel nervous when the lights go on. In contrast, at a recent luncheon in the dining room at Stonebriar Country Club in Frisco, Texas, Ralph Sorrentino, a partner at Deloitte & Touche, was thanked by his friend Barry Sullivan, for suggesting a new personnel performance evaluation system. When Sorrentino dines in the dining room, he remembers that recognition and feels good.

Some organizations spend millions of dollars on advertising campaigns designed to link the information value of a stimulus to customer purchase behavior. In a TV ad, AFLAC has successfully created a link between its duck and supplemental insurance. The duck is the unconditioned stimulus, and insurance is the conditioned stimulus. The positive feelings that buyers have toward the duck are associated with insurance, which AFLAC hopes will lead people to buy its products. Similarly, Blue Bell Creameries has linked its cow, Belle, in an award-winning TV ad. When people see Belle (unconditioned stimulus) singing in a pasture of purple flowers, they associate her with Blue Bell ice cream (conditioned stimulus). By associating the upbeat mood and dairy freshness created by the cow with its product, Blue Bell hopes to lead customers to eat its ice cream. Both organizations have successfully used the concepts of classical conditioning to increase sales of their products.

Classical conditioning isn't widely used in work settings. Employee behaviors usually don't include responses that can be changed with classical conditioning techniques. There is greater interest in the voluntary behaviors of employees and how they can be changed via operant conditioning.

Operant Conditioning

The person most closely linked with this type of learning is B. F. Skinner.[6] He coined the term operant conditioning *to refer to a process by which individuals learn voluntary behavior*. Voluntary behaviors are called *operants* because they operate, or have some influence, on the environment. Learning occurs from the consequences of behaviors, and many employee work behaviors are operant behaviors. In fact, most behaviors in everyday life (e.g., talking, walking, reading, or working) are forms of operant behavior. Table 4.1 shows some examples of operant behaviors and their consequences. Managers are interested in operant behaviors because they can influence the results of such behaviors. For example, the frequency of an employee behavior can be increased or

Table 4.1 Examples of Operant Behavior and Their Consequences

BEHAVIORS	CONSEQUENCES
The Individual	
• works and	is paid.
• is late to work and	is docked pay.
• enters a restaurant and	eats.
• enters a football stadium and	watches a football game.
• enters a grocery store and	buys food.

decreased by changing the results of that behavior. The crucial aspect of operant conditioning is what happens as a consequence of the behavior. The strength and frequency of operantly conditioned behaviors are determined mainly by consequences. Thus, managers and team members must understand the effects of different types of consequences on the task behaviors of employees. For example, at Virgin Life Care in Boston, Massachusetts, the company rewards program motivated 40 percent of its more than 940 employees to establish a habit of walking up stairs instead of taking the elevator. Thanks to the program, employees reduced their body fat by 68 percent. The company saved money on decreased medical claims and reduced absenteeism.

In operant conditioning, a response is learned because it leads to a particular consequence (reinforcement), and it is strengthened each time it is reinforced. The success of Denver's Children's Hospital motivational program to encourage perfect attendance relies on rewarding behavior (perfect attendance) or not rewarding behavior when a person calls in sick. At school, you've probably learned that if you study hard, you will receive good grades. If you keep up with your reading throughout the semester, you can cope with the stress of finals week. Thus, you've learned to operate on your environment to achieve your desired goals.

CONTINGENCIES OF REINFORCEMENT

Learning Goal

2. Describe the contingencies of reinforcement that influence behavior.

A contingency of reinforcement *is the relationship between a behavior and the preceding and following environmental events that influence that behavior*. A contingency of reinforcement consists of an antecedent, a behavior, and a consequence.[7]

An antecedent *precedes and is a stimulus to a behavior*. Antecedents are instructions, rules, goals, and advice from others that help individuals to know which behaviors are acceptable and which are not and to let them know the consequences of such behaviors. At UPS, service providers are trained on how to deliver a package. Antecedents play an essential educational role by letting service providers know in advance the consequences (rewards) of different behavior.

A consequence *is the result of a behavior, which can be either positive or negative in terms of goal or task accomplishment*. A manager's response to an employee is contingent on the consequence of the behavior (and sometimes on the behavior itself, regardless of consequence). The consequence for service providers at UPS is delivering all their packages on time and going home on time. The consequence for staff members of the sterile processing department at Children's Hospital who have perfect attendance for the quarter is they receive tote bags, their name is posted in the break room, etc.

Figure 4.2 shows an example of contingent reinforcement. First, the employee and manager jointly set a goal (e.g., selling $100,000 worth of equipment next month). Next, the employee performs tasks to achieve this goal (e.g., calling on four new customers a week, having regular lunches with current buyers, and attending a two-day training program on new methods of selling). If the employee reaches the sales goal, the manager

FIGURE 4.2 Example of Contingent Reinforcement

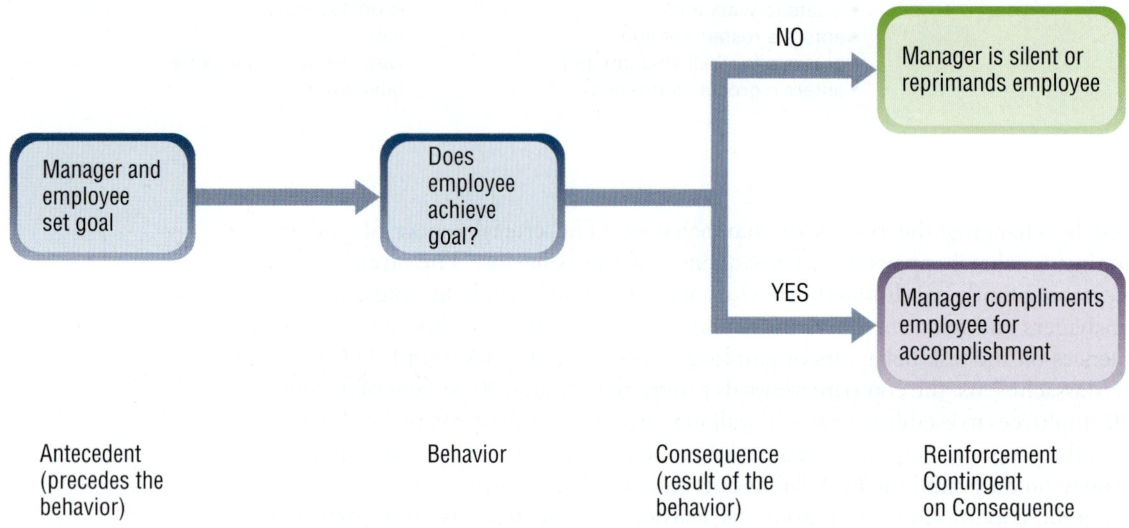

praises the employee—an action contingent on achievement of the goal. If the employee fails to reach the goal, the manager doesn't say anything or reprimands the employee.

The contingency of reinforcement concept involves three main types of contingencies. First, an event can be presented (applied) or withdrawn (removed), contingent on employee behavior. The event also may be positive or aversive. Positive events *are desirable, or pleasing, to the employee.* Aversive events *are undesirable, or displeasing, to the employee.* Figure 4.3 shows how these events can be combined to produce four types of contingencies of reinforcement. It shows whether a particular type of contingency is likely to increase or decrease the frequency of the behavior. This figure also is the basis for the following discussion of contingencies of reinforcement. Reinforcement *is a behavioral contingency that increases the frequency of a particular behavior that it follows.* Whether positive or negative, reinforcement always increases the frequency of the employee behavior. If you want a behavior to continue, you must make sure that it is being reinforced. In contrast, extinction and punishment always decrease the frequency of the employee behavior.

Positive Reinforcement

Positive reinforcement *entails presenting a pleasant consequence after the occurrence of a desired behavior* (see Figure 4.3). A manager might reward an employee's behavior that is desirable in terms of achieving the organization's goals. Dana Gibson brought a cup of coffee to Suzette Ramirez and then discussed the improved quality of her work. Suzette's work continued to improve (positive reinforcement).

Reward versus Reinforcement. The terms *reinforcement* and *reward* are often confused in everyday usage. A reward *is an event that a person finds desirable or pleasing.* A person's culture influences whether a reward acts as a reinforcer.[8] For example, praise and appreciation of employees in family-dominated cultures such as Greece, Italy, Singapore, and South Korea may mean just as much to the recipient as money. Certain material rewards can also carry unexpected consequences. In China, for example, cashiers and clerks at Wal-Mart and Sam's typically earn between 1500 and 2500 RMB per month (roughly \$200 to \$300). This is a competitive wage in China. In addition,

FIGURE 4.3 Types of Contingencies of Reinforcement

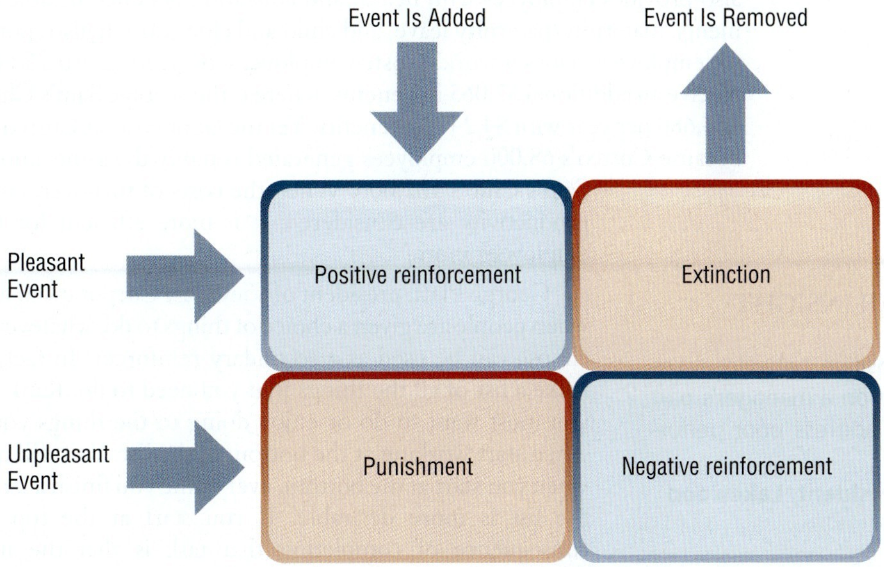

Wal-Mart distributes food to employees as holiday gifts and gives them a housing allowance. Employees in higher positions get more and better food and housing than lower level workers.[9] A manager from the United States who led a team in Japan singled out and praised a Japanese employee in front of coworkers for finding an error in the team's report. The manager believed that she was reinforcing the desired behavior. Later, however, she learned that the employee was given the silent treatment by other team members and had stopped looking for errors.[10]

To qualify as a reinforcer, a reward must increase the frequency of the behavior it follows. Money can be regarded as a positive reinforcer for a particular individual only if the frequency of the desired behavior (in this case, high performance) increases. A reward doesn't act as a reinforcer if the frequency of the behavior decreases or remains unchanged.

Primary and Secondary Reinforcers. A primary reinforcer *is an event for which the individual already knows the value.* Food, shelter, and water are primary reinforcers. However, primary reinforcers don't always reinforce. For example, food may not be a reinforcer to someone who has just completed a five-course meal.

In organizations, secondary reinforcers influence most behaviors. A secondary reinforcer *is an event that once had neutral value but has taken on some value (positive or negative) for an individual because of past experience.* Money is an obvious example of a secondary reinforcer. Although it can't directly satisfy a basic human need, money has value because an individual can use it to purchase both necessities and discretionary items. Calvert, a Bethesda, Maryland, financial firm, groups its secondary reinforcers into three categories:

- *core benefits*, such as life insurance, sick leave, holiday pay, and a retirement savings plan;
- *optional benefits*, such as dental and eye care coverage, and spending accounts for health and dependent care; and
- *other benefits*, such as tuition reimbursement, car pooling, and career planning.

At Costco, employees are offered challenging jobs and participate in the management of their own jobs. Management teaches employees quality control techniques so that they can monitor their own behavior, learn to control costs, and assume responsibility for tasks viewed traditionally as managerial prerogatives. Costco also provides employees with health and education benefits, flexible working arrangements, maternity/paternity leave, and child and elder care. It also sponsors social events for employees. Does it work? Costco employees, on average, earn $34,214 per year and receive an additional $7,065 in benefits, whereas the average Sam's Club employee earns $24,680 per year with $4,247 in benefits. Yet the labor costs at Costco are actually lower because Costco's 68,000 employees generated roughly the same amount of sales as did Sam's Club's 102,000. When the costs of turnover, employee theft, and productivity are considered, it is more efficient for Costco to pay its employees more.[11]

LEADER INSIGHT

Encouraging positive behavior takes much less effort on a manager's part than having to address poor performance issues.

Jack Gustin, President, Lakewood Hospital

George Platt, president of ViewCast Corporation, has discovered that when people are given a choice of things to do, whatever they consistently choose can be used as a secondary reinforcer. In fact, we invite you to make a list of all the things that you need to do. Rank these from things you most want to do or enjoy doing to the things you least like to do. Then start working at the bottom of the list. You will quickly notice that when you start at the bottom, every time you finish a task, the next one on the list is more desirable. If you start at the top of your list, the consequence of completing that task is that the next one is more undesirable, difficult, or boring. Using this approach, you quit. Starting from the bottom and working to the top, you don't want to quit until all tasks are done.

For several years, the percentage of leaders of color in the workplace has been increasing. With a growing proportion of the professional workforce represented by people of color, the challenge is to develop these leaders. With a traditional workforce of primarily white managers who have a shared common culture of how to act, how to lead, and how a business should be run, these new leaders bring differing cultural and racial perspectives. Organizations cannot risk the consequences of a substantial portion of their employees being left behind because they lack the managerial competencies needed for advancement. The following Diversity Competency feature highlights this topic.[12]

Diversity Competency

Coaching Leaders of Color

In dealing with the unique perspectives of people of color, the Center for Creative Leadership in Greensboro, North Carolina, has suggested that managers and coaches have a number of positive secondary reinforcers available to them to help them be successful:

- *Find similarities.* Finding similarities (children, pets, hobbies, etc.) can be an important step for working with people of color. This information often eases the strain between the coach and the person. It reduces the space between them.
- *Appreciate the social context.* For people of color, socioeconomic and political context often influences their lives. For example, a person of color who is over 55 may have experienced extreme discrimination growing up and in the workplace. In addition, these people may have questions about their upward mobility since there were few role models to point to who had moved into high managerial ranks. People from Latin America often perceived power and authority differently because of how it has been used or abused in their countries of origin.
- *Understand the organizational context.* Some organizations are relatively color-blind and some are color sensitive. Given that people of color are already

unclear about their organizational status, getting mixed messages about the need for coaching can greatly affect them. Generally people of color enter coaching experiences with less positive attitudes than whites.

- *Challenge.* The rewards of challenging assignments include developing new competencies, getting people out of their comfort zones, and mastering new knowledge. Organizational reward systems are critical. Recognition for doing a job well, educational achievements, celebrations, and salary increases are all needed to support people of color. Recognition helps establish credibility and reinforce a person's newly acquired competencies.

For more information on the Center for Creative Leadership, visit the organization's home page at www.ccl.org.

Concepts of Positive Reinforcement. Several general principles influence the effectiveness of positive reinforcement. These general principles help to explain optimum reinforcement conditions and are as follows[13]:

- The principle of contingent reinforcement *states that the reinforcer must be administered only if the desired behavior is performed.* A reinforcer administered when the desired behavior has not been performed is ineffective.
- The principle of immediate reinforcement *states that the reinforcer will be most effective if administered immediately after the desired behavior has occurred.* This is what supervisors at UPS do. The more time that elapses after the behavior occurs, the less effective the reinforcer.
- The principle of reinforcement size *states that the larger the amount of reinforcer delivered after the desired behavior, the more effect the reinforcer will have on the frequency of the desired behavior.* The amount, or size, of the reinforcer is relative. A reinforcer that may be significant to one person may be insignificant to another person. Thus, the size of the reinforcer must be determined in relation both to the behavior and the individual. ARAMARK, a supplier of food services to college campuses, gives T-shirts to workers with perfect attendance for a month and a $50 gift certificate to those with perfect attendance for a semester.
- The principle of reinforcement deprivation *states that the more a person is deprived of the reinforcer, the greater effect it will have on the future occurrence of the desired behavior.* However, if an individual recently has had enough of a reinforcer and is satisfied, the reinforcer will have less effect.

Organizational Rewards

Material rewards—salary, bonuses, fringe benefits, and the like—are obvious. Most managers also offer a wide range of other rewards, many of which aren't immediately apparent. They include verbal approval, assignment to desired tasks, improved working conditions, and extra time off. At Toyota's Camry assembly plant in Georgetown, Kentucky, management rewards employees for *kaizens*. A kaizen *is a suggestion that results in safety, cost, or quality improvements.*[14] The awards are distributed equally among all members of a team. The awards aren't cash payments; rather, they are gift certificates redeemable at local retail stores. Toyota learned that an award that could be shared by the employees' families was valued more than extra money in the paycheck. These awards instill pride and encourage other teams to scramble for new ideas and in the hope that they, too, will receive them. In addition, self-administered rewards are important. For example, self-satisfaction for accomplishing a particularly difficult assignment can be an important personal reinforcer. Table 4.2 contains an extensive list of organizational

Table 4.2 Rewards Used by Organizations

MATERIAL REWARDS	SUPPLEMENTAL BENEFITS	STATUS SYMBOLS
Pay	Company automobiles	Corner offices
Pay raises	Health insurance plans	Offices with windows
Stock options	Pension contributions	Carpeting
Profit sharing	Vacation and sick leave	Drapes
Deferred compensation	Recreation facilities	Paintings
Bonuses/bonus plans	Child-care support	Watches
Incentive plans	Club privileges	Rings
Expense accounts	Parental leave	Private restrooms
SOCIAL/INTERPERSONAL REWARDS	**REWARDS FROM THE TASK**	**SELF-ADMINISTERED REWARDS**
Praise	Sense of achievement	Self-congratulation
Developmental feedback	Jobs with more responsibility	Self-recognition
Smiles, pats on the back, and other nonverbal signals	Job autonomy/self-direction	Self-praise
Requests for suggestions	Performing important tasks	Self-development through expanded knowledge/skills
Invitations to coffee or lunch		Greater sense of self-worth
Wall plaques		

rewards. Remember, however, that such rewards will act as reinforcers only if the individuals receiving them find them desirable or pleasing.

Negative Reinforcement

Negative reinforcement (see Figure 4.3) *refers to an unpleasant event that precedes the employee behavior is removed when the desired behavior occurs.* Negative reinforcement increases the likelihood that the desired behavior will occur. Negative reinforcement is sometimes confused with punishment because both use unpleasant events to influence behavior. Negative reinforcement is used to increase the frequency of a desired behavior. In contrast, punishment is used to decrease the frequency of an undesired behavior. On NBC's TV show, the *Biggest Loser*, the station agreed to pay the person who lost the biggest percentage of his or her body weight $250,000. In this reality show, unless a contestant lost 15 pounds in two months, the show would air their photos on TV. Cynthia Nacson-Schechter explained that she knew all about the dangers of being overweight and yet these dangers and the money weren't enough to scare her into losing weight. What she feared most was the possibility that her ex-boyfriend would see her in a bikini on national TV. She lost weight and then some. It was the fear of being on national TV in a bikini that acted as a negative reinforcer for her to lose weight.

Managers and team members frequently use negative reinforcement when an employee hasn't done something that is necessary or desired. For example, air-traffic controllers want the ability to activate a blinking light and a loud buzzer in the cockpits of planes that come too close to each other. Air-traffic controllers wouldn't shut these devices off until the planes moved farther apart. This type of procedure is called *escape learning* because the pilots quickly learn to move their planes away from each other to escape the light and buzzer. Escape learning *means an unpleasant event occurs until an employee performs a behavior or terminates it.* In most instances, use of negative reinforcements generates enough behavior to escape or avoid punishment. Doing "just enough to get by" is typical.

Extinction

Extinction *is the removal of all reinforcing events.* Whereas reinforcement increases the frequency of a desirable behavior, extinction decreases the frequency of an undesirable behavior (see Figure 4.3). Managers use extinction to reduce undesirable employee behaviors that prevent achievement of organizational goals. The extinction procedure consists of three steps:

1. identifying the behavior to be reduced or eliminated,
2. identifying the reinforcer that maintains the behavior, and
3. stopping the reinforcer.

Extinction is a useful technique for reducing and eventually eliminating behaviors that disrupt normal workflow. For example, a team reinforces the disruptive behavior of a member by laughing at it. When the team stops laughing (the reinforcer), the disruptive behavior will diminish and ultimately stop.

Extinction can be regarded as a failure to reinforce a behavior positively. In this sense, the extinction of behaviors may be accidental. If managers fail to reinforce desirable behaviors, they may be using extinction without recognizing it. As a result, the frequency of desirable behaviors may inadvertently decrease.

Some managers think that doing nothing has no effect on performance. When managers do nothing following a behavior, they change the contingencies of reinforcement. If employees are taking the initiative to go beyond what is required, those behaviors will stop if they are not reinforced. If employees are taking shortcuts in areas of safety and quality and nothing is said, then extinction will cause the undesirable behaviors to continue.

Punishment

Punishment (see Figure 4.3) *occurs when an unpleasant event follows a behavior and decreases its frequency*. Remember when you tried to use a PC for the first time? You may have inadvertently deleted a document you had been working on for hours (punishment). If that happened, now you probably hit the "Save" option regularly. As in positive reinforcement, a punishment may include a specific antecedent that cues

Interpersonal punishers include a manager's oral reprimand of an employee for unacceptable behavior.

the employee that a consequence (punisher) will follow a specific behavior. A positive contingency of reinforcement encourages the frequency of a desired behavior. In contrast, punishment decreases the frequency of an undesired behavior. To qualify as a punisher, an event must decrease the undesirable behavior. Just because an event is thought of as unpleasant, it isn't necessarily a punisher. The event must actually reduce or stop the undesired behavior before it can be defined as a punisher.

Organizations typically use several types of unpleasant events to punish employees. Material consequences for failure to perform adequately include a cut in pay, a disciplinary suspension without pay, a demotion, or a transfer to a dead-end job. The final punishment is the firing of an employee for failure to perform. In general, organizations reserve the use of unpleasant material events for cases of serious behavior problems.

Interpersonal punishers are used extensively. They include a manager's oral reprimand of an employee for unacceptable behavior and nonverbal punishers such as frowns, grunts, and aggressive body language. Certain tasks themselves can be unpleasant. The fatigue that follows hard physical labor can be considered a punisher, as can harsh or dirty working conditions. However, care must be exercised in labeling a punisher. In some fields and to some employees, harsh or dirty working conditions may be considered as just something that goes with the job.

Three of the principles of positive reinforcement discussed earlier have equivalents in punishment. For maximum effectiveness:

- a punisher should be directly linked to the undesirable behavior (principle of contingent punishment);
- the punishment should be administered immediately (principle of immediate punishment); and,
- in general, the greater the size of the punisher, the stronger will be the effect on the undesirable behavior (principle of punishment size).

Negative Effects of Punishment. A criticism for using punishment is the chance that it will have negative effects, especially over long or sustained periods of time.[15] Punishment may stop an undesirable employee behavior. However, the potential negative consequences may be greater than the original undesirable behavior. Figure 4.4 illustrates some potential negative effects of punishment.

Punishment may cause undesirable emotional reactions. An employee who has been reprimanded for staying on break too long may react with anger toward the manager and the organization. Such reactions may lead to behavior detrimental to the organization. Sabotage, for example, may be a result of a punishment-oriented management system. Chapter 7 discusses aggressive behavior in the workforce more completely.

Punishment frequently leads only to short-term suppression of the undesirable behavior, rather than to its elimination. The suppression of an undesirable behavior over a long period of time usually requires continued and, perhaps, increasingly severe punishment. Another problem is that control of the undesirable behavior becomes contingent on the manager's presence. When the manager isn't around, the undesirable employee behavior is likely to recur.

In addition, the punished individual may try to avoid or escape the situation. From an organizational viewpoint, this reaction may be unacceptable if an employee avoids a particular, essential task. High absenteeism is a form of avoidance that may occur when punishment is used frequently. Quitting may be the employee's final form of escape. Organizations that depend on punishment are likely to have high rates of employee turnover. Some turnover is desirable, but excessive turnover is damaging to an organization. Todd Diener, executive vice president at Brinker International based in

FIGURE 4.4 Potential Negative Effects of Punishment

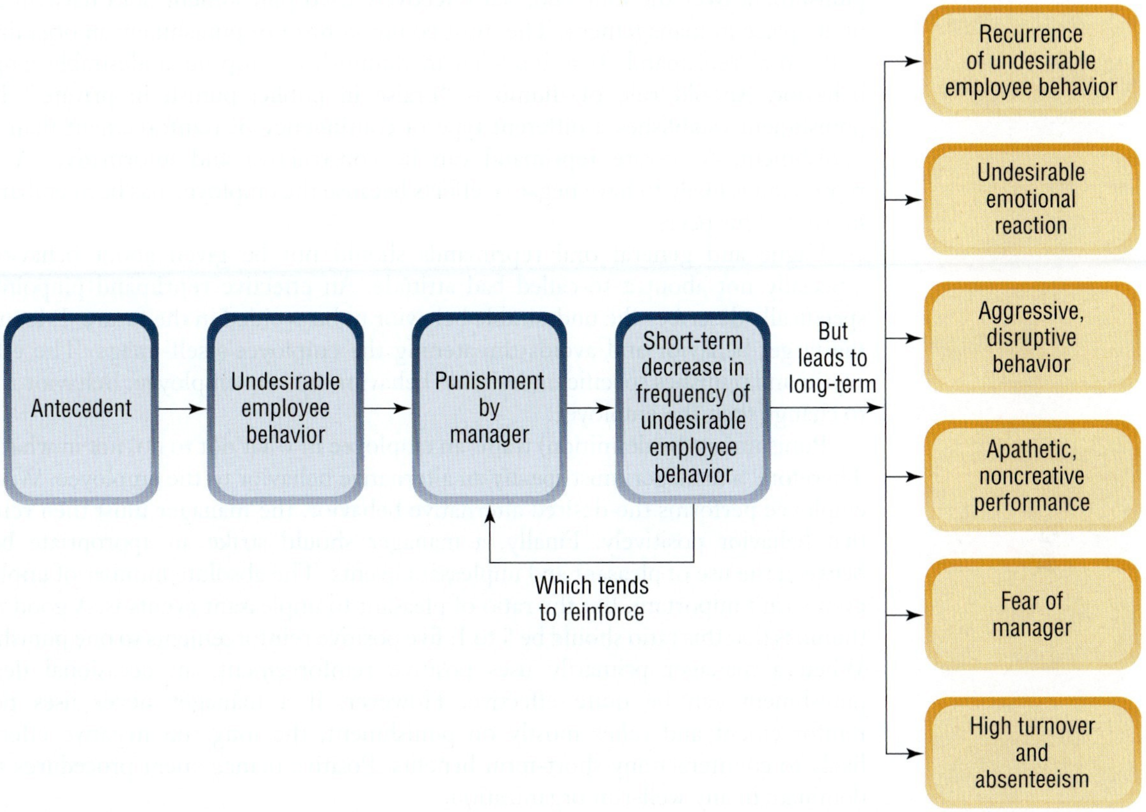

Dallas, Texas, says that recruitment and training costs average more than $600 per employee at Chili's restaurants.

Punishment suppresses employee initiative and flexibility. Reacting to punishment, many an employee has said: "I'm going to do just what I'm told and nothing more." Such an attitude is undesirable because organizations depend on the personal initiative and creativity that employees bring to their jobs. Overusing punishment produces apathetic employees who are not an asset to an organization. Sustained punishment can also lead to lower self-esteem. Lower self-esteem, in turn, undermines the employee's self-confidence, which is necessary for performing most jobs (see Chapter 2).

Punishment produces a conditioned fear of management. That is, employees develop a general fear of punishment-oriented managers. Such managers become an environmental cue, indicating to employees the probability that an aversive event will occur. So if operations require frequent, normal, and positive interaction between employees and a manager, such a situation can quickly become intolerable. Responses to fear, such as "hiding" or reluctance to communicate with a manager, may well hinder employee performance.

A manager may rely on punishment because it may produce fast results in the short run. In essence, the manager is reinforced for using punishment because the approach produces an immediate change in an employee's behavior. Thus, the manager may ignore punishment's long-term detrimental effects, which can be cumulative. A few incidents of punishment may not produce negative effects. The long-term, sustained use of punishment most often results in negative outcomes for the organization.

Effective Use of Punishment. Positive reinforcement is more effective than punishment over the long run, but effectively used punishment does have an appropriate place in management. The most common form of punishment in organizations is the oral reprimand. It is intended to diminish or stop an undesirable employee behavior. An old rule of thumb is "Praise in public; punish in private." Private punishment establishes a different type of contingency of reinforcement than public punishment. A private reprimand can be constructive and informative. A public reprimand is likely to have negative effects because the employee has been embarrassed in front of his peers.

Vague and general oral reprimands should not be given about behavior and especially not about a so-called bad attitude. An effective reprimand pinpoints and specifically describes the undesirable behavior to be avoided in the future. It focuses on the target behavior and avoids threatening the employee's self-image. The effective reprimand punishes specific undesirable behavior, not the employee. Behavior is easier to change than the employee.

Punishment (by definition) trains an employee in what not to do, not in what to do. Therefore, a manager must specify an alternative behavior to the employee. When the employee performs the desired alternative behavior, the manager must then reinforce that behavior positively. Finally, a manager should strike an appropriate balance between the use of pleasant and unpleasant events. The absolute number of unpleasant events isn't important, but the ratio of pleasant to unpleasant events is. A good rule of thumb is that this ratio should be 5 to 1: five positive reinforcements to one punishment. When a manager primarily uses positive reinforcement, an occasional deserved punishment can be quite effective. However, if a manager never uses positive reinforcement and relies mostly on punishment, the long-run negative effects are likely to counteract any short-term benefits. Positive management procedures should dominate in any well-run organization.

Positive Discipline. Richard Grote, a consultant, introduced positive discipline at Frito-Lay. It worked and the idea of positive discipline began to be used by many organizations. Grote began searching for a better management technique after a customer discovered a vulgar message written by a disgruntled employee on a corn chip. Grote gave the employee a day off with pay and called it "positive discipline." Positive discipline *emphasizes changing employee behaviors by reasoning rather than by imposing increasingly severe punishments.*[16] A key task of management is to help employees understand that the goals of the organization require certain standards of behavior and performance. One managerial task is to coach employees, issuing oral and then written reminders only when they fail to maintain behavioral and performance standards. It is the employee's responsibility to exercise self-discipline in achieving those standards. Many organizations use positive discipline to deal with problem employees and change undesirable employee behaviors. On the face of it, this approach sounds like a contradiction in terms.

General Electric's positive discipline program at its Vermont plant works as follows. An employee who comes to work late, does a sloppy job, or mistreats another employee gets an oral reminder about the behavior rather than a written reprimand. If the undesirable behavior continues, the employee is issued a written reminder. If the behavior still persists, the employee is suspended with pay for a day, called a "decision-making day." The purpose of the day is for the employee to decide whether to conform to the standards. The company pays the employee for this day to demonstrate its sincere effort to help him change. Paying the employee accomplishes two important things. First, it gives the GE managers the opportunity to inform the employee that it is serious about the problem and wants the employee to use this time to think through whether GE is the right place for her. One manager said: "But if you decide to remain with us, another disciplinary problem will result in your termination." Second, paying the employee often eliminates the anger that commonly results from a person's ultimately being fired. The purpose of the day off with pay is to send a wake-up call.

Discipline without punishment does two things. First, it communicates to the employee that the manager is serious about the matter. The specific gap between the employee's performance and the performance GE expects is highlighted. It reminds the employee of her responsibility to meet GE's standards and often gains the employee's agreement to solve this problem. Second, it sends a clear message to other employees who have been thinking about challenging the standards that the organization doesn't put up with unacceptable behavior—that GE's values and standards will not be compromised. Finally, the suspension provides tangible evidence that the employee's job is at risk.

General Electric's approach has been very successful. More than 85 percent of the employees going through the positive discipline program have changed their behaviors and stayed with GE. Since the program started, reported written warnings and reminders dropped from 39 to 23 to 12 during a recent two-year period. Employees who don't change their behaviors are fired.

Managerial Guidelines

For a positive reinforcer to cause an employee to repeat a desired behavior, it must have value to that employee. If the employee is consistently on time, the manager or team leader positively reinforces this behavior by complimenting the employee. What happens if the employee has been reprimanded in the past for coming to work late and then reports to work on time? The manager or team leader uses negative reinforcement and refrains from saying anything. Why? The employee is expected to come to work on time.

What happens if the employee continues to come to work late? The manager or team leader can use either extinction or punishment to try to stop this undesirable behavior. The team leader who chooses extinction doesn't praise the tardy employee but simply ignores the employee. The use of punishment may include reprimanding, fining, or suspending—and ultimately firing—the employee if the behavior persists.

The following guidelines are recommended for using contingencies of reinforcement in the work setting:

- Do not reward all employees in the same way.
- Carefully examine the consequences of nonactions as well as actions.
- Let employees know which behaviors will be reinforced.
- Let employees know what they are doing wrong.
- Don't punish employees in front of others.
- Make the response equal to the behavior by not cheating workers out of their just rewards.[17]

> **LEADER INSIGHT**
>
> The greatest motivation act one person can do for another is to listen.
> **Bob Nelson, President, Nelson Motivation, Inc.**

Can global managers use these guidelines to motivate employees? The following Self Competency feature illustrates how BMW managers use these basic concepts to motivate workers on its assembly line.[18]

Self Competency

Working on BMW's Assembly Line

© Photo Link/Photodisc/Getty Image

BMW relies on factory workers to find ways to cut costs and boost output in their plants.

BMW's factory located in Oxford, England, produces one of the company's new products, its 7 series. The factory has seen big changes from a few years ago, when Rover owned the factory. Then the buildings were crumbling and the plant was often half-empty. After acquiring the Rover factory, the first challenge for BMW was modernizing the facilities. They installed the newest production technology, expanded the parking lot, created more appealing landscapes, and in other ways created a more pleasant work environment. As employee Bernard Moss explained, "We had an open day for old employees and they just couldn't believe the transformation of the plant."

The improvements were badly needed, but they were costly, too. For the plant to become profitable, productivity had to improve. BMW relies on the factory workers themselves to find ways to cut costs and boost output. To motivate their employees and align their efforts with the needs of BMW, managers and union leaders designed a new pay system. It offers all employees an annual bonus of £260 (approximately $400) for their ideas. To receive the full bonus, employees must come up with an average of three ideas per employee and the ideas must save an average of £800. Other changes were also made in the way employees were paid. Under the old system, when production stopped and employees didn't come to work, they were paid anyway. When the plant was extra busy, they earned overtime pay. Now, when the plant is closed, employees are paid, but there is a new twist. Employees make up the time by putting in extra hours when needed. When things are busy, employees are expected to put in longer hours. Instead of overtime pay, they build up an account of extra time off. Each week quality reports are posted in a plaza that employees pass on their way to lunch. Employees are made aware of any quality problems.

The employees resented the new pay arrangements at first, but now they like it. According to Moss, "they [employees] are starting to see the advantages of longer holidays." Today the plant is even more productive than BMW managers had hoped for. Employees offered more than 10,000 ideas for improvements, saving the company £6 million ($7.79 million). "If people are happy, they are more efficient. If they are unhappy, they are not going to bother [making] suggestions," says Moss.

For more information on BMW, visit the organization's home page at www.bmw.com.

Learning Goal

3. Explain how positive reinforcement, negative reinforcement, punishment, and extinction can affect learning.

SCHEDULES OF REINFORCEMENT

Managers using reinforcement to encourage the learning and performance of desired behaviors must choose a schedule for applying reinforcers. The schedule of reinforcement often depends on practical considerations (e.g., the nature of the person's job and the type of reinforcer being used, deliberately or not). However, reinforcement is always delivered according to some schedule.

Continuous and Intermittent Reinforcement

Continuous reinforcement *means that the behavior is reinforced each time it occurs and is the simplest schedule of reinforcement*. An example of continuous reinforcement is dropping coins in a soft-drink vending machine. The behavior of inserting coins is reinforced (on a continuous schedule) by the machine delivering a can of soda (most of the time!). Verbal recognition and material rewards generally are not delivered on a continuous schedule in organizations. In organizations such as Mary Kay Cosmetics, Tupperware, and Amway, salespeople are paid a commission for each sale, usually earning commissions of 25 to 50 percent of sales. Although the reinforcer (money) isn't paid immediately, the salespeople track their sales immediately and quickly convert sales into amounts owed them by the organization. Most managers, however, supervise employees other than salespeople, and they seldom have the opportunity to deliver a reinforcer every time their employees demonstrate a desired behavior. Therefore, behavior typically is reinforced intermittently.

Intermittent reinforcement *refers to a reinforcer being delivered after some, but not every, occurrence of the desired behavior*. Intermittent reinforcement can be subdivided into (1) interval and ratio schedules and (2) fixed and variable schedules. In an interval schedule, *reinforcers are delivered after a certain amount of time has passed*. In a ratio schedule, *reinforcers are delivered after a certain number of behaviors have been performed*. These two schedules can be further subdivided into fixed (not changing) or variable (constantly changing) schedules. Figure 4.5 shows these four primary types of intermittent schedules: fixed interval, variable interval, fixed ratio, and variable ratio.[19]

Fixed Interval Schedule

In a fixed interval schedule, *a constant amount of time must pass before a reinforcer is provided*. The first desired behavior to occur after the interval has elapsed is reinforced. For example, in a fixed interval, one-hour schedule, the first desired behavior that occurs after an hour has elapsed is reinforced. Administering rewards according to this type of schedule tends to produce an uneven pattern of behavior. Prior to the reinforcement,

FIGURE 4.5 Four Types of Reinforcement Schedules

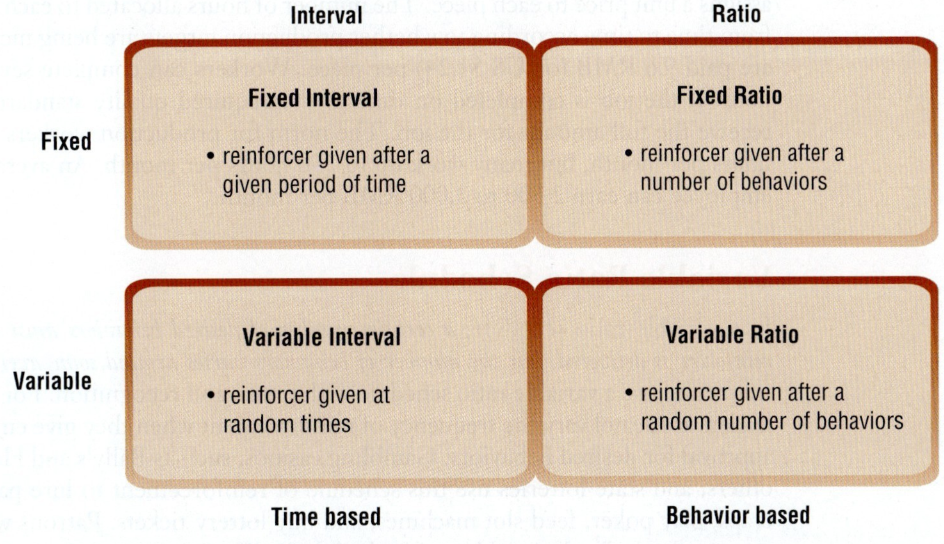

the behavior is frequent and energetic. Immediately following the reinforcement, the behavior becomes less frequent and energetic. Why? Because the individual rather quickly figures out that another reward won't immediately follow the last one—a certain amount of time must pass before it is given again. A common example of administering rewards on a fixed interval schedule is the payment of employees weekly, biweekly, or monthly. That is, monetary reinforcement comes regularly at the end of a specific period of time. Such time intervals, unfortunately, are generally too long to be an effective form of reinforcement for newly acquired work-related behavior.

Variable Interval Schedule

A variable interval schedule *represents changes in the amount of time between reinforcers.* Sherry Burnside, head of housekeeping at Presbyterian Hospital in Dallas, Texas, uses a variable interval schedule to observe and reinforce the behaviors of housekeeping personnel. A person receives $100 for perfect attendance and a score above 92 percent on 23 performance indicators (e.g., floor swept, trash baskets emptied, room dusted, etc.). To observe their behavior, Burnside announced to all housekeeping employees that, during the month, she would make seven inspections at random times. During the first week, she observed and recorded the performance of employees on Tuesday between 3:00 and 4:00 P.M. and Wednesday from 6:00 to 7:30 A.M. The following week, she made no observations. During the third week, she observed employees on Monday between 10:00 and 11:00 A.M. and Friday from 12:00 to 1:45 P.M. During the fourth week, she observed employees on Monday between 8:00 and 9:00 P.M. and from 11:00 P.M. to 12:00 A.M. and on Thursday from 2:00 to 3:30 P.M. If she didn't change her schedule, the employees would anticipate her tours and adjust their behaviors to get a reward.

Fixed Ratio Schedule

In a fixed ratio schedule, *the desired behavior must occur a specified number of times before it is reinforced.* Administering rewards under a fixed ratio schedule tends to produce a high response rate when the time for reinforcement is close, followed by periods of steady behavior. The employee soon determines that reinforcement is based on the number of responses and performs the responses as quickly as possible in order to receive the reward. The individual piece-rate system used in many manufacturing plants is an example of such a schedule. In the Northern Shipping Company in China, production workers are paid on the basis of pieces. The firm allocates a number of hours per job and assigns a unit price to each piece. The number of hours allocated to each job is reviewed from time to time according to whether production targets are being met. The workers are paid 9.6 RMB (or US $1.24) per piece. Workers can complete several pieces per hour. If the job is completed on time to the required quality standard, workers will receive the full amount for the job. The norm for production workers is to work 176 hours per month, but many work up to 250 hours per month. An average production employee can earn 2,500 to 3,000 RMB per month.[20]

Variable Ratio Schedule

In a variable ratio schedule, *a certain number of desired behaviors must occur before the reinforcer is delivered, but the number of behaviors varies around some average.* Managers frequently use a variable ratio schedule with praise and recognition. For example, team leaders at Alcatel vary the frequency of reinforcement when they give employees verbal approval for desired behaviors. Gambling casinos, such as Bally's and Harrah's, among others, and state lotteries use this schedule of reinforcement to lure patrons to shoot craps, play poker, feed slot machines, and buy lottery tickets. Patrons win, but not on any regular basis. A variable ratio schedule is effective because it creates uncertainty about when the consequence will occur. The use of this schedule makes sense for giving praise or auditing the behavior of employees. Employees know that a consequence will be delivered, but not when. To avoid consequences of either punishment or extinction, the employee keeps demonstrating the desired behaviors.

Pioneer Telephone Cooperative of Kingfisher, Oklahoma, was facing severe competition from other telephone and cable companies, such as AT&T, Cingular, and Time Warner. Management had developed the idea of a triple play—high-speed Internet, phone service, and TV service—all from one company. Management needed its sales representatives to sell this new service to its customers. The triple play provided customers with advanced video services, including pay-per-view, high-definition programming, and gaming. With only 600 employees and a little more than $100 million in sales, Pioneer Telephone is a small fish in a big pond dominated by major companies. The following Change Competency feature outlines the steps that management took to get its sales representatives to sell the triple play to its customers. Loyd Benson, Pioneer's president and chief executive officer, wanted to grow the company by 15 percent a year.[21] After reading this feature, you should be able to identify two types of reinforcement schedules management used to achieve this goal.

CHANGE COMPETENCY

PIONEER TELEPHONE COOPERATIVE

How does Pioneer get new subscribers? All employees at Pioneer are salespeople. Employees refer qualified leads to the company via Pioneer's intranet. A lead is qualified when employees, on their own time, recommend the triple play to customers and ask them to contact them at work. Employees are rewarded for each successful lead; bonuses are deposited in their company accounts and paid each quarter. Pioneer periodically offers double points for leads. To ensure that all employees are aware of the triple play, each month they receive a computer-based learning module. Each topic is designed to be an interactive experience. Employees read the information and answer 10 questions. Those who correctly answer at least 90 percent of the questions received $5. Pioneer also introduced an e-billing service. It offered a free T-shirt to the first 100 employees who enrolled in the program to learn about its e-billing service.

Pioneer used the same type of reinforcement program to get customers involved in the triple play. Called Take 5–Win $25, this program required customers to read the information in the company's newsletter, answer five questions, and send it back to Pioneer with a chance to win $25. Each month, one winner is drawn from each of Pioneer's 13 districts [13 winners each month]. Several thousand customers participated in a chance to win $25.

Loyd Benson believes that rewarding employees to promote Pioneer achieves four things: (1) It educates employees about Pioneer's products and services, (2) increases sales through solid leads, (3) reduces sales expenses, and (4) makes employees ambassadors for the company.

For more information on Pioneer Telephone Cooperative, visit the organization's home page at www.ptci.com.

Table 4.3 summarizes the four types of intermittent reinforcement schedules. The ratio schedules—fixed or variable—usually lead to better performance than do interval schedules. The reason is that ratio schedules are more closely related to the occurrence of desired behaviors than are interval schedules, which are based on the passage of time. The particular schedule of reinforcement is not as critical as the fact that reinforcement is based on the performance of desired behaviors.

Table 4.3 Comparison of Reinforcement Schedules

SCHEDULE	INFLUENCE ON PERFORMANCE	EXAMPLE
Fixed interval	Leads to average performance	Monthly paycheck
Fixed ratio	Leads quickly to high and stable performance	Piece-rate pay
Variable interval	Leads to moderately high and stable performance	Occasional praise by team members
Variable ratio	Leads to very high performance	Random quality checks with praise for zero defects

Learning Goal

4. Describe how social learning theory can be used by individuals to learn new behaviors.

SOCIAL LEARNING THEORY

Operant conditioning accurately describes some of the major factors that may influence learning. Certain aspects of learning, however, are not addressed by operant conditioning. For example, a person's feelings and thoughts aren't considered. Albert Bandura and others have demonstrated that people can learn new behavior by watching others in a social situation and then imitating their behavior.[22] Social learning theory *refers to knowledge acquisition through the mental processing of information through observing and imitating others*. The social part acknowledges that individuals learn by being part of a society, and the learning part recognizes that individuals use thought processes to make decisions. People actively process information to learn. By watching others perform a task, people develop mental pictures of how to perform the task. Observers often learn faster than those who do not observe the behaviors of others because they don't need to unlearn behaviors and can avoid needless and costly mistakes that often accompany trial-and-error learning.

FIGURE 4.6 Five Dimensions of Social Cognitive Theory

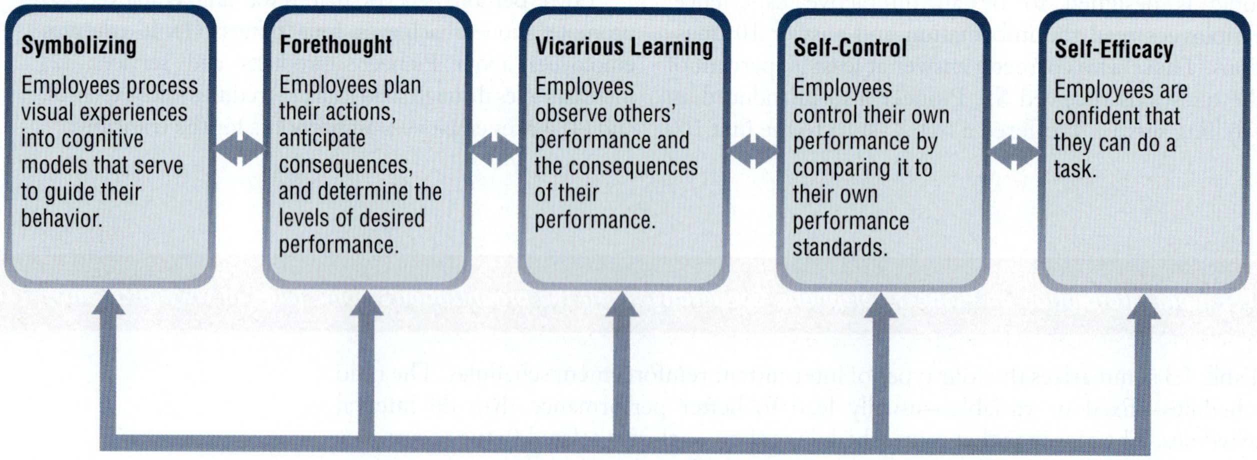
Symbolizing
Employees process visual experiences into cognitive models that serve to guide their behavior.
Forethought
Employees plan their actions, anticipate consequences, and determine the levels of desired performance.
Vicarious Learning
Employees observe others' performance and the consequences of their performance.
Self-Control
Employees control their own performance by comparing it to their own performance standards.
Self-Efficacy
Employees are confident that they can do a task.

Source: Adapted from Stajkovic, A. D., and Luthans, F. Social cognitive theory and self-efficacy. *ORGANIZATIONAL DYNAMICS*, Spring 1998, 65. Reprinted with permission.

Social learning theory has five dimensions—symbolizing, forethought, vicarious learning, self-control, and self-efficacy—as shown in Figure 4.6. These five dimensions can help you understand why different employees may behave differently when facing the same situation.

Symbolizing

Symbolizing *is the process of visualizing experiences and using the memories of them to guide behavior*. People imitate parents, friends, teachers, heroes, and others because they can identify with them. If a golfer observes the swings of Tiger Woods or Anika Sorenstam on their web pages, this observation creates an image (symbol) in that person's mind of what a good golf swing looks like. Such images or symbols help the person swing a golf club the next time she plays golf. In a social situation, when those at the head of the table at a formal dinner begin to eat, their actions let the other diners know that starting to eat now is appropriate.

Forethought

Forethought *occurs when people anticipate, plan, and guide their behaviors and actions.* For example, when a golfer who has watched an instructional video of Woods or Sorenstam getting out of a sand trap approaches the same type of shot, she recalls what she learned in the video. As a result, she adjusts her hands, feet, and body posture to the correct playing position to hit the shot. She anticipates where the ball will land and mentally plans her next shot.

Vicarious Learning

Vicarious learning *occurs when a person observes the behavior of others and the consequences of that behavior.* Employees' capacity to learn by observation enables them to obtain accurate information without having to perform these behaviors through trial and error. All self-help videos rely on vicarious learning. For vicarious learning to occur, several conditions must be met:

- The learner must observe the other person—the model—when the behavior is being performed.
- The learner must accurately perceive the model's behavior.
- The learner must remember the behavior.
- The learner must have the skills and abilities necessary to perform the behavior.
- The learner must observe that the model receives rewards for the behavior.[23]

Self-Control

Not everyone is cut out to work as a flight attendant, salesperson, construction worker, or manager. Many people never apply for particular jobs because what they see isn't consistent with their own ideas of the type of job they want. Self-control *occurs when a person selects his or her own goals and ways of reaching them to learn new behaviors.* Tina Potter, an administrative assistant at Southern Methodist University, had a new software package for graphics on her desk for a month. She knew that she had to learn how to use it even though her manager hadn't put any pressure on her to do so. She worked Saturdays on her own to learn this new technique. Potter's goal was to learn to use the graphics software to produce figures for this book—which she achieved. Her approach exhibited self-control.

Most people engage in self-control to learn behaviors both on and off the job. Mundane tasks (e.g., learning how to use e-mail) and more complex tasks (e.g., preparing a subordinate's performance appraisal) can be learned. When an employee learns through self-control, managers don't need to be controlling because the employee takes responsibility for learning and performing the desired behaviors. In fact, if a manager exercises control, it may well be redundant and counterproductive.

In recent years, the use of teams, especially self-directed teams, has taken the business world by storm. In many cases, management continues to exert too much direct control over teams. As a result, members then have few opportunities to apply self-control to their tasks. For most teams to be effective, managers must empower their members to make decisions. Empowerment *means giving employees the authority, skills, and self-control to perform their tasks.*[24] The following Teams Competency feature highlights how Steelcase Incorporated, a Minnesota manufacturer of business furniture, empowers teams to improve productivity.[25]

Teams Competency

Steelcase, Inc.

© Jack Hollingsworth/Photodisc/Getty Images

Steelcase's implementation of teams has made workers 45 percent more productive than their competitors' workers.

For 18 years, Jerry Hammond had been a spot welder, making parts of business furniture without even knowing the employees in nearby departments by name. Now, he knows his coworkers because they are a team responsible for deciding how to manufacture a part and for running as many as six different pieces of equipment. Team members are cross-trained, as time permits, during their regular shifts. Often team members stay after their shifts to watch how other employees perform certain operations.

When Steelcase's management decided to create teams and empower its employees, it realized that barriers between workers and managers would have to be removed. As a result, only customers now have reserved parking spaces. A common cafeteria is used by all employees and only a few walls remain in the plant.

Whenever new equipment is needed, a team of employees who will be responsible for running the equipment make the decision about what to buy and how it should be installed on the shop floor. A group of employees will visit the manufacturer of the equipment to learn firsthand how to use it. They also are encouraged to watch videotapes provided by the manufacturer for quality and service guidelines. Forty-one self-directed production teams and four support teams tackle day-to-day problems, such as waste, scrap, paint quality, shipping, and discipline. As a result, Steelcase has only 1 supervisor for every 33 workers, compared to a ratio of 1 to 12 for a competitor. Steelcase's workers are 45 percent more productive than its competitors, turning a customer's order into a finished product in three days instead of three weeks, thus reducing costs. Teams of employees working with suppliers also have been able to cut raw material inventory by half.

For more information on Steelcase, visit the organization's home page at www.steelcase.com.

Self-Efficacy

Self-efficacy *refers to the individual's estimate of his or her own ability to perform a specific task in a particular situation.*[26] The greater the employee's perceived ability to perform the task, the higher the employee's self-efficacy. Employees with high self-efficacy believe that (1) they have the ability needed, (2) they are capable of the effort required, and (3) no outside events will keep them from performing at a high level. If employees have low self-efficacy, they believe that no matter how hard they try, something will happen to prevent them from reaching the desired level of performance. Self-efficacy influences people's choices of tasks and how long they will spend trying to reach their goals.[27] For example, a novice golfer who has taken only a few lessons might shoot a good round. Under such circumstances, the golfer might attribute the score to "beginner's luck" and not to ability. But, after many lessons and hours of practice, a person with low self-efficacy who still can't break 100 may decide that the demands of the game are too great to justify spending any more time on it. However, a high self-efficacy individual will try even harder to improve her game. This effort might include taking more lessons, watching videotapes of the individual's own swing, and practicing even harder and longer.

Self-efficacy has an impact on learning in three ways:

- *It influences the activities and goals that individuals choose for themselves.* In a sales contest at Pioneer Telephone Cooperative in Kingfisher, Oklahoma, employees with low self-efficacy didn't set challenging, or "stretch," goals. These people weren't lazy; they simply thought that they would fail to achieve a lofty goal. The high self-efficacy employees thought that they were capable of achieving high-performance goals—and did so.
- *It influences the effort that individuals exert on the job.* Individuals with high self-efficacy work hard to learn new tasks and are confident that their efforts will be rewarded. Low self-efficacy individuals lack confidence in their ability to succeed and see their extra effort as futile because they are likely to fail anyway.
- *It affects the persistence with which a person stays with a complex task.* Because high self-efficacy people are confident that they will perform well, they are likely to persist in spite of obstacles or in the face of temporary setbacks. At IBM, low-performing employees were more likely than high-performing employees to dwell on obstacles hindering their ability to do assigned tasks. When people believe that they aren't capable of doing the required work, their motivation to do a task will be low.

Managerial Guidelines

Managers (and fellow team members) can use social learning theory to help employees learn to believe in themselves. Past experience is the most powerful influence on behavior. At work, the challenge is to create situations in which the employee may respond successfully to the task(s) required. A manager's expectations for a subordinate's performance—as well as the expectations of peers—also can affect a person's self-efficacy. If a manager holds high expectations for an employee and provides proper training and suggestions, the person's self-efficacy is likely to increase. Small successes boost self-efficacy and lead to more substantial accomplishments later. If a manager holds low expectations for an employee and gives little constructive advice, the employee is likely to form an impression that he can't achieve the goal and, as a result, perform poorly.

Guidelines for using social learning theory to influence employee behavior in organizations include the following:[28]

- Identify the behaviors that will lead to improved performance.
- Select the appropriate model for employees to observe.
- Be sure that employees are capable of meeting the technical skills required by the new behaviors.
- Structure a positive learning situation to increase the likelihood that employees will learn the new behaviors and act accordingly.
- Provide positive consequences (praise, raises, or bonuses) to employees who perform as desired.
- Develop organizational practices that maintain the newly learned behaviors.

The effective use of self-control in learning requires that several conditions be met. First, the person must engage in behaviors that he wouldn't normally want to perform. This distinguishes performing activities that the person enjoys from those involving self-control. Second, the person must be able to use self-reinforcers, which are rewards that individuals give themselves. Some self-reinforcers include buying oneself a present, going out to a "great" restaurant, playing a round of golf at a nice course, and the like. Self-reinforcers come simply from a feeling of accomplishment or achievement. Third, the person must set goals that determine when self-reinforcers are to be applied. A person high in self-control doesn't randomly reward himself, but sets goals that determine when to self-reinforce. In doing so, the person relies on his own past performance, the performance of others on similar kinds of tasks, or some standard set by others. For example, one of the authors of this book is an accomplished golfer with a single-digit handicap. After playing a round in the 70s, he frequently buys himself a golf shirt as a self-reinforcer for a good round. Finally, the person must administer the self-reinforcer only when the goal is achieved: The author buys himself a golf shirt only when he shoots a round in the 70s.

CHAPTER SUMMARY

1. Explain the role of classical and operant conditioning in fostering learning.

Classical conditioning began with Pavlov's work. He started a metronome (conditioned stimulus) at the same time food was placed in a dog's mouth (unconditioned stimulus). Quickly the sound of the metronome alone evoked salivation. Operant conditioning focuses on the effects of reinforcement on desirable and undesirable behaviors. Changes in behavior result from the consequences of previous behavior. People tend to repeat a behavior that leads to a pleasant result and not to repeat a behavior that leads to an unpleasant result. In short, when a behavior is reinforced, it is repeated; when it is punished or not reinforced, it is not repeated.

2. Describe the contingencies of reinforcement that influence behavior.

The two types of reinforcement are (1) positive reinforcement, which increases a desirable behavior because the person is provided with a pleasurable outcome after the behavior has occurred; and (2) negative reinforcement, which also maintains the desirable behavior by presenting an unpleasant event before the behavior occurs and stopping the event when the behavior occurs. Both positive and negative reinforcement increase the frequency of a desirable behavior. Conversely, extinction and punishment reduce the frequency of an undesirable behavior. Extinction involves stopping everything that reinforces the behavior. A punisher is an unpleasant event that follows the behavior and reduces the probability that the behavior will be repeated.

3. Explain how positive reinforcement, negative reinforcement, punishment, and extinction can affect learning.

There are four schedules of reinforcement. In the fixed interval schedule, the reward is given on a fixed time basis (e.g., a weekly or monthly paycheck). It is effective for maintaining a level of behavior. In the variable interval schedule, the reward is given around some average time during a specific period of time (e.g., the plant manager walking through the plant an average of five times every week). This schedule of reinforcement can maintain a high level of performance because employees don't know when the reinforcer will be delivered. The fixed ratio schedule ties rewards to certain outputs (e.g., a piece-rate system). This schedule maintains a steady level of behavior once the person has earned the reinforcer. In the variable ratio schedule, the reward is given around some mean, but the number of behaviors varies (e.g., a payoff from a slot machine). This schedule is the most powerful because both the number of desired behaviors and their frequency change.

4. Describe how social learning theory can be used by individuals to learn new behaviors.

Social learning theory focuses on people learning new behaviors by observing others and then modeling their own behaviors on those observed. The five factors emphasized in social learning theory are symbolizing, forethought, vicarious learning, self-control, and self-efficacy.

KEY TERMS AND CONCEPTS

Antecedent
Aversive events
Classical conditioning
Consequence
Contingency of reinforcement
Continuous reinforcement
Empowerment
Escape learning
Extinction
Fixed interval schedule
Fixed ratio schedule
Forethought
Intermittent reinforcement
Interval schedule
Kaizen
Learning
Negative reinforcement
Operant conditioning
Positive discipline
Positive events
Positive reinforcement
Primary reinforcer
Principle of contingent reinforcement
Principle of immediate reinforcement
Principle of reinforcement deprivation
Principle of reinforcement size
Punishment
Ratio schedule
Reinforcement
Reward
Secondary reinforcer
Self-control
Self-efficacy
Social learning theory
Symbolizing
Variable interval schedule
Variable ratio schedule
Vicarious learning

DISCUSSION QUESTIONS

1. Gambling casino owners in Las Vegas, Reno, and Atlantic City use a variable ratio reinforcement schedule. Why do people find this schedule so addictive?
2. Steven Kerr wrote an article entitled "On the Folly of Rewarding A while Hoping for B."[29] The essence of the article is that organizations often unintentionally reward behaviors that they don't want to occur. Find some examples of this behavior.
3. What schedules of reinforcement are illustrated in the Pioneer Telephone competency feature?
4. What social learning theory concepts are illustrated in the Steelcase, Inc., competency feature?
5. How do producers of self-help videos use social learning theory to change a person's behavior?
6. Visit either a local health club or diet center and schedule an interview with the manager. What types of rewards does it give its members who achieve targeted goals? Does it use punishment?
7. How can a manager or a team raise an employee's level of self-efficacy?
8. Explain the difference between negative reinforcement and punishment. Give examples of how a manager might use each.
9. What schedule(s) of reinforcement did your parent(s) use with you to reinforce good behavior at school?
10. To understand what behaviors are rewarded at UPS, visit www.sustainability.UPS.com/social/feedback/choice.html. What kinds of rewards are given to employees? What criteria are used by UPS to administer these awards?

EXPERIENTIAL EXERCISE AND CASE

Experiential Exercise: Self Competency

What Is Your Self-Efficacy?[30]

The following questionnaire gives you a chance to gain insight into your self-efficacy in terms of achieving academic excellence. Using the following five-point scale, answer the following seven questions by circling the number that most closely agrees with your thinking. An interpretation of your score follows the questions.

5 = Strongly agree
4 = Agree
3 = Moderate
2 = Disagree
1 = Strongly disagree

1. I am a good student. 5 4 3 2 1
2. It is difficult to maintain a study schedule. 5 4 3 2 1
3. I know the right things to do to improve my academic performance. 5 4 3 2 1
4. I find it difficult to convince my friends who have different view points on studying than mine. 5 4 3 2 1
5. My temperament is not well suited to studying. 5 4 3 2 1
6. I'm good at finding out what teachers want. 5 4 3 2 1
7. It is easy for me to get others to see my point of view. 5 4 3 2 1

Add your scores to questions 1, 3, 6, and 7. Enter that score here _____. For questions, 2, 4, and 5, reverse the scoring key. That is, if you answered question 2 as strongly agree, give yourself 1 point, agree is worth 2 points, and so on. Enter your score here for questions 2, 4, and 5 _____. Enter your combined score here ________. This is your *self-efficacy* score for academic achievement. If you scored between 28 and 35, you believe that you can achieve academic excellence. Scores lower than 18 indicate that you believe, no matter how hard you try to achieve academic excellence, something may prevent you from reaching your desired level of performance. Scores between 19 and 27 indicate a moderate degree of self-efficacy. Your self-efficacy may vary with the course you are taking. In courses in your major, you may have greater self-efficacy than in those outside of your major.

Case: Self Competency

Dialing for Dollars[31]

As president of Great Northern American, Joe Salatino gauges the success of this 35-year-old company by the amount of money he pays his employees. The firm's salespeople will sell more than $20 million in office, promotional, arts-and-crafts, and computer supplies to more than 60,000 businesses around the country this year. The head of this Dallas-based telemarketing company believes that spending money on commissions and bonuses is necessary to keep his 30-person sales force motivated. Great North American annually sells more than 7 million yards of packaging tape, 8 million paper clips, and 11 million BIC and Papermate pens and pencils bearing customer logos, along with about 12,000 other products. Salatino says that Great American is facing stiff competition from Internet users and constant turnover of employees.

The company's salesroom features all kinds of motivational devices. On a recent Friday morning, rotating blue lights signal that a special deal on pens is on. For the next hour, customers can get two for one on Stars and Stripes promotional pens. When the blue-light special is off, they're back up to 39 cents apiece. When the light goes off, a manager draws a large snowball on one of the large dry-erase boards to indicate another sale has ended. The noise and pace is fast and furious.

Many of Salatino's salespeople earn more than $60,000 a year, and top producers earn more than $100,000. Gary Gieb, aka John Johnson, because it's easier to spell and sounds more all-American over the phone, earned more than $100,000 last year. During a typical day, he makes 20 to 25 calls per hour. If a customer places an order, the entire sale takes just under 5 minutes. He earns commission of between 5 and 12 percent on the list price, depending on the merchandise. A salesperson usually needs a year to build up a good account base. Many employees who can't handle the self-starting selling intensity and bedlam usually leave within the first month. To establish loyal customers, many top-selling salespeople subscribe to their customer's hometown newspaper so that they can chat with the customer about local issues, such as who had a baby and who won the local football game. Peggy Gordon topped $70,000 last year selling educational supplies that police and sheriff's departments take on visits to schools. Salatino believes that employees who have established solid relationships with their customers earn significantly more money than those who have not been able to foster customer intimacy.

Questions

1. What kind of reinforcers does Salatino use to motivate his salespeople?
2. What kind of reinforcement schedule is used for paying salespeople?
3. If you were Salatino, how might the concept of self-efficacy help you hire successful salespeople?

CHAPTER 5

Motivating Employees

Learning Goals

When you have finished studying the chapter, you should be able to:

1. Explain the motivational process.
2. Describe two basic human needs approaches to motivation.
3. Explain how to design motivating jobs.
4. Describe how goal and reward expectations motivate others.
5. Explain how treating people fairly influences their motivation to work.

Learning from Experience

LIFE INSIDE GOOGLE

In 2007, Google was named the Best Company to Work For by *Fortune*. At Google you can do your laundry; drop off your dry cleaning; get an oil change, then have your car washed; work out in the gym; attend subsidized exercise classes; get a massage; study Mandarin, Japanese, Spanish, and French; and ask a personal concierge to arrange dinner reservations. You can even get haircuts on-site. Want to buy a hybrid car? The company will give you $5,000 toward that environmentally friendly car. Care to refer a friend to work at Google? Google would like that too, and it'll give you a $2,000 reward. Just have a new baby? Congratulations! Your employer will reimburse you for up to $500 in take-out food to ease your first four weeks after the baby is born. Looking to make new friends? Attend a weekly TGIF party, where there's usually a band playing. Five on-site doctors are also available to give you a checkup, free of charge.

Many Silicon Valley companies provide shuttle bus transportation from area train stations. Google operates free, Wi-Fi-enabled coaches from five Bay Area locations. Lactation rooms are common in corporate America; Google provides breast pumps so that nursing moms don't have to haul the equipment to work. Work is such a cozy place that it's sometimes difficult for Google employees to leave the office, which is precisely how the company justifies the expenses, none of which it breaks out of its administrative costs.

Even people who don't work here like to attend Google's free seminar series because of the quality of speaker Google brings to their organization. The company has become a stop on the world lecture circuit, attracting the likes of Mikhail Gorbachev, Margaret Thatcher, and Nobel laureate Muhammad Yunus. "You've got to ask yourself why these people are coming here," says 24-year-old engineer Neha Narula. "I think they come here because of the smart people."

It's easy for Google's employees to be motivated by the lavish benefits it provides to more than 10,000 employees. Just eight years old, Google has passed $10 billion in sales. Its operating margins are at 35 percent. Its stock has soared. All of which raises the question: Are Google's motivational programs the cause of its success or merely a result? Put another way: Is Google a great place to work because its stock is so high, or is its stock so high because it's a great place to work?

For more information on Google, visit the organization's home page at www.google.com.

LEARNING CONTENT

Customers can be found googling in restaurants, hotels, apartments, homes, and offices all over the world.

In its earliest days Google was a postdoctoral extension of Stanford University's computer science department, in which Larry Page and Sergey Brin were doctoral students. To this day, they jam employees into shared offices and cubicles and would do so even if Google had more space. Page, a student of "office flow," likes the idea of re-creating that university environment in which he and Brin wrote the first Google search engine.

It wasn't hard for Google's founders to break the rules of a traditional company—they had never worked full time at one. Stacy Sullivan, Google's first human resource executive, recalls that Page and Brin came to her on her second day on the job, in late 1999, and suggested that the company convert a conference room into a child-care center. Google employees had a sum total of two children at the time. Though Sullivan eventually convinced them that, because of zoning issues, the conference room was not a proper child-care facility, "they looked at me and said, 'Why not?'"

Teamwork is the norm, especially for big projects. Keith Coleman, a 26-year-old product manager who works on Gmail, oversees a 10-person secret project whose team members have taken over their own conference room. "They've given up their private offices to be crammed into this room to get things done," says Coleman. The hideaway happens to be where Gmail's chat function was created. Lounge music is usually playing, engineers wander in and out, and there's no formal daily meeting, though the team tends to congregate between five and seven in the evening. "If I could capture anything that's great about Google," says Coleman, "it's that room."[1]

Page and Brin say that their greatest challenge is to attract, develop, and manage a worldwide workforce. Many Silicon Valley types don't like working for big companies because "geeking" out and trying new things becomes a hassle. Google pays competitive salaries with experienced engineers making as much as $130,000 and receiving 800 stock options and 400 shares of restricted stock when they join. The only requirement for newly hired engineers is that they read a copy of *Essential Java* to learn Python, a software-writing language. Google has been hiring experts in many fields. For example, it recently hired Larry Brilliant, who helped eradicate smallpox, to run Google's philanthropic department. They believe that Google must provide motivational systems that will cut costs while maintaining high quality. Permitting employees to participate in incentive programs has led to greater productivity.[2]

THE BASIC MOTIVATIONAL PROCESS

Learning Goal

1. Explain the motivational process.

The question of exactly what it takes to motivate people to work has received a great deal of attention. In addressing this question, we focus on four different approaches: (1) meeting basic human needs, (2) designing jobs that motivate people, (3) enhancing the belief that desired rewards can be achieved, and (4) treating people equitably. The interrelated nature of these approaches is illustrated in Figure 5.1. Before turning our attention to these approaches, we need to define motivation.

Motivation *represents the forces acting on or within a person that cause the person to behave in a specific, goal-directed manner.*[3] Because the motives of employees affect their productivity, one of management's jobs is to channel employee motivation effectively toward achieving organizational goals. However, motivation isn't the same as performance. Even the most highly motivated employees may not be successful in their jobs, especially if they don't have the competencies needed to perform the jobs or they work under unfavorable job conditions. Although job performance involves more than motivation, motivation is an important factor in achieving high performance.[4]

FIGURE 5.1 Basics of Workplace Motivation

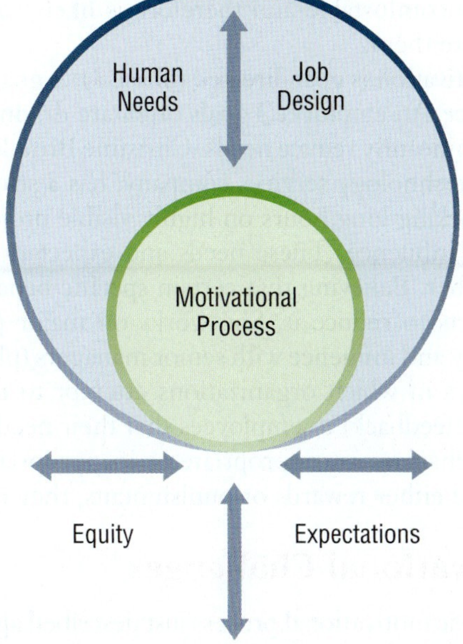

Experts might not agree about everything that motivates employees—and the effects of working conditions on their careers—but they do agree that an organization must

- attract people to the organization and encourage them to remain with it,
- allow people to perform the tasks for which they were hired, and
- stimulate people to go beyond routine performance and become creative and innovative in their work.

Thus, for an organization to be effective, it must tackle the motivational challenges involved in arousing people's desires to be productive members of the organization.

Core Phases

A key motivational principle states that performance is a function of a person's level of ability and motivation. This principle is often expressed by the following formula:

$$\text{Performance} = f(\text{ability} \times \text{motivation}).$$

According to this principle, no task can be performed successfully unless the person who is to carry it out has the ability to do so. Ability *is the person's natural talent, as well as learned competencies, for performing goal-related tasks.* Regardless of a person's competence, however, ability alone isn't enough to ensure performance at a high level. The person must also *want* to achieve a high level of performance. The multiplicative formula suggests that ability and motivation are important. If an employee is 100 percent motivated and 75 percent able to perform a task, he can probably perform the task at better than average. However, if the same individual has only 10 percent ability, no amount of motivation will enable him to perform satisfactorily. Therefore, motivation represents an employee's desire and commitment to perform and is evidenced by his performance.

The motivational process begins with identifying a person's needs, shown as phase 1 in Figure 5.2. Needs *are deficiencies that a person experiences at a particular time* (phase 1). These deficiencies may be psychological (e.g., the need for recognition), physiological (e.g., the need for water, air, or food), or social (e.g., the need for friendship). Needs often act as energizers. That is, needs create tensions within the individual, who finds them uncomfortable and therefore is likely to make an effort (phase 2) to reduce or eliminate them.

Motivation is goal directed (phase 3). A goal *is a specific result that an individual wants to achieve*. An employee's goals often are driving forces, and accomplishing those goals can significantly reduce needs. Christine Broudeau, a marketing director at EDS, a large global technology services company, has a strong drive for advancement. She expects that working long hours on highly visible projects will lead to promotions, raises, and greater influence. These needs and expectations often create uncomfortable tension within her. Believing that certain specific behaviors can overcome this tension, Broudeau acts to reduce it. She works on major problems facing EDS in order to gain visibility and influence with senior managers (phase 4). Promotions and raises are two of the ways in which organizations attempt to maintain desirable behaviors. They are signals (feedback) to employees that their needs for advancement and recognition and their behaviors are appropriate or inappropriate (phase 5). Once the employees have received either rewards or punishments, they reassess their needs (phase 6).

Motivational Challenges

The basic motivational process just described appears simple and straightforward. In the real world, of course, the process isn't as clear-cut. The first challenge is that motives can only be inferred; they cannot be seen. Claudia Aries, head of project and systems

FIGURE 5.2 Core Phases of the Motivational Process

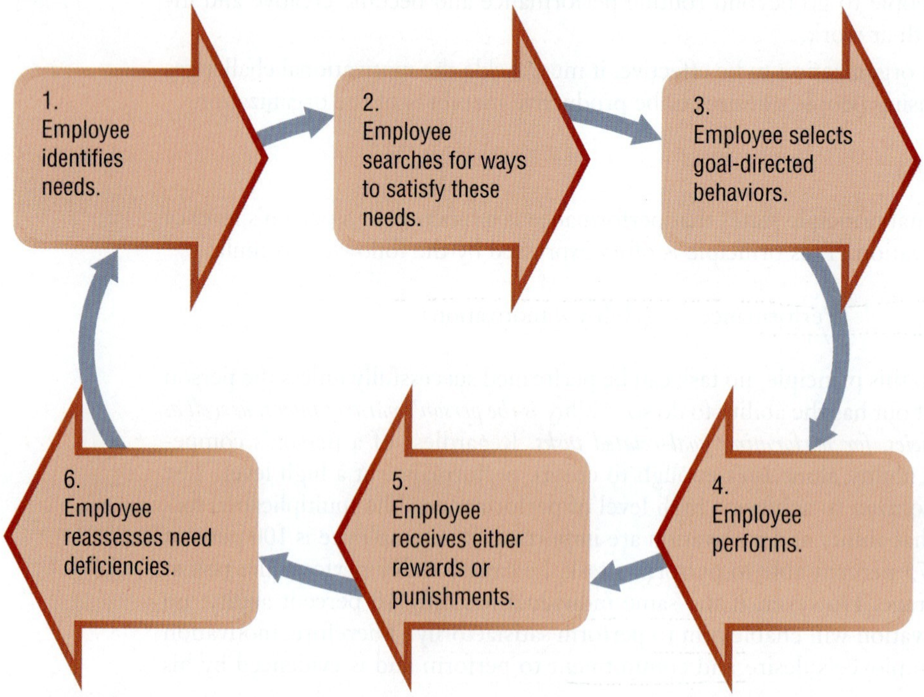

management at Celanese Chemical, observed two employees in her department who were debugging software programs that estimate service requirements for the company. She knows that both employees are responsible for the same type of work, have received similar training, have similar competencies, and have been with the organization for about five years. One employee is able to spot problems more easily and quickly than the other. Are these observable differences a result of differences in ability or motivation? Research has shown that managers tend to apply more pressure to a person if they feel the person is deliberately not performing up to their expectations due to internal, controllable events. Unfortunately, if the manager's assessment is incorrect and poor performance is related to ability rather than motivation, the response of increased pressure will worsen the problem. If poorly performing employees feel that management is insensitive to their problems, which the employees attribute to inadequate training or unrealistic time schedules, they may respond by developing a motivational problem and will decrease their commitment in response to management's insensitive actions. Therefore, before Claudia decided what actions to take, she had to deepen her understanding of why one person's output is greater than the others.

A second challenge centers on the dynamic nature of needs.[5] As we pointed out in the Learning from Experience feature, Google has developed numerous programs in its attempts to meet employee needs. Doing so is always difficult because, at any one time, everyone has various needs, desires, and expectations. Moreover, these factors change over time and may also conflict with each other. Employees who put in many extra hours at work to fulfill their needs for accomplishment may find that these extra work hours conflict directly with needs for affiliation and their desires to be with their families.

A third challenge involves the considerable differences in people's motivations and in the energy with which people respond to them. Just as different organizations produce a variety of products and offer a variety of services, different people have a variety of motivations. Curtis Harris, an engineer with Texas Instruments (TI), took an assignment with TI's plant in Sendai, Japan. He soon joined a group of American managers so he could satisfy his need to learn quickly about Japanese management practices. He discovered that Japanese do not bypass formal lines of communication. Seniority and titles are to be respected and honored and bypassing the chain of command would be a sign of disrespect.

All of these challenges are things that managers can do something about. They can determine what motivates employees and use this knowledge to channel employees' energies toward the achievement of the organization's goals. With this opportunity in mind, we devote the rest of the chapter to various approaches to motivation that managers can apply.

Before reading any further, take a few minutes to complete the questionnaire in Table 5.1. This questionnaire is designed to help you discover your skill level in motivating others.[6] The core of this chapter should help you understand why people perform as they do and provide you with tools you can use when dealing with the challenge of motivating others.

Table 5.1 **Diagnostic Survey for Motivating Others**

Please indicate the extent to which you agree with each statement using the six-point scale.

1 = Strongly disagree
2 = Disagree
3 = Slightly disagree
4 = Slightly agree
5 = Agree
6 = Strongly agree

When another person needs to be motivated:

_____1. I approach a performance problem by first establishing whether it is caused by a lack of motivation or ability.
_____2. I establish a clear standard of expected performance.
_____3. I offer to provide training and information, without offering to do tasks myself.
_____4. I am honest and straightforward in providing feedback on performance.
_____5. I use a variety of rewards to reinforce exceptional performances.
_____6. When discipline is required, I give specific suggestions for improvement.
_____7. I design assignments to make them interesting and challenging.
_____8. I provide the rewards that each person values.
_____9. I make sure that people feel fairly and equitably treated.
_____10. I make sure that people get timely feedback based on their performance.
_____11. I carefully diagnose the causes of poor performance before taking any remedial or disciplinary action.
_____12. I help people establish performance goals that are challenging, specific, and time bound.
_____13. Only as a last resort do I attempt to reassign or release a poorly performing individual.
_____14. Whenever possible, I make sure valued rewards are linked to high performance.
_____15. I discipline when effort is below expectations and below capabilities.
_____16. I combine or rotate assignments so that people can use a variety of skills.
_____17. I arrange for an individual to work with others in a team, for the mutual support of all.
_____18. I make sure that people use realistic standards for measuring fairness.
_____19. I provide immediate compliments and other forms of recognition for meaningful accomplishments.
_____20. I determine if a person has the necessary resources and support to succeed in a task.

Scoring Key

Skill Area	Item	Score
Diagnosing performance problems	11	_____
Establishing expectations and setting goals	2	_____
	12	_____
Facilitating performance	3	_____
	13	_____
	20	_____
Linking performance to rewards and discipline	5	_____
	14	_____
	6	_____
	15	_____
Using internal and external incentives	7	_____
	16	_____
	8	_____
	17	_____
Distributing rewards equitably	9	_____
	18	_____
Providing timely and straightforward performance feedback	4	_____
	10	_____
	19	_____
Total score		_____

Comparison Data

Compare your scores to three comparison standards: (1) Compare your score with the maximum possible (120). (2) Compare your scores with the scores of other students in your class. (3) Compare your scores to a norm group consisting of 500 business school students. In comparison to the norm group, if you scored

112 or above you are in the top quartile.

104–111 you are in the second quartile.

97–103	you are in the third quartile.
96 or below	you are in the bottom quartile.

Source: Adapted from Whetten, D. A., and Cameron, K. S. *Diagnosing Poor Performance and Enhancing Motivation: Developing Management Skills*, 7th ed. Upper Saddle River, NJ: Pearson Education, 2007, 328–329, 374.

MOTIVATING EMPLOYEES THROUGH SATISFYING HUMAN NEEDS

Learning Goal

2. Describe two basic human needs approaches to motivation.

Needs Hierarchy Model

The most widely recognized model of motivation is the needs hierarchy model. In this model, Abraham H. Maslow suggested *that people have a complex set of exceptionally strong needs, that can be arranged in a hierarchy.*[7] Underlying this hierarchy are the following basic assumptions:

- Once a need has been satisfied, its motivational role declines in importance. However, as one need is satisfied, another need gradually emerges to take its place, so people are always striving to satisfy some need.
- The needs network for most people is very complex, with several needs affecting behavior at any one time. Clearly, when someone faces an emergency, such as desperate thirst, that need dominates until it is gratified.
- Lower level needs must be satisfied, in general, before higher level needs are activated sufficiently to drive behavior.
- There are more ways of satisfying higher level than lower level needs.

This model states that a person has five types of needs: physiological, security, affiliation, esteem, and self-actualization. Figure 5.3 shows these five needs categories, arranged in Maslow's hierarchy.

Physiological Needs. Physiological needs *are the desire for food, water, air, and shelter.* They are the lowest level in Maslow's hierarchy. People concentrate on satisfying these needs before turning to higher order needs. Managers should understand that, to the extent employees are motivated by physiological needs, their concerns do not center on the work they are doing. They will accept any job that meets those needs. Managers who focus on physiological needs in trying to motivate subordinates assume that people work primarily for money. Hershey Foods, for example, offers insurance rebates to employees who live healthy lifestyles (e.g., physically fit nonsmokers) and raises premiums for those at greater risk. In this way, they offer incentives to encourage wellness activities.

Security Needs. Security needs *are the desire for safety, stability, and the absence of pain, threat, or illness.* Like physiological needs, unsatisfied security needs cause people to be preoccupied with satisfying them. People who are motivated primarily by security needs value their jobs mainly as defenses against the loss of basic needs satisfaction. Managers who feel that security needs are important focus on protecting workers from hazards in their environment by providing them with hard hats, goggles, and ergonomic keyboards (which are designed to prevent carpal tunnel syndrome). Psychological safety is also important. By offering health, life, and disability insurance, organizations like Google promote their employees' sense of security and well-being.

Affiliation Needs. Affiliation needs *are the desire for friendship, love, and a feeling of belonging.* When physiological and security needs have been satisfied, affiliation needs

FIGURE 5.3 Maslow's Needs Hierarchy

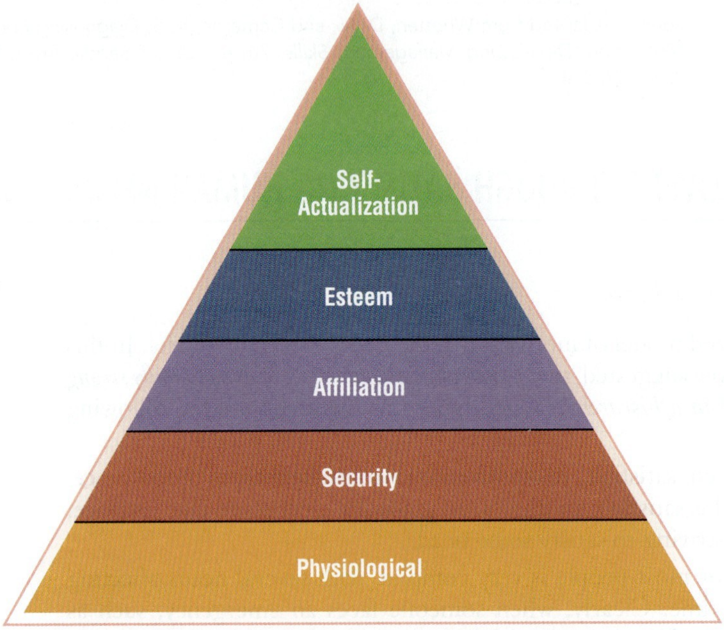

emerge. Managers should realize that when affiliation needs are the primary source of motivation, people value their work as an opportunity for finding and establishing warm and friendly interpersonal relationships. Managers and team leaders who believe that employees are striving primarily to satisfy these needs are likely to act supportively. They emphasize employee acceptance by coworkers, extracurricular activities (e.g., organized sports programs, cultural events, and company celebrations), and team-based norms. Denise Gannon, a systems engineer, dropped 48 pounds because she was inspired by her company's 10-member Slimdown team to join their fitness program and help the entire company achieve its goal of losing more than a ton of weight.[8] Page and Brin also often find engineers in the hallway at Google debating some esoteric concept at 5:30 A.M. because "there is no place that they would rather be."

Esteem Needs. *The desires for feelings of achievement, self-worth, and recognition or respect are all* esteem needs. People with esteem needs want others to accept them for what they are and to perceive them as competent and able. Managers who focus on esteem needs try to motivate employees with public rewards and recognition for achievements. Such managers may use lapel pins, articles in the company paper, achievement lists on the bulletin board, and the like to foster employees' pride in their work. Mary Kay Cosmetics rewards top performers with a pink Cadillac. According to the late Mary Kay Ash, the founder of her company, people want recognition and praise more than money.

Self-Actualization Needs. Self-actualization needs *involve people realizing their full potential and becoming all that they can become.* People who strive for self-actualization seek to increase their problem-solving abilities. Managers who emphasize self-actualization may involve employees in designing jobs, make special assignments that capitalize on employees' unique skills, or give employee teams leeway in planning and implementing their work. The self-employed often have strong self-actualization needs. When Mary

Kay Ash founded her firm in 1963, she acted on her belief that, when a woman puts her priorities in order, she can indeed have it all.

Managerial Guidelines. Maslow's needs hierarchy model also suggests the types of behaviors that will help fulfill various needs. *The three lowest categories of needs—physiological, security, and affiliation (social)—are also known as* deficiency needs. According to Maslow, unless these needs are satisfied, an individual will fail to develop into a healthy person, both physically and psychologically. In contrast, *esteem and self-actualization needs are known as* growth needs. Satisfaction of these needs helps a person grow and develop as a human being. What needs is Google satisfying for its employees?

This model provides incomplete information about the origin of needs. However, it implies that higher level needs are present in most people, even if they don't recognize or act to meet those needs. These higher level needs will motivate most people if nothing occurs to block their emergence.

The needs hierarchy is based on U.S. cultural values. In cultures that value uncertainty avoidance, such as Japan and Greece, job security and lifelong employment are stronger motivators than self-actualization. Moreover, in Denmark, Sweden, and Norway, the value and rewards of a high quality of life are more important than productivity. Thus, social needs are stronger than self-actualization and self-esteem needs in these countries. In countries such as China, Japan, and Korea that value collectivist and community practices over individual achievements, belonging and security are considerably more important than meeting growth needs. In developing East African nations that exhibit high uncertainty avoidance, low individualism, and high power distance, the community dominates. For example, their dances and worship ceremonies are focused on the community. Clearly the motivation of employees from more collective cultures differs from that of more individualistic countries. Therefore, although the needs that Maslow identified may be universal, their importance and the ways in which they are expressed vary across cultures. The rank ordering of their importance varies considerably across cultures.[9]

Maslow's work has received much attention from managers, as well as psychologists.[10] Research has found that top managers are better able to satisfy their esteem and self-actualization needs than are lower level managers; part of the reason is that top managers have more challenging jobs and opportunities for self-actualization. Employees who work on a team have been able to satisfy their higher level needs by making decisions that affect their team and organization. At the Container Store, groups of employees are trained to perform multiple tasks, including hiring and training team members—and even firing those who fail to perform adequately. As team members learn new tasks, they start satisfying their higher level needs. Employees who have little or no control over their work (e.g., assembly-line workers, toll clerks on a bridge or toll road) may not even experience higher level needs in relation to their jobs. Studies have also shown that the fulfillment of needs differs according to the job a person performs, a person's age and background, and the size of the company. "Not everyone is motivated in the same way. You shouldn't assume that it's a one-size-fits-all solution. You have to understand people's needs," says Leslie Ritter, a principal in Square Knot, LLC, a human resource consulting firm, located in Addison, Texas.

Learned Needs Model

David McClelland proposed a learned needs model of motivation that he believed to be rooted in culture.[11] He argued that everyone has three particularly important needs: for achievement, power, and affiliation. The need for achievement has been defined as *behavior toward competition with a standard of excellence*. In other words, people with a high need for achievement want to do things better and more efficiently than others have done before. The need for power can be defined as *the desire to influence people and events*. According to McClelland, there are two types of power: one that is directed toward the organization (institutional power) and one that is directed toward the self (personal power). Individuals who possess a *strong power motive* take action that affects the behaviors of others and has a strong emotional appeal. These individuals are concerned with providing status rewards to their followers. The need for affiliation has been defined as *the desire to be liked and to stay on good terms with others*. Individuals who have a *strong affiliation motive* tend to establish, maintain, and restore close personal relationships with others. A recent Gallup survey found that employees who have a best friend at work are more engaged and productive than those who do not report having a good friend at work.[12]

McClelland has studied achievement motivation extensively, especially with regard to entrepreneurship. His achievement motivation model *states that people are motivated according to the strength of their desire either to perform in terms of a standard of excellence or to succeed in competitive situations.* According to McClelland, almost all people believe that they have an "achievement motive," but probably only about 10 percent of the U.S. population is strongly motivated to achieve. The amount of achievement motivation that people have depends on their childhood, their personal and occupational

Table 5.2 Learned Needs Model

FOCUS ON	ACHIEVEMENT	AFFILIATION	POWER: PERSONALIZED POWER	POWER: SOCIALIZED POWER
Motives	Improve their personal performance and meet or exceed standards of excellence	Maintain close, friendly relationships	Be strong and influence others, making them feel weak	Help people feel stronger and more capable
Potential positive effects	Meet or surpass a self-imposed standard	Establish, restore, or maintain warm relationships	Perform powerful actions	Perform powerful actions
	Accomplish something new	Be liked and accepted	Control, influence, or persuade people	Persuade people
	Plan the long-term advancement of your career	Participate in group activities, primarily for social reasons	Impress people inside or outside the company	Impress people inside or outside the company
Potential negative effects	Try to do things or set the pace themselves	Worry more about people than performance	Be coercive and ruthless	Coach and teach
	Express impatience with poor performers	Look for ways to create harmony	Control and manipulate others	Be democratic and involve others
	Give little positive feedback	Avoid giving negative feedback	Look out for their own interests and reputations	Be highly supportive
	Give few directions or instructions			Focus on the team rather than themselves

Source: Adapted from Spreier, S. W., Fontaine, M. H., and Malloy, R. L. Leadership run amok. *Harvard Business Review*, 2006, 84(6), 75.

experiences, and the type of organization for which they work. Table 5.2 shows an application of McClelland's model to managing others.

According to McClelland's model, motives are "stored" in the preconscious mind just below the level of full awareness. They lie between the conscious and the unconscious, in the area of daydreams, where people talk to themselves without quite being aware of it. A basic premise of the model is that the pattern of these daydreams can be tested and that people can be taught to change their motivation by changing these daydreams.

Measuring Achievement Motivation. McClelland measured the strength of a person's achievement motivation with the Thematic Apperception Test (TAT). *The TAT uses unstructured pictures that may arouse many kinds of reactions in the person being tested.* Examples include an inkblot that a person can perceive as many different objects or a picture that can generate a variety of stories. There is no right or wrong answer, and the person isn't given a limited set of alternatives from which to choose. A major goal of the TAT is to obtain the individual's own perception of the world. The TAT is called a *projective method* because it emphasizes individual perceptions of stimuli, the meaning each individual gives to them, and how each individual organizes them (recall the discussion of perception in Chapter 3).

One projective test involves looking at the picture shown in Figure 5.4 for 10 to 15 seconds and then writing a short story about it that answers the following questions:

- What are people doing in this picture?
- What is being felt? What is being thought? By whom?
- How will it come out? What will happen?

FIGURE 5.4 Sample Picture Used in a Projective Test

© Manchan/Digital Vision/Getty Images

Write your own story about the picture in 75 to 100 words. Then compare it with the following story written by Susan Reed, general manager, at Innovative Hospice Care[13]:

> The four people are working as a team to accomplish the task of getting a woman over a wall. She probably couldn't make it without the help of her teammates. They all have duties—pushing, pulling, grabbing—to perform in getting her over the wall. The woman is excited about accomplishing this task and is counting on her teammates to help her. After they achieve their goal, they can relax knowing that they reached their goal of helping a teammate.

What motivational profile did you identify? Does it match this person's?

Characteristics of High Achievers. Self-motivated high achievers have three main characteristics. First, they like to set their own *goals*. Seldom content to drift aimlessly and let life happen to them, they nearly always are trying to accomplish something. High achievers seek the challenge of making tough decisions. They are selective about the goals to which they commit themselves. Hence, they are unlikely to automatically accept goals that other people, including their superiors, attempt to select for them. They exercise self-control over their behaviors, especially the ways in which they pursue the goals they select. They tend to seek advice or help only from experts who can provide needed knowledge or skills. High achievers prefer to be fully responsible for attaining their goals. If they win, they want the credit; if they lose, they accept the blame. For example, assume that you are given a choice between rolling dice with one chance in three of winning, or working on a problem with one chance in three of solving the problem in the time allotted. Which would you choose? A high achiever would choose to work on the problem, even though rolling the dice is obviously less work and the odds of winning are the same. High achievers prefer to work at a problem rather than leave the outcome to chance or to other people.

Second, high achievers avoid selecting extremely difficult goals. They prefer *moderate goals* that are neither so easy that attaining them provides no satisfaction nor so difficult that attaining them is more a matter of luck than ability. They gauge what is possible and then select as difficult a goal as they think they can attain. The game of ring toss illustrates this point. Most carnivals have ring toss games that require participants to throw rings over a peg from some minimum distance but specify no maximum distance. Imagine the same game but with people allowed to stand at any distance they want from the peg. Some will throw more or less randomly, standing close and then far away. Those with high-achievement motivation will seem to calculate carefully where they should stand to have the greatest chance of winning a prize and still feel challenged. These individuals seem to stand at a distance that isn't so close as to make the task ridiculously easy and isn't so far away as to make it impossible. They set a distance moderately far away from which they can potentially ring a peg. Thus, they set personal challenges and enjoy tasks that will stretch their abilities.

Third, high achievers prefer tasks that provide *immediate feedback*. Because of the goal's importance to them, they like to know how well they're doing. That's one reason why the high achiever often chooses a professional career, a sales career, or entrepreneurial activities. Golf appeals to most high achievers: Golfers can compare their scores to par for the course, to their own previous performance on the course, and to their opponents' scores; performance is related to both feedback (score) and goal (par). It also provides immediate feedback because a person earns an individual score and receives feedback following each shot. There are no teammates to coordinate with or cover a mistake. The ultimate responsibility for your shot is yours.

Financial Incentives. Money has a complex effect on high achievers. They usually value their services highly and place a high price tag on them. High achievers are usually self-confident. They are aware of their abilities and limitations and thus are confident when they choose to do a particular job. They are unlikely to remain very long in an organization that doesn't pay them well. Whether an incentive plan actually increases their performance is an open question because they normally work at peak efficiency. They value money as a strong symbol of their achievement and adequacy. A financial incentive may create dissatisfaction if they feel that it inadequately reflects their contributions.

When achievement motivation is operating, outstanding performance on a challenging task is likely. However, achievement motivation doesn't operate when high achievers are performing routine or boring tasks or when there is no competition against goals. An example of a high achiever is John Schnatter, CEO and founder of Papa John's. Schnatter's drive is to become number one in the $28 billion dollar pizza industry.[14]

Self Competency

John Schnatter of Papa John's Pizza

As a high school student working at a local pizza shop in Jeffersonville, Indiana, Schnatter in the early 1980s realized that there were no national pizza chains. So in 1984, he knocked out a broom closet located in the back of his father's tavern, sold his prized Z28 Camaro, purchased $1,600 worth of used restaurant equipment, and began selling pizzas to the tavern's customers. The business grew so fast that he decided to move next door. He eventually opened his first Papa John's restaurant in 1985.

Today, Papa John's is number three behind Pizza Hut and Domino's in the delivery and takeout pizza market with more than 3,000 pizzerias worldwide and sales of over $1 billion dollars. With 27 percent of the market share, Schnatter's goal is to take market share away from Pizza Hut (which has about 38 percent) and Domino's (which has about 30 percent) by having better ingredients, making a better pizza, and expanding internationally. He has achieved remarkable results by being singularly obsessive about high quality and performance. He preaches to his employees about pizza in very passionate terms. He requires all employees to memorize the company's Six Core Values, including stay focused, customer satisfaction must be superior, and people are priority No. 1 *always*—and calls on employees during meetings to stand up and shout them out. He created a Ten Point Perfect Pizza Scale that measures the quality of pizzas. For example, pieces of the toppings should not touch, there should be no "peaks or valleys" along the pizza's border, all mushrooms should be sliced to 0.25 inches, and no splotchy coloring should appear on the crust. The employee newsletter carries articles such as "The Papa John's Black Olive Story" or "The Papa John's Tomato Story." Such articles inform employees about how special ingredients are used to make Papa John's pizza.

At headquarters in Louisville, Kentucky, most employees (including Schnatter) wear Papa John's teal-blue polo shirts, with Pizza Wars embroidered across them. Employees even have their own clothing embroidered with Papa John's logo.

In 2006, Schnatter hired former Pizza Hut executive Robb Chase to develop international sales. Recognizing that international consumers have different tastes (e.g., baby lobster pizza in China) and get their pizza delivered by scooters or bicycles, Schnatter believes that Papa John's can grow by 32 percent a year in these markets. By 2010, Schnatter wants Papa John's to be the number one pizza brand in the world in terms of name recognition and by 2014, the leader in sales.

For more information on Papa John's, visit the organization's home page at www.papajohns.com.

Managerial Guidelines. McClelland and his associates at McBer and Company have conducted most of the research supporting the learned needs motivation model.[15] They have found that high needs for institutional power and achievement are critical for high-performing managers. People with these high needs are particularly good at increasing morale, creating clear expectations for performance, and getting others to work for the good of the organization. Interestingly the need for institutional power is more important for managerial success than the need for achievement. People high in need for achievement tend to be reluctant to delegate work to others and to be patient when working toward long-term objectives, behaviors often necessary for effective managers. People with a high need for achievement are often attracted to organizations that have a pay-for-performance reward system because they know if they perform, they will be financially rewarded. Finally, their research has found that successful CEOs are high in institutional power and achievement but low in affiliation needs. Why? Top managers need to make difficult decisions and cannot worry about whether they are liked by others.

> **LEADER INSIGHT**
>
> At the height of success, tear your business apart. This may not seem logical at first, but it is an important method for maintaining a thriving company and a motivated workforce.
> **Edward J. Zander, CEO and Chairman, Motorola**

The following guidelines are recommended for fostering achievement motivation in employees:

- Arrange tasks so that employees receive periodic feedback on their performance. Feedback enables employees to modify their behaviors as necessary.
- Provide good role models of achievement. Employees should be encouraged to have heroes to emulate.
- Help employees modify their self-images. High-achievement individuals accept themselves and seek job challenges and responsibilities.
- Guide employee aspirations. Employees should think about setting realistic goals and the ways in which they can attain them.
- Make it known that managers who have been successful are those who are higher in power motivation than in affiliation motivation.

One of the main problems with the learned needs motivation model is also its greatest strengths. The TAT method is valuable because it allows the researcher to tap the preconscious motives of people. This method has some advantages over questionnaires, but the interpretation of a story is more of an art than a science. As a result, the method's reliability is open to question. The permanency of the model's three needs has also been questioned. Further research is needed to explore the model's validity.[16]

Learning Goal

3. Explain how to design motivating jobs.

MOTIVATING EMPLOYEES THROUGH JOB DESIGN

Motivator—Hygiene Model

In a recent survey, more than three-fourths of employers thought that they took good care of their employees, but only 44 percent of employees agree. Two-thirds of employees think that they are loyal to their organizations, while just 41 percent of employers agree. Finally, more than 60 percent of the organizations surveyed say that they are taking steps to improve workplace morale, but just one-third of the employees agree.[17] What explains such differences?

Frederick Herzberg and his associates have found the answers to these questions. They asked people to tell them when they felt exceptionally good about their jobs and

Table 5.3 Sources of Job Satisfaction and Job Dissatisfaction

MOTIVATOR FACTORS THAT AFFECT JOB SATISFACTION	HYGIENE FACTORS THAT AFFECT JOB DISSATISFACTION
• Achievement	• Organizational rules and policies
• Advancement	• Relationships with coworkers
• Autonomy	• Relationships with supervisors
• Challenge	• Salary
• Feedback	• Security
• Responsibility	• Working conditions

when they felt exceptionally bad about their jobs. As shown in Table 5.3, people identified somewhat different things when they felt good or bad about their jobs. From this study they developed the *two-factor theory*, better known as the motivator–hygiene model, *which proposes that two sets of factors—motivators and hygienes—are the primary causes of job satisfaction and job dissatisfaction.*[18]

Motivator Factors

Motivator factors *include the work itself, recognition, advancement, and responsibility.* These factors are related to an individual's positive feelings about the job and to the content of the job itself. These positive feelings, in turn, are associated with the individual's experiences of achievement, recognition, and responsibility. They reflect lasting rather than temporary achievement in the work setting. In other words, motivators are intrinsic factors, *which are directly related to the job and are largely internal to the individual.* The organization's policies may have only an indirect impact on them. But, by defining exceptional performance, for example, an organization may enable individuals to feel that they have performed their tasks exceptionally well. Look back at the chapter-opening Learning from Experience feature and identify some of the motivators that Google uses.

Hygiene Factors

Hygiene factors *include company policy and administration, technical supervision, salary, fringe benefits, working conditions, and interpersonal relations.* These factors are associated with an individual's negative feelings about the job and are related to the environment in which the job is performed. Hygiene factors are extrinsic factors, *or factors external to the job.* They serve as rewards for high performance only if the organization recognizes high performance. Can you identify the hygiene factors used by Google to attract new employees?

Job Characteristics Model

The job characteristics model is one of the best known approaches to job design.[19] The job characteristics model uses Herzberg's recommendations of adding motivators to a person's job and minimizing the use of hygiene factors. Before reading further, complete the *Designing a Challenging Job* questionnaire at the end of the chapter (see pages 156–157).

Framework. The job characteristics model *involves increasing the amounts of skill variety, task identity, task significance, autonomy, and feedback in a job.* The model proposes that the levels of these job characteristics affect three critical psychological states: (1) experienced meaningfulness of the tasks performed, (2) experienced personal responsibility for task outcomes, and (3) knowledge of the results of task performance. If all three psychological states are positive, a reinforcing cycle of strong work motivation based on self-generated rewards is activated. A job without meaningfulness, responsibility, and feedback is incomplete and doesn't strongly motivate an employee. Figure 5.5 illustrates the elements of the job characteristic model and their relationships.

Job Characteristics. Five job characteristics hold the key to this model. They are defined as follows:

1. Skill variety—*the extent to which a job requires a variety of employee competencies to carry out the work*
2. Task identity—*the extent to which a job requires an employee to complete a whole and identifiable piece of work, that is, doing a task from beginning to end with a visible outcome*
3. Task significance—*the extent to which an employee perceives the job as having a substantial impact on the lives of other people, whether those people are within or outside the organization*

FIGURE 5.5 Job Characteristics Enrichment Model

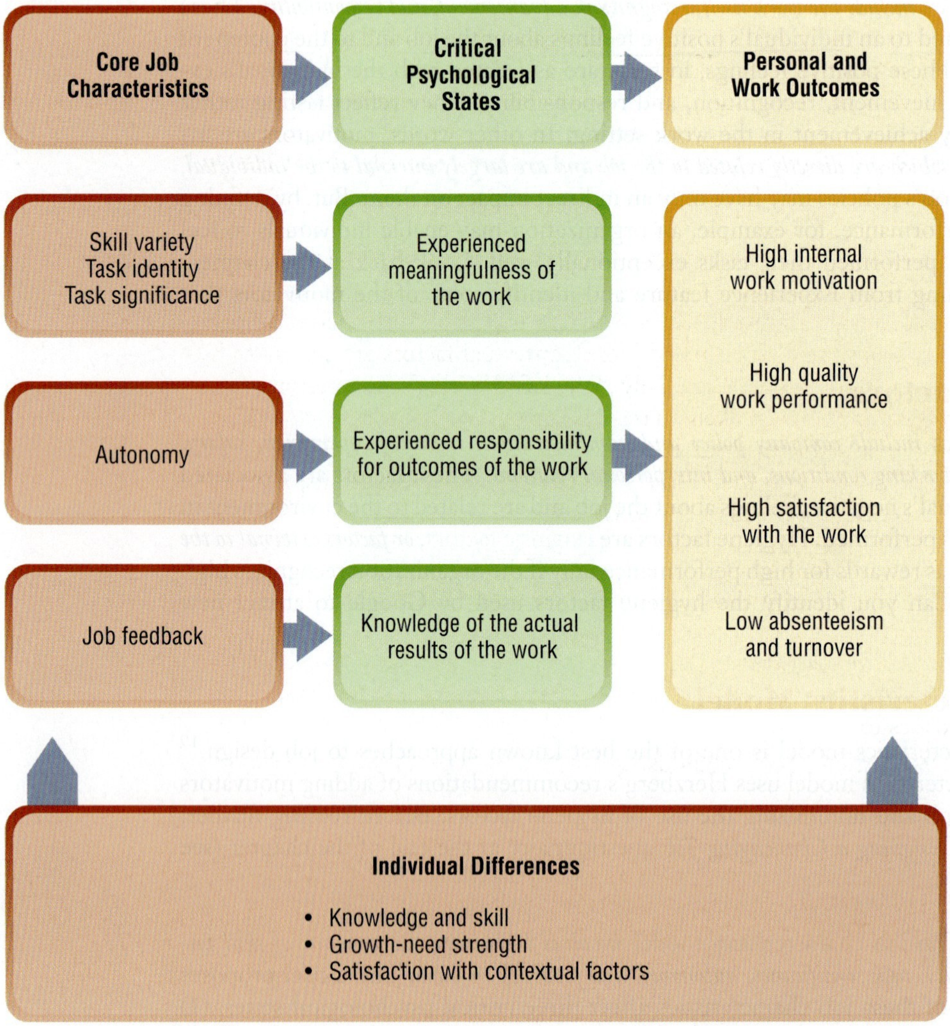

Source: J. Richard Hackman & Greg R. Oldham, WORK REDESIGN, © 1980. Reprinted by permission of Pearson Education, Inc. Upper Saddle River, NJ.

4. Autonomy—*the extent to which the job provides empowerment and discretion to an employee in scheduling tasks and in determining procedures to be used in carrying out those tasks*
5. Job feedback—*the extent to which carrying out job-related tasks provides direct and clear information about the effectiveness of an employee's performance*

Individual Differences. The individual differences (see Figure 5.5) identified in this model influence how employees respond to enriched jobs. They include knowledge and skills, strength of growth needs, and satisfaction with contextual factors. These individual differences have an impact on the relationship between job characteristics and personal or work outcomes in several important ways. Managers, therefore, should consider them when designing or redesigning jobs.

Employees with the *knowledge* and *skills* needed to perform an enriched job effectively are likely to have positive feelings about the tasks they perform. Employees unable to perform an enriched job may experience frustration, stress, and job dissatisfaction. These feelings and attitudes may be especially intense for employees who desire to do a good job but realize that they are performing poorly because they lack the necessary skills and knowledge. Accordingly, assessing carefully the competencies of employees whose jobs are to be enriched is essential. A training and development program may be needed along with an enrichment program to help such employees attain the needed competencies.

The extent to which an individual desires the opportunity for self-direction, learning, and personal accomplishment at work is called growth-need strength. This concept is essentially the same as Maslow's esteem and self-actualization needs concepts. Individuals with high growth needs tend to respond favorably to job enrichment programs. They experience greater satisfaction from work and are more highly motivated than people who have low growth needs. High growth-need individuals are generally absent less and produce better quality work when their jobs are enriched.

Contextual factors *include cultural values, organizational policies and administration, technical supervision, salary and benefit programs, interpersonal relations, travel requirements, and work conditions (lighting, heat, safety hazards, and the like).* The extent to which employees are satisfied with contextual factors at work often influences their willingness or ability to respond positively to enriched jobs. Contextual factors are similar to hygiene factors. Employees who are extremely dissatisfied with their superiors, salary levels, and safety measures are less likely to respond favorably to enriched jobs than are employees who are satisfied with these conditions. Other contextual factors (e.g., organizational culture, power and the political process, travel requirements, and team norms) also can affect employee responses to their jobs.

Managerial Guidelines. The two most used approaches for designing enriched jobs are vertical loading and the formation of natural work teams.

Vertical loading *is the delegation to employees of responsibilities and tasks that were formerly reserved for management or staff specialists.* Vertical loading includes the empowerment of employees to

- set schedules, determine work methods, and decide when and how to check on the quality of the work produced;
- make their own decisions about when to start and stop work, when to take breaks, and how to assign priorities; and
- seek solutions to problems on their own, consulting with others only as necessary, rather than calling immediately for the manager when problems arise.

The formation of *natural teams* combines individual jobs into a formally recognized unit (e.g., a section, team, or department). The criteria for the groupings are logical and meaningful to the employee and include the following:

- *Geographic:* Salespeople or information technology consultants might be given a particular region of the state or country as their territory.

- *Types of business:* Insurance claims adjusters might be assigned to teams that serve specific types of businesses, such as utilities, manufacturers, or retailers.
- *Organizational:* Word-processing operators might be given work that originates in a particular department.
- *Alphabetic or numeric:* File clerks could be made responsible for materials in specified alphabetical groups (A to D, E to H, and so on); library-shelf readers might check books in a certain range of the library's cataloging system.
- *Customer groups:* Employees of a public utility or consulting firm might be assigned to particular industrial or commercial accounts.

Many companies have used job enrichment recommendations to help them reduce turnover and absenteeism. Joseph Teno, Jr., CEO of Athleta Corporation, a sports apparel company, tells his 110 employees to put themselves and their personal needs before jobs. Athleta's turnover rate is less than 1 percent in an industry that averages 38 percent, and employees are getting their work done because each employee is cross-trained and can fill in for one another as needed.[20] Another company that has used these ideas to improve communication between employees is Sun Microsystems. The following Communication Competency feature illustrates how Sun Microsystems, a manufacturer of computer workstations, has designed jobs to save them over $250 million in real estate rent in the past four years because it no longer requires employees to come to the office every day to work. After reading this feature, you should be able to pinpoint those contextual factors and managerial guidelines found in the discussion of vertical loading.[21]

Communication Competency

Sun Microsystems iWork Program

Sun Microsystems iWork program allows employees to work from home or from an off-premise drop-in center.

The program is called iWork and according to Eric Richert, vice president of the iWork Solutions Group, the program has revolutionized the way people work. The program is based on the concept that people need far more flexibility in the way they work and where they work. Richert believes that in many instances, the conventional workplace blocks success and productivity because of contextual factors. Currently, about 43 percent of Sun's 35,000 employees in the 51 countries where Sun operates are eligible for the iWork program. Some employees are able to use iWork up to two days per week. Another 1,500 employees work from home three to five days per week. Employees who use the drop-in centers report that they save about 90 minutes in drive time and daily distraction per visit.

When an employee wants to go to work, she uses a smart card, known as Sun Ray, to log on to the network. The employee can either work from home or stop in at any one of Sun's 12 drop-in centers and 115 locations. Once the employee is logged in, she can view files and applications in a customized desktop—anytime, anywhere. Employees can view specific applications and files wherever they go—from building to building or around the world because Sun's technology links employees worldwide. No data is ever locked in an inaccessible personal computer. Sun plans to introduce the Voice-over-Internet protocol, which will further streamline communications and expand collaboration tools to make it easier to share files and work in virtual teams. Sun offers an assessment tool that helps employees determine whether they are suited to working away from the office. It provides online training programs and other tools to help managers, who initially resisted the program, to provide timely feedback to employees.

The iWork program also helps employees balance work/life issues. An employee can, for example, work at home in the morning, drop off the kids at school, and then head to a drop-in center. The employees can then pick up the kids and finish work at home. iWork has increased Sun's competitive advantage in recruiting talented engineers to work for it and has proven to be very cost effective. Job satisfaction of employees is higher, retention is up, and employee turnover is lower according to Richert.

For more information on Sun's iWork program, visit the organization's home page at www.sun.com.

Cultural Influences

One of the important themes of this book is recognizing and addressing cultural diversity in the workforce. As U.S. organizations continue to expand overseas and foreign organizations establish manufacturing operations in Canada, Mexico, and the United States, managers must be aware of cultural differences and how these differences can affect the motivation of employees. Cultural values are a part of the *contextual factors* with which managers must deal. In Chapter 2, we noted the five cultural factors—individualism/collectivism, power distance, uncertainty avoidance, gender role orientation, and long-term orientation—that impact people's attitudes. With the passage of the North American Free Trade Agreement (NAFTA), managers and employees in North America began working more closely with others who don't necessarily share similar cultural values about the motivation to work. It didn't take U.S. managers very long to realize that employees in Mexico have different attitudes toward work.[22] In the United States, workers generally favor taking the initiative, having individual responsibility, and taking failure personally. They are competitive, have high goals, and live for the future. Workers are comfortable operating in a group, with the group sharing both success and failure. They tend to be cooperative, flexible, and enjoy life as it is now.

In Mexico, employees usually are not willing to speak up and take initiative. Employees additionally prefer a management style that is more authoritarian and do not like to work in teams because of the emphasis on family rather than work teams. However, if the work team is seen as part of an individual's extended family, the team can be a powerful motivator. Employees' priorities are family, religion, and work—in that order. During the year, plant managers host family dinners to celebrate anniversaries of employees who have worked there 5, 10, 15, and 20 years. Employees may use the company clubhouse for weddings, baptisms, anniversary parties, and other family celebrations. Organizations also host a family day during which employees' families can tour the plant, enjoy entertainment and food, and participate in soccer, bowling, and other events. It is very important for families to be invited and involved.

The typical workday in Mexico is 8 A.M. to 5:30 P.M. Employees are picked up by a company bus at various locations throughout the city. Employees like to eat their main meal in the middle of the day, the cost of which is heavily subsidized (as much as 70 percent) by the company. Interestingly, managers serve the employees this meal.

Learning Goal

4. Describe how goal and reward expectations motivate others.

MOTIVATING EMPLOYEES THROUGH PERFORMANCE EXPECTATIONS

Besides creating jobs that people find challenging and rewarding, people are also motivated by the belief that they can expect to achieve certain rewards by working hard to attain them. Believing that you can get an "A" in this class by expending enough effort can be a very effective motivator. If you can clearly see a link between your study behaviors (effort) and your grade (goal), you will be motivated to study. If you see no link, why study at all? To better understand this approach to motivation, let's focus on you as we take a look at the expectancy model and explain how this model motivates you to choose certain behaviors and not others.

Expectancy Model

The expectancy model *states that people are motivated to work when they believe that they can achieve things they want from their jobs.* These things might include satisfaction of safety needs, the excitement of doing a challenging task, or the ability to set and achieve difficult goals. A basic premise of the expectancy model is that you are a rational person. Think about what you have to do to be rewarded and how much the rewards mean to you before you perform your job. Four assumptions about the causes of behavior in organizations provide the basis for this model.

First, a combination of forces in you and the environment determines behavior. Neither you nor the environment alone determines behavior. You go to work or attend school with expectations that are based on your needs, motivations, and past experiences. These factors influence how you will respond to an organization, but they can and do change over time.

Second, you decide your own behavior in organizations, even though many constraints are placed on your individual behavior (e.g., through rules, technology, and work-group norms). You probably make two kinds of conscious decisions: (1) decisions about coming to work, staying with the same organization, and joining other organizations (membership decisions); and (2) decisions about how much to produce, how hard to work, and the quality of workmanship (job-performance decisions).

Third, you and others have different needs and goals. You want particular rewards from your work, depending on your gender, race, age, and other characteristics. Of the many rewards that Google offers to its employees, which do you find attractive? Why? In five years, are these same rewards likely to be attractive to you?

Fourth, you decide among alternatives based on your perceptions of whether a specific behavior will lead to a desired outcome. You do what you perceive will lead to desired outcomes and avoid doing what you perceive will lead to undesirable outcomes.[23]

In general, the expectancy model holds that you have your own needs and ideas about what you desire from your work (rewards). You act on these needs and ideas when making decisions about what organization to join and how hard to work. This model also holds that you are not inherently motivated or unmotivated but rather that motivation depends on the situations that you face and how your responses to these situations fit your needs.

To help you understand the expectancy model, we must define its most important variables and explain how they operate. They are first-level and second-level outcomes, expectancy, instrumentality, and valence.

First-Level and Second-Level Outcomes. *The results of behaviors associated with doing the job itself are called* first-level outcomes. They include level of performance, amount of absenteeism, and quality of work. Second-level outcomes *are the rewards (either positive or negative) that first-level outcomes are likely to produce.* They include a pay increase, promotion, and acceptance by coworkers, job security, reprimands, and dismissal.

Expectancy. Expectancy *is the belief that a particular level of effort will be followed by a particular level of performance.* It can vary from the belief that there is absolutely no relationship between your effort and performance to the certainty that a given level of effort will result in a corresponding level of performance. Expectancy has a value ranging from 0, indicating you see no chance that a first-level outcome will occur after the behavior, to +1, indicating certainty that a particular first-level outcome will follow from your behavior. For example, if you believe that you have no chance of getting a good grade on the next exam by studying this chapter, your expectancy value would be 0. Having this expectancy, you shouldn't study this chapter. Good teachers will do things that help their students believe that hard work will lead you to achieve to better grades.

Instrumentality. Instrumentality *is the relationship between first-level outcomes and second-level outcomes.* It can have values ranging from –1 to +1. A –1 indicates that your attainment of a second-level outcome is inversely related to the achievement of a first-level outcome. For example, assume that you are an IBM engineer and want to be accepted as a member of your work group, but it has a norm for an acceptable level of performance. If you violate this norm, your work group won't accept you. Therefore, you limit your performance so as not to violate the group's norm. A +1 indicates that the first-level outcome is positively related to the second-level outcome. For example, if you received an A on all your exams, the probability that you would achieve your desired second-level outcome (passing this course) approaches +1. If there were no relationship between your performance on a test and either passing or failing this course, your instrumentality would be 0.

Valence. Valence *is an individual's preference for a particular second-level outcome.* Outcomes having a positive valence include being respected by friends and coworkers, performing meaningful work, having job security, and earning enough money to support a family. Valence is just not the amount of the reward you receive, but what it means to you upon receiving it. Outcomes having a negative valence are things that you want to avoid, such as being laid off, being passed over for a promotion, or being discharged for sexual harassment. An outcome is positive when it is preferred and negative when it is not preferred or is to be avoided. An outcome has a valence of 0 when you are indifferent about receiving it.

Putting It All Together. In brief, the expectancy model holds that work motivation is determined by your beliefs regarding effort–performance relationships and the desirability of various work outcomes associated with different performance levels. Simply put, you can remember the model's important features by the saying:

I exert work effort to achieve performance that leads to valued work-related outcomes.

The Expectancy Model in Action. The five key variables just defined and discussed lead to a general expectancy model of motivation, as shown in Figure 5.6. Motivation is the force that causes you to expend effort, but effort alone isn't enough. Unless you believe that effort will lead to some desired performance level (first-level outcome), you won't make much of an effort. The effort–performance relationship is based on a perception of the difficulty of achieving a particular behavior (say, working for an A in this course) and the probability of achieving that behavior. On the one hand, you may have a high expectancy that, if you attend class, study the book, take good notes, and prepare for exams, you can achieve an A in this class. That expectancy is likely to translate into making the effort required on those activities to get an A. On the other hand, you may believe that, even if you attend class, study the book, take good notes, and prepare for exams, your chances of getting an A are only 20 percent. That expectancy is likely to keep you from expending the effort required on these activities to achieve an A.

Performance level is important in obtaining desired second-level outcomes. Figure 5.6 shows six desirable second-level outcomes: self-confidence, self-esteem, personal happiness, overall GPA this semester, approval of other people, and respect of other people. In general, if you believe that a particular level of performance (A, B, C, D, or F) will lead to these desired outcomes, you are more likely to try to perform at that level. If you really desire these six second-level outcomes and you can achieve them only if you get an A in this course, the instrumentality between receiving an A and these six outcomes will be positive. But, if you believe that getting an A in this course means that you won't gain personal happiness and the approval and respect of other people, the instrumentality between an A and these outcomes will be negative. That is, if the higher the grade, the less likely you are to experience personal happiness, you might choose not to get an A in this course. Once you have made this choice, you will lessen your effort and start cutting class, not studying for exams, and so on.

Researchers are still working on ways to test this model, which has presented some problems[24]:

- The model tries to predict choice or the amount of effort an individual will expend on one or more tasks. However, there is little agreement about what constitutes choice or effort for different individuals. Therefore, this important variable is difficult to measure accurately.

FIGURE 5.6 Expectancy Model in Action

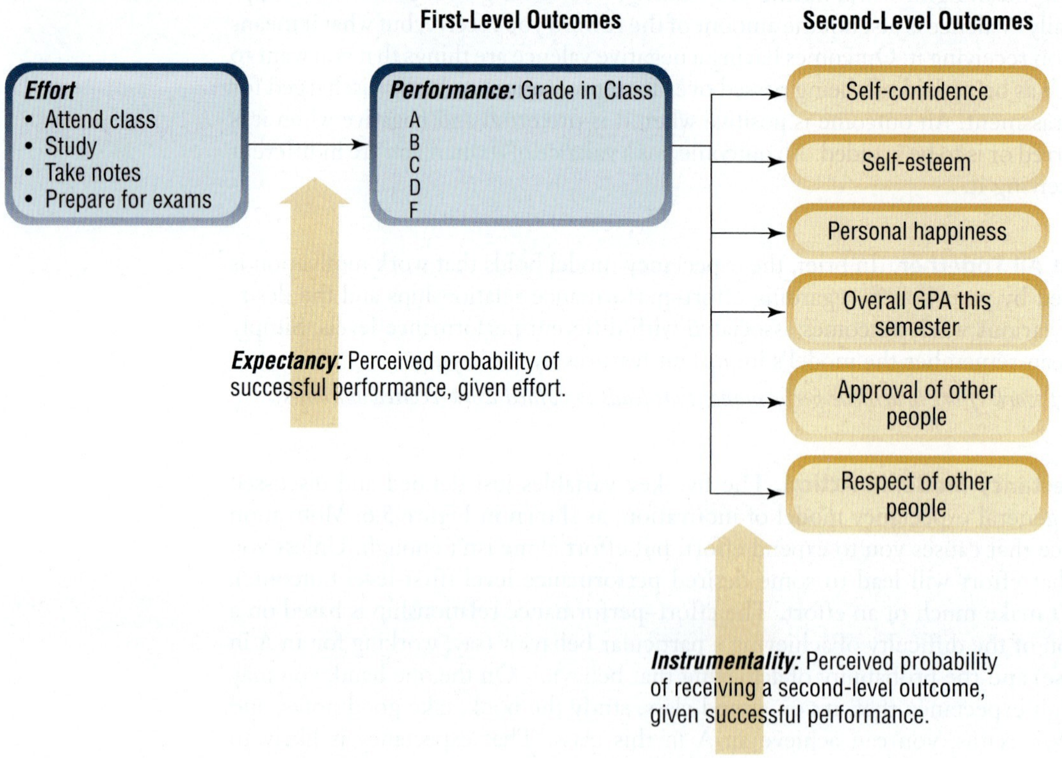

Source: VandeWalle, D., Cron, W. L., and Slocum, J. W. The role of goal orientation following performance feedback. *Journal of Applied Psychology*, 2001, 86, 629–640.

- The model doesn't specify which second-level outcomes are important to a particular individual in a given situation. Although researchers are addressing this issue, comparison of the limited results to date is often difficult because each study is unique. Take another look at the second-level outcomes in Figure 5.6. Would you choose them? What others might you choose?
- The model contains an implicit assumption that motivation is a conscious choice process. That is, the individual consciously calculates the pain or pleasure that he expects to attain or avoid when making a choice. The expectancy model says nothing about unconscious motivation or personality characteristics. In fact, people often do not make conscious choices about which outcomes to seek. Can you recall going through this process concerning your grade while taking this course?
- The model works best in cultures that emphasize internal attribution. The expectancy model works best when people in a culture believe that they can control their work environment and their own behavior, such as in the United States, Canada, and the United Kingdom.[25] In cultures where people believe the work environment and their own behavior aren't completely under their control, such as in Brazil, Saudi Arabia, Iran, Japan, and China, the assumptions of the model might not be valid. For example, a Canadian manager in Japan decided to promote one of her young female Japanese sales representatives to manager (a status and monetary reward). To her surprise, the promotion diminished the new Japanese manager's performance. Why? Japanese have a high need for harmony—to fit in with their colleagues. The promotion, an individualistic reward, separated the new manager from her colleagues, embarrassed her, and therefore diminished her work motivation.

Managerial Guidelines

The expectancy model has some important implications for motivating employees. These implications can be grouped into seven suggestions for action[26]:

1. Managers should try to determine the outcomes that each employee values. Two ways of doing so are observing employee reactions to different rewards and asking employees about the types of rewards they want from their jobs. However, managers must recognize that employees can and do change their minds about desired outcomes over time.
2. Managers should define good, adequate, and poor performance in terms that are observable and measurable. Employees need to understand what is expected of them and how these expectations affect performance. When Smith and Nephew announced a new examination table for doctors, its salespeople wanted to know what behaviors, such as cold-calling on new accounts or trying to sell the new tables to their existing accounts, would lead to more sales. To the extent that the company was able to train its salespeople in selling its new product, it was able to link salespeople's efforts with performance.[27]
3. Managers should be sure that the desired levels of performance set for employees can be attained. If employees feel that the level of performance necessary to get a reward is higher than they can reasonably achieve, their motivation to perform will be low. For example, Nordstrom tells its employees: "Respond to Unreasonable Customer Requests." Employees are urged to keep scrapbooks with "heroic" acts, such as hand-delivering items purchased by phone to the airport for a customer leaving on a last-minute business trip, changing a customer's flat tire, or paying a customer's parking ticket when in-store gift wrapping has taken longer than expected. It is hardly surprising that Nordstrom pays its employees much more than they could earn at a rival store. For those who love to sell and can meet its demanding standards, Nordstrom is nirvana.

4. Managers should directly link the specific performance they desire to the outcomes desired by employees. Recall the discussion in Chapter 4 of how operant conditioning principles can be applied to improve performance. If an employee has achieved the desired level of performance for a promotion, the employee should be promoted as soon as possible. If a high level of motivation is to be created and maintained, it is extremely important for employees to see clearly and quickly the reward process at work. Concrete acts must accompany statements of intent in linking performance to rewards.
5. Managers should never forget that perceptions, not reality, determine motivation. Too often, managers misunderstand the behavior of employees because they tend to rely on their own perceptions of the situation and forget that employees' perceptions may be different.
6. Managers should analyze situations for conflicts. Having set up positive expectancies for employees, managers must look at an entire situation to determine whether other factors conflict with the desired behaviors (e.g., the informal work group or the organization's formal reward system). Motivation will be high only when employees perceive that many rewards and few negative outcomes are associated with good performance.
7. Managers should be sure that changes in outcomes or rewards are large enough to motivate significant efforts. Trivial rewards may result in minimal efforts, if any, to improve performance. Rewards must be large enough to motivate individuals to make the effort required to substantially change performance.

LEADER INSIGHT

High performance is not a matter of chance, it is a matter of choice; it is not a thing to be waited for, it is a thing to be achieved.
Kevin Elliott, Senior Vice President, Merchandising, 7-Eleven

Rajendra Pawar has created a global chain of computer schools that graduate low-cost technicians for call centers and software firms. Pawar is the cofounder and chairman of the National Institute for Information Technology (NIIT), a company that started in 1981. The company operates in 42 countries and has an enrollment of more than 500,000 students and sales exceeding $250 million. Recently, it acquired Element K, an e-learning organization based in Rochester, New York, to offer its services in the United States. More than 3 million Indian people have graduated from NIIT. He has used many of the expectancy model's recommendations, as the following Across Cultures competency feature illustrates. Think about yourself. Why would you enter such a program?[28]

Across Cultures Competency

NIIT's McProgrammers

Crammed into a small classroom near a New Delhi shopping center, 20 of Rajendra Pawar's students practice on their keyboards, pausing slightly to look up at a whiteboard full of equations and text. The students are in their teens and most come from families whose average annual income is less than $2,000. These students expect to earn considerably more someday. This helps explain why they are so committed to learning the intricacies of and creating applications for Microsoft's . Net and Oracle's high-end databases.

Who attends NIIT? Naveen Panthary is a typical NIIT student who comes from a small town called Sagar in India. He is one of four children of a policeman whose salary topped out at about $2,000 a year. After graduating from high school, Panthary couldn't find a job. He made his way to New Delhi and enrolled in a NIIT program. Four years later, he is a trainee at an electronics company making $120 a month. Panthary expects to make more than $800 a month after he graduates and starts working full time.

The growth of NIIT has been tremendous. After watching McDonald's expand into a global fast-food chain, Pawar came up with a unique twist. The NIIT course syllabus reads like a McDonald's menu: Dollar Menu, Combo Meals, and Sides. For each menu item, there is a list of courses from which the student can choose, the number of hours required to complete the course, and the total cost for the course. The syllabus for each course is very specific with objectives assigned to each lesson. Each student gets feedback on his or her own progress by accessing the intranet. NIIT's course offerings are also offered over the Internet for as little as US $17. It also sells training manuals to Microsoft and Sun Microsystems.

Copying McDonald's notion of franchising, Pawar came up with a uniquely Indian twist. He got the most respected families in small communities to sign up as his franchisees. Indians put great emphasis on pride and respect, known as *izzat*. To lose *izzat* is to lose everything. Pawar figured if he could get respected families to be his franchisees, they'd have a powerful incentive to manage the school well—protecting their *izzat*—along with the NIIT brand name. The franchisees pay for marketing, space, desks, and computers. NIIT provides all of the course materials and selects and trains all faculty members. In return, NIIT gets royalties of 20 percent on student tuitions and is paid for all supplies. For franchisees, if well run, the profits can exceed 30 percent on their investment.

For more information on NIIT's McProgrammers, visit the organization's home page at www.niit.com\tech.

MOTIVATING EMPLOYEES THROUGH EQUITY

Learning Goal

5. Explain how treating people fairly influences their motivation to work.

Feelings of unfairness were among the most frequent sources of job dissatisfaction reported to Herzberg and his associates. Some researchers have made this desire for fairness, justice, or equity a central focus of their models. Assume that you just received a 5 percent raise. Will this raise lead to higher performance, lower performance, or no change in performance? Are you satisfied with this increase? Would your satisfaction with this pay increase vary with the consumer price index, with what you expected to get, or with what others in the organization performing the same job and at the same performance level received?

Equity Model: Balancing Inputs and Outcomes

The equity model *focuses on an individual's feelings of how fairly she is treated in comparison with others.*[29] It is based on the belief that people are motivated to maintain a fair, or equitable, relationship between themselves and others and to avoid relationships that are unfair or inequitable. It contains two major assumptions. The first is that individuals evaluate their interpersonal relationships just as they would evaluate the buying or selling of a home, shares of stock, or a car. The model views relationships as exchange processes in which individuals make contributions and expect certain results. The second assumption is that individuals don't operate in a vacuum. They compare their situations to those of the others in the organization to determine fairness. In other words, what happens to individuals is important when they compare themselves to similar others (e.g., coworkers, relatives, and neighbors).

General Equity Model. The equity model is based on the comparison of two variables: inputs and outcomes. Inputs *represent what an individual contributes to an exchange*; outcomes *are what an individual receives from the exchange.* Some typical inputs and outcomes are shown in Table 5.4. A word of caution: The items in the two lists aren't paired and don't represent specific exchanges.

According to the equity model, individuals assign weights to various inputs and outcomes according to their perceptions of the situation. Because most situations involve multiple inputs and outcomes, the weighting process isn't precise. However,

Table 5.4 Examples of Inputs and Outputs in Organizations

INPUTS	OUTCOMES
Age	Challenging job assignments
Attendance	Fringe benefits
Interpersonal skills, communication skills	Job perquisites (parking space or office location)
Job effort (long hours)	Job security
Level of education	Monotony
Past experience	Promotion
Performance	Recognition
Personal appearance	Responsibility
Seniority	Salary
Social status	Seniority benefits
Technical skills	Status symbols
Training	Working conditions

FIGURE 5.7 Inequity as a Motivational Process

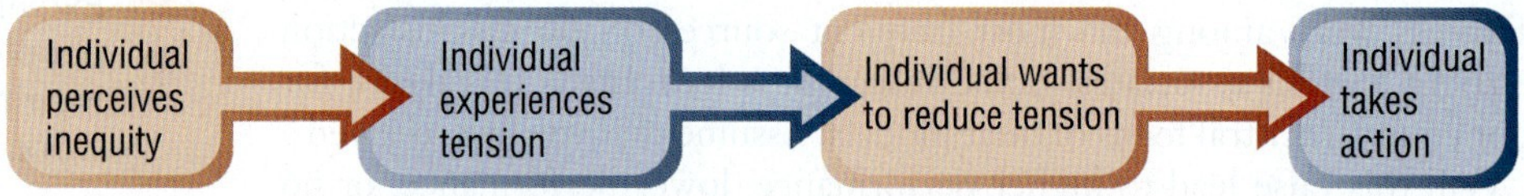

people generally can distinguish between important and less important inputs and outcomes. After they arrive at a ratio of inputs and outcomes for themselves, they compare it with their perceived ratios of inputs and outcomes of others who are in the same or a similar situation. These relevant others become the objects of comparison for individuals in determining whether they feel equitably treated.[30]

Equity exists whenever the perceived ratio of a person's outcomes to inputs equals that for relevant others. For example, an individual may feel properly paid in terms of what he puts into a job compared to what other workers are getting for their inputs. Inequity exists when the perceived ratios of outcomes to inputs are unequal. Jay Loar, a director of program engineering at Lockheed Martin, works harder than his co-workers, completes all his tasks on time even though others don't, and puts in longer hours than others, but receives the same pay raise as the others. What happens? Loar believes that his inputs are greater than those of his coworkers and therefore should merit a greater pay raise. Inequity can also occur when people are overpaid. In this case, the overpaid employees might be motivated by guilt or social pressure to work harder to reduce the imbalance between their inputs and outcomes and those of their coworkers.

Consequences of Inequity. Inequity *causes tension within and among individuals.* Tension isn't pleasurable, so people are motivated to reduce it to a tolerable level, as illustrated in Figure 5.7. To reduce a perceived inequity and the corresponding level of tension, people may choose to act in one or more of the following ways:

- People may either increase or decrease their inputs to what they feel to be an equitable level. For example, underpaid people may reduce the quantity of their production, work shorter hours, and be absent more frequently.

- People may change their outcomes to restore equity. Many union organizers try to attract nonmembers by pledging to improve working conditions, hours, and pay without an increase in employee effort (input).
- People may distort their own inputs and outcomes. As opposed to actually changing inputs or outcomes, people may mentally distort them to achieve a more favorable balance. For example, people who feel inequitably treated may distort how hard they work ("This job is a piece of cake") or attempt to increase the importance of the job to the organization ("This really is an important job!").
- People may leave the organization or request a transfer to another department. In doing so, they hope to find an equitable balance.
- People may shift to a new reference group to reduce the source of the inequity. The star high school athlete who doesn't get a scholarship to a major university might decide that a smaller school has more advantages, thereby justifying a need to look at smaller schools when making a selection.
- People may distort the inputs or outcomes of others. They may come to believe that others in a comparison group actually work harder than they do and therefore deserve greater rewards.

Keeping these six actions in mind, let's take a look at employee theft as a reaction to inequity. Employee theft is one of the most serious problems facing organizations. A recent survey conducted by Harries Interactive (www.harrisinteractive.com) found that 58 percent of U.S. employees admitted that they took items from their workplace. The most popular items stolen from work are pens and pencils (77 percent), sticky notes (44 percent), and paper clips (40 percent). Each day organizations lose an average of $9 per employee. Employee theft and shoplifting are consistently the two largest sources of inventory lost. Employee theft is the greatest in furniture shops (85 percent) and lowest in camera (5 percent) shops. Shoplifting occurs most frequently in apparel (38 percent) and is least likely in furniture (<1 percent). The National Retail Security Association estimates that employee theft costs U.S. organizations more than $40 billion a year and causes 30 percent of business failures. Billions are also stolen from retail department stores and over the Internet. Theft is up almost 25 percent a year for the past five years.[31]

Direct mail customer coupons are used by many major retailers (e.g., Sears, Wal-Mart, JCPenney, Target) to help drive customer traffic into stores. Although several types of coupons are used, the greatest abuse by employees occurs when the coupon is created without requiring a minimum purchase. That is, a $10 coupon that can be used on a $10 purchase in essence results in a free purchase of a $10 item. Many large retailers use the $10 coupon marketing tactic several times a year and mails these coupons to between 5 and 41 million customers depending on the size and type of the sale, for example, Mother's Day, Father's Day, or a Back-to-School sale. The following Ethics Competency feature indicates how some employees abused this policy and how managers stopped it.[32]

Ethics Competency

Employee Misuse of Holiday Promotional Coupons

During a recent holiday promotional event, more than 26,000 (out of 200,000 employees) employees were identified as using multiple $10 coupons at a major retailer. They used the same coupon three or more times, resulting in markdowns totaling more than $700,000. The average number of coupons redeemed was five, with some employees redeeming more than seventy $10 coupons. Further analysis determined that 300 employees used the $10 dollar coupons 20 times or more. These store employees were taking the redeemed coupons out of the cash register for their personal use.

Why did store employees engage in such behavior? The reasons varied but many felt that it was a game, it didn't really matter, they deserved a raise for putting up with hard-to-please customers, or they worked long hours and felt that they deserved a reward. Many others felt that the company policy was vague and that they didn't believe they were stealing.

Managers at headquarters knew that they had to stop such abuse, but taking action against 26,000 employees was not feasible. Therefore, they developed a script that store managers read aloud to all employees emphasizing proper handling of customer coupons. Posters were placed on the retailer's intranet and also posted in employee's break rooms in the stores. The posters outlined the seriousness and resulting loss of profits from such behaviors. A video was produced that focused on why employees abuse store privileges and reactions that employees might take when feeling mistreated by managers. A web-based reporting tool was developed that provided each store manager with a daily list of all employee coupon redemptions during a sales event. If an employee redeemed five or more coupons, his or her name would appear on the list. The names of these employees were also viewed by managers at corporate headquarters and in the human resource department.

What have been the results of these actions? The number of employees redeeming multiple coupons has dropped significantly. The number of employees who redeemed three or more coupons for a recent sale event fell by 50 percent, and for Mother's Day, coupon abuse dropped more than 60 percent.

Procedural Justice: Making Decisions Fairly

Equity theory focuses on the outcomes people receive after they have expended effort, time, or other inputs. It doesn't deal with how decisions leading to outcomes were made in the first place. Procedural justice examines the impact of the *process* used to make a decision . *The perceived fairness of rules and how decisions are made is referred to as* procedural justice.[33] Procedural justice holds that employees are going to be more motivated to perform at a high level when they perceive as fair the procedures used to make decisions about the distribution of outcomes. In organizations procedural justice is very important to most employees, who are motivated to attain fairness in how decisions are made, as well as in the decisions themselves.

Reactions to pay raises, for example, are greatly affected by employees' perceptions about the fairness of how the raises were determined. If in the minds of the employees the pay raises were administered fairly, the employees are usually more satisfied with their increases than if the employees judged the procedures used to make these increases to be unfair. The perceived fairness of the procedures used to allocate pay raises is a better predictor of satisfaction than the absolute amount of pay received.

In both the pay and evaluation situations, the individual can't directly control the decision but can react to the procedures used to make it. Even when a particular decision has negative outcomes for the individual, fair procedures help ensure that the individual feels that his interests are being protected.

Employees' assessments of procedural justice have also been related to their trust in management, intention to leave the organization, evaluation of their supervisor, employee theft, and job satisfaction. Consider some of the relatively trivial day-to-day issues in an organization that are affected by procedural justice: decisions about who will cover the phones during lunch while others are away from their desks, the choice of the site of the company picnic, or who gets the latest software for a personal computer.

Procedural justice has also been found to affect the attitudes of workers who survive a layoff. When workers are laid off, survivors (those who remain on the job) are often in a good position to judge the fairness of the layoff in terms of how it was handled. When a layoff is handled fairly, survivors feel more committed to the organization than when they believe that the laid-off workers were treated unfairly. Recently, Circuit City laid off more than 3,400 of its highest paid hourly workers and hired replacements who were willing to work for less money. The salespeople fired were not given the option of taking a pay cut. They would have to apply for their old jobs at lower pay. Circuit City said that it would hire entry-level employees for $8 dollars per hour, saving $2 to $3 dollars per hour. Greg Tarpinian, executive director of Change to Win, the union representing Circuit City employees, says that Circuit City "treats its employees as disposable commodities, put in and put out based on whatever happens to the stock price." Although the fired employees will get some severance, the question remains whether or not the newly hired salespeople will have the same level of commitment as those fired employees.[34]

Going Beyond the Call of Duty. In many organizations, employees perform tasks that are not formally required.[35] Organizational citizenship behavior *refers to employees who perform tasks that exceed formal job duties*. Examples of organizational citizenship behavior include helping coworkers solve problems, making constructive suggestions, and volunteering to perform community service work (e.g., blood drives, United Way campaigns, and charity work). Although not formally required by employers, these behaviors are important in all organizations. Helping coworkers is an especially important form of organizational citizenship behavior when it comes to computers. Every organization has its computer gurus, but often it's the secretary who doesn't go to lunch who can fix a problem easier and without insulting the struggling user. Managers often underestimate the amount of this informal helping that takes place in organizations.

© Duncan Smith/Photodisc/Getty Images

Organizational citizenship behavior may include one employee helping another with a computer problem.

Employees have considerable discretion over whether to engage in organizational citizenship behaviors. Employees who have been treated fairly and are satisfied are more likely to do so than employees who feel unfairly treated. Fairly treated employees engage in citizenship behaviors because they want to give something back to the organization. Most people desire to have fair exchanges with coworkers and others in their organization.

Howard Johnson, vice president of internal auditing for Lowe's, a national hardware store chain, developed a simple yet innovative method for acknowledging organizational citizenship behaviors at his North Carolina office. At the beginning of the year, Johnson gives each of his 10 employees a jar containing 12 marbles. Throughout the year, employees may give marbles to others who have helped them in some way or who have provided an extraordinary service. Employees are recognized throughout the year and are proud of the number of marbles they accumulate, even though they receive no monetary reward from Johnson.

Managerial Guidelines. Managers often use the equity model in making a variety of decisions, such as taking disciplinary actions, giving pay raises, allocating office and parking space, and dispensing other perquisites (perks). The equity model leads to two primary conclusions. First, employees should be treated fairly. When individuals believe that they are not being treated fairly, they will try to correct the situation and reduce tension by means of one or more of the types of actions identified previously in this section. A sizable inequity increases the probability that individuals will choose more than one type of action to reduce it. For example, individuals may partially withdraw from the organization by being absent more often, arriving at work late, not completing assignments on time, or stealing. The organization may try to reduce the inputs of such employees by assigning them to monotonous jobs, taking away some perks, and giving them only small pay increases.

Second, people make decisions concerning equity only after they compare their inputs and outcomes with those of comparable employees.[36] These relevant others may be employees of the same organization or of other organizations. The latter presents major problems for managers, who cannot control what other organizations pay their employees. For example, Ralph Sorrentino, a partner at Deloitte Consulting, hired a recent business school undergraduate for $47,500, the maximum the company could pay for the job. The new employee thought that this salary was very good until she compared it to the $55,250 that fellow graduates were getting at Boston Consulting, McKinsey, or Bain. She felt that she was being underpaid in comparison with her former classmates, causing an inequity problem for her (and the company).

The idea that fairness in organizations is determined by more than just money has received a great deal of attention from managers. Organizational fairness is influenced by how rules and procedures are used and how much employees are consulted in decisions that affect them.

CHAPTER SUMMARY

1. Explain the motivational process.

A six-stage motivational model indicates that individuals behave in certain ways to satisfy their needs. Managers have three motivational challenges—motives can only be inferred, needs are dynamic, and there are considerable differences in people's motivations.

2. Describe two basic human needs approaches to motivation.

Two human needs models of motivation are widely recognized. Maslow proposed that people have five types of needs: physiological, security, affiliation, esteem, and self-actualization and that when a need is satisfied it no longer motivates a person. McClelland believed that people have three learned needs (achievement, power, and affiliation) that are rooted in the culture of a society. We focused on the role of the achievement need and indicated the characteristics associated with high achievers, including that they like to set their own moderate goals and perform tasks that give them immediate feedback.

Herzberg claimed that two types of factors affect a person's motivation: motivator and hygiene factors. Motivators, such as job challenge, lead to job satisfaction but not to job dissatisfaction. Hygiene factors, such as working conditions, prevent job dissatisfaction but can't lead to job satisfaction. Managers need to structure jobs that focus on motivators because they lead to high job satisfaction and performance. The job characteristics model focuses on adding five motivators to the job (skill variety, task identity, task significance, autonomy, and feedback). Whether an employee responds favorably to an enriched job is dependent on her knowledge and skill, growth-need strength, and contextual factors.

3. Explain how to design motivating jobs.

The expectancy model holds that individuals know what they desire from work. They choose activities only after they decide that the activities will satisfy their needs. The primary components of this model are first- and second-level outcomes, expectancy, instrumentality, and valence. An individual must believe that effort expended will lead (expectancy) to some desired level of performance (first-level outcome) and that this level of performance will lead (instrumentality) to desired rewards (second-level outcomes and valences). Otherwise, the individual won't be motivated to expend the effort necessary to perform at the desired level.

4. Describe how goal and reward expectations motivate others.

The equity model focuses on the individual's perception of how fairly he is treated in comparison to others in similar situations. To make this judgment, an individual compares his inputs (experience, age) and outcomes (salary) to those of relevant others. If equity exists, the person isn't motivated to act. If inequity exists, the person may engage in any one of six behaviors to reduce this inequity. Both procedural justice and organizational citizenship behavior are based on the equity model and have significant implications for employees' perceptions of equity. Procedural justice examines the impact of the process (rules and procedures) used to make a decision. Organizational citizenship behaviors are employee behaviors that go above and beyond their job requirements.

5. Explain how treating people fairly influences their motivation to work.

KEY TERMS AND CONCEPTS

Ability
Achievement motivation model
Affiliation needs
Autonomy
Contextual factors
Deficiency needs
Equity model
Esteem needs
Expectancy
Expectancy model
Extrinsic factors
First-level outcomes
Goal
Growth needs
Growth-need strength
Hygiene factors
Inequity
Inputs
Instrumentality
Intrinsic factors
Job characteristics model
Job feedback
Motivating potential score (MPS)
Motivation
Motivator factors
Motivator–hygiene model
Need for achievement
Need for affiliation
Need for power
Needs
Needs hierarchy model
Organizational citizenship behavior
Outcomes
Physiological needs
Procedural justice
Second-level outcomes
Security needs
Self-actualization needs
Skill variety
Task identity
Task significance
Thematic Apperception Test (TAT)
Valence
Vertical loading

DISCUSSION QUESTIONS

1. Why is job satisfaction not strongly related to job performance?
2. Why do employees steal and/or shoplift from their employers?
3. What are your own assumptions about motivation? How do they reflect the culture in which you were raised?
4. Imagine that you have just been selected to become a new sales manager for Dell Computers in Mexico. What would you do to motivate employees to become high producers?
5. Have you worked for an organization in which employee theft was a problem? If so, what role did procedural justice play? Explain
6. What are the motivational assumptions at Sun Microsystems?
7. Focus on some aspects of your own work in which you feel your performance is below your own expectations. Using your data from the questionnaire in Table 5.1, identify particular action steps you plan to take to overcome these obstacles.
8. Why was Pawar successful in motivating employees at NIIT?
9. Phil Jackson, after winning his seventh NBA title as a coach, said: "I don't motivate my players. You cannot motivate someone. All you can do is provide a motivating environment and the players will motivate themselves." Do you agree or disagree? What's the reasoning behind your answer?
10. How could someone like John Schnatter, CEO of Papa John's, apply McClelland's learned needs model of motivation to motivate his employees?
11. To explore how Google motivates its employees, visit www.google.com. In the blank search box type in "Top 10 Reasons to Work at Google." Click on Google jobs. What basic motivational concepts are illustrated?

EXPERIENTIAL EXERCISE AND CASE

Experiential Exercise: Self Competency

Designing a Challenging Job[37]

Directions

The following list contains statements that could be used to describe a job. Please indicate the extent to which you agree or disagree with each statement as a description of a job you currently hold or have held, by writing the appropriate number next to the statement. Try to be as objective as you can in answering.

1	2	3	4	5
Strongly Disagree	Disagree	Uncertain	Agree	Strongly Agree

This job ...

_____ 1. provides much variety.
_____ 2. permits me to be left on my own to do my work.
_____ 3. is arranged so that I often have the opportunity to see jobs or projects through to completion.
_____ 4. provides feedback on how well I am doing as I am working.
_____ 5. is relatively significant in my organization.
_____ 6. gives me considerable opportunity for independence and freedom in how I do the work.
_____ 7. provides different responsibilities.
_____ 8. enables me to find out how well I am doing.
_____ 9. is important in the broader scheme of things.
_____ 10. provides an opportunity for independent thought and action.
_____ 11. provides me with a considerable variety of work.
_____ 12. is arranged so that I have the opportunity to complete the work I start.
_____ 13. provides me with the feeling that I know whether I am performing well or poorly.
_____ 14. is arranged so that I have the chance to do a job from the beginning to the end (i.e., a chance to do the whole job).
_____ 15. is one where a lot of other people can be affected by how well the work gets done.

Scoring

For each of the five scales, compute a score by summing the answers to the designated questions.

	Score
Skill variety: Sum the points for items 1, 7, and 11.	___
Task identity: Sum the points for items 3, 12, and 14.	___
Task significance: Sum the points for items 5, 9, and 15.	___
Autonomy: Sum the points for items 2, 6, and 10.	___
Job feedback: Sum the points for items 4, 8, and 13.	___
Total Score:	___

Summary Interpretation

A total score of 60–75 suggests that the core job characteristics contribute to an overall positive psychological state for you and, in turn, lead to desirable personal and work outcomes. A total score of 15–30 suggests the opposite. You can develop your own job profile by using the totals on the scales in the questionnaire, each of which has a score range of 3–15. You can calculate an overall measure of job enrichment, called the motivating potential score (MPS), as follows.

$$\text{MPS} = \frac{\text{skill variety} + \text{task identity} + \text{task significance}}{3} \times \text{autonomy} \times \text{feedback}$$

The MPS formula sums the scores for skill variety, task identity, and task significance and divides the total by 3. Thus, the combination of these three job characteristics has the same weight as autonomy and job feedback. This is because the job characteristics enrichment model requires that both *experienced responsibility* and *knowledge of results* be present for high internal job motivation. This outcome can be achieved only if reasonable degrees of autonomy and job feedback are present. The minimum MPS score is 1, and the maximum possible MPS score is 3,375. A clearly positive MPS score starts at 1,728, and a purely neutral MPS score is 729 (based on an average score of 9 per scale).

Questions

1. Visit any fast-food restaurant. Evaluate the motivating potential score of the order taker. As a manager, how might you redesign this job to increase its motivating potential score?
2. Why is a high motivating potential score more likely to lead to higher job performance than a low motivating potential score?

Case: Across Cultures Competency

Working in a Chinese Factory[38]

Yue Yuen is a city of 265,000 people that replaces the village young workers leave behind. Just like the farms from which these workers come, Yue Yuen has seasons and rhythms, but ones set by commercial dictates in countries thousands of miles away. Yue Yuen runs its own water treatment systems and power stations. Within each factory compound are dormitories and canteens, post office and phone company branches, medical clinics, and shops. One factory complex has a 100-bed hospital, a kindergarten, a 300-seat movie theater, and a performance troupe.

Zhang Qianqian, 21 years old, arrived at Yue Yuen three years ago. She says she left after 18 months because of conflicts with her boss and briefly returned home. She worked at an electronics factory last year before quitting to go home, this time for her grandmother's 80th birthday. Soon she rejoined Yue Yuen. "I've moved here and there, and I always seem to end up in this factory," she says.

One-third of the world's shoes are made in Guangdong, the province that borders Hong Kong. In this world, Yue Yuen is king. Established in 1989 by Pou Chen Corp. of Taiwan, Yue Yuen is the largest supplier to Nike, Adidas, Reebok, and other brands. The company runs three factory complexes in Gaobu, a suburb of Dongguan, and is one of the biggest employers in the province.

Yue Yuen runs some factories that make the raw materials for shoes and other factories that cut, stitch, and assemble these various parts. It employs designers to work with shoe companies to develop new styles. A Yue Yuen assembly line now takes 10 hours to make a shoe, from readying raw materials to having a finished product ready to ship, compared with 25 days four years ago.

In a world of change and uncertainty, Yue Yuen offers a stability that contrasts with the impermanence of migrant life. Many factories in the Pearl River Delta are unsafe and owe workers money. At Yue Yuen, the salary is average—about US $72 per month after deductions for room and board. The company has a reputation for long workdays and autocratic managers. But wages are paid on time. Work is capped at 11 hours a day and 60 hours a week, with Sundays off. Turnover is greater than 60 percent a year. Workers sleep 10 to a room with hot showers and adequate meals. Eighty-five percent of the workers at Yue Yuen are young women.

Factory society divides along provincial lines. Workers from the same province stick together, speaking dialects others can't understand. Local stereotypes color hiring. Many factory bosses refuse to hire people from Henan because they are considered untrustworthy, whereas those from Anhui are perceived as overly sly.

Almost all of the managers at Yue Yuen are migrants who started out on the factory floor. They're ranked by an intricate well-established hierarchy. There are 13 levels of managers, from manager trainee to managing director. There is a cafeteria exclusively for those in charge of production lines and another for chief supervisors, one step up the hierarchy. Only line leaders and higher-up managers are permitted to live inside the factory with a child.

Zhang Qianqian had come to visit friends in Room 805 from a dorm down the hall. She wore jeans and a black sports watch. Ms. Zhang recalled mornings at home when her grandmother would make breakfast. "She calls me to come eat it and sometimes I am still sleeping. Then my father says to me, 'You are lying in bed, you won't even come to eat breakfast your grandmother has made for you.'" She frowned. "At home they are always criticizing you." Most workers have complex relationships with their homes. When they aren't there, they miss it. But when they spend time in their villages, they quickly get bored and long to return to the city.

Back in their villages, families try to pressure the girls: Send money home; don't get a boyfriend; marry sooner; come back. For the most part, the girls do as they please. Many parents don't know their daughters' phone numbers inside the factory.

When the girls at Yue Yuen go home, their parents want them to rest rather than working on the farm, believing they already work too hard. The girls keep farmers' hours, rising at dawn and turning in early. But they spend most of their waking hours watching television. Time is not important in the village. At Yue Yuen, however, time is measured in precise increments. There is a plastic sign in front of every station noting how many seconds it takes that worker to complete a task. Employees are timed by supervisors with stopwatches. Productivity at Yue

Yuen is up 10 percent in the past three years. An Adidas investigation into the impact of its drive to increase efficiency found that workers initially felt more stress but over time adapted.

One production line has 470 workers. An athletic shoe may pass through 200 stations. Workers in the cutting department stamp sheets of mesh fabric into pieces. Stitchers sew logos and shoelace eyelets onto these pieces to make the shoe upper. Stock fitters glue layers of rubber and plastic to make the sole. Assemblers press the sole and upper together, insert a foot-shaped plastic mold, called a last, and glue the two parts together. A machine applies 88 pounds of pressure to each shoe. Workers remove the lasts, check for flaws, and pack the shoes in boxes. Each shoe has a "Made in China" label on its tongue. Yue Yuen has 290 production lines in factories throughout China, each turning out 157.7 million pairs of shoes annually for companies such as Nike, New Balance, Timberland, and Rockport.

The Western companies that pushed factories to improve conditions also demanded lower prices. Workers now work fewer hours but are more exhausted because tasks are precisely parceled out to ensure almost no downtime. Brands now give factories 30 days to deliver an order; three years ago it was 60 days; a decade back it was 90. Orders are getting smaller, allowing designers to respond more rapidly to fashion changes.

Questions

1. What needs are being fulfilled by employees?
2. How could you enrich the employees' jobs?
3. Would you like to work in such a factory? What's the logic behind your decision?

CHAPTER 6

Motivation through Goal Setting and Reward Systems

Learning Goals

When you have finished studying the chapter, you should be able to:

1. Explain how goal setting affects performance.
2. State the effects of goal setting on job satisfaction and performance.
3. Describe four reward programs for improving performance.

© AP Images

Learning from Experience

CONTINENTAL AIRLINES IS FLYING HIGH

When Gordon Bethune took over as CEO at Continental Airlines in 1994, the airline was in miserable shape. The company wasn't meeting its financial goals and was about to enter its third bankruptcy; employees had lost trust and confidence in top management. According to Michelle Meissner, director of human resources, "It was a horrible place to work. Programs were constantly late and on-board service was lousy." Today, Continental operates more than 3,000 flights daily from 150 U.S. cities and flies to more than 135 foreign lands.

One of Bethune's first moves was to burn the old policy manual in front of employees. He told employees to make decisions that were good for the company and its customers. Bethune also wanted to reward people for helping turn things around. The company started paying every employee an extra $65 every time Continental was ranked among the top five airlines for its monthly on-time percentage. Coming from dead last, Continental finished first three months after payments started. Why $65? Bethune told employees that Continental's poor on-time performance cost the airline $5 million a month (to feed and house people in motels, etc.). He explained that 50 percent of the savings from on-time performance would be given back to employees. A share of the $2.5 million for every employee was $65. Employees were cut separate checks for $65 and tax deductions were taken from their regular paycheck so as not to dilute the bonus. After one year, the company started paying out $100, but employees now received the bonus only if Continental ranked third or higher on its on-time percentage each month. Other airlines started copying Continental's program so Continental now ranks fifth place or higher.

In 1995, Bethune and his senior managers instituted the Go Forward Program. Although Bethune retired from Continental in 2004, the program has been continued by the airline's current CEO, Larry Kellner. The Go Forward Program measures four strategic goals:

- *Fly to Win—Achieve above-average profits for the airline industry.*
- *Fund the Future—Manage company assets to maximize stockholder value by investing in new technology to reduce costs and improve cash flow.*

For more information on Continental Airlines, visit the organization's home page at www.Continental.com.

LEARNING CONTENT

- *Make Reliability a Reality—Rank among the top airlines for on-time arrivals, baggage handling, complaint resolution, and involuntary denied boardings (overbooked flights).*
- *Working Together—Help well-trained employees build careers that focus on safety and keeping pay and benefits competitive within the airline industry.*

Every year employees receive a survey that asks questions such as "Has your leader informed you about the Go Forward Program?" and "Has your leader set measurable, specific goals based on the Go Forward Program?" Leaders who score well on these assessments are rewarded with bonuses.

Bethune also learned another lesson about choosing specific goals to reward. As on-time percentages soared, so did the number of lost bags. He realized that the on-time bonus was causing employees to focus all of their attention on getting planes out on time. A flight attendant once told Bethune to "sit down now" so the plane could take off on time. Bethune went to his seat knowing that no one was going to make Continental late. If holding a plane to get a few late bags on board threatened to cause a late departure, the bags were left behind. He addressed this need by traveling to Continental's three hubs—Houston, Cleveland, and Newark—and telling employees that lost bags weren't going to make the airline profitable. Almost immediately the message hit home and the number of lost bags dropped dramatically.[1]

To survive in today's competitive global market, setting challenging goals that take into account the crucial factors of time and quality and providing feedback to employees are no longer options. They must happen!

The motivational practices that produced the achievements at Continental are based on setting goals, developing feedback systems, and providing reward systems that get individuals to strive to reach those goals. Goals play an important part in motivating individuals to strive for high performance. The basic concepts in goal setting remain an important source for motivating employees. Regardless of the nature of their specific achievements, successful people tend to set goals. Their lives are goal oriented. This is true for politicians, students, and leaders in all sorts of organizations.[2]

In this chapter, we begin by presenting a model of goal setting and performance based on the individual. Then we focus on four commonly used reward systems that reinforce desired behaviors of employees.

Learning Goal

1. Explain how goal setting affects performance.

MODEL OF GOAL SETTING AND PERFORMANCE

Goals *are future outcomes (results) that individuals and groups desire and strive to achieve.*[3] An example of an individual goal is "I intend to graduate with a 3.2 grade point average by the end of the spring semester, 2010." Goal setting *is the process of specifying desired outcomes toward which individuals, teams, departments, and organizations will strive and is intended to increase organizational efficiency and effectiveness.*

Importance of Goal Setting

The goal-setting process is no easy task, but the effort is not only worthwhile, it is also becoming essential in the current highly competitive global business. Just as organizations strive to achieve certain goals, individuals also are motivated to strive for and attain goals. In fact, the goal-setting process is one of the most important motivational tools for affecting the performance of employees in organizations. In this section we consider one of the most widely accepted models of goal setting and indicate how goal-setting techniques can be applied to motivate individuals and teams.

Figure 6.1 presents a model of individual goal setting and performance.[4] According to this goal-setting model, goal setting has four motivational aspects:

- *Goals direct attention.* That is, they focus an employee's attention on what is relevant and important. What is important at Continental?

FIGURE 6.1 Motivational Aspects of Goal Setting

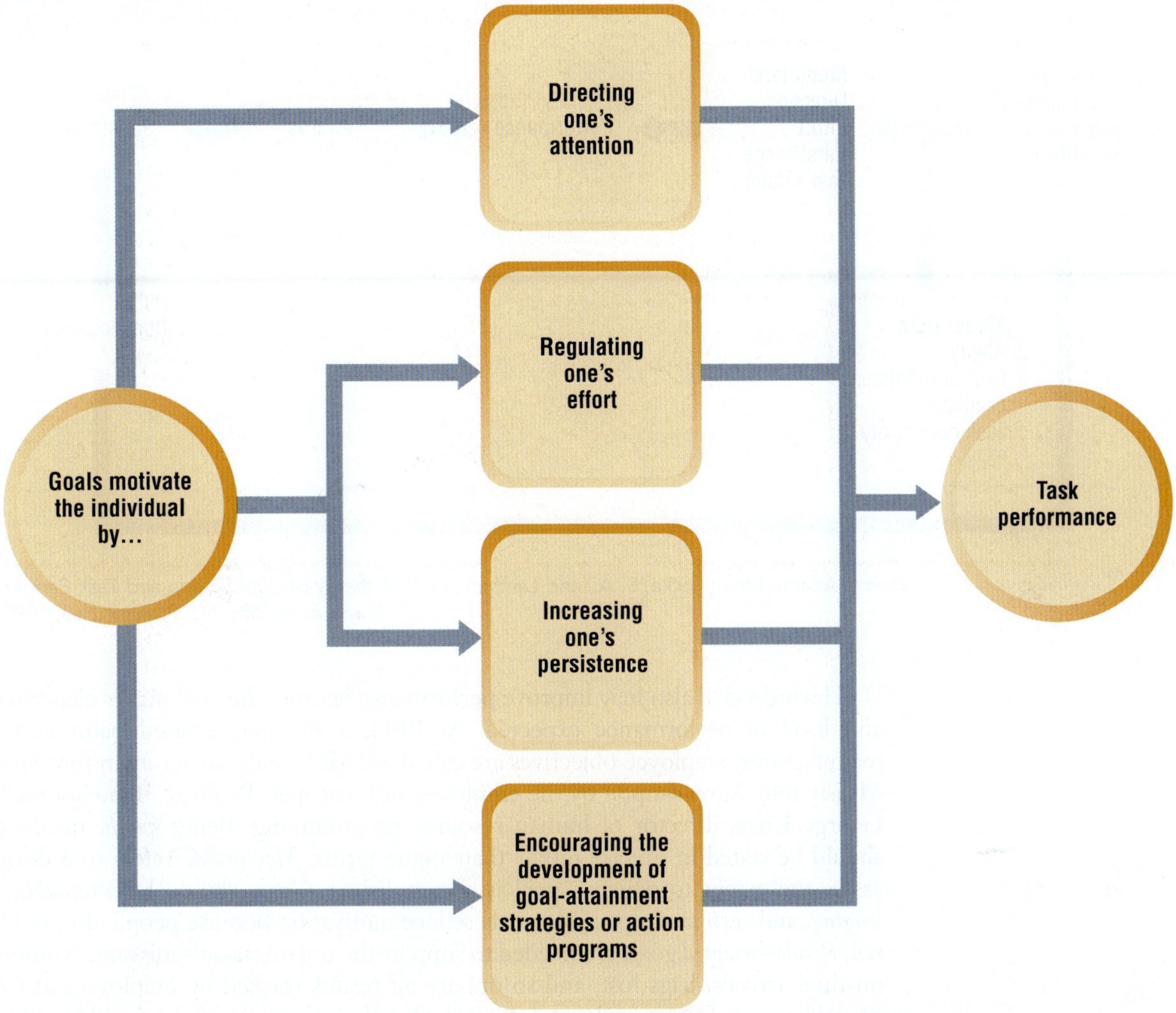

Source: E. A. Locke and G. P. Latham, *A Theory of Goal Setting and Task Performance.* Englewood Cliffs, NJ: Prentice Hall, 1990. © 1990. Adapted and reprinted by permission of Prentice Hall, Inc.

- *Goals regulate effort.* Not only do goals direct our attention, they motivate us to act. What motivates employees at Continental?
- *Goals increase persistence.* Persistence represents the effort expended on a task over an extended period of time. Persistent people find ways to overcome obstacles and avoid making excuses if they fail. What are some examples of this at Continental?
- *Goals foster strategies and action programs.* Goals encourage people to develop strategies and action programs that enable them to achieve their goals. Give an example of this at Continental?

Figure 6.2 presents a version of this model. It shows the key variables and the general relationships that can lead to high individual performance, some of which we have discussed in previous chapters. The basic idea behind this model is that a goal serves as a motivator because it allows people to compare their present performance with that required to achieve the goal. To the extent that people believe they will fall short of a goal, they will feel dissatisfied and work harder to attain it as long as they believe that it can be achieved.

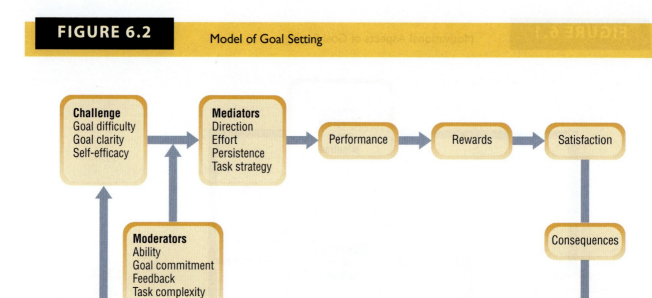

FIGURE 6.2 Model of Goal Setting

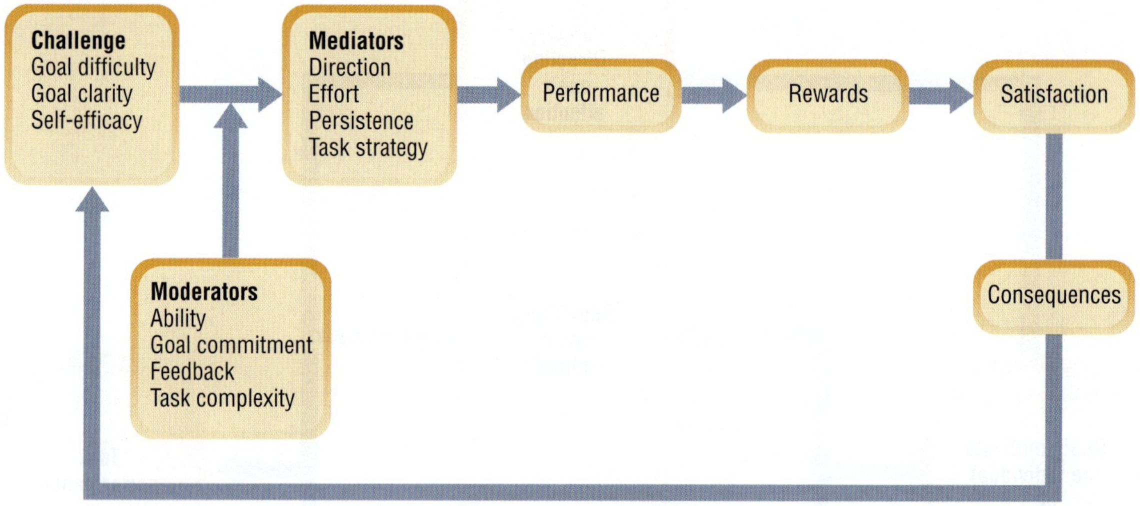

Source: Adapted from Locke, E. A., and Lantham, G. P. *A theory of Goal Setting and Task Performance.* Englewood Cliffs, NJ: Prentice Hall, 1990, 253.

Having a goal also may improve performance because the goal makes clear the type and level of performance expected. At PPG, a Pittsburgh-based paint and glass manufacturer, employee objectives are called SMART goals, an acronym for "Specific, Measurable, Agreed-upon by the employee and manager, Realistic, Timebound," says George Kock, director of human resource programming. Being *specific* means goals should be stated in precise rather than vague terms. *Measurable* refers to a device to assess the extent to which a goal is accomplished. Goals should be *attainable*, *challenging*, and *realistic*. Impossible goals reduce motivation because people do not like to fail. *Results-oriented* goals are needed to support the organization's mission. Numbers of on-time arrivals, bags lost, and so on, are all results tracked by employees at Continental because if these goals are achieved, then the organization's goal will be achieved. Finally, *timebound* means that goals need to specify target dates for completion.

Before the SMART goal system was implemented at PPG, a sales manager would be told by her boss to increase sales for the next year. Now she might be asked to develop, by September 30, three new customers in three Southeast regions with annual sales volume of $250,000 each. Using SMART, sales performance at PPG has increased by more than 25 percent.[5]

Challenge

Stated another way, goal setting is the process of developing, negotiating, and establishing targets that challenge the individual. Employees with unclear goals or no goals are prone to work slowly, perform poorly, exhibit a lack of interest, and accomplish less than employees whose goals are clear and challenging. In addition, employees with clearly defined goals appear to be more energetic and productive. They get things done on time and then move on to other activities (and goals).

Goals may be implicit or explicit, vague or clearly defined, and self-imposed or externally imposed. Whatever their form, goals serve to structure the individual's time and effort. Two key attributes of challenging goals are particularly important: goal difficulty and goal clarity.

- Goal difficulty: *A goal should be challenging but not impossible to achieve.* If it is too easy, the individual may delay or approach the goal lackadaisically. If it is too difficult, the individual may not really accept the goal and thus not try to meet it.
- Goal clarity: *A goal must be clear and specific if it is to be useful in directing effort.* The individual thus will know what is expected and not have to guess. For instance, Continental Airlines customer service agents are expected to answer customers' calls by the third ring of the phone.

Clear and challenging goals lead to higher performance than do vague or general goals. Management by objectives (MBO) *is a management system that uses goal difficulty and goal clarity as its foundation for motivating employees.* In essence, this management system involves managers and employees jointly setting goals for performance and personal development, periodically evaluating the employee's progress toward achieving these goals, and then rewarding the employee. One company that has made extensive use of management by objectives is Cardinal Health, an integrated health-care solutions provider located in Dublin, Ohio. At the beginning of each year, all 55,000 employees are asked to identify at least one performance objective that supports one of the four corporate goals of growth, operational excellence, leadership development, and customer focus. In addition, at the end of the year, managers are asked to rate employees on a set of core leadership competencies, such as self-management, teamwork, sound judgment, and relationship building. By combining the ratings from the manager with those from the employees, Cardinal has been able to show how MBO leads to both employee satisfaction and profits. Cardinal managers have found that goals that are difficult but not impossible lead to higher performance than do easy goals. However, unrealistically high goals may not be accepted or may lead to high performance only in the short run.[6] Individuals eventually get discouraged and stop trying, as predicted by the expectancy model (see Chapter 5).

LEADER INSIGHT

In soccer, you place the ball in a position not with the straightest but with the greatest number of ways to reach the goal. My job at DayJet is to help people score goals.
Jim Herriot, Vice President, DayJet

Along with goal difficulty and clarity, a third key factor that influences the establishment of challenging goals is self-efficacy. In Chapter 4, we defined *self-efficacy* as the individual's estimate of his or her own ability to perform a specific task in a particular situation. As might be expected, individuals who set high goals perform at a high level when they also have high self-efficacy. A person's self-efficacy is dependent on the task. For example, a golfer with a low handicap has high self-efficacy on the golf course. But the same person might have low self-efficacy when meeting sales quotas for a new piece of equipment that her company has just introduced.[7]

With clear and challenging goals, employee behaviors are more likely to be focused on job-related tasks, high levels of performance, and goal achievement. Table 6.1 provides a summary of the key links between goal setting and individual performance.

Table 6.1 Impact of Goals on Performance

WHEN GOALS ARE	PERFORMANCE WILL TEND TO BE
Specific and clear	Higher
Vague	Lower
Difficult and challenging	Higher
Easy and boring	Lower
Set participatively	Higher
Set by management (top down)	Lower
Accepted by employees	Higher
Rejected by employees	Lower
Accompanied by rewards	Higher
Unrelated to rewards	Lower

The following Teams Competency feature illustrates how people in teams use the basic concepts of goal challenge, goal clarity, and self-efficacy to instill teamwork. In NASCAR racing, it is often how well the pit crew performs that determines whether the driver wins the race.[8]

Teams Competency

Jeff Gordon's Rainbow Warriors

© Jared C. Tilton/Ai Wire/Landov

The Rainbow Warriors, Jeff Gordon's pit crew, work as a team with Gordon to win races.

During his career, NASCAR driver Jeff Gordon has won 75 races, four titles, and nearly $85 million in prize money. In fact, he's won more races than any other NASCAR team. Steve Letarte is considered by many NASCAR people to be a premier crew chief. Together, Gordon and Letarte give much of the credit to their pit crew, known as the Rainbow Warriors, because crew members wear rainbow-striped jumpsuits.

When the Rainbow Warriors crew was assembled, its members decided to do things differently. In the past, mechanics who had worked on a race car all week also suited up on Sunday to work as the pit crew. The car was the number one priority. The crew relied on horsepower and the driver to win the race. Pit crews didn't practice and set goals. But Letarte and Gordon knew that all drivers have essentially the same equipment. They thought the ingredient that would separate winning from losing drivers was their ability to create a team. They decided to have two crews: The first crew was responsible for the mechanics of the car (e.g., engine and suspension components); the second—the pit crew—was responsible for the car during the race.

Under Letarte and Gordon's leadership, the team hired a coach to develop specifically the teamwork competency of the pit crew. Training included rope climbing, scaling walls, wind sprints, guys carrying each other on their backs, and the like. All members of the pit crew were trained to perform all necessary tasks so that they could rotate tasks among themselves, depending on race conditions. By analyzing other NASCAR drivers, Letarte determined that if Gordon's car could leave the pit one second faster than the competition, Gordon would gain 300 feet on the competition (a car going 200 mph travels nearly 300 feet a second). The pit crew set a goal of having the car exit the pit in 13 seconds or less because races are often decided by less than 1 second between the first and second place car.

During a race, all crew members listen to each other on their scanners. They use special code words to signal whether they are changing two or four tires when Gordon pulls into the pit. The crew also determines whether to gas the car fully or just to put in enough gas to finish the race. Letarte and his crew also determine when Gordon should come in for a pit stop. Before the race, all the Rainbow Warriors sit in a circle to discuss race strategy. The circle symbolizes that the team is stronger than any individual. When Gordon wins a race, signs a personal services contact, or is paid to sign autographs, all members of both crews receive a percentage of that money.

For more information on Jeff Gordon, visit the organization's home page at www.jeffgordon.com.

Moderators

Figure 6.2 also shows four of the factors that moderate the strength of the relationship between goals and performance: ability, goal commitment, feedback, and task complexity. We begin with ability because it limits an individual's capacity to respond to a challenge.

Ability. The relation of goal difficulty to performance is curvilinear, not linear. That is, performance levels off as the limits of a person's ability are approached. In Chapter 5, we learned that motivation is an important part of a person's ability to perform. Some individuals believe that they have the ability to acquire new competencies and master new situations. They seek challenging new assignments that open their eyes to new ways of doing tasks. Others believe that their ability to complete a task is relatively stable and avoid placing themselves in a situation in which they might receive a negative evaluation.[9]

Goal Commitment. The second factor, goal commitment, *refers to an individual's determination to reach a goal, regardless of whether the goal was set by that person or someone else.*[10] What is your goal commitment in this class? Take a minute and complete the questionnaire in Table 6.2. Your commitment to achieve a goal is likely to be stronger if you make it publicly, if you have a strong need for achievement, and if you believe that you can control the activities that will help you reach that goal.

The effect of participation on goal commitment is complex. Positive goal commitment is more likely if employees participate in setting their goals, which often leads to a sense of ownership. In a study by the Corporate Leadership Council of 50,000 employees, the council found that increased commitment can lead to a 57 percent improvement in discretionary effort—employees' willingness to exceed the normal job

Table 6.2 Goal Commitment Questionnaire

	RESPONSE CATEGORY				
ITEM	STRONGLY AGREE	AGREE	UNDECIDED	DISAGREE	STRONGLY DISAGREE
1. I am strongly committed to achieving a grade of ____.	____	____	____	____	____
2. I am willing to expend the effort needed to achieve this goal.	____	____	____	____	____
3. I really care about achieving this grade.	____	____	____	____	____
4. Much personal satisfaction can be gained if I achieve this grade.	____	____	____	____	____
5. Revising my goal, depending on how other classes go, isn't likely.	____	____	____	____	____
6. A lot would have to happen to abandon my grade goal.	____	____	____	____	____
7. Expecting to reach my grade goal in this class is realistic for me.	____	____	____	____	____

Scoring:
Give yourself 5 points for each Strongly Agree response; 4 points for each Agree response; 3 points for each Undecided response; 2 points for each Disagree response; and 1 point for each Strongly Disagree response. The higher your total score, the greater is your commitment to achieve your grade goal in this class.

Source: Adapted from Cron, Wm. L., Slocum, J. W., Jr., VandeWalle, D. and Fu, F. The role of goal orientation on negative emotions and goal setting when initial performance falls short of one's performance goal. *Human Performance*, 2005, 18(1), 55–80; Hollenbeck, J. R. Williams, C. R., and Klein, H. J. An empirical examination of the antecedents of commitment to goals. *Journal of Applied Psychology*, 1989, 74, 18–23.

duties. That effort produces, on the average, a 20 percent individual performance improvement and an 87 percent reduction in a desire to leave the organization. Not expecting or wanting to be involved in goal setting reduces the importance of employee participation in terms of goal commitment. Even when a manager has to assign goals without employee participation, doing so leads to more focused efforts and better performance than if no goals are set or if a person is told simply to "do their best."[11]

The expected rewards for achieving goals play an important role in the degree of goal commitment. The greater the extent to which employees believe that positive rewards (merit pay raises, bonuses, promotions, opportunities to perform interesting tasks, and the like) are contingent on achieving goals, the greater is their commitment to the goals. At Continental, it didn't take long for employees to realize how their goals for on-time percent, bags lost, and so on, were related to their financial gain. These notions are similar to the ideas contained in the expectancy model of motivation. Similarly, if employees expect to be punished for not achieving goals, the probability of goal commitment also is higher. However, recall that punishment and the fear of punishment as the primary means of guiding behavior may create long-term problems (see Chapter 4).

Employees compare expected rewards against rewards actually received. If received rewards are consistent with expected rewards, the reward system is likely to continue to support goal commitment. If employees think that the rewards they receive are much less than the rewards they expected, they may perceive inequity. If perceived or actual inequity exists, employees eventually reduce their goal commitment.

Teamwork and peer pressures are other factors that affect a person's commitment to a goal. Health First, a nonprofit chain of hospitals in Rockledge, Florida, has successfully matched corporate goals with those of its employees. Health First management set five goals, including patient care and managing costs. Why five? Because Health First wants to keep managers focused on a handful of high-priority items that are measurable. At the beginning of the year, department heads sit down with their employees and communicate these five goals. They discuss how the employee plans to reach that goal. If the manager of the OB-GYN department needs to reduce his operating costs by 5 percent, he can log into the hospital intranet to see how costs are tracking for his department during the year. Half of a person's pay increase is based on individual and team performance. If a manager is not reaching his goal, then human resource managers give him input on how to achieve the goal. According to Bob Suttles, vice president for human resources, "The monitoring system holds managers accountable to motivate their staffs to their highest performance."[12]

Feedback. Feedback makes goal setting and individual responses to goal achievement (performance) a dynamic process. Feedback *provides information to the employee about how well he or she is doing.* It enables the individual to relate received rewards to those expected in terms of actual performance. This comparison, in turn, can influence changes in the degree of goal commitment.[13] However, some organizations are giving employees positive feedback for just showing up. Land's End, Bank of America, and the Scooter Store teach managers how to give positive feedback to employees using e-mails, prize packages, and public displays of appreciation. The 1,000-employee Scooter Store, Inc., has a manager who uses a power wheelchair to wheel around in while throwing confetti at employees. The manager also passes out 100 to 500 celebratory helium balloons once a week as a way of showing the company's appreciation for employees showing up. Such positive feedback rarely improves performance because it is not targeted at specific goals.

Task Complexity. Task complexity *refers to the cognitive processing that is needed by a person to solve the task.* For simple tasks (e.g., answering telephones at Marriott's reservation center), the effort encouraged by challenging goals leads directly to high task performance. For more complex tasks (e.g., studying to achieve a high grade), effort doesn't lead directly to effective performance. The individual must also decide where and how to allocate effort.

Mediators

Let's assume that an individual has challenging goals and that the moderating factors support achievement of these goals. How do the four mediators shown in Figure 6.2—direction, effort, persistence, and task strategy—affect performance? *Direction of attention* focuses behaviors on activities expected to result in goal achievement and steers the individual away from activities irrelevant to achieving the goals. At Continental, employees directed their attention to on-time departures, and neglected bags. That focus changed only after Bethune reminded them that lost baggage resulted in poor overall evaluation scores, which led to no financial payout for them. The *effort* a person exerts usually depends on the difficulty of the goal. That is, the greater the challenge, the greater will be the effort expended, assuming that the person is committed to reaching the goal. *Persistence* involves a person's willingness to work at the task over an extended period of time until the results are achieved. Most sports require participants to practice long and hard to hone their competencies and maintain them at a high level. Finally, *task strategy* is the way in which an individual—often through experience and instruction—decides to tackle a task. That is, what to do first.

Performance

Performance is likely to be high when (1) challenging goals have been set, (2) the moderators (ability, goal commitment, feedback, and task complexity) are present, and (3) the mediators (direction, effort, persistence, and task strategy) are operating. Destiny Health, an Oak Brook, Illinois, company that offers health programs for small businesses, offers employees a program called the Vitality Program. The Vitality Program was created to encourage employees to seek preventive medical care. This program awards points to employees who take care of themselves. For example, enrollment in a stop smoking program is worth 3,000 points, which can be redeemed for consumer electronics, movie tickets, magazine subscriptions, and vacation packages. Points can also be converted into frequent-flier miles on selected airlines. Companies whose employees each earn more than 45,000 points a year qualify for discounted health insurance.[14]

Three basic types of quantitative indicators can be used to assess performance: units of production or quality (amount produced or number of errors), dollars (profits, costs, income, or sales), and time (attendance and promptness in meeting deadlines). When such measures are unavailable or inappropriate, qualitative goals (customer satisfaction, teamwork) and indicators may be used. In addition, many organizations have developed a code of ethics to support employees in setting ethical goals and making ethical decisions. Creating ethics guidelines has several advantages that the Gap, GE, and Johnson & Johnson, among others, consider important. Some of the advantages for setting ethical goals are

- to help employees identify what their organization recognizes as acceptable behaviors,
- to legitimize the consideration of ethics as part of decision making,
- to avoid uncertainties among employees about what is right and wrong, and
- to avoid inconsistencies in decision making caused by an organizational reward system that appears to reward unethical behavior.[15]

The Gap, Inc., a $16 billion clothing manufacturer, issued a 42-page social responsibility report that spells out the problems found in its more than 3,000 factories contracted to produce clothing for the Gap, GapKids, Old Navy, and Banana Republic brands. The company has 98 percent of its clothing manufactured outside of the United States, with 22 percent of it being made in China. The company discovered persistent wage, health, and safety violations in many regions where it does business, including China, Africa, India, and Central and South America. The infractions ranged from a failure to provide proper protective equipment to physical abuse and coercion. The Gap pulled its business from 136 factories in China, India, and Pakistan due to serious labor violations and turned down bids from hundreds of others when they failed to meet the Gap's labor standards. The following Ethics Competency feature highlights what the Gap has done to improve working conditions.[16]

Ethics Competency

The Gap

© Kin Cheung/Reuters/Landov

The Gap has taken a number of measures to improve the working conditions at the factories around the world that manufacture its apparel.

What has the Gap done to improve the working conditions at the factories around the world that manufacture its apparel? First, it appointed Anne Gust, Gap's chief administrative and compliance officer, to authorize the publication of a social responsibility report. This 42-page report divulges information on the Gap's social responsibility practice to its shareholders and financial institutions. This report honestly told of the labor violations and admits that the Gap does not have all of the answers to fix them. Many of the labor problems are widespread in this industry.

Second, it built a Social Responsibility team of vendor compliance officers (VCOs) that has 90 full-time employees stationed around the world whose goal is to improve the lives of the people working in the factories. Recently, these VCOs performed more than 4,500 factory inspections in 2,100 factories. Of those, 75 percent passed inspection and were accepted into the Gap's approved supplier list. The VCOs have meetings with factory managers to help them resolve compliance issues, facilitate worker and management training sessions, and review policies and procedures. Factory monitoring is a vital part of the Gap's strategy to improve working conditions in the garment industry.

Third, it has outlined goals that each of its supplier factories are supposed to strive to achieve using the Gap's Code of Vendor Conduct, which is based on internationally accepted labor standards and published in 24 languages. Some of these standards include prohibition of child and forced (prisoners) labor and discrimination, adherence to local labor laws, workers' freedom of association, and requirements for certain wages and work hours.

Fourth, the Gap helps to foster more sustainable solutions across the industry. This includes how best to work with unions, governments, and other apparel brands and retailers to move garment manufacturers toward global and sustainable improvements in labor standards. Some of their key country-based partnerships are in Central America, where over 320 factory managers, workers, and labor inspectors have been trained in the Continuous Improvement in the Central American Workplace Program and Cambodia, where over 650 supervisors from seven garment factories have gone through a new managerial skills program.

For more information about the Gap's ethics, visit the organization's website at www.gapinc.com/public/SocialResponsibility/sr_faq.shtml.

Rewards

When an employee attains a high level of performance, rewards can become important inducements for the employee to continue to perform at that level. Rewards can be external (bonuses, paid vacations, and the like) or internal (a sense of achievement, pride in accomplishment, and feelings of success). Continental, PPG, and Jeff Gordon's

NASCAR organization all reward people for high performance. However, what is viewed as a reward in one culture may not be viewed as a reward in another. For example, doing business in Vietnam requires the exchange of gifts during the first day of a business meeting. Although they may be small and relatively inexpensive, gifts with a company logo are highly valued. The gifts should be wrapped, but white or black paper should not be used because these colors are associated with death. In contrast, exchanging gifts at a business meeting in the United States generally is not expected. Praising an individual in public for achievement in Vietnam will embarrass the individual. Rewards are not to be given in public. Conversely, public acclaim for achievement in the United States is valued.[17]

Satisfaction

Many factors—including challenging work, interesting coworkers, salary, the opportunity to learn, and good working conditions—influence a person's satisfaction with the job (see Chapter 2). However, in the goal-setting model, the primary focus is on the employee's degree of satisfaction with performance. Employees who set extremely high, difficult goals may experience less job satisfaction than employees who set lower, more easily achievable goals. Difficult goals are less frequently achieved, and satisfaction with performance is associated with success. Thus, some compromise on goal difficulty may be necessary in order to maximize both satisfaction and performance. However, some level of satisfaction is associated with simply striving for difficult goals, such as responding to a challenge, making some progress toward reaching the goals, and the belief that benefits may still be derived from the experience regardless of the outcome.

EFFECTS OF GOAL SETTING

Learning Goal

2. State the effects of goal setting on job satisfaction and performance.

What conditions increase or decrease the benefits of goal setting? Five essential conditions must come together for managers to gain the benefits of a goal-setting program:[18]

1. The employee must have the knowledge and ability to attain the goal. If the goal is to increase sales by 15 percent within the next 12 months and the employee lacks the sales competencies needed to attain it, urging them to set "stretch goals" usually isn't effective. It can make employees so anxious to reach the goal that they scramble to discover ways (ethical and unethical) to reach the goal, but do not learn the behaviors that are needed to be effective.
2. The employee must be committed to the goal, especially if the goal is difficult. Achieving a difficult goal requires a great deal of effort.
3. People need feedback on their progress toward the goal. Feedback enables employees to adjust their effort and behavior necessary for goal attainment. When employees discover that they are not reaching their goals, they typically increase their efforts because of the pride they have in their performance.
4. Tasks that are complex need to be broken down so that the employee can set subgoals that can be attained. These subgoals yield information for employees as to whether their progress is consistent with what is required for them to attain their goal.
5. Situational constraints can make goal attainment difficult. One of the primary roles of a manager is to ensure that employees have the resources necessary to attain their goals and to remove obstacles in the way of accomplishing those goals.

Impact on Performance

One of the consequences of goal setting is that it motivates individuals to achieve high performance. There are several reasons for this. First, difficult but achievable goals prompt employees to concentrate on achievement of the goals. At Enterprise Rent-A-Car, agents focus on customer satisfaction goals because they know that results are measured monthly and ranked and that these rankings affect their chances for advancement. Second, difficult goals motivate employees to spend lots of time and effort on developing methods for achieving them. At Enterprise, agents communicate with customers, sometimes at length, so that the agents understand their needs and can provide the most suitable vehicle to them, whether it is a sedan, convertible, pickup, or SUV. Customer satisfaction and loyalty are vital to the success of the business. Third, difficult goals increase people's persistence in trying to achieve them. If employees perceive that goals can be reached by luck or with little effort, they tend to dismiss the goals as irrelevant and not follow through with the actions needed to reach them.

To sum up, specific, difficult goals affect motivation and performance by

- encouraging people to develop action programs to reach these goals,
- focusing people's attention on these goal-relevant actions,
- causing people to exert the effort necessary to achieve the goals, and
- spurring people to persist in the face of obstacles.

One of the many firms that have put these actions into practice is Cincinnati's Children's Hospital Medical Center. As described in the following Communication Competency feature, communications improvements are critical for this hospital to meet its patients' goals.[19]

Communication Competency

Cincinnati Children's Hospital Medical Center

The leadership of Children's Hospital set out to establish goals for improving the effectiveness and efficiency of the hospital. For example, it set a goal for the pharmacy to deliver medicines 50 percent more efficiently at the end of a three-month period. Pharmacists found that prescriptions traveled more than 2,100 feet before they were ready for delivery. A curved shelf was flattened against the wall to permit pharmacists to work side by side. That immediately cut down the distance to 800 feet. Another goal was to deliver nonurgent medicines more quickly to patients. From their study, they found out that it took 23 hours for nonurgent medicines to reach a patient. After they studied this problem, they set a goal of 6 hours. After some trial and error, bedside nonurgent medicines were delivered in 5 hours. That in turn reduced by 50 percent the number of medicines tossed out because the patients were already discharged. These savings significantly improved the financial condition of the hospital.

Hospital Chief Jim Anderson hired Eugene Litvak to examine the number of rescheduled surgeries. The hospital normally performed 700 rescheduled surgeries a year. Litvak set a goal with the doctors of less than 10 a year. Recently, Children's performed 7 during the year. Litvak noticed that lots of beds were empty one day and the next day the hospital was overcrowded. He noted that these swings in rooms had nothing to do with infectious outbreaks, but were caused by the manner in which surgeons scheduled their surgeries. "God doesn't make people sicker on Tuesday than on Wednesday," Litvak said. Changes were made in how surgeons scheduled their surgery. Previously urgent cases, like a broken bone or an inflamed appendix, were squeezed in between surgeries that had been scheduled for months. Surgeons ended up padding the time of their operation room slots so they didn't wind up behind if a compound fracture repair went too long.

Litvak set aside 2 operating rooms just for urgent cases, leaving 18 open for scheduled procedures. An additional room was set aside for procedures that needed to be done within a week. These were the operations that were most often crammed in at the end of the day, forcing the surgeon and nurses to work late into the night. After discussing the situation with doctors and nurses, he created the "surgeon of the week" position. This person would clear his or her calendar solely to handle urgent appendectomies and bone-setting.

After these changes, he established a 45-day trial to see how the changes worked. During the 45-day trial, surgeons went home on time and were able to do more surgeries. Once the surgeons in orthopedic surgery saw the program in action, they purchased extra equipment so that they too could set aside operating rooms and institute surgeon of the week programs.

For more information on Cincinnati Children's Hospital Medical Center, visit the organization's home page at www.cincinnatichildrens.org.

Limitations to Goal Setting

Goal setting has often been shown to increase performance in a variety of settings. However, you should be aware of three limitations.[20] First, when employees lack the skills and abilities needed to perform at a high level, goal setting doesn't work. Giving an employee a goal of writing a computer program will not lead to high performance if the worker doesn't know how to write such a program. To overcome this limitation, new hires at The Ritz-Carlton, for example, are required to attend training sessions at which they are taught how to process requests and complaints, build customer loyalty, and establish relationships with restaurants, taxi services, golf courses, and others services frequently requested by guests.

Second, successful goal setting takes longer when employees are given complicated tasks that require a considerable amount of learning. Good performance on complicated tasks also requires that employees be able to direct all their attention to the tasks and not be interrupted by side issues. Steve Letarte's Rainbow Warriors pit crew is able to perform complicated tasks quickly because they are the only tasks that the crew is focusing on while the car is in the pit.

Third, goal setting can lead to major problems when it rewards the wrong behaviors. Rod Rodin is the CEO of Marshall Industries, a billion-dollar electronics distributor in Los Angeles that serves more than 30,000 customers who order more than 700,000 parts a month. He quickly recognized that the company's reward system was encouraging behaviors that led to poor service, dissatisfied customers, and, ultimately, lower profits. Rodin found that more than 20 percent of each month's sales were shipped to clients during the last three days of the month. Managers were hiding customer returns or opening bad credit accounts just to make their monthly sales goals. Divisions were hiding products from each other or saying that products had been shipped when they really had none on hand. Salespeople fought over how to split commissions on revenue from a customer who did design work in Chicago but made purchases in Cleveland. Employee and team performance were reviewed and ranked on the basis of numerical criteria, such as receivables outstanding and gross sales dollars. Rodin's solution was to scrap the incentive compensation system. He declared that there would be no more contests, prizes, or bonuses for individual achievements. Everyone at Marshall was put on a salary and shared in a companywide bonus pool if the organization as a whole met its goals. It worked.[21]

> **LEADER INSIGHT**
>
> Why should I pay you to get in the batter's box? When you hit the ball, I'll increase your pay. Results are paid for.
> **Carlos Sepulveda, CEO, Interstate Battery**

Managerial Guidelines

As you might expect, individuals who are both satisfied with and committed to an organization are more likely to stay with and accept the challenges the organization presents. Turnover and absenteeism rates for satisfied individuals are lower. This link brings us full circle to the beginning of the goal-setting model. What might happen if things go badly and an individual who had been satisfied becomes dissatisfied? Individual responses fall into at least six categories: (1) job avoidance (quitting), (2) work avoidance (absenteeism, arriving late, and leaving early), (3) psychological defenses (alcohol and/or drug abuse), (4) constructive protest (complaining), (5) defiance (refusing to do what is asked), and (6) aggression (theft or assault). Quitting is the most common outcome of severe dissatisfaction.[22]

The goal-setting model has important implications for employees, managers, and teams alike. First, it provides an excellent framework to assist the manager or team in diagnosing the potential problems with low- or average-performing employees. Diagnostic questions might include these: (1) How were the goals set? (2) Are the goals challenging? (3) What is affecting goal commitment? and (4) Does the employee know when he has done a good job? Second, it provides concrete advice to the manager on how to create a high-performance work environment. Third, it portrays the system of relationships and interplay among key factors, such as goal difficulty, goal commitment, feedback, and rewards, to achieve high performance.

Learning Goal

3. Describe four reward programs for improving performance.

REWARD PROGRAMS FOR IMPROVING PERFORMANCE

In Chapters 4 and 5 we discussed types of rewards that organizations make available to employees. From the concepts discussed in those chapters, along with the concepts presented so far in this chapter, you should by now recognize that one of the basic goals of managers should be to motivate employees to perform at their highest levels. Managers agree that tying rewards to job performance is essential. However, the actual implementation of programs designed to bring about such a relationship is often quite difficult. Questions that arise include "Should rewards be tied to the performance of an individual or team?" Recall that Rod Rodin, CEO of Marshall Industries, found that rewarding individuals created unhealthy competition among employees and destroyed morale. Deciding to reward all employees in the organization raises another question: Should the rewards be based on cost savings or profits and be distributed annually or when people retire or otherwise leave the organization? The accounting procedures required by cost savings programs are enormous and complex, but if efficient they allow rewards to be distributed relatively quickly.

Considerable research has been done on how rewards affect individual and team performance. According to the Ascent Consulting organization, the ability of rewards to motivate individuals or teams to high performance was found to depend on six factors[23]:

1. *Availability*. For rewards to reinforce desired performance, they must be available. Too little of a desired reward is no reward at all. For example, pay increases are often highly desired but unavailable. Moreover, pay increases that are below minimally accepted standards may actually produce negative consequences, including theft, falsifying records, and the like. Organizations spend an average of $850 per employee on reward and recognition programs, but there are wide variations. Fifty percent of organizations spend less than $100 per year per employee, 65 percent spend less than $500, and 10 percent spend more than $2,500 per employee annually.
2. *Timeliness*. Like performance feedback, rewards should be given in a timely manner. A reward's motivating potential is reduced to the extent that it is separated in time from the performance it is intended to reinforce. Most companies use a combination of on-the-spot awards and team/departmental performance. On-the-spot rewards are usually in the form of gift cards, excursions, causal day, time-off, and the like.
3. *Performance contingency*. Rewards should be closely linked with particular performances. If a goal is met, the reward is given. The clearer the link between goal

achievement and rewards, the better able rewards are to motivate desired behavior. Forty percent of employees nationwide believe that there is no link between their performance and rewards, such as bonuses and pay.

4. *Durability*. Some rewards last longer than others. Intrinsic rewards, such as increased autonomy, challenge, and accountability, tend to last longer than extrinsic rewards, such as pay increases.
5. *Equity*. Employees' motivation to perform is improved when they believe that the reward policies of their organization are fair and equitable.
6. *Visibility*. To promote a reward system, management must ensure that rewards are visible throughout an organization. Visible rewards, such as assignments to important committees or promotion to a new job, send signals to employees that rewards are available, timely, and based on performance.

To the extent that reward programs are used to motivate employees to achieve higher performance, we discuss four popular reward programs: gain-sharing, profit-sharing, skill-based pay, and flexible benefit programs. The strengths and limitations of each are summarized in Table 6.3.

Table 6.3 **Common Reward Programs for Improving Performance**

REWARD PROGRAMS	STRENGTHS	LIMITATONS
Gain-sharing programs	Rewards employees who reach specified production levels and control costs.	Formula can be complex; employees must trust management.
Profit-sharing programs	Rewards organizational performance.	Individuals and teams are not likely to have an impact on overall organizational performance.
Skill-based pay	Rewards employee with higher pay for acquiring new skills.	Labor costs increase as employees master more skills. Employee can "top out" at the highest wage rate.
Flexible benefits	Tailored to fit individual needs.	Administrative costs are high and the program is difficult to use with teams.

Gain-Sharing Programs

Gain-sharing programs *are designed to share with employees the savings from productivity improvements.* Productivity can be measured in terms of less downtime, quality, or safety issues. The underlying assumption of gain sharing is that employees and the employer have similar goals and thus should share in economic gains. So for every dollar paid out in gain sharing, the company saves a like amount in lower labor costs, less waste and fewer rejects, and lower workmen's compensation premiums. According to the Ascent Group, more than 25 percent of all U.S. companies have some type of gain-sharing pay program for their employees. The average payout for employees is 7.6 percent, up from 5.9 percent just a few years ago.[24]

The General Accounting Office of Congress recently concluded that gain-sharing programs are one of the most effective programs for motivating employees to better performance. Many organizations, such as DuPont, Dow Chemical, and Viking Pump, have discovered that, when designed correctly, gain-sharing programs can contribute to employee motivation and involvement. Specific formulas tailor-made for each organization are used to calculate both performance contributions and gain-sharing awards. Many gain-sharing programs encourage employees to become involved in making decisions that will affect their rewards. Gain-sharing programs are usually tied to a program, division, or department's improvement. However, prior to the establishment of any gain-sharing program, an organization needs to have a good communication system and nonconfidential performance data available to all employees.

A popular version of gain sharing is the Scanlon program, named after Joe Scanlon, a union leader in the 1930s.[25] The Scanlon program *is a system of rewards for improvements in productivity.* This program is designed to save labor costs. Incentives are calculated as a function of labor costs relative to the sales value of production. Working together, employees and managers develop a formula that bases the distribution of rewards on a ratio of total labor costs to total sales volume. If actual labor costs are less than expected, the surplus goes into a bonus pool. For example, Baltimore County workers calculated that they needed $100,000 worth of labor to generate $500,000 worth of services to residents of that county. In the following year, the same services were provided for $80,000 worth of labor. Forty percent of the $20,000 saved was then distributed to the employees, with the county keeping the balance. Employee bonuses were based on a percentage of salary.[26] In many cases, the bonus pool is equally split between the organization and employees.

Rewards for Baltimore County workers are a good example of the Scanlon program. Workers help to save on labor costs and are rewarded by being given a share of the savings.

Gain-sharing programs are better suited to certain situations than to others. Table 6.4 illustrates a list of conditions favoring this program. In general, gain-sharing programs seem suited to small organizations with a good market, simple measures of performance, and production costs that can be controlled by the employees. However, large organizations, such as DuPont and Lockheed Martin, have successfully used gain-sharing programs in their manufacturing programs. Top management should support the program and the employees should be interested in and knowledgeable about gain sharing.

Although gain-sharing programs sound good, there have been notable failures. The Fleet Financial Group recently abandoned its gain-sharing program. As part of a two-year cost-cutting effort, management had created a gain-sharing program tied to the company's ratio of expenses to revenue and its stock prices. The more costs were cut and the higher the stock rose, the more employees were supposed to be rewarded. But when Fleet's stock price remained depressed even after cost cutting, workers got the minimum payout—averaging $615 per employee. Many employees stated that, considering the

Table 6.4 Conditions Favoring Gain-Sharing Programs

ORGANIZATIONAL CHARACTERISTIC	FAVORABLE CONDITION
Size of organization	Usually fewer than 500 employees
Product costs	Controllable by employees
Organizational climate	Open, high level of trust
Style of management	Participative
Union status	No union, or one that is favorable to a cooperative effort
Communication policy	Open, willing to share financial results
Plant manager	Trusted, committed to plan, able to articulate goals and ideals of plan
Management	Technically competent, supportive of participative management style, good communication skills, able to deal with suggestions and new ideas
Workforce	Technically knowledgeable, interested in participation and higher pay, financially knowledgeable and interested

Source: Adapted from Cummings, T. G., and Worley, C. G. *Organization Development and Change*, 7th ed. Cincinnati: South-Western, 2001, 403.

blood, sweat, and tears that went into getting the bonus, it turned out to be meaningless. What further enraged employees was that top management received big bonuses that weren't tied to the same measures. Another failure occurred at Ameristeel Corporation. After seven years of using a gain-sharing program and with the worldwide overcapacity in steel production and declining prices, top management had to cancel the program. Ameristeel's gain-sharing program, which paid out largely based on productivity gains, has been replaced by a program based on employees' ability to operate efficiently by cutting costs and waste and by reducing imperfections that require steel to be rerolled.[27]

Profit-Sharing Programs

Profit-sharing programs *give employees a portion of the company's earnings.* As the name suggests, profit-sharing programs distribute profits to all employees. Average profit-sharing figures are difficult to calculate. According to some experts they typically range between 4 and 6 percent of a person's salary. Steve Watson, managing partner at Stanton Chase, an executive-recruiting firm, contends that profit sharing may have a limited impact because employees may feel that they can do little to influence the organization's overall profitability. That is, company profits are influenced by many factors (e.g., competitor's products, state of the economy, and inflation rate) that are well beyond the employees' control. However, profit-sharing programs are very popular in Japan. For example, at Seiko Instruments many managers and workers receive bonuses twice a year that equal four or five months' salary. These bonuses are based on the company's overall performance.[28]

What are the characteristics of successful profit-sharing programs? According to John Semyan, partner at TNS Associates, an executive recruiting firm, more than one-third of the companies that use profit sharing do not track the results of such programs. In addition, 28 percent indicate that their profit-sharing programs do not meet the goals. To reduce failure, the following recommendations are offered:

- Involve line managers and employees in the program's creation to ensure their support.
- Set clear goals for the program.
- Ensure that the employees understand the metrics that the program is measuring.
- Tie the program to the company's strategy.

- Give the program time to succeed. It takes two or three years for a program to change overall company performance.
- Provide up-to-date information that allows employees to see how well they are performing against their goals.[29]

The following Self Competency feature illustrates how McDonald's uses a profit-sharing program for more than 400,000 managers and senior staff members in 118 countries. For large corporations, finding the perfect balance between global consistency and cultural adaptation has become a major problem.[30]

Self Competency

McDonald's Rewards Program

In 2003, McDonald's was seeing a declining market share. The company brought its former CEO, Jim Cantalupo, out of retirement to design a reward system that would motivate managers. He announced a program, *Program to Win*, that would focus on people development. The fundamentals of the program were to provide each restaurant manager with a menu of business principles to focus on as part of the *Program to Win* approach. These principles included areas such as customer service, marketing, and restaurant image. Managers could pick three to five areas that they needed to focus on for success in their local market. For example, a manager in France who is introducing a new menu item might create business goals (e.g., number of servings, number of complaints) around that menu for the year. Human resource managers in various areas of the world would also submit their personal goals in the second half of the year for senior management's approval. At the end of the year, the human resource managers profit-sharing pool was based on how well the region (or country) met its goals as well as on the manager's operating income. A portion of the restaurant manager's annual profit-sharing payout was based on that mix.

McDonald's had traditionally used a performance system whereby only 20 percent of restaurant managers could receive the highest rating, 70 percent in the middle, and 10 percent at the bottom. By providing principles and guidance, yet allowing each local manager to customize his or her compensation program to satisfy the local markets, McDonald's has begun to see a decrease in managerial turnover. The global chain has also seen a 5 percent increase in the number of managers who say they believe that they are now paid fairly and understand their compensation and how it contributes to company goals.

For more information about McDonald's rewards program, visit the organization's home page at www.mcdonalds.com.

Skill-Based Pay Programs

Paying employees according to their value in the labor market makes a great deal of sense. After all, employees with highly developed skills and those who develop multiple skills are particularly valuable assets to the organization. As we emphasized earlier, competencies such as managing communication, team building, and change are often based on mastering a number of individual skills, such as verbal, written, and media presentations. Skill-based pay programs *are based on the number and level of job-related skills that an employee has learned.*[31] Skill-based pay compensates employees for the skills they can use in the organization, rather than for specific jobs they are performing. Pay changes do not necessarily go along with job changes. There is also little emphasis on seniority. The underlying assumption is that by focusing on the individual rather than the job, skill-based reward programs recognize learning and growth. Employees are paid according to the number of different skills they can perform.

More than 16 percent of the *Fortune* 1000 companies use skill-based pay programs to motivate employees. In the United Kingdom, the Norwich and Peterborough Building Society, a mortgage and banking business, had a 12-level reward program. It proved to be ineffective in curbing turnover, covered only some of the employees, and basically confused employees. The new program centers on 5-level job skills, such as customer service and relationship management, that are linked to pay rate changes in the market. Sixty-seven percent of employees now know that their pay progression is linked to the attainment of these 5-level job skills. As a result, employee turnover dropped to 17 percent from 25 percent, productivity increased, and customer satisfaction improved. Employees report that the new pay system is simple, transparent, and they understand what skills they need to learn to increase their pay. And managers do not have to answer the question "Why is that person earning more than I am?"[32]

Of course, skill-based pay programs have some limitations. One major drawback of skill-based pay is the tendency to "top out." Topping-out occurs when employees learn all the skills there are to learn and then run up against the top end of the pay scale, with no higher levels to attain. Some organizations, such as GE and United Technologies, have resolved the topping-out effect by installing a gain-sharing program after most employees have learned all of the required skills. Other organizations have resolved this problem by making skills obsolete, eliminating them, and adding new ones, thus raising the standards of employee competence. Other drawbacks include inadequate management commitment to the program, conflicts between the employees included in and those excluded from the skill-based pay program, inadequate training of managers, and poor program designs that increase labor costs without providing offsetting organizational benefits. Skill-based pay programs also require a heavy investment in training, as well as measurement systems capable of telling when employees have learned the new skills.

Flexible Benefit Programs

Flexible benefit programs *allow employees to choose the benefits they want, rather than having management choose for them. Flexible benefit programs often are called* cafeteria-style benefits programs. According to Leslie Ritter, a principal in Square Knot Consulting, a human resource consulting firm located in Addison, Texas, a typical corporation's benefits program currently is about 36 percent of its total employee compensation package.[33] That represents a huge cost, considering that only 3 percent or less is set aside annually for merit pay increases in most organizations. Under flexible benefit programs, employees decide—beyond a base program—which additional benefits they want, tailoring the benefits package to their needs. The idea is that employees can make important and intelligent decisions about their benefits. Some employees take all their discretionary benefits in cash; others choose additional life insurance, child or elder care, dental insurance, or retirement programs. Extensive benefit options may be highly attractive to an employee with a family. However, many benefits might be only minimally attractive to a young, single employee. Older employees value retirement programs more than younger employees and are willing to put more money into them. Employees with elderly parents may desire financial assistance in providing care for them. At Travelers Insurance Company employees can choose benefits of up to $5,000 a year for the care of dependent elderly parents.

Thousands of organizations now offer flexible benefits programs. They have become very popular because they offer three distinct advantages. First, they allow employees to make important decisions about their personal finances and to match employees' needs with their benefits programs. Second, such programs help organizations control their costs, especially for health care. Employers can set the maximum amount of benefit dollars they will spend on employees' benefits and avoid automatically absorbing cost increases. Third, such programs highlight the economic value of many benefits to employees. Most employees have little idea of the cost of benefits because the organization is willing to pay for them even though employees might not want some of them or might prefer alternatives.

Moreover, the changing workforce is causing employers to consider flexible benefits as a tool to recruit and retain employees. Starbucks Coffee Company believes that its use of flexible benefits programs has cut employee turnover from 150 to 60 percent. Starbucks calculates that hiring an employee costs $550. If so, a competitor with 300 percent turnover would have to hire three people at a cost of 3 × $550 = $1,650 per job per year, whereas Starbucks would need to spend only 0.6 × $550 = $330 per job per year.

Some limitations are associated with flexible benefit programs. First, because different employees choose different benefits packages, record keeping becomes more complicated. Sophisticated computer systems are essential for keeping straight the details of employees' records. Second, accurately predicting the number of employees that might choose each benefit is difficult. Such uncertainty may affect the firm's group rates for life and medical insurance, because the costs of such programs are based on the number of employees covered.

Managerial Guidelines

Management must make certain trade-offs when choosing among these four reward programs. Figure 6.3 provides some guidance for choosing a suitable reward program. It shows under what circumstances an individual or team program is appropriate and under what situations specific individual or team programs are most effective. If you answer the first five diagnostic questions *yes*, reward programs that permit individuals to calculate their own rewards might be of value. If you answer the first five diagnostic

FIGURE 6.3 Deciding among Alternative Reward Programs

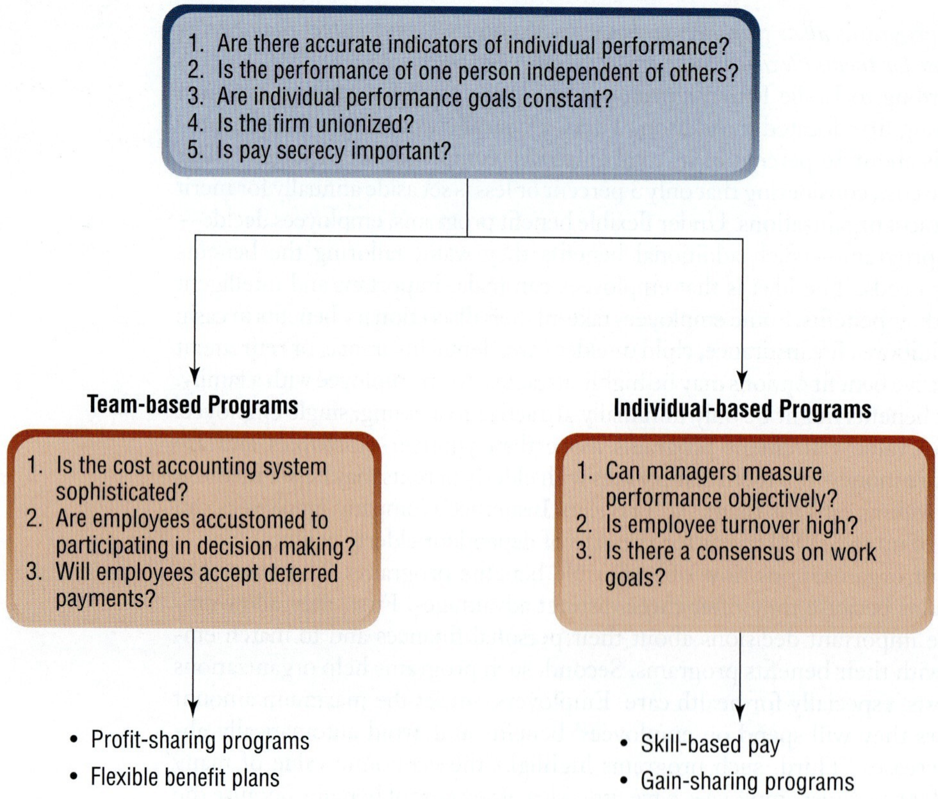

Source: Adapted from Wagner, J. A., and Hollenbeck, J. K. *Organizational Behavior*, 3rd ed. Englewood Cliffs, NJ: Simon & Schuster, 1998, 100.

questions *no*, team, department, or organization-wide reward systems might be more appropriate. If you want to reward individuals' performance, you should then ask three additional questions. If the answers to all of these questions are *yes*, a skill-based or gain-sharing program is appropriate. Similarly, if a group or team reward program seems appropriate, you should ask three additional questions. If the answers to all of these questions are *yes*, profit-sharing and flexible benefit programs are appropriate.

Reward Practices in Different Cultures

Organizations in various countries utilize different reward programs. Cultural values learned in childhood are passed down from one generation to the next and serve to differentiate one country from another. The information shown in Table 6.5 was taken from several large international studies. The researchers examined reward program differences in more than 50 cultures. In Chapter 2, we presented a framework to examine differences in thinking, feelings, ideas, and values that differentiate people of one culture from another.[34] We discussed the five dimensions that cultures can vary on: uncertainty avoidance, power distance, individualism/collectivism, gender role orientation, and long-term orientation.

Table 6.5 **Cultures and Reward Systems**

CULTURE	REWARD SYSTEM
Power distance	Pay based on individual performance
	Status symbols are important
	Pay tied to level in the organization's hierarchy
	Stock options to MBO
Individualism-collectivism	Pay based on team performance
	Profit sharing
	Little emphasis on extrinsic rewards
Gender role orientation	Extensive use of fringe benefits
	Gain sharing
	Goals set by participation linked to team achievements
	Pay equality
Uncertainty avoidance	Pay focuses on long-term orientation
	Seniority is important

Source: Adapted from Tosi, J. L., and Greckhamer, T. Culture & CEO compensation. *Organization Science*, 2004, 15, 657–670; and Hofstede, G. *Cultures Consequences*, 2nd ed. Thousand Oaks, CA: Sage, 2001.

Please reread pages 38–41 to refresh yourself with these dimensions. Using these dimensions and Table 6.5, let's explore how four of these five cultural dimensions impact differences in reward programs.[35] In high *uncertainty avoidance* cultures, reward programs emphasize seniority. There is strong loyalty to the company that leads to long-term employment. Rewards based on seniority are easy to administer and understand. These programs expose the employee to little risk because they are based on the performance of the company and not on individual and/or team efforts. There is high fear of failure. In Japan and other Asian cultures, employees receive their annual pay raise on their anniversary date (the day they joined the company). Instead of dismissing an employee for poor performance, managers move people from one department to another or into a "window seat," a job with little authority and responsibility. These practices allow the employee to save face.

In high *power distance* cultures, rewards are based on one's level within the managerial hierarchy. There are wide salary ranges between the top and lower level employees. Perquisites and status symbols are popular and expected. Profit sharing and other forms of variable compensation systems are relied on to motivate employees. Subordinates are motivated by the threat of sanctions.

In *individualistic cultures*, organizations expect individuals to look out for their own personal interests. The employee–employer compensation relationship is a business deal based on what the "labor market" will pay. Incentives are given to individuals. Therefore, skill-based programs and MBO programs are popular because they reward an individual's achievements. In collective cultures, team gain sharing is used to reinforce the team or group's achievements. At NSK, a ball-bearing manufacturer, and Toto, a toilet producer, when business slows down, these companies permit all workers to work shorter shifts and receive smaller pay checks.

In cultures that do not have a strong *gender role orientation*, equality among members is stressed. There are fewer differences in pay based on gender differences. Flexible benefits programs that allow the individual a wide choice of non–work-related benefits (e.g., child care, sabbatical leaves) are used to motivate employees to perform. For example, in Sweden, women in management take having families for granted and expect managers to find creative ways to help them work through this childbearing time.

CHAPTER SUMMARY

1. Explain how goal setting affects performance.

Goal setting is a process intended to increase efficiency and effectiveness by specifying the desired outcomes toward which individuals, departments, teams, and organizations should work. The goal-setting model developed emphasizes the challenges provided for the individual: goal difficulty, goal clarity, and self-efficacy. Setting difficult but clear and achievable goals for individuals who believe that they have the ability to complete their tasks leads to high performance. Four moderators—ability, goal commitment, feedback, and task complexity—influence the strength of the relationship between challenging goals and performance. If the individual has the ability, is committed to the goal, and is given feedback on progress toward achievement of the goal—and if the task is complex—high performance will result. All four moderators must be present to motivate a person to achieve goals. Four mediators—direction, effort, persistence, and task strategy—facilitate goal attainment. That is, these four characteristics channel or focus the person's motivational efforts. Performance, rewards, satisfaction, and consequences complete the model.

2. State the effects of goal setting on job satisfaction and performance.

Goal setting is one of the key mechanisms for increasing job satisfaction and performance because it permits employees to be self-motivated. Five requirements must be in place for goal setting to have positive benefits for the employee and organization: the employee's knowledge and ability, the employee's commitment to a goal, feedback on the task, establishment of subgoals on complex tasks, and a leader who removes obstacles that prevent employees from reaching their goals.

3. Describe four reward programs for improving performance.

Reward systems represent a powerful means for motivating high levels of individual and team performance. Four reward systems, in particular, are designed to enhance performance: gain sharing, profit sharing, skilled-based pay, and flexible benefits. Gain-sharing programs pay out regular cash bonuses to employees who increase their productivity, reduce costs, or improve quality. A similar program is profit sharing, which gives employees a portion of the organization's profits. Skilled-based pay systems pay a person according to the number and level of job-related skills that the employee masters. The value of these skills is determined by the organization. Flexible benefit programs allow employees to choose the benefits that are important to them.

KEY TERMS AND CONCEPTS

Cafeteria-style benefits programs
Feedback
Flexible benefit programs
Gain-sharing programs
Goal clarity
Goal commitment

Goal difficulty
Goal setting
Goals
Management by objectives (MBO)
Profit-sharing programs
Scanlon program
Skill-based pay programs
Task complexity

DISCUSSION QUESTIONS

1. Vivian Li, general manager at Concentric International, LLC, a company that specializes in human resource management in the Asia Pacific region, said: "If you cannot define it and measure it, you are not going to get it." What implications does this statement have for setting goals? For measuring them?
2. If a manager for American Airlines based in Dallas were transferred to Japan, what cultural issues might she encounter when rewarding employees?
3. Brenda Post, vice president of human resources at Kisco Senior Living, said that many times, managers commit the error of measuring the wrong behaviors with excruciating accuracy. What implications does this pose for managers using management by objectives?
4. How can organizations using a flexible benefit program tie its program to employee performance? What are the advantages of doing so? The disadvantages?
5. Use the goal-setting model found on page 164 to analyze Steve Letarte's NASCAR team, the Rainbow Warriors. Why is the team so effective?
6. What are the similarities and differences between gain-sharing and profit-sharing programs? Which system would motivate you to achieve greater performance? Why?
7. What factors influenced your level of goal commitment to this course? Did your level of commitment change after receiving feedback on an assignment or test? Explain.
8. What are some problems that employees might face in an organization that has adopted a skill-based pay program?
9. List your five most important personal goals. Evaluate the difficulty and clarity of each goal. Can these be measured? What are the implications, if any, of this assessment for your future?
10. What are some of the negative issues associated with goal-setting programs?
11. Visit Continental Airlines at www.continental.com. Click on "About Continental," then go to "Benefits and Incentives." How do the criteria for the various benefits and incentives illustrate the goal-setting model described in the chapter?

EXPERIENTIAL EXERCISE AND CASE

Experiential Exercise: Self Competency

Goal Setting[36]

Instructions

The following statements refer to a job you currently hold or have held. Read each statement and then select a response from the following scale that best describes your view. You may want to use a separate sheet of paper to record your responses and compare them with the responses of others.

Scale

Almost Never			**Almost Always**	
1	2	3	4	5

_____1. I understand exactly what I am supposed to do on my job.
_____2. I have specific, clear goals to aim for on my job.
_____3. The goals I have on this job are challenging.
_____4. I understand how my performance is measured on this job.
_____5. I have deadlines for accomplishing my goals on this job.
_____6. If I have more than one goal to accomplish, I know which are most important and which are least important.
_____7. My goals require my full effort.
_____8. My manager tells me the reasons for giving me the goals I have.
_____9. My manager is supportive with respect to encouraging me to reach my goals.
_____10. My manager lets me participate in the setting of my goals.
_____11. My manager lets me have some say in deciding how I will go about implementing my goals.
_____12. If I reach my goals, I know that my manager will be pleased.
_____13. I get credit and recognition when I attain my goals.
_____14. Trying for goals makes my job more fun than it would be without goals.
_____15. I feel proud when I get feedback indicating that I have reached my goals.
_____16. The other people I work with encourage me to attain my goals.
_____17. I sometimes compete with my coworkers to see who can do the best job in reaching our goals.
_____18. If I reach my goals, my job security will be improved.

_____19. If I reach my goals, my chances for a pay raise are increased.

_____20. If I reach my goals, my chances for a promotion are increased.

_____21. I usually feel that I have a suitable action program (s) for reaching my goals.

_____22. I get regular feedback indicating how I am performing in relation to my goals.

_____23. I feel that my training was good enough so that I am capable of reaching my goals.

_____24. Organization policies help rather than hurt goal attainment.

_____25. Teams work together in this company to attain goals.

_____26. This organization provides sufficient resources (e.g., time, money, and equipment) to make goal setting effective.

_____27. In performance appraisal sessions, my supervisor stresses problem solving rather than criticism.

_____28. Goals in this organization are used more to help you do your job well rather than punish you.

_____29. The pressure to achieve goals here fosters honesty as opposed to cheating and dishonesty.

_____30. If my manager makes a mistake that affects my ability to attain my goals, he or she admits it.

Scoring and Interpretation

Add the points shown for items 1 through 30. Scores of 120 to 150 may indicate a high-performing, highly satisfying work situation. Your goals are challenging and you are committed to reaching them. When you achieve your goals, you are rewarded for your accomplishments. Scores of 80 to 119 may suggest a highly varied work situation with some motivating and satisfying features and some frustrating and dissatisfying features. Scores of 30 to 79 may suggest a low-performing, dissatisfying work situation.

Questions

1. Using the concepts found in the goal-setting model, how might you increase work performance?
2. Why don't employees use goal-setting concepts in their everyday life to control their weight and personal habits?

Case: Diversity Competency

Allstate Insurance Company[37]

In today's competitive environment, companies continue to look for ways to improve their performance and achieve corporate goals. The task is not easy, but the team of human resource (HR) executives at Allstate Corporation has found that its diversity strategy has become one of the company's most important competitive weapons. It has long been Allstate's position that diversity is about neither political mandates nor legal obligation. Rather, the company's vision is stated this way: "Diversity is Allstate's strategy for leveraging differences in order to create a competitive advantage." This strategy has two major points: one internally focused and the other externally focused. According to Joan Crockett, vice president of human resources, the internal diversity focus is about "unlocking the potential for excellence in all workers by providing them the tools, resources, and opportunities to succeed." The external focus of diversity is about making certain that the workforce matches the experiences, backgrounds, and sensitivities of the markets it serves. In this context, Allstate managers view diversity not as a goal but as a process that is integrated into the daily life of the company.

All state launched its first affirmative action program back in 1969. In the early days, its commitment to diversity didn't always link recruitment, development, and retention strategies to business performance. The company focused more on affirmative action and diversity awareness through education and training. And while these initiatives were considered innovative in their day, they were not linked to Allstate's business strategy. Carlton Yearwood, director of diversity management, notes that the key question has become "How do you take this workforce of differences and bring them together in a more powerful way so that it can impact business results?" Allstate has taken four specific steps:

Step One: Succession Programming. A diverse slate of candidates is identified and developed for each key position. Allstate's management information system enables it to track and measure key drivers of career development and career opportunities for all of its more than 40,000 employees, ensuring that the company's future workforce will be diverse at all levels. Allstate's succession programming has made a difference that is easy to measure. Employment of women and minorities has grown at a rate far surpassing national averages. Today, 60 percent of Allstate's executives and managers are women and of that percent, 29 percent are Hispanics or people of color. Languages other than English, a total of 62, are spoken in more than 3,200 Allstate agencies. The company has a minority recruitment program that focuses on colleges and universities with the most diverse enrollments.

Step Two: Development. Through the company's employee development process, all employees receive an assessment of their current job skills and a road map for developing the critical skills necessary for advancement. Options include education, coaching and mentoring, and classroom training. Leaders are provided employee feedback on which they can base future development programs. In addition, all of Allstate's nonagent employees with service of more than one year have completed mandatory diversity training courses.

Step Three: Measurement. Twice a year the company takes a snapshot of all 40,000 employees through a survey called the Diversity Index. As a part of a larger online employee survey and feedback process called the Quarterly Leadership

Measurement System (QLMS), the Diversity Index taps the following questions:

1. To what extent does our company deliver quality service to customers regardless of their ethnic background, gender, age, and so on?
2. To what extent are you treated with respect and dignity at work? To what extent does your immediate manager/team leader seek out and utilize the different backgrounds and perspectives of all employees in your work group?
3. How often do you observe insensitive behavior at work, for example, inappropriate comments or jokes about ethnic background, gender, age, and so on?
4. To what extent do you work in an environment of trust where employees/agents are free to offer different opinions?

Management communicates the results of this survey via its intranet and actively solicits feedback from employees on creating action programs to solve problems and improve work processes.

Step Four: Accountability and Reward. To link compensation to the company's diversity goals, 25 percent of each manager's merit pay is based on the Diversity Index and the QLMS. Kathleen Zuzich, assistant vice president of HR, says that this sharpens the focus on the initiative. "What you measure is what people focus on. This really sends a clear signal that management of people and doing that well is really important."

To help employees maintain a balance between work and personal life, Allstate has a number of programs in place. For example, it has an on-site child-care center at its headquarters in Northbrook, Illinois, and three near-site child-care centers, all of which offer parents discount programs. It also has on-site dry cleaning, oil change, and postal and catering services and allows for flexible work arrangements for its employees. The Allstate Center for Assistive Technology (ACAT) helps employees with disabilities that include carpal tunnel syndrome, mobility impairments, and multiple sclerosis. For example, when one information technology employee began experiencing hearing problems, the ACAT team was deployed to fit him with a special home phone for use when he was on night call.

Questions

1. Using the model found on page 164, evaluate Allstate's goal-setting process. How does it work?
2. On page 171, we list some of the dimensions of an effective goal-setting program. Does Allstate meet these criteria?
3. What type of high-performance reward system should Allstate choose to motivate its employees to reach its diversity goals?

CHAPTER

7

Workplace Stress and Aggression

Learning Goals

When you have finished studying the chapter, you should be able to:

1. Explain the nature of and influences on creating stress.
2. Describe how different personalities react to stressful situations.
3. Identify the key sources of work-related stressors.
4. State the potential effects of severe stress on health, performance, and job burnout.
5. Apply individual and organizational guidelines for managing workplace stress.
6. Explain four major types of workplace aggression: bullying, sexual harassment, violence, and aggression toward the organization itself.

Learning from Experience

TRACY DAW'S STRESS AT INTEL UK

In a 2007 Court of Appeals ruling (Royal Courts of Justice in London, England), plaintiff Tracy Daw received £114,754 pounds (approximately $225,000) in personal injury compensation plus interest from Intel Incorporation (UK) Limited as a result of stress from her job that led to a nervous breakdown. Intel's U.K. headquarters office is located in Swindon, Wiltshire—about 80 miles west of London.

The Court of Appeals ruled that companies cannot rely on having a counseling service available if employees suffer ill health through overwork that results in severe stress and depression. The court found that Daw had complained 14 times about her workload and that she had three managers who made conflicting demands. Her job at Intel involved transferring payroll details from mergers and acquisitions. Daw was putting in 50- to 60-hour weeks when she had her breakdown. At the same time, she had significant parental and family responsibilities. After one of her managers found her in tears, Daw sent a lengthy e-mail explaining what the problems were and saying her feelings were similar to those she had suffered from postnatal depression. Daw was considered an "excellent" employee and Intel said it would provide another member of staff to help but failed to do so.

The company appealed the ruling, saying that it should not be liable because it provided a counseling service. But Lord Justice Pill said counseling services were not "a panacea by which employers can discharge their duty of care in all cases. The respondent, a loyal and capable employee, pointed out the serious management failings which were causing her stress and the failure to take action was that of management."

The court held that an employer's short-term counseling service could not have reduced the risk of a breakdown, since it did not reduce her workload—the cause of the stress. At most, such a service could only have advised the employee to see her own doctor. This was insufficient to discharge the employer's duty to provide a healthy working environment. Although the court recognized that Intel could not have reasonably foreseen Daw's breakdown in health by virtue of her medical history, this was not considered to be relevant.

For more information on Intel UK, visit the organization's home page at www.intel.co.uk.

LEARNING CONTENT

Tim Dixon, Daw's attorney, comments: "It has become difficult for people to sue employers for work-related stress in recent years, so this is a landmark victory. The difficulty of this type of case is that the employee has to prove not only that they were given too much work, but that the stress they were under was likely to get them ill, and that their boss knew it. Fortunately, Tracy had kept notes of every e-mail and meeting where she was asking for help. A judge initially agreed that there had been negligence. We were fairly confident that we would win on appeal."

Daw worked at Intel from 1988 through 2001, when she had a massive nervous breakdown. Daw noted that she was doing the job of nearly two people and her managers ignored pleas for help. After her breakdown, Daw indicated it was not a hard decision to take Intel to court. She states: "I was just so angry that they'd let me down and put me in this situation, even though I had done everything I could to flag up the problems I was having. Just airing it in court has been therapeutic for me."[1]

Tracy Daw's experience of stress at work is unique, but not an isolated incident, nor is the legal remedy for Daw limited to employees in the United Kingdom. The potential legal consequences for ignoring stressful conditions created by managers are anticipated to increase in the coming years in many countries.

There are several noteworthy lessons for managers and employers from this case.[2] The court made it clear that when an employee is experiencing stress related to excessive workloads, the presence of a workplace counseling service will not automatically serve to discharge the employer's duty of care in stress claims. Even if an employer has systems in place to support employees who are suffering from work-related stress, this is no substitute for putting an action plan in place to reduce their workload. Failure to do so may result in the employer being found negligent.

A failure by management to combat work-related stress is likely to lead to a finding that the employer has failed to discharge the duty of care owed to its staff. The court accepted that the employer did not have prior knowledge that the employee was susceptible to work-related depression. But despite this lack of knowledge, the employer was still held liable, because it was aware of Daw's excessive workload.

Employers must put measures in place to reduce workloads when receiving complaints from staff who cannot cope. Otherwise, they will risk paying considerable damages in claims for personal injury caused by the working environment. It is our position that proactive stress management leadership and practices are not just the thing to do to avoid lawsuits—they are the right and effective thing to do. We address some of the lessons from Daw's experience for employees later in the chapter.

Job stress is a common and costly problem in the workplace, leaving few workers untouched. For example, studies of workplace stress and aggression report the following:

- Sixty-five percent of workers said that workplace stress had caused physical and psychological difficulties, and more than 10 percent described these as having major effects.
- Twenty-five percent view their jobs as the number one stressor in their lives.
- Fourteen percent of respondents had felt like striking a coworker in the past year, but didn't.
- Twenty-five percent have felt like screaming or shouting because of job stress; 10 percent are concerned about an individual at work they fear could become violent.
- Nine percent are aware of an assault or violent act in their workplace, and 18 percent had experienced some sort of threat or verbal intimidation in the past year.
- Job stress is more strongly associated with health complaints than financial or family problems.[3]

Managers who ignore employee stress, or assign it a low priority, are likely to see declines in productivity and morale and increased legal costs. The negative consequences of stress are so dramatic that managers need to (1) take action to reduce excessive employee stress in the workplace and (2) assist employees in developing stress-coping skills. Tracy Daw experienced both physical and emotional consequences of high levels of stress at Intel.

In this chapter, we (1) explain the nature of stress, (2) discuss the role of personality differences in handling stress, (3) identify key causes of stress, (4) review the effects of stress, (5) outline actions that can be taken to help manage stress, and (6) discuss three types of workplace aggression.

NATURE OF STRESS

Learning Goal

1. Explain the nature of and influences on creating stress.

Stress *is the excitement, feeling of anxiety, and/or physical tension that occurs when the demands placed on an individual are thought to exceed the person's ability to cope.*[4] This is the most common view of stress and is often called *distress* or negative stress. Stressors *are the physical or psychological demands in the environment that cause this condition.* They can take various forms, but all stressors have one thing in common: They create stress or the potential for stress when an individual perceives them as representing a demand that exceeds that person's ability to respond.

Fight-or-Flight Response

Numerous changes occur in a person's body during a stress reaction. Breathing and heart rates increase so that the body can operate with maximum capacity for physical action. Brain wave activity goes up to allow the brain to function maximally. Hearing and sight become momentarily more acute, and muscles ready themselves for action. An animal attacked by a predator in the wild basically has two choices: to fight or to flee. The animal's bodily responses to the stressor (the predator) increase its chances of survival. The fight-or-flight response *refers to the biochemical and bodily changes that represent a natural reaction to an environmental stressor.*[5] Similarly, our cave-dwelling ancestors benefited from this biological response mechanism. People gathering food away from their caves would have experienced a great deal of stress upon meeting a saber-toothed tiger. In dealing with the tiger, they could have run away or stayed and fought. The biochemical changes in their bodies prepared them for either alternative and contributed to their ability to survive.

The human nervous system still responds the same way to stressors. This response continues to have survival value in a true emergency. However, for most people most of the time, the "tigers" are imaginary rather than real. In work situations, for example, a fight-or-flight response usually isn't appropriate. If an employee receives an unpleasant work assignment from a manager, physically assaulting the manager or storming angrily out of the office obviously is professionally inappropriate. Instead, the employee is expected to accept the assignment calmly and do the best job possible. Remaining calm and performing effectively may be especially difficult when the employee perceives an assignment as threatening and the body is prepared to act accordingly.

Medical researcher Hans Selye first used the word *stress* to describe the body's biological response mechanisms. Selye considered *stress* to be the nonspecific response of the human body to any demand made on it.[6] However, the body has only a limited capacity to respond to stressors. The workplace makes a variety of demands on people, and too much stress over too long a period of time will exhaust their ability to cope with those stressors.

Influences on the Stress Experience

A variety of factors influence how an individual experiences stress. Figure 7.1 identifies four of the primary factors: (1) the person's perception of the situation, (2) the person's past experience, (3) the presence or absence of social support, and (4) individual differences in reacting to stress.

Perceptions. In Chapter 3 we defined *perception* as the process by which people select, organize, interpret, and respond to information from the world around them. Employee perceptions of a situation can influence how (or whether) they experience stress. For example, two employees, Lenae and Richard, have their job responsibilities substantially changed—a situation likely to be stressful for many people. Lenae views the new responsibilities as an opportunity to learn new competencies. She perceives the change to be a vote of confidence from management in her ability to be flexible and take on new challenges. In contrast, Richard perceives the same situation to be extremely threatening. He concludes that management is unhappy with his performance and using this as a tactic to make him fail so that he can be fired. When given heavy work assignments by three different Intel managers, Tracy Daw did not perceive any options other than appealing to them repeatedly for extra help due to the substantial increased workload assigned to her.

Past Experiences. Richard may perceive a situation as more or less stressful based on how familiar he is with the situation and his prior experiences with the particular stressors involved. Past practice or training may allow Lenae to deal calmly and competently with stressors that would greatly intimidate less experienced or inadequately

FIGURE 7.1 Common Influences on the Stress Experienced

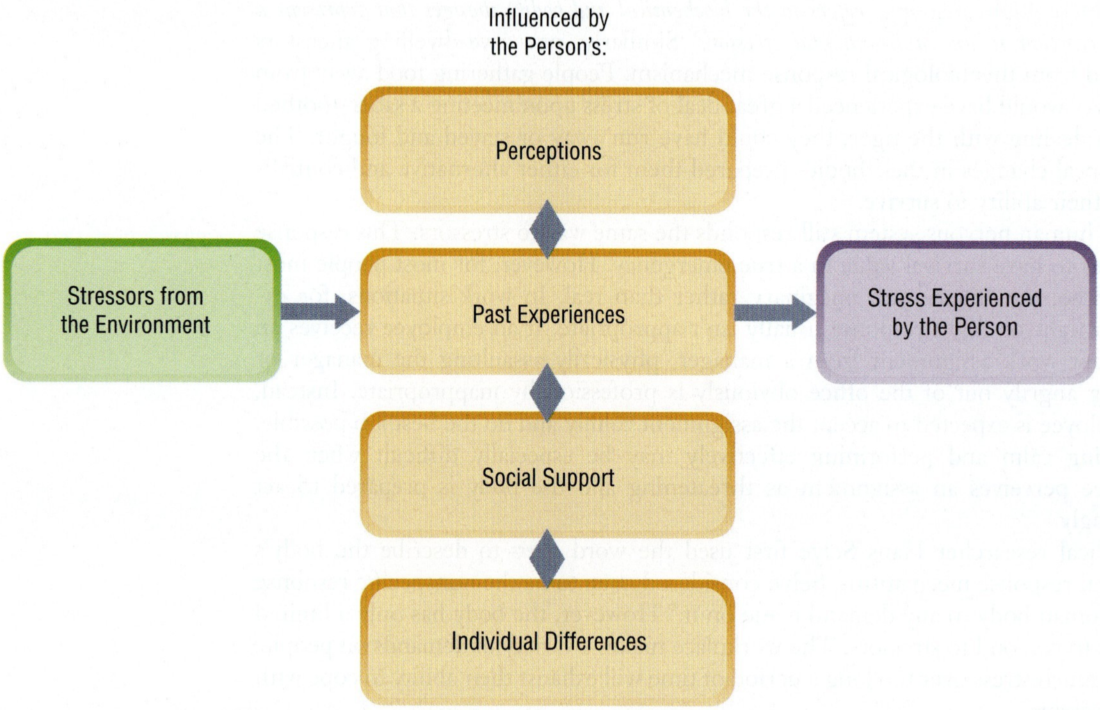

trained employees. The relationship between experiences and stress is based on reinforcement (see Chapter 4). Positive reinforcement or previous success in a similar situation can reduce the level of stress that a person experiences under certain circumstances. In contrast, punishment or past failure under similar conditions can increase stress under the same circumstances.

Social Support. The presence or absence of other people influences how individuals in the workplace experience stress and respond to stressors.[7] The presence of coworkers may increase Richard's confidence, allowing him to cope more effectively with stress. For example, working alongside someone who performs confidently and competently in a stressful situation may help Richard behave similarly. Conversely, the presence of fellow workers may irritate Lenae or make her anxious, reducing her ability to cope with stress. Also, recall that the appeals court that heard Tracy Daw's case against Intel concurred that she received no social support from the three managers who continued to pile work on her despite repeated pleas for assistance.

Individual Differences. Each person's motivation, attitudes, personality, and abilities influence the degree and nature of work stress experienced and how the individual responds.[8] Simply stated, each person is different, as we discussed in Chapters 2 and 3. What one person considers a major source of stress, another may hardly notice. Personality characteristics, in particular, may explain some of the differences in the ways in which an employee experiences and responds to stress. For example, the Big Five personality factor that we labeled *emotional stability* in Chapter 2 seems to be important in individual responses to various stressors in the work setting. Individuals at one extreme of emotional stability (described as stable, relaxed, resilient, and confident) are more likely to cope well with a wide variety of work stressors. In contrast, individuals at the other extreme (described as reactive, nervous, and self-doubting) typically have greater difficulty coping with the same stressors. We further discuss relationships between personality and stress in the following section.

PERSONALITY DIFFERENCES AND STRESS

Learning Goal

2. Describe how different personalities react to stressful situations.

Several personality traits are related to stress, including self-esteem and locus of control (personality traits discussed in Chapter 2). A personality trait may affect how a person will perceive and react to a situation or an event as a stressor.[9] For example, an individual with low self-esteem is more likely to experience stress in demanding work situations than is a person with high self-esteem. Individuals high in self-esteem typically have more confidence in their ability to meet job demands than do those with low self-esteem. Employees with high internal locus of control may take more effective action, more quickly, in coping with a sudden emergency (a stressor) than might employees with high external locus of control. Individuals high in internal locus of control are likely to believe that they can moderate the stressful situation.

Before reading further, please respond to the statements in Table 7.1. This self-assessment exercise is related to the discussion that follows.

The Type A Personality

The Type A personality *refers to a person involved in a never-ending struggle to achieve more and more in less and less time*. In contrast, the Type B personality *refers to a person who tends to be easygoing and relaxed, patient, a good listener, and takes a long-range view of things.* Characteristics of the Type A personality type include

- a chronic sense of urgency about time;
- an extremely competitive, almost hostile orientation;

Table 7.1

A Self-Assessment of Type A Personality

Choose from the following responses to answer the questions below:

A. Almost always true C. Seldom true

B. Usually true D. Never true

____	1.	I do not like to wait for other people to complete their work before I can proceed with my own.
____	2.	I hate to wait in most lines.
____	3.	People tell me that I tend to get irritated too easily.
____	4.	Whenever possible, I try to make activities competitive.
____	5.	I have a tendency to rush into work that needs to be done before knowing the procedure I will use to complete the job.
____	6.	Even when I go on vacation, I usually take some work along.
____	7.	Even when I make a mistake, it is usually due to the fact that I have rushed into the job before completely planning it through.
____	8.	I feel guilty for taking time off from work.
____	9.	People tell me I have a bad temper when it comes to competitive situations.
____	10.	I tend to lose my temper when I am under a lot of pressure at work.
____	11.	Whenever possible, I will attempt to complete two or more tasks at once.
____	12.	I tend to race against the clock.
____	13.	I have no patience for lateness.
____	14.	I catch myself rushing when there is no need.

Score your responses according to the following key:

- *An intense sense of time urgency* is a tendency to race against the clock, even when there is little reason to. The person feels a need to hurry for hurry's sake alone, and this tendency has appropriately been called "hurry sickness." Time urgency is measured by items 1, 2, 8, 12, 13, and 14. Every A or B answer to these six questions scores one point.

  Your score = ____
- *Inappropriate aggression and hostility* reveal themselves in a person who is excessively competitive and who cannot do anything for fun. This inappropriately aggressive behavior easily evolves into frequent displays of hostility, usually at the slightest provocation or frustration. Competitiveness and hostility are measured by items 3, 4, 9, and 10. Every A or B answer scores one point.

  Your score = ____
- *Polyphasic behavior* refers to the tendency to undertake two or more tasks simultaneously at inappropriate times. It usually results in wasted time due to an inability to complete the tasks. This behavior is measured by items 6 and 11. Every A or B answer scores one point.

  Your score = ____
- *Goal directedness without proper planning* refers to the tendency of an individual to rush into work without really knowing how to accomplish the desired result. This usually results in incomplete work or work with many errors, which in turn leads to wasted time, energy, and money. Lack of planning is measured by items 5 and 7. Every A or B response scores one point.

  Your score = ____

TOTAL SCORE = ____

If your score is 5 or greater, you may possess some basic components of the Type A personality.

Source: Reproduced with permission of the Robert J. Brady Co., Bowie, Maryland, 20715, from its copyrighted work *The Stress Mess Solution: The Causes and Cures of Stress on the Job*, by G. S. Everly and D. A. Girdano, 1980, 55.

- thinking about other things while talking to someone;
- an impatience with barriers to task accomplishment; and
- a sense of guilt when relaxing or taking a vacation.[10]

Two medical researchers first identified the Type A personality when they noticed a recurrent personality pattern in their patients who suffered from premature heart disease.[11] In addition to the characteristics just listed, *extreme* Type A individuals often speak rapidly, are preoccupied with themselves, and are dissatisfied with life. They tend to give quick replies to questions with no pause to deliberate before answering the questions. Type A personalities may give sarcastic, rude, and hostile responses. They may try to appear to be humorous, but with the underlying intent to be hurtful.

The questionnaire in Table 7.1 measures four sets of behaviors and tendencies associated with the Type A personality: (1) time urgency, (2) competitiveness and hostility, (3) polyphasic behavior (trying to do several things at once), and (4) a lack of planning. Medical researchers have discovered that these behaviors and tendencies often relate to life and work stress. They tend to cause stress or make stressful situations worse than they otherwise might be.

Current research suggests that the Type A personality description is too broad to predict adverse health impacts accurately. Rather, research now indicates that only certain aspects of the Type A personality—particularly anger, hostility, and aggression—may be related to severe stress and health reactions.[12] Type A individuals with these specific attributes appear to be two to three times more likely to develop adverse health impacts than are Type B individuals.

The following Self Competency feature reports on Stuart Krohn, who exhibited extreme Type A attributes and, as a result of an intense experience, engaged in a self assessment to moderate his Type A behaviors. Krohn is the coach of the Santa Monica Rugby Club. This club is made up of three teams—men, women, and youth (boys and girls) who live in the greater metropolitan Los Angeles area. The women's team and the youth squad were formed in 2005.[13]

Self Competency

Stuart Krohn's Personal Development

© PhotoLink/Photodisc/Getty Images

After years of hypercompetitiveness, former rugby player and current rugby coach Stuart Krohn finally developed the realization that rugby is just a game and that life is not a full-time competitive arena.

Under the guidance of coach Stuart Krohn since 1999, the Santa Monica Rugby Club has built a program that is the envy of other clubs. Krohn, an American whose international rugby pedigree includes captaining a world-class Hong Kong team as well as stints in France, Australia, and South Africa. A few of the achievements by the men's team over the years Krohn has been their coach include

- three consecutive appearances in the national final four,
- back-to-back national club championships in 2005 and 2006, and
- an invitation to join the Super League in 2007.

Krohn has demonstrated his competencies as a coach and, at one time, his over-the-top Type A–like hypercompetitiveness. He recalls: "Everything was a battleground—a ping-pong table, a conversation. I could feel the blood start to rush, and I could feel myself reacting to something that I shouldn't have reacted to. Even as a kid, it was all about winning." Krohn says he had to win every argument with his girlfriend, turned conversations at dinner parties into intense competitions, and nurtured a rage and hatred for other teams and referees that was sometimes overwhelming.

Krohn's competitive nature proved beneficial in some respects. He played rugby internationally for decades, winning two world championships. Now 45 years old, he led the Santa Monica club to a national championship in 2005 and 2006.

But life changed for Krohn—in his 35th year. His girlfriend dumped him, he says, because he was so intensely competitive with her. Then another thing happened that opened his eyes: A younger, less-experienced teammate was badly injured. Only miraculous medical care prevented him from being a quadriplegic. Krohn visited his teammate in the intensive care unit every day. He comments: "This guy was … fighting for his life, and I sat there with a lot of time to think. I finally realized that this is a game. I realized that everybody is not against me and life is not a full-time competitive arena."

Krohn hasn't turned into a pussycat: He's still a "yeller" at practice and on the sidelines. Team members say he pushes players sometimes to the breaking point. But he has now been happily married for years and says he approaches competition in a very different way today than he did previously.

In addition to coaching for the Santa Monica Rugby Club, he is one of the founding teachers, and of course rugby coach, at View Park Prep Charter School in the Crenshaw district. He says that they haven't won a game in three years and they attract the kids who aren't doing other sports. Krohn states: "When I'm coaching the kids, I don't focus on winning above their character development and their attitude toward the sport. They have to get that right first. I didn't get that when I was a kid."

For more information on the Santa Monica Rugby Club and Stuart Krohn, visit the organization's home page at www.santamonicarugby.com.

The Hardy Personality

What aspects of personality might protect individuals from the negative health impacts of stress? Individual traits that seem to counter the effects of stress are known collectively as the hardy personality—*a person with a cluster of characteristics that includes feeling a sense of commitment, responding to each difficulty as representing a challenge and an opportunity, and perceiving that one has control over one's own life.*[14] The hardy personality is characterized by

- a sense of personal control over events in their lives;
- a tendency to attribute one's own behavior to internal as opposed to external causes (recall the discussion of attribution in Chapter 3);
- a strong commitment to their work and personal relationships; not detaching themselves when the going gets tough; and
- an ability to view unexpected change or potential threats as challenges and opportunities for growth.[15]

A high degree of hardiness *reduces the negative effects of stressful events.* Hardiness seems to reduce stress by altering the way in which people perceive stressors. The concept of the hardy personality provides a useful insight into the role of individual differences in reactions to stressors. An individual having a low level of hardiness perceives many events or situations as stressful; an individual having a high level of hardiness perceives fewer events or situations as stressful. A person with a high level of hardiness isn't overwhelmed by challenging or difficult situations. Rather, faced with a stressor, the hardy personality copes or responds constructively by trying to find a solution—to control or influence events and situations. This behavioral response typically reduces stress reactions, moderates blood pressure increases, and reduces the probability of adverse health impacts.

Through development of the *self competency* as demonstrated by Stuart Krohn, we contend that a person may come to reflect the attributes of the hardy personality. Recall from Chapter 1 that the *self competency* involves the ability to assess your own strengths and weaknesses, set and pursue professional and personal goals, balance work and personal life, and engage in new learning—including new or changed skills, behaviors, and attitudes.

Table 7.2 provides a brief questionnaire for you to reflect on your own sense of hardiness. If you perceive your sense of hardiness is lacking, the good news is that you can do something about it. We provide suggestions in this chapter and others for developing your hardiness.

Table 7.2 Assessing Your Sense of Hardiness

Instructions:
Please respond to each of the statements below as truthfully as you can. Use the following scale:

Not like me	Seldom	Sometimes	When I think about it	Usually	Always
0	1	2	3	4	5

_____1. I have a set of things that I would like to accomplish in my life.
_____2. I spend quiet time thinking about my life and my world.
_____3. When I think about it, I wake up in the morning full of optimism and I look forward to starting my day.
_____4. I have a clear picture of what the next phase of my life will look like.
_____5. I try to learn new things.
_____6. I sleep well and am able to relax when I have free time.
_____7. I believe that I have control over most things in my life.
_____8. I look forward to the changes that happen in my life and view them as challenges.
_____9. I have goals in life and I am clear on what they are.
_____10. I am usually an optimistic person when it comes to how I view my future.
_____11. I am adventuresome, continually pushing to try new things.
_____12. I would consider myself to be very goal oriented.

Score:
Add points for items 1 through 12 = _____.

Possible Interpretations of Your Hardiness Score:

- **0–24** You likely don't feel that you can control your world and you don't spend a lot of time making plans. Your ability to handle stress is not as high as you would like.
- **25–36** You do some planning, but probably wish you did more. You tend to be "other directed" and not always in control of your life.
- **37–48** You are more self-directed and normally handle stress well. You tend to be goal oriented, though you could be more focused on setting goals.
- **49–60** You are very goal oriented and know the difference between being stressed and handling stress.

Source: Adapted from Retirement Lifestyle Centers. *How hardy is your personality?* www.retirementlifestyle.com (April 2007).

KEY SOURCES OF STRESSORS

Learning Goal
3. Identify the key sources of work-related stressors.

Employees often experience stress in both their personal and work lives. Understanding these two sources of stress and their possible interaction is important. To consider either source in isolation may give an incomplete picture of the stress that an employee is experiencing. However, our primary focus is on work-related stressors.

Work-Related Sources

Work-related sources of stress take a variety of forms. Figure 7.2 presents a framework for thinking about and diagnosing organizational sources of work-related stress. It identifies seven principal work-related stressors. This framework shows that internal individual factors influence the ways in which each employee experiences these stressors.

Workload. For some employees, having too much work to do and not enough time or resources to do it is a major stressor. Role overload *exists when the demands of the job exceed the capacity of a manager or employee to meet all of them adequately*. Some employees may be in a continuous condition of role overload. For Tracy Daw at Intel, the role overload was a major source of stress and contributor to her breakdown. Surveys commonly identify work overload or "having to work too hard" as a major source of stress.[16]

FIGURE 7.2 Sources of Work-Related Stressors and Experienced Stress

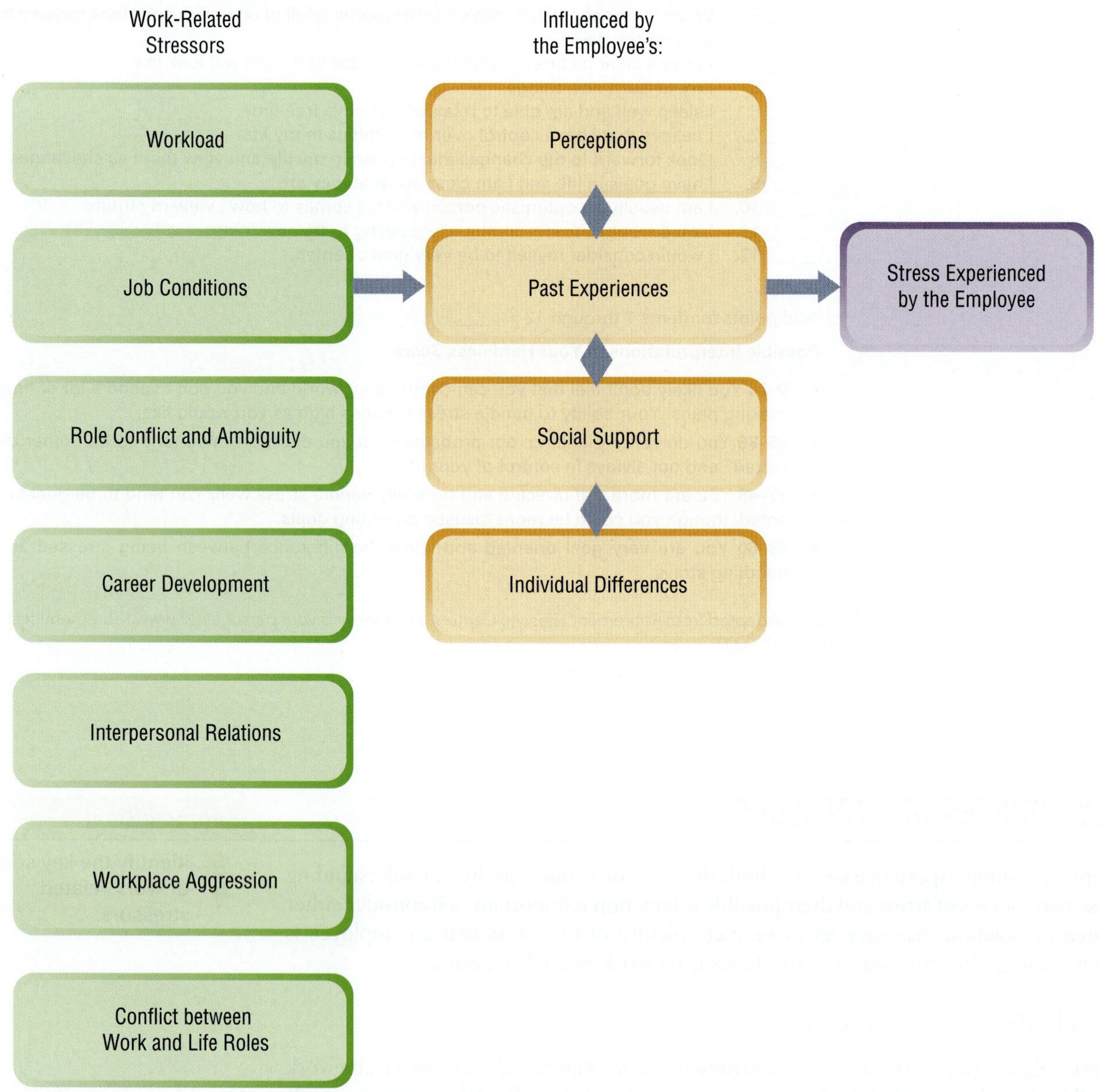

Having too little work to do also may create stress. Have you ever had a job with so little to do that the workday seemed never to end? If so, you can understand why many employees find too little work stressful. Managers sometimes are guilty of trying to do their subordinates' work, or *micromanage*, when their jobs aren't challenging enough. Micromanaging might reduce the manager's stress caused by boredom, but it is likely to increase subordinates' stress because the superior constantly watches them or second-guesses their decisions.

Job Conditions. Poor working conditions represent another important set of job stressors. Temperature extremes, loud noise, too much or too little lighting, radiation, and air pollution are but a few examples of working conditions that can cause stress in employees. Heavy travel demands or long-distance commuting are other aspects of jobs that employees may find stressful. Poor working conditions, excessive travel, and long hours all add up to increased stress and decreased performance. Recall that Tracy Daw was working 50- to 60-hour weeks prior to her breakdown and had three different managers who gave her no support—all of which contributed to her poor working conditions. At the same time, Daw had significant parental and family responsibilities.

Cutting-edge technology, while clearly of great benefit to society in general and many individuals in particular, nevertheless has created job conditions that may be quite stressful. Many employees are receiving massive volumes of e-mail, text messages, phone calls, and voice mail messages. A number of technology-assisted jobs have both maximum flexibility and maximum stress. It is often easy to perform work anytime, anyplace.[17] For some employees, this makes it difficult to draw mental boundaries between work and home.

Role Conflict and Ambiguity. Role conflict *refers to differing expectations of or demands on a person at work that become excessive.* (We discuss role conflict in detail in Chapter 12.) Role ambiguity *occurs when an employee is uncertain about assigned job duties and responsibilities.* Role conflict and role ambiguity may be particularly significant sources of job-related stress. Many employees suffer from role conflict and ambiguity, but conflicting expectations and uncertainty particularly affect managers. The responsibility for the behavior of others and a lack of opportunity to participate in important decisions affecting their job are other aspects of employees' roles that may be stressful.[18]

Career Development. Major stressors related to career planning and development involve job security, promotions, transfers, and developmental opportunities. An employee can feel stress from underpromotion (failure to advance as rapidly as desired) or overpromotion (promotion to a job that exceeds the individual's competencies). The current wave of reorganizations and downsizings may seriously threaten careers and cause stress. For example, Chrysler announced in 2007 that it plans to eliminate 13,000 blue-collar and white-collar jobs—16 percent of its workforce—by 2009. The workforce reduction represents an effort to save money, be more efficient and return to profitability.[19] When jobs, teams, departments, or entire organizations are restructured, employees often have numerous career-related concerns: Can I perform competently in the new situation? Can I advance? Is my new job secure? Typically, employees find these concerns very stressful. At Chrysler, the employees not laid off face the stress of Chrysler being spun off from DaimlerChrysler and what that might mean for their careers.

Interpersonal Relations. Teams and groups have a great impact on the behavior of employees. (We explore these dynamics in Chapter 11.) Good working relationships and interactions with peers, subordinates, and superiors are crucial aspects of organizational life, helping employees achieve personal and organizational goals. When relationships are poor, they can become sources of stress. In a recent national poll, 90 percent of respondents said they had experienced incivility at work. Of these, 50 percent said they had lost work time worrying about the incident, and 50 percent contemplated changing jobs to avoid a recurrence.[20] Incivility *refers to rudeness and employees' lack of regard for one another*. It includes the violation of workplace norms for mutual respect.[21] Consider two anonymous employee reports of workplace incivility and their feelings of distress:

- *Female employee:* "During a presentation that I was making to all of the company's international country managers and vice presidents, the division president stood up and shouted, 'No one is interested in this stuff.' His comment made me so nervous and upset that I could barely go on. I had been with this company for many years; you'd think he could have offered me a little respect for that alone."
- *Male employee:* "I was pulling off a payroll preparation cycle for a month during December, and I entered '12' (the calendar month) when I should have entered '6' (the fiscal month). The payroll cycle was garbage therefore. The accountant called me insulting names with my new boss, who was sitting right there next to me. It was humiliating and unfair. It was my first payroll preparation cycle with the company. I was new—it was an honest mistake."[22]

A high level of political behavior, or "office politics," also may create stress for managers and employees. The nature of relationships with others may influence how employees react to other stressors. In other words, interpersonal relationships can be either a source of stress or the social support that helps employees cope with stressors.

A recently uncovered source of stress for one's career relates to the desire to do the right and ethical thing in light of higher management's resistance or indifference to ethical behavior. The Society for Human Resources invited members to tell about ethical dilemmas that they encountered in the workplace. To protect the privacy of respondents, *HRMagazine* used fictitious names and omitted specific company information in reporting a sample of the stories shared by members. We share the story of Bruce in this Ethics Competency feature. Would you have done the same as Bruce in coping with the stressful dilemmas of wanting to do the right thing, caring for his family, and preserving his career options?[23]

Ethics Competency

Bruce's Stressful Dilemmas

When Bruce was recruited as the human resources director at his former employer, he was initially excited. The job offered a substantial salary increase, a car allowance, a very generous bonus plan, and the possibility of a future promotion—something not available at his previous company.

He did, however, have one qualm: He had heard rumors that this large Midwestern firm hired undocumented immigrant workers. When Bruce asked about these rumors, his interviewer admitted there had been a problem in the past. The interviewer assured Bruce that "they had cleared that situation up and I should not be concerned."

Soon after he began the new job, however, Bruce received a disquieting report from the company's new 401(k) provider. Several Social Security numbers didn't match the names of the employees who had provided them. Bruce began an investigation, but his boss quickly ordered him to stop. He explained that they couldn't afford to terminate those employees "because that would leave the company shorthanded." When Bruce expressed his concern about this deliberate violation of federal immigration laws, the company's leadership was unworried. Bruce states: "They reasoned that the INS [Immigration and Naturalization Service] had bigger fish to fry. If they were caught, the fine was an acceptable business expense since the company was making huge profits."

"I knew," says Bruce, "that [if the company got in trouble] the buck was going to stop on my desk." He also knew that his company's owners were "not the kind of folks you like to make enemies of." He believed there was a real danger that they would retaliate against him if he persisted in questioning their illegal activities. What's more, Bruce's company was privately owned by a very powerful and influential family in his community. Thus, the chances that their excesses would be "splashed all over the front page of the newspaper" were slim, he says.

Bruce opted to take a position at a new company—with a $15,000 pay cut. He also gave up a large bonus ($25,000 to $35,000) scheduled to be paid at the end of the year. Bruce comments: "The loss of $15,000 in annual income has been very difficult. [I'm] trying to raise a family and help kids through college." (Two of his five children are in college now.) Nevertheless, he says, he would make the same decision again. He and his wife believe it's their responsibility to "set examples of appropriate behavior" for their children.

Professionally, too, Bruce believes that "HR is held to a higher standard" because it is privy to so much confidential information. "I simply could not have lived with myself, knowing what I knew and not taking action." Do you think the action taken by Bruce was adequate? Explain.

Workplace Aggression. A disturbing source of stressors is workplace aggression. We discuss four types of workplace aggression in the last major part of this chapter: bullying, sexual harassment, workplace violence, and aggression toward the organization itself.

Conflict between Work and Life Roles. A person has many roles in life (e.g., employee, family member, little league coach, church volunteer, to name a few). Only one of these roles is associated with work (although some individuals may hold more than one job at a time).[24] These roles may present conflicting demands and may become sources of stress. Furthermore, work typically meets only some of a person's goals and needs. Recall the opening Learning from Experience feature in which Tracy Daw expressed conflicting pressures and stress from the demands of three different managers and in her roles as parent and spouse.

Other goals and needs may conflict with career goals, presenting an additional source of stress. For example, employees' personal desires to spend time with their families or have more leisure time may conflict with the extra hours they must work to advance their careers. The large number of dual-career couples with children has brought work and family role conflicts into sharp focus. For example, when the children are sick, who takes primary responsibility for taking them to the doctor or staying home with them?

Life Stressors

The distinction between work and nonwork stressors isn't always clear, although a primary source of stress for many employees clearly is pressures between work and family demands.[25] As Figure 7.3 illustrates, both work and family pressures may contribute to work–family stress because pressures in one area can reduce a person's ability to cope with pressures in the other. These incompatible pressures trigger stress, which, in turn, leads to work–family conflicts. These conflicts trigger possible outcomes such as dissatisfaction, frustration, and depression.

Life stressors *are tensions, anxieties, and conflicts that stem from pressures and demands in people's personal lives.* People must cope with a variety of life stressors; they deal with these stressors differently because of personality, age, gender, experience, and other characteristics. However, life stressors that affect almost everyone are those caused by significant changes: divorce, marriage, death of a family member, and the like. People have a limited capacity to respond to stressors. Too much change too quickly can exhaust the body's ability to respond and result in negative consequences for a person's physical and mental health.

Table 7.3 presents a variety of stressful events that college students may face. Based on a current social readjustment rating scale, each event is rated on a 100-point scale,[26] with 1 indicating an event that is not stressful and 100 an extremely stressful event. An

FIGURE 7.3 The Path of Work–Family Pressures, Stress, and Conflict

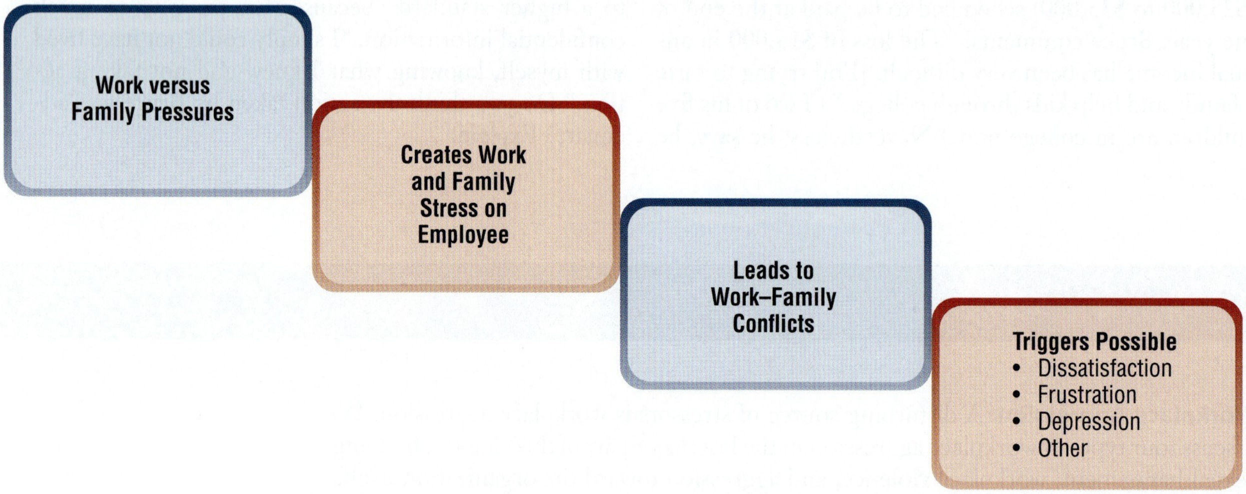

event labeled "high level of stress" might be assigned 71 to 100 points, depending on the specific stress experienced by the student. "Moderate level of stress" for an event might be scored from 31 to 70 points, and a "low level of stress" for an event may be assigned scores from 1 to 30 points by the student. During the course of a year, if a student experiences several events in the high level of stress range, there is a 50–50 chance the student will get sick as a result of the excessive stress.

Recall that stress is the body's general response to any demand made on it. The list of stressful events in Table 7.3 contains both unpleasant events, such as failing a course, and pleasant events, such as finding a new love interest. This dual nature of life stressors demonstrates that they involve both negative and positive experiences. For example,

Table 7.3 Stressful Events for College Students

EVENTS HAVING HIGH LEVELS OF STRESS	EVENTS HAVING RELATIVELY LOW LEVELS OF STRESS
• Death of parent	• Change in eating habits
• Death of spouse	• Change in sleeping habits
• Divorce	• Change in social activities
• Flunking out	• Conflict with instructor
• Unwed pregnancy	• Lower grades than expected
EVENTS HAVING MODERATE LEVELS OF STRESS	
• Academic probation	• Major injury or illness
• Change of major	• Parents' divorce
• Death of close friend	• Serious arguments with romantic partner
• Failing important course	• Outstanding achievement
• Finding a new love interest	
• Loss of financial aid	

Source: Adapted from Baron, R. A., and Byrne, D. *Social Psychology: Understanding Human Interaction*, 6th ed. Boston: Allyn & Bacon, 1991, 573.

vacations and holidays actually may be quite stressful for some people but very relaxing and refreshing for others. In addition, viewing unpleasant life events as having only negative effects is incorrect. People often can both cope with and grow from experiencing unpleasant events, as Stuart Krohn experienced as a result of his girlfriend dumping him and the near-death injury of his teammate. Of course, people typically enjoy the positive effects and stimulation of pleasurable events, such as significant accomplishments, vacations, or gaining a new family member.

EFFECTS OF STRESS

Learning Goal

4. State the potential effects of severe stress on health, performance, and job burnout.

High levels of stress can have both positive and negative effects. Our concern with high levels of work stress focuses on the negative effects because of their potential effects on individual and organizational effectiveness as well as one's health.

The potential effects of high levels of work stress occur in three main areas: physiological, emotional, and behavioral.[27] Examples of the effects of severe distress in these areas are as follows:

- Physiological effects of stress may include increased blood pressure, increased heart rate, sweating, hot and cold spells, breathing difficulties, muscular tension, gastrointestinal disorders, and panic attacks.
- Emotional effects of stress may include anger, anxiety, depression, low self-esteem, poor intellectual functioning (including an inability to concentrate and make decisions), nervousness, irritability, resentment of supervision, and job dissatisfaction.
- Behavioral effects of stress may include poor performance, absenteeism, high accident rates, high turnover rates, alcohol and substance abuse, impulsive behavior, and difficulties in communication.

The effects of work stress have important implications for organizational behavior and organizational effectiveness. We examine some of these effects in terms of health, performance, and job burnout.

Effects on Health

Health problems commonly associated with stress include back pain, headaches, stomach and intestinal problems, upper respiratory infections, and various mental problems. Although determining the precise role that stress plays in individual cases is difficult, some illnesses appear to be stress related.[28]

Stress-related illnesses place a considerable burden on people and organizations. The costs to individuals seem more obvious than the costs to organizations. This was the case for Tracy Daw, who experienced a nervous breakdown due to the excessive work demands at Intel UK. Let's review some of the organizational costs associated with stress-related disease. First, costs to employers include increased premiums for health insurance, as well as lost workdays from serious illnesses (e.g., ulcers) and less serious illnesses (e.g., headaches). Estimates are that each employee who suffers from a stress-related illness loses an average of 16 days of work a year. In addition, it is estimated that health-care costs are 50 percent higher for employees who report higher levels of stress.[29] Second, more than three-fourths of all industrial accidents are caused by a worker's inability to cope with stress-related emotional problems. Third, legal problems for employees are growing, as Intel UK managers found when they failed to address the intense stress experienced by Tracy Daw. As you may recall from the chapter-opening feature, Intel UK was ordered to pay approximately $225,000 to Tracy Daw. The number of stress-related worker compensation claims is increasing. The link between the levels of stress in the workplace and worker compensation claims is clear. When employees experience higher amounts of stress, more worker compensation claims are filed. Studies have shown similar patterns in many different industries.[30]

Post-traumatic stress disorder *is a psychological disorder brought on, for example, by horrible experiences in combat during wartime, acts of violence and terrorism, and the like.*[31] Courts are now recognizing post-traumatic stress disorder as a condition that may justify a damage claim against an employer. Employees have successfully claimed suffering from this disorder as a result of sexual harassment, violence, and other traumatic circumstances in the workplace. Awards of damages in the millions of dollars have resulted from court cases involving workplace post-traumatic stress disorder claims.

Effects on Performance

The positive and negative effects of stress are most apparent in the relationship between stress and performance. Figure 7.4 depicts the general stress–performance relationship in the shape of an arch. At low levels of stress, employees may not be sufficiently alert, challenged, or involved to perform at their best. As the curve indicates, increasing the arousal of stress may improve performance—but only up to a point. An optimal level of stress probably exists for most tasks. Beyond that point, performance begins to deteriorate.[32] At excessive levels of stress, employees are too agitated, aroused, or threatened to perform well.

Managers often want to know the optimum stress points for both themselves and their subordinates. This information, however, is difficult to pin down. For example, an employee may be absent from work frequently because of boredom (too little stress) or because of overwork (excessive stress). The curve shown in Figure 7.4 changes with the

FIGURE 7.4 Typical Relationship between Performance and Stress Arousal

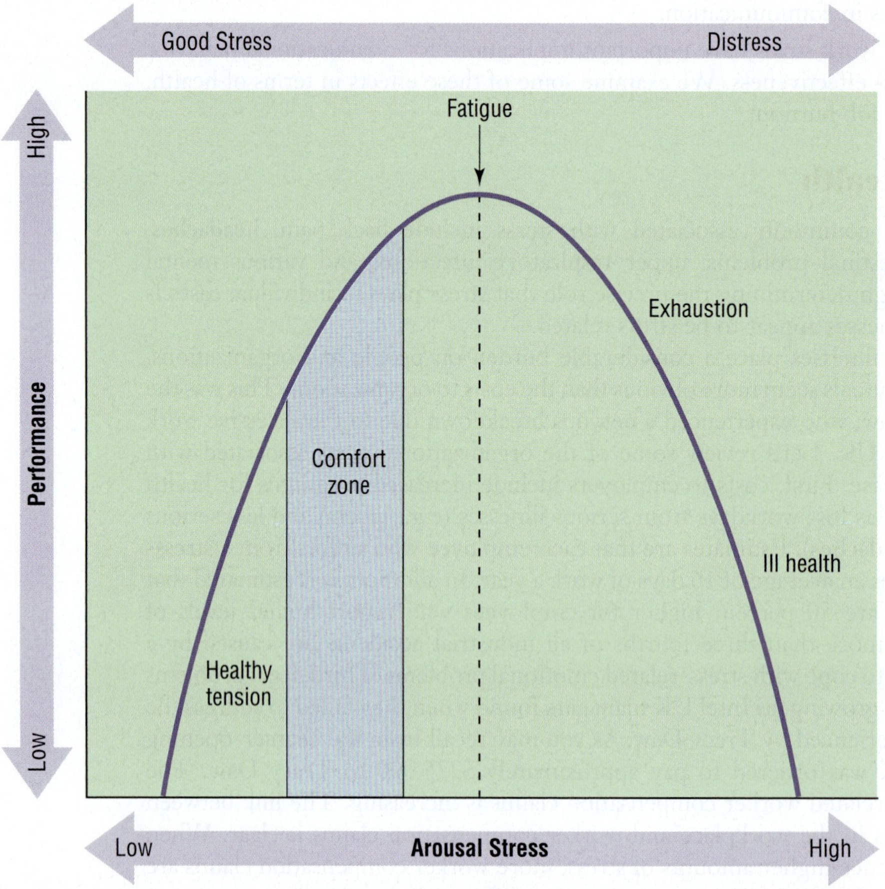

Adapted from Nixon, P. *Stress: The human function curve.* American Institute of Stress. www.stress.org (March 2007).

situation; that is, it varies for different people and different tasks. Too little stress for one employee may be just right for another on a particular task. Similarly, the optimal amount of stress for a specific individual for one task may be too much or too little for that person's effective performance of other tasks.

As a practical matter, managers should be more concerned about excessive stress than with how to add to stress. Motivating individuals to perform better is always important, but attempting to do so by increasing the level of stress is shortsighted. Studies of the stress–performance relationships in organizations often show a strong negative association between the amount of stress in a team or department and its overall performance. That is, the greater the stress employees are experiencing, the lower their productivity. This negative relationship indicates that these work settings are operating on the right-hand side (excessive stress arousal) of the curve shown in Figure 7.4. Managers and employees in these situations need to find ways to reduce the number and magnitude of stressors.

Effects of Job Burnout

Job burnout *refers to the adverse effects of working conditions under which stressors seem unavoidable and sources of job satisfaction and relief from stress seem unavailable*. Common indicators of burnout include

- emotional exhaustion—including chronic fatigue, tiredness, and a sense of being physically run down;
- depersonalization of individuals—including cynicism, negativity, and irritability toward others; and
- feelings of low personal accomplishment—including losing interest and motivation to perform, inability to concentrate, and forgetfulness.[33]

Depersonalization *refers to the treatment of people as objects*. For example, a nurse might refer to the "broken knee" in room 306, rather than use the patient's name. Doing so allows the nurse to disassociate with the patient as a person. The patient just becomes another thing to be treated according to rules and procedures.

Common indicators of job burnout include emotional exhaustion, chronic fatigue, tiredness, and a sense of being physically run down.

Most job burnout research has focused on the human services sector of the economy—sometimes called the "helping professions." Burnout is thought to be most prevalent in occupations characterized by continuous direct contact with people in need of aid. The highest probability of burnout occurs among those individuals who have both a high frequency and a high intensity of interpersonal contact. This level of interpersonal contact may lead to emotional exhaustion, a key component of job burnout.[34] Those who may be most vulnerable to job burnout include social workers, nurses, police officers, and teachers. Burnout also may affect managers or shop owners who are under increasing pressure to reduce costs, increase profits, and better serve customers.

Individuals who experience job burnout seem to have some common characteristics. Three characteristics in particular are associated with a high probability of burnout:

- experiencing a great deal of stress as a result of job-related stressors,
- tending to be idealistic and self-motivating achievers, and
- seeking unattainable goals.[35]

The burnout syndrome thus represents a combination of certain individual attributes and the job situation. Individuals who suffer from burnout often have unrealistic expectations concerning their work and their ability to accomplish desired goals, given the nature of the situation in which they find themselves. Job burnout is not something that happens overnight: The entire process typically takes a great deal of time. The path to job burnout is illustrated by Figure 7.5. One or more of the working conditions listed, coupled with the unrealistic expectations or ambitions of the individual, can lead eventually to a state of complete physical, mental, and emotional exhaustion. Under conditions of burnout, the individual can no longer cope with the demands of the job and willingness to try drops dramatically.

FIGURE 7.5 The Path to Job Burnout

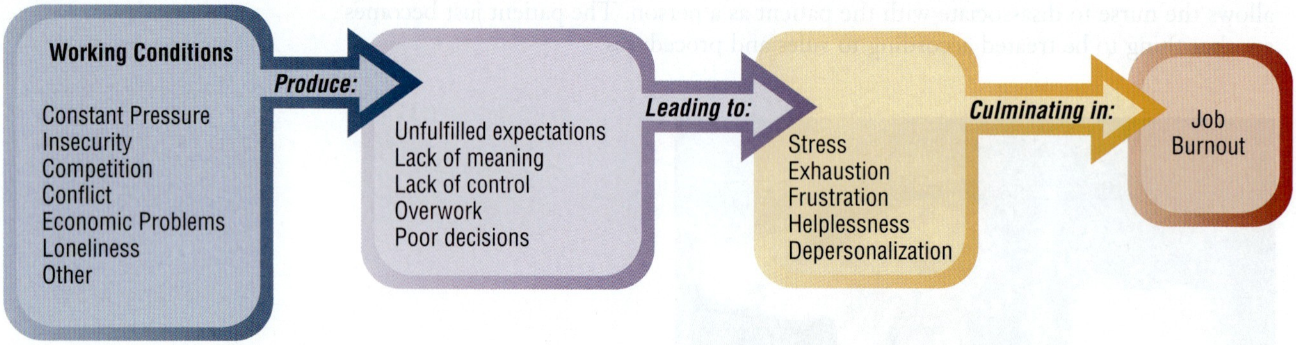

Learning Goal

5. Apply individual and organizational guidelines for managing workplace stress.

MANAGING STRESS

Individual and organizational guidelines to help managers and employees cope with stress have become increasingly popular as stress has become more widely recognized as a problem. A number of guidelines are available to individuals and organizations for managing stress and reducing its harmful effects. Stress management *refers to the actions and initiatives that reduce stress by helping the individual understand the stress response, recognize stressors, and use coping techniques to minimize the negative impact of high levels of experienced stress.*[36]

Individual Guidelines

Managing stress by an individual includes guidelines designed to (1) eliminate or control the sources of stress and (2) make the individual more resistant to or better able to cope with stress. The first step in individual stress management involves recognizing the stressors that are affecting the person's life. Next, the individual needs to decide what to do about them. Personal goals and values, coupled with practical stress management skills, can help an individual cope with stressors and reduce negative stress reactions.

Some of the guidelines for managing stress by an individual include the following:

- Plan ahead and practice good time management. Frame your aspirations (e.g., getting a job) as things you'd really like to achieve, rather than in absolute terms (e.g., I *absolutely must* get a job now).
- Get plenty of exercise, eat a balanced diet, get adequate rest, and generally take care of yourself.
- View the difficulties you encounter as opportunities to learn and challenges to be tackled, rather than as problems to be solved or difficulties to overcome.
- Recognize and minimize the tendency to be a perfectionist.
- Concentrate on balancing your work and personal life. Always take time to have fun.
- Learn relaxation techniques and maintain a sense of humor.
- Communicate with those who can provide social support and take action to help reduce the stressors.[37]

An individual can use relaxation techniques during the workday to cope with job demands. For example, a common "relaxation response" to stress is to (1) choose a comfortable position, (2) close your eyes, (3) relax your muscles, (4) become aware of your breathing, (5) maintain a passive attitude when thoughts surface, and (6) continue for a set period of time (e.g., 20 minutes).[38]

Within the work environment, the application of the knowledge, skills, and abilities of the communication competency is vital in managing stress. Consider the insights of Steve Widom, one of the founders and chief technology officer at Chordial Solutions. This firm provides enterprise software and services to businesses. It is located in Carrollton, Texas (near Dallas). In information technology (IT) jobs, Widom contends that stress is more manageable when you learn to expect the occasional 2:00 A.M. call about a system that's down. He chuckles: "If systems were perfect, we would be bored. When we signed up for IT, we knew what we were getting into." Because IT is project based, Widom emphasizes that stress comes in waves and smart stress management involves riding those waves skillfully. When those times come, he works as hard as those employees who report to him. Widom states: "When they work all night, I'm there with them. My rule of thumb is, for every all-nighter you pull, you need two days of comp time."[39]

Organizational Guidelines

As suggested in Figure 7.6, organizational stress management programs are often designed to reduce the harmful effects of stress (distress) in one or more of the following ways: (1) identify and reduce or eliminate the work stressors, (2) assist employees in changing their perceptions of the stressors and experienced stress, and (3) assist employees to cope more effectively with the outcomes from stress.

Reducing Work Stressors. Practices aimed at eliminating or modifying work stressors include

- improvements in the physical work environment;
- job redesign;
- changes in workloads and deadlines;
- changes in work schedules, more flexible hours, and sabbaticals; and
- greater levels of employee participation, particularly in planning changes that affect them.

Improvements in role clarity and role analysis can be particularly useful in removing or reducing role ambiguity and role conflict—two main sources of stress. When

FIGURE 7.6 Targets of Organizational Stress Management Programs

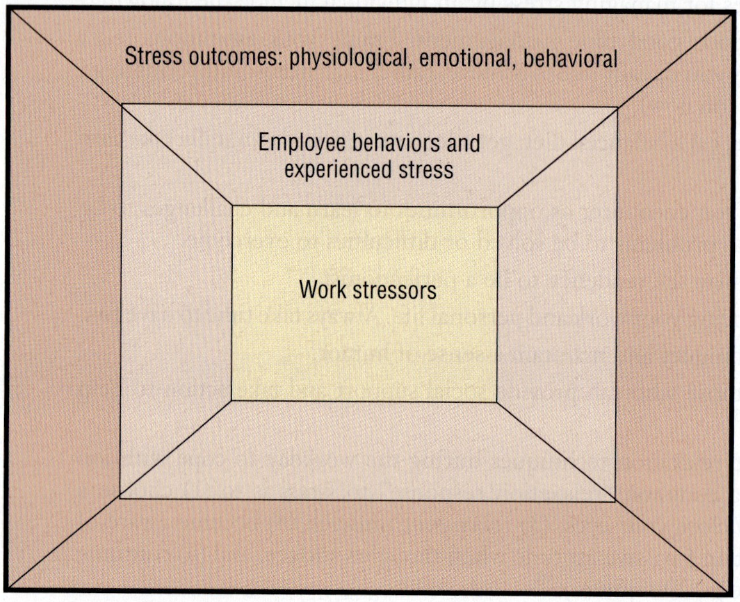

diagnosing stressors in the workplace, managers should be particularly aware that an employee's lack of control over the tasks they perform heightens stress. The greatest stress occurs when jobs are high in stressors and low in controllability, as was perceived to be the situation by Tracy Daw at Intel UK. Thus, involvement of employees in organizational changes that will affect them, work redesign that reduces uncertainty and increases control over the pace of work, and improved clarity and understanding of roles all should help reduce work stress. An important way to provide employees with more control and less stress is to give individuals more control over their time.

Larry Sanders is the chairman and chief executive of Columbus Regional Healthcare System, headquartered in Columbus, Georgia. He is the recipient of a number of awards for his leadership in health-care and civic organizations. Sanders recognizes the importance of giving employees appropriate control over their work and the need for effective communication to effectively manage stress—both his own and subordinates. Sanders comments:

> *My style of management is inclusive, open, and honest. I delegate and then expect those I left in charge to use their resources and capabilities to fulfill the responsibility. I was never micromanaged, and I don't micromanage. I was allowed to use the full range of my abilities to accomplish tasks, and I expect those who work with me and around me to do the same thing. Micromanagement kills the morale of an organization faster than anything else does.*[40]

Modifying Behaviors. Improvements targeted at behaviors and experiences of stress include

- team building,
- career counseling and other employee assistance programs,
- workshops on time management,
- workshops on job burnout to help employees understand its nature and symptoms, and
- training in relaxation techniques.

Dividing stress management programs into these categories doesn't mean that they are not related. In addition, such programs might overlap in terms of their impact on the three target areas mentioned previously. For example, a workshop dealing with role problems might clarify job descriptions and duties, reducing the magnitude of these potential stressors. At the same time, through greater knowledge and insight into roles and role problems, employees might be able to cope more effectively with this source of stress. Similarly, career counseling might reduce career concerns as a source of stress while improving the ability of employees to cope with career problems.

Creating Wellness Programs. One comprehensive remedy for improving the ability of individuals to cope with stress is a wellness program—*a health management initiative that incorporates the components of disease prevention, medical care, self-care, and health promotion.*[41] The Wellness Councils of America (WELCOA) is a nonprofit membership organization based in Omaha, Nebraska. It is dedicated to promoting healthy lifestyles. Its primary focus is on building *Well Workplaces*—organizations dedicated to the health of their employees. The council provides a blueprint to help organizations create programs that help employees make better lifestyle choices and that can have a positive impact on the organization's profits. To date, more than 600 organizations have received the Well Workplace Award. WELCOA and other wellness programs are driven by, among other factors, the continuous increases in health-care costs paid by employers and employees. The leading causes of illness are often preventable. Tobacco use, alcohol and substance abuse, sedentary lifestyles, poor nutritional habits, excessive and unnecessary

LEADER INSIGHT

There is no question that workplace wellness is worth it. The only question is whether you're going to do it today or tomorrow. If you keep saying you're going to do it tomorrow, you'll never do it. You have to get on it today.
Warren Buffett, Chairman, Berkshire Hathaway

© SW Productions/Digital Vision/Getty Images

Many organizational wellness programs focus on preventing the leading causes of illness among employees, including sedentary lifestyles and poor nutrition habits.

stressors in the workplace, and inadequate employee abilities to cope with stress are examples of targets of wellness programs.[42] The scope and features of wellness programs among organizations vary widely.

The following Change Competency feature provides an overview of Cianbro's wellness program, which has evolved over time.[43] Cianbro, headquartered in Pittsfield, Maine, is a diversified general contractor that operates in states along the U.S. Atlantic seaboard. It has 3,000 employees, who are referred to as team members. Most employees are male, blue-collar workers.

Change Competency

Cianbro's Evolving Wellness Program

Cianbro Corporation's health-care costs doubled between 1996 and 2002. Projections were that by 2012 the company's family health-care costs would be $18,000 per employee. That estimate is up from $8,200 in 2002. Rita Bubar, the firm's human resource manager, comments: "We calculated that by 2012, we would be paying over $30 million per year for health insurance costs, and we just couldn't afford that. But employees still need coverage." Cianbro implemented an employee wellness program to minimize the toll that modifiable health risks exact on its workforce productivity and bottom line. Here are some of the features of the firm's Healthy Life Style Program.

- *Voluntary participation.* Team members and spouses join the company's self-designed program voluntarily. Those who don't want to change at-risk behavior pay more for their medical coverage. Bubar comments: "We meet with our team members on the job sites, so these programs are conducted during the workday and with back-up on the phone. Most spouse interviews were done on the phone because the spouses are spread all over the place." However, she notes that the effectiveness of face-to-face meetings is higher. Thus, late-afternoon and early evening sessions were implemented at various sites for spouses in 2007.
- *Assesses at-risk behaviors.* Team members as well as spouses complete a health risk appraisal with an educator who identifies at-risk controllable behaviors (e.g., smoking, overweight, blood pressure, sedentary lifestyle, cholesterol levels, and the like).
- *Behavior modification plan.* Once the assessment is completed, the employees work with the company's health educator to develop a plan to reduce and eliminate controllable at-risk behaviors with ongoing follow-ups. Bubar remarks: "We are coordinating things in the total wellness environment and reminding people what they can do to help control their health. We have had a lot of success in our program. In tracking our risk reduction, we are pleased to say we have been able to reduce risk in all areas."
- *Monitors employee progress.* The health educators capture baseline information on each employee, give team members and spouses a summary report, set up another appointment with them, and meet several times during the year to follow up on where they are with the program. This program has been extremely successful. Bubar adds: "But wellness programs do need incentives to help make them work. People don't do things only to improve their own health." So Cianbro gives a discount off the employee's medical costs for joining the program. For a single person, the discount amounts to a little over $600 a year, and for a family, more than $1,600. At the end of 2001, the first year of the program, Cianbro had 77 percent participation; as of 2007, 86 percent.
- *Makes wellness practical.* The company distributes a monthly newsletter to employees' homes that is educational, tying wellness to its actual benefits programs, and includes a healthy recipe card. So it is not only telling people to be healthy and eat healthy, but it is also giving them tools and tips to do so. It also uses its internal website, to which employees have 24-hour access, to promote wellness activities and provides a 24-hour nurse hotline.
- *Emphasizes preventive care.* To catch things early, keep employees healthier, and hold health-care costs down, Cianbro has also designed its health-care plan to pay 100 percent of the costs for preventive care, x-rays, lab visits, and diagnostic testing both in and out-of-network.
- *Importance of wellness.* Cianbro creates "Wellness on Worksite" bulletins and distributes them to its

projects once per week. "They are designed to be read or discussed verbally by a volunteer that we have. [They are] short 10-minute bites about wellness that can be reviewed quickly as our crew is doing stretches every morning because that is part of how we start our workday," Bubar explained. There are other facets of Cianbro's ever evolving wellness initiatives and actions.

For more information on Cianbro, visit the organization's home page at www.cianbro.com.

WORKPLACE AGGRESSION

Learning Goal

6. Explain four major types of workplace aggression: bullying, sexual harassment, violence, and aggression toward the organization itself.

Workplace aggression *includes a variety of behaviors that are intended to have the effect of harming a person within or directly related to (e.g., customer, service representative, employee) the organization or the organization itself.*[44] Aggressive workplace behavior can be grouped into three broad categories: (1) hostility—abusive verbal or symbolic behaviors such as 'the silent treatment"; (2) obstructionism—behaviors that are designed to hamper the individual's performance such as refusing to provide needed resources; and (3) overt aggression—many types of assault, violence, and destruction of property.[45] Recent studies of the overall percentage and estimated number of U.S. employees who experience psychological and physical aggression show that such aggression is excessive. In one study, 41 percent of the respondents—representing 47 million U.S. employees—reported having experienced one or more forms of psychological aggression during the previous 12 months. In addition, 6 percent of respondents—representing 7 million U.S. employees—experienced one or more forms of workplace violence during the previous 12 months. In another study, nearly 45 percent of the respondents reported that they had worked for an abusive manager.[46]

Defense Mechanisms and Aggression

A variety of defense mechanisms have been identified for why some employees engage in workplace aggression. Some of the underlying defense mechanisms used by individuals to justify aggressive behaviors include the following[47]:

- Hostile attribution bias—*implicit assumption that people tend to be motivated by the desire to harm others.* This bias is used at times to explain why others behave as they do. Individuals with a strong motive to aggress may even see friendly acts by others as being driven by hidden/hostile agendas that are designed to inflict harm. This type of attribution enables aggressive persons to rationalize their own hostile behaviors as acts of self-defense intended to head off physical or verbal attack by others.
- Potency bias—*the implicit assumption by the aggressive individual that interactions with others are contests to establish dominance versus submissiveness.* This bias rationalizes the use of aggression to dominate others as demonstrating strength, bravery, control, and fearlessness. The failure to act aggressively is seen as weakness, fear, and cowardice. Thus, aggressive individuals see their behaviors as a means of gaining respect from others and feel that to show weakness is to encourage powerful others to take advantage of them.
- Retribution bias—*aggressive individuals think that taking revenge (retribution) is more important than preserving relationships.* There is a tendency to see retaliation as a more rational behavior than reconciliation. For example, aggression is seen as justifiable if it is thought to restore respect or exact retributions for a perceived wrong. Retaliation is seen by aggressive individuals as more reasonable than

forgiveness, vindication is seen as more reasonable than reconciliation, and obtaining revenge is seen as more reasonable than maintaining a relationship. This bias often underlies justification for aggressions stimulated by wounded pride, reduced self-esteem, and perceived disrespect.

- Derogation of target bias—*aggressive individuals see those they wish to make (or have made) targets of aggressions as evil, immoral, or untrustworthy.* This type of influence enables them to see the targets of aggression as deserving of it.
- Social discounting bias—*aggressive individuals believe that social customs reflect free will and the opportunity to satisfy their own needs.* They have a disdain for traditional ideals and conventional beliefs and are often cynical and critical of social events. They show a lack of sensitivity, empathy, and concern for social customs. Socially deviant behaviors intended to harm others are justified by claiming that they allow the aggressive individuals to obtain freedom of expression, relief from the cycles of social customs, and liberation from social relationships. These and other underlying mechanisms for rationalizing aggression may be seen in incidents of bullying, sexual harassment, and workplace violence.

In the remainder of this section, we present the core features of four major types of workplace aggression—bullying, sexual harassment, violence, and aggression toward the organization. As suggested in Figure 7.7, there are potential overlaps and relationships among these types of workplace aggression. For example, an employee may encounter a variety of bullying behaviors, some of which may escalate into the category of workplace violence and destruction or theft of organizational property.

Workplace Bullying

Workplace bullying *is repeated and persistent negative actions directed toward one or more individuals that involve a perceived power imbalance and create a hostile work environment.*[48] Unreasonable behavior refers to acts that a reasonable person, when considering all of the circumstances, would see as victimizing, humiliating, undermining, or threatening an employee or group of employees. Bullying often involves a misuse or abuse of power. For the employees subject to it, they can experience difficulties in defending themselves. Bullying cuts across race, religion, and gender. It involves offensive behaviors that a reasonable person would see as creating an intimidating, hostile, or abusive work environment. Normally, bullying must involve repeated incidents and a pattern of behavior.

Bullies at work engage in a variety of behaviors ranging from condescension to rage. Table 7.4 is a questionnaire that presents 24 negative acts that have been identified as

FIGURE 7.7 Potential Overlaps among Four Types of Workplace Aggression

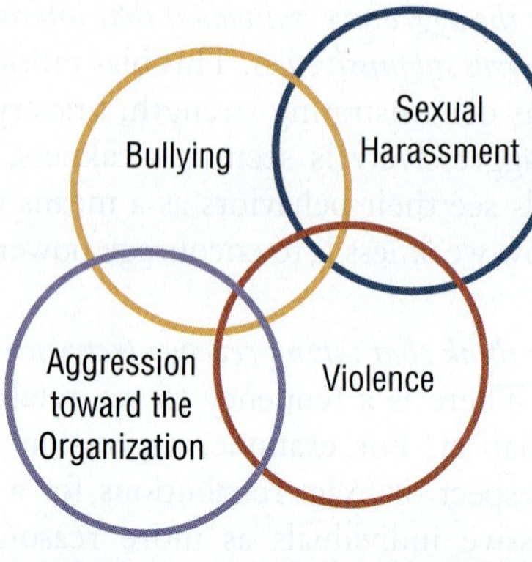

components of workplace bullying. This questionnaire enables you to assess whether you have experienced any of these bullying behaviors over the past six months and, if so, how frequently and with what intensity (cumulative number of negative acts experienced—ranges from one act to a maximum of all 24 acts). In brief, the greater the frequency of a negative act over a six-month period and the greater the number of negative acts, the more severe the degree of bullying.[49]

Women as well as men may bully others at work. Women bullies target other women an overwhelming 84 percent of the time. Men bullies target women in 69 percent of the cases. Women are most often the targets of bullying.[50]

A critical characteristic of workplace bullying is that it harms the health of the individual subjected to it. Health concerns from bullying need to be distinguished from routine office politics, teasing, incivilities, and somewhat off-color stories/jokes. All of the effects of stress identified previously may be experienced as a result of bullying. In

Table 7.4 **Negative Acts Associated with Workplace Bullying**

Instructions:
Indicate how often you may have experienced each of the negative acts associated with workplace bullying during the past six months.
Use the following scale and record your response next to each statement below:

Never	Occasionally (less than monthly)	Monthly	Weekly	Daily
0	1	2	3	4

_____1. Had information withheld that affected your performance.
_____2. Been exposed to an unmanageable workload.
_____3. Ordered to do work below your level of competence.
_____4. Given tasks with unreasonable/impossible targets/deadlines.
_____5. Had your opinions and views ignored.
_____6. Had your work excessively monitored.
_____7. Reminded repeatedly of your errors or mistakes.
_____8. Humiliated or ridiculed in connection with your work.
_____9. Had gossip and rumors spread about you.
_____10. Had insulting/offensive remarks made about you.
_____11. Been ignored, excluded, or isolated from others.
_____12. Received hints or signals from others that you should quit your job.
_____13. Been intimidated with threatening behavior.
_____14. Experienced persistent criticism of your work and effort.
_____15. Been ignored or faced hostile reactions when you approached the person.
_____16. Had key tasks removed, replaced with trivial unpleasant tasks.
_____17. Had false allegations made against you.
_____18. Subjected to excessive teasing and sarcasm.
_____19. Been shouted at or targeted with spontaneous anger (or rage).
_____20. Pressured into not claiming something to which you were entitled.
_____21. Been subjected to demeaning practical jokes.
_____22. Received unwanted sexual attention.
_____23. Received offensive remarks or behavior related to your race or ethnicity.
_____24. Experienced threats of violence or abused/attacked.

Scoring:
Total the number of points assigned. In general, the greater the *frequency* (never to daily) and the greater the intensity (none to 24 acts), the greater the degree of bullying experienced. Based on your responses to this instrument, how do you perceive and interpret the degree of bullying (if any) experienced by you?

Source: Adapted from Einarsen, S., Hoel, H., Zapf, D., and Cooper, C. L. The concept of bullying at work. In Einarsen, S., Hoel, H., Zapf, D., and Cooper, C. L. (Eds.). *Bullying and Emotional Abuse in the Workplace: International Perspectives in Research and Practice.* London: Taylor & Francis, 2003, 3–30; Lutgen-Sandvik, P., Tracy, S. J., and Alberts, J. K. Burned by bullying in the American workplace. *Journal of Management Studies*, 2007, 44, 837–862.

addition, individuals who report severe forms of bullying identify experiencing the following major symptoms:

- *General anxiety disorder*—evidenced by anxiety, excessive worry, disruptive sleep, stress headaches, and racing heart rate.
- *Clinical depression*—evidenced by loss of concentration, disruptive sleep, obsession over details at work, exhaustion (leading to an inability to function), and diagnosed depression.
- *Post-traumatic stress disorder*—evidenced by feeling edgy or irritable and constantly on guard, having recurrent nightmares and flashbacks, and needing to avoid the feelings or thoughts that remind the bullied person of the trauma.[51]

In addition to the potential terrible effects of bullying on the individual, the organization has much at stake in preventing or dealing with bullying in a direct way. A variety of organizational effects have been associated with bullying. These include (1) high absenteeism resulting from time taken off by the bullied employees, (2) reduced productivity among bullied workers, (3) stress-related illnesses that increase health-care costs to the organization, (4) reduced customer service due to bullied employees feeling less loyalty to the organization because it is not protecting them from bullying, and (5) increased employee turnover—82 percent of people targeted by a bully quit.[52]

Managerial Guidelines. Many guidelines are suggested to address bullying in the workplace. We note several of them here. As a start, management should have an anti-bullying workplace aggression policy that defines expectations for interpersonal relationships. Employees, including managers, should understand what is and is not acceptable behavior in the workplace. This will serve as one step toward creating a culture in which people treat each other with courtesy and respect. Managers encourage a culture of respect by taking corrective action against those engaged in bullying behaviors. Increasingly, employers are no longer dismissing bullying as simply a socially acceptable side effect of office politics. In addition to strong sexual harassment policies, a number of firms are developing policies that address bullying. A few examples include American Express, Burger King, and JC Penney. The failure of managers—or a supervisor if the manager is the bully—to address bullying has resulted in successful legal action against those firms.[53]

A variety of guidelines have been offered to address bullying.[54] Several of these are noted as follows:

1. Speak directly to the bully. Tell the individual that you find his or her behaviors unacceptable and to stop them. Often this is all that is needed.
2. In some cases, the bullying behaviors are not seen by others. Thus, tell a friend or work colleague. You may soon learn that you are not the only one who has been subject to the person's bullying.
3. Keep a diary of the specific behaviors and incidents of bullying and when each occurred. Many of the incidents in isolation may seem minor, but when put together, they can establish a serious pattern over time.
4. Discuss the experience of bullying with your manager. If your manager is the person who is doing the bullying, you may need to discuss the matter with a person in the human resources department or, if applicable, the appropriate person designated by organizational policy.
5. If these initial steps are not effective, it may be necessary to file a formal complaint, consistent with the organization's policies. There is no assurance that these steps will be effective.

Unfortunately, too often individuals have found it necessary to resign from their positions or seek a transfer to a different department to remove themselves from the bullying activity.

A special type of bullying in the workforce is mobbing—*the ganging up by coworkers, subordinates, or superiors to force someone out of the workplace through rumor, intimidation, humiliation, discrediting, and/or isolation*. As with the traditional form of bullying, mobbing may result in high turnover, low morale, decreased productivity, increased absenteeism, and a loss of key individuals. More broadly, it may eventually lead to diminished teamwork, trust, and a toxic workplace culture. It is estimated that about 5 percent of employees are targets of mobbing sometime in their working lives.[55]

The prime targets of mobbers are often high achievers, enthusiastic employees, those of high integrity and ethical standards, those who don't belong to the "in-group," women with family responsibilities, and even those with different religious or cultural orientations.[56] Mobbing is much more difficult for the individual to deal with than bullying. Why? The person is not simply dealing with the actions of another, but rather that of many of his or her coworkers and/or superiors. While training employee work teams, one anonymous employee reports on his witnessing mobbing: "I noticed a young man, relatively new to the company, who sat alone. Whenever he spoke, someone hurled a wisecrack his way. If he entered or left the room, jibes from his 'teammates' followed. At a break, I asked if this harassment was typical. 'Oh,' he answered, 'it's been like that since I got here. It's not everybody, just four or five guys. I guess I have to put up with it because I'm new.' I offered to address the obnoxious behavior or get help from his manager, but he refused. 'Don't,' he pleaded. 'That'll only make it worse. I just try to put up with it.'"[57]

The person subject to mobbing may find that colleagues no longer meet with her or him. Management may not provide the possibility to communicate, the person may be isolated in a work area, perhaps the individual is given meaningless work assignments, or the individual may be repeatedly left out of the information loop critical to his or her work. Taken together and repeated over time, these kinds of actions may be devastating for the individual. In too many cases, the only recourse for the individual is to seek a transfer within the organization or resign the position.

Sexual Harassment

Sexual harassment is one of the many categories of harassment that may occur in the workplace. Harassment *refers to verbal or physical conduct that denigrates or shows hostility or aversion toward an individual because of that person's race, skin color, religion, gender, national origin, age, or disability*. Harassment can also occur if conduct is directed toward a person's relatives, friends, or associates.[58] Harassment does one or more of the following:

- Has the purpose or effect of creating an intimidating, hostile, or offensive work environment.
- Has the purpose or effect of unreasonably interfering with an individual's work performance.
- Otherwise aversely affects an individual's employment opportunities.

Sexual harassment *generally refers to unwelcome sexual advances, requests for sexual favors, and other verbal or physical conduct of a sexual nature*.[59] Sexual harassment consists of two types of prohibited conduct in the United States: (1) *quid pro quo*—in which submission to harassment is used as the basis for employment decisions, and (2) *hostile environment*—in which harassment creates an offensive working environment. Consider these basic questions from a legal perspective in the United States:

- If an employee "voluntarily" has sex with a manager, does this mean that she (or he) has not been sexually harassed? Not necessarily. If an employee by her or his conduct shows that sexual advances are unwelcome, it does not matter that she (or he) eventually "voluntarily" succumbs to the harassment. In deciding whether the sexual advances are "unwelcome," the courts will often allow evidence concerning the employee's dress, behavior, and language as indications of whether the employee "welcomed" the advances.

- Is an employer liable for *quid pro quo* harassment engaged in by its managers? In general, an employer is held to be strictly liable when a manager engages in *quid pro quo* harassment.
- What is hostile environment harassment? A hostile work environment *occurs when an employee is subjected to comments of a sexual nature, offensive sexual materials, or unwelcome physical contact as a regular part of the work environment.* Generally speaking, a single isolated incident will not be considered hostile environment harassment unless it is extremely outrageous and egregious conduct. The courts look to see whether the conduct is both serious and frequent. Today, courts are more likely to find a hostile work environment as being present when the workplace includes sexual propositions, pornography, extremely vulgar language, sexual touching, degrading comments, or embarrassing questions or jokes. Supervisors, managers, coworkers, and even customers can be responsible for creating a hostile environment.
- Is an employer liable for hostile environment harassment? It depends on who has created the hostile environment. The employer is liable when supervisors or managers are responsible for the hostile environment, unless the employer can prove that it exercised reasonable care to prevent and promptly correct sexually harassing behavior and that the employee unreasonably failed to take advantage of any preventive or corrective opportunities provided by the employer.

Any harassment policy, including one on sexual harassment, should contain (1) a definition of the harassment, (2) a harassment prohibition statement, (3) a description of the organization's complaint procedure, (4) a description of disciplinary measures for such harassment, and (5) a statement of protection against retaliation.[60]

The following Diversity Competency feature provides an excellent example of a strong sexual harassment policy that was developed by the leadership team at OfficeWorksRX.[61] OfficeWorksRX is a specialized health-care staffing organization with headquarters in Tarzana, California. The firm specializes in placing medical support and medical administrative personnel. OfficeWorksRX has over 300 employees with 21 offices in four states. In addition to staffing, the firm will also provide full services, from human resources to billing, by actually running a private doctor's or medical group's office. OfficeWorksRX functions under the corporate name of Healthcare Consulting, Inc. Major excerpts from its policy include the state of California's and U.S. federal government's core regulatory requirements and prohibitions related to sexual harassment.

Diversity Competency

OfficeWorksRX Sexual Harassment Policy

OfficeWorksRX is committed to providing a work environment that is free of discrimination. In keeping with this commitment, we maintain a strict policy prohibiting unlawful harassment, including sexual harassment. Sexual harassment is prohibited by this Company and is against the law. Every employee should be aware of: (1) what sexual harassment is; (2) steps to take if harassment occurs; (3) the personal liability of harassers; and (4) prohibited retaliation for reporting sexual harassment.

What Is Sexual Harassment?

It's against the law for females to sexually harass males or other females, and for males to harass other males or females.

California Law

California law defines harassment due to sex as sexual harassment, gender harassment and harassment due to pregnancy, childbirth or related medical conditions. This includes:

- Verbal harassment—epithets, derogatory comments or slurs. *Examples*: Name-calling, belittling, sexually explicit or degrading words to describe an individual, sexually explicit jokes, comments about an employee's anatomy and/or dress, sexually oriented noises or remarks, questions about a person's sexual practices, use of patronizing terms or remarks, verbal abuse, graphic verbal commentaries about the body.
- Physical harassment—assault, impeding or blocking movement, or any physical interference with normal work or movement, when directed at an individual. *Examples*: Touching, pinching, patting, grabbing, brushing against or poking another employee's body, requiring an employee to wear sexually suggestive clothing.
- Visual harassment—derogatory posters, cartoons, or drawings. *Examples*: Displaying sexual pictures, writings or objects, obscene letters or invitations, staring at an employee's anatomy, leering, sexually oriented gestures, mooning, unwanted love letters or notes.
- Sexual favors—unwanted sexual advances which condition an employment benefit upon an exchange of sexual favors. *Examples*: Continued requests for dates, any threats of demotion, termination, etc., if requested sexual favors are not given, making or threatening reprisals after a negative response to sexual advances, propositioning an individual.

Federal Law

Under federal law, unwelcome sexual advances, requests for sexual favors, and other verbal or physical conduct of a sexual nature constitute sexual harassment when:

- Submission to such conduct is made either explicitly or implicitly a term or condition of an individual's employment.
- Submission to or rejection of such conduct by an individual is used as the basis for employment decisions affecting such individual; or
- Such conduct has the purpose or effect of unreasonably interfering with an individual's work performance creating an intimidating, hostile, or offensive working environment.

Stopping Sexual Harassment

1. When possible, simply tell the harasser to stop. The harasser may not realize the advances or behavior is offensive. When it is appropriate and sensible, simply tell the harasser the behavior or advances are unwelcome and must stop.
2. You are strongly encouraged to report sexual harassment. Contact your supervisor, another manager or your staffing coordinator. Sexual harassment or retaliation should be reported in writing or verbally. You may report such activities even though you were not the subject of harassment.
3. An investigation will be conducted. OfficeWorksRX will investigate, in a discreet manner, all reported incidents of sexual harassment and retaliation.
4. Appropriate action will be taken. Where evidence of sexual harassment or retaliation is found, disciplinary action, up to and including termination, may result.

Protection against Retaliation

Company policy and California state law forbid retaliation against any employee who opposes sexual harassment, files a complaint, testifies, assists or participates in any manner in an investigation, proceeding or hearing. …

For more information on OfficeWorksRX, visit the organization's home page at www.officeworksrx.com.

The Diversity Competency feature on OfficeWorksRX clearly sets forth the prohibition against *quid pro quo* sexual harassment and hostile work environment harassment. The behaviors associated with each are clearly developed. The course of action to stop such sexual harassment is stated in the policy by OfficeWorksRX. The potential consequences to harassers are identified. A statement of protection against retaliation is expressed. Organizations with policies such as OfficeWorksRX and, perhaps more importantly, the implementation of such policies are likely to have a reduced number of sexual harassment incidents.

Sexual harassment continues to be a serious problem in the United States.[62] In a review of a number of studies of the incidents of sexual harassment in the United States, it was found that 58 percent of the women respondents reported having experienced potentially harassing behaviors, and 24 percent report having experienced sexual harassment at work.[63] Sexual harassment continues to be a serious form of workplace aggression because it may lead to one or more of the discussed reactions outlined for bullying and in previous parts of this chapter.[64] As with bullying, management has a strong responsibility to do everything in its power to prevent sexual harassment from occurring. When it does occur, it needs to be dealt with quickly and firmly. An excellent policy statement, along with its implementation, was presented in the Diversity Competency related to the sexual harassment policy at OfficeWorksRX.

Workplace Violence

Workplace violence *is any act in which a person is abused, threatened, intimidated, or assaulted in the employment relationship and which represents an explicit or implicit challenge to the person's safety, well-being, or health.*[65]

A number of behaviors are considered to be forms of workplace violence. These include murder, rape, robbery, wounding, battering, kicking, throwing objects, biting, hitting, pushing, kicking, spitting, scratching, squeezing or pinching, stalking, intimidation, threats, leaving offensive messages, rude gestures, swearing, harassment (including sexual, racial, and other), intense bullying or mobbing, sabotage, theft, property damage, and arson.[66]

In a recent governmental study, nearly 5 percent of the 7.1 million private industry businesses in the United States reported one or more incidents of workplace violence within the 12 months prior to the survey. Half of the larger firms—those employing 1,000 or more workers—reported one or more incidents. However, it is generally recognized that numerous incidents of workplace violence are never officially reported or, if so, never formally recorded. In addition, over 70 percent of U.S. workplaces were found to have no formal policy or program that addresses workplace violence.[67]

Harm Model. As noted previously and in Figure 7.7, there are potential overlaps in the types of aggressive workplace behaviors that are considered to constitute bullying, sexual harassment, and workplace violence. These relationships and overlaps are suggested in the harm model of aggression—*a continuum that ranges from harassment to aggression to rage to mayhem.*[68] The types of conduct related to each level of aggressive or threatening behavior occur on an ascending scale, as follows:

- *Harassment.* The first level of behavior on the violence continuum is harassment. This behavior may or may not cause harm or discomfort to the individual. But, it is generally considered inappropriate conduct for the workplace. Examples of harassment include acting in a condescending way to a customer, slamming an office door, glaring at a colleague, playing frequent practical and cruel jokes, or telling a lie about a coworker.
- *Aggression.* Aggressive behaviors that cause harm to or discomfort for another person or for the organization might include shouting at a customer, slamming a door in someone's face, spreading damaging rumors about a coworker, or damaging someone's personal belongings. Clearly, all of these behaviors are inappropriate for the workplace.
- *Rage.* The third level on the continuum is rage. Rage is seen through intense behaviors that often cause fear in other persons and which may result in physical or emotional harm to people or damage to property. Rage typically makes the inappropriate behaviors physical and visible. Examples of rage can range from pushing a

customer to sabotaging a coworker's presentation or leaving hate statements on someone's desk.

- *Mayhem.* The final stage is mayhem. This stage represents physical violence against people or the violent destruction of property. Activity in this category can range from punching a customer or ransacking to physically punching a coworker or superior to destroying a facility to shooting a coworker or superior to death.

LEADER INSIGHT

When a confrontational situation develops, that's the time to back away and say 'Let's just cool off a little bit.' If the person is venting, you need to know what to do in that situation.
Robert Cartwright, Loss Prevention Manager, Bridgestone/Firestone

Warning Signs. Individuals who engage in workplace violence at the rage and mayhem levels frequently exhibit clear observable warning signs, which are often newly acquired behaviors. These warning signs include the following:

1. *Violent and threatening behavior*—including hostility and approval of the use of violence.
2. *"Strange" behavior*—becoming reclusive, deteriorating personal appearance/hygiene, and erratic behavior.
3. *Performance problems*—including problems with attendance or tardiness.
4. *Interpersonal problems*—including numerous conflicts, hypersensitivity to comments, and expressions of resentment.
5. *"At the end of his (or her) rope"*—indicators of impending suicide, the expression of an unspecified plan to "solve all problems" and the like, and statements of access to and familiarity with weapons.[69]

Triggering Events. There are identifiable sets of triggering events. The triggering event is seen to the violence-prone individual as the last straw that creates a mind-set of no way out or no more options. The most common sets of triggering events that lead to rage or mayhem are:

1. being fired, laid off or suspended, or passed over for promotion;
2. disciplinary action, poor performance review, severe criticism from one's superior or coworkers;
3. bank or court action such as foreclosure, restraining orders, or custody hearings;
4. benchmark date—the anniversary of the employee at the organization, chronological age, a date of some horrendous event (such as September 11, 2001, or the aftermath of Hurricane Katrina), and the like; or
5. failed or spurned romance or a personal crisis such as separation, divorce, or death in family.[70]

These types of triggering events are indicators that allow employers to anticipate or predict the potential of an individual who exhibits these warning signs for engaging in rage or mayhem.

Prevention Guidelines. There are a number of guidelines for organizations to help prevent workplace violence. During the hiring process, careful interviewing and background checks are essential. For the existing workforce, management's application of the foundation competencies developed throughout this book will minimize the conditions that trigger incidents of workplace violence. Employee training related to workplace violence is increasingly seen as essential. When the early warning signs of the potential for an individual to engage in workplace violence occur, the appropriate use of counseling, employee assistance program referral, sound security measures, and preventive disciplinary actions will be helpful.

A zero-tolerance violence policy that is fairly enforced and consistently communicated is a foundation guideline for minimizing and taking corrective action with respect to workplace violence.[71] First, a formal policy sends a strong signal to employees that workplace violence will not be tolerated. Second, the severity of the penalty for violent behavior should further reinforce the message. Third, a policy lets employees know exactly what conduct is prohibited.

Aggression toward the Organization

Our discussion has focused on three of the types of workplace aggression as they impact the employee or groups of employees. An employee who feels unjustly treated, whether for a good cause or self-serving rationalization, may also engage in aggressive behaviors against the organization. At times, the aggression toward the organization is seen as a way of retaliating against the person's manager or higher levels of management. Direct aggression toward management may be seen as resulting in reprisals, such as disciplinary actions or dismissal. The employee might ignore customers and their requests or be rude to them, but not to the point that the customers are likely to complain to higher management. Or, the person might say negative things as a way of blaming the customers' problems on higher management.[72]

As suggested previously, other forms of aggression against the organization may include (1) theft of equipment, supplies, or money; (2) damaging or destroying equipment and facilities; and (3) slacking off whenever possible and withholding ideas for improvements.

CHAPTER SUMMARY

1. Explain the nature of and influences on creating stress.

Stress is the excitement, feeling of anxiety, and/or physical tension that occurs when the demands placed on individuals exceed their ability to cope. This view of stress if often about negative stress. An individual's general biological responses to stressors prepare them to fight or flee—behaviors generally inappropriate in the workplace. Many factors determine how employees experience work stress, including their perception of the situation, past experiences, the presence or absence of social support, and a variety of individual differences.

2. Describe how different personalities react to stressful situations.

Several personality characteristics are related to differences in how individuals cope with stress. Individuals with a Type A personality are more prone to stress and have an increased chance of experiencing physical ailments due to it. Some dimensions of the Type A personality, such as hostility, are particularly important in terms of stress-related illness. In contrast, the collection of personality traits known as hardiness seems to reduce the effects of stress.

3. Identify the key sources of work-related stressors.

Organizational sources of stress at work often include (1) workload, (2) job conditions, (3) role conflict and ambiguity, (4) career development, (5) interpersonal relations, (6) workplace aggression, especially bullying, sexual harassment, and violence, and (7) conflict between work and life roles. In addition, significant changes or other events in an individual's personal life may also be sources of stress.

4. State the potential effects of severe stress on health, performance, and job burnout.

Stress may affect a person physiologically, emotionally, and behaviorally. Severe stress is linked to various health problems. An arch-shaped relationship exists between stress and performance. In other words, an optimal level of stress probably exists for any particular task. Less or more stress than that level may lead to reduced performance. Job burnout is a major result of unrelieved and intense job-related stress.

5. Apply individual and organizational guidelines for managing workplace stress.

Stress is a real issue for both individuals and organizations. Fortunately, various guidelines, both organizational and individual, can help managers and employees manage stress in the workplace. These guidelines often focus on identifying and removing workplace stressors as well as helping employees cope with stress. Wellness programs are particularly promising in helping employees cope with stress. Workplace aggression as discussed in the last part of the chapter requires additional organizational guidelines.

6. Explain four major types of workplace aggression: bullying, sexual harassment, violence, and aggression toward the organization itself.

Workplace aggression includes a variety of behaviors: psychological acts such as shouting or intimidating remarks, physical assault, and destruction or theft of property. Four of the more common types of workplace aggression include bullying, sexual harassment, workplace violence, and aggression toward the organization itself. There may be overlaps in the behaviors associated with each type, as suggested by the *harm model.* This model represents a continuum of levels of violence from harassment to aggression to rage to mayhem. Mayhem may include murder or destruction of organizational property. A variety of guidelines for minimizing and taking corrective action with respect to bullying, sexual harassment, and workplace violence were reviewed.

KEY TERMS AND CONCEPTS

Depersonalization
Derogation of target bias
Fight-or-flight response
Harassment
Hardiness
Hardy personality
Harm model of aggression
Hostile attribution bias
Hostile work environment
Incivility
Job burnout
Life stressors
Mobbing
Post-traumatic stress disorder
Potency bias
Retribution bias
Role ambiguity
Role conflict
Role overload
Sexual harassment
Social discounting bias
Stress
Stress management
Stressors
Type A personality
Type B personality
Wellness program
Workplace aggression
Workplace bullying
Workplace violence

DISCUSSION QUESTIONS

1. Reread the Learning from Experience opening feature on Tracy Daw's stress at Intel UK. If Daw had studied this chapter well before her breakdown, what are the two or three most important actions that she should have taken?
2. Visit the Intel website at www.intel.com/jobs/workplace. Under "Discover More," click on "The Workplace" and read the pages related to "Work/Life Balance." What inconsistencies are there between the statements on these pages and the experience of Tracy Daw?
3. Describe a personal work situation that you found stressful. Use Figures 7.1 and Figure 7.2 to identify the factors causing the stress and explain their impact on you.
4. Give an example of your use of the fight-or-flight response. In that situation, all things considered, was your response effective or ineffective?
5. How do your individual differences (e.g., motivation, attitudes, and personality) contribute to your stress? Explain.
6. Identify and list some of the stressors in a job that you have held. Which were the most difficult to deal with? Why?
7. How would you describe yourself in comparison to (a) the Type A personality, (b) the Type B personality, and (c) the hardy personality?
8. Describe a situation in which you coped well with stress. Describe another situation in which you didn't cope well with stress. How did your perception of the two situations differ?
9. Have you experienced or witnessed workplace bullying? If yes, did the management deal with it effectively? Explain.
10. Have you experienced or witnessed workplace violence? If yes, did the management deal with it effectively? Explain.

EXPERIENTIAL EXERCISE AND CASE

Experiential Exercise: Self Competency

Support in Coping with Work-Related Stress Inventory[73]

Instructions

The following statements ask about the reliability and availability of various people in providing you with support when you experience stressful problems at work. Please respond to each item by recording a number from the rating scale below next to each statement. In this way, for each statement, you will rate the combined support from your manager, your work colleagues, and your partner/family/friends in helping you with stressful issues and events at work. How much can you rely on others …

Not at all	A little	Somewhat	Much	Totally
1	2	3	4	5

Emotional Support

_____1. … to help you feel better when you experience work-related problems?

_____2. … to listen to you when you need to talk about work-related problems?

_____3. … to be sympathetic and understanding about your work-related problems?

Informational Support

_____4. … to suggest ways to find out more about a work situation that is causing you problems?

_____5. … to share their experiences of a work problem similar to yours?

_____6. … to provide information that helps to clarify your work-related problems?

Instrumental Support

_____7. … to give you practical assistance when you experience work-related problems?

_____8. … to spend time helping you resolve your work-related problems?

_____9. … to help when things get tough at work?

Appraisal Support

_____10. … to reassure you about your ability to deal with your work-related problems?

_____11. … to acknowledge your efforts to resolve your work-related problems?

_____12. … to help you evaluate your attitudes and feelings about your work-related problems?

Scoring

- Emotional support from others: Sum the points for items 1–3 = ______.
- Informational support from others: Sum the points for items 4–6 = ______.
- Instrumental support from others: Sum the points for items 7–9 = ______.
- Appraisal support from others: Sum the totals for items 10–12 = ______.

Interpretation

- A total of 12 to15 points for any of the types of support suggests you experience considerable reliability and availability in that type of support when dealing with problems that create stress.
- A total of 3 to 6 points for any of the types of support suggests that you see yourself on being on your own with respect to that type of support.

Overall

- Sum the points for all 12 items. Total scores of 48 to 60 points suggest a pattern of strong support as you deal with problems that create work-related stress. Total scores of 12 to 24 points suggest a pattern of feeling isolated and alone in dealing with problems that create work-related stress.

Questions

1. Does your score suggest that you need to take action to lower your stress level? If "yes," what actions do you think would be most effective?
2. What three competencies are likely to be most effective and important to you in managing your stress level?

Case: Ethics Competency

Ethical Dilemma at Northlake[74]

Our story opens with an irate Jim McIntosh confronting his manager of corporate reporting: "I thought we had an understanding on this issue, Frank. Tina tells me that you are threatening to go public with your stupid statements about the report. For Pete's sake, Frank, wake up and smell the coffee! You're about to damage all the important things in your life: your career, your friendships, and your company!"

Frank sat quietly in the overstuffed sofa in his V. P.'s expansive office. He thought that the pale green report lying on the desk looked innocent enough but it certainly had provided the basis for some serious turmoil. Jim stood by his desk trembling with rage. His face was bright red and mottled with anger. Frank had often seen Jim upset, but never in a temper such as this. "I'm sorry, Jim," Frank replied softly, "I know how much this means to you, but I don't think that I have a choice in this matter. I can't sit idle while you and that twit from financial analysis allow this report to go forward. You both know that these numbers have no foundation in fact."

The report, titled "Endangered Species: The Pulp and Paper Industry in the Upper Peninsula," laid out the industry's response to the new government proposals to put effluent controls on the discharge of wastewater from pulp and paper mills in environmentally sensitive regions of the province. One section of the report detailed the financial consequences of the emission controls as determined by each of the five pulp and paper companies operating in the region. Amalgamated Forest Products had taken the industry lead in developing the report, and the company president, Jean Letourneau, was scheduled to testify before a legislative subcommittee next week, giving the industry perspective on the proposed legislation.

Amalgamated had three major mills located in some of the more remote locations in the province. The firm had been facing difficult financial times due to the recession, and this had caused substantial hardship in the three small communities where the mills were located. Corporate offices were located in Northlake, a town of approximately 10,000 people.

The section of the report dealing with the dollar impact to Amalgamated Forest Products of installing the emission control equipment had been prepared by Tina Pacquette. Tina, a long-term employee of the firm, had risen through the accounting department to become the manager of financial analysis. While Tina and Frank were peers, their working relationship had not been particularly cordial. In Frank's opinion, Tina's work was barely adequate, but then, no one asked for his opinion.

"Well, Frank, your pigheadedness has really caused a problem for all of us! Wait Here! I'll get Jean Letourneau, and we'll see what he thinks about your efforts!" Jim exited the office and slammed the door.

As he waited in the silence of his boss's beautifully decorated office, Frank looked back over his 10 years with Amalgamated Forest Products. Just like his father before him, Frank started with the firm after completing high school and his first job was as a yard man culling out damaged logs before processing. That's when Frank severely damaged his right leg on the job. He had been celebrating the birth of his son the night before and he was unable to keep his footing with the dexterity required. Surgery saved the leg and he was extremely grateful that the company had brought him inside to the accounting office. An accounting clerk's salary was low compared to a yard helper's, but in a short time his natural talent for analysis brought him to the attention of the vice president of finance. Within two years, Jim McIntosh had arranged for him to go to a university, complete his Certified Management Accountants (CMA) designation after graduation, and then return to Amalgamated. The financial support provided by the firm had been adequate but not lavish by any means, and Frank had done well in his studies. He was the gold medalist for his province on the CMA examinations, and he had returned to Northlake in triumph. With three young children and a proud wife, Frank had been appointed to a new position in corporate reporting. After a year of having Jim as his mentor, he rose to the position of manager of corporate reporting.

The office door opened abruptly and Jim entered with the company president. Jean Letourneau was a distinguished man of approximately 60 years of age. He had a long history with Amalgamated and a solid reputation in the pulp and paper industry.

"What's the problem, Frank?" Jean's voice broke into the silence. "Jim tells me that you have a few concerns about the report that we're submitting to the legislative committee."

"Well, Mr. Letourneau, I think we, the company, have some major problems here. The report indicates that we'll have severe financial problems if we're forced into building a lagoon for wastewater treatment. In fact, the report says we are likely to be pushed into bankruptcy if the legislation is passed. But we all know these estimates of costs are highly inflated. There's no way that our operating costs would be raised by 30 percent. I could see our operating costs rising by only 8 to 10 percent. That's what the internal report Tina wrote a year ago predicts and there's really been no significant change. Moreover, you have to testify before the legislative committee as to the truthfulness of this report, and there's not a shred of truth in it. The other cost estimates are all high, and the prediction of our product demand is based upon a further deepening of the recession. For our internal purposes, we have been using an estimated increase of 10 percent in demand."

"Slow down, son," Letourneau's calm voice broke in, "We have to use different figures for different purposes. When we report to our shareholders, we give them numbers that are substantially altered from the internal documents, right? In this case, we have to make those dunderheads in the government see what all this regulation is doing to us. Besides, they know we're going to use the most effective numbers to justify our position."

"But this isn't simply a matter of different figures," Frank sputtered. "These numbers have been totally fabricated. And they don't take into account the damage that we're doing to the Wanawashee River. The same stuff we're dumping was cleaned up by our competition years ago. The aboriginal community downstream is still drinking this garbage. We're going to be subject to a huge lawsuit if they ever trace it to us. Then, where will we be? I've got to worry about my professional obligations as well. If this blows up, you could go to jail, and I could get my designation revoked."

"We'll cross that bridge when we come to it," Jim McIntosh interjected. "You've got to remember what's at stake here. Northlake's totally dependent on the mill for its economic survival. As the mill goes, so goes the town. It's your buddies you'd be threatening to put out of work, Frank. This legislation may not bankrupt us, but it will certainly put a squeeze on profits. If profits are gone, no more reinvestment by Chicago. Head office is putting lots of pressure on us to improve the bottom line since the takeover last year. They're talking about cutting all of that new production line equipment we requested."

"The bottom line is this, Frank," Letourneau spoke softly. "You're an important part of our team, we've invested a lot in you. Jim was talking about working you into a new role: V.P. Controller. We'd hate to let you go because of this small issue. However, we need to have everybody working on the same goal. Besides, Jim tells me this isn't even your responsibility. If you hadn't picked up the copy of the report on Tina's desk, we wouldn't have even involved you. Now take the rest of the day off, go home to Cheryl and the kids, and take out that new speed boat of yours. Think the problem through, and I'm sure you'll see the long-term benefit of what we're doing. This pollution issue is a 'Northern problem' that we can resolve here, not in some fancy legislature in the south. Besides, we've had the problem for as far back as I can remember. So a few extra years certainly won't hurt."

Questions

1. What are the likely sources (types) of stress being experienced by Frank? Give one or more indicators from the case of each source identified.
2. What are the likely sources (types) of stress being experienced by Jim McIntosh? Give one or more indicators from the case of each source identified.
3. Are there any indicators of bullying in this case? Explain.
4. Is Frank demonstrating behaviors consistent with a Type A personality, Type B personality, or hardy personality? Identify the behaviors that you think Frank exhibits consistent with the personality type selected.
5. What should Frank do? Why?

PART 3

LEADERS AND TEAMS IN ORGANIZATIONS

CHAPTER

8

Fostering Interpersonal Communication in Organizations

Learning Goals

When you have finished studying the chapter, you should be able to:

1. Describe the core elements of interpersonal communication.
2. Explain and apply the interrelated factors that enable ethical communications.
3. Describe and effectively apply nonverbal communication in interpersonal communication.
4. Describe and apply communication networks in interpersonal communication.

Learning from Experience

KEVIN SHARER, LEARNING FROM FAILURE

Kevin Sharer is the chairman, CEO, and president of Amgen, headquartered in Thousand Oaks, California. This biotechnology firm was formed in 1980. Amgen discovers, develops, and delivers human therapeutics for treating cancer, kidney disease, rheumatoid arthritis, and other diseases. Sales have increased from $1.4 billion in 2002 to over $4 billion in 2007.

In 1989, Kevin Sharer was facing failure for the first time. He was a rising star at General Electric but had recently changed jobs to join telecommunications company MCI. He anticipated that the top job in sales and marketing at MCI would lead to the CEO position within two years. "The CEO race is wide open," MCI's vice chairman assured him. But once he started work, it became clear that the chief operating officer was in line for the top slot—and didn't welcome competition from Sharer.

Nonetheless, Sharer wasted no time in developing his strategy to transform MCI—and position himself. He states: "Within six weeks, I marched into the chairman's office and proposed a restructuring of MCI's sales organization. I was at the zenith of my arrogance at that time." Sharer's proposal threatened senior executives who had spent their careers building MCI.

Moreover, he lacked experience in telecom, so he had little credibility within the organization. Sharer continues: "MCI was a crucible for me. I learned that right or not, there is a price to be paid for arrogance. The job was taking a personal toll too. It was grinding me down, and I began to retreat emotionally. My wife could not understand what I was going through because she had no corporate experience. She feared I would be fired, which only added to my feeling of isolation."

Desperate to escape MCI, Sharer telephoned Jack Welch (the CEO at GE) about returning to GE. Welch wasn't happy with the way Sharer had left GE. Welch said: "Hey, Kevin, forget you ever worked here." Sharer recalls: "At that moment, I knew I had been cast adrift in a lifeboat."

During that "gut-wrenching" time, Sharer received a letter in 1992 asking if he knew anyone who could be executive vice president of

LEARNING CONTENT

For more information on Amgen, visit the organization's home page at www.amgen.com.

Amgen, a relatively small biotech firm at that time. Having never heard of the company, he went to the public library to learn about it. He decided to nominate himself for the job and was offered the position, under the mentoring of CEO Gordon Binder. This time Sharer cast himself as a student instead of know-it-all. He worked in Amgen's labs, got tutored by its scientists, and accompanied reps on sales calls. In 2000, he was named president and CEO.

One of his first gestures as CEO was to meet individually with the top 150 people in the company and ask them for their ideas. Sharer's failure at MCI enabled him to learn that leading was not about his own success. Sharer comments: "These interviews were the single most important thing I did. They gave me the ability to create a shared reality for the company. That enabled people to align around the new vision and strategy for building Amgen."[1]

In the Learning from Experience feature, Kevin Sharer reflects on the effects of poor interpersonal communications as demonstrated in his failure at MCI—and the effects of constructive interpersonal communication he used at Amgen. There he cast himself as a student early on (asking questions, gaining knowledge, accompanying sales reps to learn about customers) and sought direct inputs through one-on-one meetings with the top 150 people after his appointment as CEO.

Recall from Chapter 1 that the *communication competency* involves the knowledge, skills, and ability to use all of the modes of transmitting, understanding, and receiving ideas, thoughts, and feelings—verbal, listening, nonverbal, written, electronic, and the like—to accurately transfer and exchange information and emotions. This chapter focuses primarily on providing a path for you to enhance your communication competency with an emphasis on interpersonal communication. Interpersonal communication *refers to a limited number of participants who (1) are usually in proximity to each other, (2) use many sensory channels, and (3) are able to provide immediate feedback.*[2] First, we discuss the process, types, and patterns of verbal, nonverbal, and other forms of communication used by employees on the job. Second, we present ways to foster ethical interpersonal dialogue in organizations. Third, we examine the nature and importance of nonverbal communication in interpersonal communication. Fourth, we review the role of communication networks in organizations, including the impacts of e-mail technology.

ELEMENTS OF INTERPERSONAL COMMUNICATION

Learning Goal

1. Describe the core elements of interpersonal communication.

For accurate interpersonal communication to take place, the thoughts, facts, beliefs, attitudes, or feelings that the sender intended to transmit must be the same as those understood and interpreted by the receiver. Recall Sharer's development of his own proposed restructuring of MCI's sales organization after being on the job for six weeks with no inputs from others prior to submitting the proposal to the chairman. His proposal was immediately interpreted as threatening by a number of senior executives and discounted because Sharer had little experience and thus little creditability in the telecommunications industry.

Figure 8.1 presents the elements of interpersonal communication involving only two people. This process is not easy, and by considering its components, you can readily see that it becomes increasingly complex as more people participate.

Sender and Receiver

Exchanges between people are an element of interpersonal communication. Labeling one person as the sender and the other as the receiver is arbitrary. These roles shift back and forth, depending on where the individuals are in the process. When the receiver

FIGURE 8.1 Elements of Interpersonal Communication

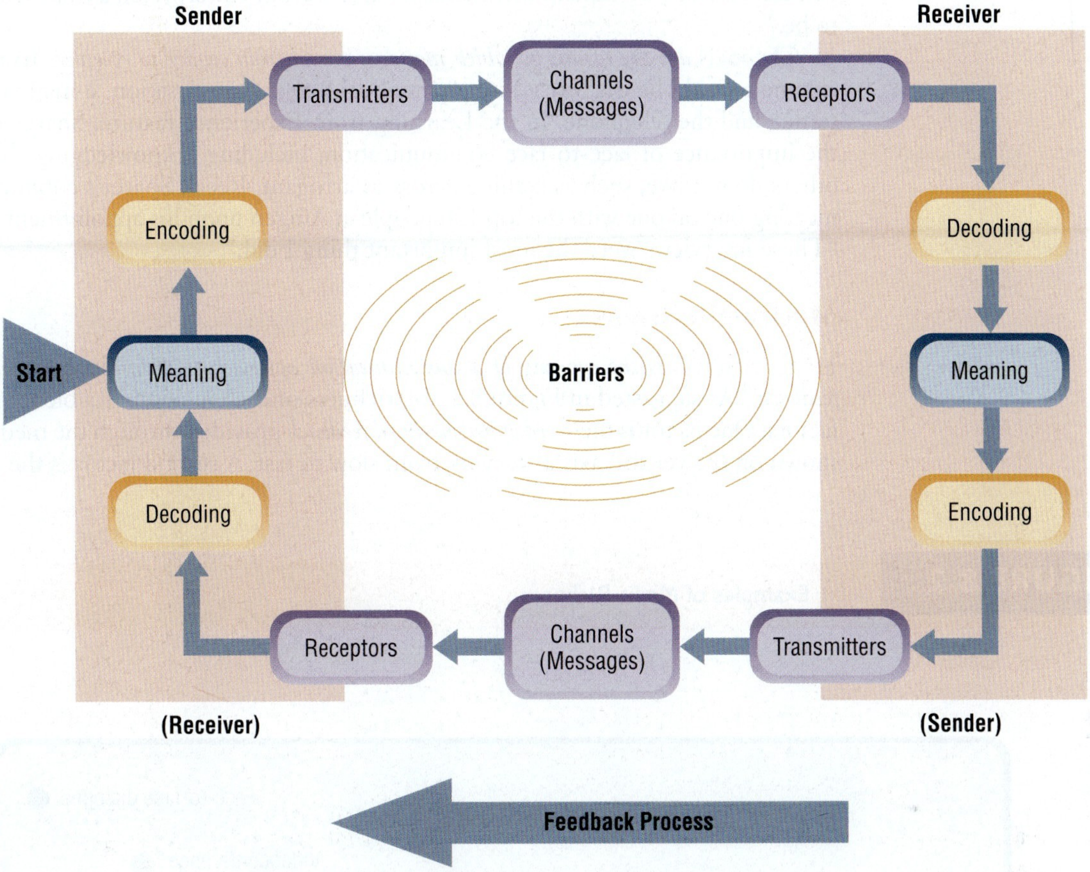

responds to the sender, the original receiver becomes the sender and the initiating sender becomes the receiver.

Transmitters and Receptors

Transmitters (*used by the sender*) and receptors (*used by the receiver*) *are the means available for sending and receiving messages*. They usually involve one or more of the senses: seeing, hearing, touching, smelling, and tasting. Transmission can take place both verbally and nonverbally. Once transmission begins, the communication process moves beyond the direct control of the sender. A message that has been transmitted cannot be brought back. How many times have you thought to yourself "I wish I hadn't said that?"

Messages and Channels

Messages *include the transmitted data and the coded (verbal and nonverbal) symbols that give particular meaning to the data*. By using both verbal and nonverbal symbols, the sender tries to ensure that messages are interpreted by the receiver as the sender intended. To understand the difference between an original meaning and a received message, think about an occasion when you tried to convey inner thoughts and feelings of happiness, rage, or fear to another person. Did you find it difficult or impossible to transmit your true "inner meaning"? The greater the difference between the interpreted meaning and the original message, the poorer will be the communication. Words and nonverbal symbols have no meaning by themselves. Their meaning is created by the sender, the receiver, and the situation or context. In our discussion of potential interpersonal and cultural barriers, we explain why messages aren't always interpreted as they were meant to be.[3]

Channels *are the means by which messages travel from sender to receiver*. Examples of channels would be the "air" during person-to-person conversation, e-mail via the Internet, and the telephone. In the Learning from Experience feature, Sharer indicated the importance of face-to-face communication, including acknowledging things that others do not like, such as coming across as arrogant. Recall Sharer's comment about meeting one on one with the top 150 people at Amgen upon his appointment as CEO: "These interviews were the most important thing I did."

Media Richness

Media richness *is the capacity of a communication approach to transmit cues and provide feedback*.[4] As suggested in Figure 8.2, the richness of each medium is a blend of several factors. One factor is the *speed of personalized feedback* provided through the medium. It is shown on the vertical axis as varying from slow to fast. A second factor is the *variety of*

FIGURE 8.2 Examples of Media Richness

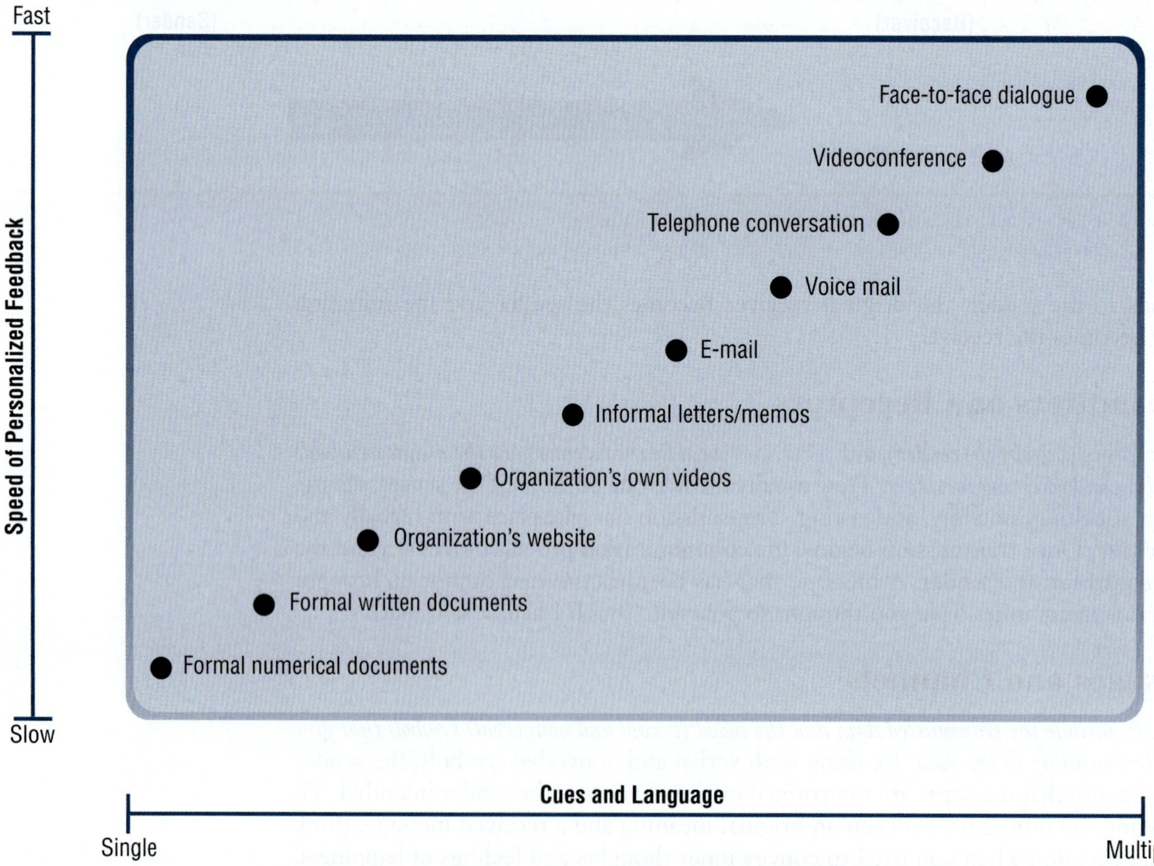

cues and language provided through the medium. It is shown on the horizontal axis as varying from single to multiple. A cue *is a stimulus, either consciously or unconsciously perceived, that results in a response by the receiver*. Figure 8.2 relates 10 different media to the combination of these two factors. Because these two factors are continual, a medium may vary somewhat in richness, depending on its use by sender and receiver. For example, e-mail may be associated with slower or quicker feedback than indicated in Figure 8.2. The speed depends on accessibility to e-mail messages and the receiver's tendency to reply immediately or later. Messages that require a long time to digest or that can't overcome biases are low in richness. Sharer, for example, made a special effort to employ rich media thru the one-on-one interviews upon becoming CEO at Amgen. Also, he noted that the business is "so complicated that no one person alone, can be maximally effective in making key decisions."[5] So that he does not forget the dangers of overconfidence, Sharer has a huge portrait of General George A. Custer, who led the doomed battle of Little Big Horn, across from his desk at Amgen. Sharer states: "It's good for those who have a job like this to look at someone who overestimated his ability, underestimated his enemy, and lost everything."[6]

Data are the output of the communication. The various forms of data include words spoken face to face and in telephone calls; words or numbers written in e-mail messages, text messages, letters, and memos; and words or numbers compiled in computer printouts. The data become information when they reinforce or change the receivers' understanding of their thoughts feelings attitudes, or beliefs. The use of groupware (various information technologies) may help such information exchange but can't always substitute for face-to-face dialogue. The reason is that, as suggested in Figure 8.2, face-to-face dialogue is the richest medium. It provides immediate feedback so that receivers can check the accuracy of their understanding and ask for clarification if they need to. It also allows sender and receiver simultaneously to observe body language, tone of voice, and facial expression. These observations add meaning to the spoken words. Finally, it enables sender and receiver to quickly identify symbols and use language that is natural and personal. Because of these characteristics, solving important and tough problems—especially those involving uncertainty and emotional content—almost always requires face-to-face dialogue.

Clearly, all the media identified in Figure 8.2 have their place and use. Moreover, a complex decision, such as Amgen's decision to enter a new market, requires the use of multiple media—ranging from formal ads to face-to-face discussions with potential users. The effective processing of a complex decision may start with face-to-face dialogue to gain an understanding and agreement on the dimensions of the decision issue and problems to be addressed. Then, some of the parties may be assigned the task of developing formal numerical documents and written documents related to the complex decision and after completion, these documents are likely to be the basis for further face-to-face dialogue.[7] Recall the failure Kevin Sharer created for himself by starting with the development of a written strategy on his own for the restructuring of the MCI sales organization. He had been on the job for six short weeks and was advancing changes to a complex issue that impacted many others.

Meaning and Feedback

The sender's message is transmitted through channels to the receiver's five senses in interpersonal communications. As Figure 8.1 suggests, received messages are changed from their symbolic form (e.g., spoken words) to a form that has meaning. Meaning *represents a person's thoughts, feelings, beliefs, and attitudes.*

Encoding *gives personal meaning to messages that are to be sent.* Vocabulary and knowledge play an important role in the sender's ability to encode. Unfortunately, some professionals have difficulty communicating with people in general. They often encode meaning in a form that only other professionals in the same field can understand. Lawyers often encode (write) contracts that directly affect consumers but use language that only other lawyers can decode. Consumer groups have pressed to have such contracts written in a language that almost everyone can understand. As a result, many banks, credit card firms, and other organizations have simplified the language in their contracts.

Decoding *gives personal, interpreted meaning to messages that are received.* Through a shared language, people can decode many messages so that the meanings received are reasonably close to the meanings transmitted. The accurate decoding of messages is often a major challenge in communicating.[8] Interpersonal communication accuracy should be evaluated in relation to an ideal state. This occurs when the sender's intended meaning and the receiver's interpretation of it are the same.[9] The transmission of factual data of a nonthreatening nature approximates the ideal state. For example, the sharing of the time, place, and procedures for a high school or college commencement ceremony generally results in easy and accurate interpersonal communication.

The interpersonal communication process during a meeting to terminate a long-term employee due to downsizing is a different and more complex matter. Consider the reflections of a seasoned manager who has had to meet with and terminate employees who were performing well:

> *If you have done it as long as I have, the challenge is that you focus on the job so much that is to be done that you ignore the individual and it can become cold. You can just race through the process. If this is the first time you have done it, you can be so caught up in the sympathetic role that one must play that you are not able to convey the message. So it is striking the appropriate balance between the two extremes.*[10]

Feedback *is the receiver's response to the message.* It lets the sender know whether the message was received as intended. Interpersonal communication becomes a dynamic, two-way process through feedback, rather than just an event.

LEADER INSIGHT

A great piece of advice came from my mentor, B. Sridhaber: 'When you are in a profession that is people related and when a lot of thinking goes behind an activity, it's better to be a process-oriented person. If the process is right, the goal will surely be met.' I realized this is true for everything that one does. I cherish this advice and make it a point to pass it on to all my associates.
SujitPatil, Manager, Corporate Communications, Tat Chemicals Ltd., Mumbai, India

Interpersonal Barriers

Barriers to interpersonal communication are numerous.[11] Let's review briefly the more important barriers that stem from individual differences and perceptions.

Individual personality traits that serve as barriers to communication include low adjustment (nervous, self-doubting, and moody), low sociability (shy, unassertive, and withdrawn), low conscientiousness (impulsive, careless, and irresponsible), low agreeableness (independent, cold, and rude), and low intellectual openness (dull, unimaginative, and literal minded). Introverts are likely to be more quiet and emotionally inexpressive (see Chapter 2) than extroverts.

Individual perceptual errors include perceptual defense (protecting oneself against ideas, objects, or situations that are threatening), stereotyping (assigning attributions to someone solely on the basis of a category in which the person has been placed), halo effect (evaluating another person based solely on one impression, either favorable or unfavorable), projection (tendency for people to see their own traits in others), and high expectancy effect (prior expectations serving to bias how events, objects, and people are actually perceived). Individuals who make the fundamental attribution error of underestimating the impact of situational or external causes of behavior and overestimating the impact of personal causes of behavior when they seek to understand why people behave the way they do are less likely to communicate effectively. This error too readily results in communicating blame or credit to individuals for outcomes. A related attribution error is the self-serving bias (communicating personal responsibility for good performance but denying responsibility for poor performance). (See Chapter 3.)

In addition to these underlying personal communication barriers, there are direct barriers, as discussed next.

Noise. Noise *represents any interference with the intended message in the channel.* A radio playing loud music while someone is trying to talk to someone else is an example of noise. Noise sometimes can be overcome by repeating the message or increasing the intensity (e.g., the volume) of the message.

Semantics. Semantics *is the special meaning assigned to words.* Thus, the same words may mean different things to different people.[12] Consider this comment by a manager to a subordinate: "How about the report for production planning? I think that they want it soon!" The manager could have intended one of several meanings in her comment:

Directing:	You should get the report to me now. That's an order.
Suggesting:	I suggest that we consider getting the report out now.
Requesting:	Can you do the report for me now? Let me know if you can't.
Informing:	The report is needed soon by production planning.
Questioning:	Does production planning want the report soon?

Consider the semantics for five words in American (U.S.) English versus British English vocabularies:

- *Pavement:* American—a hard road surface; British—footpath, sidewalk.
- *Table* (verb): American—to remove from discussion; British—to bring to discussion.
- *Tick off* (verb): American—to anger; British—to rebuke.
- *Canceled check*: American—a check paid by the bank; British—a check that is stopped or voided.
- *Ship*: American—to convey by boat, train, plane, truck, or other means; British—to convey only by boat.[13]

Language Routines. *A person's verbal and nonverbal communication patterns that have become habits are known as* language routines. They can be observed by watching how people greet one another. In many instances, language routines are quite useful because they reduce the amount of time needed to produce common messages. They also provide predictability in terms of being able to anticipate what is going to be said and how it is going to be said. The strategy of General Electric and its image is reinforced through language routines, including its slogan: "Imagination at Work." *Fortune* magazine recognized GE as number one on its list of America's most admired companies.[14] GE's slogan is supported by a related slogan to emphasize the firm's efforts to be environmentally friendly and supportive, namely, "Ecomagination: A GE Commitment."[15]

Language routines sometimes cause discomfort, offend, and alienate when they put down or discriminate against others. Many demeaning stereotypes of individuals and groups are perpetuated through language routines. For example, some years ago a manager at Texaco (now a wholly owned subsidiary of Chevron) made tapes of company conversations available to the public. These tapes contained demeaning comments made by board members and managers about minorities within the company, including blacks, Jews, other minorities, and women. Public outrage led to boycotts of Texaco, which ended up settling a racial discrimination case out of court for $176 million. After the lawsuit was settled, boycotts were called off, criticism trickled off, and Texaco's sales rebounded.[16]

Lying and Distortion. Lying *means the sender states what is believed to be false in order to seriously mislead one or more receivers.* The intention to deceive implies a belief that the receiver will accept the lie as a fact. In contrast, honesty means that the sender abides by consistent and rational ethical principles to respect the truth.[17] Everyday social flattery in conversations may not be completely honest, but it is normally considered acceptable and rarely regarded as dishonest (lying). Distortion *represents a wide range of messages that a sender may use between the extremes of lying and complete honesty.*[18] Of course, the use of vague, ambiguous, or indirect language doesn't necessarily indicate a sender's intent to mislead. This form of language may be viewed as acceptable political behavior. Silence may also be a form of distortion, if not dishonesty. Not wanting to look incompetent or make his/her manager look bad in a departmental meeting, a subordinate may remain quiet instead of expressing an opinion or asking a question.

As discussed in Chapter 3, personal distortion in interpersonal communications may occur through impression management, which represents the attempt by individuals to manipulate or control the impressions that others form about them. In Table 3.3 (pages 83–84), we reviewed five impression management tactics: self-promotion, ingratiation, intimidation, supplication, and exemplification. An additional tactic is face-saving. Face-saving often involves (1) apologizing in a way to convince others that the bad outcome isn't a fair indication of what the sender is really like as a person; (2) making excuses to others by admitting that the sender's behavior in some way caused a negative outcome, but strongly suggesting that the person isn't really as much to blame as it seems (because the outcome wasn't intentional or there were extenuating circumstances); or (3) presenting justifications to others by appearing to accept responsibility for an outcome, but denying that the outcome actually led to problems. When the opportunity is present, shifting blame for problems or a failure to meet a goal is a common means of face-saving in organizations.[19]

Impression management strategies can range from relatively harmless minor forms of distortion (being courteous to another person even if you don't like the individual), to messages that use extreme ingratiation and self-promotion to obtain a better raise or promotion than others, to intimidation. In brief, the greater the frequency of distortion tactics and the more they approach the lying end of the distortion continuum, the more they will serve as a hurdle to interpersonal communication.[20]

Cultural Barriers

Recall that *culture* refers to the distinctive ways in which different populations, societies, or smaller groups organize their lives or activities. Intercultural communication *occurs whenever a message sent by a member of one culture is received and understood by a member of another culture.*[21] The effects of cultural differences on barriers to interpersonal communication can be wide ranging. They depend on the degrees of difference (or similarity) between people in terms of language, religious beliefs, economic status, social values, physical characteristics, use of nonverbal cues, and the like. The greater the differences, the more likely it is that there will be barriers to achieving effective intercultural communication.

In Iran, there is a concept called taarof, *which is a set of social manners that seem polite or deceitful depending on one's point of view.* Taarof is a form of etiquette intended to harmonize social and communication encounters. It often involves displays of flattery and deference.[22] In interpersonal communications among Iranians, people are expected to tell you what you want to hear to avoid conflict, or to offer hope when there is none. Iranians understand such practices and are not offended by them. Nasair Hadian, a political science professor at the University of Iran, comments: "You have to guess if people are sincere, you are never sure. Symbolism and vagueness are inherent in our language." Kian Tajbakhsh, a social scientist who lived for many years in England and the United States before returning to Iran in 1996, continues: "Speech has a different function than it does in the West. In the West, 80 percent of language is explicit and as stated. In Iran 80 percent is implied." Translation: In the West, *yes* generally means "yes." In Iran, *yes* can mean "yes," but it often means "maybe" or "no." In Iran,

FIGURE 8.3 Examples of Cultures on the Cultural Context Continuum

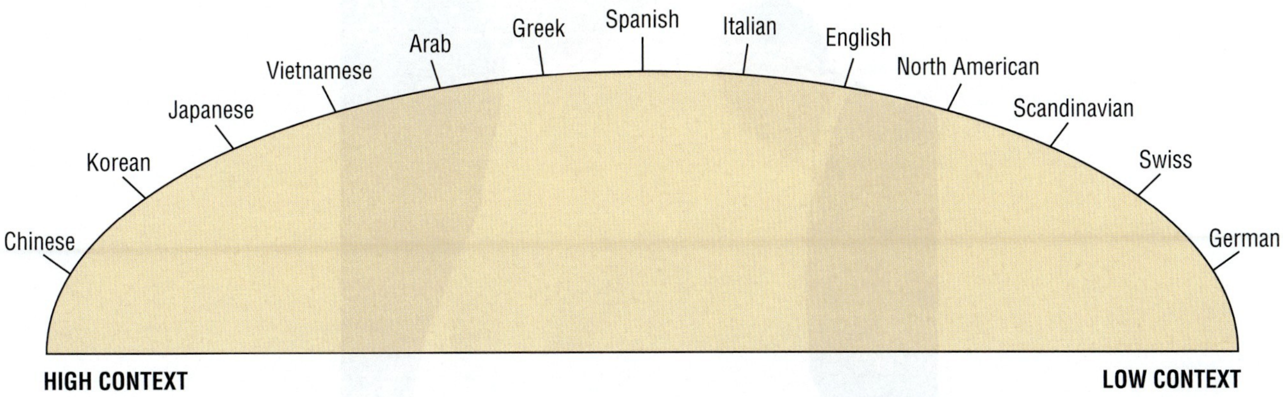

Source: Based on Hall, E. *Understanding Cultural Differences.* Yarmouth, ME: Intercultural Press, 1989; Munter, M., *Guide to Managerial Communication: Effective Business Writing and Speaking,* 5th ed. Englewood Cliffs, NJ: Prentice Hall, 1999.

"Listeners are expected to understand that words don't necessarily mean exactly what they mean."[23]

Cultural Context. *The conditions that surround and influence the life of an individual, group, or organization are its* cultural context. Differences in cultural context may represent a hurdle to communication.[24] Nations' cultures vary on a continuum from low context to high context. Figure 8.3 shows the approximate placement of various countries along this continuum.

A high-context culture *in interpersonal communication is characterized by (1) the establishment of social trust before engaging in work-related discussions, (2) the high value placed on personal relationships and goodwill, and (3) the importance of the surrounding circumstances during an interaction.* In a high-context culture, people rely on paraphrasing, tone of voice, gesture, posture, social status, history, and social setting to interpret spoken words, all of which require time to cultivate. Factors such as trust, relationships among friends and family members, personal needs and difficulties, weather, and holidays must be taken into consideration. For example, Japanese executives—when meeting foreign executives for the first time—do not immediately "get down to business." They engage in a period of building trust and getting to know each other that foreign executives often are impatient with but must conform to.

In contrast, a low-context culture *in interpersonal communication is characterized by (1) directly and immediately addressing the tasks, issues, or problems at hand; (2) the high value placed on personal expertise and performance; and (3) the importance of clear, precise, and speedy interactions.* The use of behavioral modification techniques and other reinforcement approaches discussed in Chapter 4 are based on low-context communication. Especially within low-context cultures, the purpose of communication is to often reveal actual intent, not conceal it. The individuals often ethically express what they mean and mean what they convey. In Chapter 4, we described how a manager can motivate employees with statements focusing on positive or corrective feedback and goal setting. In a heterogeneous country, such as the United States, multiple subcultures have their own unique characteristics. In contrast, the cultural context of a homogeneous country, such as China or Japan, reflects the more uniform characteristics of its people. We address

© Image Source

Differences in cultural context may represent a hurdle to communication because low-context countries, such as the United States, and high-context countries, such as Japan, have different communication norms.

the important role of nonverbal communication differences across cultures later in the chapter.

> **LEADER INSIGHT**
>
> When you go into a different country, even with all the best technology in the world, you still encounter a rich history, and that means that different people have different needs and views. Never assume you have the right answer.
>
> **David J. C.Radcliffe, CEO, Hagg Robinson Ltd., United Kingdom**

Ethnocentrism. Ethnocentrism *occurs when individuals believe that only their culture makes sense, has the "right" values, and represents the "right" and logical way to behave.*[25] This may be the greatest barrier to communication because it involves judging others from our own cultural point of view. It also involves making false assumptions about the ways others behave based on our own limited experiences. Individuals are not even aware that they are being ethnocentric because "we don't understand that we don't understand." When two highly ethnocentric people from different cultures interact, there is little chance that they will achieve a common understanding. Ethnocentric reactions to differing views may be anger, shock, or even amusement. Such people view all others as inferior and may recognize cultural diversity, but only as a source of problems. Their strategy is to minimize the sources and impacts of cultural diversity. Ethnocentric executives and managers ignore or deny that cultural diversity can lead to advantages.

The following Across Cultures Competency feature reports on how the leadership of Nokia strives to minimize ethnocentrism in the design and marketing of its cell phones.[26] Nokia, with headquarters in Espo, Finland, is a global provider of mobile devices, network technologies, and related services. The firm has approximately 60,000 employees across the world.[27] This feature is based on a more extensive interview of Jan Chipchase, who is a behavioral field researcher at the Nokia Research Center based in Tokyo.

Across Cultures Competency

Nokia's Approach to Understanding Cultural Context

Let's talk about a study we did last year [2006] on how people share objects. You can relate this to mobile phones. They're basically designed as personal objects. But if you look at usage in Africa, increasingly the phone is shared. A family might have one. A village might have one, or someone who runs a phone kiosk in a village might have one. We're thinking about how we could redesign the mobile phone and the communication experience to be more suitable for sharing.

We picked two cultures, Indonesia and Uganda. Cultural comparisons are good because they can tell you about what's similar, but also sometimes they make it easier to see obvious differences. We need a month's lead time to plan for a study. I prefer something like three or four months lead time, but we can move quite swiftly if we need to. Before we arrive, we plan the project to death. We determined where we wanted to be, and then we connected with the people in the community who could help us to arrange this. We wanted to spend time in Kampala, in a fishing village that was remote, and in villages that had no mobile connectivity. In a 12-day study, we might have an 8- to 10-member team. A fairly typical team will include two or three Nokia people, one or two good local guides, plus up to six students from local universities. Ideally, when we get somewhere, we like to be in a space where everyone can come together. Ideally, it means renting a house, having a living room space, and having stuff in a fridge.

Everyone in Nokia is coming from a different location in the world. We spend something like 10 to 12 days in a culture. Every single second and every single thing that we do should be something we can learn from. As soon as we arrive, the rules change. Maybe there's no electricity, or the guy who really absolutely said he wanted to be a part of the study won't do it. There are so many different variables. If we just go by the book when we're there, we would miss all these different opportunities for stuff that presents itself. We really try to see how people fit together and adapt.

We have maybe a dozen techniques for engaging with people from the local culture. We do street surveys, which typically involve 100-plus people. Typically, I buy a bicycle and cycle around the city with a translator. If we see something interesting, we get off and we study it. It's a breadth and depth approach to understanding the culture. Last year, I think I bought 10 bicycles. At the end of the study, we give them away to people.

When we're there, the fact is there are 101 things we would have never considered when we were planning. Some stuff is loosely related to what we're interested in, and some is just a total tangent, but we make sure we document it all. When we went to Uganda and Indonesia we thought we would deliver one report. We actually came back with five reports. We did one big one, but we delivered all these other very visual reports that we knew would interest different people in the company.

For more information on Nokia, visit the organization's home page at www.nokia.com.

ETHICAL INTERPERSONAL COMMUNICATIONS

Learning Goal

2. Explain and apply the interrelated factors that enable ethical communications.

Recall from Chapter 1 that the *ethics competency* includes the knowledge, skills, and abilities to incorporate values and principles that distinguish right from wrong in making decisions and choosing behaviors. In this section, we discuss factors that enable ethical interpersonal communications. The individual is more likely to incorporate values and principles that distinguish right from wrong in communications through effective dialogue. The barriers to effective communication—such as noise, confusing semantics, inappropriate language routines, and lying—will be reduced when effective dialogue takes place.

Dialogue *is a process whereby people suspend their defensiveness to enable a free flow of exploration into their own and others' assumptions and beliefs*. Dialogue includes (1) asking questions and listening to learn, (2) seeking shared meanings, (3) integrating multiple perspectives, and (4) uncovering and examining assumptions. As a result, dialogue can build mutual trust, common ground, and the increased likelihood of ethical interpersonal communication.[28] A necessary condition for dialogue is assertive communication. Assertive communication *means confidently expressing what you think, feel, and believe while respecting the right of others to hold different views*. Ethical dialogue requires that interacting individuals demonstrate multiple abilities and behaviors. Figure 8.4 illustrates the idea that ethical dialogue is characterized by a specific group of interrelated abilities and behaviors. They include communication openness, constructive feedback, appropriate self-disclosure, and active listening.

Through the elements of ethical dialogue and assertive communication, workplace honesty will be more prevalent. Kevin Sharer, the CEO of Amgen who is the focus of our *Learning from Experience* feature, suggests the importance of dialogue and

FIGURE 8.4 Factors That Enable Dialogue

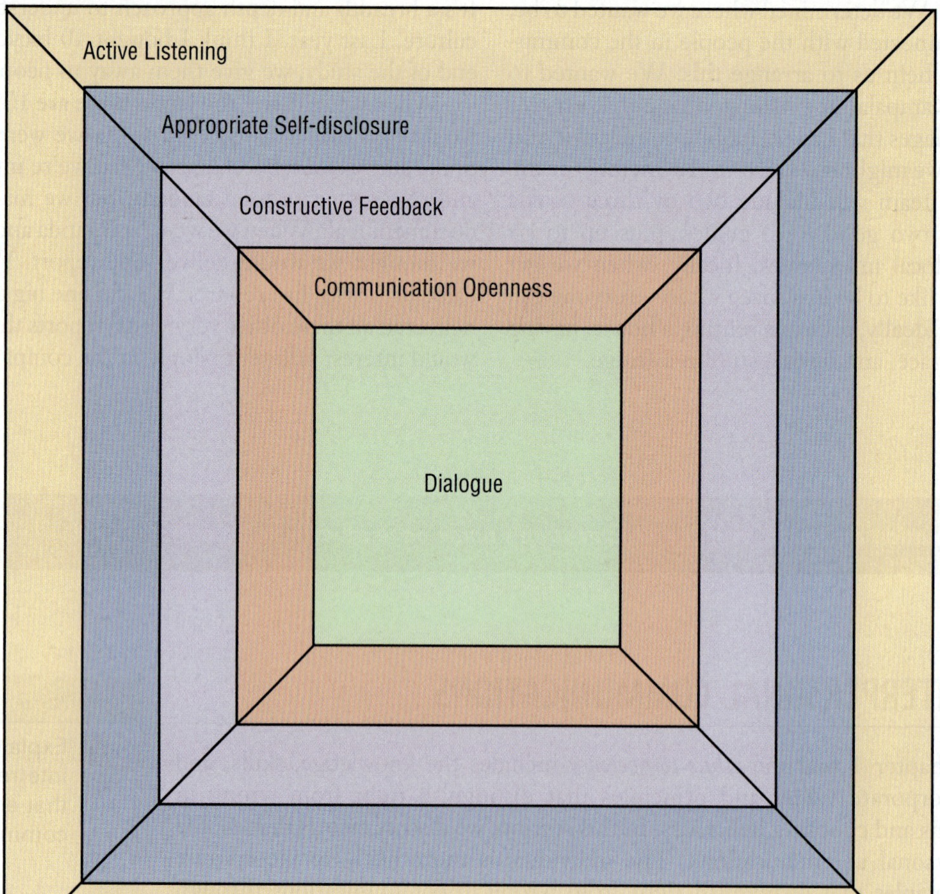

assertive communication in some of his 10 requirements for innovation. Four of those requirements are as follows:[29]

- Foster an open, risk-hungry environment that tolerates dissent and rewards the right results and behaviors.
- Get the best possible people who can work together in a supportive, team-oriented environment.
- Develop close, cross-functional collaboration across employees and the organization.
- Foster a decision-making process that is rigorous, decisive, participatory, transparent, timely, and effective.

As an organization, Amgen states eight core values, one of which is entitled "collaborate, communicate and be accountable." Consistent with our discussion of dialogue and assertive communication, this value at Amgen states:[30]

> *Leaders at Amgen seek input and involve key stakeholders in important decisions. In gathering input, strong leaders will welcome diverse opinions, conflicting views and open dialogue for serious consideration. They will clearly communicate decisions and rationales openly and in a timely manner. Once a decision is made, the leader and members of the team will all be accountable for the results and for implementing the decision rapidly.*

Communication Openness

Communication openness may be viewed as a continuum ranging from closed, guarded, and defensive to open, candid, and supportive.[31] Figure 8.5 shows that, at the extreme

FIGURE 8.5 Elements in Communication Openness

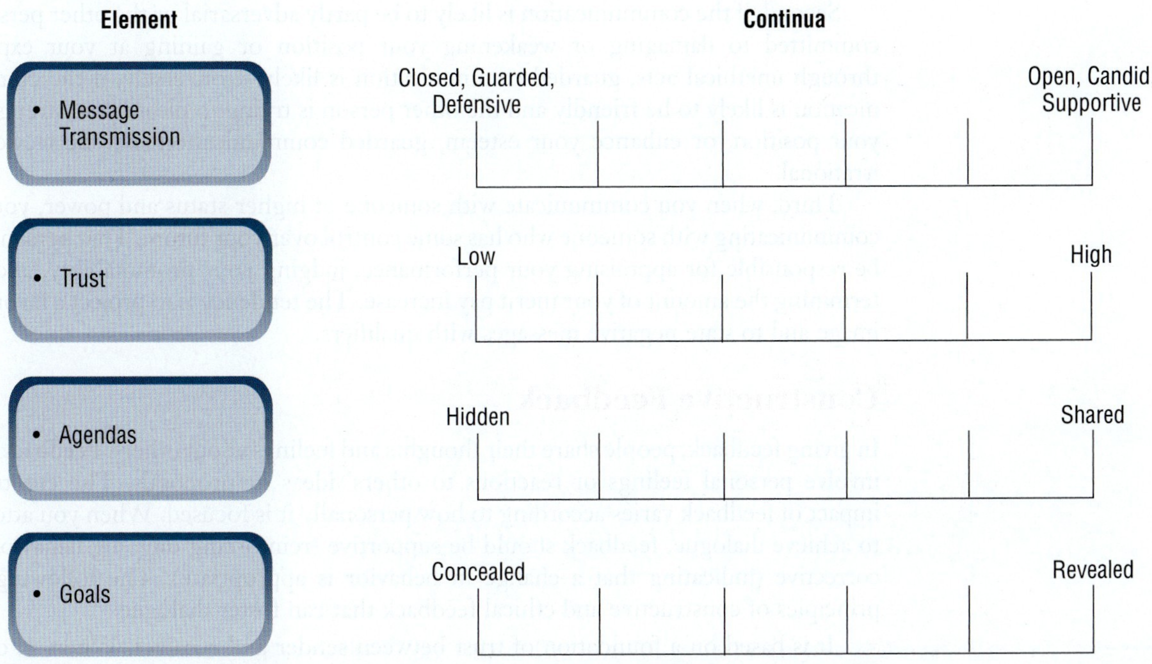

left-hand side of the continuum, messages are interpreted through low trust, hidden agendas, and concealed goals.

Communication occurs on two levels: direct and meta-communication. Meta-communication *brings out the (hidden) assumptions, inferences, and interpretations of the parties that form the basis of open messages*. In closed communication, senders and receivers consciously and purposely hide their real agendas and "messages." Game playing is rampant. Meta-communication focuses on inferences such as (1) what I think you think about what I said; (2) what I think you really mean; (3) what I really mean, but hope you don't realize what I mean; (4) what you're saying, but what I think you really mean; and (5) what I think you're trying to tell me but aren't directly telling me because . . . (you're afraid of hurting my feelings, you think being totally open could hurt your chances of promotion, and so on).

At the extreme right-hand side of the continuum in Figure 8.5, communication is open, candid, and supportive. Messages are interpreted through high trust, shared agendas, and revealed goals.[32] The words and nonverbal cues sent convey an authentic message that the sender chose without having a hidden agenda.

Breakdowns in communication at this end of the continuum are due primarily to honest errors (e.g., the different meanings that people assign to words such as *soon* or *immediately*). Communication openness usually is a matter of degree rather than an absolute. The nature of language, linguistics, and different situations (coworker to coworker, subordinate to superior, friend to friend, or spouse to spouse) creates situations that allow for degrees of shading, coloring emphasis, and deflection in the use of words and nonverbal cues as symbols of meaning.

Individual Guidelines. The degree of openness must be considered in relation to the setting. There are three important factors in a setting. First, the history of the relationship is perhaps the most significant factor affecting openness. Has the other person violated your or others' trust in the past? Has the other person been dishonest and unethical with you or others? Has the other person provided cues (verbal and/or nonverbal) soliciting or reinforcing your attempts to be open and candid? Or has the other person provided cues to the contrary? Has the history of the relationship created a level of such comfort that both you and the other person can focus on direct communication, rather than meta-communication?

Second, if the communication is likely to be partly adversarial or the other person is committed to damaging or weakening your position or gaining at your expense through unethical acts, guarded communication is likely. Conversely, if the communication is likely to be friendly and the other person is trying to please you, strengthen your position, or enhance your esteem, guarded communication may be viewed as irrational.

Third, when you communicate with someone of higher status and power, you are communicating with someone who has some control over your future. That person may be responsible for appraising your performance, judging your promotability, and determining the amount of your merit pay increase. The tendency is to project a favorable image and to state negative messages with qualifiers.

Constructive Feedback

In giving feedback, people share their thoughts and feelings about others. Feedback may involve personal feelings or reactions to others' ideas or proposals. The emotional impact of feedback varies according to how personally it is focused. When you attempt to achieve dialogue, feedback should be supportive (reinforcing ongoing behavior) or corrective (indicating that a change in behavior is appropriate). The following are principles of constructive and ethical feedback that can foster dialogue:[33]

- It is based on a foundation of trust between sender and receiver. When an organization is characterized by extreme personal competitiveness, the emphasis is on the use of power to punish and control, rigid superior–subordinate relationships, and a lack of trust for constructive and ethical feedback.

- It is specific rather than general through the use of clear and recent examples. Saying "You are a dominating person" isn't as useful as saying "Just now when we were deciding the issue, you did not listen to what others said. I felt I had to accept your argument or face attack from you."
- It is given at a time when the receiver appears to be ready to accept it. When a person is angry, upset, or defensive, that probably isn't the time for you to bring up issues.
- It is checked with the receiver to determine whether it seems valid. You can ask the receiver to rephrase and restate the feedback to test whether it matches what you intended.
- It covers behaviors that the receiver may be capable of doing something about.
- It doesn't include more than the receiver can handle at any particular time. For example, the receiver may become threatened and defensive if the feedback includes everything the receiver does that annoys you.

Individual Guidelines. Individuals, teams, and organizations all depend on feedback to improve the way they develop and perform. One approach to obtaining such feedback is through the collection and tabulation of perceptions from multiple individuals about the behaviors and performance of a single individual. For example, 360-degree feedback *is a questionnaire-based process that gathers structured feedback from a number of sources about the competencies and behaviors of an individual or team.* For a manager, questionnaires on behaviors (e.g., teamwork, leadership, goal setting) might be completed by oneself, subordinates, peers, superior, and customers. The results are compiled in a feedback report, with data from each source presented separately. These data and results are provided to the individual who then develops a plan for building strengths and improving personal performance. Normally, this discussion would take place with the person's superior or a consultant.

The use and application of 360-degree feedback is controversial. Clearly, there needs to be an ethical environment of trust and communication openness before the implementation of a formal 360-degree feedback process. It doesn't work in a highly political or bureaucratic organization. It may not work well when the feedback is used as a part of your performance review process unless specific knowledge, skills, and abilities can be linked to specific performance goals. In general, 360-degree feedback appears to work best if it is used for coaching and professional development purposes. A number of other issues and recommendations with respect to the 360-degree feedback process are beyond our scope here.[34]

Table 8.1 provides a questionnaire that can be used by you and other employees to diagnose interpersonal feedback practices within an organization. The scoring system goes from 1 point (strongly disagree) to 5 points (strongly agree) for each statement. Thus, the greater the frequency of "agree" and "strongly agree" responses to the 15 feedback practices, the greater the degree of open and, most likely ethical, interpersonal communications you perceive within the organization.

The first four items in Table 8.1 concern corrective feedback from your superiors and coworkers. Corrective feedback is not necessarily bad for the person who is receiving it. Its effectiveness is largely determined by how the feedback is given. The second section in Table 8.1 (items 5 through 8) concerns the degree to which positive feedback is given to you by individuals at higher organizational levels. Positive feedback reinforces and rewards certain behaviors so that they will be repeated in the future. The third section (items 9 through 12) concerns the degree to which positive feedback is given by your peers. Thus, the first three sections all concern the degree to which positive or negative feedback is received from sources external to you. By contrast, the fourth section (items 13 through 15) focuses on internal feedback, or

Table 8.1

Diagnosis of Feedback Practices

Read each of the following statements and record your perceptions about the feedback practices you experienced in a previous job. Respond on the continuum that ranges from strongly disagree to strongly agree, as follows:

1	2	3	4	5
Strongly Disagree	Disagree	Neutral	Agree	Strongly Agree

CORRECTIVE FEEDBACK	
1. Your manager lets you know when you make a mistake.	1 2 3 4 5
2. You receive a formal report of poor performance.	1 2 3 4 5
3. Coworkers tell you that you have done something wrong.	1 2 3 4 5
4. You are told when you should be doing something else.	1 2 3 4 5
POSITIVE FEEDBACK FROM YOUR MANAGER	
5. You receive thanks after completed jobs.	1 2 3 4 5
6. Your manager tells you when you are doing a good job.	1 2 3 4 5
7. You have a regular performance review with your manager.	1 2 3 4 5
8. The manager treats you as a mature adult.	1 2 3 4 5
POSITIVE FEEDBACK FROM PEERS	
9. Peers congratulate you for how much you accomplish.	1 2 3 4 5
10. Peers compliment you for the quality of your work.	1 2 3 4 5
11. You know more people are using the company's product or service because of your efforts.	1 2 3 4 5
12. Peers like you very much.	1 2 3 4 5
INTERNAL FEEDBACK	
13. You know when you have met your goals.	1 2 3 4 5
14. You can see the results of finding better ways of doing the job.	1 2 3 4 5
15. You know how much you can do without making a mistake.	1 2 3 4 5

the degree to which you assess yourself or other employees observe and assess themselves.

This diagnostic questionnaire clearly shows that several forms of feedback are available to employees in organizations. A lack of compatibility among these forms of feedback for you and a number of the employees may indicate serious problems in an organization's system of interpersonal communication.

Appropriate Self-Disclosure

Self-disclosure *is any information that individuals communicate (verbally or nonverbally) about themselves to others*. People often unconsciously disclose much about themselves by what they say and how they present themselves to others. The ability to express yourself to others usually is basic to personal growth and development.[35] Nondisclosing individuals may repress their real feelings because to reveal them is threatening. Conversely, total-disclosure individuals, who expose a great deal about themselves to anyone they meet, actually may be unable to communicate with others because they are too self-centered. The presence of appropriate self-disclosure, say, between superior and subordinate or team members and customers, can facilitate dialogue and sharing of work-related problems.

Individual Guidelines. A person's level in an organization often complicates self-disclosure. You are more likely to reduce self-disclosure to those having greater formal power because of their ability to punish. Even when you are able and willing to engage in "appropriate" forms of self-disclosure at work, your perception of the manager's trustworthiness in not using the revealed information to punish, intimidate, or ridicule is likely to influence the amount and form of your self-disclosure.

One of the more sensitive areas of appropriate self-disclosure relates to dating and romance with coworkers. A recent survey indicated that 39 percent of employed adults reported dating coworkers at one time or another. About 25 percent indicated their spouse is a current or former coworker.[36] A major concern in most organizations is a romantic or dating relationship between a manager and subordinate. An obvious concern and potential conflict of interest is that the manager will treat the romantic subordinate differently than other subordinates through better pay raises, promotion opportunities, and assignments. As for keeping it a secret, it's not possible. As one business relationship specialist comments: "If you think no one knows, everyone knows."[37] Increasingly, organizations require employees who are romantically involved and work in the same reporting group to disclose their relationship. Such disclosure represents one way to minimize—and, it is hoped, avoid—conflicts of many types.

Active Listening

Active listening is necessary to encourage appropriate levels of ethical feedback and openness. Active listening *involves paying attention, withholding judgment, reflecting, clarifying, summarizing, and sharing*. Listening is effective when the receiver understands the sender's message as intended.

Active listening involves paying attention, withholding judgment, reflecting, clarifying, summarizing, and sharing.

As much as 40 percent of an eight-hour workday for many employees is devoted to listening. Tests of listening comprehension suggest that people often listen at only 25 percent efficiency. Listening influences the quality of peer, manager–subordinate, and employee–customer relationships. Employees who dislike a manager may find it extremely difficult to listen attentively to the manager's comments during performance review sessions. Moreover, active listening is a necessary condition for learning. The

Greek philosopher Epictetus wisely wrote: "It is impossible for a man to learn what he thinks he already knows."

Adapted from the book *Active Listening: Improve Your Ability to Listen and Lead*, we offer the following principles to increase your active listening skills[38]:

- A primary goal of active listening is to set a comfortable tone and allow time and opportunity for the other person to think and speak. Pay attention to your frame of mind, your body language, and the other person. Be present, focus on the moment, and operate from a place of respect.
- Active listening requires an open mind. As a listener, you need to be open to new ideas, new perspectives, and new possibilities. Even when good listeners have strong views, they suspend judgment, hold their criticism, and avoid arguing or selling their point right away. Tell yourself, "I'm here to understand how the other person sees the world. It is not time to judge or give my view."
- Active listening is first about understanding the other person, then about being understood. As you gain a clearer understanding of the other person's perspective, you can then introduce your ideas, feelings, and suggestions and address any concerns. You might talk about a similar experience you had or share an idea that was triggered by a comment made previously in the conversation.
- Active listening involves the use of questions to double-check on any issue that is ambiguous or unclear, which is a component of constructive feedback. Open-ended, clarifying, and probing questions are important tools. Open-ended questions draw people out and encourage them to expand their ideas (i.e., "What are your thoughts on . . .?" or "What led you to draw this conclusion?") Clarifying questions ensure understanding and clear up confusion. Any *who, what, where, when, how*, or *why* questions can be clarifying questions, but those are not the only possibilities. You might say, "I must have missed something. Could you repeat that?" or "I am not sure that I got what you were saying. Can you explain it again another way?" By asking questions, you invite reflection and a thoughtful response instead of telling others what to do. You might ask, for example, "More specifically, what are some of the things you've tried?" or "What is it in your own style that might be contributing to the trouble with others?
- Restating key themes as the conversation proceeds confirms and solidifies your grasp of the other person's point of view. It also helps both you and other person(s) to be clear on mutual responsibilities and follow-up. Briefly summarize what you have understood as you listened (i.e., "It sounds as if your main concern is ..." or "These seem to be the key points you have expressed ..."). You could also ask the other person to summarize.

Individual Guidelines. Active listening skills are interrelated. That is, you can't practice one without improving the others. Active listening is much easier to read about than to develop and practice. The more you practice active listening skills, the more you are able to enter into effective dialogue. Moreover, the listening principles make clear that active listening is not feasible without constructive feedback.[39]

The following Change Competency feature reports on the use of active listening by Sue Powers, the chief information officer and senior vice president at Worldspan.[40] Worldspan is a major provider of travel technology services for travel suppliers, travel agencies, e-commerce sites, and corporations. The firm provides comprehensive data services linking thousands of travel suppliers around the world. Worldspan has approximately 1,700 employees.[41] In this feature, Sue Powers focuses on the communication processes used to achieve organizational changes.

Change Competency

Sue Powers' Communication Process for Introducing Change

Sue Powers relies on a communication process that she calls *socializing an idea* to nudge and encourage her colleagues to consider a new information technology system or business process. The approach is an active one. It requires more than simply running an idea up the flagpole. Socializing means practicing active listening and communication outside formal meetings, where people are less guarded. Powers notes that during casual conversations (in the hallway, in their offices, over lunch), people are more at ease and more willing to discuss change. They also are more likely to discuss their objections to an idea, making it possible to come up with solutions. In a formal setting, people can feel pushed into an idea. In informal settings, they feel they can be more honest.

For example, a few years ago Powers wondered why Worldspan couldn't get the same Internet access deal she had at home: an inexpensive DSL connection. At the time, Worldspan, which operates travel reservation systems, spent $400 to $500 a month for a fairly low-band connection linking the company to its travel agent customers. Sue Powers and David Lauderdale, the chief technology officer, began talking with Worldspan's 650-member technology team about how much more flexible and efficient a standard Internet protocol network could be. The technology team was sold, but they had to convince the rest of the company. Objections to the new technology came fast and furious. Some business managers speculated that travel agents wouldn't want to buy their own PCs and Internet service, preferring to have Worldspan provide their connectivity. Others worried about the technology transition. Salespeople said Worldspan could not get out of its contracts, which required Worldspan to provide dedicated service and equipment.

Powers and her team spent several weeks bringing the idea up again and again with employees and customers during lunch, after company meetings, at after-hours get-togethers, at company functions, and during any casual conversation. Powers didn't emphasize cost savings (although the new system would ultimately save tens of millions of dollars). Instead, she asked for reactions to the potential benefits of the change (the new system would be more reliable, easier to maintain, and simpler to use). Powers says, "The early feedback caused us to think more about what was in this for everybody, and we were able to better think through the benefits for customers and salespeople. We ended up with a better plan."

Powers used the feedback from these informal discussions to write a business case for the new system, and her plan was immediately approved. When it came time to rewrite customer contracts, the travel agents were sold on the added benefits they would get. Worldspan soon completed its rollout of the DSL network. Power notes "getting people involved early by just talking with them [through active listening] allowed us to address objections and actually have a better plan. By the time we did the business plan, we had everybody pretty much on board."

For more information on Worldspan, visit the organization's home page at www.worldspan.com.

NONVERBAL COMMUNICATION

Learning Goal

3. Describe and effectively apply nonverbal communication in interpersonal communication.

Nonverbal communication *includes the process of sending "wordless" messages by such means as facial expressions, gestures, postures, tones of voice, grooming, clothing, colors, and use or type of space.*[42] Nonverbal cues may contain many direct or hidden messages and can influence the process and outcome of "words" in communication. Even when you are silent or inactive in the presence of others, you are sending a message, which may or may not be the intended message (including boredom, fear, anger, or depression). Nonverbal signals are a rich source of information. Your own nonverbal behavior can be useful in responding to others, making stronger connections with others, and conveying certain impressions about yourself. The proportion of *emotional* reactions that are expressed through nonverbal signals may exceed 90 percent.[43]

Types of Nonverbal Cues

A framework for considering types of *personal* nonverbal cues is *PERCEIVE*, an acronym that stands for the following terms: (1) **P**roximity, (2) **E**xpressions, (3) **R**elative orientation, (4) **C**ontact, (5) **E**yes, (6) **I**ndividual gestures, (7) **V**oice, and (8) **E**xistence of adapters. A brief review of each follows[44]:

- *Proximity* is the physical distance between individuals. Generally, individuals sit, stand, and want to be near those they like. Increased proximity is usually an indication of feelings of liking and interest.
- *Expressions* are observed on the face and can last as little as 1/15th of a second. These very brief expressions occur when people are trying to hide a feeling. Interestingly, when people begin to experience an emotion, their facial muscles are triggered. If they suppress the expression, it's shown for only 1/15th of a second. If they do not suppress it, the expression will appear prominently. The six universal expressions that most cultures recognize are happiness, sadness, anger, fear, surprise, and disgust. Smiling can be real or false, interpreted by differences in the strength and length of the smile, the openness of the eyes, and the symmetry of expression.
- *Relative orientation* is the degree to which individuals face one another. Individuals sitting side by side is usually an indication that they are interested in and focused on the other person. As individuals become less interested in another person, they tend to angle their bodies away. A good way to understand relative orientation is to observe where a person's feet are placed. Often individuals will point their feet in the direction they truly want to go.
- *Contact* refers to physical contact. Generally, the amount and frequency of physical contact demonstrate closeness, familiarity, and degree of liking. A lot of touching usually indicates strong liking for another person.
- *Eyes* primarily show whom or what people are most interested in or like. One can gauge liking and interest by the frequency and duration of time spent looking. Few gestures carry more weight than looking someone in the eyes or face. Eye and face contact displays your willingness to listen and your acknowledgment of the other person's worth. Although eye contact does not indicate truthfulness or honesty (as some people believe), it does usually show interest in the other person's idea or point of view. However, prolonged and intense eye contact does not usually occur unless feelings of hostility, defensiveness, or romantic interest are present. Lack of interest may be indicated through contractions of the pupils or wandering eyes.
- *Individual gestures* can convey an image in a person's mind that is sometimes not spoken. Some typical gestures are ones that describe an emotion or experience (e.g., sobbing gesture or frenetic moving of the hands) or gestures that identify where objects are in relation to one another. Gestures also reveal how people are feeling. People tend to gesture more when they are enthusiastic, excited, and energized. People tend to gesture less when they are demoralized, nervous, or concerned about the impression they are making.
- *Voice* or speech often provides information about the demographics of a speaker (e.g., gender, age, area of origin, social class). Voice can also reveal emotions, which are transmitted through the tone of the voice, accentuation of words, rapidity of speech, and number of speech errors. Typically, speech errors indicate discomfort and anxiety. A person who begins to produce a lot of speech errors may be anxious and ill at ease.

- *Existence of adapters* is the last element of *PERCEIVE*. Adapters are small behaviors that tend to occur when people are stressed or bored with a situation. Examples are playing with rings, twirling a pen, or touching one's hair. As meetings become too long, an increasing number of adapter behaviors tend to emerge among the people in the room.

Physical Environment. Some organizations are attempting to influence interpersonal communications through the physical environment with the use of feng shui, which we introduced in Chapter 3. Feng shui is the belief that space needs to be in harmony with the environment. We noted that the Chinese phrase *feng shui* means "wind and water" to represent the flow of energy and harmony. A few of the common recommendations for office arrangements related to nonverbal communication based on feng shui include:

1. You should have a full view of the room's entrance door by merely looking up from your desk.
2. You should be able to see outside while sitting at your desk. If the office doesn't have a window, brighten up the lighting and use a picture of the outdoors.
3. Your desk should not be placed at the side of the door. You can place a screen in the space between your desk and the doorway if necessary.
4. You should have a wall at your back while seated. Presumably, it gives you a "commanding" position.[45]

Although the ability of feng shui to impact "harmony and energy" has been questioned, its principles for designing buildings and offices, including the placement of furniture and objects, are increasingly being used to varying degrees in Western societies.[46] For people in North America who are interested in feng shui, the American Feng Shui Institute is a good place to start for more details about its concepts and principles.[47]

Importance to Verbal Messages. Nonverbal communication is important to verbal communication in that neither is adequate by itself for effective dialogue. A few of the ways in which verbal and nonverbal cues can be related are as follows:

- Repeating, such as when verbal directions to some location are accompanied by pointing.
- Contradicting, such as when you say "What, me nervous?" while fidgeting and perspiring anxiously before taking a test. This is a good example of how the nonverbal message might be more believable when verbal and nonverbal signals conflict.
- Substituting nonverbal for verbal cues, such as when you return from the manager's office with a stressful expression that says "I've just had a horrible meeting with my manager"—without a word being spoken.
- Complementing the verbal cue through nonverbal "underlining," such as when you pound on a table, place a hand on the shoulder of a coworker, use a tone of voice indicating the great importance attached to the message, or give a gift as a way of reinforcing an expression of gratitude or respect.

In the following Communication Competency feature, David Gaudet reports on an experience that demonstrates the important interplay between nonverbal and verbal cues by a new employee, who showed much agility in adapting to the situation.[48] Gaudet is the executive producer and artistic director of Comedy Sportz Chicago. This organization offers a unique blend of fast, funny, and improvisational comedy that is appropriate for all ages. Although headquartered in Chicago, its touring company offers programs throughout the world.[49]

Communication Competency

Traveling with Agility

Several years ago, Dave Gaudet was doing a world tour for Intel, the computer chip company. When he and his staff arrived in Manila, one of his new hires discovered that her luggage had been lost. Gaudet states: "Because Manila was especially dangerous at the time, and the employee was very tall, very attractive and stood out like a sore thumb, [she] had to be escorted by bodyguards with machine guns on a trip to the local mall to look for substitute clothes for her. A six-foot woman with size 12 shoes isn't the easiest person to find clothes for in the Philippines. She couldn't find anything her size, so she had to improvise. She went the whole week dressed in men's clothes and didn't bat an eye." The fact that this woman was able to "adapt and roll with the punches gave Gaudet insight into her potential as an employee. He comments: "When you first hire someone, you don't know what kind of person they'll be. She turned out to be one of our star people."

Gaudet noted that the episode in Manila was not the first time he had made a management decision about a staff member based on his or her behavior on the road. He states: "Travel lets you know whether people can adapt to whatever situations they're thrust into. If someone is a hassle to travel with, I won't use that person again." He cites the example of a former employee who once "created havoc at customs in Germany for no reason whatsoever." Gaudet adds, tongue in cheek, "Instead of giving new employees training sessions or psychological evaluations, we should just put them on planes. We'd learn a whole lot more about how they adapt, how they treat other people."

When told of Gaudet's story, Dr. Susan Bailey, a leadership psychologist in New York, commented: "The employee had shown her boss she had the grace under pressure and flexibility needed for workplace advancement. The difference between being really successful versus only moderately successful at work lies in those nontechnical skills, such as interpersonal communication and social intelligence, that can come into play when you travel with your boss. That means managing your temper in frustrating situations and being aware of how you come across."

Bailey adds that a chief executive she worked with had told her he had chosen his successor based on that person's behavior during a business trip in Minneapolis, where the two ended up stranded because of a snowstorm. Bailey comments: "He said that what tipped the scales was interacting with this person at the airport while rescheduling the flight. Everyone else was rude, nasty and upset, but this fellow handled everything with grace."

For more information on Comedy Sportz Chicago, visit the organization's home page at www.comedysportzchicago.com.

Nonverbal cues have been linked to a wide variety of concepts and issues. We briefly consider two—cultural differences and status differences—in terms of the relative ranking of individuals and groups.

Cultural Differences

Throughout this book, we have noted the impact of culture on communication. Because of the many differences in nonverbal expression, people from different cultures often misunderstand each other. This is a significant barrier to cross-cultural communication.[50] Earlier in this chapter, we examined how cultural context and ethnocentrism may affect interpersonal communications. Let's now examine three forms of nonverbal cross-cultural communication: chromatics, chronemics, and body language.

Chromatics. Chromatics *is communication through the use of color*. Colors of clothing, products, packaging, or gifts send intended or unintended messages when people communicate cross-culturally. For example, in Hong Kong red signifies happiness or good luck. The traditional bridal dress is red, and at the Chinese New Year luck money is distributed in *hong bao*, red envelopes. Men in Hong Kong avoid green because of the Cantonese expression "He's wearing a green hat," which means "His wife is cheating on him." In Chile, a gift of yellow roses conveys the message "I don't like you," whereas in the Czech Republic giving red roses indicates a romantic interest.

Chronemics. Chronemics *reflects the use of time in a culture.*[51] Before reading any further, please complete the instrument in Table 8.2 to determine how you use your personal time. A monochronic time schedule *means that things are done linearly, or one activity at a time.* Time is seen as something that can be controlled or wasted by people. Time schedules are followed by employees in individualistic cultures, such as those in Northern Europe, Germany, and the United States. Being a few minutes late for a business appointment is an insult, so punctuality is extremely important. Keith Hughes is the former CEO of Associates First Capital Corporation, a consumer finance company that has been acquired by Citigroup. He used to lock the doors when a meeting was supposed to start and didn't unlock them until the meeting was over.

Table 8.2 The Polychronic Attitude Index

Please consider how you feel about the following statements. Circle your choice on the scale provided: strongly agree, agree, neutral, disagree, or strongly disagree.

	STRONGLY DISAGREE	DISAGREE	NEUTRAL	AGREE	STRONGLY AGREE
1. I do not like to juggle several activities at the same time.	5	4	3	2	1
2. People should not try to do many things at once.	5	4	3	2	1
3. When I sit down at my desk, I work on one project at a time.	5	4	3	2	1
4. I am comfortable doing several things at the same time.	5	4	3	2	1

Add up your points, and divide the total by 4. Then plot your score on the scale.

1.0	1.5	2.0	2.5	3.0	3.5	4.0	4.5	5.0
Monochronic								Polychronic

The lower the score (below 3.0), the more monochronic your organization or department is; the higher the score (above 3.0), the more polychronic it is.

Source: Adapted from Bluedorn, A. C., Kaufman, C. F., and Lane, P. M. How many things do you like to do at once? An introduction to monochronic and polychronic time. *Academy of Management Executive*, 1992, 6 (4), 17–26. Used with permission of Bluedorn, A. C., 1999.

A polychronic time schedule *means that people tend to do several things at the same time.* In everyday parlance, we call that *multitasking*. Many people may like to drive and conduct business at the same time (cars and cellular phones) or watch the news and a ball game at the same time (picture-in-picture TV). Schedules are less important than personal involvement and the completion of business. In Latin America and the Middle East, time schedules are less important than personal involvement. In Ecuador, businesspeople come to a meeting 15 or 20 minutes late and still consider themselves to be on time.

Body Language. Posture, gestures, eye contact, facial expression, touching, voice pitch and volume, and speaking rate differ from one culture to another.[52] As a simple, but potentially disastrous example, nodding the head up and down in Bulgaria means "no," not "yes." You must avoid using any gestures considered rude or insulting. For instance, in Buddhist cultures, the head is considered sacred, so you must never touch anyone's head. In Muslim cultures, the left hand is considered unclean, so never touch, pass, or receive with the left hand. Pointing with the index finger is rude in cultures ranging from the Sudan to Venezuela to Sri Lanka. The American circular "A-OK" gesture carries a vulgar meaning in Brazil, Paraguay, Singapore, and Russia. Crossing your ankle over your knee is rude in Indonesia, Thailand, and Syria. Pointing your index finger toward yourself insults the other person in Germany, the Netherlands, and Switzerland. Avoid placing an open hand over a closed fist in France, saying "tsk tsk" in Kenya, and whistling in India.

© The Studio Dog/Photodisc/Getty Images

Body language, including gestures, eye contact, facial expression, and touching, varies from one culture to another.

Prepare yourself to recognize gestures that have meaning only in the other culture. Chinese stick out their tongues to show surprise and scratch their ears and cheeks to show happiness. Japanese suck in air, hissing through their teeth to indicate embarrassment or "no." Greeks puff air after they receive a compliment. Hondurans touch a finger to the face below the eye to indicate caution or disbelief.

Finally, resist applying your own culture's nonverbal meanings to other cultures. Vietnamese may look at the ground with their heads down to show respect, not to be "shifty." Russians may exhibit less facial expression and Scandinavians fewer gestures than Americans are accustomed to, but that doesn't mean that they aren't enthusiastic. The British may prefer more distant personal and social space and might consider it rude if you move too close. Closely related is the concept of touch. Anglos usually avoid touching each other very much. In studies of touching behaviors, researchers observed people seated in outdoor cafes in each of four countries and counted the number of touches during an hour of conversation. The results were San Juan, Puerto Rico, 180 touches per hour; Paris, 110 per hour; Gainesville, Florida, 1 per hour; and London, 0 per hour.[53]

Status Differences

The following are only three of the many relationships between nonverbal cues and organizational status:

- Employees of higher status typically have better offices than do employees of lower status. For example, executive offices are typically more spacious, located on the top floors of the building, and have finer carpets and furniture than those of first-line managers. Most senior offices are at the corners, so they have windows on two sides.
- The offices of higher status employees are better "protected" than those of lower status employees. *Protected* refers to how much more difficult it would be for you to, say, arrange to visit the governor of your state than for the governor to arrange to

visit you. Top executive areas are typically least accessible and are often sealed off from others by several doors and assistants. Having an office with a door and a secretary who answers the telephone protects even lower level managers and many staff personnel.

- The higher the employee's status, the easier that employee finds it to invade the territory of lower status employees. A superior typically feels free to walk right in on subordinates, whereas subordinates are more careful to ask permission or make an appointment before visiting a superior.[54]

Carried to excess, these and other nonverbal status cues are likely to create barriers to dialogue, especially from the perspective of the employees with lower formal status. However, effective managers often use supportive nonverbal cues when meeting with subordinates, such as (1) lightly touching subordinates on the arm when they arrive and shaking hands, (2) smiling appropriately, (3) nodding to affirm what was said, (4) slightly pulling their chairs closer to subordinates and maintaining an open posture, and (5) engaging in eye contact to further demonstrate listening and interest.[55]

INTERPERSONAL COMMUNICATION NETWORKS

Learning Goal

4. Describe and apply communication networks in interpersonal communication.

An interpersonal communication network *is the pattern of communication flows, relationships, and understandings developed over time among people, rather than focusing on the individual and whether a specific message is received as intended by the sender.* Networks involve the ongoing flow of verbal, written, and nonverbal messages between two people or between one person and others. Communication networks can influence the likelihood of a match between messages as sent and as actually received and interpreted. The more accurately the message moves through the channel, the more clearly the receiver will understand it.

Individual Network

The elements of interpersonal communication shown earlier in Figure 8.1 are based on a network of only two people. Obviously, communication often takes place among many individuals and larger groups. Claudia Gonzales, a telecommunications manager for Abaco Grupo Financiero in Mexico, normally has ongoing links with many people both inside and outside her organization. Her communication network extends laterally, vertically, and externally. *Vertical networks* typically include her immediate superior and subordinates and the superior's superiors and the subordinates' subordinates. *Lateral networks* include people in the same department at the same level (peers) and people in different departments at the same level. *External networks* include customers, suppliers, regulatory agencies, pressure groups, professional peers, and friends. Thus, a person's communication network can be quite involved.

Size limits the possible communication networks within a team or informal group. In principle, as the size of a team increases arithmetically, the number of possible communication interrelationships increases exponentially. Accordingly, communication networks are much more varied and complex in a 12-person team than in a 5-person team. Although each team member (theoretically) may be able to communicate with all the others, the direction and number of communication channels often are somewhat limited. In committee meetings, for example, varying levels of formality influence who may speak, what may be discussed, and in what order. The relative status or ranking of team members also may differ. Members having higher status probably will dominate communications more than those with lower status. Even when an open network is encouraged, a team member may actually use a limited network arrangement.

A common prescription, especially for college graduates when they join an organization, is to work on developing an individual communication network. At present or in the future, how might you know if you have developed a strong inside individual network? If you are able to answer "yes" to most of the following questions, you are probably on the right track:[56]

1. Do you know people at more than one level of the organization? Do they know your name and what you do?
2. Do you know a number of the people whose work relates to yours in any way beyond your own department?
3. Are you involved in any interdepartmental activities (temporary assignments, committees, task forces, special projects, volunteer activities)?
4. Are you plugged into the grapevine? Do you find out quickly what's up?
5. Do you take every opportunity to meet face to face to define and discuss complex problems, shifting priorities, areas of responsibility?
6. Do you know and talk with others about trends that will impact your job in the future and methods to get the job done today?
7. When you become aware of a problem that involves people from various areas, do you take the initiative to indicate your willingness to work on it?
8. Do you drop by to see people—even when you don't need anything—as time permits?

Effective individual networking focuses on serving customers, streamlining internal processes, solving problems, and achieving organizational and unit goals. Networking that focuses on immediate and apparent self-serving interests and goals is often counterproductive and even more so when it serves to hurt or take advantage of others.[57] For individual network effectiveness, the individual needs political skill—*the ability to effectively understand others at work, and to use such knowledge to influence others to act in ways that enhance one's long-term personal and/or organizational goals.*[58]

The Experiential Exercise section at the end of this chapter includes a *Political Skill Inventory* on page 257.[59] You may want to complete it now. Political skill might be thought of as one side of a coin with the other side being impression management (see Chapter 3, pages 82–84).

A major study identified the primary causes of managerial failure in changing organizations. More than 1,000 successful U.S. managers participated in this study.[60] Table 8.3 shows the top 10 major themes that were cited as causes of managerial failures. Although a failed manager is likely to be characterized by several themes, it is apparent that "ineffective communication skills/practices" is cited by the vast majority (81 percent) of participants as almost always being present. The failed managers typically did not effectively share critical information with individual employees and/or work teams. Also, they failed to listen to the concerns of those around them, with potentially devastating outcomes. In essence, these failed managers were poor networkers and lacked political skill, as suggested in several of the themes identified in Table 8.3.

Table 8.3 **Themes in Causes of Managerial Failure: Perceptions of More Than 1,000 Successful Managers**

THEMES	FREQUENCY OF MENTIONS
1. Ineffective communication skills/practices	81%
2. Poor work relationships/interpersonal skills	78%
3. Person job mismatch	69%
4. Fail to clarify direction/performance expectations	64%
5. Failing to adapt and break old habits quickly	57%
6. Delegation and empowerment breakdown	56%
7. Lack of personal integrity and trustworthiness	52%
8. Unable to develop cooperation/teamwork	50%
9. Unable to lead/motivate others	47%
10. Poor planning practices/reactionary behavior	45%

Source: Adapted from Longenecker, C. O., Neubert, M. J., and Fink, L. S. Causes and consequences of managerial failure in rapidly changing organizations. *Business Horizons*, 2007, 50, 148.

Informal Group Network

An informal group network involves the communication pattern of multiple individual networks. By *informal* we mean those communication channels and messages that do not strictly follow the formal organization paths, such as when the president meets with or sends all employees an e-mail, or when a manager holds a weekly meeting with employees.

The most common form of informal group network is the grapevine—*the unofficial, and at times confidential, person-to-person or person-to-group chain of verbal, or at times e-mail, communication.*[61] The most common messages of the grapevine are rumors—unverified information, which may be of uncertain origin, that is usually spread by word of mouth or perhaps e-mail. Rumors are often a result of stress circumstances, like the perceived threats from major organizational changes. Of course, rumors themselves, especially when false, can be a source of stress and dissatisfaction. In general, the frequency of negative rumors is much greater than positive rumors in organizations.[62] Four of the major ways that messages move through grapevines in organizations are as follows[63]:

- *Single-strand chain* refers to one person telling a rumor to the next, who then tells the next person, who tells the next, and so on. As such, the rumor is told to one person at a time and passed on to others. Accuracy is lower in this type of chain than in the others because of the many alterations the story is subject to with each retelling.
- *Gossip chain* refers to only one person spreading the message, telling the story to most everyone with which the person comes in contact. This chain is likely to be the most slow moving.
- *Probability chain* refers to one person randomly contacting several others and telling them the message. Those individuals, in turn, randomly contact several others and continue to spread it. This chain is not a definite channel because the message is spread to different people, bypassing others altogether.
- *Cluster chain* refers to one person telling several close contacts who then pass it on to several people with whom they have close contacts. Regardless, people receive and transmit the message in terms of their personal biases, which results in the general theme being maintained but the details potentially being changed. It is often used to spread rumors and other news in organizations.

Informal group networks, like grapevines, cannot be eliminated by managers. In fact, managers often participate in them. The best approach is to understand grapevines and develop strategies to use in preventing and combating false or inaccurate rumors and gossip both internally and externally to the organization.[64] In an organization with low levels of communication openness, it is to be expected that informal group networks are likely to conflict with the formal employee network established by senior management. As you will recall from Figure 8.5, low communication openness is characterized by (1) closed, guarded, and defensive message transmission; (2) low trust; (3) hidden agendas; and (4) concealed goals. In this situation, it is likely that different informal group networks are likely to conflict with each other as well and be engaged in continuous power struggles. In contrast, with high levels of communication openness and other attributes of ethical interpersonal communication, individual networks, informal group networks, and formal employee networks will more often be mutually supportive and reasonably consistent with one another, thereby reducing barriers, inconsistencies, and confusion in communications within the organization.[65]

The following Self Competency feature reports on how Andres Amezuita, a senior manager at Mattel, Inc., effectively used his individual network and informal group network through a high level of communication openness.[66] Mattel, Inc., is headquartered in El Segundo, California. It is a global provider of toys and family products and has more than 30,000 employees in 43 countries.[67]

Self Competency

Andres Amezuita Develops Networks at Mattel

Andres Amezuita was promoted from the boys toy division in Latin America to a broader international role in the girls division at the company's California headquarters. While he had established an international network of personal contacts over the years at Mattel, his network beyond Latin America and the boys division was limited. He used a crisis situation in the European operations to rapidly expand the size of his network. Amezuita explains: "I knew that the business was in crisis due to a serious product delay, and I also knew that I did not have a lot of time to learn what was happening. It was a business that I was new to. Yet I needed to get my own European network alive very quickly."

Amezuita leveraged early morning walks with his dog to enhance his networking. He comments: "In California, we only have two morning hours a day that overlap with Europe's business hours. As we are waking up, they are typically heading home from work. Now, I always take my dog for a walk at 5 A.M. My dog doesn't care with whom I talk, so I decided to take that time to call the marketing and brand managers in Europe to discuss the product delay. If I call them at 5 A.M. my time, it is a surprise for them. My call is still in the middle of their workday. What I discovered was that these calls built trust and a relationship. I spent a lot of time listening to these individuals. Historically, corporate did not share things early on with the country managers, such as market research. So I decided to become very transparent. I told our European managers things more candidly."

Amezuita also began to help them out by acting as an information source about company resources. He describes what he did in those calls as matchmaking behavior: "There are many areas and resources inside the company that the country managers do not know about. They may want to use some type of media, and so I will connect them with media folks at corporate. During my early morning calls, I started identifying some of the country needs and helping them connect to the key people at corporate."

For more information on Mattel, visit the organization's home page at www.mattel.com.

Formal Employee Network

A formal employee network *is the intended pattern and flows of employee-related communication vertically—between levels—and laterally—between individuals teams, departments, and divisions.* In this chapter, we discussed several of the initiatives undertaken by Kevin Sharer at Amgen to shape, develop, and use its formal employee network. Our discussion of Nokia's approach to understanding cultural context revealed the extensive use of a formal employee network in planning for and conducting their studies in various countries. In our Change Competency feature on Sue Powers at Worldspan, she and her team used individual, informal, and formal employee networks to introduce ideas, receive feedback, and foster formal changes.

In most chapters throughout this book, we present competency features on how managers can foster or hinder the development of effective formal employee networks. Our discussion of six types of formal teams in Chapter 11—such as self-managed, virtual, and global—are examples of higher management's initiatives to form and influence various lateral and vertical formal employee networks. Also, we discuss the *network design* as one of the contemporary organizational designs in Chapter 14, *Designing Organizations*.

Sue Hagen, the senior vice president of human resources at Dole Food Company, had some concerns several years ago when the company went private. These concerns related to how talented employees would interpret this change, including whether it would be harder to recruit and retain employees. Dole is a worldwide provider of many types of food products.

Communicating with employees about what going private meant was the biggest challenge for Hagen, given the size of its workforce. Dole has 60,000 employees in 90 countries speaking 13 languages. Hagen states: "Even short, straightforward messages are complex and involved to communicate." For the two months after the change was announced, Hagen and her eight-person team worked with department heads to conduct a mass communication campaign that included small and large group meetings, e-mails, newsletters, and the company's intranet. Because only one-tenth of Dole employees work at computers on the job, Dole made sure its managers worldwide understood the change and communicated it to employees. "Managers would go out into the field and explain it to workers," Hagen says.

Dole's message centered on what it meant to be a private company instead of a public one, and reassured employees their benefits and compensation would not change. Repetition was key, she says. After the first couple of months, Hagen and her team made sure to repeat the message so that employees felt at peace with the changes. The formal employee network created by Hagen and her team was very successful and no adverse consequences resulted from going private.[68]

Managerial Guidelines

All types of networks are important for day-to-day communication in organizations.[69] First, no single network is likely to prove effective in all situations for a team or whole organization faced with a variety of tasks, problems, and goals. The apparently efficient, low-cost, and simple method of a superior instructing subordinates is likely to be ineffective if used exclusively. Dissatisfaction may become so great that members will leave the team or lose their motivation to contribute. Second, individuals and teams that face complex problems requiring a lot of discussion and coordination may deal with them ineffectively because of inadequate sharing of information, consideration of alternatives, participation, and the like. Management must consider trade-offs or opportunity costs. The use of the fully engaged formal employee network may deal poorly with simple problems and tasks that require little member coordination. For example, members may become bored and dissatisfied with meetings. They often simply come to feel that their time is being wasted. Another trade-off with the fully engaged formal network is higher labor costs. That is, employees must spend too much time on a problem and its solution in meetings when a simpler network would do well. Hence, management should use the level of networking that is most appropriate to the specific goals and tasks.

Impacts of E-Mail

E-mail impacts individual, informal group, and formal employee networks as well as interpersonal communications as a whole. In later chapters, we address other communication technologies, such as those related to teams (Chapter 11), decision making (Chapter 13), organization design (Chapter 14), and organizational change (Chapter 16).

Just as face-to-face meetings can be overused and misused in organizations, so too can e-mail. The potential perils of e-mail are greater than many assume. Research suggests as few as 50 percent of users grasp the tone or intent of an e-mail. Moreover, most people vastly overestimate their ability to relay and comprehend e-mail messages accurately. Misinterpretation is highest when the e-mail comes from the person's manager.[70] E-mail is different from live conversation in two important ways: First, you cannot modify the content of a message based on the nonverbal reaction of the other party. Second, e-mails are permanent documents. Once you send it, you cannot take it back, and you lose all control over who views your words. Unfortunately, the permanent nature of e-mail often is forgotten in the hubbub of everyday interactions and can come back to haunt the sender in unanticipated ways.

Three major challenges have been identified with the use of e-mail: First and foremost, e-mails lacks cues like facial expression and tone of voice. That makes it difficult for recipients to decode meaning well. Second, the prospect of instantaneous communication creates an urgency that pressures e-mailers to think and write quickly, which can lead to carelessness in grammar, spelling, and tone. Third, the inability to develop personal rapport over an e-mail makes relationships fragile in the face of conflict.[71] In effect, e-mail cannot adequately convey emotion. When it does, unintended emotions are often received or the sender may soon wish they could retrieve or revise the emotions sent.

The emotional dimension conveyed thru e-mail has been termed *e-body language* by one author.[72] E-body language is primarily conveyed in three main areas, as discussed next.

Tone. How you structure and phrase e-mails can play a large part in how they are interpreted. For example, the overuse of personal pronouns—*I, me, my*—makes the writer sound parochial or egotistical. Too much use of the words *we* and *they* signals a competitive atmosphere. Overuse of exclamation points, sentences in all caps and bold font, and messages marked "high importance" when that is not really so are pitfalls associated with using e-mail. These practices can easily create unintended tones and related reactions.

Timing. Because people open e-mail messages at different times, a person might reply to a message that has been superseded by another, leading to confusion. Sometimes e-mail messages arrive with an expected quick reply when the recipient is in an overload situation. In a recent survey, one-quarter of the 7,800 responding managers reported being overwhelmed by their daily communications, especially through e-mail.[73]

Tension. Interpersonal conflict may leave a bloody and ugly trail in e-mail communications. Outbursts of anger via e-mails usually make both parties look foolish, especially when individuals escalate the conflict into heated exchanges. The way to stop an online battle is to refrain from taking the bait. Don't respond to the attack in kind. Acknowledge a difference of opinion, but don't escalate the situation. Switching to a different form of communication will help avoid a trail of embarrassing messages.[74] Chapter 12 explores managing conflict and negotiating effectively.

Consider the rather drastic action in response to e-mail excess by Scott Dockter, the CEO of PBD Worldwide Fulfillment Services, headquartered in Alpharetta, Georgia. Dockter decided things were bad when he found himself continuously e-mailing his assistant, who was seated a few feet away. He suspected that overdependence on e-mail at PBD, which offers services such as call center management and distribution, was hurting productivity and perhaps sales. So, Dockter instructed the firm's 275 employees to pick up the phone or meet in person each Friday and to reduce e-mail use the rest of the time.

That was tough to digest, especially for younger employees and some senior managers. "We discovered a lot of introverts . . . who had drifted into a pattern of communicating by e-mail," Dockter says. But in less than four months, the simple directive resulted in quicker problem solving, better teamwork, and, best of all, happier customers. Cynthia Fitzpatrick of Crown Financial Ministries states "You can't get to know someone through e-mail. Our relationship with PBD is much stronger." Dockter's solution was clearly low tech, but, it influenced PBD's culture. E-mail usage dropped more than 80 percent. This prompted improved communication and more one-on-one interaction between colleagues. Clients are so impressed that they have started to visit and call his staffers more often, too. The biggest peril now? Getting trapped in telephone tag. Another partial solution may come from the Outlook e-mail system itself. In its 2007 version of Outlook, Microsoft has elevated the telephone to a prominent position. Users can click on colleagues' names, see if they're available, and use Outlook to place a call directly.[75]

CHAPTER SUMMARY

1. Describe the core elements of interpersonal communication.

The basic elements in the communication process—senders, receivers, transmitters, receptors, messages, channels, noise, meaning, encoding, decoding, and feedback—are interrelated.

Face-to-face interpersonal communication has the highest degree of information richness. An information-rich medium is especially important for performing complex tasks and resolving social and emotional issues that involve considerable uncertainty and ambiguity. Important issues usually contain significant amounts of uncertainty, ambiguity, and people-related (especially social and emotional) problems.

There are many potential challenges to effective interpersonal communication. Direct barriers include aggressive communication approaches, noise, semantics, demeaning language, and lying and distortion. The barriers stemming from cultural differences are always present. They may be especially high when the interaction takes place between individuals from high-context and low-context cultures.

2. Explain and apply the interrelated factors that enable ethical communications.

Through mastering the factors that constitute dialogue, the likelihood of engaging in ethical interpersonal communications is magnified. Dialogue includes communication openness, constructive feedback, appropriate self-disclosure, and active listening. Dialogue requires senders and receivers to play a dynamic role in the communication process. In open communication, senders and receivers are able to discuss, disagree, and search for understanding without resorting to personal attacks or hidden agendas. Feedback received from others provides motivation for individuals to learn and change their behaviors. By being an active listener, the receiver hears the whole message without interpretation or judgment. How much individuals are willing to share with others depends on their ability to disclose information.

3. Describe and effectively apply nonverbal communication in interpersonal communication.

Nonverbal cues play a powerful role in supporting or hindering dialogue. There are many types of personal nonverbal cues. They were presented through the acronym PERCEIVE, which stands for the following terms: proximity, expressions, relative orientation, contact, eyes, individual gestures, voice, and existence of adapters. The role of cultural barriers in impeding communication effectiveness was noted throughout the chapter. We examined specifically how certain nonverbal messages—the use of color, time, and gestures—can affect cross-cultural communication. Formal organizational position is often tied to status. Status symbols, office size, the floor on which the office is located, number of windows, location of a secretary, and access to senior-level employees—all influence communication patterns. We noted some cautionary comments on the need to avoid simplistic stereotypes as to the meaning of nonverbal cues employed by an individual.

4. Describe and apply communication networks in interpersonal communication.

An individual's communication network extends laterally, vertically, and externally. The development of a strong inside individual network can be determined by being able to respond "yes" to most of the eight questions presented in the chapter text, such as "Do you know a number of people whose work intersects with yours in any way beyond your own work unit?" For individual networking effectiveness, the individual needs political skill, which is a component of both our communication and self competencies. The informal group network involves the pattern of multiple individual networks. The most common form of informal group network is the grapevine, which may take the pattern of a single-strand chain, gossip chain, probability chain, or cluster chain. The formal employee network focuses on the intended pattern of employee-related communication vertically and laterally. Management needs to be proactive in creating an open and ethically based pattern to ensure that individual and employee group networks are not in conflict with the formal employee network and for the most part, supportive of it as well.

The potential impacts of e-mail technology on interpersonal communication were reviewed. We focused on the overuse and misuse of e-mail. Of course, despite its drawbacks, e-mail is vital in today's organizations and society.

KEY TERMS AND CONCEPTS

360-degree feedback
Active listening
Assertive communication
Channels
Chromatics
Chronemics
Cue
Cultural context
Decoding
Dialogue
Distortion
Encoding
Ethnocentrism
Feedback
Formal employee network
Grapevine
High-context culture
Intercultural communication
Interpersonal communication
Interpersonal communication network
Language routines
Low-context culture
Lying
Meaning
Media richness
Messages
Meta-communication
Monochronic time schedule
Noise
Nonverbal communication
Political skill
Polychronic time schedule
Receptors
Self-disclosure
Semantics
Taarof
Transmitters

DISCUSSION QUESTIONS

1. Visit Amgen's home page at www.amgen.com. Click on "About Amgen" and then "Corporate Governance." Click on "Code of Ethics-Officers" and review this statement. Kevin Sharer, who was discussed in the Learning from Experience feature, provided the leadership in developing this code for senior officers. Do you think it is an effective statement? Explain.
2. Nokia's approach to understanding cultural context is discussed in the Across Cultures Competency feature. Identify three aspects of interpersonal and cultural barriers that are not discussed in this feature and provide details.
3. How would you assess the level of ethical interpersonal communication in an organization at which you are or have been employed? Give concrete examples that serve as a basis of your assessment.
4. Based on your diagnosis of feedback practices you experienced in a current or previous job through the completion of the instrument in Table 8.1, which practices are least effective? How might they be improved?
5. In what ways can you both agree and disagree with the following statement: "The Internet and e-mail are making it easier to communicate with people from different cultures." Explain.
6. Think of a team of which you are a member. How would you assess the team's communications?
7. Why is media richness important in interpersonal communication? Do changes need to be made in the pattern and frequency of use of the various media employed by management in the organization for which you currently work or have worked? Explain.
8. Describe your individual communication network at work or at school. Is it effective? Would you like to make any changes in it? Why or why not?
9. Describe the common nonverbal cues used by someone you have worked for. Are they usually consistent or inconsistent with that person's verbal expressions? Explain.
10. What problems have you experienced with the use of e-mail?

EXPERIENTIAL EXERCISE AND CASE

Experiential Exercise: Communication Competency

Political Skill Inventory[76]

Instructions

Using the following seven-point scale, write the number in the blank before each item that best describes how much you agree with each statement about yourself.

1 = strongly disagree
2 = disagree
3 = slightly disagree
4 = neutral
5 = slightly agree
6 = agree
7 = strongly agree

_____ 1. At work, I spend a lot of time and effort networking with others.
_____ 2. At work, I know a lot of important people and am well connected.
_____ 3. I am good at using my connections and networks to make things happen at work.
_____ 4. I have developed a large network of colleagues and associates at work whom I can call on for support when I really need to get things done.
_____ 5. I spend a lot of time at work developing connections with others.
_____ 6. I am good at building relationships with influential people at work.
_____ 7. It is important that people believe I am sincere in what I say and do.
_____ 8. When communicating with others, I try to be genuine in what I say and do.
_____ 9. I try to show a genuine interest in other people.
_____ 10. I always seem to instinctively know the right thing to say or do to influence others.
_____ 11. I have good intuition or savvy about how to present myself to others.
_____ 12. I am particularly good at sensing the motivations and hidden agendas of others.
_____ 13. I pay close attention to people's facial expressions.
_____ 14. I understand people very well.
_____ 15. It is easy for me to develop good rapport with most people.
_____ 16. I am able to make most people feel comfortable and at ease around me.
_____ 17. I am able to communicate easily and effectively with others.
_____ 18. I am good at getting people to like me.

Scoring and Interpretation

Add the point values for the items related to each dimension of political skill and the sum for items 1–18.

POINTS VALUES	ITEM #
____	1
____	2
____	3
____	4
____	5
____	6

____ Total for networking ability

POINTS VALUES	ITEM #
____	10
____	11
____	12
____	13
____	14

____ Total for social astuteness

POINTS VALUES	ITEM #
____	7
____	8
____	9

____ Total for apparent sincerity

POINTS VALUES	ITEM #
____	15
____	16
____	17
____	18

____ Total for interpersonal influence

Dimensions of Political Skill

- **Networking ability**—the degree to which individuals are adept at developing and using diverse networks of people. People in these networks tend to hold assets seen as valuable and necessary for successful personal and organizational functioning. A score from 36 to 42 suggests that you see yourself as possessing strong networking ability.
- **Apparent sincerity**—the degree to which individuals appear to others as possessing high levels of integrity, authenticity, sincerity, and genuineness. They are, or appear to be, honest, open, and forthright. A score from 18 to 21 suggests you see yourself as appearing to be sincere to others.
- **Social astuteness**—the degree to which individuals are savvy observers of others and are keenly attuned to diverse social situations. They comprehend social interactions and accurately interpret their behavior, as well as that of others, in social settings. They have strong powers of discernment and high self-awareness. A score from 30 to 35 suggests you see yourself as being socially astute.
- **Interpersonal influence**—the degree to which individuals use a subtle and convincing personal style that exerts a powerful influence on those around them. Individuals high on interpersonal influence nonetheless are capable of appropriately adapting and calibrating their behavior to each situation in order to elicit particular responses from others. Because their actions are not interpreted as manipulative or coercive, individuals high in apparent sincerity inspire trust and confidence in and from those around them. A score from 24 to 28 suggests you see yourself as possessing effective interpersonal influence.

Questions

1. Based on your profile of scores, what aspects of political skill do you need to develop further?
2. How might the leadership of a manager assist or hinder you in the development of these political skills?
3. How does your personality affect your political skills?

Case: Diversity Competency

Susan's Blog and PwC's Unique People Experience Initiative[77]

My name is Susan. I am a Director in Assurance, a working mother, actively involved in the PwC (Pricewaterhouse-Coopers) women's network and a member of the parents' network. [Susan works in the Leeds, England, office of PwC.] I thought it might be worth taking the opportunity to tell you a bit about the PwC women's network and what we are up to.

PwC Women's Network

A firm-wide network for women was established around three years ago as part of the work to promote diversity. The term "diversity" covers a lot of different aspects, but the women's network not surprisingly focuses on male/female diversity. While much of the firm is 50:50, this ratio dwindles significantly at more senior levels. A primary intention of the network, therefore, was (and is) to make female role models more visible and to make positive mentoring relationships. To make support and development more accessible for women. So, three years on, how successful has it been? In some respects it is difficult to say as much of what the network sets out to achieve is fairly intangible. However, of the 74 new partners admitted in 2006, 25% were women, which has got to be a step in the right direction.

Soon after the network was launched in London, I got together with a colleague in a different department in my office, and we decided to set up a satellite women's network. We formed a committee of interested women from around the office and, since our launch, we have run a large number of internal events, some of them targeted at skills development, some informative and some purely social. Our most successful event to date in terms of getting men to attend was the session on "Doing Business with the Opposite Sex—How to Do It Better." This talked about the differences between male and female body language and how an appreciation of this can help in building better business relationships. How often does your partner's reaction to something surprise/frustrate you? It's just the same in business!

Fairly early on, we decided that we wanted to broaden the scope of the Leeds network to cover external events for entertaining female clients and targets who often get left out of the more traditional football/cricket/golf client-entertaining opportunities. Over the past couple of years, we have held a fashion show, a bonfire-themed cocktail party and a chocolate tasting evening. In December [2006] we organized our most ambitious event to date which was an evening of exclusive Christmas shopping at a large Leeds department store, along the lines of one held in London last winter.

My involvement with the local network has given me an opportunity to develop my leadership skills. Seeing the women's network in Leeds strengthen to what it is today (looking forward to such a large-scale client event), when I was involved in establishing it, gives me an immense sense of achievement. It is also fantastic to feel that you are able to input into issues which are fundamental for the firm—a Leeds representative sits on the national PwCWomen steering group. But just as importantly for me has been that I have gained a much improved network of contacts from different departments throughout the office. Relationships are, after all, what being successful in business is all about. [End of March 5, 2007, blog]

Unique People Experience (UPE)

PwC is one of the Catalyst Award winners for its Unique People Experience (UPE) initiative. Catalyst, headquartered in New York, is a leading research and advisory organization working with businesses and the professions to build inclusion environments and expanded opportunities for women at work. According to PwC, the Unique People Experience initiative was created to reduce turnover, maximize the productivity of the firm's staff, and increase the value for PwC's clients. The initiative is a philosophical approach to developing talent: Instead of treating everyone the same, the firm has customized its approach to fit the diversity of its people and create a culture of inclusion.

The first component of UPE is understanding those different needs, which is why each of the 28,000 staff is assigned a partner/leader who is charged with getting to know him or her professionally and personally, including those aspects such as race, gender, and work–life issues that can affect experiences with the firm. These conversations continue in other professional forums such as diversity leadership conferences and through PwC's networking circles for diverse groups.

The second major component of UPE is redesigning the work model to a more team-based approach. In Client Portfolio Teams (CPT), groups of partners serve a portfolio of clients and share responsibility for developing and retaining staff. This new structure was created to improve quality, reduce administrative burdens, and decrease the workload of client professionals. CPT has altered the way work gets done, resulting in greater satisfaction and lower turnover rates.

All PwC partners and staff are held accountable for UPE through an evaluation process that assesses contributions in the areas of people, quality, and profitable growth. As a main strategic area of focus, people results are critically important. Semiannual surveys track satisfaction rates, and leaders are responsible for improving scores within their businesses or geographies.

The firm's efforts have paid off: From 2001 to 2006, women's representation at the partner level increased 30 percent, from 12 to 16 percent, and voluntary turnover for client service staff has decreased from 24 to 16 percent.

Questions

1. What aspects of active listening are suggested in Susan's blog and the UPE initiative?
2. What aspects of constructive feedback are suggested in Susan's blog and the UPE initiative?
3. What aspects of supporting appropriate self-disclosure are suggested in Susan's blog and the UPE initiative?
4. What aspects of reducing interpersonal and cultural barriers are suggested in Susan's blog and the UPE initiative?

CHAPTER

9

Leading Effectively: Foundations

Learning Goals

When you have finished studying the chapter, you should be able to:

1. State the core differences between leadership and management.
2. Describe the role of power and political behavior in the leadership process.
3. Describe three legacy models of leadership: traits, Theory X/Theory Y, and behavioral.
4. Explain and apply the Situational Leadership® Model.
5. Explain and apply the Vroom–Jago time-driven leadership model.

© AP Images

Learning from Experience

STEVE BENNETT'S LEADERSHIP AT INTUIT

Steve Bennett served as the CEO of Intuit, headquartered in Mountain View, California, through 2007. Intuit is the maker of Quicken, TurboTax, ItsDeductible, and other management-related software for small businesses, accountants, and individual consumers. Bennett joined Intuit in 2000 as CEO and president. Previously, he was an executive at General Electric. When Bennett joined Intuit, the firm had 4,500 full-time employees and revenue of $1.1 billion. The firm now has 7,500 employees and revenues of $2.4 billion.

Bennett contends, "Employees who are unhappy at work won't contribute their best efforts—on the job or even at home. It will cause troubles in their personal relationships." While at Intuit, he told his managers to create a "psychological contract" with every employee. The managers were expected to spell out what was expected of employees, how well they were performing, and what they had to do to advance. Bennett adds: "I don't think command-and-control works. I think employees have a vested stake in the company's success, and they want to understand what we're doing to get better. The issue is to communicate what you're doing and why with employees. And if you get good at that, you're all on one team."

When he joined Intuit, Bennett found a company where employees didn't know how to handle differing emotions and opinions. They were afraid to counter one another at meetings and couldn't make decisions without spending hours trying to reach a consensus. He subsequently urged all employees to voice their views frankly and without fear of offending anyone. Bennett said: "We want everyone to aim for what we call True North objectives—or better short-term as well as long-term results—and we want everyone to feel enthused and connected at work. If you accept this contract and want to learn but aren't getting good results, we'll find you a job at the company where you can perform better." While at Intuit, he spent almost half of his time coaching employees.

Bennett didn't hesitate to give constructive criticism, but avoided angry attacks. At a meeting to discuss a possible acquisition, he listened while a senior manager who wasn't on the acquisition team dominated the conversation. Bennett then told him, "You know, you

For more information on Intuit, visit the organization's home page at www.intuit.com.

LEARNING CONTENT

don't know a lot about this." Bennett explains: "I tried to say it in a joking way rather than an angry way. But, I wanted the others at the meeting to know that even though the manager was at a higher rank than them, they shouldn't be swayed by him." After the meeting, Bennett met privately with the senior manager to talk further about what had happened. "His feelings were ruffled. I told him, 'You have a job and doing acquisitions isn't part of it.'"

Bennett is a strong supporter of creative and thoughtful innovations. He remarks: "You've got to be really clear on where you're going, how you're going to get there, and how everybody's role—we call it 'line of sight'—ties directly to the business outcomes we want. It's about getting things out of your brain so organizations can become more effective. A touchstone of Intuit's approach to innovation is the acceptance of failure so long as you learn from it."[1]

The Learning from Experience feature provides a few insights into Steve Bennett's effectiveness as a leader and what it means to be a leader. This and the following chapter further develop and expand on those insights. Leadership embraces the seven foundation competencies developed throughout this book, but it also goes beyond them. A team's or organization's success is greatly influenced by its leadership. Steve Bennett clearly reflects core leadership qualities.

In this chapter, we explore foundation concepts and models of leadership. First, we highlight the differences between contemporary leadership and traditional management. Second, we review the role of power and political behavior for managers. Third, we highlight three traditional leadership models. The fourth and fifth sections of this chapter present two widely used contingency models of leadership.

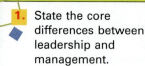

Learning Goal

1. State the core differences between leadership and management.

LEADERSHIP VERSUS MANAGEMENT

Leadership *is the process of developing ideas and a vision, living by values that support those ideas and that vision, influencing others to embrace them in their own behaviors, and making hard decisions about human and other resources.* Noel Tichy, who has studied many outstanding business leaders, describes contemporary leadership in these words:

> *Leadership is accomplishing something through other people that wouldn't have happened if you weren't there. And in today's world, that's less and less through command and control, and more and more through changing people's mindsets and hence altering the way they behave. Today, leadership is being able to mobilize ideas and values that energize other people.*[2]

A leader *is a person who exhibits the key attributes of leadership—ideas, vision, values, influencing others, and making tough decisions.* Steve Bennett at Intuit reflects these attributes. In this and the next chapter, you will discover that leadership is like a prism—something new and different appears each time you look at it from another angle. Our purpose is to identify and describe for you diverse leadership issues, ideas, and approaches. In doing so, we present various leadership perspectives and suggest some of their strengths, limitations, and applications. These chapters also are intended to give you personal insights into your own leadership abilities and those that need further development. Our assumption is simple: Leadership can be learned but not taught. Learning leadership means that you are actively seeking to make the personal changes required to become a leader.[3]

In contrast to being a leader, a traditional manager *directs, controls, and plans the work of others and is responsible for results.* Effective managers bring a degree of order and consistency to the work for their employees. To be effective, most executives and managers need to exhibit the attributes of leadership and/or management in various situations. Within business and other types of organizations, all managers are not leaders. Leaders are usually identified by such titles as *manager*, *executive*, *supervisor*, *team leader*, and the like. We use the generic title of *manager* to refer to such individuals. Regardless of title, effective managers in organizations usually accept three key functions in their roles:

- *Authority:* the right to make decisions.
- *Responsibility:* assignment for achieving a goal.
- *Accountability:* acceptance of success or failure.[4]

Table 9.1 provides an overview of the contrasts between the essentials of contemporary leadership and traditional management in terms of four major categories: thinking process, typical pattern of direction setting, approach to employee relations, and method of operation. The pairs of attributes within each category are presented as the extremes of a continuum. Most managers don't function at these extremes. However, patterns that tend toward contemporary leadership on the one hand or traditional management on the other hand are likely to emerge as managers develop and utilize their competencies.

Table 9.1 Some Comparisons between Leadership and Management

CATEGORY	CONTEMPORARY VIEW OF LEADERSHIP	TRADITIONAL VIEW OF MANAGEMENT
Thinking Process	• Originates	• Initiates
	• Focuses on people	• Focuses on things
	• Looks outward	• Looks inward
Direction Setting	• Vision	• Operational plans
	• Creates the future	• Improves the present
	• Sees forest	• Sees trees
Employee Relations	• Empowers	• Tightly controls
	• Associates	• Subordinates
	• Trusts and develops	• Directs and coordinates
Method of Operation	• Effectiveness (does the right things)	• Efficiency (does things right)
	• Creates change	• Manages change
	• Serves clients and customers	• Serves top managers

Source: Adapted from Robinson, G. Leadership versus management. *British Journal of Administrative Management*, January/February 1999, 20–21; McCartney, W. W., and Campbell, C. R. Leadership, management, and derailment: A model of individual success and failure. *Leadership & Organization Development Journal*, 2006, 27, 190–202.

As you review Table 9.1, mark the point on each continuum that reflects the relative emphasis on contemporary leadership or traditional management by a person for whom you have worked. Managers may lean more heavily toward either the contemporary leadership or the traditional management profile at various times as they face different issues and problems. However, most tend to operate primarily in terms of either the leadership or the management profile.[5]

Taken to the extreme of traditional management as shown in Table 9.1, a manager is often thought of as a "boss" in contrast to a leader. The following poem, in which the author is unknown, says it well:

> **LEADER INSIGHT**
>
> You will never get people to follow you and you will never be able to lead if you can't manage your own life and you can't act in a moral and ethical way in all environments. That doesn't mean you have to be perfect. What it means is that personal integrity is a core characteristic that will permit people to follow you.
> **Michael E. Moroone, Director, President and Chief Operating Officer, Auto Nation**

The boss drives group members; the leader coaches them.
The boss depends upon authority; the leader on goodwill.
The boss inspires fear; the leader inspires enthusiasm.
The boss says "I"; the leader says "we."
The boss assigns the task, the leader sets the pace.
The boss says, "Get there on time"; the leader gets there ahead of time.
The boss fixes the blame for the breakdown; the leader fixes the break down.
The boss knows how it is done; the leader shows how.
The boss makes work a drudgery; the leader makes it a game.
The boss says, "Go"; the leader says, "Let's go."

Learning Goal

2. Describe the role of power and political behavior in the leadership process.

POWER AND POLITICAL BEHAVIOR

All leaders use power and engage in political behavior to influence others.[6] Some leaders do so effectively and ethically. Others in managerial roles, but who do not qualify as effective leaders, use power and political behavior in ways that are ineffective and counterproductive.

Leaders' Use of Power

There are five important interpersonal sources of power—legitimate power, reward power, coercive power, referent power, and expert power—that leaders and others use in various situations.[7] Leaders use these sources of power to influence followers by appealing to one or more of their needs. Effective leadership depends as much on the acceptance of influence by the follower as on the leader's providing it. Let's review those sources of power in relation to the roles of leader and you as a follower.

Legitimate Power. Legitimate power *is an individual's ability to influence others' behaviors because of the person's formal position in the organization*. You may respond to such influence because you acknowledge the leader's legitimate right to tell you what to do. Non-managerial employees also may possess legitimate power. For example, John Ogden, a safety inspector at Lockheed Martin Vought's plant in Camden, Arkansas, has the legitimate power to shut down production if there is a safety violation, even if the plant manager objects and tries to stop the safety inspector.

Legitimate power is an important concept. Typically, a manager is given the right to make decisions within a specific area of responsibility, such as customer service, quality control, marketing, or accounting. This area of responsibility defines the activities for which the manager (and sometimes other employees) can expect to exercise legitimate power to influence behavior. The further removed managers are from their specific areas of responsibility, the weaker their legitimate power becomes. You have a zone of indifference with respect to the exercise of power by your manager.[8] The zone of indifference *is an area within which employees will accept certain directives without questioning the manager's power*. The manager may have considerable legitimate power to influence your behavior. Outside that zone, however, legitimate power disappears rapidly. For example, a secretary will type letters, answer the phone, open the mail, and do similar tasks for a manager without question. However, if the manager asks the secretary to go out for a drink after work, the secretary may refuse. The manager's request clearly falls outside the secretary's zone of indifference. The manager has no legitimate right to expect the secretary to comply. Consider this example of legitimate power:

> *My manager is Piero Di Matteo at Los Angeles Air Force Base. He believes that if you carry out your assignments on time, there will be no problem. If you get stuck, he's there to guide you.*[9]

Reward Power. Reward power *is an individual's ability to influence others' behaviors by providing valued things.* To the extent that you value the rewards that the manager can give—praise, promotions, money, time off, and so on—you may comply with requests and directives. A manager who controls the allocation of merit pay raises in a department has reward power over you and the other employees in that department. Accordingly, you may comply with some attempts by the manager to influence your behavior because you expect to be rewarded for this compliance. Consider this example of reward power:

> *Bill Weingart at First Data Merchant Services Corporation in Hagerstown, Maryland, realizes the importance of recognizing and rewarding employees when they achieve their goals. Also, he encourages education and self-improvement. He is a mentor to all who have the opportunity to work with or for him. I expect never to encounter anyone like him again in my entire working career.*[10]

Reward power is an individual's ability to influence others' behavior by providing valued things. Rewards might include awards, praise, promotions, money, or time off.

Coercive Power. Coercive power *is an individual's ability to influence others' behaviors by punishing them.* For example, you may comply with a manager's directive because you expect to be punished if you fail to do so. Punishment may take the form of reprimands, undesirable work assignments, closer supervision, tighter enforcement of work rules, suspension without pay, and the like. The organization's ultimate punishment is to fire you.

Recall, however, that punishment can have undesirable side effects (see Chapter 4). For example, the employee who receives an official reprimand for shoddy work may find ways to avoid punishment, such as by refusing to perform the task, falsifying performance reports, or being absent frequently. Coercive power doesn't necessarily encourage desired behavior, but it may stop or reduce undesirable behaviors. Consider this example of the application of coercive power:

The manager looked at me and shouted, "I don't care what your [expletive] job title is or what they [expletive] told you when you were hired. You'll do what I [expletive] tell you to do, the [expletive] way I tell you to do it, and if you don't like it, there's the [expletive] door." I had my résumé out the very next day.[11]

At times, managers do need to exercise coercive power, which is based on their legitimate power. Demoting or dismissing subordinates for poor performance, unacceptable behaviors (e.g., sexual harassment, bullying, workplace violence), and the lack of integrity (e.g., lying, deceitful conduct, and the like) may require the use of coercive power.

Referent Power. Referent power *is an individual's ability to influence others because she is respected, admired, or liked.* For example, your identification with a manager often forms the basis for referent power. This identification may include the desire by you to be like the manager. As a young manager, you might copy the leadership style of an older, admired, and more experienced manager. The senior manager, thus, has some referent power to influence your behavior.

Referent power usually is associated with individuals who possess admired personality characteristics, charisma, or a good reputation. It often is associated with political leaders, movie stars, sports figures, or other well-known individuals (hence, their use in advertising to influence consumer behavior). However, managers and employees also may have considerable referent power because of the strength of their personalities. Consider this example of the use of referent power:

Rudy Gragnani, a manager of the Coca-Cola Company bottler in Richmond, Virginia, displayed true leadership for me. An expressive customer and I were loudly discussing a problem when Rudy walked by. Later, he chewed me out for yelling at my customer. But at the next management meeting, he thanked me. Rudy understood that what he saw as an argument was just this customer's expected style of communicating. He apologized to me for misreading the situation and forwarded the thanks from the accounting area for my efforts.[12]

Expert Power. Expert power *is an individual's ability to influence others' behaviors because of recognized competencies, talents, or specialized knowledge.* To the extent that managers can demonstrate their competencies, they will acquire expert power. However, expert power often is relatively narrow in scope. For example, if you were an employee at Overhead Door Company, you might carefully follow the advice of your manager about how to program a garage door opener, yet ignore advice from the manager regarding which of three company health plans you should choose. In this instance, you recognize expertise in one area while resisting influence in another.

A lack of expert power often causes problems for new managers and employees. If you were a young accountant, you might possess a great deal of knowledge about accounting theory and procedures. Your expertise must be correctly demonstrated and applied over time to be recognized and accepted. Consider this example of the exercise of expert power:

I went to work for a manager who was one of the sharpest people I have ever worked for. The applications we worked on were some of the most intelligently constructed, flexible, reusable, modular applications I had ever seen. It was a fantastic environment for me to learn in.[13]

An effective manager who is also a leader—whether a first-line manager or top-level executive, like Steve Bennett at Intuit—uses all of these sources of power. For successful managers and organizations, the emphasis is on reward, referent, and expert power, with less reliance on coercive and legitimate power. This pattern is affected by changing technologies, increasing abilities of employees and teams to make decisions, flattening of organizational hierarchies, and changing work and personal life expectations of employees.

Use of Political Behavior

Political behavior *involves attempts by individuals to influence the behaviors of others and the course of events in the organization in order to protect their self-interests, meet their own needs, and advance their own goals.*[14] Defined in this way, almost all behavior may be regarded as political. Labeling behavior as political, however, usually implies that certain people are gaining something at the expense of others or the organization as a whole. However, a balanced understanding of political behavior and its consequences is needed. People often are self-centered and biased when labeling actions as political behavior. Employees may justify their own political behavior as defending legitimate rights or interests. Some may say it's "playing politics."

Organizational Politics. Organizational politics *involves actions by individuals, teams, or leaders to acquire, develop, and use power and other resources in order to obtain preferred outcomes.*[15] When people share power but differ about what must be done (e.g., invest in expanding in North America versus China), many decisions and actions quite naturally will be the result of a political process.

Employees are often concerned about organizational politics.[16] Typically, they also believe that an ideal work setting would be free from political behavior. Negative attitudes about political behavior and organizational politics can hinder organizational effectiveness. Examples of behaviors often seen as political are shown in Table 9.2. People tend to assume that political behavior doesn't yield the best organizational decisions or outcomes—that somehow, by pushing for their own positions, they cause

Table 9.2 Common Political Tactics

Taking counsel	The individual exercises great caution in seeking or giving advice.
Maneuverability	The individual maintains flexibility and never completely commits to any one position or program.
Communication	The individual never communicates everything. Instead information is withheld and/or at times it's released carefully.
Compromising	The individual accepts compromise only as a short-term tactic, while continuing to press ahead with one's own agenda.
Confidence	Once the individual has made a decision, he must always give the impression of knowing what he is doing, even when he does not.
Always the boss	An atmosphere of social friendship limits the power of the leader; thus the leader always maintains a sense of distance and separation from subordinates.

Source: Adapted from Buchanan, D., and Badham, R. *Power, Politics, and Organizational Change*. London: Sage 1999.

inferior actions or decisions to be made. Although this result can occur, political behavior isn't always detrimental to an organization. For example, a study involving managers in 30 organizations indicated that they were able to identify beneficial, as well as harmful, effects of political behavior.[17] Beneficial effects included career advancement, recognition and status for individuals looking after their legitimate interests, and achievement of organizational goals—getting the job done—as a result of the normal political process in the organization. Harmful effects included demotions and loss of jobs for "losers" in the political process, a misuse of resources, and creation of an ineffective organizational culture. Organizational politics may arouse anxieties that cause employees to withdraw emotionally from the organization. Their withdrawal makes creating an organization characterized by high performance and high commitment very difficult.

Political behavior, then, can meet appropriate and legitimate individual and organizational needs, or it can result in negative outcomes. In any event, leaders and employees must understand political behavior because it definitely does occur. Eliminating political behavior isn't possible—it can only be managed.

Drivers of Political Behavior. The probability of political behavior occurring typically increases in proportion to disagreements over goals, different ideas about the organization and its problems, different information about the situation, the need to allocate scarce resources, and so on.[18] If these forces didn't exist, perhaps political behavior would be minimal or wouldn't exist. However, results are never certain, resources are never infinite, and people must make difficult choices between competing goals and methods to attain them. Thus, political behavior will naturally occur as individuals, teams, and departments attempt to obtain their preferred outcomes. Managers shouldn't try to prevent the inevitable. Rather, they should try to ensure that these activities do not have negative consequences for the organization and its employees.

Managers and employees are more likely to act politically when (1) decision-making procedures and performance measures are uncertain and complex, and (2) competition for scarce resources is strong. Conversely, in less complex situations where decision-making processes are clear and competitive behavior is not rewarded, excessive political behavior is unlikely.

Even though individual differences may contribute to political behavior, such behavior is typically more strongly influenced by aspects of the situation. Managers make engaging in political behavior easier when they provide few rules or policies. Ambiguous circumstances allow individuals to define situations in ways that satisfy their own needs and desires. Further, when employees want more of a resource (e.g., equipment or office space) than is available, political behavior is likely to occur.

Political behavior is greater when managers reward it. A reward system may focus solely on individual accomplishment and minimize team contributions. When that's the case, individuals may be tempted to behave politically to ensure that they receive much more of the rewards than other team members. If their actions result in more rewards, employees are even more likely to engage in such political actions in the future. Similarly, individuals who had avoided political behavior may start behaving politically when they observe such behavior being rewarded by managers. In sum, the organizational reward system can be a significant factor in the occurrence of political behavior.

Relation to Performance Appraisal. The performance appraisal process provides a good example of a situation in which managers may stimulate political behavior among employees. Performance for employees in many departments—accounting, human resources, quality control, legal, information systems, and so on—isn't easily measured. Thus, the process used by managers results in the allocation of scarce resources (pay, bonuses, benefits, etc.) based on complex criteria.[19]

Some managers ignore the existence of politics in the appraisal process or may assume that use of a quantitative performance appraisal method (e.g., number of units sold, downtime, wastes) will minimize it. However, political behavior is a fact of life in the appraisal process. In particular, because of the ambiguous nature of managerial work, appraisals of managers by higher level leaders are susceptible to political manipulation. What is the risk, ethical or otherwise, of using performance appraisal as a political tool? Among other things, political performance appraisals by managers can

- undermine organizational goals and performance,
- compromise the link between performance and rewards,
- increase political behavior in other organizational processes and decisions, and
- expose the organization to litigation if employees are terminated.[20]

Managers should adopt the following guidelines to help cope with the problem:

- Develop goals and standards that are as clear and specific as possible.
- Link specific actions and performance results to rewards.
- Conduct structured, professional reviews, including specific examples of observed performance and explanations for ratings given.
- Offer performance feedback on an ongoing basis, rather than just once a year.
- Acknowledge that appraisal politics exists and make this topic a focus of ongoing discussions throughout the organization.[21]

The following Diversity Competency feature presents the perspectives of Carol Bartz on what it's like for women at the top and her advice to aspiring women in organizations. This feature presents excerpts from her comments on a more comprehensive set of interview questions.[22] The issues of power and political behaviors for women are clearly reflected in her comments. Bartz is currently executive chairman of Autodesk, headquartered in San Rafael, California. This firm provides 2D and 3D technologies that enable customers to visualize, simulate, and analyze the real-world performance of their ideas early in the design process. Autodesk has sales of approximately $2 billion per year.[23] Bartz was chairman, president, and CEO of Autodesk for 14 years and stepped out of those roles recently. She continues to serve in a number of other leadership roles, including the Boards of Directors of Cisco Systems, Network Alliance, and Foundation for the National Medals of Science and Technology.

Diversity Competency

Carol Bartz: Views from the Top

One piece of advice I would like to give all women, but certainly young ones, is that nobody is in charge of their career but themselves. You have to stand out and let it be known the kind of job you are doing and what you want to do in the future, and manage yourself. Point number two is everybody gets confused when they have a bad manager. They want to immediately leave the company. But instead of having your career go sideways because you are frustrated working for somebody you don't like, learn from that. The third thing I'd say is learn to be an actor. You have to learn to be confident when you are not. You have to learn to be calm when you are not and brave when you are not. Learn to be a cobra and act until you really have that confidence.

I think women should think of their careers as a pyramid, which means you need a big lateral base. Sometimes that means taking a lateral job or smaller job that gives you new experience. Men are still in control and they hire men. The people running boards, which hire the CEOs, are men. At the end of the day, that still is the disease. So we just have to get in there and keep pushing.

When you travel as a [woman] CEO, you're invited if nothing else because people are curious about you. I've been invited by presidents and senior ministers who are just curious about how I am going to act. Sometimes you get things because you have a skirt—and you have to use that instead of saying, "Oh they don't really want me." I travel extensively and I go as a technologist. In emerging countries such as China and India, it doesn't matter who you are, they just want your technology. They want to suck your brain dry. So I think younger women managers do far better in emerging economies than in Europe, for instance.

Let me add one more thing. I met with 200 female students at the biggest architectural school in Delhi [India] recently. They asked me to come to talk about women in business. At the end, they came up to me and said, "We've never been allowed to have this kind of conversation, to say what it is like for a woman managing, and managing in Indian culture." They asked me to come back, and I said they needed to start their own conversation.

For more information on Autodesk, visit the organization's home page at www.autodesk.com.

Learning Goal

3. Describe three legacy models of leadership: traits, Theory X/Theory Y, and behavioral.

LEGACY LEADERSHIP MODELS

The traits, Theory X/Theory Y, and behavioral models are probably the most basic, oldest, and most popular of the leadership models. The more recent and complex leadership models often draw on parts of these three models. Thus, these three models provide an important legacy to the contingency leadership models and the contemporary leadership literature in general.

Traits Model of Leadership

The traits model of leadership *is based on characteristics of many leaders—both successful and unsuccessful—and is used to predict leadership effectiveness.* The resulting lists of traits are then compared to those of potential managers to assess their likelihood of success or failure as leaders. There is some support for the notion that successful leaders have interests and abilities and, perhaps, even personality traits that are different from those of less effective leaders.

Key Traits. Some evidence suggests that four traits are shared by most (but not all) successful leaders:

- *Intelligence*. Successful leaders tend to have somewhat higher intelligence than their subordinates.
- *Maturity and breadth*. Successful leaders tend to be emotionally mature and have a broad range of interests.
- *Achievement drive*. Successful leaders are results oriented; when they achieve one goal, they seek another. They do not depend primarily on employees for their motivation to achieve goals.
- *Integrity*. Successful leaders, over the long term, usually have integrity. When individuals in leadership positions state one set of values but practice another set, followers quickly see them as untrustworthy. Many surveys show that honesty is the most important characteristic when employees are asked to rank and comment on the various traits of successful and unsuccessful leaders. Trust is crucial and translates into the degree of willingness by employees to follow leaders. Confusion over the leader's thinking and values creates negative stress, indecision, and personal politics.[24]

Managerial Guidelines. The traits model of leadership is inadequate for successfully predicting leadership effectiveness for at least three reasons.[25] First, in terms of personality traits, there are no consistent patterns between specific traits or sets of traits and managerial effectiveness. More than 100 different traits of successful leaders in various managerial positions have been identified. For example, the traits pattern of successful managers of salespeople includes optimism, enthusiasm, and dominance. The traits pattern of successful managers of production workers usually includes being progressive, introverted, and cooperative. These descriptions are simply generalities. Many successful managers of salespeople and production workers do not have all, or even some, of these characteristics. There also is often disagreement over which traits are the most important for an effective manager.

The second limitation of the traits model is that it often attempts to relate physical traits—such as height, weight, appearance, physique, energy, and health—to effective leadership. Most of these factors are related to situational factors that can have a significant impact on a manager's effectiveness. For example, people in the military or law enforcement must be a particular minimum height and weight in order to perform certain tasks well. Although these traits may help an individual rise to a leadership position in such organizations, neither height nor weight correlates highly with effective management. In business and other organizations, height and weight generally play no role in performance and thus are not requirements for a management position.

The third limitation of the traits model is that leadership itself is complex. A relationship between specific traits and a person's interest in particular types of jobs could well exist, which a study relating personality and effectiveness might not identify. The traits approach paints a somewhat fatalistic picture, suggesting that some people, by their traits, are more prone to be effective managers than others.

Theory X and Theory Y Model

The behavior of managers is often influenced by their assumptions and beliefs about followers and what motivates their followers. Thus, differences in the behaviors of managers can be understood by looking at the different assumptions they make. One of the most widely cited and recognized models for describing differences in these assumptions was developed by Douglas McGregor in 1957. He coined the labels "Theory X" and "Theory Y" as a way to contrast two sets of assumptions and beliefs held by managers. Theory X and Theory Y managers both understand that they are responsible for the resources in their units—money, materials, equipment, and people—in the interest of achieving organizational goals. What sets them apart are their propositions about what motivates their subordinates and what are the best ways to carry out management responsibilities.[26] Before proceeding, take a few minutes and respond to the propositions in Table 9.3.

Theory X. When McGregor developed his model, he knew many managers with the Theory X point of view. Theory X *is a composite of propositions and underlying beliefs that take a command-and-control approach to management based on a negative view of human nature.*[27] The propositions of Theory X are as follows:

- People are inherently lazy and must therefore be motivated by incentives.
- People's natural goals run counter to those of the organization; hence, individuals must be controlled by formal rules and management to ensure that they're working toward organizational goals.
- Because of irrational feelings, people are basically incapable of self-discipline and self-control.
- The average person prefers to be directed, wishes to avoid responsibility, and wants security above all.

Table 9.3 Theory X/Theory Y Propositions Instrument

Indicate your degree of agreement or disagreement with each of the eight propositions by recording the point value next to each numbered proposition. Determine the appropriate score by noting the points for the response you made to each proposition. For example, if your response to proposition 1 was strongly agree you would give yourself five points; disagree is worth two points; and so on. Add the eight scores together. Use the following scale:

STRONGLY AGREE	AGREE	UNDECIDED	DISAGREE	STRONGLY DISAGREE
(5)	(4)	(3)	(2)	(1)

_____ 1. The average human being prefers to be directed, wishes to avoid responsibility, and has relatively little ambition.

_____ 2. Most people can acquire leadership skills regardless of their particular inborn traits and abilities.

_____ 3. The use of rewards (for example, pay and promotion) and punishment (for example, failure to promote) is the best way to get subordinates to do their work.

_____ 4. In a work situation, if the subordinates can influence you, you lose some influence over them.

_____ 5. A good leader gives detailed and complete instructions to subordinates rather than giving them merely general directions and depending on their initiative to work out the details.

_____ 6. Individual goal setting offers advantages that cannot be obtained by group goal setting, because groups do not set high goals.

_____ 7. A superior should give subordinates only the information necessary for them to do their immediate tasks.

_____ 8. The superior's influence over subordinates in an organization is primarily economic.

_____ Total Score

Scoring Key:
A score of more than 32 points may indicate a tendency to manage others according to the propositions in Theory X. A score of 16 or less may indicate a tendency to manage others according to the propositions in Theory Y. A score somewhere between 16 and 32 may indicate flexibility in the management of others.

Theory X managers view management as a process that involves directing, controlling, and modifying their subordinates' behaviors to fit the needs of the organization. This perspective assumes that, without the strong intervention of managers, most employees would be passive—even resistant—to organizational needs. Therefore, employees must be persuaded, rewarded, punished, and their activities tightly controlled. Doing so is management's primary task. McGregor found that Theory X managers were everywhere in U.S. organizations when he developed his model (1957). According to him, Theory X management was largely ineffective because it ignored the social, self-esteem, and self-actualization needs of most employees.

Theory Y. McGregor concluded that a different view of managing employees was needed—one based on more adequate assumptions about human nature and human motivation. Theory Y *is a composite of propositions and beliefs that take a leadership and empowering approach to management based on a positive view of human nature*. These are the Theory Y propositions:

- The average human does not inherently dislike work. Depending on controllable conditions, work may be a source of satisfaction.

© Digital Vision/Getty Images

According to Theory Y, most employees have the capacity to exercise a relatively high degree of imagination, ingenuity, and creativity in finding solutions to organizational problems.

- Rules, top-down managerial control, and the threat of punishment are not the only means for achieving organizational goals. Employees will exercise self-direction and control in the service of goals to which they are committed.
- The average person learns, under proper conditions, not only to accept but to seek responsibility.
- The capacity to exercise a relatively high degree of imagination, ingenuity, and creativity in the solution to organizational problems is widely, not narrowly, distributed in the population.

According to the Theory Y view, employees are not *by nature* passive or resistant to organizational goals. They have become so as a result of their experiences in organizations. The motivation, the potential for development, the capacity for assuming responsibility, and the readiness to direct behavior toward organizational goals are all present in employees. Management does not put them there. It is management's responsibility to make it possible for employees to recognize and develop these human characteristics for themselves. Whereas Theory X managers attempt to gain control over their subordinates, Theory Y managers rely more on the self-control and self-direction of their subordinates.

LEADER INSIGHT

Great leaders operate more as coaches than dictators. They are clear with their direction and concise when it comes to explaining goals. However, they allow flexibility within parameters. Ego maturity is vital. Smart leaders are not infallible, but they know how to "fail fast." In other words, they are not afraid to make a mistake, learn from it, and move on.
Pamela Springer, President and CEO, ECNext, Inc.

Managerial Guidelines. McGregor's Theory X and Theory Y model spawned many new leadership models, concepts, and approaches. Compared to 50 years ago, the assumptions of Theory Y and its concern for employees are much more widely accepted in the United States nowadays among managers. Nevertheless, there are managers who find it difficult to give up some or all of the assumptions that make up the Theory X perspective and its emphasis on management's top-down approach to accomplishing goals.

McGregor's model of more than 50 years ago has been very influential in contemporary leadership and management thinking. An increasing number of managers realize that skilled and knowledgeable employees, who have been identified as the key contributors to future wealth, thrive primarily under Theory Y.[28]

Behavioral Model of Leadership

The behavioral model of leadership *focuses on what leaders actually do and how they do it*. There are several versions of this model. The model we present suggests that effective leaders help individuals and teams achieve their goals in two ways. First, they build task-centered relations with employees that focus on the quality and quantity of work accomplished. Second, they are considerate and supportive of employees' attempts to achieve personal goals (e.g., work satisfaction, promotions, and recognition). Also, they work hard at settling disputes, keeping employees satisfied, providing encouragement, and giving positive reinforcement.

The greatest number of studies of leader behavior has come from the Ohio State University leadership studies program, which began in the late 1940s. This research was aimed at identifying leader behaviors that are important for attaining team and organizational goals. These efforts resulted in the identification of two main dimensions of leader behavior: consideration and initiating structure.[29] Our review of the behavioral model is based on that leadership studies program. Table 9.4 provides the opportunity for you to diagnose your own leadership style according to the behavioral style of leadership.

Table 9.4 **Behavioral Leadership Style Questionnaire**

The following statements can help you diagnose your leadership style according to the behavioral model of leadership. Read each item carefully. Think about how you usually behave when you are the leader (or if you were in a leader role). Then, using the following, record the letter that most closely describes your style next to the item.

A = Always
O = Often
? = Sometimes
S = Seldom
N = Never

_____ 1. I take time to explain how a job should be carried out.
_____ 2. I explain the part that others are to play in the team.
_____ 3. I make clear the rules and procedures for others to follow in detail.
_____ 4. I organize my own work activities.
_____ 5. I let people know how well they are doing.
_____ 6. I let people know what is expected of them.
_____ 7. I encourage the use of uniform procedures for others to follow in detail.
_____ 8. I make my attitude clear to others.
_____ 9. I assign others to particular tasks.
_____10. I make sure that others understand their part in the team.
_____11. I schedule the work that I want others to do.
_____12. I ask that others follow standard rules and regulations.

_____13. I make working on the job more pleasant.
_____14. I go out of my way to be helpful.
_____15. I respect others' feelings and opinions.
_____16. I am thoughtful and considerate of others.
_____17. I maintain a friendly atmosphere in the team.
_____18. I do little things to make it more pleasant for others to be a member of my team.
_____19. I treat others as equals.
_____20. I give others advance notice of change and explain how it will affect them.
_____21. I look out for others' personal welfare.
_____22. I am approachable and friendly toward others.

Scoring:
The point values for Always (A), Often (O), Sometimes (?), Seldom (S), and Never (N) are as follows: A=5; O=4; ?=3; S=2; and N=1. Sum the point values for items 1 through 12. Then, sum the point values for items 13 through 22.

Point values for initiating structure:
_____ 1, _____ 2, _____ 3, _____ 4, _____ 5, _____ 6, _____ 7, _____ 8, _____ 9, _____ 10, _____ 11, _____ 12 = Total _____

Point values for consideration:
_____ 13, _____ 14, _____ 15, _____ 16, _____ 17, _____ 18, _____ 19, _____ 20, _____ 21, _____ 22 = Total _____

Interpretation:
Items 1 through 12 reflect an initiating structure or task leadership style. A score greater than 47 indicates that you describe your leadership style as high on initiating or task structure. You see yourself as planning, directing, organizing, and controlling the work of others. Items 13 through 22 reflect a considerate or relationship style. A score greater than 40 indicates that you see yourself as a considerate leader. A considerate leader is one who is concerned with the comfort, well-being, and personal welfare of her subordinates. In general, individuals rated high on initiating structure and at least moderate on consideration tend to be in charge of more productive teams than those whose leadership styles are low on initiating structure and high on consideration.

Source: Schriesheim, C. *Leadership Instrument.* Used by permission, Miami, Florida: University of Miami, 2005.

Consideration. Consideration *is the extent to which the leader has relationships with subordinates that are characterized by mutual trust, two-way communication, respect for employees' ideas, and empathy for their feelings.* This style emphasizes the satisfaction of employee needs. The manager typically finds time to listen, is willing to make changes, looks out for the personal welfare of employees, and is friendly and approachable. A high degree of consideration indicates psychological closeness between manager and subordinates; a low degree shows greater psychological distance and a more impersonal leader.

When is consideration effective? The most positive effects of manager consideration on effectiveness and job satisfaction occur when (1) the task is routine and denies employees little, if any, satisfaction from the work itself; (2) followers are predisposed toward participative leadership; (3) team members must learn something new; (4) employees feel that their involvement in the decision-making process is legitimate and affects their job performance; and (5) employees feel that strong status differences should not exist between them and their leader.

Initiating Structure. Initiating structure *is the extent to which a leader defines and prescribes the roles of subordinates in order to set and accomplish goals in their areas of responsibility.* This style emphasizes the direction of team or individual employee activities through planning, communicating, scheduling, assigning tasks, emphasizing deadlines, and giving orders. The manager sets definite standards of performance and expects subordinates to achieve them. In short, a manager with a high degree of initiating structure concerns himself with accomplishing tasks by setting performance goals, giving directions, and expecting them to be followed.

When is initiating structure effective? The most positive effects of manager initiating structure on effectiveness and job satisfaction occur when (1) a high degree of pressure for output is imposed by someone other than the leader; (2) the task satisfies employees; (3) employees depend on the manager for information and direction on how to complete the task; and (4) employees are psychologically predisposed toward being instructed in what to do, how to do it, and when it should be achieved.

Figure 9.1 suggests that the dimensions of consideration and initiating structure are not necessarily mutually exclusive and, in fact, may be related in various ways. A manager may be high, low, or moderate on both consideration and initiating structure, as suggested in Figure 9.1. Steve Bennett, the CEO of Intuit, appears to be a manager who is high on consideration and moderate to high on initiating structure, depending on the leadership issue. Consider three of his perspectives in the Learning from Experience feature:

- "We want everyone to feel enthused and connected at work." (consideration)
- "Employees who are unhappy at work won't contribute their best efforts on the job or even at home. It will cause troubles in their personal relationships." (consideration)
- Bennett tells Intuit managers to create a "psychological contract" with every employee, spelling out what is expected of them, how well they are performing, and what they must do to advance (initiating structure).

Managerial Guidelines. Some studies suggest that a manager who emphasizes initiating structure generally improves productivity, at least in the short run. However, managers who rank high on initiating structure and low on consideration generally have large numbers of grievances, absenteeism, and high employee turnover rates. The view now widely accepted is that effective managers can have high consideration and initiating structure at the same time. Showing consideration is beneficial insofar as it leads to high levels of team morale and low levels of turnover and absenteeism. At the same time,

FIGURE 9.1 Behavioral Leadership Grid

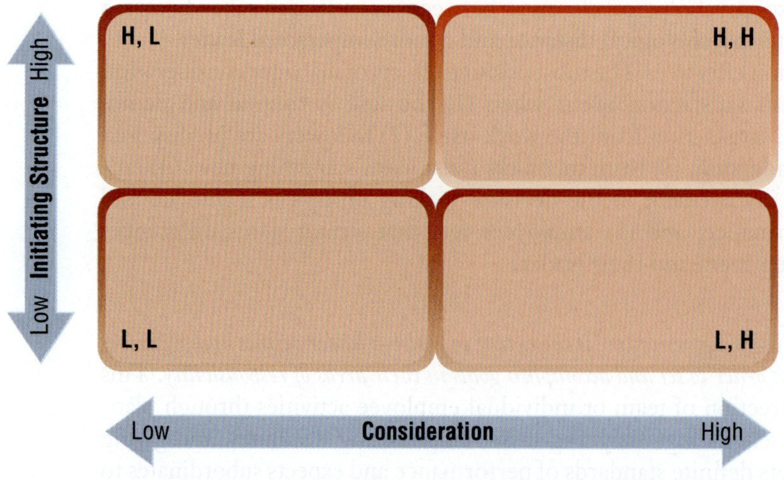

high levels of initiating structures are useful in promoting high levels of efficiency and performance.

Perhaps the main limitation of the behavioral model was the lack of attention it gave to the effects of the situation. It focused on relationships between managers and employees but gave little consideration to the situation in which the relationships occurred. A better understanding of behavior usually results when both the person and the situation are examined.

The following Self Competency feature on Douglas R. Conant, the CEO of Campbell Soup, provides additional insights into the effective application of both high consideration and initiating structure.[30] Campbell's, headquartered in Camden, New Jersey, is a global manufacturer and marketer of high-quality simple meals, including soup, baked snacks, vegetable-based beverages, and premium chocolate products. The company has more than $7.5 billion in annual sales and a portfolio of more than 20 brands, including *Campbell's*, *Pepperidge Farm*, *Arnott's*, *VI*, and *Godiva*.[31]

Self Competency

Douglas Conant, CEO of Campbell Soup

© AP Images

Since Douglas R. Conant became the president and CEO of Campbell Soup Co. in 2001, he has sought to improve the business by cost cutting, innovations, and a concentrated effort to reinvigorate the workforce.

Douglas R. Conant became the president and CEO of Campbell's in 2001, after 25 years of extensive experience in other food companies. In less than 7 years, he led the transformation of Campbell's from a widely criticized old brand that was threatened with being purchased to one of the industry's best performers. The turnaround has been achieved by cost cutting, innovations, and a concerted effort to reinvigorate the workforce. "We're hitting our stride a little bit more [than our peers]," says Conant, in his understated style. Conant did not shake up the firm through in-your-face control and domination. He readily gives others credit and deflects praise.

When Conant first assessed employee engagement with a widely distributed and anonymously submitted survey, Campbell's workforce ranked at the bottom. This was in comparison to other firms that had employees complete the survey from the Gallup Organization. Conant set about reinvigorating the employees and firm through initiatives such as these:

- *Using a personal touch.* In his time at Campbell, Conant has sent out more than 16,000 handwritten thank-you notes to employees, from the chief investment officer to the receptionist at headquarters. These notes are often found hanging in people's offices or above their desks. "In business, we're trained to find things that are wrong, but I try to celebrate what's right," says Conant.
- *Setting expectations.* All managers must meet with direct reports each quarter to update their progress on clearly articulated goals. However, given the poor state of leadership at Campbell's when he arrived, Conant led the process over a six-year period of replacing 300 of the company's 350 managers. Half of the replacements were from within and half from outside the firm.
- *Featuring communications.* Every six weeks, Conant has lunch with a group of a dozen or so employees to hear about problems and get feedback. Conant knows he doesn't have all the answers, admitting

mistakes with a simple but meaningful "I can do better." Harvey Golub, Campbell's chairman and the former head of American Express Co., comments: "He's an extraordinary leader who behaves with the utmost integrity. People follow him and believe in him. He's an Eagle Scout." One of Conant goals is to have a management team that builds trust and fosters engagement.

- *Developing professional opportunities and learning.* Conant encourages movement among employees and has created a CEO Institute to develop the pipeline of talent. Conant is a devout reader of leadership-related books. He has scores of books in his office on shelves and piled up in corners. He keeps extra copies on hand to share with colleagues. Conant started a book club for top executives.
- *Stimulating innovation.* Conant knows that Campbell must keep developing new products and ideas to maintain its momentum. So he has focused on innovation, the lifeblood of any consumer packaged-goods company. He has homed in on three key areas: healthy, convenient, and premium goods. Take soup, for example. It's still Campbell's mainstay, accounting for half of sales. Simple innovations such as pop-top cans helped lift sales of condensed soup 8 percent in 2005 and 5 percent in 2006 after more than a decade of declines. In 2007, Campbell launched 40 new or reformulated soups, including 14 that use sea salt to reduce sodium.

For more information on the Campbell Soup Company, visit the organization's home page at www.campbellsoupcompany.com.

Developers of the legacy leadership models—traits, Theory X/Theory Y, and behavioral—sought to find characteristics and personal attributes that apply to most leadership situations. In contrast, situational (contingency) leadership models identify variables that permit certain leadership characteristics and behaviors to be effective in given situations. In the next two sections, we present two contingency models of leadership: the Situational Leadership® Model, and the Vroom–Jago leadership model.

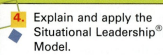

Learning Goal

4. Explain and apply the Situational Leadership® Model.

SITUATIONAL LEADERSHIP® MODEL

The Situational Leadership® Model *states that the style of leadership should be matched to the level of readiness of the followers.*[32] Like other contingency models of leadership, this one contains three basic components: a set of several possible leadership styles, a description of several alternative situations that leaders might encounter, and recommendations for which leadership styles are most effective in each situation.

Leadership Styles

According to the model, managers can choose from among four leadership styles. These four leadership styles involve various combinations of task behavior and relationship behavior. Task behavior is similar to initiating structure and relationship behavior is similar to consideration as described in the behavioral model. More specifically, task behavior *includes using one-way communication, spelling out duties, and telling followers what to do and where, when, and how to do it.* An effective manager might use a high degree of task behavior in some situations and only a moderate amount in other situations. Relationship behavior *includes using two-way communication, listening, encouraging, and involving followers in decision making, and giving emotional support.* Again, an effective manager may sometimes use a high degree of relationship behavior, and at other times less. By combining different amounts of task behavior with different amounts of relationship behavior, an effective manager may use four different leadership styles. The four leadership styles are called *telling, selling, participating,* and *delegating*. These styles are shown in Figure 9.2.[33]

FIGURE 9.2 The Situational Leadership® Model

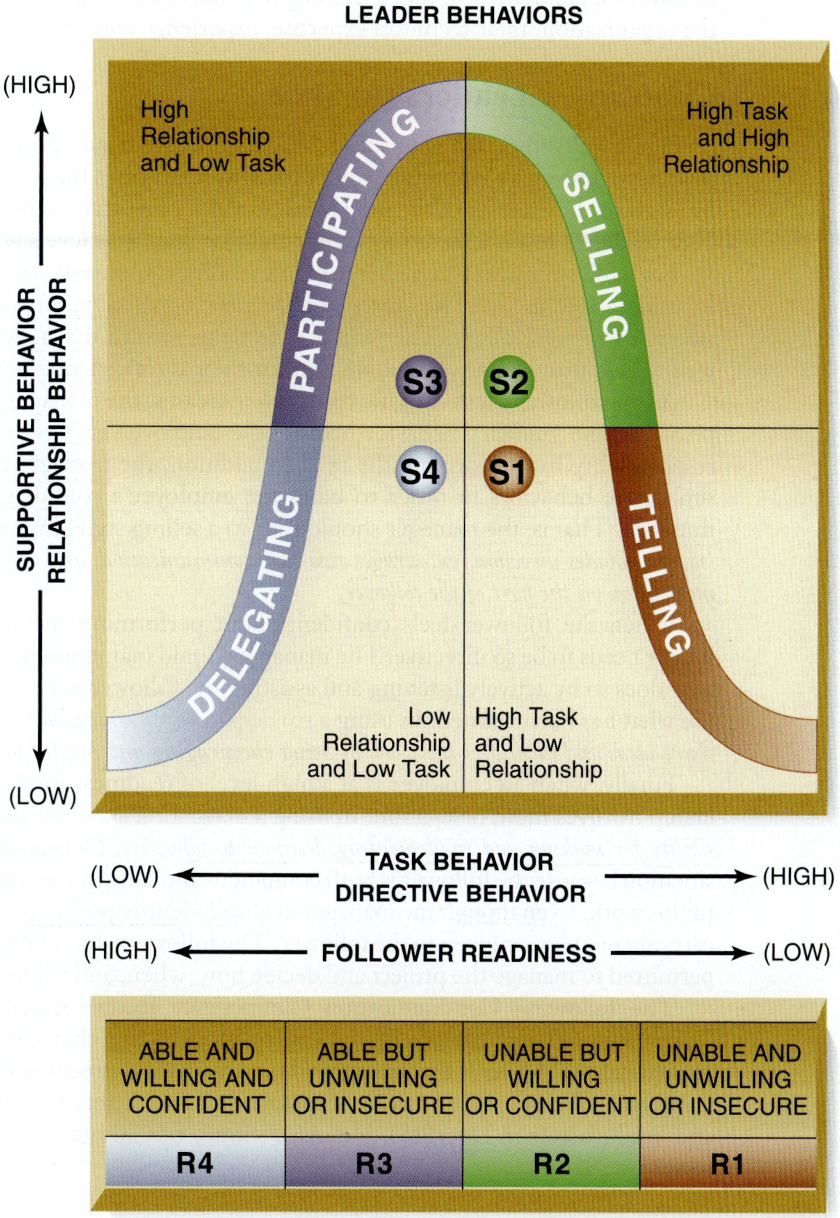

Situational Contingency

According to this model, a manager should consider the situation before deciding which leadership style to use. The situational contingency in this model is the degree of follower readiness. Readiness *is a follower's ability to set high but attainable task-related goals and a willingness to accept responsibility for reaching them*. Readiness is not a fixed characteristic of followers—it depends on the task. The same group of followers may have a high degree of readiness for some tasks, but a low degree of readiness for others. The readiness level of followers depends on how much training they have received, how committed they are to the organization, their technical expertise, experience with the specific task, and so on.

Choosing a Leadership Style

As Figure 9.2 shows, the appropriate leadership style depends on the level of follower readiness. The curve running through the graph indicates the leadership style that best fits each readiness level of the individual or team. Note that at the bottom of the figure high readiness levels appear on the left and low readiness levels appear on the right.

For a follower who is at the stage of low readiness for a task, a telling style is effective. In using a telling style, *the leader provides clear instructions, gives specific directions, and supervises the work closely*. The telling style helps ensure that new employees perform well, which provides a solid foundation for their future success and satisfaction.

As the follower's task-specific readiness increases, the manager needs to continue to provide some guidance behavior because the employee isn't yet ready to assume total responsibility for performing the task. In addition, the manager needs to begin using supportive behaviors in order to build the employee's confidence and maintain enthusiasm. That is, the manager should shift to a selling style. In using a selling style, *the leader provides direction, encourages two-way communication, and helps build confidence and motivation on the part of the follower*.

When the follower feels confident about performing the task, the manager no longer needs to be so directive. The manager should maintain open communication but now does so by actively listening and assisting the follower as he or she makes efforts to use what has been learned. In using a participating style, *the leader encourages followers to share ideas and facilitates the work by being encouraging and helpful to subordinates*.

Finally, when an employee is at a high level of readiness for the task, effective leadership involves more delegation. In using a delegating style, *the leader turns over responsibility for making and implementing decisions to followers*. Delegating is effective in this situation because the follower is both competent and motivated to take full responsibility for his work. Even though the manager may still identify problems, the responsibility for carrying out plans is given to the follower. The follower who is fully ready for a project is permitted to manage the project and decide how, when, and where tasks are to be done.

The following Communication Competency feature reports on how Michelle Miller adjusted her leadership style in relation to the characteristics of one of her subordinates.[34] Miller is the manager who opened a Walgreens store in Redondo Beach, California. Walgreens is a major drugstore and health service chain with 5,700 stores and headquarters in Deerfield, Illinois, a suburb of Chicago. It plans to operate 7,000 stores by 2010.[35]

Communication Competency

Michelle Miller of Walgreens

Michelle Miller's wall of her back office is papered with work schedules. Miller's store in Redondo Beach, California, employs people with sharply different skills and perspectives. A critical part of her job, therefore, is to put people into roles and shifts that will allow them to shine—and to avoid putting clashing personalities together. At the same time, she attempts to find ways for individuals to grow.

There's Jeffrey, for example, a "goth rocker" whose hair is shaved on one side and long enough on the other side to cover his face. Miller almost didn't hire him because he couldn't quite look her in the eye during his interview. But he wanted the hard-to-cover night shift, so she decided to give him a chance. After a couple of months, she noticed that when she gave Jeffrey a vague assignment, such as "Straighten up the merchandise in every aisle," what should have been a two-hour job would take him all night—and wouldn't be done very well. But if she gave him a more specific task, such as "Put up all the risers for Christmas," all the risers would be in line, with the right merchandise on each one, perfectly priced, labeled, and "faced" (turned toward the customer). Give Jeffery a general task, he would struggle. Give him one that forced him to be accurate and analytical, and he would excel. Miller concluded that this was Jeffrey's strength. So, as a good manager, she told Jeffrey what she had learned about him and praised him for his good work.

Miller knew she could get more out of Jeffrey. So she devised a plan to reassign responsibilities across the entire store to capitalize on his unique strengths. In every Walgreens, there is a responsibility called "resets and revisions." A reset involves stocking an aisle with new merchandise, a task that usually coincides with a predictable change in customer buying patterns (at the end of summer, for example, the stores will replace sun creams and lip balms with allergy medicines). A revision is a less time-consuming but more frequent version of the same thing: Replace these cartons of toothpaste with this new and improved variety. Display this new line of detergent at this end of the row. Each aisle requires some form of revision at least once a week.

In most Walgreens stores, each employee "owns" one or more aisles. This employee is responsible not only for serving customers but also for "facing" the merchandise, keeping the aisle clean and orderly, tagging items with a Telxon gun, and conducting all resets and revisions. This arrangement is simple, efficient, and affords each employee a sense of personal responsibility. But Miller decided that since Jeffrey was so good at resets and revisions—and didn't enjoy interacting with customers—this should be his full-time job, in every single aisle.

It was a challenge. One week's worth of revisions requires a binder three inches thick. But Miller reasoned that not only would Jeffrey be excited by the challenge and get better and better with practice, but other employees would be freed from what they considered a chore and have more time to greet and serve customers. The store's performance proved her right. After the reorganization, Miller saw not only increases in sales and profit but also in that most critical performance metric, customer satisfaction. In subsequent months, her store netted perfect scores in Walgreens' mystery shopper program.

For more information on Walgreens, visit the organization's home page at www.walgreens.com.

Managerial Guidelines

The Situational Leadership® Model helps managers recognize that the same leadership style may be effective in some situations but not others. Furthermore, it highlights the importance of considering the followers' situation when choosing a leadership style as Michelle Miller did. This model has generated quite a bit of interest among practitioners and researchers. The idea that managers should be flexible with respect to the leadership style they use is appealing.[36] An inexperienced employee may perform as well as an experienced employee if properly directed and closely supervised. Michelle Miller demonstrated this in her leadership of Jeffrey. An appropriate leadership style should also help followers gain more experience and become more competent. Thus, as a manager helps followers develop to higher levels of readiness, the manager's style also needs to evolve. Therefore, this model requires the manager to be constantly monitoring the readiness level of followers in order to determine the combination of task and relationship behaviors that is most appropriate.

Like other contingency models, this one assumes that managers can accurately assess each situation and change their leadership styles to match different situations. Some managers can read situations and adapt their leadership style more effectively than others. For those who can't, what are the costs of training them to be able to do so? Do these costs exceed the potential benefits? Before an organization adopts a management training program to teach managers to use this model of leadership, they need to answer questions such as these.

Learning Goal

5. Explain and apply the Vroom–Jago time-driven leadership model.

VROOM–JAGO LEADERSHIP MODEL

Victor Vroom and Arthur Jago developed a model that focuses on the leadership role in decision-making situations.[37] Victor Vroom revised this model to (1) give greater consideration to ranges that may exist in situational variables, (2) clarify the presentation of the five leadership styles in the earlier model, and (3) further emphasize the time-driven dimension to the choice of leadership style in relation to decision-making situations. The Vroom–Jago time-driven leadership model *prescribes a leader's choice(s) among five leadership styles based on seven situational factors, recognizing the time requirements and costs associated with each style.*[38]

Leadership Styles

There are five core leadership styles that vary in terms of the levels of empowerment and participation available to the leader's subordinates. These styles are summarized here in increasing levels of empowerment and participation:

- Decide style—*the leader makes the decision alone and either announces or sells it to the team.* The leader uses personal expertise and collects information from the team or others who can help solve the problem. The role of employees is clearly one of providing specific information that is requested, rather than generating or evaluating solutions.
- Consult individually style—*the leader presents the problem to team members individually, getting their ideas and suggestions and then makes the decision without bringing them together as a group.* This decision may or may not reflect their influence.
- Consult team style—*the leader presents the problem to team members in a meeting, gets their suggestions, and then makes the decision.* It may or may not reflect their influence.
- Facilitate style—*the leader presents the problem to the team in a meeting, acts as a facilitator, defines the problem to be solved, and sets the boundaries within which the decision must be made.* The goal is to get agreement on a decision. Above all, the leader takes care to ensure that her ideas are not given any greater weight than those of others simply because of her position. The leader's role is much like that of chairperson, coordinating the discussion, keeping it focused on the problem, and being sure that the essential issues are discussed. The leader doesn't try to influence the team to adopt "her" solution. The leader is willing to accept and implement any solution that has the support of the entire team.
- Delegate style—*the leader permits the team to make the decision within prescribed limits.* The team undertakes the identification and diagnosis of the problem, developing alternative procedures for solving it and deciding on one or more alternative solutions. The leader doesn't enter into the team's deliberations unless explicitly asked, but plays an important role by providing needed resources and encouragement. This style represents the highest level of subordinate empowerment.

Situational Variables

The Vroom–Jago time-driven leadership model focuses on seven situational factors (contingency variables) that should be assessed by the leader to determine which of the five leadership styles to use. An implicit assumption is that a manager has the ability to use any one of the styles, as the situation factors suggest. Victor Vroom developed a Windows-based computer program called Expert System that enables the leader to record judgments on a five-point scale as to the extent to which a factor is present in a particular situation. Specifically, 5 = high presence, 3 = moderate presence, and 1 = low presence. Following our presentation of the seven situational factors, we demonstrate their use with a simplified "high" or a "low" presence evaluation.

- *Decision significance*—the degree to which the problem is highly important and a quality decision is imperative. In brief, how important is the technical quality of the decision?
- *Importance of commitment*—the degree to which subordinates' personal willingness to support the decision has an impact on the effectiveness of implementation. In brief, how important is subordinate commitment to the decision? Employees are more likely to implement enthusiastically a decision that is consistent with their goals, values, and understanding of the problem.
- *Leader expertise*—the degree to which the leader has relevant information and competencies to understand the problem fully and select the best solution to it. In brief, does the leader believe that he has the ability and information to make a high-quality decision?
- *Likelihood of commitment*—the degree to which subordinates will support the leader's decision if it is made. Followers who have faith and trust in the judgments of their leaders are more likely to commit to a decision, even if the subordinates were not heavily involved in making it. In brief, if the leader were to make the decision, would subordinate(s) likely be committed to it?
- *Team support*—the degree to which subordinates relate to the interests of the organization as a whole or a specific unit in solving the problem. In brief, do subordinates share the goals to be achieved by solving this problem?
- *Team expertise*—the degree to which the subordinates have the relevant information and competencies to understand fully the problem and select the best solution to it. In brief, does the leader think that subordinates have the abilities and information to make a high-quality decision?
- *Team competence*—the degree to which team members have the abilities needed to resolve conflicts over preferred solutions and work together in reaching a high-quality decision. In brief, are team members capable of handling their own decision-making process?

Solution Matrix

The solution matrix shown in Table 9.5 represents the basic features of the Vroom–Jago time-driven leadership model. This matrix begins on the left where you evaluate the significance of the situation—high (H) or low (L). The column headings denote the situational factors that may or may not be present. You progress across the matrix by selecting high (H) or low (L) for each relevant situational factor. After you determine the significance of the decision, you then evaluate the degree (high or low) to which employee commitment is important to implementation of the decision. As you proceed across the matrix, record a value (H or L) for only those situational factors that call for a judgment, until you reach the recommended leadership style.

Decision-Time Penalty. The decision-time penalty *is the negative result of decisions not being made when needed.* Managers often must make decisions when time is of the essence. For example, air traffic control managers, emergency rescue squad leaders, and nuclear energy plant managers may have little time to get inputs from others before having to make a decision. The time penalty is low when there are no severe pressures on the manager to make a quick decision.

Table 9.5 **Vroom–Jago Time-Driven Leadership Model**

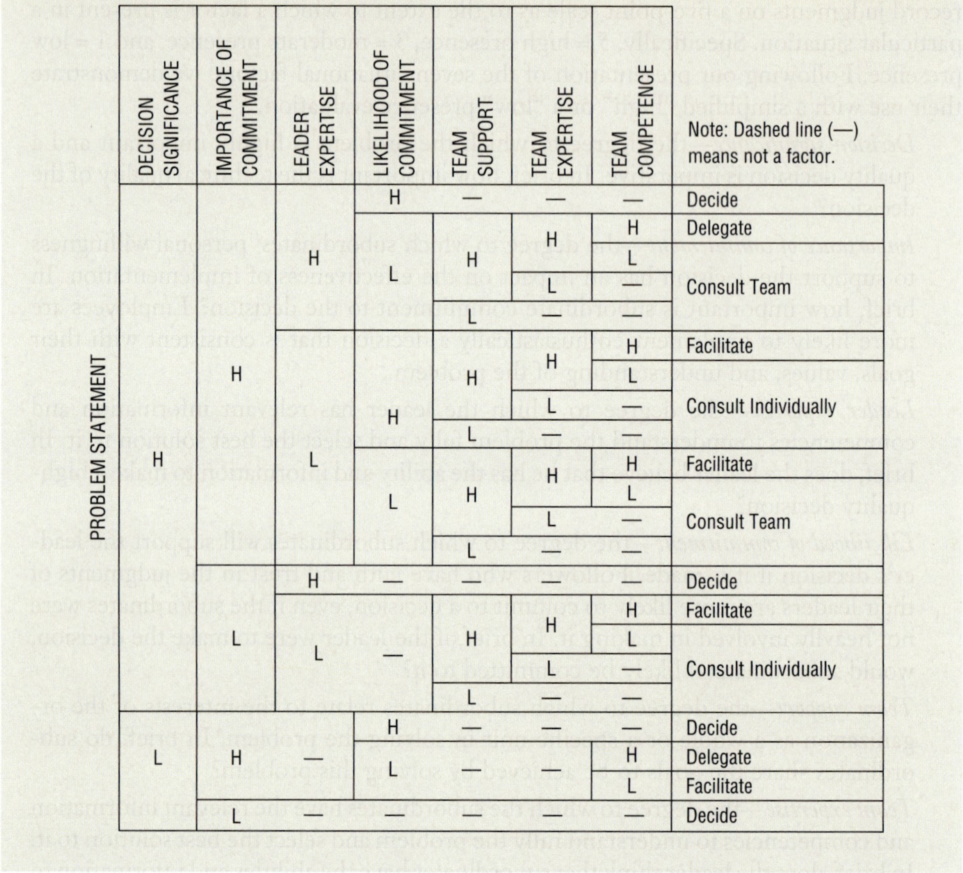
PROBLEM STATEMENT
DECISION SIGNIFICANCE
IMPORTANCE OF COMMITMENT
LEADER EXPERTISE
LIKELIHOOD OF COMMITMENT
TEAM SUPPORT
TEAM EXPERTISE
TEAM COMPETENCE
Note: Dashed line (—) means not a factor.
Decide
Delegate
Consult Team
Facilitate
Consult Individually
Facilitate
Consult Team
Decide
Facilitate
Consult Individually
Decide
Delegate
Facilitate
Decide

Source: Vroom, V. H. Leadership and decision-making. *Organizational Dynamics*, Spring 2000, 82–94.

Negative effects on "human capital" occur because the delegate and consult styles (especially the consult team version) use time and energy, which can be translated into costs even if there are no severe time constraints. Many managers spend almost 70 percent of their time in meetings and that time always has a value, although the precise costs of meetings vary with the reasons for them. For example, while Sandra Swann, vice president of human resources at ViewCast, is in a meeting, other decisions are being delayed. What's the cost to ViewCast for these delays? One cost, obviously, is the value of time lost through the use of participative decision making. Benefits gained from employees participating in meetings include being members of a team, strengthening their commitment to the organization's goals, and contributing to the development of their leadership capabilities (mainly as related to the self and communication competencies). Thus, the cost of holding a meeting must be compared to the cost of not holding a meeting.

Although participation can have negative effects on human capital, it can also have positive effects. As we emphasize throughout this book, participative leader behaviors help develop the technical skills and managerial competencies of employees, build teamwork, and foster loyalty and commitment to organizational goals. The Vroom–Jago model considers the trade-offs among four criteria by which a leader's decision-making style can be evaluated: decision quality, employee commitment to implementation, costs, and employee development. The consult and delegate styles are viewed as most supportive of employee development.

This model is applied in the following Change Competency feature.[39] We ask you to assume the role of executive director of a repertory theater and select the leadership style that you would use.

Change Competency

How Would You Lead?

You are the executive director of a repertory theater affiliated with a major university. You are responsible for both financial and artistic direction of the theater. You recognize that both sets of responsibilities are important, but you have focused your efforts where your own talents lie—on ensuring the highest level of artistic quality to the theater's productions. Reporting to you is a group of four department heads responsible for production, marketing, development, and administration, along with an assistant dean, who is responsible for the actors who are also students in the university. They are a talented set of individuals, and each is deeply committed to the theater and experienced in working together as a team.

Last week you received a comprehensive report from an independent consulting firm commissioned to examine the financial health of the theater. You were shocked by the major conclusion of the report: The expenses of operating the theater have been growing much more rapidly than income, and by year's end the theater will be operating in the red. Unless expenses can be reduced, the surplus will be consumed, and within five years the theater might have to be closed.

You have distributed the report to your staff and are surprised at the variety of reactions that it has produced. Some dispute the report's conclusions, criticizing its assumptions or methods. Others are more shaken, but even they seem divided over steps that should be taken and when. None of them or, in fact, anyone connected with the theater wants it to close. It has a long and important tradition both in the university and the surrounding community.

As executive director—and armed with the solution matrix shown in Table 9.5—what leadership style should you choose when making a decision about how to lead? Start with *decision significance* on the left-hand side of the matrix. This first column requires that you make a decision about the importance of the issue. After you make that decision, go to the next column, *importance of commitment*. Again, you must make a decision about the importance of having staff members committed. After you make this decision, you face another decision and then another. As you make each decision, follow the columns across the matrix. Eventually, at the far right-hand side of the matrix, you will arrive at the recommended best style of leadership to use, which is based on your previous seven decisions.

We used this method and obtained the results shown below. Based on this analysis, we selected the style of leadership that we recommend for this situation. Do you agree?

Problem Statements in Table 9.5	Our Answers
Decision significance	High
Importance of commitment	High
Leader expertise	Low
Likelihood of commitment	Low
Team support	High
Team expertise	High
Team competence	High

We recommend that you use the facilitate style with the teams. A different answer to one or more of these situational factors would probably result in a different recommended leadership style.

Managerial Guidelines

The Vroom–Jago time-driven leadership model is consistent with work on group and team behaviors, as we will discuss in Chapter 11. If managers can diagnose situations correctly, choosing the best leadership style for those situations becomes easier. These choices, in turn, enable them to make high-quality, timely decisions. If the situation requires delegation, the manager must learn how to establish the desired goals and limitations and then let employees determine how best to achieve the goals within those limitations. If the situation calls for the manager alone to make the decision, the manager should be aware of potential positive and negative consequences of not asking others for their input.

The model does have some limitations. First, subordinates in various countries may have a strong desire to participate in decisions affecting their jobs, regardless of the model's recommendation of a style for the manager to use. If subordinates aren't involved in the decision, they may become frustrated and not be committed to the decision. Recall, of course, our framework of work-related values in Chapter 2—individualism/collectivism, power distance, uncertainty avoidance, gender role orientation, and long-term orientation. We noted that in societies high in power distance and uncertainty avoidance, there is often a much greater employee acceptance of taking orders without participation in decision making. Second, certain competencies of the manager play a key role in determining the relative effectiveness of the model. For example, in situations involving conflict, only managers skilled in communication and conflict resolution may be able to use the kind of participative decision-making strategy suggested by the model. A manager who hasn't developed such abilities may obtain better results with a more directive style, even though this leadership style is different from the style that the model proposes. Third, the model is based on the assumption that decisions involve a single process. Often, decisions go through several cycles and are part of a solution to a bigger problem than the one being addressed at the time.

Choosing the most appropriate leadership style can be difficult. A theme of employee empowerment has begun to prevail in many leading business organizations. Evidence shows that this leadership style can result in productive, healthy organizations. Participative management is not appropriate for all situations, as the model in Table 9.5 suggests.

CHAPTER SUMMARY

1. State the core differences between leadership and management.

Leadership is the process of developing ideas and a vision, living by values that support those ideas and that vision, influencing others to embrace them in their own behaviors, and making hard decisions about human and other resources. Thus, contemporary leadership includes the seven foundation competencies developed throughout this book and more. In contrast, the traditional view of management focuses on looking inward, improving the present, tight controls, directing, coordinating, efficiency, and the like. Both contemporary leaders and traditional managers must accept three key functions to be effective: authority, responsibility, and accountability.

2. Describe the role of power and political behavior in the leadership process.

Leaders draw on five sources of power to influence the actions of followers: legitimate, reward, coercive, referent, and expert. All managers engage in political behavior to influence others—sometimes ineffectively. Political behavior and organizational politics focus on efforts to protect or enhance self-interests, goals, and preferred outcomes. The drivers of political behavior were noted with special emphasis on how managers can foster or minimize political behaviors of subordinates in relation to the performance appraisal process.

3. Describe three legacy models of leadership: traits, Theory X/Theory Y, and behavioral.

Three of the legacy leadership models are the traits, Theory X/Theory Y, and behavioral models. The traits model emphasizes the personal qualities of leaders and attributes success to certain abilities, skills, and personality characteristics. This model fails to explain why certain managers succeed and others fail as leaders. The primary reason is that it ignores how traits interact with situational variables. The Theory X/Theory Y model is based on the premise that the behavior of managers is often influenced by their assumptions and beliefs about followers and what motivates their followers. Theory X is a composite of propositions and underlying beliefs that take a command-and-control approach to management based on a negative view of human nature. In contrast, Theory Y is a composite of propositions and beliefs that take a leadership and empowering approach to management based on a positive view of human nature. The behavioral model emphasizes leaders' actions instead of their personal traits. We focused on two leader behaviors—initiating structure and consideration—and how they affect employee performance and job satisfaction. The behavioral model tends to ignore the situation in which the manager is operating. This omission is the focal point of the two contingency models of leadership that we reviewed. The contingency approach emphasizes the importance of various situational factors for leaders and their leadership styles.

4. Explain and apply the Situational Leadership® Model.

The Situational Leadership® Model states that managers should choose a style that matches the readiness of their subordinates to follow. If subordinates are not ready to perform a task, a directive leadership style will probably be more effective than a relationship style. As the readiness level of the subordinates increases, the manager's style should become more participative and less directive.

5. Explain and apply the Vroom–Jago time-driven leadership model.

The Vroom–Jago model presents a manager with choices among five leadership styles based on seven situational (contingency) factors. Time requirements and other costs associated with each style are recognized in the model. The leadership styles lie on a continuum from decide (leader makes the decision) to delegate (subordinate or team makes the decision). A solution matrix (Table 9.5) is used to diagnose the situation and arrive at the recommended leadership style.

KEY TERMS AND CONCEPTS

Behavioral model of leadership
Coercive power
Consideration
Consult individually style
Consult team style
Decide style
Decision-time penalty
Delegate style
Delegating style
Expert power
Facilitate style
Initiating structure
Leader
Leadership
Legitimate power
Manager
Organizational politics
Participating style
Political behavior
Readiness
Referent power
Relationship behavior
Reward power
Selling style
Situational Leadership® Model
Task behavior
Telling style
Theory X
Theory Y
Traits model of leadership
Vroom–Jago time-driven leadership model
Zone of indifference

DISCUSSION QUESTIONS

1. Visit Intuit's home page at www.intuit.com. Click on "About Intuit" and then "Intuit Operating Values." Read the 10 operating values. What leadership concepts presented in this chapter are illustrated in these operating values? Are these operative values consistent with the discussion of Steve Bennett in the Learning from Experience feature? Explain.
2. Based on the five sources of power presented in the chapter text, which ones are illustrated in the Learning from Experience feature on Steve Bennett? Relate his

specific comments or remarks about him to each source of power identified.

3. Think of a manager for whom you have worked. How would you assess this manager in terms of the contemporary view of leadership versus traditional view of management based on the dimensions shown in Table 9.1?
4. Think of an organization for which you have worked. What drivers of political behavior can you identify?
5. Think of a manager for whom you have worked. Did this manager engage in political performance appraisals or do things to minimize politics in the performance appraisal process? Explain with specific examples.
6. Based on the Self Competency feature related to Doug Conant, what specific examples of Theory X and/or Theory Y propositions can you identify for him? Justify your interpretations.
7. In the Diversity Competency feature, we presented excerpts of Carol Bartz's views of what it's like for women at the top and her advice to aspiring women in organizations. Based on the Situational Leadership® Model, what style or styles of leadership does she represent? Relate her specific comment(s) to each style identified.
8. Based on the Communication Competency feature related to Michelle Miller, what behaviors and decisions by her reflected elements of the Situational Leadership® Model?
9. Based on a problem situation in which you were a team member or leader, was the appropriate leadership style used according to an assessment of the situational variables in the Vroom–Jago time-driven leadership model? Use Table 9.5 to guide your assessment.
10. Assume that you have been selected as a team leader for four other classmates. The team's assignment is to develop a 10-page paper on the behavioral model of leadership and then present the paper to the class. This project represents 30 percent of the course grade. How might the Vroom–Jago time-driven leadership model be helpful to you as the team leader? What limitations does this model impose on you as team leader?

EXPERIENTIAL EXERCISE AND CASE

Experiential Exercise: Self Competency

Personal Power Inventory[40]

Instructions

Think of a group of which you are a member. For example, it could be a team at work, a committee, or a group working on a project at your school. Use the following scale to respond to the numbered statements:

1 = Strongly disagree
2 = Disagree
3 = Slightly disagree
4 = Neither agree nor disagree
5 = Slightly agree
6 = Agree
7 = Strongly agree

_____1. I am one of the more vocal members of the group.
_____2. People in the group listen to what I have to say.
_____3. I often volunteer to lead the group.
_____4. I am able to influence group decisions.
_____5. I often find myself on "center stage" in group activities or discussions.
_____6. Members of the group seek me out for advice.
_____7. I take the initiative in the group for my ideas and contributions.
_____8. I receive recognition in the group for my ideas and contributions.
_____9. I would rather lead the group than be a participant.
_____10. My opinion is held in high regard by group members.
_____11. I volunteer my thoughts and ideas without hesitation.
_____12. My ideas often are implemented.
_____13. I ask questions in meetings just to have something to say.
_____14. Group members often ask for my opinions and input.
_____15. I often play the role of scribe, secretary, or note taker during meetings.
_____16. Group members usually consult me about important matters before they make a decision.
_____17. I clown around with other group members.
_____18. I have noticed that group members often look at me, even when not talking directly to me.
_____19. I jump right into whatever conflict the group members are dealing with.
_____20. I am very influential in the group.

Scoring and Interpretation

Visibility		**Influence**	
Item	Your Score	Item	Your Score
1.	_______	2.	_______
3.	_______	4.	_______
5.	_______	6.	_______
7.	_______	8.	_______
9.	_______	10.	_______
11.	_______	12.	_______
13.	_______	14.	_______
15.	_______	16.	_______
17.	_______	18.	_______
19.	_______	20.	_______
Total	_______	Total	_______

FIGURE 9.3 Power Matrix

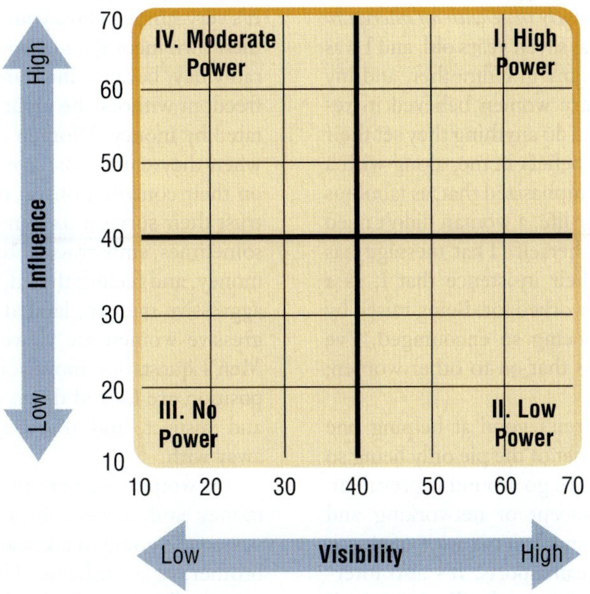

Source: Adapted from Reddy, W. B., and Williams, G. The visibility credibility inventory: Measuring power and influence. In J. W. Pfeiffer (ed.), *The 1988 Annual: Developing Human Resources*. San Diego: University Associates, 1988,124.

Use the scores calculated and mark your position on the power matrix shown in Figure 9.3. The combinations of visibility and influence shown are described as follows:

1. *High power*. Individuals in quadrant I exhibit behaviors that bring high visibility, and they are able to influence others. In organizations, these individuals may be considered to be on the "fast track."
2. *Low power*. Individuals in quadrant II are highly visible but have little real influence. This condition could reflect their personal characteristics but also could indicate that formal power resides elsewhere in the organization. Often these people may hold staff, rather than line, positions that give them visibility but that lack "clout" to get things done.
3. *No power*. Individuals in quadrant III, for whatever reason, are neither seen nor heard. Individuals in this category may have difficulty advancing in the organization.
4. *Moderate power*. Individuals in quadrant IV are "behind-the-scenes" influencers. These individuals often are opinion leaders and "sages" who wield influence but are content to stay out of the limelight.

Case: Diversity Competency

Georgette Mosbacher, CEO and President of Borghese[41]

Georgette Mosbacher is the CEO and president of Borghese, Inc., which is headquartered in New York City. The firm manufactures and markets luxury cosmetics, skin care, and fragrance products internationally. Mosbacher has led several entrepreneurial ventures and is active in a number of volunteer and advocacy pursuits. She is the author of *It Takes Money, Honey*, a guide written to help women achieve financial freedom, and *Feminine Force*, an inspirational book designed to assist women in achieving their full potential. This case is based on excerpts from an in-depth interview of Mosbacher.

What accounts for your success in so many areas? I have always been curious and I've always been an achiever. I'm very tenacious, as well; I don't give up on things. Furthermore, it's just my nature to be adventurous. I'm very willing to go out and try new ventures.

What insights into the process of buying a firm can you offer? If I had to stress one central theme, it would be this: An entrepreneur has to persevere. This involves beating the bushes to raise the funds necessary to make the purchase, developing a comprehensive business plan, having a vision and a plan of action, and then going out and selling the idea. You must convince potential investors that you can accomplish that which you envision for the business, and that their investments will pay off. Financing is the first challenge an entrepreneur faces in the process of buying a firm. Obviously, money is necessary to get a company going. The second challenge is being able to deliver on your vision and your business plan. Entrepreneurs have to turn over every stone, analyze every possibility, and must not let rejection get them down. Tenacity is the key to success.

What is it that motivates you to devote your time and resources to the development of women, particularly those with an interest in business? My father died when I was seven years old, and I was raised by my great-grandmother, my grandmother, and my mother. These three extraordinary women believed in responsibility and that a person could do anything they set their mind to do. They instilled these beliefs in me, along with a belief in myself. Moreover, they emphasized that, as fabulous as it could be to have a man in her life, a woman didn't need one to create a fulfilling life for herself. That message has always empowered me, as has their insistence that I, as a woman, could achieve anything I worked for. Being raised by these three strong women and being so encouraged, I've always felt a responsibility to pass that on to other women; I've made it a personal mission.

Additionally, women often aren't good at helping one another; unfortunately, the mind-set of the pie only being so big and there only being so much to go around is prevalent. Men seem to have a better concept of networking and partnering to accomplish goals, and I think a lot of this is owed to men's participation in team sports. It's also interesting that men can argue and disagree and still turn to each other for help and support as if nothing ever happened. Women, on the other hand, when they've argued or even perceive a slight, typically will not only refrain from asking for assistance, they won't talk to that person in the future. Sadly, this sort of behavior prevents women from achieving the same kind of camaraderie that men attain and utilize to their advantage in the business world. The "Old Boys Club" truly does exist, and the members are very good at being loyal and helpful to one another. Women don't do that, and it is unfortunate. I hope that my participation in activities that support women helps overcome this mentality and helps women appreciate the value in supporting each other.

In light of this, do you think it is important for women in business to find effective mentors? I think that is helpful, but I firmly believe that you can be your own mentor. This can be achieved through believing in one's self, the attitude that anything can be accomplished, and abandoning fears, including the fear of ridicule, and the fear of failure. Fear is the most debilitating, paralyzing emotion, and it has to be tamed in order for a person to succeed. An individual that believes she can pick herself up and go forward, even in the face of adversity, is positioned for success. As long as something isn't illegal or immoral, it is fair game; you go for it. The worst that can happen is you fail. In my opinion, "failure" isn't a dirty word and it isn't a stop sign; rather, it's a detour.

You are also passionate about women's financial freedom, as outlined in your book, It Takes Money, Honey. *What is the most important piece of financial advice you like to share with women?* It's very simple: Have your own money. Women have to earn their own incomes, manage that money, and put it away for a rainy day, because that rainy day always comes. There is no freedom without the ability to survive, and survival is facilitated by money. Women often abdicate that basic principle when they enter marriage because they don't put any value on their contributions to the partnership. As such, they entrust their survival to someone else. I also think women are sometimes embarrassed by talking about money, wanting money, and feeling they deserve to be compensated. Strong, aggressive men are lauded as path-breakers, but strong, aggressive women are viewed, and often termed, negatively. Men's quests for money are admired; women in the same position are looked down upon. It's considered unfeminine and suspect, and that's an attitude that has to be done away with.

As women, we're not brought up to think that we deserve money and success. Instead, we're raised to believe that someone's going to take care of us, whether that be a father, a brother, or a husband. That might sound comforting, but statistically that doesn't happen. Many women who live comfortably before divorces fall below the poverty line after marital splits. Why is that? Because they relied on someone to take care of them and were set adrift when the situation changed. Ultimately, whose fault is that? It can't be blamed on someone else. We're all responsible for our own well-being.

*For more information on Borghese, visit the organization's home page at **www.borghese.com.***

Questions

1. How would you characterize Mosbacher in terms of the contemporary view of leadership versus the traditional view of management. Use Table 9.1 in developing your assessment.
2. What types of interpersonal sources of power are reflected in Mosbacher's comments? Give specific examples of her remarks that are related to each type of power identified.
3. Based on the Theory X/Theory Y model of leadership, how would you describe Mosbacher?
4. How would you assess Mosbacher in relation to the behavioral model of leadership?

CHAPTER 10

Leading Effectively: New Perspectives

Learning Goals

When you have finished studying the chapter, you should be able to:

1. Explain and apply the characteristics of the transactional leadership model.
2. Discuss and apply the attributes of the authentic leadership model.
3. Explain and apply the essentials of the transformational leadership model.
4. Explain the core features of the Global Leadership and Organizational Behavior Effectiveness (GLOBE) model.

© Fred Prouser/Reuters/Landov

Learning from Experience

NURTURING LEADERS AT GE

General Electric (GE) is consistently recognized as one of the best and most admired firms in the world. Less well known is GE's reputation as one of the best companies in the world for developing leadership talent. A key executive in developing leadership talent at GE has been William J. Conaty. He recently retired after 40 years at GE, including 13 years as head of human resources. Most of this opening feature reflects on his advice for nurturing leaders. This advice is presented in five areas:

Differentiate. The continuous assessment of employees, including all levels of management, builds organizational vitality and fosters a true performance-based culture in Conaty's view. Employees should be constantly assessed on their performance. Conaty contends differentiation is what drives GE. He states: "You have to know who are the least effective people on your team—and then you have to do something about them."

Improving Performance. Managers at GE are expected to continually seek to improve performance, both their own and their team members'. Conaty comments: "One of the reasons managers fail at GE is they stop learning. The job grows, the accountability grows, and the people don't grow with it." Continuous learning is so valued that GE training courses are considered high-profile rewards. Getting selected to go to Crotonville, the 53-acre executive training center in New York's Hudson River Valley, is a signal that someone is poised to go to the next level. Conaty states: "Crotonville is one of the best tools we have in our arsenal." GE invests about $1 billion annually on training and development programs—from assembly line workers through executives at a variety of training centers.

Become Easy to Replace. At GE, great leaders, in part, are viewed as those who develop excellent succession plans. Insecure leaders are intimidated by them. Conaty notes: "I can go business by business and tell you where we're strongest and weakest on succession. It all comes down to having an executive who doesn't want to admit someone else could do their job. If they kill two or three viable successors along the way, you have to start looking at the person who's doing the killing." At GE, leaders are judged on the strength of their team and are rewarded

LEARNING CONTENT

For more information on GE, visit the organization's home page at www.ge.com.

for mentoring people throughout the organization. Conaty takes pride in the fact that his own successor is someone that he helped develop within the HR function at GE.

Keep Focused. "You can't move 325,000 people with mixed messaging and thousands of initiatives," according to Conaty. Leaders at GE succeed by being consistent and straightforward about a handful of core messages. And the best don't get derailed when times turn tough. Conaty notes: "I'd say 70% of our leaders handle adversity well, and 30% let it overwhelm them. If you can't take a punch and you don't have a sense of humor, you don't belong in this company. Everyone experiences failure now and then. It's how you handle it that matters."

Ethical Leadership. In addition to its formal ethics programs, procedures, rules, and the like, GE develops and demands ethical leadership to ensure a seamless consistency between leaders' personal attributes (like honesty), their public and private statements, and their direct and indirect actions. Jeff Immelt, the CEO, begins and ends each annual meeting of GE's 200 officers and its 600 senior managers by restating the company's fundamental integrity principles: "GE's business success is built on our reputation with all stakeholders for lawful and ethical behavior. Commercial considerations *never* justify cutting corners. Upholding this standard is the specific responsibility of the leaders in the room." For any serious lapse, the warning is clear: One strike and you're out. GE's senior managers and officers know the CEO is serious because every year or so, a senior manager who knowingly or recklessly violated company ethics for commercial or personal reasons is terminated.[1]

Recall our comment from Chapter 9 that the understanding of leadership is like that of a prism—there is something new and different each time you look at it from a new angle. In this chapter, we present additional lenses for understanding and addressing the range of leadership issues and the pressures on leaders in particular situations. Our focus is on new perspectives and models of leadership: transactional, authentic, transformational, and GLOBE (an acronym for Global Leadership and Organizational Behavior Effectiveness).

Leadership is future oriented. It involves influencing people to move from where they are (here) to some new place (there).[2] Clearly, the leadership of GE has a significant influence in continuously transforming the firm. GE is lauded for its ability to change direction quickly. Jeff Immelt, GE's CEO, comments: "Most people inside GE learn from the past but have a healthy disrespect for our business history. They have the ability to live in the moment and not be burdened by the past, which is extremely important."[3] In the Learning from Experience feature, this future orientation is also illustrated in Conaty's remark: "One of the reasons managers fail at GE is they stop learning. The job grows, the accountability grows, and the people don't grow with it." However, different leaders define or perceive *here* and *there* differently. For some, the journey between here and there is relatively routine, like driving a car on a familiar road. Others see the need to chart a new course through unexplored territory. Such leaders perceive fundamental differences between the way things are and the way things can or should be. They recognize the shortcomings of the present situation and offer a sense of passion and excitement to overcome them. Recall Conaty's comment: "Leaders succeed at GE by being consistent and straightforward about a handful of core messages. And the best don't get derailed when times turn tough."

TRANSACTIONAL LEADERSHIP MODEL

Learning Goal

1. Explain and apply the characteristics of the transactional leadership model.

Transactional leadership *involves motivating and directing followers primarily through appealing to their own self-interest.* The transactional leadership model focuses on a carrot (and sometimes a stick) approach, setting performance expectations and goals and providing feedback to followers. The primary power of transactional leaders comes from their formal authority in the organization. They focus on the basic management processes of controlling, organizing, and short-term planning.

Key Components

Three primary components of the transactional leadership model are usually viewed as prompting followers to achieve their performance goals[4]:

- *Provides contingent rewards.* Transactional leaders identify paths that link the achievement of goals to rewards, clarify expectations, exchange promises and resources for support, arrange mutually satisfactory agreements, negotiate for resources, exchange assistance for effort, and provide commendations for successful performance. These leaders set and clarify detailed goals to obtain short-term and measurable results.
- *Exhibits active management by exception.* Transactional leaders actively monitor the work performed by subordinates, take corrective actions if deviations from expected standards occur, and enforce rules to prevent mistakes.
- *Emphasizes passive management by exception.* Transactional leaders intervene after unacceptable performance or deviations from accepted standards occur. They may wait to take action until mistakes are brought to their attention. Corrective actions and possibly punishment are used as a response to unacceptable performance.

The transactional leadership model is best viewed as necessary but insufficient in developing maximum leadership potential. One leadership expert makes the following point:

> *Without the transactional base, expectations are often unclear, direction is ill-defined, and the goals you are working toward are too ambiguous. . . . Transactions clearly in place form the base for more mature interactions.*[5]

Managerial Guidelines

Effective transactional leaders are likely to engage in the following five practices:

- They ask: "What needs to be done?"
- They ask: "What is right for the organization?
- They develop action plans.
- They take responsibility for decisions.
- They take responsibility for communicating.[6]

A transactional leader may tend to overemphasize detailed and short-term goals, standard operating procedures, rules, and policies. This emphasis may tend to stifle creativity and the generation of new ideas. The pure form of the transactional leadership model may work only where organizational problems and goals are clear and well defined. There may be a tendency for transactional leaders to not reward or ignore ideas that do not fit with the manager's plans and goals.

The transactional leader attempts to influence others by exchanging good performance for extrinsic rewards, such as wages, financial incentives, benefits, and status symbols, such as a larger office. The failure to perform is often followed by punishment. Also, transactional leaders may be quite effective in guiding efficiency initiatives designed to cut costs and improve productivity in the short term.[7] They tend to be highly directive and action oriented, if not dominating. The relationships between transactional leaders and followers tend to be transitory and not based on emotional bonds.

The following Change Competency feature reports on what appears to be the excessive reliance on transactional leadership by Robert Nardelli, who was removed as the CEO of Home Depot in 2007.[8] At one time, Nardelli's major restructuring of Home Depot and other changes was interpreted as an example of his leadership acumen. Home Depot, with headquarters in Atlanta, Georgia, is a major home improvement specialty retailer with approximately 2,200 stores.[9]

Change Competency

Robert Nardelli's Transactional Leadership at Home Depot

Robert Nardelli's role as CEO of Home Depot from 2001 to January 2007 may be best remembered by the public for his $210 million severance package upon dismissal. It created a firestorm of criticism. Nardelli changed Home Depot's internal and external dynamics.

His transactional, and some would say arrogant, leadership did not engender loyalty among Home Depot's shareholders, customers, and employees. In the end, his failure to understand and listen to them proved fatal. Of course, Nardelli might still be CEO if Home Depot's stock had not declined almost 9 percent during his period as CEO, while shares of Lowe's increased 186 percent over the same period. Let's consider some of the actions associated with his transactional leadership.

Almost immediately upon becoming CEO in 2001, Nardelli embarked on an aggressive plan to centralize decision making of the nation's second-largest retailer after Wal-Mart Stores Inc. He invested more than $1 billion in new technology, such as self-checkout aisles and inventory management systems that generated reams of data. He decided that he wanted to measure virtually everything that happened at each store and division to hold managers strictly accountable for meeting their numbers.

All this was new at a relatively laid-back organization known for the independence of its store managers and the folksy, entrepreneurial style of retired cofounders Bernard Marcus and Arthur Blank. One of Nardelli's favorite sayings is "Facts are friendly." He seemed less concerned about being friendly to people. Some saw this as a strength. "This guy is maniacal about goals, objectivity, accomplishments within the boundaries of the values of the company," stated Kenneth G. Langone, the third cofounder of Home Depot, a member of its board of directors, and a strong Nardelli ally.

But among many of Home Depot's employees, especially rank-and-file workers in its stores, there was little sympathy as Nardelli's actions were followed by declining financial results. They resented the replacement of many thousands of full-time store workers with legions of part-timers. This was one aspect of a relentless cost-cutting program Nardelli used to drive gross margins from 30 percent in 2000 to about 34 percent by 2006. As the news of his dismissal spread through Home Depot's Atlanta headquarters and reached stores, some employees text-messaged each other with happy faces and exclamation points. "I think that it is being received well. Most people believed that Bob was autocratic and stubborn," said an assistant manager in an Atlanta store who asked not to be named. A corporate office manager commented: "It's amazing the reaction of people on my floor. People are openly ecstatic. High-fiving. There's a group talking about going to happy hour at noon."

Nardelli's data-driven, in-your-face management style grated on many seasoned executives, resulting in massive turnover in Home Depot's upper ranks. "He would say that you're just not leadership material, you're just not Home Depot material, you're just not the type of person we need," says a former senior executive.

For more information on Home Depot, visit the organization's home page at www.homedepot.com.

Learning Goal

2. Discuss and apply the attributes of the authentic leadership model.

AUTHENTIC LEADERSHIP MODEL

Authentic leadership *refers to individuals who (1) know and understand themselves, (2) know what they believe and value, and (3) act on their values and beliefs through open and honest communications with subordinates and others.*[10] As a result of these attributes, subordinates are more willing to trust and follow the authentic leader. These leaders can be directive or participative. The person's leadership style is not what distinguishes inauthentic leaders from authentic leaders. Authentic leaders build credibility and win the respect of followers by encouraging and respecting diverse viewpoints. They seek to foster

An authentic leader wins the respect of followers by encouraging and respecting diverse viewpoints and in general by fostering collaborative relationships.

collaborative and trusting relationships with followers, customers, shareholders, and other stakeholders.

These leaders convey a genuine desire to serve rather than primarily control others through their leadership. These leaders strive to find ways to empower employees in the pursuit of making a difference. Authentic leaders recognize and value individual differences in goals and competencies. They also have the ability and desire to identify the underlying talents of subordinates and to help build them into workable strengths and competencies.

Key Components

The model of authentic leadership includes the following interrelated components discussed next and shown in Figure 10.1.[11]

Stimulates Follower Identification. Authentic leaders influence followers' attitudes and behaviors, which, in turn, positively affects their self-esteem. These leaders are able to determine their followers' strengths and develop them. Authentic leaders help followers link their strengths to a common purpose or mission. This is accomplished through leading by example and setting high moral standards of honesty and integrity. They are open, positive, and highly ethical. There is an orientation toward doing "what is right and fair" for the leader and followers.

Authentic leaders identify with their followers by being up front, openly discussing their own and followers' limitations while constantly nurturing the growth of followers.

Authentic leaders have a clear sense of how their roles require them to act responsibly, ethically, and in the best interests of others. Through their high moral values, honesty, and integrity, followers' social identification with the work team, department, or organization is increased. Followers are able to connect and identify with the leader over time. The followers' self-concept and related self-control become identified with or tied to the purpose or mission of the organization.

Creates Hope. Authentic leaders create positive motivations for followers by fostering goal setting and helping them identify how to achieve their goals. The role of hope was discussed in Chapter 2. We noted that *hope* involves a person's willpower (determination) and waypower (road map) to achieve goals. Followers accept and become

FIGURE 10.1 Key Components of Authentic Leadership Model

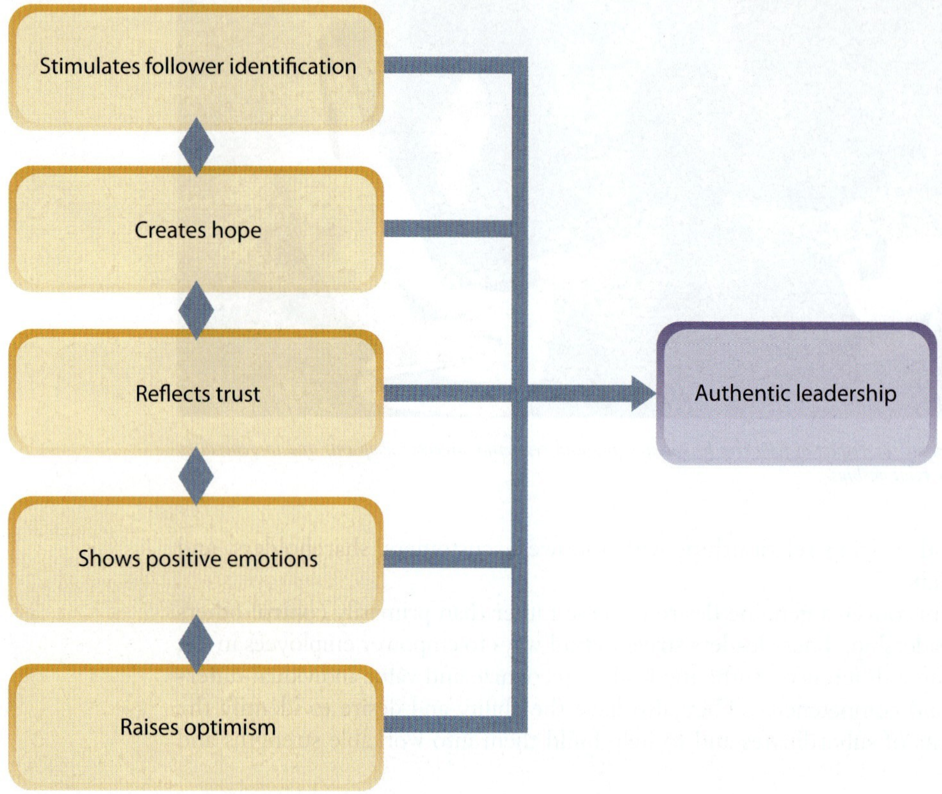

Source: Based on Avolio, B. J., Gardner, W. L., Walumbwa, F. O., Luthans, F., and May, D. R. Unlocking the mask: A look at the process by which authentic leaders impact follower attitudes and behaviors. *Leadership Quarterly*, 2004, 15, 801–823.

committed to the goals that can be achieved. Also, they believe that successful plans can be developed to achieve these goals. Authentic leaders are able to enhance followers' sense of hopefulness by (1) showing high levels of commitment, sharing, and openness; (2) communicating important information needed for them to reach the goals; and (3) encouraging questioning and open discussions.

Reflects Trust. Based on reviews of their attributes, authentic leaders are more likely to be trusted by followers and others. They build trust by (1) encouraging open two-way communications, (2) sharing critical information—the bad and the good, and (3) revealing their perceptions and feelings about the people with whom they work—the good and the bad in a constructive way. Followers come to know what the leader values and stands for. In turn, the leader comes to know what the followers value and stand for.

Shows Positive Emotions. The positive emotions of authentic leaders broaden followers' thoughts on how to achieve goals and solve problems, discover novel ways for doing things, and foster creative thinking. They are more likely to stimulate positive feelings among followers and a sense of identification with the purposes being championed.

Raises Optimism. Authentic leaders tend to be optimists and stimulate a sense of optimism among followers. Optimists persevere in the face of obstacles or difficulties, assess personal failures and setbacks as temporary, and exhibit high levels of work motivation, performance, and job satisfaction. Optimism includes the assumption that individuals can do something to change situations for the better. Pessimism includes the assumption that probably nothing individuals do will make much of a difference. Optimists want to take action, which increases the likelihood that goals will be set, pursued, and achieved. That's how optimism may create a self-fulfilling outcome. Optimists are less stressed by ordinary ups and downs. They tend to see bad situations as temporary and specific—as something they can address.

Managerial Guidelines

Authentic leaders influence followers' attitudes and behaviors through identification, hope, trust, positive emotions, and optimism. The focus is on the positive attributes and strengths of people—not on their weaknesses. Authentic leadership focuses on understanding enough about yourself to be able to make confident statements such as these:

- *I know what I'm good at and what I'm not so good at. I will build on my strengths and shore up my weaknesses.*
- *I will surround myself with people who are good, really good at what I neither have the time for or the ability to do myself. I will build a truly diversified team who can get the job done, who can achieve the focus.*
- *When I mess up I will fess up. I will forgive myself and move on. I will do the same with other committed team players. I recognize that when I trip up and fall, it's because I am moving, and that without movement there can be no progress.*
- *I will be myself at all times. I will not wear a mask.*

The leader is, in part, a "servant" to followers.[12] The leader is called on to engage employees' hearts and minds in a purpose greater than any of them. Authentic does not mean being "soft." Tough assignments, accountability, and high standards of performance are part of being an authentic leader.

This model suggests that such leadership will, over the long run, result in superior organizational performance. Although this may prove to be the case, data on this perspective are limited. Moreover, many factors and forces are likely to influence the leadership process. Some of these include organizational power and politics, organizational structure, and organizational culture. Top executives may be able to shape and influence many of these factors. However, that may not be as feasible for first- and middle-level managers who must work at developing their own authentic leadership style if their top-level executives do not exhibit or model this kind of leadership.

The following Diversity Competency feature presents a few of the perspectives of Marilyn Carlson Nelson, who is now chairman of Carlson, on leadership and diversity. As you read this feature, her authentic leadership behaviors will become clear.[13] Nelson has received many awards and forms of recognition for both her corporate and civic leadership. She was selected by *U.S. News and World Report* as one of "America's Best Leaders" and in 2007, for the fourth consecutive year, she was named one of "The World's 100 Most Powerful" by *Forbes* magazine. Privately owned Carlson, headquartered in Minneapolis, Minnesota, specializes in hotel, restaurant, travel, cruise, and marketing services. Carlson brands and services include: Regent Hotels & Resorts, Radisson Hotels & Resorts, Country Inn & Suites By Carlson, T.G.I. Friday's and Pick Up Stix restaurants, Carlson Wagonlit Travel, and Carlson Marketing. Based in Minneapolis, Carlson's brands and services employ more than 190,000 people in nearly 150 countries. Carlson's 2006 systemwide sales, including franchised operations, totaled \$37.1 billion.[14]

LEADER INSIGHT

Without self-discipline, you can't gain the respect of your followers. Most people profess to having good values but lack the discipline to convert those values into consistent actions. Authentic leaders have the self-discipline to show their values through their actions. When they fall short, they admit their mistakes.

Bill George, former CEO of Metronics and author of *Authentic Leadership* and *True North: Discover Your Authentic Leadership*

Diversity Competency

Marilyn Carlson Nelson on Leadership and Diversity

© Courtesy of Carlson

Marilyn Carlson Nelson, who was CEO of Carlson until 2008 and now serves as Chairman of the Board, has made strides toward redefining leadership and creating a more diverse workplace.

It's been said that people deserve the leadership they get, and I think it means perhaps we need to redefine success. If in our personal lives we think of success as power, or prestige, or money, then perhaps we shouldn't expect that our leadership is going to reflect different values. Some people think, 'You're the CEO. That must be the most liberating thing in the world. You can rule your world!' The fact is, you actually have to subordinate your own emotions, your own desires, even make decisions on behalf of the whole that might conflict with what you would do on an individual basis. Sometimes you have to let someone go that you care about deeply.

Beyond being a moral and political imperative, having the most diverse, most exciting workplace possible is also a strategic imperative. Not just because we have this dream of creating a world where everyone has equal opportunity and there's justice for all and shared prosperity but because we have an amazing role to play. We can model to a world increasingly divided that the American melting pot is still a goal; that we can work together for the collective good; that we are a model of goodness; and that as a nation we will continue to be good. So, we accept that diversity is part of our personal agenda, not just a corporate agenda. Every one of us has freedom and the personal accountability that goes with freedom. One person can make a difference, and it can be you. Don't ever say "they." Say "I." You can change them. You can change you—and you must keep pursuing it. Don't look around. I look at you, and you look at me. Let's hold ourselves accountable. Today, smart minds don't come in any one color, shape, or gender. They come in all ranges of diversity. What are we doing to change the workplace at Carlson?

- First, we now have nearly 40 percent women in our executive ranks. I recognized that we didn't have a high percentage of women in executive roles, but every year when we did our succession planning many women were named as backups to some of our key roles. Still, when it came to the moment of truth, when someone would be promoted, the women didn't get the job. I asked, What is the barrier? Why do these women look so great until the day we make a decision? They'd always say, Well she's not very strong financially—as if that were congenital! So, we started identifying their developmental needs earlier and then training them faster.
- Sometimes people needed better people skills. Often, when women and minorities work really hard, they are seen by others as aggressive when they need to be seen as assertive. People skills training can help.
- We're members of groups that allow us to share best practices in diversity. We support these groups because we want a network, we want to learn.
- We have a pilot program with a dedicated diversity recruiter. We hadn't done that before, hoping that we could just recruit the best of the best, and diversity would just happen. But we forget how easy it is to pick someone like ourselves, even though that isn't our intention.
- We believe in mentoring and have developed a program of mentorship for women. We need to make sure more minority mentoring goes on in our companies. Through the National Women's Business Council, I've learned that mentoring is a powerful differentiator for success.

For more information on Carlson, visit the organization's home page at www.carlson.com.

TRANSFORMATIONAL LEADERSHIP MODEL

Learning Goal

3. Explain and apply the essentials of the transformational leadership model.

Transformational leadership *involves anticipating future trends, inspiring followers to understand and embrace a new vision of possibilities, developing others to be leaders or better leaders, and building the organization or group into a community of challenged and rewarded learners.*[15] Transformational leadership may be found at all levels of the organization: teams, departments, divisions, and the organization as a whole. *Visionary, inspiring, daring,* and *ethical* are words that describe transformational leaders. They are assertive risk takers who seize or create new opportunities. They are also thoughtful thinkers who understand the interactions of technology, culture, stakeholders, and external environmental forces.

As suggested in Figure 10.2, the transformational leadership model is challenging to implement. As you will see, there are some similarities between the transformational and authentic leadership models.

Key Components

The key interrelated components of the transformational leadership model include individualized consideration, intellectual stimulation, inspirational motivation, and idealized influence.[16]

Shows Individualized Consideration. Individualized consideration *is the degree to which the leader attends to followers' needs, acts as a mentor or coach, and listens to followers' concerns.* In particular, transformational leaders provide special attention to each follower's needs for achievement and growth. Followers and colleagues are encouraged to develop to successively higher levels of their potential. Individual differences are embraced and rewarded to enhance creativity and innovation. An open dialogue with followers is encouraged and "management by continuous engagement" is standard

FIGURE 10.2 Key Components of the Transformational Leadership Model

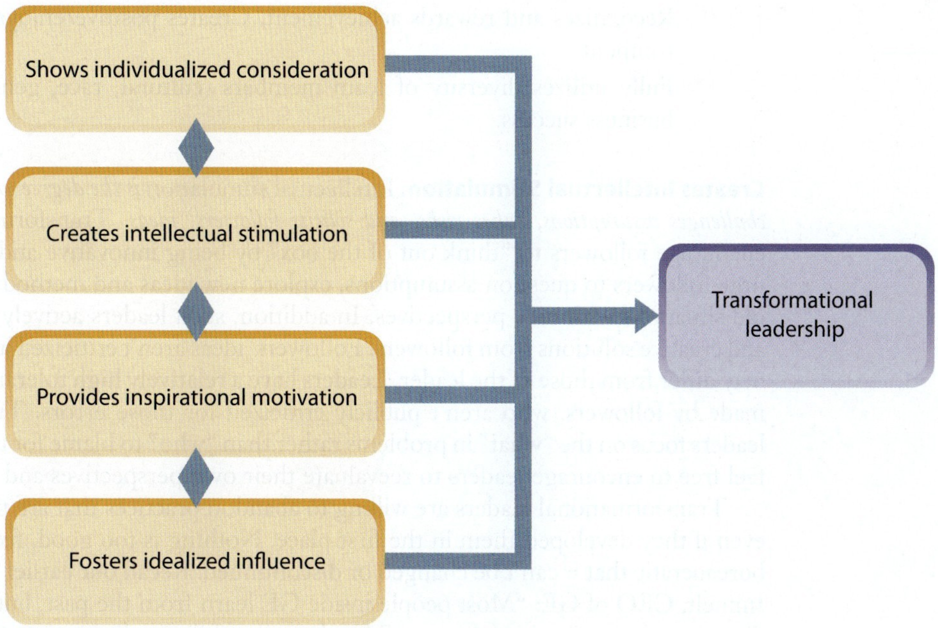

Source: Based on Bass, B. M., and Riggio, R. E. *Transformational Leadership*, 2nd ed. Florence, KY: Lawrence Erlbaum Associates, 2005.

practice. Listening skills are sharp and reflect this observation: It's not what you tell them, it's what they hear.

Transformational leaders empower followers to make decisions. At the same time, they monitor followers to determine whether they need additional support or direction and to assess progress. With trust in leaders' intentions, followers think, "This person is trying to help me by noting mistakes, as opposed to pointing a finger at me in some accusatory way." Moreover, trust is important in leading change as change itself requires risk taking. As we have noted in a number of places, a foundation for trust lies in consistency between a person's words and actions. Individuals are often willing to take considerable risks for their leader if she practices what she preaches.

Several dimensions used to assess GE managers through the *GE Leadership Survey* reflect the concept of individualized consideration. Managers are rated on performance criteria within general characteristics through a scale that ranges from:

Significant development needs 1 2 3 4 5 Outstanding strength.[17]

The general characteristics and specific performance criteria that GE considers most closely related to individualized consideration follow:

- *Communication/Influence*:
  - Communicates in open, candid, clear, complete, and consistent manner—invites response/dissent.
  - Listens effectively and probes for new ideas.
  - Uses facts and rational arguments to influence and persuade.
  - Breaks down barriers and develops influential relationships across teams, functions, and layers.
- *Team Builder/Empowerment*:
  - Selects talented people; provides coaching and feedback to develop team members to fullest potential.
  - Delegates whole task; empowers team to maximize effectiveness. Is personally a team player.
  - Recognizes and rewards achievement. Creates positive/enjoyable work environment.
  - Fully utilizes diversity of team members (cultural, race, gender) to achieve business success.

Creates Intellectual Stimulation. Intellectual stimulation *is the degree to which the leader challenges assumptions, takes risks, and solicits followers' ideas.* Transformational leaders encourage followers to "think out of the box" by being innovative and creative. They urge followers to question assumptions, explore new ideas and methods, and approach old situations with new perspectives. In addition, such leaders actively seek new ideas and creative solutions from followers. Followers' ideas aren't criticized just because they may differ from those of the leader. Leaders have a relatively high tolerance for mistakes made by followers, who aren't publicly criticized for those errors. Transformational leaders focus on the "what" in problems rather than "who" to blame for them. Followers feel free to encourage leaders to reevaluate their own perspectives and assumptions.

Transformational leaders are willing to abandon practices that are no longer useful even if they developed them in the first place. Nothing is too good, fixed, political, or bureaucratic that it can't be changed or discontinued. Recall our earlier quote from Jeff Immelt, CEO of GE: "Most people inside GE learn from the past, but have a healthy disrespect for our business history. They have the ability to live in the moment, and not be burdened by the past, which is extremely important." The prevailing view of transformational leaders is that it is better to question ourselves than to leave all of the questioning about us to our competitors. They view risk taking as necessary and desirable for the long-term development and success of the organization. In brief, they promote creativity, rationality, and thoughtful problem solving from multiple points of view.

The general characteristics and specific performance criteria related to intellectual stimulation that are used to assess the leadership effectiveness of GE managers follow:

- *Knowledge/Expertise/Intellect*:
  - Possesses and readily shares functional/technical knowledge and expertise. Constant interest in learning.
  - Demonstrates broad business knowledge/perspective with cross-functional/multicultural awareness.
  - Makes good decisions with limited data. Applies intellect to the fullest.
  - Quickly sorts relevant from irrelevant information; grasps essentials of complex issues and initiates action.
- *Shared Ownership/Boundaryless*:
  - Self-confidence to share information across traditional boundaries and be open to new ideas.
  - Encourages/promotes shared ownership for team vision and goals.
  - Trusts others; encourages risk taking and boundaryless behavior.
  - Encourages everyone to be heard. Open to ideas from anywhere.
- *Initiative/Speed*:
  - Creates real and positive change. Sees change as an opportunity.
  - Anticipates problems and initiates new and better ways of doing things.
  - Hates/avoids/eliminates "bureaucracy" and strives for brevity, simplicity, clarity.
  - Understands and uses speed as a competitive advantage.

Provides Inspirational Motivation. Inspirational motivation *is the degree to which leaders articulate a vision that is appealing to followers*. Of course, the transformational leader requires more than a vision to foster change. A vision *expresses fundamental aspirations and purpose, usually by appealing to peoples' emotions and minds*. The leader needs the competencies to translate abstract and intangible concepts of a broad vision into understandable and concrete goals with which followers can associate and identify required actions. What vision was expressed by Marilyn Carlson Nelson in the Diversity Competency feature? How is she attempting to translate it into concrete and understandable goals?

In effect, transformational leaders guide followers by providing them with a sense of meaning and challenge. Such leaders get followers involved in, and eventually committed to, a vision of a future that may be significantly different from the present. They inspire others by what they say and do. These leaders appeal to followers' sense of pride, self-esteem, and other intrinsic motivators. The framing and inspirational promotion of a consistent vision and set of values is the foundation of transformational leadership. One leadership expert sums it up this way:

> *Transformational leaders are shapers of values, creators, interpreters of institutional purpose, exemplars, makers of meanings, pathfinders, and molders of organizational culture. They are persistent and consistent. Their vision is so compelling that they know what they want from every interaction. Their visions don't blind others, but empower them.*[18]

The general characteristics and specific performance criteria for assessing the leadership effectiveness of GE managers that are related to inspirational motivation follow:

- *Vision*:
  - Has developed and communicated a clear, simple, customer-focused vision/direction for the organization.
  - Is forward thinking, stretches horizons, challenges imaginations.

    - Inspires and energizes others to commit to vision. Captures minds. Leads by example.
    - As appropriate, updates the vision to reflect constant and accelerating change impacting the business.
- *Customer/Quality Focus*:
    - Listens to customers and assigns the highest priority to customer satisfaction, including internal customers.
    - Inspires and demonstrates a passion for excellence in every aspect of work.
    - Strives to fulfill commitment to quality in total product/service offering.
    - Lives customer service and creates service mind-set throughout organization.

Fosters Idealized Influence. Idealized influence *is the degree to which leaders behave in charismatic ways that cause followers to identify with them.* Charisma *involves motivating and directing followers by developing in them a strong emotional commitment to a vision and set of shared values.* Transformational leaders demonstrate the behaviors that followers strive to mirror. Followers typically admire, respect, and trust such leaders. They identify with these leaders as people, as well as with the vision and values that they are advocating. Positive idealized influence allows followers to feel free to question what is being advocated. The goals of followers are often personally meaningful and consistent with their self-concepts. They willingly give extra effort because of the intrinsic rewards obtained from performing well, not just because of the potential for receiving greater monetary and other extrinsic rewards. Immediate short-term goals are viewed as a means to the followers' commitments to a greater vision.

To further earn such idealized influence, transformational leaders often consider the needs and interests of followers over their own needs. They may willingly sacrifice personal gain for the sake of others. Transformational leaders can be trusted and demonstrate high standards of ethical and moral conduct. Followers come to see such leaders as operating according to a pattern of open communication. Thus, they can be very direct and challenging to some followers (e.g., poor performers) and highly empathetic and supportive of others (e.g., those with a seriously ill family member).

Although transformational leaders minimize the use of power for personal gain, they will use all of the sources of power—expert, legitimate, reward, referent, and coercive—at their disposal to move individuals and teams toward a vision and its related goals. As an example of referent power, followers often describe transformational leaders as individuals who have had a major impact on their own personal and professional development.

When assessing the leadership effectiveness of GE managers, the following general characteristics and specific performance criteria that relate to idealized influence are used:

- *Integrity*:
    - Maintains unequivocal commitment to honesty/truth in every facet of behavior.
    - Follows through on commitments; assumes responsibility for own mistakes.
    - Practices absolute conformance with company policies embodying GE's commitment to ethical conduct.
    - Actions and behaviors are consistent with words. Absolutely trusted by others.
- *Accountability/Commitment*:
    - Sets and meets aggressive commitments to achieve business objectives.
    - Demonstrates courage/self-confidence to stand up for the beliefs, ideas, coworkers.
    - Fair and compassionate, yet willing to make difficult decisions.
    - Demonstrates uncompromising responsibility for preventing harm to the environment.

- *Global Mind-Set*:
  - Demonstrates global awareness/sensitivity and is comfortable building diverse/global teams.
  - Values and promotes full utilization of global and workforce diversity.
  - Considers the global consequences of every decision. Proactively seeks global knowledge.
  - Treats everyone with dignity, trust, and respect.

Managerial Guidelines

Faced with increasing turbulence in their environments, organizations need transformational leadership more than ever—and at all levels, not just at the top. The need for managers of vision, confidence, and determination, whether they are leading a small team or an entire organization, is increasing rapidly. Such managers are needed to motivate others to assert themselves, to join enthusiastically in team efforts, and to have positive feelings about what they're doing. Top managers must come to understand, appreciate, and support as never before employees who are willing to make unpopular decisions, who know when to reject traditional ways of doing something, and who can accept reasonable risks. A "right to fail" must be nurtured and be an integral part of an organization's culture. This leadership is vital to the most difficult, complex, and vague organizational threats, opportunities, and weaknesses.

Transformational leadership fosters synergy. Synergy *occurs when people together create new alternatives and solutions that are better than their individual efforts.* The greatest chance for achieving synergy is when people don't see things the same way; that is, differences present opportunities. Relationships don't break down because of differences but because people fail to grasp the value of their differences and how to take advantage of them. Synergy is created by people who have learned to think win–win, and who listen in order to understand the other person.

> **LEADER INSIGHT**
>
> Leaders need to have people follow them. They need to energize people so that they rally behind a vision and take leadership roles themselves in bringing that vision to life. Understanding what motivates employees in different cultures and environments is key to running a successful multinational company.
>
> **Cynthia Tragge-Lakra, Senior Vice President for Human Resources, GE Consumer Finance**

The following Self Competency feature reports on Sir Richard Branson, chairman of the Virgin Group, headquartered in London.[19] It extends our discussion of Richard Branson presented in Chapter 2, especially as related to the Learning from Experience feature on him. This feature gives special emphasis to his idealized influence as a transformational leader. The Virgin Group consists of 200 companies in 30 countries in such diverse industries and related companies as travel and tourism (e.g., Virgin Games and Virgin Experience Days), shopping (e.g., Virgin Books and Virgin Digital), social and environment (e.g., Virgin Earth and Virgin Fuels), and media and telecommunications (e.g., Virgin Media and Virgin Mobile). Virgin has more than 40,000 employees.[20] Branson founded Virgin as a mail-order record retailer in 1970.

Self Competency

Richard Branson, Chairman of the Virgin Group

Many executives focus on creating shareholder value and devote their attention primarily to customers. As noted in Chapter 2, Branson believes that the correct pecking order is employees first, customers next, and then shareholders. His logic is this: If your employees are happy, they will do a better job. If they do a better

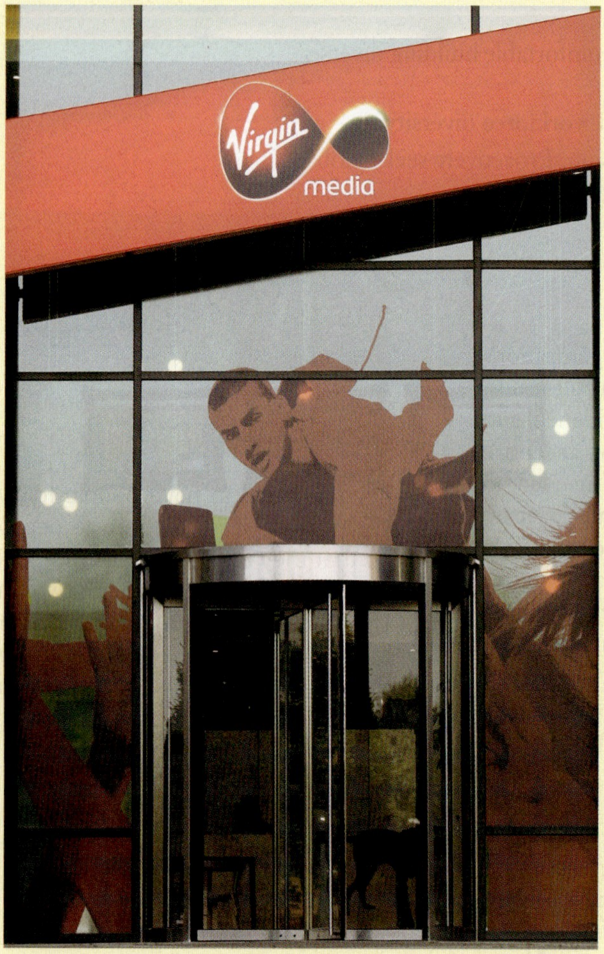

The Virgin Group, led by Richard Branson, consists of diverse industries including travel and tourism, shopping, social and environment, and media and telecommunications.

job, the customers will be happy, and thus business will be good and the shareholders will be rewarded.

In a recent survey of 700 corporate directors in Great Britain, they were asked whose leadership and values they most admired. Branson was at the top of the survey. David Rooke, a managing consultant at Harthill Consultants, states: "Branson is the consummate people's man. He is not a smooth operator that people may feel inclined to distrust, but a genuine strategist, who thinks outside the box, who achieves, and given some of his crazier pastimes, someone who manifestly enjoys life." In an article entitled *Integrity to What Matters Most*, three leadership experts make this comment, among others, about Branson: "Steadfast integrity to his unique sense of personal meaning has always been one of Branson's values."

In a recent visionary commitment, Branson pledged as much as $3 billion during the next 10 years (through 2017) to tackle global warming. The money is an estimate of his anticipated personal profits from his airlines and rail company, so the amount is not precise. But anything close would be a dramatic investment in a cleaner environment through developing new and cleaner sources of energy. Branson states: "We must not be the generation responsible for irreversibly damaging the environment." In another entrepreneurial decision, Branson offered a $25 million prize from his own money to anyone who figures out how to remove a billion tons of carbon dioxide per year from the atmosphere. These are just a couple of the environmental initiatives to which Branson is providing leadership. Let's peruse a few of the ideas on leadership and management by this transformational leader:

> *Ultimately, the entrepreneur will only succeed if he or she has good people around them and listens to their advice. My colleagues know me as Dr. Yes because I always find it hard to say "No" to new ideas and proposals. I rely on them to guide me but ultimately, I'm also prepared to trust my intuition, as long as I feel it is well informed. It is impossible to run a business without taking risks. Virgin would not be the company it is today if risks had not been taken.*
>
> *I think one of the reasons for our success is the core values which Virgin aspires to. This includes those that the general public thinks we should aspire to, like providing quality service. However, we also promise value for money, and we try to do things in an innovative way, in areas where consumers are often ripped-off, or not getting the most for their money. I believe we should do what we do with a sense of fun and without taking ourselves too seriously, too! If Virgin stands for anything, it should be for not being afraid to try out new ideas in new areas.*
>
> *Whenever I experience any kind of setbacks, I always pick myself up and try again. I prepare myself to have another stab at things with the knowledge I've gained from the previous failure. My mother always taught me never to look back in regret, but to move on to the next thing. The amount of time that people waste on failures, rather than putting that energy into another project, always amazes me. I have fun running the Virgin businesses, so a setback is never a bad experience, just a learning curve.*
>
> *Loyalty means a lot to me. Working with people I know and trust makes me feel secure. I guess that's why I prefer to promote from within. People who join Virgin know that there are plenty of opportunities to progress in their careers.*

For more information on the Virgin Group Ltd., visit the organization's home page at www.virgin.com.

GLOBE MODEL

Learning Goal

4. Explain the core features of the Global Leadership and Organizational Behavior Effectiveness (GLOBE) model.

The Global Leadership and Organizational Behavior Effectiveness (GLOBE) model *examines the interrelationships between societal culture, organizational culture, and organizational leadership*. Approximately 170 social scientists and management scholars from 62 cultures/countries representing all major regions throughout the world are engaged in a long-term study of cross-cultural leadership.[21] The 62 "societal cultures" are grouped into 10 societal clusters. Four of these clusters and some of the countries in each cluster are as follows: Anglo (Australia, Canada, United States); Arabic (Egypt, Morocco, Kuwait); Germanic (Austria, Germany, Switzerland); and Southern Asia (India, Indonesia, Malaysia).

© Ryan McVay/Photodisc/Getty Image

The GLOBE model addresses leadership qualities within cultural clusters, and makes recommendations on how managers should conduct business in cultural clusters other than their own.

The GLOBE model draws on data from more than 17,000 managers in almost 1,000 organizations in 62 societies. It addresses leadership qualities within those cultural clusters, and makes recommendations on how managers should conduct business in cultural clusters other than their own. Given the massive research efforts within the GLOBE model, it is only possible to provide illustrative highlights of this project here. For comprehensive discussions of the many facets, findings, and recommendations with respect to the GLOBE model, the interested reader should see the references cited.[22]

Let's begin with a few definitions in this model:

- Organizational leadership—*the ability of an individual to influence, motivate, and enable others to contribute toward the effectiveness and success of the organizations of which they are members.*
- Societal culture—*shared motives, values, beliefs, identities, and interpretations or meanings of significant events that result from common experiences of members of collectives and are transmitted across generations.*

Key Components

According to this model, individuals have implicit beliefs, convictions, and assumptions about the attributes and behaviors that distinguish leaders from others: effective leaders from ineffective ones, and moral leaders from evil ones. Implicit leadership models influence the importance that individuals place on selected leader behaviors and attributes.

Dimensions of Culture. In our discussion of culture in Chapter 2, we used a framework of culture based on five value orientations: individualism/collectivism, power distance, uncertainty avoidance, gender role orientation, and long-term orientation. Also, recall our discussion of McClelland's learned needs motivation model in Chapter 5. It too is based on culture, including the need for power, need for affiliation, and need for achievement. The GLOBE model of cultural dimensions has been adapted and expanded from these two models. As presented in Table 10.1, the GLOBE model includes nine cultural dimensions. The meaning of each dimension is presented in this table.

A significant aspect of GLOBE's nine cultural dimensions is that each one is defined in two ways: *practices* (or "as is") and *values* (or "should be"). *Practices* reflect the respondents' day-to-day realities. *Values* reflect their aspirations and ideals. The 17,370 managers were asked about both practices and values. Their answers led to some intriguing findings. The values score ("should be") in most cases was noticeably different

Table 10.1 Cultural Dimensions of the GLOBE Model

CULTURAL DIMENSION	DEFINITION
1. Assertiveness	• The degree to which individuals are bold, forceful, dominant, confrontational, or demanding in relationships with others.
2. Collectivism–group	• The degree to which individuals express and show pride, loyalty, and cohesiveness to their organizations or families.
3. Collectivism–societal	• The degree to which organizational and societal institutional (such as government) practices encourage and reward collective (joint) distribution of resources (such as under socialism) and collective action.
4. Future orientation	• The degree to which a society encourages and rewards behaviors such as planning, investing in the future, and delaying gratification.
5. Gender egalitarianism	• The degree to which a society minimizes differential treatment between men and women, such as through equal opportunity based on ability and performance.
6. Humane orientation	• The degree to which a society or organization encourages and rewards individuals for being fair, altruistic, generous, caring, and kind to others.
7. Performance orientation	• The degree to which a society encourages and rewards group members for performance improvement, excellence, high standards, and innovation.
8. Power distance	• The degree to which members of a society accept and endorse the equal (lower power distance) or unequal (higher power distance) distribution of authority, control, and status privileges (such as a class structure).
9. Uncertainty avoidance	• The degree to which a society, organization, or group relies on social norms, formal rules, and formal procedures to alleviate the unpredictability of future events.

Source: Based on House, R. J., Hanges, P. J., Javidan, M., Dorfman, P., and Gupta, V. (Eds.). *Culture, Leadership, and Organizations: The GLOBE Study of 62 Societies.* Thousand Oaks, CA: Sage, 2004.

from the practices score ("as is"). The values score was often higher than the practices score. For example, managers worldwide valued gender egalitarianism more than they said they were experiencing it in practice.

Another surprising finding emerged. A high value score was often associated with a low practice score on a cultural dimension. This is contrary to conventional wisdom that people behave in a certain way because they hold certain values in high esteem. However, if employees "in practice" experience a low degree of something perceived as good, its absence may lead them to value ("should be") it all the more. But if employees in practice have a high degree of something perceived as good, the value they put on it doesn't need to be high.[23]

When it came to examining the societal culture dimensions in relation to the leadership dimensions, the GLOBE researchers thoughtfully concluded:

> *When individuals think about effective leader behaviors, they are more influenced by the value ("should be") they place on the desired future than their perception of current realities ("as is"). Our results, therefore, suggest that leaders are seen as the society's instruments for change. They are seen as the embodiment of the ideal state of affairs.*
>
> *In general, cultural dimension values, not practices, are related to the cultural leadership dimensions. Both values and leadership dimensions represent desired end states; values reflect culture; the other leadership attributes.*[24]

Impacts of Culture on Leadership. The GLOBE model, more than the others we have reviewed, emphasizes the central role of societal culture through its values and beliefs in understanding what leadership styles and practices will be seen by subordinates as effective and desirable. A few of the GLOBE findings on the relationships between culture and leadership are as follows:

- Societal cultural values and practices affect what leaders do.
- Societal cultural values and practices affect organizational culture and practices.
- Organizational culture and practices also affect what leaders do.
- A leader's acceptance by followers is influenced by the interaction of cultural and organizational factors in relation to the leader's attributes and behaviors.
- A leader's effectiveness is influenced by the interaction of the leader's attributes and behaviors in relation to organizational and cultural factors.

GLOBE Leadership Dimensions. The GLOBE model has six dimensions of leadership. To obtain a personal sense of your leadership style, complete the GLOBE questionnaire that appears in the Experiential Exercise and Case section at the end of this chapter (page 314).

The six global leadership dimensions and their basic definitions are as follows:

- *Charismatic/value based*—visionary, inspirational, decisive, has integrity.
- *Team oriented*—collaborative, diplomatic, considerate.
- *Self-protective*—self-centered, status conscious, face-saver.
- *Participative*—democratic, delegator, values group needs.
- *Human oriented*—modest, helps others, displays empathy to others.
- *Autonomous*—individualistic, independent, unique.

Leadership across Cultures. There is no question that one of the most important facets of a global leader's job is to effectively influence people from other parts of the world. Effective leadership requires the ability to listen, to frame the message in a way that is understandable to the receiver, and to accept and use feedback. Effective global leadership involves finding solutions in a way that allow decisions to be implemented by members of diverse cultures. Although this may sound simple, it can be quite complicated.

The U.S. respondents in the GLOBE study reported very high performance-oriented values. To a typical American manager, effective leadership means direct and explicit directions. Facts and figures are important. Effective leaders focus their attention and thinking on rational means of solving problems. To these leaders, leadership means delivering the results. People from cultures with lower performance-oriented values, such as Russia or Greece, are not comfortable with strong results-oriented leaders. In these cultures, facts and figures are often hard to come by and are not taken seriously when they are available. Therefore, to a Greek employee, effective leaders do not necessarily rely on facts and figures. Their approach to discussions and explorations of issues tend to be without any clear commitment to explicit results.

Employees from countries with lower assertive values, such as Sweden and the Netherlands, say they prefer leaders to use two-way communication. They want to participate in decisions that will impact them. Employees want leaders who not only deliver results, but improve the interpersonal relations between them.

In cultures with higher gender-differentiated values, such as South Korea and Japan, employees expect effective leaders to use different language for males and females. For females, the leadership style is more paternalistic and one way and most of the time it is initiated by the leader. In Denmark, Sweden, and other countries with gender-egalitarian values, women are offended if they are patronized or in any way treated differently from men.

Effective leadership was also found to differ by power distance values in a culture. In countries like Russia or Thailand with high power distance values, effective leadership is mostly one way, top to bottom (Theory X or transactional). The effective leader is expected to know more than his employees. Input or feedback from subordinates is seldom asked for and, in fact, may be seen as impolite and disloyal.

A culture's uncertainty avoidance values also influences leaders' behaviors. In countries with high levels of uncertainty avoidance values, such as Switzerland and Austria, the leader's message needs to be clear and explicit and based on facts. The leader needs to be very clear on what needs to be done and the rules to follow to get things done. Meetings are planned in advance with a clear agenda, highly structured, and formal. Leaders are not likely to use a participative style of leadership. In countries with lower uncertainty avoidance values, like Russia or Greece, people are not used to highly structured procedures. Effective leaders, therefore, are not expected to announce agendas in advance and meetings can last for hours without any clear decision being made.

In cultures with strong collectivist values, the leader is expected to stress group harmony and cohesion. An effective leader's influence is soft and indirect. Conflict is to be avoided. Both charismatic/valued-based leaders and team-oriented leaders are usually found in such societies. Therefore, the effective leader tends to use indirect language to influence employees and wants employees to enter into discussions about issues facing them.

Finally, in countries like the Philippines and Malaysia, which are high on the humane-oriented values, the effective leader is seen as being caring and paternalistic. The leader's influence is focused on being supportive rather than leading others based on facts. The process is more important than the result because it helps build group cohesiveness. On the other hand, countries like France or Spain, which are lower on the humane-oriented values, people do not expect their leaders to be highly supportive or caring. Generosity is not important. Employees want their leader to give them clear, simple directions.

Managerial Guidelines

Our presentation is just a snapshot of the many findings with respect to leadership behaviors across cultures from the GLOBE model. One implication of the GLOBE model is that leadership is in the eye of the beholder. That is, *leader* is a term applied by observers (think of them as followers, at least potentially) to someone whose behaviors and characteristics match the observers' implicit leadership preferences.[25]

The GLOBE researchers set out to demonstrate that possessing an implicit leadership model is true of groups as well as individuals. The researchers' main contention was that each societal culture is associated with a specific set of beliefs by followers about leadership. Put another way, the researchers wanted to show that societal and organizational culture influence the kind of leadership found to be outstanding by people within that culture—and that is what they found.

But this isn't the only finding about leadership that the research team hoped to demonstrate. They expected that any individual's implicit leadership model would include beliefs about unacceptable and ineffective leadership as well as beliefs about acceptable and effective leadership. So another question was "Are both the positive and the negative attributes of leadership shared by the members of a cultural cluster?" They confirmed that it was. The GLOBE team identified which leadership attributes are positive, negative, and different across cultural clusters. A few of the findings with managerial guidelines for 4 of the 10 societal clusters are as follows:

- *Anglo Cluster* (Australia, Canada, England, Ireland, New Zealand, South Africa [white sample], and United States): The outstanding leader demonstrates charismatic influence and inspiration while encouraging participation. Outstanding leaders are viewed as being diplomatic, delegating authority, and allowing everyone to have their say.
- *Arabic Cluster* (Egypt, Morocco, Turkey, Kuwait, and Qatar): Outstanding leaders need to balance a paradoxical set of expectations. On one hand, they are expected to be charismatic and powerful, but on the other, they are expected not to differentiate themselves from others and to have modest styles. Leaders are also expected to have a great deal of power and control and to direct most decisions and actions.
- *Germanic Cluster* (Austria, Germany, the Netherlands, and Switzerland): The outstanding leader is one who is charismatic, highly team oriented, and participative.
- *Southern Asia Cluster* (India, Indonesia, Iran, Malaysia, the Philippines, and Thailand): The outstanding leader is humane, participative, and charismatic. Leaders are expected to be benevolent while maintaining a strong position of authority.

The following Across Cultures Competency feature provides insights and emerging themes related to leadership and culture in Mexico based on the GLOBE model. This feature draws from an extensive presentation of leadership and culture in Mexico.[26]

Across Cultures Competency

Leadership and Culture in Mexico: Emerging Themes

A corollary of the high assertiveness (tough and dominating) and high power distance of traditional Mexican culture is that individuals with little formal power have had very little influence and involvement in determining organizational policies and practices. This was shown in the GLOBE data where *participative leadership* approaches in Mexico were ranked 59th out of 62 GLOBE countries in importance. Historically, participative leadership has generally had little impact on followers' attitudes and performance in Mexico.

The traditional view of participation, however, may be changing. In several industrial centers, including the urban border areas shared with the United States, there is an increased interest in participative management approaches. This corresponds with the increasing number of joint ventures and *maquiladora* operations in Mexico, where popular international management styles are being tried with some apparent success. The participative approach in Mexico differs from approaches that are popular in the United States and Europe. But it seems to be similar to that found in Asian countries (which are often high in power distance). With the developing participative approach, leaders in Mexico make decisions and develop strategies, which they then discuss with followers who will eventually carry them out. There is an active give and take between leaders and followers regarding how decisions and strategies are implemented. These discussions may jump from one issue to another, but the skillful leader can apparently manage multiple discussions at one time. The key point of these discussions is that all individuals who are involved have an opportunity to provide input related to the implementation of strategies and decisions made by leaders.

Leaders in Mexico who obtain follower input with this approach represent a significant change from the autocratic leadership practices that have been traditionally followed in Mexico. The increasing popularity of a participative approach is suggested by the GLOBE culture data, which show that Mexicans believe there should be much less emphasis on power distance in their society. The changing portrait of Mexican society and organizations is likely to include more participative leadership of some type in the future.

The increasing importance of collective/team efforts inside Mexican organizations is indicated by the high score for *team-oriented leadership* in the GLOBE data. Team-oriented leadership is rated the highest of the leadership factors that contribute to outstanding leadership in Mexico. This leadership includes being diplomatic, collaborative, integrative, and administratively competent. Both directive and participative leadership approaches can be important in producing team effectiveness. Directive leadership is often useful early in a team's development, whereas participative leadership becomes effective later on as the team starts performing. A team orientation shows recognition of the importance of collective effort to compete in Mexico's changing economy and may be an organizational extension of the collectivism–group factor in Mexico.

GLOBE respondents from Mexico also expressed a strong desire for more *performance orientation* and *future orientation* in their institutions and organizations. This probably reflects the many changes occurring in Mexican society as Mexico becomes an increasingly important member of the international business community. Mexicans increasingly recognize the importance of planning and performance in order to compete successfully in international markets.

CHAPTER SUMMARY

1. Explain and apply the characteristics of the transactional leadership model.

The transactional leadership model calls for managers to influence followers primarily through contingent reward-based exchanges. Managers attempt to identify clear goals for followers, the specific paths for achieving the goals, and the rewards that will be forthcoming for achieving them. A follower's performance is monitored and corrective actions are taken if there are deviations from the expected path. The emphasis is on exchanging units of work for units of rewards (salary, bonuses, size of office, etc.).

2. Discuss and apply the attributes of the authentic leadership model.

Authentic leadership involves influencing followers' attitudes and behaviors through the core interrelated processes of stimulating follower identification, creating hope, reflecting trust, showing positive emotions, and raising optimism. Managers who are authentic leaders know and understand themselves, know what they believe and value, and act on their values and beliefs through open and honest communications with subordinates and others. They are highly ethical managers.

3. Explain and apply the essentials of the transformational leadership model.

Transformational leadership involves influencing followers through a complex and interrelated set of behaviors and abilities. Managers who are transformational leaders anticipate the future, inspire relevant stakeholders (especially followers) to embrace a new vision or set of ideas, develop followers to be leaders or better leaders, and guide the organization or group into a community of challenged and rewarded learners. This model extends and incorporates features of authentic leadership. The components of the transformational leadership model that primarily relate to followers include showing individualized consideration, creating intellectual stimulation, providing inspirational motivation, and fostering idealized influence. Transformational managers are both challenging and empathetic—and they are people of integrity.

4. Explain the core features of the Global Leadership and Organizational Behavior Effectiveness (GLOBE) model.

The GLOBE model examines the interrelationships between societal culture, organizational culture, and organizational leadership. We provided a snapshot of the concepts and findings with respect to the interrelationships between the nine cultural dimensions and six global leadership dimensions in the GLOBE model. This model provides many insights on why and how individual managers need to cope with and adjust to cross-cultural issues when leading organizations.

KEY TERMS AND CONCEPTS

Assertiveness
Authentic leadership
Charisma
Collectivism–group
Collectivism–societal
Future orientation
Gender egalitarianism
Global Leadership and Organizational Behavior Effectiveness (GLOBE) model
Humane orientation
Idealized influence
Individualized consideration
Inspirational motivation
Intellectual stimulation
Organizational leadership
Performance orientation
Power distance
Societal culture
Synergy
Transactional leadership
Transformational leadership
Uncertainty avoidance
Vision

DISCUSSION QUESTIONS

1. Visit GE's home page at www.ge.com. Click on "Our Company" and then "Leadership." Read the profiles of any five of the GE corporate executives. Based on the Learning from Experience feature, what insights on becoming a leader at GE seem to be illustrated in these profiles?
2. Robert Nardelli's extensive reliance on transactional leadership was a key factor in his dismissal as the CEO of Home Depot. Why do you think this leadership model is an inadequate foundation to the change competency? To address this question, please review our discussion of the knowledge, skills, and abilities that comprise the change competency presented in Chapter 1.
3. In what three ways did a manager you have worked for use transactional leadership?
4. Based on the manager identified in Question 3, in what ways did that person exhibit or fail to exhibit each of the components of authentic leadership?
5. Review the Diversity Competency feature to determine which of the various perspectives of Marilyn Carlson Nelson suggest that she is an authentic leader. Identify specific comments by Carlson Nelson that reflect specific components of authentic leadership.
6. Assume that you have just taken a job at a large manufacturing facility. What insights provided in this chapter can help you be an effective "follower" in this situation?
7. Think of a person that you know who comes closest to exhibiting transformational leadership. Describe three behaviors of this person that are consistent with being a transformational leader.
8. Review the Self Competency feature on Richard Branson. Identify specific statements by and about Branson that reflect specific components of transformational leadership.
9. Review the nine cultural dimensions in the GLOBE model (see Table 10.1). How would you describe your societal culture as you understand it with respect to each of these dimensions? In what ways do you think your experiences with leaders reflect this cultural profile?

EXPERIENTIAL EXERCISE AND CASE

Experiential Exercise: Self Competency

GLOBE Leader Behaviors Instrument[27]

Introduction

The GLOBE leader behaviors instrument presented here represents an adapted and much shortened version of the leadership instruments used in the GLOBE project. This adapted instrument is for instructional purposes only. It is designed to give you a more personal understanding of each of the six global leadership dimensions and a profile of what you think represents an outstanding leader.

Instructions

You are probably aware of people who are exceptionally skilled at motivating, influencing, or enabling you, others, or groups to contribute to the success of an organization or task. We might call such people "outstanding leaders." This instrument presents behaviors and characteristics that can be used to describe these leaders. Each behavior or characteristic is accompanied by a short definition to clarify its meaning. Using the description of outstanding leaders as a guide, rate the behaviors and characteristics on this instrument. On the line next to each behavior or characteristic, write the number from the scale below that best describes how important that behavior or characteristic is to you for a leader to be considered as outstanding.

Scale:

1 = This behavior or characteristic *greatly inhibits* a person from being an outstanding leader.
2 = This behavior or characteristic *somewhat inhibits* a person from being an outstanding leader.
3 = This behavior or characteristic *slightly inhibits* a person from being an outstanding leader.
4 = This behavior or characteristic *has no impact* on whether a person is an outstanding leader.
5 = This behavior or characteristic *contributes slightly* to a person being an outstanding leader.
6 = This behavior or characteristic *contributes somewhat* to a person being an outstanding leader.
7 = This behavior or characteristic *contributes greatly* to a person being an outstanding leader.

		Behavior or Characteristic	Definition
_____	1.	Diplomatic	Skilled at interpersonal relations, tactful
_____	2.	Evasive	Refrains from making negative comments to maintain good relationships and save face
_____	3.	Listener	Seeks inputs from subordinates in an authentic way
_____	4.	Intragroup competitor	Tries to exceed the performance of others in his or her group
_____	5.	Autonomous	Acts independently, does not rely on others
_____	6.	Independent	Does not rely on others; self-governing
_____	7.	Improvement oriented	Seeks continuous performance improvement
_____	8.	Inspirational	Inspires emotions, beliefs, values, and behaviors of others, inspires others to be motivated to work hard
_____	9.	Anticipatory	Anticipates, attempts to forecast events, considers what will happen in the future
_____	10.	Trustworthy	Deserves trust, can be believed and relied on to keep his or her word
_____	11.	Worldly	Interested in temporal events; has a world outlook
_____	12.	Just	Acts according to what is right or fair
_____	13.	Win–win problem-solver	Able to identify solutions that satisfy individuals with diverse and conflicting interests
_____	14.	Self-interested	Pursues own best interests
_____	15.	Integrator	Integrates people or things into cohesive, working whole
_____	16.	Calm	Not easily distressed
_____	17.	Loyal	Stays with and supports friends even when they have substantial problems or difficulties
_____	18.	Unique	An unusual person; has characteristics of behaviors that are different from most others
_____	19.	Collaborative	Works jointly with others
_____	20.	Encouraging	Gives courage, confidence, or hope through reassuring and advising
_____	21.	Democratic	Makes decisions in a joint way
_____	22.	Secretive	Tends to conceal information from others
_____	23.	Asocial	Avoids people or groups; prefers own company
_____	24.	Generous	Willing to give time, money, resources, and help to others
_____	25.	Formal	Acts in accordance with rules, convention, and ceremonies
_____	26.	Modest	Does not boast; presents self in a humble manner
_____	27.	Consultative	Consults with others before making plans or taking action
_____	28.	Loner	Works and acts separately from others
_____	29.	Compassionate	Has empathy for others;

inclined to be helpful or show mercy

_____ 30. Intellectually stimulating — Encourages others to think and use their minds; challenges beliefs, stereotypes, and attitudes of others

_____ 31. Balanced orientation — Places appropriate value on both individual and group needs

_____ 32. Egalitarian — Believes that individuals should have equal rights and privileges

_____ 33. General manager — An agile manager, one who does not insist on making all decisions

_____ 34. Delegator — Willing and able to relinquish close control of projects or tasks

_____ 35. Self-effacing — Presents self in a modest way

_____ 36. Patient — Has and shows patience

_____ 37. Individualistic — Behaves in a different manner than peers

Scoring

Sum the scores for each item shown within each global leadership dimension and divide by the number of items to obtain an average score on that dimension. These average scores reflect your model of what it means to be an outstanding leader.

- Charismatic/value based

____7; ____8; ____9; ____10; ____12; ____20; ____30 = Total _____ ÷ 7 = _____ = Average score on charismatic/value based

- Team oriented

____1; ____11; ____13; ____15; ____17; ____19; ____27 = Total _____ ÷ 7 = _____ = Average score on team oriented

- Self-protective

____2; ____4; ____14; ____22; ____23; ____25; ____28 = Total _____ ÷ 7 = _____ = Average score on self-protective

- Participative

____3; ____21; ____31; ____32; ____33; ____34 = Total _____ ÷ 6 = _____ = Average score on participative

- Humane oriented

____16; ____24; ____26; ____29; ____35; ____36 = Total _____ ÷ 6 = _____ = Average score on humane oriented

- Autonomous

____5; ____6; ____18; ____37 = Total _____ ÷ 4 = _____ = Average score on autonomous

Interpretation

The six average scores represent your model of what it means to be an outstanding leader. An average score that ranges from 1 to 3.5 suggests that you think the global leadership dimension inhibits, to varying degrees, the person from being an outstanding leader. An average score that ranges from 3.6 to 4.9 suggests that you think the leadership dimension has little to no impact on whether a person is an outstanding leader. An average score that ranges from 5 to 7 suggests that you think the leadership dimension slightly to greatly contributes to a person being an outstanding leader. In the GLOBE research, the charismatic/value-based leadership dimension emerged as the most strongly endorsed contributor, worldwide, to acceptable and effective leadership. Is your score on this leadership dimension consistent with this finding? The team-oriented leadership dimension is also endorsed worldwide as a strong contributor to outstanding leadership.[28] Is your score on this leadership dimension consistent with this finding?

Case: Change Competency

Meg Whitman, CEO of eBay[29]

Founded in 1995 and headquartered in San Jose, California, eBay is the leading online marketplace for the sale of goods and services by a diverse community of individuals and businesses. eBay has more than 220 million registered users and is the most popular shopping site on the Internet.

eBay's mission is to provide a global trading platform where practically anyone can trade practically anything. It features a variety of international sites, specialty sites, 50,000 categories of merchandise, and services that aim to provide users with the necessary tools for efficient online trading in both auction-style and fixed-price formats. Recent innovations in trading formats, such as *Want It Now* and *Best Offer*, provide new ways for shoppers to find and buy what they want on the website. Europe, Asia, and cross-border trade are major areas of growth for eBay. The firm offers localized sites in 24 countries. On any given day, millions of items are listed on eBay in thousands of categories. People from all over the world buy and sell on eBay. Since becoming the CEO of eBay in 1998, Meg Whitman has led the acquisition of companies that are compatible with eBay's core business. These acquisitions include the following:

- *PayPal.* PayPal enables any individual or business with an e-mail address to securely and quickly send and receive payments online. PayPal's service builds on the existing financial infrastructure of bank accounts and credit and uses proprietary fraud prevention systems to create a safe payment solution.
- *Skype.* Skype is a fast-growing Internet communication offering, allowing people everywhere access to unlimited voice and video communication for free between the users of Skype software. Skype is available in 27 languages and is used in almost every country around the world. Skype generates revenue through its premium offerings such as

making and receiving calls to and from landline and mobile phones. Skype was acquired by eBay in 2005.

- *Shopping.com*. Shopping.com pioneered online comparison shopping and is one of the fastest growing shopping destinations on the Internet. It was acquired by eBay in 2005.
- *Rent.com*. Rent.com is the most visited online apartment listing service in the United States. It was acquired by eBay in 2005.
- *Online Classifieds*. Designed to help people meet, share ideas, and trade on a local level, eBay's online classifieds websites are available in hundreds of cities and regions around the world.
- *StubHub*. StubHub is a ticket marketplace, enabling customers to buy and sell tickets at fair market value to a vast selection of sporting, concert, theater and other live entertainment events, even those that are "sold out." It was acquired by eBay in 2007.

Whitman is many things—a mom, wealthy, and, as many say, one of the best CEOs in America. One thing she isn't is the stereotype of a new-economy executive. A one-time Procter & Gamble brand manager, Bain consultant, and Hasbro division manager, Whitman is a person with experience and discipline. The casual work environment at eBay only goes so far in explaining her leadership style.

This company looks like a dotcom, but its approach is corporate. Whitman's executives handle categories (e.g., toys, cars, and collectibles) like brand managers at P&G handle Bounty, Crest, or Tide. They dwell on data, following every transaction and customer nuance just as executives do at P&G. Whitman is considered one of eBay's strengths. She is thought to be the reason why eBay is the only startup among all of its once promising peers that hasn't died or been acquired by others. Whitman is positioning it to become a full-service Internet retailer—far more than just an auction site. This is suggested through the acquisitions by eBay in recent years. Whitman comments: "I'm a better leader, a better manager, a better executive than when I arrived as a youngster. I have learned how to manage a company that reinvents itself every couple of years."

When Whitman arrived at eBay, she promised to transform the company from an online auction house into a much bigger, general-purpose shopping destination—the first place people turn when they want to buy anything. eBay owns no inventory or warehouses, which helps make it highly profitable. It has cleverly used e-mail, message boards, and its virtual community to forge bonds with customers and to police the behavior of its buyers and sellers. Its website enables small sellers to participate in a vast marketplace—and lets eBay collect fees on even the tiniest of transactions. A key element in the firm's growth strategy is to continuously expand the eBay marketplace and new services to communities around the world.

A fundamentally business-like quality permeates eBay. Employees are cheerful and informal. Their cubicles are littered with sports souvenirs, Godzilla figurines, and Beanie Babies. There are free sodas in the break rooms. But when you talk to eBay people, you don't hear much about fun and games. You hear about plans, systems, numbers, and results.

Whitman has a craving for statistics and, more specifically, for bottom-line results. Asked what it is like reporting to Whitman, one manager says, "I have numbers. I know them. They're very clear. And the expectations are high." Another manager comments: "Several years ago we were a secondary collectibles marketplace. Now we're a trading platform." In plain English, that means eBay has diversified, offering not just old ceramic plates and baseball cards but a wide array of products from bigger brand-name stores, including new items at set prices. "We want people to think of eBay first when they're in shopping mode, the way they might think of Wal-Mart," says a marketing executive.

Whitman has provided a number of insights and perspectives on her leadership. "One of the reasons I believe eBay has been so successful is that we have stuck to our business plan from inception. At eBay, we work every day to be the world's most compelling commerce platform on the Internet." The firm stays focused on its goals. Those goals include attracting more customers; expanding the goods traded on the site; spreading eBay to more global markets; making the user experience more fun, exciting, and easier; and acquiring Internet companies to become a full-service retailer.

"I think at all good companies, employees are excited by the mission of the company. And at eBay the mission is about creating this global online marketplace where your next-door neighbor's chance of success is equal to a large corporation's. We look for people who are energized by the mission of the company. Once they're here, we want to make sure that they have a chance to understand the company in a really deep way. I said to our head of strategy when he came to work for us: 'Don't do anything for three months. Just absorb, understand, get the counterintuitive nature of the business.' We give people a chance to settle in, and then we make sure that they are well managed, that they are focused on high-impact projects, and that they understand the results that they are going to be accountable for.

"To keep up with our growth, we have reorganized early and often. That keeps people fresh; it brings a new set of eyes to problems. It keeps people excited because they get repotted into new opportunities. That's something we've done since the beginning of the company. We've probably made about 10 to 12 changes in how we have structured the organization. Some were major, some were more evolutionary.

"We come up with a lot of good ideas, but we will not be the fountain of all good ideas. Users that have good ideas about how to make the platform more effective can tap into it through our API [application programming interface]. We now have 10,000 outside developers; not long ago it was just 400. We think it's important to open up the platform because it makes eBay better, it makes eBay stronger, as other people develop applications to the platform. And it's not only software. It's also businesses that grow up to support eBay."

Whitman's free-market philosophy goes only so far. Sometimes she has had to play censor of items traded on the site. "We crossed the Rubicon in 1999," she says. That's when she decided to ban firearms, alcohol, and tobacco. She also outlawed murder memorabilia less than a century old. (You can sell Lizzie Borden's ax but not Jeffrey Dahmer's refrigerator on eBay.) Selling a simple lunch date is permitted. A lunch with Warren Buffett went for $202,000, prompting Buffett to remark to Whitman, "It's always interesting to see what your market value is in real time."

She struggled most over her decision to ban Nazi memorabilia. Several years ago Starbucks chairman Howard Schultz, an eBay director at the time, returned from a trip to Auschwitz and passionately urged Whitman to take Nazi items off the site. The debate inside the company was intense. As some execs and board members clung to eBay's libertarian values, Whitman recalls, "I finally said, 'Okay, I know, but I can't stand this.'" She banned all Nazi items except documents, coins, and copies of historical books like *Mein Kampf*. "This decision doesn't yield to analysis," she says. "It's a judgment call. There has to be one person making the decision, and it's the CEO."

Employees at eBay like to tell this story about Whitman. She was on a flight to India with three other eBay employees when one of them developed a dangerous gastrointestinal problem somewhere near Tehran, Iran. Whitman pulled out an atlas and decided Istanbul, Turkey, was the nearest, safest city in which they could land. She called an air emergency service and arranged for an ambulance to be waiting on the tarmac when the plane landed. Whitman rode in the ambulance with the ill executive and stayed with him for hours in the hospital, talking to his wife on the phone. Once the executive was stabilized, Whitman flew with him to a hospital in London in the corporate jet. She and the other eBay employees flew a commercial flight to India, leaving the corporate jet for the executive to fly home to California. "She will exert herself personally, far and above the call of duty," says Rajiv Dutta, head of eBay's PayPal business. "She makes you want to do the right thing."

For more information on eBay, visit the organization's home page at ***www.ebay.com/aboutebay.***

Questions

1. What aspects of Meg Whitman's leadership reflect transactional leadership? Explain.
2. What aspects of Meg Whitman's leadership reflect authentic leadership? Explain.
3. What aspects of Meg Whitman's leadership reflect transformational leadership? Explain.

CHAPTER

11

Developing and Leading Teams

Learning Goals

When you have finished studying the chapter, you should be able to:

1. State the basic features of groups and teams.
2. Describe the attributes of common types of work-related teams.
3. Explain the stages of team development.
4. Describe the core factors that influence team effectiveness.
5. Explain five of the potential dysfunctions of teams.

Learning from Experience

IT LEADERSHIP TEAM AT REGIONS FINANCIAL

The basic activities of Regions Financial Corporation, headquartered in Birmingham, Alabama, are mortgage banking, traditional full-service banking services, and other financial services. Regions serves customers in 16 states across the South, Midwest, and Texas. Regions operates 1,900 AmSouth and Regions Bank banking offices. Its brokerage subsidiary, Morgan Keegan & Co., has 450 branch offices.

When you look at the information technology (IT) leadership team at Regions Financial, you see a diverse group of individuals. The vice president of application delivery advanced through the ranks, as did the chief information officer (CIO). The other five team members have had solid careers in IT. The vice president of technology risk management is known for his strategic and broad technical knowledge. The vice president of telecommunications has a more tactical, get-it-done approach. The vice president of production services is a communicator who connects well with people throughout the organization. The director of information management and enterprise architecture came from outside the banking industry and has a strong data management background. The vice president of the project management office has been at Regions for more than 25 years, with management experience in several technical areas.

But the team members also bear some strong similarities. Most would score off the charts on an analytical-thinking test. All are excellent problem-solvers. They see IT as a department that needs to be run as a business. There's no question in their minds that their common goal is to support the bank's strategy.

"When you combine all these differences and similarities in a team, the group becomes stronger than the sum of its parts," says John Dick, the CIO. This can be invaluable when problems arise. For instance, a downturn in the performance of the bank's online banking system prompted the leadership team members to jump in and apply their various approaches and skills rather than leave the problem to the application delivery group. Dick thinks many leaders have yet to learn about the strength diversity brings to a team. He states: "You see it all the time—people selecting leaders who are exactly like themselves,

For more information on the Regions Financial Group, visit the organization's home page at www.regions.com.

LEARNING CONTENT

whether they're heavily analytical or very creative. And while homogeneous teams can accomplish a lot in a short amount of time, to take it to the next level, you need a team with diverse experience and backgrounds."

The IT leadership team didn't always perform at such a high level. When the group was formed, its members were more focused on their individual functions, Dick notes. That meant he needed to spend more of his own time bringing the right mix of resources to bear when issues arose.

But now, especially as the IT group takes on higher impact projects that cross many functional areas of the bank, Dick notes: "There's been a shift. Now, everyone knows each other's skills and capabilities, and everyone gets engaged in problem-solving, decision-making and fact-finding around lots of different topics."[1]

The Learning from Experience feature illustrates two important points about effective teams: (1) Individual performance by committed and competent individuals is crucial, and (2) individuals working together as a team can often achieve more than if they work alone.

In this chapter, we primarily focus on one of the seven core competencies introduced in Chapter 1. Recall that the *teams competency* includes the knowledge, skills, and abilities to develop, support, facilitate, and lead groups to achieve organizational goals. Throughout the chapter, we discuss ways to understand and increase the effectiveness of groups and teams. We focus on (1) the basic features of groups and teams; (2) the types of teams commonly used in organizations; (3) the ways in which team members develop and learn; (4) the principal factors that influence team effectiveness; and (5) the potential dysfunctions of teams if not effectively developed, used, and led.

INTRODUCTION TO GROUPS AND TEAMS

Learning Goal

1. State the basic features of groups and teams.

For our purposes, a group *is any number of people who share goals, often communicate with one another over a period of time, and are few enough so that each individual may communicate with all the others, person to person.*[2]

Classifications of Groups

Most individuals belong to various types of groups, which can be classified in many ways. For example, a person concerned with obtaining membership in a group or gaining acceptance as a group member might classify groups as open or closed to new members. A person evaluating groups in an organization according to their primary goals might classify them as friendship groups or task groups. A friendship group *evolves informally to meet its members' personal security, esteem, and belonging needs.* A task group *is created by management to accomplish certain organizational goals.* Of course, a single group in the workplace may serve both friendship and task purposes. The primary focus of this chapter is on types of task groups, commonly known today as teams, such as the IT leadership team at Regions Financial Corporation.

Informal Group

An informal group *is one that develops out of the day-to-day activities, interactions, and sentiments that the members have for each other.* Informal groups typically satisfy their members' security and social needs. Informal groups can provide their members with desirable benefits (e.g., security and protection). An informal group can also provide positive feedback to other members.

At work, informal groups may oppose higher management and organizational goals, reinforce and support such goals, or simply be unrelated to the organizational goals. The organization often has considerable influence on the development of informal groups through the physical layout of work, the leadership practices of managers, and the types of technology used.[3] For example, 7-Eleven found that moving its employees from one headquarters building to a new building had an impact on who belonged to informal groups. The physical distance between members may make face-to-face communication difficult and cause groups to disband or reform themselves. In contrast, a new manager taking over a department and telling its employees to "shape up or ship out" may cause an informal group to form, with its members uniting against the manager.

Some managers believe that close-knit informal groups have undesirable effects on an organization. They view groups as a potential source of antiestablishment power, as a way of holding back information when the group doesn't identify with organizational goals, or as a means of pressuring individuals to slow production. For instance, an informal group might set production limits for their members, fearing that management might use an outstanding worker as a standard for output and that increased production might lead to some workers being laid off. The all-too-common belief that higher productivity will work against the interests of workers is kept alive and enforced by some informal groups within organizations.[4]

Informal groups can also exercise undesirable power over individual members. Such power usually falls into two categories. First, a group may be able to use rewards and punishments to pressure members to conform to its standards. Second, a group may restrict the ways by which social needs can be satisfied on the job. Informal groups have been known to ridicule certain members or give them the silent treatment for not conforming to group standards of "acceptable" behavior. This treatment may threaten the individual's safety, social, and esteem needs. Managers should probably try to minimize the undesirable effects of informal groups rather than try to eliminate them.[5] Informal groups in organizations can't be classified simply as positive or negative. They may exhibit both characteristics from time to time, depending on the circumstances or issues facing the organization.[6]

Team

A team *is a small number of employees with complementary competencies who are committed to common performance goals and working relationships for which they hold themselves mutually accountable.*[7] The heart of any team is a shared commitment by its members for their joint performance. Team goals could be as basic as responding to all customers' calls within 24 hours or as involved as reducing defects by 20 percent during the next 6 months. The key point is that such goals can't be achieved without the cooperation and communication of team members. When a team is formed, its members must have (or quickly develop) the right mix of competencies to achieve the team's goals. Also, its members need to be able to influence how they will work together to accomplish those goals. The IT leadership team at Regions Financial has the common general goal of supporting the bank's strategy and shared commitment to run it as a business. The team is relatively small and brings together a range of capabilities to achieve optimal results.

Effective Teams

To make teams more effective, managers must know how to recognize effective and ineffective teams. An effective team or group has the following core characteristics. Its members

- know why it exists and have shared goals,
- support agreed-on guidelines or procedures for making decisions,
- communicate freely among themselves,
- receive help from one another and give help to one another,

- deal with conflict openly and constructively, and
- diagnose its own processes and improve their own functioning.[8]

The degree to which a team lacks one or more of these characteristics determines whether—and to what extent—it is ineffective. These basic characteristics apply to all teams. Recall the experience in the development of the IT leadership team at Regions Financial. Dick, the CIO, noted that his team didn't initially perform at a high level. When formed, the team members were focused on their individual functions. Dick noted: "There's been a shift. Now everyone knows each other's skills and capabilities, and everyone gets engaged in problem-solving, decision-making and fact finding around lots of different topics." At Regions, teamwork is so important that a couple of people with business expertise and strong technology capabilities were actually let go because "they fought the team environment," Dick says. "They wanted to be the Lone Ranger and get all the credit for their own group, and that's not tolerated here."[9]

Team Empowerment

All types of teams and groups need the degree of empowerment that will help them achieve their goals. Accordingly, team empowerment *refers to the degree to which its members perceive the group as (1) being competent and able to accomplish work-related tasks (potency), (2) performing important and valuable tasks (meaningfulness), (3) having choice (autonomy) in how they carry out their tasks, and (4) experiencing a sense of importance and significance (impact) in the work performed and goals achieved.*[10] You may relate the key dimensions of empowerment—*potency, meaningfulness, autonomy*, and *impact*—to your own experience by responding to the brief questionnaire in Table 11.1. To obtain your team empowerment score, follow the directions in the table.

Our discussion of the IT leadership team at Regions Financial suggests that it is both effective and empowered. Of course, such teams can operate at all levels of an organization, not just among high-level managers. The following Teams Competency feature reports on problems solved by an assembly team at the Toyota car factory in Georgetown, Kentucky.[11] Each day this factory makes approximately 2,000 Camrys, Avalons, and Solaras. Toyota is famous for its emphasis on continuous improvement and the use of teams to do so throughout the organization.[12]

Teams Competency

A Toyota Assembly Team's Simple Solution

Howard Artrip stood at the assembly line alongside a rack of blue plastic totes filled with sun visors and seat belts. Just beyond Artrip and the rack of totes, a line of Camrys and Avalons passed by—no engines, no dashboards, no seats.

Artrip, a manager in the assembly area, tells the story of how the totes—ordinary Rubbermaid carryalls—solved a problem. "There used to be eight racks of parts here," he says. The racks crowded the workstation, but gave the team member ready access to all possible parts. The operator would eyeball the car coming up the line, step to the racks of visors and seat belts, and "grab the right parts and run to the car." He or she would step into the slowly advancing car, bolt belts and visors in place, step back onto the factory floor—and do it again. All in 55 seconds, the time each slowly moving car spends at each workstation.

The problem was that there were 12 possible combinations of sun visors and nine variations of seat belts. So just deciding which parts to snatch had become a job in itself. In every shift, 500 cars passed the racks, each car needing four specific parts: 2,000 opportunities to make an error. Even with 99 percent perfection, 5 cars per shift would get the wrong sun visors or seat belts. The

© Andy Rain/Bloomberg News/Landov

Toyota made a simple change to their assembly line to make the process run more smoothly and to eliminate meaningless tasks.

job—installing parts—had become cluttered with meaningless tasks.

A team of assembly associates considered the problem and made a decision. Don't make the associate pick the parts; let him or her focus on installing them. The idea seems obvious in retrospect: Deliver a kit of presorted visors and seat belts—one kit per car, each containing exactly the right parts. The team applied the simplest technology available, the blue Rubbermaid caddy. Artrip states: "We went just down the road to Wal-Mart and bought them." Now, the employee just grabs the handle of the blue tote like a lunch pail and steps into the car to bolt the part to it.

In the case of the blue tote, the change came out of a routine analysis of dozens of assembly line jobs at Georgetown. When the simplification effort started several years ago, Artrip's team found 44 jobs where assemblers had to make 1 or 2 decisions as they installed parts. They found 23 workstations that required between 7 and 11 decisions. Any jobs requiring 7 to 11 decisions in 55 seconds were going to cause problems. Now, 85 line jobs require just 1 or 2 meaningful decisions. Not a single job requires 7 or more decisions. In the eyes of the team members, they made the work easier for themselves and created better results—fewer errors.

For more information on Toyota, visit the organization's home page at www.toyota.com.

Table 11.1 **Team Empowerment Questionnaire**

Instructions: Think of a team that you have been (or are) a member of in a work setting. Respond to each statement below by indicating the degree to which you agree or disagree with it in terms of the team identified. The scale is as follows.

1	2	3	4	5
Strongly Agree	Agree	Undecided/ Neutral	Disagree	Strongly Disagree

Place the appropriate number value next to each item.

Potency Items

_____ 1. The team had confidence in itself.

_____ 2. The team believed that it could be very good at producing high-quality work.

_____ 3. The team expected to be seen by others as high performing.

_____ 4. The team was confident that it could solve its own problems.

_____ 5. The team viewed no job as too tough.

Meaningfulness Items

_____ 6. The team cared about what it did.

_____ 7. The team thought that its work was valuable.

_____ 8. The team viewed its group goals as important.

_____ 9. The team believed that its projects were significant.

_____ 10. The team considered its group tasks to be worthwhile.

Autonomy Items

_____ 11. The team could select different ways to do its work.

_____ 12. The team determined how things were done.

_____ 13. The team had a lot of choice in what it did without being told by management.

_____ 14. The team had significant influence in setting its goals.

_____ 15. The team could rotate tasks and assignments among team members.

Impact Items

_____ 16. The team assessed the extent to which it made progress on projects.

_____ 17. The team had a positive impact on other employees.

_____ 18. The team had a positive impact on customers.

_____ 19. The team accomplished its goals.

_____ 20. The team made a difference in the organization.

Total: Add points for items 1 through 20. This total is your perceived team empowerment score. Scores may range from 20 to 100. Scores of 20 through 45 suggest low team empowerment. Scores of 46 through 74 indicate moderate levels of team empowerment. Scores of 75 through 100 reveal a state of significant to very high team empowerment.

Source: Adapted from Kirkman, B. L., and Rosen, B. Beyond self-management: Antecedents and consequences of team empowerment. *Academy of Management Journal*, 1999, 42, 58–74; Kirkman, B. L., and Rosen, B. Powering up teams. *Organizational Dynamics*, Winter 2000, 48–65.

When to Use Teams

Different types of goals, problems, and tasks confronting an organization require varying degrees of cooperation among individuals and teams. Some require both individual and team problem solving. Organizations can incur excessive costs if either individual or team decision making is used improperly. The unnecessary use of teams is wasteful because the employees' time could have been used more effectively on other tasks; it creates boredom, resulting in a feeling that time is being wasted, and reduces motivation. Conversely, the improper use of individual problem solving can result in poor coordination, little creativity, and numerous errors. In brief, team problem solving is likely to be superior to individual problem solving when

- the greater diversity of information, experience, and approaches to be found in a team is important to the task at hand;
- acceptance of the decisions arrived at is crucial for effective implementation by team members;
- participation is important for reinforcing the values of representation versus authoritarianism and demonstrating respect for individual members through team processes; and
- team members rely on each other in performing their jobs.

Our discussions of the IT leadership team at Regions Financial Corporation and the Toyota assembly team provide practical examples of the effective use of team decision making.

Learning Goal

2. Describe the attributes of common types of work-related teams.

TYPES OF WORK-RELATED TEAMS

Of the many types of work-related teams, we consider six of the most common: functional teams, problem-solving teams, cross-functional teams, self-managed teams, virtual teams, and global teams. As suggested in Figure 11.1, all of these types of teams may be found in a single organization. It is quite possible that a single employee may work in all of these types of teams over a period of time.

FIGURE 11.1 Common Types of Work-Related Teams

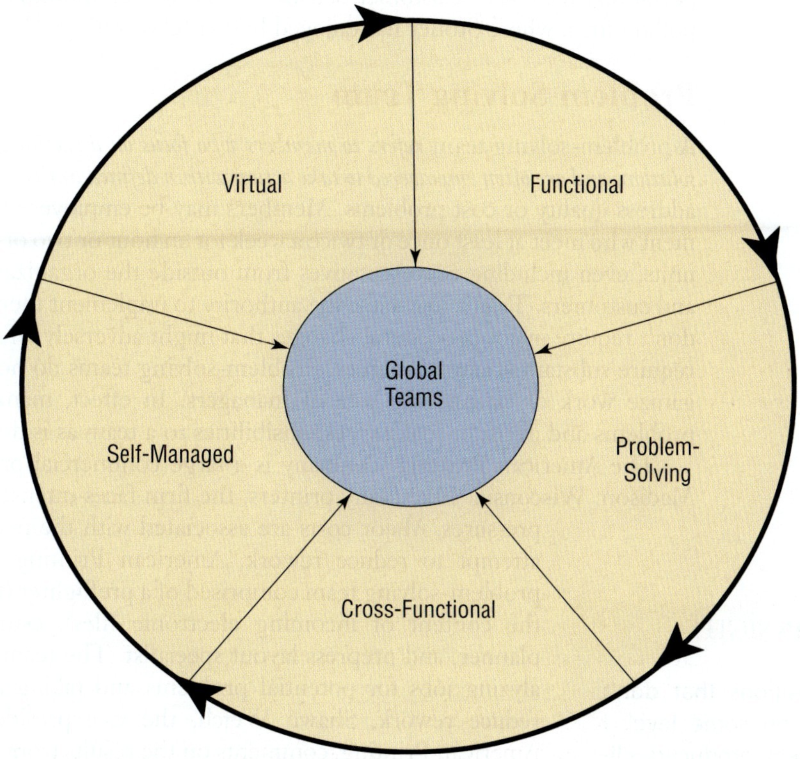

Functional Team

A functional team *usually includes employees who work together daily on similar tasks and must coordinate their efforts*. These teams often exist within functional departments: marketing, purchasing, production, engineering, finance, auditing, human resources, and the like. Within a human resource department, one or more functional teams could perform recruiting, compensation, benefits, safety, training and development, affirmative action, industrial relations, and similar functions.

Stoner, Inc., is headquartered in Quarryville, Pennsylvania, and has 54 full- and part-time employees. The firm manufactures more than 300 cleaning, lubrication, and coating products for other businesses. The firm is run on two operational levels: the leadership team and six functional teams. The functional teams include (1) inside sales; (2) manufacturing, warehousing, and purchasing; (3) technology; (4) sales; (5) marketing; and (6) accounting, logistics, and information technology. Stoner's functional teams are connected to the leadership team through representatives, but each has the authority to make a variety of decisions related to its functions.

Stoner team members are both empowered and rewarded to fulfill the needs of customers and meet performance goals. Guidance is provided by a core set of company principles: Exceed Customer Expectations, Motivated Teams, Safety/Health/Environmental Responsibility, Innovation, and Continuous Improvement. Performance-based bonus incentives, both financial and nonmonetary, allow team members to share in the success of the company along with other Stoner stakeholders. "We try to hire the best, give responsibility and freedom, and share the rewards," says General Manager Rob Marchalonis.

Feedback from customers who are dissatisfied is recorded in what is known as the "Below Expectations Log." Each customer's feedback is reviewed weekly by the entire leadership team, and by functional teams where appropriate, to determine corrective actions. Less than 1.5 percent of all Stoner customer transactions result in below expectations feedback. Customer satisfaction is further monitored by an independent polling firm, where Stoner has enjoyed best-in-class ratings.[13]

Problem-Solving Team

A problem-solving team *refers to members who focus on a specific issue, develop a potential solution, and are often empowered to take action within defined limits.* These teams frequently address quality or cost problems. Members may be employees from a specific department who meet at least once or twice a week for an hour or two or members from several units, even including representatives from outside the organization, such as suppliers and customers. Teams may have the authority to implement their own solutions if they don't require major procedural changes that might adversely affect other operations or require substantial new resources. Problem-solving teams do not fundamentally reorganize work or change the role of managers. In effect, managers delegate certain problems and decision-making responsibilities to a team as is done at Toyota.[14]

The American Printing Company is a large commercial printing firm located in Madison, Wisconsin. Like many printers, the firm faces intense competition and cost pressures. Major costs are associated with the need to rework jobs. To attempt to reduce rework, American Printing formed a five-person problem-solving team comprised of a preflighter (the person who checks the content of incoming electronic files), estimator, scheduler, job planner, and prepress layout specialist. The team was charged with analyzing jobs for potential problems and taking action to prevent and reduce rework. Shawn Welch, the vice president of operations for American Printing, comments on the results from this team's and related efforts: "We reduced the rework rate from over 3% of sales to below 2%. It is not zero-defect, but it is closer to where we want to be."[15]

LEADER INSIGHT

There are few positions that don't require teamwork on some level. I work with developers, producers, client operations, sales, and executive leadership. Teamwork is expected. If you can't work well with others you're never going to make it very far.
Bryan Stoehs, Channel Manager, Gartner News, Gartner, Inc.

Cross-Functional Team

A cross-functional team *refers to members from various work areas who identify and solve mutual problems.* Cross-functional teams draw members from several areas to deal with problems that cut across departmental and functional lines. Cross-functional teams may operate on an extended basis. This is illustrated by the diverse group of members on the IT leadership team at Regions Financial Corporation. Also, the leadership team at Stoner, Inc., is cross-functional—consisting of Rob Ecklin, the president, and a representative from each of the six functional teams. Cross-functional teams may be disbanded after the problems they addressed have been solved and their goals achieved.

Cross-functional teams are frequently used to foster innovation, speed, and a focus on responding to customer needs. They may design and introduce quality improvement programs and new technology, meet with customers and suppliers to improve inputs or outputs, and link separate functions (e.g., marketing, finance, manufacturing, and human resource) to increase product or service innovations.[16] Increasingly, such teams include members from outside the organization such as customer representatives, consultants, and suppliers.

Motorola, headquartered in Schaumburg, Illinois, is a global provider of wireless, broadband, network, enterprise, computer, and related products and services for consumers, businesses, and governments. It makes extensive use of cross-functional teams. For example, the selection of suppliers is done by cross-functional sourcing teams that are headed up by the purchasing department. The teams have discussions with the company's chief technology officer and product development teams. The teams set strategies for the commodities that Motorola buys and aligns them with Motorola's suppliers. The idea is to choose the technologies, components, and suppliers up front before design takes place. Rita Lane, the chief procurement officer of Motorola, comments: "We run a strategic sourcing process that we call rapid sourcing initiative. We select strategic sources for a longer term period. Ideally, we would like those sources to be part of the new product process. The cross-functional teams look at multiple facets of technologies to try and get a long-term three- to five-year plan for strategic sources and map them to our technology road maps."[17]

Lonnie Bernardoni, corporate vice president of new product innovation, adds: "Purchasing is involved very early in the design process including when the initial proposal for a product is announced. At the earliest stage, purchasing starts the sourcing process as a team. We are ramping faster to a higher number while in that same time we saw a 40% improvement in our quality metrics. Quality from suppliers improved 51% by working with them and having them as part of our team."[18]

Self-Managed Team

A self-managed team *refers to highly interdependent, competent, and empowered members who work together effectively on a daily basis to manufacture an entire product (or major identifiable component) or provide an entire service to a set of customers.*[19]

Self-managed teams are often empowered to perform a variety of managerial tasks, such as (1) scheduling work and vacations by members, (2) rotating tasks and assignments among members, (3) ordering materials, (4) deciding on team leadership (which can rotate among team members), (5) setting key team goals within overall organizational goals, (6) budgeting, (7) hiring replacements for departing team members, and (8) sometimes even evaluating one another's performance. Each member may even learn all tasks that have to be performed by the team.[20]

The impact of self-managed teams on productivity has been considerable. In some cases, they have raised productivity 30 percent or more and have substantially raised quality. They fundamentally change how work is organized and leadership is practiced.[21] The introduction of self-managed teams typically eliminates one or more managerial levels, thereby creating a flatter organization. Even if a managerial level is not eliminated, the role of management and supervision changes. Consider this typical pattern when self-managed teams are adopted in manufacturing settings. Traditional supervision is eliminated. The once-supervisor (if he or she still exists) serves in the same role as functional specialists such as process specialists or quality specialists. Supervisors (usually called something else such as team development coordinator) are often viewed as training coordinators. They manage a process to ensure that each team member is constantly learning new information and skills about the manufacturing process. Functional experts also serve as trainers providing hands-on training to team members. The team development coordinators often provide mentoring and coaching of individual team embers.[22]

Managerial Guidelines. Self-managed teams aren't necessarily right for every situation or organization. Both costs and benefits accompany such a system. A number of questions need to be addressed in considering the introduction of self-managed teams, including the following.

1. Is the organization fully committed to aligning all management systems with empowered work teams, including selection of leaders, team-based rewards, and open access to information?
2. Are organizational goals and the expected results from the teams clearly specified?
3. Will the teams have access to the resources they need for high performance?
4. Will team members carry out tasks that require a high degree of coordination and communication?

5. Do employees have the necessary maturity levels to effectively carry out peer evaluations, selection and discipline decisions, conflict management, and other administrative tasks?
6. Are employee competency levels sufficient for handling increased responsibility and, if not, will increased training result in appropriate competency levels?[23]

Virtual Team

Functional, problem-solving, cross-functional, and even self-managed teams may operate as virtual teams. A virtual team *refers to members who collaborate through various information technologies on one or more tasks while geographically dispersed at two or more locations and who have minimal face-to-face interaction.*[24] Unlike teams that operate primarily in person-to-person settings with members of the same organization, virtual teams work primarily across distance (any place), across time (any time), and increasingly across organizational boundaries (members from two or more organizations). Accordingly, some of the potential benefits of virtual teams include these:

- Members can work from anywhere at anytime.
- Members can be recruited for their competencies, not just the physical location where they primarily work and live.
- Members with physical handicaps that limit travel can participate.
- Expenses associated with travel, lodging, and leasing or owning physical space may be reduced.

The core features of a virtual team are goals, technology links, and people. Goals are important to any team, but especially so to a virtual team. Clear, precise, and mutually agreed-on goals are the glue that holds a virtual team together. The ability to hire and fire by a superior and reliance on rules and regulations are minimized in effective virtual teams.

As in all teams, people are at the core of effective virtual teams, but with some unique twists. Everyone in a virtual team needs to be autonomous and self-reliant while simultaneously working collaboratively with others. This duality requires a certain type of person and a foundation of trust among team members. The most apparent feature of a virtual team is the array of technology-based links used to connect members and enable them to carry out its tasks. Virtual teams are increasingly common because of rapid advances in computer and telecommunications technologies.[25]

Technology Links. Three broad categories of technologies are often used in the operation of virtual teams: desktop videoconferencing systems, collaborative software systems, and Internet/intranet systems.[26] Virtual teams can function with only simple e-mail and telephone systems, including voice mail. However, *desktop videoconferencing systems* (DVCSs) re-create some of the aspects of face-to-face interactions of conventional teams. This technology makes possible more complex communication among team members. The DVCS is a relatively simple system for users to operate. A small camera mounted atop a computer monitor provides the video feed to the system; voice transmissions operate through an earpiece–microphone combination or speakerphone. Connection to other team members is managed through software on the user's computer. With improvements in bandwidth-related technologies and reduced costs, videoconferencing systems—increasingly referred to as *telepresence systems*—are starting to provide another tool for creating more face-to-face like meetings for all types of teams where the members are physically dispersed. The cost of these systems vary greatly—typically from $80,000 to $500,000 for equipping a room. In addition, there is the cost of purchasing high-speed bandwidth.[27]

Collaborative software systems (group support systems) comprise the second category of technologies that enable the use of virtual teams. Collaborative software is designed for both independent and interactive use. For example, Lotus Notes, a dominant collaborative software product, is designed specifically for communication and data sharing when team members are working at different times, at the same time, independently, or interactively. It combines scheduling, electronic messaging, and document and data sharing. Although Lotus Notes and other such software may be used to support teamwork in a traditional work environment, they are vital to the operation of empowered virtual teams. Instant messaging (IM) is a virtual Post-it note. It is informal and interactive. IM helps to keep tabs on each other's availability.

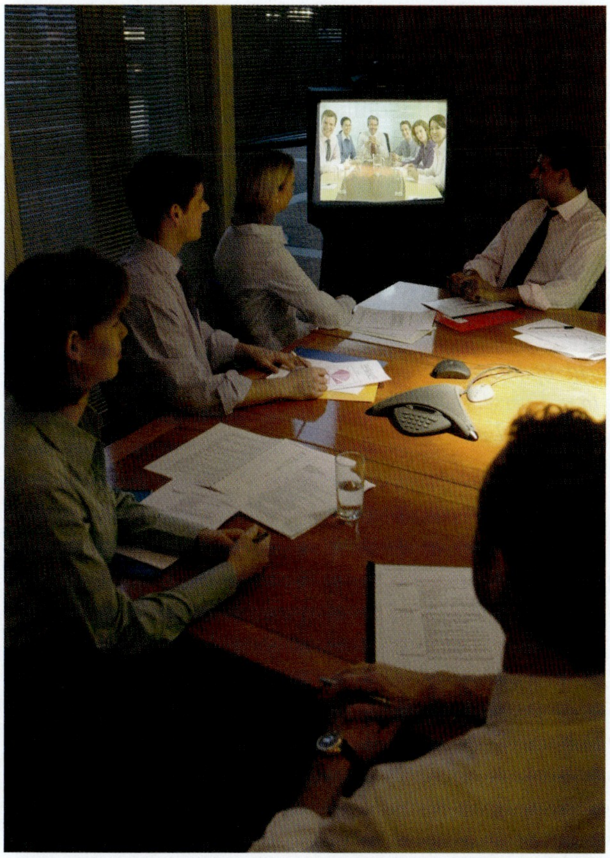

Desktop videoconferencing systems re-create some of the aspects of face-to-face interactions of conventional teams.

Internet and intranet technologies represent the third main enabler of virtual teams. Intranets give organizations the advantage of using Internet technology to disseminate information and enhance interemployee communication while maintaining system security. They allow virtual teams to archive text, visual, audio, and numerical data in a user-friendly format. The Internet and intranets also allow virtual teams to keep other organizational members and important external stakeholders, such as suppliers and customers, up to date on a team's progress.[28]

Managerial Guidelines. A variety of managerial guidelines have been offered for enhancing the *people* dimension of virtual teams.[29] We share five of them here:

- Develop clear and specific goals in collaboration with the team members.
- If feasible, bring the members together for an initial face-to-face session. This could last one to three days depending on the scope and complexity of the team's responsibilities and goals. Members need to be given adequate time to get to know one another. This initial session may include team-building activities. Work-related goals, team member roles, and team responsibilities should be thoroughly discussed in this session. With advances in communication technologies, there are some who hold the view that an initial face-to-face session may not be essential and could be too

costly for team members located around the world. This view may be more applicable to teams that have a relatively short duration.

- For long-term or permanent teams, establish a schedule of periodic face-to-face meetings—quarterly, semiannual, or annual—if feasible.
- Agree on what, when, and how information, issues, and problems will be shared as well as on how team members will respond to them. For example, at McDonald's, all e-mails need to be answered within 24 hours.
- Establish clear norms and procedures for reducing, surfacing, and resolving conflicts. Pamela Kandela, an occupational psychologist who conducts research on virtual teams for Cisco, comments: "Technology, if not well used, can lead to misunderstandings and destructive conflict. Conflict tends to be more prolific in virtual teams because team members are less likely to have had a history of working together. This coupled with the impersonal nature of virtual communication, means that such teams have much weaker interpersonal bonds than do face-to-face teams. Best practices need to be established to minimize these tendencies."[30]

The special managerial challenges associated with virtual teams are reflected in the following (anonymous) quote by a team leader at Boeing-Rocketdyne:

> *I must be a diplomat to help teams overcome cultural differences, an ambassador to keep sponsors around the world updated on the team's progress, a psychologist to provide a variety of rewards to a diverse and often isolated group of team members, an executive, a coach, and a role model all at the same time.*[31]

Global Team

A global team *has members from a variety of countries who are, therefore, often separated significantly by time, distance, culture, and language.*[32] As suggested in Figure 11.1, global teams may operate like any of the other types of teams we have discussed—functional, problem solving, cross-functional, self-managed, and virtual. Global teams typically conduct a substantial portion of their tasks as virtual teams.

Four of the principal reasons for the use of global teams are as follows:[33]

1. The desire to develop goods and services in a variety of countries with a minimum level of customization. In this circumstance, global teams help to define common features of goods and services that will appeal to customers in different countries. Procter & Gamble and 7-Eleven use global teams to market their products.
2. In contrast to reason 1 just given, there is a desire to develop goods or services that are tailored to the unique needs and requirements of local markets. The global team members from different countries can provide insight into and input about these unique market needs and requirements for specific attributes of goods and services.
3. Global teams enable organizations to leverage and capitalize on expertise that exists in different countries. This eliminates the need to bring the required expertise to a single country by relocating team members and encountering all of the costs of doing so, including the costs of removing team members from family and friends or relocating entire families.
4. For organizations such as Celanese Chemicals and Elsevier Publishing, the location of manufacturing facilities, distribution centers, and marketing units in various countries requires the use of global teams. The teams serve as a mechanism for coordinating these dispersed resources. Global teams allow companies to take advantage of lower manufacturing costs in one country, the central location of a distribution center in another, and "on-site" marketing units by bringing together individuals virtually. These global teams usually need to meet face to face only on occasion.

Managerial Guidelines. Global virtual teams face a variety of special managerial challenges relative to most virtual or face-to-face teams because of differences in the members' cultures and native languages as well as significant time zone differences in their normal working hours.[34] For example, virtual teams with members from China, Germany, Japan, France, and the United States are more culturally, socially, and linguistically diverse (even if the work-related communications are undertaken in English) than virtual teams with members from California, Colorado, Florida, Massachusetts, and New York. In a number of chapters, we discuss the special challenges associated with differences across cultures and the suggested managerial guidelines related to them.

With respect to time, the normal working hours for global virtual team members may vary by 12 or more hours due to differences in the time zones where members reside. Moreover, the cultural meaning of *time* may vary among team members in different societies, which we discussed in more detail in Chapter 8. Cultural orientations about time may affect team members' perceptions of schedules and deadlines. In some cultures, for instance, the Germanic and Scandinavian countries, schedules and deadlines are seen as absolutes. In other countries, such as Mexico and Italy, they are often seen as guidelines. In recognition of the potential for different views of time among global virtual team members, managers should (1) create an awareness of the different views members may have with respect to time after the formation of the team; (2) facilitate the development of agreed-on norms and expectations with respect to time; and (3) encourage the use of precise language with respect to time and avoid the use of time-related language such as "Wait a minute," "I'll be in touch shortly," and "Let's keep in contact as time permits." Of course, all of the managerial guidelines for virtual teams apply to global virtual teams as well.

LEADER INSIGHT

You virtually have a never-ending business day. One of the biggest challenges is very early-morning and late-night meetings. But there's no way to avoid it. On the upside, our stakeholders are quite pleased that we've shortened the time-to-market and delivered early.

Kathleen Gillam, Manager, Enterprise Web Development Team for Human Resource Solutions, Intel

The following Across Cultures Competency feature provides an example of the successful use of a global virtual team by Logitech.[35] Logitech designs a broad portfolio of interface devices, such as computer mice and keyboards, that represent the "last inch" between consumers and their PCs, console games, and digital music or home entertainment systems. Logitech International is a Swiss public company with headquarters in Fremont, California. The firm has approximately 7,500 employees worldwide.[36]

Across Cultures Competency

Logitech's Global Virtual Team

The flagship mouse that Logitech introduced in 2007 is truly the result of global collaboration. The mechanical engineering and design took place in Ireland; electrical engineering in Switzerland; corporate marketing, software engineering, and quality assurance at the company's Fremont, California, headquarters; tooling in Taiwan; and manufacturing in China.

The far-flung design team is as good a representative as any of the "follow the sun" model of engineering now taking hold in the electronics industry. The shortage of good local talent drives companies to create geographically distributed project teams with members strategically located in regions that begin their days when others' end. To shorten time-to-market for their employers' products, these teams share the burden of a 24-hour work cycle.

For Peter Sheehan, creative director at Design Partners in Bray, Ireland, Logitech's external design team, the group working on the Logitech Revolution mouse was a "dream team." Communication problems were rare, he said, because the team met in person at the beginning of the project and once a month thereafter in the countries of team members.

Although the team experienced the inevitable cultural differences, the more challenging issues related to professional fields. Sheehan comments: "My colleagues are fond of saying that in most design reviews, everybody follows their script. Engineers are trained to follow one script, which is to be logical, rational and relatively conservative in how they innovate. The designers are there to inspire and capture the essence of an idea as well as to make it into a rational, finished product. And the marketing people read from their script, which is to push everyone to create a compelling story for the consumer. Country of origin notwithstanding, everyone plays their script."

The Logitech–Design Partners collaborators put in an unusual amount of face time, but its value cannot be overstated. Sheehan comments: "It's a recharging of the batteries of the relationships. There's very little that can replace it when it comes to the details of the design process, in terms of the interaction between disciplines."

For Sheehan, some of the big mistakes in leading global virtual teams include

- assuming from an e-mail or an instant message that you are on the same page with your colleague in a time zone 12 hours different from yours;
- failure to take advantage of the many collaborative tools available;
- managers who don't trust that their remote employees are actually working;
- failure to take advantage of the best skilled workers simply because they are in a vastly different time zone; and
- intruding too frequently on team members for status reports and the like.

For more information on Logitech, visit the organization's home page at www.logitech.com.

Learning Goal

3. Explain the stages of team development.

STAGES OF TEAM DEVELOPMENT

The development of an effective team is not automatic. Various conditions for success or failure occur throughout a team's life. To provide a sense of these conditions, we present a basic five-stage developmental sequence that a team may go through: forming, storming, norming, performing, and adjourning.[37] The types of work-related and socially related behaviors that may be observed differ from stage to stage. Figure 11.2 shows the five stages on the horizontal axis and the level of team maturity on the vertical axis. It also indicates that a team can fail and disband during a stage or when moving from one stage to another. Pinpointing the developmental stage of a team at any specific time is difficult. Nevertheless, managers and team members need to understand these developmental stages because each can influence a team's effectiveness. In the following discussion, we describe behaviors that might occur at each stage. Of course, a team or group does not necessarily develop in the straightforward manner depicted in this model.[38] Team members with high levels of the seven core competencies presented throughout this book are likely to speed up and alter the stages of development presented here.

Forming Stage

Team members often focus on defining goals and developing procedures for performing their jobs in the forming stage. Team development in this stage involves getting acquainted and understanding leadership and other member roles. In terms of social behaviors, it should also deal with members' feelings and the tendency of most members to depend too much on one or two of the team's members. Otherwise, individual members might (1) keep feelings to themselves until they know the situation; (2) act more secure than they actually feel; (3) experience confusion and uncertainty about what is expected of them; (4) be nice and polite, or at least certainly not hostile; and (5) try to size up the personal benefits relative to the personal costs of being involved with the team or group.

Researchers investigated the impact of a collaborative software system on the development and performance of corporate teams.[39] They were fortunate in having access to an organization whose top managers were very interested in the results of the study.

FIGURE 11.2 Stages of Team Development

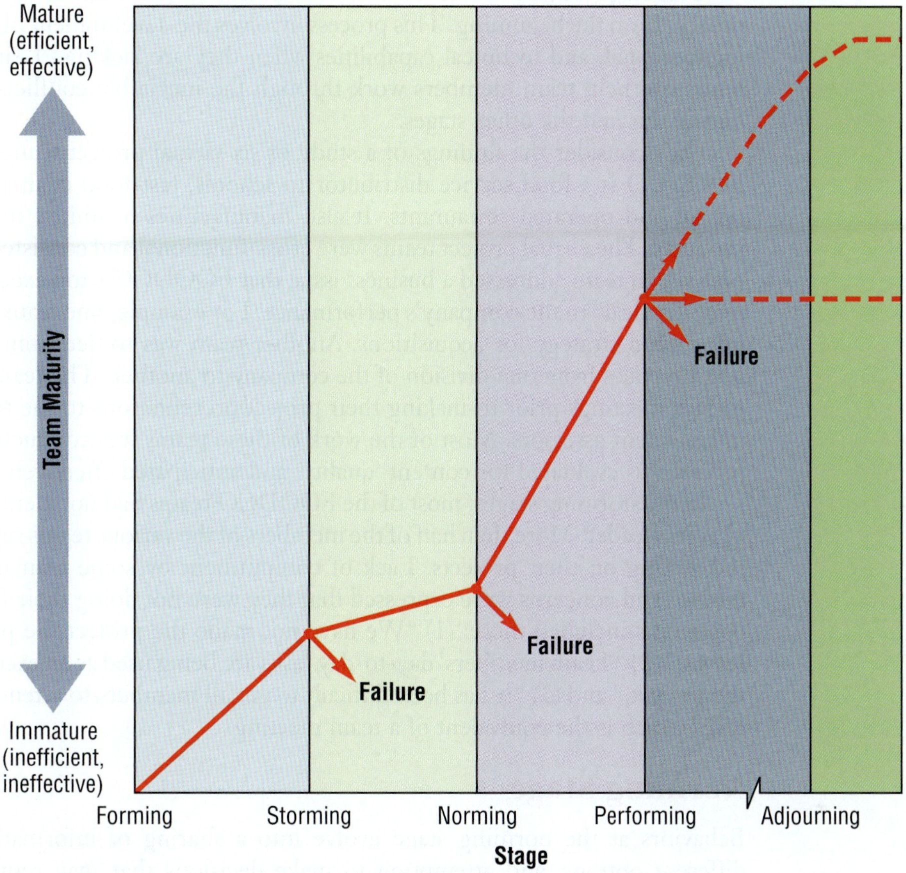

Source: Adapted from Tuckman, B. W., and Jensen, M. A. C. Stages of small-group development revisited. *Groups and Organization Studies*, 1977, 2, 419–442; Kormanski, C. Team interventions: Moving the team forward. In J. W. Pfeiffer (ed.). *The 1996 Annual: Volume 2 Consulting*. San Diego: Pfeiffer and Company, 1996, 19–26.

This interest allowed the investigators to study the two teams in detail, using meeting transcripts and individual interviews. One team studied had used a collaborative software system from the start, whereas the second team used the system only after the team had met a few times. The investigators' findings indicated that the two teams developed and performed quite differently. The team that started with the collaborative system improved faster than the other team at each stage of development. The researchers found that a collaborative software system can help a group get started (forming), but only when the group considers that use of the system to be important to the task at hand.

Storming Stage

The storming stage is characterized by conflicts over work, relative priorities of goals, who is to be responsible for what, and the directions of the team leader. Social behaviors are a mixture of expressions of hostility and strong feelings. Competition over the leadership role and conflict over goals may dominate this stage. Some members may withdraw or try to isolate themselves from the emotional tension generated. The key is to manage conflict during this stage, not to suppress it or withdraw from it. The team can't effectively move into the third stage if its members do not handle conflict effectively. Suppressing conflict will likely create bitterness and resentment, which will last long after team members attempt to express their differences and emotions. Withdrawal may cause the team to fail.

This stage may be shortened or mostly avoided if the members use a team-building process from the beginning. This process involves the development of decision-making, interpersonal, and technical capabilities when they are lacking. Team-building facilitators can help team members work through the inevitable conflicts that will surface during this and the other stages.

Let's consider the findings of a study of six virtual project teams at FOODCO.[40] FOODCO is a food service distributor to schools, fast-food chains, and individually owned and operated restaurants. It also manufactures a limited number of its own products. The virtual project teams were cross-functional and consisted of five members each. Each team addressed a business issue that FOODCO's top executives considered to be "critical" to the company's performance. For example, one team was to develop an integration strategy for acquisitions. Another team was to determine how to transfer best practices from one division of the company to another. The teams had three face-to-face meetings prior to making their project presentations to the top executives and independent assessors. Most of the work of these teams was conducted virtually. Each project was evaluated for content, quality, and anticipated effectiveness.

In the storming stages, most of the FOODCO teams had not identified or agreed on a project leader. More than half of the members of the various teams reported difficulties in working on their projects. Lack of commitment by some team members became evident and concerns were expressed that they were not doing their fair share. Typical comments included these: (1) "We have not made the project the priority that it deserves," (2) "Team members' day-to-day tasks are being used as an excuse to avoid doing the project," and (3) "It has been difficult to get all members to attend each conference call," which is the equivalent of a team meeting.

Norming Stage

Behaviors at the norming stage evolve into a sharing of information, accepting of different options, and attempting to make decisions that may require compromise. During this stage, team members set rules by which the team will operate. For teams that become effective, relations-oriented behaviors often focus on empathy, concern, and positive expressions of feelings that lead to a sense of cohesion. Cooperation and a sense of shared responsibility develop among members of effective teams.

Returning to FOODCO, by the end of the third face-to-face meeting of the six virtual project teams, most of them had recognized the need for reaching agreement on how they would operate in the future. The teams reconsidered (and reinforced) existing norms or established new norms regarding information collection, document sharing, task responsibilities, acceptable attendance at conference calls, and team commitment. Teams discussed ways in which members could be held more accountable for timely delivery of project assignments and openly confronted problems that might interfere with the completion of their projects. Most teams expressed some regret about their initial passivity, lack of initiative, and delays in collecting information. The comments by members of several teams suggested that they continued to struggle with issues of commitment and trust during the norming stage. It was believed that this adversely impacted their effectiveness in the performing stage.[41]

Performing Stage

Team members show how they can achieve results together during the performing stage. The roles of individual members are accepted and understood. The members have learned when they should work independently and when they should help each other. The two dashed lines in Figure 11.2 suggest that teams may differ after the performing stage. Some teams continue to learn and develop from their experiences, becoming more efficient and effective. Other teams may perform only at the level needed for their survival. Excessive self-oriented behaviors, development of norms that inhibit task completion, poor leadership, or other factors may hurt productivity.

In the performing stage of the six FOODCO virtual project teams, the differences among the teams became even more evident. These differences emerged with respect to team commitment, higher executive-level sponsor involvement and support, coordination, intrateam trust, and member "loafing." Teams that perceived greater amounts of resource availability at the onset of their projects performed better at the end of the project. Teams with greater mission clarity, more time to examine work process effectiveness, and higher levels of executive sponsor support were more effective.

A profile of the "best" team shows that at each stage of development it was proactive, focused, resourceful, and unafraid to seek support and guidance as needed The best team, as compared to the least effective team, developed a much stronger consensus regarding its team's mission. The best team reported greater levels of executive sponsor support and more frequent assessments by team members of its own processes than the least effective team. Members of the best team realized they needed to revise their work processes to meet the deadline and perform well. In contrast, members of the least effective team continued to struggle to the end of the project on how they could best accomplish their mission. In the performing stage, the best team, as compared to the least effective team, saw themselves as having a high level of mission clarity, communication, commitment, and trust among team members. Various other findings surfaced in terms of the stages of development for the six virtual project teams at FOODCO, but they are beyond the scope our discussion.[42]

Adjourning Stage

The termination of work behaviors and disengagement from social behaviors occur during the adjourning stage. A problem-solving team or a cross-functional team created to investigate and report on a specific issue within six months has well-defined points of adjournment. After the presentations were made to the top executives and several other assessors by the six virtual project teams at FOODCO, they were disbanded. The reports and presentations represented the "output" from their projects. Top management accepted these projects as "input" for their consideration and possible implementation by others. Another example of a team with a specific adjournment stage is the Logitech global virtual team discussed in the Across Cultures Competency feature. After the design team completed the work on the new mouse, it was disbanded.

The IT leadership team at Regions Financial Corporation, as discussed in our Learning from Experience opening feature, will continue for an undetermined period to address continuing and new issues over time. Presumably, this team will "adjourn" if John Dick, the CIO, or his successor decides to alter or eliminate the current team process. Of course, even on this IT team, some degree of adjourning occurs in terms of relation-oriented behaviors as team members are transferred, promoted, or leave the organization. The Toyota assembly team is an example of an ongoing team that needs to continuously work on adapting to maintain or improve its effectiveness.[43] Our presentation in the following section presents key factors that influence team effectiveness from the "get go" and over time.

The developmental stages of teams—regardless of the framework used to describe and explain them—are not easy to move through. Failure or reduced effectiveness can occur at any point in the sequence, as indicated in Figure 11.2. Our discussion of FOODCO's virtual project teams suggested some of the factors that influence team effectiveness.

Learning Goal

4. Describe the core factors that influence team effectiveness.

CORE INFLUENCES ON TEAM EFFECTIVENESS

The factors that influence team and group effectiveness are interrelated. Figure 11.3 identifies eight of the core factors. Each factor needs to be analyzed separately and in relation to each other. This approach fosters a fuller understanding of team dynamics and effectiveness—and helps to develop the competencies needed to be an effective team member and leader.

Context

The context *refers to the external conditions within which a team works.* Moreover, the context can directly affect each of the seven other factors that affect a team. Examples of a team's context include technology, physical working conditions, management practices, and organizational rewards and punishments.[44] Our discussion of virtual teams illustrated the contextual influence of technology. We also noted the contextual influence of the differences in executive sponsor involvement and support among the virtual project teams at FOODCO.

If the members of a team are more focused on themselves than their peers, perhaps the organization's reward system (a contextual factor) should be tailored so that individuals see how their own interests are being served by being strong team contributors. This notion is based on three perspectives:

1. Motivation primarily comes from the individual, not the team.
2. The development of competencies, such as those emphasized in this book, are individual undertakings.
3. Fairness in dealing with teams does not necessarily mean equal pay for all members of the team.

The team system at the Mayo Clinic considers these perspectives in its recruitment and selection process (a contextual factor) by not hiring physicians and others who want to maximize their own personal income. A physician at the Mayo Clinic states:

> *The Mayo culture attracts individuals who see the practice of medicine best delivered when there is an integration of medical specialties functioning as a team. It is what we do best, and most of us love to do it. What is most inspiring is when a case is successful because of the teamwork of a bunch of docs from different specialties; it has the same feeling as a home run in baseball.*[45]

FIGURE 11.3 Core Influences on Team Effectiveness

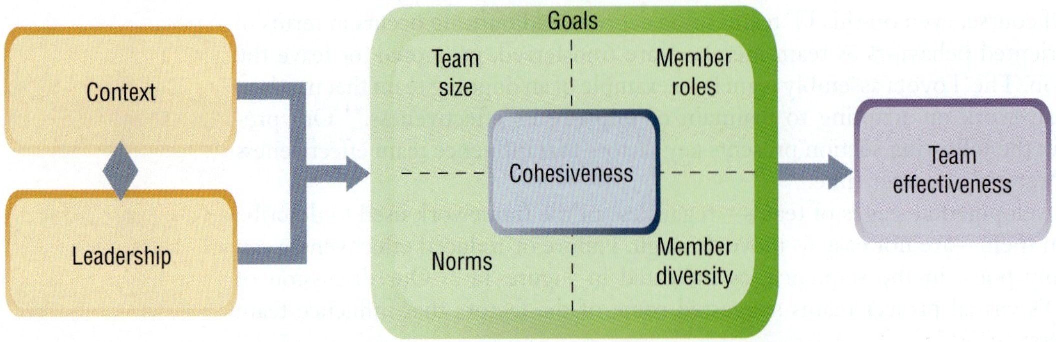

© Ryan McVay/Photodisc/Getty Images

In an office, the placement and types of furniture and work spaces can influence the social interaction of teams.

In office settings, the placement and types of furniture, work spaces, conference rooms, halls, and the like (all contextual factors) can influence and/or regulate the social interaction of teams. Recall our discussion of interpersonal communication networks in Chapter 8 and the potential impacts of physical settings. With respect to the physical environment for individuals and teams, it is suggested that:

> *Today's work environment needs to support a variety of work styles, technologies, and activities. Workers need to collaborate and work alone. They need open spaces to casually socialize with colleagues and they need quiet places to perform solo work, reflect, and allow ideas to incubate.*[46]

Leadership

In Chapters 9 and 10, we discussed leadership in depth. Much of that discussion applies to the leadership of teams as well. Team leaders may be formally designated to their roles, as were John Dick, the CIO and team leader of the IT leadership team at Regions Financial Corporation, and Peter Sheehan, creative director at Design Partners and the team leader of the Logitech global virtual team that designed the new computer mouse. In other cases, informal leaders emerge to develop and guide the team or group in accomplishing, or perhaps changing, its goals. An informal leader *is an individual whose influence in a team grows over time and usually reflects a unique ability to help the team reach its goals.*

Multiple Leaders. Team leadership is often thought of in terms of one person. Because a team often has both interpersonal relations-oriented and task-oriented tasks and goals, it may have two or more leaders. These two categories of tasks and goals may require different skills and leadership styles, creating a total set of demands that one person may have difficulty satisfying. Informal task-related leaders of teams aren't likely to emerge unless the formal leader ignores task-related responsibilities or lacks the necessary skills to carry them out. In contrast, relations-oriented leaders of teams may well emerge informally.

Impact of Team Leaders. As suggested in Figure 11.3, team leaders may influence virtually all aspects of a team (e.g., goals, size, member roles, diversity, norms, cohesiveness, and even context).[47] A leader often assumes a key role in the relations between the team and external groups, such as customers or suppliers, and often influences the selection of new members. Even when the team heavily participates in the selection process, the team leader may screen potential members, thereby limiting the number and range of candidates, as is done at the Mayo Clinic.

The following Self Competency feature reports on the team leadership and impact of Brian Catalde as he assumed the presidency of the National Association of Home Builders (NAHB).[48] NAHB is a 225,000-member trade association whose mission is to enhance the climate for housing and the building industry. It is headquartered in Washington, D.C.[49] Catalde is the president and chief operating officer of Paragon Communities, a single-family home and multifamily land developer and builder, which is headquartered in El Segundo, California. The firm develops and builds about 500 houses and condo units a year.[50]

Self Competency

Brian Catalde's Team Leadership of NAHB

When he was the incoming president of the National Association of Home Builders, Brian Catalde committed to work with the executive team to develop mutually agreed-on long-term goals and projects for the NAHB. He states: "I've adopted the mentality that leading the NAHB is not about me. It's about giving the team the right information and encouraging them to make the right decisions for the NAHB's future."

Before becoming president, Catalde served six years on the NAHB board of directors. He became quite familiar with the multiple issues the organization tackled. Catalde quickly realized that the association's goals lacked continuity from one year to the next. As part of the preparation for his new role, Catalde reviewed the notes from every presidential planning meeting held during the previous six years. He states: "There was a lot of jumping around because each new president wanted to pursue goals that were different from what the outgoing president had pursued. Working on goals and issues for just a year—that lack of a long-term commitment—was a problem."

Catalde gathered the executive team in a retreat setting. He encouraged them to share what they hoped to focus on during their own eventual presidencies. He led the team in an extensive discussion of each member's interests and merged them into a reasonable number of long-term goals and issues that needed to be addressed over a period of years. The executive team reached a consensus on the pertinent goals, which was a first. He states: "By establishing long-term priorities and goals, we all know what we need to do. We all want to be something bigger than just individuals. We want to be part of a great, record-setting team."

During his stint as president of the NAHB, Catalde decided to focus on team building and achieving common goals. To that end, he encouraged each member of the executive team to serve as a leader of the agreed-on long-term goal and project that was of greatest interest to that person. In effect, Catalde established multiple leader roles around specific long-term goals and projects. He hopes that this process will help the NAHB ultimately achieve much more than would otherwise be possible. The team agreed that the key general and internal goals that require a multiyear commitment include (1) communicating better with members, (2) encouraging greater member diversity, and (3) reaching out to more prospective members through the restructuring of membership levels.

Catalde hopes that his efforts will change the NAHB executive team's processes and norms. He admits that implementing this kind of new process and long-term team-based goal setting requires a certain level of finesse and self-sacrifice. "To do this, you have to give up autonomy as the president and work together for common goals. You can't get people to buy in if you're king for a day."

For more information on the National Association of Home Builders, visit the organization's home page at www.nahb.com.

Goals

Team goals *are the outcomes desired for the team as a whole, not just goals of the individual members*. Our Self Competency feature related to Brian Catalde reported on his efforts to lead the organization's executive team in the establishment of long-term goals and projects for the NAHB. Recall his comment: "To do this, you have to give up autonomy as the president and work together for common goals. You can't get people to buy in if you're king for a day."

Many aspects of goals are discussed in Chapter 6. Throughout the book, we focus on how goals influence individual, team, and organizational effectiveness. Obviously, individual and organizational goals are likely to influence team goals and behaviors in pursuit of these goals.[51] Both compatible and conflicting goals often exist within a team. Moreover, teams typically have both relations-oriented and task-oriented goals. Effective work-related teams spend two-thirds or more of their time on task-oriented issues and roughly one-third or less of their time on relations-oriented issues. The pursuit of only one or the other type of goal over the long run can hurt performance, increase conflicts, and cause a team to disband. The influence of goals on group dynamics and outcomes becomes even more complex when the possible compatibilities and conflicts among member goals, broader team goals, and even broader organizational goals are considered.

One mechanism for dealing with these issues is the use of superordinate goals, *which two or more individuals, teams, or groups might pursue but can't be achieved without their cooperation*. These goals do not replace or eliminate individual or team goals and may be either qualitative or quantitative. An example of a qualitative goal is "We need to pull together for the good of the team." An example of a quantitative goal is "We need to work together if we are to reach our goal of launching a new line within nine months." Superordinate goals may have a more powerful effect on the willingness of individuals or teams to cooperate if they are accompanied by team rewards established by higher management. Team rewards are given to team members and are determined by the results of their joint efforts. Team rewards may also be in the form of a sense of mutual satisfaction and accomplishment for having performed well by serving customers, achieving high quality, and making a difference.

At times, the way the organization's principles and values are expressed and implemented may serve as superordinate goals. For example, the core principles set forth by Dr. William J. Mayo late in his life continue to serve as superordinate goals at the Mayo Clinic. They include, among others,

- continuing pursuit of the ideal of service and not profit,
- continuing primary and sincere concern for the care and welfare of each individual patient, and
- continuing interest by every member of the staff in the professional progress of every other member.[52]

In Chapter 4, we discussed self-efficacy—the individual's estimate of his or her own ability to perform a specific task in a particular situation. In a similar sense, collective efficacy *is a team's or group's shared perception of its capability to successfully perform specific tasks*. The performance of such tasks is necessary to achieve team goals. If a team lacks in collective efficacy, the impact of setting team goals will be diminished.[53] Great NBA basketball teams, like the San Antonio Spurs, the Chicago Bulls with Michael Jordan, or the Boston Celtics with Larry Bird, demonstrate collective efficacy year after year.

Team Size

The effective size of a team can range from 3 members to a normal upper limit of about 16 members.[54] Collaborative software systems, the Internet, and other technologies are enabling larger teams to work effectively on some tasks. Twelve members probably is the largest size that allows each member to interact easily with every other member face to

Table 11.2 Typical Effects of Size on Teams

	Team Size		
Dimension	2–7 Members	8–12 Members	13–16 Members
1. Demands on leader	Low	Moderate	High
2. Direction by leader	Low	Moderate	Moderate to high
3. Member tolerance of direction by leader	Low to moderate	Moderate	High
4. Member inhibition	Low	Moderate	High
5. Use of rules and procedures	Low	Moderate	Moderate to high
6. Time taken to reach a decision	Low	Moderate	High

Source: I. D. Team size and technology fit: Participation, awareness, and rapport in distributed teams. Professional Communication, 2005, 48, 68–77.

face, especially when the team members are not highly interdependent in performing their tasks on a day-to-day basis.[55] This is the situation with the Toyota assembly team that we discussed in the Team Competency feature. Table 11.2 shows six dimensions of teams that change as team size increases. The likely effects of team size on each dimension are highlighted. Note that members of teams of 7 or fewer interact differently than do members of teams or groups of 13 to 16. A 16-member board of directors will operate differently from a 7-member board. Large boards of directors often form committees of 5 to 7 members to consider specific matters in greater depth than can the entire board.

As with all influences on teams, the effects identified in Table 11.2 need to be qualified. For example, adequate time and sufficient member commitment to a team's goals and tasks might lead to better results from a team of seven to nine than from a hurried and less committed team of five members. If a team's primary task is to tap the knowledge of the members and arrive at decisions based primarily on expertise rather than judgment, a larger team won't necessarily reflect the effects identified in Table 11.2. Of course, many teams that are formed with professionals (experts and managers) are intended to integrate expertise and judgments.

The effective IT leadership team at Regions Financial Corporation, presented in the Learning from Experience opening feature, consisted of seven members. The effective Logitech global virtual team that designed the new computer mouse, presented in the Across Cultures Competency, also consisted of seven members. The senior leadership team of the NAHB, discussed in the Self Competency feature on Brian Catalde, consists of six members. In contrast, the production teams at a Volvo plant that manufactures truck cabins in the Netherlands consist of 11 to 13 members. The members of these teams are not highly interdependent throughout the workday in performing their relatively routine tasks. The Volvo teams are effective with the relatively large size.[56]

Member Roles

A universally agreed-on framework of team roles does not exist.[57] For our purposes, member roles in teams can be classified as to whether they are task-oriented, relations-oriented, or self-oriented roles. Each member has the potential for performing each of these roles over time.[58] This classification underlies most other models of team member roles.[59]

Task-Oriented Role. The task-oriented role *of a team member involves facilitating and coordinating work-related behaviors and decision making*. This role may include

- *initiating* new ideas or different ways of considering team problems or goals and suggesting solutions to difficulties, including modification of team procedures;
- *seeking information* to clarify suggestions and obtain key facts;

- *giving information* that is relevant to the team's problem, issue, or task;
- *coordinating* and clarifying relationships among ideas and suggestions, pulling ideas and suggestions together, and coordinating members' activities; and
- *evaluating* the team's effectiveness, including questioning the logic, facts, or practicality of other members' suggestions.

Relations-Oriented Role. The relations-oriented role *of a team member involves fostering team-centered attitudes, behaviors, emotions, and social interactions.* This role may include

- *encouraging* members through praise and acceptance of their ideas, as well as indicating warmth and solidarity;
- *harmonizing* and mediating intrateam conflicts and tensions;
- *encouraging* participation of others by saying: "Let's hear from Susan" or "Why not limit the length of contributions so all can react to the problem?" or "Juan, do you agree?";
- *expressing* standards for the team to achieve or apply in evaluating the quality of team processes, raising questions about team goals, and assessing team progress in light of these goals; and
- *following* by going along passively or constructively and serving as a friendly member.

Self-Oriented Role. The self-oriented role *of a team member involves the person's self-centered attitudes, behaviors, and decisions that are at the expense of the team or group.* This role may include

- *blocking progress* by being negative, stubborn, and unreasoningly resistant—for example, the person may repeatedly try to bring back an issue that the team had considered carefully and rejected;
- *seeking recognition* by calling attention to oneself, including boasting, reporting on personal achievements, and in various ways avoiding being placed in a presumed inferior position;
- *dominating* by asserting authority, manipulating the team or certain individuals, using flattery or proclaiming superiority to gain attention, and interrupting the contributions of others; and
- *avoiding* involvement by maintaining distance from others and remaining insulated from interaction.

Effective teams often are composed of members who play both task-oriented and relations-oriented roles over time. A particularly adept individual who reveals behaviors valued by the team probably has relatively high *status*—the relative rank of an individual in a team. A team dominated by individuals who exhibit mainly self-oriented behaviors is likely to be ineffective because the individuals don't adequately address team goals or engage in needed collaboration.

Table 11.3 provides a questionnaire for evaluating some of your task-oriented, relations-oriented, and self-oriented behaviors as a team member. The questionnaire asks you to assess your tendency to engage in each role, on a scale of 1 to 5 (or almost never to almost always). Member composition and roles greatly influence team or group behaviors. Either too much or too little of certain member behaviors can adversely affect team performance and member satisfaction.[60]

Member Diversity

The growing diversity of the workforce adds complexity—beyond individuals' personalities and team roles—to understanding team behavior and processes. We have discussed how the composition of the workforce is undergoing continued change in terms of primary and secondary categories of diversity, which are increasingly reflected in the membership of teams. As you may recall from Chapter 1, primary categories, over which individuals have little influence, include age, race, ethnicity, gender, physical

Table 11.3 Assessing Your Role-Oriented Behavior as a Team Member

Instructions: Assess your behavior on each item for the team that you selected by using the following scale.

1	2	3	4	5
Almost Never	Rarely	Sometimes	Often	Almost Always

Place the appropriate number value next to each item.

Task-oriented behaviors: In this team, I ...

______ 1. initiate ideas or actions.
______ 2. facilitate the introduction of facts and information.
______ 3. summarize and pull together various ideas.
______ 4. keep the team working on the task.
______ 5. ask whether the team is near a decision (determine consensus).

Relation-oriented behaviors: In this team, I ...

______ 6. support and encourage others.
______ 7. harmonize (keep the peace).
______ 8. try to find common ground.
______ 9. encourage participation.
______ 10. actively listen.

Self-oriented behaviors: In this team, I ...

______ 11. express hostility.
______ 12. avoid involvement.
______ 13. dominate the team.
______ 14. free ride on others.
______ 15. take personal credit for team results.

Total: Add points for items 1 through 15.

Interpretation: Scores of 20–25 on task-oriented behaviors, 20–25 on relations-oriented behaviors, and 5–10 on self-oriented behaviors probably indicate that you are an effective team member. This conclusion assumes that other team members perceive you as you see yourself.

abilities and qualities, and sexual orientation. In contrast, the secondary categories include education, work experiences, job position, income, marital status, religious beliefs, geographical location, parental status, ways of thinking, personal style, seniority, and the like. It is common to think of the primary categories as sources of difficulties in team functioning. The general assumption is that people like to work on teams with people who are similar to themselves. In the initial time period of members working together, this is often the case. However, as team members work together over time, these primary categories in the U.S. work environment appear to become less important to understanding team difficulties. In contrast, the secondary categories often become more important to understanding difficulties in team functioning, such as the formation of subgroups in a team based on age, seniority, job position, specialty, and the like. Recall John Dick's reflection on the IT leadership team at Regions Financial. When the group was formed, its members initially were more focused on their individual functions. Also, Peter Sheehan, who led Logitech's global virtual team in developing the computer mouse, found the greatest divisions related to professional field, not cultural differences—although there were some. Sheehan stated: "My colleagues are fond of saying that in most design reviews, everyone follows their script."[61]

The existence of subgroups in teams refers to fault lines—*the process by which teams divide themselves into subgroups based on one or more attributes.*[62] In general, the development of strong fault lines works *against* a good decision-making team. Teams without strong fault lines become aware of more issues, perceive issues in different and deeper ways, propose more novel and creative courses of action, and engage in constructive task-related conflict.[63] Our many years of experience with numerous student teams who have had to analyze complex cases or complete challenging projects suggests that diverse teams who do not form strong fault lines typically develop more effective cases or projects. Team effectiveness will be hampered if members hold false stereotypes about each other.[64] Although attitudes are changing, diversity all too often still is viewed more negatively than positively. This negative reaction may be due, in large part, to four underlying attitudes involving stereotypical false assumptions, as follows:

- Diversity poses a threat to the organization's effective functioning.
- Expressed discomfort with the dominant group's values is perceived as oversensitivity by minority groups.
- Members of all groups want to become and should be more like the dominant group.
- Equal treatment means the same treatment.

Renée Wingo, the chief people officer at Virgin Mobile USA, thoughtfully expresses her view on diversity with respect to teams this way:[65]

> *The power of any group or team of people is the power of the mix. You may do all right, but you're not going to create any magic as a manager unless you bring together people with diverse perspectives who aren't mini versions of you.*

The goal of achieving diversity creates unique challenges in making it work *for* rather than *against* the long-term interests of individuals, teams, and organizations.[66] Once an "us versus them" distinction is perceived through strong fault lines in a team, subgroups tend to discriminate against other team members who are different. Moreover, they tend to perceive these other team members as inferior, adversarial, and competitive.[67]

One of the ways leading organizations are attempting to be proactive in preventing or resolving diversity-based conflicts in teams and other work settings is through the acceptance and support of affinity groups—sometimes called employee networks, advocacy groups, support groups, or resource groups.[68] Within organizations, affinity groups *are typically voluntary, employee-driven groups that are organized around a particular shared interest, background, or goal.* These groups are usually initiated by employees and typically focus on a shared interest or characteristic such as race, ethnicity, gender, or sexual orientation. Each group's main goals are to create an open forum for idea exchange, employee-related interests, and goals to higher management. They frequently serve as advisory groups to higher management. They are open to all employees of the organization. Each group usually has a structure with leaders, periodic meetings, and goals.[69]

The following Diversity Competency feature reports on the use of affinity groups to prevent, reduce, and resolve diversity-related issues at Johnson & Johnson.[70] This firm is widely recognized for its best practices with employees. J&J is a comprehensive and broadly based manufacturer of health-care products, as well as provider of related services for the consumer, pharmaceutical, and medical devices and diagnostics markets. J&J has 250 operating companies and employs approximately 121,000 individuals in 57 countries.[71]

Diversity Competency

Johnson & Johnson's Affinity Groups

Affinity Groups are voluntary, employee-driven associations within the Johnson & Johnson Family of Companies organized around shared interests or characteristics. These grass-roots groups emerge for individuals to share experiences, provide advice and address unique member concerns. As they have grown, Affinity Groups have become more prominent and involved in initiatives that go beyond simply serving their membership.

Today, Affinity Groups play an integral role in advancing diversity and inclusion throughout the Johnson & Johnson companies. They not only provide valuable insight into market opportunities within the groups they represent, they also serve as a resource for orienting new employees, offering employees a forum for the exchange of ideas and providing personal and professional leadership development opportunities.

To be officially recognized as an Affinity Group, each proposed group must meet a series of criteria. Such requirements include developing a formal group structure by appointing an executive committee and defining the group's purpose and intended activities. Some of these activities include professional development, workplace enhancement, diverse talent recruitment, and community initiatives. Every affinity group must be open to any and all employees of the Johnson & Johnson Family of Companies, regardless of age, gender, race, religion, national origin, physical ability, sexual orientation, thinking style, background and all other attributes that make each person unique.

The scope and role of two of Johnson & Johnson's affinity groups follows:

- *African American Leadership Council (AALC).* The mission of the African American Leadership Council is to take a leadership role in making our companies the employers of choice for African American talent at every level. The organization works to support an environment where African Americans are included, challenged and supported while maximizing their personal potential and value to the Johnson & Johnson Family of Companies.
- *Hispanic Organization for Leadership and Achievement (HOLA).* The Hispanic Organization for Leadership and Achievement is intended to act as a catalyst for ideas to develop the leadership of Hispanics at Johnson & Johnson companies and to contribute to the growth of their businesses. Its vision is to be recognized as an organization that values, optimizes and leverages the internal and external resources of its Hispanic community for the global benefit of the Johnson & Johnson Family of Companies.

For more information on Johnson & Johnson, visit the organization's home page at www.jnj.com.

Norms

Norms *are the rules and patterns of behavior that are accepted and expected by members of a team or whole organization.* They help define the behaviors that members believe to be necessary to help them reach their goals. Over time, every team establishes norms and enforces them on its members.[72] Norms often are more rigidly defined and enforced in informal groups—by peer pressure—than in formally organized teams. Such norms may further or inhibit achievement of organizational goals.

Norms Versus Organizational Rules. Norms differ from organizational rules. Managers may write and distribute formal organizational rules to employees in the form of manuals and memoranda. At times, employees refuse to accept such rules or simply ignore them. In contrast, norms are informal, often unwritten expectations that are enforced by team members. If a member consistently violates these norms, the other members sanction the individual in some way. Sanctions may range from physical abuse to threats to ostracism to positive inducements (rewards) for compliance. Those who consistently adhere to the team's norms typically receive praise, recognition, and acceptance from the other members.

Team members may be only vaguely aware of some of the norms that are operating, but they should be made aware of these norms for at least two reasons. First, awareness increases the potential for individual and team freedom and maturity. Second, norms can positively or negatively influence the effectiveness of individuals, teams, and organizations. For example, team norms of improving quality are likely to reinforce an organization's formal quality standards. Or, team norms toward absenteeism may affect the level of absence behavior by members.[73]

Relation to Goals. Teams often adopt norms to help them attain their goals. Moreover, some organizational development efforts are aimed at helping members evaluate whether their team's norms are consistent with, neutral with respect to, or conflict with organizational goals. For example, a team may claim that one of its goals is to become more efficient. However, the team members' behaviors might be inconsistent with this stated goal; that is, members take long lunch breaks, let products that are not quite up to quality standards pass to customers, ignore some quality control steps in the production process, and the like.

Even if team members are aware of such norms, they may think of them as being necessary in order to achieve their own goals. Members may claim that producing more than the norm will "burn them out" or reduce product or service quality, resulting in lower long-term effectiveness. If a team's goals include minimizing managerial influence and increasing the opportunity for social interaction, its members could perceive norms restricting employee output as desirable.

Enforcing Norms. Teams don't establish norms for every situation. They generally form and enforce norms with respect to behaviors that they believe to be particularly important. Members are most likely to enforce norms under one or more of the following conditions:[74]

- Norms aid in team survival and provide benefits. For instance, a team might develop a norm not to discuss individual salaries with other members in the organization to avoid calling attention to pay inequities.
- Norms simplify or make predictable the behaviors expected of members. When coworkers go out for lunch together, there can be some awkwardness about how to split the bill at the end of the meal. A group may develop a norm that results in some highly predictable way of behaving: split the bill evenly, take turns picking up the tab, or individually pay for what each ordered.
- Norms help avoid embarrassing interpersonal situations. Norms might develop about not discussing romantic involvements in or out of the office (so that differences in moral values don't become too obvious) or about not getting together socially in members' homes (so that differences in taste or income don't become too obvious).

Norms express the central values and goals of the team and clarify what is distinctive about its identity. Employees of the Cavalry advertising agency wear unconventional but stylish clothing. Managers at EDS and J.C. Penney may view their doing so as deviant behavior. However, Jan Deatherage from the advertising agency says, "We think of ourselves as trendsetters. Being fashionably but informally dressed conveys that to our clients and the public."

Conforming to Norms. Conformity may result from the pressure to adhere to norms. The two basic types of conformity are compliance and personal acceptance. Compliance conformity *occurs when a person's behavior reflects the team's desired behavior because of real or imagined pressure*. In fact, some individuals may conform for a variety of reasons, even though they don't personally agree with the norms. They may think that the appearance of a united front is necessary for success in accomplishing team goals. On a more personal level, someone may comply in order to be liked and accepted by others. Meeting this need may apply especially to members of lower status in relation to those of higher status, such as a subordinate and a superior. Finally, someone may comply because the costs of conformity are much less than the costs of nonconformity, which could threaten the personal relationships in the team.

The second type of conformity is based on positive personal support of the norms. In personal acceptance conformity, *the individual's behavior and attitudes are consistent with the team's norms and goals*. This type of conformity is much stronger than compliance conformity because the person truly believes in the goals and norms.[75]

All of the preceding helps explain why some members of highly conforming teams may easily change their behavior (compliance type of conformity), whereas others may oppose changes and find them highly stressful (personal acceptance type of conformity). Without norms and reasonable conformity to them, teams would be chaotic and few tasks could be accomplished. Conversely, excessive and blind conformity may threaten expressions of individualism and a team's ability to change and learn.

Cohesiveness

Cohesiveness *is the strength of the members' desire to remain in a team and their commitment to it.* Cohesiveness is influenced by a variety of factors, especially the degree of compatibility between team goals and individual members' goals—in terms of both task-related goals and relations-oriented goals. Members who have a strong desire to remain in a team and personally accept its goals often form a highly cohesive team.[76]

This relationship between cohesiveness and conformity isn't a simple one. Low cohesiveness usually is associated with low conformity. However, high cohesiveness doesn't exist only in the presence of high conformity. High-performing teams may have high member commitment and a desire to stick together, while simultaneously respecting and encouraging individual differences. This situation is more likely to develop when cohesiveness arises from trusting relationships and a common commitment to performance goals.[77]

In confronting problems, members of a cohesive team are likely to encourage and support nonconformity. For example, a hot group *usually is small, and its members are turned on by an exciting and challenging goal.* A hot group completely engages its members, capturing their attention to the exclusion of almost everything else. For its members, the characteristics of a hot group are the same: vital, absorbing, full of debate and laughter, and very hard working.[78] Hot groups may arise from the need to deal with major challenges and changes, innovation, complex projects, or crises. For example, the development of the Boeing 777 jetliner spawned several hot groups. The most distinguishing characteristic of any hot group is the total commitment and preoccupation with its task-related goal(s).

Impact on Effectiveness. Team performance and productivity can be affected by cohesiveness. Cohesiveness and productivity can be related, particularly for teams having high performance goals. If the team is successful in reaching those goals, the positive feedback of its successes may heighten member commitment and satisfaction. For example, a winning basketball team is more likely to be cohesive than one with a losing record, everything else being equal. Also, a cohesive basketball team may be more likely to win games. Conversely, low cohesiveness may interfere with a team's ability to win games. The reason is that members aren't as likely to communicate and cooperate to the extent necessary to reach the team's goals. Rudy Tomjanovich, former coach of the NBA Houston Rockets, told his team before the playoffs to remember that "teams win NBA playoffs, individuals don't." High team cohesiveness actually may be associated with low efficiency if team goals conflict with organizational goals. Team members might think that the boss holds them accountable rather than that they hold themselves accountable to achieve results. Therefore, the relationships among cohesiveness, productivity, and performance can't be anticipated or understood unless the team's goals and norms are also known.

Learning Goal

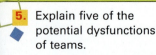

5. Explain five of the potential dysfunctions of teams.

POTENTIAL TEAM DYSFUNCTIONS

If a team's members and its leader are not savvy to the concepts, models, and issues discussed in this and other chapters, a variety of team dysfunctions may come into play, especially in the performing stage of team development.[79] To enrich your understanding

FIGURE 11.4 Potential Team Dysfunctions

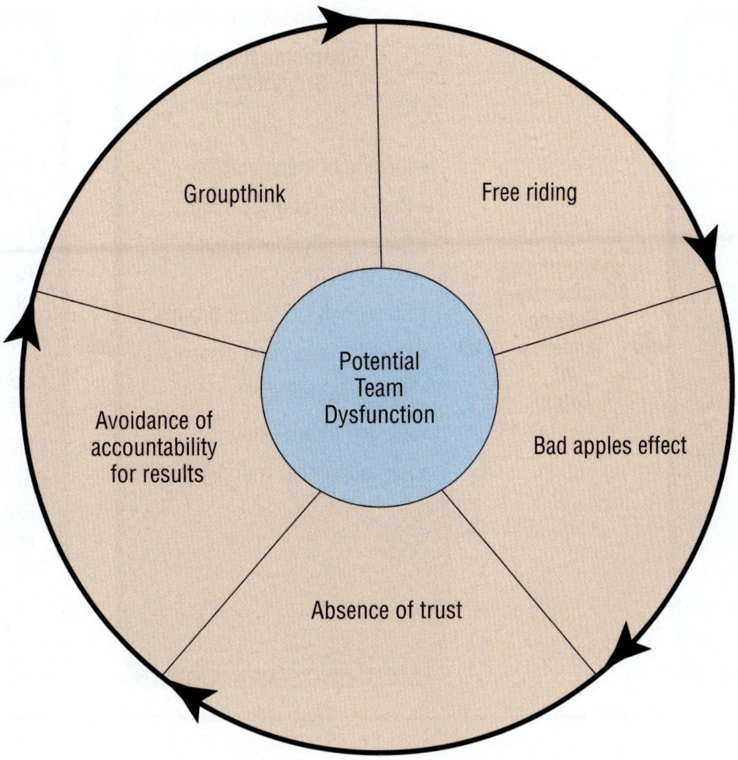

of the potential sources of team ineffectiveness noted in this and previous chapters, we focus here on five potential team dysfunctions: groupthink, free riding, bad apples effect, absence of trust, and avoidance accountability for results. As suggested in Figure 11.4, a poorly performing team is likely to suffer from more than one dysfunction.

Groupthink

Groupthink *is an agreement-at-any-cost mentality that results in ineffective group or team decision making and poor decisions.* Irving L. Janis, who coined the term *groupthink*, focused his research on high-level governmental policy groups faced with difficult problems in a complex and dynamic environment. Of course, team or group decision making is quite common in all types of organizations. When a team is faced with a highly stressful and anxiety-provoking situation, the possibility of groupthink exists in private sector organizations as well as those in the public sector. Figure 11.5 outlines the initial conditions that are likely to lead to groupthink, its characteristics, and the types of defective decision making that result from it.

The characteristics of groupthink include the following:[80]

- An *illusion of invulnerability* is shared by most or all team members, which creates excessive optimism and encourages extreme risk taking. Statements such as "No one can stop us now" or "the other group has a bunch of jerks" may be made by members suffering from an illusion of invulnerability.
- *Collective rationalization* discounts warnings that might lead the members to reconsider their assumptions before committing themselves to major policy decisions. Statements

FIGURE 11.5 The Groupthink Process

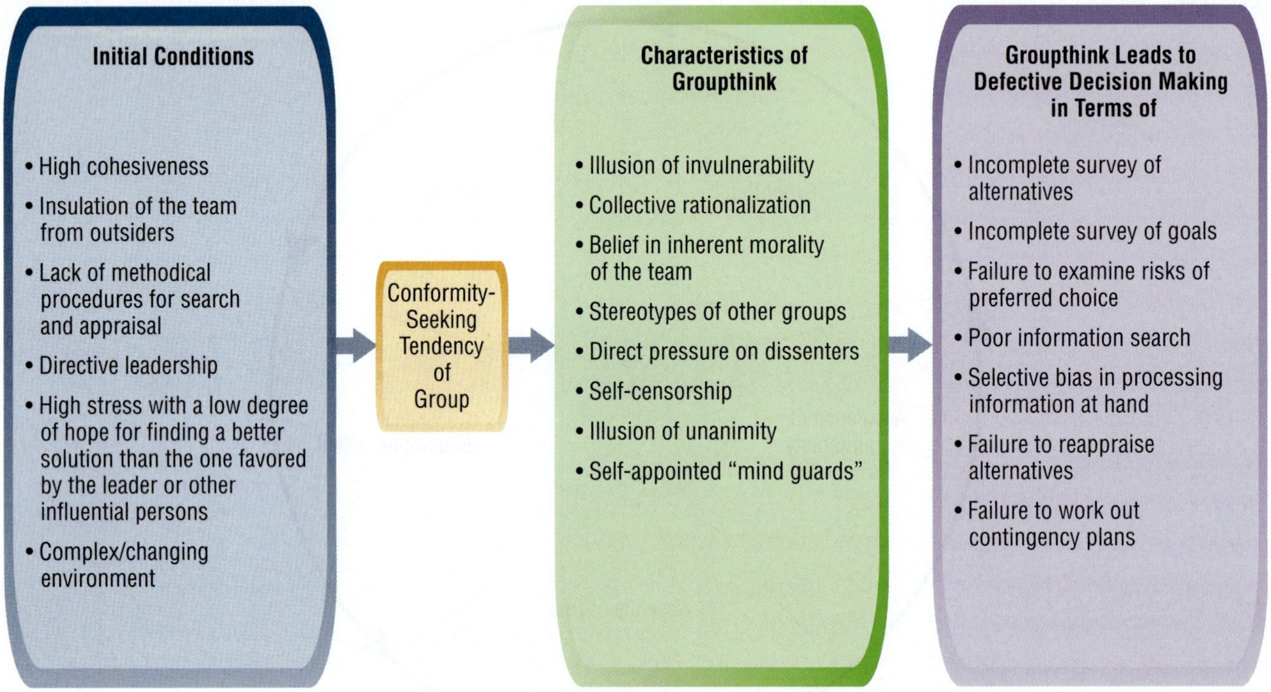

such as "We are confident that only a small segment of auto buyers are willing to buy fuel-efficient autos" were made by U.S. auto executives until recent years.

- An *unquestioned belief* in the team's inherent morality leads members to ignore the ethical or moral consequences of their decisions.
- *Stereotypical views* of rivals and enemies (other groups) picture them as too evil to warrant genuine attempts to negotiate or too weak or stupid to counter whatever attempts are made to defeat their purpose.
- *Direct pressure* is exerted on any member who expresses strong arguments against any of the team's illusions, stereotypes, or commitments, making clear that such dissent is contrary to what is expected of all loyal members. The leader might say, "What's the matter? Aren't you a team member anymore?"
- *Self-censorship* of deviations from any apparent team consensus reflects the inclination of members to minimize the importance of their doubts and not present counterarguments. A member might think, "If everyone feels that way, my feelings must be wrong."
- A *shared illusion of unanimity* results, in part, from self-censorship and is reinforced by the false assumption that silence implies consent.
- The emergence of *self-appointed "mind-guard"* members serves to protect the team from adverse information that might shatter the shared complacency about the effectiveness and morality of their decision. Example: "Those studies don't apply to our issue."

Some research suggests that the strongest triggers leading to groupthink are (1) a strong and directive leader who expresses early endorsement for a particular solution to the problem at hand, and (2) the lack of methods and established processes for making decisions. The directive leader, verbally and/or nonverbally, often discourages diverse perspectives and promotes a favored solution early in the team deliberations. Also, the stress and anxiety being experienced by the team members in considering their complex and unique problem is reduced through premature concurrence seeking. Much research suggests that high levels of anxiety are a possible cause of premature concurrence seeking, which is associated with a desire to conform.[81]

Free Riding

The potential for conflicting team and individual interests is suggested by the free-rider concept. A free rider *is a team member who obtains benefits from membership but does not bear a proportional share of the responsibility for generating the benefit.*[82] *Free riding* is referred to by some as *shirking* or *social loafing*. Students sometimes experience the free rider problem when an instructor assigns a group project for which all of the members receive the same (group) grade. Let's assume that there are five students on the team and that one member makes little or no contribution. This noncontributing member obtains the benefit of the team grade but does not bear a proportional share of the demands in earning the team grade.

When team members fear that one or more other members may free ride, a phenomenon may occur known as the sucker effect, *which refers to one or more individuals in the team deciding to withhold effort in the belief that others (the free riders) are planning to withhold effort.* The sucker role is repulsive to many team members for three reasons. First, the free riding of others violates an equity standard: Members don't want others receiving the same levels of rewards for less input or effort. Second, it violates a standard of social responsibility: Everyone should do their fair share. Third, the free riding of others may violate a standard of reciprocity or exchange.[83] A team is doomed to ineffectiveness with both free riders and other members acting on the basis of the sucker effect.

Bad Apples Effect

The bad apples effect *refers to negative team or group members who withhold effort, express negative feelings and attitudes, and violate important team norms and behaviors.*[84] We already addressed one aspect of the "bad apple" in the form of withholding effort in our discussion of free riding. The common saying "a bad apple spoils the barrel" captures the basic idea of one or more negative individuals on a team having a disproportionate and adverse effect on other members of the team and, as a result, reducing its effectiveness. Bad apples may even be "destroyers" of team processes and effectiveness through their persistent negative behaviors and communications. These individuals have even been characterized as being like a cancer that spreads throughout the team or even the larger workforce.[85]

The types of negative feelings and attitudes expressed by a bad apple are reflected in our discussion of the self-oriented role. You will recall that this role includes such things as expressing hostility, avoiding involvement at one extreme or dominating the team at the other extreme, blocking progress by being stubborn and unreasonably resistant, taking personal credit for team results, and so on. The violation of important team norms and behaviors is seen at the extreme through forms of workplace aggression, as discussed in Chapter 7. Recall our discussion of workplace bullying, which includes a variety of behaviors that typically violate the norms and behaviors endorsed by most team members. These negative behaviors and communications range from condescension to threats of violence or actual attacks. (See Table 7.4 on page 211 for a list of 24 negative acts associated with workplace bullying.)

Absence of Trust

The absence of trust among team members can severely hamper its effectiveness.[86] Members of teams with an absence of trust tend to act in these ways:

- Conceal their weaknesses and mistakes from one another.

- Hesitate to ask for help or provide constructive feedback.
- Hesitate to offer help outside their own areas of responsibility.
- Jump to conclusions about the intentions and aptitudes of others without attempting to clarify them.
- Fail to recognize and tap into one another's skills and experiences.[87]

The important role of trust and how to increase it in teams and organizations was addressed in Chapters 8 and 10.

Avoidance of Accountability for Results

When teams don't commit to a clear set of goals and plan of action, even the most committed individuals may hesitate to confront their peers on counterproductive actions and behaviors. Team members may put their own needs (ego, career, recognition) ahead of the goals of the team when individuals aren't held accountable. If members lose sight of the need to achieve results, the team's effectiveness suffers.[88] For example, Gary Boomer, a CPA and president of Boomer Consulting in Manhattan, Kansas, contends:

> *Often accountants (CPA firms) are focused on effort rather than results. This often comes from the emphasis on chargeable hours. Don't misunderstand; accounting is a business that requires a significant investment of one's time. However, improved standards, processes and procedures can help firms reduce time requirements while improving client satisfaction.*[89]

In the following chapter, *Managing Conflict and Negotiating Effectively*, we discuss approaches for reducing avoidance of conflict, especially those that might be triggered by efforts to hold individuals or teams as a whole accountable.

As we commented at the start of this section, the potential team dysfunctions discussed here are just that—*potential.* They are not inevitable. Even if one or more of them begins to develop, this chapter and others have suggested ways for diagnosing and resolving them.

CHAPTER SUMMARY

1. State the basic features of groups and teams.

We focused on developing the *teams competency*—the ability to develop, support, facilitate, and lead groups to achieve team and organizational goals. Groups and teams are classified in numerous ways. In organizations, a basic classification is by the group's primary purpose, including informal groups and task groups (now commonly called teams). Informal groups develop out of the day-to-day activities, interactions, and sentiments of the members for the purpose of meeting their security or social needs. Informal groups may support, oppose, or be indifferent to formal organizational goals. Effective groups, formal or informal, have similar basic characteristics. We reviewed the core characteristics of effective teams. The degree to which a team lacks in one or more of these characteristics determines whether—and to what extent—it is ineffective. For a team to operate, it must have some degree of empowerment, which is reflected in terms of the teams' degree of potency, meaningfulness, autonomy, and impact. We noted that problem-solving teams are not always appropriate in our discussion of when to use teams. Four factors were identified for understanding when team problem solving is likely to be superior to individual problem solving.

2. Describe the attributes of common types of work-related teams.

Functional teams include members from the same functional department, such as marketing, production, or finance. Problem-solving teams include individuals from a particular area of responsibility who address specific problems such as cost overruns or a decline in quality. Cross-functional teams include individuals from a number of specialties and departments who deal with problems that cut across areas. Self-managed teams include employees who must work together daily to manufacture an entire product (or major identifiable component) or provide an entire service to a set of customers. For maximum effectiveness, self-managed teams need to be empowered; that is, have a strong sense of potency, meaningfulness, autonomy, and impact. A variety of organizational, team, and individual factors must be satisfied for introduction of self-managed teams. Any type of task group could function somewhat or primarily as a virtual team, which collaborates through various information technologies. Global teams refer to members from a variety of countries and are, therefore, often separated significantly by time, distance, culture, and native language.

3. Explain the stages of team development.

The five-stage developmental model focuses on forming, storming, norming, performing, and adjourning. The issues and challenges a team faces change with each stage. Teams do not necessarily develop in the straightforward manner presented in this model, especially when the members possess strong team management and related competencies. Several other models are available to aid in understanding the developmental sequence of teams.

4. Describe the core factors that influence team effectiveness.

Team dynamics and effectiveness are influenced by the interplay of context, leadership, goals, size, member roles, member diversity, norms, and cohesiveness. One type of changing contextual influence on how teams work and network with other teams is that of information technology, especially the rapid developments in collaborative software systems. Other contextual influences are the nature of the organization's reward system and how it fits the basic value orientations of team members, especially in terms of individualism and collectivism. Team leaders may be appointed or emerge informally. They are often in a position to affect a number of the other influences on team effectiveness. Team members need to clearly understand and accept team goals as outcomes desired by each member of the team as a whole. Team size can substantially affect the dynamics among the members and the ability to create a sense of mutual accountability. Teams of about 16 or more members typically break into smaller task groups. Members may assume task-oriented, relationship-oriented, or self-oriented roles. Member diversity often enhances the effectiveness of teams by bringing more divergent insights into the causes of problems and their potential solutions. Of course, if not handled thoughtfully, member diversity may also be a source of conflict and poor communication among team members through the development of fault lines. Norms differ from rules in important ways and can have a positive or negative impact on performance. The pressures to adhere to norms may result in either compliance conformity or personal acceptance conformity. Another factor having an impact on the effectiveness of teams is cohesiveness. Of course, high cohesiveness is usually helpful to work-related teams if it improves their ability to perform tasks and achieve goals.

5. Explain five of the potential dysfunctions of teams.

The potential team dysfunctions are just that—*potential.* They are not inevitable as we indicate in this and previous chapters. Team members and leaders need to be mindful of the potential or actual development of team dysfunctions. They include groupthink, free riding, the bad apples effect, absence of trust, and the avoidance of accountability for results.

KEY TERMS AND CONCEPTS

Affinity groups
Bad apples effect
Cohesiveness
Collective efficacy
Compliance conformity
Context
Cross-functional team
Fault lines

Free rider
Friendship group
Functional team
Global team
Group
Groupthink
Hot group
Informal group
Informal leader
Norms
Personal acceptance conformity
Problem-solving team
Relations-oriented role
Self-managed team
Self-oriented role
Sucker effect
Superordinate goals
Task group
Task-oriented role
Team
Team empowerment
Team goals
Virtual team

DISCUSSION QUESTIONS

1. Visit Regions Financial Corporation's home page at www.regions.com. Click on "About Regions" and then "Corporate Governance." Read the section on "Raising Ethical Issues/Reporting Code Violations/Governance." Would any of the potential team dysfunctions presented in the chapter work against this code? Explain.
2. Think of one work-related team of which you are or have been a member during the past two years. In terms of the types of teams presented in this chapter, how would you classify it? Did it appear to be of more than one type? Explain.
3. For the team you identified in Question 2, how would you evaluate it in terms of the basic characteristics of effective teams?
4. Based on your answers to the questions in Table 11.1, what actions are needed to increase the degree of empowerment for this team? Are those actions feasible?
5. Review the Teams Competency feature on the Toyota assembly team's simple solution. In our discussion of self-managed teams, we presented eight managerial tasks that may be representative of the degree of empowerment in a self-managed team. Which of those managerial tasks are illustrated in the Toyota assembly team feature? Which of those tasks would be difficult to assign to a team in an assembly line situation? Explain.
6. Assume that you had to complete a class project as a member of a virtual team that could meet face to face only twice. What are four special challenges that your virtual team would face in undertaking the project?
7. Think of a new team or group in which you participated during the past two years. Describe and explain the degree to which the development of this team or group matched the five-stage model of team development discussed in this chapter.
8. What were the formal and informal goals of the team or group you identified in Question 7? Were the informal goals consistent and supportive of the formal goals? Explain.
9. Review the Self Competency feature on Brian Catalde's team leadership of NAHB. In what ways do the following key influences play a role for Brian Catalde in diagnosing and influencing this leadership team: context, goals, team size, norms, and member roles?
10. We identified five potential team dysfunctions. What are the likely special challenges in dealing with these potential team dysfunctions for a leader of a virtual team or global virtual team?

EXPERIENTIAL EXERCISE AND CASE

Experiential Exercise: Teams Competency

Team Assessment Inventory[90]

Instructions

Think of a student or work-related team in which you have been a member and that was formed to achieve one or more goals. This team could be associated with a specific course, student organization, or job.

1. Evaluate the *success* of your team on each *item* in this instrument. Use the following scale and assign a value from 1 to 5 to each item. Record the number next to each numbered item. How successful do you think your team was on each of the items?

1 = Not at all successful (well below expectations)
2 = Somewhat successful (though below expectations)
3 = Moderately successful (meets expectations)

4 = Fairly high level of success (exceeds expectations)
5 = Very high level of success (far exceeds expectations)

2. Based on the item assessments and any other related dimensions for each factor, evaluate the *overall success* of your team on each of the seven summary *factors*. Sum the item scores for each factor. Divide the sum (total) by the number of items in that factor.

I. Goals Factor

_____1. Team members understood the goals and scope of the team.

_____2. Team members were committed to the team goals, and took ownership of them.

Overall Goals Factor:
Add the scores for items 1 through 2 and divide by 2 = _______.

II. Team Performance Management Factor

_____3. Individual roles, responsibilities, goals, and performance expectations were specific, challenging, and accepted by team members.

_____4. Team goals and performance expectations were specific, challenging, and accepted by team members.

_____5. The workload of the team was shared more or less equally among team members.

_____6. Everyone on my team did his or her fair share of the work.

_____7. No one on my team depended on other team members to do his or her work.

_____8. Nearly all the members on my team contributed equally to the work.

Overall Team Performance Management Factor:
Add the scores for items 3 through 8 and divide by 6 = _______.

III. Team Basics Factor

_____9. My team had enough members to handle the tasks assigned (i.e., small enough to meet and communicate frequently and easily, and yet not too small for the work required of the team).

_____10. The team as a whole possessed the competency levels required to achieve its goals.

_____11. The team members possessed the complementary competencies required to achieve the team's goals.

Overall Team Basics Factor:
Add the scores for items 9 through 11 and divide by 3 = _______.

IV. Team Processes Factor

_____12. My team was able to solve problems and make decisions.

_____13. My team was able to encourage desirable conflict and discourage undesirable team conflict.

_____14. My team members were able to communicate, listen, and give constructive feedback.

_____15. Team meetings were conducted effectively.

_____16. Members of my team were very willing to share information with other team members about our work.

_____17. Members of my team cooperated to get the work done.

_____18. Being on my team gave me the opportunity to work on a team and to provide support for other team members.

_____19. My team increased my opportunities for positive social interaction.

_____20. Members of my team helped each other when necessary.

Overall Team Processes Factor:
Add the scores for items 12 through 20 and divide by 9 = _______.

V. Team Spirit Factor

_____21. Members of my team had great confidence that the team could perform effectively.

_____22. My team took on the tasks assigned and completed them.

_____23. My team had a lot of team enthusiasm.

_____24. My team had high morale.

_____25. The team developed norms (i.e., expectations concerning team member behavior) that contributed to effective team functioning and performance.

_____26. Team members invested energy intensely on behalf of the team.

Overall Team Spirit Factor:
Add the scores for items 21 through 26 and divide by 6 = _______.

VI. Team Outcomes Factor

_____27. The team attained measurable results (if objective or quantifiable measures were available).

_____28. The product or service delivered by the team met or exceeded the expectations of those receiving it.

_____29. My team carried out its work in such a way as to maintain or enhance its ability to work together on future team tasks.

_____30. Generally, the team experience served to satisfy, rather than frustrate, the personal needs of team members.

Overall Team Outcomes Factor:
Add the scores for items 27 through 30 and divide by 4 = _______.

VII. Team Learning Factor

_____31. We took time to figure out ways to improve team processes.

_____32. Team members often spoke up to test assumptions about issues under discussion.

_____33. Team members got all the information they needed from others.

_____34. Someone always made sure that we stopped to reflect on the team's processes.

_____35. The team as a whole asked for feedback from others as it progressed.

_____36. The team actively reviewed its own progress and performance.

Overall Team Learning Factor:
Add the scores for items 31 through 36 and divide by 6 = ______.

Interpretation

An overall score of 4–5 on a factor suggests considerable success (exceeding expectations and success). An overall score of 3 on a factor suggests a satisfactory level of success and a feeling of just "okay." An overall score of 1–2 on a factor suggests that the team processes needed considerable improvement. You might consider all seven factors as a whole to arrive at a final summary assessment. Insights for the action steps needed are likely to be learned through each factor and the specific items that are in it.

Questions

1. Based on this inventory, what specific changes do you propose to improve the effectiveness of this team?
2. Are any team dysfunctions suggested by your scores on one or more of the seven team factors? Explain. If none are identified, why do you think that was the case for this team?

Case: Teams Competency

Patrice Zagamé's Team Leadership of Novartis Brazil[91]

Novartis Brazil is an operating unit of Novartis, which is a major developer and provider of products to protect and improve health. Patrice Zagamé became the president of Novartis Brazil in 2002. When he arrived, Zagamé found a company with poor financial performance for two consecutive years and losing market share following four consecutive layoff rounds. Employee morale was low. There was a top-down culture with employees showing low accountability for the overall results. Also, the members of the leadership team were not accustomed to challenging each other.

Zagamé contends that "team-based decisions [have] better quality." His leadership style is to openly challenge proposed decisions and encourage the expression of different opinions. When any employee disagrees with his perspective, Zagamé's natural inclination is a willingness to understand. So, he asks the employee to explain his or her opinion. In team meetings, he brings a topic up for discussion and waits for members to express their perspectives before closing the topic. Even when he needs to give an order, Zagamé makes sure to first listen to the employee and then use a tone of voice that is respectful but, at the same time, firm. As a leader, he models an invitation to "speak up."

With the head of human resources, Ney Suva, Zagamé started a number of initiatives to develop a program called *Speak Up*. They started by working with the leadership team members. Zagamé requested that he and Suva prediscuss an issue with each other before bringing a proposal to the executive team meeting, fostering horizontal debate. Zagamé also emphasized that it was the responsibility of each member of the leadership team to model the culture expected in his or her functional area. To enable that behavior, the team focused on the leadership style of each member and identified what that person had to modify to leverage the whole process.

From an organizational perspective, the team also created a program called *Four Cultural Pillars* (innovation, customer focus, teamwork, and fun) based on employee feedback. Those pillars made explicit the expected behaviors. After a massive communication campaign, a yearly award ceremony was held to honor the individuals or teams that role-modeled the pillars.

To support the program, workshops for 12 functional teams were conducted, starting again with the cross-functional leadership team. Each team reviewed the processes it was using, how it related to the other teams, and how established assumptions and norms influenced the way the team members worked together. The findings from one of those off-site workshops follow:

- Some members valued authority and hierarchy, and they considered *Speak Up* as a challenge to those norms.
- Some members assumed that any CEO idea in a meeting was to be implemented. In contrast, Zagamé thought that some meetings were brainstorming sessions and expected ideas to be challenged.
- Some members thought that they were promoted because of their good ideas. Thus, they should continue being the main idea generators. They were challenged by colleagues who had a fundamental belief that team decisions were better. The latter individuals were much more open to their direct reports speaking up, because they considered it a way to improve the decision-making process.
- Finally, the functional leaders found that the manner in which they communicated controversial decisions to their teams had an influence on the members' "speak-up capacity." To model the desired behaviors, when Zagamé makes a decision that contradicts the opinion of one of his direct reports (after discussion), he says, "I hope you can understand me, but please do this." His tone and genuine concern for the person make it easier to accept the decision.

Based on *Speak Up*, the *Four Cultural* Pillars, the workshops, and Zagamé modeling the desired behaviors, the team members and leaders throughout the company changed the way they operated. This resulted in more open and cooperative relationships.

The results can be seen throughout the company. In a recent communication session with all employees, there were 10 spontaneous questions or comments from the audience. One employee openly shared her emotional reaction to the *Four Cultural Pillars* program (from anger to understanding) and expressed that the workload was very high in her area. Zagamé acknowledged that the team still had to achieve progress on that front and publicly recognized her for the courage to speak up.

For two consecutive years, Novartis Brazil has exceeded its financial goals and its market share has stabilized. It was named —two years in a row—as one of the 100 Best Companies to work for in Brazil. The firm is now admired in the marketplace and recognized as one of the successful subsidiaries of Novartis. Also, Novartis Brazil is now able to attract top talent for key positions.

For more information on Novartis, visit the organization's home page at ***www.novartis.com.***

Questions

1. What team dysfunctions appeared to exist at Novartis Brazil when Patrice Zagamé arrived as the president?
2. What norms appeared to exist upon Zagamé's arrival and what norms did he work on changing and adding?
3. Why is Zagamé an effective team leader?
4. How was member diversity valued by Patrice Zagamé and Ney Suva, the head of human resources?

1- Team dysfunctions - groupthink - avoidance of accountability for results
- bad apples effect

2- Norms (before) - Top down culture and low accountability.
(after) - open and cooperative culture (through speak up programe)

3- Effective leadership - Relations - oriented member role
- openness to questions and suggestions
- listening ear
- Respective tone.

CHAPTER 12

Managing Conflict and Negotiating Effectively

Learning Goals

When you have finished studying the chapter, you should be able to:

1. Describe the primary levels of conflict in organizations.
2. Explain and use the common interpersonal conflict-handling styles.
3. Discuss and apply the core stages, strategies, and influences in negotiations.
4. State several of the unique aspects of and recommendations for negotiating across cultures.

Learning from Experience

SUE PESCHIN AND AMY GEARING

Sue Peschin is an executive coach in Rockville, Maryland. She is able to use her past experiences to help clients. One issue, in fact, came up repeatedly in her career. She recalls the time her manager at an association in the Washington, D.C., area had a conflict with a manager in New York who was higher up in the organization. As can happen in such situations, each manager asked Peschin to do something different—and they wouldn't let go of their demands, leaving Peschin stuck in the middle.

She decided to lay it all out: Peschin told her D.C. manager what the New York manager wanted. She went back to the New York manager and explained that there was a conflict in what she was being told to do. Peschin told them both they had to work it out and let her know what they decided. She stated: "I can't choose for you." She went back to doing her work while they worked it out. Peschin advises her clients to do as she did: "If two different people are barking in your ear, it's fine to be direct with them about it: 'One manager is telling me this, you're telling me that. I need to know what the priority is here.' You don't want to just sit and stew about it."

But sometimes speaking out isn't so easy. Not long after Amy Gearing began work at a research firm based in Columbia, Maryland, she noticed her manager and her manager's manager did not agree on much. Every time the two managers had a meeting, Gearing's manager would come back to the office upset. And soon enough, the senior manager openly discounted things that Gearing's manager said. So what Gearing said or did was also discounted. The senior manager would undercut both Gearing and her manager in front of other staff members and managers.

Gearing got along and worked closely with her immediate manager. Her manager's superior observed this close working relationship and didn't like it. As a result, she was caught up in the dispute on a personal level. She was eventually laid off—which Gearing looks back on as a lucky event. She got an MBA and landed a job she loves. Gearing reflects: "It was really hard. I knew no matter what work I did, the senior manager would find a way to discount it. My manager being so wonderful was really the only thing that kept me at the job."[1]

LEARNING CONTENT

Conflict and the need to manage it occurs every day in organizations. Conflict *is a process in which one party (person or group) perceives that its interests are being opposed or negatively affected by another party.*[2] This definition implies incompatible concerns among the people involved and includes a variety of conflict issues and events. Conflict management *refers to the diagnostic processes, interpersonal styles, and negotiation strategies that are designed to avoid unnecessary conflict and reduce or resolve excessive conflict.* The ability to understand and correctly diagnose conflict is essential to managing it.

In this chapter, we examine conflict and negotiation from several perspectives. First, we present the core dimensions of conflict and note different attitudes about it. Second, we identify the primary levels of conflict found in organizations. Third, we discuss five interpersonal styles in conflict management and the guidelines under which each style may be appropriate. Fourth, we address the types of negotiation and basic negotiation strategies, and highlight the role of third-party mediation in the negotiation process. Fifth, we discuss some of the complications and recommendations for negotiations across cultures.

Our attitude is that conflict may sometimes be desirable and at other times destructive. In Chapter 7, we reviewed a variety of destructive conflicts that were related to high levels of stress and workplace aggression. Although some types of conflict can be avoided and reduced, other types of conflict have to be properly managed. The balanced approach is sensitive to the consequences of conflict, ranging from negative outcomes (loss of skilled employees, sabotage, low quality of work, stress, and even violence) to positive outcomes (creative alternatives, increased motivation and commitment, high quality of work, and personal satisfaction). In the Learning from Experience feature, Sue Peschin was successful in resolving the conflicting priorities she received from two managers. She surfaced the issue and pressed them to resolve the inconsistent demands they were placing on her. Amy Gearing was not as successful and actually considered being laid off as a lucky event for her. She moved on to obtain an MBA and landed a great job that she loves.

The balanced approach recognizes that conflict occurs in organizations whenever interests collide. Sometimes, employees will think differently, want to act differently, and seek to pursue different goals. When these differences divide individuals, they must be managed constructively.[3] How easily or effectively conflict can be managed depends on various factors, such as how important the issue is to the people involved and whether strong leadership is available to address it. Table 12.1 identifies some of the dimensions that distinguish conflict situations that are difficult to resolve from conflict situations that are easier to resolve.

Table 12.1 **Effects of Various Dimensions of Conflict**

DIMENSION	DIFFICULT TO RESOLVE	EASY TO RESOLVE
• The issue itself	A matter of principle or values	Simply clarifying misperceptions
• Size of the stakes	Large	Small
• Continuity of interaction	Single transaction	Long-term relationship
• Attitudes	Negative toward each other	Neutral to positive toward each other
• Communication competency	Weak, poor listening	Strong, active listening
• Characteristics of participants' "groups"	Disorganized, with weak leadership	Cohesive, with strong leadership
• Involvement of third parties	No neutral third party available	Trusted, prestigious, neutral third party available

Source: Adapted from Lewicki, R. J., Saunders, D. M., and Barry, B. *Negotiation*, 5th ed. Boston: McGraw-Hill/Irwin, 2006.

LEVELS OF CONFLICT

Learning Goal

1. Describe the primary levels of conflict in organizations.

Four primary levels of conflict may be present in organizations: intrapersonal (within an individual), interpersonal (between individuals), intragroup (within a group), and intergroup (between groups). Figure 12.1 suggests that these levels are often cumulative and interrelated. For example, an employee struggling with whether to stay on a certain job may show hostility toward coworkers, thus triggering interpersonal conflicts.

Intrapersonal Conflict

Intrapersonal conflict *occurs within an individual and usually involves some form of goal, cognitive, or affective conflict.* It is triggered when a person's behavior results in outcomes that are mutually exclusive. Inner tensions and frustrations commonly result, as Amy Gearing experienced. Gearing became a victim of the disputes between her manager and his manager. Recall her comment: "It was really hard. I knew no matter what work I did, the senior manager would find a way to discount it. My manager being so wonderful was the only thing that kept me at the job."

A graduating senior may have to decide between jobs that offer different challenges, pay, security, and locations. Trying to make such a decision may create one (or more) of three basic types of intrapersonal goal conflict:

1. *Approach–approach conflict* means that an individual must choose between two or more alternatives, each of which is expected to have a positive outcome (e.g., a choice between two jobs that appear to be equally attractive).
2. *Avoidance–avoidance conflict* means that an individual must choose between two or more alternatives, each of which is expected to have a negative outcome (e.g., relatively low pay or extensive out-of-town traveling).
3. *Approach–avoidance conflict* means that an individual must decide whether to do something that is expected to have both positive and negative outcomes (e.g., accepting an offer of a good job in a bad location).

Many decisions involve the resolution of intrapersonal goal conflict.[4] The intensity of intrapersonal conflict generally increases under one or more of the following

FIGURE 12.1 Primary Levels of Conflict in Organizations

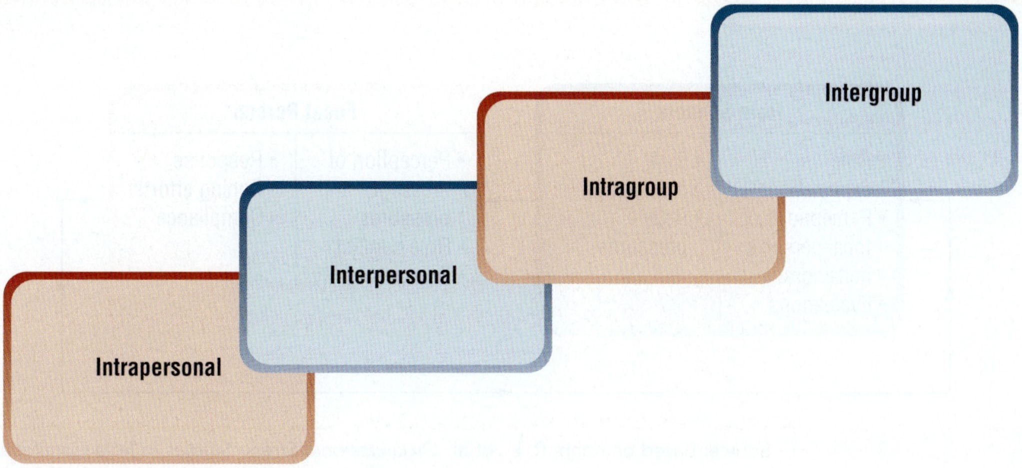

conditions: (1) Several realistic alternative courses of action are available for handling the conflict, (2) the positive and negative consequences of the alternative courses of action are roughly equal, or (3) the source of conflict is important to the individual. Sue Peschin and Amy Gearing seemed to experience these conditions. Peschin was able to resolve these conditions, but that was not the outcome for Gearing while employed. Gearing being laid off triggered the resolution and subsequent decisions to move on to new opportunities.

Severe unresolved intrapersonal conflict within employees, customers, or others may trigger intense interpersonal conflict. As discussed in Chapter 7, much violence and aggression in the workplace has its source in severe intrapersonal conflict.

Interpersonal Conflict

Interpersonal conflict *occurs when two or more individuals perceive that their attitudes, behaviors, or preferred goals are in opposition.* As with intrapersonal conflict, much interpersonal conflict is based on some type of role conflict or role ambiguity.

Role Conflict. A role *is the set of interconnected tasks and behaviors that others expect a person to perform.* Figure 12.2 presents a role episode model, which involves role senders and a focal person. Role senders are individuals who have expectations of how the focal person should behave. A role episode begins before a message is sent because role senders have expectations and perceptions of the focal person's behaviors. These, in turn, influence the actual role messages that the senders transmit. The focal person's perceptions of these messages and pressures may then lead to role conflict. Role conflict *occurs when a focal person responds with behaviors that serve as inputs to the role senders' process.* A role set *is the group of role senders that directly affect the focal person.* A role set might include the employee's manager, other team members, close friends, immediate family members, and important clients or customers.

Four types of role conflict may occur as a result of incompatible messages and pressures from the role set:

- *Intrasender role conflict* may occur when different messages and pressures from a single member of the role set are incompatible, for example, when a manager wants a routine goal achieved more quickly, at a lower cost, and with higher quality.

FIGURE 12.2 Role Episode Model

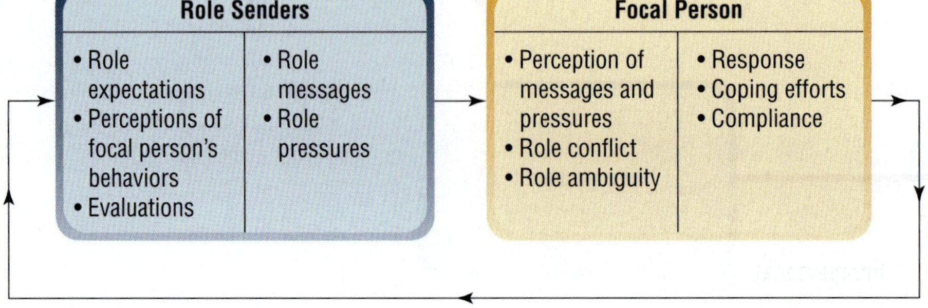

Source: Based on Kahn, R. L., et al. *Organizational Stress: Studies in Role Conflict and Ambiguity.* New York: John Wiley and Sons, 1964, 26.

- *Intersender role conflict* may occur when the messages and pressures from one role sender oppose messages and pressures from one or more other senders.
- *Interrole conflict* may occur when role pressures associated with membership in one group are incompatible with pressures stemming from membership in other groups.
- *Person–role conflict* may occur when role requirements are incompatible with the focal person's own attitudes, values, or views of acceptable behavior. Intrapersonal conflict typically accompanies this type of role conflict.[5]

Role Ambiguity. Role ambiguity *is the uncertainty and lack of clarity surrounding expectations about a single role.* Like role conflict, severe role ambiguity causes stress and triggers subsequent coping behaviors. These coping behaviors often include (1) taking aggressive action (e.g., verbal abuse, theft, and violence) and hostile communication, (2) withdrawing, or (3) attempting joint problem solving. Research findings suggest that high levels of role conflict and role ambiguity have numerous dramatic effects, including stress reactions, aggression, hostility, and withdrawal behaviors (turnover and absenteeism).[6] Stress is a common reaction to severe role conflict and role ambiguity (see Chapter 7). However, effective managers and professionals possess the ability to cope with the many ambiguities inherent in their roles.

Intragroup Conflict

Intragroup conflict *refers to disputes among some or all of a group's members, which often affect a group's dynamics and effectiveness.* For example, family-run businesses—like the Robert Mondavi Corporation, whose principal business is to produce and market table wines—can be especially prone to intragroup and other types of conflict. Such conflicts typically become more intense when an owner–founder approaches retirement, actually retires, or dies. Only 3 in 10 family-run businesses make it to the second generation, and only 1 in 10 survives into the third generation. The biggest obstacles to succession are the relationships among the family members who own the business and bear responsibility for keeping it alive for another generation. What determines whether a family business soars or nosedives? It depends, in large part, on the respect that family members give each other in the workplace, their willingness to take on roles at work different from those they have at home, and their ability to manage conflict effectively.[7]

Siblings can have the most volatile and complex family relationships—and the issues become magnified in a business. The conflicts are often practical. Can one sibling work for another? Should birth order determine hierarchy? Should siblings give in to the one who whines the most to preserve peace, then work around him or her?

The answers depend on the situation. Ongoing factors often underlie these problems. Although they share parents and many memories, siblings often must come to grips with having different attitudes and preferences because they grew up at different times in a changing family environment. The fact that parents try to interest their children in the family business but give them little assistance in understanding how to work with each other puts the siblings in a double bind: an obligation with no road map.[8] The insights provided in this chapter and throughout this book provide at least a portion of the needed road map.

There are many other types of intragroup conflicts in organizations as we have discussed in previous chapters, especially in the previous chapter on developing and leading teams.

Intergroup Conflict

Intergroup conflict *refers to opposition, disagreements, and disputes between groups or teams.* At times, intergroup conflict is intense, drawn out, and costly to those involved. Under high levels of competition and conflict, the groups develop attitudes toward each other that are characterized by distrust, rigidity, a focus only on self-interest, failure to listen, and the like.

Intergroup conflict within organizations can occur horizontally across teams, departments, or divisions, and vertically between different levels of the organization, such as between top management and first-level employees. At Ford, American Airlines, and other companies, this type of vertical conflict is clearly seen in union–management disputes through collective bargaining. Horizontal conflicts often occur between manufacturing and marketing or internal auditors and the other business functions.

Let's consider four of the various sources of intergroup conflict:[9]

- *Perceived goal incompatibility.* Goal incompatibility is probably the greatest source of intergroup conflict. The potential conflicts between marketing and manufacturing are significant in many organizations because some of the goals for these two functions may be at odds. For example, at Jostin's—a provider of class rings, yearbooks, and the like—one of the top marketing goals that will help maximize sales (for which bonuses and commissions are received) is to satisfy the unique requests of customers. Manufacturing has the priority goal of long lead times to maximize efficiency. Accordingly, marketing may state: "Our customers demand variety." Manufacturing may counter: "All of the orders for pictures and rings don't arrive until late April or early May. We cannot meet the demand for these orders by late May. We need longer lead times to maximize efficiency."
- *Perceived differentiation.* The greater the number of ways in which groups see themselves as different from each other (e.g., the Millennial generation versus generation Y), the greater the potential for conflicts between them. These differences may actually be sources of strength, such as the specialized expertise and insights that those from different functions and backgrounds contribute to achieve the organization's goals. Unfortunately, these differences too often serve as the base for stimulating distrust and conflicts between the groups or teams.
- *Task interdependency.* Task interdependency *refers to the interrelationships required between two or more groups in achieving their goals.* For example, marketing needs manufacturing to produce the required products on a timely and cost-effective basis. Manufacturing needs marketing to generate sales of those products that it is able to produce. In general, as task interdependency increases, the potential for conflict between the groups increases. Of course, task interdependency also occurs among organizations, such as between General Motors and its suppliers.
- *Perceived limited resources.* Limited resources create the condition for groups competing and engaging in conflict over the available resources. At 7-Eleven, the opening of 500 7-Eleven stores in Beijing, China, before the start of the Olympic games meant delaying the needed renovation of many older 7-Eleven stores in the United States. Organizations have limited money, physical facilities, and human resources to allocate among different groups. The groups may think they need more of the resources than are available to meet the goals for which they will be held accountable.

The following Teams Competency feature reports on IBM's cross-team workouts to manage conflicts between teams and groups.[10] The International Business Machines Corporation (IBM), with headquarters in Armonk, New York, is one of the world's major providers of computer products and services. IBM's service arm accounts for more than half of its sales. IBM has approximately 355,000 employees worldwide.[11]

Teams Competency

IBM's Cross-Team Workouts

A few years ago, IBM's sales and delivery organization became increasingly complex as the company brought together previously independent divisions and reorganized itself to provide customers with full solutions of bundled products and services. Senior executives soon recognized that managers in different units were not dealing with conflicts. The relationships among them were strained because they failed to consult and coordinate around cross-unit issues. This led to the creation of a forum called the Market Growth Workshop. This forum was designed to send a message throughout the company that getting cross-unit conflict resolved was critical to meeting customer needs and, in turn, growing market share. Monthly conference calls brought together managers, salespeople, and frontline product specialists from across the company. They discussed and resolved cross-unit conflicts that were hindering important sales—for example, the difficulty salespeople faced in getting needed technical resources from overstretched product groups.

The Market Growth Workshop evolved into a more structured approach to managing escalated conflict known as Cross-Team Workouts. Designed to make conflict resolution more transparent, the workouts are weekly meetings in person and via conference calls of people across the organization who work together on sales and delivery issues for specific accounts. The sessions provide a public forum for resolving conflicts over account strategies, solution configurations, pricing, and delivery. Those issues that cannot be resolved at the local level are escalated to regional workout sessions attended by managers from product groups, services, sales, and finance. Attendees then communicate and explain the resolutions to their reports.

Issues that cannot be resolved at the regional level are escalated to an even higher level workout session attended by cross-unit executives from a larger geographic region, such as the Americas or Asia Pacific. The session is chaired by the general manager of the region presenting the issue. The most complex and strategic issues reach this global forum. Attendance at these sessions overlaps—the managers who chair one level of a cross-team workout session attend the session at the next higher level. This overlap allows them to observe the decision-making process at the higher level, which further enhances the transparency of the process among different levels of the company.

IBM has further formalized the process for the direct resolution of conflicts between services and product sales on large accounts by designating a managing director in sales and a global relationship partner in IBM global services as the ultimate point of resolution for escalated conflicts. By explicitly making the resolution of complex conflicts part of the job descriptions for both managing director and global relationship partner—and by making that clear to others in the organization—IBM has reduced ambiguity, increased transparency, and increased the efficiency with which conflicts are resolved.

For more information on IBM, visit the organization's home page at www.IBM.com.

INTERPERSONAL CONFLICT-HANDLING STYLES

Learning Goal

2. Explain and use the common interpersonal conflict-handling styles.

Individuals handle interpersonal conflict in various ways.[12] Figure 12.3 presents a model for understanding and comparing five interpersonal conflict-handling styles. The styles are identified by their locations on two dimensions: *concern for self* and *concern for others*. The desire to satisfy your own concerns depends on the extent to which you are *assertive* or *unassertive* in pursuing personal goals. Your desire to satisfy the concerns of others depends on the extent to which you are *cooperative* or *uncooperative*. The five interpersonal conflict-handling styles thus represent different

FIGURE 12.3 Interpersonal Conflict-Handling Styles

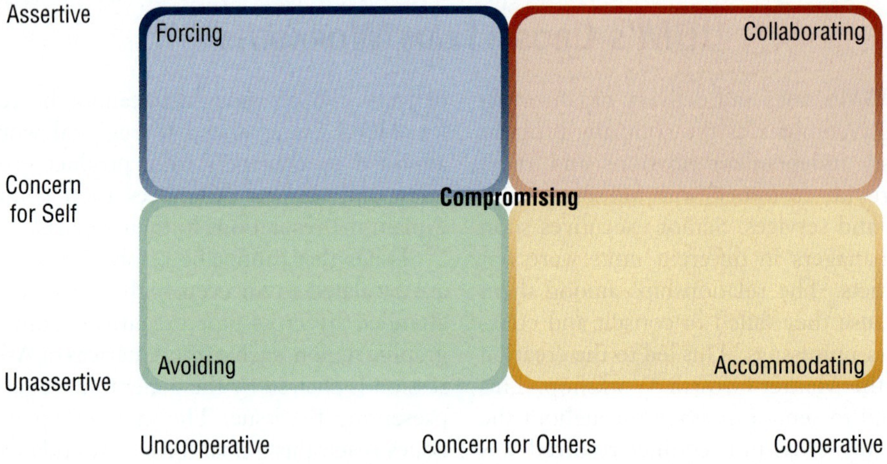

combinations of assertiveness and cooperativeness. Although you may have a natural tendency toward one or two of the styles, you may use all of them as the situation and people involved change. For example, the style you use in working through a conflict with a good friend may be quite different from the style you use with a stranger after a minor auto accident. The experiential exercise at the end of this chapter contains a questionnaire on page 384 that you can use to assess your own styles for handling conflict. We suggest that you complete this questionnaire now.

LEADER INSIGHT

You have to be willing to temporarily upset a lot of people in order to save a company. You have to withstand a lot of conflict, histrionics, screaming at meetings, and toughness on all sides.
Debra Cafaro, CEO, Ventas, Inc.

Avoiding Style

The avoiding style *refers to unassertive and uncooperative behaviors*. A person uses this style to stay away from conflict, ignore disagreements, or remain neutral. The avoidance approach reflects an aversion to tension and frustration and may involve a decision to let a conflict work itself out. Because ignoring important issues often frustrates others, the consistent use of the avoidance style usually results in unfavorable evaluations by others. The following statements illustrate the avoiding style:

- If there are rules that apply, I cite them. If there aren't, I leave the other person free to make her own decision.
- I usually don't take positions that will create controversy.
- I shy away from topics that are sources of disputes with my friends.
- That's okay. It wasn't important anyway. Let's leave well enough alone.

Individual Guidelines. When unresolved conflict gets in the way of accomplishing goals, the avoiding style will lead to negative results for the organization. This style may be desirable under some situations, such as when (1) the issue is minor or only of passing importance and thus not worth the individual's time or energy to confront the conflict, (2) the individual doesn't have enough information to deal effectively with the conflict at that time, (3) the individual's power is so low relative to the other person's that there's little chance of causing change (e.g., disagreement with a new strategy approved by top management), and (4) others can resolve the conflict more effectively.

Forcing Style

The forcing style *refers to assertive and uncooperative behaviors and represents a win–lose approach to interpersonal conflict*. Those who use the forcing approach try to achieve their own goals without concern for others. This style relies on coercive power, which we explained in Chapter 9. It may help a person achieve individual goals, but, like avoidance, forcing tends to result in unfavorable evaluations by others. The following statements illustrate the forcing style:

- I like to put it plainly: Like it or not, what I say goes.
- I convince the other person of the logic and benefits of my position.
- I insist that my position be accepted during a disagreement.
- I usually hold onto my solution to a problem after the controversy starts.

Those who use forcing style try to achieve their own goals without concern for others, sometimes threatening demotion, dismissal, and other punishments.

Forcing-prone individuals assume that conflict resolution means that one person must win and the other must lose. When dealing with conflict, forcing-style managers may threaten or actually use demotion, dismissal, negative performance evaluations, or other punishments to gain compliance. When conflict occurs between peers, employees using the forcing style might try to get their way by appealing to their manager. This approach represents an attempt to use the manager to force the decision on the opposing individual.

Individual Guidelines. Overreliance on forcing by a manager lessens employees' work motivation because their interests haven't been considered. Relevant information and other possible alternatives usually are ignored. In some situations the forcing style may be necessary, such as when (1) emergencies require quick action, (2) unpopular courses of action must be taken for long-term organizational effectiveness and survival (e.g., cost cutting and dismissal of employees for unsatisfactory performance), and (3) the individuals need to take action for self-protection and to stop others from taking advantage of them.

At times, personal decisions can escalate to the point at which each or one of the party's—employer versus employee—uses the forcing style. When the conflict is escalated and unresolved, one of the parties may even appeal to the legal system to force the preferred solution on the other party through court-mandated orders. The following incident demonstrates the need for employers to use consistent and authentic reasons for adverse employment decisions, such as dismissing an employee, who, in this case, was a manager.[13] Generally, this will reduce the likelihood of employees resorting to the court system to attempt to address and resolve their conflicts.

Darrell L. Burrell, an African-American male, began his employment with the Dr Pepper/Seven Up Bottling Group LP (Dr Pepper) as corporate purchasing manager. Burrell initially worked for Penny Soriano, Dr Pepper's vice president of purchasing. When Soriano resigned, she recommended that Burrell replace her. Burrell sought the position and temporarily filled the job while Dr Pepper looked for a replacement. Ultimately, Dr Pepper sought a replacement from outside the company. Dr Pepper hired Ted Koester, a white male, to fill the vacant position. Koester did not have purchasing experience.

Burrell and Koester clashed from the outset. During their first telephone conversation, Burrell became concerned about Koester's qualifications when Koester allegedly admitted that he lacked purchasing experience and asked Burrell to teach him purchasing. For his part, Koester alleged that Burrell engaged in various insubordinate acts. The conflict accelerated when Koester gave Burrell a negative performance review. When Burrell delivered a written response to Koester's evaluation, Dr Pepper terminated Burrell's employment. After receiving a right-to-sue letter from the Equal Employment Opportunity Commission (EEOC), Burrell filed suit in U.S. district court alleging unlawful discrimination for refusal to promote, unlawful discrimination for termination based on race, and unlawful retaliation for termination based on previous complaints of race discrimination.

The district court ruled in favor of Dr Pepper's summary judgment for dismissal. After appeal by Burrell to the 5th U.S. Circuit Court of Appeals, the court ruled that Dr Pepper put forth a legitimate nondiscriminatory claim for Burrell's termination: his on-the-job insubordination. Ironically, this court also remanded Burrell's failure-to-promote discrimination claim for trial. Why? To the EEOC and the district court, Dr Pepper asserted that it hired Koester for his purchasing experience, but he had none. In the circuit court of appeal, Dr Pepper changed the rationale for hiring Koester, namely, his experience in the bottling industry. As of this writing, it is not known if Burrell will elect to go to trial over the discrimination claim.

Accommodating Style

The accommodating style *refers to cooperative and unassertive behaviors*. Accommodation may represent an unselfish act, a long-term strategy to encourage cooperation by others, or just complying with the wishes of others. Individuals using the accommodating style are typically evaluated favorably by others, but they may also be perceived as weak and submissive. The following statements illustrate the accommodating style:

- Conflict is best managed through the suspension of my personal goals in order to maintain good relationships with others.
- If it makes other people happy, I'm all for it.
- I like to smooth over disagreements by making them appear less important.
- I ease conflict by suggesting that our differences are trivial and then show goodwill by blending my ideas into those of the other person.

Individual Guidelines. When using the accommodating style, an individual may act as though the conflict will go away in time and appeal for cooperation. The person will try to reduce tensions and stress by providing support. This style shows concern about the emotional aspects of conflict but little interest in working on its substantive issues. The accommodating style simply results in the individual covering up or glossing over personal feelings. It is generally ineffective if used consistently. The accommodating style may be effective in the short run when (1) the individual is in a potentially explosive emotional conflict situation, and smoothing is used to defuse it; (2) maintaining harmony and avoiding disruption are especially important in the short run; and (3) the conflicts are based primarily on the personalities of the individuals and cannot be easily resolved.

Collaborating Style

The collaborating style *refers to strong cooperative and assertive behaviors*. It is the win–win approach to interpersonal conflict handling. The person using collaboration desires to maximize joint results. An individual who uses this style tends to (1) see conflict as natural, helpful, and leading to a more creative solution if handled properly; (2) exhibit trust in and candor with others; and (3) recognize that when conflict is resolved to the satisfaction of all, commitment to the solution is likely. An individual who uses the collaborating style is often seen as dynamic and evaluated favorably by others. The following statements illustrate the collaborating style:

- I first try to overcome any distrust that might exist between us. Then I try to get at the feelings that we mutually have about the topics. I stress that nothing we decide is cast in stone and suggest that we find a position for which we can do a trial run.
- I tell the others my ideas, actively seek out their ideas, and search for a mutually beneficial solution.
- I like to suggest new solutions and build on a variety of viewpoints that may have been expressed.
- I try to dig into an issue to find a solution good for all of us.

Individual Guidelines. With this style, conflict is open and evaluated by all concerned. Sharing, examining, and assessing the reasons for the conflict should lead to development of an alternative that effectively resolves it and is acceptable to everyone involved. Collaboration is most practical when (1) a high level of cooperation is needed to justify expending the extra time and energy needed to make working through the conflict worthwhile; (2) sufficient parity in power exists among individuals so that they feel free to interact candidly, regardless of their formal status; (3) the potential exists for mutual benefits, especially over the long run, for resolving the dispute through a win–win process; and (4) sufficient organizational support is given for investing the necessary time and energy in resolving disputes in this manner. The norms, rewards, and punishments of the organization—especially those set by top management—provide the framework for encouraging or discouraging collaboration.

> **LEADER INSIGHT**
>
> The best conflict management executives lead by example. They are candid and encourage candor in their interactions with others, stepping up and calling out dysfunctional behavior when they see it. They really listen to what others have to say: don't resort to passive-aggressive or bullying tactics to get their way, and give and receive feedback in a healthy, depersonalized way.
>
> **Howard Guttman, Principal, Guttman Development Strategies, and author, *When Goliaths Clash: Managing Executive Conflict to Build a More Dynamic Organization***

Compromising Style

The compromising style *refers to behaviors at an intermediate level of cooperation and assertiveness*. The individual using this style engages in give-and-take concessions. Compromising is commonly used and widely accepted as a means of resolving conflict. The following statements illustrate the compromising style:

- I want to know how and what others feel. When the timing is right, I explain how I feel and try to show them where they are wrong. Of course, it's often necessary to settle on some middle ground.
- After failing to get my way, I usually find it necessary to seek a fair combination of gains and losses for all of us.
- I give in to others if they are willing to meet me halfway.
- As the old saying goes, half a loaf is better than nothing. Let's split the difference.

An individual who compromises with others tends to be evaluated favorably. Various explanations are suggested for the favorable evaluation of the compromising style, including that (1) it is seen primarily as a cooperative "holding back," (2) it reflects a pragmatic way of dealing with conflict, and (3) it helps maintain good relations for the future.

Individual Guidelines. The compromising style shouldn't be used early in the conflict resolution process for several reasons. First, the people involved are likely to compromise on the stated issues rather than on the real issues. The first issues raised in a conflict often aren't the real ones, and premature compromise will prevent full diagnosis or exploration of the real issues. For example, students telling professors that their courses are tough and challenging may simply be trying to negotiate an easier grade. Second, accepting an initial position is easier than searching for alternatives that are more acceptable to everyone involved. Third, compromise is inappropriate to all or part of the situation when it isn't the best decision available. That is, further discussion may reveal a better way of resolving the conflict.

Compared to the collaborating style, the compromising style doesn't maximize mutual satisfaction. Compromise achieves moderate, but only partial, satisfaction for each person. This style is likely to be appropriate when (1) agreeing enables each person to be better off, or at least not worse off than if no agreement were reached; (2) achieving a total win–win agreement simply isn't possible; and (3) conflicting goals or opposing interests block agreement on one person's proposal.

Effectiveness of Styles

Studies conducted on the use of different interpersonal conflict-handling styles indicate that the collaborating style tends to be characteristic of (1) more successful rather than less successful individuals and (2) high-performing rather than medium- and low-performing organizations. People tend to perceive collaboration in terms of the constructive use of conflict. The individual's use of collaboration seems to result in positive feelings by others, as well as favorable evaluations of performance and abilities. In contrast to collaboration, the forcing and avoiding styles often have negative effects. These styles tend to be associated with a less constructive use of conflict, more negative feelings, and unfavorable evaluations of performance and abilities. The effects of the accommodating and compromising styles appear to be mixed. The use of accommodation sometimes results in positive feelings from others. But these individuals do not form favorable evaluations of the performance and abilities of those using the accommodating style. The use of the compromising style generally is followed by positive feelings from others.[14]

The following Self Competency feature reports on the conflict management capabilities of Kathryn G. Correia, the senior vice president for hospital administration of ThedaCare, Inc., which is headquartered in Appleton, Wisconsin.[15] ThedaCare is a community health system in northeast Wisconsin with approximately 5,300 employees. It consists of four hospitals, a home and senior services division, several joint ventures, and related health services and facilities.[16]

Self Competency

Kathryn Correia, Managing Conflicts at ThedaCare

© Comstock Images/Jupiter Images

Kathryn Correia has worked to create a culture at ThedaCare in which employees are encouraged to adopt conflict resolution based on collaboration and compromise.

Kathryn Correia faced several key issues upon being promoted to senior vice president of hospital administration at ThedaCare. She resolved to turn these issues into workable solutions for ThedaCare and looked toward collaborative resolutions. Correia's first issue involved two competing surgeons. One surgeon wanted to be the exclusive provider of bariatric surgeries. This approach was initially rejected by the other surgeon. When she realized neither surgeon would bend, Correia hired a professional mediator and held sessions with the surgeons. In the end, a new strategy was developed in which the surgeons would coexist—one was put in charge of bariatric care; the other took on a new role in another area of the hospital. Both surgeons were pleased with the results. Correia comments: "I could not change the physicians' behaviors or styles, but I could find ways to change my behavior and engage the medical staff as much as possible to find a solution that was in line with the organization's goals."

Correia also led the efforts to resolve conflict between the pharmacy and nursing departments. Nurses were complaining about the pharmacy's process and inefficiency in filling prescriptions. They felt the pharmacists did not understand their hectic schedules. The pharmacists complained that nurses were sending incomplete orders. No process was in place and the question remained, "Whose job is it?" Correia led a weeklong rapid improvement event by forming a group of frontline staff—stakeholders and employees from other areas—and engaging a trained facilitator.

After evaluating the process, they devised a new order and redistribution system by the following week. New responsibilities were given to pharmacy technicians who were redistributed on two hospital floors to make sure orders were complete and filled on time. Nurses making their rounds during the day had easy access to technicians.

Correia states: "Instead of pointing fingers, we found collaboration. This leads to a safe and effective patient experience; our patient flow time has decreased and the nurses and pharmacists have partnered to make their jobs more manageable. The most beneficial thing learned from conflict training is taking a proactive approach to understanding the habit of reframing issues and knowing there are always other options."

Through these and other initiatives, Correia has modeled and fostered the creation of a culture where the employees are encouraged to adopt a conflict resolution approach based on collaboration and, when necessary, compromise.

For more information on ThedaCare, visit the organization's home page at www.thedacare.org.

NEGOTIATION IN CONFLICT MANAGEMENT

Learning Goal

3. Discuss and apply the core stages, strategies, and influences in negotiations.

Negotiation *is a process in which two or more interdependent individuals or groups, who perceive that they have both common and conflicting goals, state and discuss proposals and preferences for specific terms of a possible agreement.* Negotiation often includes a combination of compromise, collaboration, and possibly some forcing on vital issues. A negotiation situation is one in which

- two or more individuals or groups must make decisions about their combined goals and interests,
- the individuals are committed to peaceful means for resolving their disputes, and
- there is no clear or established method or procedure for making the decisions.[17]

Stages of Negotiation

Negotiations can be viewed as a process with a series of distinct stages. Table 12.2 provides a list of a few of the questions that might be presented in each of the four stages of negotiations, as discussed next:

- The first stage is (1) assessing the situation to ensure that it is appropriate for negotiation, (2) preparing to enter into negotiations, and (3) determining that the other party has some reason to negotiate with you. A critical issue to address in this stage is for each party to establish its BATNA. BATNA *refers to the **Best Alternative To a Negotiated Agreement** and refers to the negotiator's absolute bottom line.* If an agreement isn't better than the BATNA, it actually makes the negotiator worse off. To protect negotiators from escalating to irrational commitments during negotiations, they need to identify and assess the alternatives if an agreement is not reached.
- The second stage is establishing and agreeing on the process by which the negotiations will proceed. Matters that require discussion and prior agreement between the parties include the scope of the issues, who will participate, deadlines, and understandings regarding how the negotiators will approach the problem and each other.

Table 12.2 **Sample Questions in Each Stage of Negotiations**

Stage 1: Assessing the Situation
- Are you clear on your interests and priority issues?
- Have you defined the criteria by which you will determine whether or not you will enter into an agreement?
- Have you defined your BATNA (Best Alternative To a Negotiated Agreement)? That is, do you know what you will do if there is no agreement?
- Have you considered the interests and constraints of the other party?

Stage 2: Establishing the Process
- Have you agreed on the scope of the issues?
- Do you understand how agreements will be approved or ratified?
- Are you in agreement on time frames and deadlines?
- Have you discussed what information may be required and how it will be acquired and managed (e.g., confidentiality)?

Stage 3: Negotiating the Agreement
- Are you entering negotiations committed to meet your interests—not your positions?
- Are you identifying and addressing the interests of the other party?
- Are you jointly identifying mutual interests and expanding the "pie"?
- Are you building a relationship that will support the agreement?

Stage 4: Implementing the Agreement
- Are all of the agreements clearly understood and perhaps spelled out in writing?
- Does the agreement spell out the responsibilities of the parties in the implementation of the agreement?
- Is there a provision for assessing the implementation of the agreement and improving it as necessary?
- Are there procedures for jointly resolving disputes under the agreement in a timely manner?

Source: Adapted from Cormick, G. W. *Negotiation Skills for Board Professionals.* Mill Creek, WA: CSE Group, 2005; Dietmeyer, B. *Strategic Negotiation: A Breakthrough Four-Step Process for Effective Business Negotiation.* Chicago: Dearborn Trade, 2004.

- The third stage is negotiating the substantive agreement. In this stage, the negotiators will make a number of strategic decisions regarding tactics and acceptable outcomes.
- The fourth stage is implementing the agreement. It is important that the agreement reached will be and can be implemented. Experienced negotiators will consider what understandings need to be reached to ensure timely and effective implementation.[18]

Distributive Negotiations Strategy

Distributive negotiations *involve traditional win–lose situations in which one party's gain is the other party's loss.* This strategy often occurs over economic issues, such as the negotiating by Ford (and other U.S. automakers) with the United Auto Workers over the costs and support of health benefits and retirement plans. Communications are guarded, and expressions of trust are limited. Threats, distorted statements, and demands are common. In short, the parties are engaged in intense, emotion-laden conflict. The forcing and compromise conflict-handling styles characterize distributive negotiations.[19]

Some individuals and groups believe in distributive (win–lose) negotiations. Negotiators have to be prepared to counter them. Awareness and understanding probably are the most important means for dealing with win–lose negotiation ploys by the other party. Four of the most common win–lose strategies that you might face as a negotiator are the following:[20]

- *I want it all.* By making an extreme offer and then granting concessions grudgingly, if at all, the other party hopes to wear down your resolve. You will know that you have met such a negotiator when you encounter the following tactics: (1) The other party's first offer is extreme; (2) minor concessions are made grudgingly; (3) you are pressured to make significant concessions; and (4) the other party refuses to reciprocate.
- *Time warp.* Time can be used as a powerful weapon by the win–lose negotiator. When any of the following techniques are used, you should refuse to be forced into an unfavorable position: (1) The offer is valid only for a limited time; (2) you are pressured to accept arbitrary deadlines; (3) the other party stalls or delays the progress of the negotiation; and (4) the other party increases pressure on you to settle quickly.
- *Good cop, bad cop.* Negotiators using this strategy hope to sway you to their side by alternating sympathetic with threatening behavior. You should be on your guard when you are confronted with the following tactics: (1) The other party becomes irrational or abusive; (2) the other party walks out of a negotiation; and (3) irrational behavior is followed by reasonable, sympathetic behavior.
- *Ultimatums.* This strategy is designed to try to force you to submit to the will of the other party. You should be wary when the other party tries any of the following: (1) Presents you with a take-it-or-leave-it offer; (2) the other party overtly tries to force you to accept its demands; (3) the other party is unwilling to make concessions; and (4) you are expected to make all of the concessions.

Distributive negotiations between management and labor are most visible when labor unions go on strike. Goodyear and the United Steelworkers, which represents 12,000 employees at 12 U.S. plants, attempted to negotiate a new labor agreement for many months. Although the previous contract expired in July 2006, the parties continued to negotiate without a contract until October 5, 2006, the day the members of the United Steelworkers went on strike. The strike lasted almost 12 weeks with a negotiated agreement being reached in late December 2006. The striking employees returned to work on January 2, 2007.[21]

The parties were at extreme odds over job security, plant closings, retiree health care, and related issues. The strike was associated with bitterness and hostility. Wayne

Ranick, a union spokesperson, commented: "In 2003, we accepted cuts in wages, pension and health care benefits, and we allowed them to close one facility. Now they want more plant closures. By hiring replacement workers (during the strike), Goodyear is making coming to an agreement much more difficult." In contrast, Ed Markey, a Goodyear spokesperson, stated: "We won't accept a contract that puts us at a cost or competitive disadvantage."[22] Goodyear insisted the proposed cuts and savings were necessary to remain competitive.

Distributive negotiations dominated the process with Goodyear "winning" on most of their demands and compromising on some issues. The agreement will help save Goodyear $70 million in 2007, $240 million in 2008, and $300 million in 2009. In addition, the Tyler, Texas, plant will be shut down in 2008 rather than in 2007, as initially proposed by Goodyear.[23] The union was in a weak bargaining power position because of the threat and ability of Goodyear to relocate much tire production abroad.

Integrative Negotiations Strategy

Integrative negotiations *involve joint problem solving to achieve results that benefit both parties*. With this strategy, the parties identify mutual problems, identify and assess alternatives, openly express preferences, and jointly reach a mutually acceptable solution. Rarely perceived as equally acceptable, the solution is simply advantageous to both sides.[24] Although most of the negotiations between Goodyear and the United Steelworkers union were distributive in terms of cost savings demands, the parties did employ some integrative negotiations as well. For example, incentive systems were designed to improve productivity that also enabled additional earnings by union members. Second, Goodyear agreed to invest $500 million over three years to modernize its North American plants rather than relocate this production capacity to other countries. This modernization, while reducing per-unit production costs, improves job security for union workers by keeping operations in North America. Third, Goodyear agreed to profit sharing of up to $25 million in 2009 and up to $30 million in 2010. Thus, as company profits improve, there is an opportunity for higher compensation to union employees—another win–win outcome.[25]

Principled Negotiations. A variety of principles and actions are recommended for successful integrative (win–win) negotiations. Principled negotiations *refer to the prescribed ways in which the parties should negotiate to resolve disputes*. It suggests that *how* the negotiation is accomplished may be as important as *what* they are negotiating about to achieve mutually satisfactory outcomes. Many individuals, especially when employing distributive negotiations, focus their attention on the *what*, thereby neglecting the *how* of negotiations. The framework and prescriptions of principled negotiations evolved out of work being done since 1979 by associates of the Harvard Negotiation Project.[26]

Principled negotiations advocate the following four principles to increase the likelihood of successful integrative negotiations:[27]

- *Separate the people from the problem*. The first principle in reaching a mutually agreeable solution is to disentangle the substantive issues of the negotiation from the interpersonal relationship issues between the parties and deal with each set of issues separately. Negotiators should see themselves as working side by side, dealing with the substantive issues or problems, instead of attacking each other.
- *Focus on interests, not positions*. People's egos tend to become identified with their negotiating positions. Furthermore, focusing only on stated positions often obscures what the participants really need or want. Rather than focusing only on the positions taken by each negotiator, a much more effective strategy is to focus on the underlying human needs and interests that had caused them to adopt those positions.
- *Invent options for mutual gains*. Designing optimal solutions under pressure in the presence of an adversary tends to narrow people's thinking. Searching for the one

right solution inhibits creativity, particularly when the stakes are high. These blinders can be removed by establishing a forum in which various possibilities are generated before decisions are made about which action to take.

- *Insist on using objective criteria.* The parties should discuss the conditions of the negotiation in terms of one or more standards, such as market value, expert opinion, custom, or law. This principle steers the focus away from what the parties are willing or unwilling to do. By using objective criteria, neither party has to give in to the other, and both parties may defer to a fair solution.

Ron Shapiro is coauthor of *The Power of Nice: How to Negotiate So Everyone Wins—Especially You* and CEO of the Shapiro Negotiation Institute. He has negotiated numerous agreements, ranging from real estate acquisitions to corporate mergers, from major financial packages to home loans, from settling symphony orchestra and umpire strikes to completing contracts for professional athletes. Consistent with integrative and principled negotiations, he suggests:

> *Don't negotiate as if you'll never again do business with the person across the table. . . . Forget about conquerors and victims. Negotiation is not war. It isn't about getting the other side to wave a flag and surrender. Don't think hurt. Think help. Don't demand. Listen. The best way to get most of what you want is to help the other side get some of what it wants. . . . On the surface, negotiation may seem to be about winning and losing. After all, to the victor belong the spoils. Can it be true that only the hardest, toughest and meanest negotiators will be the most successful? . . . These types of negotiators will undoubtedly achieve success in deals, but most will fall short in the long run. I believe that you can be "nice" and still get what you are after. In fact, you often get better results, achieve more of your goals, and build long-term relationships with even greater returns. Win–win simply means the best way to get what you want is to help them get what they want.*[28]

Table 12.3 provides a concise summary of the differences between integrative negotiations and distributive negotiations in terms of five core characteristics.

Common Influences on Negotiation Strategies

In this section, we highlight the following four common influences on the distributive and integrative negotiation strategies: attitudinal structuring, intraorganizational negotiations, negotiator's dilemma, and mediation.

Attitudinal Structuring. Attitudinal structuring *is the process by which the parties seek to establish feelings and relationships.* Throughout any negotiations, the parties reveal certain attitudes (e.g., hostility or friendliness and competitiveness or cooperativeness) that influence their communications. Recall our previous quote from Ron Shapiro related to

Table 12.3 **Integrative versus Distributive Negotiations**

CHARACTERISTIC	INTEGRATIVE NEGOTIATIONS	DISTRIBUTIVE NEGOTIATIONS
• Outcome sought	Win–win	Win–lose
• Motivation	Joint gain	Individual gain
• Interests	Congruent	Opposed
• Time horizon emphasis	Long term	Short term
• Issues	Multiple issues	Single or few issues

Source: Adapted from La Piana Associates. The difference between integrative and distributive negotiation. www.lapiana.org (July 2007).

the attitudes that he thinks the parties should hold to establish effective negotiations. Reflect on his statement: "I believe that you can be 'nice' and still get what you are after."

William Ury is a well-known scholar on negotiations and heads the Global Negotiation Project at Harvard. We share a few of his remarks related to attitudinal structuring in negotiations:

> *Deal with the people and their emotions first. Be soft on the people so that you can be hard on the problem. . . . It's important not to react without thinking, but instead to "go to the balcony," a mental place of calm and perspective where you can step back and remember what your interests are. The truth is that we can't have a whisper of a chance of influencing the other side until we are able to influence ourselves. . . . It's important to put yourself in the other side's shoes, understand their interests and how they feel. Negotiation is an exercise in influence. You're trying to influence another person. You can't influence their mind unless you know where their mind is right now. Try to be inventive. Open up to other options besides your position.*[29]

Intraorganizational Negotiations. Groups often negotiate through representatives. For example, representatives of OPEC nations set oil prices for the cartel. However, these representatives first have to obtain agreement from the leaders of their respective nations before they can work out an agreement with each other. Intraorganizational negotiations *involve negotiators building consensus for agreement and resolving intragroup conflict before dealing with the other group's negotiators.*[30] The negotiators of the United Steelworkers, when negotiating with Goodyear, had to negotiate with the local union officials at the 12 Goodyear plants as to the priority issues and their demands as well as the concessions to make to Goodyear. Initially, several of the locals were strongly opposed to some of the terms in the tentative agreement.

Negotiator's Dilemma. Negotiators increasingly realize the importance of cooperatively creating value by means of integrative negotiations. However, they must also acknowledge the fact that both sides may eventually seek gain through the distributive process. The negotiator's dilemma *is a situation in which the tactics of self-gain tend to repel moves to create greater mutual gain.* An optimal solution results when both parties openly discuss the problem, respect each other's substantive and relationship needs, and creatively seek to satisfy each other's interests. However, such behavior doesn't always occur because of the exclusive focus on self-serving outcomes and the extensive use of questionable political and communication tactics.[31]

Win–win negotiators are vulnerable to the tactics of win–lose negotiators. As a result, negotiators often develop an uneasiness about the use of integrative strategies because they expect the other party to use distributive strategies. This mutual suspicion often causes negotiators to leave joint gains on the table. Moreover, after win–win negotiators have been stung in several encounters with experienced win–lose strategists, they soon "learn" to become win–lose strategists. Finally, if both negotiators use distributive strategies, the probability of achieving great mutual benefits is virtually eliminated. The negotiations will likely result in both parties receiving only minimal benefits.

Graphically, the integrative and distributive negotiation strategies may be placed on vertical and horizontal axes, representing the two negotiating parties. Then, a matrix of possible outcomes emerging from the negotiating process can be developed to illustrate the negotiator's dilemma, as shown in Figure 12.4 for person A and person B.

Mediation. At times, the parties engaged in negotiations get stuck and are not able to resolve one or more issues. As you would expect, this situation occurs more frequently with the distributive negotiations strategy than with the integrative negotiations strategy. In this situation, the parties may elect to use some form of alternative dispute resolution. For example, mediation *is a process by which a third party helps two (or more) other parties resolve one or more conflicts.* Most of the actual negotiations occur directly

FIGURE 12.4 Matrix of Negotiated Outcomes

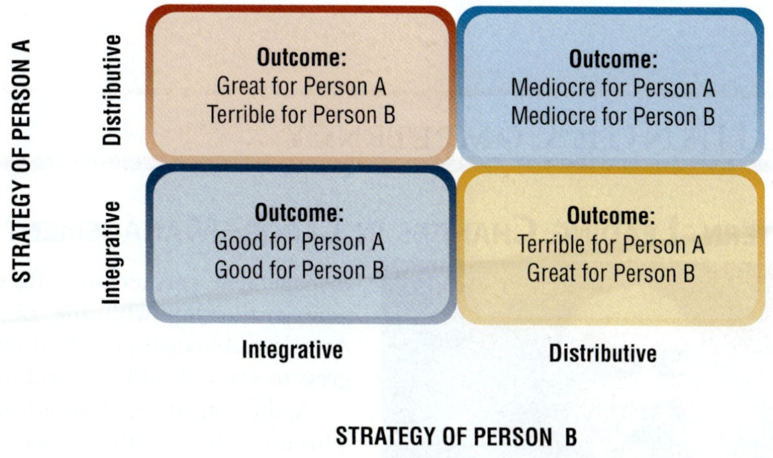

Source: Adapted from Anderson, T. Step into my parlor: A survey of strategies and techniques for effective negotiation. *Business Horizons*, May–June 1992, 75.

between the involved individuals. But, when the parties appear likely to become locked in win–lose conflict, a mediator, acting as a neutral party, may be able to help them resolve their differences.[32] Recall the Self Competency feature on Kathryn Correia, a leader at ThedaCare. She successfully used a professional mediator to resolve the conflict between two competing surgeons.

Mediators need special competencies. They must (1) be able to diagnose the conflict, (2) be skilled at breaking deadlocks and facilitating discussions at the right time, (3) show mutual acceptance, and (4) have the ability to provide emotional support and reassurance. In brief, an effective mediator must instill confidence in and acceptance by the parties in conflict.

Key tasks in the mediator's role include the following:

- *Ensure mutual motivation.* Each party should have incentives for resolving the conflict.
- *Achieve a balance of power.* If the power of the individuals isn't equal, establishing trust and maintaining open lines of communication may be difficult.
- *Coordinate confrontation efforts.* One party's positive moves must be coordinated with the other party's readiness to do likewise. A failure to coordinate positive initiatives and readiness to respond can undermine future efforts to work out differences.
- *Promote openness in dialogue.* The mediator can help establish norms of openness, provide reassurance and support, and decrease the risks associated with openness.
- *Maintain an optimum level of tension.* If the threat and tension are too low, the incentive for change or finding a solution is minimal. However, if the threat and tension are too high, the individuals involved may be unable to process information and envision creative alternatives. They may begin to polarize and take rigid positions.[33]

The following Change Competency feature reports on how Andy Stern, the president of the Service Employees International Union (SEIU), is leading changes in how the union represents the members and negotiates with management.[34] He places considerable emphasis on integrative negotiations through principled negotiations and positive attitudinal structuring. The SEIU is a North American Union with 1.8 million members. Its members come from four sectors: hospital systems, long-term care, property services, and public services. It is headquartered in Washington, D.C.[35]

Change Competency

Andy Stern, Leading Changes in Labor–Management Relations

© John Gress/Reuters/Landov

Andy Stern, president of the Service Employees International Union, wants to remake the labor movement by creating more labor–management partnerships.

As president of SEIU, Andy Stern has become one of the most recognizable and powerful labor leaders in the United States. In 2005, Stern pulled his union out of the AFL-CIO in dramatic fashion at its convention. Since then, he has helped form the rival Change to Win federation, which represents about 6 million workers. Stern says he wants to remake the labor movement by shedding its old adversarial image and creating more labor–management partnerships. Recently, he announced a new partnership with the Business Roundtable and American Association of Retired Persons to push Congress to act on health-care reform.

At the same time, SEIU is feared by many employers. This union has a high success rate at waging aggressive organizing campaigns (e.g., for janitors at the headquarters of Nationwide Insurance, Procter & Gamble, and Eli Lilly). The campaigns often include support from elected officials, clergy, and activists. We share a few of Stern's thoughts on changes being pursued by his union and leadership.

"I think the need for unions is far greater today than almost at any time since the 1930s and '40s. I think American workers want a voice on their job. And the question is: Will unions change to become better partners with employers to respond to what is now a global economy, where more people went to work today in the U.S. in retail than in manufacturing?

"What we know is that most people believe now that their children will be financially worse off than they are. Seven out of 10 Americans are living paycheck to paycheck and do feel like an organization, an association, or even a union would be helpful in changing that situation. At the same time, unions have an image of being old, not effective, in some cases not looking like the new workforce. So we have an image problem. I would say the only way to change your image is to change reality.

"I think unions need to appreciate [that] there are ways in which we add value to employers and there are ways that we make them less competitive. So we need to understand markets, we need to understand their competition, we need to appreciate where we can be helpful, like increasing financing, or leveling the playing field so competition is about entrepreneurial activity, about quality, about efficiency and not about who can pay the least. We want to find a 21st century new model that may look more like a European model, that is less focused on individual grievance, more focused on industry needs. But I think the employers are rather scared and unimaginative—it's too much about cost and bottom lines and not enough about people and human relations.

"Most critics of me come from outside the union. I don't hear our members say that I am too quick to collaborate with management. People don't go to work to have a fight. They go to work to provide a service, to build a community, to take care of their family. I don't hear most people say 'I can't wait to go to work to have a fight with that boss.'

"I'm never satisfied, because I think our union and the labor movement—I'd say even a lot of our employers—are really slow in making the change to a global economy, a very fast-paced 24/7 economy. We don't see our employers as enemies. We don't want to be attached to any single political party. Our attitude now is we need to build successful employers as part of that, you need to be involved and have a voice, and that everyone needs to share in the success of an employer, not just the shareholders and the executives."

Whether one supports unions or the views of Andy Stern, one thing is certain—he is striving to lead a number of fundamental changes, primarily through integrative and principled negotiations. Consistent with principled negotiations, here are Stern's stated views on how labor and management can work together better:

- Relationships are not a matter of chance, they are a matter of choice.
- Approach partnerships by making finding a solution a higher priority than placing blame.
- Learn to disagree without being disagreeable.
- Offer incentives that encourage others to take risks.
- Keep an open mind rather than an open mouth, be willing to change, keep focused on shared goals.

For more information on SEIU, visit the organization's home page at www.seiu.org.

NEGOTIATING ACROSS CULTURES

Learning Goal

4. State several of the unique aspects of and recommendations for negotiating across cultures.

The most obvious aspect of international business negotiations is the effect of different cultures on the process. There are two common perspectives about cross-cultural negotiations:

- Negotiations in one country are totally different from negotiations in any other country. Global negotiations are likely to be completely different from domestic transactions.
- Negotiating globally is essentially the same as negotiating domestically. They're all business transactions.[36]

Both perspectives are inadequate, if not wrong. Cultural differences are critical. However, the core concepts of conflict management and negotiations addressed in previous sections of this chapter are useful and important across cultures as well. In this section, we focus on those aspects of negotiations that are unique in cross-cultural negotiations.

Differences in Negotiators

The issues and complexities relevant to all negotiations are increased—sometimes dramatically—when negotiators are from different cultures.[37] Table 12.4 provides a framework for understanding a person's negotiating style and approach based on 10 dimensions. These dimensions have been used to explain how the orientations of negotiators vary across cultures.

We want to emphasize that there can be substantial differences among negotiators within a culture—at least based on self-assessments of their own negotiating style. For example, Table 12.5 reports on the percentage distributions for respondents from India and Mexico on the 10 dimensions of negotiating style listed in Table 12.4.[38] Although some differences in relative negotiating orientations are evident between respondents in

Table 12.4 Dimensions of Negotiating Style

Dimension		Scale (1–5)	
1. Goal	Contract	1 2 3 4 5	Relationship
2. Attitudes	Win–Lose	1 2 3 4 5	Win–Win
3. Personal style	Informal	1 2 3 4 5	Formal
4. Communications	Direct	1 2 3 4 5	Indirect
5. Time sensitivity	High	1 2 3 4 5	Low
6. Emotionalism	High	1 2 3 4 5	Low
7. Agreement form	Specific	1 2 3 4 5	General
8. Agreement building	Bottom up	1 2 3 4 5	Top down
9. Team organization	One leader	1 2 3 4 5	Consensus
10. Risk taking	High	1 2 3 4 5	Low

Source: Adapted from Salacuse, J. W. Negotiating: The top ten ways that culture can affect your negotiation. *Ivey Business Journal, March/June 2005*, 1–6; Salacuse, J. W. Ten ways that culture affects negotiating style: Some survey results. *Negotiation Journal*, July 1998, 221–240.

India and Mexico, the within-culture differences are very apparent in Table 12.5. For example, 39 percent of the respondents in India expressed a strong contract goal orientation versus 34 percent who expressed a strong relationship orientation. Also, 41 percent expressed a desire for a one-leader team organization versus 39 percent who emphasized a consensus orientation. Within Mexico, there were wide variations along the entire continuum for a number of dimensions. The bottom line is that when negotiating across cultures, you need to come prepared to learn about the cultures and predispositions of the specific negotiators, while also appreciating and being open to their possible predispositions based on their own culture.

Let's consider a few examples of negotiator orientations based on cultural influences from other studies. In one study,[39] 100 percent of the respondents from Japan emphasized win–win in their approach to negotiations. In contrast, only 37 percent of the Spanish negotiators utilized a win–win approach. A negotiator from Germany with a very formal style might insist on addressing individuals by their titles, avoid the use of personal stories and anecdotes, and avoid any mention of private or family life. In contrast, a negotiator from the United States with an informal style might use first names as a form of address, strive to develop a personal relationship with other parties, and dress more casually on purpose. The contrast between direct and indirect communications has to do primarily with how straightforward and to the point communication typically is during the negotiations. Indirect communication consists of heavy use of nonverbal communication (see Chapter 8) and many vague statements. German and U.S. negotiators are typically viewed as relatively direct in their negotiations. French and Japanese negotiators are viewed as relatively more indirect, relying a great deal on nonverbal cues to help understand the negotiations.

The traditional assumptions and generalizations about cross-cultural negotiations may not apply when long-term and insider relationships have been established. This situation applies particularly to negotiations by the Japanese with each other, whom they view as insiders. Almost by definition, Japanese businesspeople consider Westerners to be outsiders. Thus, Westerners often incorrectly assume that the Japanese never use direct or confrontational approaches to conflict resolution and negotiation. In fact, they

Table 12.5 Percentage Distributions on 10 Dimensions of Negotiating Style for Respondents from India and Mexico

	SCALE									
	INDIA					MEXICO				
	1	2	3	4	5	1	2	3	4	5
1. *Goal:* contract (1) versus relationship (5)	39%	12%	10%	5%	34%	27%	25%	23%	11%	15%
2. *Attitudes:* win–lose (1) versus win–win (5)	27	5	5	4	59	5	6	6	20	63
3. *Personal style:* Informal (1) versus formal (5)	28	6	13	7	45	7	13	25	28	28
4. *Communications:* Direct (1) versus indirect (5)	71	11	9	1	8	54	31	8	3	3
5. *Time sensitivity:* high (1) versus low (5)	59	15	6	5	15	49	31	12	5	3
6. *Emotionalism:* high (1) versus low (5)	24	9	19	7	41	16	26	27	17	14
7. *Agreement form:* specific (1) versus general (5)	55	11	6	3	25	39	30	16	7	8
8. *Agreement building:* bottom up (1) versus top down (5)	43	11	10	8	27	22	15	20	18	26
9. *Team organization:* one leader (1) versus consensus (5)	41	8	5	6	39	14	31	17	17	21
10. *Risk taking:* high (1) versus low (5)	49	12	16	4	19	13	34	36	12	6

Source: Adapted from Metcalf, L. E., Bird, A., Shankarmahesh, M., Aycan, Z., Larimo, J., and Valdelamar, D. D. Cultural tendencies in negotiation: A comparison of Finland, India, Mexico, Turkey, and the United States. *Journal of World Business*, 2006, 41, 387.

often are very direct in resolving differences of opinion with other Japanese. They explicitly state the principal differences among group members and state demands, rejections, and counteroffers directly with each other.[40]

Cross-Cultural Emotional Intelligence

Negotiators and others are likely to be more effective if they possess emotional intelligence. We discussed emotional intelligence (EI) in Chapter 2. Let's extend that discussion by noting the relationship of the components of EI with the specific skills and abilities that increase cross-cultural effectiveness for negotiators. The components and relationships include the following:

- *Self-awareness:* acknowledging differences between home and host cultures; realizing the impact of cultural values on performance, recognizing initial difficulties in adjusting to new cultural norms and seeking assistance; being open to new perspectives; managing uncertainties by seeking cultural coaching; resisting the urge to impose one's own values on the host culture; understanding the link between the host culture and cross-cultural conflicts; and being flexible and patient when uncomfortable situations arise during negotiations;
- *Self-motivation*: maintaining optimism in the face of new challenges; effectively handling stress; seeking new ways of achieving goals during negotiation impasses;

and consciously balancing the advantages of global negotiations against challenges and stressors in such negotiations;

- *Social empathy*: developing good listening skills; being sensitive to differences; asking questions and seeking to understand before reacting; being willing to change so as to show respect for other negotiators; openly sharing information that provides others with more understanding; and respecting opposing viewpoints; and
- *Social skill*: being outgoing and friendly; building relationships; seeking common ground despite cross-cultural differences; being open minded and engaging in discussion rather than immediately passing judgment; and communicating informally to build rapport and future cooperation in negotiations.[41]

A mastery of these components of EI provides the foundation for becoming an effective negotiator in cross-cultural work situations. Moreover, EI enables the negotiator to avoid applying simplistic stereotypes to specific negotiators from other cultures.[42]

Consistent with the characteristics of EI and the competencies emphasized throughout this book, a good approach is to focus on the individual differences of specific negotiators to gain a deeper appreciation and understanding of their cultural context. This will short circuit the natural tendency toward simplistic stereotypes and erroneous attributions.

Negotiation Process

Many features of the negotiation process, such as the key questions in each stage of negotiations, are similar across cultures. We note here a few of the features that are unique or require tailoring to across culture negotiations:[43]

- *Dealing with people*. It is essential to take adequate time to get to know the other negotiators as professionals and people. More time is needed than in domestic business negotiations, because cultural, as well as personal, knowledge has to be acquired. Almost every negotiation involves a face-saving situation. The successful international negotiator avoids making people uncomfortable. To save face, the negotiator needs to avoid arrogance, be careful in the choice of words so as not to offend the other party, and treat the other negotiators with respect. This will help generate trust. When people trust one another, they communicate more openly and are more receptive to each other's proposals and point of view.
- *Time*. Allow plenty of time. In particular, give time to think—do not respond too quickly to new proposals. The timing of verbal exchanges is crucial in negotiations. Some Westerners find gaps or pauses in conversations to be disturbing, whereas people from other cultures (e.g., Japan, China) prefer to leave a moment of silence between statements. Patience is an asset in global negotiations, but can be destroyed by time pressures.
- *Managing issues*. Be flexible with the negotiation agenda if the other party does not stick to it. It may be somewhat frustrating when a negotiation agenda has been agreed on and then slowly eroded bit by bit. Such a situation may mean that the other party prefers a global rather than a step-by-step negotiation; the other party may not see negotiation as a linear process in which issues are addressed one after the other and settled before proceeding to the next issue.
- *Communication process*. The basic guideline for effective communication in international negotiations is to be ready for different communication styles. Be cautious when interpreting silence, emotions, threats, and any kind of manipulative communication. Start by assessing as accurately as possible the intercultural obstacles, such as language and problems of communication in general. Businesspeople often underestimate or even completely overlook this point, because they often share a technical or business culture with their negotiators. Beware that what is explicitly

said is not necessarily what is implicitly meant. Check, verify. Spend time on checking communication accuracy, especially when the stakes are high.

- *Developing relationships*. The agreement should foster the development of the relationship and be flexible enough to deal with expected and unexpected changes. A major concern is to balance the *relationship* and *deal orientations*. The ultimate goal of negotiation is to establish a mutually trustworthy relationship. This is, of course, true in all negotiations, but especially so in cross-cultural negotiations where so many things can and do go wrong. With trust, the parties are more able to work through the inevitable problems.

The following Across Cultures Competency feature provides a glimpse into the complexities of negotiating in one culture, namely, China.[44] This feature includes the views of Hewlett-Packard (HP) executives on their experiences in negotiating with the Chinese. China is one country where cultural influences are important to the negotiating process. Remember, in addition to those presented here, there are many other cultural aspects to negotiating with the Chinese.

Across Cultures Competency

Negotiating with the Chinese and Views of HP Executives

A variety of cultural norms and practices reflect modern negotiations in Chinese settings. We provide brief snapshots of a few of them in this feature.

Guanxi. The Chinese call interpersonal connections or social capital *guanxi*. *Guanxi* connotes more than the typical relationship between Western people; it is a special relationship between individuals in which each can make strong and often nearly unlimited demands on the other. *Guanxi* exists among family members but can also arise among unrelated people who have close interactions or common experiences. In China, the *people* involved in the negotiation can be as or even more important than the information or facts involved.

This suggests that when several companies compete for a contract from a Chinese customer, the company with the best *guanxi* will often win the contract. The responsibility for introducing the parties usually falls on a company's local representative. One Chinese manager who represents Hewlett-Packard in negotiations states, "Because our U.S. decision-maker and negotiator come from the top of the company, they know less about the business rules in Asia. We serve as the locals who understand what Chinese suppliers are talking about, what their intention (really is)."

Although China is growing rapidly and becoming more open, without Chinese intermediaries, strangers—especially if one party is a foreigner—will usually be unable to make deals in China. The negotiation between strangers is only the beginning of *guanxi*; closing a deal requires much more.

Paternal Leadership. Chinese leadership and decision-making practices flow from the hierarchical nature of Chinese society. In most Chinese organizations, key decisions are left to an individual leader. In many Western companies, where different managers may be responsible for different parts of the negotiation, decisions are often reached through consultation and consensus, which can lead to a slower decision-making process. One HP manager with negotiating experience in China comments:

> *U.S. teams will often include a high-level manager (such as a VP), a supply manager, and perhaps managers from financial and legal departments. The big difference between Chinese and Western teams is that in China decisions can often be made faster because they depend on only one or two key individuals within the company. ... If one looks at the Western [approach] ... it can take much longer, because it depends on a more structured process [and] they tend to go through more layers of people.*

"Face" Considerations. In Chinese culture, a person's reputation and social standing depend on "saving face," a notion similar to Western concepts of dignity and prestige. Face considerations are critical to the process of formulating and modifying negotiation proposals. For most Chinese leaders, to be seen as "soft" by subordinates means to risk losing face. Most Chinese negotiation

concessions will be made by team leaders, so gaining concessions often depends on enabling the leader to save face. One HP manager with negotiating experience in China comments:

> *Usually the small group discussions will be limited, with no more than three team members accompanying each business leader. Our side will also be a very small group. During this stage, we can discuss sensitive topics. … It is true that having compelling data can increase your powers of persuasion. But the final result may be determined by other quite strategic considerations. In my opinion, data accounts for 60–70 percent of persuasive power, while other dynamics in the negotiation, including managing status concerns, will account for the other 30–40 percent.*

Holistic Thinking. In the initial stages of negotiation, Chinese teams tend first to establish agreement on general principles before moving to more specific issues, in order to avoid or postpone direct conflict. This practice can conflict with Western negotiators who want to move to concrete and specific details. One HP executive with negotiating experience in China and other Asian countries comments:

> *In negotiation, Westerners and Asians will focus on different aspects of the topic. The judgment of Asians depends more on feelings of friendship or long-term relations. [Asians] will talk informally about things … [for example,] "once upon a time they did us a favor." They combine topics together. Westerners are more logical. Their judgment is based on data. They are practical and realistic … business is only business. Although they may have argued very confrontationally, they will forget the argument when they finish the negotiation.*

Reciprocity. A basic Chinese bargaining strategy is the appeal to reciprocity. As one manager states: "Negotiation is a process of relationship building. The needs of both sides need to be satisfied in the long run." Chinese negotiators readily accept reciprocity as a criterion for dividing gains or resolving disagreements. Concessions made by one party on one issue demand a reciprocal concession on another issue, but timing is important: making concessions during the early stages of a negotiation may be seen as a sign of weakness by Chinese counterparts. According to this view, Chinese negotiators prefer to make concessions at the end of a negotiation.

For more information on China's culture and business practices, visit websites such as www.index-china.com and www.chineseculturesite.com.

CHAPTER SUMMARY

1. Describe the primary levels of conflict in organizations.

Conflict occurs at four different levels within organizations: intrapersonal, interpersonal, intragroup, and intergroup. Intrapersonal conflict occurs within the individual. Interpersonal conflict occurs when someone's wishes or desires are perceived to be in opposition to another's. Intragroup conflict occurs between or among group members. Intergroup conflict occurs between groups or teams.

2. Explain and use the common interpersonal conflict-handling styles.

The five styles for handling interpersonal conflict are avoiding, forcing, accommodating, collaborating, and compromising. An individual may have a natural preference for one or two of these styles. Most individuals are likely to use all of them over time when dealing with various interpersonal conflict situations. As a reminder, an instrument for measuring your own conflict-handling style is presented in the Experiential Exercise and Case section at the end of this chapter.

3. Discuss and apply the core stages, strategies, and influences in negotiations.

Negotiation is a component in conflict management. It is a process by which two or more interdependent individuals or groups, who perceive that they have both common and conflicting goals, state and discuss proposals and preferences for specific terms of a possible agreement. The four core stages of negotiation include (1) assessing the situation, (2) establishing the process, (3) negotiating the agreement, and (4) implementing the agreement. provides examples of questions that need to be addressed in each stage. The two major negotiating strategies are distributive (focus is on win–lose outcomes) and integrative (focus is on win–win outcomes). Principled negotiations focus on the *how* or process of negotiations to increase the likelihood of positive outcomes for all parties. Four of the influences that affect the selection or implementation of each of these strategies are attitudinal structuring, intraorganizational negotiations, the negotiator's dilemma, and mediation when stalemates occur over particular issues.

4. State several of the unique aspects of and recommendations for negotiating across cultures.

Negotiators across cultures may differ with respect to (1) negotiating attitude with a focus on the win–lose (distributive) strategy versus win–win (integrative) strategy, (2) personal style with a formal versus informal approach, (3) communication style with a direct versus indirect approach, and (4) agreement form with a preference for a set of general versus highly specific provisions or understandings. Global negotiators are likely to be more effective if they possess emotional intelligence, which increases their cross-cultural adaptation ability in the components of self-awareness, self-motivation, social empathy, and social skill. Aspects of the negotiation process that may be unique when negotiating across cultures include dealing with people, allowing enough time, managing issues, handling the communication process, and developing relationships over time.

KEY TERMS AND CONCEPTS

Accommodating style
Attitudinal structuring
Avoiding style
BATNA
Collaborating style
Compromising style
Conflict
Conflict management
Distributive negotiations
Forcing style
Integrative negotiations
Intergroup conflict
Interpersonal conflict
Intragroup conflict
Intraorganizational negotiations
Intrapersonal conflict
Mediation
Negotiation
Negotiator's dilemma
Principled negotiations
Role
Role ambiguity
Role conflict
Role set
Task interdependency

DISCUSSION QUESTIONS

1. Visit the Wikipedia home page at www.en.wikipedia.org. In the search box, enter the word "Conflict" and click. Read the pages under the major section on "Causes of Conflict." Reread the experiences of Sue Peschin and Amy Gearing, as discussed in the chapter-opening Learning from Experience feature. What concepts from this section would they have likely identified as the causes of their conflict situations?
2. What conflict-handling styles appeared to be used by Sue Peschin, Amy Gearing, and their managers in the Learning from Experience feature? Explain.
3. Reread the Self Competency feature related to Kathryn Correia at ThedaCare. What types of role conflict were evident for her and others in these conflict situations? Explain.
4. Give personal examples of (a) approach–approach conflict, (b) avoidance–avoidance conflict, and (c) approach–avoidance conflict.
5. Provide examples of (a) intrasender role conflict, (b) intersender role conflict, (c) interrole conflict, and (d) person–role conflict that you have experienced.
6. Think of a current or past relationship with someone who had much more power than you. How would you describe that person's relative use of the five interpersonal conflict management styles? How would you evaluate that person's conflict management effectiveness?
7. Reread the Teams Competency feature on IBM's cross-team workouts. What levels of conflict were addressed through this conflict management approach? Explain. What interpersonal conflict-handling styles are illustrated? Explain.
8. Have you been involved in negotiations in which the other party used the distributive negotiations strategy? Describe the situation. What did you do in response to the tactics used with this strategy? How did you feel? What was the outcome?

9. How would you evaluate yourself on the components of emotional intelligence in relation to your ability to be an across-cultures negotiator? Turn to the experiential exercise *What's Your Emotional IQ?* in Chapter 2, page 64. If you have not done so, complete this self-assessment. What are the implications of this self-assessment for you with respect to across culture negotiations?

EXPERIENTIAL EXERCISE AND CASE

Experiential Exercise: Self Competency

Conflict-Handling Styles[45]

Instructions

Each numbered item contains two statements that describe how people deal with conflict. Distribute 5 points between each pair of statements. The statement that more accurately reflects your likely response should receive the highest number of points. For example, if response (a) strongly describes your behavior, then record

5 a.
0 b.

However, if responses (a) and (b) are both characteristic, but (b) is slightly more characteristic of your behavior than (a), then record

2 a.
3 b.

1. _____ a. I am most comfortable letting others take responsibility for solving a problem.
   _____ b. Rather than negotiate differences, I stress those points for which agreement is obvious.
2. _____ a. I pride myself on finding compromise solutions.
   _____ b. I examine all the issues involved in any disagreement.
3. _____ a. I usually persist in pursuing my side of an issue.
   _____ b. I prefer to soothe others' feelings and preserve relationships.
4. _____ a. I pride myself in finding compromise solutions.
   _____ b. I usually sacrifice my wishes for the wishes of a peer.
5. _____ a. I consistently seek a peer's help in finding solutions.
   _____ b. I do whatever is necessary to avoid tension.
6. _____ a. As a rule, I avoid dealing with conflict.
   _____ b. I defend my position and push my view.
7. _____ a. I postpone dealing with conflict until I have had some time to think it over.
   _____ b. I am willing to give up some points if others give up some too.
8. _____ a. I use my influence to have my views accepted.
   _____ b. I attempt to get all concerns and issues immediately out in the open.
9. _____ a. I feel that most differences are not worth worrying about.
   _____ b. I make a strong effort to get my way on issues I care about.
10. _____ a. Occasionally I use my authority or technical knowledge to get my way.
    _____ b. I prefer compromise solutions to problems.
11. _____ a. I believe that a team can reach a better solution than any one person can working independently.
    _____ b. I often defer to the wishes of others.
12. _____ a. I usually avoid taking positions that would create controversy.
    _____ b. I'm willing to give a little if a peer will give a little, too.
13. _____ a. I generally propose the middle ground as a solution.
    _____ b. I consistently press to "sell" my viewpoint.
14. _____ a. I prefer to hear everyone's side of an issue before making judgments.
    _____ b. I demonstrate the logic and benefits of my position.
15. _____ a. I would rather give in than argue about trivialities.
    _____ b. I avoid being "put on the spot."
16. _____ a. I refuse to hurt a peer's feelings.
    _____ b. I will defend my rights as a team member.
17. _____ a. I am usually firm in pursuing my point of view.
    _____ b. I'll walk away from disagreements before someone gets hurt.
18. _____ a. If it makes peers happy, I will agree with them.
    _____ b. I believe that give-and-take is the best way to resolve any disagreements.
19. _____ a. I prefer to have everyone involved in a conflict generate alternatives together.
    _____ b. When the team is discussing a serious problem, I usually keep quiet.
20. _____ a. I would rather openly resolve conflict than conceal differences.
    _____ b. I seek ways to balance gains and losses for equitable solutions.
21. _____ a. In problem solving, I am usually considerate of peers' viewpoints.
    _____ b. I prefer a direct and objective discussion of my disagreement.
22. _____ a. I seek solutions that meet some of everyone's needs.
    _____ b. I will argue as long as necessary to get my position heard.
23. _____ a. I like to assess the problem and identify a mutually agreeable solution.
    _____ b. When people challenge my position, I simply ignore them.

24. ____ a. If peers feel strongly about a position, I defer to it even if I don't agree.
____ b. I am willing to settle for a compromise solution.

25. ____ a. I am very persuasive when I have to be to win in a conflict situation.
____ b. I believe in the saying, "Kill your enemies with kindness."

26. ____ a. I will bargain with peers in an effort to manage disagreement.
____ b. I listen attentively before expressing my views.

27. ____ a. I avoid taking controversial positions.
____ b. I'm willing to give up my position for the benefit of the group.

28. ____ a. I enjoy competitive situations and "play" hard to win.
____ b. Whenever possible, I seek out knowledgeable peers to help resolve disagreements.

29. ____ a. I will surrender some of my demands, but I have to get something in return.
____ b. I don't like to air differences and usually keep my concerns to myself.

30. ____ a. I generally avoid hurting a peer's feelings.
____ b. When a peer and I disagree, I prefer to bring the issue out into the open so we can discuss it.

Scoring

Record your responses (number of points) in the space next to each statement number and then sum the points in each column.

Column 1	Column 2	Column 3	Column 4	Column 5
3 (a) ____	2 (a) ____	1 (a) ____	1 (b) ____	2 (b) ____
6 (b) ____	4 (a) ____	5 (b) ____	3 (b) ____	5 (a) ____
8 (a) ____	7 (b) ____	6 (a) ____	4 (b) ____	8 (b) ____
9 (b) ____	10 (b) ____	7 (a) ____	11 (b) ____	11 (a) ____
10 (a) ____	12 (b) ____	9 (a) ____	15 (a) ____	14 (a) ____
13 (b) ____	13 (a) ____	12 (a) ____	16 (a) ____	19 (a) ____
14 (b) ____	18 (b) ____	15 (b) ____	18 (a) ____	20 (a) ____
16 (b) ____	20 (b) ____	17 (b) ____	21 (a) ____	21 (b) ____
17 (a) ____	22 (a) ____	19 (b) ____	24 (a) ____	23 (a) ____
22 (b) ____	24 (b) ____	23 (b) ____	25 (b) ____	26 (b) ____
25 (a) ____	26 (a) ____	27 (a) ____	27 (b) ____	28 (b) ____
28 (a) ____	29 (a) ____	29 (b) ____	30 (a) ____	30 (b) ____
Total ____	Total ____	Total ____	Total ____	Total ____

Next carry over the totals from the column totals and then plot your total scores on the following chart to show the profile of your conflict-handling styles. A total score of 36 to 45 for a style may indicate a strong preference and use of that style. A total score of 0 to 18 for a style may indicate little preference and use of that style. A total score of 19 to 35 for a style may indicate a moderate preference and use of that style.

	Total	0 10 20 30 40 50 60
Column 1 (Forcing)	____	__ __ __ __ __ __ __
Column 2 (Compromising)	____	__ __ __ __ __ __ __
Column 3 (Avoiding)	____	__ __ __ __ __ __ __
Column 4 (Accommodating)	____	__ __ __ __ __ __ __
Column 5 (Collaborating)	____	__ __ __ __ __ __ __
		0 10 20 30 40 50 60

Questions

1. Are you satisfied with this profile? Why or why not?
2. Is this profile truly representative of your natural and primary conflict-handling styles?
3. What actions, if any, do you propose for improving your conflicting handling styles?

Case: Communication Competency

Lee Johnson and Chris' Performance Review[46]

Lee Johnson is the manager of the printing department for the Human Resource Training Facility (HRTF), a federal agency that provides human resource training to other government agencies as well as companies in the private sector. Lee's department prints the training manuals, brochures, classroom materials, and any other print jobs required by other HRTF departments. Lee's shop also contracts their printing services to outside organizations (both public and private) to bring in additional revenue. Despite the fact that the HRTF is a government operation, it collects fees for its services and is run like any other business. Consequently, the printing operation must adhere to strict business practices such as quality control, customer satisfaction, revenue generation, timely delivery, and cost containment.

Lee manages a dozen employees in the print shop. Each employee is responsible for a variety of tasks such as acquiring new clients, servicing client needs, designing print layouts, producing the required number of print materials at a reasonable cost, quality control of the print jobs, and timely delivery of the order. The employees often must work in teams to deliver an order, especially if it is a large job.

Each employee gets a performance review once a year. Lee must evaluate his employees on six performance dimensions that are standard across the HRTF. These dimensions are:

1. revenue generation,
2. client satisfaction,
3. cost efficiency,
4. quality control,
5. timely delivery, and
6. work attitude.

Lee has the authority to weight each of these dimensions in any way that seems appropriate. However, the HRTF requires that each employee be rated on all dimensions so comparisons can be made across different departments. Lee does not particularly enjoy this annual review process. He takes the task seriously because the results are used to determine salary increases, promotions, merit pay, skill training opportunities, and, in rare cases, termination of employment. The employees do not particularly care for the annual review either, because the stakes are high and no one wants to risk looking bad to the boss or coworkers. Lee conducts these performance reviews over several days at the end of the fiscal year. Lee does a performance evaluation on a standardized form prior to the review, and then calls in each employee individually to discuss the ratings and written comments.

Today, Chris West is being reviewed. Chris has worked in the print department for three years and knows how the review process works. Chris is not the top performer in the group, but does good work. This year Chris has had trouble getting the print jobs to the clients on time. This is the key issue that Lee must address in the performance review. Chris enters Lee's office.

Chris: I have been anticipating this review, but I am a bit nervous about it.

Lee: Never mind that. It's all here in your performance evaluation, and it should be very clear. We are here to determine your annual pay increase. I see that you were always here at work on time, and that the work that you did was of good quality and well received by clients. However, I also see that you were not always on time with all of your projects, and have caused delays in getting projects out on time. This is not good.

Chris: Yes, I see that, and I agree with what you are saying. However, I am late on my projects because of legitimate reasons. I am not comfortable sending out projects to clients unless they are ready to go. I also have trouble getting the rest of my team to get things in on time and it slows my process down.

Lee: Forget about the team. We are only concerned with your performance and how it impacts our clients. We believe in meeting the client's needs in every way, and that is a critical element for success both internally and externally. The fact that you perform quality work does not help this agency satisfy clients' deadlines.

Chris: Yes. I hear what you are saying, and I do understand that my job is not just related to the quality of work, but also intimately tied to meeting deadlines. I see the value of getting projects out on time. However, I am torn between getting them out to clients as acceptable versus exactly on time. I value and care about my job and hope to maintain a future here.

Lee: Obviously there is a balance between timeliness and acceptable quality. You should know about the importance of deadlines. Your pay raises are based on meeting these timelines. I decide the pay increases, and meeting deadlines is a big factor.

Chris: Yes. Meeting deadlines is vital. I do understand that my job is not just related to the quality of work, but also intimately tied to meeting deadlines. But I am not clear on why good work that is a little late doesn't warrant my annual increase?

Lee: Our customers need to be able to depend on receiving work within an acceptable time frame, and the quality of the work is a separate issue; you are not meeting those deadline requirements. How can you expect me to reward you for not meeting expectations? Failing to consistently meet client deadlines impacts the ability of this organization to uphold and honor our client contracts. In determining an employee's annual pay increase, I look at those areas that are deficient in an employee's performance.

Chris: I understand what you are saying.

Lee: So in conclusion, you must do a better job next year. You will not be receiving an annual increase.

Questions

1. What levels of conflict are evident in this case? Explain.
2. What types of role conflict are evident in this case? Explain.
3. What interpersonal conflict styles are employed by Lee and Chris? Explain.
4. Was Lee an effective manager in handling this performance review session? Explain.
5. Was Chris effective in this performance review session? Explain.

PART 4

THE ORGANIZATION

CHAPTER

13

Making Ethical and Managerial Decisions

Learning Goals

When you have finished studying the chapter, you should be able to:

1. Explain and apply the core concepts and principles for making ethical decisions.
2. Describe and use four models for making managerial decisions.
3. Explain organizational creativity and how to foster it.

© AP Images

Learning from Experience

THE ETHICS OF JIM SINEGAL, COFOUNDER AND CEO OF COSTCO

Jim Sinegal is the cofounder, president, and CEO of Costco Wholesale. Jeff Brotman, the other cofounder, is chairman of the board. Costco is headquartered in Issaquah, Washington, near Seattle. Costco is a leading warehouse-club operator with 510 warehouses worldwide, 376 of which are in the United States. It may open up to 500 new stores by 2020, with as many as 40 new stores in 2008. The firm has 132,000 employees and approximately 17.5 million gold star members and 5.3 million business members, each paying $45 per year to join. Costco has an 87 percent membership renewal rate. A typical Costco store stocks 4,000 types of items, with a limited number of each type—such as four brands of toothpaste.

Unlike the stereotypical CEO, Sinegal doesn't try to distance himself from his employees. He even wears a name tag—but not one that says "Jim, the CEO" or "Jim, Costco Founder." It just says "Jim." He easily could be mistaken for a stock clerk.

His management philosophy is simple. He states: "We have said from the very beginning: 'We're going to be a company that's on a first-name basis with everyone.'" That also includes answering his own phone. He continues: "If a customer's calling and they have a gripe, don't you think they kind of enjoy the fact that I picked up the phone and talked to them?" Sinegal and Brotman recently wrote: "We remain committed to running our company and living conscientiously by our Code of Ethics every day: to obey the law; take care of our members; take care of our employees; respect our suppliers; and reward you, our shareholders."

Many executives think shareholders are best served if they do all they can to hold down costs, including the costs of labor. Costco's approach is different. In terms of how it treats its employees, Sinegal says, "It absolutely makes good business sense. Most people agree that we're the lowest-cost provider. Yet we pay the highest wages. So it must mean we get better productivity. It's axiomatic in our business—you get what you pay for." Wages at Costco start at $10 an hour, rising to $18.32, excluding twice-a-year bonuses of between $2,000 and

LEARNING CONTENT

For more information on Costco, visit the organization's home page at www.costco.com.

$3,000 for those at the top wage for more than a year. Its average hourly wage is $17 an hour. Sinegal remarks: "Obviously it's not just wages that motivate people. How much they are respected, and whether they feel they can have a career at a company, are also important."

Costco's chief financial officer, Richard Galanti, speaks the same language. "One of the things Wall Street chided us on is that we're too good to our employees. ... We don't think that's possible. Costco is not going to make money at the expense of what's right." Costco's senior vice president for human resources, John Matthews, echoes the same sentiment. "When Jim [Sinegal] talks to us about setting wages and benefits, he doesn't want us to be better than everyone else. He wants us to be demonstrably better."

One of Sinegal's cardinal rules is that no branded item, such as a Xerox printer, can be marked up by more than 14 percent and no private-label item, such as Costco gasoline, by more than 15 percent. In contrast, supermarkets generally mark up merchandise by 25 percent and department stores by 50 percent or more. The secret to Costco's profit is simple. Its margin on each item isn't very high—but Sinegal says they make it up on volume. Some Wall Street analysts think Costco is also overly generous to its customers. One analyst states: "At Costco, it's better to be an employee or a customer than a shareholder." Another analyst asserts: "Whatever goes to employees comes out of the pockets of shareholders." Sinegal replies: "On Wall Street, they're in the business of making money between now and next Thursday. I don't say that with any bitterness, but we can't take that view. We want to build a company that will still be here 50 and 60 years from now." Interestingly, Costco stock has done very well.

For the past several years, Sinegal has received a salary of $350,000, excluding stock options. That is low for a CEO of a $60 billion-per-year business. By comparison, the typical CEO of a large American company makes more than 430 times the pay of the average worker. Sinegal states, "I figured that if I was making something like 12 times more than the typical person working on the floor, that was a fair salary." Of course, as a cofounder of the company, Sinegal owns a lot of Costco stock—more than $150 million worth. He's rich, but only on paper.[1]

Ethical concepts and issues are increasingly recognized as key components in all types of decision making in leading organizations, such as Costco and Johnson & Johnson. The remarks by Jim Sinegal in the Learning from Experience feature provide a glimpse into the efforts by the leadership of Costco to instill and shape an ethical environment. It is the obligation of the top leaders to model the firm's core values and ethical principles in their decisions.

The issues related to making ethical and managerial decisions have been presented in a number of previous chapters. In this chapter, we expand on them. First, we discuss core concepts and principles that are fundamental to ethical decision making and behavior. Next, we review the features of four models for making managerial decisions. Then, we conclude with a presentation of two approaches for stimulating creativity in decision making.

MAKING ETHICAL DECISIONS

Learning Goal

1. Explain and apply the core concepts and principles for making ethical decisions.

Decisions and behaviors by employees in organizations have an underlying foundation of ethical concepts, principles, and rules.[2] Because of the importance of ethics in management, we recognize it throughout this book in the Ethics Competency features. As you will recall from Chapter 1, the *ethics competency* involves the knowledge, skills, and abilities to incorporate values and principles that distinguish right from wrong in making decisions and choosing behaviors. We also noted in that chapter that *ethics* are values and principles that distinguish right from wrong. In the broadest sense, ethics refers to the study of moral values, principles, and rules, including the determination of standards of conduct and obligations for individuals and organizations. Ethical issues in organizations are common and complex. In fact, ethical issues influence the decisions that employees make daily. Some ethical issues involve factors that blur the distinction between "right" and "wrong." As a result, employees may experience ethical dilemmas.

In some situations, there are no simple rules for making ethical decisions. Our goal here is to help further develop your competency in applying ethical concepts to decision making. Your assessment of alternatives will be improved by examining five key components that comprise the basics of ethical decision making: ethical intensity, decision-making principles and decision rules, concern for affected individuals, benefits and costs, and determination of rights. As suggested in Figure 13.1, these basic components are interrelated and need to be considered as a whole in order to make ethical decisions.

FIGURE 13.1 Basics for Making Ethical Decisions

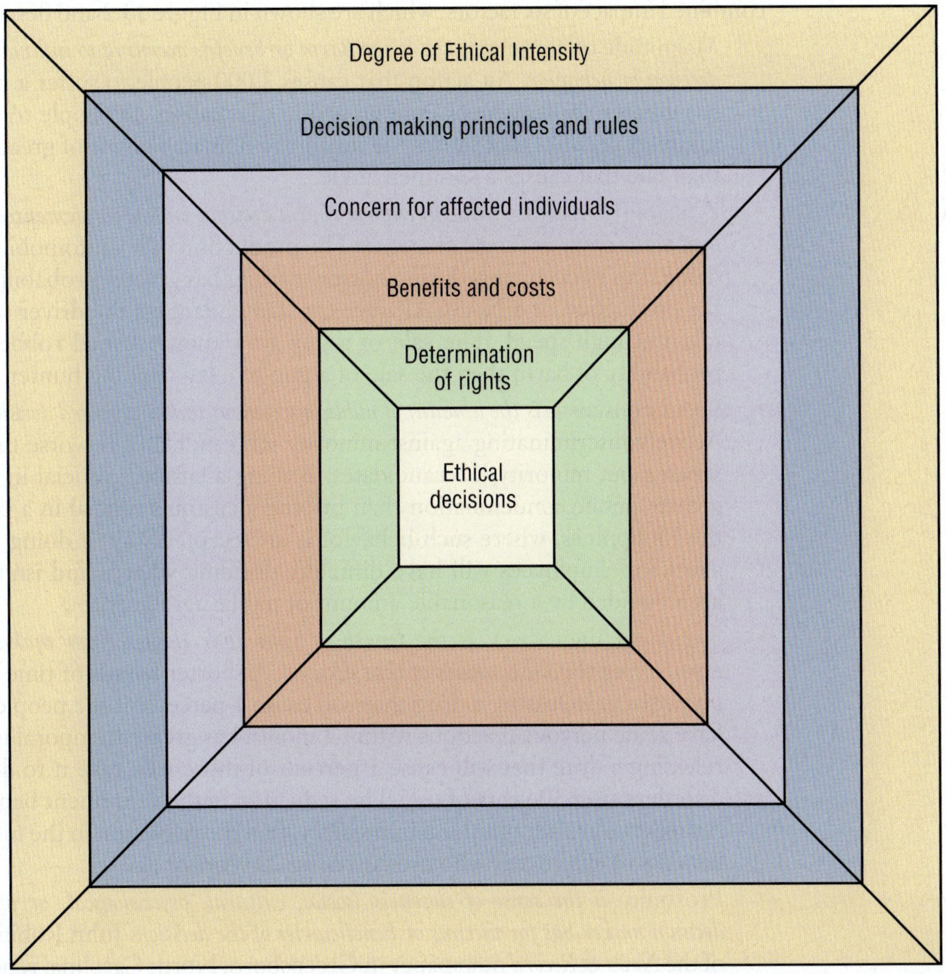

The Ethics Resource Center, headquartered in Washington, D.C., conducts ethical surveys of workers in the United States. In their most recent survey, more than half of the American employees surveyed observed at least one type of ethical misconduct in the workplace despite an increase in employee's awareness of formal ethics programs. Another key finding of the survey is the importance of having an ethical culture in organizations. Employees in organizations with a weak ethical culture reported a much higher level of observing at least one type of misconduct than employees in an organization with a strong ethical culture (70 percent compared to 34 percent). Those employees in organizations with a strong ethical culture were more likely to report the misconduct than those in weak-culture organizations (79 percent compared to 48 percent). Culture had a stronger impact on the results reported by employees than did an organization's formal ethics and compliance programs. Patricia Harned, the president of the Ethics Resource Center, comments: "Creating a strong ethical environment should be a top priority of all companies. We know formal programs are critical and work well initially, but we must now focus greater attention on building the right culture in which programs operate. This data shows, for example, that management needs to lead by example to set the right tone throughout the whole organization."[3] Jim Sinegal and the other top executives at Costco appear to be committed to a strong ethical culture through leading by example.

Ethical Intensity

Ethical intensity *is the degree of moral importance given to an issue.*[4] It is determined by the combined impact of six factors, which are shown in Figure 13.2 and described as follows.

- Magnitude of consequences *is the harm or benefits accruing to individuals affected by a decision or behavior.* An action that causes 2,000 people to suffer a particular injury has greater consequences than an action that causes 20 people to suffer the same injury. A decision that causes the death of a human being is of greater consequence than one that causes a sprained ankle.
- Probability of effect *is the likelihood that a decision will be implemented and that it will lead to the harm or benefit predicted.* The production of an automobile that would be dangerous to occupants during normal driving has greater probability of harm than the production of a NASCAR race car that endangers the driver when curves are taken at high speed. The sale of a gun to a known armed robber has a greater probability of harm than the sale of a gun to a law-abiding hunter.
- Social consensus *is the amount of public agreement that a proposed decision is bad or good.* Actively discriminating against minority job candidates is worse than not actively seeking out minority job candidates. Bribing a customs official in Canada evokes greater public condemnation than bribing a customs official in a country, such as the Philippines, where such behavior is an accepted way of doing business. Managers and employees will have difficulty deciding what is and isn't ethical if they aren't guided by a reasonable amount of public agreement.
- Temporal immediacy *is the length of time that elapses from making a decision to experiencing the consequences of that decision.* A shorter length of time implies greater immediacy. Releasing a drug that will cause 1 percent of the people who take it to have acute nervous reactions within 1 month has greater temporal immediacy than releasing a drug that will cause 1 percent of those who take it to develop nervous disorders after 30 years of use. The reduction in the retirement benefits of current retirees has greater temporal immediacy than the reduction in the future retirement benefits of employees who are currently 22 years of age.
- Proximity *is the sense of closeness (social, cultural, psychological, or physical) that the decision maker has for victims or beneficiaries of the decision.* John Robinson, the editor of the *News & Record* newspaper in Greensboro, North Carolina, reported the layoff of 41 people in 2007. This left 100 people in the news department.[5] This action had a greater impact on them than the personal impact they feel when reporting on layoffs of employees at other companies.
- Concentration of effect *is the inverse function of the number of people affected by a decision.* A change in an insurance policy denying coverage to 40 people with claims of $30,000 each has a more concentrated effect than a change denying coverage to 4,000 people with claims of $400 each. Cheating an individual or small group of individuals out of $10,000 has a more concentrated effect than cheating an organization, such as the IRS, out of the same sum.

FIGURE 13.2 Determinants of Ethical Intensity

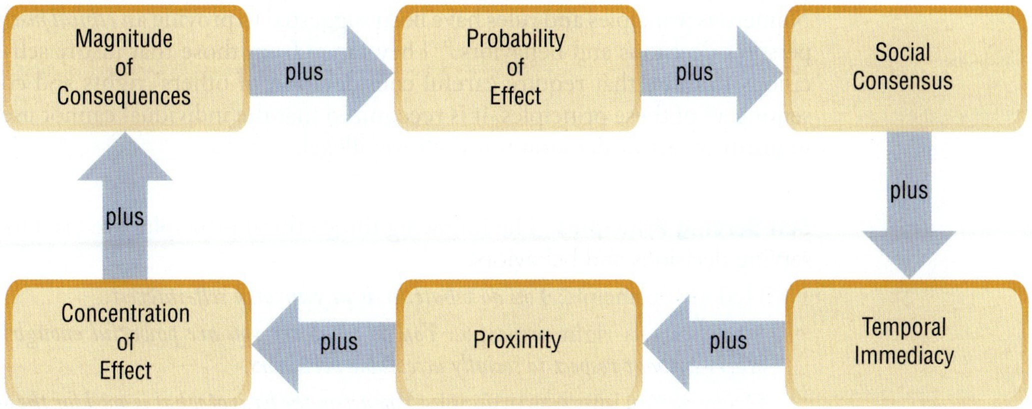

Individual Guidelines. The six factors of ethical intensity are influenced by the characteristics of the decision issue itself. Ethical intensity rises with increases in one or more of its factors and declines with reductions in one or more of these factors, assuming that all other conditions remain constant. However, you may rate the ethical intensity of the same decision differently than another person because you place different values on the principles and rules of ethics in decision making. Table 13.1 provides a questionnaire for your use in rating the ethical intensity of 10 different behaviors.

Table 13.1 **Ethical Intensity of Selected Behaviors**

Instructions: Evaluate each of the 10 behaviors shown in this questionnaire in terms of its ethical intensity. The overall scale of ethical intensity varies from –5, which indicates highly unethical behavior, to +5, which indicates a highly acceptable and ethical behavior. Write down the number on each scale at or near the point that reflects your assessment. What factors were most important in arriving at your rating of the ethical intensity for each behavior?

	ETHICAL INTENSITY		
BEHAVIORS	UNETHICAL/ NEGATIVE –5	NEUTRAL 0	ETHICAL/ POSITIVE +5

_____ 1. Covering up mistakes by coworkers.
_____ 2. Giving a favor to a client out of friendship.
_____ 3. Giving a favor to a client for a bribe.
_____ 4. Discriminating against an employee on the basis of race.
_____ 5. Presenting misleading information to a customer.
_____ 6. Presenting only positive features of your organization's products to a customer.
_____ 7. Manipulating performance data and indicators to give the appearance of reaching your goals.
_____ 8. Rewarding people differently based on differences in performance.
_____ 9. Bending the rules to help the organization.
_____10. Using an office PC for personal use.

Decision-Making Principles and Decision Rules

There are no universally accepted principles and rules for resolving all of the ethical issues that arise when faced with complex managerial situations. In addition, individuals and groups differ over what influences ethical and unethical behaviors and decisions. Numerous principles and rules have been suggested to provide an *ethical justification* for a person's decisions and behaviors.[6] They range from those that justify self-serving decisions to those that require careful consideration of others' rights and costs. In presenting all of these principles, it is recognized that the individual cannot use a principle to justify an act or decision if it is clearly illegal.

Self-Serving Principles. The following three ethical principles are used to justify self-serving decisions and behaviors.

- Hedonist principle: *You do whatever is in your own self-interest.*
- Might-equals-right principle: *You do whatever you are powerful enough to impose on others without respect to socially acceptable behaviors.*
- Organization interests principle: *You act on the basis of what is good for the organization.*

Some of the statements and thoughts that might reflect self-serving principles include the following: (1) "This act really won't hurt anybody"; (2) "I don't feel comfortable doing this, but if this is what it takes to get ahead (via money/work/promotion/prestige), I should probably do it"; (3) "Everybody else does it, so why shouldn't I"; (4) "Because _____ is my boss and told me to do this, I have no choice but to comply"; and (5) "Since this is such a small matter to most people and it will help our organization, who will notice."[7]

Balancing Interests Principles. The following three ethical principles are used to justify decisions intended to balance the interests of multiple individuals or groups[8]:

- Means–end principle: *You act on the basis of whether some overall good justifies a moral transgression.*
- Utilitarian principle: *You act on the basis of whether the harm from the decision is outweighed by the good in it—that is, the greatest good for the greatest number.*
- Professional standards principle: *You act on the basis of whether the decision can be explained before a group of your peers.*

These principles provide the ethical foundation for many decisions in organizations. They create the basis for helping to resolve ethical dilemmas. For example, organizations—Goodyear, Ford, and others—are able to justify employee layoffs for the good of the organization. However, they recognize certain responsibilities for providing career counseling and severance packages for the employees affected.

The Internet, new surveillance technologies, privacy issues, and governmental legislation in the United States and many other countries have created major concerns in the attempt to balance the interests of individuals, organizations, and the public at large.[9] The growing perception is that employees and consumers have lost too much of their privacy to employers, marketers, and governmental agencies. Although a variety of U.S. laws have been passed that attempt to protect the privacy of individuals in their roles as citizens, an employee's legal rights to privacy in the workplace is quite limited.[10]

Privacy issues in the workplace pose ethical dilemmas in terms of (1) distribution and use of employee data from computer-based human resource information systems; (2) increasing use of paper-and-pencil honesty tests, resulting from polygraph testing being declared illegal in most situations; (3) procedures and bases for substance abuse and AIDS testing; and (4) genetic testing. The ethical dilemmas in each of these areas revolve around balancing the rights of the individual, the needs and rights of the employer, and the interests of the community at large.[11]

Most employers claim to want to ensure a reasonable degree of employee privacy even when they are not legally obligated to do so. This claim and perspective is based on the balancing interests ethical principles. There is, however, wide consensus that employers must protect against the actions of employees who download pornography or copyrighted music, send harassing e-mail, reveal company secrets, disclose personal information, sell drugs, or even slack off on their jobs because of the time they spend surfing the Internet. New technologies make it possible for employers to monitor many aspects of their employees' jobs, especially on telephones, computer terminals, through electronic and voice mail, and when employees are using the Internet. Monitoring of employees by employers is virtually unregulated by the U.S. government. Therefore, unless company policy specifically states otherwise (and even this is not assured), there are no legal prohibitions against an employer listening, watching, and reading almost all workplace communications by employees.[12]

Concern for Others Principles. The following three ethical principles focus on the need to consider decisions and behaviors from the perspective of those affected and the public as a whole:

- Disclosure principle: *You act on the basis of how the general public would likely respond to the disclosure of the rationale and facts related to the decision.*
- Distributive justice principle: *You act on the basis of treating an individual or group equitably rather than on arbitrarily defined characteristics (e.g., gender, race, age).*
- Golden rule principle: *You act on the basis of placing yourself in the position of someone affected by the decision and try to determine how that person would feel.*

These three ethical principles are often *imposed* on certain categories of decisions and behaviors through laws, regulations, and court rulings. In effect, governments impose ethical principles and rules that organizations are expected to comply with in certain situations. For example, U.S. civil rights laws forbid organizations from considering personal characteristics—such as race, gender, religion, or national origin—in decisions to recruit, hire, promote, or fire employees. These laws are based on the ethical principle of distributive justice, which requires the same (or substantially the same) treatment of individuals regardless of age, disability, race, national origin, religion, and sex. For example, employees who are similar in relevant respects should be treated similarly, and employees who differ in relevant respects should be treated differently in proportion to the differences between them. On this basis, the U.S. Equal Pay Act of 1963 asserts that paying women and men different wages is illegal when their jobs in the same organization require substantially equal skills, effort, and responsibility and are performed under similar working conditions. The idea of working conditions encompasses two factors: (1) physical surroundings such as temperature, fumes, and ventilation and (2) hazards. This act applies to organizations with 15 or more employees. There are limited exceptions for pay differentials when an employer can show that:

- the difference is due to a seniority or merit system; or
- the difference is due to an employee's education, training, and experience.[13]

The scenario in Table 13.2 lets you choose a course of action based on the nine ethical principles just described. If you were Ray, what would you do?

Managerial Guidelines. As noted previously, no single factor influences the degree to which decisions and behaviors are likely to be ethical or unethical. However, the following actions can help integrate ethical decision making into the day-to-day life of an organization:[14]

- Top managers must demonstrate their commitment to ethical behaviors and decisions made by other managers and employees. Recall the remark of Jim Sinegal, the CEO of Costco, in the Learning from Experience feature: "We remain committed to running our company and living conscientiously by our Code of Ethics

Table 13.2

Ethical Assessment of a Scenario

Scenario

Ray manages a unit in a company that calls itself a "total quality" organization. Part of the organization's mission statement says that employees should strive to continually improve their performance. Lately, Ray's unit has been extremely busy trying to get its work done on several important projects. Ray asked his vice president for advice about how to meet all of the deadlines, and the VP basically told him that his unit would have to cut corners on quality in order to get everything done on time. The VP also told Ray that meeting deadlines is the best way to keep clients off their backs, and that the clients rarely complain about substandard work because its effects show up much later. However, Ray knows that doing substandard work for clients will only hurt the company's reputation in the long run.

Questions

1. What should Ray do?
2. How would you evaluate the ethics of your decision with respect to the degree to which it is based on each of the following ethical principles?

Ethical Principle

HIGH DEGREE		UNCERTAIN/ UNDECIDED		LOW DEGREE (NONE)
5	4	3	2	1

To what degree is your decision based on this ethical principle:

1. Hedonist	5	4	3	2	1
2. Might-equals-right	5	4	3	2	1
3. Organization interests	5	4	3	2	1
4. Means-end	5	4	3	2	1
5. Utilitarian	5	4	3	2	1
6. Professional standards	5	4	3	2	1
7. Disclosure	5	4	3	2	1
8. Distributive justice	5	4	3	2	1
9. Golden rule	5	4	3	2	1

Source: Scenario adapted from Loviscky, G. E., Treviño, L. K., and Jacobs, R. R. Assessing managers' ethical decision-making: An objective measure of managerial moral judgment. *Journal of Business Ethics*, 2007, 73, 263–285.

every day: to obey the law; take care of our members; take care of our employees; respect our suppliers; and reward you, our shareholders."

- A clear code of ethics should be developed and followed. Costco has a clearly stated code of ethics with sections that address obeying the law, members, employees, suppliers, and shareholders. The section entitled "Obey the Law" states:

  > The law is irrefutable! Absent a moral imperative to challenge a law, we must conduct our business in total compliance with the laws of every community where we do business. We pledge to: (1) Comply with all laws and other legal requirements. (2) Respect all public officials and their positions. (3) Comply with safety and security standards for all products sold. (4) Exceed ecological standards required in every community where we do business. Comply with all applicable wage and hour laws. Comply with all applicable anti-trust laws. (5) Conduct business in and with foreign countries in a manner that is legal and proper under United States and foreign laws. (6) Not offer, give, ask for, or receive any form of bribe or kickback to or from any person or pay to expedite government action or otherwise act in violation of the Foreign Corrupt Practices Act. (7) Promote fair, accurate, timely, and understandable disclosure in reports filed with the Securities and Exchange Commission and in other public communications by the Company.[15]

- A whistle-blowing and/or ethical concerns procedure should be established and followed. Costco addresses this and the following guidelines in its code of ethics, as follows:

> (1) The Code of Ethics applies to all directors, offices, and employees of the Company. (2) All persons are encouraged to promptly report actual or suspected violations of the Code. Federal law and other laws protect employees from retaliation if complaints are honestly made. Violation involving employees should be reported to the responsible Executive Vice President, who shall be responsible for taking prompt and appropriate action to investigate and respond. Other violations should be reported to the General Counsel (999 Lake Drive, Issaquah, WA 98027), who shall be responsible for taking prompt and appropriate action to investigate and respond. (3) Conduct that violates the Code will constitute grounds for disciplinary action, ranging from reprimand to termination and possible criminal prosecution.[16]

- Managers and employees alike should be involved in the identification of ethical problems to arrive at a shared understanding of them and to help solve them.
- The performance appraisal process should include consideration of ethical issues.
- The organizational priorities and efforts related to ethical issues should be widely publicized. Costco's code of ethics concludes:

> What do Costco's mission statement and code of ethics have to do with you? EVERYTHING! The continued success of our company depends on how well each of Costco's employees adheres to the high standards mandated by our Code of Ethics. And a successful company means increased opportunities for success and advancement for each of you. No matter what your current job, you can put Costco's Code of Ethics to work everyday. It's reflected in the energy and enthusiasm you bring to work, in the relationships you build with your management, your co-workers, your vendors and your members.[17]

This theme is presented and repeated many times throughout Costco and by its leadership. For example, the career opportunities section of Costco's website emphasizes that it is "A workplace focused on ethics and obeying the law."

Concern for Affected Individuals

The highest form of ethical decision making involves a careful determination of who will receive benefits or incur costs as a consequence of a decision. For major decisions, this assessment may include a variety of stakeholders—shareholders, customers, lenders, suppliers, employees, and governmental agencies, among others.[18] The more specific an individual or group can be identified about who may benefit and who may incur costs from a particular decision, the more likely it is that ethical implications will be fully considered.

UN Global Compact. Launched in 2000, the UN Global Compact is the largest "corporate citizenship" initiative in the world.[19] This voluntary initiative includes more than 3,000 companies from 100 countries as well as 700 civil societies, labor organizations, and academic institutions. Several of the business member organizations include UBS, AG (Switzerland), Alcatel-Lucent (France), Bayer AG (Germany), Cisco Systems (USA), and Nike Inc. (USA). This compact represents a partnership between the private sector and other sectors to promote responsible corporate citizenship as one means of encouraging business to be part of the solution to a more sustainable and inclusive global economy. The Global Compact works to advance 10 universal principles in the areas of human rights, labor standards, the environment, and anticorruption. These principles are presented in Table 13.3. The specific ethical guidelines and suggested decisions for each universal principle are presented on the website of the UN Global Compact at www.unglobalcompact.org.

The UN Global Compact promotes responsible corporate citizenship, encouraging business to be part of the solution to a more sustainable and inclusive global economy.

Table 13.3 UN Global Compact Principles

Human Rights
Businesses should:

- *Principle 1*: Support and respect the protection of internationally proclaimed human rights.
- *Principle 2*: Make sure that they are not complicit in human rights abuses.

Labor Standards
Businesses should:

- *Principle 3*: Uphold the freedom of association and the effective recognition of the right to collective bargaining.
- *Principle 4*: Uphold the elimination of all forms of forced and compulsory labor.
- *Principle 5*: Uphold the effective abolition of child labor.
- *Principle 6*: Uphold the elimination of discrimination in respect of employment and occupation.

Environment
Businesses should:

- *Principle 7*: Support a precautionary approach to environmental challenges.
- *Principle 8*: Undertake initiatives to promote greater environmental responsibility.
- *Principle 9*: Encourage the development and diffusion of environmentally friendly technologies.

Anti-Corruption
Businesses should:

- *Principle 10*: Work against corruption in all its forms, including extortion and bribery.

Note: Specific ethical guidelines and suggested decisions for each principle are presented at www.unglobalcompact.org.

Source: The ten principles of the UN Global Compact. www.unglobalcompact.org (September 2007).

The UN Global Compact is not a regulatory agency—it does not "police," enforce, or measure the behavior or actions of companies. Rather, the Global Compact relies on public accountability, transparency, and the enlightened self-interest of companies to initiate and share the actions they take in pursuing the principles on which the Global Compact is based. Accordingly, we are not suggesting that all of the 3,000 member companies fully implement these principles.

> **LEADER INSIGHT**
>
> The Global Compact is a universal commitment across our business to key principles. It offers a strategic and operational framework for organizing corporate social responsibility and, as a global initiative with local networks around the world, allows us to act consistently, wherever we operate.
> **Neville Isdell, CEO, Coca-Cola Company**

Employment at Will. Employment at will *is an employment relationship in which either party can terminate the employment relationship at will with no liability if there was not an express contract for a definite term governing the employment relationship.*[20] Although employment at will allows an employee to quit for no reason, it is also used when an employer wants to fire an employee at any time for any reason or no reason. At-will employment is a creation of U.S. law.

All 50 states recognize retaliatory discharge as an exception to the at-will rule. Under the retaliatory discharge exception, an employer may not fire an employee if it would violate a state or federal statute. For example, an employee who reported illegal behavior by the organization to a government agency cannot be fired. Most states also recognize an implied contract as an exception to at-will employment. Implied employment contracts are most often found when an employer's personnel policies or handbooks indicate that an employee will not be fired except for good cause. If the employer fires the employee in violation of an implied employment contract, the employer may be found liable for breach of contract.[21]

The employment-at-will doctrine increasingly has been challenged successfully in alleged wrongful termination cases in the courts. These challenges are based on the distributive justice principle and the golden rule principle. Before 1980, companies in the United States were free to fire most nonunion employees "at will." Employees were fired for any reason without explanation and rarely went to court to challenge a termination. The vast majority who did had their suits dismissed. However, the courts have recently ruled in favor of exceptions to the employment-at-will doctrine, especially if questionable termination procedures were followed.[22]

Benefits and Costs

An assessment of the ethical implications of the benefits and costs of a decision or issue requires a determination of the interests and values of those affected by the decision(s). Those affected might be the organization as a whole, all employees or specific groups of employees, customers, suppliers, a community, society as a whole, and other affected parties. *Benefits* refer to whatever a party considers desirable. *Costs* refer to whatever a party considers undesirable. Benefits and costs can refer to monetary or nonmonetary effects. A low-cost, coal-burning power plant (monetary effect) that produces high levels of pollution (nonmonetary effect) results in a benefit to the firm and a cost to the public.

The rub comes in considering the implications, including ethical implications, of the benefits and costs of particular decisions through the interests and "eyes" of those affected. One party's benefits in a decision may create or be perceived to create costs for one or more other parties. A few of these potential tensions with ethical implications are briefly noted as follows:

- Greater profits for shareholders versus higher wages for employees. Within the United States, the legally mandated minimum wage for workers was recently raised with subsequent required increases in 2008 and 2009. The concern for others ethical principles were presented as the rationale for the minimum wage that should be paid by U.S. employers, with a few exceptions.

- Increased production of electrical energy with lower per unit costs versus the need for lower levels of pollution. Traditionally, electric utilities used the organization interests principle to suggest that if greater pollution would lower production costs and increase profits, it was justifiable. Today, an increasing number of business leaders are recognizing the need to proactively address pollution problems and not simply wait for government regulatory agencies and laws that require them to do so. This is consistent with the views expressed in the UN Global Compact and endorsed on a voluntary basis by its 3,000 member organizations.
- Higher prices needed by suppliers (especially those in developing countries) to pay better wages, provide a safer work environment, and pollute less versus providing lower prices to consumers. The self-serving principles suggest the firm should solely seek to obtain products or services from suppliers at the lowest possible cost with the highest possible quality from any source in the world. Again, the UN Global Compact, among others, attempts to moderate these self-serving principles with balancing interests principles.
- Survival of the business through layoffs and reduced compensation versus the desires of stakeholders for greater job security and increased compensation for employees. Various combinations of ethical principles often come into play in such situations, including self-serving, balancing interests, and concern for others.

Care must be taken to guard against assuming that all stakeholders attach the same importance or ethical principles to the costs versus benefits of particular decisions. Conflicting assessments can lead to different interpretations of ethical responsibilities. For example, Greenpeace and other environmental groups emphasize the benefits of "preservation of nature" and that the costs of doing so are well worth it. John Passacantando, the executive director of Greenpeace USA, comments:

> *In the end, protecting the environment is about very clear choices. We can either stand up for what is right—our health, humanity, and heritage on this planet of ours—or we can sit by and watch while decisions are made that threaten to destroy our collective future.*[23]

The Computer TakeBack Campaign is dedicated to reducing e-waste and to encouraging the recycling or taking back of computers by computer manufacturers.

In 2007, Apple came under heavy criticism from environmental groups, such as Greenpeace and the Computer TakeBack Campaign, for its lack of dedication to reducing e-waste, its use of toxic chemicals in manufacturing products, and the restrictions it places on recycling and taking back its computers, iPods, and other products. Steve Jobs, Apple's CEO, responded with an open letter to the public about Apple's commitment to the environment. As part of his five-page statement, Jobs concludes:

> *Today is the first time we have openly discussed our plans to become a green Apple. It will not be the last. We will be providing updates of our efforts and accomplishments at least annually, most likely around this time of the year (May). And we plan to bring other environmental issues to the table as well, such as the energy efficiency of the products in our industry. We are also beginning to explore the overall carbon "footprint" of our products, and may have some interesting data and issues to share.*[24]

Steve Smith, a Greenpeace spokesman, replied to Jobs statement: "Apple's new commitment to environmental transparency and the phase out of the worst chemicals in its product range are genuine steps forward."[25] However, representatives in Greenpeace and the Computer TakeBack Campaign still have concerns about Apple's policy on shipping e-waste to other countries. They contend lax regulations and even more lax enforcement have resulted in mountains of toxic e-waste that cause severe health and environmental problems.

Managerial Guidelines. The utilitarian principle is a common approach by managers to weighing of benefits and costs of organizational decisions. Utilitarianism emphasizes the greatest good for the greatest number in judging the ethics of a decision. For example, a manager who is guided by utilitarianism considers the potential effect of alternative actions on employees who will be affected and then selects the alternative benefiting the greatest number of employees. The manager accepts the fact that this alternative may harm others. As long as potentially positive results outweigh potentially negative results, the manager considers the decision to be both good and ethical.

According to some critics, such as Greenpeace, utilitarianism has been misused by managers in U.S. organizations. They suggest that there is too much short-run maximizing of personal advantage and too much discounting of the long-run costs of disregarding ethics. Those costs are claimed to include rapidly widening gaps in income between rich and poor, creation of a permanent underclass with its hopelessness, and harm done to the environment. These critics believe that too many people and institutions are acquiring wealth for the purpose of personal consumption and power and that the end of acquiring wealth justifies any means of doing so. As a result, these critics suggest that trust of leaders and institutions, both public and private, has declined.[26] A recent Harris Interactive Poll found only 13 percent of respondents expressed a great deal of confidence in business leaders who are running major companies.[27] Perhaps more individuals such as Jim Sinegal or Irene Rosenfeld, the CEO of Kraft Foods, would help to increase trust in the ethics of leaders and institutions. Also, greater transparency in decisions that affect others, as illustrated in our discussion of Apple and Steve Jobs, would enhance a sense of trust in the leadership of corporations. Of course, a reduction in the fraudulent and unethical decisions by some top executives, which receive widespread publicity and shapes the public's general negative stereotype of top leaders, would also increase a sense of trust in leaders.[28]

Determination of Rights

The notion of rights also is complex and continually changing. One dimension of rights focuses on who is entitled to benefits or participation in decisions. If rights change, then the mix of benefits and costs change. Union–management negotiations frequently involve conflicts and dilemmas over management's rights to hire, promote, fire, reassign union employees, and outsource work. Slavery, racism, gender and age discrimination, and invasion of privacy often have been challenged by appeals to values based on concepts of fundamental rights, especially in terms of the distributive justice and golden rule principles.

Managerial Guidelines. Issues of responsibilities and rights in the workplace are numerous and vary greatly over time. A few examples include unfair and reverse discrimination, sexual harassment, employee rights to continued employment, employer rights to terminate employment "at will," employee and corporate free speech, due process, the right to test for substance abuse and acquired immune deficiency syndrome (AIDS), and the right to privacy. Some experts believe that workplace rights and the establishment of trust with employees is a crucial internal issue facing organizations today.[29]

Recall our discussion of the universal principles of the UN Global Compact. These principles address concern for affected individuals, benefits and costs, and determination of rights. The following Ethics Competency feature presents a portion of the ethical guidelines and suggested decisions for principle 1, namely "Businesses should support and respect the protection of internationally proclaimed human rights."[30] As noted previously, 3,000 major companies worldwide have agreed to advance this and the other nine universal principles.

Ethics Competency

UN Global Compact: Human Rights Principle

Why Human Rights Are Important for Business

The responsibility for human rights does not rest with government or nation-states alone. Human rights issues are important both for individuals and the organizations that they create. As part of its commitment to the Global Compact, the business community has a responsibility to uphold human rights both in the workplace and more broadly within society. There is a growing recognition that a good human rights record can support improved business performance.

Bringing Human Rights into Company Policy and Culture

A key starting point is for individuals within companies to develop an understanding of the issues, for example, by making reference to the Universal Declaration of Human Rights. This document, published by the United Nations, was developed with input from a number of stakeholders, including major private sector organizations. Companies also need to ensure that they are respecting existing national laws in the countries where they operate, and identify how these may vary according to local culture. Equally important is that respect for human rights is embedded in the core values and culture of the organization.

The development and implementation of a human rights policy should take into account any appropriate guidelines and, where possible, include input from and consultation with relevant stakeholder groups. Some ideas for bringing human rights into company policy include:

- developing a company policy and strategy to support human rights,
- developing a health and safety management system,
- providing staff training on human rights issues and how they are affected by business,
- providing staff training on internal company policies as they relate to human rights,
- performing human rights impact assessments of business activities and reviewing them regularly,
- discussing human rights impacts with affected groups, and
- working to improve working conditions in consultation with the workers and their representatives.

Organizations can improve or ensure human rights through their daily workplace activities in a number of ways; for example, by:

1. providing safe and healthy working conditions,
2. guaranteeing freedom of association,
3. ensuring nondiscrimination in personnel practices,
4. ensuring that they do not use directly or indirectly forced labor or child labor, and
5. providing access to basic health, education, and housing for the workers and their families, if these are not provided elsewhere.

For more information on the UN Global Compact, visit the organization's home page at www.unglobalcompact.org.

MAKING MANAGERIAL DECISIONS

Learning Goal

2. Describe and use four models for making managerial decisions.

In previous chapters, we have presented a variety of concepts and models that are important to understanding individual, team, and managerial decision making. In this section, we describe the main features of four managerial decision-making models: the rational, bounded rationality, evidence-based, and political models. In doing so, we introduce you to the different ways in which managerial decision making is viewed. Each model is useful for gaining insights into the complex array of managerial decision-making situations in an organization.

Rational Model

The rational model *involves a process for choosing among alternatives to maximize benefits to an organization.* This includes comprehensive problem definition, thorough data collection and analysis, and a careful assessment of alternatives. The criteria for evaluating alternatives are well known and agreed on. The generation and exchange of information among individuals presumably happen in an unbiased and accurate way. Individual preferences and organizational choices are a function of the best alternative for the entire organization.[31] Thus, the rational model of decision making assumes that:

1. all available information concerning alternatives has been obtained,
2. these alternatives can be ranked according to agreed-on criteria, and
3. the alternative selected will provide the maximum gain possible for the organization.

An implicit assumption is that ethical dilemmas do not exist in the decision-making process. The means–end and utilitarian principles often dominate the consideration of ethical issues.

Xerox's Six-Stage Process. The Xerox Business Research Group (XBRG) developed a six-stage rational process for guiding decision making. It is presented in Table 13.4. Column 1 shows the six stages, column 2 identifies the key question to be answered in each stage, and column 3 indicates what's needed to proceed to the next stage. Managers and employees receive extensive training to help them work through these stages.[32]

Table 13.4 Xerox's Rational Decision-Making Process

STAGE	CORE QUESTION	TO GO TO THE NEXT STEP, DEVELOP:
1. Identify and select problem	What do we want to change?	Identification of the gap; "desired state" described in observable terms
2. Analyze problem	What's preventing us from reaching the "desired state"?	Key cause(s) documented and ranked
3. Generate potential solutions	How could we make the change?	Solution list
4. Select and plan the solution	What's the best way to do it?	Plan for making and monitoring the change; measurement criteria to evaluate solution effectiveness
5. Implement the solution	Are we following the plan?	Solution in place
6. Evalute the solution	How well did it work?	Verification that the problem is solved, or agreement to address continuing problems

Source: Adapted from Xerox consensus matrix. Available at http://www.xbrg.com (accessed June 2005).

The rational model puts a premium on logical thinking.[33] Sophie Vandebroek is the chief technology officer at Xerox. She sees innovation as a combination of a creative process and a rational decision-making process. Vandebroek comments:

> *We do research on six S's. We constantly want to make our systems simpler, speedier, smaller (because smaller means less expensive), smarter (like remote diagnostics, remote prognostics, making sure our customers don't need to deal with their systems because Xerox knows the status of the machine), more secure, and socially responsible (meaning more green technologies).*[34]

Managerial Guidelines. Clearly, a desirable feature of the rational model is that it helps keep people from jumping to premature conclusions about the nature of the problem and course of action to take. It encourages more deliberation, including the search for critical pieces of information. Of course, it provides no guarantee of success, especially with decision situations that involve a high degree of risk or uncertainty.[35]

One limitation of the rational model is that it can take a considerable amount of time. The resources required to use the rational model may exceed the benefit from it. This approach requires considerable data and information, which may be hard to obtain. Moreover, if the situation keeps changing, the decisions selected may quickly become obsolete. Another limitation is that managers may have to act when goals are vague or conflicting. Even when the rational process is used, decision makers may simply change the stated goals, criteria, or weights if a favored alternative doesn't come out on top. In brief, we suggest using the rational model to the extent feasible but don't expect it to be the sole or even primary guide in making many managerial decisions.[36]

The following Change Competency feature reports on the rational decision making at St. Vincent's Hospital to eliminate medical errors and improve efficiency.[37] This not-for-profit hospital, located in Birmingham, Alabama, is part of the Ascension Health Corporation.[38]

Change Competency

St. Vincent's Rational Initiatives

At St. Vincent's, medical data are literally in the air. X-rays, CAT scans, and lab results can be retrieved immediately off of the hospital's wireless network, saving doctors time. But St. Vincent's Wi-Fi network has been turned toward an even more important purpose: eliminating medical errors. The goal is zero preventable errors.

That's a hard goal to achieve. One study showed that one in five hospital medications is given in error. Medical mistakes, including those that occur during surgery and at other stages of patient care, may kill 100,000 people a year in the United States. Significantly reducing such mistakes could save more lives than curing diabetes.

Consistent with the rational model, St. Vincent has adopted state-of-the-art technologies to prevent mistakes. Robot arms often perform surgery with precision. Machines measure out doses of medicine. Surgical tools have bar codes so that they can be tracked—ensuring that they are properly maintained and never left inside patients. Nurses use scanners to check bar codes on patients' armbands so that drugs are given as doctors prescribed. Physicians can download an x-ray in a few minutes. Lab results come across as soon as they're ready, not hours later. With a tablet PC, physicians can show patients images of their broken bones or tumors. They can even compare new images to old ones.

Prescribing drugs by computer has been a huge time saver for physicians. The pharmacy information system includes electronic order entry and advanced clinical screening that checks for drug/drug, drug/allergy, and therapeutic class duplications. St. Vincent also deployed automated dispensing cabinets, featuring locked, sealed pockets that prevent clinician access to nonprescribed medications based on order information received from the pharmacy system.

At St. Vincent's, the medical staff can also check every patient test, order, and procedure via an electronic results viewer, which is accessible from wireless tablets. Approximately 1,500 personal computers (PCs) are deployed throughout patient rooms and nursing stations across the six-building hospital campus. In patient rooms, medical devices, such as blood pressure monitors and heart monitoring machines, are connected to each bedside PC, so vital sign information doesn't have to be reentered. Through dual-monitor computers at each nursing station, providers can review digital radiographic images alongside current clinical data, such as medication orders, patient allergies, laboratory results, and other clinical observations.

For more information on St. Vincent's Hospital Birmingham, visit the organization's home page at www.stv.org.

Bounded Rationality Model

The bounded rationality model *describes the limitations of rationality and emphasizes the decision-making processes often used by individuals or teams.* This model helps to explain why different individuals or teams may make different decisions when they have exactly the same information. This model also recognizes the reality that complete information—concerning available alternatives or the outcome of some course of action—may be impossible for an individual or team to obtain, regardless of the amount of time and resources applied to the task. As portrayed in Figure 13.3, the bounded rationality model reflects the individual's or team's tendencies to

1. select less than the best goal or alternative solution (that is, to *satisfice*),
2. undertake a limited search for alternative solutions, and
3. cope with inadequate information and control of external and internal environmental forces influencing the outcomes of decisions.[39]

Satisficing. Satisficing *is the tendency to select an acceptable, rather than an optimal, goal or decision. Acceptable* might mean easier to identify and achieve, less controversial, or otherwise safer than the best alternative. For example, profit goals are often stated as a percentage, such as a 15 percent rate of return on investment or a 5 percent increase in profits over the previous year. These goals may not be the optimal attainable. They may,

FIGURE 13.3 Bounded Rationality Model

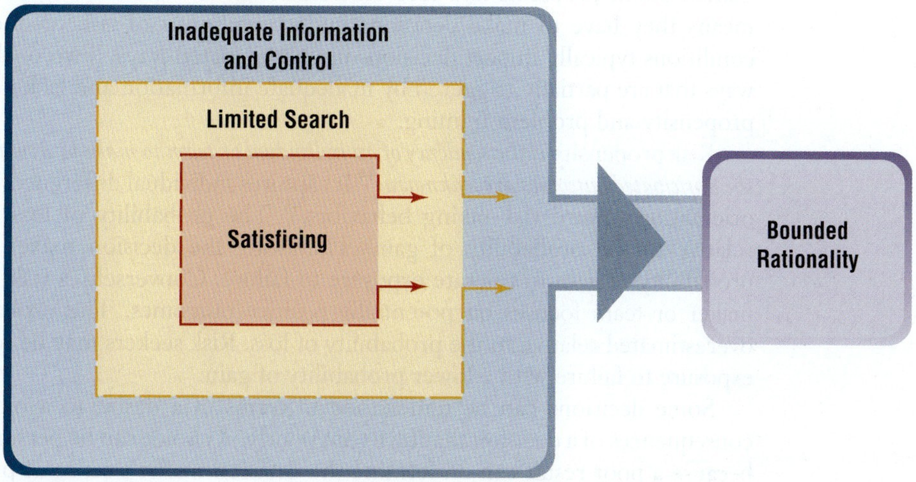

in fact, reflect little more than top management's view of reasonable goals that are challenging but not impossible to achieve. Herbert Simon, who introduced the bounded rationality model, comments:[40]

> *Satisficing doesn't necessarily mean that managers have to be satisfied with what alternative pops up first in their minds or in their computers and let it go at that. The level of satisficing can be raised—by personal determination, setting higher individual or organizational standards, and by the use of an increasing range of sophisticated management science and computer-based decision-making and problem-solving techniques.*
>
> *As time goes on, you obtain more information about what's feasible and what you can aim at. Not only do you get more information, but in many, if not most, companies there are procedures for setting targets, including procedures for trying to raise individuals' aspiration levels [goals]. This is a major responsibility of top management.*

Limited Search. Individuals and teams often make a limited search for possible goals or solutions to a problem, considering alternatives only until they find one that seems adequate. For example, in choosing the "best" job, you won't be able to evaluate every available job in your particular field. You might hit retirement age before obtaining all of the information needed for a decision! In the bounded rationality model, an individual or team stops searching for alternatives as soon as an acceptable ("good-enough") goal or solution is discovered.[41]

One form of limited search is escalating commitment—*a process of continuing or increasing the allocation of resources to a course of action even though a substantial amount of feedback indicates that the choice made is wrong*. This process, in terms of capital investment decisions, is often called "throwing good money after bad." One of the explanations for escalating commitment is that individuals feel responsible for negative consequences, which motivates them to justify previous choices. Individuals may become committed to a choice simply because they believe that consistency in action is a desirable form of behavior.[42] Also, this process may be more likely if groupthink exists, which was discussed in Chapter 11. A number of years ago, there was an escalating commitment to a single, integrated baggage-handling system for all airlines at the Denver International Airport. Although numerous problems with the integrated system continued after repeated and expensive failed efforts to resolve them, the managers continued for more than a year to increase their commitment to making it work. They refused to recognize that the problem was the system itself. Finally, as a result of increased pressures from various stakeholders to open the new airport, the integrated baggage-handling system was scrapped.[43]

Inadequate Information and Control. Decision makers often have inadequate information about problems and face environmental forces that they can't control. This means they have to make decisions under conditions of risk or uncertainty. These conditions typically impact decisions in unanticipated ways. Two of the unanticipated ways that are partially triggered by inadequate information and lack of control are risk propensity and problem framing.

Risk propensity *is the tendency of an individual or team to make or avoid decisions in which the anticipated outcomes are unknown*.[44] It captures individual differences in the individual orientation toward risk-taking behaviors.[45] The probability of loss is overestimated relative to the probability of gain. Therefore, the decision maker requires a high probability of gain to tolerate exposure to failure. Conversely, a risk-seeking decision maker or team focuses on potentially positive outcomes. The probability of gain is overestimated relative to the probability of loss. Risk seekers may be willing to tolerate exposure to failure with a lower probability of gain.

Some decisions can be understood in terms of a desire to avoid the unpleasant consequences of a decision that turns out poorly. A choice can be personally threatening because a poor result can undermine the decision maker's sense of professional competence, create problems for the organization, and even get the decision maker demoted or fired. Many individuals have a low propensity for risk. They purchase many types of insurance to avoid the risk of large but improbable losses. They invest in savings accounts, CDs, and money market funds to avoid the risk of extreme fluctuations in stocks and bonds. Generally, they prefer decision alternatives that produce satisfactory results more than risky decisions that have the same or higher expected outcomes.[46]

Problem framing *is the tendency to interpret issues and options in either positive or negative terms*. Individuals or teams in favorable circumstances tend to be more risk averse because they think that they have more to lose. In contrast, individuals or teams in unfavorable situations tend to think that they have little to lose and therefore may be more risk seeking. Focusing on potential losses increases the importance of risk. In contrast, focusing on potential gains lessens the importance of risk. Thus, a positively framed situation fosters risk taking by drawing managerial attention to opportunities rather than the possibility of failure. An example of positive versus negative framing is that of the certainty of winning $6,000 or the 80 percent probability of winning $10,000. Most people prefer the certain gain to the uncertain chance of larger gain. Which would you choose? Although risk aversion commonly is assumed to hold for most decisions, many exceptions have been documented. For example, people tend to prefer taking risks when making a choice between a certain loss and a risky loss.[47]

Managerial Guidelines. Decision rules are a part of the bounded rationality model. They are often referred to as *heuristics*. They provide quick and easy ways for managers to reach a decision without a detailed analysis and search. They are written down, easily applied, and sometimes thought of as "rules of thumb." One type of heuristic is the dictionary rule, *which involves ranking items the same way a dictionary does: one criterion (analogous to one letter) at a time*. The dictionary rule gives great importance to the first criterion. It is valid in decision making only if this first criterion is known to be of overriding importance.[48]

Consider what can happen when management too hastily uses the dictionary rule. The director and his staff at the Ohio Department of Claims experienced a growing backlog of social benefit appeals. They implemented a change in handling procedures. Their brief analysis led to a pooling idea that grouped similar claims for mass handling. However, the analysis failed to focus on the reason for the growing number of claims. After the backlog grew to the point that claims took a year to process, the director discovered a loophole in the legislation that had inadvertently eased eligibility requirements. The director made the legislature aware of the oversight and the loophole was closed. In the meantime, the agency was subjected to constant criticism and legal action for its slow, error-prone claims management. As the incident suggests, managers often want to find out quickly what is wrong and fix it immediately. The all-too-common result is poor problem definition and a choice of criteria that proves to be misleading. Symptoms are analyzed while more important concerns may be ignored.[49]

Recall one of the comments by Herbert Simon in the previous quote: "The level of satisficing can be raised—by personal determination, setting higher individual or organizational standards, and by the use of an increasing range of sophisticated management science and computer-based decision-making and problem-solving techniques." Knowledge management has emerged as one way for doing so.

Knowledge management *is the art of adding or creating value by systematically capitalizing on the know-how, experience, and judgment found both within and outside an organization*. Knowledge management is a means of raising the level of satisficing. Knowledge is different from data and information. *Data* represent observations or facts that have no context and are not immediately or directly useful. *Information* results from placing data within some meaningful context, often in the form of a message. *Knowledge* is that which a person comes to believe and value on the basis of the systematic organized accumulation of information through experience, communication, and inference. Knowledge can be viewed both as a *thing* to be stored and manipulated and as *process* of applying expertise.[50]

Knowledge can be either tacit or explicit. Tacit knowledge *is developed from direct experience and usually is shared through conversation and storytelling*. The campus food director at Pennsylvania State University telling a new manager how to handle abusive students or a sales manager at the Four Seasons Hotel telling a catering person about the habits of a particular client are examples of conveying tacit knowledge. In contrast, explicit knowledge *is more precise and formally expressed*, such as a computer database and software program that creates information and analyses on customer purchasing habits or a training manual describing how to close a sale.

Evidence-Based Management Model

The evidence-based management model *proceeds from the premise that using better, deeper diagnosis and employing facts to the extent possible enables managers to do their jobs better.*[51] Its roots are in evidence-based medicine, a quality movement designed to apply the scientific method to medical practice.[52] Moreover, this model embraces the core elements of the rational model, but in an expanded and applied version to managerial decision making. This model also recognizes and attempts to reduce the problems identified through the bounded rationality model.

Jeffrey Pfeffer and Robert Sutton, two of the leading developers of the evidence-based management model, comment:

> *As with medicine, management is and will likely always be a craft that can be learned only through practice and experience. Yet, we believe that managers (like doctors) can practice their craft more effectively if they are routinely guided by the best logic and evidence—and if they relentlessly seek new knowledge and insight, from both inside and outside their companies, to keep updating their assumptions, knowledge, and skills.*[53]

This model emphasizes the dangers of being "seduced" by the "quick fix" or "fad." It reminds us that managerial decision making is often complex and time consuming, and it requires a tough, disciplined mind-set. Beware of easy and simpleminded answers.[54] According to this model, one way to help managers avoid simpleminded quick fixes is to carefully consider these critical diagnostic questions:[55]

1. What assumptions does the idea or practice make about people and organizations? What would have to be true about people and organizations for the idea or practice to be effective?
2. Which of these assumptions seem reasonable and correct to you and your colleagues? Which seem wrong and suspect?
3. Could this idea or practice still succeed if the assumptions turned out to be wrong?
4. How might you and your colleagues quickly and inexpensively gather some data to test the reasonableness of the underlying assumptions?
5. What other ideas or management practices can you think of that would address the same problem or issue and be more consistent with what you believe to be true about people and organizations?

The evidence-based management model helps to reduce mental blinders that prevent managers from seeing, seeking, using, or sharing relevant and accessible information during the decision-making process.[56] The most problematic aspect of the failure to seek information occurs when a manager is motivated or biased to favor a particular course of action. As a result, there is often an absence of seeking out or listening to disconfirming evidence.

Managerial Guidelines. The evidence-based management model presents a number of guidelines for improving managerial decision making. The overarching prescription for evidence-based management is much broader than any single guideline, namely, the need for *wisdom*. Pfeffer and Sutton suggest:

> *... wisdom means "knowing what you know and knowing what you don't know," especially striking a balance between arrogance (assuming you know more than you*

do) and insecurity (believing that you know too little to act). This attitude enables people to act on their present knowledge while doubting what they know. It means they do things now, as well as keep learning along the way.[57]

Evidence-based management involves learning principles, models, and concepts (knowing what) as well as processes and procedures (knowing how).[58] This book has implemented this learning process through the presentation of models and concepts (knowing what) and their application (knowing how) through the Learning from Experience features, competency features, experiential exercises, and cases. In their day-to-day decision making, managers are well served by learning from books such as this one and the key sources we have cited as they address issues and problems related to perceptions, stress, conflict, communication, culture, leadership, organization design, change, decision making, and the like.

Let's consider a few of the guidelines advanced by Pfeffer and Sutton for using evidence-based management:

- Managers should be cautious about blindly embracing and implementing practices and ideas that are sold as new and novel, but are really old ideas and practices under new labels. Employees subjected to such "new" ideas and practices soon discover that higher management is simply advancing "old wine in a new bottle," which creates cynicism, skepticism, and distrust toward management.
- Managers should constructively question the *big* idea or technique that is claimed to create breakthroughs for the organization. In general, most claimed breakthroughs—or "silver bullets"—represent incremental improvements in the best case scenario or counterproductive changes if they do not fit the context and tasks performed by employees in specific units.
- Managers should be cautious of celebrating and embracing lone "geniuses" or gurus. Knowledge that effectively guides decision making is rarely generated by a lone guru. Moreover, gurus too often oversimplify management challenges and the decision context in prescribing their ready-made solutions.
- Managers should recognize and diagnose the potential drawbacks, not just virtues, of a particular *new* idea or practice both before and during its implementation. In medicine, few drugs are without potential negative side effects, and few surgical procedures are without potential risks and problems. These potential downsides are typically made explicit in the practice of medicine, but rarely so in the "selling" of a new idea, technique, or program that is claimed to solve one or more problems in organizations.

LEADER INSIGHT

A good decision maker will always weigh the evidence. Although it's clear that we all rely on our personal experiences and values to guide our decision making, leaders who differentiate themselves time and again are the ones who trust their intuition but also use properly researched evidence to make decisions. That does not mean that their well-honed intuition is without value, but it should drive their demands for evidence, rather than replace it altogether.
Chris Hyman, CEO, Serco Group

Let's now turn to a few of the limitations in the use of the evidence-based management model. First, the notions of "substituting facts for conventional wisdom" and "being committed to fact-based decision making" can be a challenge to put in practice. For example, it can be challenging "... to define what a fact is—who decides which facts count, get included, get dismissed, and so forth?"[59] The managers and other stakeholders may disagree on which goals, data, evidence, and logic are relevant for or should be used in the decision-making process. For example, the fact that new home sales by Centex, a home builder, are declining may be interpreted by marketing managers as a pricing issue, whereas construction managers might see it as building the wrong types of houses in a market, while finance managers think it is due to rising interest rates. Second, evidence-based management does not adequately address the value of intuition and judgment, especially when the decision-making situation involves high risk, uncertainty, or novelty due to the lack of "facts" that can "predict" the outcome of decision alternatives.[60] Strategic decisions made by managers often involve uncertainty because data and evidence look backward, even though the decisions made today with that data are about the future, which may or may not be influenced by the past when the competitive environment is highly complex and rapidly changing. Third, evidence for managerial decision making, especially under conditions of uncertainty, may be contradictory, not always easy to make sense of, and subject to different interpretations among managers as well as influential stakeholders. While recognizing these potential limitations, the evidence-based management model, which we have only highlighted here, has much to offer for improving the day-to-day managerial decision making that takes place in organizations.

The following Self Competency feature on Diane Schueneman, the senior vice president and head of Merrill Lynch's Global Infrastructure Solutions Group, talks about some of the ways that she implements the evidence-based management model.[61] This feature also reflects her change and team competencies. Merrill Lynch, headquartered in New York, is a major wealth management, capital markets, and advisory company. It has offices in 38 countries and territories with total client assets of approximately $1.7 trillion. Merrill Lynch has approximately 62,000 employees.[62] This feature provides selected excerpts of an extensive interview with Diane Schueneman. The group she leads includes approximately 13,000 employees.

Self Competency

Diane Schueneman, Senior VP and Head of Merrill Lynch's Global Infrastructure Solutions Group

© Stockbyte/Getty Images

Diane Schueneman of Merrill Lynch believes that it is the integration of technology and operations, from beginning to end, that allows for effective customer service.

I try to remember that we're not a technology company; we're a financial-services company that supplies solutions to our customers around their financial needs—simple as that. Customers don't say, "You do a really great job creating an equity product." They ask, "How well do you deliver it to me?" and "Does it meet my needs?"

So the whole reason to combine technology and operations rests on the customer's needs. And to deliver against those needs requires the best operational processes and the best technology. But you can't start with one and graft on the other. It's the integration of technology and operations, from beginning to end, that really allows you to serve customers effectively, anywhere in the world. It's one example of how we're transforming our organization to think differently from the ways that financial-services companies have thought in the past—which is to say you have to move beyond an individual silo mentality.

If I can rally my organization around the customer's vantage point, I can deliver higher productivity and greater effectiveness. What is interesting is that this also drives employee satisfaction. When managers ask, "How do we get people in a support group like IT or operations to feel like they're part of the business?" the answer seems to be: connect people to the company's value proposition and to customers. People want to feel like they're valued, and there's nothing like the customer telling you that you're valued to make you feel good about your contribution. Sometimes people think that customer value is all on the front line, the face. But if the technology behind the scenes can't process the requests, the customer is not going to be happy. So I need to have the IT and operations staff recognizing how the end goal is dependent on their contribution. Everybody's got a role to play and everybody needs to understand the value of their role.

I think anytime you ask people to change, they wonder if they've done something wrong. To move past that, you explain the rationale and the vision of where you want to go—in our case, moving from an internal focus to an external one centered on the customer's perspective. Once you get people excited about change and give them the freedom to think, you unleash their intellectual capabilities. They do amazing things, and that's how you get innovation.

Our global support model initiative is one example. This is where our infrastructure team got together to basically rethink and reinvent what our entire technology platform should look like. How do we become more efficient, agile, and scalable than we are today? How do we train our people so they have the best skills in the business? How do we organize ourselves so we are delivering all of the firm's capabilities to clients in the ways clients want them delivered?

Another thing that I focus on very heavily is creating learning and development opportunities for employees, because if you don't do that, then you can't ask them to take risks. We have to teach them how to take risks, how to make change happen. We've started a six-month technology innovation program, which grew out of a successful innovation program one of our groups was running. It combines periodic classroom training with an ongoing contest where ten teams will each create a business proposal and compete to have it funded by our technology-investment committee.

For more information on Merrill Lynch, visit the organization home page at www.ml.com.

Political Model

The political model *describes decision making by individuals, groups, or units when the parties perceive that they have separate and different interests, goals, and values.* It stands in contrast to the evidence-based management model because of its focus on self-interest goals. Those may not change as new information is learned. Problem definition, data search and collection, information exchange, and evaluation criteria are methods used to bias the outcome in favor of the individual, group, or unit.[63]

The distribution of power in an organization and the effectiveness of the tactics used by managers and employees influence the impact of the decisions.[64] The political model doesn't explicitly recognize ethical dilemmas. However, it often draws on two of the self-serving ethical principles discussed previously: (1) the hedonistic principle—do whatever you find to be in your own self-interest; and (2) the might-equals-right principle—you are strong enough to take advantage without respect to ordinary social customs.

The political model is found in organizations throughout the world. For example, French culture values relatively high power distance. Relationships between superiors and subordinates are unequal, with different levels of status and privilege. The political model in French organizations, such as Altedia, Société Allen SA, and Group Ares, is based on various underlying assumptions and expected behaviors, three of which follow:

- Power, once attained, should not be shared except with a small group of senior managers. Some people are born to lead and others to follow; it is difficult for people to change. Secretaries are there to follow orders. Middle managers need to consult with their bosses as well as many others in the organization before making a decision.
- If individuals have been recognized as having top-management competencies, it does not matter if they are put in a job where they have no experience. They should be able to learn how to do their jobs with experience because of their competencies.
- It is harmful to reveal information unnecessarily because then the decision-making process cannot be controlled. When, where, and how to communicate information is a delicate question that often only the upper echelons can decide.[65]

Managerial Guidelines. The political model as seen in organizations focuses on individuals and groups to exert power or influence others' behaviors. The influence methods

Table 13.5 Influence Strategies

INFLUENCE STRATEGY	DEFINITION
• Rational persuasion	Use logical arguments and factual evidence.
• Inspirational appeal	Appeal to values, ideals, or aspirations to arouse enthusiasm.
• Consultation	Seek participation in planning a strategy, activity, or change.
• Ingratiation	Attempt to create a favorable mood before making request.
• Exchange	Offer an exchange of favors, share of benefits, or promise to reciprocate at later time.
• Personal appeal	Appeal to feelings of loyalty or friendship.
• Coalition	Seek aid or support of others for some initiative or activity.
• Legitimating	Seek to establish legitimacy of a request by claiming authority or by verifying consistency with policies, practices, or traditions.
• Pressure	Use demands, threats, or persistent reminders.

Source: Adapted from Yukl, G., Guinan, P. J., and Sottolano, D. Influence tactics used for different objectives with subordinates, peers, and superiors. *Group & Organization Management*, 1995, 20, 275; Buchanan, D., and Badham, R. *Power, Politics and Organizational Change.* London: Sage, 1999, 64.

presented at the top of Table 13.5—rational persuasion, inspirational appeal, and consultation—often are the most effective in many workplace situations. The least effective methods seem to be coalition, legitimating, and pressure. To assume that certain methods will always work or that others will always fail is a mistake. Differences in effectiveness occur when attempts to influence are downward rather than upward in the organizational hierarchy. Differences in effectiveness appear when various methods are used in combination rather than independently. The influence process is complex. To understand fully the effectiveness of various influence strategies, you need to know the power sources available, the direction of attempts to influence (i.e., upward, downward, or laterally), the goals being sought, and the cultural values of the organization.

Having the *capacity* (power) to influence the behaviors of others and effectively using it aren't the same thing. Managers who believe that they can always effectively influence the behaviors of others by acquiring enough power simply to order other people around generally are ineffective. The ineffective use of power has many negative implications, both for the individual and the organization. For example, the consequences of an overreliance on the pressure method are often negative. Managers who are aggressive and persistent with others—characterized by a refusal to take *no* for an answer, reliance on repeated reminders, frequent use of face-to-face confrontations, and the like—usually suffer negative consequences. Compared to others, the managers who rely heavily on the pressure method typically (1) receive the lowest performance evaluations, (2) earn less money, and (3) experience the highest levels of job tension and stress.[66] Also, recall our discussion of *impression management* strategies—ingratiation, self-promotion, and face-saving—and *political skill* in Chapters 3 and 8.

Learning Goal

3. Explain organizational creativity and how to foster it.

STIMULATING CREATIVITY IN ORGANIZATIONS

Nature of Organizational Creativity

Organizational creativity *is the generation of unique and useful ideas by an individual or team in an organization.* Innovation builds on unique and useful ideas.[67] Creativity helps

FIGURE 13.4 Potential Roadblocks to Creativity and Innovation

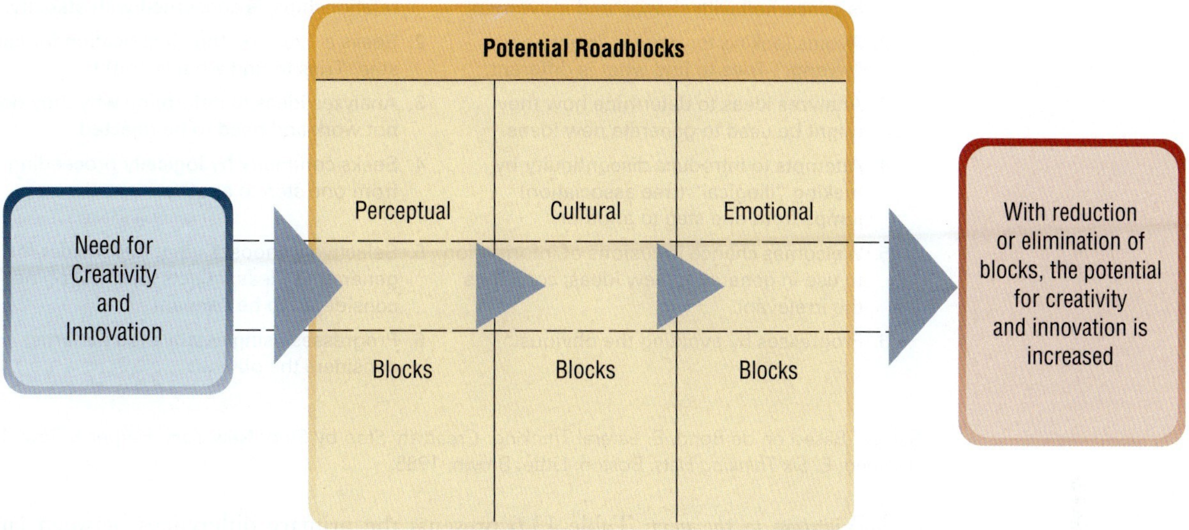

employees uncover problems, identify opportunities, and make novel choices in solving problems. The stimulation of creativity is in the hands of managers as they think about and establish the work environment. For example, poorly designed motivational and reward systems are likely to result in ineffective team approaches. One creativity expert comments: "The thing about creativity is that you can't tell at the outset which ideas will succeed and which will fail. ... Now, leaders pay a lot of lip service to the notion of rewarding failure. ... Often, they have a forgive-and-forget policy. Forgiveness is crucial but it's not enough. In order to learn from mistakes, it's even more important to forgive and *remember*."[68] We have discussed various ways of reducing roadblocks to creativity and innovation. As suggested in Figure 13.4, three broad categories are perceptual, cultural, and emotional blocks[69]:

1. *Perceptual blocks* include such factors as the failure to use all of the senses in observing, failure to investigate the obvious, difficulty in seeing remote relationships, and failure to distinguish between cause and effect.
2. *Cultural blocks* include a desire to conform to established norms, overemphasis on competition or conflict avoidance and smoothing, the drive to be practical and narrowly economical above all else, and a belief that indulging in fantasy or other forms of open-ended exploration is a waste of time.
3. *Emotional blocks* include the fear of making a mistake, fear and distrust of others, grabbing the first idea that comes along, and the like. For many organizations, fostering creativity and innovation is essential to their ability to offer high-quality products and services.

There are numerous methods for fostering creativity with an individual or team. We address two of them here: the lateral thinking method and brainstorming method.

Lateral Thinking Method

The lateral thinking method *is a deliberate process and set of techniques for generating new ideas by changing an individual's or team's way of perceiving and interpreting information.* We can best explain this method by contrasting it with the vertical thinking method, *which is a logical step-by-step process of developing ideas by proceeding continuously from one bit of*

Table 13.6 Characteristics of Lateral versus Vertical Thinking

LATERAL THINKING	VERTICAL THINKING
1. Tries to find new ways for looking at things; is concerned with change and movement.	1. Tries to find absolutes for judging relationships; is concerned with stability.
2. Avoids looking for what is "right" or "wrong." Tries to find what is different.	2. Seeks a "yes" or "no" justification for each step. Tries to find what is "right."
3. Analyzes ideas to determine how they might be used to generate new ideas.	3. Analyzes ideas to determine why they do not work and need to be rejected.
4. Attempts to introduce discontinuity by making "illogical" (free association) jumps from one step to another.	4. Seeks continuity by logically proceeding from one step to another.
5. Welcomes chance intrusions of information to use in generating new ideas; considers the irrelevant.	5. Selectively chooses what to consider for generating ideas; rejects information not considered to be relevant.
6. Progresses by avoiding the obvious.	6. Progresses using established patterns; considers the obvious.

Source: Based on de Bono, E. *Lateral Thinking: Creativity Step by Step*. New York: Harper & Row, 1970; de Bono, E. *Six Thinking Hats*. Boston: Little, Brown, 1985.

information to the next. Table 13.6 presents the primary differences between lateral thinking and vertical thinking. Edward de Bono, the British physician and psychologist who developed the lateral thinking method, stated that the two processes are complementary and not at odds with each other.

Lateral thinking fosters the generation of unique ideas and approaches. Vertical thinking is useful for assessing them. Lateral thinking enhances the effectiveness of vertical thinking by offering it more from which to select. Vertical thinking improves the impact of lateral thinking by making good use of the ideas generated. You probably use vertical thinking most of the time, but when you need to use lateral thinking, vertical thinking capabilities won't suffice.[70]

The lateral thinking method includes a variety of techniques for (1) developing an awareness of current ideas and practices, (2) stimulating alternative ways for identifying or looking at a problem, and (3) aiding in the development of new ideas. Here, we consider only three of the techniques for fostering the development of new ideas: reversal, analogy, and cross-fertilization.

Reversal Technique. The reversal technique *involves examining a problem by turning it completely around, inside out, or upside down*. Engineers at Conoco asked, "What's good about toxic waste?" By so doing, they discovered a substance in refinery waste that they now are turning into both a synthetic lubricant and—they hope—a promising new market. Ronald Barbaro, president of Prudential Insurance, considered the idea, "You die before you die," and came up with "living benefit" life insurance. It pays death benefits to people suffering from terminal illnesses before they die. Prudential has sold more than a million such policies.[71]

Analogy Technique. The analogy technique *involves developing a statement about similarities among objects, persons, and situations*. Some examples of analogies are "This organization operates like a beehive" or "This organization operates like a fine Swiss watch." The technique involves translating the problem into an analogy, refining and developing the analogy, and then retranslating the problem to judge the suitability of the analogy. If an analogy is too similar to the problem, little will be gained. Concrete and specific analogies should be selected over more abstract ones. Analogies should describe a specific, well-known issue or process in the organization. For an organization that is ignoring increased environmental change, an analogy might be "We are like a flock of ostriches with our heads buried in the sand."

Cross-Fertilization Technique. The cross-fertilization technique *involves asking experts from other fields to view the problem and suggest methods for solving it from their own areas of expertise.* For the technique to be effective, these outsiders should be from fields entirely removed from the problem. An attempt can then be made to apply new methods to the problem. Each year, Hallmark Cards brings to its Kansas City headquarters 50 or more speakers who might provide fresh ideas to the firm's more than 700 artists, designers, writers, editors, and photographers. Hallmark staffers often go from Hallmark's mid-town headquarters to a downtown loft, where teams of writers and artists get away from phones to exchange ideas. They also may spend days in retreat at a farm in nearby Kearney, Missouri, taking part in fun exercises.[72]

Brainstorming Method

Traditional brainstorming *is a process whereby individuals state as many ideas as possible during a 20- to 60-minute period.* It is usually done with 5 to 12 people. Guidelines for brainstorming include (1) the wilder the ideas the better, (2) don't be critical of any ideas, (3) hitchhike on or combine previously stated ideas, and (4) quantity is wanted. In the past, traditional brainstorming was assumed to generate many more and better ideas than if the same number of individuals worked alone.[73] Some research indicates that traditional brainstorming may not be nearly as effective as once thought.[74] This is especially true if the types of perceptual, cultural, and emotional blocks noted previously are prevalent in the day-to-day work environment. It is critical that the process and guidelines for conducting a traditional brainstorming session be followed. These guidelines are set forth in Table 13.7.

Table 13.7 **Guidelines for Conducting a Traditional Brainstorming Session**

Basic Facilitator

- Make a brief statement of the four basic rules.
- State the time limit for the session.
- Read the problem and/or related question to be discussed and ask, "What are your ideas?"
- When an idea is given, summarize it by using the speaker's words insofar as possible. Have the idea recorded by a recorder or on an audiotape machine. Number each idea. Follow your summary with the single word "Next. "
- Say little else. Whenever the facilitator participates as a brainstormer, group productivity usually falls.
- Consider asking participants to spend 10 minutes on doing individual brainstorming prior to the start of the session by having them record their initial ideas on cards that are provided.

Handling Issues

- When someone talks too long, wait until he or she takes a breath (everyone must stop to inhale sometime), break into the monologue, summarize what was said for the recorder, point to another participant, and say "Next. "
- When someone becomes judgmental or starts to argue, stop him or her.
- When the discussion stops, relax and let the silence continue. Say nothing. The pause should be broken by the group and not the facilitator. This period of silence is called the mental pause because it is a change in thinking. All the obvious ideas are exhausted; the participants are now forced to rely on their creativity to produce new ideas.
- When someone states a problem rather than idea, repeat the problem, raise your hand with five fingers extended, and say, "Let's have five ideas on this problem. " You may get only 1 or you may get 10, but you're back in the business of creative thinking.
- Strongly enforce the rule that only one person speaks at a time.
- Provide note cards for people who get ideas while someone else is speaking to minimize production blocking.

Source: Adapted from Wilson, C. E. Brainstorming pitfalls and best practices. *Interactions*, September/October 2006, 50–53; Dharmarajan, K. *Eightstorm: Eight Step Brain Storming for Innovative Managers.* Las Vegas, NV: BookSurge Publishing, 2007.

To brainstorm effectively is to think of an idea, express it, and get on with thinking of and expressing more new ideas. In face-to-face brainstorming, however, people may be prevented from doing so because someone else is talking. As a result, team members may get bogged down waiting for other people to finish talking. Team members also may be anxious about how others will view them if they express their ideas. This problem may be particularly acute when ideas can be interpreted as critical of current practice or when it is part of a politically hot topic. Withholding ideas for these reasons defeats the purpose of brainstorming.[75]

Electronic brainstorming *involves the use of collaborative software technology to anonymously enter and automatically disseminate ideas in real time to all team members, each of whom may be stimulated to generate other ideas*. For example, GroupSystems, headquartered in Broomfield, Colorado, is one of the leading providers of electronic brainstorming software. For this approach to work, each team member must have a computer terminal that is connected to all other members' terminals. The software allows individuals to enter their ideas as they think of them. Every time an individual enters an idea, a random set of the team's ideas is presented on each person's screen. The individual can continue to see new random sets of ideas by pressing the appropriate key.[76]

Research on electronic brainstorming is encouraging. It tends to produce more novel ideas than traditional brainstorming. It also removes the main barrier of traditional brainstorming: Members seeing and hearing which ideas are whose. Electronic brainstorming permits anonymity and lets team members contribute more freely to idea generation. They need not fear they will "sound like a fool" to other employees and managers when spontaneously generating ideas. These advantages appear to be greater for teams of seven or more people or where there is distrust among team members.[77]

The following Teams Competency feature reports on Funcom's use of teams to foster organizational creativity.[78] Funcom is an independent developer and publisher of computer and console games. It has released 26 games, including Dreamfall, the Longest Journey, and Anarchy Online—The Notum Wars. Funcom N.V. is incorporated in the Netherlands with major offices in Durham, North Carolina; Oslo, Norway; and Dübendorf, Switzerland.[79]

Teams Competency

Funcom's Teams Foster Organizational Creativity

At Funcom, the focus of team members is primarily on the game they are developing. Individuals are motivated to deliver the best within their specific responsibility, but they also need to connect with other team members, whose skills may fall into a radically different area. A visual artist who is creating a fantasy world set 30,000 years in the future might need to connect with a software engineer whose primary concern is how the detailed programming will work. Both have to be willing and capable of learning from each other and to solve problems together without reducing efficiency. In describing how creativity is stimulated at Funcom, founder Gaute Godager says, "It's innovative, self-examining (not taking anything for granted), and cooperative, and it involves teamwork. Everyone says they like to work in teams, but we're 110 percent dependent on them. For a product to work, there needs to be one person in each area who knows what's going on. There needs to be creative discipline, but within that framework there also needs to be a lot of freedom. Meeting these two demands is quite difficult."

The key factor that Godager and his managers recognize is that effective teamwork and the management of tensions can be realized only through trust. To achieve this, the company tries to recruit people with high levels of skill in their specific disciplines. This is important, because team members need to have trust in one another's capabilities—no one person can micromanage the detail. Godager sees his own role as one of inspiring people about the game idea and setting the boundaries of creativity. He knows he doesn't have the technical expertise to oversee the specifics, so Funcom's employees are allowed as much creative freedom as they can handle. The value in this is that the individual team members feel a strong sense of project ownership, since it is their own individual and collective creativity that defines the game. Funcom needs people who can cover broad areas and input their creativity into the detail. It is also an issue of philosophy—a view that the ability to express creativity is fulfilling.

Funcom allows team members to work flexibly within broad constraints. This balance enables diversity within a work environment that is fundamentally homogeneous in terms of core values, goals, and systems. Individual needs are met and managed within a framework of shared values and goals that facilitate trust.

For more information on Funcom, visit the organization's home page at www.funcom.com.

CHAPTER SUMMARY

Individuals often experience ethical dilemmas when making decisions. We addressed five important issues, which can be stated as questions, in ethical decision making: What is the ethical intensity? What are the principles and rules? Who is affected? What are the benefits and costs? Who has rights?

1. Explain and apply the core concepts and principles for making ethical decisions.

The rational, bounded rationality, evidence-based management, and political models are commonly used to explain managerial decision making. Each model explains some aspects of managerial decision-making situations and processes. All four models are needed to grasp the complexity and entire range of decision making. Managerial guidelines related to the use of each model were presented.

2. Describe and use four models for making managerial decisions.

Creativity is needed in changing, complex, and uncertain environments. This situation often results in ambiguity and disagreement over both the goals to be achieved and the best course of action to pursue. Organizational creativity and innovation are crucial to the discovery and implementation of unique and useful ideas. We reviewed common roadblocks to creativity that surface in organizations, including perceptual, cultural, and emotional blocks. Two of many approaches for stimulating organizational creativity are the lateral thinking method and brainstorming method.

3. Explain organizational creativity and how to foster it.

KEY TERMS AND CONCEPTS

Analogy technique
Bounded rationality model
Concentration of effect
Cross-fertilization technique
Dictionary rule
Disclosure principle
Distributive justice principle
Electronic brainstorming
Employment at will
Escalating commitment
Ethical intensity
Evidence-based management model
Explicit knowledge
Golden rule principle
Hedonist principle
Knowledge management
Lateral thinking method
Magnitude of consequences
Means–end principle
Might-equals-right principle
Organization interests principle
Organizational creativity
Political model
Probability of effect
Problem framing
Professional standards principle
Proximity
Rational model

Reversal technique
Risk propensity
Satisficing
Social consensus
Tacit knowledge
Temporal immediacy
Traditional brainstorming
Utilitarian principle
Vertical thinking method

DISCUSSION QUESTIONS

1. Go to www.costco.com. In the search box, type in "investor relations" and then click on "corporate governance." Open the document entitled "Vendor Code of Conduct." Identify at least three of the ethical principles that are reflected in this document. What is a specific provision that illustrates each of the principles identified?
2. Go to Table 13.3 in this chapter. It presents 10 UN Global Compact principles. Evaluate any three of these principles in relation to each of the six factors that make up ethical intensity.
3. What are the likely benefits and costs to the employment-at-will concept from the perspective of employers, employees, and society at large?
4. What are the differences between the organization interests principle and the utilitarian principle?
5. Think of an organization in which you are or have been an employee. Describe a decision situation that seemed to be based on the bounded rationality model in relation to the concepts of satisficing, limited search, and inadequate information and control.
6. What are the differences between the evidence-based management model and the political model?
7. Review the Self Competency feature on Diane Schueneman, senior VP and head of Merrill Lynch's Global Infrastructure Solutions Group. This feature primarily reflects her use of the evidence-based management model. What specific aspects of this model are illustrated through this feature?
8. Describe a specific problem that you have experienced that was probably affected by the problem framing bias.
9. Review the Teams Competency on how Funcom's teams foster organizational creativity. In what ways does this feature illustrate ways to reduce perceptual, cultural, and emotional blocks to creativity?

EXPERIENTIAL EXERCISE AND CASE

Experiential Exercise: Ethics Competency

You Make the Decision[80]

Instructions

Mark the preferred decision for each of the four incidents and reply to the two questions that follow each incident.

Ethical Incidents

1. Barbara is a sales representative for Global Fashions Inc. One of her best customers, George, places a large order for linen jackets for the coming spring season. Barbara knows that Global has had production and delivery problems with these jackets. She also knows that George's order will assure her year-end bonus. Should she:

____ A Take the order. There's no guarantee that Global won't meet the deadline, and George is sophisticated enough to know that sometimes problems happen in manufacturing.

____ B Warn George of the risk and put the sale at risk before taking the order, if George still wants to place it.

____ C Refuse the order, since she's likely to disappoint a long-time customer by promising something that may not happen.

Questions
1. What ethical principle or principles reflect your decision?
2. How would you assess the ethical intensity in this situation?

2. Jose is a general manager of a division of Global Operations. In that capacity, he knows that his company is planning on making layoffs soon. Juan, a good friend in another division, tells Jose he is about to buy a new house that is much more expensive, but he's confident that he can make the higher payments, because his career at Global is going well. Jose doesn't know if Juan will be laid off but is concerned. Should he:

____ A Warn Juan of the upcoming layoffs.

____ B Encourage Juan to hold off on buying the house because "something is up" and he can't say more.

____ C Let Juan's direct supervisor know what Juan is doing.

_____ D Stay out of the issue. Since Jose doesn't know what's going to happen to Juan, there's really nothing to do.

Questions
1. What ethical principle or principles reflect your decision?
2. How would you evaluate the ethical intensity in this situation?

3. Don is a sales representative for a local moving company. His friend Adam works as an auto salesman. Adam informs Don that people who move are surprisingly likely to buy new cars shortly thereafter because their commute has now changed. He tells Don, "I'll tell you what. Give me the names of people you meet with to discuss moving. I'll send them a welcome-to-the-neighborhood note. If any of them buy a car, I'll give you a piece of my commission." Don should:

_____ A Give Adam the names—there's no harm done.
_____ B Offer to take Adam's cards and give them to customers.
_____ C Decline the offer.

Questions
1. What ethical principle or principles reflect your decision?
2. How would you assess the ethical intensity in this situation?

4. You've been a manager at your company for five years and have developed an excellent reputation. Your future looks bright, which is a good thing since you have a family to support. Yesterday a fellow employee, Kim, came to you with a problem. Kim, an African-American woman who used to report to you, had just been turned down for a promotion. You believe she was very qualified for the position and perfectly capable of doing it with excellence. The candidate chosen was a white male with good qualifications but not as much experience or, in your opinion, capability as Kim. Steve, the manager who did not select Kim, happens to be "a rising star" whom you've known for years and with whom you get along pretty well. Steve couldn't make you CEO and couldn't get you fired, but he is in a position to help or hinder your career. What do you do?

_____ A Encourage Kim to speak to HR and offer to speak to them as well about your excellent opinion of Kim.
_____ B Talk to Steve.
_____ C Tell Kim that many (legitimate) factors go into a promotion decision and that such a decision can't be judged from the outside.
_____ D Talk to Steve's supervisor.

Questions
1. What ethical principle or principles reflect your decision?
2. How would you assess the ethical intensity in this situation?

Case: Communication Competency

Bruce Moeller, CEO of DriveCam, Inc.—The Way I Work[81]

Headquartered in San Diego, California, DriveCam reduces claims costs and saves lives by improving the way people drive. DriveCam lessens risk by improving driver behavior and assessing liability in collisions. Combining sight and sound, expert analysis, and driver coaching, DriveCam's approach has reduced vehicle damages, workers' compensation, and personal injury costs by 30 to 90 percent in more than 70,000 commercial, government, and consumer vehicles. DriveCam, launched in 1998, operates in North America, Europe, Africa, Australia, and Asia. This case presents excerpts of Bruce Moeller's own description of his patterns of communicating and decision making. He is the president, CEO, and member of the Board of Directors of DriveCam.[82] Moeller comments:

The first thing I do when I get up [is] grab my BlackBerry and see what the issues are. Then I'll go through all my e-mails. In total, I get 80 or 100 a day, and I have to know what's okay or what isn't okay. Some mornings it's a struggle to get dressed before you're writing back different e-mails on the BlackBerry. I get to work about 7:30. When I get in, I put my PC, which I've brought from home, into the docking station. I'm compulsive about my e-mail. That's one of my primary communication tools with the rest of the enterprise. It's a one-to-many communication, so it's more efficient.

Then I'll start walking around and going to visit each of my direct reports: marketing, sales, engineering, operations, finance. The COO (chief operating officer) and I also have a meeting that lasts half an hour or an hour every morning—it might be, there's a compliment about this level of service, or somebody dropped the ball on this. I might also meet with the CFO (chief financial officer). We just raised around $28 million, so there's plenty of cash, but there might be a receivable issue. Usually he's just making me aware of issues so I see the little warning flags if someone's not paying. Sometimes he's escalating it to me, saying could you call their CEO and request the payment, or ask their COO under what conditions they could pay. It's really just what's going on in everyone's world; all of us debrief on anything that's new. This is a pretty fast-paced place. We joke here if you miss half a day you've got to get caught back up.

I'm a kind of hub-and-spoke guy, so it's me with this person or me with that one. But because of that hub and spoke, various guys were having difficulty communicating with each other. I'm feeling totally in the loop, of course, getting updates on everything and everybody, but it became apparent that the different functions might not be aware of what the others were doing. So I just agreed to do a meeting with my direct reports every week. We go off-site from 3 p.m. to 8 p.m. We call it Tuesdays with Moeller.

I like to keep my schedule fairly open so that I can be in the moment with whatever the hot issue is—a customer problem or some opportunity. During the day I'll typically have only two or three scheduled meetings. I just like to be very fluid and to force the organization to stay externally focused. If you spend a lot of scheduled time, you get fooled into thinking you're working when you're just playing with each other on internal stuff. When you could've been externally focused on the marketplace.

I like one-on-one meetings anyway. I like to be able to read people, read their eyes, and probe if I'm sensing they're pulling back on something or afraid of something. I'm reading signals all the time. Group meetings are problematic because people perform for audiences. Especially with the CEO in the room it hampers full-flowing conversation because people don't want to look stupid and you tend to get managed information. To combat that, I tell them you never shoot the messenger. Whatever you're feeling, you don't show it. By reacting emotionally you're putting a brand on that news, and you're subliminally shaping behavior. Even when I'm happy, I try to control my emotions. Otherwise I would be telling people not to come to me unless it's with good news.

I encourage free-flowing conversation with other little things, too. A lot of times I'll dress really casually and speak very casually with the employees, trying to be just one of the guys—of course, realizing that I'm not and they don't see me that way. I also have an open-door policy, and my office tends to be a gathering place. I put candy and nuts in here to encourage people to come in, grab a handful of M&M's, and talk. Everyone here knows that even if there are three people in here talking about something, you can come in and join in the meeting, too. If we're talking about marketing and you're an engineer, you might have a good idea. If someone walks in, especially if I think he would be interested or could enhance the conversation, I'll take a quick 60 seconds to update him on what we're talking about. And if he's not interested or doesn't have time to talk, that's okay.

I've always resisted having a secretary. I like to do all the stuff myself and not have somebody keep me insulated from anyone else. Unless I'm really busy, I do my own travel. Expense reports—that's the one liberty I do take. I don't do expense reports. I take all my receipts and walk them down to accounting and say, here, this is from a speech I gave in New Orleans. And that's as far as I go.

I'm almost fully digital, so there's no paper at all on my desk. I do have a little desk calendar with a different French word every day. But I'm not a big note-taker. I think it distracts from really listening to and absorbing what somebody said. If notes are required, I make sure our COO or somebody else is there to take them. I just listen, engage, and remember what the salient points are. I find I'd miss certain nuances of the inflection in the voice, or body language, if I were taking notes.

Client meetings are pretty easy and I enjoy those the most. I come in with a very open and honest approach—I'm not trying to sell you anything. In reality, obviously, I am, but only if it fits. First, I establish a connection if we don't already have one: a sports team, a city we both used to live in, a school. Now, bingo, we're connected. Then I ask myself why the person's here in the first place: If I were him, I'd be coming in because of this problem or that. So I have a theory. And often I'll say, if I were you, the only reason I'd come here is because I have a crash-cost problem, or I just don't trust my employees. You watch them when you throw out your theory, and they'll light up and say, "Yes, but our main fear was that the union wouldn't accept this." I've disarmed them now. If I'm wrong, I can watch that body language—"No, no, no, no, not at all. I wouldn't be here if I thought that. But it's between you and that other company, and I'm here to do due diligence," or whatever they're gonna say. In any conversation, I'm asking 80 percent of the questions, even though they're out to find out about me.

*For more information on DriveCam, visit the organization's home page at **www.drivecam.com**.*

Questions

1. In what specific ways does Moeller's communication competency influence decision making at DriveCam?
2. What comments by Moeller reflect ethical principles? Relate the specific comments to the specific ethical principles.
3. Does Moeller appear to practice any of the concepts that are part of the evidence-based management model? Explain.
4. How does Moeller's leadership help to create an environment that fosters organizational creativity? Explain.

CHAPTER

14

Designing Organizations

Learning Goals

When you have finished studying the chapter, you should be able to:

1. Explain how environmental, strategic, and technological factors affect the design of organizations.
2. State the differences between mechanistic and organic organizations.
3. Describe four foundation organization designs: functional, place, product, and multidivisional.
4. Describe two contemporary organization designs: multinational and network.

Learning from Experience

LOWE'S COMPANIES, INC.

In 1946, Carl Buchan transformed his North Wilkesboro Hardware store in North Carolina into Lowe's by eliminating some general merchandise and focusing on hardware and building materials. By the mid-1950s, the number of stores had grown and he coined the slogan "Lowe's low prices." He expanded his stores into a chain of 15 by 1960 that operated in North Carolina, Tennessee, and West Virginia. He sold lumber, power tools, and hardware to building contractors in these three states. Today, Lowe's Companies has evolved to become a nationwide chain of home improvement stores with more than 185,000 employees, selling more than 40,000 products and generating revenues of more than $47 billion. More than 12 million customers a week visit its 1,380 stores. It has recently expanded in Canada and plans to have 100 stores open in Canada in the near term. It also plans to open stores in Monterrey, Mexico, in 2009 (rival Home Depot already has 55 stores in Mexico). Home Depot, the leader in the home improvement industry, has sales that exceed $91 billion from its more than 2,000 stores.

When Buchan started Lowe's, he focused on small and medium-sized markets. Today, Lowe's has expanded into major metropolitan markets with populations of 500,000 or more. But the company is not forgetting its roots and plans to open half of its 150 new stores in rural markets to serve farmers and small business owners. To improve its nationwide sales, Lowe's purchased a 38-store chain, Eagle Hardware and Garden. To supply these stores, Lowe's is expanding its distribution network. Recently, Lowe's spent $2.4 billion on building new warehouses in Oregon, Georgia, Indiana, Missouri, and North Carolina.

Lowe's is trying to take advantage of four major trends in the marketplace. First, Lowe's is putting an emphasis on installation services in more than 40 categories, such as flooring, cabinets, and appliances. Lowe's second goal is trying to appeal to female urban shoppers. Female shoppers make about 80 percent of the home improvement decisions. These shoppers want installation services in major categories, such as cabinets and flooring. In 2004, Lowe's opened its first urban store, with a focus on satisfying the home improvement needs of inner-city dwellers and building superintendents in New York City. Third, to retain the professional builder as a customer, Lowe's entered into a

LEARNING CONTENT

For more information on Lowe's, visit the organization's home page at www.lowes.com.

joint venture with Kobalt-brand professional mechanics' tools manufactured by Snap-on. Finally, Lowe's wants to attract more baby boomers who want less hassle, one-stop shopping, and someone they can trust to help them with home improvement projects.[1]

The basis for any successful organization is for people to work together and understand how their actions interrelate with the actions of others to support the organization's strategy. Yet, talented people in even the best managed organizations are sometimes left groping to understand how their own activities contribute to their organization's success. An organization's design is crucial in clarifying the roles of the managers and employees who hold the organization together. Organization design *is the process of selecting a structure for the tasks, responsibilities, and authority relationships within an organization.*[2] An organization's design influences communication patterns among individuals and teams and what person or department has the political power to get things done. The structure of an organization influences the behavior of employees. Therefore, an organization's design plays a critical role in the success of an organization.

The formal connections among various divisions or departments in an organization can be represented in the form of an organization chart. An organization chart *is a representation of an organization's internal structure, indicating how various tasks or functions are interrelated.* How is Lowe's organized to compete in the home improvement industry? Figure 14.1 shows an abridged organization chart for Lowe's. Each box represents a specific job, and the lines connecting them reflect the formal lines of communication between individuals performing those jobs. That is, the senior vice president for the North Central Division reports to the executive vice president for store operations, who reports to the CEO.

An organization chart provides several benefits. First, it gives some insight into how the entire organization fits together. Everyone presumably knows who reports to whom and where to go with a particular problem. Second, the chart may indicate gaps or duplication of activities. Unfortunately, the chart doesn't show how things really get done in an organization or who really has the political clout to make things happen.

Organization design decisions often involve the diagnosis of multiple factors, including an organization's culture, power and political behaviors, and job design. Organization design represents the outcomes of a decision-making process that includes environmental factors, strategic choices, and technological factors. Specifically, organization design should:

- promote the flow of information and speed decision making in meeting the demands of customers, suppliers, and regulatory agencies;
- clearly define the authority and responsibility for jobs, teams, departments, and divisions; and
- create the desired balance of integration (coordination) among jobs, teams, departments, and divisions, with built-in procedures for fast response to changes in the environment.

We frequently refer to departments and divisions as we discuss organization design. The term *department* typically is used to identify a specialized function within an organization, such as human resources, production, accounting, and purchasing. In contrast, the term *division* typically is used to identify a broader, often autonomous part of an organization that performs many, if not all, of the functions of the parent organization with respect to a product or large geographic area.

In this chapter, we first note how environmental factors, strategic choices, and technological factors can influence the design of an organization.[3] Then, we introduce and compare mechanistic and organic organizations and show how each type reflects a

FIGURE 14.1 Organization Chart for Lowe's

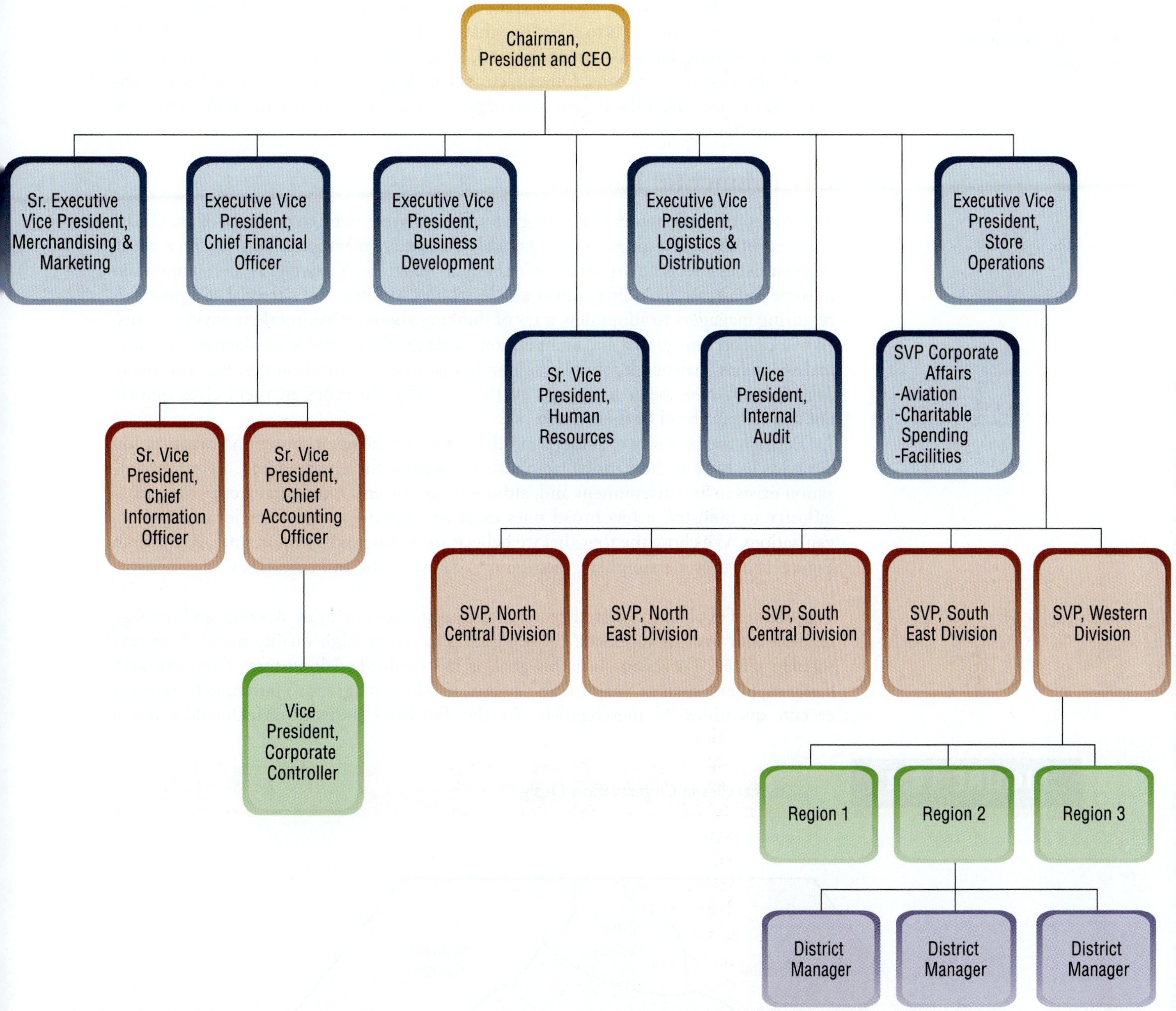

basic design decision. Strategic choices made by top managers also influence the structure of the organization. Next, we describe the functional, place, product, and multidivisional bases of design and the requirements for their integration. Finally, we describe two emerging approaches to organization design: multinational and network organizations. These designs are intended to overcome the limitations of the others in the face of complex, diverse, and changing environments, technologies, and business strategies.

Learning Goal

1. Explain how environmental, strategic, and technological factors affect the design of organizations.

KEY FACTORS IN ORGANIZATION DESIGN

Every organization design decision (e.g., greater decentralization and empowerment of employees) solves one set of problems but creates others. By definition, the choice of organization design entails a set of trade-offs because every organization design has some drawbacks. The key is to select one that minimizes the drawbacks. Figure 14.2 lists the three primary factors—environmental, strategic, and technological—that impact organization design decisions. Other factors (e.g., suppliers, customers, and new competitors) can also affect the design of an organization, but we have chosen these three as most important.

Environmental Factors

The environmental factors that managers and employees need to be aware of are (1) the characteristics of the present and possible future environments and (2) how those characteristics affect the organization's ability to function effectively. Hypercompetition in some industries, including consumer electronics, airlines, and personal computers, is requiring managers to adopt new ways of thinking about managing their environments. As markets become global and competition escalates, the quest for productivity, quality, and speed has spawned a remarkable number of new organization designs. Yet, many organizations have been frustrated by their inability to redesign themselves quickly enough to stay ahead of their rivals.

Perhaps the best way to understand the impact of the environment on organization design is to look at the various factors that comprise the environment. Every organization exists in an environment and, although specific environmental factors vary from industry to industry, a few broad ones exert an impact on the strategies of most organizations. We chose the four that we believe are among most important.[4] As shown in Figure 14.3, they are suppliers, distributors, competitors, and customers.

Suppliers. To obtain required materials, an organization must develop and manage relationships with its suppliers. Lowe's goal is to secure high-quality materials at reasonable prices. To accomplish this goal, it has established long-term contracts with many suppliers, such as Snap-on and Lenox, in which it agrees to purchase from them certain quantities of merchandise. In the fast-food industry, McDonald's has a

FIGURE 14.2 Key Factors in Organization Design

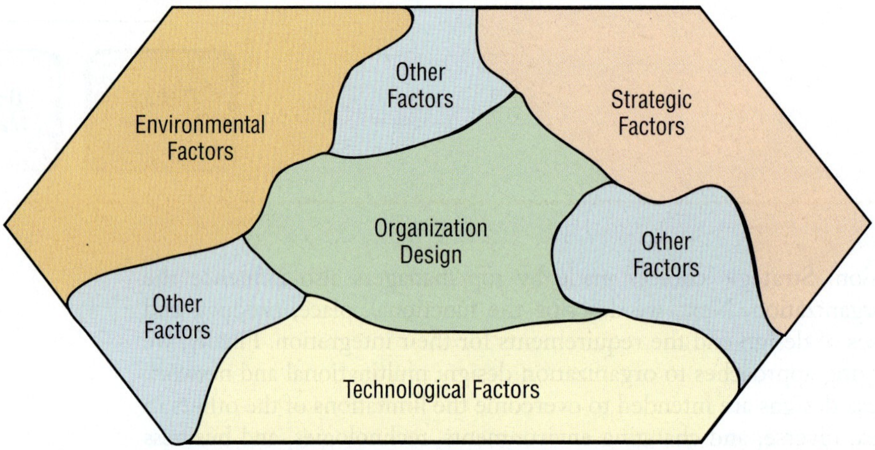

FIGURE 14.3 Forces in an Organization's Environment

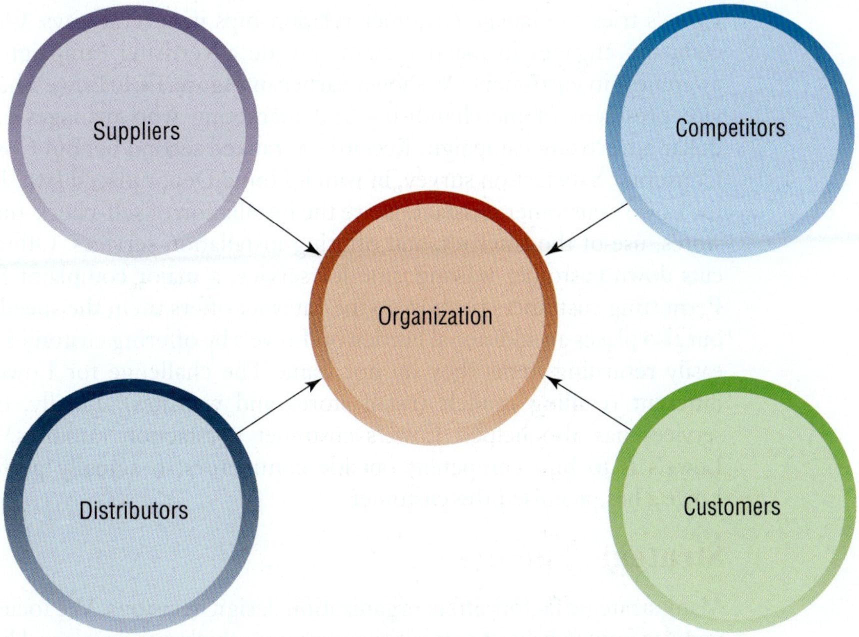

long-term contract with J. R. Simplot to supply the chain with potatoes. To supply McDonald's, Simplot has contracts with more than 1,000 potato growers throughout the world. Such long-term contracts ensure product uniformity, cost stability, and delivery reliability. Customers are drawn to familiar brands and expect reasonable cost and product consistency.

Distributors. An organization must establish channels of distribution that give it access to customers. Distributors are the various organizations that help other organizations deliver and sell its products. Manufacturers, such as Lenox and Whirlpool, do not typically distribute their products directly to the customer; instead, they deliver their products to one of Lowe's 14 regional warehouses, which then fill store orders.

In other businesses, store managers can develop personalized relationships with customers and devise ways to offer them good quality in both sales and service. Sam Su, who heads up Pizza Hut's China operations, has found distribution in Shanghai to be vastly different than in the United States. Because traffic is so congested, pizza delivery is usually made by drivers on motor scooters who weave and dodge through snarled terrific or by delivery people who use peddle bikes with warming ovens strapped onto their bike to deliver pizzas to customers. Orders are received from customers primarily via cell phones. He recently has converted apartments into pizza parlors and simply has delivery people deliver pizza to residents of multistory apartment buildings.

Competitors. Competitors can also influence the design of an organization because they drive the organization to become more productive. The major competitors of Lowe's are Home Depot, Sears, and Menard. To compete at low cost requires organization designs that are simple and easy to manage. Cost savings must be gained at every step of the process, including labor, raw materials, acquisition of land, logistics, and human resources. For example, Lowe's turns over its store inventory about 4.5 times a year, compared to Home Depot's 5.0 and holds goods in inventory about 10 days longer than

Home Depot. Lowe's is trying to turn its inventory faster and reduce the number of days goods are in inventory to remain cost competitive with Home Depot and Sears.

Customers. Relationships with customers are vital. Customers can easily evaluate the costs of various products and easily switch buying habits with minimal inconvenience. Lowe's tries to manage customer relationships in several ways. On a global level, the company engages in massive country-wide advertising campaigns to create product awareness in customers. As shown earlier in Figure 14.1, Lowe's has a senior executive vice president of merchandising and marketing who manages Lowe's multimillion dollar advertising campaign. Recently, it ranked second behind Costco in an American Consumer Satisfaction survey, in which Home Depot placed last. Three of the reasons for Lowe's customer satisfaction are the installation of self-check-outs in more than 750 stores, use of the Internet, and offering installation services. Offering self-check-outs cuts down customer waiting time for service, a major complaint for most customers. Permitting customers to shop on the Internet offers them the speed of Internet service, but also places an additional burden on Lowe's by offering customers the convenience of easily returning items they do not want. The challenge for Lowe's is to bridge two different retailing models (retail stores and websites). Finally, offering installation services has also helped Lowe's customer satisfaction rankings. The challenge for Lowe's is to hire competent outside contractors to actually perform the work that Lowe's has promised the customer.

Strategic Factors

Many strategic factors affect organization design decisions. We focus on one of the most popular frameworks of competitive strategy, which was developed by Michael Porter of Harvard University. According to Porter, organizations need to distinguish and position themselves differently from their competitors in order to build and sustain a competitive advantage.[5] Organizations have attempted to build competitive advantages in various ways, but three underlying strategies appear to be essential to doing so: cost leadership (that is, a low-cost strategy), differentiation, and focused strategies, which are illustrated in Figure 14.4.

FIGURE 14.4 Strategies Model

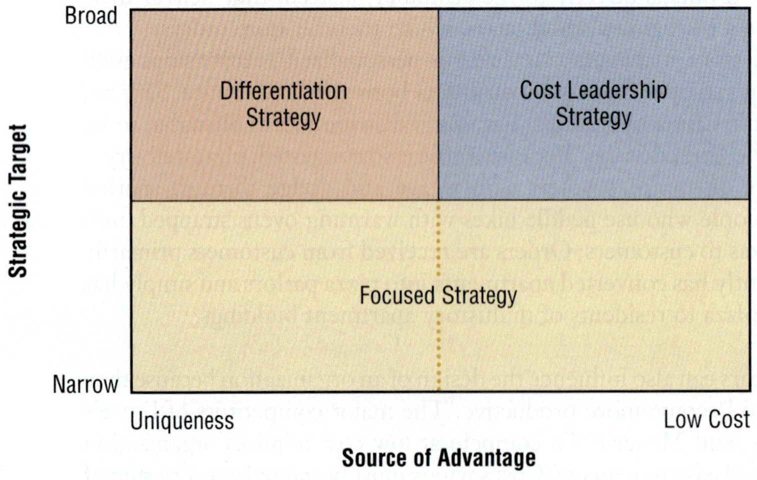

Source: Adapted with permission of The Free Press, a Division of Simon and Schuster Adult Publishing Group, from *Competitive Strategy: Techniques for Analyzing Industries and Competitors* by Michael E. Porter. Copyright © 1980, 1998 by The Free Press. All rights reserved.

Low-Cost Strategy. A low-cost strategy *is based on an organization's ability to provide a product or service at a lower cost than its rivals.* An organization that chooses the low-cost strategy seeks to gain a significant cost advantage over other competitors and pass the savings on to consumers in order to gain market share. Such a strategy aims at selling a standardized product that appeals to an "average" customer in a broad market. Customers buy from these companies because they feel that these companies have been around for a long time and are less risky to buy from than others. The organization must attain significant economies of scale in key business activities (e.g., purchasing and logistics). Because the environment is stable, few product modifications are needed to satisfy customers. The organization's design is functional, with accountability and responsibility clearly assigned to various departments. Lowe's has adopted a low-cost business strategy.

LEADER INSIGHT

Failure to factor the environmental issue into corporate strategy greatly increases the probability that the company strategy will turn into a nightmare for many firms. A company needs to think proactively about how to create a reputation for a clean company that helps develop the economy in environmentally sustainable ways.

Elizabeth Economy, Senior Fellow, U.S. Council on Foreign Relations

© AP Images

An organization that chooses a low-cost strategy, such as Dollar General, seeks to gain cost advantage over competitors and to pass the savings on to consumers.

Other organizations that have successfully used a low-cost strategy include Dollar General, BIC in ballpoint pens, and Wal-Mart in discount stores. The risks involved in following this strategy are (1) getting "locked in" to a technology and organization design that is expensive to change, (2) the ability of competitors to copy the strategy (e.g., Target copying Wal-Mart), or, most important, (3) management not paying attention to shifts in the environment (e.g., customer demand for different types of products and/or services and losing market share, as happened at Kmart).

The low-cost strategy is based on locating and taking advantage of opportunities for an organization to seek cost-based advantages in all of its activities. Tune Hotels operates hotels in Kuala Lumpur, Malaysia. It builds rooms for $22,000, a cost that includes land. Competitors' rooms cost three times as much. The rooms, which cost as little as US $16 per night, come with a King Koil mattress, an electronic door lock, one power outlet, and a bathroom with a shower. Some rooms have a window and others do not. Hooks hang on the walls instead of closets, a saving that allows more rooms per floor. The floors are concrete. There are no towels, soap, phone, or radio. Towels and soap can be purchased in the hotel's 24-hour store. Air-conditioning and televisions also cost extra. Only the toilet paper is free says Tony Fernandes, the CEO for Tune Hotels. To keep rates low, Tune leases space to a fast-food restaurant on the first floor and sells advertising space on room walls, room keys, in hallways, and in the lobby. The hotels run about 92 percent occupancy.[6]

Differentiation Strategy. A differentiation strategy *is based on providing customers with something unique that makes the organization's product or service distinctive from its competition.* This is the strategy chosen by Starbucks, The Ritz-Carlton Hotels, and Maytag Corporation, among others. An organization that uses a differentiation strategy typically uses a product organization design whereby each product has its own manufacturing, marketing, and R&D departments. The key managerial assumption behind this strategy is that customers are willing to pay a higher price for a product that is distinctive in some way. Superior value is achieved through higher quality, technical superiority, or some special appeal. Organizations pursuing differentiation must still control expenses to balance somewhat higher costs with a distinctive edge in key activities, such as manufacturing. Therefore, an organization selecting a differentiation business strategy must aim at achieving cost parity by keeping costs low in areas not related to differentiation and by not spending too much to achieve differentiation.

In almost all differentiation strategies, attention to product quality and service represents the ways in which organizations build their competitive advantage. For example, Toyota's strategy with Lexus is based on exceptional manufacturing quality, the use of genuine wood paneling, advanced sound systems, high engine performance, and comparatively high fuel economy (for luxury cars). After-sales service is hard to duplicate by other dealers. Other organizations that have successfully used a differentiation strategy include American Express in credit cards, Nordstrom in department stores, and Krups in coffeemakers and espresso makers. The biggest disadvantage that these organizations face is maintaining a price premium as the product becomes more familiar to customers. Price is especially an issue when a product or service becomes mature. Organizations may also overdo product differentiation, which places a burden on their R&D departments, as well as a drain on their financial and human resources.

A firm that has succeeded in implementing the differentiation strategy is Starbucks. The following Communication Competency feature illustrates how Starbucks uses a differentiation strategy to create high value for its customers.[7]

Communication Competency

Starbucks Coffee

Wake up and smell the coffee—Starbucks is everywhere. The world's number one coffee retailer, Starbucks Coffee grew at an annual rate exceeding 30 percent during the 1990s and early 2000s. Once a Seattle-based coffee-bean retailer that pioneered the concept of uniquely blended coffees, Starbucks now has over 13,000 coffee shops in more than 35 countries employing more than 115,000 people. It opens a new outlet every day of the year. More than 33 million customers worldwide visit one of its stores each week. The company also owns Seattle's Best Coffee and Torrefazione Italia coffee brands. In addition, Starbucks markets its coffee through grocery stores and licenses its brand for other food and beverage products. Revenues exceed $8 billion. The company plans to have more than 40,000 locations by 2010.

Starbucks charges premium prices for its coffees and ice tea drinks. It recently rolled out breakfast items and other hot food items to entice customers to spend more time in its outlets. Time spent in the store is critical because the Starbucks mystique is to create a community of coffee drinkers who share stories about their lives with each other on a regular basis. To remain ahead of its competitors, such as Dunkin' Donuts and Caribou Coffee and smaller local coffee houses, it continuously rolls out new products that capture and retain its premium image.

It has begun selling CDs and other lifestyle products at many of its locations as part of its strategy to branch out beyond coffee. It has entered into an agreement with PepsiCo to develop new vending machines to deliver premium coffees to customers on the go, while licensing an agreement with Beam Global Spirits and Wine to produce a line of Starbucks coffee liqueurs. It has also entered into an agreement with Kraft Foods to provide food (sandwiches) at airports and other locations.

Starbucks has also initiated a program to help coffee growers improve their crops to meet the company's exacting quality standards. By choosing not to franchise its operations, Starbucks is in a much better position to closely monitor the operations of its stores to ensure their quality. Starbucks keeps employee morale high by offering health-care benefits and stock options to all those who work more than 20 hours a week.

For more information on Starbucks, visit the organization's home page at www.starbucks.com.

Focused Strategy. A focused strategy *is designed to help an organization target a specific niche in an industry*, unlike both the low-cost and differentiation strategies, which are designed to target industry-wide markets. An organization that chooses a focused strategy may utilize any of a variety of organization designs, ranging from functional to product to network, to satisfy its customers' preferences. The choice of organization design reflects the niche of a particular buyer group, a regional market, or customers who have special tastes, preferences, or requirements. The basic idea is to specialize in ways that other organizations can't effectively match. A major assumption for companies who adopt a focus strategy is that they can attract a growing number of new customers and continue to attract repeat buyers. Attracting repeat buyers is very important because they are knowledgeable about the firm's offerings and are less likely to be price sensitive. Repeat buyers often become emotionally attached to the firm's products/services and act as spokespeople for the firm. Harley Davidson has captured this emotional appeal. Can you recall another firm that has customers with tattoos advertising their product?

Organizations that have successfully used a focused strategy include Karsten Manufacturing, Blue Bell Creameries, and Chaparral Steel. Karsten Manufacturing has implemented its focused strategy by designing and producing a line of golf clubs under the Ping label. It was able to carve out a defensible niche in the hotly contested golf equipment business. Karsten uses ultrasophisticated manufacturing equipment and composite materials to make golf clubs almost on a customized basis.

The greatest disadvantage that an organization faces in using a focused strategy is the risk that its underlying market niche may gradually shift toward a broader market. Distinctive customer tastes may "blur" over time, thus reducing the defensibility of the niche. For example, when Calloway Golf introduced its own line of golf equipment, it targeted the same customers that Karsten had targeted. In an attempt to differentiate Ping from Calloway, Karsten introduced a broader line of clubs that would appeal to the wider golfing public, thus losing its distinctive niche in the marketplace. Another risk faced by firms pursuing a focused strategy is that of expanding its distribution channels too quickly. To be successful pursuing a focused strategy, customers must love the firm's products so that they become buyers. For more than 15 years, Krispy Kreme Doughnuts was able to create a cultlike group of customers who were willing to stand in line at 5:00 A.M. for high-priced, fresh-from-the-oven doughnuts. Krispy Kreme diluted its premium image by selling its doughnuts in gas stations, large supermarket chains, and even in Target stores. As a result, customers felt less desire to pay the high price of a Krispy Kreme doughnut after it had lost its special appeal.

Technological Factors

Technology *is a process by which an organization changes inputs into outputs.* Although there are literally hundreds of technologies, we focus on how technology in general influences the design of an organization. The coordination of teams and departments, the delegation of authority and responsibility, and the need for formal integrating mechanisms are all influenced by the degree to which units must communicate which each other to accomplish their goals. The way in which a firm communicates and shares information directly impacts how well it can design products customers want. In turn, this knowledge of customer needs is fed directly into the organization's information system, which ties together all functional activities that are needed to provide the product.

Task Interdependence. Task interdependence *refers to the extent to which work performed by one person or department affects what other members do.*[8] Three types of task interdependence have been identified—pooled, sequential, and reciprocal—and are shown in Figure 14.5.

- *Pooled interdependence* occurs when departments or teams are relatively autonomous and make an identifiable contribution to the organization. For example, the many sales and services offices of Farmers Insurance don't engage in day-to-day decision making, coordination, and communication with each other. The local Farmers agents operate their offices without much interaction with other agents. Managers in regional offices coordinate, set policies, and solve problems for agents in their territories. The performance of each agent and regional office is readily identifiable.

FIGURE 14.5 Types of Task Interdependence in Organization Design

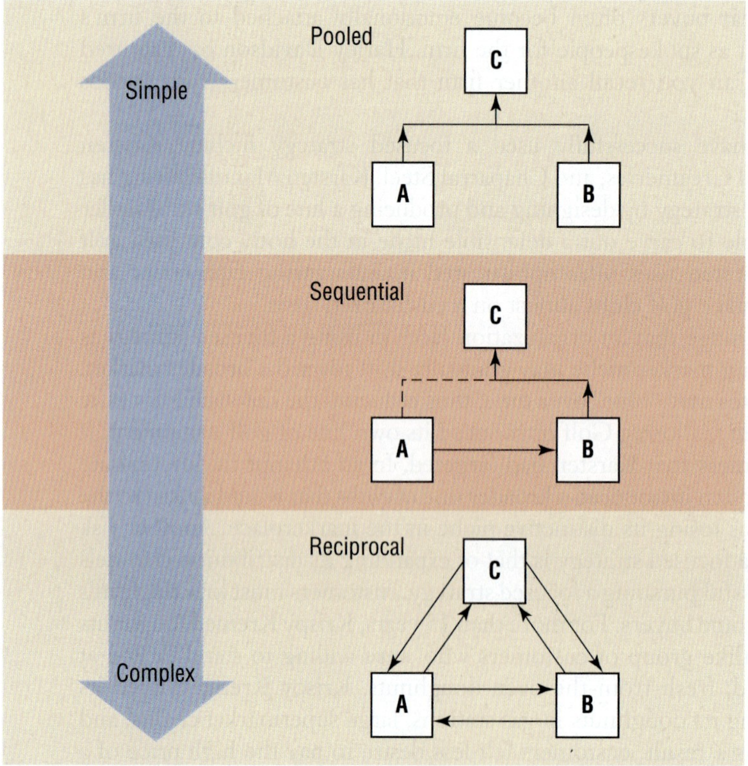

Pooled interdependence exists when the performance of one person has no direct impact on that of another. Golf and tennis teams rely on pooled interdependence. The scores of the players on each team are added at the end of the match to arrive at the team's total, even though the players on each team may not see or talk with their teammates during play.

At Brinker International, each global division (such as Chili's, Romano's Macaroni Grill, Maggiano's Little Italy, and On the Border) is a profit center and responsible for its own casual-dining restaurants, R&D, human resources, and marketing. When a company, such as Brinker, uses a pooled technological interdependence, responsibility for coordinating products is in the hands of product managers. Product managers coordinate the activities of different functions to deliver what the customer wants.

- *Sequential interdependence* occurs when one team or department must complete certain tasks before one or more other teams or departments can perform their tasks. Football teams use sequential interdependence. When the offense is on the field, the defense is resting, waiting to return to the field. Exxon/Mobil uses sequential interdependence to deliver gasoline and other products to a variety of consumers. This process starts with exploration (the search for crude oil and natural gas), production (drilling of wells for retrieval of gas and oil), supply (transport of the raw material via ship and/or pipeline to refineries), refining (the breakdown of hydrocarbons into various by-products), distribution (transportation of product by pipeline, truck, or rail), and marketing (the sale of products to the customer). The flow of materials is always the same. A predetermined order or flow of activities defines sequential interdependence.
- *Reciprocal interdependence* occurs when the outputs from one team or department become the inputs for another team or department and vice versa. Basketball, soccer, hockey, and volleyball teams rely on reciprocal interdependence. Essentially, reciprocal interdependence exists when all units within an organization depend on one another to produce an output. Figure 14.5 shows that reciprocal interdependence is the most complex type and that pooled interdependence is the simplest type of technological interdependence. The greater the interdependence among teams or departments, the greater the need for coordination. Placing reciprocally interdependent teams or departments under one executive often improves integration and minimizes information processing costs within a unit. For example, at Presbyterian Hospital, the Emergency Room is operated in a reciprocally interdependent manner. When a patient arrives at the room, a series of qualified medical personnel are assembled to analyze the patient's condition. Once a diagnosis is made, a team of specialists is assembled to tackle problems in their area(s) of expertise—coronary, pulmonary, respiratory, etc. As each team performs its services, they discover new information that needs to be communicated with members of the next team to ensure the patient's recovery.

MECHANISTIC AND ORGANIC ORGANIZATIONS

Learning Goal

2. State the differences between mechanistic and organic organizations.

A mechanistic organization *is designed so that individuals and functions will behave in predictable ways.* A reliance on formal rules and regulations, centralization of decision making, narrowly defined job responsibilities, and a rigid hierarchy of authority characterize this organization.[9] In a mechanistic organization, the emphasis is on following procedures and rules. If you've ever worked at McDonald's, you probably know how highly standardized each step of the most basic operations must be. For example, boxes of fries are stored two inches from the wall and one inch apart. The operations are the same, whether in Tokyo or Dallas.

In contrast, an organic organization *is characterized by low to moderate use of formal rules and regulations, decentralized and shared decision making, broadly defined job responsibilities, and a flexible authority structure with fewer levels in the hierarchy*. The degree of job specialization is low; instead, a broad knowledge of many different jobs is required. Self-control is expected and there is an emphasis on reciprocal technological interdependence among employees. Recently, more organizations have started to move toward an organic management approach to promote managerial efficiency and to improve employee satisfaction. Many employees and teams heavily involved in R&D at Adobe Systems, Electronic Arts (a developer of computer and video games), and Hewlett-Packard, among others, are likely to enjoy decision-making autonomy.

Top management typically makes decisions that determine the extent to which an organization will operate mechanistically or organically. At Brinker International, the four groups of causal-dining restaurants operate throughout the world with relative autonomy (pooled interdependence). At YUM! Brands, until top management decided to merge some of these operations (e.g., KFC, Pizza Hut, Taco Bell) into one at major self-service gas stations in the United States, each brand operated independently. The move to have several restaurants operating out of one location created the need for more coordination of operations between these brands.

A mechanistic organization is essentially a bureaucracy. Max Weber, a German sociologist and economist in the early 1900s, defined a bureaucracy as an organization having the following characteristics:

- The organization operates according to a body of rules or laws intended to tightly control the behavior of employees.
- All employees must carefully follow extensive impersonal rules and procedures in making decisions.
- Each employee's job involves a specified area of expertise, with strictly defined obligations, authority, and powers to compel obedience.

Organic systems, such as SAS, emphasize employee competence and empower employees to make decisions.

- The organization follows the principle of hierarchy; that is, each lower position is under the tight control and direction of a higher one.
- Candidates for jobs are selected on the basis of "technical" qualifications. They are appointed, not elected.
- The organization has a career ladder. Promotion is by seniority or achievement and depends on the judgment of superiors.[10]

A bureaucracy *is a system of rules and regulations designed to enhance an organization's efficiency*. The word *bureaucracy* often brings to mind rigidity, incompetence, red tape, inefficiency, and ridiculous rules. In principle, though, the basic characteristics of a mechanistic system may make a bureaucratic organization design feasible or even desirable in some situations. Any discussion of a mechanistic organization must distinguish between the way it should ideally function and the way some large-scale organizations actually operate.

The degrees to which organizations emphasize a mechanistic or an organic system can vary substantially, as suggested in Figure 14.6. Lowe's and Home Depot have relatively mechanistic organizations in terms of the selected dimensions. They are represented by organization B in Figure 14.6. Electronic Arts, Deloitte Consulting, and SAS, a software design/integration firm in North Carolina, place more emphasis on the dimensions that represent an organic system. They are represented by organization A. The organic system emphasizes employee competence, rather than the employee's formal position in the hierarchy, as a basis for rewards, including promotion. This type of organization has a flexible hierarchy and empowers employees to make decisions.

FIGURE 14.6 Organic and Mechanistic Design Features

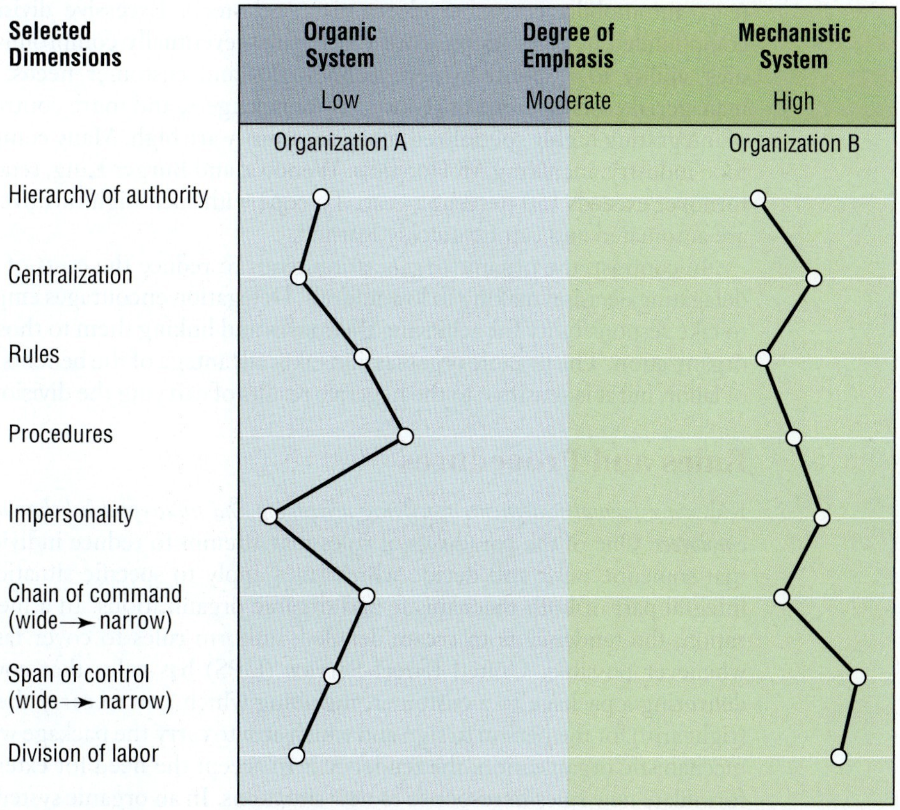

Hierarchy of Authority

Hierarchy of authority *indicates who reports to whom.* For example, the Lowe's organization chart (see Figure 14.1) shows that the vice president/corporate controller reports to the senior vice president/chief accounting officer, who then reports to the executive vice president/chief financial officer. In a mechanistic system, higher level departments set or approve goals and detailed budgets for lower level departments and issue directives to them. A mechanistic organization has as many levels in its hierarchy as necessary to achieve tight control. An organic organization has few levels in its hierarchy, which makes coordination and communication easier and fosters innovation.

The hierarchy of authority is closely related to centralization. Centralization *means that all major, and oftentimes many minor, decisions are made only at the top levels of the organization.* Centralization is common in mechanistic organizations, whereas decentralization and shared decision making between and across levels are common in organic organizations. At Jiffy Lube, Wendy's, and Pier 1 Imports, top executives make nearly all decisions affecting store operations, including hours of operation, dress codes for employees, starting salaries, advertising, location, and the like. Rules and regulations are sent from headquarters to each store, and detailed reports (e.g., sales and employee attendance) from the stores are sent up the hierarchy.

Division of Labor

Division of labor *refers to the various ways of dividing up tasks and labor to achieve goals.* A mechanistic organization typically has a high division of labor. In theory, the fewer tasks a person performs, the better he may be expected to perform them. However, a continued increase in the division of labor may eventually become counterproductive. Employees who perform only very routine and simple jobs that require few skills may become bored and frustrated. The results may be low quality and productivity, high turnover, and high absenteeism. This situation developed in numerous U.S. industries (e.g., automobile, consumer electronics, and steel). Excessive division of labor was compounded by rigid union work rules, which eventually compromised these companies' ability to respond to new technologies and customer needs. In addition, the managerial costs (volume of reports, more managers, and more controls to administer) of integrating highly specialized functions usually are high. Many companies in the fast-food industry, including McDonald's, Wendy's, and Burger King, report that employee turnover exceeds 150 percent a year. To cope with such high turnover, most processes are automated and can be quickly learned.

In contrast, the organic organization tends to reduce the costs of high turnover by delegating decision making to lower levels. Delegation encourages employees and teams to take responsibility for achieving their tasks and linking them to those of others in the organization. The organic organization takes advantage of the benefits from the division of labor, but it is sensitive to the negative results of carrying the division of labor too far.

Rules and Procedures

Rules *are formal statements specifying acceptable and unacceptable behaviors and decisions by employees.* One of the paradoxes of rules that attempt to reduce individual autonomy is that someone must still decide which rules apply to specific situations. Rules are an integral part of both mechanistic and organic organizations. In a mechanistic organization, the tendency is to create detailed, uniform rules to cover tasks and decisions whenever possible. United Parcel Service (UPS) has rules that cover all aspects of delivering a package to a customer, including which arm to carry the clipboard under (right arm) for the person to sign and which arm to carry the package with (left arm). In a mechanistic organization, the tendency is to accept the need for extensive rules and to formulate new rules in response to new situations. In an organic system, the tendency is to create rules only when necessary (e.g., safety rules to protect life and property).

Procedures *are preset sequences of steps that managers and employees must follow when performing tasks and dealing with problems*. Procedures often comprise rules that are to be used in a particular sequence. For example, to obtain reimbursement for travel expenses in most organizations, employees must follow specific reporting procedures, including submission of receipts. Procedures have many of the same positive and negative features that characterize rules, and they often proliferate in a mechanistic organization. Managers in organic systems usually know that rules and procedures can make the organization too rigid and thus dampen employee motivation, stymie innovation, and inhibit creativity. Employee input is likely to be sought on changes in current rules and procedures or on proposed rules and procedures when they are absolutely necessary. Employees at all levels are expected to question, evaluate, and make suggestions about such proposals, with an emphasis on collaboration and communication. In a mechanistic system, rules and procedures tend to be developed at the top and issued via memoranda. Such memos may convey the expectation of strict compliance and the adverse consequences of not complying.

Impersonality

Impersonality *is the extent to which organizations treat their employees, customers, and others according to objective, detached, and rigid characteristics*. Managers in a highly mechanistic organization are likely to emphasize matter-of-fact indicators (college degrees, certificates earned, test scores, training programs completed, length of service, and the like) when making hiring, salary, and promotion decisions. Although managers may consider these factors in an organic organization, the emphasis is likely to be on the actual achievements and professional judgments of individuals rather than on rigid quantitative indicators.

Kisco Senior Living, a company that operates senior living housing in North Carolina and California, operates as an organic organization. A college graduate applying for a job at Kisco goes through an extensive interview process. It may involve several managers, many (if not all) of the employees with whom the applicant would work, and even a casual and informal "interview" by a group of residents. The person responsible for filling the open position solicits opinions and reactions from these people before making a decision. In most instances, the manager calls a meeting of those who participated in the interview process to discuss a candidate.

Chain of Command

Early writers on organization design stressed two basic ideas about who reports to whom and who has what authority and responsibility.[11] First, the chain of command *refers to the hierarchical arrangement of authority and responsibility*. Authority and responsibility flow in a clear, unbroken vertical line from the highest executive to the lowest employee. Clarity of direction is the basis for the chain. Second, the unity of command ***holds that no subordinate should receive direction from more than one superior***. Although some organizations don't rigidly follow unity of command in their designs, overlapping lines of authority and responsibility can make managing a more difficult task than it should be. Without unity of command, who may direct whom to do what becomes cloudy and confusing. Lowe's senior vice president and chief information officer (CIO) has the authority to make decisions about management information systems. These would include decisions about suppliers, type of operating systems, service contracts with vendors, and the like. The CIO reports directly to the executive vice president and chief financial officer, who can hold the CIO responsible and accountable for the operations of that department.

Span of Control

Span of control *reflects the number of employees reporting directly to one manager*. When the span of control is broad, relatively few levels exist between the top and bottom of the organization, as in many R&D labs. At Lowe's, Robert Niblock, the president and chief operating officer, has a span of control of eight (see Figure 14.1). Conversely, in a military unit, the span of control is narrow because officers and noncommissioned officers need tight control over soldiers in order to get them to respond quickly and precisely. Although there is no "correct" number of subordinates that a manager can supervise effectively, the competencies of both the manager and employees, the similarity of tasks being supervised, and the extent of rules and operating standards all influence a manager's span of control.

In tomorrow's global environment many firms will find that, in order to stay competitive, they must change how they manage. Management blunders at Eastman Kodak and Ford Motor Company have occurred because of management's inability to adapt to the speed and turbulence of a changing environment. In some cases, even after massive high-tech investments, management is only beginning to make the organizational changes needed to transform their organizations.

When managers from the United States arrive in China, they instantly notice that they have crossed more than an international border. The forces that drive business success in the United States are different than those in China because of the differences in values, traditions, and expectations; that is, cultural differences. As we have pointed out in various sections of this book, culture colors the way managers view their world. Using the organization design concepts we have presented, the following Across Cultures Competency feature highlights some of the organizational design differences between operating in China versus the United States.[12]

Across Cultures Competency

How to Make Factories Play Fair

It is obvious to most U.S. managers that auditing of Chinese management practices is failing to stop widespread abuse of labor standards, such as poor working conditions and child labor, and the manufacture of products (e.g., dog food, toys, cribs, toothpaste) that fail to conform to U.S. specifications. Such practices have led several U.S. firms, such as Mattel and Graco, to issue massive product recalls. The Fair Factories Clearinghouse, a joint effort started in 2006 by L. L. Bean, Reebok, Timberland, and other companies, is gathering social-compliance information from thousands of factories. All U.S. companies have agreed to use a single set of standards rather than competing corporate codes. Once a plant has been certified, buyers know that the factory uses satisfactory labor standards. This information is shared with other companies. If a factory fails the certification process, companies give the factory time to become compliant before cutting it off as a supplier.

Nike uses a balanced scorecard. When evaluating suppliers, Nike looks at labor code compliance along with measures such as price, quality, and delivery times. Nike is also streamlining its methods of designing shoes, working with factories to develop more efficient production techniques, and placing orders only with certified suppliers. By reducing bottlenecks, Nike hopes to eliminate overtime, a major source of labor abuse. Eric Sprunk, Nike's vice president for global footwear operations, believes that through innovation and efficiency, Chinese factories can be made more profitable.

The question is whether or not these changes will improve the average worker's life. Issues like the nonpayment of wages, overtime without extra pay, and refusal to let workers organize unions are complex problems because of Chinese laws. Local governmental officials don't enforce Chinese labor laws.

FOUNDATION ORGANIZATION DESIGNS

Learning Goal

3. Describe four foundation organization designs: functional, place, product, and multidivisional.

Now that we have examined the various factors that affect managers' choices of an organization design, let's consider some of the design choices available. As we discuss them, we refer to the factors that influence a particular choice of design.

Organizational Design Options

Figure 14.7 illustrates six commonly used approaches to organization design. These approaches, and the conditions under which they are most likely to be effective, are contrasted in terms of the key factors in organization design. Although every design gives rise to its own set of trade-offs, management's ability to work around some of their disadvantages is critical. In well-managed organizations, such as Lowe's and General Electric (GE), senior managers can use effective designs to enhance decision making and information flow and ease strategy implementation. In poorly run organizations, such as US Airways and Ford Motor Company, oftentimes the organization's design is one of the critical problems leading to a lack of efficiency.

LEADER INSIGHT

Knowing when to use each design may be a greater source of competitive advantage than knowing how to flawlessly execute them. The choice of design is influenced by the strategy that the firm chooses to follow.

Andrew Kohlberg, President, Kisco Senior Living

Environmental forces comprise a continuum on the vertical axis of Figure 14.7, ranging from few to many. Technological interdependence comprises a continuum on the horizontal axis, ranging from pooled to reciprocal. At one end of the continuum is a cluster of choices that reflect uniformity in customers, technologies, and geographic markets, represented by firms such as Avis Rent-a-Car, Allstate Insurance Company, and Motel 6. At the other end of the continuum are

FIGURE 14.7 Organization Design Options

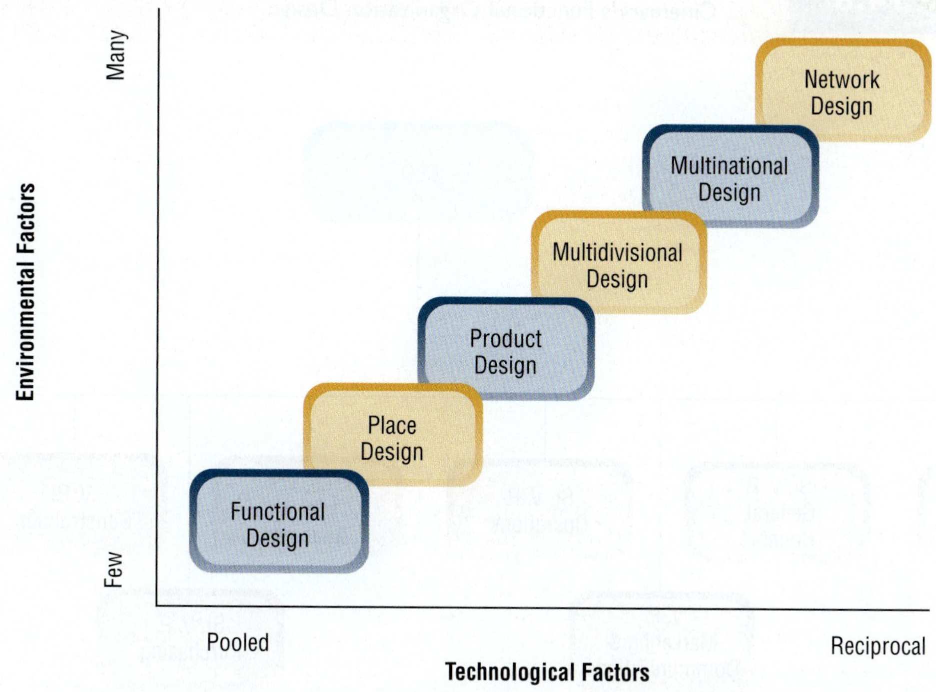

organization design choices that reflect diversity in customers, technologies, and geographic markets, represented by firms such as DuPont and General Electric.

The comparative framework broadly portrays how the design of an organization may differ and change as a result of various patterns of environmental and technological factors. The simplest environment (lower left) implies that some version of the functional organization design is likely to be appropriate. The most complex environment (upper right) implies that a network organization design is likely to be appropriate. In general, designs become more complex as an organization moves from a functional design to a network design. Moreover, the designs require more coordination among people and activities as they become increasingly complex.

Functional Design

Functional design *involves the creation of positions, teams, and departments on the basis of specialized activities.* Functional grouping of employees is the most widely used and accepted form of departmentalization (see Lowe's organization chart in Figure 14.1). Although the functions vary widely, grouping tasks and employees by function can be both efficient and economical. A common theme of functional design is the desirability of standardizing repetitive tasks and automating them whenever possible. This approach helps reduce errors and lowers costs. Management then concentrates on exceptions to eliminate gaps or overlaps.

Key Features. Departments of a typical manufacturing firm with a single product line often are grouped by function: engineering, human resource, manufacturing, shipping, purchasing, sales, and finance. Tasks also are usually divided functionally by the process used: receiving, stamping, plating, assembly, painting, and inspection (sequential interdependence). Figure 14.8 shows how Cinemark Theaters uses this organization design. Cinemark has more than 400 movie theaters (4,500 screens) in the United States and Latin America. Cinemark operates its multiplex theaters in smaller cities and suburban areas of major metropolitan markets.[13]

FIGURE 14.8 Cinemark's Functional Organization Design

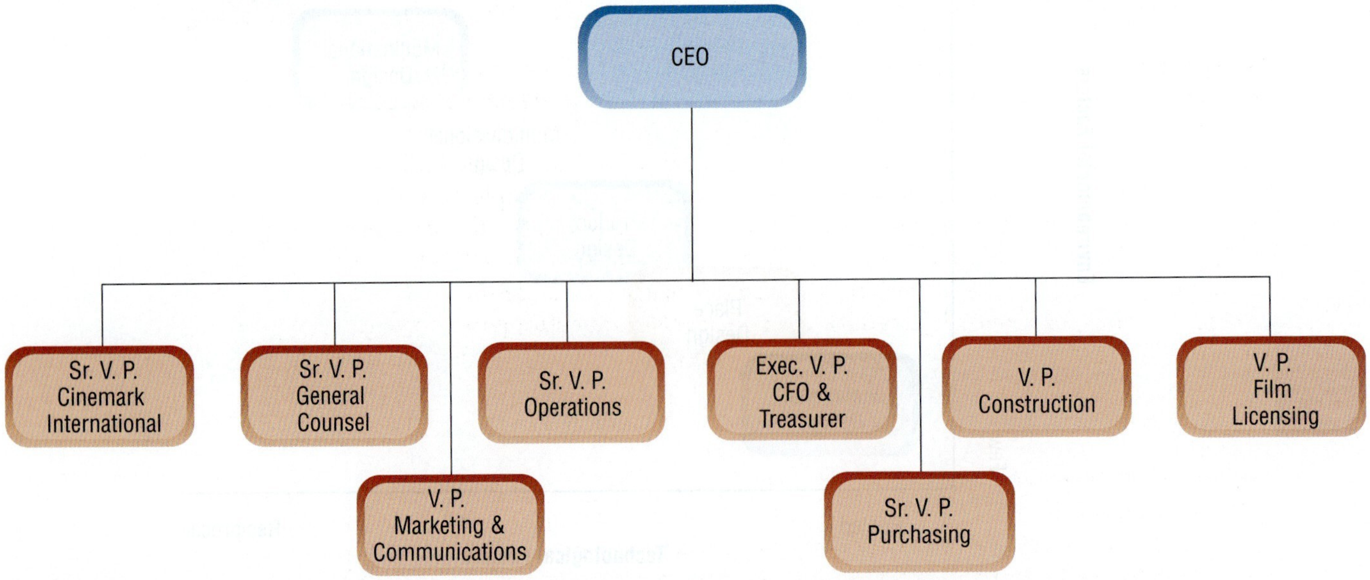

Source: www.hoovers.com (June 2007).

Managerial Guidelines. A functional design has both advantages and disadvantages. On the positive side, it permits clear identification and assignment of responsibilities, and employees easily understand it. People doing similar tasks and facing similar problems work together in a functional design. This increases the opportunities for communication, mutual support, and centralization of decision making. Functional designs hold down administrative costs because everyone in a department shares the training, experiences, and resources needed to perform that function. This allows senior management to easily identify employees and promote those employees who have the necessary technical expertise to manage their particular function.

A disadvantage is that a functional design fosters a limited point of view that focuses on a narrow set of tasks. Employees tend to lose sight of the organization as a whole. Coordination across functional departments often becomes difficult as the organization increases the number of geographic areas served and the range of goods or services provided. Employees within each function tend to identify with that function rather than the entire organization. Thus, a big disadvantage of a functional design is that each function is likely to have its own set of priorities, goals, and even time perspectives on what constitutes an urgent versus routine matter. Finally, with the exception of marketing, most employees in a functionally designed organization have no direct contact with customers and often lose touch with the need to meet or exceed customer expectations.

A functional design may be effective when an organization has a narrow product line, competes in a uniform environment, pursues a low-cost or focused business strategy, and doesn't have to respond to the pressures of serving different types of customers. The addition of staff departments, such as legal or quality assurance, to a functional design may enable an organization to deal effectively with changes in the organization's environment. As shown earlier in Figure 14.7, functional design is the most basic type of organization design and often represents a base from which other types of designs evolve.

Place Design

Place design *involves establishing an organization's primary units geographically while retaining significant aspects of functional design.* All functional groups for one geographic area are in one location. Coca-Cola Enterprises uses a place design. The regions are managed by regional vice presidents who are accountable for the operations and profitability of agents in their areas. Many companies that are marketing intensive and need to respond to local market conditions or customer needs typically use place designs.

Key Features. Many of the functions required to serve a geographic territory are placed under one manager, rather than assigning different functions to different managers or consolidating many of the functions in a central office. Many international firms use place design to address cultural and legal differences in various countries and the lack of uniformity among customers in different geographic markets. For example, Coca-Cola Enterprise, Inc., bottles and distributes soft drinks around the world. It sells soft drinks in the United States, Canada, and Europe. It is organized into four regions (Central and North America, Eastern North America, Western North America, and Europe). North America accounts for about 75 percent of Coca-Cola sales, while Europe accounts for the rest. The place design enables Coca-Cola to sell products that fit customers' tastes. For example, Coca-Cola sells Appletise, Buxton, and Five-Alive, among 15 other types of drinks, in Europe, but not in the United States.[14]

Managerial Guidelines. Place design has several potential advantages. Each department or division is in direct contact with customers in its locale and can adapt more readily to their demands. Managers in a particular market become specialists in a region and are quickly able to learn about local labor practices, government requirements, and cultural norms. Finally, a place design puts the firm's operations close to its customers or suppliers. Therefore, it can reduce logistical costs by locating unique resources closer to customers. Coca-Cola learned that it was much cheaper to build bottling plants in Belgium than to bottle Coke in England and then ship it across the English Channel. For Celanese Chemical Corporation, opening a new plant in Singapore to serve the growing demand for its products in the Far East saved it millions of dollars in shipping costs (from the United States).[15] For marketing, locating near customers might mean lower costs and/or better service. Salespeople can spend more time selling and less time traveling. Being closer to the customer may help them pinpoint the marketing tactic most likely to succeed in that particular region.

Organizing by place clearly increases control and coordination problems because of duplication of functions. A major disadvantage of the place design is that it duplicates in each place all of the functional activities needed to serve that region. Also, if regions have their own marketing, human resources, manufacturing, and distribution policies, headquarters management may have difficulty achieving coordination. It can be especially difficult and costly to coordinate departments that are thousands of miles apart and whose managers have limited contact with each other. Further, regional and district managers may want to control their own internal activities to satisfy local customers. Employees may begin to emphasize their own geographically based unit's goals and needs more than those of the organization as a whole. To help ensure uniformity and coordination, organizations such as Wendy's, Domino's Pizza, and Burger King insist that all managers serve their products at a quality standard that is uniform across regions. Headquarters managers therefore need to develop extensive rules and regulations to ensure quality across regions.

Product Design

Product design *involves the establishment of self-contained units, each capable of developing, producing, marketing, and distributing its own goods or services*. As the organization expands into new products, the functional structure often loses many of its advantages. Product diversity often leads to serving many types of customers involving multiple different technologies. The product design therefore divides the organization into self-contained units responsible for developing, producing, distributing, and selling their own products and services. Most companies in the *Fortune 500* use some form of product design. Figure 14.9 illustrates the product design of United Technologies.

Key Features. Unlike functional structures, in which specialization is based on the activities of tasks (e.g., marketing, human resources, manufacturing), product divisions are organized in such a way that managers and employees become experts about the products they develop, produce, and sell. A product type of organization design, therefore, encourages functional activities to support a particular product.

Elisha Graves Otis, who invented the elevator in 1853, provided the foundation for what is today United Technologies.[16] Throughout its existence, various companies having widely different product lines, as illustrated in Figure 14.9, have been bought and sold. Today, United Technologies is a $47 billion company organized around six distinct product lines. Note that, although these six product lines are all involved in technology, there is little overlap among them in terms of customers, distribution channels, and technology. That is, customers such as Boeing buy Pratt & Whitney jet engines but do no business with Otis. Each product line faces a different set of competitors and has crafted its business strategy to compete in its particular business environment. Pratt & Whitney has developed a *focused business strategy* to compete in its market. For its Sikorsky product line, it has developed helicopters for major oil companies, which use helicopters to shuttle crews to and from offshore oil platforms; hospitals, which use them to move accident victims and the critically ill to their facilities; and the armed forces of the United States, which use them for troop movement.

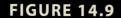

FIGURE 14.9 United Technologies' Product Design Organization

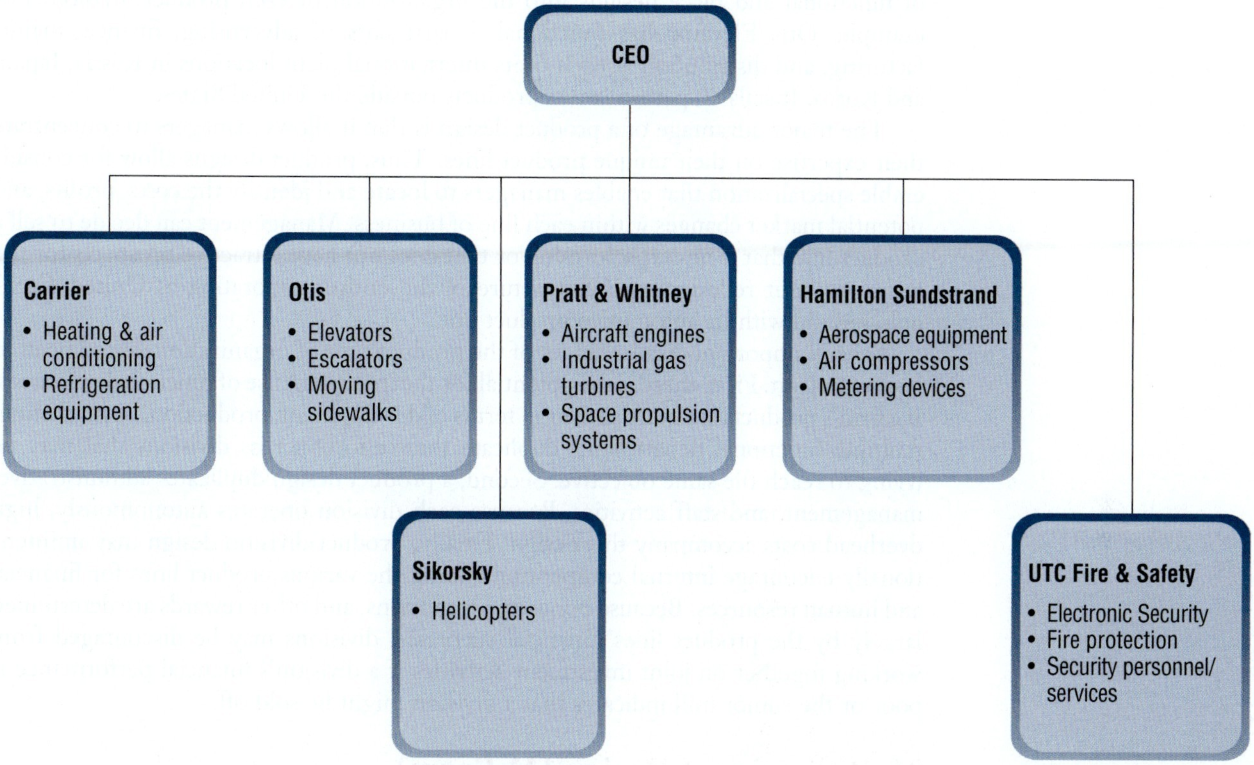

Source: www.hoovers.com (June 2007).

Managers handling this product line have little need to communicate with those manufacturing elevators as part of the Otis product line.

Managerial Guidelines. Most organizations that produce multiple goods or services, such as GE, United Technologies, and Boeing, utilize a product design. Such a design reduces the information overload that managers face in a purely functional organization design. Under that type of design, the vice president of marketing at United Technologies would have to be able to market a wide variety of products, understand the competitive forces in many industries, and focus on crafting a business strategy to compete in each industry. When the diversity of goods or services and types of customers reaches a certain point, the creation of multiple marketing vice presidents (one vice president for each product line) to handle the complexity of the business can be the most effective approach. Each division is then evaluated on its own performance. At United Technologies, Carrier contributed 28 percent of the total revenues generated; Otis, 22 percent; Pratt and Whitney, 23 percent; UTC Fire & Security, 10 percent; Hamilton Sundstrand, 10 percent; and Sikorsky, 7 percent.

Organizations that use a product type of design usually begin with a functional design and then add some place design features as they begin to serve new geographic markets. Eventually, serving multiple customers creates management problems that can't be effectively dealt with by a functional or place design alone. The addition of new product lines, diverse customers, and technological advances also increases the complexity and uncertainty of the organization's business environment. Recently United Technologies sold its Automotive Division and acquired the Chubb group, a London-based security group. Chubb then acquired Kidde PLC, a manufacturer of fire-fighting equipment in the United Kingdom, and changed the product division's name to UTC Fire & Security.

When changing to a product design, however, companies usually don't completely discard functional or place designs. Instead, the product design may incorporate features of functional and place designs into the organization of each product division. For example, Otis Elevator has functional departments of advertising, finance, manufacturing, and distribution at each of its international plant locations in Russia, Japan, and Korea. It sells 80 percent of its products outside the United States.

The major advantage of a product design is that it allows managers to concentrate their expertise on their unique product lines. Thus, product designs allow for considerable specialization that enables managers to locate and identify the costs, profits, and potential market changes within each line of business. Management can decide to sell a product line that is underperforming or that does not have attractive prospects for the future without redesigning the structure of the entire corporation as United Technologies did with its automotive product line.

Several important disadvantages of the product type of organization design need to be pointed out. First, there is the potential for the inefficient use of functional resources. If a firm's products are quite similar in terms of development, production, or marketing, multiple functional departments duplicate their efforts across divisions that may be trying to reach the same objective. Second, a product design duplicates administrative, management, and staff activities. Because each division operates autonomously, high overhead costs accompany this design. Finally, product division design may unintentionally encourage internal competition among the various product lines for financial and human resources. Because bonuses, promotions, and other rewards are determined largely by the product lines' financial successes, divisions may be discouraged from working together on joint investment activities if a division's financial performance is poor or the rumor mill indicates that a division might be sold off.

Multidivisional Design (M-Form)

A variation of the product design is the multidivisional design, sometimes referred to as the M-form.[17] In multidivisional design (M-form), *tasks are organized by division on the basis of the product or geographic markets in which the goods or services are sold.* Divisional managers are primarily responsible for day-to-day operating decisions within their units. Freed from these day-to-day operating responsibilities, top-level corporate managers can concentrate on strategic issues, such as allocating resources to the various divisions, assessing new businesses to acquire and divisions to sell off, and communicating with shareholders and others. These top-level managers often are supported by elaborate accounting and control systems and specialized staff. Top-level corporate management may also delegate to product divisions the authority to develop their own strategic plans.

Key Features. A multidivisional design eases problems of coordination by focusing expertise and knowledge on specific goods or services. A department or division thoroughly familiar with a product line and its set of customers can best handle that line. Such a design clearly meets the needs of a company such as Unilever, which provides diverse products to diverse customers in geographic locations throughout the world. Unilever, a British/Dutch provider of household goods, personal care products, foods, and other items, uses this design to meet its customers' needs. It provides more than 20 brands of black tea in order to meet the different tastes of individuals in different countries.

One disadvantage of the multidivisional design is that a firm must have a large number of managerial personnel to oversee all of the product lines. Another disadvantage is the higher cost that results from the duplication of various functions by the divisions.

Managerial Guidelines. To be effective, headquarters managers need to transfer decision-making authority, responsibility, and accountability to local managers who are scattered around the globe. This approach is expensive because these managers typically do not share resources or help each other out. Managers tend to work in their local country and do not interact with managers located in other regions. Therefore, interunit coordination can become a major issue if both units are dealing with a similar customer. The advantage of this design is that employees in a product-based unit can focus on one product line, rather than be overextended across multiple product lines. As with a functional design, an organization with a multidivisional design can deal with complex environments by adding horizontal mechanisms, such as linking roles, task forces, integrating roles, and cross-functional teams.

CONTEMPORARY ORGANIZATION DESIGNS

Learning Goal

4. Describe two contemporary organization designs: multinational and network.

For organizations to function effectively, their designs must not be static; designs have to change to reflect new environmental challenges, threats, and opportunities. The best design for an organization depends on the nature of the environment, the strategy chosen by top managers, and the degree of technological interdependence needed by various parts of the organization. During the past decade, several new forms of organization design have been introduced and used by organizations. In particular, two types of organization design—multinational and network—have emerged in response to certain deficiencies in traditional organization designs and to rapid changes in the environment.[18]

Multinational Design

A multinational design *attempts to maintain coordination among products, functions, and geographic areas.*[19] Meeting the need for this extensive three-way cooperation is especially difficult because operating divisions are separated by distance and time. A further complication is that managers often are separated by culture and language. A "perfect" balance, if such were possible, requires a complex design. Hence, most multinational designs focus on the relative emphases that should be given to place and product design options.

Large multibusiness firms, such as Exxon/Mobil, Nestlé, and BP, operate in various countries, each of which has its own set of customers, governmental officials, and the like. On the one hand, local managers face pressures to be "local insiders"; that is, to design organizations that follow rules and regulations accepted as legitimate by locals. On the other hand, managers face pressures to be "company insiders"; that is, to design organizations that minimize coordination problems with company units in other countries, manage a diverse set of customers, and adhere to rules and regulations viewed as appropriate by the company. The problem of operating companies in many countries presents enormous challenges for managers.

Key Features. Multinational organizations *produce and sell products and/or services in two or more countries.* A company can be global without necessarily being multinational. Boeing, for example, produces planes in the United States only, but it works with a worldwide network of suppliers and subcontractors and sells planes all over the world. Companies can become multinational by setting up their own subsidiaries in other countries, by establishing joint ventures in other countries with local partners, or by acquiring companies in other countries. IBM, for example, has built up its worldwide network of subsidiaries by setting up wholly owned companies in a large number of countries. To become fully established in the U.S. auto market, Toyota entered into a joint venture with General Motors in California and then set up a wholly owned subsidiary three years later in the United States. It now produces cars and trucks at several U.S. locations.

Managerial Guidelines. The forces generating global integration in many industries include (1) the growing presence and importance of global competitors and customers, (2) the global rise in market demand for products, (3) new information technologies, and (4) efficient factories that can manufacture goods for customers throughout the world.[20] Worldwide product divisions in firms dealing with such forces are likely to dominate decisions, overpowering the interests of geographically based divisions. Pressures from national governments and local markets also may be strong, often requiring multinational corporations to market full product lines in all of the principal countries they serve. Marketing opportunities, however, may not be open to companies unless they negotiate terms with host governments. Therefore, a worldwide product-line division may not be as effective at opening new markets as a geographically organized division because, under the latter type of organization, local managers can respond more effectively to local governments' concerns. A division operating under a place design often can establish relations with host governments, invest in distribution channels, develop brand recognition, and build competencies that no single product-line division could afford. Thus, valid reasons still exist for a country or regional (Europe, North America, Latin America, Central Asia, the Pacific Rim, and the Middle East) organization design.

The following Change Competency feature illustrates how Procter & Gamble (P&G) realigned its organization design to be more competitive around the world. P&G is the world's number one maker of household products with sales exceeding $69 billion dollars. Few of you go a day without using at least one product made by P&G. The company has more than 300 brands available in more than 180 countries. During the past few years, P&G bought Gillette and sold its Spin Brush, Right Guard, and Soft & Dri Dry Idea product lines to satisfy antitrust regulations. It also laid off more than 6,000 employees to improve its bottom line.[21]

Change Competency

Procter & Gamble's Organizational Realignment

Here Robert McDonald, vice chairmen-global operations for the Procter & Gamble Co., speaks to reporters. When it acquired Gillette, P&G realigned all of its products into one of three global business units: household care, beauty and health care, and Gillette.

Since the 1930s, P&G used a product design to spur internal innovation, organize its marketing campaigns, and make acquisitions. This design facilitated the growth of major products, such as Crest, Tide, and Iams, because each manager could oversee all aspects of his or her product. In the 1990s and early 2000s, as sales growth in the United States started to slow, rising incomes abroad made P&G products more affordable. Unfortunately, managing expansive global operations became very complex from its headquarters in Cincinnati. For example, Tide detergent needed to be formulated differently in each part of the world according to local water chemistry and other factors. Distribution and marketing requirements also varied significantly across regions. As the number of P&G products grew, so did the responsibilities of the regional managers. The sheer number of P&G products in any given country or region meant that managers could not devote sufficient time and resources to managing them effectively.

In 1999, P&G reorganized under a plan called Organization 2005. With the acquisition of Gillette, P&G realigned all of its products into one of three global business units: household care, beauty and health care, and Gillette, as shown in Figure 14.10. Each global business unit oversees multiple product categories that share a common customer or marketing need. The purpose for the reorganization was to achieve significant economies of scale and cost effectiveness by ensuring that innovations would be spread around the globe. Under the previous design, country managers were responsible for managing all of the products within their country. With the new multinational structure, a product innovation will cut across regional markets much faster. Technical innovations and new products are shared across regions of the world. Each global business unit will have the responsibility for making all decisions regarding product manufacturing and sourcing of raw materials. Employees have the responsibility for developing a deep understanding of the specific customer needs and unique distribution requirements and for nurturing relationships with retailers and local governments.

P&G believes that the new design will enable local managers to manage their distribution channels more effectively and work closer with retailers to promote their

FIGURE 14.10 Procter & Gamble

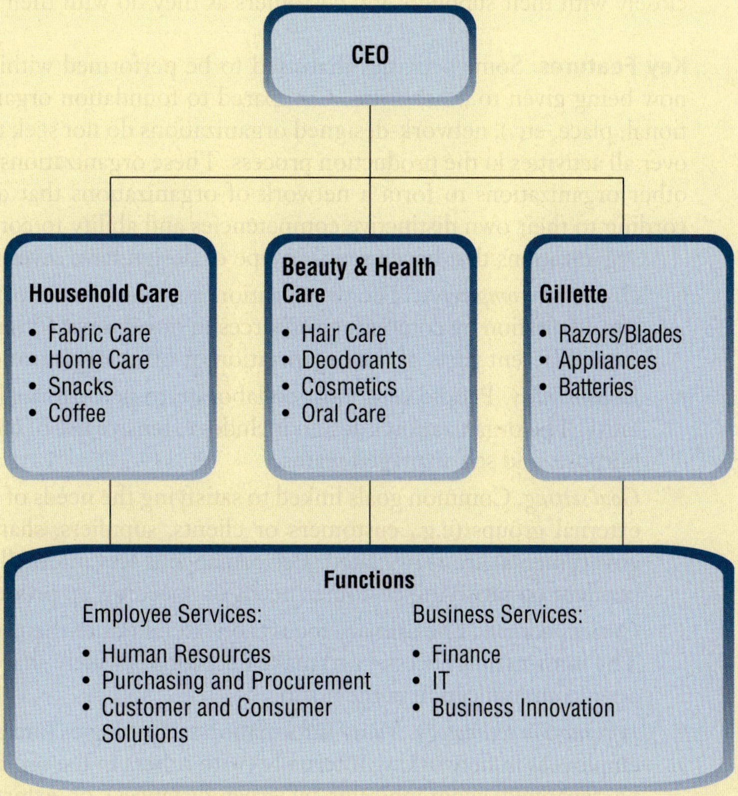

Source: Abridged from Piskorski, M. J. and Spadini, A. *Procter & Gamble: Organization (2005).* Boston, MA: Harvard Business School Case #9-707-402, 5.

products. As shown in Figure 14.10, functional experts in employee services (e.g., human resources, purchasing) and business services (e.g., finance, management information systems, facilities) report to global business units. Some of these functions (e.g., market research, logistics) are shared across global business units.

According to Alan Lafley, chairman, president, and CEO of P&G, he wants P&G to be global and local, big and small, and decentralized with centralized reporting and control. He hopes that this new design will enable P&G to continue its success.

For more information on Procter & Gamble, visit the organization's home page at www.pg.com.

Network Design

All organizations seek to combine the stability and efficiency of their existing designs with a capability for fast response and flexibility. However, relying on foundation organization designs (functional, place, etc.) to attain such a balance has proven very difficult, if not impossible. Therefore, many organizations have designed a new structure, called a network design, to achieve these goals. A network design *subcontracts some or many of its operations to other firms and coordinates them to accomplish specific goals.*[22] Sometimes also called a *virtual organization*, managers need to coordinate and link people (from many organizations) to perform activities in many locations. Contacts and working relationships in the network are facilitated by electronic means, as well as through face-to-face meetings. The use of computer-based technologies permits managers to coordinate suppliers, designers, manufacturers, distributors, and others on an instantaneous, real-time basis. Often, managers in a network design will work as closely with their suppliers and customers as they do with their own employees.

Key Features. Some activities that used to be performed within the organization are now being given to other firms. Compared to foundation organization designs (functional, place, etc.), network-designed organizations do not seek to maintain full control over all activities in the production process. These organizations seek partnerships with other organizations to form a network of organizations that divide up the work according to their own distinctive competencies and ability to contribute.

Organizations that have used this type of design have seven key features:

- *Distinctive competence*. The organization maintains superiority through innovation and adaptation by combining resources in novel ways. Often these resources come from different parts of the organization or other organizations.
- *Responsibility*. People who must collaborate to perform their tasks share responsibility. The organization's design includes extensive use of cross-functional, special-purpose, and self-managed teams.
- *Goal setting*. Common goals linked to satisfying the needs of one or more important external groups (e.g., customers or clients, suppliers, shareholders, lenders, and governments) are formulated. Performance is less internally driven and more dependent on satisfying customer needs or speeding up product development.
- *Communication*. The primary focus is on lateral rather than vertical communication. The information necessary to make decisions is widely shared and distributed, and open communication is the norm.
- *Information technology*. Many information technologies (including groupware) assist employees in networking internally (with others in the organization who may even be separated geographically by great distances) or externally (with customers, suppliers, regulatory agencies, and others). Typical information technologies and related groupware include e-mail, special PC software decision aids, voice mail, cell

phones, fax, telecommuting, teleconferencing, and local-area and wide-area computer networks.

- *Organization system.* The design has a bias toward an organic system with as few organizational levels as possible. A network design supports individual initiative and collaboration among individuals in teams.
- *Balanced view.* Individuals, teams, departments, and divisions do not view themselves as isolated islands having only their unique goals and ways of doing things. They view themselves in relation to others with common goals and rewards. Forms of cooperation and trust evolve over time, based on a history of past performance. The basic assumption of trust is that each person, team, or department depends on resources controlled by others and that mutual gains are obtained by pooling resources and finding win–win solutions for all.[23]

By connecting people regardless of their location, the network design enhances fast communications so that people can act together. Numerous organizations in the fashion, toy, publishing, software design, and motion picture industries use this design. Organizing on a network basis allows the organization to compete on the basis of speed and ability to quickly transfer knowledge.

The production of movies has for a long time illustrated many characteristics of a network design. Filmmakers, directors, producers, actors, agents, makeup artists, costume designers, special-effects artists, technicians, and lawyers come together from many different organizations and agencies to produce a film. Although they are all independent, the producer and director need to closely orchestrate and communicate with each of these groups to produce a film according to very exact specifications. After the production is complete and the film is released, these various people disband and then regroup (often with different people) to produce another film with a different set of actors, producers, directors, and so forth. Thus, the movie industry is actually composed of many different specialized organizations, each of which is critically dependent on the people, knowledge, and skills of other organizations to create a product that is often beyond the scope, capabilities, and means of any one firm.

Managerial Guidelines. The network design offers many advantages for an organization.[24] First, the organization brings together the special knowledge and skills of others to create value rather than hiring permanent employees to perform this task. The network design enables managers to focus on one set of activities and rely on others to contribute. For example, Medical City of Dallas uses doctors from many specialty practices, such as radiology, oncology, and plastic surgery, to serve its patients. The idea of coordinating the actions of employees with highly specialized capabilities from many locations to focus on a core task captures the essence of a network organization. Employees or teams participating in the network oftentimes become extremely specialized in a narrow range of tasks. Second, the network design has the advantage of bringing together people with different insights into teams that work exclusively on a given project. Thus, network designs enhance the search for new ideas and creative solutions. It is important for employees working on such a project to have strong self-management, teamwork, communication, diversity, and change competencies. Third, organizations choosing a network design can work with a wide variety of different suppliers, customers, and other organizations. This gives managers a high degree of flexibility to respond to different circumstances. When a given project is completed, the teams making up the network will be disassembled.

With many people working from different locations and often linked by electronic means, some problems can surface. First, other organizations can sometimes fail to live up to the deadlines that were established. Because network designs work in real time, a delay in one part of the process has ripple effects throughout the system. How many times have you waited for a doctor in an office for an opinion? In instances where time is critical, delays can be very costly because the entire system must wait until a decision is made. Thus, dependence on other organizations can create an operational risk. Often, additional resources or coordination is needed, thus increasing the cost to the organization. Second, since the network design does not provide managers with knowledge to complete the process on their own, they must constantly monitor the quality of work provided by those in other organizations. Because knowledge resides in people's minds, the network organization is only as competitive as the quality and resources assigned to the project by another organization. Assigning employees with weak communication and team competencies, for example, can lead to failure. Third, employees in the outsourced organization may not commit to the same values and sense of time urgency to which employees in the networked organization are committed. Therefore, it is crucial that all people working in a network organization understand the critical nature of the project. Last, because the network design requires managers to work with many organizations, the lines of authority, responsibility, and accountability are not always clear. Therefore, projects are delayed and cost overruns do occur.

The following Change Competency feature illustrates how FedEx uses a network design to deliver packages around the globe. In a world where there are no borders, just time zones, FedEx provides services to people in more than 220 countries. According to Fred Smith, chairman, president, and CEO of FedEx, FedEx spends about $1.5 billion annually on information technology used to support his network organizational design. Why? On a usual business day, FedEx handles about 3,000 transactions every second, as well as 1,000 questions about the location of a package. Instructions go out to 70,000 handheld devices carried by carriers and customers. Everyday, FedEx handles roughly 6 million shipments around the globe. These are delivered through an organization that operates more than 680 aircraft and 70,000 trucks. The complexity of the FedEx network organization design is best captured in a story Smith tells about a shipment of roses. After reading this feature, you should be able to identify how FedEx uses the seven key characteristics of a network design to satisfy its customers.[25]

Change Competency

FedEx

Every organization wants to come up with an organization design that ties the customer closer to its business. FedEx designed the department of Ship Manager to help customers as they weigh packages, calculate shipping charges, and print shipping labels. Each time a customer uses FedEx, the Ship Manager department is held accountable and responsible for ensuring that the customer's information is correct and automatically loaded into the FedEx database. An employee from that department then contacts the customer and integrates these data into the customer's billing system. The integration provided by this department makes the customer less likely to switch to a competitor.

How does this all work? According to Fred Smith, let's suppose that you're in New York City, and your mom lives in Phoenix. You go online to place an order for two dozen roses online from ProFlowers, indicating that these should be delivered within 48 hours. ProFlowers is headquartered in San Diego, California, but gets its roses from Rio de Janeiro. The roses clear customs in Miami, Florida. ProFlowers generates a shipping label and notifies FedEx Express, which assigns the order a tracking number and dispatches a courier who scans the number. This triggers a notification to FedEx, ProFlowers, and the customer that the roses have been picked up in ProFlowers' distribution center. Once the flowers are in FedEx's hands, the flowers will be sent to FedEx's World Hub in Memphis. The Hub handles more than 400 flights and 1.5 million packages every day. Your mom's roses have a distinct bar code that signals they're headed for Phoenix. At the Hub the roses are scanned and sorted so they can be flown to Phoenix. The flowers arrive in Phoenix on time in a little less than 24 hours. The Ship Manager department then enters all of this data into its system and updates ProFlowers' database with the name of the customer, type of flowers orders, etc.

For more information on FedEx, visit the organization's home page at www.fedex.com.

The dominant themes of current design strategies are (1) how the factors in the environment affect how the organization must compete for scarce resources, (2) the importance of choosing a strategy to gain a competitive edge in the industry, and (3) how technological interdependence can influence the type of design chosen. Unfortunately, there is no "one best way" to design an organization. Managers must consider multiple factors and design their organization accordingly.

CHAPTER SUMMARY

1. Explain how environmental, strategic, and technological factors affect the design of organizations.

The environment facing an organization consists of external stakeholders. We indicated that four groups in particular—suppliers, distributors, competitors, and customers—can affect how an organization operates. Strategic factors and the choice of business strategy—low cost, differentiation, focused—have a direct impact on an organization's design. Organizations pursuing a low-cost strategy usually seek designs that emphasize functional departments (e.g., accounting, finance, marketing). Differentiation strategies are based on the organization's ability to provide customers with a unique product or service. These organizations are typically organized along product lines. Focused strategies are intended to help an organization target a specific niche within an industry. Organizations pursuing this strategy are typically organized by product. Technological factors determine the degree of coordination needed among individuals, teams, and departments to reach the organization's goals. Three types of interdependence—pooled, sequential, and reciprocal—were identified and discussed.

2. State the differences between mechanistic and organic organizations.

If top management supports tight, centralized control of day-to-day decisions, a mechanistic organization is more likely to be used than an organic one. Mechanistic organizations are bureaucratic and function effectively when the environment is stable. Organic organizations have fewer rules and regulations and function effectively in rapidly changing environments and ambiguous situations. People gain influence by contributing to the resolution of issues and solution of problems.

3. Describe four foundation organization designs: functional, place, product, and multidivisional.

A functional design separates the organization along various departmental lines, such as marketing, finance, and human resources, and top managers may integrate departments as needed. In place departmentalization, the different geographical areas served by the organization present different environmental conditions. All functions are usually performed at each place. A product design emphasizes the nature of the organization's products and/or services. Each product is unique and requires special attention by top management. A multidivisional form (M-form) is useful to organizations that offer a wide array of products in geographically dispersed markets.

4. Describe two contemporary organization designs: multinational and network.

A multinational design attempts to maintain three-way organizational capabilities among products, functions, and geographic areas. Production in several countries presents enormous coordination problems for managers who must adhere to headquarters policies and local customs at the same time. A network design emphasizes horizontal coordination for managing complex task interdependencies. This type of design also features the use of various information technologies that enable the organization to process vast amounts of data. Mainly used in high-tech and filmmaking organizations, this type of design cannot be effectively implemented without adequate electronic capabilities.

KEY TERMS AND CONCEPTS

Bureaucracy
Centralization
Chain of command
Differentiation strategy
Division of labor
Focused strategy
Functional design
Hierarchy of authority
Impersonality
Low-cost strategy
Mechanistic organization
Multidivisional design (M-form)
Multinational design
Multinational organizations
Network design
Organic organization
Organization chart
Organization design
Place design
Procedures
Product design
Rules
Span of control
Task interdependence
Technology
Unity of command

DISCUSSION QUESTIONS

1. To learn more about Lowe's organization's design and business strategy, visit www.lowes.com and click on "About Lowe's," then "Investors," and then "Annual Report." Read the Letter to Shareholders. What strategy is Lowe's pursing to reach its goals? How is it organized?
2. Using what you learned about Lowe's in Question 1, explain what business strategy Lowe's uses.
3. What impact does the choice of strategy by Starbucks' top managers have on how this organization is designed?
4. How does technological interdependence affect the organization design of FedEx?
5. What is an organic organization? A mechanistic organization? How does the environment influence organic and mechanistic structures?
6. The following are some reasons for organizational ineffectiveness:
   - *Lack of goal clarity*—strategic goals are not clear or linked to particular aspects of the organization's design.
   - *Lack of internal alignment*—the design of the organization is internally inconsistent.
   - *Ineffective links to customers*—the design does not effectively integrate the demands of customers.
   - *Lack of external fit*—the design does not fit the needs of the environment.

   Identify and describe briefly one organization (Kmart, Krispy Kreme, etc.) whose ineffectiveness you believe reflects these reasons.
7. Global managers must be capable of balancing the often-contradictory pulls of being locally responsive and globally efficient. If P&G were going to open a manufacturing plant in Wuhan, China, what are some of the issues that their managers would need to address?
8. ARAMARK Corporation, a global provider of managed services, is organized by product line, including campus dining, business dining, uniform rentals, corrections (feeding prisoners), and sports and recreation (managing concessions at various sports arenas). What are some likely organization design problems that Joe Neubauer, ARAMARK'S CEO, faces?
9. What practices typically found in a functional organization design have to be changed when top management chooses a network design?
10. What are some of the challenges facing managers of a network organization?

EXPERIENTIAL EXERCISE AND CASE

Experiential Exercise: Communication Competency

Analyzing Your Organization's Design[26]

Instructions

Listed are statements describing an organization's design. Indicate the extent to which you agree or disagree with each statement as a description of an organization you currently work for or have worked for in the past. Circle the appropriate number next to the statement.

PERFORMANCE MANAGEMENT CONTEXT

Managers in my organization ...	Not at all			Neutral			To a very great extent
Set challenging/aggressive goals.	1	2	3	4	5	6	7
Issue creative challenges to their people instead of narrowly defining tasks.	1	2	3	4	5	6	7
Make a point of stretching their people.	1	2	3	4	5	6	7
Use business goals and performance measures to run their businesses.	1	2	3	4	5	6	7
Hold people accountable for their performance.	1	2	3	4	5	6	7
Encourage and reward hard work through incentive compensation.	1	2	3	4	5	6	7

Average score for performance management context ________________

SOCIAL SUPPORT CONTEXT

Managers in my organization ...	Not at all			Neutral			To a very great extent
Devote considerable effort to developing subordinates.	1	2	3	4	5	6	7
Push decisions down to the lowest appropriate level.	1	2	3	4	5	6	7
Have access to the information they need to make good decisions.	1	2	3	4	5	6	7
Quickly replicate best practices across organizational boundaries.	1	2	3	4	5	6	7
Treat failure in a good effort as a learning opportunity, not as something to be ashamed of.	1	2	3	4	5	6	7
Are willing and able to take prudent risks.	1	2	3	4	5	6	7

Average score for social support context ________________

PLOT SCORES ON THE GRAPH

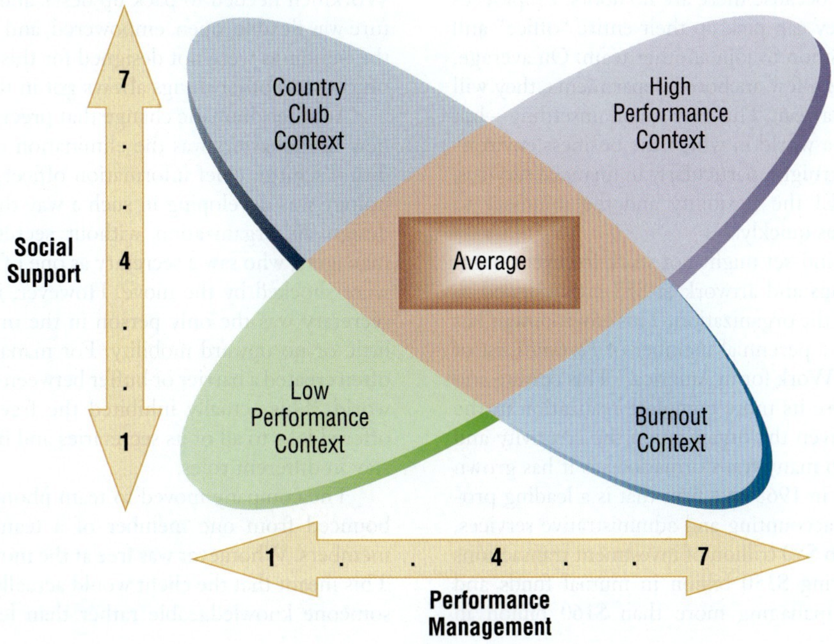

Questions

1. Using the data you plotted, how is your organization designed?
2. What are some consequences for employees working in a country club–designed organization? A burnout-designed organization?
3. What managerial decisions are needed to make your organization's design more effective?

Case: Change Competency

The Organization on Wheels: SEI[27]

Joining SEI, a financial services provider, is an unusual experience for new hires. The new hire is given a map and sent down to a storeroom on the lower floor of the main building. There, the employee is issued a chair and desk, both on wheels, with a computer and phone on the desktop. The map shows where in the complex of nine barn-like buildings on the corporate campus in Oaks, Pennsylvania, the new hire will initially be located. The employee then rolls the desk through the buildings, into the oversized elevators designed for this purpose, and past hallways filled with a provocative (and sometimes shocking) collection of contemporary art. In a large, open room (filled with similar desks on wheels), the employee finds the spot on the map, nudges neighboring desks aside and pulls down a thick, red wire that snakes down from the ceiling, containing computer, phone, and electrical connections. Once this "python" is plugged in, the company computer recognizes the new employee and routes calls or visitors to the location.

The message from Day One is clear. This is an organization that is flexible, creative, and ready for constant transformation. The company is open and not hierarchical. The atmosphere and dress code are business casual. There are no corner offices—or offices at all. There is no need for an open-door policy because there are no doors. Employees are empowered. They can pick up their entire "office" and move to another location to join another team. On average, with the exception of a few anchored departments, they will relocate about twice a year. This may sound unsettling—but that is the point. In a world in which the business environment can change overnight, particularly in financial services, this design gives SEI the flexibility and the mind-set to transform itself just as quickly.

Although this mind-set might not work for every organization, the buildings and artwork at SEI are designed to reflect the culture of the organization. This environment has helped to make SEI a perennial member of *Fortune's* list of "Best Companies to Work for in America." This culture and approach, even before its more complete realization in the Oaks offices, have given the organization the creativity and flexibility to undergo many transformations as it has grown from a small startup in 1968 to a firm that is a leading provider of investment accounting and administrative services, processing more than $50 trillion of investment transactions annually, administering $350 billion in mutual funds and pooled assets, and managing more than $160 billion in investments. SEI operates 22 offices in 12 countries and has revenues of over $1.2 billion.

The SEI Environment

Just before its move to its Oaks headquarters, SEI had undergone a significant reinvention of the organization. Reinventions are necessary for success and survival. As companies grow, Alfred West, SEI's CEO, believes a certain hardening of the arteries sets in. Organizational designs often create blinders that make it hard to see emerging opportunities and threats. People become fixed in their ways, ignoring the changes in the business environment. Silos develop. Costs tend to escalate. Companies become arrogant and markets become mature.

Transformation

One of the major shifts in the organization was the emphasis on teams. Teams were a way to break the traditional silos and bring together the diverse players needed to spark creativity and execute innovations. However, while teamwork increased, the reality was that to move a worker from one team to another meant about $1,400 in reconstruction costs and days of lost productivity. Walls literally had to be torn down. Workmen needed to pack up desks and furniture. The culture was flexible, open, empowered, and nonhierarchical, but the buildings were not designed for this. Hallways, cubicles, offices, and other things always got in the way.

Another dramatic change that preceded the move to the new headquarters was the elimination of all secretaries. Judith Tschirgi, chief information officer, believed that technology was developing in such a way that it was possible to design an organization without secretaries. Some senior managers, who saw a secretary as one of the perks of the job, were shocked by the move. However, it was clear that the secretary was the only person in the organization who had little or no upward mobility. For managers, the secretaries often created a barrier or buffer between the manager and the world. This actually inhibited the free flow of ideas. SEI offered jobs to all of its secretaries and half of them chose to stay in different roles.

The company moved to team phones, where a call that bounced from one member of a team went to all other members. Whomever was free at the moment would pick up. This meant that the client would actually be able to speak to someone knowledgeable rather than leaving a message. It also meant that all members of the team would be aware of the entire business. The elimination of secretaries created the need for more direct access to managers and other employees. Yet the organization was still in offices. This was yet another area of tension between the emerging culture and structure and the company's existing workspace.

Design Principles

The best way to explore the design of SEI offices is to explain why specific design choices were made. Instead of fitting an organization into a preexisting "box" of standard corporate architecture, the decision by senior managers was to create an organizational design that truly reflected the needs of the organization. Among the principles reflected in SEI's design are the following:

- **Egalitarianism**—Ideas are more important than hierarchy. The organization flattened the hierarchy and eliminated secretaries, but the new office literally leveled the playing field. There are no offices. The desks are in large barn-like spaces, with high ceilings and open spaces, surrounded by more private conference rooms. Alfred West has the same desk and office furniture as everyone else in the company. Personal space is not used to distinguish individuals. Titles and seniority do not matter. With its relatively flat organization, there is no hierarchy in the building and this sets the tone for work there. This is a signal that any individual's ideas are as good as anyone else's. In addition to the office design, the dress code is casual, and there are no assigned parking spaces.
- **Empowerment**—Employees are encouraged to act as owners. This is clearly communicated by both the offices on wheels and the ability of the employees to change their location in the organization without an edict from on high. Although senior managers set the overall vision and strategy, employees are empowered to take themselves to another team in the organization on their own.
- **Transparency**—In an office without walls, there are no secrets. The overall impact of open architecture is openness. There are no private conversations. A manager can take the temperature of the team just by listening and thus knows when to jump in before a situation gets out of hand. This leads to a lot more openness and interaction, and mentoring and learning. Everyone also has to become skilled at body language, respecting space and signals such as someone working intently with his or her eyes down, versus eyes up indicating the person is open for conversation.
- **Flexibility**—The open office design means that teams can be reconfigured on the fly. When SEI moved to its new office, each employee was limited to just two boxes for his or her belongings. Every year there is a competition among business units to see who can throw away the most material during "cleanup day." This ensures that employees are ready to move. Creating a space for a new team or initiative is as simple as rolling desks to a new location, hooking up the infrastructure connections, and getting to work.
- **Teamwork and interaction**—The barn-like open rooms encourage fluid and informal interactions. There is open communication, with everything in the line of sight and nothing higher than a desk to block the interaction. There is no need to gather around the water cooler to exchange information and ideas. It happens everywhere. There is no executive dining room, just a large cafeteria that is in use as a central meeting place throughout the day. There are also small sitting areas throughout the building for spontaneous meetings and informal interactions. A health club on the campus helps make the office an engaging and fun place to work. The only closed-door areas are the conference rooms and there are not too many of them.

The Impact of the Design

Although SEI has not formally measured the impact of its design on the bottom line, the environment has affected the business in many ways. The company's financial performance took off after its move to the new offices, with earnings growth of almost 30 percent per year from 1996 to 2006, with no increase in workforce. Its average annual return since the move was 28 percent. Even during the dramatic downturn in the investment industry since 2001, SEI has been able re-strategize every one of its businesses and continue to post strong performance gains.

With greater interaction of employees, decisions can be made more quickly, which increases efficiency and effectiveness. These offices, and the culture they reflect, have helped the company grow to become a leader in its market and, as mentioned, to be consistently recognized by *Fortune* as one of the best places to work in America. This result, based on employee surveys, is a sign that the employees who are with the company find this environment engaging and stimulating. Of course, as noted, the environment is a screening mechanism for new employees, so those who join the company appreciate and like the culture reflected in its office design.

Questions

1. Is SEI using an organic or mechanistic design? Provide support for your answer.
2. What kinds of technological interdependence are present at SEI?
3. What type of organization design would work best for SEI? Why?

CHAPTER

15

Cultivating Organizational Culture

Learning Goals

When you have finished studying the chapter, you should be able to:

1. Explain how an organization's culture is formed, sustained, and changed.
2. Describe four types of organizational culture.
3. Discuss how organizational culture can influence ethical behaviors of managers and employees.
4. Explain why fostering cultural diversity is important.
5. Describe the process of organizational socialization and its effect on culture.

Learning from Experience

TDINDUSTRIES

Many organizations claim that people are their most important assets, but TDIndustries lives it. For the past 25 years, this organization has practiced servant leadership. According to its chairman and founder Jack Lowe, this has made TDIndustries, a $250-million-plus mechanical/electrical/plumbing company, one of the most unique companies in the industry. It has consistently been ranked by *Fortune* magazine as one of America's top 100 companies to work for. TDIndustries employs more than 1,500 people, many of whom have been with the company for more than 10 years. Jack Lowe and Harold MacDowell, the CEO, believes that TDI's success can be credited to its mission and culture and its practice of servant leadership.

TDI employees work with their customers in a partnership to fulfill TDI's mission: "We are committed to providing outstanding career opportunities by exceeding our customer's expectations through continuous improvement." This mission statement is carried out by creating a culture that values individual differences, fairness, high ethical standards, honesty, and a concern for and belief in the individual. The central reason for creating the TDI culture is the servant leadership model. Servant leadership means that every person can become a leader by first serving and then by choice, leading. This means that leaders (servants) coach employees (leaders) by serving their needs. In his servant role, MacDowell answers his own phone, has no reserved parking, and works in an 8- × 11-foot cubicle just like everyone else.

Some of the principles of servant leadership as practiced at TDI are as follows:

- People should work together to grow the company. If an organization lives up to its mission, all people have the ability to become leaders.
- Leaders are teachers, are people builders, and have faith in people.
- Leaders have a sense of humor. They can laugh at themselves.
- Leaders keep their eyes on high goals. They are both dreamers and doers.
- Leaders have to learn to trust the judgment of employees.

To keep servant leadership central to TDI's culture, new employees are assigned to servant leadership discussion groups. These groups meet weekly for six weeks to discuss various aspects of servant leadership, such as sharing power, listening, and trusting, and how these

LEARNING CONTENT

For more information on TDIndustries, visit the organization's home page at www.tdindustries.com.

basic concepts can be applied to their jobs at TDI. TDI has a mentoring program designed to give all new employees a positive start in the company. A mentor adopts a new employee for the first six months. This relationship continues as long as both of them work together at the same location.

At the same time, all new employees are enrolled in servant leadership classes. They enter the first phase of a two- or three-week field assignment designed to acquaint them with jobs and working conditions at a construction site. The second phase is an intensive four-week, trade-specific classroom training program. The final phase consists of six weeks of mentored on-the-job training during which the new employees must earn certification in a variety of skills.[1]

The competencies and values of employees and managers play a large role in determining the effectiveness and success of an organization. As illustrated by the Learning from Experience feature, the style, character, and ways of doing things at TDI are driven by the servant leadership model. Fully understanding the soul of an organization requires plunging below the charts, financial numbers, machines, and buildings into the world of organizational culture.[2]

In this chapter, we examine the concept of organizational culture and how cultures are formed, sustained, and changed. We also explore some possible relationships between organizational culture and performance, the relationship between organizational culture and ethical behavior, the challenge of managing a culturally diverse workforce, and, finally, how organizations socialize individuals into their particular cultures. We begin with a brief overview of what organizational culture is and how organizational cultures are formed, sustained, and changed.

DYNAMICS OF ORGANIZATIONAL CULTURE

Learning Goal

1. Explain how an organization's culture is formed, sustained, and changed.

Organizational culture *reflects the shared and learned values, beliefs, and attitudes of its members.*[3] Organizational cultures evolve slowly over time. Unlike mission and vision statements, they are not usually written down, but are the soul of an organization. A culture is a collection of unspoken rules and traditions that operate 24 hours a day. Culture plays a large part in determining the quality of organizational life. Some managers have sought to replicate the strong cultures of successful companies like Southwest Airlines, Mayo Clinic, and TDI, whereas others have tried to engineer their own culture in the hope of increasing loyalty, productivity, and/or profitability. Culture is rooted in the countless details of an organization's life and influences much of what happens to employees within an organization. The culture of an organization influences who gets promoted, how careers are either made or derailed, and how resources are allocated. Each of these decisions conveys some unique aspect of an organization's culture. Although leaders are aware of their organization's culture(s), they are often unsure about how to influence it. If cultures are powerful influencers of behavior, they must be created and managed. More specifically, organizational culture includes:

- routine ways of communicating, such as organizational rituals and ceremonies and the language commonly used;
- the norms shared by individuals and teams throughout the organization, such as no reserved parking spaces;
- the dominant values held by the organization, such as product quality or customer service;
- the philosophy that guides management's policies and decision making, including determining which groups are included or consulted on decisions;

- the rules of the game for getting along in the organization, or the "ropes" that a newcomer must learn in order to become an accepted member; and
- the feeling or climate conveyed in an organization by the physical layout and the way in which managers and employees interact with customers, suppliers, and other outsiders.[4]

None of these components individually represents the culture of the organization. Taken together, however, they reflect and give meaning to the concept of organizational culture. Using these six attributes, how would you describe the culture of TDI?

As indicated in Figure15.1, organizational culture exists on several levels, which differ in terms of visibility and resistance to change. Just like peeling an onion, the least visible, or deepest, level of organizational culture is that of *shared assumptions and philosophies*, which represent basic beliefs about reality, human nature, and the way things should be done. For example, one key assumption at TDI is that employees should be committed to a philosophy of servant leadership.

The next level is that of organizational cultural values, *which represent collective beliefs, assumptions, and feelings about what things are good, normal, rational, and valuable.*[5] Cultural values can be quite different from organization to organization. In some cultures, employees may care deeply about money, but in others they may care more about technological innovation or employee well-being. These values tend to persist over time, even when organizational membership changes.

The next level is that of shared behaviors, *including norms, which are more visible and somewhat easier to change than values.* Servant leadership provides a framework for understanding what behaviors are shared by employees at TDI.

The most superficial level of organizational culture consists of symbols. Cultural symbols *are words (jargon or slang), gestures, and pictures or other physical objects that carry a particular meaning within a culture.*[6] Someone entering a New York City Police Department precinct station encounters symbols of authority and spartan surroundings, including physical barriers between officers and civilians; the attire of the duty officer; emblems of authority, such as the American flag, seals, certificates, photos of various city leaders, and signs prohibiting certain behaviors; and hard straight chairs, vending machines, and instructions. In contrast, someone entering the lobby of a Ritz-Carlton hotel encounters warmth, including comfortable chairs and soft couches, decorative pictures, plants and flowers, and reading materials. Harold MacDowell, CEO at TDI, sits in an

FIGURE 15.1 Layers of Organizational Culture

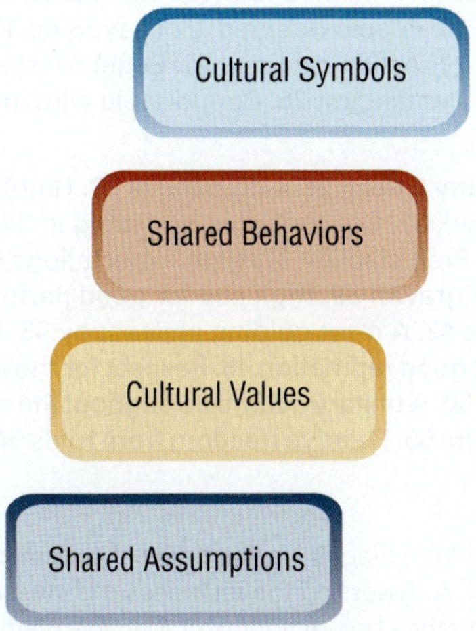

open cubicle like all other managers and has no reserved parking. Such arrangements symbolize that all employees are equal.

The cultural symbols of McDonald's also convey a standard meaning. McDonald's restaurants are typically located in rectangular buildings with large windows to let the sun in and with neatly kept surroundings. Parking lots are large and paved; there is rarely any visible litter. A drive-in window indicates that speedy service is available. The most prominent symbol is the golden arch sign that towers over the building, where zoning laws permit. Inside, bright colors and plants create a homey atmosphere. Glistening stainless steel appliances behind the counter provide an up-to-date, efficient, and sanitary appearance. Above all, everything is *clean*. Cleanliness is achieved by endless sweeping and mopping of floors, rapid removal of garbage, instant collecting of dirty trays and cleaning of spills, washing of windows to remove smudges and fingerprints, cleaning of unoccupied tables, and constant wiping of the counter. Both the interior and exterior convey cultural symbols of predictability, efficiency, speed, courtesy, friendliness, and cleanliness.

Organizational culture is important for employees and managers alike. Achieving a good match between the values of the organization and those of the employee first requires that a potential employee figure out what an organization values and second that she find an organization that shares her personal values. You can address the first task by making a list of the 8 values that are most characteristic of you and a company that you would like to work for and eight values that are least characteristic of your company and you as shown in Table 15.1. Then return to the Learning from Experience

Table 15.1

What Do You Value at Work?

We have listed 54 values below. These are divided into two groups of 27 each. Select four values in the **YOU ARE** group and four values from the **YOUR COMPANY** group that you desire. Place these in your top eight choices. Next, take four values that are least descriptive of you and four values that are least descriptive of your company and place these in your bottom eight choices. Is there a match?

Top Eight Choices

Bottom Eight Choices

The Choice Menu

You Are: 1. Flexible 2. Adaptable 3. Innovative 4. Able to seize opportunities 5. Willing to experiment 6. Risk-taking 7. Careful 8. Autonomy-seeking 9. Comfortable with rules 10. Analytical 11. Attentive to detail 12. Precise 13. Team-oriented 14. Ready to share information 15. People-oriented 16. Easygoing 17. Calm 18. Supportive 19. Aggressive 20. Decisive 21. Action-oriented 22. Eager to take initiative 23. Reflective 24. Achievement-oriented 25. Demanding 26. Comfortable with individual responsibility 27. Comfortable with conflict

Your Company Offers: 28. Competitive 29. Highly organized 30. Results-oriented 31. Having friends at work 32. Collaborative 33. Fitting in 34. People enthusiastic about their jobs 35. Stability 36. Predictability 37. High expectations of performance 38. Opportunities for professional growth 39. High pay for good performance 40. Job security 41. Praise for good performance 42. A clear guiding philosophy 43. A low level of conflict 44. An emphasis on quality 45. A good reputation 46. Respect for the individual's rights 47. Tolerance 48. Informality 49. Fairness 50. A unitary culture throughout the organization 51. A sense of social responsibility 52. Long hours 53. Relative freedom from rules 54. The opportunity to be distinctive, or different from others

Source: Adapted from Siegel, M. The perils of culture conflict. *Fortune*, November 9, 1998, 259; Chatman, J. A. and Jehn, K. A. Assessing the relationship between industry characteristics and organizational culture: How different can they be? *Academy of Management Journal*, 1994, 37, 522–553.

feature and answer the question "What are TDI's values?" Would you like to work for this organization?

Forming a Culture

An organizational culture forms in response to two major challenges that confront every organization: (1) external adaptation and survival and (2) internal integration.[7]

External adaptation and survival *refer to how the organization will find a niche in and cope with its constantly changing external environment.* How managers respond to their external environment is partly based on the cultural values of society. In Chapter 2, we indicated how a country's cultural values (e.g., power distance, gender role orientation, uncertainty avoidance, long-term orientation, and individualism/collectivism) can influence employees' behavior. The pressures for employees to conform to their country's culture cannot be ignored by managers.[8] Managers in Indonesia, Italy, and Japan, for example, believe that the purpose of an organization's design is to let everyone know who his or her boss is. Managers in the United States and Great Britain, on the other hand, believe that an organization's design is intended to coordinate group behavior. Siemens is an organization based in Germany, a country with a high uncertainty avoidance–based culture. Managers at Siemens strive to survive and adapt to changes in its external environment by closely following rules and regulations of Germany. In Germany long-term employment is common because job security is highly valued. Laying off employees during a slight economic downturn is not seen as a likely option by Siemens to reduce its costs. Employees in high power distance and low uncertainty avoidance countries, such as Singapore and the Philippines, tend to view their organizations as traditional families, with the father protecting the family members both physically and economically. For example, employees at Behn Meyer Chemical or ADC Krone based in Singapore expect their bosses to take care of them in exchange for their loyalty. Thus, these organizations need to adapt to changes in their competitive situation without laying off employees.

Managerial Guidelines. External adaptation and survival involve addressing the following issues:

- *Mission and strategy*: Identifying the primary purpose of the organization and selecting strategies to pursue this mission.
- *Goals*: Setting specific targets to achieve.
- *Means*: Determining how to pursue the goals, including selecting an organizational structure and reward system.
- *Measurement*: Establishing criteria to determine how well individuals, teams, and departments are accomplishing their goals.

Internal integration *refers to the establishment and maintenance of effective working relationships among the members of an organization.* Internal integration involves addressing the following issues:

- *Language and concepts*: Identifying methods of communication and developing a shared meaning of key values.
- *Group and team boundaries*: Establishing criteria for membership in groups and teams.
- *Power and status*: Determining rules for acquiring, maintaining, and losing power and status.
- *Rewards and punishments*: Developing systems for encouraging desirable behaviors and discouraging undesirable behaviors.[9]

An organizational culture emerges when members share knowledge and assumptions as they discover or develop ways of coping with issues of external adaptation and internal integration. Figure 15.2 shows a common pattern in the

FIGURE 15.2 How Cultures Emerge

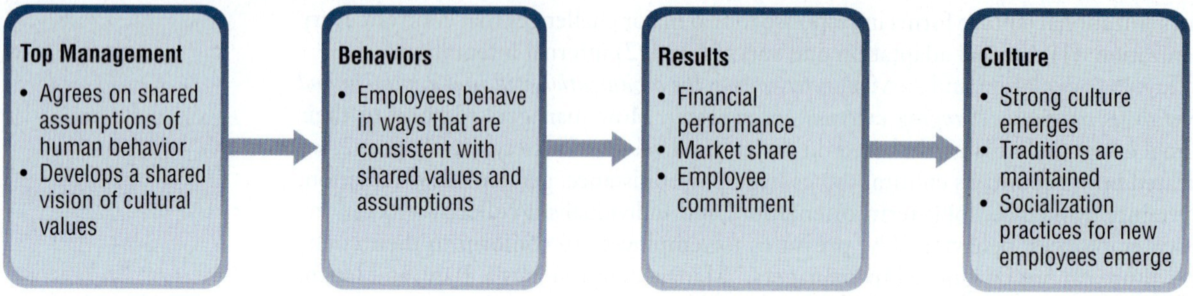
Top Management
• Agrees on shared assumptions of human behavior
• Develops a shared vision of cultural values
Behaviors
• Employees behave in ways that are consistent with shared values and assumptions
Results
• Financial performance
• Market share
• Employee commitment
Culture
• Strong culture emerges
• Traditions are maintained
• Socialization practices for new employees emerge

emergence of organizational cultures. In fast growing organizations, such as Akami Technologies, iMergent, or CyberSource, the founder or a few key individuals may largely influence the organization's culture. Later in the life of the organization, its culture will reflect a complex mixture of the assumptions, values, and ideas of the founder or other early top managers and the subsequent experiences of managers and employees.

Societal and Organizational Cultures. Throughout this book, we have indicated that a country's cultural values, customs, and societal norms are critically important for managers to understand in order to motivate, lead, build high-performance teams, and handle conflict in their organizations more effectively. The dominant value of a country's culture also affects an organization's culture.

LEADER INSIGHT

I wanted to create a unique corporate culture. I knew that I had only one chance to establish a culture that would set the norms, expectations, and performance standards for the entire organization.
Andreas Renschler, CEO, Mercedes-Benz

Mercedes-Benz decided to build a new plant in Vance, Alabama, to manufacture its M-Class SUV. Andreas Renschler, CEO of Mercedes-Benz, believed that if he could combine the very best engineers and managers from Germany, Japan, and the United States, he could build an award-winning car. He gambled that building a car with employees from three different countries might lead to "creative conflict," which might produce a world-class car. Senior Japanese managers and engineers from Toyota, Honda, and Nissan, along with managers from Saturn and the Big Three in the United States, and from Mercedes-Benz in Germany formed the top management team. He also worked with minority groups, women, and the Alabama Black Caucus to bring much needed diversity to solve problems.

Before we read about the plant in Alabama, however, let's quickly review some of the basic cultural values of the three countries (for a more in-depth analysis, see Chapter 2). In the German culture, individualism is prized, along with formal credentials that signify expertise. Contractual relationships govern how the organization will manage the employee. In Japan, collectivism is important. Relations are based on interpersonal trust. Integrative (holistic or systems) thinking is highly valued along with experience (seniority). In the United States, individualism is important. Directness and informality in superior–subordinate relations are prized. There is a strong work ethic that anything is possible. Contractual relations between individuals and the organization are free and open, meaning the employees are likely not to be committed to the organization. The following Across Cultures Competency feature talks more about the three cultures and describes what Renschler learned about managing employees from them.[10]

Across Cultures Competency

Mercedes-Benz's Multicultural Plant

© Skip Nall/Photodisc/Getty Images

The Mercedes-Benz factory in Alabama is moving toward egalitarian relationships between production workers and managers. For example, all employees wear the same uniform.

Germans are strongly influenced by the medieval guild system. Power is hidden in the functional structure of the organization. Senior managers engage in top-down decision making. The worker is highly trained in an apprentice system by a *Meister* (master craftsman). The apprentice system establishes their expertise and hierarchical position in the production system. The apprentice shows strong deference to the authority of the *Meister*. Compliance is preferred over consensus. Once apprentices learn their tasks, they prefer to be left alone to carry them out without interference from a supervisor. The relationship between manager and subordinates is distant. Employees regard themselves as craftsmen and as such, should only be given broad responsibilities. Teams are regarded only as loosely knit groups of individuals with clearly defined roles and strong expertise. The employee's relationship to the organization is based on the law and the strength of the union.

In contrast to the German system, the Japanese system focuses on positional authority (rather than authority based on expertise) and functional relationships (not hierarchical ones). Well-trained problem-solving teams make decisions in specific areas of responsibility. Japanese employees work collaboratively to seek solutions that improve output. The Japanese work system is characterized by (1) work being highly specified as to content, sequence, timing and outcome; (2) simple production systems, (3) working collaboratively with suppliers; (4) a strong emphasis on details; (5) continuous experimentation and feedback by following the scientific method; (6) consensus-based and shared decision making in teams; and (7) rewards based on seniority and plant-wide performance.

The American culture of pragmatism is goal oriented rather than problem focused. There is an extensive division of labor where employees are given limited, but clear, responsibilities and authority. Employees think about the short term. Americans are driven to get things done, which can result in risk taking. Getting things done means pushing things along without having detailed plans thought out very clearly.

After the Mercedes-Benz factory in Alabama had been operating for some time, Renschler found that the German-rooted superior–subordinate relationship was still in place. Much of the technical training was done by Germans who continued to have the informal designation of *Meister*. Many elements of the Japanese production system were being used, including assigning teams responsibilities for continuous quality improvement. The plant's manufacturing system is moving toward egalitarian relationships between production workers and managers. All employees wear the same uniform. Renschler and his senior management team have begun to organize groups of employees to focus on team-based problem-solving methods that hopefully will resolve cultural differences.

For more information on Mercedes-Benz, visit the organization's home page at www.mbusa.com.

Sustaining a Culture: Managerial Guidelines

The ways in which an organization functions and is managed may have both intended and unintended consequences for maintaining and changing organizational culture.

FIGURE 15.3 Methods of Maintaining Organizational Culture

Figure 15.3 illustrates a basic approach for maintaining an organization's culture: (1) The organization hires individuals who seem to fit its culture and (2) the organization maintains its culture by removing employees who consistently or markedly stray from accepted behaviors and activities.

Specific methods of maintaining organizational culture, however, are a great deal more complicated than just hiring the right people and firing those who don't work out. The most powerful indicators of the organization's culture are (1) what managers and teams pay attention to, measure, and control; (2) the ways in which managers (particularly top managers) react to critical incidents and organizational crises; (3) managerial and team role modeling, teaching, and coaching; (4) criteria for allocating rewards and status; (5) criteria for recruitment, selection, promotion, and removal from the organization; and (6) organizational rites, ceremonies, and stories.[11]

What Managers and Teams Pay Attention To. One of the more powerful methods of maintaining organizational culture involves the processes and behaviors that managers, individual employees, and teams pay attention to—that is, the events that get noticed and commented on. Dealing with events systematically sends strong signals to employees about what is important and expected of them. For example, Tom Salonek, president of Go-e-biz.com, an e-business consulting firm, holds a 15-minute meeting every morning at 7:25 A.M. sharp with his salespeople, who use cell phones to call in from the road. They share their challenges and results from the previous day. Salonek closely monitors sales contacts they have made, giving them an extra $20 a day for making their daily contact goal quotas.

Reactions to Incidents and Crises. When an organization faces a crisis such as terrorism attacks or loss of a major customer, the handling of that crisis by managers and employees reveals a great deal about its culture. The manner in which the crisis is dealt with can either reinforce the existing culture or bring out new values and norms that change the culture in some way. Gary Kelly, CEO of Southwest Airlines, tells a story about a customer who had gotten gasoline on her clothes while refueling her rental car. The customer was (understandably) stopped by TSA officials, who won't allow anyone on a plane with gas-soaked clothing. Stephanie Gamble, a Southwest supervisor, took down the customer's clothing and shoe size, and left for a nearby department store to buy her something to wear. On the flight home with her new clothes the customer, who had left money in an envelope for the supervisor to mail her items back, was handed the same envelope with this note: "Stephanie won't take your money for clothes or postage. Have a good flight." This incident says a lot about the caring and nurturing culture that Southwest Airlines has created for its customers.[12]

Role Modeling, Teaching, and Coaching. Aspects of an organization's culture are communicated to employees by the way managers treat them. At The Ritz-Carlton Hotels and Resorts, all new trainees are shown films that emphasize customer service. Managers also demonstrate good customer or client service practices in their interactions with customers. For example, the story is told of the beach attendant who was busy stacking chairs for an evening event when he was approached by a guest who asked to leave two chairs out because he wanted to return to the beach that evening with his girlfriend and propose. Although the beach attendant was going off duty, he didn't just have two chairs on the beach; he put on a tuxedo and brought flowers, champagne, and candles. He met the couple when they arrived at the beach later that evening. He escorted them to the chairs, presented the flowers, lit the candles, and served the champagne to them. The repeated emphasis on good customer relations in both training and day-to-day behavior helps create and maintain a customer-oriented culture throughout The Ritz-Carlton Hotel and Resorts chain.[13]

Allocation of Rewards and Status. Employees also learn about an organization's culture through its reward system. The rewards and punishments attached to various behaviors convey to employees the priorities and values of both individual managers and the organization. At TDIndustries, employees are eligible for a 401(k) plan after just 90 days and can earn up to $7,000 for referring a new hire to the company. All employees are cross-trained to perform a variety of tasks to reduce production bottlenecks and status differences among the plumbing, electrical, mechanical, and other trades. At Sara Lee, the baked goods company, programs encourage managers at different levels to own stock in the company. The rationale is that managers should have a stake in the financial health of the firm, based on its overall performance.

In many organizations the status system maintains certain aspects of its culture. The distribution of perks (a corner office on an upper floor, executive dining room, carpeting, a private secretary, or a private parking space) demonstrates which roles and behaviors are most valued by an organization. At Chase Manhattan Bank in New York City, Jim Donaldson was promoted to vice president for global trusts. His new office was well furnished with most of the symbols of relatively high status. Before he was allowed to move in to his new office, however, his boss ordered the maintenance department to cut a 12-inch strip from the entire perimeter of the carpet. At Chase Manhattan, wall-to-wall carpeting is a status symbol given only to senior vice presidents and above.

An organization may use rewards and status symbols ineffectively and inconsistently. If so, it misses a great opportunity to influence its culture. An organization's reward practices and its culture are strongly linked in the minds of its members. In fact, some authorities believe that the most effective method of influencing organizational culture may be through the reward system. Within NASA, the crash of the space shuttle *Columbia* and the explosion in space over Texas of the *Challenger* have been attributed to a change in the reward system from one that rewarded space safety and technical brilliance to a reward system that focused on efficiency and reuse of the space shuttle. NASA's motto of "faster, better, and cheaper" put an emphasis on meeting schedules and avoiding cost overruns. This motto became a symbol of how rewards were allocated.[14]

Recruitment, Selection, Promotion, and Removal. As Figure 15.3 suggests, one of the fundamental ways in which organizations maintain a culture is through the recruitment process. In addition, the criteria used to determine who is assigned to specific jobs or positions, who gets raises and promotions and why, who is removed from the organization by firing or early retirement, and so on, reinforce and demonstrate basic aspects of an organization's culture. These criteria become known throughout the organization and can maintain or change an existing culture.

Organizational Rites and Ceremonies. Organizational rites and ceremonies *are planned activities or rituals that have important cultural meaning to employees.* Certain managerial or employee activities can become rituals that are interpreted as part of the organizational culture. Rites and ceremonies that sustain organizational culture include rites of passage, degradation, enhancement, and integration. Table 15.2 contains examples of each of these four types of rites and identifies some of their desirable consequences.[15]

A ceremony used at Mary Kay Cosmetics Company provides a good example of rites of enhancement. During elaborate awards ceremonies, gold and diamond pins, fur stoles, and pink Cadillac's are presented to salespeople who achieve their sales quotas. Music tends to arouse and express emotions, and all the participants know the Mary Kay song, "I've Got that Mary Kay Enthusiasm." It was written by a member of the organization to the tune of the hymn "I've Got that Old Time Religion." This song is a direct expression of the Mary Kay culture and is fervently sung during the awards ceremonies. The ceremonies are reminiscent of a Miss America pageant, with all of the participants dressed in glamorous evening clothes. The setting is typically an auditorium with a stage in front of a large, cheering audience. The ceremonies clearly are intended to increase the identity and status of high-performing employees and emphasize the company's rewards for excellence.[16]

Organization Stories. Many of the underlying beliefs and values of an organization's culture are expressed as stories that become part of its folklore. These stories transmit the existing culture from old to new employees and emphasize important aspects of that culture—and some may persist for a long time. The Mayo Clinic in Rochester, Minnesota, is famous for its patient care. A story is told about the critically ill mother of a bride. The bride told the physicians how much she wanted her mother to be part of her wedding ceremony. The physicians conveyed this message to the critical care manager. A team of physicians worked hard to stabilize her mother's condition. Within hours, the hospital atrium was transformed for the wedding service, complete with flowers, balloons, and confetti. Staff members provided a cake, and nurses arranged for the mother's hair and makeup, dressed her, and wheeled her bed to the atrium. A volunteer played the piano and the chaplain performed the ceremony. On every floor, hospital staff and visiting family members ringed the atrium balconies "like angels from above" to quote

Table 15.2 Organizational Rites and Ceremonies

TYPE	EXAMPLE	POSSIBLE CONSEQUENCES
Rites of passage	Basic training, U.S. Army	Facilitate transition into new roles; minimize differences in way roles are carried out
Rites of degradation	Firing a manager	Reduce power and identity; reaffirm proper behavior
Rites of enhancement	Mary Kay Cosmetics Company ceremonies	Enhance power and identity; emphasize value of proper behavior
Rites of integration	Office party	Encourage common feelings that bind members together

Source: Adapted from Trice, H. M., and Beyer, J. M. *The Cultures of Work Organizations.* Englewood Cliffs, NJ: Prentice-Hall, 1993, 111.

the bride. This scene not only provided evidence of caring to the patient and her family, but a strong reminder to the staff that patient's needs come first.[17]

Changing a Culture: Managerial Guidelines

The same basic methods used to maintain an organization's culture may be used to modify it. That is, culture might be modified by changing (1) what managers and teams pay attention to, (2) how crises are handled, (3) criteria for recruiting new members, (4) criteria for allocating rewards, (5) criteria for promotion within the organization, and (6) organizational rites, ceremonies, and stories.

> LEADER INSIGHT
>
> Culture change does not occur in a vacuum. All employees must embrace the change. Senior managers need to celebrate behaviors that reinforce and reward the new culture's values.
> **David Novak, CEO, YUM! Brands**

Changing organizational culture can be tricky because accurately assessing organizational culture in itself is difficult. Most large, complex organizations actually have more than one culture. The Gainesville (Florida) Police Department, for example, has distinctly different cultures based on the shifts to which officers are assigned and their rank. *When multiple cultures are present within an organization, they are referred to as* subcultures. Often, if an organization has subcultures they will reflect the following three types: an operating culture (line employees), an engineering culture (technical and professional people), and an executive culture (top management). Each culture stems from very different views typically held by these groups of individuals.[18] Faced with a variety of subcultures, management may have difficulty (1) accurately assessing them and (2) effecting needed changes, especially when these subcultures are based in units in different locations.

Why is changing a culture so hard? There are at least three reasons.[19] First, cultures give employees an organizational identity. It tells customers and others what the organization stands for. Southwest Airlines, for example, is known as a fun place to work that values customer satisfaction and customer loyalty before corporate profits. The story told by Gary Kelly about helping a woman who soaked her clothes with gasoline helps give Southwest Airlines its distinctive identity with passengers and employees. Second, culture provides stability. Southwest is known for having parties and celebrating. Therefore, each city in which Southwest operates has a budget for parties. These parties and celebrations reflect its positive and reinforcing work environment. Third, culture helps focus its employees' behaviors. One of the functions of a culture is to help employees understand why the organization does what is does and how it intends to accomplish its long-term goals. When Southwest Airlines was created in 1971, its goals were to be the best short-haul, low-fare, high-frequency, point-to-point carrier in the United States. Employees knew that they had to achieve exceptional service to keep costs down to compete with the automobile and Greyhound. Those goals haven't changed much in more than three decades.

Despite obstacles to changing an organization's culture, change is feasible. In the case of failing organizations or significant shifts in an organization's external environment, changing the culture is essential. Successfully changing organizational culture requires

- understanding the old culture first because a new culture can't be developed unless managers and employees understand where they're starting from;
- providing support for employees and teams who have ideas for a better culture and are willing to act on those ideas;
- finding the most effective subculture in the organization and using it as an example from which employees can learn;
- not attacking culture head on but finding ways to help employees and teams do their jobs more effectively;
- treating the vision of a new culture as a guiding principle for change, not as a miracle cure;
- recognizing that significant organization-wide cultural change takes 5 to 10 years; and

- living the new culture because actions speak louder than words.

The transformation of Harley-Davidson is one example of how a company changed its culture, as discussed in the following Change Competency feature. To change a company's culture, its reward systems, leader behaviors, and organizational structures must be changed.[20]

Change Competency

Harley-Davidson

© AP Images

Harley-Davidson CEO Jim Ziemer has worked hard to sustain the Harley culture that his predecessor, Richard Teerlink, created.

When Richard Teerlink took over as president of Harley-Davidson in 1987, the differences in quality between Harley-Davidson and its competitors were striking. For example, only 5 percent of Honda's motorcycles failed to pass inspection; more than 50 percent of Harleys failed the same test. Honda's value added per employee was three times that of Harley's. Harley's relations with its dealers were poor because they were forced to provide customers with free service because of factory defects. So what did Teerlink do? He set out to change the culture of Harley-Davidson, which he accomplished before retiring in 1999.

First, he emphasized that although Harley was a manufacturer of motorcycles, it was also in the "experience business." He said that the real product is not a machine, but a lifestyle, an attitude, a way of being, a perspective on life that had its beginnings before Bill Harley and Arthur Davidson built the first motorized bicycle in 1901. It is the strength and courage that come from feelings of individuality. Therefore, riding a Harley is the stuff adventure and legends are made of.

Second, he began emphasizing organizational and individual learning at all levels through a Leadership Institute. The institute was designed to introduce new workers to Harley's goals and culture while providing current workers with a better understanding of the organization's design and effects of competition on Harley's performance. Managers prepared a series of nontechnical explanations of how cash flow and flexible production affect financial success. Line workers were taught how products, sales, and productivity affect profitability. Substantial changes in employee job descriptions, responsibilities, and production processes were undertaken in an effort to increase job enrichment and worker empowerment. These efforts were implemented through cross-training and expansion of job responsibilities. Teerlink eliminated the positions of vice presidents of marketing and operations because these jobs didn't add value to the product. Teams of employees, such as a "create-demand team," which is in charge of producing products, and a "product-support team," now make marketing and operations decisions. Employees formed quality circles that became a source of bottom-up ideas for improving quality. Employees created a peer review system to evaluate each other's performance instead of relying solely on first-line supervisors' evaluations. These evaluations help determine employees' pay.

Third, to recapture the Harley mystique, Teerlink revitalized the Harley Hogs, a customer group formed to get people more actively involved in motorcycling. To attract female riders, the Ladies of Harley group was formed to increase ridership and interest among young female motorcyclists. Teerlink and his staff regularly attended road rallies and helped clubs sponsor various charitable events. Harley also issued a credit card to thousands of riders and encouraged them to use the card for the purchase of a motorcycle, service, and accessories. The sale of merchandise, including T-shirts, clothing, jewelry, small-leather goods, and numerous other products, permits customers to identify with the company. As Teerlink noted, "There are very few products that are so exciting that people will tattoo your logo on their body."

Since Teerlink's retirement, CEO James Ziemer has worked hard to sustain Harley's culture. With recent sales exceeding $6 billion and more than 9,000 employees, it appears that Ziemer has been able to sustain the culture Teerlink and his predecessor Jeff Bluestein created.

For more information on Harley-Davidson, visit the organization's home page at www.harley-davidson.com.

We cover planned organizational change extensively in Chapter 16. Many of the specific techniques and methods for changing organizational behaviors presented in that chapter also may be used to change organizational culture. Indeed, any comprehensive program of organizational change, in some sense, is an attempt to change the culture of the organization.

We can't overemphasize how difficult deliberately changing organizational cultures may be. In fact, the incompatibility of organizational cultures and their resistance to change has been one of the most significant barriers to successful corporate mergers. It is estimated that 60 percent of all mergers fail to achieve their financial goals because of cultural differences. For a merger to be effective, at least one (and sometimes both) of the merging organizations may need to change its culture.

TYPES OF ORGANIZATIONAL CULTURE

Learning Goal

2. Describe four types of organizational culture.

Cultural elements and their relationships create a pattern that is distinct to an organization (e.g., the culture of TDIndustries versus that of Harley-Davidson). However, organizational cultures do have some common characteristics.[21] One proposed framework is presented in Figure 15.4. The vertical axis reflects the relative control orientation of an organization, ranging from stable to flexible. The horizontal axis reflects the relative focus of attention of an organization, ranging from internal functioning to external functioning. The extreme corners of the four quadrants represent four pure types of organizational culture: bureaucratic, clan, entrepreneurial, and market. In a culturally homogeneous organization such as Mary Kay, one of these basic types of culture will dominate. Marriott, Capital One, the New York City and other large police departments, and other organizations have subcultures.

As is true of organization designs, different organizational cultures may be appropriate under different conditions, with no one type of culture being ideal for every situation. However, some employees may prefer one culture to others. As you read about each type of culture, consider which best fits your preferences. Employees who work in an organization with a culture that fits their own view of an ideal culture tend to be committed to the organization and optimistic about its future. Also, a culture should reflect the organization's goals.

Bureaucratic Culture

An organization that practices formality, rules, standard operating procedures, and hierarchical coordination has a bureaucratic culture. Recall from Chapter 14 that the goals of a bureaucracy are predictability, efficiency, and stability. Its members highly value standardized goods and customer service. Behavioral norms support formality over

FIGURE 15.4 Framework of Types of Culture

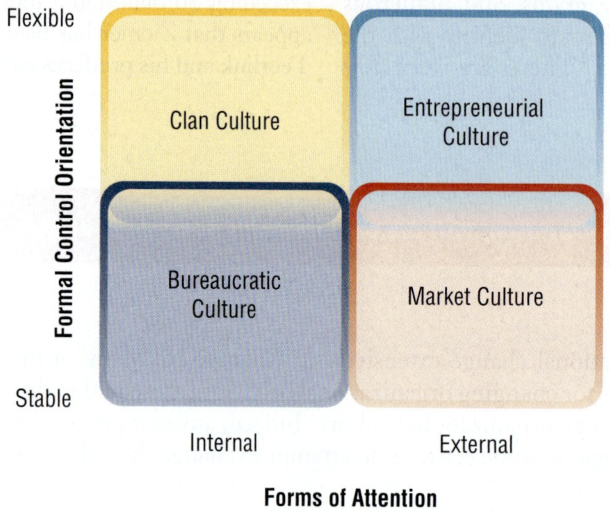

Source: Adapted from Hooijberg, R., and Petrock, F. On cultural change: Using the competing values framework to help leaders execute a transformational strategy. *Human Resources Management*, 1993, 32, 29–50; Quinn, R. E., *Beyond Rational Management: Mastering the Paradoxes and Competing Demands of High Performances.* San Francisco: Jossey-Bass, 1988.

informality. Managers view their roles as being good coordinators, organizers, and enforcers of written rules and standards. Tasks, responsibilities, and authority for all employees are clearly defined. The organization's many rules and processes are spelled out in thick manuals, and employees believe that their duty is to "go by the book" and follow legalistic procedures.

When Carol Bernick took over as CEO of Alberto-Culver in 1994, it was a $350 million company that was losing money. She stated that one of the biggest problems facing the company wasn't its product line or competition, but its bureaucratic culture. Employees didn't have a sense of ownership and urgency, and weren't rewarded for making decisions or taking risks. Employees simply waited to get their marching orders from their bosses and ignored many customer complaints because their boss didn't ask them to solve the complaints. Performance evaluations were based on the personal likes and dislikes of a manager and not on results. Her parents, founders of the company, kept the financial aspects of the business from the employees so employees had no knowledge about the problems confronting the business. Bernick was able to change the bureaucratic culture by changing its reward system, its organization's design, and the technology it uses. Today, it sales exceed $3.7 billion dollars.[22]

Clan Culture

Tradition, loyalty, personal commitment, extensive socialization, teamwork, self-management, and social influence are attributes of a clan culture. Its members recognize an obligation beyond the simple exchange of labor for a salary. They understand that contributions to the organization (e.g., hours worked per week) may exceed any contractual agreements. The individual's long-term commitment to the organization (loyalty) is exchanged for the organization's long-term commitment to the individual (security). Because individuals believe that the organization will treat them fairly in terms of salary increases, promotions, and other forms of recognition, they hold themselves accountable to the organization for their actions. Organizations such as YUM! Brands, State Farm

Insurance Company, and Southwest Airlines have developed strong clan cultures. Herb Kelleher, the former chairman of Southwest Airlines, stated: "Culture is one of the most precious things a company has so you must work harder at it than anything else." For organizations with clan cultures, this is especially true.

A clan culture achieves unity by means of a long and thorough socialization process. Long-time clan members serve as mentors and role models for newer members. The clan is aware of its unique history and often documents its origins and celebrates its traditions in various rites. Members have a shared image of the organization's style and manner of conduct. Public statements and events reinforce its values. In the restaurant support center (i.e., the headquarters) of YUM! Brands, which owns the KFC, Pizza Hut, and Taco Bell chains among others, there hangs a plaque with the "Founding Truth" and "How We Work Together Principles" proudly displayed for all to see. Statements on these plaques communicate the culture of YUM!, such as "Great operations and marketing drive sales," "No finger pointing," and "The restaurant manager is #1, not senior management."[23]

In a clan culture, members share feelings of pride in membership. They have a strong sense of identification and recognize their common fate in the organization. The up-through-the-ranks career pattern results in an extensive network of colleagues whose paths have crossed and who have shared similar experiences. Shared goals, perceptions, and behavioral tendencies foster communication, coordination, and integration. A clan culture generates feelings of personal ownership of a business, a product, or an idea. In addition, peer pressure to adhere to important norms is strong. The richness of the culture creates an environment in which few areas are left totally free from normative pressures. Depending on the types of its norms, the culture may or may not generate risk-taking behavior or innovation. Success is assumed to depend substantially on sensitivity to customers and concern for people. Teamwork, participation, and consensus decision making are believed to lead to this success.

Entrepreneurial Culture

High levels of risk taking and creativity characterize an entrepreneurial culture. There is a commitment to experimentation, innovation, and being on the leading edge. This culture doesn't just quickly react to changes in the environment—it creates change. Many of today's hi-tech companies, such as Apple, 37signals, and Get Digital, have developed entrepreneurial cultures. Effectiveness means providing new and unique products and rapid growth. Individual initiative, flexibility, and freedom foster growth and are encouraged and well rewarded.

Entrepreneurial cultures usually are associated with small to midsized companies that are still run by a founder. Innovation and entrepreneurship are values held by the founder. The following Teams Competency feature illustrates 37signals entrepreneurial culture.[24]

Teams Competency

37signals

At 37signals, a company with just eight employees whose web-based collaboration software is used by thousands of small businesses, there isn't time to sit around a conference room sipping lattes and deconstructing memos. There isn't even a company conference room. There are just a couple of cubicles, loads of brainpower, and three simple goals: Make useful business software, make it easy to run, and make money selling it.

Founder and president Jason Fried, age 33, decided early on that he didn't need to be in Silicon Valley,

California, to design cool software. Half his team works out of a plain-vanilla Chicago office that 37signals shares with a design studio. A tiny crew, only three of whom graduated from college, has built software that many users consider the best for small-business collaboration. Unconventional organizing is proving to be one of 37signals' biggest assets. The company creates programs that facilitate teamwork, and it ends up relying on the very same tools it builds. "We are growing in the same way a lot of our customers are, so we build products that we need to run our own business," Fried says. "We just build stuff we want to use. If we need it, they need it."

The 37signals team manages its products remotely. When a problem pops up, it can be fixed without having to recall software or ask customers to install a patch. If a new product isn't quite what customers wanted, 37signals can respond immediately. When the company launched Highrise, a contact-management tool, customers pleaded for a specific format for freelancers. Within 36 hours, 37signals expanded its offering. "They implement a mix of what's on their own road map and what people suggest," says subscriber Chris Busse, a web developer.

Fried admits that the 37signals team is stretched thin handling its users' demands. But he insists that the bigger a staff gets, the slower it moves. "A lot of teams have problems with overcollaboration," he says. "Too much teamwork, too many cooks in the kitchen, too many people making decisions." Simplicity is one of 37signals' guiding principles, in programming as well as management. For most technical issues that arise, simple workarounds will address 95 percent of the need with 10 percent of the effort that would be required to cover everything. For example, when designing Writeboard, for collaborative writing, the team wanted to let people track how much a document had changed over time. They pored over Ph.D. theses and complex algorithms to find an answer. Ace programmer David Hansson worked out a "cheat" software to track the number of characters in each document. The evolving total could be conveyed visually using dots of different sizes. With that clever solution, 37signals reduced what could have been a months-long programming project to a day's work.

On the company blog, Signal vs. Noise, Fried shares what he's learned about teamwork with more than 65,000 readers. First, kill all your meetings; they waste employees' time. "Interruption is the biggest enemy of productivity," he says. "We stay away from each other as much as we can to get more stuff done." Use e-mails and software instead to exchange information, ideas, and solutions. Next, dump half your projects to focus on the core of your business. Too much time and effort are wasted on second-tier objectives. Third, let your employees decide when and where to work so they can be both efficient and happy. As long as their fingers are near a keyboard, they could as easily be in Caldwell, Idaho, as in Chicago.

For more information on 37signals, visit this organization's home page at www.37signals.com.

Market Culture

The achievement of measurable and demanding goals, especially those that are financial and market based (e.g., sales growth, profitability, and market share), characterize a market culture. PepsiCo, Bank of America, and AIG, among others, have many of the characteristics found in market cultures. Hard-driving competitiveness and a profit orientation prevail throughout the organization. CEO Christos Cotsakos describes the market culture of E*Trade this way: "At E*Trade we're an attacker. We're predatory. We believe in the God-given right to market share."

In a market culture, the relationship between individual and organization is contractual. That is, the obligations of each party are agreed on in advance. In this sense, the control orientation is formal and quite stable. The individual is responsible for some level of performance, and the organization promises a specified level of rewards in return. Increased levels of performance are exchanged for increased rewards, as outlined in an agreed-on schedule. Neither party recognizes the right of the other to demand more than was originally specified. The organization doesn't promise (or imply) security, and the individual doesn't promise (or imply) loyalty. The contract, renewed annually if each party adequately performs its obligations, is utilitarian because each party uses the other to further its own goals. Rather than promoting a feeling of membership in a social system, the market culture values independence and individuality and encourages members to pursue their own financial goals.

In market cultures, superiors' interactions with subordinates largely consist of negotiating performance–reward agreements and/or evaluating requests for resource allocations. Managers aren't formally judged on their effectiveness as role models or mentors. The absence of a long-term commitment by both parties results in a weak socialization process. Social relations among coworkers aren't emphasized, and few economic incentives are tied directly to cooperating with peers. Managers are expected to cooperate with managers in other departments only to the extent necessary to achieve their performance goals. As a result, they may not develop an extensive network of colleagues within the organization. The market culture often is tied to monthly, quarterly, and annual performance goals based on profits. At PepsiCo, managers are driven to make their numbers (sales quotas). The emphasis is on fixing problems quickly and moving up the organization's hierarchy.[25]

Culture–Performance Relationships

Organizational culture has the potential to enhance organizational performance, individual satisfaction, the sense of certainty about how problems are to be handled, and so on. However, if an organizational culture gets out of step with the changing expectations of internal and/or external stakeholders, the organization's effectiveness can decline. Organizational culture and performance clearly are related, although the evidence regarding the exact nature of this relationship is mixed. Studies show that the relationship between many cultural attributes (featured in the popular press as being important for performance) and high performance hasn't been consistent over time.[26] Based on what we know about culture–performance relationships, a contingency approach seems to be a good one for managers and organizations to take. Further investigations of this issue are unlikely to discover one "best" organizational culture (either in terms of strength or type).

We do know the following about the relationships between culture and performance:

- Organizational culture can have a significant impact on a firm's long-term economic performance.
- Organizational culture will probably be an even more important factor in determining the success or failure of firms during the next decade.
- Organizational cultures that inhibit strong long-term financial performance are not rare; they develop easily, even in firms that are filled with reasonable and intelligent people.
- Although tough to change, organizational cultures can be made more performance enhancing if managers understand what sustains a culture.[27]

Managerial Guidelines. We can summarize the effects of organizational culture on employee behavior and performance with four key ideas. First, knowing the culture of an organization allows employees to understand both the firm's history and current methods of operation. This knowledge provides guidance about expected future behaviors. Second, organizational culture can foster commitment to corporate philosophy and values. This commitment generates shared feelings of working toward common goals. Third, organizational culture, through its norms, serves as a control mechanism to channel behaviors toward desired behaviors and away from undesired behaviors. Finally, certain types of organizational cultures may be related directly to greater effectiveness and productivity than others.

The need to determine which attributes of an organization's culture should be preserved and which should be modified is constant. In the United States during the 1980s, many organizations began changing their cultures to be more responsive to customers' expectations of product quality and service. During the late 1990s, many organizations began to reassess how well their cultures fit the expectations of the workforce. The U.S. workforce has changed to become much more diverse. More and more employees have begun to feel that organizational cultures established decades ago are out of step with contemporary expectations. We address the challenge of adjusting established organizational cultures to meet the expectations of a diverse workforce in the remainder of this chapter.

Learning Goal

3. Discuss how organizational culture can influence ethical behaviors of managers and employees.

ETHICAL BEHAVIOR AND ORGANIZATIONAL CULTURE

From the insider trading scandals of the 1980s and loan scandals of the 1990s to the more widespread fraud and manipulation of financial information, organizations experience chronic breakdowns in ethical conduct. The fact that the problem is enduring despite considerable public outcry, governmental action, and business attempts to create new structures and programs suggests underlying problems. Ethical problems in organizations continue to concern managers and employees greatly. One organization, Deloitte Touche Tohmatsu, a professional-service firm, has created a web-based ethics course for all employees in the 150 countries in which it operates. It has the kind of 1-800 hotline mandated by the Sarbanes-Oxley Act of 2002 for the anonymous reporting of wrongdoings. It has also customized its ethics program on a country-by-country basis since in some cultures having a 1-800 hotline would not be culturally acceptable.[28]

Impact of Culture

Organizational culture involves a complex interplay of formal and informal systems that may support either ethical or unethical behavior. As discussed previously, formal systems include leadership, structure, policies, reward systems, orientation and training programs, and decision-making processes. Informal systems include norms, heroes, rituals, language, myths, sagas, and stories. Organizational culture appears to affect ethical behavior in several ways.[29] For example, a culture that emphasizes ethical norms provides support for ethical behavior. In addition, top management plays a key role in fostering ethical behavior by exhibiting the correct behavior. Organizations identified as having strong moral cultures include Ben & Jerry's, Canon, Hewlett Packard, Medtronic, Patagonia, and Tom's of Maine. Top managers in these organizations have a culture that rewards moral priorities and influences how employees behave. If lower level managers observe top-level managers sexually harassing others, falsifying expense reports, diverting shipments to preferred customers, misrepresenting the organization's financial position, and other forms of unethical behavior, they assume that these behaviors are acceptable and will be rewarded in the future. Thus, the presence or absence of ethical behavior in managerial actions both influences and reflects the culture. The organizational culture may promote taking responsibility for the consequences of actions, thereby increasing the probability that individuals will behave ethically. Alternatively, the culture may diffuse responsibility for the consequences of unethical behavior, thereby making such behavior more likely. In short, ethical business practices stem from ethical organizational cultures.

Employees might take various steps to reduce unethical behavior, including

- secretly or publicly reporting unethical actions to a higher level within the organization,
- secretly or publicly reporting unethical actions to someone outside the organization,
- secretly or publicly threatening an offender or a responsible manager with reporting unethical actions, or
- quietly or publicly refusing to implement an unethical order or policy.

Whistle-Blowing

Whistle-blowing *is the disclosure by current or former employees of illegal, immoral, or illegitimate organizational practices to people or organizations that may be able to change the practice.* The whistle-blower lacks the power to change the undesirable practice directly and so appeals to others either inside or outside the organization.[30]

The collapse of Enron started when Sherron Watkins sat down at her computer on August 14, 2001, and began typing a questioning and now famous memo to her boss, Kenneth Lay. "I am incredibly nervous that we will implode in a wave of accounting scandals," she wrote. Watkins' seven-page memo became the smoking gun in an investigation of alleged financial misdealing at Enron and Arthur Andersen, an auditing firm, that ultimately led to the collapse of both firms. Watkins found herself confronting fraudulent behavior that was illegal and could be related to individuals. Her concerns also had to do with the mismanagement of information and ineffective leadership. She acted when the evidence became overwhelming that a significant wrongdoing had occurred, even though she feared retaliation.

What do you consider a whistle-blowing offense? The following Ethics Competency feature asks you to decide what a wrongdoing is, and asks you if you would blow the whistle on a person who you observed engaging in a certain practice. We also ask you to indicate whether the types of retaliation listed would happen to you if you reported such a wrongdoing to top management and/or the organization's ethics officer. For the purpose of this illustration, you may assume that the average cost of the wrongdoing is $35,000 and that you had observed this wrongdoing frequently. We realize that oftentimes a dollar amount is difficult to place on a wrongdoing (e.g., a safety violation, sexual harassment, mismanagement). On page 488, you can compare your answers to those of people who have actually blown the whistle at work.[31]

Ethics Competency

What Would You Do?

We realize that the eight types of wrongdoing presented will be significantly affected by the cost of the wrongdoing. The cost, quality of evidence, and frequency of activity of the wrongdoing are all related to whether you would actually blow the whistle or just threaten to do so. The type of retaliation also varies by the type of wrongdoing and the cost. We want you to indicate the type of retaliation most likely suffered by the whistle-blower.

Type of Wrongdoing	**Would You Report to Management?**	
Stealing	YES	NO
Waste	YES	NO
Mismanagement	YES	NO
Safety problems	YES	NO
Sexual harassment	YES	NO
Unfair discrimination	YES	NO
Legal violation	YES	NO
Financial reporting	YES	NO

Type of Retaliation	**Would This Happen to You?**	
Coworkers not associating with person	YES	NO
Pressure from coworkers to stop complaint	YES	NO
Withholding of information needed to perform job	YES	NO
Poor performance appraisal	YES	NO
Verbal harassment or intimidation	YES	NO
Tighter scrutiny of daily work by management	YES	NO
Reassignment to a different job	YES	NO
Reassignment to a different job with less desirable duties	YES	NO
Denial of a promotion	YES	NO

Managerial Guidelines

The following leadership actions by managers can help create an organizational culture that encourages ethical behavior:

- Be realistic in setting values and goals regarding employment relationships. Do not promise what the organization cannot deliver.
- Encourage input from throughout the organization regarding appropriate values and practices for implementing the culture. Choose values that represent the views of both employees and managers.
- Opt for a *strong* culture that encourages and rewards diversity and dissent, such as grievance or complaint mechanisms or other internal review procedures.
- Provide training programs for managers and teams on adopting and implementing the organization's values. These programs should stress the underlying ethical and legal principles and cover the practical aspects of carrying out procedural guidelines.

An effective organizational culture should encourage ethical behavior and discourage unethical behavior. Admittedly, ethical behavior may "cost" the organization and individuals. A global firm that refuses to pay a bribe to secure business in a particular country may lose sales. An individual may lose financially by not accepting a kickback. Similarly, an organization or individual might seem to gain from unethical actions. An organization may flout U.S. law by quietly paying bribes to officials in order to gain entry to a new market. A purchasing agent for a large corporation might take kickbacks for purchasing all needed office supplies from a particular supplier. However, such gains are often short term.

In the long run, an organization can't successfully operate if its prevailing culture and values aren't similar to those of society. That is as true as the observation that, in the long run, an organization cannot survive unless it provides high-quality goods and services that society wants and needs. An organizational culture that promotes ethical behavior is not only compatible with prevailing cultural values in the United States, but it also makes good business sense.

Learning Goal

4. Explain why fostering cultural diversity is important.

FOSTERING CULTURAL DIVERSITY

Diversity *represents individual differences and similarities that exist among people.* There are three important issues about diversity.[32] First, there are many different dimensions of diversity. Diversity is not about age, gender, or race. It is also not about being gay, heterosexual, or lesbian, or having certain religious beliefs. Diversity pertains to all those individual differences that make each one of us unique. Second, diversity is not synonymous with differences. Diversity encompasses both similarities and differences. For the manager, this means managing both similarities and differences among employees. Finally, diversity includes all differences and similarities and not just pieces. In Chapter 2, we discussed how various personality dimensions, such as openness, conscientiousness, self-esteem, and locus of control, contribute to each person's unique personality. Managers need to deal not only with these dimensions, but also with a person's attitudes, cultural values, and the like.

Organizations are becoming increasingly diverse in terms of gender, race, ethnicity, and nationality. More than half of the U.S. workforce consists of women, minorities, and recent immigrants. The growing diversity of employees in many organizations can bring substantial benefits, such as more successful marketing strategies for different types of customers, improved decision making, and greater creativity and innovation. The U.S. Department of Labor forecasts that 60 percent of all new employees entering the U.S. workforce during the period from 2000 to 2010 will be women or people of color. Whether motivated by economic necessity or choice, organizations will be competing in this marketplace for talent. At DuPont, a group of African-American workers recently opened promising new markets for the firm by focusing on black farmers. A multicultural team gained the company about $45 million in new business by changing the way DuPont designs and markets decorating materials (e.g., countertops) in order to appeal more to overseas customers. CEO Bob Ulrich of Target says that "Our ability to offer an exceptional shopping experience depends on team members who understand the diverse communities we serve." Forty-one percent of Target employees are classified as diverse. Target offers all employees a series of classes on appreciating differences, communication styles, managing inclusion, and the multicultural workforce.[33]

Challenges

Along with its benefits, cultural diversity brings costs and concerns, including communication difficulties, intraorganizational conflict, and turnover. Effectively fostering cultural diversity promises to continue to be a significant challenge for organizations for a long time. For example, programs such as day care and elder care, flexible work schedules, paternal leaves, and management of contingent workers are major issues facing organizations. United Technologies, an organization we covered in Chapter 14 (see pages 442–444), uses a variety of diversity management approaches. During succession planning, a diversity manager participates to ensure that a diverse pool of employees is considered for career advancement. The company also provides performance appraisal training to help managers make judgments that accurately reflect each person's efforts and contributions. It sponsors forums for women and minorities and encourages membership in employee mentoring networks, such as the Society for Women Engineers, National Society of Black Engineers, and the National Society for Hispanic MBAs. The challenge for United Technologies is to ensure that all employees working for the company feel comfortable and committed to its goals.[34]

Diversity Programs: Managerial Guidelines

There are no easy answers to the challenges of fostering a culturally diverse workforce. However, there are some common characteristics in organizations with effective diversity management programs. These characteristics have been distilled into the following helpful guidelines:

- Managers and employees must understand that a diverse workforce will embody different perspectives and approaches to work and must truly value variety of opinion and insight.
- Managers must recognize both the learning opportunities and the challenges that the expression of different perspectives presents for the organization.
- The organizational culture must create an expectation of high standards of performance and ethics from everyone.
- The organizational culture must stimulate personal development.
- The organizational culture must encourage openness.
- The organizational culture must make workers feel valued.
- The organization must have a clearly stated and widely understood mission.[35]

Table 15.3 contains a questionnaire that you can use to examine your awareness of diversity issues. Take a moment to complete it now. What did you learn about yourself?

Table 15.3 Diversity Questionnaire

Directions
Indicate your views by placing a T (true) or F (false) next to each of these nine statements.

1. I know about the rules and customs of several different cultures. ____
2. I know that I hold stereotypes about other groups. ____
3. I feel comfortable with people of different backgrounds from my own. ____
4. I associate with people who are different from me. ____
5. I find working on a multicultural team satisfying. ____
6. I find change stimulating and exciting. ____
7. I enjoy learning about other cultures. ____
8. When dealing with someone whose English is limited, I show patience and understanding. ____
9. I find that spending time building relationships with others is useful because more gets done. ____

Interpretation
The more true responses you have, the more adaptable and open you are to diversity. If you have five or more true responses, you probably are someone who finds value in cross-cultural experiences.

If you have less than five true responses, you may be resistant to interacting with people who are different from you. If that is the case, you may find that your interactions with others are sometimes blocked.

Source: Adapted from Gardenswartz, L., and Rowe, A. What's your diversity quotient? *Managing Diversity Newsletter*, New York: Jamestown (undated).

Learning Goal

5. Describe the process of organizational socialization and its effect on culture.

SOCIALIZATION OF NEW EMPLOYEES

Socialization *is the process by which older members of a society transmit to younger members the social skills and knowledge needed to function effectively in that society.* Similarly, organizational socialization *is the systematic process by which an organization brings new employees into its culture.*[36] In other words, it involves the transmission of an organization's cultural values from managers and senior employees to new employees, providing the social knowledge and skills needed to perform organizational roles and tasks successfully. In other words, socialization takes an outsider and turns that person into an insider by promoting and reinforcing the organization's core values and beliefs. It is during the organizational socialization process that the newcomer reaches a psychological contract with the organization. A psychological contract *refers to a person's overall set of expectations regarding what they will contribute to the organization and what the organization will provide in return.* Unlike a business contract, a psychological contract is not written on paper, nor are its terms clearly defined. It is an understanding reached between the person and the organization. In the Learning from Experience feature, we noted how TDI's servant leadership program is the cornerstone of its socialization program. Thus, if you choose to work at TDI, you need to accept the servant leadership program as a part of your psychological contract with TDI.

Organizational socialization provides the means by which new employees learn which "ropes" to pay attention to and which to ignore. It includes learning work group, departmental, and organizational values, rules, procedures, and norms; developing social and working relationships; and developing the skills needed to perform a job.

Organizational Socialization Process

Figure 15.5 presents an example of an organizational socialization process. It doesn't represent the socialization process of every organization. However, many firms with strong cultures—such as Disney, TDIndustries, and Interstate Battery—frequently follow at least some of these steps in socializing new employees:

Step 1. Entry-level candidates are selected carefully. Trained recruiters use standardized procedures and seek specific capabilities that are related to the success of the business.

Step 2. Challenging early work assignments in the first year on the job are critical. For years, KeySpan Energy, a gas utility company in Brooklyn, New York, held a three-day executive retreat at a resort in Seaview, New Jersey. Newly hired employees had to be nominated by their manager to attend this retreat. After a day of playing golf, fishing, and so forth, and a night of dinner and cards, the next morning, at breakfast the CEO would pick a new employee to lead the group in discussion of a current issue confronting the company. The employee would have 90 minutes or so to prepare and make the presentation shortly thereafter. Careers were made or broken on these presentations. Those who successfully survived this "baptism by fire" were given plum job assignments in powerful departments.

Step 3. Tough on-the-job training leads to mastery of one of the core disciplines of the business. Promotion is then tied to a proven track record. At KFC, for example, many restaurant managers have been greeters, a member of the bus staff, waiters, chefs, and so forth.

Step 4. Careful attention is given to measuring results and rewarding performance. Reward systems are true indicators of the values that underlie an organization's culture. At KFC, David Novak passes out floppy rubber chickens (all of which

FIGURE 15.5 Steps in Socialization Process

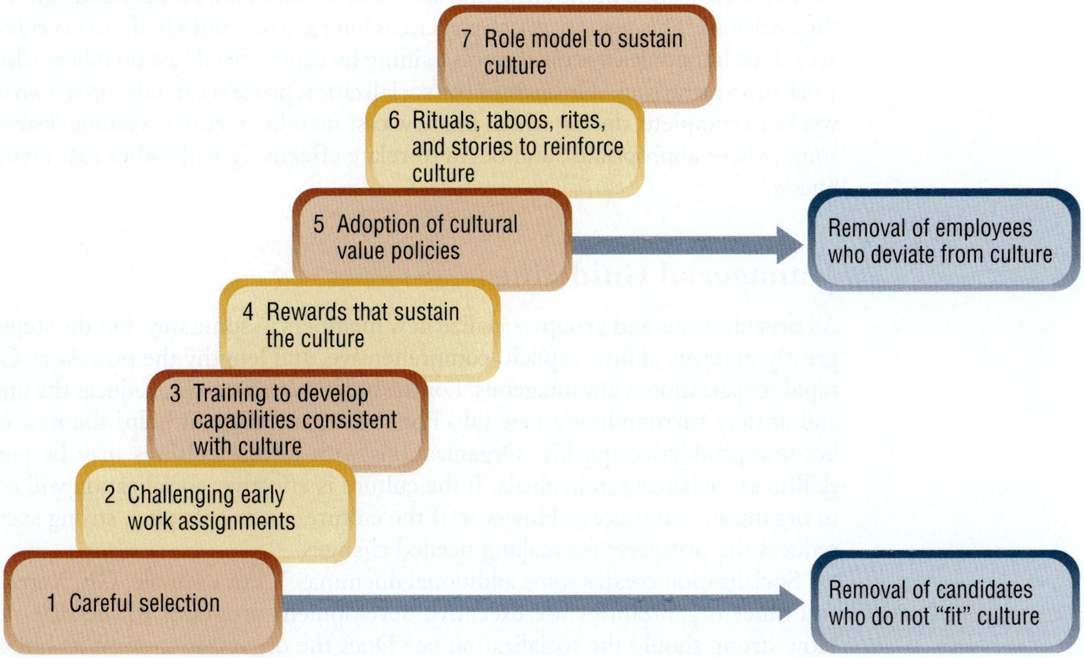

are numbered and have a personal note on them) as a reward and to recognize employees for their outstanding contributions to KFC.

Step 5. Adherence to the organization's values is emphasized. Identification with common values allows employees to justify the personal sacrifices caused by their membership in the organization.

Step 6. Reinforcing folklore provides legends and interpretations of important events in the organization's history that validate its culture and goals. Folklore reinforces a code of conduct for "how we do things around here."

Step 7. Consistent role models and consistent traits are associated with those recognized as being on the fast track to promotion and success.[37]

How effectively have you been socialized by either your current or past employer? Take a few minutes and answer the questions found in Table 15.4 on page 481. How does your degree of socialization affect your job satisfaction? Job performance?[38]

Disney World has an effective socialization process that uses some of these seven steps to help ensure that tens of thousands of visitors a day will have fun.[39] Disney annually hires more than 2,000 people and employs more than 27,500 at Disney World. Those who cannot afford housing around the Disney World site are housed in a separate Disney gated complex. Disney carefully screens all potential members (Step 1). After recruits complete their applications, they are screened for criminal records. Those who have a record are dropped from consideration.

All workers at Disney World must strictly follow Disney rules (e.g., no mustaches, visible tattoos, or dangling body piercing items, and no hair color outside of the "normal" colors) and norms (such as always taking the extra step to make sure guests have a good experience) and behave in a certain way. To learn these rules, norms, and behaviors, new cast members (recruits) receive formal training at Disney University in groups of 45 and follow a rigid program. During the Tradition I program, which lasts a day and a half, new cast members learn the Disney language and the four Disney values: safety, courtesy, show or entertainment, and efficiency. They also receive training in how to answer guests' questions no matter how simple or difficult the question (Step 5). About 40 percent of new cast members complete Tradition I training. Many simply quit when they understand what their jobs and the rules entail.

Once the cast members have completed the Tradition I phase, they move on to further socialization in the attraction areas (Adventureland, Fantasyland, and so on) that they will join. This session, which can last as long as a day and a half, covers rules for each area. Last but not least is on-the-job training by experienced cast members who actually work in an attraction. This part of the socialization process can take up to two and a half weeks to complete, during which the new cast members wear a costume, learn to sing a song (where appropriate), and begin to relate effectively with other cast members and guests.

Managerial Guidelines

All organizations and groups socialize new members in some way, but the steps can vary greatly in terms of how explicit, comprehensive, and lengthy the process is. Generally, rapid socialization is advantageous. For the individual, it quickly reduces the uncertainty and anxiety surrounding a new job. For the organization, it helps the new employee become productive quickly. Organizations with strong cultures may be particularly skillful at socializing individuals. If the culture is effective, socialization will contribute to organizational success. However, if the culture needs changing, strong socialization reduces the prospects for making needed changes.

Socialization creates some additional dilemmas.[40] For example, GE, Xerox, Disney, and other organizations use executive development programs to socialize new hires. How strong should the socialization be? Does the organization want its hires to think alike, at least in terms of a certain level of logic and intelligent analysis? To have the same

Table 15.4 How Effectively Have You Been Socialized?

Instructions Complete the following survey items by considering either your current job or one you held in the past. If you have never worked, identify a friend who is working and ask that individual to complete the questionnaire for his or her organization. Read each item and circle your response by using the rating scale shown below. Remember, there are no right or wrong answers. On completion, compute your total score by adding up your responses and compare it to the scoring norms.

	Strongly Disagree	Disagree	Neutral	Agree	Strongly Agree
1. I have been through a set of training experiences that are specifically designed to give newcomers a thorough knowledge of job-related skills.	1	2	3	4	5
2. This organization puts all newcomers through the same set of learning experiences.	1	2	3	4	5
3. I did not perform any of my normal job responsibilities until I was thoroughly familiar with departmental procedures and work methods.	1	2	3	4	5
4. There is a clear pattern in the way one role leads to another, or one job assignment leads to another, in this organization.	1	2	3	4	5
5. I can predict my future career path in this organization by observing other people's experiences.	1	2	3	4	5
6. Almost all of my colleagues have been supportive of me personally.	1	2	3	4	5
7. My colleagues have gone out of their way to help me adjust to this organization.	1	2	3	4	5
8. I received much guidance from experienced organizational members as to how I should perform my job.	1	2	3	4	5
9. In the last several months, I have been extensively involved with other new recruits in common, job-related activities.	1	2	3	4	5
10. I am gaining a clear understanding of my role in this organization from observing my senior colleagues.	1	2	3	4	5

Total score = ______

Scoring Norms
10–20 = Low socialization
21–39 = Moderate socialization
40–50 = High socialization

business values and sense of professionalism? In some sense, the answer to these questions has to be *yes*. Yet, oversocialization runs the risk of creating rigid, narrow-minded corporate men and women. The goal of most organizations' socialization

Table 15.5 Possible Outcomes of the Socialization Process

SUCCESSFUL SOCIALIZATION IS REFLECTED IN	UNSUCCESSFUL SOCIALIZATION IS REFLECTED IN
• Job satisfaction	• Job dissatisfaction
• Role clarity	• Role ambiguity and conflict
• High work motivation	• Low work motivation
• Understanding of culture, perceived control	• Misunderstanding, tension, perceived lack of control
• High job involvement	• Low job involvement
• Commitment to organization	• Lack of commitment to organization
• Tenure	• Absenteeism, turnover
• High performance	• Low performance
• Internalized values	• Rejection of values

processes is to develop independent thinkers committed to what they believe to be right, while at the same time helping them become collaborative team players who have good interpersonal skills. This goal poses a challenge for socialization, which, to be effective, must balance these two demands.

The socialization process may affect employee and organizational success in a variety of ways. Table 15.5 lists some possible socialization outcomes. These outcomes aren't determined solely by an organization's socialization process. For example, job satisfaction is a function of many things, including the nature of the task, the individual's personality and needs, the nature of supervision, opportunities to succeed and be rewarded, and the like (see Chapter 2). Note that successful socialization may contribute to job satisfaction, whereas unsuccessful socialization may contribute to job dissatisfaction.

CHAPTER SUMMARY

1. Explain how an organization's culture is formed, sustained, and changed.

Organizational culture is the pattern of beliefs and expectations shared by members of an organization. It includes a common philosophy, norms, and values. In other words, it expresses the "rules of the game" for getting along and getting things done and ways of interacting with outsiders, such as suppliers and customers. Some aspects of organizational culture are cultural symbols, heroes, rites, and ceremonies. Organizational culture develops as a response to the challenges of external adaptation and survival and of internal integration. The formation of an organization's culture also is influenced by the culture of the larger society within which the organization must function.

The primary methods for both sustaining and changing organizational culture include (1) identifying what managers and teams pay attention to, measure, and control; (2) recognizing the ways in which managers and employees react to crises; (3) using role modeling, teaching, and coaching; (4) developing and applying fair criteria for allocating rewards; (5) utilizing consistent criteria for recruitment, selection, and promotion within the organization and removal from it; and (6) emphasizing organizational rites, ceremonies, and stories.

Although all organizational cultures are unique, four general types are identified and discussed: bureaucratic, clan, entrepreneurial, and market. They are characterized by differences in the extent of formal controls and focus of attention.

2. Describe four types of organizational culture.

Organizational culture also can have a strong effect on ethical behavior by managers and employees alike. One concept linking culture to ethical behavior is organizational dissent. Cultures that encourage dissent and permit whistle-blowing provide guidelines for ethical behaviors.

3. Discuss how organizational culture can influence ethical behaviors of managers and employees.

Fostering cultural diversity is expected to be one of the principal challenges facing the leaders of organizations for years to come. How leaders respond to this challenge will determine the effectiveness of culturally diverse teams, an organization's communication process, and employees' personal development.

4. Explain why fostering cultural diversity is important.

Socialization is the process by which new members are brought into an organization's culture. At firms having a strong culture, socialization steps are well developed and the focus of careful attention. All organizations socialize new members, but depending on how it is done, the outcomes could be either positive or negative in terms of job performance, satisfaction, and commitment to the organization. We presented a seven-step process for socializing new employees.

5. Describe the process of organizational socialization and its effect on culture.

KEY TERMS AND CONCEPTS

Bureaucratic culture
Clan culture
Cultural symbols
Diversity
Entrepreneurial culture
External adaptation and survival
Internal integration
Market culture
Organizational cultural values
Organizational culture
Organizational rites and ceremonies
Organizational socialization
Psychological contract
Shared behaviors
Socialization
Subcultures
Whistle-blowing

DISCUSSION QUESTIONS

1. To further explore the concept of servant leadership at TDIndustries, visit TDI's website (www.tdindustries.com). Go to "About Us" and click on "Servant Leadership." Why has this concept worked so well at TDIndustries?
2. Provide two examples of how organizational culture is expressed at your college or university.
3. Describe how the organizational culture at your college or university affects your behavior.
4. What are the primary methods that Richard Teerlink used to change the culture of Harley-Davidson?
5. Describe how organizations use symbols and stories to communicate value and beliefs. Give some examples of organizations' symbols or stories with which you are familiar.
6. Use the phrases in Table 15.1 to describe the culture of an organization with which you are familiar. How does its organizational culture affect the type of employee who chooses to work there?
7. What role does teamwork play in sustaining 37signals' entrepreneurial culture?
8. How might an organization use its culture to increase the probability of ethical behavior and decrease the probability of unethical behavior by its managers and employees?
9. In what type of organizational culture would you prefer to work? Why? Table 15.1 can help you understand your own values.
10. George Platt, CEO of ViewCast, a video encoding company, says that changing a culture is among the hardest things he has ever done. Why is changing a culture so difficult?

EXPERIENTIAL EXERCISE AND CASE

Experiential Exercise: Self Competency

Assessing the Culture of Your Organization[41]

Instructions

Think of an organization that you currently work for or used to work for. This questionnaire will help you look at some aspects of that organization's culture. The following 40 statements indicate some organizational values. If these values are held by top management, they generally will be shared by other members of the organization. Read each statement and indicate in the blank to the left of the statement how much the behavior contained in the statement is valued in that organization. Use the following key for your responses:

4 = Very highly valued in the organization.
3 = Valued in the organization.
2 = Given rather low value in the organization.
1 = Not valued in the organization.

_____ 1. Free communication among employees, each respecting the feelings, competence, and judgment of others.
_____ 2. Facing problems, not shying away from them.
_____ 3. Offering moral support and help to employees and colleagues in crisis.
_____ 4. Match between feelings and expressed behavior.
_____ 5. Preventive action on most matters.
_____ 6. Employees taking independent action relating to their jobs.
_____ 7. Teamwork and team spirit.
_____ 8. Employees trying out innovative ways of solving problems.
_____ 9. Genuine sharing of information, feelings, and thoughts in meetings.
_____ 10. Going deeper rather than doing surface-level analysis of interpersonal problems.
_____ 11. Interpersonal contact and support among employees.
_____ 12. Tactfulness, cleverness, and even a little manipulation to get things done.
_____ 13. Superiors encouraging their subordinates to think about their development and take action in that direction.
_____ 14. Close supervision and direction of employees regarding their behaviors.
_____ 15. Accepting and appreciating help offered by others.
_____ 16. Encouraging employees to take a fresh look at how things are done.
_____ 17. Free discussion and communication among superiors and subordinates.
_____ 18. Facing challenges inherent in the work situation.
_____ 19. Confiding in superiors without fear that they will misuse the trust.
_____ 20. "Owning" mistakes made.
_____ 21. Considering both positive and negative aspects before taking action.
_____ 22. Obeying and checking with superiors rather than being concerned about larger organizational goals.
_____ 23. Performing immediate tasks rather than being concerned about larger organizational goals.
_____ 24. Making genuine attempts to change behavior on the basis of feedback received.

Use the following key for the remainder of your responses:

4 = This belief is very widely shared in the organization.
3 = This belief is fairly well shared in the organization.
2 = Only some people in the organization share this belief.
1 = Few or no people in the organization share this belief.

_____ 25. Effective managers suppress their feelings.
_____ 26. Pass the buck to others tactfully when there is a problem.
_____ 27. Trust begets trust.
_____ 28. Telling a polite lie is preferable to telling the unpleasant truth.
_____ 29. Prevention is better than cure.
_____ 30. Freedom for employees breeds lack of discipline.
_____ 31. Emphasis on teamwork dilutes individual accountability.
_____ 32. Thinking and doing new things are important for organizational vitality.
_____ 33. Free and candid communication among various levels helps in solving problems.
_____ 34. Surfacing problems is not enough; we should find the solution.
_____ 35. When the situation is urgent and has to be dealt with, you have to fend for yourself.
_____ 36. People are what they seem to be.
_____ 37. A stitch in time saves nine.
_____ 38. A good way to motivate employees is to give them autonomy to plan their work.
_____ 39. Employee involvement in developing the organization's mission and goals contributes to productivity.
_____ 40. In today's competitive situation, consolidation and stability are more important than experimentation.

Organizational Cultural Values Profile

The Organizational Cultural Values Profile assesses eight dimensions of an organization's culture. Each dimension is listed, along with the items related to it. For each aspect, add the ratings you assigned to the item numbers indicated.

Important: For each bold item with an asterisk, you must convert your rating as follows: 1 becomes 4; 2 becomes 3; 3 becomes 2; and 4 becomes 1.

Openness		**Proaction**	
Items 1	_______	Items 5	_______
9	_______	13	_______

17	________	21	________
25*	________	29	________
33	________	37	________
Total	________	*Total*	________
Confrontation		**Autonomy**	
Items 2	________	Items 6	________
10	________	**14***	________
18	________	**22***	________
26*	________	**30***	________
34	________	38	________
Total	________	*Total*	________
Trust		**Collaboration**	
Items 3	________	Items 7	________
11	________	15	________
19	________	**23***	________
27	________	**31***	________
35*	________	39	________
Total	________	*Total*	________
Authenticity		**Experimentation**	
Items 4	________	Items 8	________
12*	________	16	________
20	________	24	________
28*	________	32	________
36	________	**40***	________
Total	________	*Total*	________

Organizational Cultural Values Interpretation Sheet

The eight organizational cultural values are **O**penness, **C**onfrontation, **T**rust, **A**uthenticity, **P**roaction, **A**utonomy, **C**ollaboration, and **E**xperimentation. The following definitions may help to clarify the values:

1. **O**penness: Spontaneous expression of feelings and thoughts and sharing of these without defensiveness.
2. **C**onfrontation: Facing—not shying away from—problems; deeper analysis of interpersonal problems; taking on challenges.
3. **T**rust: Maintaining confidentiality of information shared by others and not misusing it; a sense of assurance that others will help when needed and will honor mutual obligations and commitments.
4. **A**uthenticity: Match between what one feels, says, and does; owning one's actions and mistakes; unreserved sharing of feelings.
5. **P**roaction: Initiative; preplanning and preventive action; calculating payoffs before taking action.
6. **A**utonomy: Using and giving freedom to plan and act in one's own sphere; respecting and encouraging individual and role autonomy.
7. **C**ollaboration: Giving help to, and asking for help from, others; team spirit; working together (individuals and groups) to solve problems.
8. **E**xperimentation: Using and encouraging innovative approaches to solve problems; using feedback for improving; taking a fresh look at things; encouraging creativity.

Norms for the Organizational Culture Value Profile

	Low	High
1. Openness	13	17
2. Confrontation	10	16
3. Trust	10	16
4. Authenticity	10	14
5. Proaction	12	18
6. Autonomy	11	16
7. Collaboration	13	17
8. Experimentation	11	16

Based on the studies of the value profile so far, these are the high- and low-scoring norms.

High scores indicate a strong belief in the values and, thus, a strong organizational culture. Low scores illustrate a weak set of cultural values. If the average or mean score for your organization is low, the questions on the profile can be used as the basis for action planning to improve the organization's culture and to increase openness, creativity, and collaboration. Remember that items 12, 14, 22, 23, 25, 26, 28, 30, 31, 35, and 40 are reverse scored.

Questions

1. What approaches might you use to change these cultural values?
2. Using these eight values, analyze the culture at TDIndustries. What is its profile and how does it influence employees' behaviors?

Case: Change Competency

Ford's CEO Leads Cultural Change[42]

After losing $12.7 billion in 2006, Ford had to pledge its factories, headquarters, and the rights to its blue oval logo to the banks and bondholders. This was required just to get enough capital to finance its turnaround plan. Those were all tough decisions. But these are difficult times for the U.S. auto industry. With Cerberus Capital Management taking over at Chrysler, the status quo is no longer an option at Ford.

Ford once exemplified corporate efficiency. It is the birthplace of the assembly line and home of the celebrated Whiz Kids, who pioneered many modern management techniques in the 1960s. In recent years, it degenerated into a symbol of inefficiency. Some automobile experts claim corporate lifers became all too comfortable with the idea of losing money. Mediocrity was acceptable. The company's complacency showed up in the very language it used internally to rate its own models. Ford used the designations "L" for Leader, "AL" for Among Leaders, and "C" for Competitive. Too many executives simply strived for Cs, asserted William C. "Bill"

Ford, Jr., executive chairman of the board. When asked about the grading system, the great-grandson of Henry Ford jokingly put a gun to his head and pulled the trigger. "We still do that?" he asked in disbelief. "I don't know where that came from."

The Old Ford Way

Bill Ford, Jr., had served as chief executive for nearly five years. He concluded that an insider could no longer fix Ford. The job required an outsider. Alan Mulally, the former head of Boeing Co.'s commercial airlines division, was hired as CEO in September 2006. Mulally is working hard to change work habits that took years to develop. He wants managers to think more about customers than their own careers. For Ford to have any chance of becoming profitable by 2009, a cost-saving contract with the United Auto Workers (UAW) is required. Ford will also likely sell Jaguar or Mercury. But the salvation of Ford will require more than simply cutting costs. One way or another, the company has to figure out how to produce more vehicles that consumers actually want. That will require Mulally to address the most fundamental problem of all: Ford's defeatist culture.

Mulally has made it a top priority to encourage his leadership team to admit mistakes, to share more information, and to cooperate across divisions. He's holding everybody's feet to the fire with tough oversight and harsh warnings about Ford's predicament. "We have been going out of business for 40 years," Mulally told a group of 100 information technology staffers at a "town meeting." He has repeated the message to every employee group that he has addressed.

Mulally has yet to convince stakeholders that Ford can reach its goals. History provides ample basis for such skepticism. Historically Ford has been a place that's notorious for destroying auto industry outsiders. Despite Bill Ford's strong backing, Mulally has run into plenty of resistance. Nearly all of the Ford managers have spent their entire careers at Ford. Some of them grimaced when Mulally received a $28 million paycheck for his first four months of work. On Mulally's first meeting with his inherited team, one manager asked: "How are you going to tackle something as complex and unfamiliar as the auto business when we are in such tough financial shape?" Unfazed by the question, Mulally looked the manager directly in the eye and said: "An automobile has about 10,000 moving parts, right? An airplane has two million, and it has to stay up in the air."

Although Mulally lacks in-depth auto industry knowledge, he is free of many of the cultural habits that have gotten Ford into so much trouble. "He doesn't know what he doesn't know," says Ford Americas President Mark Fields. When Mulally was reviewing the company's 2008 product line, for example, he was told that Ford loses close to $3,000 every time a customer buys a Focus compact. "Why haven't you figured out a way to make a profit?" he asked. Executives explained that Ford needed the high sales volume to maintain the company's corporate average fuel economy rating and that the plant that makes the car is a high-cost UAW factory in Michigan. He shot back: "That's not what I asked. I want to know why no one figured out a way to build this car at a profit, whether it has to be built in Michigan or China or India, if that's what it takes." Nobody had a good answer.

How did Ford evolve from one of the most admired companies in the world into one where losing money was okay? Until the mid-1960s, Ford was considered a model of management excellence. Under U.S. Defense Secretary Robert S. McNamara, one of a group of military veterans at the company dubbed the Whiz Kids, Ford developed scientific consumer research techniques that are now commonplace throughout the business world. But after McNamara left in 1961, Henry Ford II (Bill's uncle) gradually assumed a bigger role in management. He built a culture where rising stars like successive Ford Presidents Lee Iacocca and Semon "Bunkie" Knudson were often pitted against one another like gladiators in Rome's coliseum to prove themselves. As the auto industry's growth slowed, limiting career opportunities for managers, executives turned on one another. They also became more cautious. "The bureaucracy at Ford grew, and managers took refuge in the structure when things got tough rather than innovate or try new ideas that seemed risky," stated Allan Gilmour, a retired chief financial officer at Ford.

Personal ties with the Ford family, always important at the company, sometimes trumped performance in promotion decisions. Some ambitious managers focused increasingly on developing their political skills with Ford family members instead of focusing on financial results. Critics also blame the family members, who emphasized dividend payments because it was their primary source of income instead of long-term financial results. This encouraged a focus on current profits rather than long-term planning over the decades.

Organization Design Issues

The company's unusual approach to grooming leaders discouraged collaboration. Ford had a long tradition of rapidly cycling executives through new posts every two years or so. In fact, managers used to refer to their posts as "assignments" rather than jobs. One consequence was that managers needed to make their goals in a short time period. This discouraged cooperation with other divisions and regions, whose products were often on a different timetable. Also engineers did not get rewarded or recognized for carrying over their predecessor's design or idea—even if it saved big money. Mulally has moved to lengthen job tenures. "You can't hold somebody accountable for a job they've held for nine months."

Ford's organization design was complex. It had four parallel operating units worldwide, each with its own costly bureaucracy, factories, and product development staff. No two vehicles in Ford's lineup shared the same mirrors, headlamps, or even such mundane pieces as the springs and hinges for the hood. That left Ford at a big cost disadvantage in engineering and parts compared with General Motors, Chrysler, Toyota, and Honda. Mulally wants to get that number of different engineering platforms down to five or six platforms, similar to Honda. "There's no global company I know of that can succeed with the level of complexity we have at Ford," he says.

In the previous organization hierarchy at Ford, an elaborate system of employment grades clearly established an employee's rank in the pecking order. The grades also had the unintentional effect of quashing ideas and keeping information tightly controlled. Ford Americas President Fields arrived at the company from IBM in 1989. He couldn't make a lunch date with an executive who held a higher grade. People asked him what his grade was "as a condition of including me or socializing with me," Fields recalls. Also, he was discouraged from airing problems at meetings unless his boss approved first.

There are many examples of Ford losing opportunities because of its organization design. One recent example involved Sync, a system that allows voice-command control of a cell phone and MP3 player. It was a big success in 2007 at the North American International Auto Show. Ford developed it with Microsoft Corp. and rolled it out in 2008. Volvo and Land Rover want to offer Sync as well. However, neither can use it because the electrical systems of the Swedish and British cars are incompatible with Ford's. Mulally found that to be incomprehensible, considering that Ford has owned the European brands for nearly a decade.

The New Ford Way

To try to eliminate all of Ford's unnecessary duplication, Mulally has taken more control over the product line. Now he personally approves every new vehicle worldwide. Production is now coordinated by Derrick M. Kuzak, Ford's first-ever chief of global product development. Kuzak's team is designing cars that can be easily adapted to appeal to worldwide markets. They've developed a global small car that Ford will build in two or three plants starting in 2010. It is expected to sell in the United States for $10,000 to $12,000. This car will differ only slightly from the version that will be sold in South America, Europe, and Asia. Another key goal in the near future is to create a midsize sedan that could serve both North America and Europe. Today, for example, the European Mondeo sedan and the North American Fusion are built independently of one another. Kuzak is overseeing an attempt to coordinate the future designs of those vehicles.

Mulally knows that changing the organizational design won't cure Ford. The company's deeply ingrained hierarchical culture is being fundamentally changed. For the first time, Mulally is requiring every operating group to share all of its financial data with every other group. That information used to be closely guarded. Shortly after he ordered the change, three separate executives called him to make sure they had heard right. Mulally stated: "You can't manage a secret."

To spread the cultural revolution, Mulally has changed how a number of things are done at Ford. A summary of these changes is shown here.

	Before Mulally	After Mulally
Organization	Regional fiefdoms. Every global market had its own strategy and products.	Mulally wants to break down geographic hierarchies and create a single worldwide organization.
Meetings	Held monthly. Lots of happy talk. Little information sharing.	Held weekly. Discussing problems is encouraged. A goal is to spot red flags early.
Strategic Vision	To diversify away from the Ford brand, the company acquired underperforming luxury brands.	Strengthen the traditional blue oval Ford brand. Sell off or close poor-performing brands.
Promotions	Managers changed jobs frequently to develop their skills.	Executives stay in place, winning only promotions that are deserved.

Mulally has turned the traditional monthly meeting of divisional chiefs into weekly meetings. Every executive has to attend in person or by videoconference. No subordinates can be sent. To ensure focus, the BlackBerries that used to be common at these meetings are now banned. So are side conversations that often took place when someone else was talking, even if by video link. The most radical change is that operating chiefs are now expected to bring a different subordinate to every meeting. This is a big step at a company where subordinates were not privy to sensitive financial and marketing data. Mulally wants staffers to start talking about ideas through unofficial e-mail, blog, and watercooler channels.

He is also taking symbolic steps to treat white-collar and blue-collar employees more equitably. In 2007, many workers on the shop floor received bonuses of $300 to $800, based on a new formula that is also being applied to executives. Of course, his endorsement by union workers will depend a lot on contract negotiations with the UAW.

Mulally is fond of talking about how he is breaking long-standing company taboos. For example, there is a taboo about never admitting when you don't know something. At one meeting, an executive went on for several minutes trying to answer a question to which he clearly did not have the answer. After the meeting, Mulally asked Fields why the executive spoke for so long. "Because 'I don't know' isn't in Ford's vocabulary," Fields explained. Now it is. To reinforce the point, Mulally has actually banned the thick background binders executives used to bring to the weekly meetings. That means they sometimes can't immediately summon the necessary details to answer Mulally's questions. That's fine with him: "I know that if they don't have the answer one week, they'll have it next week," he says.

Questions

1. How would you describe the culture at Ford?
2. What specific management practices helped create and maintain this culture?
3. Can Mulally succeed in changing Ford's culture?

ANSWERS TO ETHICS COMPETENCY

What Would You Do?

Types of Wrongdoings	Percentage of People Who Would Report the Wrongdoing to Management
Stealing	25%
Waste	17
Mismanagement	42
Safety problems	23
Sexual harassment	40
Unfair discrimination	27
Legal violations	53
Financial reporting	52

Type of Retaliation	Percentage Who Experienced It
Coworkers not associating with person	12%
Pressure from coworkers to stop complaint	5
Withholding of information needed to perform job	10
Poor performance appraisal	15
Verbal harassment or intimidation	12
Tighter scrutiny of daily work by management	14
Reassignment to a different job	8
Reassignment to a different job with less desirable duties	7
Denial of a promotion	7

CHAPTER

16

Guiding Organizational Change

Learning Goals

When you have finished studying the chapter, you should be able to:

1. Identify key pressures for change.
2. Discuss the nature of planned organizational change.
3. Identify common reasons for individual and organizational resistance to change.
4. Discuss methods for promoting change.

Learning from Experience

MICROSOFT IN CHINA

In the mid-1990s, Microsoft sent a couple of sales managers to mainland China. Their goal was to sell software at the same prices the company charged elsewhere in the world. Microsoft simply announced to potential customers that it was open for business. It didn't work. According to Ya-Qin Zhang, a Microsoft executive, the problem wasn't market share, but getting revenue. Chinese people were using Windows software, but no one was paying to use it because they were using counterfeit copies that were selling on the street for a few dollars.

Microsoft fought to protect its intellectual property. It sued companies for using its software illegally, but lost these suits in China's courts. Microsoft's managers came and left China because they couldn't generate the revenues that Bill Gates, its CEO, and others wanted. Beijing's city government retaliated against Microsoft by installing free open-source Linux operating systems on workers' PCs. This version, called Red Flag Linux, was to be the official system used by all Chinese governmental officials. Security and military personnel who depended on Microsoft software questioned whether or not the technology developed by Microsoft was being used by U.S. agents to spy on China. According to Craig Mundie, Microsoft's top executive who now guides its China strategy, "Our business was broken in China. We needed a change. Our business practices didn't reflect the importance of taking a collaborative approach with the government."

Mundie and others began talking with Chinese government personnel to convince them that Microsoft's software was not a secret tool of the U.S. government. It permitted Chinese software engineers to look at the fundamental source code for its Windows operating system and to substitute certain portions with their own software—something that Microsoft never allowed in the past. At the same time, Gates and other executives became convinced that China's weak intellectual property laws meant that its usual pricing strategies were doomed. Gates recognized that, although it was terrible that the Chinese government let people pirate software, if they were going to pirate software, he wanted them to pirate Microsoft's. He knew that he had to change the perception that Microsoft was just going to sue people for pirating software. Microsoft's top managers knew that if it could help the government's

LEARNING CONTENT

For more information on Microsoft, visit the organization's home page at www.microsoft.com.

social agenda, the Chinese government would support you even if they didn't like you.

Microsoft decided to assist local Chinese officials with their decisions about which software to use—Linux or Microsoft. The firm committed more than $150 million to this effort. As a result of Microsoft's efforts, the Chinese government required central, provincial, and local governments to begin using legal Microsoft software, but at a much lower price. Beijing's city employees now pay for software that they had previously pirated. The Chinese government recently required local PC manufacturers to load legal software on their computers. Lenovo, the market leader in China, is selling its PCs with legal software. The number of PCs shipped with legal software now is approaching 40 percent, a sharp contrast to the less than 10 percent a few years ago.

How did this change occur? To do business in China, managers have to work closely with the government. Investments have to be made with the blessings of governmental officials at all levels. Microsoft worked with personnel in the Department of Education to finance computer classrooms in rural areas. It also has begun extensive training programs for teachers and software entrepreneurs for free. Although Microsoft's revenue in China averages less than $7 for every PC compared to $100-200 in other countries, Gates believes that these numbers will converge. Microsoft estimates that Windows is used in 90 percent of China's 120 million PCs.[1]

Understanding and managing organizational change are tasks that present complex challenges. Planned change may not work, or it may have consequences far different from those intended. Today, organizations must have the capacity to adapt quickly and effectively in order to survive. Often the speed and complexity of change severely test the capabilities of managers and employees to adapt rapidly enough. When organizations fail to change, the cost of that failure may be quite high. Hence, managers and employees must understand the nature of the changes needed and the likely effects of alternative approaches to bring about that change.

Because organizations exist in changing environments, bureaucratic organizations are increasingly ineffective. Organizations with rigid hierarchies, high degrees of functional specialization, narrow and limited job descriptions, inflexible rules and procedures, and impersonal, autocratic management can't respond adequately to demands for change. As we pointed out in Chapter 14, organizations need designs that are flexible and adaptive. Organizations also need reward systems and cultures that allow greater participation in decisions by employees and managers alike.

In this chapter, we examine the pressures on organizations to change, types of change programs, and why accurate diagnosis of organizational problems is crucial. We explore the difficult issue of resistance to change at both the individual and organizational levels and examine ways to cope with that inevitable resistance. In addition, we identify three methods for promoting organizational and behavioral changes.

PRESSURES FOR CHANGE

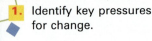

Learning Goal

1. Identify key pressures for change.

Why Change?

As Bill Gates and his executives discovered at Microsoft, change can be difficult and takes time. Despite the challenges, many organizations successfully make needed changes, but failure also is common. There is considerable evidence that adaptive, flexible organizations have a competitive advantage over rigid, static organizations.[2] As a result, managing change has become a central focus of managers in most organizations.

Most organizations around the world have tried to change themselves—some more than once—during the past decade. Yet for every successful change, there is an equally prominent failure. Wal-Mart's dramatic performance improvement stands in stark contrast to a string of disappointments that have plagued Kmart. The rise of Target and Kohl's as leaders in the retailing industry merely emphasizes Kmart's inability to reverse its declining market share in retailing.

Organizations that are well positioned to change will prosper, but those that ignore change will flounder. For example, several years ago, Sun Microsystems lost tremendous market share to its competitors, HP, IBM, and Dell. It failed to develop a server to run the next version of Microsoft's Windows and instead tried to develop its own software called Solaris. To regain market share, Scott McNealey, Sun's CEO, is focusing on what he calls "disruptive innovation." While most of Sun's competitors make plain-vanilla computers and compete on price, he plans to change the rules of the game by developing "throughput computing" chips that can handle dozens of tasks at the same time. Although this change strategy sounds appealing, it calls for Sun to move in two directions at once: Build bare-bones servers, while inventing cutting-edge technologies. As a result, Sun will spend 17 percent of its current budget on R&D, compared to 2 percent at Dell. The results of this change strategy have yet to be determined.[3]

There is an almost infinite variety of *pressures for change*. In this section, we examine four of the most significant ones: (1) globalization of markets, (2) technology, (3) social networks, and (4) generational differences.

Globalization

Organizations today face global competition on an unprecedented scale. Globalization *means that many markets are worldwide and are served by international or multinational corporations*. These firms create pressures on domestic corporations to internationalize and redesign their operations. Global markets now exist for most products, but to compete effectively in these markets, firms often must transform their cultures, structures, and operations. Lenovo has now become a dominant user of software in the PC market after Lenovo purchased IBM's laptop manufacturing facilities. Until this purchase, few people outside of China had ever heard of Lenovo.

In his book, *The World Is Flat*, Thomas Friedman, outlined the most important global forces that managers faced in the late 20th and early 21st centuries:[4]

- the fall of the Berlin Wall and the opening of Eastern European markets,
- the start of the Internet,
- development of software to manage Internet communications,
- development of self-organizing communities via the Internet,
- outsourcing, and
- the founding of Google, Yahoo, and MSN web search engines.

These and other powerful globalization forces required domestic firms to abandon "business as usual" in order to remain competitive. In some industries, such as steel, apparel, and shoes, global strategies are replacing country-by-country approaches. Although globalization strategies aren't easy to implement, many organizations have effectively moved outside their domestic markets. Procter & Gamble, YUM! Brands (KFC, Pizza Hut, Taco Bell, Long John Silver's, and A&W Root Beer), and Mary Kay Cosmetics have highly successful Asian operations. Mary Kay will sell more products in China by 2010 than in the United States. KFC and Pizza Hut serve more customers in China and earn more profits from these operations than anywhere else in the world. Procter & Gamble and Gillette merged to form a $68 billion consumer products company that serves customers in more than 80 countries and employees more than 138,000 people. Together, they hope to do what each has struggled to do on its own—ramp up sales in the developing markets of China and Eastern Europe, bring global products to market more quickly, increase their leverage over Wal-Mart and Costco, and gain savings with media companies from which they buy advertising.[5]

© Courtesy of Campbell Soup Company

Highly decentralized organizations, such as Campbell Soup, have operating units and sell products throughout the world.

Going global does not mean that the firm provides exactly the same goods or services in all countries. For example, Campbell Soup Company has long wanted to sell its soups in Russia. In the early 1990s, however, it gave up trying to sell canned soups in Russia because women weren't buying them. To understand why women weren't buying their soup, Campbell hired cultural anthropologists to visit homes in Russia to watch how consumers prepare and eat soup. What did they learn? Russians eat soup more than five times a week, compared with America's once-a-week habit. Russians consume more than 32 billion bowls annually, compared to just 14 billion in the United States. The anthropologists also found that Russians consider themselves to be the world's foremost experts on soup. Russians have words that they use only for soup. Armed with this information, Campbell now plans to sell a beef broth soup with pieces of meat, onions, and potatoes; a chicken broth with chicken, onions, and potatoes; and a mushroom soup with large pieces of mushrooms, onions, and seasonings. Campbell's strategy is to encourage Russians to use these soups as a base for their homemade soups. Campbell also knows that for century's mothers have done the bulk of the soup preparation, with daughters helping out by cutting vegetables. Therefore, instead of trying to change this tradition, it is targeting newlywed women as they take on the role of soup-maker. Campbell gives out discount coupons and recipes at buildings where couples register their marriages.[6]

Technology

Coping with global competition requires a flexibility that many organizations often do not possess. Fortunately, the revolution in information technology (IT) permits organizations to develop the needed flexibility. IT is having a profound impact on individual employees, teams, and organizations. For example, experts who have studied its impact on organizations have observed that IT:

- changes almost everything about an organization—its structure, its products, its markets, and its manufacturing processes;
- increases the value of invisible assets, such as knowledge, competencies, and training;
- democratizes a company because employees have more information and can communicate with anyone else in the organization;
- increases the flexibility of work by allowing more employees to work at home, on the road, or at hours that suit them; and

- allows organizations to unify their global operations and to work a 24-hour day spanning the world.[7]

Imagine a team of employees that works 16 hours a day, seven days a week, are never sick or late, and demand no benefits or health insurance. They spend every minute maximizing their productivity. Who are these employees? Robots. Staples, an office supply chain, use robots to fill orders in its 500,000-square-foot warehouse in Chambersburg, Pennsylvania. Staples realized that the order fulfillment process was the weakest link in its supply-chain management system. The company had traditionally used a conveyor belt where employees gathered goods just like you do when shopping at a grocery store. Instead of a shopping cart, employees put their goods on the conveyor belt and then additional employees packaged them for shipment. Today, when an order is received, the computer tells the robots where to find the rack with the goods. Through the use of bar-code stickers on the floor, the robot goes to the rack and waits for an employee to pull the correct items and place them in a box. When the order is completed, the robot packs the box and puts on a shipping label. A central computer instructs the robot where to leave the package for delivery. Before robots arrived, the warehouse processed 13,000 orders daily. With the use of robots, it now handles 18,000 orders daily.[8]

However, the potential effects of IT aren't uniformly positive. Organizations that rely on sophisticated information technologies are more vulnerable to sabotage, espionage, and vandalism. Moreover, IT can create new social divisions (e.g., the computer literate versus the nonuser and the educated versus the uneducated) even as it brings people together. If the full potential of IT is to be realized, employees must be better educated, better trained, and better motivated than at any time in history. However, wisdom and intuition remain essential for good management, and having more information, faster, cannot replace good judgment and common sense.

The globalization phenomenon and information technologies are linked in interesting ways. Highly decentralized organizations, such as Procter & Gamble and Campbell Soup, with operating units scattered throughout the world, face some significant challenges in terms of coordination and cooperation. However, advanced computer and telecommunication technologies provide mechanisms to link employees in ways only imagined in the past. For example, many multinational corporations rely on the use of virtual teams to accomplish their work. *Virtual teams* are groups of geographically and/or organizationally dispersed coworkers who are assembled via a combination of telecommunications and information technologies to accomplish organizational tasks. Such teams rarely meet or work together face to face. Virtual teams may be set up on a temporary basis and used to accomplish a specific task, or they may be relatively permanent and used to address ongoing strategic planning issues. The membership of virtual teams may be quite fluid, with members changing according to task demands even for those teams with an ongoing assignment.[9]

Social Networks

The Internet has also changed social networking. Facebook, a popular social networking website founded in 2004, claims to sign up more than 150,000 new members each day. MySpace, another social networking site, claims that it adds 250,000 a day, and LinkedIn, a business networking site, adds thousands of new members each day. All of these forms of social networking are changing the way people communicate, search for jobs, and form groups. Managers must understand these forms of social networking in order to be effective. Why? Social networking allows employees to ignore the rules and find solutions to problems without going through the organization's chain of command. For example, Bell Canada uses social networks in which managers freely share ideas about best practices. These networks also work on problems identified as hindering business, such as managing people from different generations and the bureaucracy associated with hiring new employees. Bell Canada found that employees' job satisfaction rose when they participated in such groups and even helped bring out needed changes.

Generational Differences

Along with 85 million baby boomers in the United States (those born between 1946 and 1964) and 50 million Gen X'ers (those born between 1965 and 1977), there has been an influx of 76 million younger Millennials (those born between 1978 and 1999) into the workforce.[10] Most Millennials have never experienced life without a microwave, computer, ATM card, or a television remote. They will be the first generation to have used e-mail, instant messaging, and cell phones since childhood. Due to a variety of factors, instant gratification is causing some Millennials to have unrealistic expectations about their careers. Many are unwilling to work hard and make personal sacrifices to get ahead. Millennials' impatience to want things yesterday may cause them to become inefficient, says Barbara Dwyer, CEO of the Job Journey. The disadvantage is that they lack the patience to work through a complex problem. E-mail and instant messaging also reduce the opportunity for employees to develop strong interpersonal competencies, which could derail their careers in the future.

Motivating these three generations of employees requires managers to adapt their management styles. At IBM, Kari Barbar offers different learning venues to different generations. Boomers are accustomed to learning in a classroom with a teacher and want to work through the problem. Gen X'ers prefer web courses so they can learn by themselves and at their own pace. Networking-prone Millennials enjoy working on blogs with others to solve a problem. Some organizations are also tailoring programs to retain and attract all generations. For example, Millennials are opting out of putting in the long hours common for boomers, and have high expectations for personal growth on the job. More than half of the Millennials have college degrees, but many take time off to travel before they start to look for a job, which used to be a "red flag" for baby boomers back when managers were considering hiring them.[11]

With more career options, Millenial employees are nudging some organizations to think more creatively about the work/life balance. Deloitte Consulting has created programs that help Millennial employees think about their careers. It learned that Millenial employees are motivated by friendship and will choose a job just to be with friends and Gen X'ers. Boston-based Gentle Moving once hired an entire athletic team. "It looked like a great work environment because of the people," said Niles Kuronen, a rower. "It was huge to be able to work with friends." Millennial employees use their BlackBerries or iPods to check in with their friends, and they want flexibility during the week. Today's technologies allow employees to be perpetually connected with their peers.

The line between work and friends is blurred for the Millennials who look to their friends for advice and career direction. For baby boomers going to college, a student called home once a week, maybe. Boomers couldn't wait to claim their independence from their parents. Today, students call their parents three or four times a day to keep in contact with them. Sun Microsystems's telecommuting program was started to appeal to Millennial employees and more than half of all employees are now on this program.

Millennial employees are also searching for meaning in their work. More than half of the workers in their twenties prefer employment in companies that provide volunteer opportunities. Employees at Salesforce.com, for example, will do 50,000 hours of community service in 2007. According to Marc Benioff, its CEO, this has helped attract and retain employees.

The following Diversity Competency feature illustrates some of the management challenges associated with managing across generations. Understanding these differences is important to increase managers' ability to attract and retain high-quality employees.[12]

Diversity Competency

Managing across Generations

What attracts Millennials to an organization? According to Jared Larrabee of Deloitte Consulting, Millennials bring to the job several desirable features:

- *Tech-savvy*. They can locate details about anything in seconds because they have grown up with the Internet.
- *Adept at global and diversity issues*. Through online social networks, they have found ways to reach beyond the confirms of their own geography and have established relationships with others through Facebook, MySpace, and other social networking portals.
- *Team oriented*. Millennials measure their accomplishments by their peers.
- *Multitaskers*. Most Millennials feel that listening to an iPod while working improves their job satisfaction and productivity.
- *Focus on work/life balance*. Having flexibility about when and where to work is very important for keeping them loyal to their organization.

Millennials also bring some behaviors that organizations need to be aware of:

- *Lack of independence*. Because they are so connected to others, including their parents, they often need more direction than Gen X'ers or boomers.
- *Lack of discretion*. Because many of the Millennials have discussed everything from musical tastes to dating habits with their friends, this lack of confidentiality can have a major impact on the organization. There will be no secrets between manager and subordinate. Millennials will need to adopt acceptable standards of behavior. They will have to figure out what they can share with their friends and what they should not share.
- *Unrealistic expectations*. Millennials believe that they can change the world quickly. The problem is that they lack the experience and political savvy to make it happen.
- *Impatience*. Millennials have played video games that show players how they are doing instantly. In organizations, they will need to learn to wait for semiannual or annual performance reviews that rely on a manager's subjective evaluations in the areas of leadership, teamwork, and communications.
- *Relaxed work ethic*. Many are unwilling to work hard and make personal sacrifices to get ahead.
- *Weak interpersonal competencies*. E-mail and instant text-messaging reduce opportunities for face-to-face communications, but strong interpersonal competencies are required to be successful in most organizations.

Compared to baby boomers or Gen X'ers, Millennials spend 50 percent more time than others on their computers either socializing or blogging. The use of electronic social interactions with friends has replaced face-to-face interactions. Technology has made it easier to maintain a network of valued friendships. Therefore, Millennials often do not recognize a manager's authority in the same way as boomers and Gen X'ers do. They are more inclined to discuss an instruction with friends before obeying it. They want to be treated as equals, partnering with their manager and coworkers in making decisions that affect them.

PLANNED ORGANIZATIONAL CHANGE

Learning Goal

2. Discuss the nature of planned organizational change.

Distinguishing between change that inevitably happens to all organizations and change that is deliberately planned by members of an organization is important. Our focus is primarily on intentional, goal-oriented organizational change. Planned organizational change *represents a deliberate attempt by managers and employees to improve the functioning of teams, departments, divisions, or an entire organization in some important way.*[13]

Table 16.1 Approaches to Change

MEANS	ECONOMIC	ORGANIZATIONAL DEVELOPMENT
Purpose	Profit	Develop employees' competencies
Leadership	Top-down	Participative
Focus	Structure and strategy	Culture
Motivation	Incentives lead performance	Incentives lag performance

Two radically different approaches are used to achieve organizational change: economic and organizational development.[14] Each approach is guided by a different set of assumptions about the purpose and means for change. We have highlighted these differences in Table 16.1.

Economic Approach

The economic approach *refers to creating change for the purpose of creating shareholder value*. Change is driven by top management, whose members use financial incentives to motivate employees to change their behaviors. Change is planned and focused. Leaders who create change using this approach set goals based on expectations of the financial markets. They do not involve their management team or employees in discussing ways to reach financial goals. These change agents focus on decisions that affect the strategy, structure, and systems of their organization. The economic approach is mainly used by turnaround artists, and not by people who want to build the organization.

> LEADER INSIGHT
>
> Changing a successful company is hard because you have to persuade people that they have to do something differently. In changing a poor performing company, you just start kicking butt, taking names, and changing things.
>
> **Michael Jordan, Chairman, EDS**

When Michael Jordan took over as CEO of EDS, a systems and management services company, in 2003, the company was losing market share and was in bad shape financially.[15] The Board of Directors hired him to turn around the company fast. Jordan developed a one–two punch to stop the financial bleeding, retain customers, and bring financial results to shareholders. EDS was losing more than $1 billion dollars a year and more than $800 million on a Navy contract alone. New business wasn't coming in and old customers were leaving because EDS couldn't deliver what it had promised. To turn around EDS, Jordan fired many executives and surrounded himself with 20 of EDS's best and brightest employees. "If you've got a crisis, you go internally and get the best people who know the business and take a risk on them." In 2004, EDS and the Navy signed a new contract and established a positive relationship. Jordan's biggest problem, however, were EDS employees. "There were a lot of people in their foxholes with their helmets pulled down over their ears," Jordan says. Divisions were fragmented and employees in different divisions didn't talk to each other. There was a morale problem, some of which was caused by the company's new severance package, which was reduced to a maximum of 4 weeks of salary from the industry norm of 26 weeks. Jordan demanded accountability, but appreciated employees who took risks. Today, there is consistency, a business strategy for each product division, best practices are shared between divisions, and the company's financial shape is positive. Employees are even wearing knit polo shirts with the EDS logo embroidered on it.

Organizational Development Approach

The organizational development approach *refers to developing employees' competencies to solve problems by enabling them to identify and become emotionally committed to improving the performance of the firm*. By focusing on the effectiveness and efficiency with which employees carry out their jobs, this approach focuses on building partnerships, trust, and employee commitment. If commitment is developed, it is assumed that the extensive use of rules and regulations will be unnecessary. Simply changing the organization's design does not change the way people behave. The organizational development approach requires management to engage people emotionally in examining why the existing structure and systems are not meeting the new challenges facing the organization.

Wegman's grocery store, a $3.8 billion company headquartered in Rochester, New York, has 70 grocery stores in the Northeast.[16] It uses the organizational development approach to empower employees to make changes. It has created a work environment where employees' contributions count and there are few rules. Wegman's knows that shoppers who are emotionally connected to a store spend 46 percent more at the checkout stand than those who aren't. It is each employee's job to create this emotional bond for the shopper by changing the way Wegman's does business. Wegman's selects people who are passionate about customer service, have a genuine interest in food, and are capable of making decisions on their own. When Kelly Shoeneck completed an analysis on a competitor's shopper loyalty program, she handed it to her manager. He told Shoeneck that she would have to make the presentation to Robert Wegman, CEO, herself. To instill the Wegman's approach to change, all management employees go through a store manager training program, where they learn how to greet customers, sweep floors, gut fish, bake bread, walk a customer to the car, and the like. All members of the Wegman's family have also been through the same training program.

Sequencing of Approaches

Jeff Immelt, CEO of General Electric and his top leadership team, have used a combination of approaches to change the strategic direction of GE.[17] When Immelt took over from Jack Welch in September 2001, he faced a period of intense uncertainty—from the September 11, 2001, terrorist attacks through new regulations and a shaky economy. Top management needed to create an agenda for transforming GE to compete successfully in the 21st century. One of Immelt's favorite sayings is that "Too many companies have lost the ability to innovate because they have become 'business traders' rather than 'business creators.'" To become a business creator, he knows that GE must become a more customer-driven, global, and diverse company—one that rewards innovation, embraces technology, and grows products internally in a slow-growth global economy. As a result, an increasing number of GE executives have marketing, as opposed to engineering, backgrounds because he believes that marketing will carry GE through economic slumps. GE has sold off slow-growth businesses, such as insurance. GE has bought companies such as Vivendi Universal's entertainment assets and Amersham PLC, a British diagnostics and biotech firm. GE hopes that these businesses will sharpen GE's innovative capabilities in the media and medical industries.

GE Capital, which finances equipment and processes company credit cards, has been broken down into four separate businesses, making each business more accountable for its own profits. In comparison to Jack Welch, who rotated key managers through divisions to develop generalists, Immelt wants to keep managers in place to develop leaders as specialists. These specialists must also be excellent teachers. A leader's two primary roles are to be able to work with people who do not necessarily agree with you and to share what he or she has learned. Whereas Welch grew GE through acquisition, Immelt wants to grow GE through innovation. Immelt's central idea is this: "We have to make our own growth."

Managerial Guidelines

Managers who face major changes need to think through the long-term consequences of using either the economic approach or the organizational development approach. Moreover, finding managers with the managerial competencies needed to sequence change properly is difficult.

Most successful change approaches share some common characteristics. For example, effective change programs typically involve:

- motivating change by creating a readiness for the change among managers and employees and attempting to overcome resistance to change (which we discuss in detail shortly);
- creating a shared vision of the desired future state of the organization;
- developing political support for the needed changes;
- managing the transition from the current state to the desired future state; and
- sustaining momentum for change so that it will be carried to completion.

The initiatives required to address each of these aspects of a change program are summarized in Figure 16.1.

FIGURE 16.1 Initiatives Contributing to Effective Change Management

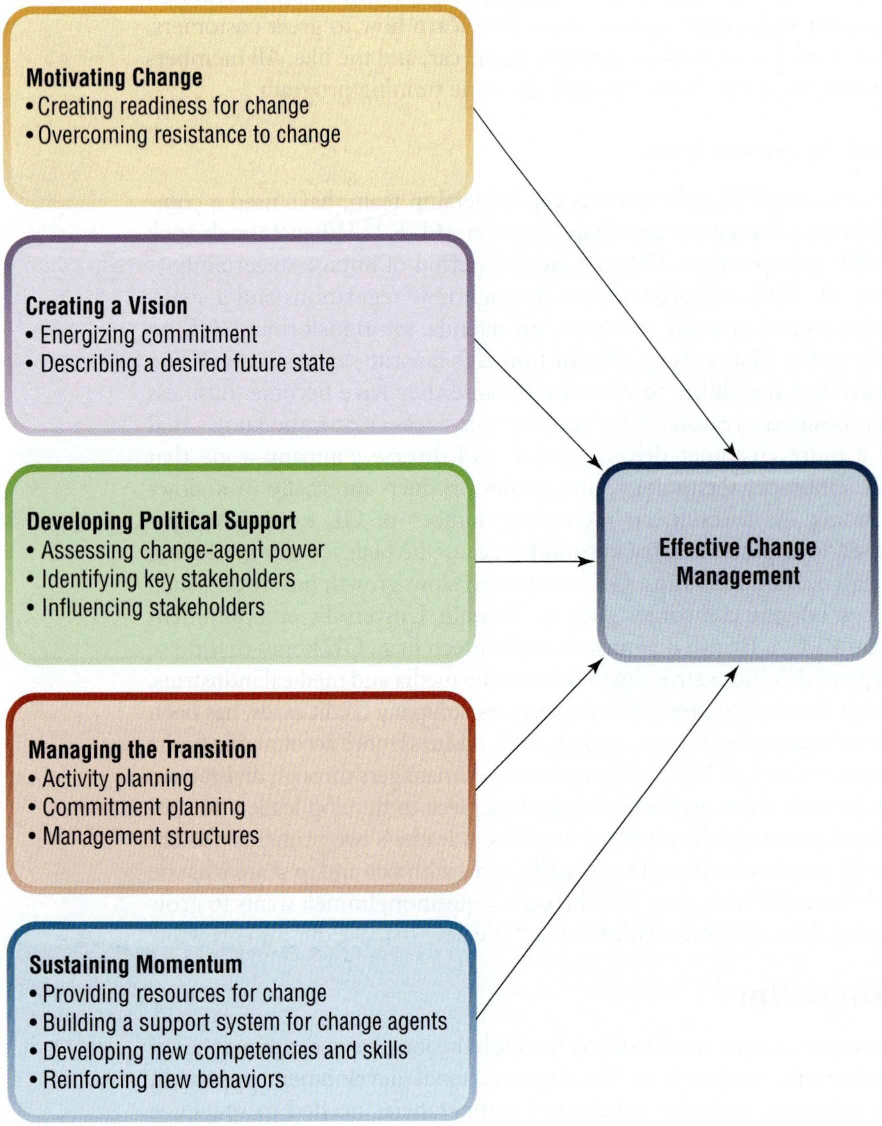

Source: Reprinted with permission from Cummings, J. G., and Worley, C. G. *Organizational Development and Change*, 6th ed. Cincinnati, OH: South-Western, 1997, 154.

Similarly, the conditions necessary for successfully carrying out effective change programs include the following:

- The organization's members must be the key source of energy for change, not some party external to the team or organization.
- Key members of the organization must recognize the need for change and be attracted by the potentially positive outcomes of the change program.
- A willingness to change norms and procedures must exist.

Economic and organizational development programs and the conditions necessary for their use are similar in certain respects. Change must come from within the organization. People must be aware of the need for change, believe in the potential value of the proposed changes, and be willing to change their behaviors in order to make the team, department, or organization more effective. Absent these beliefs and behaviors, effective organizational change is problematic. Managers must be open to trying different approaches at different times, as Jeff Immelt does at GE.

RESISTANCE TO CHANGE

Learning Goal

3. Identify common reasons for individual and organizational resistance to change.

Change involves moving from the known to the unknown. Because the future is uncertain and may negatively affect people's careers, salary, and competencies, organization members generally do not support change unless compelling reasons convince them to do so. Resistance to change often is baffling because it can take so many forms. Overt resistance may be expressed through strikes, reduced productivity, shoddy work, and even sabotage. Covert resistance may be expressed by increased tardiness and absenteeism, requests for transfers, resignations, loss of motivation, lower morale, and higher accident or error rates. One of the most damaging forms of resistance is passive resistance by employees—a lack of participation in formulating change proposals and ultimately a lack of commitment to the proposals, even when they have had an opportunity to participate in making such decisions.

As Figure 16.2 shows, resistance to change occurs for a variety of reasons. Some are traceable to individuals, but others involve the nature and structure of organizations. The combination of these two sources of resistance can be devastating to change. Managers and employees need to understand the reasons for resistance to change and its sources.

Individual Resistance

The six reasons for individual resistance to change shown in Figure 16.2 aren't the only reasons why individuals might resist workplace change, but they are the most common.

Perceptions. In Chapter 3, we discussed the notion of perceptual defense—a perceptual error whereby people tend to perceive selectively those things that fit most comfortably with their current view of the world. Once individuals have established an understanding of reality, they may resist changing it. Among other things, people may resist the possible impact of change on their lives by (1) reading or listening only to what they agree with, (2) conveniently forgetting any knowledge that could lead to other viewpoints, and (3) misunderstanding communication that, if correctly understood, wouldn't fit their existing attitudes and values. For example, managers enrolled in management training programs at Exxon/Mobil are exposed to different managerial philosophies and techniques. In the classroom, they may competently discuss and answer questions about these new ideas, yet carefully separate in their minds the approaches that they believe wouldn't work from those that they believe would work or that they already practice.

FIGURE 16.2 Sources of Resistance to Change

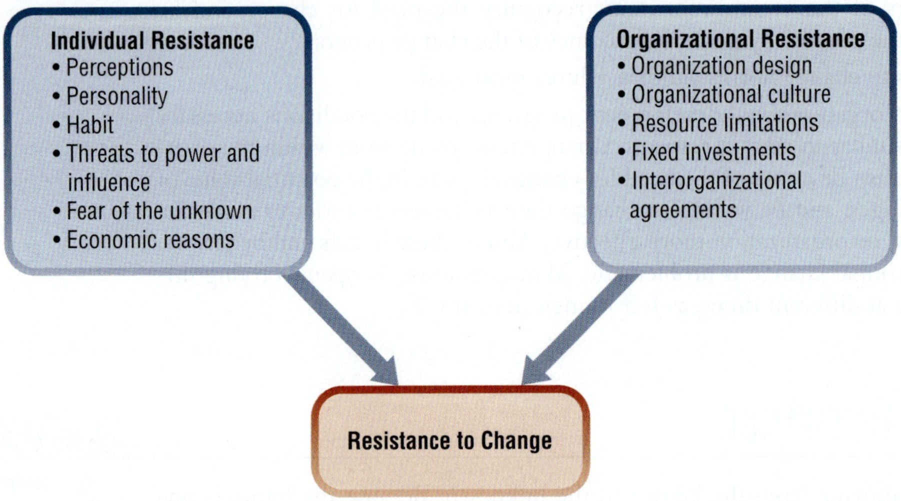

Personality. Some aspects of an individual's personality may predispose that person to resist change. In Chapter 2, we indicated that self-esteem is an important personality characteristic that determines how a person behaves in an organization. People with low self-esteem are more likely to resist change than those with high self-esteem because low self-esteem people are more likely to perceive the negative aspects of change than the positive aspects. Low self-esteem people are not as likely as high self-esteem people to work hard to make change succeed.[18] Another personality characteristic is adjustment (see the Big Five personality profile in Chapter 2). People who are nervous, self-doubting, and moody typically have a difficult time changing their behaviors. They may resist change until those people they depend on endorse it. These employees are highly dependent on their supervisors for performance feedback. They probably won't accept any new techniques or methods for doing their jobs unless their supervisors personally support the changes and indicate how these changes will improve performance and/or otherwise benefit the employees.[19]

Managers must be careful to avoid overemphasizing the role played by personality in resistance to change because they can easily make the fundamental attribution error (see Chapter 3). There is a tendency to "blame" resistance to change in the workplace on individual personalities. Although personality may play a role (as we have just discussed), it seldom is the only important factor in a situation involving change.

Habit. Unless a situation changes dramatically, individuals may continue in their usual ways. A habit can be a source of comfort, security, and satisfaction for individuals because it allows them to adjust to the world and cope with it. Whether a habit becomes a primary source of resistance to change depends, to a certain extent, on whether individuals perceive advantages from changing their behaviors. For example, if, on Michael Jordan's first day as CEO of EDS, he suddenly announced that all employees would immediately receive a 10 percent pay raise, few would object even though the pay raise might result in changes in behavior because it would allow employees to pursue a more expensive lifestyle. However, when Michael Jordan announced that EDS employees' severance pay would be reduced from 26 to 4 weeks, many employees felt betrayed. Those let go from EDS would not have the luxury of taking time to find a job because of pressing personal financial issues—mortgage and car payments, credit card bills, etc.

Threats to Power and Influence. Some people in organizations may view change as a threat to their power or influence. The control of something needed by others, such as information or resources, is a source of power in organizations. Once a power position has been established, individuals or teams often resist changes that they perceive as reducing their ability to influence others. One of Michael Jordan's major hurdles to overcome when he took over as CEO from Dick Brown was to get divisions to share information with each other. Started by Ross Perot in 1962, EDS had built a culture of rugged individualism. "Fix the problem yourself" was a saying frequently heard in the hallways of EDS. A large statue of an American bald eagle in its corporate headquarters symbolized this culture. Each of its divisions rarely shared information or technology. One division would invest time and money to create a new system only to learn that another division already had such a system in place. EDS's management could not send an e-mail directly to all 132,000 employees because the company used 16 different e-mail systems. Sales results were available only after the finance department closed its books at the end of each quarter. Jordan needed to revamp EDS and did so by consolidating data centers, organizing EDS around four services, and cutting costs.[20]

Fear of the Unknown. Confronting the unknown makes most people anxious. Each major change in a work situation carries with it an element of uncertainty. When Sri Lanka tea producer Dilmah Fernando decided to invest in tea shops to compete in the $70 billion global hot-beverage market, people thought he was crazy. Dilmah's major competitors, like Unilever whose Lipton brand has a 15 percent share of the world's tea market, and Associated British Foods, second with its Twinings tea at 6 percent market share, had tried and failed to compete successfully against Starbucks and other coffee shops. Dilmah's "T-Bars," as he named them, are stand-alone chic and trendy outlets targeting the Buddha bar set. He opened 65 T-Bars in Poland, Belarus, Kazakhstan, and other places where Starbucks had a lesser presence. He had to face many unknown factors, such as how to get the tea from the plantations to the shops in countries where roads are in poor conditions. He also found that in Colombo, roads were shut down for military security checks at random times, increasing the time it took tea to travel from the plantation to the shop. Oftentimes, a 100-mile trip took seven or more hours, making the tea less fresh because of the excessive heat. Similarly, worried shippers have abandoned Sri Lanka out of fear that their trucks will be attacked by warring tribes

Dilmah Fernando has had to face many unknown factors to make his "T-Bars" successful in the world market.

engaged in this country's civil war. Although Dilmah has successfully overcome these unknowns, he is sure that he will face others.[21]

Economic Reasons. Money weighs heavily in people's considerations, and they certainly can be expected to resist changes that might lower their incomes. In a very real sense, employees have invested in the status quo in their jobs. That is, they have learned how to perform their work well, how to get good performance evaluations, and how to interact effectively with others. Changes in established work routines or job duties may threaten their economic security. Employees may fear that, after changes are made, they won't be able to perform as well and thus may not be as valuable to the organization, their supervisors, or their coworkers. Since Nestlé bought Perrier in 1992, it has struggled to finds ways to increase the productivity of its French employees. The average Perrier worker produces 600,000 bottles a year compared with 1.1 million bottles per worker at San Pellegrino and Evian, Nestlé's two major competitors. The French employees have resisted change because they will need to take a cut in pay and increase the number of hours worked per week from 35 to 40. Nestlé maintains that when the French employees are not on strike, they earn an average annual salary of $32,000, which is good money for the southern part of France. Nestlé has promised to cut 15 percent of the workforce unless changes are made.[22]

Sometimes the problems and dissatisfaction in a company are so serious that a general readiness for change exists. For instance, at Ford Motor Company, GM, and Chrysler, employees knew that major changes in medical and retirement benefits were necessary if their organizations were to survive. However, the real challenge is for managers to create a sense of readiness for change while things seem to be going well instead of after a company begins to experience problems. The following Self Competency feature can help you assess your readiness for change.[23] If your readiness score is low, what competencies do you need to develop to increase your readiness for change?

Self Competency

Are You Ready to Change?

Instructions

Read each of the following statements and then use the scale shown to reflect your opinion. Record your answer in the blank at the left of the question's number.

1	2	3	4	5	6	7
Completely disagree			Neither agree nor disagree			Completely agree

_____1. I believe that an expert who doesn't come up with a definitive answer probably doesn't know too much.

_____2. I think it would be fun to live in a foreign country for a period of time.

_____3. The sooner we all agree on some common values and ideals, the better.

_____4. A good teacher is one who makes you wonder about your way of looking at things.

_____5. I enjoy parties where I know most of the people more than ones where all or most of the people are strangers.

_____6. A manager who hands out a vague assignment gives me a chance to show initiative and originality.

_____7. People who lead even, regular lives—in which few surprises or unexpected events arise—really have a lot to be grateful for.

_____8. Many of our most important decisions are actually based on insufficient information.

_____9. There is really no such thing as a problem that can't be solved.

_____10. People who fit their lives to a schedule probably miss most of the joy of living.

_____11. A good job is one in which what is to be done and how it is to be done are always clear.

_____12. It is more fun to tackle a complicated problem than to solve a simple one.

_____13. In the long run, it is possible to get more done by tackling small, simple problems than large, complicated ones.

_____14. Often the most interesting and stimulating people are those who don't mind being different or original.

_____15. What we are used to is always preferable to what is unfamiliar.

_____16. People who insist on a "yes" or "no" answer just don't know how complicated things really are.

Interpretation

To get your total score, you need to do several things. First, sum your responses to the *odd*-numbered items and write your score here: _____. Second, add 64 points to that score to create the first subtotal and record it here: _____. Third, sum your responses to the *even*-numbered items and write your score here: _____. Then subtract that number from the subtotal for the odd-numbered items to determine your overall score.

Your overall score is _______. Total scores may range from 16 to 112. The lower your overall score, the more willing you may be to deal with the uncertainty and ambiguity that typically go with change. Higher scores suggest a preference for more predictable and structured situations and indicate that you may not respond as well to change. Research data show scores typically range from 20 to 80, with a mean of 45. How does your score compare to these norms?

Organizational Resistance

To a certain extent, the nature of organizations is to resist change. Organizations often are most efficient at doing routine tasks and tend to perform more inefficiently, at least initially, when doing something for the first time. Thus, to ensure operational efficiency and effectiveness, some organizations may create strong defenses against change. Moreover, change often opposes vested interests and violates certain territorial rights or decision-making prerogatives that departments, teams, and informal groups have established and accepted over time. Again, Figure 16.2 shows several of the more significant reasons for organizational resistance to change.

Organization Design. Many managers believe that organizations need stability and continuity in order to function effectively. Indeed, the term *organization* implies that the individual, team, and department have a certain structure. Individuals have assigned roles, established procedures for getting the job done, consistent ways of getting needed information, and the like. However, this legitimate need for structure also may lead to resistance to change. Bureaucratic organizations may have narrowly defined jobs, clearly identified lines of authority and responsibility, and limited flows of information from top to bottom.[24] This was a problem facing Michael Jordan at EDS. The use of a rigid design and an emphasis on the authority hierarchy caused employees to use only certain specific channels of communication and to focus narrowly on their own duties and responsibilities. Typically, the more mechanistic the organization, the more numerous are the levels through which an idea must travel (see Chapter 14). This type of design, then, increases the probability that any new idea will be screened out because it threatens the status quo. More adaptive and flexible organizations are designed to reduce the resistance to change created by rigid organizational structures.

Organizational Culture. Organizational culture plays a key role in change. Cultures are not easy to modify and may become a major source of resistance to needed changes (see Chapter 15). One aspect of an effective organizational culture is whether it has the flexibility to take advantage of opportunities to change. An ineffective organizational culture (in terms of organizational change) is one that rigidly socializes employees into the old cultural values even in the face of evidence that it no longer works.

Cultural synergy is important when merging two companies. When Chrysler and Mercedes-Benz merged, immediately there were cultural clashes. Bob Eaton, CEO of Chrysler, proposed that the name of the new company be ChryslerDaimler-Benz. Daimler-Benz CEO Jürgen Schrempp told him that the name was a deal breaker and that a merger was impossible. Why? Daimler would hold 57 percent of the stock in the new company and all strategic decisions would be made in Stuttgart, Germany. Therefore, the two companies would never be equals. All news releases for the company would be written in German and translated into English. A joke around Auburn Hills in Michigan was "How do you pronounce DaimlerChrysler?" The answer: "Daimler. The Chrysler is silent." Second, Mercedes was a mechanistic organization and had developed a bureaucratic culture, with layers of committees and subcommittees reviewing decisions. Chrysler was an organic organization and had developed an entrepreneurial culture. Its divisions were lean and market driven. Mercedes employees were driven by perfection and its managers were used to reading stacks of black books to justify even a minor decision. With the disappointing sales of the Chrysler Crossfire, a car heralded to be a cross between German design and American marketing, many top American managers left Chrysler. In May 2007, Daimler sold 80.1% of Chrysler to Cerberus Capital Management for $7.4 billion. Cereberus named Robert Nardelli, former CEO of Home Depot, as its CEO.[25]

Resource Limitations. Some organizations want to maintain the status quo, but others would change if they had the resources to do so. Change requires capital, time, and individuals with a lot of competencies. At any particular time, an organization's managers and employees may have identified changes that could or should be made, but they may have had to defer or abandon some of the desired changes because of resource limitations. When Jay Grinney took over as CEO of the HealthSouth Corporation, one of the nation's largest health-care providers, which is based in Birmingham, Alabama, he needed to immediately make changes after former CEO Richard Scrushy allegedly inflated earnings. In 2005, Scrushy was acquitted of most charges, but 15 other HealthSouth executives pled guilty to fraud charges. Grinney slashed 250 management jobs; sold unprofitable rehabilitation and diagnostic centers, such as the Doctors Hospital in Coral Gables, Florida; sold five nursing homes in Massachusetts; and also sold 10 private planes and one helicopter to pay down a $3.3 billion dollar debt. As a result, HealthSouth has returned to profitability and its revenues have exceeded $3 billion dollars. Grinney wants to move HealthSouth into inpatient services that will be much in demand in the future, such as skilled nursing.[26]

Fixed Investments. Resource limitations aren't confined to organizations with insufficient assets. Goodyear Tire and Rubber Company had invested its financial resources to establish more than 5,300 authorized dealers. These dealers mainly sell replacement tires, which account for 70 percent of the company's sales. However, with the proliferation of retail formats—from discounters and convenience stores to warehouse clubs and online shops—the retail loyalty that it earned from its dealers has been lost. Pressured to boost sales, Goodyear had little choice but to sell tires through mass merchandisers (e.g., Discount Tires, Costco, Wal-Mart, Sears). These merchandisers demanded and received bulk discounts. The result was that some of its authorized dealers, who were expected to honor warranties and recalls, were paying more for their tires than what Sears charged at retail. As a result, Goodyear dealers are selling other replacement brand tires about 60 percent of the time. A Goodyear authorized tire dealer for more than 35 years was kicked out of its dealer network because he wasn't buying enough tires. Robert Keegan, Goodyear's CEO, admits that "We lost sight of the fact that it's in our interest that our dealers succeed."[27]

Fixed investments aren't limited to physical assets; they also may be expressed in terms of people. For example, consider employees who no longer are making a significant contribution to an organization but have enough seniority to maintain their jobs. Unless they can be motivated to perform better or retrained for other positions, their salaries and fringe benefits represent, from the organization's perspective, fixed investments that can't easily be changed.

Interorganizational Agreements. Agreements between organizations usually impose obligations on them that can restrain their actions. Labor negotiations and contracts provide some examples. Nike's relationship with colleges and various NFL teams precludes Adidas and other sporting apparel manufacturers from negotiating with them until the current contract expires. Some universities have recently dropped Nike because of their ability to negotiate better terms with Adidas. Ways of doing things that once were considered the rights of management (the right to hire and fire, assign tasks, promote and demote, and the like) may become subject to negotiation and fixed in a union–management contract. Other types of contracts also may constrain organizations. For example, proponents of change may face delay because of arrangements with competitors, commitments to suppliers and other contractors, and pledges to public officials in return for licenses, permits, financing, or tax abatement. Several years ago when the Dallas Cowboys football team announced that it had plans to move from its home in Irving, Texas, to a new location in 2009, the city of Arlington, Texas, gave the team $325 million dollars as an inducement to choose Arlington to build their new $1.2 billion, 80,000-seat stadium. The city issued a bond for that amount. This arrangement requires that the Cowboys stay in the city for at least the next 30 years, play all their home games at that stadium, and pay $2 million dollars in rent (with increases depending on inflation) a year for the duration of the contract.[28]

Force Field Analysis

Realistically, resistance to change will never cease completely. Managers and employees, however, can learn to identify and minimize resistance and thus become more effective change agents. People often have difficulty with clearly understanding situations that involve change. Part of the reason is that even analyzing a change problem may be quite complex when a large number of variables must be considered.

Kurt Lewin, a pioneering social psychologist, developed a way of looking at change that has been highly useful for managers and employees when faced with the challenge of change. Lewin viewed change not as an event but rather as a dynamic balance of forces working in opposite directions. His approach, called force field analysis, *suggests that any situation can be considered to be in a state of equilibrium resulting from a balance of forces constantly pushing against each other*. Certain forces in the situation—various types of resistance to change—tend to maintain the status quo. At the same time, various pressures for change are acting opposite to these forces. The combined effect of these two sets of forces is illustrated in Figure 16.3.[29]

To initiate change, an organization must take one or more of three actions to modify the current equilibrium of forces:

- increasing the strength of pressure for change;
- reducing the strength of the resisting forces or removing them completely from the situation; and/or
- changing the direction of a force—for example, by changing a resistance into a pressure for change.

Using force field analysis to understand the process of change has two primary benefits. First, managers and employees are required to analyze the current situation. By becoming competent at diagnosing the forces pressing for and resisting change, individuals should be able to understand better the relevant aspects of a change situation. Second, force field analysis highlights the factors that can be changed and those that can't be changed. People typically waste time considering actions related to forces over

FIGURE 16.3 Force Field Analysis

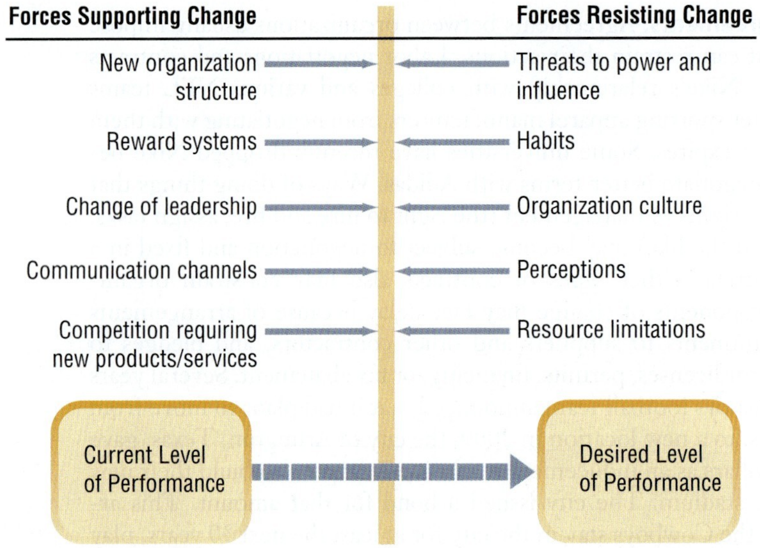

which they have little, if any, control. When individuals and teams focus on the forces over which they do have some control, they increase the likelihood of being able to change the situation.

Of course, careful analysis of a situation doesn't guarantee successful change. For example, people in control have a natural tendency to increase the pressure for change to produce the change they desire. Increasing such pressure may result in short-run changes, but it also may have a high cost: Strong pressure on individuals and teams may create conflicts that disrupt the organization. Often the most effective way to make needed changes is to identify existing resistance to change and focus efforts on removing resistance or reducing it as much as possible.

An important part of Lewin's approach to changing behaviors consists of carefully managing and guiding change through a three-step process:

1. *Unfreezing*. This step usually involves reducing those forces that are maintaining the organization's behavior at its present level. Unfreezing is sometimes accomplished by introducing information to show discrepancies between behaviors desired by employees and behaviors they currently exhibit.
2. *Moving*. This step shifts the organization's behavior to a new level. It involves developing new behaviors, values, and attitudes through changes in organizational structures and processes.
3. *Refreezing*. This step stabilizes the organization's behavior at a new state of equilibrium. It is frequently accomplished through the use of supporting mechanisms that reinforce the new organizational state, such as organizational culture, norms, policies, and structures.

The following Change Competency feature illustrates how three friends from Boulder, Colorado, went sailing in the Caribbean and started Crocs. One of the friends was wearing a foam clog that he had bought in Canada. The others tried the Crocs and wanted to buy a pair for themselves. With no one to fund them, they started selling the

LEADER INSIGHT

Changing the attitude and behavior of hundreds of thousands of people is very, very hard to accomplish. You cannot mandate it, or engineer it. What you can do is create the conditions for transformation by providing incentives, defining marketplace realities and goals. But at some point you must trust.

Lou Gerstner, Chairman, Carlyle Team

multicolored Crocs—with their Swiss-cheese perforations, cushy orthotic beds, and odor-preventing materials—in 2003 from a warehouse in Florida. Today it is a more than $400 million dollar company.[30]

Change Competency

Crocs

© AP Images

Factors including comfort of the product, ease of ordering for retailers, and an endorsement from the American Podiatric Medical Association have contributed to the success of Crocs shoes.

Croc's founders—Lyndon Hanson, Scott Seamans, and George Boedecker—returned from their Caribbean sailing vacation and leased a warehouse in Florida with the idea of selling the comfortable clogs one of the friends had gotten them hooked on. They ordered the product from Finproject, a Canadian manufacturer that made Crocs and owned the formula for the special resin that gave the soles their unusual comfort and their odor resistance. They sold shoes first to sailing enthusiasts but soon gained a word-of-mouth following among doctors, nurses, gardeners, and other people who had to be on their feet all day.

The founders hired Ron Snyder, who worked in manufacturing, as the CEO to get their new company off the ground. Snyder was convinced that they could make a nice profit if they could sell the Crocs for around $30. This would let people buy multiple pairs. After distributing the Crocs for awhile, Snyder decided to buy Finproject. Since buying the Canadian manufacturing plant, they have added manufacturing plants in China, Italy, Mexico, and Romania. At first, the four men thought that international sales would make up about 10 percent of Crocs' sales. Currently, international sales make up about 30 percent. Crocs' workforce has expanded from 3 in 2003 to more than 3,200 in 2007 and its shoes are sold in more than 17,500 outlets in 80 countries.

Store buyers knew Crocs were comfortable, but Crocs needed to convince the buyers to change their way of thinking—and also get the endorsement of the medical community—to overcome large retail stores' resistance to the shoe. Why? Usually retailers have to purchase shoes in bulk at least six months in advance. Crocs managers had to convince these buyers that they could reorder as few as 24 pairs of Crocs at a time and have them delivered in a matter of weeks, not months. Such a reordering system was unheard of in the retail footwear departments. They also worked on gaining an endorsement from the American Podiatric Medical Association. This endorsement gained them credibility and an opportunity to advertise Crocs in more than 1,000 doctors' offices. Once Crocs gained the doctors' endorsements, Crocs began distributing their shoes to retailers in the United States, including Dillard's, Nordstrom's, REI, and Sports Authority.

To extend its reach into the children's market, it purchased a business started by Sheri Schmeizer, a stay-at-home mom. In the summer of 2005, Schmeizer decided to use clay and rhinestones to make charms that would fit snugly into the holes of her daughter's Crocs. She immediately saw the potential to sell charms that would fit into the holes of Crocs. Within weeks, Schmeizer and her husband started Jibbitz, a company that made the charms. During the first six months, the couple sold more than 250,000 charms; 6 million within the first year. They outsourced manufacturing to Asia and opened a warehouse in Boulder. The Crocs management team saw the revenue potential and bought the company for $10 million.

Crocs is now sponsoring volleyball tournaments and producing special branded Crocs for companies like Google and Tyco. It has partnered with colleges so students can order Crocs in school colors. In 2006, it reached an agreement with the NFL and NHL to give them rights to use all team logos on their shoes. Crocs has also reached an agreement with Disney to make a limited edition of Crocs footwear named Disney by Crocs, and will soon offer shoes with icons of legendary superhero characters such as Batman, Superman, and Wonder Women.

For more information on Crocs, visit this organization's home page at www.crocs.com.

Learning Goal

4. Discuss methods for promoting change.

PROMOTING CHANGE

Organizational Diagnosis

Organizational diagnosis *is the process of assessing the functioning of the organization, department, team, or job to discover the sources of problems and areas for improvement.* It involves collecting data about current operations, analyzing those data, and drawing conclusions for potential change and improvement. An accurate diagnosis of organizational problems and functioning is absolutely essential as a starting point for planned organizational change.[31]

Information needed to diagnose organizational problems may be gathered by questionnaires, interviews, or observation—and from the organization's records. Typically, some combination of these data gathering methods is used. An advantage of the information collecting process is that it increases awareness of the need for change. Even with widespread agreement on the need for change, people may have different ideas about the approach to be used and when, where, and how it should be implemented.

To diagnose an organization, managers need to have an idea about what information to collect and analyze. Choices on what to look for invariably depend on managers' perceptions, the leadership practices used, how the organization is structured, its culture, and the like. Potential diagnostic models provide information about how and why certain organizational characteristics are interrelated. We illustrate one such model in Figure 16.4. Based on concepts presented throughout this book, this model illustrates how a change in one element usually affects others. For example, a change in an organization's reward system from one based on individual performance to a team-based system will affect the type of individuals joining the organization. ViewCast Corporation undertook such a reward system change because it reflected the needs employees wanted to satisfy on the job, how leaders made decisions, the type of decisions that teams could make, the structure of the department or division, and the culture of the organization. The new reward system required that managers from various product lines frequently communicate with each other and share best practices. It also helped change the culture from a market one to a clan culture.

Any planned change program also requires a careful assessment of individual and organizational capacity for change. Two important aspects of individual readiness for change are the degree of employee satisfaction with the status quo and the perceived personal risk involved in changing it. Figure 16.5 shows the possible combinations of these concerns. When employees are dissatisfied with the current situation and perceive little personal risk from change, their readiness for change probably would be high. In contrast, when employees are satisfied with the status quo and perceive high personal risk in change, their readiness for change probably would be low. When Michael Jordan was brought into EDS by its Board of Directors, he faced a situation where many employees perceived a high personal risk from his changes and high level of dissatisfaction with the current situation (lower right corner of Figure 16.5). By adopting the economic approach to change, he tried to move the EDS employees' readiness to the upper left-hand corner of Figure 16.5 (high readiness for change).

FIGURE 16.4 Diagnostic Model of Change

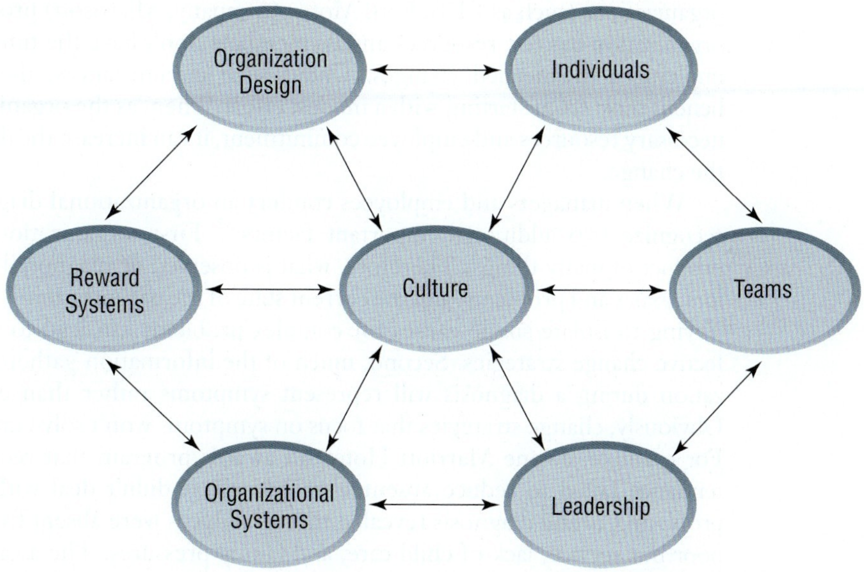

FIGURE 16.5 Employee Readiness for Change

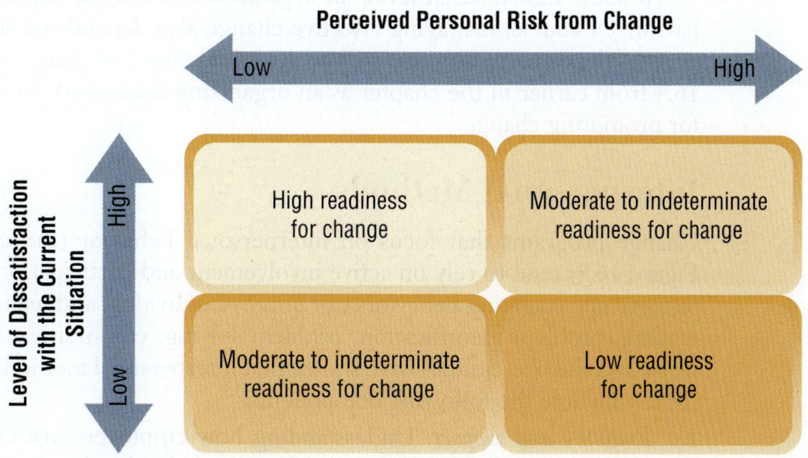

Source: Adapted from Zeira, Y., and Avedisian, J. Organizational planned change: Assessing the chances for success. *Organizational Dynamics*, Spring 1989, 37.

With regard to individual readiness for change, another important aspect is employee expectations regarding the change effort because expectations play a crucial role in behavior. If people expect that nothing of significance will change, regardless of the amount of time and effort they might devote to making it happen, this belief can become a self-fulfilling prophecy. And when employee expectations for improvement are unrealistically high, unfulfilled expectations can make matters worse. Ideally, expectations regarding change should be positive yet realistic.

In addition, the organization's capacity for change must be accurately assessed. Approaches that require a massive commitment of personal energy and resources from organizations (such as EDS, Ford Motor Company, Microsoft) probably will fail if the organization has few resources and its members don't have the time or opportunity to implement the needed changes. Under such circumstances, the organization may benefit most from starting with a modest effort. Then, as the organization develops the necessary resources and employee commitment, it can increase the depth and breadth of the change.

When managers and employees conduct an organizational diagnosis, they need to recognize two additional important factors.[32] First, organizational behavior is the product of many things. Therefore, what is observed or diagnosed—employee behaviors, issues and problems, and the current state of the organization—has multiple causes. Trying to isolate single causes for complex problems can lead to simplistic and ineffective change strategies. Second, much of the information gathered about an organization during a diagnosis will represent symptoms rather than causes of problems. Obviously, change strategies that focus on symptoms won't solve underlying problems. For example, at one Marriott Hotel, an awards program that recognized perfect attendance failed to reduce absenteeism because it didn't deal with the causes of the problem. Careful diagnosis revealed that employees were absent from work because of poor bus service, lack of child care, and family pressures. The awards offered weren't sufficient to change employee behaviors and, more important, didn't address the employees' real problems.

Potential resistance to change represents another important aspect of readiness and motivation for change. Both individual and organizational resistance to change must be diagnosed. The main objective of planned organizational change is to alter the behavior of individuals within the organization. In the final analysis, organizations survive, grow, prosper, decline, or fail because of the things that employees do or fail to do. Behavior, therefore, should be a primary target of planned organizational change. In other words, to be successful, change programs must have an impact on employee roles, responsibilities, and working relationships.

At some fundamental level, all organizational change depends on changes in behavior. Of course, managing effective change also depends on identifying specific aspects of the organization that will be the initial target of change efforts. We use Figure 16.4 from earlier in the chapter as an organizing framework to explore these methods for promoting change.

Interpersonal Methods

Change programs that focus on interpersonal behavior (the *individual's* variable in Figure 16.4) tend to rely on active involvement and participation by many employees. Successfully changing behaviors can improve individual and team processes in decision making, problem identification, problem solving, communication, working relationships, and the like. Studies have shown that interpersonal methods for achieving change usually include the following components:[33]

1. *Empathy and support*. Understanding how employees are experiencing change is useful. It helps identify those who are troubled by the change and helps management to understand the nature of their concerns. When employees feel that those managing change are open to their concerns, they are more willing to provide

information. This openness, in turn, helps establish collaborative problem solving, which may overcome barriers to change.

2. *Communication*. People are more likely to resist change when they are uncertain about its consequences. Effective communication can reduce gossip, rumors, and unfounded fears. Adequate information helps employees prepare for change.
3. *Participation and involvement*. Perhaps the single most effective strategy for overcoming resistance to change is to involve employees directly in planning and implementing change. Involved employees are more committed to implementing the planned changes and more likely to ensure that they work than are employees who have not been involved.

One popular approach to focus on people who are having problems fitting in with others or dealing with change is to use survey feedback. We examine that approach next.

Survey Feedback. In survey feedback *information is (1) collected (usually by questionnaire) from members of an organization, department, or team; (2) organized into an understandable and useful form; and (3) fed back to the employees who provided it.*[34] In Chapter 8, we discussed how 360-degree feedback is used by managers to improve the performance of employees; 360-degree feedback is just one form of survey feedback. It leads to a comprehensive assessment of an employee's performance and usually leads to change methods that increase the likelihood that the person's competencies will be taken into account. This information provides the basis for planning actions to deal with specific issues and problems. The primary objective of all interpersonal methods is to improve the relationships among team members through the discussion of common problems, rather than to introduce a specific change, such as a new computer system. Survey feedback also is frequently used as a diagnostic tool to identify team, department, and organizational problems. Because of its value in organizational diagnosis, survey feedback often is utilized as part of large-scale, long-term change programs in combination with other approaches and techniques.

Take a few minutes to complete the questionnaire found in Table 16.2. This survey feedback instrument is designed to help you discover your competency in leading change. When leading change, most people rely on what they know best and avoid areas where they struggle. What are your best areas? Where might you improve? You might want to identify 20 people who know you well and ask each of these people to take this survey assessing your attitudes and behaviors. When you have obtained their feedback, you will then be able to develop an accurate self-portrait based on this feedback.[35]

Table 16.2 **Leading Positive Change**

Instructions: Please use the following rating scale to discover your change competency ability. Your answers should reflect your attitudes and behaviors as they are now, not as you would like them to be. Be honest.

Rating Scale:

1 = Strongly disagree

2 = Disagree

3 = Slightly disagree

4 = Slightly agree

5 = Agree

6 = Strongly agree

Assessment:

_____ 1. I create positive energy in others when I interact with them.

_____ 2. I know how to unlock the positive energy in other people.

_____ 3. I express compassion toward people who are facing pain or difficulty.

_____ 4. I help promote compassionate responses in others when it is appropriate.

_____ 5. I usually emphasize a higher purpose or meaning associated with the work I do.

_____ 6. I forgive others for the harm they may have produced or the mistakes they made.
_____ 7. I maintain high standards of performance, even though I am quick to forgive.
_____ 8. The language I use encourages virtuous actions by people.
_____ 9. I express gratitude frequently and conspicuously, even for small acts.
_____ 10. I keep track of things that go right, not just things that go wrong.
_____ 11. I frequently give other people positive feedback.
_____ 12. I emphasize building on strengths, not just overcoming weaknesses.
_____ 13. I use a lot more positive comments than negative comments.
_____ 14. I compare my own (or my group's) performance against the highest standards.
_____ 15. When I communicate a vision, I capture people's hearts as well as their heads.
_____ 16. I work to close abundance gaps—the difference between good performance and great performance.
_____ 17. I exemplify absolute integrity.
_____ 18. I know how to get people to commit to my vision of the change.
_____ 19. I take advantage of a small-wins strategy in all my change initiatives.
_____ 20. I have developed a teachable point of view for subjects I care about.

Scoring Key:

Score	**Quartile**
100 or above	Top quartile
81–99	2nd quartile
60–80	3rd quartile
Below 60	4th quartile

Subscales for Changed Competency Ability	**Items**
Personal capability to lead positive change	2, 3, 5, 6, 7, 9, 10, 12, 13, 16, 17, 20
Ability to mobilize others toward positive change	1, 4, 8, 11
Capacity to create positive deviance in organizations	14, 15, 18, 19

Team Methods

As the name suggests, the purpose of team methods is to get a handle on team performance problems.[36] As illustrated in Figure 16.6, team performance is influenced by the competencies of its members, organizational structure, the organization's reward system, organizational culture, and other factors. Team methods are designed to improve relations among team members and their team's performance. You might wish to review the materials in the chapter on teams, Chapter 11, for more information on the characteristics of successful teams and how managers can change the behaviors of team members to become more effective.

Team Building. In team building, *team members diagnose how they work together and plan changes to improve their effectiveness*. Team building begins when members recognize a problem.[37] An effective team can recognize barriers to its own effectiveness and design and take actions to remove them. During team building, members of the team contribute information concerning their perceptions of issues, problems, and working relationships. Usually information is gathered during team meetings or prior to meetings, using interviews or questionnaires. Managers then analyze the information and diagnose work-related problems. Using problem diagnosis as the starting point, team members plan specific actions and assign individuals to implement them. At some later stage, team members evaluate their plans and progress to determine whether their actions solved the problems identified. As team effectiveness grows, the potential impact on organizational performance increases. Another good way to define team building is that it consists of the activities designed to move the team up the performance curve shown in Figure 16.6.

The goal of many team-building methods is to change the culture of the organization. In Chapter 15 we explored changing organizational culture and pointed out just how difficult such changes can be. Among other issues and problems, just assessing

FIGURE 16.6 The Team Performance Curve

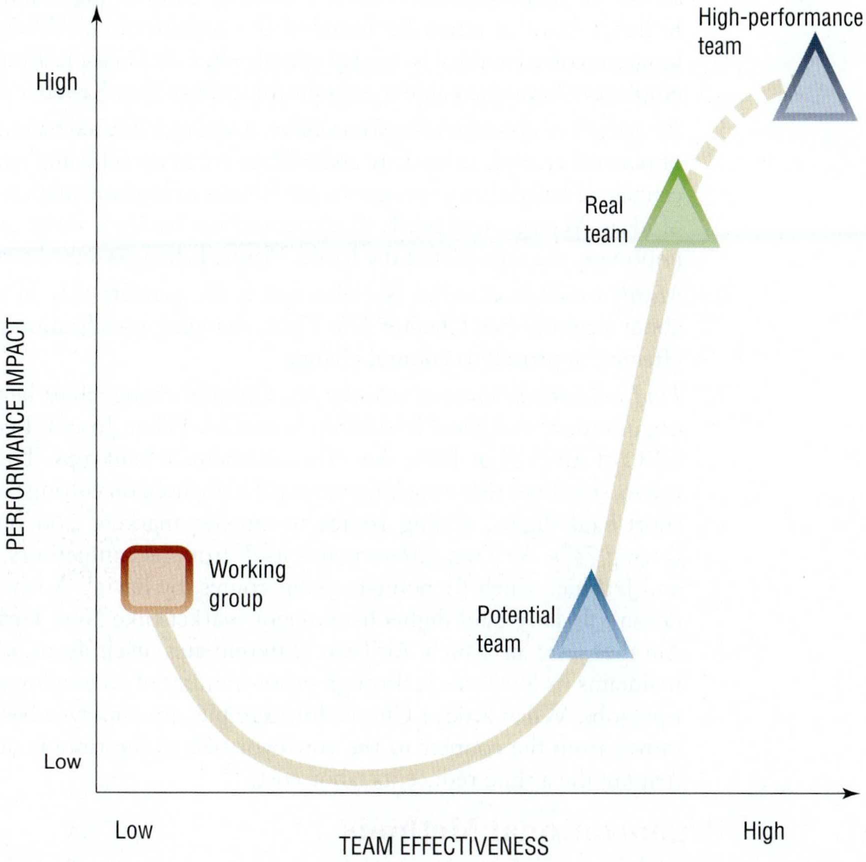

Source: Adapted from Katzenbach, J. R., and Smith, D. K. *The Wisdom of Teams.* Boston: Harvard Business School Press, 1993, 84.

accurately the organization's culture before any plans for changes can be developed may be a daunting task. In addition, some aspects of culture (e.g., the deepest core values shared by employees) may be almost impossible to change. Despite these challenges, some organizations have successfully changed their cultures. How did they do it? A detailed examination of successful cultural change suggests that the odds for success can be increased by giving attention to seven main issues:

1. *Capitalize on dramatic opportunities.* The organization needs to take advantage of the moment when obvious problems or challenges that are not being met "open the door" to needed change. When Michael Jordan took over as CEO of EDS, many of EDS's problems focused on the internal design of the organization and loss of customers.
2. *Combine caution with optimism.* Managers and employees need to be optimistic with regard to the advantages of cultural change; otherwise they will be unwilling to make the attempt. Yet, because cultural change can have negative impacts, the organization needs to proceed with caution. Expectations for improvement must be positive, yet realistic.
3. *Understand resistance to cultural change.* Resistance to change needs to be diagnosed. Identifying and reducing sources of resistance is valuable in cultural change as well as in other change programs.

4. *Change many elements but maintain some continuity.* "Don't throw the baby out with the bathwater" is a common saying that sums up the importance of recognizing what is of value and retaining it. Southwest Airlines, a firm that we have examined in other chapters in this book, has grown and prospered since its founding in the early 1970s, yet it managed to retain a core of cultural ideas and beliefs that Herb Kelleher instilled when he founded the organization. Although Kelleher is no longer involved in the day-to-day operations, CEO Gary Kelly and other long-time employees have been able to sustain the culture that Kelleher created.
5. *Recognize the importance of implementation.* A survey indicated that more than 90 percent of planned changes in strategy and culture are never fully implemented. A large percentage of failed change programs are failures of implementation rather than failures of ideas. Management needs to recognize that having a vision and a plan, although important, are only part of the battle. Planned changes must be carried through.
6. *Modify socialization tactics.* Socialization is the primary way in which people learn about a culture (see Chapter 15). Thus, changing socialization processes can be an effective approach to cultural change.
7. *Find and cultivate innovative leadership.* Cultural change must begin at the top of the organization, and good leadership is crucial. When Joseph Leonard took over as CEO of AirTran in 1999, the airline was almost bankrupt. Today, it is one of the low-cost airlines that is making money. He focused on cutting costs, flying lucrative short-haul flights, adding routes to smaller markets, and buying fuel-efficient Boeing 737s. AirTran differentiates itself from its competitors, such as Southwest and JetBlue, which fly point-to-point routes, by having Atlanta as its hub. It also doesn't fly long-haul flights from major markets like New York and Los Angeles. Another way in which AirTran differentiates itself from its competitors and maintains its low costs is through cross-training of its employees to perform multiple jobs. When Zakiya Cheris, for example, an employee based in Philadelphia, moves from the counter to the conveyor belt to the runway at the airport, she is helping the airline reduce its labor costs.[38]

Organizational Methods

In the past decade, a large number of organizations have radically changed how they operate to satisfy customers' demands. Increased competition has forced many organizations to downsize, become leaner and more efficient, and be flexible. Organizations are unlikely to undertake major organizational changes unless there are compelling reasons to do so. Power, habit, culture, and vested interests are organization-wide norms that are difficult to change. Many organizations, such as Ford Motor Company, Kmart, and Tyco, had to experience a severe threat to their survival before they were motivated to undertake such change.

Organization-wide change programs frequently are aimed at changing an organization's design, reward systems, culture, and organizational systems. Approaches to change that focus on organizational methods involve redefining positions or roles and relationships among positions and redesigning departmental, divisional, and/or organizational structure. Unfortunately, implementing design or structural change has sometimes been used as an excuse for organizations simply to downsize their workforces without identifying and exploring the reasons for inefficiency and poor performance.

A key feature of organizational change methods is the active role of top management in all phases of the change process. Because top managers are responsible for the strategic direction and operation of the organization, they decide when to initiate such changes, what the change should be, how it should be implemented, and who should be responsible for implementing it. In organizations undergoing organization-wide changes, senior managers need to play three roles:

- *Envisioning.* Top management must articulate a clear and credible vision for the change. They must also set new standards of performance.

- *Energizing*. Top management must demonstrate personal excitement for the changes and model behaviors that are expected of others. They must constantly communicate with all employees.
- *Enabling*. Top management must provide the resources necessary for undertaking significant change and use rewards to reinforce new behaviors.[39]

The following Communications Competency feature illustrates how top management played all three roles at IBM to bring about change in its policies about hiring gay, lesbian, bisexual, and transgender (GLBT) employees. In 1953, Thomas J. Watson, Jr., the president of IBM, issued a written policy promising that the company would hire people based on their ability, "regardless of race, color, or creed." This was a bold statement, coming as it did a year before the U.S. Supreme Court's *Brown v. Board of Education* decision and 11 years before the passage of the Civil Rights Act. IBM was planning to build plants in Kentucky and North Carolina, and Watson wanted to make sure they were integrated. Watson's vision for IBM was a company where the work environment was free from all forms of discrimination and harassment. Since that statement, IBM has been on the cutting edge of promoting GLBT rights.[40]

Communication Competency

Personnel Policy Changes at IBM

IBM has three major areas in which it focuses its diversity programs: equal opportunity, affirmative action, and work/life. IBM senior managers have taken the following actions to support the diversity of its more than 134,000 employees:

- It is a major financial supporter of gay rights groups in the United States.
- To export its culture of openness, IBM supports GLBT groups in 23 countries.
- In 2005, it convened a group of gay college students at the Human Rights Campaign to form a national organization of students in science and technology.
- IBM persuaded Marci Bowers, one of the world's leading sex-reassignment surgeons and herself a transgendered person, to participate in the company health insurance program.

In 1995 under the leadership of its CEO Louis Gerstner, IBM formed six executive-level task forces, one each for women, African Americans, Hispanics, Native Americans, people with disabilities, and employees with work/life issues. Each task force was asked four questions: How can IBM attract the most talented people from your group? How can the company keep them engaged and productive? How should IBM market to them? Which groups outside IBM should become IBM partners?

Sam Palmisano, IBM's current CEO, noted that IBM looks very different than when he joined the company. The number of women executives worldwide has increased 490 percent since 1995. The number of GLBT individuals has grown even faster and the number of executives with disabilities has tripled. IBM now buys $2.1 billion of goods and services from suppliers owned by women, minorities, or GLBT individuals and it sells more than $500 million of goods and services to those groups. Palmisano knows that effective management of GLBT individuals is an important strategic objective at IBM.

IBM has received many awards from GLBT associations. For example, recently, it scored 100 percent on the Human Rights Campaign, was named second on the top 100 employers for lesbian and gay staff in Britain according to the Workplace Equality Index in the United Kingdom, and was named as one of the top 50 Latina companies for providing career advancement opportunities and diversity policies for Latinas.

For more information on IBM, visit the organization's home page at www.ibm.com and search for "Valuing Diversity."

CHAPTER SUMMARY

1. Identify key pressures for change.

A rapidly changing environment places many demands on managers and employees, including the need to plan for and manage organizational change effectively. Pressures for change stem from globalization, the increasing use of information technology as a communication channel, the rise in the number of powerful social networking groups, and different generations of employees in many organizations. Each of these pressures for change requires managers to adapt their behaviors in order to achieve their organization's goals.

2. Discuss the nature of planned organizational change.

There are two major approaches to achieving planned organizational change: economic and interpersonal. The economic approach focuses on changing the organization's design, reward system, and technology to achieve change and improve stockholder value. The organizational development approach focuses on the development of employee's interpersonal competencies. This approach requires employees and managers to become emotionally involved with the organization and be committed to its values and goals. Many successful planned change programs sequence these two basic approaches, starting first with the economic and then shifting to the organizational development approach.

3. Identify common reasons for individual and organizational resistance to change.

Individuals may resist change because of their perceptions or personalities. In addition, habits, threats to established power and influential relationships, fear of the unknown, and economic insecurities may generate further resistance to change. Organizational resistance to change may be caused by organizational design and culture, resource limitations, fixed investments that are not easily altered, and interorganizational agreements. By performing a force field analysis, various resistances to change can be explored in more detail.

4. Discuss methods for promoting change.

Three methods are available for promoting organizational change: interpersonal, team, and organizational. The interpersonal method focuses on changing employees' behaviors so that they can become more effective performers. This method usually involves some use of survey feedback. As the name suggests, the team method focuses on ways to improve the performance of entire teams, and team-building activities are its foundation. The organizational method is aimed at changing the organization's structure, reward system, level at which decisions are made, and the like.

KEY TERMS AND CONCEPTS

Economic approach
Force field analysis
Globalization
Organizational development approach
Organizational diagnosis
Planned organizational change
Survey feedback
Team building

DISCUSSION QUESTIONS

1. Go to Microsoft's website (www.microsoft.com) and type in "Annual Report." Pick the latest annual report and read "Shareholder Letter." What are the key pressures for change reported in this statement?
2. From Table 16.1, what change approach did Gates use in China to gain access to the Chinese consumer?
3. Why is organizational diagnosis essential to the success of any change effort?
4. Think of a situation in which someone asked you to change your behavior. Did you change? Why or why not?
5. Based on your answers to the Leading Positive Change questionnaire in Table 16.2, what competencies do you need to develop? How will you develop these?
6. Rosabeth Kanter, a leading authority on change, stated that trying to change an organization is like trying to

teach elephants to dance. Why is changing an organization's direction so difficult?

7. Based on the force field analysis, why is it hard for people to lose weight and keep it off?
8. From your own experience, describe a team, department, or organization that needed to change. Which of the change approaches presented was used? Was it successful?
9. Identify and describe an ethical dilemma or issue created by some organizational change effort with which you are familiar. How was the ethical problem handled? What, if anything, would you do differently?

EXPERIENTIAL EXERCISE AND CASE

Experiential Exercise: Self Competency

Assessing an Organization's Readiness for Change[41]

Instructions

This questionnaire is designed to help you understand the level of support or opposition to change within an organization. Please respond to each of the 16 items according to how true it is in terms of an organization with which you are familiar. Circle the appropriate number on the scale that follows the question.

3 = Yes
2 = Somewhat
1 = No

1. Is the change effort being sponsored by top management? 3 2 1
2. Are all levels of management committed to the change? 3 2 1
3. Does the organization's culture encourage change? 3 2 1
4. Does the organization reward continuous improvement? 3 2 1
5. Has top management clearly stated the reason for change? 3 2 1
6. Has top management presented a clear vision of the future? 3 2 1
7. Does the organization use objective indicators to measure its performance? 3 2 1
8. Does the change effort support other major ongoing activities in the organization? 3 2 1
9. Has the organization benchmarked itself against world-class organizations? 3 2 1
10. Do all employees understand the customers' needs? 3 2 1
11. Does the organization reward employees for being innovative and looking for causes of problems? 3 2 1
12. Is the organization's design adaptable? 3 2 1
13. Do senior managers communicative effectively to all employees? 3 2 1
14. Has the organization recently implemented a successful change? 3 2 1
15. Do employees assume responsibility for their own behavior? 3 2 1
16. Do senior managers make decisions quickly? 3 2 1

Norms:

40–48 = High readiness for change
24–29 = Moderate readiness for change
16–23 = Low readiness for change

Questions

1. What type of change program (economic or organizational development) might work best in your organization?
2. Depending on your score, what are some individual and organizational resistances to change that you might encounter when making changes in your organization? How do you plan to overcome these?
3. What ethical problems might you face when implementing changes in your organization?

Case: Change Competency

Changing of the Guard at HP[42]

In the aftermath of the corporate spy scandal that wracked Hewlett-Packard (HP) with a wave of resignations, a lawsuit, and a long list of investigations, CEO Mark Hurd has managed to turn HP around. HP sales are over $100 billion with a profit of $9 billion. In this industry, growth is an obsession. For HP to keep pace with other competitors in the tech industry, it must add $6 billion of revenue each year. He compares HP sales of $41,320 per employee against IBM's $28,840 and thinks that HP can still do better.

Hurd is a sharp contrast to his predecessor, Carly Fiorina. He arrived without making bold proclamations or sweeping plans. He walks the factory floor, talks with employees, leaves 50 voice mails a day, and gets quick updates by cell phone as he goes from one meeting to another. He studied the financial books, chatted with senior staff he inherited and then set out to fix HP. "Without execution," he says "*vision* is just another word for *hallucination*. The day you feel like you've won, you need to drive out of the parking lot and not come back." He focuses on processes and execution and has been known to go through every detail to get a clear answer.

When Hurd arrived at HP after Fiorina was fired on February 9, 2005, he didn't do any ads, no voiceovers, and didn't hang his portrait in the lobby. He didn't go to the World Economic Forum but instead spent time at Best Buy in Palo Alto, California, talking with customers to learn how customers liked/disliked HP's products. Hurd quickly realized that he was in charge of a demoralized staff and had an organization with high costs and little direction. After having dozens of meetings with his staff, shop floor employees, and customers, he asked them "Where can HP grow?" Hurd also had memorized hundreds of metrics—prices, costs, margins, discounts, growth rates, revenues—and used them in follow-up meetings with employees. Quickly employees knew that Hurd was all business. The word quickly spread that when meeting with Hurd, you better have your facts and figures at your fingertips. You had better know how revenue moves through your business and how your business fits into HP business strategy. Ann Livermore, a 25-year HP employee, says "He drives operational excellence because he believes in business basics, including a focus on cost reduction, so HP can win on price."

Hurd soon learned that executives had little control over their budgets. Under Fiorina, HP had three product lines (printers, PCs, servers). The units for these product lines were responsible for designing and building their own products, but most of the marketing and selling were run by a different unit, the Customer Solutions Group (CSG). This division was created to unite the autonomous product line fiefdoms that HP had always had. Under this organization design, 80 different products were assigned to CSG. What actually happened is that this organization design blocked direct feedback from the sales force to the product designers. It pitted divisions against one another. Each division pushed CSG to dedicate more sales staff to selling their product line over another division's product. This design let each group avoid accountability and assign blame.

Hurd immediately handed budget control to the product division heads and disbanded the CSG so managers could make better decisions faster. Only a few services, such as human resource management and finance, are done by headquarters staff. Now product heads control their own profit and loss, sales, marketing and suppliers. Accountability is assigned at the product level.

At the same time, Hurd laid off 15,000 employees with no loss in revenues. The watchword became "simplify." He also changed the reward system. There had been a complex bonus system built around revenue, profitability, and subjective evaluations, such as "total customer experience." Hurd's plan bases bonuses solely on the company's profitability and growth.

Hurd also hired Randall Mott from Wal-Mart to track inventory and forecast sales. This was an immerse task since HP had 85 data centers. Mott designed an inventory system that enables HP to track the performance of more 100,000 suppliers. If they fail to perform up to HP standards, they are dropped. Mott also closed 79 data centers, thereby saving millions of dollars. HP now deploys more than 6,900 consultants and programmers in India and China to convert customers' software into new languages used by HP computers.

The problem with IT is that unless HP can achieve integration of its IT systems, HP's costs will be too high. Specifically, HP spent 80 percent of its IT money just to keep the system running and 20 percent of its money testing new ideas. The goal is to spend 70 percent on innovation and 30 percent on maintenance. Mott believes that one of the keys to HP's success is not the technology, but is about answering more than 800 million customer questions each year to their satisfaction.

Questions

1. What methods of planned change were used by Hurd? Explain.
2. What aspects of the change competency (see Chapter 1) are demonstrated by Hurd?
3. Do you think Hurd's changes at HP will improve HP's financial performance?

PART 5

INTEGRATING CASES

INTEGRATING CASES

BMW'S Dream Factory and Culture

BMW, with more than $60 billion in sales, is much smaller than its American rivals. However, the U.S. auto giants could still learn some things from BMW. Detroit's rigid bureaucracies have been slow to respond to competitive threats and market trends. In contrast, BMW's management system is flat, flexible, entrepreneurial—and fast.

Few companies have been as consistent as BMW at producing an ever-changing product line, with near flawless quality, that consumers like. BMW has redefined luxury design with its 7 Series, created enthusiasm for its Mini, and maintained some of the highest profit margins in the auto industry. A sporty four-wheel-drive coupe and a stylish minivan called the Luxury Sport Cruiser rolled off the production line in 2008. These models promise to continue BMW's run of cool cars under its new chief executive, Norbert Reithofer. (His predecessor, Helmut Panke, stepped down upon reaching the mandatory retirement age of 60. Panke once insisted that all six members of the management board take an advanced driving course so they would have a better feel for BMW cars.) Says Reithofer: "We push change through the organization to ensure its strength. There are always better solutions."

Virtually everyone at BMW is expected to help find those solutions. When demand for the 1 Series compact soared, plant manager Peter Claussen volunteered to temporarily use the brand new factory in Leipzig, Germany—which had been designed for the 3 Series—to produce 5,000 of the compacts. Claussen and his associates quickly figured out how to do it while maintaining high quality. Recently, line workers in Munich, Germany, suggested adding a smaller diesel engine in the 5 Series. They contended that it would have enough power to handle like a Bimmer (a nickname for BMW cars, unlike the "beemer" or "beamer" nicknames used for BMW motorcycles) and be a big seller among those on a tighter budget. They were right.

Culture Much of BMW's success stems from an entrepreneurial culture that is rare in corporate Germany. Management in Germany is usually top-down, and the cultural gulf between workers and managers is significant. BMW's 106,000 employees, however, have become a network of committed associates with few hierarchical barriers to hinder innovation. From the moment they set foot inside the company, associates experience a sense of place, history, and mission. Individuals from all levels of BMW work side by side. They create informal networks where even the most unorthodox ideas for making better Bimmers or boosting profits can be voiced. BMW buyers may not know it, but when they slide behind the wheel, they are driving a vehicle born of thousands of impromptu brainstorming sessions. BMW, in fact, might just be the chattiest auto company ever. Claussen comments: "The difference at BMW is that [managers] don't think we have all the right answers. Our job is to ask the right questions."

That's not to say this freewheeling idea factory hasn't made its share of blunders over the years. In 2001, BMW alienated customers with its iDrive control system. The device was designed to help drivers quickly move through hundreds of information and entertainment functions with a single knob. It proved incomprehensible to many buyers. Rival Audi is narrowing the gap with BMW in Europe by producing a new generation of stylish, high-performance cars that have topped consumer polls. Toyota's Lexus also has BMW in its sights as it makes a move to gain market share in Europe with sportier, better handling cars. Reithofer comments: "We will be challenged—no question. We have to take Lexus seriously."

In BMW's favor is an enduring sense that things can go wrong. New hires quickly learn that the BMW world as they know it began in 1959. That's when the company nearly went bankrupt and was just a step away from being acquired by Mercedes. This long-ago trauma remains the pivotal moment in BMW folklore. Reithofer continues: "We never forget 1959. It's in our genes, and it drives our performance." BMW wouldn't exist today if it weren't for a bailout by Germany's wealthy Quandt family—still the controlling shareholder, with a 47 percent stake—and a pact with labor to keep the company afloat. "Near-death experiences are very healthy for companies," says David Cole, a partner at the Center for Automotive Research in Ann Arbor, Michigan. "BMW has been running scared for years."

The story of 1959 is told and retold at each orientation of new plant associates. Works Council Chief Manfred Schloch, a 26-year veteran, holds up old, grainy black-and-white photos of two models from the 1950s. The big one was too pricey for a struggling postwar Germany. The other, a tiny two-seater, looked like a toy and was too small to be practical, even by the standards of that era. The company badly misjudged the market, he says. Schloch pulls out a yellowed, typewritten 1959 plan for turning the company around with a new class of sporty sedans. Schloch then hands out photos of Herbert Quandt and the labor leader of the period, Kurt Golda. Schloch states: "I explain how we rebuilt the company with Quandt's money and the power of the workforce. And I tell them that's the way it works today, too."

Motivated Workers, Better Cars BMW derives much of its strength from an almost unparalleled labor harmony rooted in that long-ago pact. In 1972 and years before the rest of European companies began to think about pay for performance, the company included all employees in profit sharing. It set up a plan that distributes as much as one and a half months' extra pay at the end of the year, provided BMW meets financial targets. In return, employees are flexible. When a plant is introducing new technology or needs a volume boost, it's not uncommon for associates from other BMW factories to move into temporary housing far from home for months and put in long hours on the line. Union leaders have made it easy for BMW to quickly adjust output to meet demand. Without paying overtime, the company can increase the production schedule to as much as 140 hours a week (20 hours per day, 7 days a week) or scale it back to as little as 60 hours. The system enables BMW to provide a high level of job security, and no one can remember any layoffs—ever. Since 2000, BMW has hired 12,000 new associates even as General Motors and Ford Motor have slashed tens of thousands of jobs.

BMW's human resources department receives more than 200,000 applications annually. Those who make it to an interview undergo elaborate daylong drills in teams that screen out big egos. For the lucky few who are hired, a Darwinian test of survival ensues. BMW promotes talented managers rapidly and provides little training along the way. It requires them to reach out to others to learn the ropes. With no one to formally coach them in a new job, managers need to stay humble and work closely with subordinates and their peers. This minimizes traditional corporate turf battles. Anyone who wants to push an innovative new idea learns the key to success fast. "You can go into fighting mode or you can ask permission and get everyone to support you," says Stefan Krause, BMW's 44-year-old chief financial officer. "If you do it without building ties, you will be blocked."

Work Environment The construction of the Leipzig factory is a testament to the power of such ties. When plant manager Claussen first proposed a competition to lure top architects, executives at headquarters were taken back. Krause comments: "People said to me, 'What's wrong with these guys in Leipzig? We don't need beautiful buildings, we need productive buildings.'" Claussen convinced Krause and others that the unconventional approach wouldn't just produce a pretty factory but one whose open, airy spaces would improve communications between line workers and managers and create an environment that helps the company build cars better.

Even before Claussen began pushing his architectural vision, others were busy designing the inner workings of the plant. Jan Knau, an engineer, was only 27 when he was asked to come up with a flexible assembly line for the factory. Knau, then just a junior associate, contacted BMW's top 15 assembly engineers. He invited them to a two-day workshop at a BMW retreat near the Austrian Alps. After a series of marathon sessions that included discussions of every facet of the ideal assembly line, Knau sketched a design with four "fingers," or branches, off the main spine. The branches could extend to add equipment needed to build new models. This made it possible to keep giant robots along the main line in place rather than moving them for each production change, an expensive and time-consuming process.The Leipzig plant opened in 2005. It represents Claussen's vision of teamwork enhanced through design by Knau's creative engineering concepts. With pillars of sunlight streaming through soaring glass walls, architect Hadid's design looks more like an art museum than a car factory. Open workspaces cascade over two floors. Unfinished car bodies move along a track with enhanced lighting that runs above offices and an open cafeteria. If the pace of the half-finished cars slows, engineers know it immediately and can quickly investigate the problem. The weekly quality audits—in a plaza workers pass on their way to lunch—ensure that everyone is quickly aware of any production snafus. The combination of togetherness and openness sparks impromptu dialogue among line workers, logistics engineers, and quality experts. Knau states: "They meet simply because their paths cross naturally. And they say, 'Ah, glad I ran into you, I have an idea.'"

Flexibility and Innovation The flexibility of BMW's factories allows for a wide range of variations on basic models. At Leipzig, for instance, parts ranging from dashboards and seats to axles and front ends snake onto overhead conveyer belts to be lowered into the assembly line in precise sequence according to customers' orders. BMW buyers can select everything from engine type to the color of the gear-shift box to a seemingly limitless number of interior trims—and then change their mind and order a completely different configuration as little as five days before production begins. Customers request some 170,000 changes a month in their orders, mostly higher priced options such as a bigger engine or a more luxurious interior. There are so many choices that line workers assemble exactly the same car only about once every nine months.

This kind of customization would swamp most automakers with budget-busting complexity. But BMW has emerged as a sort of anti-Toyota. Toyota excels in simplifying automaking. BMW excels in mastering complexity and tailoring cars to customers' tastes. That's what differentiates BMW from Lexus and the rest of the premium pack. "BMW drivers never change to other brands," says Yoichi Tomihara, president of Toyota Deutschland. He concedes that Toyota lags behind BMW in the sort of customization that creates emotional appeal.

Bottom-up ideas help keep BMW's new models fresh and edgy year after year. Young designers in various company studios from Munich headquarters to DesignWorks in Los Angeles are constantly pitted against one another in constructive competitions. Unlike many car companies, where a design chief dictates a car's outlines to the staff, BMW designers are given only a rough goal. Otherwise, they are free to come up with their best concepts.

To get the most out of its associates, BMW likes to bring together designers, engineers, and marketing experts to work intensively on a single project. The redesign of the Rolls-Royce Phantom, for instance, was dubbed "The Bank." The 10 team members worked out of an old bank building at London's Marble Arch, where dozens of Rolls Royces roll by daily. "We took designers from California and Munich and put them in a new environment" to immerse them in the Rolls Royce culture, says Ian Cameron, Rolls's chief designer. The result was the new Phantom, a 19-foot vehicle that remains true to Rolls's DNA, but with 21st-century lines and BMW's technological sophistication under the hood. With sales of the $350,000 car running at about 700 a year, the Phantom is the best seller in the super-luxury segment, outstripping both the Bentley Arnage and the Mercedes Maybach.

Much of BMW's innovation doesn't come via formal programs such as The Bank, however. In 2001, management decided to pull the plug on the disappointing Z3 sports coupe. That didn't stop a 33-year-old designer named Sebastian Trübsbach from doodling a sketch of what a Z3 successor might look like. Ulrich Bruhnke, head of BMW's high-performance division, loved it. In Trübsbach's drawing, Bruhnke saw a car that could rival Porsche's Cayman S in performance but at a lower price. He persuaded a few designers and engineers to carve out some time for the renegade project. Next, Bruhnke gathered a team to map out the business case. The small group worked for 10 months to build a prototype.

The moment of truth came in 2004 at a top-secret test track near Munich. Cars were lined up so the Board of Directors could examine their styling and proportions in natural light. Only one was covered by a tarp. Panke approached the mystery model. "What is this interesting silhouette?" he asked Bruhnke, who invited his boss to take a look. Panke yanked back the cloth, exposing a glittering, bronze metallic prototype for what would become the Z4 coupe. Bruhnke breathed a sigh of relief when he saw Panke's eyes light up as they viewed the car's design. Panke and the Board of Directors quickly gave the go ahead. The Z4 coupe sped to production in just 17 months, hitting showrooms in 2007.

To take a virtual tour of how each model of the Z4 is manufactured, go to www.bmwusfactory.com. Click on "Virtual Tour." The virtual tour is at BMW's state-of-the art Spartanburg, South Carolina, manufacturing plant. A moderator describes each step of the production process.

For more information on the BMW Group, visit the organization's home page at ***www.bmwgroup.com.***

Questions

1. How would you describe the culture at BMW?
2. What model of leadership is illustrated at BMW? How does this impact BMW's culture?
3. Using the concepts illustrated in the job characteristics model (see Chapter 5), analyze why employees derive high job satisfaction at BMW.
4. What attributes of organizational creativity are fostered at BMW?

Source: Adapted from Edmondson, G. BMW's dream factory. *Business Week*, October 16, 2006, 70–80; Kurylko, D. T. Job swap works for BMW. *Automotive News*, July 9, 2007, 48; Cokayne, R. BMW plan offers workers stable income. *BusinessReport*, September 3, 2007; Pries, L. Emerging production systems in the transnationalization of German carmakers: Adaptation, application or innovation? *New Technology: Work and Employment*, 2003, 18, 82–100; BMW Group. www.bmwgroup.com (September 2007).

ROWE Program at Best Buy

Jennifer Janssen works in the finance department at the headquarters of Best Buy, located in Minneapolis, Minnesota. One of Best Buy's electronics suppliers is furious because he claims he has not been paid. Janssen states: "He told me, 'I'm not going to ship any more products to your company unless I get this issue resolved.' " She has to resolve the problem by the end of the day. The mother of twins also has to pick up her children from day care. What choices does she have? Perhaps Janssen makes a call to her husband, asking if he could skip out early while she puts out the fire at work. (Again?) Maybe Janssen scrambles to find someone who can handle the issue in time for her to leave at 4:00 P.M. (Did anyone see me?) Or perhaps, after another late night, Janssen spends the car ride home wondering whether she should just quit. (This time, I swear!)

But Janssen is calm as she figures out what happened to her vendor's payment, Janssen knows that she can leave the office at 4:00—without guilt, without looking over her shoulder. Because even if a solution isn't found by then, she can keep working on it from her laptop at home. No one remarks that she's leaving and no one notices. Janssen is part of the program to solve the problem of overwork at Best Buy. Like many other U.S. companies, Best Buy strives to meet the demands of its business—how to do things better, faster, and cheaper than its competitors—with an increasingly stressed-out workforce.

The company's culture used to embrace long hours and sacrifice. One manager even gave a plaque to the employee "who turned on the lights in the morning and turned them off at night." Darrell Owens, a Best Buy veteran, once stayed up for three days in a row to write a report that was suddenly due. He received a bonus and a vacation. But, Owens stated: "I ended up in the hospital." Cali Ressler, a human resources executive, had noticed an alarming trend: Women were accepting the reduced pay and status of a part-time position but doing the same work because it was the only way to get the family flexibility they needed. Ressler states: "If we keep moving the way we're moving, women are going to be in the same place we were 40 years ago."

ROWE Program The number of people in the United States who say they are overworked has been rising, from 28 percent of Americans in 2001 to 44 percent, according to the Families and Work Institute. Instead of launching a "work/life balance" program, Best Buy rethought the very concept of work. Under the *Results-Only Work Environment* program, or ROWE, employees can work when and where they like, as long as they get the job done.

As of 2007, the program was only four years old and was started at Best Buy's Minneapolis headquarters, which has 4,000 employees. Recently, Best Buy started introducing the ROWE program to its 100,000 employees in retail stores. The firm is still figuring out how the program can be applied in stores, because retail requires "time clocks" and working to schedules, which are against the program's operating philosophy.

The ROWE program is based on 13 principles and rules. The key ones include:

- There are no work schedules in the traditional sense.
- Every meeting is optional, with a few key exceptions.
- Employees are not to judge how colleagues spend their time. Thus, there is to be no focus on "how many hours did you work."
- Work is not a place you go, it's something you do.
- As long as the work gets done, employees do whatever they want whenever they want.
- In brief, ROWE is all about results. No results, no job. It's that simple.

Entire departments join at once, so that no single employee is left out and made to feel less dedicated. Thus far, 75 percent of the 4,000 employees at Best Buy's headquarters are in the ROWE program. Each group finds a different way to keep flexibility from turning into chaos. The public relations team has pagers to make sure someone is always available in an emergency. Janssen has software that turns voice mail into e-mail files accessible from anywhere, making it easier for her to work at home. Many teams realized that they needed only one regular weekly or monthly staff meeting, so they eliminated the unproductive ones.

Early Results Results from and reactions to ROWE have been encouraging. Productivity has increased an average of 35 percent within six to nine months in Best Buy units implementing ROWE. Voluntary turnover has dropped between 52 percent and 90 percent in three Best Buy divisions that have implemented ROWE. The three divisions were chosen because they were otherwise unaffected by company reorganizations or other initiatives. This voluntary turnover figure is viewed as an indication that employees who once would have left Best Buy decided to stay put after ROWE was implemented. One procurement division saw voluntary turnover drop from 37 percent a year to less than 6 percent annually.

Jody Thompson helped introduce ROWE and is now a principal of Culture Rx, a division of Best Buy. Culture Rx offers customized consulting services tailored to the needs of clients with ROWE at the core of its philosophy. A Culture Rx study of attitudes of ROWE participants found that feelings of pressure and a sense of working too hard have changed. Thompson states: "They feel happier about work. They feel more ownership of their work. They feel clearer about what they're doing for the company, and they see ROWE as a benefit that's almost more important than any other. They talk about it as if to say, 'Someone else could offer me more money, but I wouldn't go because I now have control over my time.' "

Change Process The ROWE experiment started quietly. Cali Ressler used to manage Best Buy's work/life balance programs and is now a principal with Thompson at Culture Rx. She helped a troubled division of the retail group in Minneapolis deal with poor employee morale. Ressler encouraged the manager to try flexible scheduling, trusting his team to work as it suited them. As she recalls: "He said, 'Well, trust doesn't cost me anything.' " The innovation was that the whole team did it together. Although the sample size was fewer than 300 employees, the early results were promising. Turnover in the first three months of employment fell from 14 percent to zero, job satisfaction rose 10 percent, and their team-performance scores rose 13 percent.

When Jody Thompson, who then led Best Buy's "organizational change" initiatives, heard about Ressler's work, she pushed the company's top management to make total flexibility available to everyone. No one is forced into it; teams sign up when they're ready. Best Buy expects that ROWE one day will apply to the whole company in one form or another.

The transition to a flexible workplace in Minneapolis was slow. "There was a lot of trepidation," says Traci Tobias, who manages travel reimbursements for Best Buy. "A lot of 'Can I really do this? Do I need to stop and tell someone? What will people think of me?' " Each ROWE team had to deal with those fears. "We took baby steps," Tobias says. The first step was an online calendar in which everyone entered exactly where they were at any given time. After a few weeks, the employees abandoned the calendar and now just use an ad hoc combination of out-of-office messages and trust. "There is no typical day," Tobias says. On a recent Wednesday, she slept in, went to a doctor's appointment, and arrived in the office around 10 A.M.

When Tobias needs to find people, she checks the whiteboards hanging outside their cubes, where she and her coworkers write down where they are on any given day: "In the office today." "Out of the office this afternoon, available by e-mail." The impromptu meetings are gone, but business done by cell phone is way up. Because she no longer assumes that everyone is around, Tobias makes more of an effort to catch up with her colleagues by phone or e-mail instead of just dropping by someone's office. "You can still have those conversations," she says, just not always in person. She noticed that e-mails have gotten more concise and meaningful, with much less "FYI." And as everyone started to rethink their priorities, Tobias stated: "We spent a lot less time in meetings." They used to have a two-hour weekly staff meeting that often devolved into chitchat. Now, if they don't need to meet, they don't.

The transition required a lot of changing of old attitudes, and it produced a lot of stress. Some employees broke down and cried in ROWE training sessions. Ressler states: "People in the baby-boom generation realize what they gave up to get ahead in the workplace, and a lot of times it's their families. They realize that it doesn't have to be that way." In particular, men thank her and Thompson, who run the sessions, for giving them permission to spend more time with their families. "They know now they can do it and not be judged," says Thompson.

The change also has exposed some ugly attitudes among managers. When Thompson proposed extending flexibility to hourly workers, the managers resisted, arguing that "there are certain people that need to be managed differently than other people. 'Because we believe that administrative assistants need to be at their desk to 'serve' their bosses,' " she says. That issue is not yet resolved, but Thompson says ROWE is requiring the company to confront it.

Denise LaMere, a Best Buy corporate strategist, has struggled to figure out how to prove herself in the new environment. "It made me very nervous," LaMere says. Without children, she once had an advantage—she could always be the first one in and the last one out. She states: "I had all this panic. Everything we knew about success was suddenly changing."

The change begins with what Best Buy calls "sludge sessions." These sessions are where employees dig out the cultural barriers to change—the jokes and comments that reinforce overwork. Tobias comments: "It's like, coming in at 10 o'clock and someone says, 'Wow, I wish I could come in at 10.' It's really hard to let that bounce off and not be defensive." LaMere admits that she used to gossip about who was taking an extra-long lunch break. "We were all watching each other. You don't want to be seen eating in the cafeteria." LaMere always ate at her desk.

During the first few weeks in ROWE, employees call "sludge" out loud when they hear an offending comment. They try to keep a sense of humor about it—some teams put a dollar into a kitty for every sludge infraction. Yes, it sounds weird, but it can help people break their bad habits, says Phyllis Moen, a sociologist at the University of Minnesota who has studied Best Buy's ROWE employees. "These are all examples of the way we use time to say how valuable we are," she says.

Sources of Resistance Managers have put up the most resistance. The hardest part of the transition to ROWE, says Tom Blesener, one of the first to go through it, was accepting responsibility for the stress his employees felt. "It was me," he says. "That was hard." Blesener also had to learn how to stop treating his employees as if they were "unruly children," he says. Blesener manages 27 people who handle the company's extended-warranty services. His 20 hourly employees told him they were sick of punching time clocks. "They felt it was almost inhumane," he says. Now these data-entry clerks and claims processors focus on how many quality forms they get through in a week, rather than when they do it. They still count their hours (Best Buy has to follow governmental overtime rules for hourly workers), but they have more freedom to schedule their work around their families' needs.

In the end, Blesener had to give up some of his control. When a client needed someone to be available on Saturdays, Blesener left it up to his team to decide how to handle the coverage. Under ROWE, he can't stop by his employees' desks and spring deadlines on them—they might not be there. He now plans his whole team's work more carefully and meets with each of his direct reports weekly. "It requires you to get to know your people on a much deeper level," he says.

Total flexibility may not be for everyone. For instance, Best Buy's legal department so far has resisted the new way of working, partly because the in-house attorneys are worried that it will reduce their pay, says one of them, Jane Kirshbaum. Best Buy's lawyers are compensated in part based on how well they serve their clients—other departments that have legal issues—and they are not connected to any revenue-generating part of the business. Kirshbaum wonders if they will be criticized as unresponsive if they take off one afternoon. She admires the freedom the employees in the ROWE program seem to enjoy. She changed to a four-day schedule after the birth of her second child and struggles every day with the push of work and the pull of family. Still, she is not convinced that ROWE will work for her. She already checks e-mail and voice mail on her "day off." Will ROWE push even more work into her downtime? Without everyone in the office, she asks, "How do you make sure that the person who's left is not the person who's dumped on?"

In exchange for more autonomy, Best Buy employees give up the guidelines that signal where work ends and leisure begins. Janssen says the hardest adjustment was "not working 24 hours a day. Because you have that ability now. I had to learn when enough is enough." Moen says the old rigid system is comforting for routine-loving workers. ROWE, she says, "could be harder for people who want order in their lives."

Despite all the challenges, employees who have already made the switch say the benefits of "ROWE-ing," as they call it, are profound. Tobias says she has stopped avoiding her children. "I was getting up in the morning, rushing to get out of the door before my kids were awake," she says. If her children saw her, they would beg her to stay for breakfast. Now, because her quarterly goals are very clearly spelled out, she knows exactly what she has to finish in a given week—negotiate a rental-car contract or audit expense reports, for example. She can decide how and when to do it. If she wants to have a leisurely breakfast, she will. "My kids have stopped saying every morning, 'Mommy, I don't want you to go to work,'" she says. It isn't perfect. "The family doesn't always win," she says. But the family doesn't always lose either. "I don't feel guilty anymore."

Janssen, for her part, had considered leaving when she was pregnant. "Now, it's not even an issue," she says. As for Blesener, the retail supervisor, he went to his first parent–teacher conference, a task that had always fallen to his wife, a stay-at-home mother to their two sons. Joe Pagano, a vice president who works in merchandising, looks back in sadness at all the sacrifices he made. His wife stayed at home with their son and daughter. He states: "I basically worked every Saturday, and some Sundays. It's one of the biggest regrets of my life." After his department switched to the new system, he started taking an afternoon here and there to play golf. He went to Special Persons Day at his grandson's school. Pagano continues: "If things had been different, I probably would have been a better father and husband, and a better manager. I'm doing this so other people do not do what I did wrong."

Key Rationale The corporate management team, led by CEO Brad Anderson, was initially skeptical about the ROWE program and whether it should be expanded. The initial experiments with ROWE showed that it helped to reduce voluntary turnover, improve productivity, and increase employee morale. As a result of these outcomes, top management allowed managers throughout corporate headquarters to adopt the ROWE program at their discretion. As noted, experiments with the introduction of ROWE in retail stores are in the early phase.

Ultimately, for Best Buy, the new approach to work is about staying competitive, not just helping its employees. Like many other companies facing global competition, Best Buy expects more training, more initiative, and more creativity from all of its employees. The company doesn't guarantee job security: Management has realized that it can't expect so much from its employees without giving something in return. "We can embrace that reality and ride it, or we can try to fight it," says Shari Ballard, an executive vice president.

*For more information on Best Buy, visit the organization's home page at **www.bestbuy.com**.*

Questions

1. What approach to organizational change does the ROWE program illustrate?
2. Identify some resistances, both organizational and individual, that the ROWE program had to overcome.
3. What sources of stress are apparent in this case?
4. How would you describe the culture of Best Buy? How has the culture helped the change?
5. In what ways does the introduction of the ROWE program reflect the evidence-based management model (see Chapter 13)?

Source: Adapted from Thottan, J. Reworking work: An inside look at Best Buy's bold experiment. *Time*, July 25, 2005. www.time.com (September 2007); Conlin, M. Smashing the clock: No fixed schedules. No mandatory meetings. Inside Best Buy's radical reshaping of the workplace. *Business Week*, December

11, 2006, 60ff; Halkias, M. It comes from the job. *Dallas Morning News*, February 21, 2007, D1, D6; Brandon, J. Rethinking the time clock. *Business 2.0*, March 2007, 24; Jossi, F. Clocking out. *HRMagazine*, 2007, 52(6), 46–50; About Culture Rx. www.culturerx.com (September 2007).

How Personal Can Ethics Get?

This is a true case. Names have been changed to protect identities.

Valerie Young was a marketing manager at an international cosmetics and fragrance company, Wisson, which is headquartered in Chicago. Wisson underwent a major reorganization due to cost cutting. Valerie's department was downsized from 25 to 10 people the year before. They did survive as a small team though, and their role within the organization was unique—acting as an agency, delivering designs for bottles and packaging and developing the fragrances for their brands.

Valerie's manager, Lionel Waters, had been with the department for 14 years. He was hired by Wisson's CEO at the time, after he had worked for big names in the fragrance industry. He had launched one of the most successful female fragrances in the industry several years before. Waters joined the company in order to start new product lines for the company in the mass fragrance market. He then hired two close friends as executives with salaries well above industry standards and gave them each six weeks annual vacation. Teams were formed around them quickly and after three years, each team had its own line of fragrances that were launched worldwide.

Nature of Work Valerie was hired to contribute organizational, financial, and marketing skills. The rest of the team was mainly comprised of creative individuals who had basically no interest whatsoever in the dry theoretical world of calculating numbers and strategies. Valerie had not worked in the beauty industry before, but was eager to learn everything about the world of scents and how they were developed. At that time, the department worked with many different perfumers from several fragrance companies. The perfumers themselves, or their representatives, came to present their creations for new projects, or the Wisson teams went to their suppliers' offices in France to conduct so-called "fragrance sessions."

It takes time to develop a fragrance product that will end up being a perfect creation on the counters of the world's department stores. The name, concept, design of the bottle and packaging, advertising, and, last but not least, the fragrance has to be put together to create an innovative and uniquely new product. Fragrance development itself takes a tremendous amount of time.

First, the perfumers are briefed about the new project so that they can base their creations on already firm ideas about the end product. Then, for every new project in the department, at least 300 to 400 samples are submitted by the perfumers. The majority of those samples are usually discarded right away after "smelling" for the first time because the scent did not match the concept or simply did not smell good enough. Some are set aside, smelled again and again, and during that process, the perfumers get feedback about what to change. Sometimes Valerie's team got 20 reworked submissions for one scent and it often happened that after all that work, the original was picked as the best choice. In the final phase, three to four fragrances remain and only those few go on to the market research testing phase.

During Valerie's first year at the company, the team worked with as many as eight different fragrance companies to have a good diversity of new scent ideas. After a while, they began using only perfumers from two fragrance companies for their projects. She was wondering why they stopped working with the other perfumers, because their submissions were not bad at all and they also successfully supply Wisson's competitors. Why were these perfumers not good enough for Wisson? It did not take long for the team members to realize that Waters was not to be questioned. The team then went forward and developed great relationships with the perfumers of the two remaining fragrance houses.

The Incident And then one day, it all became clear to Valerie. She had some copies to make and walked to the copy room in the office area. As she was putting her originals in the copy machine, she saw that there was a paper jam, and the person who caused it left without taking care of it. She started to open the drawers of the paper supply and checked the output tray. There were some sheets that someone must have forgotten and she was going to throw them in the recycling container next to the copy machine. As soon as she grabbed the sheets, she saw that they looked like her boss's private company's stationary (he had a consulting company on the side). So Valerie looked closer and realized that what was in her hand were invoices from Waters to the two fragrance companies Wisson worked with that listed "commissions and fees" totaling almost $35,000 per month! So that was the reason Wisson stopped working with other companies—they probably refused to pay Waters' kickbacks!

Valerie was stunned. She was left shocked and speechless. Almost as if it were like a reflex action, she took all her papers and the invoices and walked back to her office. Sitting there for a while, she tried to calm down. So many questions were running through her head: "Does anyone else know about this? Are other people on our team involved? Is this normal in the industry? Should I talk to anyone about it?"

All kinds of thoughts were spinning inside her, and she spent the rest of that workday walking around as if she was in a cloud. Fortunately her boss was not in that day. He was probably on vacation, just like the 20 other weeks per year of time off he grants himself.

When Valerie came home the night of her discovery, she told her boyfriend about it. This is one of those situations when you have to tell somebody; otherwise you think you are going to explode. Her boyfriend was not directly affected by this, so she could confide in him and be sure of his honest opinion. First, he did not quite understand what she was saying because it sounded so outrageous, but then he realized what had happened. He asked her if she had told anyone else about it, and when she assured him that she had not, he recommended that she keep this information to herself for the time being, not because he is not an ethical person himself, but because he knew that her career in Chicago could be in danger if something happened to her boss. After all, her boss was in charge of the department and if he were gone, the already small team might not survive either.

Valerie's Dilemmas Valerie did not have a U.S. green card, only a special working visa, which allows non–U.S. citizens with unique skills to work in this country for a certain amount of time. This kind of visa is completely dependent on the "fairness" of the company someone is working for, and means that Valerie could lose the right to work, or even the right to stay in the United States if she did not have this job any longer.

And that was not all. She had just been accepted for the master's of science program at the University of Chicago and was looking forward to starting it. Her tuition would be reimbursed by the company if she got A's and B's in her classes. This was a huge opportunity to gear her career toward greater challenges and successes.

But what about ethics? What about her own values? In this situation, there was so much more at stake than just right or wrong. The decision she had to make would influence other people's lives as well as her own. Her colleagues had become her friends, and even though her boss disregarded good management and leadership principles, these individuals formed friendships among themselves, particularly since they had been reduced to only a handful of people. Instead of joining his team in building up not only professional but also friendly relationship with his employees, Waters preferred to look for only one goal—to enrich himself. He did not care about relationships with other fragrance companies either. Perfumers are somewhat like artists; they sometimes work well under pressure and they are often inspired by their customers as well. To have the greatest diversity of fragrance submissions, Waters should have worked with perfumers from more than only two companies. This would have given Wisson's products a big competitive advantage.

Waters was a constant example of how not to be ethical in handling business and employees. Instead of being a leader who would help activate ethics mindfulness in others, he was the polar opposite. He seemed to have made it one of his goals to spend as much of the company's money as possible. Launch events went overboard with extravagances and expenses; on one occasion, just to show off his horseback riding talent, he rented an entire stable outside of Chicago for one hour. The cost: $25,000—and he expensed it to the company.

Usually he showed up late for meetings or canceled them entirely even when the attendees were already in the office. Or, he would tell someone "something really important" came up, and then relate a completely different version to somebody else. Waters' team did all the work and had to make most decisions without him because he was rarely around. Mondays and Fridays he usually stayed home or at his other office, and with some traveling and all that vacation time, there was never much opportunity to actually work with him. So they learned to be efficient and productive by themselves without the person who was supposed to be their team leader, teacher, and supervisor. It finally deteriorated to the point that even the most positive colleagues realized that Waters contributed nothing to either the work level or to morale, both of which were already low. And that was without even being burdened with the things Valerie now knew!

Could she let her boss get away with this? Was she not obligated to report this? After all, in the company's policies it was clearly stated:

> *Personal payments, bribes or kickbacks to customers or suppliers or the receipt of kickbacks, bribes or personal payments by employees are absolutely prohibited.*

How could she even work with Waters any longer under these circumstances? She felt her anger toward him growing stronger. What kind of person was this man? Was he just a greedy human being? Didn't he make enough money already? He has always acted as if he were the most naïve person in the office, and now she's discovered this! She wished she had never seen those papers. It would have been much easier for her to continue her work and conduct "business as usual."

Valerie's Decision and Rationale What Valerie had to do, or not do, somehow became an easy decision for her. It was clear that she was unable to report this before she had another job or even before she graduated from the master's program, which was her ultimate short-term goal. Getting another job is not easy without a green card. The Immigration and Naturalization Service has made it more difficult for non–U.S. citizens to work in the United States, so companies hesitate to hire people like Valerie because it means a lot of paperwork and expenses for them. Also, workers with Valerie's type of visa have only 30 days to find a new job in the event they lose theirs; otherwise, they are required to leave the country.

Basically, Valerie did not really have a choice if she did not want to become a martyr for the ethics cause. She decided to wait for a while before bringing these findings to light, at least until she was close to graduating from the master's program so that she could receive her degree. It seemed that the highly ethical stance would be to report this right away, but it also seemed silly to sacrifice herself and her own future for the sake of "outing" someone who had been so unethical. Did she act morally and ethically correctly? She felt that she put her own interests before ethics for now, and that bothered her deeply, but she knew she was going to do what had to be done as soon as her circumstances allowed for it.

Valerie's discovery changed everything, and nothing. She still had to set up meetings with their long-time perfumers, and participate and act as if she knew nothing about what happened. She did try talking to Waters about involving other fragrance companies again. Her stated reason to him was that Wisson only receives approximately 100 submissions per project now, instead of the 300 to 400 in prior years. He was not willing to discuss that topic at all though, which obviously did not surprise her. She wondered whether the perfumers knew about these sweet deals too, or if they believed that their hard work won them their projects. Every time Waters said something regarding the importance of keeping the fragrance development as this team's responsibility, she said to herself, "Yes, and I know why!"

What Next? When the timing is right, and Valerie makes this crucial information "public," of course, Waters and his future will be affected. He will certainly lose his job, could possibly face criminal charges, and his reputation in the industry will be destroyed. For the team, the question will be if it can survive without him. The teams do have a very strong brand manager among them, who has an excellent reputation within the Wisson organization. Perhaps he will be able to take over the team and restart this department the right way.

Questions

1. What ethical concepts and dilemmas are facing Valerie?
2. If you were Valerie, what would you do? Why?
3. What types of stressors are being experienced by Valerie?
4. How would you evaluate Waters in relation to each dimension of the authentic leadership model (see Chapter 10)?

Source: Dench, S. How personal can ethics get? *Journal of Management Development*, 2006, 10, 1013–1017. Used with permission through the Copyright Clearance Center. Rightsholder: Emerald Group Publishing Limited.

Was Firing Him Too Drastic?

Michael Kalinsky is the founder of Empyrean Management Group, which provides a full-service consultative approach to meeting the human resource needs of clients. It is headquartered in a suburb of Philadelphia, Pennsylvania. Kalinsky was feuding with a vice president, David Kenworthy, who also happened to be his former brother-in-law. The conflicts were becoming all too frequent, mostly because Kalinsky and Kenworthy disagreed over how much autonomy Kenworthy had for making decisions that involved the company's biggest client, Capital One.

Family Ties But complicating matters even further was the fact that the father of the vice president/ex-brother-in-law—Kalinsky's former father-in-law, Bruce Kenworthy—was Empyrean's biggest investor. Regardless of family ties, Kalinsky was beginning to wonder if it was time to take radical action and confront his former brother-in-law.

The family had endured its share of turmoil since Kalinsky cofounded Empyrean with a childhood friend, Allen Jordan, in 2000. Soon after depositing a check for $100,000 from Empyrean's original investor, Kalinsky received a call from his then father-in-law, an officer at the bank, who told him that the check had bounced. The investor had changed his mind, but Bruce Kenworthy was familiar with Empyrean's business plan and offered to bankroll the new company with $100,000 from his retirement account. "I saw a chance to build a business for the family that we could pass on to the next generation," Bruce says. There was a catch: Under the terms of the loan, Kalinsky would have to appoint Bruce's son, David, to the position of vice president and make him a minority shareholder.

IRS Audit Eager to open for business, Kalinsky readily agreed to the terms. Empyrean quickly landed business with blue-chip clients, including Sun Trust Bank and Capital One, and began building a staff of recruiters. Then the problems started. In August 2001, Kalinsky received a shocking notice from the Internal Revenue Service (IRS) informing him that Empyrean had failed to pay its payroll taxes that year. Jordan, who, as the company's chief financial officer, was responsible for handling payroll taxes, had quit a few months earlier to become a consultant. Kalinsky was devastated. He faced the prospect of a long IRS investigation that could sink the company, and to make matters worse, his wife, Margaret, asked him for a divorce that summer. "I couldn't believe what was happening," he says. "I was losing my wife, my best friend, and my company all at the same time."

Bruce continued to be a supportive counsel for Kalinsky after the divorce, and even invited him to live in his home for a few months. Kalinsky's relationship with his former brother-in-law, however, began to unravel after the younger Kenworthy moved to Richmond, Virginia, to manage the Capital One account at the bank's headquarters. With hundreds of miles between them, the pair worked independently and rarely saw each other, keeping in touch mainly through infrequent phone calls and e-mails. They drifted further apart during the next two years, as Kenworthy focused on the Capital One account, while Kalinsky devoted most of his time to the IRS investigation.

Finally, in 2003, the IRS completed its audit. It demanded $250,000 in back taxes from Empyrean and required Allen Jordan, who had retained his stake in the company, to pay off roughly 20 percent of the debt. Kalinsky and Jordan worked out repayment plans with the IRS. With the troubles behind him, Kalinsky began to refocus his efforts on growth. By the end of 2003, the company was back on track, posting about $2.9 million in annual sales and turning a profit. But Kalinsky wanted Empyrean to tackle bigger jobs and take more risks. He pushed Kenworthy to expand the relationship with Capital One and bring in new accounts. He also asked him to spend more time at headquarters in Blue Bell, Pennsylvania. Kenworthy, in turn, requested a promotion and a larger ownership stake.

Incident with Capital One Kalinsky was considering the request when he received alarming news from Capital One in early 2004. The bank, which represented 40 percent of Empyrean's revenue, had decided to give the contract to a larger firm. Kalinsky had no idea that the account was even in jeopardy. "I never saw it coming," he says. And he blamed Kenworthy for not alerting him: "I just couldn't understand how he could allow the situation to go so far without letting me know."

A few weeks later, the competitor pulled out, granting Empyrean a chance to win back the contract. Kalinsky immediately made plans to hop on a plane to Capital One's headquarters in Richmond. Then he received a call from Kenworthy, who made it clear that he resented the interference. "He claimed he had the situation well in hand," Kalinsky says. Kalinsky chose not to make the trip, but he did call several other Empyrean employees based at Capital One to find out what was happening. Some of the employees told him that Kenworthy often criticized Kalinsky's decisions and questioned his leadership in front of both them and Capital One staff. "It was clear that there wasn't a great deal of mutual respect between Mike and Dave," says Thomas Brady, a former staffing director at Empyrean who worked with Kenworthy in Richmond for seven months. "They each had their own ideas about how to run the business."

Now, instead of promoting Kenworthy, Kalinsky was thinking about firing him. It seemed like every conversation they had turned into a battle, Kalinsky says. Bruce noticed the strain as well. "It seemed like the stress of the situation really created a conflict between Mike and Dave's personalities," Bruce says. "To this day I'm not really sure why they grew to dislike each other."

One thing that would keep Kalinsky from firing Kenworthy was concern about his relationship with Bruce. In addition to being Empyrean's biggest investor, Kalinsky's former father-in-law had continued to be a trusted business adviser and confidant through the divorce and the IRS troubles. Firing Bruce's son was bound to damage that relationship. What's more, David had been integral to keeping the company afloat during the IRS investigation. Should Kalinsky try to work this out, or should he act?

The Decision One night shortly after a phone call with his ex-brother-in-law, Kalinsky drove to Bruce's house and laid out the facts as he saw them: David's open criticism of him and seeming inability to retain a key client were jeopardizing Empyrean's future. Bruce told Kalinsky that the decision was up to him. Bruce states: "I asked Mike whether this was a personal or business decision. When he told me it was all about business, I said he needed to do what he thought was best."

Kalinsky put off calling Kenworthy for a few days. When he finally dialed David's number, Kalinsky was surprised by his terse tone. Bruce had alerted his son to the fact that he was about to be fired. Kalinsky was caught off guard but stood by his decision. Not surprisingly, the conversation was heated and ended badly. Kalinsky states: "It was quite obvious that Dave wasn't very happy with me. I understand why Bruce did it, but in hindsight it would have gone better if I had talked to Dave first."

Kalinsky felt drained but relieved. He had fired Kenworthy and regained control of his company. He also received a hopeful sign from Capital One, which agreed to keep a few Empyrean recruiters on-site while the bank mulled over its next step. But the euphoria quickly deteriorated. With emotions running high and no buyout provisions in place, Kalinsky and Kenworthy disagreed on how to cash out Kenworthy's shares. That August, Kenworthy sued Kalinsky and Empyrean, seeking a cash settlement equal to his stock holdings, in addition to damages for wrongful termination. To Kalinsky's surprise, Bruce was also listed as a plaintiff and wanted to cash out his stake. Bruce states: "Though I didn't think about it at the time, once Mike let Dave go, I needed to leave the company as well. It would have been a prickly situation any other way."

That December, Kalinsky sat down with his ex-in-laws and their lawyers for the first of many mediation sessions. Both sides hired appraisers to value the company. They reached a settlement three months later. Empyrean agreed to pay the Kenworthys for their shares of the business, in addition to the $100,000 loan from Bruce, within two years. The wrongful termination charge was dropped.

For more information on the Empyrean Group, visit the organization's home page at ***www.hiresmartpeople.com.***

Questions

1. Should Kalinsky have fired his former brother-in-law? Explain.
2. Were the styles of conflict management used in this case effective? Explain.
3. Were integrative negotiations employed through the process of principled negotiations? Explain.
4. What concepts in the bounded rationality model (see Chapter 13) of decision making are illustrated by this case? Explain.
5. What communication problems and issues are illustrated in this case?

Source: Dahl, D. Was firing him too drastic? *INC. Magazine*, October 2006, 51–54. Used with permission through the Copyright Clearance Center. Rightsholder: Mansueto Ventures LLC.

Changes at Scout Mortgage

John Mangels and Steve Walsh had been dreading the decision for years. But the nature of their industry had changed, and now to stay healthy the business had to somehow change, too. Just a few years ago, Mangels and Walsh loved their top salespeople so much they awarded them trophies. Now these very same star performers were causing a crisis. What was the best way out?

Walsh and Mangels had built Scout Mortgage of Scottsdale, Arizona, by paying their loan officers on commission, the standard form of compensation in the industry. Four years ago, when the real estate market was booming, paying employees as much as $300,000 a year didn't seem outrageous. But in recent years the market had cooled. Scout's business dropped by more than half from 2004 through 2006, and those lavish commissions started to look excessive.

The work changed too. Selling that once depended on developing leads had become passive, a matter of taking phone calls generated by newspaper ads and direct mailings. So Walsh and Mangels considered something radical: paying their loan officers salaries—relatively low ones—instead of commissions. They knew the decision could cause friction, maybe chase their best salespeople out the door. It could bring turmoil to a company facing a tight market. But something had to give.

Walsh and Mangels had met while working together at another mortgage company and founded their own brokerage in 2000. Scout grew quickly, fueled by Arizona's real estate boom and a wave of refinancing. In 2004, the company funded more than $600 million in mortgages and employed 25 loan officers, plus an equal size support staff. "With higher volume, you can really survive under just about any model," says Mangels.

In the mortgage industry, the overwhelming majority of loan officers work on commission. Traditionally, a salesperson works to generate a lead—often through contacts with real estate agents or builders—finds a lender, and does the paperwork. Loan officers typically earn a percentage of the loan amount (1 percent when borrowers have good credit) plus miscellaneous fees and premiums. In some cases, they can earn higher commissions by persuading the customer to accept a higher interest rate, though Walsh and Mangels say their reps weren't steering people with bad credit to risky loans, as some involved in the subprime loan mess apparently were.

For Scout's loan officers, it was great. Each mortgage generated a commission of $4,000 to $7,000, which was split 50–50 between the loan officer and the company. A rep could do quite well closing just three loans a week. In 2006, the firm's four top loan officers made between $250,000 and $300,000 each.

Changes in Markets and Technology But business slowed down when interest rates edged up in early 2004. By 2006, volume had dropped to about $240 million in mortgages funded. Much of the company's share of that was eaten up by payroll taxes, benefits, and marketing costs. "We were working for tips as owners of the company" says Walsh.

It wasn't just the housing market that was evolving. Using search engines, loan officers easily could scan hundreds of lenders to find the best deals. With automated underwriting software, files could be processed in seconds. The process of approving a loan became automatic, as software programs printed out approvals or denials of loans based on credit scores and other data. Working with loan shoppers who came in over the transom as prospects, Scout's team of loan officers began to seem like a highly paid phone bank. "They would come in and say, 'What's for lunch?'" Walsh says. "One of them said we'd have to pay him a higher commission to actually get out of his chair and go out and get business."

Human Resource Issues The solution seemed clear: Replace the commissioned staff with cheaper salaried ones. But it wasn't that simple. Making the switch meant bucking the basic paradigm of the industry. And losing the company's most experienced employees could hurt customer service. Some of the top performers were stars who closed more than 20 loans a month. There was Chris, the superstar salesman with a knack for finding ways to close with problematic borrowers such as people with little equity or poor credit. There was Nancy, the grandmother who worked 13-hour days and stayed by her phone until 9 or 10 at night. And there was Marcy, not only a top performer but a generous host who frequently invited the staff to parties at her house.

Most painful of all, there were personal ties. These loan officers were friends with families. They socialized after work and played with one another's children at Christmas parties. "How do you tell someone they're overpaid and they're no longer needed?" says Mangels.

They tried to avoid layoffs with a halfway measure. They began hiring salaried loan officers starting at $40,000 and kept existing staffers on commission. But it just led to tension. When the new hires realized the grass was much greener on the other side of the cubicle, some began asking to switch to commissions. Says Mangels, "There was whispering, 'Why are you guys working for $4,000 per month when you could be making $12,000?'" After initially thinking they'd been too draconian, the owners began to wonder if they hadn't gone far enough.

The Decision In April 2007, Walsh and Mangels decided to make major changes. "Basically, what we really needed to do was just scrape down to the foundation and start over," says Mangels. They eliminated sales commissions and switched entirely to a salaried staff. They decided to break the news at the end of the week, looked at the calendar, and groaned—it would be Friday, April 13, 2007.

When the day arrived, Walsh and Mangels sat down in a conference room and summoned the employees one by one. A glass window overlooked the cubicles on the office floor. Employees stole glances toward the conference room. In the days beforehand, the owners had tried to soften the blow by leaking hints of the coming changes. Some employees urged them to reconsider: One even tried to change Walsh's mind by approaching Walsh's brother.

They had decided to fire five commissioned loan officers plus three members of the support staff. Walsh and Mangels considered offering the commissioned employees salaried positions but decided there would be too much bad blood. It seemed clear no one would stay for maybe half of what he or she made in the past.

Chris, Nancy, Marcy, and others were gone. Six of the newer salaried officers were allowed to stay. Under the new policies, mortgage officers would earn a base salary of $36,000 per year plus a flat commission of $100 for closing a loan. Depending on productivity and volume of business (which fluctuates with interest rates), they might earn $60,000 to $120,000 a year.

The staff changes were part of a larger rethinking of the business that the owners hope will attract business: Walsh and Mangels will pass savings to customers by covering closing costs.

In the fall of 2007, Scout rolled out a website on which customers are able to compare mortgages. Walsh and Mangels are betting that the industry is approaching a day when customers will be able to shop for mortgages online much as a person can shop for airline tickets on Orbitz. They expect to be licensed in all 50 states by 2009. In the fall, Scout also rolled out an aggressive ad campaign of direct mail, Google ads, TV and radio spots, and billboards. New ads promote the idea that Scout reps have no incentive to steer customers toward high-interest or risky loans. Walsh asserts: "Unless you separate compensation from the program, you cannot get honest advice from anybody."

Scout hopes higher volume will outweigh lower margins. Walsh comments: "If we can offer absolutely the lowest rate possible, will we gain market share? It has to be a yes. It could be the greatest or best decision we ever made, or the worst. Only time will tell."

*For more information on Scout Mortgage, visit the organization's home page at **www.scoutmortgage.com**.*

Questions

1. What is your assessment of the ethical intensity (see Figure 13.2) of the changes made by Walsh and Mangels? Explain.
2. What decision-making model or models were used by Walsh and Mangels to dismiss employees and make the other changes? Explain.
3. What approach to change is illustrated in the case? Explain.

Source: Denison, K. Could Scout Kill Commissions? *INC.*, September 2007, 55–57.

Whole Foods Market

Whole Foods Market was founded in 1980 as one small store in Austin, Texas. It is now a leading retailer of natural and organic foods, with more than 270 stores in North America and the United Kingdom. Whole Foods Market has a focused mission. It is highly selective about what it sells and is dedicated to stringent quality standards. The firm is committed to sustainable agriculture. In 2007, Whole Foods acquired Wild Oats Markets, a natural and organic foods retailer with 109 stores.

John Mackey John Mackey founded Whole Foods Market and currently serves as the company's CEO and president. He is known for being casual, opinionated, and very direct. On a scale of CEO directness, Mackey might rate an 8 or 9. On a scale of CEO competitiveness, he is off the charts as judged by most observers.

Current and former colleagues describe Mackey as spiritual and calculating, forthright and aloof, humble and arrogant, good-natured and prickly, rebellious and open-minded, and impatient and impetuous. Mackey himself does little to dispel the contradictions. He says he is pro-employee but is avowedly anti-union. Mackey calls himself pro-customer but acknowledges that he runs a store with higher profit margins (and prices, often) than almost any other grocer. He is avowedly pro-capitalism but also pro-love. Asked once to list the principles he lives by, Mackey commented: "Love is the only reality. Everything else is merely a dream or illusion."

Mackey remarks: "Americans love to shop, right? We love to shop. And Americans love to eat. We're the fattest nation on earth. But, paradoxically, we don't love to shop for food. Grocery shopping in America, for the most part, is a chore." Mackey tried to address this problem before almost anybody else. Yet, he began as a food entrepreneur not so much to introduce style into the supermarket aisles as to influence the health and eating habits of the next generation of Americans. His original stores were big on nuts and grains and loaves dense as doorstops. It was food that took some serious chewing. Mackey comments: "The produce often came from farmers who showed up unannounced at the backdoor with muddy boots and battered pickup trucks. Tomatoes, turnips, carrots, basil—it might be local, it might be organic, it might be both: it just depended on the day."

Mackey's next project, after more than two decades spent trying to reinvent the supermarket, is to change the value and reputation of business in America. He remarks: "Business is always painted as the bad guys. They're the ones who are greedy, selfish, the ones who despoil the environment. They're never the heroes. Business has done a terrible job of portraying itself as invaluable. And it never will be accepted by society as long as business says it has no responsibility except for maximizing profits." Mackey's efforts at rehabilitating the good name of business have involved speaking to college students and talking up the Whole Foods "stakeholder" philosophy, which emphasizes the importance of satisfying customers and employees before shareholders. His argument is that a responsible business benefits all its stakeholders, including the local community and the environment; he also asserts that such a business will naturally enjoy a higher stock price.

In the meantime, he intends to make some waves. Tired of the way Wall Street's analysts enlist corporate executives in the setting of important quarterly earnings targets—often with the effect of punishing the stock of companies that fail to meet them—Mackey has decided Whole Foods will not play the short-term expectations game. "It's stupid," he says.

In November 2006, Mackey sent a letter to all team members at Whole Foods Market. It stated, in part:

> *The tremendous success of Whole Foods Market has provided me with far more money than I ever dreamed I'd have and far more than is necessary for either my financial security or personal happiness. . . . I am now 53 years old and I have reached a place in my life where I no longer want to work for money, but simply for the joy of the work itself and to better answer the call to service that I feel so clearly in my own heart. Beginning on January 1, 2007, my salary will be reduced to $1, and I will no longer take any other cash compensation. . . . My intention is for the board of directors to donate all of the future stock options I would be eligible to receive to our two company foundations.*

Working at Whole Foods Market Whole Foods Market slowly opens larger stores in labor markets where untraditional management practices may seem, simply, weird. Whole Foods opened a store in Manhattan, within the new Time Warner building at Columbus Circle. It is the largest supermarket in Manhattan, with 59,000 square feet. The ceilings are airy, the café is sky lit, the aisles are so wide that two shopping carts and a baby stroller—three abreast—can easily slide past one another. The Columbus Circle Whole Foods provides an array of choices. The prepared-foods area includes a sushi bar, staffed at lunch with 11 people; a pizza bar with 14 kinds of pizza; a coffee and tea bar; a salad bar with 40 items; and a daily hot-lunch bar that includes separate arrays of Asian, Indian, and Latin food. The produce section recently offered 15 different varieties of organic greens, including dinosaur kale; the meat case held four dozen kinds of meat. The store has 30 checkout stations, a single bank-style line, and a line monitor to speed customers to the next open cashier. Columbus Circle opened with 292 people on staff, which means some of the 14 teams had 50 or more members, a hard group to stay focused on their goal. Of those 292 staff members, 70 came from other stores. With their understanding of the company, they were the starter culture; in Mackey's metaphor, a yogurt culture. The store has a team leader and two associate store team leaders, both of whom were previously running their own stores in Georgetown, Maryland, and Albuquerque, New Mexico, before coming to New York. Three months after it opened, Columbus Circle had 468 team members, including 140 people on the cashier/front-end team alone—more people than used to work in a whole store.

Aaron Foster came to Columbus Circle from a Philadelphia Whole Foods. He's a cheese buyer, and standing at the cheese display, he's pondering the tension in Whole Foods' values—as he puts it, to "further the goals of sustainable agriculture and natural food production while being as big as we are and growing as fast as we are." A customer comes up to Foster. She states: "Excuse me. I'm looking for a certain cheese. It begins with a C. It's one syllable." Foster focuses on the roster of C cheeses in his brain. "I bought it yesterday at Dean & DeLuca!" the customer comments. Foster replies: "Comte cheese." "That's it!" the customer says, and they head off to get her some.

Barry Keenan is working the fresh seafood case. He calls out the weights of the salmon and the shrimp he is selling before the scale can display them. He states: "I shopped at the Whole Foods in Chelsea all the time. I figured I'd put in my application, they hired me in September."

Chris Hitt, who was at Whole Foods for 16 years and left as president in 2001, says, "Customers experience the food and the space, but what they really experience is the work culture. The true hidden secret of the company is the work culture. That's what delivers the stores to the customers."

Wendy Steinberg has worked at Whole Foods since 1992 (her husband works at Whole Foods, too), and she is now one of the associate team leaders at Columbus Circle. She has a story from her first year at the company, when she was working in a store in Providence, Rhode Island:

> *I was on break, in the break room. I hadn't been a team member more than six months, and there was this guy in the break room. He was sitting there, with his hands crossed, with this big 1970s style Afro, just checking things out. We talked. He asked me a lot of questions. I had no idea who he was. I figured he was just another team member. Finally, she says "I was like, who are you, anyway?" He answers "John Mackey."*

Market/Cultural Shifts Mackey says he thinks Whole Foods benefits from the fact that the American culture, and especially the food culture, is shifting profoundly. The old idea was A&P and Shop Rite. The milk always in one place and the meat in another; the Muzak and fluorescent lights and wheels rolling over linoleum producing a supermarket trance that was exactly the same in Connecticut as in California. The old idea was Mom going to the store once a week and rarely reading labels. The old idea was male grocery executives and store managers and a clientele that was almost exclusively women.

In Mackey's view, consumer evolution requires a change in the look and feel of grocery stores. It obliges retailers to understand that a sizable portion of consumers (up to 65 percent) are willing to pay more for organic food. It demands a new kind of empathy for an American family that has changed its eating habits (cooking less, shopping more often, and buying more prepared foods) and its makeup (more single parents, fewer children). A large number of women hold executive positions within Whole Foods, Mackey points out, and store designs depend greatly on women's preferences. "We have a lot more feminine energy here," he says.

Whole Foods has also been helped by the entrepreneurs who have been driving the organic and natural-foods movement for the past three decades. The company has incorporated ideas and employees from the chains it has bought—Bread & Circus and Fresh Fields in the Northeast, Mrs. Gooch's in the West, Wellspring in North Carolina—even as many of its vendors have followed the same path from fringe to hip to the edge of mainstream. There seems to be some agreement among Mackey and businessmen like Steve Demos, the president of White Wave, which makes Silk soy milk. They contend that the battles for consumer attention (good tastes, recognizable brands), as well as the fight for agricultural validation (sustainable farming, no antibiotics), have largely been won. It's the push to get their ideas about socially responsible business into the mainstream that is just beginning. Demos says: "Wall Street —that's where the fun begins. They only measure one thing, the bottom line. My goal is to demonstrate that the principle-based business model is more profitable than its counterpart, and when we do, Wall Street will chase us instead of the other way around."

Mackey, of course, is just as fervent a capitalist—or neocapitalist, as he calls himself, since he characterizes his early political views as socialist and says his commitment to free markets came late in life. He simply maintains that there is no conflict between an aggressively capitalistic enterprise and a socially responsible enterprise like Whole Foods Market. He is steadfast that his company will never compromise with Wall Street on its values—the 5 percent of profits given every year to charity, the installation of solar panels on the tops of some stores, the payment to employees for their community service. At the same time, Mackey says the company won't compromise its intentions to make as much money as possible along the way. Mackey comments: "One of the things that's held back natural foods for a long time is that most of the other people in this business never really embraced capitalism the way I did."

It irks Mackey that some of his oldest customers don't accept that the road to profitability runs directly into the mainstream. He comments: "I don't know how many letters we get from people who resent that. 'You've sold out,' they say, or 'Don't forget about the little people who supported you when you were nothing.'" He adds: "It's interesting that when an idea that began on the fringe hits the mainstream, it's no longer hip and cool, even if it preserves its integrity and values. America has a love affair with small businesses. But when they get to be big, they're no longer good, they must be evil." Mackey's commitment, along with the team members at Whole Foods Market, to multiple stakeholders is suggested in the firm's formal statement of its "Declaration of Interdependence."

Declaration of Interdependence With the support and leadership of Mackey, the Declaration of Interdependence was created originally in 1985 by 60 team members who volunteered their time. This was five years after Mackey founded the firm. It was updated in 1988, 1992, and 1997, and the 1997 version remains in effect. We present excerpts of that declaration here:

Our motto—Whole Foods, Whole People, Whole Planet—emphasizes that our vision reaches far beyond just being a food retailer. Our success in fulfilling our vision is measured by customer satisfaction, team member excellence and happiness, return on capital investment, improvement in the state of the environment, and local and larger community support. Our ability to instill a clear sense of interdependence among our various stakeholders (the people who are interested and benefit from the success of our company) is contingent upon our efforts to communicate more often, more openly, and more compassionately. Better communication equals better understanding and more trust.

Natural and Organic Products. We appreciate and celebrate that great food and cooking improve the lives of all of our stakeholders. Breaking bread with others, eating healthfully and eating well—these are some of the great joys of our lives.

Our goal is to sell the highest quality products that also offer high value for our customers. High value is a product of high quality at a competitive price. Our product quality goals focus on ingredients, freshness, taste, nutritive value, safety and/or appearance. While we have very high standards for product quality, we believe that it is important to be inclusive and open minded, and not overly restrictive or dogmatic.

Customers. Our customers are the most important stakeholder in our business. Therefore, we go to extraordinary lengths to satisfy and delight our customers. We want to meet or exceed their expectations on every shopping trip. We know that by doing so we turn customers into advocates for whole foods. We guarantee our customers 100% product satisfaction or their money will be refunded.

Outstanding customer service is a result of both our team members' competencies and enthusiasm in serving our customers and their in-depth knowledge and excitement about the products we sell. We nurture a quality business relationship with our customers by daily demonstrating our customer service beliefs:

- Customers are the lifeblood of our business and we are interdependent on each other.
- Customers are the primary motivation for our work—they are not an interruption of our work.
- Customers are people who bring us their wants and desires and our primary objective is to satisfy them as best we can—they are *not* people to argue or match wits with.
- Customers are fellow human beings with feelings and emotions like our own; they are equals to be treated with courtesy and respect at all times.

We continually experiment and innovate in order to raise our retail standards. We create store environments that are inviting, fun, unique, informal, comfortable, attractive, nurturing, and educational. We want our stores to become community meeting places where our customers come to join their friends and to make new ones. Our stores are "inclusive." Everyone is welcome, regardless of race, gender, sexual orientation, age, beliefs, or personal appearance. We value diversity—whole foods are for everyone.

Team Members. Our success is also dependent upon the collective energy and intelligence of all our team members. In addition to receiving fair wages and benefits, belief in the value of our work and finding fulfillment from our jobs is a key reason we are part of Whole Foods Market. Therefore, we design and promote safe work environments where motivated team members can flourish and reach their highest potential. And no matter how long a person has worked or plans to work with us, each and every team member is a valued contributor. There are many team members in our company who "work behind the scenes" to produce product, distribute product and generally support our retail team members and customers. Although they are not as visible as our retail team members, they are integral to the success of our business. Achieving unity of vision about the future of our company, and building trust between team members is a goal of Whole Foods Market. At the same time, diversity and individual differences are recognized and honored. We aim to cultivate a strong sense of community and dedication to the company. We also realize how important leisure time, family, and community involvement outside of work are for a rich, meaningful and balanced life. We must remember that we are not "Whole Life Market."

We strive to build positive and healthy relationships among team members. "Us versus them" thinking has no place in our company. We believe that the best way to do this is to encourage participation and involvement at all levels of our business. Some of the ways we do this are:

- Self-Directed Teams that meet regularly to discuss issues, solve problems and appreciate each other's contributions.
- Increased communication through Team Member forums and Advisory Groups, and open book, open door, and open people practices.
- Labor gainsharing and other Team Member incentive programs.
- Team Member Stock Options and Stock Purchase Plan.
- Commitment to make our jobs more fun by combining work and play and through friendly competition to improve our stores.
- Continuous learning opportunities about company values, food, nutrition and job skills.
- Equal opportunity for employment, with promotion mostly from within the company.

Profits and Growth. We earn profits every day through voluntary exchange with our customers. We know that profits are essential to create capital for growth, job security and overall financial success. Profits are the "savings" every business needs in order to change and evolve to meet the future. They are the "seed corn" for next year's crop. We are the stewards of our shareholder's investments and we are committed to increasing long-term shareholder value.

As a publicly traded company, Whole Foods Market intends to grow. We will grow at such a pace that our quality of work environment, team member productivity and excellence, customer satisfaction, and financial health continue to prosper.

There is a community of self interest among all of our stakeholders. We share together in our collective vision for the company. To that end, we have a salary cap that limits the maximum cash compensation (wages plus profit incentive bonuses) paid to any team member in the calendar year to 14 times the company-wide annual average salary of all full-time team members.

Our Communities. Our business is intimately tied to the neighborhood and larger community that we serve and in which we live. The unique character of our stores is a direct reflection of the customers who shop with us. Without their support, both financial and philosophical, Whole Foods Market would not be in business. Our interdependence at times goes beyond our mutual interest in quality food, and where appropriate, we will respond.

- We donate 5% of our after-tax profits to not-for-profit organizations.
- We have a program that financially supports team members for doing voluntary community service.

Environmental Stewardship. We see the necessity of active environmental stewardship so that the earth continues to flourish for generations to come. We seek to balance our needs with the needs of the rest of the planet through the following actions:

- Supporting sustainable agriculture. We are committed to greater production of organically and biodynamically grown foods in order to reduce pesticide use and promote soil conservation.
- Reducing waste and consumption of non-renewable resources. We promote and participate in recycling programs in our communities. We are committed to re-usable packaging, reduced packaging, and water and energy conservation.
- Encouraging environmentally sound cleaning and store maintenance programs.

Balance and Integration. Satisfying all of our stakeholders and achieving our standards is our goal. One of the most important responsibilities of Whole Foods Market's leadership is to make sure the interests, desires and needs of our various stakeholders are kept in balance. We recognize that this is a dynamic process. It requires participation and communication by all of our stakeholders. It requires listening compassionately, thinking carefully and acting with integrity. Any conflicts must be mediated and win–win solutions found. Creating and nurturing this community of stakeholders is critical to the long-term success of our company.

Is Whole Foods Market's Declaration of Interdependence too good to be true? One indicator that it is more than a public relations statement is the recognition in 2007—the tenth year in a row—that its 50,000 team members have ranked their company as one of *Fortune* magazine's "100 Best Companies to Work For." Other indicators are the continuing and strong increases within store sales and the opening of new stores—a reflection of customer satisfaction. Sales increased to over $7 billion in 2007, including sales of approximately $1.2 billion due to the acquisition of Wild Oats Markets.

Mackey's View of Stakeholders Consistent with Whole Foods declaration of interdependence, Mackey has expressed his sense of obligation to multiple stakeholders and the special leadership challenges that go with this value in these words:

> *I think the hardest part of my job is the way Whole Foods Market views itself philosophically. We are a business dedicated to serving all of the various stakeholders of the company. And by stakeholders we mean customers, team members, stockholders, community, and the environment. Sometimes what is in the best interest of one stakeholder may not be in the best interest of another stakeholder and, as the CEO, I have to balance the various interests of the different constituencies and stakeholders to create win, win, win scenarios. That can sometimes be very difficult to do. Everybody wants something from the CEO.*

For more information on Whole Foods Market, visit the organization's home page at ***www.wholefoodsmarket.com.***

Questions

1. Using the Big Five personality dimensions (see Chapter 2), describe John Mackey's personality. How does his personality impact his running of Whole Foods?
2. What is motivating John Mackey?
3. Using the dimensions of authentic leadership (see Chapter 10), describe Mackey's leadership style.
4. What aspects of self-managed teams are illustrated in this case?
5. What are the cultural characteristics of Whole Foods?

Source: Adapted from Gertner, J. The virtue in 6 heirloom tomatoes. *New York Times*, June 6, 2004, 44–50; Lubove, S. Food porn. *Forbes*, February 14, 2005, 102–112; Fishman, C. The anarchist's cookbook. *Fast Company*, July 2004, 70–78; Mackey, J. I no longer want to work for money. *Fast Company*, February 2007, 112–113; Gray, S. Boss talk: John Mackey. *Wall Street Journal*, December 4, 2006, B1; John Mackey quotes. www.woopidoo.com/business_quotes (September 2007); About Whole Foods Market. www.wholefoodsmarket.com (September 2007).

The Road to Hell

John Baker, chief engineer of Caribbean Bauxite Company Limited of Barracania in the West Indies, was making his final preparations to leave the island. His promotion to production manager of Keso Mining Corporation near Winnipeg—one of Continental Ore's fast-expanding Canadian enterprises—had been announced a month before, and now everything had been attended to except the last vital interview with his successor, the able young Barracanian Matthew Rennalls. It was vital that his interview be a success and that Rennalls leave Baker's office uplifted and encouraged to face the challenge of his new job. A touch on the bell would have brought Rennalls walking into the room, but Baker delayed the moment and gazed thoughtfully through the window, considering just exactly what he was going to say and, more particularly, how he was going to say it.

Baker, an English expatriate, was 45 years old and had served his 23 years with Continental Ore in many different places: the Far East, several countries of Africa; Europe; and for the last two years, the West Indies. He had not cared much for his previous assignment in Hamburg and was delighted when the West Indian appointment came through. Climate was not the only attraction. Baker had always preferred working overseas in what were called the "developing countries" because he felt he had an innate knack—more than most other expatriates working for Continental Ore—of knowing just how to get on with regional staff. After only 24 hours in Barracania, however, he realized that he would need all of his innate knack if he were to deal effectively with the problems in this field that now awaited him.

Matthew Rennalls At Baker's first interview with Glenda Hutchins, the production manager, the whole problem of Rennalls and his future was discussed. Then and there, it was made quite clear to Baker that one of his important tasks would be the grooming of Rennalls as his successor. Hutchins had pointed out that not only was Rennalls one of the brightest Barracanian prospects on the staff of Caribbean Bauxite—at London University, he had taken first-class honors in the B.Sc. engineering degree—but, being the son of the minister of finance and economic planning, he also had political pull.

Caribbean Bauxite had been particularly pleased when Rennalls decided to work for it, rather than for the government in which his father had such a prominent post. The company ascribed his action to the effect of its vigorous and liberal regionalization program that, since World War II, had produced 18 Barracanians at the middle management level and had given Caribbean Bauxite a good lead in this respect over all other international concerns operating in Barracania. The success of this timely regionalization policy had led to excellent relations with the government—a relationship that gained added importance when Barracania, three years later, became independent, an occasion that encouraged a critical and challenging attitude toward the role foreign interests would play in the new Barracania. Hutchins, therefore, had little difficulty convincing Baker that the successful career development of Rennalls was of prime importance.

The interview with Hutchins was now two years in the past, and Baker, leaning back in his office chair, reviewed just how successful he had been in the grooming of Rennalls. What aspects of the latter's character had helped, and what had hindered? What about his own personality? How had that helped or hindered? The first item to go on the credit side, without question, would be the ability of Rennalls to master the technical aspects of his job. From the start, he had shown keenness and enthusiasm, and he had often impressed Baker with his ability in tackling new assignments and the constructive comments he invariably made in departmental discussions. He was popular with all ranks of Barracanian staff and had an ease of manner that stood him in good stead when dealing with his expatriate seniors.

Those were all assets, but what about the debit side? First and foremost was his racial consciousness. His four years at London University had accentuated this feeling and made him sensitive to any sign of condescension on the part of expatriates. Perhaps to give expression to this sentiment, as soon as he returned home from London, he threw himself into politics on behalf of the United Action Party, which was later to win the pre-independence elections and provide the country with its first prime minister.

The ambitions of Rennalls—and he certainly was ambitious—did not, however, lie in politics. Staunch nationalist that he was, he saw that he could serve himself and his country best—was not bauxite responsible for nearly half the value of Barracania's export trade?—by putting his engineering talent to the best use possible. On this account, Hutchins found that she had an unexpectedly easy task in persuading Rennalls to give up his political work before entering the production department as an assistant engineer.

It was, Baker knew, Rennalls' well-represented sense of racial consciousness that had prevented their relationship from being as close as it should have been. On the surface, they could not have seemed more agreeable. Formality between the two was minimal. Baker was delighted to find that his assistant shared his own peculiar "shaggy dog" sense of humor, so jokes were continually being exchanged. They entertained one another at their houses and often played tennis together—and yet the barrier remained invisible, indefinable, but ever present. The existence of this screen between them was a constant source of frustration to Baker, since it indicated a weakness that he was loath to accept. If successful with people of all other nationalities, why not with Rennalls?

At least he had managed to break through to Rennalls more successfully than had any other expatriate. In fact, it was the young Barracanian's attitude—sometimes overbearing, sometimes cynical—toward other company expatriates that had been one of the subjects Baker raised last year when he discussed Rennalls' staff report with him. Baker knew, too, that he would have to raise the same subject again in the forthcoming interview, because Martha Jackson, the senior person in charge of drafting, had complained only yesterday about the rudeness of Rennalls. With this thought in mind, Baker leaned forward and spoke into the intercom: "Would you come in, Matt, please? I'd like a word with you." Rennalls came in, and Baker held out a box and said "Do sit down. Have a cigarette."

Baker and Rennalls' Meeting Baker paused while he held out his lighter and then went on. "As you know, Matt, I'll be off to Canada in a few days' time, and before I go, I thought it would be useful if we could have a final chat together. It is indeed with some deference that I suggest I can be of help. You will shortly be sitting in this chair doing the job I am now doing, but I, on the other hand, I am ten years older, so perhaps you can accept the idea that I may be able to give you the benefit of my longer experience."

Baker saw Rennalls stiffen slightly in his chair as he made this point, so he added in explanation, "You and I have attended enough company courses to remember those repeated requests by the human resources manager to tell people how they are getting on as often as the convenient moment arises, and not just the automatic once a year when, by regulation, staff reports have to be discussed."

Rennalls nodded his agreement, so Baker went on, "I'll always remember the last job performance discussion I had with my previous boss back in Germany. She used what she called the 'plus and minus technique.' She firmly believed that when managers seek to improve the work performance of their staff by discussion, their prime objective should be to make sure the latter leave the interview encouraged and inspired to improve. Any criticism, therefore, must be constructive and helpful. She said that one very good way to encourage a person—and I fully agree with her—is to discuss good points, the plus factors, as well as weak ones, the minus factors. So I thought, Matt, it would be a good idea to run our discussion along these lines."

Rennalls offered no comment, so Baker continued, "Let me say, therefore, right away, that as far as your own work performance is concerned, the pluses far outweigh the minuses. I have, for instance, been most impressed with the way you have adapted your considerable theoretical knowledge to master the practical techniques of your job—that ingenious method you used to get air down to the fifth shaft level is a sufficient case in point. At departmental meetings, I have invariably found your comments well taken and helpful. In fact, you will be interested to know that only last week I reported to Ms. Hutchins that, from the technical point of view, she could not wish for a more able person to succeed to the position of chief engineer."

"That's very good indeed of you, John," cut in Rennalls with a smile of thanks. "My only worry now is how to live up to such a high recommendation."

"Of that I am quite sure," returned Baker, "especially if you can overcome the minus factor which I would like now to discuss with you. It is one that I have talked about before, so I'll come straight to the point. I have noticed that you are more friendly and get on better with your fellow Barracanians than you do with the Europeans. In point of fact, I had a complaint only yesterday from Ms. Jackson, who said you had been rude to her—and not for the first time, either.

"There is, Matt, I am sure, no need for me to tell you how necessary it will be for you to get on well with expatriates, because until the company has trained sufficient personnel of your caliber, Europeans are bound to occupy senior positions here in Barracania. All this is vital to your future interests, so can I help you in any way?"

While Baker was speaking of this theme, Rennalls sat tensed in his chair, and it was some seconds before he replied. "It is quite extraordinary, isn't it; how one can convey an impression to others so at variance with what one intends? I can only assure you once again that my disputes with Jackson—and you may remember also Godson—have had nothing at all to do with the color of their skins. I promise you that if a Barracanian had behaved in an equally peremptory manner, I would have reacted in precisely the same way. And again, if I may say it within these four walls, I am sure I am not the only one who has found Jackson and Godson difficult. I could mention the names of several expatriates who have felt the same. However, I am really sorry to have created this impression of not being able to get on with Europeans—it is an entirely false one—and I quite realize that I must do all I can to correct it as quickly as possible. On your last point, regarding Europeans holding senior positions in the company for some time to come, I quite accept the situation. I know that Caribbean Bauxite—as it has been doing for many years now—will promote Barracanians as soon as their experience warrants it. And, finally, I would like to assure you, John—and my father thinks the same, too—that I am very happy in my work here and hope to stay with the company for many years to come."

Rennalls had spoken earnestly, and Baker, although not convinced by what he had heard, did not think he could pursue the matter further except to say, "All right, Matt, my impression may be wrong, but I would like to remind you about the truth of that old saying 'What is important is not what is true, but what is believed.' Let it rest at that."

But suddenly Baker knew that he did not want to "let it rest at that." He was disappointed once again at not being able to break through to Rennalls and at having again had to listen to his bland denial that there was any racial prejudice in his makeup.

Baker, who had intended to end the interview at this point, decided to try another tack. "To return for a moment to the plus and minus technique I was telling you about just now, there is another plus factor I forgot to mention. I would like to congratulate you not only on the caliber of your work but also on the ability you have shown in overcoming a challenge that I, as a European, have never had to meet.

"Continental Ore is, as you know, a typical commercial enterprise—admittedly a big one—that is a product of the economic and social environment of the United States and Western Europe. My ancestors have all been brought up in this environment for the past two or three hundred years, and I have, therefore, been able to live in a world in which commerce (as we know it today) has been part and parcel of my being. It has not been something revolutionary and new that has suddenly entered my life. In your case," went on Baker, "the situation is different, because you and your forebears have only had some fifty and not two or three hundred years. Again, Matt, let me congratulate you—and people like you—on having so successfully overcome this particular hurdle. It is for this very reason that I think the outlook for Barracania—and particularly Caribbean Bauxite—is so bright."

Rennalls had listened intently, and when Baker finished, he replied, "Well, once again, John, I have to thank you for what you have said, and, for my part, I can only say that it is gratifying to know that my own personal effort has been so much appreciated. I hope that more people will soon come to think as you do."

There was a pause, and, for a moment, Baker thought hopefully that he was about to achieve his long-awaited breakthrough. But Rennalls merely smiled back. The barrier remained unbreached. There were some five minutes' cheerful conversation about the contrast between the Caribbean and Canadian climates and whether the West Indies had any hope of beating England in a soccer game before Baker drew the interview to a close. Although he was as far as ever from knowing the real Rennalls, he was nevertheless glad that the interview had run along in this friendly manner and, particularly, that it had ended on such a cheerful note.

Rennalls' Memo This feeling, however, lasted only until the following morning. Baker had some farewells to make, so he arrived at the office considerably later than usual. He had no sooner sat down at his desk than his secretary walked into the room with a worried frown on her face. Her words came fast. "When I arrived this morning, I found Mr. Rennalls already waiting at my door. He seemed very angry and told me that he had a vital letter to dictate that must be sent off without any delay. He was so worked up that he couldn't keep still and kept pacing about the room, which is most unlike him. He wouldn't even wait to read what he had dictated. Just signed the page where he thought the memo would end. It has been distributed, and your copy is in your tray."

Puzzled and feeling vaguely uneasy, Baker opened the envelope marked "confidential" and read the following memo:

FROM: Assistant Engineer
TO: Chief Engineer Caribbean Bauxite Limited
SUBJECT: Assessment of Interview between Messrs. Baker and Rennalls

It has always been my practice to respect the advice given to me by seniors, so after our interview, I decided to give careful thought once again to its main points and to make sure that I had understood all that had been said. As I promised you at the time, I had every intention of putting your advice to the best effect.

It was not, therefore, until I had sat down quietly in my home yesterday evening to consider the interview objectively that its main purpose became clear. Only then did the full enormity of what you said dawn on me. The more I thought about it, the more convinced I was that I had hit upon the real truth—and the more furious I became. With a facility in the English language which I—a poor Barracanian—cannot hope to match, you had the audacity to insult me (and through me every Barracanian worth his salt) by claiming that our knowledge of modern living is only a paltry fifty years old, while yours goes back two hundred to three hundred years. As if your materialistic commercial environment could possibly be compared with the spiritual values of our culture! I'll have you know that if much of what I saw in London is representative of your most boasted culture, I hope fervently that it will never come to Barracania. By what right do you have the effrontery to condescend to us? After all, you Europeans think us barbarians, or, as you say amongst yourselves, we are "just down from the trees."

Far into the night I discussed this matter with my father, and he is as disgusted as I. He agrees with me that any company whose senior staff think as you do is no place for any Barracanian proud of his culture and race. So much for all the company claptrap and specious propaganda about regionalization and Barracania for the Barracanians.

I feel ashamed and betrayed. Please accept this letter as my resignation, which I wish to become effective immediately.

cc: Production Manager
Managing Director

Questions

1. What were Baker's intentions in the conversation with Rennalls? Were they fulfilled or not, and why?
2. Was Baker alert to nonverbal signals? What did both Baker and Rennalls communicate to one another by nonverbal means?
3. How did Baker's view of himself affect the impression he formed of Rennalls?
4. What kind of interpersonal relationship had existed between Baker and Rennalls prior to the conversation described in the case? Was the conversation consistent or inconsistent with that relationship?
5. What, if anything, could Baker or Rennalls have done before, during, or after the conversation to improve the situation?
6. How would you characterize the personality attributes of Baker and Rennalls?
7. What perceptual errors and attributions (see Chapter 3) are evident?

Source: Prepared and adapted with permission from G. Evans, late of Shell International Petroleum Co. Ltd., London, for Shell-BP Petroleum Development Company of Nigeria, Limited.

A Novice Manager's Tale of Woe

"Now what do I do?" Tricia Monet, the store director at Personal Reflections, was sitting in her kitchen wondering what happened. "Once I was made store director things began so well. We all got along well together; in fact, we even met the store sales quota on more than one occasion. I don't know what happened. All of us got along, but once they knew I might leave, everyone was fighting. I hadn't decided to leave; I was just exploring the option of returning to college. Now Lori won't speak to me except when absolutely necessary. What am I going to do now? How can I get things to run smoothly again?"

Background Personal Reflections, a national chain of personal care and household products, had a store in a mall in Sioux City, Iowa. Tricia, who was 23, had recently moved to Sioux City with her fiancé who was transferred by his firm. Before looking for a job, Tricia did some soul searching and decided that she wanted to try something other than accounting for a career.

Tricia had completed a bachelor's degree in accounting a year before. After graduation, she worked in an accounting firm for just under a year. Tricia determined she liked interacting with people, but her accounting job kept her working primarily with numbers. She had originally been attracted to accounting because she liked the structure, organization, and "neatness" of accounting. Other than the accounting job, her work experience was limited to jobs to work her way through school. She had no supervisory or managerial experience.

Tricia was from a large, very close-knit family in an Illinois city near St. Louis, Missouri. The family enjoyed being together and spent as much time as they could with each other even though several members no longer lived in the immediate area. Tricia has both older and younger sisters and brothers.

Tricia saw an ad in the Sioux City newspaper in mid-June and applied for an assistant director position at the Personal Reflections store in the mall. Three weeks later, she interviewed with the district manager, was offered the job within two hours, and accepted the job two days later. A week later, Tricia attended a two-week training class in another city. The company seemed great, the benefits were good, the people were helpful, and Tricia believed the training taught her a lot. However, once the initial training was completed, Personal Reflections provided little additional information or support for their store directors.

Setup of the Store Most Personal Reflections stores in the district had one store director and two assistant directors. However, this district manager had hired a third assistant director in one of her other stores, and that store had seen marked improvements. Productivity and efficiency had increased by 20 percent, and the turnover for assistant store directors decreased by 33 percent. Because it was so successful in the other store, the district manager decided to try three assistant directors in the Sioux City store as well.

Throughout the year, the assistant store directors were scheduled in 9-hour shifts and on many days the shifts overlapped by several hours. On weekends and other busy days, the shifts for assistant store directors were 8:00 A.M. to 5:00 P.M., 10:00 A.M. to 7:00 P.M., and 1:00 P.M. to 10:00 P.M. Even with lunch and dinner breaks as well as scheduled meetings, there were periods when all three assistant directors were working at the same time. The assistant store directors' shifts varied; they did not always get the same shift time. The store director developed the work schedule for two weeks at a time. The store director's work schedule varied so that she was there during each shift several times each week.

Initially, the Sioux City store had a store director, Heather Munson, and two assistant directors, including Tricia. The district manager was still recruiting one more assistant director. All the other employees were part-timers. During the fall and winter holiday season, there were 30 or more part-time employees. During times other than the holiday season, there were generally 10 to 12 part-timers. While Personal Reflections considered current employees for promotion, in the Sioux City store no part-time employee was interested in becoming a full-time employee or being promoted. In the Sioux City store, only four of the part-time employees had worked at the store for two years or more. One employee had worked in the store seven years, while another employee had worked in the store for four years. Two employees had been with the Sioux City store for two years.

Personal Reflections ranked its stores based on sales. There were four levels. Level 1 stores had the largest sales volume; the Sioux City store was a level 3. The corporation ran contests periodically. There were monetary bonuses for the stores with the largest sales volume. The sales quotas during those contests were set so high that it was virtually impossible for the smaller stores to meet the quota and receive the bonus. The company believed that active competition between stores, directors, and district managers was good. Practically, what this meant was that only the largest stores, their directors, and district managers achieved the rewards. Separate contests were not held for the smaller stores. Following is an example of a company-wide contest. During December, if a store in the district made its weekly sales quota, then the district manager won a trip to Florida and the store manager won a computer. The assistant managers would receive a monetary gift of $1,000. However, the sales quotas were rarely ever achieved, and many districts included a combination of store levels, so smaller stores had a hard time keeping up with the larger volume stores.

Tricia's First Three Months Tricia's first day at the Sioux City store was August 1. It was company policy that once new assistant store directors were trained, they were assigned to a store without the store director being involved in the decision. Heather Munson resented being excluded from hiring decisions. Tricia and Munson clashed from the very beginning. Tricia felt like she was being interrogated whenever she interacted with Munson.

The store that Tricia was assigned to had consistently failed to meet its sales goals. In addition, the store seemed cluttered and messy. The back room, which was small, served as both break room and storeroom. Most of the merchandise was jammed into the store area. It was difficult for store employees to find merchandise on the store floor, and the customers had an even more difficult time finding what they wanted. When Tricia tried to organize the merchandise on the floor, Munson yelled at her for doing something Munson had not told her to do.

Within a week, the other assistant director gave her two-weeks' notice. Once she was gone, the relationship between Tricia and Munson became even more confrontational. After only a month, Tricia was ready to quit. She went home every day for a week thinking that there was no way on earth that she could work with *that woman*, Heather Munson. By September, Tricia was ready to give her notice. Before she could quit, Munson came to work and said she had back problems and would be going on disability leave.

As a result, Tricia was required to act as the store director with barely a month of experience. She was left alone to open and close the store and make all the bank deposits 7 days a week. Excited by the possibilities, she took up the challenge. Within a week or two things began to turn around and the store appeared neater and uncluttered. At the end of September, the district manager told Tricia that Munson would not be returning to her position of store director at Personal Reflections.

Throughout September, the district manager was recruiting and hiring assistant managers for the store. By October 1, she had hired three assistant managers. During the first two weeks of October, they were sent to the training session. By the middle of October, the Sioux City store had a complete complement of assistant store directors—Amy, Lori, and Tammy. Tricia was officially offered the store director position at the end of October. During the month of October, the three assistant store directors and Tricia seemed to get along well together.

When the announcement was made that Tricia was store director, the assistant store directors were excited for Tricia. In return, Tricia was excited about having assistant store directors to help run the store. Tricia thought to herself, "We have a team now and we can really turn the store around." Tricia said that she could not have imagined a better work environment. All four seemed to share many of the same ideas and goals and even went to dinner one night after work together. Tricia knew the holiday season rush was coming, and it was the busiest time of year. Since all the management staff was relatively new, she wondered how they would do. She knew the next months would be difficult.

The three assistant store directors had varying experiences. Lori had only a high school degree. However, she had prior experience in retail and had even been an assistant manager in a retail store. Amy had an associate's degree and had been an assistant manager before. Amy was from Sioux City, had never left her hometown, and did not plan to in the future. Tammy had a degree in social work and had a great deal of life experience. When she was in social work, she had even been in a supervisory position. She liked things to be very structured and did not like tasks that required creativity. All three were very interested in careers in retail. All three were highly motivated as it related to store goals and doing the best work they could, while Lori and Tammy were also competitive with each other.

Getting Ready for the Holiday Rush As November began, Tricia made judgments about the capabilities of the three new assistant store directors, Lori, Amy, and Tammy. Lori clearly had the highest motivation and drive for success. She wanted to achieve everything she could for herself. Tricia quickly made Lori her "right-hand person" and consulted her whenever there were problems. Lori found it easy to do all the paperwork and never made errors. Amy was the most amicable and perhaps the easiest of all to get along with. She did not have much self-confidence and was not at all assertive. She wanted everything to run smoothly and wanted everyone to like her. Amy rarely had any problems with the paperwork and the job responsibilities. Tammy was older than Lori and Amy and more resistant to learning and trying new things. Tammy was struggling with learning to do the forms and getting along in a new environment. Just before working at Personal Reflections, she had worked for six years in a different national retail chain where she had had little authority. As Tricia watched Tammy, she realized that Tammy made frequent mathematical errors on the paperwork she had to complete as part of her position, and sometimes the paperwork was not completed on time. Tammy did not seem to understand the importance of completing the forms efficiently or accurately. She did not understand that errors could mean the store could run out of popular merchandise and thus lose sales. Tricia tried to explain this to Tammy, who said she understood but still made errors on the paperwork.

The district manager made it clear that the individual pay structure at Personal Reflections was strictly confidential. Even Tricia as the store director did not know the salaries of the assistant store directors. However, they all felt that they had a good idea about what the others were making, based on comments each of them had made. In a conversation the second week of November, Tammy told Tricia what she was making and that it was more than either Lori or Amy. Tammy, Lori, and Amy had all told each other what they were earning. Tammy was earning \$2,000 more than Lori and \$4,000 more than Amy. Tricia realized that she herself made only $2,000 more per year than Tammy. She didn't feel that it was fair—after all, she was in charge of the store and was responsible for the bank deposits and stock orders. In addition, Tricia felt that Tammy was the weakest of the three assistant store directors.

Tricia's strategy as store director was to create an atmosphere where they were all equals. Tricia always valued their input and comments and used them whenever possible. She set challenging goals for Lori, laughed with Amy, and held Tammy's hand. Tricia believed she had established a congenial work environment while actively working to change the image of the store. She met daily with each assistant store director and weekly with all three. She solicited ideas about how to improve the performance of the store. There were no evident interpersonal conflicts between any of the employees.

Tricia valued the assistant store directors' input. Tricia offered an example. "At the beginning, there was a problem with the props for the window display. We were having difficulty fitting it into smaller window space and were at a loss. Lori and I had put the unit together, and we were very proud of ourselves. Tammy brought it to our attention that it wasn't going to fit, and Amy noticed that the cord would not reach the outlet." In complete shock, Lori and Tricia did not want to see their hard work go to waste. Tricia stepped back and wondered how they were going to work together to solve this issue. Lori was getting very defensive about Tammy's view of the project and time was running out. So Tricia said, "Tammy, Lori—let's improvise. You two work together to cut-and-paste the display so that it fits in the area. Amy, let's find an extension cord and an alternate route to the plug end." By the end of the night, they had worked together to accomplish the task.

Tricia's Leadership and Goals Before Tricia became store director, the Sioux City store was messy and disorganized. The store floor was cluttered and the back room was a maze. There was no room to receive shipments. With a back room the size of a large walk-in closet and a loft above the bathroom, no one could ever locate what they needed. Tricia had again involved the assistant store directors in the process.

"The store had a problem with running neatly. The back room was not organized at all and no one cared. I had condensed and straightened the back room so that everyone could see what we had. However, the problem was not organizing it, but keeping it that way. Therefore, I assigned each assistant manager to a section of the back room. Each was to label the products, put like items together, and maintain her area. I even had bins brought in to better organize the areas for the back room." Tricia would inspect the back room weekly and determine what needed to be addressed and who was accomplishing this task. By the end, everyone knew each other's section and maintenance was no longer an issue. Tricia also knew the organizing plan had been successful because of the feedback from the part-time employees. The appearance of the sales floor and the back room amazed the four employees who had been at the store the longest. Tricia gained confidence in her abilities. She was proud of the success the store was attaining.

Tricia began running daily contests for things such as highest sales for the day, most creative product display, and most helpful associate. Only the part-time employees were eligible for the contests. She involved the assistant store directors in developing and administering the contests. Tricia and her team developed a Fishbowl contest, which was whenever any of the part-time sales associates did a certain type of demonstration on a customer, they were allowed to draw a fish on the poster shaped like a fishbowl. Whoever had the most fish in the bowl at the end of the day received some sort of small prize such as a free pretzel from the local pretzel store or a trial size of the store's product to take home. Another type of contest was called the Zone. The store was zoned into five sections, where part-timers were variously assigned. Whenever a part-timer approached a customer and demonstrated a product on her, and the customer bought a product within that zone, the employee's name was written down and put into a hat. At the end of the day, a member of management would draw a name and a small prize would be awarded.

Tricia also was allowed to have special employee parties. She could open the store early and "the employees could shop at ease. At these events, we would always award door prizes, give special discounts, and sometimes have snacks and beverages for the associates to enjoy. One time right before the holidays, we opened at 7:00 A.M. for our employees and had a morning buffet. We bought donuts, bagels, fruit, and beverages for this event, and all employees were given an additional 15 percent off their regular discount."

While enjoying the challenge, Tricia wanted to go back to college. She commented to her district manager that she was interested in going back to get her MBA. Immediately before Thanksgiving, Tricia had a management meeting to talk about the upcoming holiday season in the store. At the end of the meeting, Tricia told the assistant store directors that she was thinking of going back to school in January but had not made her decision yet. She was surprised that they seemed sad and disgruntled by her statement. Amy and Tammy both said that they did not want Tricia to leave. Lori said that if she were Tricia, she would not make the decision to leave, but that Tricia should do what was best for her.

Once the three knew what Tricia was considering, the collegial team atmosphere disappeared. Lori started ordering Tammy around and Tammy was ready to quit. Tricia met with each of them about the problem and told them to work it out between the two of them. Soon after, they appeared to be getting along better than before. When Tammy became upset about the benefits program, Tricia directed her to call the company's benefits coordinator.

These events occurred as they entered the holiday season, which was the busiest time of the year. The average non-holiday volume of shipments received was from 50 to 100 boxes over six days. During the holiday season, the store received 100 to 150 boxes over six days. The store's sales increased from approximately $20,000 a week to $60,000 a week. The week before the holiday, the store's sales were $130,000!

After the Announcement During the first weekly meeting in December, the tone of the meeting changed. Before the meeting, Lori and Amy had met to decide what to say. They chose to tell Tricia about all the things they did not like about her work. One example was that she would not always take lunch and would then leave "early." Tricia reasoned that, as a salaried employee, she was not required to take a lunch so when she put in her hours, she could leave. In addition, if she had to work late one day to cover for employees, then the next day she would leave early. Tricia knew she was one level above them in the hierarchy and therefore had more privileges. The assistant store directors did not think that was fair. Tricia's frequent statements about all of them being equals encouraged the women to feel justified in watching Tricia's activities and recording whenever she did things differently than they did.

Tricia's feelings were hurt and she reacted defensively. She said, "I would never have watched my boss and confronted her about her quitting times, and, since I am your boss, you don't supervise me—I supervise you." Tricia reminded the three women of the hierarchical system at Personal Reflections. She reminded them that directions flowed downward, not upward. By the time the meeting ended, everyone left with feelings of animosity and resentment.

Two days after the meeting, Tricia found out that Tammy had gone over Tricia's head and contacted the district manager about the store director position. This particularly upset Tricia because she had been very sensitive to Tammy's needs and protective of her in the work environment. Tricia admitted to herself that she was furious. Amy had told Tricia of Tammy's actions, and also that Lori and Tammy were already plotting to get Tricia's position since she was considering leaving. Amy also told her that Tammy asked for Amy's help in getting the store director position whether or not Tricia left in January. Amy said she refused because she would not betray Tricia.

Throughout November and December, the district manager was silent. She did not interact with Tricia at all. However, she did not encourage Lori and Tammy to talk directly to her. She spoke with Tammy, who had called her complaining about Tricia. Tammy also lobbied for the district manager to give her the store director position when Tricia left. The district manager never personally notified Tricia of the conversation. Nor did the district manager come to the store or try to help the individuals resolve their differences.

Each of the assistant store directors reacted differently to Tricia after she told them of her thoughts about returning to school. Lori and Tricia went from allies to enemies. In one instance, Tricia had spent two days developing the work schedule. It took two days because of the 25 temporary, part-time employees hired for the holiday season as well as the company forms that needed to be completed to ensure optimum coverage. The company forms frequently necessitated revisions to the work schedule. The day after completing the schedule, Tricia had a day off. Lori rewrote part of the schedule because a part-timer wanted a change in her schedule. Lori made the change and never told Tricia. The next day Tricia did not recheck the schedule because it was completed. On the day in question, they were one employee short. The employee was scheduled to be a front greeter, which was a very important position. Tricia questioned all the assistant managers and finally Lori admitted to changing it. Tricia reprimanded Lori and explained to her that other forms were consulted before changes to the schedule could be done and she needed to be kept informed. Animosity between the two heightened.

By this time, Tricia was no longer trying to interact with Lori and Tammy except for necessary work issues. She became authoritative in all her dealings with the two. However, she gave Amy additional responsibilities and, in effect, trained Amy to be store director. Tricia even went to the extreme of ensuring that her shift in the store overlapped with Lori's as little as possible. Lori spoke to Tricia only when absolutely necessary. Generally, Lori completely ignored Tricia and acted as if she were not even present.

At home, Tricia started asking herself questions. "What had happened to the team? Where do I go from here? How do I get things back on track at the store? What do I do about all this conflict? I don't want to leave the store with things in such a mess. I want to resolve the conflict."

Questions

1. Using organizational behavior modification, include a plan to change Tammy's behavior concerning paperwork.

2. Using equity theory (see Chapter 5), discuss the equity comparisons made by Tricia, Lori, and Tammy.
3. How does Tricia's attitude toward the situation, her coworkers, and herself influence her motivation? Use expectancy theory (see Chapter 5) to determine what relationship would be most affected (effort-to-performance, performance-to-outcome, or reward valence).
4. Using the five different styles of reacting to conflict—avoiding, forcing, accommodating, collaborating, and compromising (see Chapter 12)—analyze the behavior of Tricia, Lori, Tammy, and Amy.
5. Were any team dysfunctions evident in this case? Explain.

Source: This case was prepared by Sally Dresdow, Joy Benson, and Sheila Herbert, *A Novice Manager's Tale of Woe*. Case appeared in John Venable (ed.), *Annual Advances in Business Cases—2001*, 156–163. Published by Society for Case Research. This case is intended to be used as a basis for class discussion. The views presented here are those of the case authors and do not necessarily reflect the views of the Society for Case Research. The names of the organization, individuals, location, and financial information have been disguised to preserve anonymity. Edited for *Organizational Behavior*, 12th edition, and used with permission.

Bob Knowlton

Bob Knowlton was sitting alone in the conference room of the laboratory. The rest of the group had gone. One of the secretaries had stopped and talked for a while about her husband's coming induction in the Army, and had finally left. Knowlton, alone in the laboratory, slid a little farther down in his chair, looking with satisfaction at the results of the first test run of the new photon unit.

He liked to stay after the others had gone. His appointment as project head was still new enough to give him a deep sense of pleasure. His eyes were on the graphs before him, but in his mind he could hear Dr. Jerrold, the head of the laboratory, saying again. "There's one thing about this place that you can bank on. The sky is the limit for a person who can produce." Knowlton felt again the tingle of happiness and embarrassment. Well, dammit, he said to himself, he had produced. He had come to Simmons Laboratories two years ago. During a routine testing of some rejected Clanson components he had stumbled on the idea of the photon correlator, and the rest just happened. Jerrold had been enthusiastic; a separate project had been set up for further research and development of the device, and he had gotten the job of running it. The whole sequence of events still seemed a little miraculous to Knowlton.

He had shrugged off his reverie and bent determinedly over the sheets when he heard someone come into the room behind him. He looked up expectantly. Jerrold often stayed late himself, and now and then dropped in for a chat. This always made his day's end especially pleasant. But it wasn't Jerrold. The man who had come in was a stranger. He was tall, thin, and rather dark. He wore steel-rimmed glasses and had on a very wide leather belt with a large brass buckle. The stranger smiled and introduced himself. "I'm Simon Fester. Are you Bob Knowlton?" Bob said "yes," and they shook hands. "Doctor Jerrold said I might find you in. We were talking about your work, and I'm very much interested in what you're doing." Knowlton waved him to a chair. Fester didn't seem to belong in any of the standard categories of visitors: customers, visiting fireman, shareholder. Bob pointed to the sheets on the table. "These are the preliminary results of a test we're running. We've got a new gadget by the tail and we're trying to understand it. It's not finished, but I can show you the section that we're testing." He stood up, but Fester was deeply engrossed in the graphs. After a moment he looked up with an odd grin. "These look like plots of a Jennings surface. I've been playing around with some autocorrelation functions of surfaces—you know that stuff." Knowlton, who had no idea what Fester was referring to, grinned back and nodded, and immediately felt uncomfortable. "Let me show you the monster," he said, and led the way to the workroom.

After Fester left, Knowlton slowly put the graphs away, feeling vaguely annoyed. Then, as if he had made a decision, he quickly locked up and took the long way out so that he would pass Jerrold's office. But the office was locked. Knowlton wondered whether Jerrold and Fester had left together.

The next morning Knowlton dropped into Jerrold's office, mentioned that he had talked with Fester, and asked who he was.

"Sit down for a minute," Jerrold said. "I want to talk to you about him. What do you think of him?" Knowlton replied truthfully that he thought Fester was very bright and probably very competent. Jerrold looked pleased.

"We're taking him on," he said. "He has a very good background at a number of laboratories, and he seems to have ideas about the problems we're tackling here." Knowlton nodded in agreement, instantly wishing that Fester not be placed with him.

"I don't know yet where he will finally land," Jerrold continued, "but he seems interested in what you're doing. I thought he might spend a little time with you by way of getting started." Knowlton nodded thoughtfully. "If his interest in your work continues, you can add him to your group.

"Well, he seemed to have some good ideas even without knowing exactly what we are doing." Knowlton answered. "I hope he stays; I'd be glad to have him."

Knowlton walked back to the lab with mixed feelings. He told himself that Fester would be good for the group. He was no dunce; he'd produce. Knowlton thought again of Jerrold's promise when he had promoted him: "The person who produces gets ahead in this outfit." The words now seemed to him to carry the overtones of a threat.

The next day, Fester didn't appear until mid-afternoon. He explained that he had had a long lunch with Jerrold, discussing his place in the lab. "Yes," said Knowlton, "I talked with him yesterday morning about it, and we both thought you might work with my group for a while.

Fester smiled in the same knowing way that he had smiled when he mentioned the Jennings surfaces. "I'd like to," he said.

Knowlton introduced Fester to the other members of the lab. Fester and John Link, the mathematician of the group, hit it off well together. They spent the rest of the afternoon discussing a method of analysis of patterns that Link had been worrying over for the last month.

It was 6:30 when Knowlton finally left the lab that night. He had waited almost eagerly for the end of the day to come—when all the lab personnel would all be gone and he could sit in the quiet room, relax, and think it over. Think what over? He asked himself. He didn't know. Shortly after 5:00 they had all gone except Fester, and what followed was almost a duel. Knowlton was annoyed that he was being cheated out of his quiet period, and finally resentful, determined that Fester should leave first.

Fester was sitting at the conference table reading, and Knowlton was sitting at his desk in the little glass-enclosed office that he used during the day when he needed to be undisturbed. Fester had gotten last year's progress reports out and was studying them carefully. Time dragged. Knowlton doodled on a pad, the tension growing inside him. What the hell did Fester think he was going to find in the reports?

Knowlton finally gave up, and they left the lab together. Fester took several of the reports with him to study that evening. Knowlton asked him if he thought the reports gave a clear picture of the lab's activities.

"They're excellent," Fester answered with obvious sincerity. "They're not only good reports; what they report is damn good too!" Knowlton was surprised at the relief he felt, and grew almost jovial as he said good-night.

Driving home, Knowlton felt more optimistic about Fester's presence in the lab. He had never fully understood the analysis that Link was attempting. If there was anything wrong with Link's approach, Fester would probably spot it.

And if I'm any judge, he thought, he won't be especially diplomatic about it.

He described Fester to his wife, Lucy, who was amused by the broad leather belt and the brass buckle.

"It's the kind of belt the Pilgrims must have worn," she laughed.

"I'm not worried about how he holds his pants up," Knowlton laughed with her. "I'm afraid that he's the kind that just has to make like a genius twice each day. And that can be pretty rough on the group."

Knowlton had been asleep for several hours when he was jarred awake by the telephone. He realized it had rung several times. He swung off the bed, muttering about damn fools and telephones. It was Fester. Without any excuses, apparently oblivious of the time, he plunged into an excited recital of how Link's patterning problem could be solved.

Knowlton covered the mouthpiece to answer his wife's stage whisper, "Who is it?" "It's the genius."

Fester, completely ignoring the fact that it was 2:00 in the morning, proceeded excitedly to explain a completely new approach to certain of the photon lab problems that he had stumbled onto while analyzing some past experiments. Knowlton managed to put some enthusiasm in his own voice and stood there, still half-dazed and very uncomfortable, listening to Fester talk endlessly, it seemed, about what he had discovered. He said that he not only had a new approach but also an analysis that showed how inherently weak the previous experiment was. He finally concluded by saying that further experimentation along that earlier line certainly would have been inconclusive.

The following morning, Knowlton spent the entire morning with Fester and Link, the usual morning group meeting having been called off so that Fester's work of the previous night could be gone over intensively. Fester was very anxious that this be done, and Knowlton wasn't too unhappy to call the meeting off for reasons of his own.

For the next several days, Fester sat in the back office that had been turned over to him and did nothing but read the progress reports of the work that had been done in the last six months. Knowlton caught himself feeling apprehensive about the reaction that Fester might have to some of his work. He was a little surprised at his own feelings. He had always been proud—although he had put on a convincingly modest face—of the way his team had broken new ground in the study of photon measuring devices. Now he wasn't sure. It seemed to him that Fester might easily show that the line of research they had been following was unsound or even unimaginative.

The next morning, as was customary, the members of Knowlton's group, including the secretaries, sat around the table in the conference room for a group meeting. He had always prided himself on the fact that the team as a whole guided and evaluated its work. He would point out that, often what started out as a boring recital of fundamental assumptions to a naïve listener uncovered new ways of regarding these assumptions that wouldn't have occurred to the lab member who had long ago accepted them as a necessary basis for the research he was doing. These group meetings also served another purpose. He admitted to himself that he would have felt far less secure if he had had to direct the work completely on his own. Team meetings, as a principle of leadership, justified the exploration of blind alleys because of the general educative effect of the team. Fester and Link were there, as were Lucy Martin and Martha Ybarra. Link sat next to Fester, the two of them continuing their conversation concerning Link's mathematical study from yesterday. The other group members, Bob Davenport, George Thurlow, and Arthur Oliver, sat there waiting quietly.

Knowlton, for reasons that he didn't quite understand, brought up a problem that all of them had previously spent a great deal of time discussing. The team had come to an implicit conclusion that a solution was impossible and that there was no feasible way of treating it experimentally. Davenport remarked that there was hardly any use of going over it again. He was satisfied that there was no way of approaching the problem with the equipment and the physical capacities of the lab.

This statement had the effect of a shot of adrenaline on Fester. He said he would like to know in detail what the problem was. Fester walked to the whiteboard and began to discuss the problem with the others and simultaneously list the reasons why it had been abandoned. Very early in the description of the problem it became evident that Fester was going to disagree about the impossibility of solving it. The group realized this and finally the descriptive materials and their recounting of the reasoning that had led to its abandonment dwindled away. Fester began his analysis, which as it proceeded might have well been prepared the previous night although Knowlton knew that to be impossible. He couldn't help being impressed with the organized and logical way that Fester was presenting ideas that must have occurred to him only a few minutes before.

However, Fester said some things that left Knowlton with a mixture of annoyance, irritation, and, at the same time, a rather smug feeling of superiority in at least one area. Fester was of the opinion that the way that the problem had been analyzed was typical of what happened when such thinking was attempted by a team, and with an air of sophistication that made it difficult for a listener to dissent, he proceeded to make general comments on the American emphasis on team ideas, satirically describing the ways in which they led to a "high level of mediocrity."

Knowlton observed that Link stared studiously at the floor and was conscious of George Thurlow's and Bob Davenport's glances at him at several points during Fester's little speech. Inwardly, Knowlton couldn't help feeling that this was one point at least in which Fester was off on the wrong foot. The whole lab, following Dr. Jerrold's lead, talked, if not actually practiced, the theory of small research teams as the basic organization for effective research. Fester insisted that the problem could be solved and that he would like to study it for a while himself.

Knowlton ended the session by remarking that the meetings would continue and that the very fact that a supposedly insoluble experimental problem was now going to get another look was yet another indication of the value of such meetings. Fester immediately remarked that he was not at all averse to meetings for the purpose of informing the group of the progress of its members. He went on to say that the point he wanted to make was that creative advances were seldom accomplished in such meetings, that they were made by the individual "living with" the problem closely and continuously, forming a sort of personal relationship with it. Knowlton responded by saying that he was glad Fester had raised these points and that he was sure the team would profit by reexamining the basis on which they had been operating. Knowlton agreed that individual effort was probably the basis for making major advances but that he considered the group meetings useful primarily because of the effect they had on keeping the team together and on helping the weaker members of the team keep up with the advances of the ones who were able to move more easily and quickly when analyzing problems.

As days went by and the meetings continued, Fester came to enjoy them because of the direction the meetings soon took. Typically, Fester would hold forth on some subject, and it became clear that he was, without question, more brilliant and better prepared on the topics germane to the problems being studied. He probably was more capable of going ahead on his own than anyone there, and Knowlton grew increasingly disturbed as he realized that his leadership of the team had been, in fact, taken over. In Knowlton's occasional meetings with Dr. Jerrold, whenever Fester was mentioned, he would comment only on Fester's ability and obvious capacity for work, somehow never quite feeling that he could mention his own discomforts. He felt that they revealed a weakness on his own part. Moreover, Dr. Jerrold was greatly impressed with Fester's work and with the contacts he had with Fester outside the photon laboratory.

Knowlton began to feel that the intellectual advantages that Fester had brought to the team might not quite compensate for evidences of a breakdown in the cooperative spirit that had been evident in the group before Fester's coming. More and more of the morning meetings were skipped. Fester's opinion concerning the abilities of others of the team, with the exception of Link's, was obviously low. At times during morning meetings or in smaller discussions, he had been rude, refusing at certain times to pursue an argument when he claimed that it was based on the other person's ignorance of the facts involved. His impatience with the others also led him to make remarks of this kind to Dr. Jerrold. This Knowlton inferred from a conversation he had had with Jerrold. The head of the lab had asked whether Davenport and Oliver were going to be retained, but he hadn't mentioned Link. This conversation led Knowlton to believe that Fester had had private conversations with Jerrold.

Knowlton had little difficulty making a convincing case regarding whether Fester's brilliance actually was sufficient recompense for the beginning of his team's breaking up. He spoke privately with Davenport and Oliver. Both clearly were uncomfortable with Fester's presence. Knowlton didn't press the discussion beyond hearing them in one way or another say that they sometimes felt awkward around Fester. They said that sometimes they had difficulty understanding the arguments he advanced. In fact, they often felt too embarrassed to ask Fester to state the grounds on which he based such arguments. Knowlton didn't talk to Link in this manner.

About six months after Fester's coming to the photon lab, meetings were scheduled at which the sponsors of much of the ongoing research were going to be briefed on progress. At special meetings, project heads customarily presented the research being conducted by their groups. The other members of the laboratory groups were invited to other, more general meetings later in the day and open to all. The special meetings usually were restricted to project heads, the head of the laboratory, and the sponsors. As the time for his special meeting approached, Knowlton felt that he must avoid the presentation at all costs. He felt that he couldn't present the ideas that Fester had advanced—and on which some work had been done—in sufficient detail and answer questions about them. However, he didn't feel that he could ignore these newer lines of work and present only the work that had been started or completed before Fester's arrival (which he felt perfectly competent to do). It seemed clear that keeping Fester from attending the meeting wouldn't be easy in spite of the fact that he wasn't on the administrative level that had been invited. Knowlton also felt that it wouldn't be beyond Fester, in his blunt and undiplomatic way, if he was present at the meeting, to comment on Knowlton's presentation and reveal the inadequacy that he felt.

Knowlton found an opportunity to speak to Jerrold and raised the question. He remarked to Jerrold that, of course, with the interest in the work and Fester's contributions he probably would like to come to these meetings. Knowlton said that he was concerned about the feelings of the others in the group if Fester were invited. Jerrold brushed this concern aside by saying that he felt the group would understand Fester's rather different position. He thought that, by all means, Fester should be invited. Knowlton then immediately said that he had thought so too and further that Fester should make the presentation because much of it was work that he had done. As Knowlton put it, this would be a nice way to recognize Fester's contributions and to reward him because he was eager to be recognized as a productive member of the lab. Jerrold agreed, and so the matter was decided.

Fester's presentation was very successful and, in some ways, dominated the meeting. He held the interest and attention of those attending, and following his presentation the questions persisted for along period. Later that evening at the banquet, to which the entire laboratory was invited, a circle of people formed about Fester during the cocktail period before the dinner. Jerrold was part of the circle and discussion concerning the application of the theory Fester was proposing. Although this attention disturbed Knowlton, he reacted and behaved characteristically. He joined the circle, praised Fester to Jerrold and the others, and remarked how able and brilliant some of his work was.

Knowlton, without consulting anyone, began to consider the possibility of a job elsewhere. After a few weeks, he found that a new laboratory of considerable size was being organized in a nearby city. His training and experience would enable him to get a project-head job equivalent to the one he had at the lab, with slightly more money.

When it was offered, he immediately accepted the job and notified Jerrold by letter, which he mailed on a Friday night to Jerrold's home. The letter was brief, and Jerrold was stunned. The letter merely said that Knowlton had found a better position; that there were personal reasons why he didn't want to appear at the lab anymore; that he would be glad to come back later (he would be only 40 miles away), to assist if there were any problems with the past work; that he felt sure that Fester could, however, supply any leadership that was required for the group; and that his decision to leave so suddenly was based on some personal problems (he hinted at family health problems involving his mother and father, which was fictitious). Dr. Jerrold took it at face value but still felt that Knowlton's behavior was very strange and quite unaccountable. Jerrold had always felt that his relationship with Knowlton had been warm; that Knowlton was satisfied and, as a matter of fact, quite happy and productive.

Jerrold was considerably disturbed because he had already decided to place Fester in charge of another project that was going to be set up soon. He had been wondering how to explain this decision to Knowlton in view of the obvious help, assistance, and value Knowlton had been getting from Fester and the high regard in which Knowlton held him. In fact, Jerrold had considered letting Knowlton add to his staff another person with Fester's background and training, which apparently had proved so valuable.

Jerrold did not make any attempt to contact Knowlton. In a way, he felt aggrieved about the whole thing. Fester, too, was surprised at the suddenness of Knowlton's departure and when Jerrold, in talking to him, asked him whether he preferred to stay with the photon group rather than to head the Air Force project that was being organized, he chose the Air Force project and moved into that job the following week. The photon lab was hard hit. The leadership of the photon group was given to Link, with the understanding that it would be temporary until someone else could be brought in to take over.

Questions

1. One might say that there was a "personality" clash between Knowlton and Fester. What personality model could you use to describe it?
2. What leadership style did Knowlton need from Dr. Jerrold after Fester arrived? Did he receive this? Explain.
3. Was Knowlton's team effective before Fester arrived? After Fester arrived? Why or why not?
4. What changes in conflict management should Dr. Jerrold make to prevent another Knowlton problem?

Source: This case was developed by Dr. Alex Bavelas. It was edited for *Organizational Behavior*, 12th edition, and used with permission.

8 Mile

Jimmy "B-Rabbit" Smith, Jr. (Eminem), wants to succeed as a rapper and to prove that a white man can create moving sounds. His job at the North Detroit Stamping (NDS) plant fills his days while he pursues his music at night—and sometimes on the plant's grounds. The film's title refers to Detroit's northern city boundary, well known to local people. *8 Mile* is a gritty look at Detroit's hip-hop culture in 1995 and Jimmy's desire to be accepted by it. Eminem's original songs "Lose Yourself" and "8 Mile" received several award nominations. "Lose Yourself" won the 2003 Academy Award for best original song.

The scene has two parts. It is an edited composite of two brief NDS plant sequences that appear in different places in the film. Part 1 of the scene appears early in the film in the sequence "The Franchise." Part 2 appears in the last 25 minutes of the film in the "Papa Doc Payback" sequence. Jimmy arrives late for work in the first part of the scene, after riding the city bus because his car did not start. The second part occurs after his beating by Papa Doc (Anthony Mackie) and Papa Doc's gang. The film continues to its end with Jimmy's last battle (a rapper competition).

What to Watch For and Ask Yourself

1. What is your perception of the quality of Jimmy's job and his work environment?
2. What is the quality of Jimmy's relationship with Manny (Paul Bates), his foreman? Does it change? If it does, why?
3. How would you react to this type of work experience?

The Breakfast Club

John Hughes's careful look at teenage culture in a suburban Chicago high school focuses on a group of teenagers from the school's different subcultures. They start their Saturday detention with nothing in common, but over the course of a day, they learn each other's innermost secrets. The highly memorable characters—the Jock, the Princess, the Criminal, the Kook, and the Brain—leave lasting impressions. If you have seen the film, try to recall which actor or actress played each character.

The scene from *The Breakfast Club* is an edited version of the "Lunchtime" sequence that appears in the first third of the film. Carefully study each character's behavior to answer the following questions. The rest of the film shows the growing relationships among the detainees as they try to understand each other's personalities.

What to Watch For and Ask Yourself

1. Which Big Five personality dimensions describe each character in this scene?
2. Which characters show positive affect? Which show negative affect?

Mr. Baseball

The New York Yankees trade aging baseball player Jack Elliot (Tom Selleck) to the Chunichi Dragons, a Japanese team. This lighthearted comedy traces Jack's bungling entry into Japanese culture and exposes his cultural misconceptions, which almost cost him everything—including his new girlfriend Hiroko Uchiyama (Aya Takanashi). Unknown to Jack, Hiroko's father is "The Chief" (Ken Takakura), the Chunichi Dragons' manager. After Jack slowly begins to understand Japanese culture and Japanese baseball, his teammates finally accept him. This film shows many examples of Japanese culture, especially its love for baseball.

The *Mr. Baseball* scene takes place after "The Chief" has removed Jack from a baseball game. It shows Jack dining with Hiroko and her grandmother (Mineko Yorozuya), grandfather (Jun Hamamura), and father. The film continues with a dispute between Jack and Hiroko. Jack also learns from "The Chief" what he must do to succeed on the team.

What to Watch For and Ask Yourself

1. Does Jack Elliot behave as if he had cross-cultural training before arriving in Japan?
2. Is he culturally sensitive or insensitive?
3. What do you propose that Jack Elliot do for the rest of his time in Japan?

Seabiscuit

Combine a jockey who is blind in one eye with an undersized, ill-tempered thoroughbred and an unusual trainer. The result: the Depression Era champion race horse Seabiscuit. This engaging film shows the training and development of Seabiscuit by trainer "Silent" Tom Smith (Chris Cooper) and jockey Red Pollard (Tobey Maguire). The enduring commitment of owner Charles Howard (Jeff Bridges) ensures the ultimate success of Seabiscuit on the racing circuit. Based on *Seabiscuit: An American Legend*, the best-selling book by Laura Hillenbrand, *Seabiscuit* received seven 2003 Academy Award nominations, including Best Picture.

The *Seabiscuit* scene is an edited composite from DVD Chapters 21 and 22 toward the end of the film. In earlier scenes, Red severely injured a leg and cannot ride Seabiscuit in the competition against War Admiral. Samuel Riddle (Eddie Jones), War Admiral's owner, described any new rider as immaterial to the race's result. The scene begins with Red giving George Wolff (Gary Stevens), Seabiscuit's new jockey, some tips about riding him. Red starts by saying to George, "He's got a strong left lead, Georgie. He banks like a frigg'n airplane." The film continues to its exciting and unexpected ending.

What to Watch For and Ask Yourself

1. Does Red set clear performance goals for George? If he does, what are they?
2. Does Red help George reach those performance goals? How?
3. Does Red give George any positive reinforcement while he tries to reach the performance goals?

For Love of the Game

Billy Chapel (Kevin Costner), a 20-year veteran pitcher for the Detroit Tigers, learns just before the season's last game that the team's new owners want to trade him. He also learns that his partner, Jane Aubrey (Kelly Preston), intends to leave him. Faced with these daunting blows, Chapel wants to pitch a perfect final game. Director Sam Raimi's love of baseball shines through in some striking visual effects.

The scene from *For Love of the Game* is a slightly edited version of the "Just Throw" sequence that begins the film's exciting closing scenes. In this scene, Tigers' catcher Gus Sinski (John C. Reilly) comes out to the pitching mound to talk to Chapel. It is the beginning of Chapel's last game.

What to Watch For and Ask Yourself

1. At what level are Billy Chapel's esteem needs at this point in the game?
2. Do you expect Gus Sinski's talk to have any effect on Chapel? If it will, what effect do you expect it to have?
3. What rewards potentially exist for Billy Chapel? Remember, this is the last baseball game of his career.

Meet the Parents

Greg Focker (Ben Stiller) hopes his weekend visit to his girlfriend Pam's (Teri Polo) home will leave a positive impression on her parents. Unfortunately, Jack (Robert De Niro), Pam's father, immediately dislikes him. Jack's fondness does not improve after Greg accidentally breaks the urn holding Jack's mother's ashes. Other factors do not help the developing relationship: Greg is Jewish, while Jack is a WASP ex-CIA psychological profiler. These factors blend well to cause the continuous development of stress and the stress responses of all parties involved.

The scene from *Meet the Parents* comes from the "Bomb's the Word" segment in the last quarter of the film. Greg has boarded his flight to return home after his excruciating weekend visit with Pam's family. By this time, he has experienced an almost endless stream of stressors: meeting Pam's parents for the first time, taking a polygraph test administered by Jack, adjusting to Jinx the Himalayan cat's odd behavior, and . . . the film continues to a predictable happy ending.

What to Watch For and Ask Yourself

1. Does Greg experience the stress response during this scene? What evidence appears in the scene?
2. Does he experience distress or eustress?
3. Why does Greg respond so harshly to the simple request to check his bag?

U-571

This action-packed World War II thriller shows a U.S. submarine crew's efforts to retrieve an Enigma encryption device from a disabled German submarine. After the crew gets the device, a German vessel torpedoes and sinks their submarine. The survivors must now use the disabled German submarine to escape from the enemy with their prize.

The *U-571* scene is an edited composite of the "To Be a Captain" sequence early in the film and the "A Real Sea Captain" sequence in about the middle of the film. A "chalkboard" (title screen) that reads "Mr. Tyler, permission to speak freely?" separates the two parts. You can pause and separately study each part of the scene.

The first part occurs before the crew boards the disabled German U-boat. The second part occurs after the crew of survivors board the U-boat and try to return to England. Andrew Tyler (Matthew McConaughey), formerly the executive officer, is now the submarine's commander following the drowning death of Mike Dahlgren (Bill Paxton), the original commander. Just before this part of the scene, Tyler overheard some crewmen questioning his decision about taking a dangerous route to England. They also question why Chief Petty Officer Henry Klough (Harvey Keitel) is not the commander. The film continues with a German reconnaissance airplane circling their submarine and a crewman challenging Tyler's authority.

What to Watch For and Ask Yourself

1. What aspects of leadership does Dahlgren describe as important for a submarine commander?
2. Which leadership behaviors or traits does Klough emphasize?
3. Are the behaviors or traits emphasized in Question 2 right for this situation? Why or why not?

The Emperor's Club

William Hundert (Kevin Kline), a professor at Saint Benedict's Academy for Boys, believes in teaching his students about living a principled life. He also wants them to learn his beloved classical literature. New student Sedgewick Bell (Emile Hirsch) challenges Hundert's principled ways. Bell's behavior during the 73rd annual Mr. Julius Caesar Contest causes Hundert to suspect that Bell leads a less than principled life, a suspicion reinforced years later during a repeat of the competition.

This scene appears at the end of the film. It is an edited portion of the Mr. Julius Caesar Contest reenactment at former student Sedgewick Bell's (Joel Gretsch) estate. Bell wins the competition, but Hundert notices Bell's earpiece. Earlier in the film, Hundert had suspected that young Bell also wore an earpiece during the original competition. Bell announced his candidacy for the U.S. Senate just before talking to Hundert in the bathroom. In his announcement, he described his commitment to specific values he would pursue if elected.

What to Watch For and Ask Yourself

1. Does William Hundert describe a specific type of life that one should lead? If so, what are its elements?
2. Does Sedgewick Bell lead the type of life described by Hundert in Question 1? Is he committed to any specific ethics view or theory?
3. What consequences or effects do you predict for Sedgewick Bell because of the way he chooses to live his life?

Apollo 13

This superb film dramatically shows the NASA mission to the moon that had an in-space disaster. Innovative problem solving and decision making amid massive ambiguity saved the crew. *Apollo 13* has many examples of problem solving and decision making.

The scene from the film shows day 5 of the mission, about two-thirds of the way through *Apollo 13*. Earlier in the mission, Jack Swigert (Kevin Bacon) stirred the oxygen tanks at mission control's request. An explosion in the spacecraft happened shortly after this procedure, causing unknown damage to the command module. Before this scene takes place, the damage has forced the crew to move into the LEM (Lunar Exploration Module), which becomes their lifeboat for return to earth.

What to Watch For and Ask Yourself

1. What triggers the conflict in this scene?
2. Is this intergroup conflict or intragroup conflict? What effects can such conflict have on the group dynamics on board *Apollo 13?*
3. Does mission commander Jim Lovell (Tom Hanks) successfully manage the group dynamics to return the group to a normal state?

Casino

Martin Scorsese's lengthy, complex, and beautifully photographed study of 1970s Las Vegas gambling casinos and their organized crime connections completes his trilogy that includes *Mean Streets* (1973) and *Goodfellas* (1990). Ambition, greed, drugs, and sex destroy the mob's gambling empire. The film includes strong performances by Robert De Niro, Joe Pesci, and Sharon Stone. The violence and expletive-filled dialogue give *Casino* its R rating.

The *Casino* scene is part of "The Truth about Las Vegas" sequence early in the film. It follows the scenes of deceiving the Japanese gambler. It starts with a close-up of Sam "Ace" Rothstein (Robert De Niro) standing between his two casino executives (Richard Amalfitano, Richard F. Strafella). His voiceover says, "In Vegas, everybody's gotta watch everybody else." The scene ends after Sam Rothstein describes the ex-cheaters who monitor the gambling floor with binoculars. The film continues with the introduction of Ginger (Sharon Stone).

What to Watch For and Ask Yourself

1. Which type or form of organizational design does this scene show?
2. Does this scene show the results of the differentiation and integration organizational design processes?
3. Does this scene show any behavioral demands of organizational design? What are they?

Backdraft

Two brothers follow their late father, a legendary Chicago firefighter, and join the department. Stephen "Bull" McCaffrey (Kurt Russell) joins first and rises to the rank of lieutenant. Younger brother Brian (William Baldwin) joins later and becomes a member of Bull's Engine Company 17. Sibling rivalry tarnishes their work relationships, but they continue to successfully fight Chicago fires. Add a plot element about a mysterious arsonist, and you have the basis for an extraordinary film. The intense, unprecedented special effects give the viewer an unparalleled experience of what it is like to fight a fire.

The scene appears early in *Backdraft* as part of "The First Day" sequence. Brian McCaffrey has graduated from the fire academy, and the fire department has assigned him to his brother's company. This scene shows Engine Company 17 preparing to fight a garment factory fire. The film continues with Brian receiving some harsh first-day lessons as Engine Company 17 successfully fights the fire.

What to Watch For and Ask Yourself

1. What parts of the Chicago Fire Department culture does this scene show? Does the scene show any cultural artifacts or symbols? If it does, what are they?
2. Does the scene show any values or norms that guide the firefighters' behavior? If it does, what are they?
3. What does Brian McCaffrey learn on his first workday?

Field of Dreams

Ray Kinsella (Kevin Costner) hears a voice while working in his Iowa cornfield that says, "If you build it, he will come." Ray concludes that "he" is legendary "Shoeless Joe" Jackson (Ray Liotta), a 1919 Chicago White Sox player suspended for rigging the 1919 World Series. With the support of his wife Annie (Amy Madigan), Ray jeopardizes his farm by replacing some corn fields with a modern baseball diamond. "Shoeless Joe" soon arrives, followed by the rest of the suspended players. This charming fantasy film, based on W. P. Kinsella's novel *Shoeless Joe*, shows the rewards of pursuing a dream.

The scene is part of the "People Will Come" sequence toward the end of *Field of Dreams*. By this time in the story, Ray has met Terrence Mann (James Earl Jones). They have traveled together from Boston to Minnesota to find A. W. "Moonlight" Graham (Burt Lancaster). At this point, the three are at Ray's Iowa farm.

This scene follows Mark's (Timothy Busfield) arrival to discuss the foreclosure of Ray and Annie's mortgage. Mark, who is Annie's brother, cannot see the players on the field. Ray and Annie's daughter Karin (Gaby Hoffman) has proposed that people will come to Iowa City and buy tickets to watch a baseball game. Mark does not understand her proposal. The film continues to its end.

What to Watch For and Ask Yourself

1. Who is the target of change in this scene?
2. What are the forces for change? Are the forces for change internal or external to the change target?
3. Does the scene show the role of leadership in organizational change? If it does, who is the leader? What does this person do to get desired change?

Scarface

In the film *Scarface*, Antonio "Tony" Montana (Al Pacino) is a Cuban cocaine trafficker who comes to Florida for political asylum via the Mariel Boatlift. Once in the United States, Montana achieves new levels of decadence as he winds his way around Miami's underworld of drugs and violence. In Greek tragedy fashion, the film chronicles Tony Montana's rise to the top of the Mob—and his subsequent downfall.

Originally released in 1983 without fanfare, *Scarface* developed a cult following over the years, and many critics today consider the Brian De Palma classic to be the ultimate gangster film. DePalma ratchets up the tension in each scene, delivering tragic betrayals and ferocious violence—most notably with chainsaws. *Scarface* plays like a long cocaine rush, as Tony gets rich selling the narcotic then lost in a murderous frenzy from it.

In the film's "Shakedown" scene, Tony Montana sits with a law enforcement boss, sharing a drink and discussing bribes to keep the police off his case. The liaison informs Montana that the Supreme Court has granted police the right to invade his privacy. For the right price, however, the fuzz will leave him alone, and perhaps even support him. "How do I know you're the last cop I'm going to have to grease?" Pacino asks. The police liaison replies, "Do you think I want this conversation going any farther than this table? My guys got families, they're legitimate cops.... If they are embarrassed they're going to suffer. And if they suffer they're going to make you suffer. Comprende?"

What to Watch For and Ask Yourself

1. Who has legitimate power in this scene? Explain.
2. How are coercive power and reward power being applied in the discussion between Tony Montana and the agent?
3. In what way does the discussion constitute political behavior, and what ethical issues arise during the conversation?

Reality Bites

In the 1994 comedy *Reality Bites*, Lelaina Pierce (Winona Ryder) is a videographer filming a documentary (also called *Reality Bites*) about the disenfranchised lives of her Generation X friends and roommates. One close friend, Troy Dyer (Ethan Hawke), is a starving artist and grunge musician who works dead-end minimum-wage jobs while chasing musical pipe dreams. Other friends are shown to be equally directionless, as the film proceeds to chronicle the many career and relationship struggles common to Gen Xers fresh out of college during the 1990s.

In the movie's "Wiener Dude" scene, a Wiener Schnitzel crew captain (David Spade) explains to the perplexed Lelaina that the hot dog chain's cashier position is a juggling act. "You got people coming at you from the front, coming at you from the back, from the sides ... people at the condiment exchange, people at the drive-thru, kids on bikes—and they're all depending on [you]. Hey, you got time to lean, you got time to clean, buddy, all right? You gotta be 150% on your toes, 150% of the time."

What to Watch For and Ask Yourself

1. Is Lelaina's relationship with her crew captain at Wiener Schnitzel a motivator factor or a hygiene factor, according to Herzberg's motivator–hygiene model?
2. Based on the job characteristics model, will Lelaina experience high motivation and quality work performance as a cashier at Wiener Schnitzel? Explain.
3. What might management at Wiener Schnitzel do to enrich Lelaina's job experience?

Back to the Future II

In this first of two sequels to the 1985 hit movie *Back to the Future*, returning characters Marty McFly (Michael J. Fox), Emmett "Doc" Brown (Christopher Lloyd), and Jennifer Parker (Elisabeth Shue) travel back and forth between the years 2015, 1985, and 1955 in a silver time-traveling DeLorean. As the three begin tinkering around with events and family members in the future and in time past, they endanger themselves and alter history with near disastrous results. In a mind-bending twist, Marty must repeat his 1955 visit from the first *Back to the Future* film to prevent disastrous changes to 1985, yet without interfering with his first trip. In the end, the original course of history is restored and the characters' lives are rescued from historical oblivion.

In the scene "Looking into the Future," an aged Marty McFly sits at a futuristic family dinner with his gadget-wearing children, when coworker Douglas J. Needles breaks in on the videophone to propose an underhanded money scheme at work. McFly's reluctant compliance in the swindle leads to an immediate dismissal from the company, as corporate boss Ito Fujitsu monitors the entire transaction and fires Marty on the spot. As seen in the clip, Red Hot Chili Peppers bassist Flea makes a cameo appearance as the unscrupulous Douglas J. Needles.

What to Watch For and Ask Yourself

1. What forces of change will shape the future of organizations during the next decade, as envisioned in the movie *Back to the Future II*?
2. Why is diversity an important managerial concept for the future of organizations?
3. Explain why ethical leadership is increasingly important to the future of organizations.

Brazil

In the cult classic film *Brazil*, a common housefly causes a bureaucratic glitch that sparks terrorism, false arrests, and an escapist fantasy romance between lead character Sam Lowry (Jonathan Pryce) and dream girl Jill Layton (Kim Greist). As the 1985 dark comedy progresses, Lowry, a low-level Ministry of Information clerk, grows increasingly conflicted about his job within an overreaching, machine-run bureaucracy and comes to despise the system while living out a heroic second life in his dreams.

Directed by Monty Python's Terry Gilliam and British playwright Tom Stoppard, *Brazil* is at once funny and disturbing—even Orwellian. The film tops many critics' all-time favorite lists and features an amusing cameo from Robert De Niro as Archibald "Harry" Tuttle. Observers note that the film mirrors the much-publicized "Battle of Brazil" that pitted Gilliam against bureaucratic forces at Universal Studios, which thought *Brazil* was long and overly cynical.

In the movie's "Employee DZ-015" scene, Sam Lowry is seen reporting for his first day on the job. The experience teeters between dreary melancholy and pulsating frenzy, as Lowry—known to the organization only as employee number DZ-015—is led awkwardly and hurriedly to his lonely, 30th floor office space by detached government coworkers.

What to Watch For and Ask Yourself

1. What organizational values and norms did Sam Lowry learn from his first socialization encounter at the government's Ministry of Information?
2. At what stage of the organizational socialization process would you place Sam Lowry, and what important formative experiences take place during this stage?
3. Which of the four types of organizational cultures is depicted in the scene, and what cultural symbols of the organization help inform your answer?

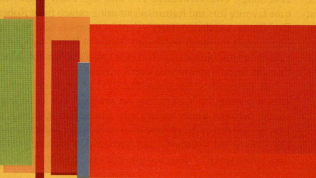

REFERENCES

CHAPTER 1

1. *Adapted from* About us, our philosophy, world famous fun stuff. www.pikeplacefish.com (January 2008); Yokoyama, J., and Michelli, J. *When Fish Fly: Lessons for Creating a Vital and Energized Workplace—From the World Famous Pike Place Fish Market*. New York: Hyperion, 2004; Bauman, M. Good times mean good business at Pike Place. *Knight Ridder Tribune Business News*, November 26, 2006, 1–2.
2. *Adapted from* Organizational Behavior Division domain statement of the Academy of Management. www.aomonline.org (February 2007).
3. Naquin, S. S., and Holton, E. Leadership and managerial competency models: A simplified process and resulting model. *Advances in Developing Human Resources*, 2006, 8, 144–165; For discussions of the uses and limitations of competency frameworks, see Levenson, A. R., van der Stede, W. A., and Cohen, S. G. Measuring the relationship between managerial competence and performance. *Journal of Management*, 2006, 32, 360–380; Ruth, D. Frameworks of managerial competence: Limits, problems, and suggestions. *Journal of European Industrial Training*, 2006, 30, 206–226; Ven, J., and Chuang, C. The development of a competency ontology. *Journal of American Academy of Business*, 2007, 11, 275–279.
4. Corporations that have benefited from ITG competency models. www.itg.com (February 2007).
5. *Adapted from* Rossetti, D. Flying fish—Islander shares personal strategies for developing a successful business. *Mercer Island Reporter*, September 16, 2004, 2–3; Burns, H. Making work work. *Innsbrook Today*, November 2004, 1.
6. Harrington, B., and Hall, D. T. *Career Management & Work/Life Integration: Using Self-Assessment to Navigate Contemporary Careers*. Thousand Oaks, CA: Sage, 2007.
7. Inkson, K. *Understanding Careers: The Metaphors of Working Lives*. Thousand Oaks, CA: Sage, 2006; Heslin, P. A. Experiencing career success. *Organizational Dynamics*, 2005, 34, 376–390.
8. Hunt, J. M., and Weintraub, J. R. *The Coaching Organization: A Strategy for Developing Leaders*. Thousand Oaks, CA: Sage, 2006.
9. This section draws from Zaremba, A. *Organizational Communication: Foundations for Business and Collaboration*. Belmont, CA: Wadsworth/Thomson Higher Education, 2006; Wood, J. A. *Communication Mosaics: An Introduction to the Field of Communication*. Belmont, CA: Wadsworth, 2008.
10. Yokoyama, J., and Bergquist, J. The world famous Pike Place Fish story: A breakthrough for managers. *Retailing Issues Newsletter*. College Station, TX: Center for Retailing Studies, Texas A&M University, November 2001, 2.
11. *Adapted from* Hymowitz, C. Two Super Bowl coaches offer lessons for screaming managers. *Wall Street Journal Online*, January 31, 2007. http://online.wsj.com (February 2007); Derrick, J. C. Lovie's success began as a youngster. www.newsjournal.com (February 3, 2007); Tony Dungy. *Wikipedia: The Free Encyclopedia*. http://en.wikipedia.org (February 2007).
12. This section draws from April, K., and Shockley, M. L. (Eds.). *New Realities in a Changing World*. New York: Palgrave Macmillan, 2007; Page, S. E. *Difference: How the Power of Diversity Creates Better Groups, Teams, Schools, and Societies*. Princeton, NJ: Princeton University Press, 2007; Clegg, S. R., Carter, C., Kornberger, M., and Messner, M. *Business Ethics in Practice: Representation Discourse and Performance*. Northampton, MA: Edward Elgar Publishing, 2007.
13. Salett, E. P. Defining multiculturalism. *Washington Post*, May 24, 2001, 16A; Salett, E. P., and Koslow, D. R. (Eds.). *Race Ethnicity and Self: Identity in Multicultural Perspectives*, 2nd ed. Washington, DC: National Multicultural Institute, 2003.
14. Konrad, A. M., Prasad, P., and Pringle, J. *Handbook of Workplace Diversity*. Thousand Oaks, CA: Sage, 2006; Bilimoria, D., and Piderit, S. K. *Handbook on Women in Business and Management*. Northampton, MA: Edward Elgar Publishing, 2007.
15. *Adapted from* Dial, J. Retiring the generation gap—10 principles for working across generations. *Leading Effectively Newsletter*, January 2007. www.ccl.org (February 2007).
16. Rowh, M. Managing younger workers. *Office Solutions*, 2007, 24(1), 29–31.
17. *Adapted from* Pomeroy, A. She's still lovin' it. *HR Magazine*. December 2006, 8, 58–61; Palmer, A. T. Interview: Patricia Harris—Close to the action. *Chicago Tribune*, June 26, 2006, 5–6.
18. This section draws from Thiroux, J., and Krasemann, K. *Ethics: Theory and Practice*, 9th ed. Upper Saddle River, NJ: Prentice-Hall, 2006; Lovell, A., and Fisher, C. *Business Ethics and Values*, 2nd ed. Upper Saddle River, NJ: Prentice-Hall, 2006.
19. McNamara, C. *Complete Guide to Ethics Management: An Ethics Toolkit for Managers*. 2006. www.managementhelp.org/ethics (February 2007); Geva, A. A typology of moral problems in business: A framework for ethical management. *Journal of Business Ethics*, 2006, 69, 133–147.
20. Treviño, L. K., and Nelson, K. *Managing Business Ethics: Straight Talk About How to Do It Right*. New York: Wiley, 2006.
21. Cohen, M. *101 Ethical Dilemmas*, 2nd ed. New York: Routledge, 2007.
22. *Adapted from* Liberman, V. Corporate ethics are in the eye of the beholder, says Ron Brown. *Across the Board*,

January/February 2006, 45–47; CEO's Corner. Center for Ethical Business Cultures. www.cebcglobal.org (February 2007).

23. Harris, P. R., Moran, R. T., and Moran, S. *Managing Cultural Differences: Global Strategies for the 21st Century*, 6th ed. New York: Elsevier, 2005; Fatehi, K. *Managing Internationally: Succeeding in a Culturally Diverse World.* Thousand Oaks: CA: Sage, 2007.
24. Adler, N. J., and Gunderson, A. *International Dimensions of Organizational Behavior*, 5th ed. Mason, OH: Thomson South-Western, 2008.
25. Copeland, M. J., and Schuster, C. P. *Global Business Practices: Adapting for Success.* Mason, OH: Thomson South-Western, 2006.
26. *Adapted from* Fowler, G. A. In China's offices, foreign colleagues might get an earful. *Wall Street Journal*, February 13, 2007, B1.
27. Levi, D. *Group Dynamics for Teams*, 2nd ed. Thousand Oaks, CA: Sage, 2007; LaFasto, F. M. J., and Larson, C. E. *When Teams Work Best: 6000 Team Members and Leaders Tell What It Takes to Succeed.* Thousand Oaks, CA: Sage, 2002; Ancona, D., and Bresman, H. *X-Teams: Leadership in Action.* Boston: Harvard Business School Press, 2007.
28. *Adapted from* Ludin, S. Go fish. *T&D*, August 2001, 70–72.
29. Scearce, C. *100 Ways to Build Teams.* Thousand Oaks, CA: Sage, 2007.
30. Larry Richman named president & CEO of LaSalle Bank. About us—LaSalle Bank. January 18, 2007. www.lasallebank.com (February 2007).
31. *Adapted from* Dalton, C. M. A man you can bank on: An interview with Larry D. Richman, LaSalle Bank, N.A. *Business Horizons*, 2007, 50(1), 11–15; Saulig, R. R. Why we do what we do. *BOMA Chicago.* March 1, 2005. www.boma-chicago.org (February 2007).
32. This section draws from Lawler, E. E., Worley, C. G., and Porras, J. *Built to Change: How to Achieve Sustained Organizational Effectiveness.* New York: Wiley, 2006; Cameron, K. S., and Quinn, R. E. *Diagnosing and Changing Organizational Culture: Based on the Competing Values Framework.* New York: Wiley, 2006; Burke, W. W. *Organizational Change: Theory and Practice*, 2nd ed. Thousand Oaks, CA: Sage, 2007.
33. Nadler, D. A. The CEO's 2nd act. *Harvard Business Review*, 2007, 85(1), 66–72. Burke, R. J., and Cooper, C. L. (Eds.). *Inspiring Leaders.* New York: Routledge, 2006.
34. Neal, J. *Edgewalkers: People and Organizations That Take Risks, Build Bridges, and Break New Ground.* Westport, CT: Greenwood Publishing, 2007.
35. This section draws from Chesbrough, H. *Open Business Models: How to Thrive in the New Innovation Landscape.* Boston: Harvard Business School Press, 2007; Allen, T. J., and Henn, G. *Organization and Architecture: Managing the Flow of Technology.* Burlington, MA: Elsevier Sciences & Technology Books, 2007; Tapscott, D., and Williams, A. D. *Wikinomics: How Mass Collaboration Changes Everything.* New York: Penguin, 2007.
36. Davis, S., and Meyer, C. *Blur: The Speed of Change in the Connected Economy.* New York: Warner Books, 1999, 5; Davis, S. *Lessons from the Future: Making Sense of the Blurred World.* Mankato, MN: Capstone Press, 2001.
37. Sherman, L. M. Rapid prototyping: Pretty soon, you won't be able to get along without it. *Plastics Technology*, 2001, 47(2), 62–67; The people behind the technology. www.santineng.com (February 2007); Buss, D. D. Embracing speed. *Nation's Business*, June 1999, 12–17.
38. *Adapted from* Morgan, G. Chiquita and the Rainforest Alliance. *Corporate Citizen*, 2006, 34–37; Corporate responsibility. *Chiquita Brands International, Inc. 2005 Annual Report*, 21–22. www.chiquita.com (February 2007); Alsever, J. Chiquita cleans up its act. *Fortune*, November 27, 2006, 73–74; Bucheli, M. *Bananas and Business.* New York: New York University Press, 2005; Chiquita admits to paying terrorists. www.msnbc.com (March 2007); Apuzzo, M. Chiquita agrees to $25 million fine. *Houston Chronicle*, March 15, 2007, D6; Otis, J. For banana giant, a matter of protection or profit? *Houston Chronicle*, April 2, 2007, A1, A12.

CHAPTER 2

1. *Adapted from* www.virgin.com (February 2007); Kirkpatrick, D. Rich geeks in paradise. *Fortune*, December 11, 2006, 49–50; Elkind, P. Branson gets grounded. *Fortune*, February 5, 2007, 13–14; Mogul: Save the earth, win $25 M. *Dallas Morning News*, February 10, 2007, 12A.
2. Judge, T. A., Jackson, C. L., and Shaw, J. C. Self-efficacy and work-related performance: The role of individual differences. *Journal of Applied Psychology*, 2007, 92, 101–127; Payne, S. C., Youngcourt, S. S., and Beaubien, J. M. A meta-analytic examination of the goal orientation nomological net. *Journal of Applied Psychology*, 2007, 92, 128–150.
3. Matthias, M. R., Gosling, S. D., and Pennebaker, J. W. Personality in its natural habitat: Manifestations and implicit folk theories of personality in daily life. *Journal of Personality and Social Psychology*, 2006, 90, 862–877.
4. Nettle, D. The evolution of personality variation in humans. *American Psychologist*, 2006, 61, 6522–631.
5. Turkheimer, E. Heritability and biological explanation. *Psychological Review*, 1998, 105, 782–791.
6. Furnham, A., Petrides, K. V., Tsaousis, I., Pappas, K., and Garrod, D. A cross-cultural investigation into the relationship between personality and work values. *Journal of Psychology*, 2005, 139, 5–33.
7. Kitayama, B. M., and Karasawa, M. Cultural affordance and emotional experience. *Journal of Personality and Social Psychology*, 2006, 91, 890–904.
8. Hofstede, G. *Cultures Consequences*, 2nd ed. Thousand Oaks, CA: Sage, 2001.
9. Bing, J. W. Hofstede consequences: The impact of his work on consulting and business. *Academy of Management Executive*, 2004, 18(1), 80–88; Shipper, F., Hoffman, R. C., and Rotondo, D. M. Does the 360 feedback process create actionable knowledge equally across cultures? *Academy of Management Learning & Education*, 2007, 6, 33–50.

10. Halawah, J. The effect of motivation, family environment and student characteristics on academic achievement. *Journal of Instructional Psychology*, 2006, 33(2), 91–100; Feist, G. J. How development and personality influence scientific through interest and achievement. *Review of General Psychology*, 2006, 16, 173–182.
11. *Adapted from* Arnoult, S. New horizons for JetBlue. *Air Transport World*, 2005, 42(11), 73–75; Neeleman, D. Lessons from the slums of Brazil. *Harvard Business Review*, 2005, 83(1), 24; Newman, R. Preaching JetBlue. *Chief Executive*, October 2004, 26–30; Brodsky, N. Street smarts: Learning from JetBlue. *Inc.*, March 2004, 59ff.
12. Felps, W., Mitchell, T. R., and Byington, E. How, when and why bad apples spoil the barrel: Negative group members and dysfunctional groups. *Research in Organizational Behavior*, 2006, 27, 175–222.
13. Daniels, C. Does this man need a shrink? *Fortune*, February 5, 2001, 205.
14. *Adapted from* Donnellan, M. B., Oswald, F. L., Baird, B. M., and Lucas, R.E. The mini-IPIP scale: Tiny-yet-effective measures of the Big Five factors of personality. *Psychological Assessment*, 2006, 18, 192–203; http://en.wikipedia.org/wiki/Big_Five_personality_traits (February 2007).
15. The discussion of the personality characteristics have been drawn from Big Five personality trait discussions: http://en.wikipedia.org/wiki/Big_Five_personality_traits, February, 2007; Barrick, M. R., and Mount, M. K. The big five personality dimensions and job performance: A meta-analysis. *Personnel Psychology*, 1991, 44, 1–26; Grant, S., and Langan-Fox, J. Personality and the occupational stressor-strain relationship: The role of the Big Five. *Journal of Occupational Health Psychology*, 2007, 12, 20–33; Mount, M. K., Barrick, M. R., Scullen, S. M., and Rounds, J. Higher-order dimensions of the Big Five personality traits and the big six vocational interest types. *Personnel Psychology*, 2005, 58, 447–479; Mueller, B., and Plug, E. Estimating the effect of personality on male and female earnings. *Industrial and Labor Relations*, 2006, 60, 3–22.
16. Gale, S.F. Three companies cut turnover with tests. *Workforce*, 2002, 81(4), 66–69; Gales, S. F. Putting job candidates to the test. *Workforce*, 2003, 82 (4), 64–68; Hogan, R. *Personality and the Fate of Organizations*. Mahwah, NJ: Lawrence Erlbaum Associates 2006.
17. Seery, M. D., Blascovich, J., and Weisbuch, M. The relationship between self-esteem level, self-esteem stability and cardiovascular reactions to feedback. *Journal of Personality and Social Psychology*, 2004, 87, 133–145; Judge, T. A., and Bono, J. E. Relationship of core self-esteem traits-self-esteem, general self-efficacy, locus of control, and emotional stability-with job satisfaction and job performance: A meta-analysis. *Journal of Applied Psychology*, 2001, 86, 80–92.
18. Tay, C., Soon, A., and Dyne, L. V. Personality, biographical characteristics and job interview success: A longitudinal study of the mediating effects of interviewing self-efficacy and the moderating effects of internal locus of control. *Journal of Applied Psychology*, 2006, 91, 446–454.
19. Ibid.
20. Goleman, D. *Working with Emotional Intelligence*. New York: Bantum Press 1998.
21. Cote, S., and Miners, C. T. H. Emotional intelligence, cognitive intelligence, and job performance. *Administrative Science Quarterly*, 2005, 51, 1–29; Law, K. S., Wong, C., and Lynda, J. S. The construct and criterion validity of emotional intelligence and its potential utility for management studies. *Journal of Applied Psychology*, 2004, 89, 483–497.
22. Personal interview with C. Jarnagin, Consultant, Lattice Consulting, LLP, February 2007.
23. Ford, M. T., Heinen, B. A., and Langkamer, K. L. Work and family satisfaction and conflict: A meta-analysis of cross-domain relations. *Journal of Applied Psychology*, 2007, 91, 57–80; Kreiner, G. E., Hollensbe, E. C., and Sheep, M. L. Where is the "Me" among the "We"? Identity work and the search for optimal balance. *Academy of Management Journal*, 2006, 49, 1031–1057.
24. Snyder, C. R., Berg, C., and Woodward, J. T. Hope against the cold. *Journal of Personality*, 2005, 73, 287–312; Youssef, C. M., and Luthans, F. Positive organizational behavior in the workplace: The impact of hope, optimism, and resilience. *Journal of Management*, 2007, 33, 321–349; Stajkovic, A. D. Development of a core confidence-higher order construct. *Journal of Applied Psychology*, 2006, 91, 1208–1224.
25. Luthans, F., and Youssef, C. M. Positive workplaces. In Snyder, C. R., and Lopez, S. (Eds.). *Handbook of Positive Psychology*, 2nd ed. Oxford, UK: Oxford University Press, in press. O'Neil, S. L., and Chapman, E. N. *Your Attitude Is Showing*. Upper Saddle River, NJ: Pearson, 2008.
26. Luthans, F., Avolio, B. J., Avey, J. B., and Norman, S. M. Positive psychological capital: Measurement and relationship with performance and satisfaction. *Personnel Psychology*, 2007, 60, 541–572; Luthans, F., and Youssef, C. M. Emerging positive organizational behavior. *Journal of Management*, 2007, 33, 321–349.
27. Bowling, N. A. Is the job satisfaction–job performance relationship spurious? A meta-analytic examination. *Journal of Vocational Behavior*, 2007, 167–185; Chan, D. Interactive effects of situational judgment effectiveness and proactive personality on work perceptions and work outcomes. *Journal of Applied Psychology*, 2006, 91, 475–481.
28. www.containerstore.com (March 2007); Halkias, M. Container Store put on the market. *Dallas Morning News*, February 17, 2007, D1–D6; Erickson, T. J., and Gratton, L. What it means to work here. *Harvard Business Review*, March 2007, 104–112; Appleson, G. The Container Store. *St. Louis-Post Dispatch*, October 11, 2006, B1; Powers, V. Finding workers who fit the Container Store built a booming business for neatniks who turned out to be their best employees. *Business 2.0*, November 2004, 74ff.
29. Cooper-Hakim, A., and Viswesvaran, C. The construct of work commitment: Testing an integrative framework.

Psychological Bulletin, 2005, 131, 241–259; Mowday, R. T., Porter, L. W., and Steers, R. M. *Employee–Organization Linkages: The Psychology of Commitment, Absenteeism, and Turnover*. New York: Academic Press, 1982.

30. Bowler, W., and Brass, D. J. Relational correlates of interpersonal citizenship behavior: A social network perspective. *Journal of Applied Psychology*, 2006, 91, 70–82.
31. The seminal work in the field was done by Lazarus, R. *Emotion and Adaption*. New York: Oxford University Press, 1991. Also see Cron, W. L., Slocum, J. W., Jr., VandeWalle, D., and Fu, F. The role of goal orientation on negative emotions and goal setting when initial performance falls short of one's goal. *Human Performance*, 2005, 18, 55–80; Fong, C. T. The effects of emotional ambivalence on creativity. *Academy of Management Journal*, 2006, 49, 1016–1030.
32. Bagozzi, R. P., Wong, N., and Yi, Y. The role of culture and gender in the relationship between positive and negative emotions. *Cognition and Emotion*, 1999, 16, 641–672.
33. Kakuchi, S. Put on a happy face. *Asian Business*, 2000, 36, 56; Barger, P. B., and Grandey, A. A. Service with a smile and encounter satisfaction: Emotional contagion and appraisal. *Academy of Management Journal*, 2006, 49, 1229–1238; Laabs, J. J. Hotels train to help Japanese guests. *Personnel Journal*, 1994, 73(9), 28–32.
34. Illies, R., Scott, B. A., and Judge, T. A. The interactive effects of personal traits and experienced states on intraindividual patterns of citizenship behavior. *Academy of Management Journal*, 2006, 49, 561–575.
35. *Used by permission from* Dorfman, P., and Howell, J. *Cultural Values Questionnaire*. Las Cruces, NM: New Mexico State University, 2007.
36. *Adapted from* Schutte, N. S., Malouff, J. M., Hall, L. E., Haggerty, D. J., Cooper, J. T., Golden, C. J., and Dornheim, L. Development and validation of a measure of emotional intelligence. *Personality and Individual Differences*, 1998, 25, 167–177.

CHAPTER 3

1. *Adapted from* For Estée Lauder's Thia Breen, a successful career is made up of "people, passion and performance." http://knowledge.wharton.upenn.edu (January, 2007); Born, P. Lauder brightens 59th street. Bloomingdale's. *WWD*, November 22, 2006, 8; Naughton, J. Thia Breen promoted at Lauder. *WWD*, August 11, 2006, 5.
2. Shanock, L. R., and Eisenberger, R. When supervisors feel supported: Relationships with subordinates' perceived supervisor support, perceived organizational support, and performance. *Journal of Applied Psychology*, 2006, 91, 689–695.
3. Talley-Sejin, M. How to Feng-Shui your retail showroom. *In Furniture*, October 16, 2006, 30. Also see http://en.wikipedia.org/wiki/Feng_shui (February 2007).
4. *Adapted from* Yap, J. Prosperous spaces: Singapore's skyline boasts the gloss of modernity. But under closer scrutiny. *Business Traveller Asia Pacific*, 2005, 26(5), 26–31.
5. Personal communication with Alberto de La Guardia, Manager, Frito-Lay Company, Plano, TX, February 2007.
6. Rosen, C. C., Levy, P. E., and Hall, R. J. Placing perceptions of politics in the content of the feedback environment, employee attitudes and job performance. *Journal of Applied Psychology*, 2006, 91, 221–232.
7. *Adapted from* Henderson, P. W., Giese, J. L., and Cote, J. A. Impression management using typeface designs. *Journal of Marketing*, 2004, 68(4), 60–72.
8. Diener, E. What is positive about positive psychology: The curmudgeon and Pollyanna. *Psychology Inquiry*, 2003, 14(2), 115–120.
9. Heslin, P. A., Latham, G. P., and VandeWalle, D. The effect of implicit person theory on performance appraisals. *Journal of Applied Psychology*, 2005, 90, 842–856; Heslin, P. A., VandeWalle, D., and Latham, G. P. Keen to help? Manager's implicit person theories and their subsequent employee coaching. *Personnel Psychology*, 2006, 59, 871–902.
10. McCrae, R. R., and Terracciano, A. Universal features of personality traits from the observer's perspective: Data from 50 cultures. *Journal of Personality and Social Psychology*, 2005, 88, 547–561.
11. Young, J. *Global Relocation Trends Survey*. Woodridge, IL: GMAC Relocation Services, 2006.
12. The entire issue of the *Journal of World Business*, 2005, 40, 340–430, is dedicated to exploring foreign assignments and career opportunities. For an overview, see Thomas, D. C., Lazarova, M. B., and Inkson, K. Global careers: New phenomenon or new perspectives. *Journal of World Business*, 2005, 40, 340–347; Collings, D. G., Scullion, H., and Morley, M. J. Changing patterns of global staffing in the multinational enterprise: Challenges to the conventional expatriate assignment and emerging alternatives. *Journal of World Business*, 2007, 42, 198–213.
13. Luthans, F., Wischun, Z., and Avolio, B. J. The impact of self-efficacy on work attitudes across cultures. *Journal of World Business*, 2006, 41, 121–132.
14. Janssens, M., Cappellen, T., and Zanoni, P. Successful female expatriates as agents: Positioning oneself through gender, hierarchy, and culture. *Journal of World Business*, 2006, 41, 133–148; Verma, A., Toh, S. M., and Budhwar, P. A new perspective on the female expatriate experience: The role of host country national categorization. *Journal of World Business*, 2006, 41, 112–120.
15. *Adapted from* www.traderscity.com/abcg/culture8.htm (May 2005).
16. Walberg, M. Yes, first impressions still mean a lot. mwalberg@bellsouth.net; Sears, G. J., and Rowe, P. M. A personality-based similar-to-me effect in the employment interview: Conscientiousness affect versus competence-mediated interpretations and the role of job relevance. *Canadian Journal of Behavioural Science*, 2003, 35(1), 13–34; Brtek, M. D., and Motowidlo, S. J. Effects of procedure and outcome accountability on interview validity. *Journal of Applied Psychology*, 2002, 87, 185–191.

17. Cable, D. M., and Judge, T. A. The effect of physical height on workplace success and income: Preliminary test of a theoretical model. *Journal of Applied Psychology*, 2004, 89, 428–441; Siegel, P. A., and Brockner, J. Individual and organizational consequences of CEO claimed handicapping: What's good for the CEO may not be good for the firm. *Organizational Behavior and Human Decision Processes*, 2005, 96, 1–22.
18. Morsch, L. Do pretty people earn more? www.CareerBuilder.com (January 2007); Biddle, J. E., and Hamermesh, D. S. Beauty, productivity, and discrimination: Lawyers' looks and lucre. *Journal of Labor Economics*, 1998, 16(1), 172–201.
19. Heuzé, J., Nicolas, R., and Manual, M. Relations between cohesion and collective effectiveness within male and female professional basketball teams. *Canadian Journal of Behavioural Science*, 2006, 38(1), 81–91.
20. Shapiro, J. R., King, E. B., and Quiñones, M. A. Expectations of obese trainees: How stigmatized trainee characteristics influence training effectiveness. *Journal of Applied Psychology*, 2007, 92, 239–249.
21. Sprott, D. E., Spangenberg, E. R., and Fisher, R. The importance of normative beliefs to the self-fulfilling prophecy. *Journal of Applied Psychology*, 2003, 88, 423–431; McNatt, D. B. Ancient Pygmalion joins contemporary management: A meta-analysis of the result. *Journal of Applied Psychology*, 2000, 85, 314–322.
22. Davidson, O. B., and Eden, D. Remedial self-fulfilling prophecy: Two field experiments to prevent Golem effects among disadvantaged women. *Journal of Applied Psychology*, 2000, 85, 386–398.
23. Harris, K. J., Kacmar, K. M., and Zivuska, S. The impact of political skills on impression management effectiveness. *Journal of Applied Psychology*, 2007, 92, 278–285; Bolino, M. C., Varela, J. A., Bande, B., and Turnley, W. H. The impact of impression-management tactics on supervisory rating of organizational citizenship behavior. *Journal of Organizational Behavior Management*, 2006, 27, 281–298; Bolino, M. C., and Turnley, W. H. Measurement of impression management: A scale development based on Jones and Pittman taxonomy. *Organizational Research Methods*, 1999, 2, 187–206.
24. Ibid.
25. Hirschberger, G. Terror management and attributions to blame innocent victims. *Journal of Personality and Social Psychology*, 2006, 91, 832–845.
26. Speer, S. A. The interactional organization of the gender attribution process. *Sociology*, 2005, 39, 67–88.
27. Ployhart, R. E., Ehrhart, K., Holcombe, and Hayes, S. C. Using attributions to understand the effects of applicant reactions. *Journal of Applied Social Psychology*, 2005, 35, 259–296.
28. Forgas, J. P. On being happy and mistaken: Mood effects on the fundamental attribution error. *Journal of Personality and Social Psychology*, 1998, 25, 318–331.
29. Nurcan, E., and Murphy, S. E. Cross-cultural variations in leadership perceptions and attribution of charisma to the leader. *Organizational Behavior and Human Decision Processes*, 2003, 92(1–2), 52–66.
30. *Adapted from* Varchaver, N. Long Island confidential. *Fortune*, November 27, 2006, 172–184; Kumar, S., and Abraham A. Bridging the gap: People and process with content in context. *KMWorld*, 2007, 16(1), S14–S16.
31. Dixon, A. L., and Schertzer, S. M. B. Bouncing back: How salesperson optimism and self-efficacy influence attributions and behaviors following failure. *Journal of Personal Selling & Sales Management*, 2005, 25, 361–370.
32. Hochwarter, W. A., Witt, L. A., and Treadway, D. C. The interaction of social skill and organizational support on job performance. *Journal of Applied Psychology*, 2006, 91, 482–489; Treadway, D. C., Ferris, G. R., and Hochwarter, W. The role of age in the perceptions of politics-job performance relationship: A three study constructive replication. *Journal of Applied Psychology*, 2005, 90, 872–881.
33. Bivens, L. J., and Weller, C. E. The "job-loss" recovery: Not new, just worse. *Journal of Economic Issues*, 2006, 40, 603–629; Armstrong-Stassen, M. Coping with downsizing: A comparison of executive-level and middle managers. *International Journal of Stress Management*, 2005, 12, 117–141.
34. *Adapted from* Fandt, P.M. *Management Skills: Practice and Experience*. Minneapolis, MN: West Publishing, 1994. Reprinted with permission.
35. *Adapted from* Gardenwartz, L., and Rowe, A. *Diverse Teams at Work*. New York: McGraw-Hill, 1994, 169.

CHAPTER 4

1. *Adapted from* www.pressroom.ups.com (March 2007); personal communication with Cal Peveto, Business Manager, UPS, Southwest Region, Dallas, TX (March 2007).
2. www.ascentgroup.com (March 2007).
3. Weiss, H. M. Learning theory and industrial and organizational psychology. In Dunnette, M. D., and Hough, L. M. (Eds.), *Handbook of Industrial & Organizational Psychology*, 2nd ed. Palo Alto, CA: Consulting Psychologist Press, 1990, 170–221; Bouton, M. E. *Learning and Behavior: A Contemporary Synthesis*. Sunderland, MA: Sinauer Associates, 2006.
4. Oaks, S. Absenteeism: Positive reinforcement works. *ASHCSP Angle*, March 2007, 4. For other examples, see Roberson, J. Healthier workers, healthier profit. *Dallas Morning News*, May 3, 2007, 1D–8D.
5. Kanfer, R. Motivation theory and industrial and organizational psychology. In Dunnette and Hough, *Handbook of Industrial & Organizational Psychology*, 75–169; Daniels, A. C. *Bringing Out the Best in People*, 2nd ed. New York: McGraw-Hill, 2000, 25–78.
6. Skinner, B. F. *About Behaviorism*. New York: Knopf, 1974; Martin, G., and Pear, J. *Behavior Modification: What It Is and How to Do It*. Upper Saddle River, NJ: Pearson Education, 2006.
7. Thompson, H., Iwata, B. A., Hanley, G. P., Dozier, C. L., and Samaha, A. The effects of extinction, noncontingent reinforcement, and different reinforcement

of other behavior as control procedures. *Journal of Applied Behavior Analysis*, 2003, 36, 221–239; Rawe, J. Fat chance. *Time*, June 11, 2007, 62; Cullen, L. T. The company doctor. *Time*, June 25, 2007, Global 4.
8. Thang, L. C., Rowley, C., Quang, T., and Warner, M. To what extent can management practices be transferred between countries? The case of human resource management in Vietnam. *Journal of World Business*, 2007, 42, 113–127.
9. Bland, C., Brown, J., Ewing, J., Kavi, S., Morehead, G., and Sims, C. *Wal-Mart China* (unpublished Executive MBA paper). Dallas, TX: Cox School of Business, Southern Methodist University, March 2007.
10. Paik, Y., and Sohn, J. D. Expatriate managers and MNC's ability to control international subsidiaries: The case of Japanese MNCs. *Journal of World Business*, 2004, 39, 61–70.
11. O'Toole, J., and Lawler, E. E., III. The choices managers make or don't make. *The Conference Board*, September/October 2006, 24–29.
12. *Adapted from* Livers, A. B. Coaching leaders of color. In Ting, S., and Scisco, P. (Eds.), *The CCL Handbook of Coaching*. San Francisco: Jossey-Bass, 2006, 92–121.
13. Daniels, *Bringing Out the Best*, 59–60; Deeprose, D. *How to Recognize and Reward Employees: 150 Ways to Inspire Peak Performance*. New York: AMACOM, 2006.
14. Besser, T. L. Rewards and organizational goal achievement: A case study of Toyota Motor manufacturing in Kentucky. *Journal of Management Studies*, 1995, 32, 383–401; Lustgarten, A. Elite factories. *Fortune*, September 6, 2004, 240ff; Takeda, H. *Synchronized Production System: Going Beyond Just in Time through Kaizen*. London: Kogan Page, 2006.
15. Wayne, S. J., Shore, L. M., and Bommer, W. H. The role of fair treatment and rewards in perceptions of organizational support and leader-member exchange. *Journal of Applied Psychology*, 2002, 87, 590–598.
16. Grote, D. F. Discipline without punishment. *Across the Board*, September/October 2001, 52–57.
17. Luthans, F., Avolio, B. J., Avey, J. B., and Norman, S. M. Positive psychological capital: Measurement and relationship with performance and satisfaction. *Personnel Psychology*, 2007, 60, 541–572.
18. *Adapted from* Mackintosh, J. How BMW put the Mini back on track. *Financial Times*, March 19, 2003, 14.
19. Latham, G. P., and Huber, V. L. Schedules of reinforcement: Lessons from the past and issues for the future. *Journal of Organizational Behavior Management*, 1992, 12, 125–150.
20. Smyth, R., Wang, J., and Deng, X. Equity-for-debt swaps in Chinese big business: A case study of restructuring in one large state-owner enterprise. *Asia Business Review*, 2004, 10(3/4), 382–401; Selmer, J. Cultural novelty and adjustment: Western business expatriates in China. *International Journal of Human Resource Management*, 2006, 17, 1209–1222.
21. *Adapted from* Sims, S. Truly a pioneer. *US Business Review*, November 2006, 116–117 (March 2007). For a different example, see Rodriguez, D. A., Targa, F., and Belzer, M. H. Pay incentives and truck driver safety: A case study. *Industrial and Labor Relations Review*, 2006, 59 (2), 205–225.
22. Bandura, A. *Social Learning Theory*. Upper Saddle River, NJ: Prentice Hall, 1977; Bandura, A. *Self-Efficacy: The Exercise of Self-Control*. New York: W. H. Freeman, 1997.
23. Duffy, J. Boundaryless psychology: A discussion. *Canadian Psychology*, 2003, 44, 249–256.
24. Ahearne, M., Mathieu, J., and Rapp, J. To empower or not to empower your sales force? An empirical examination of the influence of leadership empowerment behavior on customer satisfaction and performance. *Journal of Applied Psychology*, 2005, 90, 945–955.
25. *Adapted from* www.steelcase.com (March 2007); Hackett, J. P. Preparing for the perfect product lunch. *Harvard Business Review*, April 2007, 45–50; Hawthorne, C. Steelcase house. *Architecture*, November 2000, 67.
26. Judge, T. A., Jackson, C. L., and Shaw, J. C. Self-efficacy and work-related performance: The integral role of individual differences. *Journal of Applied Psychology*, 2007, 92, 107–127; Tasa, K., Taggar, S., and Seijts, G. H. The development of collective efficacy in teams: A multilevel and longitudinal perspective. *Journal of Applied Psychology*, 2007, 92, 17–27.
27. Stajkovic, A. D. Development of a core confidence-higher order construct. *Journal of Applied Psychology*, 2006, 91, 1208–1224.
28. Yeo, G. B., and Neal, A. An examination of the dynamic relationship between self-efficacy and performance across levels of analysis and levels of specificity. *Journal of Applied Psychology*, 2006, 91, 1088–1101.
29. Kerr, S. On the folly of rewarding A, while hoping for B. *Academy of Management Journal*, 2005, 18, 769–783.
30. *Adapted from* Lee, C., and Bobko, P. Self-efficacy beliefs: Comparison of five measures. *Journal of Applied Psychology*, 1994, 79, 364–370; Maurer, T. J., and Pierce, H. R. A comparison of Likert scale and traditional measures of self-efficacy. *Journal of Applied Psychology*, 1998, 83, 324–330.
31. Personal communication with Joe Salatino, President, Great Northern American, Dallas, TX, March 2007.

CHAPTER 5

1. *Adapted from* Lashinsky, A. Search and Joy. *Fortune*, January 22, 2007, 70–82; Helft, M. Google, master of online traffic helps its workers beat the rush. *New York Times*, March 10, 2007, A1–A3; Gog, S. K. At Google, hours are long, but the company is free. *Washington Post*, January 24, 2007, F1ff.
2. Goffee, R., and Jones, G. Leading clever people. *Harvard Business Review*, March 2007, 72–79; Latham, G. P., and Ernst, C. T. The new world of work and organizations: Keys to motivating tomorrow's workforce. *Human Resource Management Review*, 2006, 16(2), 181–198.
3. LePine, J. A., LePine, M. A., and Jackson, C. L. Challenge and hindrance stress: Relationships with exhaustion, motivation to learn and learning performance. *Journal of Applied Psychology*, 2004, 98, 883–891.

4. Maurer, T. J., Weiss, E. M., and Barbeite, F. G. A model of motivation in work-related learning and development activity: The effects of individual, situational, motivational, and age variables. *Journal of Applied Psychology*, 2003, 88, 707–724; Wright, T. A., and Bonett, D. G. Job satisfaction and psychological well-being as nonadditive predictors of workplace turnover. *Journal of Management*, 2007, 33, 141–160.
5. Halbesleben, J. R. B., and Bowler, W. M. Emotional exhaustion and job performance: The mediating role of motivation. *Journal of Applied Psychology*, 2007, 92, 93–106.
6. Whetton, D. A., and Cameron, K. S. *Developing Management Skills*, 7th ed. Upper Saddle River, NJ: Pearson, 2007, 328–329.
7. Maslow, A. H. *Motivation and Personality*. New York: Harper & Row, 1970. For an excellent overview of motivation models, see Ambrose, M. L., and Kulik, C. T. Old friends, new faces: Motivation research in the 1990s. *Journal of Management*, 1999, 25, 231–237.
8. Culp, M. Work programs boost weight loss. *Dallas Morning News*, March 25, 2007, J1–J8.
9. Lovett, S., and Coyle, T. Job satisfaction and technology in Mexico. *Journal of World Business*, 2004, 39, 217–232; Schuler, R. S., and Jackson, S. E. A quarter-century review of human resource management in the U.S. *Management Revue*, 2005, 16(1), 1–25.
10. Koltko-Rivera, M. E. Rediscovering the later version of Maslow's hierarchy of needs. *Review of General Psychology*, 2006, 10, 302–317.
11. McClelland, D. C., and Burnham, D. H. Power is the great motivator. *Harvard Business Review*, March/April 1976, 100–111; Payne, D. K. *Training Resources Group*. Boston: McBer & Company, 1998.
12. Rath, T. *Vital Friends*. New York: Gallup Press, 2006.
13. Personal communication with Susan Reed, General Manager, Innovative Hospice Care, Fort Worth, TX, March 2007.
14. *Adapted from* www.papajohns.com (March 2007); Walkup, C. International expansion is a big slice of pizza chain's plans. *Nation's Restaurant News*, February 19, 2007, 8–9.
15. Choi, J. A motivational theory of charismatic leadership. *Journal of Leadership and Organizational Studies*, 2006, 13, 24–43; Spreier, S. W., Fontaine, M. H., and Malloy, R. L. Leadership run amok: The destructive potential overachievers. *Harvard Business Review*, 2006, 84(6), 72–83.
16. Collins, C. J., Hanges, P. J., and Locke, E. A. The relationship of achievement motivation to entrepreneurial behavior: A meta-analysis. *Human Performance*, 2004, 17, 95–117.
17. Manager Joanne Reichardt, www.randstad.com (March 2007).
18. Herzberg, F. I., Mausner, B., and Snyderman, B. B. *The Motivation to Work*. New York: John Wiley & Sons, 1959; Bryne, M. The implications of Herzberg's "motivation-hygiene" theory for management in Irish Health sector. *The Health Care Manager*, January/March 2006, 4–12.
19. Hackman, J. R., and Oldham, G. R. *Work Redesign*. Reading, MA: Addison-Wesley 1980; Reb, J., and Cropanzona, R. Evaluating dynamic performance: The influence of salient Gestalt characteristics on performance ratings. *Journal of Applied Psychology*, 2007, 92, 490–499; Butler, A. B. Job characteristics and college performance and attitudes: A model of work–school conflict and facilitation. *Journal of Applied Psychology*, 2007, 92, 500–510.
20. www.athleta.com (March 2007).
21. *Adapted from* www.sun.com (March 2007); Greengard, S. Sun's shining example. *Workforce Management*, March 2005, 48.
22. Gómez, C. The influence of environmental, organizational, and HRM factors on employee behaviors in subsidiaries: A Mexican case study of organizational learning. *Journal of World Business*, 2004, 39, 1–11.
23. Vroom, V. H. *Work and Motivation*. New York: John Wiley & Sons, 1964.
24. Chapman, D. S., and Uggerslev, K. L. Applicant attraction to organizations and job choice: A meta-analytic review of the correlates of recruiting outcomes. *Journal of Applied Psychology*, 2005, 90, 928–944; Erez, A., and Isen, A. M. The influence of positive affect on the components of expectancy motivation. *Journal of Applied Psychology*, 2002, 87, 1055–1067.
25. Adler, N. *International Dimensions of Organizational Behavior*, 4th ed. Mason, OH: South-Western, 2002, 179–182.
26. Rhoades, L., and Eisenberger, R. Perceived organizational support: A review of the literature. *Journal of Applied Psychology*, 2002, 87, 698–714.
27. Personal interview with T. Johnson, Clinical Therapy Representative, Smith and Nephew, Corpus Christi, TX, March 2007.
28. *Adapted from* Frauenheim, E. NIIT raises U.S. presence with element K deal. *Workforce Management*, August 14, 2006, 12; Malik, O. McProgrammers. *Business 2.0*, August 2004, 97–102.
29. Adams, J. S. Toward an understanding of inequity. *Journal of Abnormal and Social Psychology*, 1963, 67, 422–436.
30. Shore, T. H., Tashchian, A., and Jourdan, L. Effects of internal and external pay comparisons on work attitudes. *Journal of Applied Social Psychology*, 2006, 36(10), 2578–2599.
31. Employee thefts of office supplies can add up to big costs. *HR Focus*, 2006, 83(9), 9; Gillentine, A. Knowing is half the battle for new hires. *Daily Record*, March 27, 2006, NA.
32. *Adapted from* Molzahn, J. *Education and reinforcement to modify workforce behavior* (unpublished paper). Dallas, TX: Cox School of Business, Southern Methodist University, December 2007.
33. Barsky, A., and Japlan, S. A. If you feel bad, it's unfair: A quantitative synthesis of affect and organizational justice perceptions. *Journal of Applied Psychology*, 2007, 92, 286–296; Li, H., Bingham, J. B., and Umphress, E. E. Fairness from the top perspective: Perceived procedural justice and collaborative problem solving in new

product development. *Organization Science*, 2007, 18, 200–216.

34. Thau, S., Aquino, K., and Wittek, R. An extension of uncertainty management theory to the self: The relationship between justice, social comparison orientation and antisocial work behaviors. *Journal of Applied Psychology*, 2007, 92, 250–258; Riolli, L., and Savicki, V. Impact of fairness, leadership and coping on strain, burnout and turnover in organizational change. *International Journal of Stress Management*, 2006, 13, 351–377; Grubb, III, W. L. Procedural justice and layoff survivor's commitment: A quantitative review. *Psychological Reports*, 2006, 99(2), 515–531; Niessen, C. Age and learning during unemployment. *Journal of Organizational Behavior*, 2006, 27, 771–792; Circuit City firing 3,400 workers. *Dallas Morning News*, March 29, 2007, 2D; Dalton, F. Bottom line: It's a business. *USA Today*, April 3, 2007, A14.
35. Kamdar, D., McAllister, D. J., and Turban, D. B. All in a day's work: How follower individual differences and justice perceptions predict OCB role definitions and behavior. *Journal of Applied Psychology*, 2006, 91, 841–855.
36. Hoffman, B. J., Blair, C. A., and Meriac, J. P. Expanding the criterion domain? A quantitative review of the OCB literature. *Journal of Applied Psychology*, 2007, 92, 555–566.
37. J. Richard Hackman and Greg R. Oldham, *WORK REDESIGN*, copyright 1980. Reprinted by permission of Pearson Education, Inc., Upper Saddle River, NJ.
38. *Adapted from* www.yueyuen.com (March 2007); Chang, L. T. In Chinese factory, rhythms of trade replace rural life. *Wall Street Journal*, December 31, 2004, A1–A5.

CHAPTER 6

1. *Adapted from* www.continentalairlines.com; Nohria, N., Mayo, A. J., and Benson, M. *Gordon Bethune at Continental Airlines*. Boston, MA: Harvard Business School Case, 9-406-073; Continental gains attitude. *Business Week Online*, April 4, 2007; Grensing-Pophal, L. Follow me. *HRMagazine*, 2000, 45(2), 36–39.
2. Rewards & recognition best practices. www.ascentgroup.com (May 2007).
3. Stajkovic, A. D., Locke, E. A., and Blair, E. S. A first examination of the relationships between primed subconscious goals, assigned conscious goals, and task performance. *Journal of Applied Psychology*, 2006, 91, 1172–1180; Latham, G. P. The motivational benefits of goal-setting. *Academy of Management Executive*, 2004, 18, 126–129.
4. Locke, E. A., and Latham, G. P. *A Theory of Goal Setting and Task Performance*. Englewood Cliffs, NJ: Prentice-Hall, 1990; Locke, E. A., and Latham, G. P. Building a practically useful theory of goal setting and task motivation: A 35-year odyssey. *American Psychologist*, 2002, 57, 705–717.
5. Latham, G. P. A five step approach to behavior change. *Organizational Dynamics*, 2003, 32, 309–318. For a good example, see Stock, H. Ways to motivate advisers to meet team goals. *American Banker*, 2007, 172(61), 9ff.
6. Moss, B. These workers heed their health, then reap rewards. *Dallas Morning News*, December 19, 2004, D7ff; Mullich, J. Get in line. *Workforce Management*, 2003, 82(13), 43–47; Erez, A., and Judge, T. A. Relationship to core self-evaluations to goal setting, motivation and performance. *Journal of Applied Psychology*, 2001, 86, 1270–1279.
7. Bandura, A., and Locke, E. A. Negative self-efficacy and goal effects revisited. *Journal of Applied Psychology*, 2003, 88, 87–99; Wolters, C. A. and Daugherty, S. G. Goal structures and teachers' sense of efficacy: Their relation and association to teaching experience and academic level. *Journal of Educational Psychology*, 2007, 99, 181–193.
8. *Adapted from* www.jeffgordon.com (May 2007); Anderson, L. NASCAR. *Sports Illustrated*, April 9, 2007, 84.
9. Cron, W. L., Slocum, J. W., VandeWalle, D., and Fu, F. The role of goal orientation, negative emotions and goal setting when initial performance falls short of one's performance goal. *Human Performance*, 2005, 18, 55–50; Seijts, G. H., Latham, G. P., Tasa, K., and Latham, B. W. Goal setting and goal orientation: An integration of two different yet related literatures. *Academy of Management Journal*, 2004, 47, 227–240.
10. *Adapted from* Wright, P. M., O'Leary-Kelly, A. M., Cortina, J. M., Klein, H. J., and Hollenbeck, J. R. On the meaning and measurement of goal commitment. *Journal of Applied Psychology*, 1994, 79, 795–808; Klaus-Helmut, S. Organizational commitment: A further moderator in the relationship between work stress and strain. *Journal of Stress Management*, 2007, 14, 26–40.
11. Mullich, J. Get in line. *Workforce Management*, 2003, 82 (13), 43–47.
12. Gossage, B. Lose weight, get a toaster. *Inc.*, January 2005, 24.
13. Zaslow, J. The most-praised generation goes to work. *Wall Street Journal*, May 6, 2007; Remus, I., and Judge, T. A. Goal regulation across time: The effects of feedback and affect. *Journal of Applied Psychology*, 2005, 90, 453–467; Mellalieu, S. D., Sheldon, H., and O'Brien, M. The effects of goal setting on rugby performance. *Journal of Applied Behavior Analysis*, 2006, 39(2), 257–262.
14. www.desstinyhealth.com (May 2007).
15. Locke and Latham. Building a practically useful theory.
16. *Adapted from* www.gapinc.com (May 2007).
17. Borton, L. Working in a Vietnamese voice. *Academy of Management Executive*, 2000, 14(4), 20–31; Smith, E. D., Jr., and Pham, C. Doing business in Vietnam: A cultural guide. *Business Horizons*, May/June 1996, 47–51.
18. Latham, G. P. The motivational benefits of goal-setting. *Academy of Management Executive*, 2004, 18(4), 125–126; Goldman, B. M., Masterson, S. S., and Locke, E. A. Goal-directedness and personal identity as correlates of life outcomes. *Psychological Reports*, 2002, 91, 152–166.
19. *Adapted from* Herper, M. Special surgery. *Forbes*, April 7, 2007, 51–55; www.cincinnatichildrens.org (May 2007).

20. Latham, G. P., and Locke, E. A. Enhancing the benefits and overcoming the pitfalls of goal setting. *Organizational Dynamics*, 2006, 35, 332–341.
21. *Adapted from* Dess, G. P., and Picken, J. C. *Beyond Productivity*. New York: American Management Association, 1999, 164–167.
22. Locke, E. A. Setting goals for life and happiness. In Snyder, C. R., and Lopez, S. J. (Eds.), *Handbook of Positive Psychology*. London: Oxford University Press, 2002, 299–312; Kerr, S., and Landauer, S. Using stretch goals to promote organizational effectiveness and personal growth: General Electric and Goldman Sachs. *Academy of Management Executive*, 2004, 18, 134–138.
23. www.ascentgroup (May 2007); Kalleberg, A. L., Marsden, P. V., Reynolds, J., and Knoke, D. Beyond profit? Sectoral differences in high-performance work practices. *Work and Occupations*, 2006, 33(3), 271–303.
24. Imberman, A. A. Gild your bottom line. www.pcimag.com (May 2007).
25. Tyler, L. S., and Fisher, B. The Scanlon concept: A philosophy as much as a system. *Personnel Administrator*, July 1983, 33–37.
26. Fox, J., and Lawson, B. Gain-sharing program lifts Baltimore employees' morale. *American City and County*, September 1997, 112(10), 93–94; Spevak, C. Gain-sharing revisited. *Physician Executive*, 2006, 32(2), 64–68.
27. Scott, K. D. Scanlon & skill: Two compensation plans for difficult times. *Pay for Performance*, December 2002, 1ff; personal conversation with Steve Watson, Managing Director, Stanton Chase, Dallas, TX, May 2007.
28. Mullich, J. Get in line, *Workforce Management*, 2003, 82 (13), 43–47.
29. Personal conversation with John Semyan, Partner, TSN, Dallas, May 2007. Also see Williams, M. L., McDaniel, M. A., and Nguyen, N. T. A meta-analysis of the antecedents and consequences of pay level satisfaction. *Journal of Applied Psychology*, 2006, 91, 392–413.
30. *Adapted from* Marquez, J. McDonald's rewards program leaves room for some local flavor. *Workforce Management*, April 10, 2006, 26.
31. Lee, C., Law, K. S., and Bobko, P. The importance of justice perceptions on pay effectiveness: A two-year study of a skilled-based pay plan. *Journal of Management*, 1999, 25, 851–873.
32. Guthrie, J. P. Alternative pay practices and employee turnover: An organization economics perspective. *Group & Organization Management*, 2000, 25, 419–439.
33. Personal conversation with Leslie Ritter, Principal, Square Knot, Addison, TX, May 2007.
34. Hofstede, G. *Cultures Consequences*, 2nd ed. Thousand Oaks, CA: Sage, 2001.
35. Tosi, H. L., and Greckhamer, T. Culture and CEO compensation. *Organization Science*, 2004, 15, 657–670. Carlo, G., Roesch, S. C., and Knight, G. P. Between or within cultural variation: Cultural group as a moderator of the relations between individual differences and resource allocation preferences. *Journal of Applied Development Psychology*, 2001, 22, 559–579.
36. *Adapted from* Locke and Latham. *A Theory of Goal Setting and Task Performance*, 355–358.
37. *Adapted from* www.allstate.com (May 2007); Allstate: 3rd time on the top 50 diversity list. *American Banker*, April 20, 2004, 9.

CHAPTER 7

1. *Adapted from* Milar, M., and Fuller, G. Stressed HR woman wins massive payout. *Personnel Today*, August 8, 2006, 3; Counseling: No compensation for manager failings. *BusinessZONE*, February 13, 2007, 1; Walker, E. Intel to pay for stress. *Swindon Advertiser*, February 8, 2007; Intel Incorporation and Tracy Ann Daw Ruling—Case No: B3/2006/1302. Strand, London: Royal Courts of Justice, February 7, 2007.
2. Delaney, M. Employers must act on workplace stress. *Personnel Today*, February 7, 2007, 1.
3. American Institute of Stress. Job stress. www.stress.org (January 2008).
4. Barling, J., Kelloway, E. K., and Frone, M. R. (Eds.). *Handbook of Work Stress*. Thousand Oaks, CA: Sage, 2005.
5. Fink, G. (Ed.). *Encyclopedia of Stress*. New York: Elsevier, 2007.
6. Selye, H. History of the stress concept. In Goldberger, L., and Breznitz, S. (Eds.) *Handbook of Stress*, 2nd ed. New York: Free Press, 1993, 7–20; Friedman, H. S., and Silver, R. C. (Eds.). *Foundations of Health Psychology*. New York: Oxford University Press, 2007.
7. Sundin, L., Bildt, C., Lisspers, J. Hochwalder, J., and Setterlind, S. Organizational factors, individual characteristics and social support: What determines the level of social support? *Work*, 2006, 27, 45–56.
8. Grant, S., and Langan-Fox, J. Personality and the occupational stressor–strain relationship: The role of the big five. *Journal of Occupational Health Psychology*, 2007, 12, 20–33.
9. Bettencourt, B. A., Talley, A., Benjamin, A. J., and Valentine, J. Personality and aggressive behavior under provoking and neutral conditions: A meta-analytic review. *Psychological Bulletin*, 2006, 132, 751–777.
10. Olson, K. R. A literature review of social mood. *Journal of Behavioral Science*, 2006, 7, 193–203.
11. Friedman, M., and Rosenman, R. *Type A Behavior and Your Heart*. New York: Knopf, 1974.
12. Cooper, C. L. (Ed.). *Handbook of Stress Medicine*. Boca Raton, FL: CRC Press, 2005
13. *Adapted from* Szegedy-Maszak, M. Competition freaks. *Los Angeles Times*, November 28, 2005, F1–F2; Santa Monica Rugby Club. www.santamonicarugby.com (February 26, 2007).
14. Maddi, S. R., Harvey, R. H., Khoshaba, D. M., Lu, J. L., Persico, M., and Brow, M. The personality construct of hardiness, III: Relationships with repression, innovativeness, authoritarianism, and performance. *Journal of Personality*, 2006, 74, 575–597.
15. Turnipseed, D. L. Hardy personality: A potential link with organizational citizenship behavior. *Psychological*

Reports, 93, 2003, 529–543; Jacobs, G. D. Truestar Health. www.truestarhealth.com (February 2007); Hardiness Institute for Performance Enhancement and Leadership Training. The hardiness concepts. www.hardinessinstitute.com (April 2007); Maddi, S. R., and Khoshaba, D. M. *Resilience at Work*. New York: Amacom, 2006.

16. Gryna, F. M. *Work Overload: Redesigning Jobs to Minimize Stress and Burnout*. Milwaukee, WI: ASQ Quality Press, 2004; Warr, P. *Work, Happiness, and Unhappiness*. New York: Psychology Press, 2007.
17. Richmond, A., and Skitmore, M. Stress and coping: A study of project managers in a large ICT organization. *Project Management Journal*, 2006, 37, 5–17.
18. Wong, S., DeSanctis, G., and Staudenmayer, N. The role relationship between task interdependency and role stress: A revisit of the job-demands control model. *Journal of Management Studies*, 2007, 44, 285–303; Daniels, K. Rethinking job characteristics in work stress research. *Human Relations*, 2006, 59, 267–290.
19. Maynard, M., Bunkley, N., and Austen, I. Detroit's slump could break up Chrysler group. *New York Times*, February 15, 2007, A1, A3.
20. Chao, L. Not-so-nice costs: As stress mounts, rise in office rudeness weighs on productivity. *Wall Street Journal*, January 17, 2006, B4.
21. Porath, C. L., and Erez, A. Does rudeness really matter? The effects of rudeness on task performance and helpfulness. *Academy of Management Journal*, 2007, 50, 1181–1197.
22. Pearson, C. M., Andersson, L. M., and Porath, C. L. Assessing and attacking workplace incivility. *Organizational Dynamics*, 2000, 29(2), 123–137.
23. *Adapted from* Pomeroy, A. The ethics squeeze. *HRMagazine*, 2006, 51(3), 48–55.
24. Aziz, S., and Zickar, M. J. A cluster analysis investigation of workaholism as a syndrome. *Journal of Occupational Health Psychology*, 2006, 11, 52–62; Jones, F., Burke, R. J., and Westman, M. (Eds.). *Work–Life Balance: A Psychological Perspective*. New York: Psychology Press, 2006.
25. Kossek, E. E., and Lambert, S. J. (Eds.). *Work and Life Integration: Organizational, Cultural, and Individual Perspective*. Mahwah, NJ: Lawrence Erlbaum Associates, 2005.
26. Hobson, C. J., Kamen, J., Szostek, J., Nethercut, C. M., Tiedman, J. W., and Wojnarowicz, S. Stressful life events: A revision and update of the social readjustment rating scale. *International Journal of Stress Management*, 1998, 5, 1–23.
27. Clarke, S., and Cooper, C. (Eds.). *Managing the Risk of Workplace Stress*. New York: Routledge, 2003; Ashforth, B. E., Kreiner, G. E., Clark, M. A., and Fugate, M. Normalizing dirty work: Managerial tactics for countering occupational taint. *Academy of Management Journal*, 2007, 50, 149–174.
28. Arnetz, B. B., and Ekman, R. (Eds.). *Stress in Health and Disease*. New York: Wiley, 2006.
29. Gillentine, A. Health care costs are 50 percent higher due to reports of high levels of stress. *Colorado Springs Business Journal*, May 26, 2006, 1; Conlin, M. Get healthy—or else. *Business Week*, February 26, 2007, 58–69.
30. Haines, J., Williams, C. L., and Carson, J. Workers' compensation for psychological injury: Demographic and work-related correlates. *Work*, 2006, 26, 57–66.
31. *Post-Traumatic Stress Disorder: A Real Illness*. Washington, DC: National Institute of Mental Health, 2005.
32. Josi, V. *Stress: From Burnout to Balance*. Thousand Oaks, CA: Sage, 2005; LeFevre, M., Kolt, G. S., and Matheny, J. Eustress, distress, and their interpretation in primary and secondary occupational stress interventions: Which way first? *Journal of Managerial Psychology*, 2006, 21, 547–565.
33. Reinardy, S. It's gametime: The Maslach burnout inventory measures burnout of sports journalists. *Journalism and Mass Communication Quarterly*, 2006, 83, 397–412.
34. Halbesleben, J. R., and Bowler, M. Emotional exhaustion and job performance: The mediating role of motivation. *Journal of Applied Psychology*, 2007, 92, 93–106.
35. Toppinen-Tanner, S., Kalimo, R., and Mutanen, P. The process of burnout in white-collar and blue-collar jobs: Eight-year prospective study of exhaustion. *Journal of Organizational Behavior*, 2002, 23, 555–567.
36. Seward, B. L. *Managing Stress: Principles and Strategies for Health and Well-Being*, 4th ed. Sudbury, MA: Jones & Bartlett, 2004.
37. Luskin, F., and Pelletier, K. *Stress Free for Good: 10 Scientifically Proven Life Skills for Health and Happiness*. San Francisco: HarperSanFrancisco, 2005; Shelton, A. *Transforming Burnout: A Simple Guide to Self Renewal*. Tacoma, WA: Vibrant Press, 2006.
38. Gamow, D., and Gamow, K. *Freedom from Stress: How to Take Control of Your Life*. Lakewood, CO: Glenbridge Publishing, 2006.
39. *Adapted from* Jacobs, M. IT is most stressful job, survey says. *Dallas Morning News*, January 21, 2007, 1J, 6J; Chordial Solutions. www.chordial.com (March 2007).
40. Grazier, K. L. Interview with Larry Sanders. *Journal of Healthcare Management*, 2006, 51(4), 212–214.
41. Halton, C. Health risk management: Well being for the employee and the bottom line. *Benefits Quarterly*, 2005, 21(3), 7–10; Milano, C. What ails wellness programs? *Risk Management*, 2007, 54(6), 30–37.
42. For extensive information on wellness programs, go to the website for the Wellness Councils of America at www.welcoa.org (January 2008); also see Murta, S. G., Sanderson, K., and Oldenburg, B. Process evaluation in occupational stress management programs: A systematic review. *American Journal of Health Promotion*, 2007, 21, 248–254.
43. *Adapted from* Cianbro's wellness plan cuts healthcare costs. *Contractor's Business Management Report*, February 2007, 1, 11–14; About Cianbro. www.cianbro.com (February 2007).
44. *Adapted from* Martinko, M. J., Douglas, S. C., and Harvey, P. Understanding and managing workplace aggression. *Organizational Dynamics*, 2006, 35, 117–130; Geddes, D., and Roberts Callister, R. Crossing the line

(s): A dual threshold model of anger in organizations. *Academy of Management Review*, 2007, 32, 721–746.

45. Schat, A. C. H., and Kelloway, E. K. Workplace aggression. In Barling, J., Frone, M., and Kelloway, E. K. (Eds.). *Handbook of Work Stress*. Thousand Oaks, CA: Sage, 2005, 189–218.
46. Schat, A. C. H., Frone, M. R., and Kelloway, E. K. Prevalence of workplace aggression in the U.S. workforce. In Kelloway, E. K., Barling, J., Hurrell, Jr., J. J. (Eds.). *Handbook of Workplace Violence*. Thousand Oaks, CA: Sage, 2006, 47–91; Leonard, B. Study: Bully bosses prevalent in U.S. *HRMagazine*, 2007, 52(5), 22, 28.
47. James, L. R., and Associates. A conditional reasoning measure for aggression. *Organizational Research Methods*, 2005, 8, 69–99; Cavell, T. A., and Malcolm, K. T. (Eds.). *Anger, Aggression, and Interventions for Interpersonal Violence*. Mahwah, NJ: Lawrence Erlbaum Associates, 2007.
48. Salin, D. Ways of explaining workplace bullying: A review of enabling, motivating and precipitating structures and processes in the work environment. *Human Relations*, 2003, 56, 1213–1232; Heames, J., and Harvey, M. Workplace bullying: A cross-level assessment. *Management Decision*, 2006, 44, 1214–1230.
49. Lutgen-Sandvik, P., Tracy, S. J., and Alberts, J. K. Burned by bullying in the American workplace. *Journal of Management Studies*, 2007, 44, 837–862.
50. Workplace Bullying Institute. Workplace bullying-related research. www.bullyinginstitute.org (March 2007); Kilmartin, C., and Allison, J. *Men's Violence against Women: Theory, Research, and Activism*. Mahwah, NJ: Lawrence Erlbaum Associates, 2007.
51. Tracy, S. J., Lutgen-Sandvik, P., and Alberts, J. K. Nightmares, demons, and slaves: Exploring the painful metaphors of workplace bullying. *Management Communication Quarterly*, 2006, 20, 148–185; Hodson, R., Roscigno, V. J., and Lopez, S. H. Chaos and the abuse of power: Workplace bullying in organizational and interactional context. *Work and Occupations*, 2006, 33, 382–416.
52. Canada Safety Council. Bullying in the workplace. www.safety-council.org (March 2007).
53. Von Bergen, C. W., Zavaletta, J. A., and Soper, B. Legal remedies for workplace bullying: Grabbing the bully by the horns. *Employee Relations Law Journal*, 2006, 32(3), 14–40; Meglich-Sepico, P., Faley, R. H., and Erdos Knapp, D. Relief and redress for targets of workplace bullying. *Employee Responsibilities and Rights Journal*, 2007, 19, 31–43.
54. Harvey, M. G., Heames, J. T., Richey, R. G., and Leonard, N. Bullying: From the playground to the boardroom. *Journal of Leadership & Organizational Studies*, 2006, 12(4), 1–11; Ferris, G. R., Zinko, R., Brouer, R. L., Buckley, M. R., and Harvey, M. G. Strategic bullying as a supplementary, balanced perspective on destructive leadership. *Leadership Quarterly*, 2007, 18, 195–206.
55. Westhues, K. Summary of workplace mobbing conference. Brisbane, Australia: Workplace Mobbing Conference, October 14–15, 2004.
56. Davenport, N., Schwartz, R. D., and Elliott, G. P. *Mobbing: Emotional Abuse in the American Workplace*, 3rd ed. Ames, IA: Civil Society Publishing, 2005.
57. Gates, G. Bullying and mobbing. *Pulp & Paper*, 2004, 78 (10), 31–33.
58. Bowling, N. A., and Beehr, T. A. Workplace harassment from the victim's perspective: A theoretical model and meta-analysis. *Journal of Applied Psychology*, 2006, 91, 998–1012; Harassment. http://en.wikipedia.org (March 2007).
59. This discussion is based on Sexual harassment. http://en.wikipedia.org (March 2007); Division for Public Education, American Bar Association. Sexual harassment. www.abanet.org (April 2007); Boland, M. L. *Sexual Harassment in the Workplace: What You Need to Know and What You Can Do*. Naperville, IL: Sourcebooks, 2006.
60. Equal Opportunity Commission. Sexual harassment. www.eeoc.gov (March 2007); Gordon-Howard, L. *The Sexual Harassment Handbook*. Franklin Lakes, NJ: Career Press, 2007.
61. *Adapted from* OfficeWorksRX sexual harassment policy. www.officeworksRX.com (March 2007).
62. Walsh, D. J. *Employment Law for Human Resource Practice*, 2nd ed. Mason, OH: Thomson/South-Western, 2007.
63. Ilies, R., Hauserman, N., Schwochau, S., and Stibal, J. Reported incidence rates of work-related sexual harassment in the United States. *Personnel Psychology*, 2003, 56, 607–632.
64. Daniel, T. D. Developing a "culture of compliance" to prevent sexual harassment. *Employment Relations Today*, 2003, 30(3), 33–42.
65. Workplace violence. http://en.wikipedia.org (March 2007).
66. Canadian Centre for Occupational Health and Safety. Violence in the workplace. www.ccohs.ca (March 2007); Cappell, D., and DiMartino, V. *Violence at Work*, 3rd ed. Geneva, Switzerland: International Labour Organization, 2006.
67. Survey of workplace violence prevention. Washington, DC: United States Department of Labor, October 27, 2006.
68. Geffner, R., Baverman, M., Galasso, J., and Marsh, J. (Eds.). *Aggression in Organizations: Violence, Abuse, and Harassment at Works and Schools*. Binghamton, NY: Haworth Press, 2004.
69. Hershcovis, M. S., Turner, N., Barling, J., Arnold, K. A., Dupré, K. E., Inness, M., LeBlanc, M. M., and Sivanathan, N. Predicting workplace aggression: A meta-analysis. *Journal of Applied Psychology*, 2007, 92, 228–238.
70. Perline, I. H., and Goldschmidt, J. *The Psychology and Law of Workplace Violence*. Springfield, IL: Charles C. Thomas, 2004; Galperin, B. L., and Leck, J. D. Understanding the violent offender in the workplace. *Journal of American Academy of Business*, 2007, 10, 114–120.
71. Lucero, M. A., and Allen, R. E. Implementing zero tolerance policies: Balancing strict enforcement with fair treatment. *S.A.M. Advanced Management Journal*, 2006, 71(1), 35–42; Martinko, M. J., Douglas, S. C., Harvey, P., and Joseph, C. Managing organizational aggression.

In Kidwell, R., and Martin, C. (Eds.). *Managing Organizational Deviance*. Thousand Oaks, CA: Sage, 2005, 237–259.

72. Olson, B. J., Nelson, D. L., and Parayitam, S. Managing aggression in organizations: What leaders must know. *Leadership & Organization Development Journal*, 2006, 27, 384–398; Viollis, P., Roper, M. J., and Dicker, K. Avoiding the legal aftermath of workplace violence. *Employee Relations Law Journal*, 2005, 31(3), 65–70.
73. *Adapted and modified from* Lawrence, S. A., Garner, J., and Callan, V. J. The support appraisal work stressors inventory: Construction and initial validation. *Journal of Vocational Behavior*, 2007, 70, 172–204.
74. Russell, G. *Ethical dilemma at Northlake.* Used with permission of author. Grant Russell is director of the Bachelor of Accounting & Financial Management Program, School of Accountancy, University of Waterloo: Waterloo, Ontario, 2005.

CHAPTER 8

1. *Adapted from* George, G. *True North: Discover Your Authentic Leadership*. Hoboken, NJ: Wiley 2007; George, B. What is your true north? *Fortune*, March 19, 2007, 125–130; About Amgen. www.amgen.com (March 2007). Hollon, J. 10 steps for innovation. *Workforce Management*, February 27, 2006, 50–51.
2. De Vito, J. A. *Interpersonal Messages: Communication and Relationship Skills*. Boston: Allyn & Bacon, 2008; Beebe, S. A., Beebe, S. J., and Redmond, M. V. *Interpersonal Communication: Relating to Others*, 5th ed. Boston: Allyn & Bacon, 2008.
3. Bokeno, R. M. Dialogue at work? What it is and isn't. *Development and Learning in Organizations*, 2007, 21, 9–11.
4. Boyle, M. Growing against the grain. *Fortune*, May 3, 2004, 148–152.
5. Biography: Kevin W. Sharer. www.referenceforbusiness.com (March 2007).
6. Russ, G. S., Draft, R. L., and Lengel, R. H. Media selection and managerial characteristics in organizational communications. *Management Communication Quarterly*, 1990, 4, 151–175; Robert, L. P., and Dennis, A. R. Paradoxes of richness: A cognitive model of media choice. *IEE Transactions on Professional Communication*, 2005, 48, 10–21: Sheer, V. C., and Chen, L. Improving media richness theory. *Management Communication Quarterly*, 2004, 18, 76–93.
7. Shepherd, M. M., and Martz, Jr., W. B. Media richness theory and the distance education environment. *Journal of Computer Information Systems*, 2006, 47, 114–122.
8. Jensen, A., and Trenholm, S. *Interpersonal Communication*, 6th ed. New York: Oxford University Press, 2007.
9. Stetts, D. K. Learning to work with emotions during an internship. *Business Communication Quarterly*, 2006, 4, 446–449.
10. *Adapted from* Molinsky, A., and Margolis, J. The emotional tightrope of downsizing: Hidden challenges for leaders and their organizations. *Organizational Dynamics*, 2006, 35, 145–159.
11. Hamlin, S. B. *How to Talk So People Listen: Connecting in Today's Workplace*. New York: HarperCollins, 2006.
12. Adler, R. B. Rodman, G., and Elmhorst, J. *Understanding Human Communication*, 9th ed. New York: Oxford University Press, 2006.
13. Scott, J. C. Differences in American and British vocabulary: Implications for international business. *Business Communication Quarterly*, December 2000, 27–39.
14. Fisher, A. America's most admired corporations. *Fortune*, March 19, 2007, 88–94.
15. Ecomagination. www.ge.ecomagination.com (January 2008).
16. Brinson, S. L., and Benoit, W. L. The tarnishing star. *Management Communication Quarterly*, 1999, 12, 483–510; Labich, K. No more crude at Texaco. *Fortune*, September 6, 1999, 205–212.
17. Spitzberg, B. H., and Cupach, W. R. *The Dark Side of Interpersonal Communication*. Mahwah, NJ: Lawrence Erlbaum Associates, 2007.
18. Marshak, R. J. *Covert Processes at Work: Managing the Five Hidden Dimensions of Organizational Change*. San Francisco: Berrett-Kohler, 2007.
19. Keil, M., Im, G. P., and Mähring, M. Reporting bad news on software projects: The effects of culturally constituted views of face-saving. *Information Systems Journal*, 2007, 17, 59–87.
20. Vigoda-Gadot, E., and Drory, A. (Eds.). *Handbook of Organizational Politics*, North Hampton, MA: Edward Elgar Publishing, 2006.
21. Beamer, L., and Varner, I. *Intercultural Communication in the Global Workplace*, 4th ed. New York: McGraw-Hill, 2008.
22. Mozveni, A. Solving the riddles of Iran. www.martinfrost.ws (March 2007).
23. Slackman, M. The fine art of hiding what you mean to say. *New York Times*, August 6, 2006, 4–5.
24. Eckert, G. *Intercultural Communication*. Mason, OH: Thomson/South-Western, 2006; Tuleja, E. A. *Intercultural Communication for Business*. Mason, OH: Thomson/South-Western, 2005.
25. Ethnocentrism. http://en.wikipedia.com (March 2007); Gudykunst, W. B. (Ed.). *Theorizing about Intercultural Communication*. Thousand Oaks, CA: Sage, 2005.
26. *Adapted from* Hempel, J. Nokia's design research for everyone. BusinessWeek.com, www.businessweek.com (March 17, 2007).
27. Nokia. www.nokia.com (March 2007); Chipchase, J. Always on: An introduction to design research for everyone. www.janchipchase.com (January 2008).
28. Kohlrieser, G. The power of authentic dialogue. *Leader to Leader*, Fall 2006, 36–40; Bokeno. Dialogue at work?; Conklin, J. *Dialogue Mapping: Building Shared Understanding of Wicked Problems*. New York: Wiley, 2006.
29. *Adapted from* Hollon. Ten steps for innovation, 50.
30. Amgen: Our mission and values. www.amgen.com (March 2007).
31. Ucok, O. Transparency, communication and mindfulness. *Journal of Management Development*, 2006, 25 1024–1028; Balton, J. The candor imperative. *Industrial and*

Commercial Training, 2006, 7, 342–349; Jablin, F. M. Courage and courageous communication among leaders and followers in groups, organizations, and communities. *Management Communication Quarterly*, 2006, 20, 94–1101.

32. Covey, S. M. R., and Merrill, R. R. *The Speed of Trust: The One Thing that Changes Everything*. New York: Free Press, 2006; Bachmann, R., and Zaheer, A. (Eds.). *Handbook of Trust Research*. Northampton, MA: Edward Elgar Publishing, 2007.
33. London, M. *Job Feedback: Giving, Seeking, and Using Feedback for Performance Improvement*, 2nd ed. Mahwah, NJ: Lawrence Erlbaum Associates, 2003.
34. Atwater, L. E. 360-degree feedback to leaders: Does it relate to changes in employee attitudes? *Groups & Organization Management*, 2006, 31, 578–600; Bradley, T. P., Allen, J. M., Hamilton, S., and Filgo, S. K. Leadership perception: Analysis of 360-degree feedback. *Performance Improvement Quarterly*, 2006, 19, 7–23.
35. Petrino, S. (Ed.). *Balancing the Secrets of Private Disclosures*. Mahwah, NJ: Lawrence Erlbaum Associates, 2000; Kirkpatrick, D. C., Duck, S., and Foley, M. K. *Relating Difficulty: The Process of Constructing and Managing Difficult Interactions*. Mahwah, NJ: Lawrence Erlbaum Associates, 2006.
36. Sixel, L. M. How to deal when cupid strikes at work. *Houston Chronicle*, February 15, 2007, D1–D2.
37. Nierenberg, A. *Million Dollar Networking: The Sure Way to Find, Keep and Grow Your Business*. Sterling, VA: Capital Books, 2006.
38. *Adapted from* Hoppe, M. *Active Listening: Improve Your Ability to Listen and Lead*. Greensboro, NC: Center for Creative Leadership, 2006; Brownell, J. *Listening: Attitudes, Principles, and Skills*, 3rd ed. Boston: Allyn & Bacon, 2006.
39. Compton, M. Communications 101. *Women in Business*, 2006, 58(5), 13–13; Raines, C., and Ewing, L. *The Art of Connecting: How to Communicate Effectively with Anyone*. New York: Amacom, 2006.
40. *Adapted from* Holmes, A. The art of influence: Without it you'll never get anything done. *CIO*, 2006, 20(3), 1–5.
41. About Worldspan. http://worldspan.com (March 2007).
42. Center for Nonverbal Studies. Nonverbal communication. http://members/aol.com/nonverbal2/center.htm (January 2008).
43. Hickson, M., Stacks, D. W., and Moore, N. *Nonverbal Communication: Studies and Applications*. New York: Oxford University Press, 2007. Manusov, U., and Patterson, M. L. (Eds.). *The SAGE Handbook of Nonverbal Communication*. Thousand Oaks, CA: Sage, 2006.
44. *Adapted from* Beall, A. E. Body language speaks. *Communication World*, March/April 2004, 18–20; Knapp, M. L., and Hall, J. A. *Nonverbal Communication in Human Interaction*, 6th ed. Belmont, CA: Wadsworth, 2006.
45. Zeer, D. *Office Feng Shui: Creating Harmony in Your Work Space*. San Francisco: Chronicle Books, 2004.
46. Tsang, E. W. Toward a scientific inquiry into superstitious business decision-making. *Organization Studies*, 2004, 25, 923–946; Smith, V., and Stewart, B. L. *Feng Shui: A Practical Guide for Architects and Designers*, New York: Kaplan Publishing, 2006.
47. American Feng Shui Institute. www.amfengshui.com (March 2007).
48. *Adapted from* Welch, S. J. Traveling with the boss. *New York Times*, July 18, 2006, C7–C8.
49. Comedy Sportz Chicago. www.comedysportzchicago.com (March 2007).
50. Bowe, H., and Martin, K. *Communication across Cultures: Mutual Understanding in a Global World*. New York: Cambridge University Press, 2007; Newsom, D. *Bridging the Gaps in Global Communication*. Boston: Blackwell Publishing, 2007.
51. Bluedorn, A. C., Kaufman, C. F., and Lane, P. M. How many things do you like to do at once? An introduction to monochronic and polychronic time. *Academy of Management Executive*, 1992, 6(4), 17–26; Kaufman-Scarborough, C., and Lindquist, J.D. Time management and polychronicity comparisons, contrasts, and insights for the workplace. *Journal of Managerial Psychology*, 1999, 14, 288–312; Crossan, M., Cunha, M. P., Vera, D., and Cunha, J. Time and organizational improvisation. *Academy of Management Review*, 2005, 30, 129–145.
52. Samovar, L. A., Porter, R. E., and McDaniel, E. R. *Communication between Cultures*, 6th ed. Belmont, CA: Thompson/Wadsworth Publishing, 2007.
53. Latane, B., Liu, J. H., Nowak, A., Bonevento, M., and Zheng, L. Distance matters: Physical space and social impact. *Personality and Social Psychology Bulletin*, 1995, 21, 795–805.
54. Aquino, K., Brover, S. L., Bradfield, M., and Allen, D. G. The effects of negative affectivity, hierarchical status, and self-determination on workplace victimization. *Academy of Management Journal*, 1999, 42, 260–272.
55. Pease, B., and Pease, A. *The Definitive Book of Body Language*. New York: Bantam, 2006.
56. *Adapted from* Baber, D., and Wayman, L. Internal networking: The key to influence. *Canadian HR Reporter*, June 17, 2002, 12–13.
57. Amand, N., and Conger, J. A. Capabilities of the consummate networker. *Organizational Dynamics*. 2007, 36, 13–27; Ng, I., and Chow, I. H. Does networking with colleagues matter in enhancing job performance? *Asia Pacific Journal of Management*, 2005, 22, 405–421.
58. Ahearn, K. K., Ferris, G. R., Hochwarter, W. A., Douglas, C., and Ammeter, A. P. Leader political skill and team performance. *Journal of Management*, 2004, 30, 309–327.
59. Ferris, G. R., Treadway, D. C., Kolodinsky, R. W., Hochwarter, W. A., Kacmar, C. J., Douglas, C., and Frank, D. D. Development and validation of the political skill inventory. *Journal of Management*, 2005, 31, 128; also see Treadway, D. C., Hochwarter, W. A., Kacmar, C. J., and Ferris, G. R. Political will, political skill, and political behavior. *Journal of Organizational Behavior*, 2005, 26, 229–246.
60. Longenecker, C. O., Neubert, M. J., and Fink, L. S. Causes and consequences of managerial failure in rapidly changing organizations. *Business Horizons*, 2007, 50, 145–155.

61. Trenholm, S. *Thinking through Communication: An Introduction to the Study of Human Communication*, 5th ed. Boston: Allyn & Bacon, 2007.
62. Bordia, P., Jones, E., Gallois, C., and Difonzia, N. Management are aliens! Rumors and stress in organizational change. *Groups and Organization Management*, 2006, 31, 601–621.
63. *Adapted from* Burke, L. A., and Morris Wise, J. The effective care, handling and pruning of the office grapevine. *Business Horizon*, 2003, 46(3), 71–76.
64. Kemmel, A. J. *Rumors and Rumor Control: A Manager's Guide to Understanding and Combatting Rumors*. Mahwah, NJ: Lawrence Erlbaum Associates, 2004.
65. Michelson, G., and Mouly, V. S. Do loose lips sink ships? The meaning, antecedents and consequences of rumor and gossip in organizations. *Corporate Communications: An International Journal*, 2004, 9, 189–201.
66. *Adapted from* Amand, N., and Conger, J. A. Capabilities of the consummate networker. *Organizational Dynamics*, 2007, 36, 13–27.
67. Mattel: Investor Relations. www.mattel.com (April 2007).
68. *Adapted from* Marquez, J. Private concerns. *Workforce Management*, 2006, 85(18), 1, 41–43.
69. Cross, R., Thomas, B., Dutra, A., and Newberry, C. Using network analysis to build a business. *Organizational Dynamics*, 2007, 36, 345–362; Belasen, A. T. *The Theory and Practice of Corporate Communication: A Competing Values Perspective*. Thousand Oaks, CA: Sage, 2007.
70. Epley, N., & Kruger, J. When what you type isn't what they read: The perseverance of stereotypes and expectancies over e-mail. *Journal of Experimental Social Psychology*, 2005, 41, 414–422; Kruger, J., Epley, N., Parker, J., and Ng, Z. Egocentrism over e-mail: Can people communicate as well as they think? *Journal of Personality and Social Psychology*, 2005, 89, 925–936.
71. Enemark, D. It's all about me: Why e-mails are so easily misunderstood. *Christian Science Monitor*, May 15, 2006, 13–14.
72. Whipple, R. T. *Understanding E-Body Language: Building Trust Online*. Rochester, NY: Productivity Publications, 2006; Byron, K. Carrying too heavy a load? The communication and miscommunication of emotion by email. *Academy of Management Review*, 2008, 33, in press.
73. Chatzky, J. Confessions of an e-mail addict. *Money*, March 2007, 28–29.
74. Whipple, R. E-body language: Decoded. *T & D*, February 2006, 20–22.
75. *Adapted from* E-mail. Can we talk. *Business Week*, December 4, 2006, 109.
76. *Adapted from* Ferris, G. R., Treadway, D. C., Kolodinsky, R. W., Hochwarter, W. A., Kacmar, C. J., Douglas, C., and Frink, D. D. Development and validation of the political skill inventory. *Journal of Management*, 2005, 31, 126–152. Used with permission.
77. *Adapted from* Susan on relationship building and the women's network. http://pwc.blogs.com/pwcpeople/2007/ (April 1007); PricewaterhouseCoopers named 2007 Catalyst Award winner. www.catalyst.org (April 2007); About us: Diversity. www.pwc.com (April 2007).

CHAPTER 9

1. *Adapted from* Hymowitz, C. Business is personal so managers need to harness emotions. *Wall Street Journal*, November 13, 2006, B1; Vara, V. After GE: Intuit's Steve Bennett on why some General Electric alumni succeed—and some don't. *Wall Street Journal*, April 16, 2007, R3; Kirkpatrick, D. Throw it to the wall and see if it sticks. *Fortune*, December 12, 2005, 142–146; Shinn, S. Think smart, move fast. *BizED*, May/June 2007, 20–24. About Intuit. www.intuit.com (January 2008).
2. Tichy, N. M. The teachable point of view. *Journal of Business Strategy*, January/February 1998, 29–33; Tichy, N. M. *The Cycle of Leadership: How Great Leaders Teach Their Companies to Win*. New York: HarperBusiness, 2004; Tichy, N. M., and DeRose, C. Leadership judgment at the front line. *Leader to Leader*, Summer 2006, 31–37.
3. McCartney, W. W., and Campbell, C. R. Leadership, management, and derailment: A model of individual success and failure. *Leadership & Organization Development Journal*, 2006, 27, 190–202.
4. White Stag Leadership Development. Principles of leadership. www.whitestag.org (April 2007).
5. Northouse, P. G. *Leadership: Theory and Practice*, 4th ed. Thousand Oaks, CA: Sage, 2007.
6. Ferris, G. R., Davidson, S. L., and Perrewe, P. L. *Political Skill at Work: Impact on Work Effectiveness*. Mountain View, CA: Davies-Black Publishing, 2005; Glaser, J. E. Power and influence. *Leadership Excellence*, 2006, 23(3), 16–18.
7. French, J. R. P., and Raven, B. The bases of social power. In Cartwright, D. (Ed.). *Studies in Social Power*. Ann Arbor: University of Michigan Institute for Social Research, 1959, 150–167.
8. See, for example, the classic work by Barnard, C. I. *The Functions of the Executive*. Cambridge, MA: Harvard University Press, 1938, 110.
9. Fryer, B. Bosses from heaven—and hell! *Computerworld*, August 9, 1999, 46–47; also see de Reuver, R. The influence of organizational power on conflict dynamics. *Personnel Review*, 2006, 35, 589–603.
10. Ibid.; also see Chen, H.-M., and Hsieh, Y.-H. Key trends of the total reward system in the 21st century. *Compensation and Benefits Review*, 2006, 38(6), 64–71.
11. Ibid.; also see Troutwine, R. Ruling by fear and intimidation. *T&D*, 2006, 60(1), 14–15.
12. Ibid.; also see Fedor, D. B., and Ramsay, R. J. Effects of supervisor power on preparer's responses to audit review: A field study. *Behavioral Research in Accounting*, 2007, 19, 91–105.
13. Fryer, Bosses from heaven—and hell!
14. Scarnati, J. T. The godfather theory of management: An exercise in power and control. *Management Decision*, 2002, 40, 834–841; Blass, F. R., and Ferris, G. R. Leader reputation: The role of mentoring, political skill, contextual learning, and adaptation. *Human Resource Management*, 2007, 46, 5–19.

15. Cross, R., Parker, A., and Cross, R. L. *The Hidden Power of Social Networks: Understanding How Work Really Gets Done in Organizations*. Boston: Harvard Business School Press, 2004; Harvard Business Essentials. *Power, Influence, and Persuasion*. Boston: Harvard Business School Press, 2005.
16. Poon, J. M. Trust-in-supervisor and helping coworkers: Moderating effect of perceived politics. *Journal of Managerial Psychology*, 2006, 21, 518–532; Treadway, D. C., Hochwarter, W. A., Ferris, G. R., Kacmar, C. J., Douglas, C., Ammeter, A. P., and Buckley, M. R. Leader political skill and employee reactions. *Leadership Quarterly*, 2004, 15, 493–513.
17. Madison, D. L., Allen, R. W., Porter, L. W., Renwick, P. A., and Mayes, B. T. Organizational politics: An exploration of managers' perceptions. *Human Relations*, 1980, 33, 79–100; Finkelstein, S. *Why Smart Executives Fail: What You Can Learn from Them*. Bergenfield, NJ: Penguin, 2003.
18. Valle, M. The power of politics: Why leaders need to learn the art of influence. *Leadership in Action*, 2006, 26 (2), 8–12; Broom, M. F. *The Infinite Organization: Celebrating the Positive Use of Power in Organizations*. Palo Alto, CA: Davies-Black, 2002.
19. Higgins, C., Judge, T. A., and Ferris, G. R. Influence tactics and work outcomes. A meta-analysis. *Journal of Organizational Behavior*, 2003, 24, 89–106.
20. Hochwarter, W. A., Ferris, G. R., Gavin, M. B., and Perrewé, P. L. Political skill as neutralizer of felt accountability—job tension effects on job performance ratings: A longitudinal investigation. *Organizational Behavior and Human Decision Processes*, 2007, 102, 226–254; Ferris, G. R., Treadway, D. C., Perrewé, P. L., Brouer, R. L., Douglas, C., and Lux, S. Political skill in organizations. *Journal of Management*, 2007, 33, 290–330; Akella, A. *Unlearning the Fifth Discipline: Power, Politics, and Control in Organizations*. Thousand Oaks, CA: Sage, 2004.
21. Catano, V. M., Darr, W., and Campbell, C. A. Performance appraisal of behavior-based competencies: A reliable and valid procedure. *Personnel Psychology*, 2007, 60, 60–89; Bennett, Jr., W., Lance, C. E., and Wolhr, D. J. *Performance Measurement: Current Perspectives and Future Challenges*. Mahwah, NJ: Laurence Erlbaum Associates, 2006.
22. *Adapted from* View from the top: Leading women executives talk about how they got where they are—and why their ranks are so thin. *Wall Street Journal*, November 20, 2006, R6–R7.
23. Autodesk: Company information. www.autodesk.com (April 2007).
24. Yukl, G. A. *Leadership in Organizations*, 6th ed. Upper Saddle River, NJ: Pearson Prentice-Hall, 2006; Sidle, C. The five intelligences of leadership. *Leader to Leader*, Winter 2007, 19–25.
25. Bass, B. M. *Bass and Stogdill's Handbook of Leadership*, 3rd ed. New York: Free Press, 1990; Zaccaro, S. J. Traits-based perspective of leadership. *American Psychologist*, 2007, 62, 6–16.
26. McGregor, D. The human side of enterprise. *Management Review*, 46(11), 1957, 22–28, reprinted in *Reflections: The SOL Journal*, Fall 2000, 6–14; Heil, G., Stephens, D. C., McGregor, D., and Bennis, W. G. *Douglas McGregor, Revisited: Managing the Human Side of the Enterprise*. New York: John Wiley & Sons, 2000.
27. McGregor, D., *The Human Side of the Enterprise*. New York: McGraw-Hill, 1960.
28. Survey: The X and Y factors. *Economist*, January 21, 2006, 19–20.; Locander, W. B., and Luechauer, D. L. The leadership equation. *Marketing Management*, 2005, 14(5), 42–44; Kellaway, L. The infinite potential to…get out of bed in the morning. *Financial Times*, September 5, 2005, 10.
29. Judge, T. A., Piccolo, R. F., and Ilies, R. The forgotten ones? The validity of consideration and initiating structure in leadership research. *Journal of Applied Psychology*, 2004, 89, 36–51; Fleishman, E. A., and Harris, E. E. Patterns of leadership behavior related to employee grievances and turnover: Some post hoc reflections. *Personnel Psychology*, 1998, 51, 825–834; Fleishman, E. A. Consideration and structure: Another look at their role in leadership research. In Damserau, F., and Yammarino, F. J. (Eds.). *Leadership: The Multi-Level Approaches*. Greenwich, CT: JAI Press, 1998, 285–302.
30. *Adapted from* Carter, A. Lighting a fire under Campbell: How Doug Conant's quiet, cerebral style got things bubbling again. *BusinessWeek*, December 4, 2006, 96–101; Brubaker, H. Souper saver. *Knight Ridder Tribune Business News*, July 26, 2006, 1, 2.
31. Our Company: Campbell Soup Company. www.campbellsoupcompany.com (April 2007).
32. Hersey, P., et al. *The Management of Organizational Behavior: Leading Human Resources*, 8th ed. Escondido, CA: Center for Leadership Studies, 2001.
33. *Source:* Hersey, P., Blanchard, K. H., and Johnson, D. E. *The Management of Organizational Behavior: Leading Human Resources*. © 2001 Center for Leadership Studies. Used with permission.
34. *Adapted from* Buckingham, M. What great managers do. *Harvard Business Review*, 2005, 83(3), 70–79; Buckingham, M. *The One Thing You Need to Know*. New York: Free Press, 2005.
35. Walgreens: Fast facts. www.walgreens.com/about (April 2007).
36. Vecchio, R. P., and Boatwright, K. J. Preferences for idealized styles of supervision. *Leadership Quarterly*, 2002, 13, 327–337; Houghton, J. D., and Yoho, S. K. Toward a contingency model of leadership and psychological empowerment: When should self-leadership be encouraged? *Journal of Leadership and Organizational Studies*, 2005, 11(4), 65–83; Yun, S., Cox, J., and Sims, Jr., H. P. The forgotten follower: A contingency model of leadership and follower self-leadership. *Journal of Managerial Psychology*, 2006, 21, 374–388; Avery, G. C., and Ryan, J. Applying situational leadership in Australia. *Journal of Management Development*, 2002, 21, 242–262; Zigarmi, D., Blanchard, K. H., Cooper, M., and Edeburn, C. *The Leader Within: Knowing Enough about Yourself to Lead Others*. Escondido, CA: Ken Blanchard Companies, 2004.

37. Vroom, V. H., and Jago, A. G. *The New Leadership*. Englewood Cliffs, NJ: Prentice-Hall, 1988; also see Sternberg, R. J., and Vroom, V. The person versus the situation in leadership. *Leadership Quarterly*, 2002, 13, 321–323.
38. The discussion of the revised model is based on Vroom, V. H. New developments in leadership and decision making. *OB News*. Briarcliff Manor, NY: Organizational Behavior Division of the Academy of Management, headquartered at Pace University, Spring 1999, 4–5; Vroom, V. H. Leadership and the decision-making process. *Organizational Dynamics*, Spring 2000, 82–93; Vroom, V. H. Educating managers for decision making and leadership. *Management Decision*, 2003, 41, 968–978.
39. *Adapted from* Vroom, V. H. *Leadership and the decision-making process*, 90–91. Also see Duncan, W. J., LaFrance, K. G., and Ginter, P. M. Leadership and decision making: A retrospective application and assessment. *Journal of Leadership & Organizational Studies*, 2003, 9, 1–20.
40. *Adapted from* Reddy, W. B., and Williams, G. The visibility/credibility inventory: Measuring power and influence. In Pfeiffer, J. W. (Ed.). *The 1988 Annual: Developing Human Resources*. San Diego: University Associates, 1988, 115–124; also see Ferris, G. R., Treadway, D. C., Kolodinsky, R. W., Hochwarter, W. A., Kacmar, C. J., Douglas, C., and Frink, D. D. Development and validation of the political skill inventory. *Journal of Management*, 2005, 31, 126–152
41. *Adapted from* Dalton, C. M. The business of beauty, a beauty in business: An interview with Georgette Mosbacher, CEO and president of Borghese. *Business Horizons*, 2006, 49, 269–273; Borghese: About us. www.borghese.com (April 2007).

CHAPTER 10

1. *Adapted from* Brady, D. Secrets of an HR superstar—On the eve of retiring, GE's Bill Conaty offers tips on nurturing leaders in your organization. *BusinessWeek*, April 9, 2007, 66–67; Heineman, Jr., B. W. Avoiding integrity and land mines: An inside look at how GE has worked to build a culture that sustains both high performance and high integrity. *Harvard Business Review*, 2007, 85(4), 100–108; Colvin, G. What makes GE great? *Fortune*, March 6, 2006, 90–94; Morris, B. The GE mystique. *Fortune*, March 6, 2006, 98–102; General Electric: Company information. www.ge.com (April 2007).
2. Puccio, G. J., Murdock, M. C., and Mance, M. *Creative Leadership: Skills That Drive Change*. Thousand Oaks, CA: Sage, 2006.
3. Colvin, What makes GE great?, 90–93.
4. Bass, B. M. Does the transactional-transformational leadership paradigm transcend organizational and national boundaries? *American Psychologist*, 1997, 52, 130–139; Leadership. www.changingminds.org (April 2007).
5. Avolio, B. J. *Leadership Development in Balance: Made/Born*. Mahwah, NJ: Lawrence Erlbaum Associates, 2005, 15.
6. Drucker, P. F. What makes an effective executive. *Harvard Business Review*, 2004, 82(6), 58–63; Hackman, J. R., and Wageman, R. Ask the right questions about leadership: Discussion and conclusions. *American Psychologist*, 2007, 62, 43–47.
7. Bryant, S. E. The role of transformational and transactional leadership in creating, sharing and exploiting organizational knowledge. *Journal of Leadership & Organizational Studies*, 2003, 9(4), 32–44; Judge, T. A., and Piccolo, R. F. Transformational and transactional leadership: A meta-analytic test of their relative validity. *Journal of Applied Psychology*, 2004, 89, 755–768.
8. *Adapted from* Grow, B. Out at Home Depot. *BusinessWeek*, January 15, 2007, 56–62; Forester, M. Culture shock at Home Depot. *Chain Store Age*, February 2007, 12–13; Zimmerman, A. Home Depot executives close to Nardelli resign. *Wall Street Journal*, February 2, 2007, B5.
9. All about us: Home Depot. www.homedepot.com (April 2007).
10. Avolio, A. B., and Luthans, A. *The High Impact Leader: Authentic Resilient Leadership That Gets Results and Sustains Growth*. New York: McGraw-Hill, 2005; Luthans, F., Youssef, C. M., and Avolio, B. J. *Psychological Capital: Developing the Human Competitive Edge*. New York: Oxford University Press, 2006.
11. This discussion draws from Avolio, B. J. Promoting more integrative strategies for leadership theory-building. *American Psychologist*, 2007, 62, 25–33; Novicevic, M. M., Harvey, M. G., Buckley, M. R., Brown-Radford, J. A., and Evans, R. Authentic leadership: A historical perspective. *Journal of Leadership and Organizational Studies*, 2006, 13, 64–75; Avolio, B. J., Gardner, W. L., Walumbwa, F. O., Luthans, F., and May, D. R. Unlocking the mask: A look at the process by which authentic leaders impact follower attitudes and behaviors. *Leadership Quarterly*, 2004, 15, 801–823; Gardner, W. L., and Schermerhorn, J. R. Unleashing individual potential: Performance gains through positive organizational behavior and authentic leadership. *Organizational Dynamics*, 2004, 33, 270–281; George, B., with Sims, P. *True North: Discover Your Authentic Leadership*. New York: Wiley, 2007.
12. Barbuto, Jr., J. E., and Wheeler, D. W. Scale development and construct clarification of servant leadership. *Group & Organization Management*, 2006, 31, 300–326.
13. *Adapted from* Kopf, B., and Birleffi, B. Not her father's chief executive. *U.S. News & World Report*, October 30, 2006, 64–65; Carlson Nelson, M. On the path: Businesses' unfinished journey to diversity. *Vital Speeches of the Day*, March 15, 2004, 336–339; Marilyn Carlson Nelson receives Sharing Diversity Leadership Award from Multicultural Development Center. Available at Carlson: For the Media 2006. www.carlson.com (April 2007).
14. Carlson: about us. www.carlson.com (April 2007).
15. Anderson, T. D. *Transforming Leadership: Equipping Yourself and Challenging Others to Build the Leadership Organization*, 2nd ed. Boca Raton, FL: CRC Press, 1998.
16. This section draws from Bass, B. M., and Riggio, R. E. *Transformational Leadership*, 2nd ed. Florence, KY:

Lawrence Erlbaum Associates, 2005; Boerner, S., Eisenbeiss, S. A., and Griesser, D. Follower behavior and organizational performance: The impact of transformational leaders. *Journal of Leadership and Organizational Studies*, 2007, 13, 15–26; Piccolo, R. F., and Colquitt, J. A. Transformational leadership and job behaviors: The mediating role of core job characteristics. *Academy of Management Journal*, 2006, 49, 327–340; Hoffman, B. J., and Frost, B. C. Multiple intelligences of transformational leaders: An empirical examination. *International Journal of Manpower*, 2006, 27, 37–51; McGuire, D., and Hutchings, K. Portrait of a transformational leader: The legacy of Dr. Martin Luther King Jr. *Leadership & Organization Development Journal*, 2007, 28, 154–166; Cole, M. S., Bedeian, A. G., and Field, H. S. The measurement equivalence of web-based and paper-and-pencil measures of transformational leadership. *Organizational Research Methods*, 2006, 9, 339–368; Nemanich, L. A., and Keller, R. T. Transformational leadership in an acquisition: A field study of employees. *Leadership Quarterly*, 2007, 18, 49–62; Rafferty, A. E., and Griffin, M. A. Dimensions of transformational leadership: Conceptual and empirical extensions. *Leadership Quarterly*, 2004, 15, 329–354.

17. GE leadership effectiveness survey. www.1000ventures.com (April 2007).
18. Egan, G. *Change Agent Skills*. Monterey, CA: Brooks/Cole, 1985, 204.
19. *Adapted from* About Virgin: Richard Replies. www.virgin.com (April 2007); Levinson, E. Preaching green with the zeal of a convert. *Fortune*, April 2, 2007, 28; Tierney, J. A cool $25 million for a climate backup plan. *New York Times*, February 13, 2007, F1; Beatty, S. Giving back: Branson's big green investment. *New York Times*, September 22, 2006, W2; Thomson, M., Emery, S., and Porras, J. Integrity to what matters. *Association Now*, December 2006, 39–43; Coleman, A. Make me good, but not yet. . . . *Director*, 2007, 60(9), 46–50; Guthrie, J. Ask the expert: How to be the ultimate entrepreneur. *FT.com*, March 8, 2006, 1–2; Kets de Vries, M. F. R. *The New Global Leaders: Richard Branson, Percy Barnevik, and David Simon*. San Francisco: Jossey-Bass, 1999; Wells, M. Red baron. *Forbes*, July 3, 2000, 151–160.
20. About us: Virgin Group Ltd. www.virgin.com (April 2007).
21. Global Leadership and Organizational Behavior Effectiveness (GLOBE) project. www.thunderbird.edu (May 2007). We express appreciation to Mansour Javidan (Thunderbird School of Global Management) and Peter Dorfman (New Mexico State University) for their review and constructive inputs on a draft of our discussion of the GLOBE model. Their inputs have been incorporated in this presentation.
22. This section is based on Chhokar, J. S., Brodbeck, F. C., and House, R. J. (Eds.). *Culture and Leadership across the World: The GLOBE Book of In-Depth Studies of 25 Societies*. Florence, KY: Lawrence Erlbaum Associates, 2007; House, R. J., Hanges, P. J., Javidan, M., Dorman, P. W., and Gupta, V. (Eds.). *Culture, Leadership, and Organizations: The GLOBE Study of 62 Societies*. Thousand Oaks, CA: Sage, 2004; House, R. J., Javidan, M., Dorfman, P. W., and de Luque, M. S.. A failure of scholarship: Response to George Graen's critique of GLOBE. *Academy of Management Perspectives*, 2006, 20(4), 102–114; Javidan, M. House, R. J., Dorfman, P. W., Hanges, P. J., and de Luque, M. S. Conceptualizing and measuring cultures and their consequences: A comparative review of GLOBE's and Hofstede's approaches. *Journal of International Business Studies*, 2006, 37, 897–914.
23. *Based on* Grove, C. N. Worldwide differences in business values and practices: Overview of GLOBE research findings. GLOVELL LLC. www.glovell.com (May 2007).
24. House et al, *Culture, Leadership, and Organization*, 275–276.
25. Grove, Worldwide differences in business values and practices.
26. *Adapted from* Howell, J. P., DelaCerda, J., Martinez, S. M., Prieto, L., Bautista, J. A., Ortiz, J., Dorfman, P., and Mendez, M. J. Leadership and culture in Mexico. *Journal of World Business*, 2007, 42, 449–462; also see Matviuk, S. Cross-cultural leadership behavior expectations: A comparison between United States managers and Mexican managers. *Journal of American Academy of Business*, 2007, 11, 253–260.
27. *Adapted from* Leader Behaviors (Sections 2 and 4). GLOBE Research Survey: Form Alpha. The research-based versions of these leadership and culture scales within the GLOBE project are available on the GLOBE website at the Thunderbird School of Global Management: www.thunderbird.edu (May 2007). This adapted instrument is from House et al., *Culture Leadership and Organizations*, Chapter 8. Used, adapted, and shortened with permission of Mansour Javidan, President and CEO of GLOBE and Director of the Garvin Center for Cultures and Languages of International Management, Thunderbird School of Global Management (June 1, 2007).
28. Grove, Worldwide differences in business values and practices.
29. *Adapted from* Lashinsky, A. Building eBay 2.0. *Fortune*, October 16, 2006, 160–162; Brown, E. What would Meg do? *Forbes*, May 21, 2007, 94–98; eBay CEO Meg Whitman interview. *Finance Wire*, April 19, 2007, 1; Waters, R. eBay revives core e-commerce activity. *Financial Times*, January 25, 2007, 27; Sellers, P. eBay's secret. *Fortune*, October 18, 2004, 160–168; Schonfeld, E. The world according to eBay. *Business 2.0*, January/February 2005, 76–80; Schonfeld, E. How to manage growth. *Business 2.0*, December 2004, 98–99; Malone, M. S. Meet Meg Whitman. *Wall Street Journal*, March 16, 2005, A24, A26; About eBay. www.ebay.com (May 2007).

CHAPTER 11

1. *Adapted from* Brandel, M. The team at the top. *Computerworld*, October 23, 2006, 40–42; About Regions Financial Corporation. www.regions.com (May 2007).
2. Homans, G. C. *The Human Group*. New York: Harcourt, Brace and World, 1959, 2.

3. Levi, D. *Group Dynamics for Teams*, 2nd ed. Thousand Oaks, CA: Sage, 2007; Edmondson, A. C. *Teams That Learn: What Leaders Must Do to Foster Organizational Learning*. New York: Wiley, 2006.
4. Wheelan, S. A. *Creating Effective Teams: A Guide for Members and Leaders*, 2nd ed. Thousand Oaks, CA: Sage, 2005.
5. Morton, S. C., Brookes, N. J., Smart, P. K., Backhouse, C. J., and Burns, N. D. Managing the informal organization: Conceptual model. *International Journal of Productivity and Performance Management*, 2004, 53, 214–227.
6. Oh, H., Labianca, G., and Chung, M. A multilevel model of group social capital. *Academy of Management Review*, 2006, 31, 569–582.
7. LaFasto, F., and Larson, C. *When Teams Work Best*. Thousand Oaks, CA: Sage, 2001.
8. Herrenkohl, R. C. *Becoming a Team: Achieving a Goal*. Mason, OH: Thomson/South-Western, 2004.
9. Brandel, The team at the top, 42.
10. Kirkman, B. I., and Rosen, B. Beyond self-management: Antecedents and consequences of team empowerment. *Academy of Management Journal*, 1999, 42, 58–74; Chen, G., Kirkman, B. L., Kanfer, R., Allen, D., and Rosen, B. A multilevel study of leadership, empowerment, and performance in teams. *Journal of Applied Psychology*, 2007, 92, 331–346; Mathieu, J. E., Gilson, L. L., and Rudy, T. M. Empowerment and team effectiveness: An empirical test of an integrated model. *Journal of Applied Psychology*, 2006, 91, 97–108.
11. *Adapted from* Fishman, C. No satisfaction. *Fast Company*, December 2006/January 2007, 82–91.
12. Liker, J. K. *The Toyota Way: 14 Management Principles from the World's Greatest Manufacturer*. New York: McGraw-Hill, 2003.
13. *Adapted from* Johnson, K. Stoner: Built on a strong foundation. *Quality Progress*, August 2004, 40–47; Stoner: 60 years of innovation. www.stonersolutions.com (May 2007).
14. Marín, J. A., del Val, P. A., and Bonavia, T. The impact of ad hoc teams in the automobile industry. *Team Performance Management*, 2006, 12, 278–284.
15. *Adapted from* Cross, L. Combating rework. *Graphic Arts Monthly*, August 2004, 34–37; About us: American Printing Company. www.americanprintingco.com (May 2007).
16. Dubinsky, R., Druskat, V. U., Mangino, M., and Flynn, E. What makes good teams work better: Research-based strategies that distinguish top-performing cross-functional drug development teams. *Organization Development Journal*, 2007, 25, 179–186; Applebaum, S. A., and Gonzalo, F. Effectiveness and dynamics of cross-functional teams: A case study of Northerntranspo Ltd. *Journal of American Academy of Business*, 2007, 10(2), 36–44; Gebert, D., Boerner, S., and Kearney, E. Cross-functionality and innovation in new product development teams: A dilemmatic structure and its consequences for the management of diversity. *European Journal of Work and Organizational Psychology*, 2006, 15, 431–458; Mohamed, M., Stankosky, M., and Murray, A. Applying knowledge management principles to enhance cross-functional team performance. *Journal of Knowledge Management*, 2004, 8, 127–140.
17. *Adapted from* Carbone, J. Time-to-market is key. *Purchasing*, March 15, 2007, 30–32.
18. Ibid., 31; also see Avery, S. Pathways to convergence. *Purchasing*, April 5, 2007, 52–54.
19. Douglas, C. Martin, J. S., and Krapels, R. H. Communication in the transition to self-directed work teams. *Journal of Business Communication*, 2006, 43, 295–321; Tata, J., and Prasad, S. Team self-management, organizational structure, and judgments of team effectiveness. *Journal of Managerial Issues*, 2004, 16, 248–266.
20. Kauffeld, S. Self-directed work groups and team competence. *Journal of Occupational and Organizational Psychology*, 2006, 79, 1–21; Cooney, R. Empowered self-management and the design of work teams. *Personnel Review*, 2004, 33, 677–690.
21. Van Mierlo, H., Rutte, C. G., Kompier, M. A., and Doorewaard, H. A. Self-managing teamwork and psychological well-being: Review of a multicultural research domain. *Group & Organization Management*, 2005, 30, 211–235.
22. Kent, T. W. A process for identifying the skills needed for operating in a self-directed work team in a manufacturing setting. *Team Performance Management*, 2006, 12, 258–271.
23. *Teamwork and High Performance Work Organization*. Dublin, Ireland: European Foundation for the Improvement of Living and Working Conditions, 2006. Available in electronic format only. www.eurofound.eu.int (May 2007); Kirkman, B. L., and Rosen, B. Powering up teams. *Organizational Dynamics*, 2000, 28(3), 48–66; Langfred, C. W. Too much of a good thing? Negative effects of high trust and individual autonomy in self-managing teams. *Academy of Management Journal*, 2004, 47, 385–399.
24. Hertel, G., Kondradt, U., and Voss, K. Competencies for virtual teamwork: Development and validation of a web-based selection tool for members of distributed teams. *European Journal of Work and Organizational Psychology*, 2006, 15, 477–504; Powell, A., Piccoli, G., and Ives, B. Virtual teams: A review of current literature and directions for future research. *Database for Advances in Information Systems*, 2004, 35, 6–37.
25. Edwards, A., and Wilson, J. R. *Implementing Virtual Teams*. Abingdon, Oxon, UK: Gower Publishing, 2004; Jones, R., Oyung, R., and Pace, L. *Working Virtually: Challenges of Virtual Teams*. Hershey, PA: IRM Press, 2005.
26. This presentation is based primarily on Brown, M. K., James-Tanny, C., and Huettner, B. *Managing Virtual Teams: Getting the Most from Wikis, Blogs, and Other Collaborative Tools*. Plano, TX: Wordware Publishing, 2007; Townsend, D. M., DeMarie, S. M., and Hendrickson, A. R. Virtual teams: Technology and the workplace of the future. *Academy of Management Executive*, 1998, 12(3), 17–29; Malhotra, A., and Majchrzak, A. Virtual workspace technologies. *Sloan Management Review*, 2005, 46(2), 11–14.

27. Buckley, W. M. Better virtual meetings. *Wall Street Journal*, September 28, 2006, B1, B5.
28. Denton, D. K. Using intranets to make virtual teams effective. *Team Performance Management*, 2006, 12, 253–257; Sadowski-Rosters, G., Duysters, G., and Sadowski, B. M. *Communication and Cooperation in the Virtual Workplace: Teamwork in Computer-Mediated-Communication*. Northampton, MA: Edward Elgar Publishing, 2007.
29. This presentation is based on Duarte, D. L., and Snyder, N. T. *Mastering Virtual Teams: Strategies, Tools, and Techniques That Succeed*, 3rd ed. San Francisco: Jossey-Bass, 2006; De Luca, D., and Valacich, J. S. Virtual teams in and out of synchronicity. *Information Technology & People*, 2006, 19, 323–344; Bergiel, B. J., Bergiel, E. B., and Balsmeier, P. W. The reality of virtual teams. *Competition Forum*, 2006, 4, 427–432; Jones, R., Oyung, R., and Pace, L. *Working Virtually: Challenges of Virtual Teams*. Hershey, PA: Idea Group Publishing, 2005.
30. Cane, A. Virtual teams: Recent advances. *Financial Times*, February 12, 2007, 9.
31. Malhotra, A., Majchrzak, A., and Rosen, B. Leading virtual teams. *Academy of Management Perspective*, 2007, 21(1), 60–70.
32. Golden, T. D., and Veiga, J. F. Spanning boundaries and borders: Toward understanding the cultural dimensions of team boundary spanning. *Journal of Managerial Issues*, 2005, 17, 178–198; Symons, J., and Stenzel, C. Virtually borderless: An examination of culture in virtual teaming. *Journal of General Management*, 2007, 32, 1–17.
33. Barczak, G., McDonough, E. F., and Athanassiou, N. So you want to be a global project leader? *Research Technology Management*, 2006, 49(3), 28–35; Gatlin-Watts, R., Carson, M., Horton, J., Maxwell, L., and Maltby, N. A guide to global virtual teaming. *Team Performance Management*, 2007, 13, 47–52.
34. Kankanhalli, A., Tan, B. C., and Wei, K. K. Conflict and performance in global virtual teams. *Journal of Management Information Systems*, 2006/2007, 23(3), 237–274; Anawati, D., and Craig, A. Behavioral adaptation within cross-cultural virtual teams. *IEEE Transactions on Professional Communication*, 2006, 49, 44–56; Kiessling, T. S., Marino, L. D., and Richey, R. G. Global marketing teams: A strategic option for multinationals. *Organizational Dynamics*, 2006, 237–250; Saunders, C., Van Slyke, C., and Vogel, D. R. My time or yours? Managing time visions in global virtual teams. *Academy of Management Executive*, 2004, 18(1), 19–31; Hildebrand, C. Cross-cultural collaboration. *PM Network*, 2007, 21(3), 46–54.
35. *Adapted from* Schiff, D. Global teams rock around the clock. *Electronic Engineering*, August 7, 2006, 12–14.
36. About Logitech. www.logitech.com (June 2007).
37. Tuckman, B. W. Development sequence in small groups. *Psychological Bulletin*, 1965, 62, 384–399; Tuckman, B. W., and Jensen, M. A. Stages of small group development revisited. *Group & Organization Studies*, 1977, 2, 419–427; Obert, S. L. Developmental patterns of organizational task groups: A preliminary study. *Human Relations*, 1983, 36, 37–52.
38. Akrivou, K., Boyatzis, R. E., and McLeod, P. L. The evolving group: Towards a prescriptive theory of intentional group development. *Journal of Management Development*, 2006, 25, 689–706; Tran, V. N., and Latapie, H. M. Four strategies for team and work structuring in global organizations. *Business Review*, 2006, 5, 105–110.
39. Caouette, M., and O'Connor, B. The impact of group support systems on corporate teams' stages of development. *Journal of Organizational Computing and Electronic Commerce*, 1998, 8, 57–81; also see Lee-Kelley, L., Grossman, A., and Cannings, A. A social interaction approach to managing the "invisibles" of virtual teams. *Industrial Management & Data Systems*, 2004, 104, 650–657.
40. *Adapted from* Furst, S. A., Reeves, M., Rosen, M., and Blackburn, R. S. Managing the life cycle of virtual teams. *Academy of Management Executive*, 2004, 18(2), 6–20.
41. Ibid.
42. Ibid.
43. Burke, C. S., Stagl, K. C., Salas, E., Pierce, L., and Kendall, D. Understanding team adaptation: A conceptual analysis and model. *Journal of Applied Psychology*, 2006, 91, 1189–1207.
44. Doolen, T. L., Hacker, M. E., Van Aken, E. Managing organizational context for engineering team effectiveness. *Team Performance Management*, 2006, 12, 138–154.
45. Berry, L. L. Leadership lessons from Mayo Clinic. *Organizational Dynamics*, 2004, 33, 228–242.
46. Hase, B., and Heerwagen, J. H. Phylogenetic design: A new approach for workplace environments. *Journal for Quality & Participation*, 2000, 23(5), 27–31; also see Wickhorst, V., and Geroy, G. Physical communication and organization development. *Organization Development Journal*, 2006, 24(3), 54–63.
47. Burke, C. S., Stagl, K. C., Klein, C., Goodwin, G. F., Salas, E., and Halpin, S. M. What type of leadership behaviors are functional in teams?: A meta-analysis. *Leadership Quarterly*, 2006, 17, 288–307; Morgeson, F. P., and DeRue, D. S. Event criticality, urgency, and duration: Understanding how events disrupt teams and influence team leader intervention. *Leadership Quarterly*, 2006, 17, 271–287.
48. *Adapted from* Popovec, J. Gathering wisdom: New NAHB president Brian Catalde highlights teamwork and long-term goals. *Builders*, January 2007, 109–111.
49. NAHB: Our organization. www.nahb.org (June 2007).
50. Paragon Communities corporate fact sheet. www.paragoncommunities.com (June 2007).
51. O'Hara, D., and Maglieri, K. A. Goal statements and goal directed behavior: A relational frame account of goal setting in organizations. *Journal of Organizational Behavior Management*, 2006, 26, 131–170.
52. About Mayo Clinic: Mission, values, and core principles. www.mayoclinic.org (June 2007).
53. Tasa, K., Taggar, S., and Seijts, G. H. The development of collective efficacy in teams: A multilevel and longitudinal perspective. *Journal of Applied Psychology*, 2007, 92, 17–27; Gibson, C. B., and Early, P. C. Collective cognition in action: Accumulation, interaction, examination, and accommodation in the development and operation of group

efficacy beliefs in the workplace. *Academy of Management Review*, 2007, 32, 438–458.
54. Mueller, J. S. Is your team too big? Too small? What's the right number? June 14, 2006; http://knowledge.wharton.upenn.edu (June 2007).
55. Tohidi, H., and Tarokh, M. J. Productivity outcomes of teamwork: Effect of information technology and team size. *International Journal of Production Economics*, 2006, 103, 610–615; Bradner, E., Mark, G., and Hertel, I. D. Team size and technology fit: Participation, awareness, and rapport in distributed teams. *IEEE Transactions on Professional Communication*, 2005, 48, 68–77.
56. Kuipers, B. S., and de Witte, M. C. Teamwork: A case study on development and performance. *International Journal of Human Resource Management*, 2005, 16, 185–201.
57. Aritzeta, A., Swailes, S., and Senior, B. Belbin's team role model: Development, validity and applications for team building. *Journal of Managerial Studies*, 2007, 44, 96–118; Manning, T., Parker, R., and Pogson, G. A revised model of team roles and research findings. *Industrial and Commercial Training*, 2006, 38, 287–296.
58. Bales, R. F. *Interaction Process Analysis*. Cambridge, MA: Addison Wesley, 1950; Klein, K. J., Lim, B., Saltz, J. L., and Mayer, D. M. How do they get there? An examination of the antecedents of centrality in team networks. *Academy of Management Journal*, 2004, 47, 952–963.
59. Stewart, G. L., Fulmer, I. S., and Barrick, M. R. An exploration of member roles as a multilevel linking mechanism for individual traits and team outcomes. *Personnel Psychology*, 2005, 58, 343–365.
60. Kelly, J. R., and Spoor, J. R. Naïve theories about the effects of mood in groups: A preliminary investigation. *Group Processes & Intergroup Relations*, 2007, 10, 203–222.
61. Harrison, D. A., and Klein, K. J. What's the difference? Diversity constructs as separation, variety, or disparity in organizations. *Academy of Management Review*, 2007, 32, in press.
62. Barkema, H. G., and Shvyrkov, O. Does top management team diversity promote or hamper foreign expansion? *Strategic Management Journal*, 2007, 28, 663–680.
63. Rico, R., Molleman, E., Sánchez-Manzannes, M., and Van der Vegt, G. S. The effects of diversity faultlines and team task autonomy on decision quality and social integration. *Journal of Management*, 2007, 33, 111–132; Hambrick, D. C. Upper echelons theory: An update. *Academy of Management Review*, 2007, 32, 334–343.
64. Hobman, E. V., Bordia, P., and Gallois, C. Perceived dissimilarity and work group involvement: The moderating effects of group openness to diversity. *Group & Organization Management*, 2004, 29, 560–587.
65. Hymowitz, C. Managers can't limit hiring to clones of themselves. *Career Journal*. www.careerjournal.com (June 2007).
66. Jackson, S. E., and Joshi, A. Diversity in social context: A multi-attribute, multilevel analysis of team diversity and sales performance. *Journal of Organizational Behavior*, 2004, 25, 675–702; van Knippenberg, D., De Dreu, C. K., and Homan, A. C. Work group diversity and group performance: An integrative model and research agenda. *Journal of Applied Psychology*, 2004, 89, 1008–1022.
67. Kang, H., Yang, H., and Rowley, C. Factors in team effectiveness: Cognitive and demographic similarities of software development team members. *Human Relations*, 2006, 59, 1681–1710; Staples, D. S., and Zhao, L. The effects of cultural diversity in virtual teams versus face-to-face teams. *Group Decision and Negotiation*, 2006, 15, 389–406.
68. Society for Human Resource Management. Employee affinity groups. www.shrm.org/diversity (June 2007).
69. Hankin, H. *The New Workforce*. New York: AMACOM, 2005.
70. *Adapted from* Affinity groups: Johnson & Johnson. www.jnc.com (June 2007).
71. Fast facts: Johnson & Johnson. www.jnj.com (June 2007).
72. Taggar, S., and Ellis, R. The role of leaders in shaping formal team norms. *Leadership Quarterly*, 2007, 18, 105–120; Ehrhart, M. G., and Naumann, S. E. Organizational citizenship behavior in work groups: A group norms approach. *Journal of Applied Psychology*, 2004, 89, 960–974.
73. Bamberger, P., and Biron, M. Group norms and absenteeism: The role of peer referent others. *Organizational Behavior and Human Decision Processes*, 2007, 103, 179–196.
74. Feldman, D. C. The development and enforcement of group norms. *Academy of Management Review*, 1984, 9, 47–53.
75. Besser, T. L. *Team Toyota*. Ithaca: State University of New York Press, 1996; Ehrhart, M. G., and Naumann, S. E. Organizational citizenship behavior in work groups: A group norms approach. *Journal of Applied Psychology*, 2004, 89, 960–974.
76. Spoor, J. R., and Kelly, J. R. The evolutionary significance of affect in groups: Communication and group bonding. *Group Processes and Interpersonal Relations*, 2004, 7, 398–412; Man, D. C., and Lam, S. The effects of job complexity and autonomy on cohesiveness in collectivistic and individualistic work groups: A cross-cultural analysis. *Journal of Organizational Behavior*, 2003, 24, 979–1001.
77. Knouse, S. B. Task cohesion: A mechanism for bringing together diverse teams. *International Journal of Management*, 2006, 23, 588–596; Forrester, W. R., and Tashchian, A. Modeling the relationship between cohesion and performance in student work groups. *International Journal of Management*, 2006, 23, 458–464.
78. Lipman-Blumen, J., and Leavitt, H. J. *Hot Groups: Seeding Them, Feeding Them, and Using Them to Ignite Your Organization*. New York: Oxford University Press, 1999; also see Gratton, L. *Hot Spots: Why Some Teams, Workplaces and Organizations Buzz with Energy and Others Don't*. San Francisco: Berrett-Kohler, 2007.
79. Lencioni, P. M. *The Five Dysfunctions of Teams: A Leadership Fable*. San Francisco: Jossey-Bass, 2002; Lencioni, P. M. *Overcoming the Five Dysfunctions of a Team: A Field Guide for Leaders, Managers, and Facilitators*. San Francisco: Jossey-Bass, 2005; Harris, T. E., and Sherblom, J. C.

Small Group and Team Communication, 4th ed. Boston: Allyn & Bacon, 2007.

80. Janis, I. L. *Groupthink*, 2nd ed. Boston: Houghton Mifflin, 1982; Whyte, G. Groupthink reconsidered. *Academy of Management Review*, 1989, 14, 40–56; Brownstein, A. L. Biased decision processing. *Psychological Bulletin*, 2003, 129, 545–591.
81. Chapman, J. Anxiety and defective decision making: An elaboration of the groupthink model. *Management Decision*, 2006, 44, 1391–1404; Schültz, P., and Bloch, B. The "silo-virus": Diagnosing and curing departmental groupthink. *Team Performance Management*, 2006, 12, 31–43; McAvoy, J., and Butler, T. The impact of the Abilene paradox on double-loop learning in an agile team. *Information and Software Technology*, 2007, 49, 552–563.
82. Albanese, R., and Van Fleet, D. D. Rational behavior in groups: The free-riding tendency. *Academy of Management Review*, 1985, 10, 244–255; Chen, X., and Bachrack, D. G. Tolerance of free-riding: The effects of defection size, defection pattern, and social orientation in a repeated public good dilemma. *Organizational Behavior and Human Decision Processes*, 2003, 90, 139–147.
83. Schnake, M. E. Equity in effort: The "sucker effect" in co-acting groups. *Journal of Management*, 1991, 17, 41–55; Murphy, S. M., Wayne, S. J., Liden, R. C., and Erdogan, B. Understanding social loafing: The role of justice perceptions and exchange relationships. *Human Relations*, 2003, 56, 61–84.
84. Felps, W., Mitchell, T. R., and Byington, E. How, when, and why bad apples spoil the barrel: Negative group members and dysfunctional groups. *Research in Organizational Behavior*, 2006, 27, 175–222.
85. Tyler, K. One bad apple: Before the whole bunch spoils train managers to deal with poor performance. *HRMagazine*, 2004, 49(12), 77–86.
86. Mooradian, T., Renzl, B., and Matzler, K. Who trusts? Personality, trust and knowledge sharing. *Management Learning*, 2006, 37, 523–540.
87. Cottrell, C. A., Li, N. P., and Neuberg, S. L. What do people desire in others? A sociofunctional perspective on the importance of different valued characteristics. *Journal of Personality and Social Psychology*, 2007, 92, 208–231; Brodbeck, F. C., Kerschreiter, R., Mojzisch, A., and Schulz-Hardt, S. Group decision making under conditions of distributed knowledge: The information asymmetries model. *Academy of Management Review*, 2007, 32, 459–478.
88. Lencioni, P. M. Team dysfunction: Identify the cause and cure. *Leadership Excellence*, 2006, 23(12), 6.
89. Boomer, L. G. Build a winning team and fight firm dysfunction. *Accounting Today*, February 24–March 16, 2003, 1, 21.
90. *Adapted from* The Student Audit Instrument. Developed by Jon M. Werner, a faculty member in the Department of Management at the University of Wisconsin–Whitewater. Also see Senior, B., and Swailes, S. Inside management teams: Developing a teamwork survey instrument. *British Journal of Management*, 2007, 18, 138–153; Wageman, R., Hackman, J. R., and Lehman, E. Team diagnostic survey: Development of an instrument. *Journal of Applied Behavioral Science*, 2005, 373–398.
91. *Based on* Novartis builds "speak-up" in Brazil. *T+D*, 2005, 59(7), 40–41 (no author stated); Novartis to increase Brazil investments by 70 million, July 3, 2006; http://news.notiemail.com (June 2007).

CHAPTER 12

1. *Adapted from* Joyce, A. Head butting: When the bosses fight, you might get hurt. *Washington Post*, July 16, 2006, F6, F7.
2. Rahim, M. A. *Managing Conflict in Organizations*, 3rd ed. Westport, CT: Quorum Books, 2001.
3. Kellett, P. M. *Conflict Dialogue: Working with Layers of Meaning in Practice*. Thousand Oaks, CA: Sage, 2007; Druckman, D., Fast, L., and Cheldelin, S. (Eds.). *Conflict*, 2nd ed. New York: Continuum International Publishing Group, 2008; Cahn, D. D., and Abigail, R. A. *Managing Conflict through Communication*, 3rd ed. Boston: Allyn & Bacon, 2006.
4. Amabile, T. M., and Kramer, S. J. Inner work life: Understanding the subtext of business performance. *Harvard Business Review*, 2007, 85(5), 72–83.
5. Mohr, A. T., and Puck, J. F. Role conflict, general manager job satisfaction and stress, and the performance of IJVs. *European Management Journal*, 2007, 25, 25–35; Judge, T. A., Illies, R., and Scott, B. A. Work–family conflict and emotions: Effects at work and at home. *Personnel Psychology*, 2006, 59, 779–814.
6. Wong, S., De Sanctis, G., and Staudenmayer, N. The relationship between task interdependency and role stress: A revisit of the job-demands control model. *Journal of Management Studies*, 2007, 44, 284–303; Fogler, J. P., Poole, M. S., and Stutman, R. K. *Working through Conflict: Strategies for Relationships, Groups, and Organizations*, 5th ed. Boston: Allyn & Bacon, 2005.
7. Spector, B. (Ed.). *Family Business Conflict Resolution Handbook*. Philadelphia: Family Business, 2005; also see Dechurch, L. A., Hamilton, K. L., and Haas, C. Effects of conflict management strategies on perceptions of intragroup conflict. *Group Dynamics: Theory, Research, and Practice*, 2007, 11, 66–78.
8. Pervin, A. Managing the relationships that bind or bond. www.pervinfamilybusiness.com (June 2007); Fisher, A. Working for your kids. *Fortune*, June 25, 2007, 130–138.
9. Daft, R. L. *Organization Theory and Design*, 9th ed. Mason, OH: Thomson/South-Western, 2007; Umphress, E. E., Smith-Crowe, K., Brief, A. P., Dietz, J., and Watkins, M. B. When birds of a feather flock together and when they do not: Status composition, social dominance orientation, and organizational attractiveness. *Journal of Applied Psychology*, 2007, 92, 396–409.
10. *Adapted from* Weiss, J., and Hughes, J. Want collaboration? Accept—and actively manage—conflict. *Harvard Business Review*, 2005, 83(3), 93–101; Frausnheim, E. A leader in leadership, *Workforce Management*, May 21, 2007, 19–23.

11. IBM. *Hoovers*. www.hoovers.com (June 2007).
12. Thomas, K. W. Conflict and negotiation processes in organizations. In Dunnette, M. D., and Hough, L. M. (Eds.). *Handbook of Industrial and Organizational Psychology*, Vol. 3, 2nd ed. Palo Alto, CA: Consulting Psychologists Press, 1992, 651–717; Hede, A. Toward an explanation of interpersonal conflict in work groups: *Journal of Managerial Psychology*, 2007, 22, 25–39; Chan, C. A., Monroe, G., Ng, J., and Tan, R. Conflict management styles of male and female junior accountants. *International Journal of Management*, 2006, 23, 289–295.
13. *Adapted from* Fox, J. Burrel versus Dr Pepper/Seven Up Bottling Group Inc. *Executive Legal Adviser*, May/June 2007, 8–9; Case 06–10267. 5th U.S. Circuit Court of Appeals (March 20, 2007).
14. Gross, M. A., and Guerrero, L. K. Managing conflict appropriately and effectively: An application of the competence model to Rahim's organizational conflict styles. *International Journal of Conflict Management*, 2000, 11, 200–226; Tjosvold, D., Law, K. S., and Sun, H. Effectiveness of Chinese teams: The role of conflict types and conflict management approaches. *Management and Organization Review*, 2006, 2, 231–252; de Reuver, R. The influence of organizational power on conflict dynamics. *Personnel Review*, 2006, 35, 589–603; Aritzeta, A., Ayestaran, S., and Swailes, S. Team role preference and conflict management styles. *International Journal of Conflict Resolution*, 2005, 16, 157–182.
15. *Adapted from* Dreachslin, J. L., and Kiddy, D. From conflict to consensus: Managing competing interests in your organization. *Healthcare Executive*, 2006, 21(6), 9–14; Robert Wood Johnson Foundation and Institute for Healthcare Improvement. *A New Era in Nursing: Transforming Care at the Bedside*. www.rwjf.org (June 2007).
16. About ThedaCare. www.thedacare.org (June 2007).
17. Lewicki, R. J., Barry, B., and Saunders, D. M. *Negotiation*, 5th ed. Boston: McGraw-Hill/Irwin, 2006; Lewicki, R. J., and Hiam, A. *Mastering Business Negotiation: A Working Guide to Making Deals and Resolving Conflict*. San Francisco: Jossey-Bass, 2006.
18. Masters, M. F. *Business of Negotiating*. Upper Saddle River, NJ: Prentice Hall, 2008; Raiffa, H. *Negotiation Analysis: The Science and Art of Collaborative Decision Making*, 2nd ed. Cambridge, MA: Belknap Press, 2007.
19. Walton, R. E., and McKersie, R. B. *A Behavioral Theory of Labor Negotiations: An Analysis of a Social Interaction System*, 2nd ed. Ithaca, NY: ILR Press, 1991; Walton, R. E., Cutcher-Gershenfield, J. E., and McKersie, R. B. *Strategic Negotiations: A Theory of Change in Labor–Management Relations*. Ithaca, NY: ILR Press, 2000.
20. Fisher, R., and Ury, W. *Getting to Yes: Negotiating Agreement without Giving In*, 2nd ed. New York: Penguin Books, 1991; Spector, B. Introduction: An interview with Roger Fisher and William Ury. *Academy of Management Executive*, 2004, 18(3), 101–108; Fisher, R., and Shapiro, D. *Beyond Reason: Using Emotions as You Negotiate*. New York: Penguin, 2006.
21. Kosdrosky, I. Goodyear union plans to terminate contract Thursday. *Wall Street Journal*, October 3, 2006, A10; Tentative pact may end Goodyear strike. *New York Times*, December 23, 2006, C4; Kiel, F. Goodyear resumes tire production as union approves new 3-year deal. *Transport Topics*, January 8, 2007, 2–3.
22. Masquez, J. Goodyear fight hints at rough road ahead for unions. *Workforce Management*, 2006, 85(12), 12–13.
23. Lin-Fisher, B. Healing will take time at Goodyear. *Knight Ridder Tribune Business News*, January 3, 2007, 1–2; USW ratifies agreement with Goodyear; Pact provides company substantial cost savings. December 29, 2006. www.goodyearnegotiations.com (June 2007).
24. Ertl, D., and Gordon, M. *The Point of the Deal: How to Negotiate When Yes Is Not Enough*. Boston: Harvard Business School Press, 2007; Deutsch, M., Coleman, P. T., and Marcus, E. C. (Eds.). *The Handbook of Conflict Resolution: Theory and Practice*, 2nd ed. San Francisco: Jossey-Bass, 2006; Kim, P. H., Pinkley, R. L., and Fragale, A. R. Power dynamics in organizations. *Academy of Management Review*, 2005, 30, 799–822.
25. USW ratifies agreement with Goodyear. www.goodyearnegotiations.com (June 2007).
26. Program on Negotiation: Harvard Negotiation Project. www.pon.harvard.edu/hnp (June 2007).
27. Fisher and Ury, *Getting to Yes*; Malhotra, D., and Bazerman, M. *Negotiation Genius: How to Overcome Obstacles and Achieve Brilliant Results at the Bargaining Table and Beyond*. New York: Bantam, 2007.
28. *Adapted from* Powers of persuasion. *Fortune*, October 12, 1998, 160–164; Shapiro, R., and Jankowski, M. *The Power of Nice: How to Negotiate So Everyone Wins—Especially You*, rev. ed. New York: John Wiley & Sons, 2002; Shapiro Negotiation Institute. www.shapironegotiations.com (June 2007).
29. *Excerpts from* Tyler, K. The art of give-and-take. *HR Magazine*, November 2004, 107–116; also see Beasor, T. *Great Negotiators: How the Most Successful Negotiators Think and Behave*. London: Gower Publishing, 2006.
30. Beacon, N., and Blyton, P. Conflict for mutual gains. *Journal of Management Studies*, 2007, 44, 814–834.
31. Katz, H., Kochan, T. A., and Colvin, A. J. *An Introduction to Collective Bargaining & Industrial Relations*, 4th ed. New York: McGraw-Hill/Irwin, 2008; Friedman, R. A. *Front Stage Backstage: The Dynamic Structure of Labor Negotiations*. Cambridge, MA: The MIT Press, 1994; Rousseau, D. M., and Batt, R. Global competition's perfect storm: Why business and labor cannot solve their problems alone. *Academy of Management Perspectives*, 2007, 21(2), 16–23.
32. Chatterjee, C. *Alternative Dispute Resolution*. New York: Routledge, 2008.
33. Kressel, K. The strategic style in mediation. *Conflict Resolution Quarterly*, 2007, 24, 251–283; Honoroff, B., and Optow, S. Mediation ethics: A grounded approach. *Negotiation Journal*, 2007, 23, 155–172.
34. *Adapted from* Maher, K. Are unions relevant? SEIU president Andy Stern thinks so. But he also sees a need for attitude adjustment. *Wall Street Journal*, January 22, 2007, R5; Rayasam, R. *SEIU's Andy Stern: Going global.*

June 6, 2007. www.usnews.com (July 2007); Bai, M. The new boss. *New York Times*, January 30, 2005. www.nytimes.com (July 2007).
35. What is SEIU? www.seiu.org (July 2007).
36. Culture and negotiation. www.negotiations.org (July 2007); Brett, J. M. *Negotiating Globally: How to Negotiate Deals, Resolve Disputes, and Make Decisions across Cultural Boundaries*, 2nd ed. San Francisco: Jossey-Bass, 2007.
37. Salacuse, J. W. Ten ways that culture affects negotiating style: Some survey results. *Negotiation Journal*, 1998, 14, 221–240; Salacuse, J. W. Negotiating: The top ten ways that culture can affect your negotiation. *Ivey Business Journal*, March/April 2005, 1–6; Katz, L. *Negotiating International Business: The Negotiator's Reference to 50 Countries Around the World*. Charleston, SC: BookSurge Publishing, 2007.
38. Metcalf, L. E., Bird, A., Shankarmahesh, M., Aycan, Z., Larimo, J., and Valdelamar, D. D. Cultural tendencies in negotiation: A comparison of Finland, Mexico, Turkey, and the United States. *Journal of World Business*, 2006, 41, 382–394.
39. Salacuse, J. W., Johnson, J. P., Lenartowicz, T., and Apud, S. Cross-cultural competence in international business: Toward a definition and a model. *Journal of International Business Studies*, 2006, 37, 525–543.
40. Brett, J. M., and Ukumura, T. Inter- and intracultural negotiation: U.S. and Japanese negotiators. *Academy of Management Journal*, 1998, 41, 495–510; Peltokorpi, V. Knowledge sharing in a cross-cultural context: Nordic expatriates in Japan. *Knowledge Management Research & Practice*, 2006, 4, 138–148; Moriomoto, I., Saijo, M., Nohara, K., Takagi, K., Otsuka, H., Suzuki, K., and Okumura, M. How do ordinary Japanese reach consensus in group decision making?: Identifying and analyzing "naïve negotiation." *Group Decision and Negotiation*, 2006, 15, 157–169.
41. *Adapted from* Jassawalla, A., Truglia, C., and Garvey, J. Cross-cultural conflict and expatriate manager adjustment: An exploratory study. *Management Decision*, 2004, 42, 837–849; Schmidt, W. V., Conaway, R. N., Easton, S. S., and Wardrope, W. J. *Communicating Globally: Intercultural Communication and International Business*. Thousand Oaks, CA: Sage, 2007; Rudd, J. E., and Lawson, D. R. *Communicating in Global Business Negotiations*. Thousand Oaks, CA: Sage, 2007.
42. Griffin, T. J., and Daggatt, W. R. *The Global Negotiator: Building Strong Business. Relationships Anywhere in the World*. New York, 1992, HarperBusiness, 29–30.
43. *Adapted from* Ghauri, P., and Usunier, J. (Eds.). *International Business Negotiations*. New York: Pergamon, 2006; Boyer, M. A. *Negotiating in a Complex World: An Introduction to International Negotiation*, 2nd ed. London: Littlefield Brown Publishers, 2005; Brett, J., Behfar, K., and Kern, M. C. Managing multicultural teams. *Harvard Business Review*, 2006, 84(1), 84–91.
44. *Adapted from* Movius, H., Matsuura, M., Yan, J., and Kim, D. Tailoring the mutual gains approach for negotiations with partners in Japan, China, and Korea. *Negotiation Journal*, 2006, 22, 389–435; also see Ma, Z. Negotiating into China: The impact of individual perceptions on Chinese negotiation styles. *International Journal of Emerging Markets*, 2006, 1, 64–83; Fang, T. Negotiation: The Chinese style. *Journal of Business & Industrial Marketing*, 2006, 21, 50–60; March, R. M., and Wu, S.-H. *The Chinese Negotiator: How to Succeed in the World's Largest Market*. Tokyo: Kodansha International Ltd., 2007.
45. *Adapted from* Baskerville, D. M. How do you manage conflict? *Black Enterprise*, May 1993, 63–66; Thomas, K. W., and Kilmann, R. H. *The Thomas-Kilmann Conflict Mode Instrument*. Tuxedo, NY: Xicom, 1974; Rahim, M. A. A measure of styles of handling interpersonal conflict. *Academy of Management Journal*, 1983, 26, 368–376.
46. *Adapted from* Tatum, B. C., and Eberlin, R. J. Organizational justice and conflict management styles: Teaching notes, role playing instructions, and scenarios. *International Journal of Conflict Management*, 2006, 17, 66–81. Used with permission, through Copyright Clearance Center. Copyright © 2006, International Journal of Conflict Management. June 29, 2007.

CHAPTER 13

1. *Adapted from* Cascio, W. F. Decency means more than "Always Low Prices": A comparison of Costco to Wal-Mart's Sam Club. *Academy of Management Perspectives*. 2006, 20(3), 26–37; Bary, A. Everybody's store. *Barron's*, February 12, 2007, 29–32; *Costco Wholesale Corporation 2006 Annual Report*. www.costco.com (July 2007); Costco: Our Code of Ethics. www.costco.com (July 2007); Greenhouse, S. How Costco became the anti-Wal-Mart. *New York Times*, July 17, 2005. www.nytimes.com. Click on "Articles: 1981–present" or search by entering "How Costco became the anti-Wal-Mart (July 2007); *Costco Wholesale: 3rd quarter results, FY 2007*. www.costco.com (July 2007); Dhiman, S. Running successful organizations humanly: Lessons from the trenches. *Journal of Global Business Issues*, 2007, 1, 53–58; Shalfi, M. The Costco commitment. *Retail Merchandiser*, 2007, 47(1), 8–11; Hudson, K. Boss talk. *Wall Street Journal*, August 27, 2007, A1, A7.
2. Ferrell, O. C., Fraedrich, J., and Ferrell, L. *Business Ethics: Ethical Decision Making and Cases*, 7th ed. Boston: Houghton Mifflin, 2008; Feldman, S. P. Moral business cultures: The keys to creating and maintaining them. *Organizational Dynamics*, 2007, 33, 156–170; Loviscky, G. E., Treveño, L. K., and Jacobs, R. R. Assessing managers' ethical decision-making: An objective measure of managerial moral judgment. *Journal of Business Ethics*, 2007, 73, 263–285.
3. *Adapted from* Ethics Resource Center. National business ethics survey. www.ethics.org (January 2008); also see Brown, M. T. *Corporate Integrity: Rethinking Organizational Ethics and Leadership*. New York: Cambridge University Press, 2005; Gibson, K. *Ethics and Business: An Introduction*. New York: Cambridge University Press, 2007.
4. The framework for this section is based primarily on James, T. M. Ethical decision making by individuals in organizations: An issue-contingent model. *Academy of*

Management Review, 1991, 16, 366–395; May, D. R., and Paul, K. P. The role of moral intensity in ethical decision making. *Business and Society*, 2002, 41, 84–118; Watley, L. D., and May, D. R. Enhancing moral intensity: The roles of personal and consequential information in ethical decision-making. *Journal of Business Ethics*, 2004, 49, 105–126; McMahon, J., and Harvey, R. J. The effect of moral intensity on ethical judgment. *Journal of Business Ethics*, 2007, 72, 335–357; Leitsch, D. L. Using dimensions of moral intensity to predict ethical decision making in accounting. *Accounting Education: An International Journal*, 2006, 15, 135–149; Goles, T., White, G. B., Beebe, N., Dorantes, C. A., and Hewitt, B. Moral intensity and ethical decision-making: A contextual extension. *The DATABASE for Advances in Information Systems*, 2006, 37, 86–95.

5. Robinson, J. Bad news gets personal. *News & Record Staff Blogs*, June 10, 2007. www.blog.news-record.com (July 2007).
6. Kolbe, R. W. (Ed.). *Encyclopedia of Business Ethics and Society*. Thousand Oaks, CA: Sage, 2008; DeGeorge, R. *Business Ethics*, 6th ed. Upper Saddle River, NJ: Prentice Hall, 2006.
7. Bauer, C. An ethics self-exam. *Internal Auditor*, June 2004, 27–31; Michael, M. L. Business ethics: The law of rules. *Business Ethics Quarterly*, 2006, 16, 475–504; also see McCloskey, D. N. *The Bourgeois Virtues: Ethics for an Age of Commerce*. Chicago: University of Chicago Press, 2006.
8. Weiss, J. W. *Business Ethics: A Stakeholder and Issues Management Approach*, 4th ed. Mason, OH: Thomson/South-Western, 2006; Reynolds, S. J., Schultz, F. C., and Hekman, D. R. Stakeholder theory and managerial decision-making: Constraints and implications of balancing stakeholder interests. *Journal of Business Ethics*, 2006, 64, 285–301.
9. Staples, W. G. (Ed.). *Encyclopedia of Privacy: Are U.S. Civil Rights Under Siege?* Westport, CT: Greenwood Press, 2007.
10. O'Harrow, R. *No Place to Hide: Behind the Scenes of Our Emerging Surveillance Society*. New York: Free Press, 2005; Solove, D. J. *The Digital Person: Technology and Privacy in the Information Age*. New York: New York University Press, 2005.
11. Howard, G. *Vetting and Monitoring Employees: A Guide for HR Practitioners*. Aldershot, Hampshire, UK: Gower Publishing, 2007; Privacy Rights Clearinghouse. Workplace privacy. www.privacyrights.org (July 2007).
12. Etzioni, A. *The Limits of Privacy*. New York: Basic Books, 2000; Cohn, M. *101 Ethical Dilemmas*. New York: Routledge, 2003; Bennett, C., and Raab, C. *The Governance of Privacy: Policy Instruments in Global Perspective*. Boston: MIT Press, 2006; Swire, P. P., and Bermann, S. *Information Privacy: Official Reference for the Certified Information Privacy Professional*. York, ME: International Association of Privacy Professionals, 2007.
13. U.S. Equal Employment Opportunity Commission. Discrimination by type: Facts and guidance. www.eeoc.gov (July 2007).
14. Crane, A., and Matten, D. *Business Ethics*. New York: Oxford University Press, 2007; Kitson, A., and Campbell, R. *The Ethical Organization*. New York: Palgrave Macmillan, 2008.
15. Costco's code of ethics. www.costco.com (July 2007).
16. Ibid.
17. Ibid.
18. Lawrence, A. T., and Weber, J. *Business and Society: Stakeholders, Ethics, Public Policy*. Burr Ridge, IL: McGraw-Hill/Irwin, 2007.
19. *Adapted from* United National Global Compact. www.unglobalcompact.org (July 2007).
20. Cushway, B. *The Employer's Handbook*, 5th ed. London: Kogan Page Ltd., 2007.
21. Repa, B. K. *Your Rights in the Workplace*, 8th ed. Berkeley, CA: NOLO, 2007.
22. Stone, K. V. Revisiting the at-will employment doctrine: Imposed terms, implied terms, and the normative world of the workplace. *Industrial Law Journal*, 2007, 36, 84–101.
23. Greenpeace: About Us. www.greenpeace.org/usa (July 2007).
24. Jobs, S. *A greener apple*. May 3, 2007. www.apple.com (July 2007).
25. Steve Jobs addresses Apple's enviro-critics. *Greener-Computing*, May 3, 2007. www.greenercomputing.com (July 2007).
26. Heisler, W. J. Ethical choices in the design and administration of executive compensation programs. *Business Horizons*, 2007, 50, 277–290; Duran, M. A. Norm-based behavior and corporate malpractice. *Journal of Economic Issues*, 2007, 41, 221–241; Uhl-Bien, M., and Carsten, M. K. Being ethical when the boss is not. *Organizational Dynamics*, 2007, 36, 187–201.
27. Brown, M. E. Misconceptions of ethical leadership: How to avoid potential pitfalls. *Organizational Dynamics*, 2007, 36, 140–155.
28. Zahra, S. A., Priem, R. L., and Rasheed, A. A. Understanding the causes and effects of top management fraud. *Organizational Dynamics*, 2007, 36, 122–139.
29. Jasper, M. *You've Been Fired: Your Rights and Remedies*. New York: Oxford University Press, 2007; Repa, *Your Rights in the Workplace*.
30. United Nations Global Compact. www.gln.org (July 2007).
31. Anderson, D. R., Sweeney, D. J., Williams, T. A., and Martin, R. K. *An Introduction to Management Science: Quantitative Approaches to Decision Making*, 12th ed. Mason, OH: Cengage Learning/South-Western, 2008.
32. *Adapted from* Xerox Consensus Matrix. www.xbgr.com (August 2007).
33. Pollock, J. L. *Thinking about Acting: Logical Foundations for Rational Decision Making*. New York: Oxford University Press, 2006.
34. Colvin, G. Xerox's inventor-in-chief. *Fortune*, July 9, 2007, 65, 69–72.
35. Hodgkinson, G. P., and Starbuck, W. H. (Eds.). *The Oxford Handbook of Organizational Decision Making*. New York: Oxford University Press, 2008.
36. Kahneman, D., and Tversky, A. (Eds.). *Choices, Values, and Frames*. New York: Cambridge University Press,

2000; Marnet, O. History repeats itself: The failure of rational choice models in corporate governance. *Critical Perspectives on Accounting*, 2007, 18, 191–210.
37. *Adapted from* Solovy, A. Ten lessons from the top 100 most wired hospitals and health systems. www.hhnmag.com. (July 2007); Herper, M. Doctors, untethered. Forbes. *com*, June 21, 2004, 20–21; Gruman, G. Caging wireless. *CIO Magazine*, July 15, 2004, 14; Williams, C. T. Inside a closed loop medication strategy. *Nursing Management*, October 2004, 89, 24.
38. About St. Vincent Hospital. www.stv.org (August 2007).
39. Simon, H. A. *Administrative Behavior: A Study of Decision-Making Processes in Administrative Organizations*, 4th ed. New York: Free Press, 1997; also see Clegg, S. The bounds of rationality: Power/history/imagination. *Critical Perspectives on Accounting*, 2006, 17, 847–863.
40. Roach, J. M. Simon says: Decision making is "satisficing" experience. *Management Review*, January 1979, 8–9; also see deBoer, L., Gaytan, J., and Arroyo, P. A satisficing model of outsourcing. *Supply Chain Management: An International Journal*, 2006, 11, 444–455.
41. Knudsen, T., and Levinthal, D. A. Two faces of search: Alternative generation and alternative evaluation. *Organization Science*, 2007, 18, 39–54; Tiawana, A., Wang, J., Keil, M., and Ahluwalia, P. The bounded rationality bias in managerial evaluation of real options: Theory and evidence from IT projects. *Decision Sciences*, 2007, 38, 157–181.
42. Staw, B. M. The escalation of commitment to a course of action. *Academy of Management Review*, 1981, 6, 577–587; Street, M., and Street, V. L. The effects of escalating commitment on ethical decision-making. *Journal of Business Ethics*, 2006, 64, 343–356.
43. Montealegre, R., and Keil, M. Deescalating information technology projects: Lessons from the Denver International Airport. *MIS Quarterly*, 2000, 24, 417–447; Denver International Airport. http://en.wikipedia.org/wiki/Denver_International_Airport (August 2007).
44. Brockman, B. K. Becherer, R. C., and Finch, J. H. Influences on an entrepreneur's perceived risk: The role of magnitude, likelihood, and risk propensity. *Academy of Entrepreneurship Journal*, 2006, 12, 107–126; Hillson, D. and Murray-Webster, R. *Understanding and Managing Risk Attitude*. Aldershot, Hampshire, UK: Gower Publishing, 2007.
45. Coleman, L. Risk and decision making by finance executives. *International Journal of Managerial Finance*, 2007, 3, 108–128.
46. Cho, J., and Lee, J. An integrated model of risk and risk-reducing strategies. *Journal of Business Research*, 2006, 59, 112–120. For a discussion of the relationship between escalating commitment and risk propensity, see Wong, K. F. The role of risk in making decisions under escalation situations. *Applied Psychology: An International Journal*, 2005, 54, 584–607.
47. Kahneman, D. A perspective on judgment and choice: Mapping bounded rationality. *American Psychologist*, 2003; 58, 697–720.
48. Schoemaker, P. J. H., and Russo, J. E. A pyramid of decision approaches. *California Management Review*, Fall 1993, 9–31; Walker, E. D., and Cox III, J. F. Addressing ill-structured problems using Goldratt's thinking processes. *Management Decision*, 2006, 44, 137–154; Browne, G. J., Pitts, M. G., and Wetherbe, J. C. Cognitive stopping rules for terminating information search in online tasks. *MIS Quarterly*, 2007, 31, 89–104.
49. Nutt, P. C. Expanding the search for alternatives during strategic decision-making. *Academy of Management Executive*, 2004, 18(4), 13–28; Nutt, P. C. Intelligence gathering for decision making. *Omega*, 2007, 35, 604–622; Gilovich, T., Griffin, D., and Kahneman, D. *Heuristics and Biases: The Psychology of Intuitive Judgment*. New York: Cambridge University Press, 2002.
50. Turner, K. L., and Makhija, M. V. The role of organizational controls in managing knowledge. *Academy of Management Review*, 2006, 31, 197–217; Patriotta, G. *Organizational Knowledge in the Making: How Firms Create, Use, and Institutionalize Knowledge*. New York: Oxford University Press, 2005.
51. This section is based on Pfeffer, J., and Sutton, R. I. Management half-truths and nonsense: How to practice evidence-based management. *California Management Review*, 2006, 46(3), 77–100; Pfeffer, J., and Sutton, R. I. *Hard Facts, Dangerous Half-Truths & Total Nonsense: Profiting from Evidence-Based Management*. Boston: Harvard Business School Press, 2006.
52. Shortell, S. M. Promoting evidence-based management. *Frontiers of Health Services Management*, 2006, 22(3), 23–29.
53. Pfeffer, J., and Sutton, R. I. Evidence-based management. *Harvard Business Review*, 2006, 84(1), 2.
54. Baack, S. Book review of *Hard Facts, Dangerous Half-Truths & Total Nonsense: Profiting from Evidence-Based Management. Academy of Management Learning & Education*, 2007, 6, 139–140.
55. Pfeffer and Sutton, *Hard Facts, Dangerous Half-Truths & Total Nonsense*, 22.
56. Bazerman, M. H., and Chugh, D. Decisions without blinders. *Harvard Business Review*, 2006, 84(1), 88–97.
57. Pfeffer and Sutton, Management half-truths and nonsense, 96–97.
58. Rousseau, D. M., and McCarthy, S. Educating managers from an evidence-based perspective. *Academy of Management Learning & Education*, 2007, 6, 84–101.
59. Baack, Book review of *Hard Facts. . . . Academy of Management Learning & Education*, 2007, 6, 139–141; also see other reviews of this book in the same issue by Miller, S., Williams, J., Dierdorff, E. C., and Bielmeier, P., 141–149. These reviews address the strengths and potential limitations of the evidence-based management model.
60. Gigerenzer, G. *Gut Feelings: The Intelligence of the Unconscious*. New York: Viking Press, 2007; Dane, E., and Pratt, M. G. Exploring intuition and its role in managerial decision making. *Academy of Management Review*, 2007, 32, 33–54.
61. *Adapted from* Weinburg, A. L. Focusing on the customer: An interview with the head of Merrill Lynch's operations and IT. *McKinsey Quarterly*, August 2007, 1–7.
62. Merrill Lynch: About Us. www.ml.com (August 2007).

63. Vigoda-Gadot, E., and Drory, A. (Eds.). *Handbook of Organizational Politics*. Northampton, MA: Edward Elgar Publishing, 2006; Kramer, R. M., and Neale, M. A. (Eds.). *Power and Influence in Organizations*. Thousand Oaks, CA: Sage, 1998.
64. Lencioni, P. Silos, politics, and turf wars: Don't turn colleagues into competitors. *Leadership Excellence*, 2006, 23(2), 3–4.
65. Funk, S. Risky business. *Across the Board*, July/August 1999, 10–12.
66. Gilley, J. W. *The Manager as Politician*. Westport, CT: Praeger, 2006.
67. Hamel, G., Gould, S. J., and Weick, K. E. *On Creativity, Innovation and Renewal*. San Francisco: Jossey-Bass, 2002; Jeffcutt, P., and Pratt, A. *Creativity and Innovation in the Cultural Economy*. New York: Routledge, 2008.
68. La Barre, P. Weird ideas that work. *Fast Company*, January 2002, 68–73.
69. George, J. M. Creativity in organizations. In Walsh, J. P., and Brief, A. P. (Eds.). *The Academy of Management Annals*. Florence, KY: Taylor & Francis, 2007, in press; De Fillippi, R., Grabher, G., and Jones, C. Introduction to paradoxes of creativity: Managerial and organizational challenges in the cultural economy. *Journal of Organizational Behavior*, 2007, 28, 511–521; Bolton, C. *Management and Creativity: From Creative Industries to Creative Management*. Malden, MA: Blackwell, 2006.
70. de Bono, E. *Serious Creativity: Using the Power of Lateral Thinking to Create New Ideas*. New York: HarperCollins, 1993; Fisher, J. R., Jr. The need for lateral thinking in the new century. *National Productivity Review*, Spring 2000, 1–12; Edward de Bono personal website. www.edwarddebono.com (August 2007); Adair, J. *The Art of Creative Thinking: How to Be Innovative and Develop Great Ideas*. London: Kogan Page, 2007.
71. Amabile, T. M. How to kill creativity. *Harvard Business Review*, September/October 1998, 77–87; Gogatz, A. and Mondejar, R. *Business Creativity: Breaking the Invisible Barriers*. New York: Palgrave Macmillan, 2005.
72. Gryskiewicz, S. S., and Epstein, R. Cashing in on creativity at work. *Psychology Today*, September/October 2000, 62–67; Maurzy, J., and Harriman, R. A. Three climates for creativity. *Research Technology Management*, 2003, 46, 27–31.
73. Osborn, A. F. *Applied Imagination*, rev. ed. New York: Scribner, 1957.
74. Paulus, P. B., and Njstad, B. A. (Eds.). *Group Creativity: Innovation through Collaboration*. New York: Oxford University Press, 2003.
75. Sandberg, J. Brainstorming works best if people scramble for ideas on their own. *Wall Street Journal*, June 13, 2006, B1.
76. For a description of the wide array of collaborative software products and services offered by GroupSystems, visit this organization's home page at www.groupsystems.com (September 2007).
77. Dennis, A. R., and Reinicke, B. A. Beta versus VHS and the acceptance of electronic brainstorming technology. *MISQuarterly*, 2004, 28, 1–20; Reing, B. A., Briggs, R. O., and Nunamaker, Jr., J. F. On the measurement of ideation quality. *Journal of Management Information Systems*, 2007, 23, 143–161.
78. *Adapted from* Ind, N., and Watt, C. Teams, trust and tribalism. *Design Management Review*, 2006, 17(3), 41–47.
79. Company Info: Funcom. www.funcom.com (August 2007).
80. *Adapted from* Liberman, V. Scoring on the job. *Across the Board*, November/December 2003, 47–51; Vogt, P. Test your business ethics. http://resources.monster.com/tools/quizzes (August 2007); Right versus right: Ethical dilemmas in business. http://www.globalethics.org. Click on "Dilemmas" (August 2007).
81. *Adapted from* Moeller, B., and Clifford, S. The way I work. *Inc. Magazine*, July 2007, 88, 90–91. Used with permission. Copyright Clearance Center. Copyright 2007.
82. About DriveCam. www.drivecam.com (September 2007).

CHAPTER 14

1. *Adapted from* www.lowes.com (June 2007); personal conversation with H. Johnson, Vice President, Internal Auditing, Lowe's, June 2007.
2. Pitts, R. A., and Lei, D. *Strategic Management: Building and Sustaining Competitive Advantage*, 4th ed. Mason, OH: Thomson/South-Western, 2006, 442.
3. Lei, D., and Slocum, J. W. Strategic and organizational requirements for competitive advantage. *Academy of Management Executive*, 2005, 19, 31–45.
4. Suarez, F. F., and Lanzolla, G. The role of environmental dynamics in building a first mover advantage theory. *Academy of Management Review*, 2007, 32, 377–392; Daft, R. *Organization Theory and Design*, 9th ed. Mason, OH: Thomson/South-Western, 2007, 136–169.
5. Porter, M. *Competitive Strategy*. New York: Free Press, 1980.
6. Doebele, J. Proletariat capitalist. *Forbes*, 2007, June 18, 128–130; www.tunehotels.com (July 2007); Akan, O., Allen, R. S., Helms, M. M., and Spralls, S. A., III. Critical tactics for implementing Porter's generic strategies. *Journal of Business Strategy*, 2006, 27(1), 43–54.
7. www.starbucks.com (June 2007); Harrison, J. S., Chang, E., Gauthier, C., Joerchel, T., Nevarez, J., and Wang, M. Exporting a North American concept to Asia: Starbucks in China. *Cornell Hotel & Restaurant Administration Quarterly*, 2005, 46(2), 275–284.
8. Thompson, J. D. *Organizations in Action*. New York: McGraw-Hill, 1967; Van der Vegt, G. S., and Janseen, O. Joint impact of interdependence and group diversity on innovation. *Journal of Management*, 2003, 29, 729–752.
9. Burns, T., and Stalker, G. *The Management of Innovation*. London: Social Science Paperbacks, 1961, 96–125.
10. *Adapted from* Weber, M. *The Theory of Social and Economic Organization* (trans. Parsons, T.). New York: Oxford University Press, 1947, 329–334.
11. Hellriegel, D., Jackson, S. J., and Slocum, J. W., Jr. *Managing: A Competency-Based Approach*, 11th ed. Cincinnati, OH: Cengage Learning/South-Western, 2008,

39–69; Brisco, F. From iron cage to iron shield: How bureaucracy enables temporal flexibility for professional service workers. *Organization Science*, 2007, 18, 297–314.
12. *Adapted from* Engardio, P., and Roberts, D. How to make factories play fair. *Business Week*, November 27, 2006, 58.
13. www.cinemark.com (June 2007); personal conversation with E. Albright, Lease Administration, Cinemark Theaters, Plano, TX, June 2007.
14. www.coca-cola.com (June 2007).
15. Personal conversation with C. Arias, Director, International Sales, Celanese Corporation, Dallas, TX, June 2007.
16. www.utc.com (June 2007).
17. Harris, M., and Raviv, A. Organization design. *Management Science*, 2002, 48, 852–866.
18. Luo, Y., and Shenkar, O. The multinational corporation as a multilingual community. *Journal of International Studies*, 2006, 37(3), 321–340.
19. Christmann, P. Multinational companies and the natural environment: Determinants of global environmental policy standardization. *Academy of Management Review*, 2004, 47, 747–759.
20. Vance, C. M., and Paik, Y. Forms of host-country national learning for enhanced MNC absorptive capacity. *Journal of Managerial Psychology*, 2005, 20, 590–606.
21. *Adapted from* Piskorski, M. J., and Spadini, A. *Procter & Gamble: Organization* 2005(B). Boston, MA: Harvard Business School, Case 9-707-402, 5; www.pg.com (June 2007).
22. Joshi, A. The influence of organizational demography on the external networking behavior of teams. *Academy of Management Review*, 2006, 31, 583–595.
23. Kim, T., Oh, H., and Swaminathan, A. Framing interorganizational network exchange: A network inertia perspective. *Academy of Management Review*, 2006, 31, 704–720.
24. Martins, L. L., Gilson, L. L., and Maynard, M. T. Virtual teams: What do we know and where do we go from here? *Journal of Management*, 2004, 30, 805–836; Markus, M. L., Manville, B., and Agres, C. E. What makes a virtual organization work? *Sloan Management Review*, 2000, 42(1), 13–27.
25. *Adapted from* Babcock, C. FedEx integration wins customers for keeps. *Informationweek.com*, September 11, 2006, 112–114; Smith, F. W. A budding network. *Forbes*, May 7, 2007, 64–66; www.fedex.com. (June 2007); www.wikipedia.org/wiki/ProFlowers (June 2007).
26. *Adapted from* Birkinshaw, J., and Gibson, C. Building ambidexterity into an organization. *MIT Sloan Management Review*, 2004, 45(4), 47–55.
27. *Adapted from* West, A. P., Jr., and Wind, Y. Putting the organization on wheels: Workplace design at SEI. *California Management Review*, 2007, 49, 138–153; www.sei.com (June 2007).

CHAPTER 15

1. www.tdindustriesI.com (July 2007); Personal conversation with Bob Ferguson, Director, TDI, Plano, TX, June 2007; McLaughlin, C. A strong foundation. *Training*, 2001, 38(3), 80ff.
2. Jarnagin, C., and Slocum, J. W., Jr. Creating corporate cultures through mythopoetic leadership. *Organizational Dynamics*, 2007, 36, 288–302.
3. Organizational culture. www.en.wikipedia.org (July 2007); Mason, R. Lessons in organizational ethics from the *Columbia* disaster: Can a culture be lethal? *Organizational Dynamics*, 2004, 33, 128–142.
4. Kim, T., Cable, D. M., and Kim, S. Socialization tactics, employee proactivity and person–organization fit. *Journal of Applied Psychology*, 2005, 90, 232–233; Morgan G. *Images of Organization*, updated edition, Thousand Oaks, CA: Sage, 2007.
5. Gibson, C. B., and Zellmer-Bruhn, M. E. Metaphors and meaning: An intercultural analysis of the concept of teamwork. *Administrative Science Quarterly*, 2001, 46, 274–298.
6. Schein, E. H. *Organizational Culture and Leadership*. San Francisco: Jossey-Bass, 1985.
7. Ibid., 49–84.
8. Gelfand, M. J., Nishii, L. H., and Raver, J, L. On the nature and importance of cultural tightness-looseness. *Journal of Applied Psychology*, 2006, 91, 1225–1244; Molinsky, A. Cross-cultural code-switching: The psychological challenges of adapting behavior in foreign cultural interactions. *Academy of Management Review*, 2007, 32, 595–621.
9. Chatman, J. A., Polzer, J. T., Barsade, S. G., and Neale, M. A. Being different yet feeling similar: The influence of demographic composition and organizational culture on work process and outcomes. *Administrative Science Quarterly*, 1998, 43, 749–779.
10. *Adapted from* Apfelthaler, G., Muller, H. J., and Rehder, R. R. Corporate global culture as a competitive advantage: Learning from Germany and Japan in Alabama and Austria. *Journal of World Business*, 2002, 37, 108–118.
11. Schein, E. H. *Organizational Culture and Leadership; O'Donovan, G. The Corporate Culture Handbook: How to Plan, Implement and Measure a Successful Culture Change Programme*. Dublin, Ireland: Liffey Press, 2006.
12. Maxon, T. Supervisor goes above and beyond. *Dallas Morning News*, May 20, 2007, D5.
13. Morris, B. The new rules. *Fortune*, 2006, July 24, 70–84.
14. Schein, E. H. Organizational culture. *American Psychologist*, 1990, 45, 109–119.
15. Trice, H. M., and Beyer, J. M. *The Cultures of Work Organizations*. Englewood Cliffs, NJ: Prentice-Hall, 1993, 111.
16. Personal conversation with Fred Flores, Director, Mary Kay Cosmetics, Dallas, TX, July 2007.
17. Berry, L. L. Leadership lessons from the Mayo Clinic. *Organizational Dynamics*, 2004, 33, 228–242.
18. Sorensen, J. B. The strength of corporate culture and the reliability of firm performance. *Administrative Science Quarterly*, 2002, 47, 70–91.
19. Jarnagin and Slocum, Creating corporate cultures through mythopoetic leadership; Whitely, A., and

Whitely, J. *Core Values and Organizational Change*. Singapore: World Scientific Publishing, 2007.

20. *Adapted from* www.harley-davidson.com (July 2007); Rollin, B. E. *Harley-Davidson and Philosophy: Full-Throttle Aristotle*. Portland, OR: Open Court Publishing, 2006.
21. Kerr, J., and Slocum, J. W., Jr. Managing corporate cultures through reward systems. *Academy of Management Executive*, 1987, 1(2), 99–108.
22. www.albertoculver.com (July 2007); Murphy, H. L. Lavin & Bernick: Personal care, beauty products, Melrose Park. *Crain's Chicago Business*, October 17, 2005, 90ff.
23. Barry, M., and Slocum, J. W., Jr. Changing culture at Pizza Hut and YUM! Brands, Inc. *Organizational Dynamics*, 2003, 32, 319–330.
24. *Adapted from* Caplan, J. Small is essential. *Time*, May 28, 2007, Global 8–10; see also www.37signals.com (July 2007).
25. Barry and Slocum, Changing culture at Pizza Hut and YUM! Brands, Inc.
26. Sorensen, J. B. The strength of corporate culture and the reliability of firm performance. *Administrative Science Quarterly*, 2002, 47, 70–91.
27. Balthazard, P. A., Cooke, R. A., and Potter, R. E. Dysfunctional culture, dysfunctional organization: Capturing the behavioral norms that form organizational culture and drive performance. *Journal of Managerial Psychology*, 2006, 21, 709–732.
28. Personal communication with Ralph Sorrentino, Partner, Deloitte Consulting, Dallas, TX, July 2007.
29. Feldman, S. P. Moral business cultures: The keys to creating and maintaining them. *Organizational Dynamics*, 2007, 36, 156–170; Elci, M., Kitapci, H., and Erturk, A. Effects of quality culture and corporate ethical values on employee work attitudes and job performance. *Total Quality Management & Business Excellence*, 2007, 18(3–4), 285–303; Organ, D. W., Podsakoff, P. M., and MacKenzie, S. B. *Organizational Citizenship Behavior: Its Nature, Antecedents and Consequences*. Thousand Oaks, CA: Sage, 2006.
30. Near, J. P., Rehg, M. T., VanScotter, J. R., and Miceli, M. P. Does type of wrongdoing affect the whistle-blowing process? *Business Ethics Quarterly*, 2004, 14, 219–242; Nam, D., and Lemak, D. J. The whistle-blowing zone: Applying Barnard's insights to a modern ethical dilemma. *Journal of Management History*, 2007, 13, 33–42; Moorhead, D. T. SOX and whistleblowing. *Michigan Law Review*, 2007, 15, 1757–1780.
31. *Adapted from* Near et al., ibid.
32. Umphress, E. E., Smith-Crowe, K., and Brief, A. P. When birds of a feather flock together and when they do not: Status composition, social dominance orientation and organizational attractiveness. *Journal of Applied Psychology*, 2007, 92, 396–409.
33. www.gov.census (July 2007); Roberson, Q. M., and Stevens, C. K. Making sense of diversity in the workplace. *Journal of Applied Psychology*, 2006, 91, 379–391; Roberson, L., and Kulik, C. Stereotype threat at work. *Academy of Management Perspectives*, 2007, 21(2), 24–40; Caminiti, S. Moving up the ranks. *Fortune*, June 25, 2007, S2–S6.
34. www.utc.com (July 2007).
35. Pendry, L. F., Driscoll, D. M., and Susannah, C. T. Diversity training: Putting theory into practice. *Journal of Occupational and Organizational Psychology*, 2007, 80, 27–51.
36. Kim, T., Cable, D. M., and Kim, S. Socialization tactics, employee proactivity and person–organizational fit. *Journal of Applied Psychology*, 2005, 90, 232–241.
37. Rollag, K. The impact of relative tenure on newcomer socialization dynamics. *Journal of Organizational Behavior*, 2004, 25, 853–873.
38. *Adapted from* Cable, D., and Parsons, C. Socialization tactics and person–organization fit. *Personnel Psychology*, 2001, Spring, 1–23.
39. www.disney.com (July 2007); Brannen, M. Y. When Mickey loses face: Recontextualization, semantic fit and semiotics of foreignness. *Academy of Management Review*, 2004, 29, 593–616.
40. Bowen, D. E., and Ostroff, C. Understanding HRM-firm performance linkages: The role of the "strength" of the HRM system. *Academy of Management Review*, 2004, 29, 203–221.
41. From *The 1994 Annual: Developing Human Resources*. Reprinted by permission of John Wiley & Sons, Inc.
42. *Adapted from* Kiley, D. The new heat on Ford. *Business Week*, 2007, June 4, 33ff; Kiley, D. Mulally: Ford's most important new model. *Business Week Online*, January 9, 2007; Wilson, A. Ford CVEO: It's all about leveraging assets. *Automotive News*, April 30, 2007, 1ff; Webster, S. A. Mulally works on leadership: Ford CEO hopes to recreate product line, cut complexity. *Knight Ridder Tribune Business News*, April 1, 2007, 1ff; Webster, S. A. Sky's the limit, says Ford down-to-earth chief. *Knight Ridder Business News*, April 1, 2007, 1ff.

CHAPTER 16

1. *Adapted from* Kirkpatrick, D. How Microsoft conquered China. *Fortune*, July 23, 2007, 78–84; www.microsoft.com (August 2007); Microsoft in China: Clash of titans; Kanellos, M. Microsoft gets diplomatic in China. (www.news.com/Microsoft+gets+diplomatic+in+China/2100-1001_3-932927.html).
2. Marshak, R. J. *Covert Process at Work: Managing the Five Hidden Dimensions of Organizational Change*. San Francisco, CA: Berrett-Koehler Publishers, 2007.
3. www.sun.com (July 2007); also see Kersetter, J., and Burrows, P. A CEO's last stand. *Business Week*, July 26, 2004, 64ff.
4. Friedman, T. L. *The World Is Flat*. New York: Farrar, Straus and Giroux, 2005; Harvey, M. G., and Novicevic, M. M. The world is flat: A perfect storm for global business? *Organizational Dynamics*, 2006, 35, 207–220; Penn, M. J. *Microtrends*. New York: Twelve Hachette Book Company, 2007.
5. Piskorski, M. J., and Spadini, A. L. *Procter & Gamble: Organization (A)*. Boston, MA: Harvard Business School, Case # 9–707–401.

6. Jargon, J. Can M'm, M'm good translate? *Wall Street Journal*, July 9, 2007, A16.
7. Arnott, S. The Brown era begins as challenges for IT increase. *Computing*, June 28, 2007, 6.
8. West, E. These robots play fetch. *Fast Company*, July/August 2007, 49–50.
9. Greenbery, P. S., Greenbery, R. H., and Antonucci, Y. L. Creating and sustaining trust in virtual teams. *Business Horizons*, 2007, 50, 325–334; Bosch-Sijtsema, P. The impact of individual expectations and conflict of expectations of virtual teams. *Group and Organization Management*, 2007, 23, 358–388.
10. Tyler, K. The tethered generation. *HRMagazine*, May 2007, 41–46.
11. Dominiak, M. "Millennials" defying the old models. *Television Week*, May 7, 2007, 68–69; Trunk, P. What Gen Y really wants. *Time*, July 16, 2007, Global 8; Hymowitz, C. Managers find ways to get generations to close culture gaps. *Wall Street Journal*, July 10, 2007, B1; Frey, W. H. *Mapping the Growth of Older America: Seniors and Boomers in the Early 21st Century*. Washington, DC: The Brookings Institute, May 2007.
12. *Adapted from* Larrabee, J. The virtuous cycle of community involvement. *Strategic HR Review*, May/June 2007, 24–27; Rowh, M. Managing younger workers. *Office Solutions*, 2007, 24(1), 29–31.
13. Cummings, T. G., and Worley, C. G. *Organizational Development and Change*, 8th ed. Mason, OH: Thomson/South-Western, 2008.
14. Beer, M., and Nohria, N. Resolving the tension between theories E and O of change. In Beer, M., and Nohria, N. (Eds.). *Breaking the Code of Change*. Boston: Harvard Business School Press, 2000, 1–34.
15. Hall, C. Captain turnaround. *Dallas Morning News*, July 22, 2007, D1ff.
16. Boyle, M. The Wegman's way. *Fortune*, January 24, 2005, 61–68.
17. Sonnenfeld, J. A. A return to the power of ideas. *Sloan Management Review*, 2004, 45(2), 30–33; Useem, J. Another boss, another revolution. *Fortune*, April 5, 2004, 112–118.
18. Beer, M., Voelpel, S. C., Leibold, M., and Tekie, E. B. Strategic management as organizational learning: Developing fit and alignment through a disciplined process. *Long Range Planning*, 2005, 38, 445–466.
19. Duckworth, A. L., Peterson, C., and Mathews, M. D. Grit: Perseverance and passion for long-term goals. *Journal of Personality and Social Psychology*, 2007, 92, 1087–1101.
20. EDS executive says job isn't over. *Dallas Morning News*, January 21, 2005, 1D.
21. Ellis, E. Vintage Ceylon. *Fortune*, July 23, 2007, 61–62.
22. Tomlinson, R. Troubled waters at Perrier. *Fortune*, November 24, 2004, 173ff.
23. *Adapted from* Nutt, P. C. *The Tolerance for Ambiguity and Decision Making*. Columbus, OH: Fisher School of Business, 2007.
24. Hoetker, G., and Agarwal, R. Death hurts, but it isn't fatal: The postexit diffusion of knowledge created by innovative companies. *Academy of Management Journal*, 2007, 50, 446–467.
25. Iacocca, L., and Whitney, C. The worst decision I ever made. *The Conference Board Review*, July/August 2007, 46–48.
26. www.Healthsouth.com (August 2007).
27. Kelleher, K. Giving dealers a raw deal. *Business 2.0*, December 2004, 82–84.
28. www.dallascowboys.com (August 2007).
29. Lewin, K. *Field Theory in Social Science*. New York: Harper & Row, 1951.
30. *Adapted from* Anderson, D. When Crocs attack. *Business 2.0*, November 2006, 51–53; www.crocs.com (August 2007).
31. Swann, W. B., Chang-Schneider, C., and Katie, L. M. Do people's self-views matter? Self-concept and self-esteem in everyday life. *American Psychologist*, 2007, 62 (2), 84–94.
32. Cummins and Worley, *Organizational Development and Change*; Berry, C. M., Ones, D. S., and Sackett, P. R. Interpersonal deviance, organizational deviance and their common correlates: A review and meta-analysis. *Journal of Applied Psychology*, 2007, 92, 410–424.
33. Ramos, C. M. Organizational change in a human service agency. *Journal of Consulting Psychology: Practice and Research*, 2007, 59, 41–53.
34. Cummings and Worley, *Organizational Development and Change*.
35. *Adapted from* Whetten, D. A., and Cameron, K. S. *Developing Management Skills*, 7th ed. Upper Saddle River, NJ: Pearson/Prentice Hall, 2007, 538–539.
36. Cummings and Worley, *Organizational Development and Change*, 230–252; Lantz, G. Team building blocks and breakthroughs. *Human Resource Planning*, 2007, 30(2), 12–14.
37. Serva, M. A., Fuller, M. A., and Mayer, R. C. The reciprocal nature of trust: A longitudinal study of interacting teams. *Journal of Organizational Behavior*, 2005, 26, 625–649.
38. www.airtran.com (August 2007).
39. Cummings and Worley, *Organizational Development and Change*, 501.
40. www.IBM.com (August 2007); Gunther, M. Queer Inc. *Fortune*, December 11, 2006, 94ff.
41. *Adapted from* Stewart, T. A. Rate your readiness to change. *Fortune*, February 7, 1994, 106–110.
42. *Adapted from* Hardy, Q. The Uncarly. *Forbes*, March 12, 2007, 80–88; Lee, L. *HP sees a gold mine in data mining. Business Week*, April 30, 2007, 30ff; Lee, L. HP bests Dell again. *Business Week Online*, February 21, 2007; personal communication with Barbara Thomas, HP Corporate Accounts Segment Director, Dallas, TX, September 2007.

SUBJECT AND ORGANIZATIONAL INDEX

D

M

Q

R

AUTHOR INDEX

In the entry "Adair, J., R-26n.70 (414)": R-26 refers to page R-26 in the References section; n.70 refers to note 70 on that page; and (414) refers to the *text* page where the note is called out. Page numbers followed by "f" indicate figures; "t", tables.

C

D

E

I

J

K

L

M

N

O

P

Q

R

S

T

U

V

W

Y

Z

Instant Access to Powerful eResources for:

Organizational Behavior

Twelfth Edition

by Hellriegel/Slocum

eResources Included:

- **Organizational Behavior Competencies Self-Assessment Test**
  Seven foundation competencies all employees, managers, and leaders need to have are Self Competency, Communication, Diversity, Ethics, Across Cultures, Teams and Change. Use the online test to assess abilities, set benchmarks, consider goals, clarify expectations, and advance fundamental competence across these seven interrelated sets of key skills, behaviors, attitudes, and knowledge.
- **Student Companion Site**
  Additional study aids

Tear out card missing?

If you did not buy a new textbook, the tear-out portion of this card may be missing or the Access Code on this card may have already been used. Access Codes can be used only once and are not transferable.

ISBN-13: 978-0-324-58737-1
ISBN-10: 0-324-58737-6

SOUTH-WESTERN
CENGAGE Learning™

TO GET STARTED:

1. Launch a web browser and go to **academic.cengage.com**
2. Click on "Create an Account" under Student eResource Registration.
3. Enter the Access Code below exactly as it appears.

ACCESS CODE

PP3HMNVP3WV5DT

4. Follow the prompts to create your account.
5. Record your email address and password for future visits.

Email:

Password:

NOTE: The duration of your access to the eResources begins when registration is complete.

For technical support, go to

academic.cengage.com/support